Programming Microsoft®
Visual Basic® .NET
Version 2003

Francesco Balena

PUBLISHED BY
Microsoft Press
A Division of Microsoft Corporation
One Microsoft Way
Redmond, Washington 98052-6399

Library of Congress Cataloging-in-Publication Data
Balena, Francesco, 1960-
        Programming Microsoft Visual Basic .NET version 2003 / Francesco Balena.
            p. cm.
        Includes index.
        ISBN 0-7356-2059-8
        1. Microsoft Visual BASIC.   2. BASIC (Computer program lanuage)   3. Microsoft
        .NET.   I. Title.

    QA76.73.B3B348   2003
    005.2'768--dc22   2003058666

Printed and bound in the United States of America.

3 4 5 6 7 8 9   QWT   8 7 6 5

Distributed in Canada by H.B. Fenn and Company Ltd.

A CIP catalogue record for this book is available from the British Library.

Microsoft Press books are available through booksellers and distributors worldwide. For further information about international editions, contact your local Microsoft Corporation office or contact Microsoft Press International directly at fax (425) 936-7329. Visit our Web site at www.microsoft.com/mspress. Send comments to *mspinput@microsoft.com*.

Acquisitions Editor: Danielle Bird Voeller
Project Editor: Kathleen Atkins
Technical Editor: Jeff Webb
Indexer: Virginia Bess

Body Part No. X10-21789

To Adriana, the love of my life

Contents

Part II   Object-Oriented Programming

Class Fundamentals   98

Inheritance   **129**

Interfaces, Delegates, and Attributes   **171**

11   Regular Expressions   307

12   Threading   326

Acknowledgments

I love having the opportunity to thank all the people who helped me make the first and second editions of *Programming Microsoft Visual Basic .NET*.

Let's begin with Jeffrey Richter, for writing such a friendly foreword for the first edition and for helping me understand what happens behind the .NET curtain. Even though he was busy writing his own *Applied Microsoft .NET Framework Programming*—a book that all .NET developers should have on their desks—he always found the time to reply to my weirdest queries. (I gave Jeffrey a hand in making the Visual Basic .NET version of that book, entitled *Applied Microsoft .NET Framework Programming with Microsoft Visual Basic .NET*.)

Next comes Giuseppe Dimauro, whose deep knowledge of Windows, COM, and SQL Server programming—and the speed at which he can translate all this knowledge into fully working, bug-free applications—continues to astonish me after so many years. Giuseppe is my partner in Code Architects, an Italian .NET-focused software and consulting company, and he spends a lot of his time speaking at MSDN conferences and consulting for Microsoft Italy.

I don't have to introduce Dino Esposito, probably the most prolific writer in the developer community as well as cofounder of the *www.vb2themax.com site*. The great thing about Dino is his attitude in going beyond the usual programming clichés that often kill creativity. Don't miss Dino's latest books, *Applied XML Programming for .NET* and *Programming ASP.NET*, also from Microsoft Press.

This is the right place to thank all the other brains at Wintellect, including Jeff Prosise, John Robbins, Kenn Scribner, Brent Rector, Jason Clark, and John Lam. Being a Wintellectual is such an enriching experience that I feel very proud to be part of this group. And thanks to Lewis Frazer and Jim Bail for letting me complete both editions before throwing me again in the .NET training arena.

Finding documentation about the Framework isn't a problem today, but it was as scarce as gold (and almost as precious) when the product was in early beta version. My gratitude goes to my friend Francesco Albano of Microsoft Italy for sharing his knowledge and helping me find great technical material when I badly needed it.

A big thank you goes to the trainers and experts at Code Architects. Marco Bellinaso and Alberto Falossi patiently proofread all the chapters in the first edition. The new chapters on COM+, remoting, and security wouldn't be as rich and valuable as they are without the support from Enrico Sabbadin. I am very proud we put together such a great team!

My friend Giovanni Librando is the acquisition editor in Mondadori, the Italian publisher that translates my Microsoft Press books. But above all, he is an experienced teacher with a keen talent for finding the comic side of programming. I had never realized how much fun speaking at a developers' conference could be until I gave my first four-hand session with him.

I know for sure that my writing style owes a lot to Kathleen Atkins, the editor who has worked with me in the last five years. Apparently, I managed to convince heads at Microsoft Press that all sorts of things might go wrong if I work with another editor, so they keep assigning Kathleen to my book projects. If you had seen the original manuscript before she reviewed it, you'd understand why I feel so grateful to Kathleen and to the other great editors who assisted her in this edition, Brenda Pittsley and Jennifer Harris.

Danielle Bird Voeller has been the acquisition editor for this book, and she did her job in the best way possible. She always had an immediate answer to all my requests and had all Visual Studio .NET beta versions sent to me no later than a couple of days after their release. (Quickly enough, if you consider that I live nine time zones away.)

I can't help being grateful to the technical editors at Microsoft Press who have worked on this book. Jack Beaudry did a superb job on the first edition, whereas Jeff Webb helped me adapt the material for .NET 1.1, checked the new chapters, and gave me some great tips. Without them this book wouldn't be so accurate and filled with details.

I feel a bit silly thanking the two people who have helped more than anyone else. How can I just say *thank you* to my wife Adriana and my son Andrea for their love? You are the driving force behind this and other books—and pretty much all else I do.

—Francesco

Foreword from *Programming Microsoft Visual Basic .NET*

When Microsoft has some new technology its developers want to start getting feedback about, it holds a System Design Review (SDR). In October 1999, I was fortunate enough to be invited to an SDR for what was then called COM+ 2.0. In my career, I've always been much more interested in Win32 APIs than in COM, so I normally wouldn't go to such an event. However, since I didn't have too much else going on during the days of the SDR, I decided to attend and see what new stuff Microsoft had planned for COM. Well, let me tell you—I was blown away! COM+ 2.0 wasn't just some enhancements added to COM; this new COM was a totally different way of developing software and components.

To me, it was obvious: this new COM was the future of almost all software development. When Microsoft developers realized that what they were building was so much more than a new version of COM, the company changed the name of the technology from COM+ 2.0 to the Microsoft .NET Framework—which is how this new development platform is known today. The .NET Framework allows developers to create robust applications quickly and easily. This new platform also solves a lot of the problems that have plagued Windows for years: DLL Hell, security issues, memory leaks, memory corruption, inconsistent APIs and error handling, and so on.

Immediately after the SDR, I became a consultant on the .NET Framework team and have been programming to this new platform almost exclusively for more than two years. I must say I love it! And I never want to go back to my old C and C++ ways. If you plan on having a software development career, you should definitely start learning how to use the .NET Framework today.

Currently Microsoft offers many different technologies that accomplish different tasks:

- To create dynamic Web sites, you must learn Visual Basic Scripting Edition or JScript.

- To create high-performance databases, you must learn T-SQL.

- To create scalable memory-efficient components, you must use C/C++ and optionally MFC and ATL.

- To automate personal productivity applications (such as Microsoft Word and Excel), you must learn Visual Basic for Applications.

- To rapidly build GUI applications, you must learn Visual Basic.

Today's "solutions" are built by developers using many of these technologies. For example, many dynamic Web sites use scalable components that access a database, which means that many programmers must be fluent in all these different technologies and in all the different programming languages. Obviously, this is an enormous amount of work, and very few people (if any) are able to become masters of all these technologies and programming languages.

Because the .NET Framework can be used to accomplish every one of the tasks I just listed, we'll see all the current technologies collapse into one technology—The .NET Framework. The .NET Framework enables developers to build dynamic Web sites and scalable, memory-efficient components, and it will enable them to build GUI applications rapidly. Shortly after its initial release, the .NET Framework will be used by Microsoft SQL Server to offer high-performance database access. Further down the road, we should see productivity applications such as Microsoft Word and Excel using the .NET Framework to process macros that automate these applications. Learning the .NET Framework today will give you a huge head start in knowing how to perform all these tasks. It will really be possible for someone to become fluent in all these technologies.

Francesco's book is a great first step toward understanding the .NET Framework. His book covers all the main topics that every .NET Framework developer will need to know. To explain and demonstrate these topics, Francesco has chosen the popular Visual Basic .NET programming language. Programmers already familiar with Visual Basic will find this book a big help when migrating their existing code because Francesco clearly points out where things have changed from Visual Basic 6 to Visual Basic .NET. But developers who aren't familiar with Visual Basic will still find this book to be a great way to get started learning the .NET Framework because the concepts explained apply to all programming languages that target the .NET Framework.

Francesco also presents the material in a unique bottom-up approach—that is, he starts with the basic programming language and common language runtime concepts (such as classes, delegates, events, garbage collection, and serialization). After you understand the basics, he explains how these concepts and technologies are applied to enterprise solutions (such as ADO.NET and ASP.NET Web Forms and XML Web services). Finally, after reading this book, you'll find it a valuable reference guide that you'll be able to turn to time and time again to get answers to your nagging problems as you develop your .NET Framework applications.

I have no doubt that Francesco's book will quickly become an indispensable resource for any .NET Framework developer.

Jeffrey Richter

http://www.Wintellect.com

January 2002

Introduction

The first edition of *Programming Visual Basic .NET* has been one of the most popular .NET books since its release in April 2002. Many readers have reviewed it on Amazon.com, citing it as one of the best .NET Framework books they've encountered. It is often the only Visual Basic book in Amazon's list of top sellers in the Computer and Internet category. Being on that list for 18 months is in itself quite remarkable, considering that books of this type typically become obsolete in a couple of months.

Which leads us to this question: why write a completely revised second edition if readers seem so satisfied with the original book? After all, I could have just uploaded some new material on my *www.vb2themax.com* Web site, as I've done for minor fixes and typo reports.

As a matter of fact, when Microsoft released Visual Studio .NET 2003 and version 1.1 of the .NET Framework in spring 2003, I thought that a new edition of the book was unnecessary and that making some notes available online would suffice. Like many developers, I initially perceived the new versions as minor upgrades from previous ones, but then I realized that many applications written for version 1.0 behave differently (or don't work at all) under the new version. The truth is many areas of the .NET Framework changed remarkably in version 1.1—most notably ASP.NET and Web services—and both Visual Studio .NET and Visual Basic .NET themselves have evolved from its initial 2002 release. Not being aware of the new features means missing an opportunity to make your code run faster and more reliably, plus it means wasting a lot of time and energy tweaking the code to have it run under .NET Framework version 1.1.

These kinds of problems became more critical with the release of Windows Server 2003, which improves on Windows 2000 Server in areas such as Component Services, Internet Information Services, and security. If you write enterprise-level applications, you should absolutely take advantage of the improved robustness, scalability, and security in Windows Server 2003. Alas, some of the information provided in the first edition of the book—especially in the chapters on ASP.NET—is outdated and of little use under the newest version of the operating system. (This holds true for most books based on version 1.0 of the .NET Framework.)

The last—and decisive—factor that convinced me to write a completely new book was the opportunity to cover a few important topics that I left out in the first edition—namely, PInvoke, COM Interop, COM+, remoting, code access security, and Windows Forms applications over HTTP—and to illustrate techniques that I learned after the first edition was published. A new edition also allows me to improve chapters with new descriptions and more focused code examples.

Why a Book This Large

Granted, I could have written two or three books with the material you can find in these pages—for example, a book on Visual Basic .NET, another on Win32 applications and database applications, and a third on Web Forms, Web services, and other Internet-related topics. I even suspect that smaller books might have been a wiser decision from a business perspective. Why didn't I do that then?

In my opinion, the revolutionary aspect of the .NET initiative is that it lets developers adopt a unified programming paradigm, regardless of the language they're using or the type of application they're building. All the objects in the .NET class library are closely interrelated, and you can't create great applications by focusing on a small portion of the Framework and ignoring the rest. For example, programmers working on client-side solutions should learn about the Windows Forms portion of the Framework, but also about multithreading and GDI+. Programmers working on Web Forms should know about .NET data types, collections, and regular expressions. XML Web services programs require familiarity with object serialization and asynchronous delegates. Finally, you must master class inheritance, interfaces, assembly binding, and low-level details on memory management and garbage collection to write *any* type of .NET application.

For all these reasons, I believe that a single volume can cover all the many facets of .NET programming better than many smaller books, which would inevitably overlap in their explanations of .NET fundamentals. And only a book from a single author can ensure that there are neither repetitions nor glaring omissions as it provides the big .NET picture.

By the way, those of you who already own the first edition of *Programming Microsoft Visual Basic .NET* might notice that this edition has fewer pages than its predecessor, and then conclude that the new edition doesn't cover topics in the same depth. That isn't the case; the page count is different only because the publisher used a different layout style for the text. The word count command in Microsoft Word doesn't lie: both editions contain about 3 million characters.

To make room for new material in this edition, I moved some topics from the previous edition to separate files and made them available on the companion CD. You'll find a mention of this extra material where appropriate.

Check Out the E-Book, Too

Many readers asked me why the first edition of *Programming Microsoft Visual Basic .NET* wasn't provided in electronic format on the companion CD, unlike its *Programming Microsoft Visual Basic 6* predecessor. I had to make this decision when I realized that the Visual Basic 6 e-book was freely available for download on several Web sites.

Needless to say, this questionable practice had a huge cost in terms of lost sales. The only possible line of defense was to not offer *Programming Microsoft Visual Basic .NET* as an e-book.

On the other hand, I realize that many readers would like to have an electronic and searchable version of the books they buy. This is especially true for large books like this one and for reference books that are meant to help developers in their everyday activity.

For these reasons—but especially because I don't want to hinder *all* readers because a small number of them behave unethically—I decided to include an e-book of this edition of *Programming Microsoft Visual Basic .NET Version 2003* on the companion CD, cross my fingers, and hope for the best.

I can't protect the material on the CD from illegal copying, and I wouldn't do it even if it were possible because I dislike treating readers as if they were potential misbehavers. I can only ask you to think twice before sharing the CD contents with other people and imagine how you would feel if you worked for months on an application only to see it freely downloadable from the Internet.

Let me summarize what you're going to find on the companion CD:

- *Programming Microsoft Visual Basic .NET Version 2003* (this book) in fully searchable e-book format.

- *Programming Microsoft Visual Basic 6* in fully searchable e-book format.

- Additional documents about Visual Basic .NET and the .NET Framework (over 200 printed pages).

- All the code samples, grouped by the chapter to which they refer.

You can run code samples on any computer capable of running Microsoft Visual Studio .NET 2003. For serious development, you should have a system based on Pentium III or higher and running Windows 2000, Windows XP, or Windows Server 2003. (Windows NT is OK for Windows Forms projects, but not for developing ASP.NET applications.) Ensure that you have installed Internet Information Services (IIS) before installing Visual Studio .NET and the .NET Framework, if you want to develop ASP.NET solutions. You need about 2.5 gigabytes free on your disk to install Visual Studio .NET (about 500 megabytes of which must be available on the system drive) and 384 megabytes of RAM (even though at least 512 megabytes are necessary to work on real-world projects).

Who Should Read This Book?

Let me make another point clear up front. This book isn't for beginner developers wishing to learn Visual Basic .NET. Rather, it's for experienced Visual Basic developers who want to leverage the full potential of Microsoft .NET. If you don't feel at ease with

Visual Basic and its forms, if you don't know how to work with classes and objects, or if you've never developed a database application using ADO, this isn't the book for you. There are no step-by-step instructions about creating projects, no tutorials describing a variable, a class, or a database connection.

Visual Basic .NET is a new language, but fortunately you can still leverage much of your experience with previous language editions. For example, ADO.NET evolved from ADO, so you need to know what a connection string is and how to build it. Even if Windows Forms controls are more powerful than their Visual Basic 6 cousins, many of the techniques you've developed in recent years are still useful. For those who need to refresh their memory, I have included the full electronic version of *Programming Microsoft Visual Basic 6* on the companion CD. For example, you can have a look at it for a tutorial of object-oriented concepts (Chapters 6 and 7), the SQL language (Chapter 8), the ADO object model (Chapter 13), and Active Server Pages and IIS applications (Chapter 20). The CD is fully searchable, so you can find what you're looking for in a matter of seconds. Links to specific topics are provided when it's useful to do so.

Because *Programming Microsoft Visual Basic .NET 2003* is aimed at experienced developers, it contains few complete, ready-to-run applications. Instead, I focused on shorter code examples that illustrate how a specific .NET feature works. Most of the listings in this book are one page or shorter, and include only the relevant portions of complete examples provided on the CD. For example, I don't waste precious pages to include the complete listings of related examples that differ only in a handful of statements or to include the tons of statements that a Visual Studio designer creates when you drop a few controls on a Windows form. Shorter code listings mean improved readability, and I can use the saved space for something more interesting.

A Bottom-Up Approach to the .NET Framework

Although I spend most of my time consulting and writing applications, I also do a lot of teaching in public seminars and on-site workshops. I teach my .NET programming classes both in the United States and Europe, and I regularly give sessions and full-day workshops at conferences such as VBITS, WinSummit, and DevWeek.

Teaching Visual Basic .NET while writing the first edition of *Programming Microsoft Visual Basic .NET* was an enriching and useful experience because I could refine the structure and content of the book based on the feedback from attendees and students. For example, I changed the sequence of a few chapters when I realized it made the comprehension of later topics easier. I also used my teaching experience to further refine the book in this second edition, replacing several code examples with more effective versions and addressing the most common questions that attendees ask during a seminar.

This book follows a bottom-up approach that starts with an introduction to the Microsoft .NET initiative and language basics (Part I), then progresses through inheritance and new features such as delegates and attributes (Part II), and continues with a thorough description of the base classes in the .NET Framework (Part III). At this point, readers have all the necessary background to understand what comes next, such as Windows Forms and GDI+ (Part IV), database programming with ADO.NET and XML (Part V), and ASP.NET applications (Part VI). The last group of chapters (Part VII) was written specifically for the second edition and covers advanced topics, such as PInvoke, COM Interop, COM+, remoting, security, and Internet-related features.

I suggest that you read this book without jumping back and forth from chapter to chapter because each chapter builds on those that come before it. This dependency of continuity is especially true for chapters in Parts I, II, and III. After you've become familiar with .NET foundations, you can decide to focus on Win32 applications, on database applications, or on ASP.NET applications, depending on your priorities. You should approach Part VII only if you have a solid understanding of topics covered in previous parts.

As I did with the first edition, I will upload corrections and new content to the Web site of my Code Architects company, *www.codearchitects.com*, where you can also find useful programming tools for Visual Basic .NET developers.

Microsoft Press also provides corrections and additional content for its books through the World Wide Web at

http://www.microsoft.com/learning/support/

If you have problems, comments, or ideas regarding this book or the companion CD, please send them to Microsoft Press as well as to me. Send e-mail to

mspinput@microsoft.com

Or send postal mail to

Microsoft Press
Attn: Programming Series Editor
One Microsoft Way
Redmond, WA 98052-6399

Please note that support for the Visual Studio .NET software product itself isn't offered through the preceding address. For help using Visual Studio .NET, visit *http://www.microsoft.com/support*.

Programming Microsoft Visual Basic .NET 2003 is my attempt to write a book that explains how you can build great, robust, easily maintainable, real-world applications with Visual Basic .NET and Visual Studio .NET. I wanted to demonstrate what I consider the best coding practices in the .NET environment, as well as provide you with a reference to the most important classes of the .NET Framework, a collection of tips for high-performance and scalable applications, and many code examples that you can reuse in your programs.

The first edition of this book took me one year to write—most of which was spent fighting against beta versions that refused to work as documented—and I spent three more months on this second edition. It cost me a fortune in espresso coffee and I canceled a couple of summer vacations, but I am very proud of the result. *Programming Microsoft Visual Basic .NET Version 2003* is the book I wanted to write, and I hope it will help you become an expert Visual Basic .NET developer in a fraction of the time I needed to complete it and, above all, without the headaches and all the caffeine.

Francesco Balena

fbalena@vb2themax.com

Part I
The Basics

1 Introducing Microsoft .NET

Virtually all books about a programming language start with an introductory chapter that praises that language, offers a first working example, describes some cool feature of the language, or mixes all three approaches. Microsoft Visual Basic .NET calls for a different treatment, however. Before you can fully appreciate the features of this new, almost revolutionary version of the language, you must understand what the .NET architecture is all about.

.NET as a Better Programming Platform

At the risk of oversimplifying, you can think of the .NET initiative as the convergence of several distinct but loosely tied goals, the most important of which are overcoming the limitations of the COM programming model and finding a common programming paradigm for Internet-related applications.

Leveling Windows Platforms

Microsoft .NET offers an object-oriented view of the Windows operating system and includes hundreds of classes that encapsulate all the most important Windows kernel objects. For example, a portion of .NET named GDI+ contains all the objects that create graphic output in a window. Depending on the specific Windows version, in the future these objects might use Windows GDI functions, the DirectX library, or even OpenGL, but as far as the developer is concerned there is only one programming model to code against.

Security is built into .NET, so you don't have to worry much about the underlying operating system's security model. .NET security goes further than Windows security. For example, the administrator can grant or revoke individual applications the right to access the registry or the file system, among many other things. This security model is independent of the specific version of Windows the application is running on.

.NET components and applications are also inherently safer than COM components and "old-style" Windows applications. For example, .NET components are automatically checked to ensure that their code hasn't been altered. You can also sign a .NET application with a digital signature and use a technology such as Authenticode to let users know who the author of the application is.

.NET as a Better COM

You can look at .NET as the next generation of COM if you like, in that the two programming models let you solve more or less the same problems and promote component-based development. Behind the scenes, however, they're completely different, and .NET is superior to COM in many respects.

First and foremost, a .NET application can consist of one or more assemblies. Each assembly is usually an individual EXE or DLL executable file. An assembly can also include other files, such as .html, .gif, or other nonexecutable files. Assemblies are the unit of versioning in the sense that all the files in an assembly have the same version number. The assembly is also the smallest unit of logical deployment because you never deploy a subset of the files that make up the assembly. Typically, an application uses several external assemblies, including those belonging to the .NET Framework itself.

.NET doesn't use the registry to store any information about assemblies (even though it still uses the registry to store information about the .NET Framework itself). In general, all the information related to an application and the components it uses are stored in configuration files held in the application's main directory. A configuration file uses XML syntax to store hierarchical data and therefore is more flexible than, say, .ini files. For example, an entry in this configuration file might contain the connection string to the main database used by the application so that the administrator can change it with an editor as simple as Notepad.

Let's see how .NET solves the component versioning problem, which has plagued COM-based applications for years. There are two kinds of .NET components: private and shared. Private components are stored in the application's main directory (or in one of its subdirectories) and aren't visible to other applications. So each application uses its private components, and distinct applications can use different versions of these components because they're stored in different directories. Shared components, on the other hand, are visible to all .NET applications and are typically stored in a central repository named global assembly cache (GAC), located under the C:\Windows\Assembly directory. Each component in the GAC is kept in a separate directory, and different versions of the shared component can coexist on a computer. Each application compiled against version X.Y of a given component continues to work correctly even if the user installs a newer (or older) version of the same component.

Versioning even extends to the .NET Framework itself. When a new version of the .NET Framework becomes available, you can install it on a computer without removing previous versions of the framework and applications using the previous versions will continue to work. As a matter of fact, the computer I use for development has both versions 1 and 1.1 of the .NET Framework installed.

.NET versioning is more flexible than COM versioning. In fact, a developer or a system administrator can use a configuration file to redirect a request for a given component to another version of the same component. So the component author can release a new version that fixes a few bugs or that's more efficient and thus indirectly improve the robustness and speed of all the applications that use that component without introducing version incompatibility problems.

.NET solves another tough problem: deployment. Because .NET applications can use private assemblies only if they're stored in the applications' own directory trees, you can install most .NET applications by using the so-called XCOPY deployment, that is, by copying all the files to a directory on the target system. The fact that you can use this simple installation method doesn't mean that real-world .NET applications don't need an installation procedure, however; you usually need to create shortcuts on the Start menu or let the end user select which portions of the applications will be installed. In addition, the installation routine might need to install shared components in the GAC. Even considering these ancillary tasks, however, installing a .NET application is much simpler than installing a similar COM application because fewer things can go wrong.

Unlike COM, the .NET Framework is designed around the concept of inheritance. All the objects in the .NET Framework form a hierarchy with a single root, the System.Object class, from which all the other classes derive. These classes provide functionality in almost any conceivable area, including the user interface, data access, Internet programming, XML processing, security, and cross-machine communication.

Most of the time, programming under .NET means extending one of these classes. For example, you can create a text box control that accepts only numbers by deriving a new class from the System.Windows.Forms.TextBox class and adding all the necessary code that rejects invalid entries. Classes that don't inherit from a specific .NET class implicitly inherit from System.Object and therefore benefit in other ways from being part of the .NET object hierarchy. Needless to say, this approach encourages code reuse.

All .NET Languages Are Born Equal

.NET moves most of the functionality from the language to the .NET Framework itself. For example, the .NET Framework includes classes for opening, reading, and writing text and binary files, so there is no point in having this functionality embedded in programming languages. Another example: a portion of the .NET Framework named Windows Forms offers classes that can create windows and controls. (You can think of this portion as the heir of forms in Visual Basic 6.) All .NET languages can use these classes, and therefore all languages have the same capabilities in creating applications with a rich user interface, without having to resort to low-level, advanced techniques such as subclassing.

Microsoft provides several languages with .NET, including Visual Basic .NET, C#, Managed C++, Visual J#, and JScript. Many C++ developers have switched or are expected to switch to C#, which is considered the best language for .NET applications. C# is actually a great language that takes the best ideas from other languages, such as C++ and Java. But the truth is that C# and Visual Basic .NET are roughly equivalent, and both of them let you tap the full power of the .NET Framework. The two languages have the same potential, so you are free to choose the one that makes you more productive. Execution speed is also equivalent for all practical purposes, because the C# and Visual Basic compilers generate more or less the same code.

If you've worked with previous editions of Visual Basic, my advice is that you should use Visual Basic .NET to explore the .NET Framework way of doing things, such as working with files, databases, the user interface, XML, HTTP, and so on, until you feel comfortable. Then you might want to have a look at C#—you'll be surprised by how easily you learn it. The C# language consists of only a handful of keywords, the majority of which have close counterparts in Visual Basic .NET. The real difficulty in learning C# directly from Visual Basic 6 is that you have to absorb complex concepts, such as inheritance and structured exception handling, so making a two-step transition is surely less traumatic.

Another interesting point to consider is that both the Visual Basic and C# compilers belong to the .NET Framework, not to the Visual Studio package. In theory, you can write and compile Visual Basic .NET applications using any editor—yes, including Notepad—and compile the applications using the vbc.exe compiler provided with the .NET Framework. As a matter of fact, some portions of the framework—the XML parser, for example—actually rely on the presence of the C# compiler to dynamically create and compile code on the fly, a technique that provides stunning performance.

Because all the objects you work with belong to the .NET object hierarchy—or extend objects in that hierarchy—you can easily manipulate such objects with any .NET language. This approach offers a degree of cross-language interoperability that's simply impossible using COM. For example, you can inherit a Visual Basic .NET class from a C# class, and you can define an interface with Visual Basic and write a C# class that implements it. .NET maintains a degree of compatibility with COM-based languages thanks to a portion of the .NET Framework known as COM Interoperability.

Web Forms, the Successor to Active Server Pages

ASP.NET is arguably the most important portion of the .NET Framework, or at least the main reason why all serious Internet developers should think about migrating to the new platform. ASP.NET is a dream come true for anyone who has ever built (or attempted to build) large-size applications using Active Server Pages (ASP) or any comparable server-side technology.

Broadly speaking, ASP.NET comprises two distinct but tightly related technologies: Web Forms and XML Web services. Web Forms are used for Internet applications with a user interface and are meant to replace ASP applications, although you can still run ASP and ASP.NET on the same computer. Web services are for Internet applications without a user interface and are discussed in the next section.

ASP.NET applications are written in full-featured, compiled languages such as Visual Basic .NET and C#, so ASP.NET code runs faster than the equivalent ASP script code. Even more important in my opinion is that you can now use early binding and strongly typed variables (which reduce the number of run-time errors) and have full access to components and functions in the Windows API. ASP.NET is available for Windows 2000, Windows XP, and Windows 2003 Server.

Unlike its predecessor, ASP.NET offers the gamut of debugging features, including breakpoints set inside the IDE and the ability to print tracing and profiling information about pages being browsed. Debugging an ASP.NET application isn't much different from debugging a standard Visual Basic application, and it might be even easier, thanks to the new trace facilities.

Another step forward from ASP is that ASP.NET truly permits and promotes separation between the user interface (that is, the HTML code) and the code that makes the application work (written in C#, Visual Basic, or any other .NET language). Thanks to the concept of code behind modules, you can split an ASP.NET page into two distinct files, one containing the HTML code and controls and the other containing the source code. The first time the page is requested by a browser, the ASP.NET infrastructure passes the source code file to the proper compiler and dynamically ties the compiled code with events produced by the user interface controls. You can still intermix UI code and application logic code in the same file if you prefer, and you can precompile the code-behind file if you don't want to distribute your source code.

Speaking of events, ASP.NET is based on the familiar event-driven programming model that millions of Visual Basic developers know so well. For example, when an ASP.NET page is loaded your code receives a Page_Load event, and so forth. This does not mean that you can easily move code from a traditional client-side application into a server-side ASP.NET application (this wasn't a goal of the ASP.NET initiative), but you don't have to learn yet another programming model for working with Web programs.

Because ASP.NET uses compiled code, you probably won't need to write components as frequently as you did under ASP. However, you might need to write a component to gather common functionality in a single place (to improve code reuse) or to take advantage of COM+ transactional features. An important new feature of ASP.NET is that you can overwrite a component even while an application is using it. This is possible thanks to a feature known as shadow copying. An ASP.NET application doesn't load the component from its original file; instead, it copies the file into a temporary directory and loads the component from there. The original file isn't locked, and you can overwrite it at will. All subsequent requests to the pages that use that component will use the new instance instead of the old one. If you consider that all the configuration values of an ASP.NET application are stored in an XML file in the application's main directory, you see that you can upgrade an ASP.NET application by simply copying the new files over the old ones, without having to stop and restart the IIS application.

ASP.NET supports a more flexible version of the Session object. Under ASP.NET, Session variables can be held on the machine that hosts IIS (as in traditional ASP), on another machine in the same network, or inside a SQL Server database. The latter two arrangements make it possible to access those variables from any machine on the LAN, so you can distribute an application over Web farms with little effort. Just as important, you can decide to create Session objects that don't rely on client-side cookie support, so ASP.NET applications can work even with browsers that have their cookie support disabled.

ASP.NET expands on traditional ASP in many other areas as well. For example, ASP.NET pages that don't vary frequently can be cached, a technique that delivers much better performance, especially if the page is built from data stored in a database. Another great feature of ASP.NET is its open architecture, which makes it possible to create custom handlers associated with files with a given extension. (Accomplishing the same in pre-.NET days required mastery of the Internet Services API [ISAPI] programming model and a lot of C++ wizardry.)

Web Services, the Programmable Internet

Rather than just delivering a better ASP, the .NET initiative is trying to shape how the Internet works in the future. A problem with today's Internet is that there's no integration among the millions of sites around the world because there isn't a standard way to query them and get the information they store. Microsoft and other software companies are now trying to remedy this situation by introducing Web services. A Web service is nothing but an application that listens to requests coming to a TCP socket and reacts to the commands each request contains. For example, a Web service that provides foreign currency exchange rates presumably will react to requests containing the name of the source currency, the amount of money, and the name of the target currency. The Web service will then do the conversion from source to target currency and return the result to the client. Both the requests and the result are sent and received using SOAP, and there will be no ambiguity about the meaning of each piece of information sent through the wire.

An important point about Web services is that they aren't based on any proprietary technology. Clients need only to format a SOAP request and send it through HTTP, and the server needs only to decode the request and send the result. All the protocols and technologies used by Web services—such as SOAP, XML, HTTP, and TCP/IP—are open standards. Microsoft doesn't own any of these standards, though it's working with other companies and with the W3C to shape them. As a matter of fact, you can implement a Web service on operating systems other than Microsoft Windows.

Because Web services are based on off-the-shelf technologies, you don't need .NET to implement them. In fact, you can create a Web service using Visual Basic 6 and the SOAP Toolkit. However, the more you learn about the .NET Framework, the more you realize that you can be much more productive creating and consuming Web services using .NET than you can using traditional technologies. For example, you can invoke a Web service asynchronously with just a handful of statements in Visual Basic .NET.

The Microsoft .NET Framework

By now you should be convinced that the .NET initiative isn't just marketing hype. It delivers real benefits to developers and users alike. It's time to have a closer look at the new architecture.

Requirements

As of this writing, you can run the .NET Framework only on a Windows computer. All Windows versions are supported, with the notable exception of Windows 95. You can use Windows 98, Windows 98 SE, Windows Me, Windows NT 4, Windows 2000, Windows XP, and Windows 2003, in all their Home, Professional, and Server variants.

You can download the .NET Framework from the Microsoft Web site and install it to make the systems discussed here .NET-compliant. However, since this book is about Visual Basic .NET, I assume that you'll install the .NET Framework from Visual Studio .NET CDs. The complete framework takes up about 20 MB on the hard disk, but because individual .NET applications reuse much of the code in the .NET class hierarchy, you can expect them to have a smaller footprint than their COM counterparts. For example, Visual Basic applications don't need any extra DLLs as they did until Visual Basic 6. Windows XP and Windows 2003 include the .NET Framework, so you don't have to install it to run your applications on these systems.

The framework contains the compilers and other command-line utilities to link modules together and install .NET components in the GAC. Technically speaking, no additional development tools are needed to develop .NET applications. In practice, however, you need Visual Studio .NET (or a similar environment from another vendor) to do serious programming. For example, Visual Studio contains the designers for creating Windows Forms and Web Forms applications visually and a tool for exploring the methods that a Web service exposes using a standard object browser.

.NET Architecture

The best way to understand how .NET works is to look at the many layers in the .NET Framework, as shown in Figure 1-1. Let me describe each individual layer, starting from the bottom.

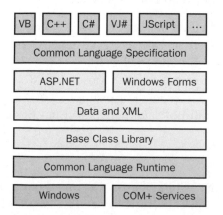

Figure 1-1   The layers in the .NET Framework

At the bottom of the hierarchy sits the Windows API. .NET offers an object-oriented view of the operating system's functions, but doesn't replace them, so you shouldn't forget that most calls into the .NET Framework are ultimately resolved as calls into one of the Windows kernel DLLs.

You might be surprised to find COM+ Services at this level of the .NET hierarchy. Microsoft believed that rewriting the COM+ kernel from scratch would have been too much for this initial release of .NET, so they decided to have the .NET Framework rely on Component Services. You can therefore create .NET components that take advantage of the transaction, synchronization, and security services offered by COM+, even though this approach adds overhead because execution must flow from .NET to COM (each time execution crosses this border). In most applications, this overhead is negligible, however. On the plus side, all the same concepts apply (even though the syntax used to achieve those services is different). This means .NET programmers can continue to write enterprise-level applications using the programming model they already know and leverage the same services they used under COM+.

The common language runtime is the first layer that belongs to the .NET Framework. This layer is responsible for .NET base services, such as memory management, garbage collection, structured exception handling, and multithreading. If .NET is ever to be ported to non-Windows architectures—as of this writing, a few projects are pursuing this goal—writing a version of the common language runtime for the new host must be the first step. The runtime is contained in the MSCorEE.dll file, and all .NET applications call a function in this DLL when they begin executing.

The Base Class Library (BCL) is the portion of the .NET Framework that defines all the basic data types, such as System.Object (the root of the .NET object hierarchy), numeric and date types, the String type, arrays, and collections. The BCL also contains classes for managing .NET core features, such as file I/O, threading, serialization, and security. The way types are implemented in the BCL follows the Common Type System (CTS) specifications. For example, these specifications dictate how a .NET type exposes fields, properties, methods, and events; it also defines how a type can inherit from another type and possibly override its members. Because all .NET languages recognize these specifications, they can exchange data, call into each other's classes, and even inherit from classes written in other languages. The BCL is contained in the MSCorLib.dll component.

The Data And XML layer contains the .NET classes that work with databases and with XML. Here you can see that support for XML is built right into the .NET Framework, rather than accessed through external components, as is the case with pre-.NET languages. In fact, XML can be considered the format that .NET uses to store virtually any kind of information. All the .NET configuration files are based on XML, and any object can be saved to XML with just a few statements. Of course, the .NET Framework comes with a powerful and fast XML parser.

The Data portion of this layer—what is commonly called ADO.NET—is the .NET counterpart of the ActiveX Data Objects (ADO) technology. In spite of their similar names, ADO and ADO.NET are very different. Whereas classic ADO covers virtually all the database techniques available—including server-side and client-side cursors, disconnected resultsets, and batch updates—ADO.NET focuses mainly on disconnected resultsets (called DataSets in ADO.NET terminology) and currently offers no support for server-side cursors. The DataSet object is much more powerful than the ADO Recordset object and can store data coming from multiple tables, in the same database or different databases. You can create relationships among different data tables, and you can import or export both the data and the metadata as XML.

The next two layers are ASP.NET and Windows Forms, which are located at the same level in the diagram. These portions of the framework contain all the classes that can generate the user interface—in a browser in the former case and using standard Win32 windows in the latter case. As I explained earlier, ASP.NET comprises both Web Forms and Web services. Even though these two portions appear at the same level in the diagram, and in spite of their similarities, these technologies are very different. Web Forms run on the server and produce HTML code that's rendered in a browser on the client (which can run on virtually any operating system), whereas Windows Forms run on the client (and this client must be a Windows machine). However, you can mix them in the same application, to some extent at least. For example, you can have a .NET application that queries a remote Web service through the Internet and displays its result using Windows Forms.

The .NET Framework class library consists of a collection of assemblies, each one comprising one or more DLLs. For example, ADO.NET is contained in the System.Data.dll assembly, and the XML portion of the framework is contained in the System.Xml.dll assembly. You can see all the assemblies that make up the .NET Framework class library by browsing the Assembly directory under the main Windows directory, as you can see in Figure 1-2.

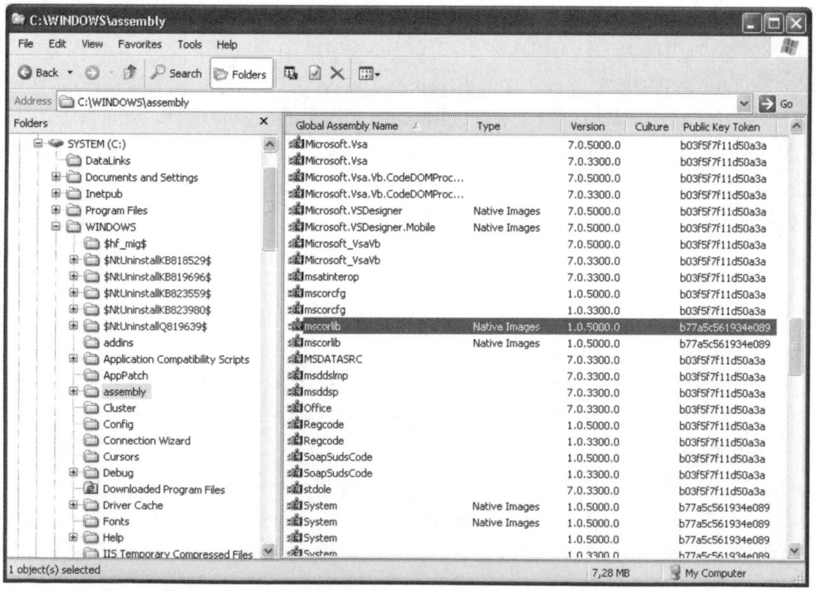

Figure 1-2   The Windows\Assembly directory of a computer on which both versions 1.0 and 1.1 of the .NET Framework have been installed

.NET Languages and Tools

The Common Language Specification (CLS) is a set of specifications that Microsoft has supplied to help compiler vendors. These specifications dictate the minimum group of features that a .NET language must have, such as support for signed integers of 16, 32, or 64 bits, zero-bound arrays, and structured exception handling. A compiler vendor is free to create a language that exceeds these specifications—for example, with unsigned integers or arrays whose lowest index is nonzero—but a well-designed application should never rely on these non-CLS-compliant features when communicating with other .NET components because the other component might not recognize them. Interestingly, Visual Basic .NET matches the CLS specifications almost perfectly, so you don't have to worry about using non-CLS-compliant features in your applications. C# developers can use a Visual Studio .NET option to ensure that only CLS-compliant features are exposed to the outside.

At the top of the diagram in Figure 1-1 are the Programming languages that comply with CLS. Microsoft offers the following languages: Visual Basic .NET, C#, Managed C++, Visual J#, and JScript. Many other languages have been released by other vendors or are under development, including Perl, COBOL, Smalltalk, Eiffel, Python, Pascal, and APL, plus a few that—to be honest—I've never heard of.

All the .NET languages produce managed code, which is code that runs under the control of the runtime. Managed code is quite different from the native code produced by traditional compilers, which is now referred to as unmanaged code. Of all the new language offerings from Microsoft, only C++ can produce both managed and unmanaged code, but even C++ developers should resort to unmanaged code only if strictly necessary—for example, for doing low-level operations or for performance reasons—because only managed code gets all the benefits of the .NET platform.

Because all the .NET languages—from Microsoft or other vendors—target the CLS and use the classes and the data types in the .NET Framework, they're more similar than languages used to be in the past. For example, all .NET languages handle errors using structured exception handlers and support 16-bit, 32-bit, and 64-bit signed integers. Another example: because the common language runtime and the CTS support only single inheritance (which means that a type can inherit only from one type), all languages support single inheritance; there's no room for multiple inheritance in the .NET world. The similarity among all languages has three important consequences.

First, the execution speed of all languages tends to be the same, as I have already explained, so your choice of language should be based on other factors, such as productivity. Second, language interoperability is ensured because all the languages use the same data types and the same way to report errors, so you can write different portions of an application with different languages without worrying about their integration.

Third, and maybe most important from the perspective of us developers: learning a new .NET language is surprisingly effortless if you've already mastered another .NET language. Developers who know both Visual Basic .NET and C# (and possibly other languages as well) will undoubtedly have more job opportunities, so .NET is also a great opportunity for all professionals and consultants. I believe that all Windows developers should start working with the new version of the language they know better—Visual Basic .NET if they've worked with Visual Basic 6, or C# if they've worked with C++ or Java—and then learn the other language as soon as they feel comfortable with the .NET way of doing things.

The Visual Basic .NET Compiler

Before we continue with our exploration of the .NET world, let's create our first Visual Basic program, compile it, and run it. In the process, you'll learn several interesting things about the .NET architecture. In this first example, I use Notepad to create a simple program and the command-line vbc.exe compiler to produce an executable. In most real cases, you'll use Visual Studio .NET and its integrated editor, but I don't want you to be distracted by that environment during this first experiment.

Launch Notepad (or any other text editor), and type the following code:

```
Module Module1
    Sub Main()
        Dim x As Double, res As Double
        x = 12.5
        res = Add(x, 46.5)
        System.Console.Write("The result is ")
        System.Console.WriteLine(res)
    End Sub

    Function Add(ByVal n1 As Double, ByVal n2 As Double) As Double
        Add = n1 + n2
    End Function
End Module
```

Even though the syntax is different from Visual Basic 6, it should be clear what this program does. The only new statements are the calls to the Write and WriteLine methods of the System.Console object, which send their argument to the console window. (The WriteLine method also appends a newline character.) Save this source file with the name Test.vb, next open a command window and move to the directory in which you saved the Test.vb file, and then run the VBC compiler and pass it the Test.vb file. The vbc.exe file is located in this directory:

C:\Windows\Microsoft.NET\Framework\vx.y.zzzz

where *Windows* is the main Windows directory and *x.y.zzzz* is the complete version number of the runtime in use. Version 1 of the .NET Framework has a complete version number 1.0.3705, whereas the .NET Framework version 1.1 corresponds to version number 1.1.4322. For example, on my system this is the command I have to type to run the Visual Basic 2003 compiler:

C:\Windows\Microsoft.NET\Framework\v1.1.4322\vbc Test.vb

If you don't want to type this long path to the VBC compiler, just open a command window by invoking the Visual Studio .NET Command Prompt command in the Visual Studio .NET Tools submenu under the main Visual Studio .NET menu that you reach from the Start button.

The preceding VBC command creates an executable file named Test.exe, which you can run from the command prompt. If everything goes well, you see the result in the console window and the prompt appears again:

```
The result is 59
```

Congratulations! You just created your first Visual Basic .NET program. More precisely, you created a console application, which can take its input from the keyboard and can output its results in the console window. Needless to say, you'll write few (if any) commercial programs as console applications. In fact, Visual Basic .NET can also deliver standard Windows EXE applications and DLL components. Creating an executable from multiple source files is also very simple because you simply need to pass all the filenames on the command line. (You can even use * and ? wildcards.)

```
vbc main.vb test.vb functions.vb
```

The name of the executable files is derived from the name of the first file passed on the command line (it would be main.exe in the preceding example), but you can select a different name using the /out option, as here:

```
vbc *.vb /out:myapp.exe
```

Unlike traditional compilers—but like all other .NET languages—the Visual Basic .NET compiler doesn't produce .obj files that you later assemble into an executable file by using a linker. The .NET Framework comes with a linker, the Assembly Linker (AL) utility, but you will rarely need it. One task for which you need this linker is to produce an assembly made up of modules authored with different programming languages. Read the .NET SDK documentation for more details about the VBC compiler.

The Intermediate Language Disassembler (ILDASM)

Unlike traditional programming languages, .NET compilers don't produce native code that can be directly fed to and executed by the CPU. Instead, they produce the so-called Microsoft Intermediate Language (MSIL or just IL) code, which is a sort of machine language for a virtual processor that doesn't correspond to any commercial CPU available today. While the IL code is lower level than most modern programming languages, it's higher level than pure Intel assembly language. IL is a stack-oriented language that doesn't directly address CPU registers and is aware of high-level concepts such as exceptions and object creation.

Looking at the IL code is quite simple because the .NET Framework gives you a tool named ILDASM (Intermediate Language Disassembler), which can display the IL code stored inside any executable produced by a .NET compiler. This utility can run both as a command-line program and as a standard Windows application with its own user interface. For now, let's use it as a command-line utility to disassemble the Test.exe file we created in the preceding section:

```
Ildasm Test.exe /Out=Test.il
```

(This command assumes that Ildasm.exe is on the system path.) This is the abridged content of the Test.il file produced by the disassembler:

```
.assembly extern mscorlib
{
  .publickeytoken = (B7 7A 5C 56 19 34 E0 89 )   // .z\V.4..
  .ver 1:0:5000:0
}
.assembly extern Microsoft.VisualBasic
{
  .publickeytoken = (B0 3F 5F 7F 11 D5 0A 3A )   // .?_....:
  .ver 7:0:5000:0
}
.assembly Test
{
  .hash algorithm 0x00008004
  .ver 0:0:0:0
}
.module Test.exe
// MVID: {04008867-1531-4A47-B05E-F4E1C9245472}
.imagebase 0x00400000
.subsystem 0x00000003
.file alignment 512
.corflags 0x00000001
// Image base: 0x03090000
.class private auto ansi sealed Module1
       extends [mscorlib]System.Object
{
  .custom instance void [Microsoft.VisualBasic]Microsoft.VisualBasic.Globals/
    StandardModuleAttribute::.ctor() = ( 01 00 00 00 )
  .method public static void  Main() cil managed
  {
    .entrypoint
    .custom instance void [mscorlib]System.STAThreadAttribute::.ctor()
     = ( 01 00 00 00 )
    // Code size       43 (0x2b)
    .maxstack  2
    .locals init (float64 V_0, float64 V_1)
    IL_0000:  ldc.r8     12.5
    IL_0009:  stloc.1
    IL_000a:  ldloc.1
    IL_000b:  ldc.r8     46.5
    IL_0014:  call       float64 Module1::Add(float64, float64)
    IL_0019:  stloc.0
    IL_001a:  ldstr      "The result is "
    IL_001f:  call       void [mscorlib]System.Console::Write(string)
    IL_0024:  ldloc.0
    IL_0025:  call       void [mscorlib]System.Console::WriteLine(float64)
    IL_002a:  ret
  } // end of method Module1::Main
```

```
.method public static float64  Add(float64 n1, float64 n2) cil managed
{
  // Code size       6 (0x6)
  .maxstack  2
  .locals init (float64 V_0)
  IL_0000:  ldarg.0
  IL_0001:  ldarg.1
  IL_0002:  add
  IL_0003:  stloc.0
  IL_0004:  ldloc.0
  IL_0005:  ret
} // end of method Module1::Add

} // end of class Module1
```

I won't comment on each line of this IL listing, but I want to draw your attention to a few important details. First, the .assembly extern statements declare to the external DLLs that this program is going to use mscorlib as the main .NET component, in which the main types are defined. Microsoft.VisualBasic is the component that provides support for most Visual Basic statements. These references include the assembly's version, and .NET will look for the correct version even if multiple versions of the same assembly are registered in the GAC. This feature ensures, for example, that .NET 1 and 1.1 applications can run on the same system.

Second, the IL sees floating-point numbers and strings as native types. The ldc.r8 statement loads a Double value onto the stack, and the ldstr statement loads a string onto the stack. This is another example of the higher-level nature of the IL when compared with native assembly code.

Finally, the .method public static void Main() cil managed statement marks the beginning of the IL code produced by the Sub Main procedure in the original Visual Basic code. IL has retained the name of this and the Add procedures, so these names are visible to whoever disassembles your code. In general, an IL disassembly is much more descriptive than the code that you get by running a traditional disassembler on a standard Windows executable. Calls to methods—both to internal methods such as Add and to external methods such as System.Console::Write—store the method name because the address of those methods is evaluated at run time. If you worry about your users or other programmers seeing the names of your classes, fields, and methods, you can run your assembly through an *obfuscator* utility, such as the one provided for free with Visual Studio .NET 2003, or a commercial tool such as Demeanor (*www.wiseowl.com*).

The Just-in-Time (JIT) Compiler

The first thing that all .NET executables do once launched is load the MSCorEE.dll file that's the actual .NET runtime and then call the _CorMainExe function that this DLL exposes. The code in _CorMainExe then looks into the metadata stored inside the executable file to retrieve the address of the application's entry point (most often, the Sub Main procedure). Next, the IL code in the entry point procedure is handed to the just-in-time (JIT) compiler, which is located in the .NET runtime, converted to native code, and then executed.

As the main procedure invokes other methods, the .NET runtime uses the JIT compiler to transform the IL code in those methods into native code and then executes the native code. This on-the-fly compilation is done only once per method in the application's lifetime because the native code is kept in memory and reused when that specific method is called again.

Even if there's an increase in overhead caused by the compilation of each method, most .NET applications run as fast as native code. Don't confuse the JIT compiler with traditional interpreters, such as those provided with early versions of Java. Additionally, the application is never compiled all at once, so the start-up time is usually negligible even for large applications. Only applications that make many method calls as soon as they run might suffer from a perceivable increase in overhead. (This is the case with large Windows Forms programs.)

An interesting consequence of the JIT compilation approach is that a .NET compiler doesn't need to adopt aggressive and time-consuming low-level optimization techniques—such as registry allocations—and can deliver an executable faster than a traditional compiler, also because no link step is needed. A faster compilation step means that you'll spend less time watching the monitor and waiting for the compiler to finish.

To be honest, however, Visual Basic developers have lost an important feature in the transition from Visual Basic 6 to .NET, which is interpreted p-code. You can't run or debug an application before you compile it to IL and then JIT-compile it to native code. This "innovation" makes Visual Basic more similar to other programming languages and is going to disappoint many long-time Visual Basic developers. On the plus side, debugging capabilities in Visual Studio .NET are much better than those in the Visual Basic 6 debugger, and you don't have to worry about minor differences between the p-code and native code.

Many developers are worried about the quality of the code produced by the JIT compiler and assume that it will run slower than the code produced by a traditional optimizing compiler. I was skeptical about the JIT compiler myself until I made some benchmark studies and examined the .NET internals more carefully—it's time to debunk a few popular beliefs.

Most optimization techniques adopted by traditional compilers are (or can be) still used by .NET compilers; for example, loop unrolling, constant folding, and common subexpression elimination. The IL code that the JIT compiler converts to native code has already been digested by the Visual Basic compiler or whatever .NET compiler you're using.

The JIT compiler has a deeper knowledge of the executing environment than a traditional compiler. For example, the JIT compiler can emit code for a specific CPU instead of generating code for a generic Intel x86 microprocessor, so it can take advantage of the Intel P4 or Itanium, AMD Athlon, and new processors as they are released. (Of course, the runtime has to be updated with a new version of the JIT compiler to leverage the new processors' features.) Because all applications are compiled when they run, even old applications benefit from the adoption of a new CPU—a benefit you don't enjoy with traditional compiled applications.

There are other runtime-only optimization techniques that traditional compilers can't use. For example, the JIT compiler can optimize method calls even across different components because it can control the entire execution environment. Another example: method calls in the COM world work through indirection and use function pointers in the vtable; methods must work this way because the compiler doesn't know where the target object is loaded at run time. On the contrary, a JIT compiler knows where the target object is in memory and can get rid of those indirections by directly calling the method with a single and faster CALL assembly opcode.

A JIT compiler can make its optimizations more effective by monitoring the main application's behavior. For example, the JIT compiler might decide to perform method inlining (an optimization technique that gets rid of method calls by moving the code from the called procedure into the caller routine) only for the routines that are called more frequently. The JIT compiler's current capabilities in flow-control analysis are minimal, but they will surely improve in forthcoming versions.

The Native Image Generator (NGEN)

So far, I've described the JIT compiler that you will use most frequently on Windows systems. You should be aware that the .NET Framework comes with a Native Image Generator (NGEN) utility that can compile an entire application at installation time instead of at run time. This approach improves the load time of a .NET application or component, so it's especially useful with shared class and function libraries. Not surprisingly, Microsoft uses this utility for some key portions of the framework itself, such as MSCorLib.dll. In Windows Explorer, such precompiled .NET Framework class library components are marked with the Native Image label, as you can see in Figure 1-2.

Before you decide to use NGEN to precompile all your applications, you should consider that this approach reduces start-up time for only a small number of applications, most notably those that make a lot of method calls when they start. In some cases, precompiling an application can worsen performance because NGEN has no knowledge about the run-time environment and can't use optimization techniques such as adaptive method inlining and cross-assembly optimization. Finally, remember that you can't use NGEN to convert IL to native code and run the executable on another system. As a result, you can't use this tool to make the reverse engineering of your .NET applications more difficult.

Working with Assemblies

The .NET Framework supports the creation of several kinds of applications: Windows console applications (also known as Character User Interface, or CUI, applications),

Windows Forms (standard Windows GUI applications), Windows Services (previously known as Windows NT Services), Components (reusable objects conceptually similar to COM components), Web Forms (server-side Web applications with user interface), and Web Services (server-side Web applications that can be queried programmatically).

Regardless of its type, a .NET application is deployed in the form of one assembly. You can also decide to split an application into multiple assemblies, for example, if you want to reuse code in other applications more easily. An assembly can include one or more executable files, each of which is individually known as a managed module. A managed module contains both IL code and metadata that describes both the types that the module exposes and the types that the module references.

Single-File and Multiple-File Assemblies

Most .NET compilers, including the Visual Basic and the C# compilers, transform one or more source files into a single-module assembly:

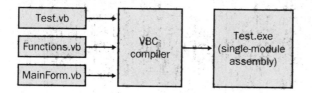

If the assembly contains managed modules written in different languages or if the assembly contains nonexecutable files, such as .html, .doc, .gif, or .jpg files, you must create a multifile assembly by using a tool named Assembly Linker (AL.EXE). In this case, you must use the /target:module option to inform the VBC compiler that it must output a managed module that will be later passed to the AL utility:

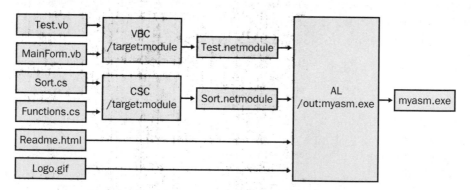

In the case depicted in the preceding diagram, the resulting assembly consists of five files: Myasm.exe, Test.netmodule, Sort.netmodule, Readme.html, and Logo.gif. When you assemble resource files, you can decide whether the resource file is included in the output file (using the / embed AL option) or just referenced by the assembly (using the /linkres AL option).

Neither Visual Studio .NET nor Visual Studio .NET 2003 can create multifile assemblies, so you're forced to use AL from the command line to link multiple modules in one assembly.

Metadata and the Manifest

The metadata included in each managed module completely describes each type defined in the module: name, public members, and the signature of each distinct method, down to the type of its private variables. Metadata also records information about every type that this module uses, including the name of the assembly that contains that type.

In short, you can think of metadata as a superset of type libraries used under COM, with an important difference: you can't separate IL from its metadata. (By comparison, you can create stand-alone type libraries.) While you can do COM programming without using a type library, you can't invoke code inside a .NET assembly if you can't access its metadata (and therefore the assembly file itself because the metadata is always stored inside the assembly's modules).

The most important use of metadata is in ensuring that methods and fields are accessed in a correct way; that is, you must pass the correct number of arguments of the right type and assign the return value to a variable of the proper type. When referencing a type in another assembly, the metadata makes certain that the correct version of the assembly is used. Remember that a given system can host multiple versions of the same assembly.

Another good thing about metadata is that it makes a managed module self-describing. By looking at metadata, BCL knows exactly what an assembly needs to run (such as a specific version of the .NET runtime), which external assemblies it references, and so on. No additional information is to be stored outside the assembly—for example, in the system registry—and you can install the assembly by making a simple XCOPY of its files in a directory on the hard disk. (As you already know, this simplified scenario doesn't account for shared assemblies, which also require registration in the GAC.)

More generally, the entire .NET architecture is based on metadata. For example, the .NET memory manager uses metadata to calculate how much memory must be allocated when a .NET object is created. Metadata is also used when your code is serializing the state of an object to a file or a database field and also when your code is remoting an object (which occurs when the runtime serializes an object and sends its state to another workstation, where a perfect copy of the object can be re-created). IntelliSense in Visual Studio also exploits metadata to list members of a given type, as does the Object Browser tool to display all the types contained in an assembly and their members. The action of reading metadata to retrieve information about types in an assembly is known as reflection.

The file you specify with the /out option of AL—or the only executable file that you have when you create single-file assemblies with the VBC compiler—contains the assembly's manifest. The manifest is a special metadata section that lists the names of all the files that make up the assembly and of all the types that the assembly exposes to the outside.

When a .NET application instantiates or uses a type from an assembly, the runtime loads the module that contains the manifest and determines which module contains the IL code for that specific type. If the requested type is in another module, the runtime loads it, compiles the IL code of the method being invoked (or the constructor method if the type is being instantiated), and finally runs it. Of course, execution is faster if the runtime doesn't need to load a different module. Therefore, you should arrange a multimodule assembly so that all the types used most frequently are defined in the module that contains the manifest.

Code Verification

Metadata and JIT compilation make it possible to achieve one of the most important features of the .NET platform: code security and verification. As you'll see in a moment, these features have far-reaching consequences.

Verification is the process through which the runtime checks that each method is called with the correct number and type of arguments, that all pointers point to the correct data type, and that in general the application doesn't read or modify memory that doesn't belong to it. For example, verification ensures that data and code aren't misused and that the application won't be stopped because of fatal errors caused by pointers that contain bogus values. An incorrect pointer is one of the most frequent causes of GPF errors in C/C++ applications (and even in Visual Basic 6 applications if you play low-level tricks with API functions).

Verification guarantees that .NET applications are inherently more robust than non-.NET ones, an important factor that will decrease the total cost of software production, debugging, and support. But verification has another important benefit: because the runtime can guarantee that applications won't read or modify memory they don't own, you can run multiple applications inside the same address space (that is, the same Win32 process).

As you might know already, Windows processes offer code isolation at the expense of memory and other resources. Windows NT and later versions have a good reputation for robustness because their processes are better isolated than, say, under Windows 95 or Windows 98, which in turn are much more robust than old 16-bit Windows 3.1, whose processes share the same address space. If each process is completely isolated, it can crash without affecting any other process or the operating system as a whole.

In spite of the process isolation provided by Windows, a clever programmer working in the unmanaged world can read and modify memory belonging to another application and can even write code that runs in the context of the other application (for example, by using a technique known as DLL injection). This security breach opens up the door to malicious pieces of code, such as viruses and Trojan horses.

By comparison, .NET applications enjoy far more robust isolation than traditional Windows programs. This is because there's absolutely no way for managed code to affect another program, no matter how hard it tries. A system administrator can install a managed application and be reasonably sure that it won't harm the system. (More follows on this topic in the next section.)

AppDomains

While traditional Windows applications can be isolated by being loaded in separate address spaces (and therefore in different processes), isolation under .NET doesn't rely on virtual memory features offered by the CPU. This means that multiple .NET applications can run inside the same Windows process without compromising their robustness.

Because application and process aren't synonyms in the .NET world, a new concept has been coined: Application Domain, or AppDomain. An AppDomain is a logical managed application that runs inside a physical Windows process. (See Figure 1-3.) A Windows process can host multiple AppDomains, which can be multiple copies of the same application or different applications. In general, you load multiple AppDomains in the same physical process only if they run related applications.

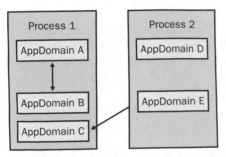

Figure 1-3   AppDomains are logical applications running in the same physical Windows process.

AppDomains have at least two major advantages. First, they use less memory and fewer resources than Windows processes, so they're launched and destroyed faster and they scale better. Second, communication between AppDomains hosted in the same process is much faster than between traditional Windows programs because the AppDomains share the same address space and can simply call into one another (after verifying the method signature and checking that the caller has the right to call the method). For example, communication between AppDomain A and AppDomain B in Figure 1-3 is much faster than communication between AppDomain C and AppDomain E.

AppDomains are especially convenient when you load multiple copies of an assembly in a single physical Windows process. In this case, the code for the application is JITcompiled and loaded only once—the first time the assembly is launched—so you save both start-up time and memory. (This optimization works only with assemblies marked as *domain neutral*.)

The .NET Framework Class Library

I've already explained that the .NET Framework class library is a collection of classes that managed applications use to access the operating system, the file system, databases, and any other resource. In this section, I'll briefly introduce the most interesting portions of the .NET class library.

To better organize the hundreds of classes in the library, the .NET Framework supports namespaces. Namespaces are similar to directories on disk: just as a directory can contain files and other directories, a namespace can contain classes and other (nested) namespaces. For example, all the classes that have to do with database programming are grouped in the System.Data namespace. The System namespace is arguably the most important namespace because all the basic types are defined there, including numeric, data, and string types.

A namespace can be split into more DLLs; in fact, the logical organization of the types in an assembly is distinct from its physical organization. For example, you can put types that are used less frequently into a separate DLL so that they aren't loaded if they aren't used.

You're already familiar with the goal of a few namespaces—for example, System.Windows.Forms (for creating client-side Win32 applications), System.Web (for creating ASP.NET applications with a user interface), and System.Web.Services (for creating Web services). A glance at the other namespaces offers a quick way to learn about other important features of the framework.

ADO.NET

System.Data and its nested namespaces include types for working with databases. The classes in these namespaces make up the portion of the .NET Framework known as ADO.NET. Compared with "classic" ADO, ADO.NET is more focused on client-side data processing and doesn't offer support for server-side cursors such as keysets and dynamic cursors, at least not in its first version.

There are a few slightly different flavors of ADO.NET, depending on whether you're connecting to a SQL Server database (version 7 or 2000), an Oracle database, an OLE DB source, or an ODBC source. Unlike ADO, which attempts to promote independence from a specific database, ADO.NET recognizes that most developers work with a single database server and want to take advantage of all its features. ADO.NET is further subdivided into namespaces, each one corresponding to a given database. For example, even if you don't plan to take advantage of specific SQL Server features, you should use classes in the System.Data.SqlClient namespace when working with SQL Server because they interact with the database engine using more efficient communication channels than System.Data.OleDb or System.Data.Odbc classes. The System.Data.OleDb classes use the standard OLE DB Provider for SQL Server, whereas the System.Data.Odbc classes use the ODBC driver for SQL Server. Therefore, classes in these two namespaces have to traverse more software layers to get to the data.

GDI+

Windows programmers have used Graphics Device Interface (GDI) functions for years to create graphic shapes, bitmaps, metafiles, color palettes, and so on. Types in the System.Drawing namespace give you a way to access these functions using an object-oriented programming model, which simplifies graphic programming enormously and minimizes the risk of resource leaking (a serious problem with all graphic-intensive applications).

Typically, you'll use GDI+ classes in Windows Forms, but nothing prevents you from working with them in server-side ASP.NET applications. For example, you might create an ASP.NET application that creates a chart on the server and sends it to the client in an HTML page, or a Web service application that performs sophisticated graphic processing on bitmaps submitted in input.

Platform Invoke and COM Interoperability

Even if Microsoft is actively helping developers jump on the .NET bandwagon, they don't expect that the thousands of applications written in recent years should be tossed aside. More realistically, large applications will be ported to .NET gradually, for example, as developers write new components that interact with the existing code.

Another problem that developers have to face is that all the devices from third-party hardware manufacturers are provided as traditional or COM DLLs, so there must be a way to access them from managed code. This holds true also for functions in Windows DLLs that haven't yet been encapsulated in .NET classes.

The .NET Framework gives you a couple of technologies that help you write code that interacts with the so-called legacy applications, written as traditional DLL or COM components. The portion of the runtime known as Platform Invoke or *PInvoke* is in charge of calling functions embedded in traditional DLLs, including Windows DLLs. The portion of the runtime known as COM Interoperability is in charge of exchanging data with COM components. COM Interoperability works in both directions: you can consume a COM component from a .NET application, but you can also expose a .NET component to a COM application, for example, an application authored with Visual Basic 6.

.NET Remoting

In a nutshell, remoting is the managed code counterpart of Distributed COM (DCOM); it lets you access objects located on another machine. More precisely, remoting lets you access and code against objects located in a different AppDomain—whether the other AppDomain is running on the same or another computer.

.NET doesn't use COM; communication with the other process or machine occurs through channels of a different nature, such as TCP or HTTP channels. The classes that help you manage remoting are located in the System.Runtime.Remoting namespace or in one of its nested namespaces.

Other Namespaces

While the bulk of managed classes are in the System namespace or one of the namespaces nested inside System, you might find yourself working with other classes that don't belong to this namespace.

Classes in the Microsoft.Win32 namespace are specific to the Windows platform and will never be ported to other operating systems. These classes encapsulate Windows-specific objects, such as the registry or system events.

The Microsoft.VisualBasic namespace gathers classes that help you write Visual Basic .NET code with a syntax as close to Visual Basic 6 as possible. In most cases, classes in this namespace duplicate functionality offered by other classes in the .NET Framework, so you have a choice. You can use them to retain the good old Visual Basic flavor, or you can opt for the more generic classes in the System namespace. The former approach minimizes time spent in producing real-world .NET applications, while the latter one is preferable if you plan to learn other .NET languages, such as C#. In this book I'll use both approaches, starting with the classes in the Microsoft.VisualBasic namespace and then exploring in depth the more generic .NET classes, which are often more powerful and versatile.

I know it has been a long chapter—and you have read a lot of new concepts and seen very little code. Believe me, I needed this chapter to introduce the most important features of .NET. You'll see plenty of code in the following chapters, starting with the next chapter, in which you'll learn about new syntax and data types in Visual Basic .NET.

2 Modules and Variables

In my opinion, the best way to approach Visual Basic .NET is to consider it a brand-new language whose syntax is only vaguely compatible with versions 1 through 6. On the other hand, it's unmistakably Visual Basic. Even novice Visual Basic programmers will find themselves comfortable with Visual Basic .NET, although they might need some time to get familiar with the new language features and the many syntax changes. If you're a longtime Visual Basic developer, keep in mind that these changes are for the good and are intended to make Visual Basic more similar to other .NET programming languages. A consequence of this approach is that switching to another .NET language, such as C#, will be relatively simple because you don't have to significantly change your practices.

Modules and Namespaces

The first important new characteristic of all Visual Basic .NET files is that they have the same .vb extension. This detail might be disorienting at first if you have a lot of experience with Visual Basic 6 and earlier versions, in which you could count at least six different file extensions, such as .frm for forms, .bas for standard modules, and .cls for class modules. The reason Visual Basic .NET uses just one file extension for all its files is that there aren't many differences between, say, a module file and a class file. More precisely, the need for a module file and class file has disappeared under Visual Basic .NET because now a file can contain multiple modules and multiple classes, and even a combination of the two.

A file can also contain a form, but remember that Visual Basic .NET forms are nothing but classes that inherit from the System.Windows.Forms.Form class defined in the .NET Framework. From the developer's perspective, forms are classes with which a designer has been associated. A designer is just a tool that lets you visually design the user interface of a form (or a UserControl)—for example, by dropping controls from the Toolbox and modifying their properties at design time from within the Properties window. Visual Basic 6 and earlier versions offer designers for forms with an important difference: form and control properties are saved in the .frm file but are invisible in the code window. By comparison, all the Visual Basic .NET designers produce code that can be browsed in the code window; in fact, you might theoretically define the appearance of a form and its control without even using the designer.

The developer decides how modules, classes, and forms (and other types of components, such as UserControls) are distributed among the files in the current project. For example, you can use a file for a form and all the classes the form uses, which can be a good solution, especially if no other form uses those classes. Similarly, you can gather all the (nonevent) procedures that a form uses in a module and include both the form and the module in the same file.

Finally, a single file can even include two or more forms—or other classes with an associated designer. In practice, however, you rarely want to organize your forms that way because the Visual Studio .NET integrated development environment (IDE) can associate the designer with only one class in a given file, which means that you can visually edit only one of the forms in the file. All the other forms can be edited by manually writing code, but you forgo one of the most productive features of the environment.

Modules

The module block is delimited by the Module and End Module keywords and can contain any number of variables, subs, and functions. Here's an example of a module named MathFunctions that contains a constant that's visible to the entire project, a variable that's visible only to the code inside the block, and a Public function:

```
Module MathFunctions
    ' A public constant
    Public Const DoublePI As Double = 6.28318530717958
    ' A private array
    Private factValues(169) As Double

    ' Return the factorial of a number in the range 0-169.
    Public Function Factorial(ByVal n As Integer) As Double
        ' Evaluate all possible values in advance during the first call.
        If factValues(0) = 0 Then
            Dim i As Integer
            factValues (0) = 1
            For i = 1 To 169
                factValues(i) = factValues(i - 1) * CDbl(i)
            Next
        End If

        ' Check the argument.
        If n >= 0 And n <= 169 Then
            ' Return the value in the array if argument is in range.
            Factorial = factValues(n)
        Else
            ' Raise an error otherwise.
            Err.Raise(6, , "Overflow")
        End If
    End Function
End Module
```

The code in the Factorial function checks whether factValues(0) is 0, in which case it fills the factValues array with all the possible factorial values for numbers in the range 0 through 169. (The Factorial function won't work for negative numbers, and the factorial for numbers higher or equal to 170 can't be stored in a Double variable.)

Using the Public keyword allows you to access both the DoublePI constant and the Factorial function from elsewhere in the project, like this:

```
Circumference = radius * DoublePI
```

The Sub New Procedure

As you see, Module…End Module blocks are similar to modules in previous Visual Basic versions in that they work as containers for procedures and variables. They have additional features, however, such as the New constructor method. If a module contains a Sub New procedure, the runtime calls this procedure before running any code inside the module itself. You can take advantage of this detail to simplify (and slightly optimize) the code in the Factorial function by moving the initialization code for the factValues array to inside the Sub New procedure:

```
Module MathFunctions
    ' A public constant
    Public Const DoublePI As Double = 6.28318530717958
    ' A private array
    Private factValues(169) As Double

    Sub New()
        ' Evaluate all possible values in advance.
        Dim i As Integer
        factValues(0) = 1
        For i = 1 To 169
            factValues(i) = factValues(i - 1) * CDbl(i)
        Next
    End Sub

    ' Return the factorial of a number in the range 0-169.
    Function Factorial(ByVal n As Integer) As Double
        If n >= 0 And n <= 169 Then
            ' Return the value in the array if argument is in range.
            Factorial = factValues(n)
        Else
            ' Raise an error otherwise.
            Err.Raise(6, , "Overflow")
        End If
    End Function
End Module
```

An important detail: the runtime invokes the Sub New procedure the very first time a variable or a procedure in the module is referenced by the running project. The Sub New procedure doesn't run when a constant defined in the module is accessed.

The Sub Main Procedure

As with previous Visual Basic versions, you can decide whether your application starts with a given visible object (typically a form) or by executing a Sub Main procedure defined in a module. A problem that occurs with previous language versions is that only one module in your application can contain a Sub Main procedure because otherwise an ambiguity might result—that is, the Visual Basic compiler will be unable to decide which Sub Main procedure is the entry point for the program. With Visual Basic .NET, you can select which module contains the Sub Main procedure that runs when your program starts from inside the project Property Pages dialog box, which you bring up with the Properties command on the Project menu or by selecting the project name in the Solution Explorer window and then clicking the Properties button near the top border of the window. (See Figure 2-1.) If you select the generic Sub Main entry in the list, however, you get a compilation error if two or more modules (or no module at all) contain a Sub Main procedure. Similarly, you get a compilation error if you specify the name of a module that doesn't contain a Sub Main procedure.

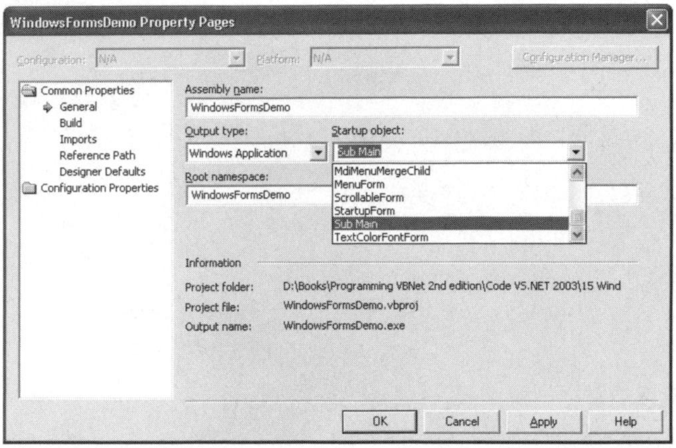

Figure 2-1 The project Property Pages dialog box

If you're writing a Windows Forms application, you don't strictly need a Sub Main because you can designate the start up form for the program, unless you want to execute a block of code before displaying the main form. In this case, you must invoke the Run method of the System.Windows.Forms.Application object as in the following code snippet:

```
Module MainModule
    Sub Main()
        ' Call a procedure that does the initialization (not shown here).
        InitializeAllVariables()
        ' Initialize the form library and display the form.
        System.Windows.Forms.Application.Run(New Form1)
    End Sub
End Module
```

In a difference from previous versions of the language, the Sub Main procedure can take arguments and even return a value. To take advantage of this feature, which is especially useful when you're writing utilities meant to be launched from the command prompt, you must declare a Sub Main procedure that takes an array of strings as an argument:

```
' A simple utility that displays the sum of
' numbers passed on the command line
Sub Main(ByVal args() As String)
    Dim res As Double, i As Integer
    For i = 0 To UBound(args)
        res = res + CDbl(args(i))
    Next
    Console.WriteLine(res)
End Sub
```

You can debug an application that takes command-line arguments from inside Visual Studio .NET, by entering the command line in the Debugging page of the project Property Pages dialog box, which you display by clicking Properties on the Project menu. Notice that a sequence of characters enclosed within double quotes is correctly considered a single argument on the command line.

Utilities that are designed to run from inside a batch file often return an error code, which the batch file can test by means of an IF ERRORLEVEL statement. In this case, you just need to transform the procedure into a Function that returns an Integer, as in

```
' A simple utility that displays the sum of numbers passed on the
' command line, and returns ERRORLEVEL=1 if any error
Function Main(ByVal args() As String) As Integer
    On Error Goto ParseError
    Dim res As Double, i As Integer
    For i = 0 To UBound(args)
        res = res + CDbl(args(i))
    Next
    Console.WriteLine(res)
    Return 0
ParseError:
    Console.WriteLine("One or more arguments are not valid numbers")
    Return 1
End Sub
```

Notice the use of the new Return keyword to return a value from a function and exit the function itself at the same time.

Classes

I'll talk about Class modules in detail in Chapter 4, so here I'll simply outline a few basic syntactical guidelines that you need for understanding other portions of this chapter.

A Visual Basic .NET class is defined by the code inside a Class...End Class block. A class can contain Private and Public variables (or fields, in the .NET terminology) and procedures. The following code defines a simple Person class that exposes one constant, two fields, and one method:

```
Public Class Person
    Public Const Title As String = "Mr. "
```

```
        Public FirstName As String
        Public LastName As String

        Function CompleteName() As String
            CompleteName = FirstName & " " & LastName
        End Function
End Class
```

Naming guidelines in the .NET documentation suggest that you use Pascal case in class names—for example, PartTimeEmployee—and that you *not* use a C character as a prefix in class names.

Using the Person class elsewhere in the application is straightforward:

```
Dim aPerson As New Person()
aPerson.FirstName = "Joe"
aPerson.LastName = "Doe"
Console.WriteLine(aPerson.Title & aPerson.CompleteName)   ' => Mr. Joe Doe
```

A class can expose public constants of any type, such as the Title string constant in the preceding code. This capacity makes Visual Basic .NET classes more flexible than classes in previous language versions, which can contain only private constants.

The most anticipated innovation in classes is the Visual Basic .NET support for class inheritance. All you need to inherit a new class from Person is an Inherits statement immediately after the Class statement:

```
Class Employee
    Inherits Person

    Public BirthDate As Date                ' A new field

    Function ReverseName() As String        ' A new method
        ReverseName = LastName & ", " & FirstName
    End Function
End Class
```

This code demonstrates that the new class inherits all the properties in the base class and also shows how you can make your code less verbose using the With block, as you do in Visual Basic 6:

```
Dim anEmployee As New Employee()
With anEmployee
    .FirstName = "Robert"
    .LastName = "Smith"
    ' Use the new (noninherited) members.
    .BirthDate = #2/5/1960#
    Console.WriteLine(.ReverseName)          ' => Smith, Robert
End With
```

I'll describe inheritance in depth in Chapter 5, even though I make use of inheritance before that chapter. Inheritance is so central to the .NET architecture that it's impossible to explain several key concepts without mentioning it.

Forms

I'll cover Windows Forms in detail in Chapter 15. In this section, I'll just acquaint you with what a Windows Form is. Under .NET, a form is simply a class that inherits from the System.Windows.Forms.Form class in the .NET Framework. When you create a form inside the Visual Studio .NET environment, the following code is generated:

```
Public Class Form1
    Inherits System.Windows.Forms.Form

#Region " Windows Form Designer generated code "
    Public Sub New()
        MyBase.New()
        'This call is required by the Windows Form Designer.
        InitializeComponent()
        'Add any initialization after the InitializeComponent() call.
    End Sub

    'Form overrides dispose to clean up the component list.
    Protected Overloads Overrides Sub Dispose(ByVal disposing As Boolean)
        If disposing Then
            If Not (components Is Nothing) Then
                components.Dispose()
            End If
        End If
        MyBase.Dispose(disposing)
    End Sub

    'Required by the Windows Form Designer
    Private components As System.ComponentModel.Container

    'NOTE: The following procedure is required by the Windows Form Designer.
    'It can be modified using the Windows Form Designer.
    'Do not modify it using the code editor.
    <System.Diagnostics.DebuggerStepThrough()> _
    Private Sub InitializeComponent()
        '
        'Form1
        '
        Me.AutoScaleBaseSize = New System.Drawing.Size(5, 13)
        Me.ClientSize = New System.Drawing.Size(292, 273)
        Me.Name = "Form1"
        Me.Text = "Form1"
    End Sub
#End Region

End Class
```

The Inherits keyword tells you that this Form1 class inherits from System.Windows.Forms.Form and therefore can be considered a Windows Form. As the comments in the code clearly indicate, the code inside the InitializeComponents procedure is under the direct control of the form designer, and you shouldn't modify it directly in the code editor. Better yet, you should leave the #Region block in a collapsed state so that you don't modify its contents accidentally. (Regions are a Visual Studio .NET feature that lets you expand and collapse selected blocks of code.)

Namespaces

Modules and classes live in namespaces. The thousands of classes defined in the .NET Framework are grouped in namespaces—for instance, the System namespace that gathers the basic type classes, such as Integer, String, and Array.

Namespace Blocks

All the classes and modules in your Visual Basic .NET project belong to the default namespace defined in the Root Namespace field in the project Property Pages dialog box (see Figure 2-1). However, you can create explicit Namespace...End Namespace blocks anywhere in your source files. For example, you can define the HumanBeings namespace as a container for the Person class defined previously:

```
Namespace HumanBeings
    Public Class Person
        ⋮
    End Class
End Namespace
```

If a piece of code references a class or procedure in another namespace, it must include the complete namespace of the referenced element, as you see here:

```
' Use the Person class from another namespace.
Dim p As New HumanBeings.Person
p.FirstName = "Joe"
```

You can't define variable declarations or procedures directly inside a Namespace block. For example, the following code snippet won't compile:

```
Namespace MyNamespace
    Function MyFunction()
        ⋮
    End Function
End Namespace
```

A Namespace block—defined either in code or on the General page of the project Property Pages dialog box—can contain only five types of blocks: Module, Class, Structure, Interface, and Enum. I've already shown you the Module and Class blocks. Enum blocks are described in the "Constants and Enums" section later in this chapter and in more depth in Chapter 7. I'll talk about Structure blocks at the end of this chapter. I cover Interface blocks in Chapter 6.

Interestingly, you can have multiple Namespace blocks with the same name in a project, in the same or in a different source file. This feature lets you keep the logical organization of your source code entities completely distinct from the physical structure. For example, you can have a file that contains multiple namespaces, or you can have all the elements of a namespace scattered in different source files. In fact, all the source files in your project belong to the root namespace defined in the project Property Pages dialog box.

Nested Namespaces

Namespaces can be nested. The System.Collections namespace, for example, contains several collectionlike classes, and the System.IO namespace includes classes that let you read from and write to files. There is no theoretical limit to nesting namespaces, and namespaces nested at three or more levels are quite common in the .NET Framework, so you might see, for example, System.Xml.Schema or System.Windows.Forms.ComponentModule.Com2Interop.

You can create nested namespaces in your Visual Basic .NET projects simply by nesting Namespace…End Namespace blocks. For example, the following code defines the Animals.Mammals.Dog, Animals.Mammals.Cat, and Animals.Reptiles.Lizard classes:

```
Namespace Animals
    Namespace Mammals
        Class Dog
            ⋮
        End Class

        Class Cat
            ⋮
        End Class
    End Namespace

    Namespace Reptiles
        Class Lizard
            ⋮
        End Class
    End Namespace
End Namespace
```

The scope rules for referencing classes and functions in other namespaces can be easily extended to nested namespaces. For example, the code inside the Dog class can directly reference the Cat class, but it needs to go through the Reptiles namespace to reach the Lizard class:

```
Class Dog
    Dim aCat As New Cat()
    Dim aLizard As New Reptiles.Lizard()
    ⋮
End Class
```

The Imports Statement

When working with nested namespaces, you can make your code remarkably less verbose by using the Imports statement. In practice, each Imports statement tells the compiler that the code in the source file can access all the classes, procedures, and structures defined in a given namespace, without your having to specify the name of the namespace itself. For example, consider the following Imports statements:

```
Imports System.Drawing
Imports System.Windows.Forms
Imports System.ComponentModel
```

These three Imports statements let you use more concise code to refer to elements in those namespaces:

```
Dim bmp As Bitmap        ' Same as System.Drawing.Bitmap
Dim ctrl As Control      ' Same as System.Windows.Forms.Control
Dim comp As Component     ' Same as System.ComponentModel.Component
```

You can save some typing even if you don't have an Imports statement that matches exactly the namespace of the element you want to reference. For example, the following Imports statement for the System namespace lets you make most of your external references more concise because many important objects are in the System namespace or in a namespace nested in System:

```
Imports System
⋮
Dim bmp As Drawing.Bitmap        ' same as System.Drawing.Bitmap
```

You can run into problems if you have distinct Imports statements referring to namespaces that contain classes with the same name. For example, say that both the Animals.Mammals namespace and the Computers.Accessories namespace expose a class named Mouse. In this situation, the following code won't compile because the Mouse reference is ambiguous:

```
' *** This code doesn't compile.
Imports Animals.Mammals
Imports Computers.Accessories
⋮
Sub TestImports
    Dim m As Mouse
    ⋮
End Sub
```

Even in this case, you can use the Imports statement to reduce your labor by specifying an alias for one of the conflicting namespaces:

```
Imports Animals.Mammals
Imports Acc = Computers.Accessories
⋮
Sub TestImports
    Dim m As Mouse      ' Same as Animals.Mammals.Mouse
    Dim m2 As Acc.Mouse ' Same as Computers.Accessories.Mouse
    ⋮
End Sub
```

Notice that Imports statements must always include the *complete* namespace you're importing. If you import a namespace defined somewhere in the current project, remember to account for the root namespace.

You can use an Imports statement only if the current application has a reference to the target namespace and so permits the namespace to appear in the Object Browser. New Visual Basic .NET projects have a reference to the most important classes in the Framework, but not all. If the namespace you're interested in isn't listed in the Solution Explorer, you must add a reference to it by right-clicking References in the Solution Explorer and clicking Add Reference on the shortcut menu. (See Figure 2-2.) Or you can use the Add Reference command on the Project menu. The Add Reference dialog box (Figure 2-3) lists all the .NET components as well as all the Component Object Model (COM) components registered in the system.

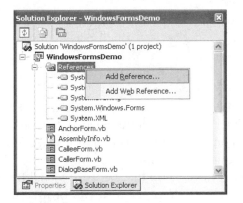

Figure 2-2   The References subtree of the Solution Explorer

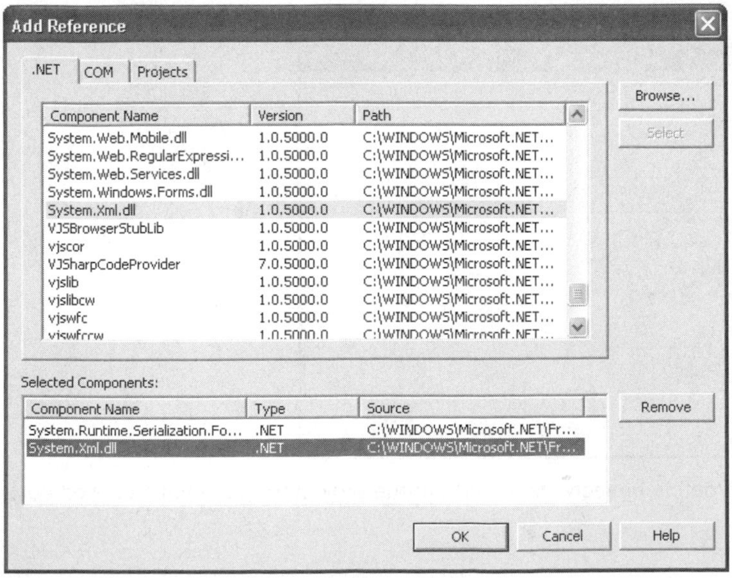

Figure 2-3   The Add Reference dialog box

Visual Basic lets you specify the name of a class in an Imports statement, a feature that lets you access the static members of a class without prefixing them with the class name. Consider this class, defined in the ModulesDemo root namespace:

```
Class NumericConstants
    Public Const Zero As Integer = 0
    Public Const One As Integer = 1
End Class
```

Here's how your application can access the two constants as if they were globally defined:

```
' This statement imports a class, not a namespace.
Imports ModulesDemo.NumericConstants

Module MainModule
    Sub Main()
        Dim value As Integer = One       ' Assigns 1.
    End Sub
End Module
```

Projectwide Imports

Most Visual Basic .NET projects rely heavily on a few namespaces in the .NET Framework, such as the System namespace, which contains all the basic data types, and the Microsoft.VisualBasic namespace, which contains all the Visual Basic statements, functions, and constants. Repeatedly importing these namespaces into all the files of a project is a nuisance. Fortunately, you don't have to do that because Visual Basic .NET applications can define a number of projectwide imports. You can browse the list of predefined imports, as well as add your own, in the project Property Pages dialog box. (See Figure 2-4.)

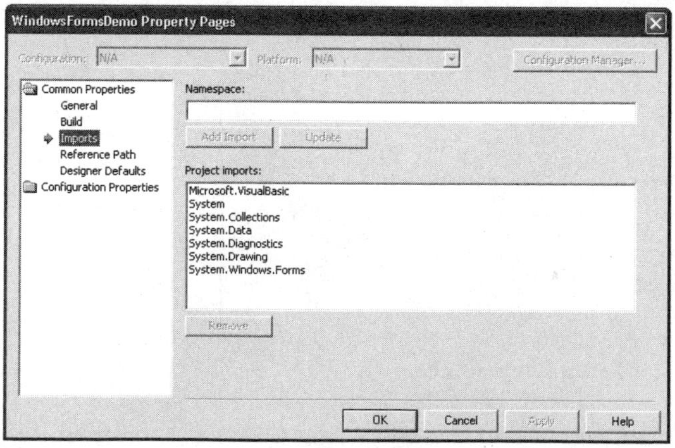

Figure 2-4   You can define projectwide imports in the project Property Pages dialog box.

Variables

Visual Basic .NET programs declare and use their variables in ways that are similar to previous language versions. Under the surface, however, there are many important differences, and you need to be aware of all of them to fully exploit the potential of .NET and not be trapped in subtle conversion issues when you're porting your code from Visual Basic 6.

Declarations

You can declare a variable using the Dim, Private, Public, or Static keyword. The scope rules are simple and are similar to Visual Basic 6 scope rules:

- You use Dim inside a procedure to declare a local (dynamic) variable, which is visible only inside that procedure.

- You use Dim or Private outside procedure blocks—but inside a Class or Module block—to create variables that can be accessed from anywhere inside that class or module but not from elsewhere in the project. (A Dim inside a Structure has a Public scope, however.)

- You use Public inside a Module block to create global variables—that is, variables that exist for the entire program's lifetime and that can be accessed from anywhere in the current project.

- You use Public inside a Class block to create a public field for that class.

- You use the Static keyword to declare static variables inside a procedure. (Note that you can't use the Static keyword in a procedure declaration to make all the variables in the procedure Static as you can in Visual Basic 6.)

The following piece of code demonstrates the five types of variables:

```
Module MyModule
    ' This global variable is visible to the entire application.
    Public myGlobalVar As String
    ' These variables are visible only inside the current module.
    Private myModuleVar As String
    Dim myModuleVar2 As String

    Sub MyProcedure()
        ' This private variable is visible only inside this procedure.
        Dim myPrivateVar As String
        ' This static variable maintains its value between
        ' consecutive calls to this procedure.
        Static counter As Integer
        ⋮
    End Sub
End Module
```

Naming Guidelines

The .NET documentation comes with a set of clear rules about naming procedures, variables, arguments, and other programming entities. These are just guidelines, so you may adhere to them or ignore them. Here's a brief summary:

- Don't use so-called Hungarian notation for variables and parameters. Visual Studio .NET lets you browse the declaration of a variable by simply moving the mouse cursor over it, so you don't need a prefix to make the variable's type explicit, as in lngValue.

- Parameters are lowercase or camelCase—for example, firstName or currentValue.

- Private variables should be camelCase, whereas public fields in classes that appear as properties to clients should be Pascal case.

Personally, I like these guidelines because they are similar to those I've come to use in recent years, and I adopted them for the code samples in this book. For example, I have never been fond of Hungarian notation, which I think makes your code *less* readable than usual. (Incidentally, my dislike for prefixes in variable names allowed me to move my Visual Basic 6 code to .NET without having to change prefixes for Integer, Long, and Variant variables.) I use Hungarian notation sparingly in this book, however, when I want to draw your attention to the type of a variable.

The Option Explicit and Option Compare Statements

Visual Basic .NET supports the Option Explicit statement, but its syntax is different from that in previous language versions because it can be followed by an On or Off qualifier:

```
' Force explicit declaration of all the variables in the module.
Option Explicit On
Option Explicit        ' The On clause can be omitted.

' Make variable declarations optional in the current module.
Option Explicit Off
```

Visual Basic .NET continues to support the Option Compare statement, whose syntax hasn't changed from previous language versions:

```
' Make string comparisons in the module work in a case-sensitive way.
Option Compare Binary

' Make string comparisons in the module work in a case-insensitive way.
Option Compare Text
```

In a difference from Visual Basic 6, you can select the default setting in the project Property Pages dialog box for all the modules of the project that don't contain an Option Explicit or Option Compare statement. (See Figure 2-5.)

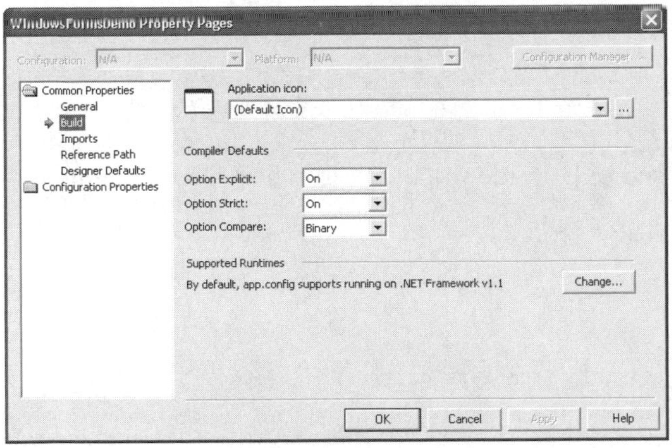

Figure 2-5   Projectwide settings for Option Explicit, Option Strict, and Option Compare

Multiple Declarations

As in previous language versions, you can declare multiple variables in the same Dim, Private, or Public statement. However, the syntax is different because you can use one single As clause for multiple variables of the same type:

```
' Declare three Long variables.
Dim x, y, z As Long
```

The semantics are different from previous Visual Basic versions as well in that all the variables in the statement are of the same type (Long, in the preceding code snippet). By comparison, under Visual Basic 6 the same statement declares one Long variable and two Variant variables (or whatever was the default type established by a Defxxx statement). This behavior will disorient many developers, but it makes Visual Basic resemble other languages, such as C# and C++. As in Visual Basic 6, you can have multiple As clauses in the same statement:

```
' Declare three variables of different types.
Dim i As Long, k As Integer, s As String
```

Visual Basic .NET doesn't support Defxxx statements—that is, DefInt A-Z—which is good news. Those statements were left over from the GW-Basic days about 20 years ago. Among their many unfortunate qualities, they make code reuse problematic because you can't move a code block to another module without also worrying about the Defxxx in use in the source and target modules.

Block-Scoped Variables

Visual Basic .NET also supports the so-called block variables, a special type of dynamic variables that you declare using Dim inside a For...Next, Do...Loop, or While...End While block of code:

```
Dim x As Integer
For x = 1 To 10
    Dim y As Integer     ' A block variable
    ⋮
Next
```

These variables can be used only inside the block in which they're defined:

```
' *** This code doesn't compile.
For x = 1 To 10
    Dim y As Integer     ' A block variable
    ⋮
Next
x = y           ' y isn't accessible from outside the For block.
```

Block variables improve the readability of your code because they make clear where a variable is used. But Visual Basic .NET raises a compilation error if the same variable is declared at the procedure level, as in this code:

```
' *** This code doesn't compile.
Dim y As Integer      ' Procedure variable with the same name
For x = 1 To 10
    Dim y As Integer   ' Block variable
    ⋮
Next
```

It's OK to have a block variable with the same name as a variable declared outside the procedure at the class level or globally in the application. If you have two distinct non-nested blocks in the same procedure, you can declare the same variable in both blocks and even use a different type for the two instances:

```
For x = 1 To 10
    Dim y As Integer       ' A block variable
    ⋮
Next
Do
    Dim y As Long          ' Another block variable
    ⋮
Loop
```

One important detail about block variables: although their scope is the block in which they are declared, their lifetime coincides with the procedure's lifetime. In other words, if you reenter the same block, the variable isn't initialized again and contains the value it had the last time the block was exited. For example, consider this code:

```
For z = 1 To 2
    Dim y As Long
    For x = 1 To 2
        y = y + 1
        Console.WriteLine(y)
    Next
Next
```

After you run the preceding code, the console window contains the values 1 2 3 4. If this behavior isn't exactly what you meant to achieve, you must reinitialize the variable inside the block by using an explicit assignment or by using an initializer, which I explain later in this chapter.

Data Types

Visual Basic .NET supports most of the data types available under previous versions of Visual Basic, including Single, Double, and String. Things aren't smooth at all in this area, though, because many important under-the-covers changes have been made and will affect you, especially if you're porting legacy applications to Visual Basic .NET.

The Object Data Type

First and foremost, the Variant type isn't supported any longer. The .NET data type closest to Variant is the System.Object type. The Object type has become the one-size-fits-all data type under Visual Basic .NET in that it can contain *any* type and therefore is significantly different from the Object data type that you find in previous language versions. Object variables can be assigned any type because, in the .NET Framework, *everything* is an object, including Integer and String values. More precisely, all the basic data types are defined in the System namespace and directly inherit from the System.Object. As you will see in greater detail in Chapter 5, a variable can always be assigned a value whose type inherits from the variable's class. Therefore, the following statements are legal under Visual Basic .NET:

```
Dim o As Object, s As String
s = "ABCDE"
o = 123          ' Assign an integer to an Object variable.
o = s            ' Assign a string to an Object variable.
```

You might argue that using an object to hold a scalar value such as a string or an integer sounds like a waste of memory and that the practice can slow down your application considerably. This is partly true, but you should consider that Visual Basic .NET objects take fewer resources and are inherently more efficient than Visual Basic 6 objects. There's more to learn about this topic, as you'll see in the "Value Types and Reference Types" section later in this chapter.

Integer Data Types

Visual Basic .NET Long variables hold 64-bit integer values—and are therefore ready for 64-bit CPUs and operating systems—while Integer variables hold 32-bit values and therefore should replace Long variables when you're porting Visual Basic 6 applications. The new Short data value can accommodate 16-bit values, while the Byte data type still works with unsigned 8-bit values. For example, let's see how you can convert a group of variable declarations from Visual Basic 6 to Visual Basic .NET:

```
' A Visual Basic 6 group of variable declarations
Dim b As Byte
Dim i As Integer
Dim l As Long

' The corresponding Visual Basic .NET code fragment
Dim b As Byte
Dim i As Short
Dim l As Integer
```

Most of the time, you can keep the Integer and Long data types when you're converting a legacy application to Visual Basic .NET, and the resulting code will work as it used to. However, 64-bit integer operations map to multiple assembly opcodes on 32-bit processors, so unnecessarily using Long can hurt performance.

Visual Studio .NET 2003 comes with a handy utility, which you can reach by selecting the Upgrade Visual Basic 6 Code command in the Tools menu. This command brings up a dialog box in which you can type or paste Visual Basic 6 code. If this code uses external COM libraries, you should add a reference to the libraries in the References tab. (See Figure 2-6.) You can then click the Upgrade button to have this code converted to Visual Basic .NET and pasted in the code window. While you can't use this utility to convert entire applications, it is useful for short code snippets and is a valuable learning tool as well, as you can use it to quickly see how most statements can be converted to Visual Basic .NET from earlier versions of the language.

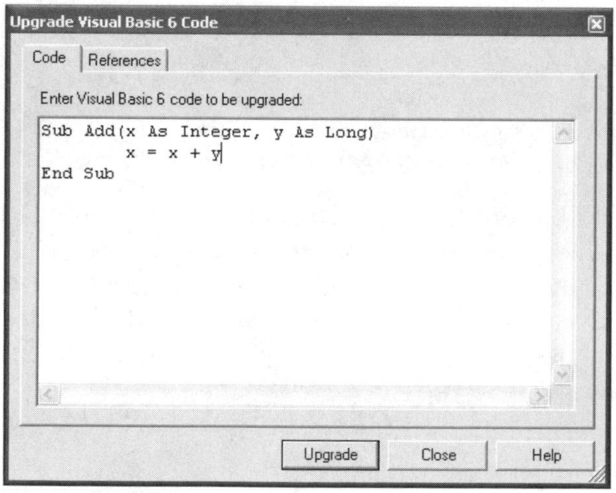

Figure 2-6   The Upgrade Visual Basic 6 Code dialog box

The Boolean Data Type

The Boolean data type survived the transition from Visual Basic 6 to Visual Basic .NET, but there are two points to consider. First, the new Boolean type takes 4 bytes instead of 2, so large Boolean arrays take more memory and tax your application's performance.

Second, whereas in the .NET runtime the True value is rendered as 1, Visual Basic .NET uses the value -1 for better compatibility with previous versions of the language. The True value is automatically converted to 1 when passed from Visual Basic to other languages, so language interoperability shouldn't be seriously affected by this decision.

Most Visual Basic programs don't depend on how True values are rendered because you typically use Boolean values from comparison operators in If and Do expressions, as in this code:

```
' The expression (x < 100) creates a temporary Boolean value.
If x < 100 Then x = x + 1
```

The internal value of True becomes important when you use comparison operators inside assignment statements. For example, a Visual Basic 6 developer can replace the preceding statement with the following one, which is more concise even though not necessarily faster:

```
' Increment x if it is less than 100.
x = x - (x < 100)
```

The preceding expression works correctly under Visual Basic .NET as well. However, you must convert the Boolean expression to an Integer explicitly if Option Strict is on. (I cover the Option Strict statement later in this chapter.)

```
 ' (This works also when Option Strict is on.)
x = x - CInt(x < 100)
```

The Decimal Data Type

The Currency data type isn't supported in the .NET Framework and has been replaced by the Decimal type, which offers wider range and better precision. Indirect evidence that the Decimal type is meant to replace the Currency type shows up in the trailing @ symbol (once reserved for Currency values) that you now use to tell the compiler that you're actually working with a Decimal value:

```
Dim d As Decimal
⋮
' Make it clear that you're adding a Decimal constant.
d = d + 123.45@
```

The Decimal data type is different from the Decimal subtype available under Visual Basic 6, which allows you to store Decimal values only in Variant variables. The Decimal type holds a number in fixed-point format and is useful for preventing rounding and truncating problems; it can hold values in the range + or - 79,228,162,514,264,337,593,543,950,335 with no decimal point, or + through - 7.9228162514264337593543950335 with 28 places to the right of the decimal. The smallest nonzero number that you can represent with this data type is + or - 0.0000000000000000000000000001.

The Char Data Type

The Char data type is a new entry in the list of data types that Visual Basic supports. A Char variable can hold a single Unicode character and therefore takes 2 bytes. When assigning a literal character to a Char variable, you should use a trailing c to let Visual Basic .NET know that the literal character must be converted to a Char before the assignment:

```
Dim ch As Char
ch = "A"c          ' Note the trailing "c" character.

' *** The following line raises a compilation error.
ch = "ABC"c        ' More than one character
```

You can explicitly ask for a conversion from String to Char data type using the new CChar function:

```
ch = CChar(Mid("Francesco", 3, 1))
```

The CChar function is mandatory in conversion from String to Char when Option Strict is on, as I explain later in this chapter. You can use the Chr or ChrW function to convert a Unicode code to a character, as in this code snippet:

```
ch = Chr(65)     ' This is the "A" character.
```

In case you're wondering why you should use the more limited Char variable instead of a full-featured String value, the answer is simple: better performance. The reasons for this, however, will be clear only when I discuss garbage collection later in this chapter.

Mapping .NET Data Types

Visual Basic .NET supports a subset of all the data types defined in the .NET Framework, as summarized in Table 2-1 (taken from the .NET Framework Developers Guide). The correspondence is perfect, and you can even declare your variables using the .NET data type if you prefer:

```
' Declare a String and a Date the .NET way.
Dim s As System.String      ' Equivalent to As String
Dim d As System.DateTime    ' Equivalent to As Date
```

Table 2-1   Data Types Supported Under Visual Basic .NET and Their Corresponding .NET Framework Types

Visual Basic Type	.NET Runtime Type	Storage Size	Value Range
Boolean	System.Boolean	4 bytes	True or False
Byte	System.Byte	1 byte	0 to 255 (unsigned)

Table 2-1   Data Types Supported Under Visual Basic .NET *(continued)*
and Their Corresponding .NET Framework Types

Visual Basic Type	.NET Runtime Type	Storage Size	Value Range
Char	System.Char	2 bytes	0 to 65535 (unsigned)
Date	System.DateTime	8 bytes	January 1, 1 CE to December 31, 9999
Decimal	System.Decimal	12 bytes	+/- 79,228,162,514,264,337,593,543,950, 335 with no decimal point; +/- 7.9228162514264337593543950335 with 28 places to the right of the decimal; smallest nonzero number is +/- 0.0000000000000000000000000001
Double	System.Double	8 bytes	-1.79769313486231E308 to -4.94065645841247E-324 for negative values; 4.94065645841247E-324 to 1.79769313486232E308 for positive values
Integer	System.Int32	4 bytes	-2,147,483,648 to 2,147,483,647
Long (long integer)	System.Int64	8 bytes	-9,223,372,036,854,775,808 to 9,223,372,036,854,775,807
Object	System.Object (class)	4 bytes	Any type can be stored in a variable of type Object
Short	System.Int16	2 bytes	-32,768 to 32,767
Single	System.Single	4 bytes	-3.402823E38 to -1.401298E-45 for negative values; 1.401298E-45 to 3.402823E38 for positive values
String	System.String (class)	10 bytes + (2 * string length)	0 to approximately 2 billion Unicode characters
User-Defined Type (Structure block)	(Inherits from System. ValueType)	Sum of the size of its members	Each member of the structure has a range determined by its data type and is independent of the ranges of the other members

Fixed-length strings aren't supported by Visual Basic .NET, therefore this statement doesn't compile:

```
Dim s As String * 30          ' *** Invalid under Visual Basic .NET
```

To help you port Visual Basic 6 code that uses fixed-length strings, the Microsoft.Visual-Basic.Compatibility.VB6 namespace offers the FixedLengthString class. See the language manuals for more details on this class.

Assignments and Operators

Visual Basic .NET has several new features that change the way you assign values to variables. The most important of these is field initializers.

Initializers

Under Visual Basic .NET, you can declare and initialize a variable or a class-level field in one statement. This long-awaited feature lets you simplify your code and improve its readability:

```
' Three examples of variable initializers
Dim width As Single = 1000
Dim firstName As String = "Francesco"
Dim startDate As Date = Now()
```

As the last statement shows, the value being assigned doesn't have to be constant. Note that you can initialize a variable only if it's the sole variable declared in the Dim, Public, or Private statement:

```
' *** This line doesn't compile.
Dim x, y, z As Long = 1
```

Initializers are especially useful for class-level variables and global variables because they offer a simple way to provide default values for fields and properties:

```
Class Person
    Public Country As String = "USA"
End Class
```

Initializers are especially useful with block variables to ensure that the variable is correctly reinitialized to a given value whenever the block is reentered. This is the only case in which it makes sense to use initializers to assign a variable its default value (0 for numbers, empty string for String variables, and so on):

```
For z = 1 To 2
    ' Ensure that the y variable always starts at 0.
    Dim y As Long = 0
    For x = 1 To 2
        ⋮
    Next
Next
```

Initializers also work with variables holding object references. For example, the following statements declare and create an ADO.NET DataSet object:

```
Dim ds As System.Data.DataSet
ds = New System.Data.DataSet
```

You can make your code more concise as follows:

```
Dim ds As System.Data.DataSet = New System.Data.DataSet
```

Even better, Visual Basic .NET supports a special syntax that lets you get rid of the repeated class name:

```
Dim ds As New System.Data.DataSet
```

The preceding statement looks like a Visual Basic 6 declaration, but don't let the resemblance confuse you. Under previous language versions, the As New syntax creates a so-called auto-instancing object variable. The compiler generates code that checks such a variable before each reference to it, and it automatically creates an object of the corresponding type if the variable is found to be Nothing. As a result, no object is ever created if the variable is never referenced during the execution path. Under Visual Basic .NET, the preceding statement is simply a special form of a variable initializer, and an object is always created when the Dim statement is executed. Visual Basic .NET doesn't support any syntax form that corresponds to the Visual Basic 6 auto-instancing variables.

Initializers also support object constructors that take parameters. (I cover constructors in Chapter 4.) For example, the constructor for the DataSet object supports a string argument to which you pass the name of the DataSet object itself:

```
Dim ds As New System.Data.DataSet("Publishers")
```

The >> and << Operators

Visual Basic .NET 2003 introduces two new binary operators for bit shifting. The << operator shifts its first operand to the left by a number of bits specified by its second operand. For example

```
Console.WriteLine(34 << 2)      ' => 136
```

Similarly, the >> operator shifts its first operand to the right by a number of bits specified by its second operand:

```
Console.WriteLine(34 >> 2)      ' => 8
```

If you are unfamiliar with bit operations, these operators might look quite unpredictable, if not completely useless. To understand how they perform, you must convert the left-hand operator to its binary representation. For example, the binary representation of 34 is 00100010. If you shift this number two digits to the left, you get 10001000 (the binary equivalent of 34), whereas you get 00001000 (that is, 8) if you shift it two digits to the right. (Notice that the rightmost 1 digit is "pushed out" of the number and is lost, without any error.)

Because they work on binary numbers, the << and >> operators take only integer values—that is, Byte, Short, Integer, Long, or Enum values—as their left-hand operand, whereas the right-hand operand must be Byte, Short, or Integer. When you shift a value to the right, the sign bit is retained, which means that shifting a negative value to the right produces another negative value:

```
Dim N As Short = -8      ' -8 decimal = 11111111 11111000 binary
Console.Write(N >> 2)    ' -2 decimal = 11111111 11111110 binary
```

This type of right shifting is known as arithmetical shifting, to differentiate it from the logical shifting that shifts bits without caring for the sign bit. Visual Basic .NET does logical shifting only when the left-hand operand is a Byte value because there is no sign bit in this case. With other data types, to perform right shifting without sign extension you must mask the result with an And operator:

```
' Notice the "S" suffix to force a Short hex constant.
Console.Write(N >> 2 And &H4FFFS)   ' 20472 decimal = 00111111 11111110 binary
```

If the second operand is a variable and you don't know in advance the number of bits by which the number is going to be shifted, you should use the >> operator twice, as in the following code:

```
' Logical shift of N to the right for K times
' (Assumes that N is Short and K is higher than zero.)
Console.Write(N >> K And (&H7FFFS >> K - 1))
```

The << and >> operators have the lowest priority among Visual Basic operators, so you don't need to enclose the k   1 expression in parenthesis, but you need to enclose (&H7FFFS >> k   1) inside parenthesis to have the >> operator be evaluated before the And operator. Notice that you should use the &H7FFFFFFF mask for Integer operands, and the &H7FFFFFFFFFFFFFFF mask for Long operands.

Be aware that Visual Basic uses only the least significant bits of the second operand in an attempt not to perform too many time-consuming shift operations. For example, it ANDs the right-hand operand with 7 (binary 00000111) when shifting Byte values, 15 (binary 00001111) when shifting Short values, 31 (binary 00011111) when shifting Integer values, and 63 (binary 00111111) when shifting Long values. This behavior can cause unexpected results. For example, you might not be prepared for this result:

```
Console.Write(2 << 33)          ' => you expect 0, but is 4
```

You get this result because the second operand (33, binary 0010001) is ANDed with 31 (binary 00011111), which gives 00000001 and therefore the number is shifted to the left by just one bit.

You often need to do bit shifting when you are interacting with hardware devices that require bit-coded values, or when calling Windows API functions that take or return integers containing packed values. The << operator can be useful for performing multiplications by a power of 2. For example, shifting a value to the left by 5 bits is the same as multiplying it by 32, except that you can ignore overflow errors. Similarly, shifting a value 2 bits to the right is the same as dividing it by 4, and it works even with negative numbers because Visual Basic .NET does arithmetic shifts.

If the operand is a Long, a shift operation is more than 25 times faster than the equivalent multiplication or division because it maps to a single CPU opcode instead of many. (Conversely, shifting Integer or Short values isn't significantly faster than multiplying or dividing them because in both cases only one CPU opcode is needed.)

The << operator becomes useful to set, clear, toggle, or test an individual bit in an integer value, as the following routines demonstrate:

```
' (All these routines assume that N is in the range 0-31.)
' Set the N-th bit of a value.
Function BitSet(ByVal value As Integer, ByVal n As Integer) As Integer
    Return value Or (1 << n)
End Function

' Clear the N-th bit of a value.
Function BitClear(ByVal value As Integer, ByVal n As Integer) As Integer
    Return value And Not (1 << n)
End Function

' Toggle the N-th bit of a value.
Function BitToggle(ByVal value As Integer, ByVal n As Integer) As Integer
    Return value Xor (1 << n)
End Function

' Test the N-th bit of a value.
Function BitTest(ByVal value As Integer, ByVal n As Integer) As Boolean
    Return CBool(value And (1 << n))
End Function
```

With a little additional effort, you can also rotate integer values to the left or to the right without using a loop:

```
' Rotate an integer value N bits to the left. (N in the 0-31 range)
Function RotateLeft(ByVal value As Integer, ByVal n As Integer) As Integer
    Return (value << n) Or ((value >> 32 - n) And Not (-1 << n))
End Function

' Rotate an integer value N bits to the right. (N in the 0-31 range)
Function RotateRight(ByVal value As Integer, ByVal n As Integer) As Integer
    Return ((value >> n) And Not (-1 << 32 - n)) Or (value << 32 - n)
End Function
```

(Understanding how these routines work is left as an exercise to you, the reader.)

The .NET Framework offers the BitVector32 class for easy manipulation of bit-coded integers, and the BitArray class for dealing with arrays of bits. I cover these classes in Chapter 7.

The Option Strict Statement

One defect of Visual Basic mentioned by many detractors was the lack of control over conversions between different types. For example, in Visual Basic 6 the following code is perfectly legal:

```
Dim s As Single, d As Double
d = 1 / 3
s = d
```

The problem with this code is that when you assign a Double variable or expression to a Single variable, you're going to lose precision and might even incur an overflow error. This type of conversion is also known as narrowing conversion. Other examples of narrowing conversions are from Long to Integer or to Byte, or from Double to Long. A conversion in the opposite direction—for example, from Single to Double—is known as widening conversion and should always be allowed because you can't lose precision or cause overflow errors.

Visual Basic .NET supports the new Option Strict compiler directive, which you can set to On to disable implicit narrowing conversions. For example, the following code doesn't compile:

```
' At the top of the source file
Option Strict On              ' Same as Option Strict
  ⋮
' Later in the same source file...
Dim d As Double = 1.123
Dim s As Single
s = d       ' Narrowing conversion raises compilation error.
```

Note that you can omit the On keyword because Option Strict is sufficient to activate this feature. You don't need to include this directive in all your modules because you can set a projectwide setting in the project Properties Page dialog box. (See Figure 2-5.)

By default, Option Strict is set to Off at the project level, presumably in order to facilitate importing of Visual Basic 6 projects. However, I strongly suggest that you turn it on—at least for all new projects—so that you can take advantage of this new feature. You'll spend more time writing code because you have to manually convert values to the target type, but this extra effort pays off nicely at debug time when you don't have to worry about subtle conversion bugs.

If Option Strict is on for the entire project, you can turn it off locally by inserting the following statement at the top of individual source files:

```
Option Strict Off
```

When Option Strict is off, you can implicitly convert between strings and dates, string and Boolean values, and string and numeric values, as you did in Visual Basic 6. If Option Strict is on, you must explicitly state your intention by using a conversion function, such as CInt, CLng, or CSng:

```
' This code works regardless of the current Option Strict setting.
Dim d As Double = 1.123
Dim s As Single = CSng(d)
```

The Option Strict On statement implicitly forces you to declare all your variables; in other words, Option Strict On implies Option Explicit On. If Option Strict is on, any undeclared variable raises a compilation error. Another side effect of the Option Strict option is to disallow late binding operations:

```
' If Option Strict is on, the following code doesn't compile.
Dim o As Object
o = New Form1
o.Show                 ' Late binding method call
```

You must disable Option Strict to assign a Boolean value to a Short, an Integer, or a Long variable. This behavior is a bit disconcerting at first because a Boolean variable can hold only the values 0 and 1, so an assignment of this kind is never a narrowing conversion and you might not see the need for setting Option Strict to Off:

```
Dim s As Short, b As Boolean
' This line doesn't compile if Option Strict is on.
s = b
' This line always compiles. (Note the new CShort conversion function.)
s = CShort(b)
```

You must use the CChar conversion function when you're converting a string to a Char variable because such an assignment is correctly considered a narrowing conversion. The Option Strict On statement has other effects on what your code can do:

■ You can't use the integer division operator \ with floating-point numbers because this operator silently converts its operands to Long (a narrowing conversion).

■ The ∧ operator always returns a Double value, so you can't assign its result to anything other than a Double variable.

■ Because conversions from integer types to Boolean are forbidden, you can't use an integer variable by itself in an If expression as a concise way to determine whether it's equal to 0:

```
' This statement doesn't work if Option Strict is on.
If intValue Then Console.WriteLine("intValue is <> 0")
' The preferred syntax under Visual Basic .NET
If intValue <> 0 Then Console.WriteLine("intValue is <> 0")
```

Assigning Object Values

One of the major syntax changes in Visual Basic .NET is that the Set keyword is no longer needed to assign an object reference to an object variable, and in fact the Set keyword isn't valid in variable assignments. To understand the reason for this change, you must consider that the Set keyword was necessary under previous versions of the language only to solve the ambiguity caused by default properties—for example, the Text property of TextBox objects:

```
Dim tb As TextBox       ' This is Visual Basic 6 code.
tb = Text1              ' Assign the Text1.Text to tb.Text
Set tb = Text1          ' Assign a reference to Text1 to tb.
```

Visual Basic .NET solves this ambiguity in a completely different, more radical way: default members are not supported under .NET, period. In other words, neither .NET classes nor classes that you define in your code can expose a default property or method. So you don't need a special keyword to deal with those default values in assignments, and you assign scalar values and object references in the same way:

```
' In Visual Basic .NET, this is always an object assignment.
Dim tb As TextBox
tb = Text1

' You can also use initializers.
Dim tb2 As TextBox = Text1
```

Whereas the equal sign works for object assignments, you must still use the Is operator to test whether two object variables point to the same object in memory.

There is one exception to the rule that classes can't have a default member. A property or method can be the default member for its class if it accepts one or more arguments. Take the Collection object as an example:

```
' The .NET version of the Collection object
Dim col As New Microsoft.VisualBasic.Collection()
' Add two elements.
col.Add("Francesco", "FirstName")
col.Add("Balena", "LastName")
' The following statements are equivalent. (Item is the default member.)
Console.WriteLine(col.Item(1))            ' => Francesco
Console.WriteLine(col(1))                 ' => Francesco
' The following statements are equivalent. (Item is the default member.)
Console.WriteLine(col.Item("LastName"))   ' => Balena
Console.WriteLine(col("LastName"))        ' => Balena
```

The reason for this exception to the general rule is that the presence of arguments makes the syntax unambiguous:

```
' This can only mean you're accessing the default Item method.
Dim o As Object = col(1)
' This can only mean you are assigning a reference to the Collection.
Dim o2 As Object = col
```

Shorthand for Common Operations

Visual Basic .NET supports a variation of the standard assignment operation, which you can use when you're performing a math or string operation on a variable and are going to store the result in the variable itself. This shorthand is especially useful when you're incrementing or decrementing a variable or when you're appending a string to a string variable:

```
Dim x As Long = 9
Dim y As Double = 6.8
Dim s As String

x += 1          ' Increment x by one (same as x = x + 1).
y -= 2          ' Decrement y by two (same as y = y - 2).
x *= 2          ' Double x (same as x = x * 2).
x \= 10         ' Divide x by ten (same as x = x \ 10).
```

```
y /= 4          ' Divide y by four (same as y = y / 4).
y ^= 3          ' Raise y to the 3rd power (same as y = y ^ 3).
s &= "ABC"      ' Append o a string (same as s = s & "ABC").
```

If you're working with Visual Basic .NET 2003, you can use similar shortcuts for the new << and >> operators:

```
x <<= 2         ' Shift x two bits to the left (same as x = x << 2).
x >>= 1         ' Shift x one bit to the right (same as x = x >> 1).
```

If Option Strict is on, you can use neither the \= operator with floating-point variables (because the \ operator converts its operands to Long) nor the ^= operator with anything but a Double variable (because the ^ operator returns a Double value).

Value Types and Reference Types

You can group all the data types that the .NET Framework supports—both the native types and the types you create—in two broad categories of reference types and value types. In a nutshell, reference types behave like objects, whereas value types behave like scalar types (Integer or Single). You need to understand the differences between the two, or risk introducing subtle bugs into your code.

In the .NET Framework, everything is an object, and most data types are reference types. When you declare a variable of a reference type, you're allocating a pointer variable (a 32-bit integer value on current Windows platforms) that points to the actual object. The object itself is stored in a memory area called the managed heap and is under the supervision of the .NET Framework runtime, whereas the pointer variable can be stored elsewhere (for example, on the stack if it's a dynamic variable declared inside a procedure). After all the pointer variables that point to a given object go out of scope or are explicitly set to Nothing, the object undergoes a process known as garbage collection, and the memory it takes in the heap is freed. Unlike Visual Basic 6 and COM objects, the memory allocated for .NET objects isn't released immediately after all the pointer variables are destroyed because garbage collection occurs only when the .NET runtime runs out of memory in the managed heap. This phenomenon is also known as nondeterministic finalization, and I'll talk about it in greater detail in Chapter 5.

Value types inherit from System.ValueType. This class inherits from System.Object (as do all the classes defined in the .NET Framework, either directly or indirectly) but redefines its methods. Value types aren't allocated in the managed heap, and the corresponding variable *holds* the value rather than *points* to it. The actual location in which a value type is stored depends on its scope. For example, local value type variables are allocated on the stack. All .NET numeric types are value types, as are Enums and the types you define with a Structure…End Structure block. .NET strings and arrays are reference types, as are all the objects you define with a Class…End Class block. If you're in doubt as to whether a .NET type is a class or a structure, just read the documentation or view it in the object browser (which displays different icons for classes and structures).

You'll learn more about value types in Chapter 5, but you need at least these basics to understand a few topics in this and the next chapter. In general, value types are faster than similar reference types, for two reasons: there is no need to dereference a pointer to get to the actual data, and, more important, the .NET Framework doesn't need to allocate and then release memory in the managed heap. If a value type variable is held on the stack, as shown in the illustration, the variable is automatically destroyed and no time-consuming cleanup operation is needed when you exit the procedure.

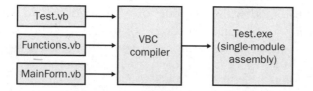

You must pay attention to whether you're dealing with a reference or a value type for two reasons. First and foremost, the assignment operation works differently in the two cases. When you assign a reference type to a variable, you're actually assigning the pointer so that the target variable will now point to the original value. No data is duplicated, and you can modify the original data through both the original and the new variable. This is typical object behavior, and includes objects that you instantiate from classes defined in your application:

```
' Person is a class defined in the current application.
Dim p1 As New Person
p1.FirstName = "Francesco"
' Assign to another Person variable.
Dim p2 As Person = p1
' You can modify the original object through the new variable.
p2.FirstName = "Joe"
Console.WriteLine(p1.FirstName)    ' => Joe
```

Conversely, when you assign a value type—such as a numeric data type—to a variable of the same type, a *copy* of the original data is assigned, and therefore the original data and the new variable are completely unrelated.

An important detail: the .NET String class is a reference type, as the following code snippet demonstrates:

```
Dim s1 As String = "Francesco"
Dim s2 As String = s1
' Prove that the two variables point to the same String object.
Console.WriteLine(s2 Is s1)            ' => True
```

The second reason you must pay attention to the nature of the data you process—reference type or value type—concerns performance. As I've explained, value types are usually faster. In addition, sometimes a value type is converted to a reference type and back without your being aware of this internal conversion that silently slows down your code.

To refine this explanation, whenever you pass a value type to a method that takes an Object argument, the value is converted to a reference type: the .NET runtime allocates a block of memory in the managed heap, copies the value in that area, and passes the method a pointer to that memory location. This operation is known as boxing. For example, you have a hidden boxing operation when you pass a number to the Debug.Write method because that method can take only an Object or a String argument.

The simplest example of a boxing operation occurs when you assign a value type—an integer, for example—to an Object variable:

```
Dim i As Integer = 1234
' The next statement causes the following sequence of operations:
' (1) a block of memory is allocated in the heap;
' (2) the original integer value is copied in that memory block;
' (3) the address of the block is assigned to the Object variable.
Dim o As Object = i
```

As you might guess, boxing a value is a time-consuming activity. Likewise, you waste CPU time when you reassign a boxed value back to a variable of a value type—an operation known as unboxing:

```
' ...(Continuing the previous example)...
' The next statement causes the following sequence of operations:
' (1) the pointer in the o variable is used to locate the data;
' (2) the integer is copied into the target variable;
' (3) the heap memory used by the o variable is garbage collected
'      (eventually, some time after the o variable is set to Nothing).
' (Next statement doesn't compile if Option Strict is on.)
Dim i2 As Integer = o
```

Note that the previous code snippet works only if Option Strict is disabled. If Option Strict is on, you must rewrite the last statement this way:

```
Dim i2 As Integer = CInt(o)
```

Here's the bottom line: always use value types rather than reference types if you have a choice. For example, use Char variables instead of String variables if you're working with one-character strings. And enable Option Strict at the application level so that an unboxing operation can't go unnoticed.

There's more to reference types, value types, boxing, and unboxing, as you'll learn in Chapter 5.

The CType Keyword

As you know, the Option Strict On statement prevents the programmer from carelessly inserting code that might fail at run time because of a failed conversion. For this reason, when you're unboxing a value from an Object variable to a value type variable, you need an explicit conversion operator (CInt in the following statement):

```
' obj is an Object variable.
Dim i As Integer = CInt(obj)
```

Whereas you can always assign a Person object to an Object variable without any particular precaution—because this assignment can never fail at run time—the opposite assignment might fail if the object isn't compatible with the type of the target variable. Because this assignment is a narrowing conversion, you must tell the compiler that you know what you're doing if Option Strict is on. You do this by manually converting (or coercing or casting) the object to the target type, using the CType operator:

```
' obj is an Object variable.
Dim pers As Person = CType(obj, Person)
```

Note that the second argument of the CType operator is the name of the target class and isn't enclosed in quotes. If the argument can't be directly cast to the target type, CType attempts to convert it. For example, the following statement successfully converts the string to the integer, even if it means dropping the fractional portion of the original number embedded in the string:

```
Dim res As Integer = CType("123.45", Integer)      ' => 123
```

If the argument cannot be converted to the target type, CType causes a runtime error and throws an InvalidCastException object.

The DirectCast Keyword

The DirectCast keyword offers yet another way to convert between types. This keyword has the same syntax as CType but differs from the latter in a few important details. First, DirectCast works only with arguments of reference types and attempts to pass value types are flagged as compilation errors. (CType works with both reference and value types.)

Second, CType always attempts to convert the argument to the target type and is therefore able to convert a string into a numeric type (if the string actually contains a number, of course); DirectCast works only if the source argument can be cast to the target type and throws an InvalidCastException object otherwise. (DirectCast is unable to perform even widening conversions from Short to Integer or Single to Double.)

Third, DirectCast is slightly faster than CType, so you should use the former when you want to cast rather than convert a value. In practice, however, the speed difference between these operators is negligible. Summarizing, you can use the DirectCast keyword on two occasions:

- When casting a variable of a base class to a variable of a derived class—for example, a Person variable to an Employee variable or an Object variable to another reference type

- When casting an object variable to an interface variable

Constants and Enums

In a difference from previous language versions, Visual Basic .NET classes can expose public constants, which are seen from outside the class as read-only fields. Except for this detail, their syntax is similar to that in Visual Basic 6. If Option Explicit is enabled, constants require an explicit type declaration:

```
' This works only if Option Explicit is off.
Public Const DefaultPassword = "mypwd"
' This works always and is the recommended syntax.
Public Const DefaultPassword As String = "mypwd"
```

Enum blocks can appear anywhere in a source file: inside a module, class, or structure block or directly at the namespace level.

```
Enum Shape
    Triangle        ' This takes a zero value.
    Square          ' 1
    Rectangle       ' 2
    Circle          ' 3
    Unknown = -999  ' (Values don't need to be sorted.)
End Enum

' A variable that can be assigned an Enum type
Dim aShape As Shape = Shape.Square
```

In another difference from Visual Basic 6, which implicitly used 32-bit integers for Enum values, you can choose among the Byte, Short, Integer, and Long data types, where Integer is the default type if omitted. (You should use Integer unless you have a good reason to do otherwise because it matches the 32-bit registers in Intel CPUs.) You can't omit the name of the Enum when you're using an enumerated constant:

```
' 16 bits are enough for this Enum, so we can use Short.
Enum Shape As Short
    :
End Enum

' *** The following line doesn't compile because you
'      must use the complete name Shape.Square.
Dim aShape As Shape = Square
```

If no explicit value is provided, the first member inside the Enum block is assigned the value 0, the second member is assigned the value 1, and so on. Even though Enum values are internally stored as integers, by default you aren't allowed to assign a number to an Enum variable if Option Strict is on, and you must convert the number to the proper Enum type before assigning it an Enum variable:

```
aShape = CType(1, Shape)
```

Arrays

Arrays have undergone many changes in the migration to Visual Basic .NET. First of all, arrays are always zero-based:

```
' This statement always declares an array of 11 elements.
Dim arr(10) As Integer
```

Because the first element of all arrays has a zero index, the To keyword inside a Dim statement is forbidden, and the Option Base statement is no longer supported.

An interesting new feature of arrays is that you can expose them as public members of a class, which means that the following code—which would raise a compiler error under previous versions of the language—is legal under Visual Basic .NET:

```
Class Person
    ' Provide up to 4 lines for address.
    Public Address(4) As String
    ⋮
End Class
```

Under Visual Basic 6, you achieve a similar result by creating a property that takes a numeric index argument and set or return the corresponding element of a private array. The Visual Basic .NET solution is more concise and efficient.

The ReDim Statement

As in Visual Basic 6 and previous versions, you can declare an array with the Dim statement and actually allocate memory for it with a subsequent ReDim statement. Under Visual Basic .NET, however, the ReDim statement can't be used to declare an array— in other words, you can't have a ReDim statement without a Dim statement for a given array. Because ReDim can never declare the type of an array, it doesn't support the As clause:

```
' Declare the array.
Dim arr() As Integer
⋮
' Create the array.
ReDim arr(100)          ' Note that no As clause is used here.
```

One problem that the Visual Basic 6 compiler copes with is that the ReDim statement can change the number of dimensions in the array; this feature keeps the compiler from producing the most efficient code possible because it must always check how many dimensions an array has before accessing its elements.

To let the compiler produce more efficient code, Visual Basic .NET introduces the concept of rank, that is, the number of dimensions in an array. New syntax rules dictate that ReDim can change the number of elements in an array but can't change the rank of the array itself. You indicate the rank of an array in a Dim statement by inserting the appropriate number of commas inside the parentheses:

```
' Declare a two-dimensional array.
Dim arr2(,) As String
' Declare a three-dimensional array.
Dim arr3(,,) As String
⋮
' Create the arrays.
ReDim arr2(10, 10)
ReDim arr3(10, 10, 10)
```

You can re-create the array as many times as you need, provided you don't change the rank of the array. You can also use ReDim Preserve if you want to keep values already in the array. As in Visual Basic 6 and previous versions, ReDim Preserve lets you change only the number of elements in the last dimension:

```
' ...(Continuing the previous code snippet)...
ReDim Preserve arr2(10, 20)
ReDim Preserve arr3(10, 10, 20)

'*** The following statements raise an
'    ArrayTypeMismatchException exception at run time.
ReDim Preserve arr2(20, 10)
ReDim Preserve arr3(10, 20, 20)
```

Array Initializers

Initializers also work with arrays, and you can initialize the values in an array by using a comma-delimited list of values enclosed by curly braces:

```
' Declare and create an array of 5 integers.
Dim arr() As Integer = {0, 1, 2, 3, 4}
```

You must omit the number of elements in the Dim statement if you use an initializer. When creating multidimensional arrays, however, you must indicate the rank of the array and use nested blocks of curly braces:

```
' Declare and create a two-dimensional array of strings
' with two rows and four columns.
Dim arr2(,) As String = { {"00", "01", "02", "03"}, _
                          {"10", "11", "12", "13"} }
```

Copying Arrays

Starting with Visual Basic 6, you can assign one array to another:

```
' In Visual Basic 6, this line copies arr1 elements to arr2.
arr2() = arr1()
```

Visual Basic .NET also supports array assignment, but the result is different from what you might expect because the Visual Basic .NET array is a reference type—in other words, it's more akin to an object than to an old-style array. See what a difference the reference nature of an array can make:

```
' *** Visual Basic .NET code
Dim arr1() As Integer = {0, 111, 222, 333}
 ' Create another reference to the array.
Dim arr2() As Integer = arr1
' Modify the array through the second variable.
arr2(1) = 9999
' Check that the original array has been modified.
Console.WriteLine(arr1(1))            ' => 9999
```

Does this mean that Visual Basic .NET can't copy arrays? Of course not, but you have to use a different syntax. Being objects, arrays expose several methods. One of these methods is Clone, which creates a *copy* of the original array and returns a reference to that copy. Let's rewrite the previous example to use the Clone method:

```
Dim arr3() As Integer = {0, 111, 222, 333}
' Create a copy (clone) of the array.
' (This code assumes that Option Strict is off.)
 Dim arr4() As Integer = arr3.Clone()
' Modify an element in the new array.
arr4(1) = 9999
' Check that the original array hasn't been affected.
Console.WriteLine(arr3(1))            ' => 111
```

If Option Strict is on, the preceding code fragment fails because the Clone method returns an Object value and the assignment results in a narrowing conversion. Note the empty pair of parentheses that you must use in the second argument of the CType or DirectCast operator when converting to an array of types:

```
' (This code works regardless of current Option Strict setting.)
arr4 = DirectCast(arr3.Clone(), Integer())
```

In general, if you're converting a value to an array, the second argument of the CType or DirectCast operator must specify the rank of the target array, which you can do by using zero or more commas inside the pair of parentheses:

```
Dim arr5(,) As Integer = {{0, 1, 2, 3}, {0, 10, 20, 30}}
' Create a copy of the 2-dimensional array.
Dim arr6(,) As Integer = DirectCast(arr5.Clone(), Integer(,))
```

If Option Strict is off, you can also assign an array to an Object variable and access the array's element through late binding:

```
' ...(Continuing the preceding code fragment)...
' (This code assumes that Option Strict is off.)
Dim o As Object = arr5
Console.WriteLine(o(1, 1))            ' => 10
```

Surprisingly, if you have an array of object elements (as opposed to value types, such as numbers and structures), you can even assign the array to an Object array. For example, because the Visual Basic .NET String type is an object type, the following code runs flawlessly:

```
Dim strArr() As String = {"00", "11", "22", "33", "44"}
Dim objArr() As Object = strArr
Console.WriteLine(objArr(2))          ' => 22
```

This is a particular case of a more general rule, which states that you can assign an array of type X to an array of type Y if the X type derives from Y. Because all classes inherit from Object, you can always assign an array of object types to an Object array. (Option Strict doesn't have to be off for this assignment to succeed.) However, this kind of assignment works only if X is a reference type. For example, it works with strings and with classes you define but fails with numeric arrays and arrays of user-defined Structure types. (Read on to learn about Structure types.)

The Array object exposes many other intriguing methods, as you will learn in Chapter 8.

Alternative Syntaxes for Arrays

Visual Basic .NET supports an alternative, undocumented syntax for declaring arrays, in which the pair of parenthesis follows the type name rather than the array name:

```
Dim arr As Integer()
Dim arr2 As Integer() = {1, 2, 3}
```

This syntax makes Visual Basic .NET more similar to C#, but there are other advantages as well. For example, you can reassign an array without a ReDim keyword:

```
arr2 = New Integer() {1, 2, 3, 4}
```

This syntax becomes handy when you need to create an array of values and pass it to a method because it saves you the declaration of an array variable for the sole purpose of passing it as an argument:

```
' Create an array on-the-fly and pass it as a method argument.
MyObject.MyMethod(New Integer() {1, 2, 3, 4})
```

Notice that you can't specify the number of elements between the two parentheses. The only way to create an array with a given number of elements is by specifying all its elements between curly braces.

Empty Arrays

Visual Basic .NET lets you create two types of "empty" arrays: uninitialized arrays and arrays that contain zero elements. An uninitialized array is just an array variable set to Nothing, whereas a zero-element array is a non-Nothing variable that points to an array with zero elements. Here is the (undocumented) method for creating zero-element arrays:

```
Dim arr(-1) As Integer           ' Or whatever type you need...
```

If you have a routine that returns an array, you can decide whether you want to return Nothing or a zero-element array when an empty array should be returned. In general, returning a zero-element array makes for more linear code in the caller. Consider this routine, which returns all the indices of a given substring in a longer string:

```
Function Matches(ByVal Text As String, ByVal Search As String) As Integer()
    ' Return Nothing if Search isn't found in Text.
    If InStr(Text, Search) = 0 Then Return Nothing
    ' Else return an array containing the indices of all occurrences.
    Dim res() As Integer
    :
    Return res
End Function
```

The caller of the previous routine must discern the Nothing case from the regular case, as follows:

```
Dim res() As Integer = Matches(aLongString, "abc")
If res Is Nothing Then
    Console.WriteLine("Found 0 matches")
Else
    ' The {0} place holder is replaced by the value after the comma.
    Console.WriteLine("Found {0} matches", UBound(res) + 1)
End If
```

Now, consider what happens if you modify the Matches routine:

```
' Return a zero-length array if Search isn't found in Text.
Dim res(-1) As Integer
If InStr(Text, Search) = 0 Then Return res
```

Now the caller requires less code because it doesn't have to check for Nothing first:

```
Dim res() As Integer = Matches(aLongString, "abc")
Console.WriteLine("Found {0} matches", Ubound(res) + 1)
```

Structures

The Type…End Type block isn't supported in Visual Basic .NET and has been replaced by the Structure…End Structure block, which offers many additional features and is actually more similar to classes than to the user-defined types (or UDTs) allowed in previous language versions. You can have a structure at the namespace level, inside a Class or Module block, or even inside another structure.

Members inside a structure must be prefixed with an accessibility (visibility) qualifier, as in this code:

```
Structure PersonStruct
    Dim FirstName As String          ' Dim means Public here.
    Dim LastName As String
    Public Address As String
    Private SSN As String
End Structure
```

The declaration of the structure's data members can neither include initializers nor use the As New declaration syntax. As comments in the preceding example suggest, the default accessibility level for structures—that is, the visibility level implied by a Dim keyword—is Public (unlike classes, where the default level is Private). Visual Basic .NET unifies the syntax of classes and structures, and structures support most of the functionality of classes, including methods:

```
Structure PersonStruct
    Dim FirstName As String
    Dim LastName As String
    Public Address As String
    Private SSN As String

    Function CompleteName() As String
        CompleteName = FirstName & " " & LastName
    End Function
End Structure
```

Like classes, structures can also embed properties. (For more information, read the "Properties" section of Chapter 4.) Unlike classes, however, structures are value types rather than reference types. Among other things, this means that Visual Basic .NET automatically initializes a structure when you declare a variable of that type; in other words, the following statements are all equivalent:

```
Dim p As PersonStruct
Dim p As PersonStruct = New PersonStruct()    ' Verbose initializer
Dim p As New PersonStruct                      ' Shortened syntax
```

Each structure implicitly defines a parameterless constructor, which initializes each member of the structure to its default value (0 for numeric members, null string for String members, and Nothing for object members). It's illegal to define an explicit parameterless constructor or a destructor for the structure. But you can define a New constructor method with arguments, as follows:

```
Structure PersonStruct
    Dim FirstName As String
    Dim LastName As String
    Public Address As String
    Private SSN As String

    ' A constructor for this structure
    Sub New(ByVal FirstName As String, ByVal LastName As String)
        ' Note how you can use the Me keyword.
        Me.FirstName = FirstName
        Me.LastName = LastName
    End Function
    :
End Structure
```

(See Chapter 4 for more information about constructor methods.)

A consequence of the value type nature of Structure variables is that the actual data is copied when you assign a structure variable to another variable, whereas only a pointer to data is copied when you assign a reference value to a variable. Also note that the equality operator isn't supported for structures. This code summarizes the differences between classes and structures:

```
' This code assumes you have a PersonClass class, with the same members
' as the PersonStruct structure.

' Creation is similar, but structures don't require New.
Dim aPersonObject As New Person()
Dim aPersonStruct As PersonStruct          ' New is optional.

' Assignment to members is identical.
aPersonObject.FirstName = "Joe"
aPersonObject.LastName = "Doe"
aPersonStruct.FirstName = "Joe"
aPersonStruct.LastName = "Doe"

' Method and property invocation is also identical.
Console.WriteLine(aPersonObject.CompleteName())          ' => Joe Doe
Console.WriteLine(aPersonStruct.CompleteName())          ' => Joe Doe

' Assignment to a variable of the same type has different effects.
Dim aPersonObject2 As Person = aPersonObject
' Classes are reference types; hence, the new variable receives
' a pointer to the original object.
aPersonObject2.FirstName = "Ann"
' The original object has been affected.
Console.WriteLine(aPersonObject.FirstName)     ' => Ann
'
Dim aPersonStruct2 As PersonStruct = aPersonStruct
' Structures are value types; hence, the new variable receives
' a copy of the original structure.
aPersonStruct2.FirstName = "Ann"
' The original structure hasn't been affected.
Console.WriteLine(aPersonStruct.FirstName)     ' => Joe
```

A few other features of classes aren't supported by structures in Visual Basic .NET. For example, structures implicitly inherit all the methods of the Object class, but they can neither explicitly inherit from another structure nor can they be inherited from.

After this first exposure to the most important syntax changes in how modules, classes, and variables are declared and used, you're ready to see what has changed in the language and how you can control execution flow under Visual Basic .NET.

3 Control Flow and Error Handling

Even with the many changes in the core language syntax, Visual Basic .NET code continues to look like Visual Basic. Most of the differences are in the details, which means sometimes you must dig far into the language specifications to find what's new in Visual Basic.

That you must look carefully is especially true of statements that have to do with flow control, such as procedure definitions and execution flow statements, which I cover in the first part of this chapter. Later in this chapter, I show you which Visual Basic commands have been preserved in the transition to Visual Basic .NET and which have been replaced by something else. Finally, the last portion of this chapter explains what exceptions are and the .NET way of handling errors.

Execution Flow Control

Visual Basic .NET has inherited the syntax of most execution flow statements, such as the If, For, and Do loops, but a few old-style instructions have been dropped, such as GoSub. Most syntax changes are related to how procedures are defined and invoked.

Procedures

As in previous versions, Visual Basic .NET supports Sub and Function procedures, which can be Private, Public, or Friend. A procedure's definition can include ByVal and ByRef parameters, Optional parameters, and ParamArray arguments. However, there are a few important differences that you must take into account when porting a legacy application to avoid subtle bugs and when building an application from scratch to avoid unnecessary performance hits.

A major syntax change under Visual Basic .NET is that the list of arguments being passed to a procedure must be enclosed in brackets, whether you're calling a Sub or a Function procedure:

```
' A call to a Sub procedure
MySubProc(first, second)
```

Note that this rule applies to procedure calls but not to language keywords, such as Throw or AddHandler. Conveniently, the Visual Studio .NET editor puts a pair of parentheses around the argument list if you forget to add them yourself. If Option Strict is on, you can't rely on implicit narrowing conversions when you're passing arguments to a procedure. For example, when passing a Double variable to a Single argument you must make the conversion explicit by using the CSng function:

```
Dim d As Double = 1.23
MyProc(CSng(d))

Sub MyProc(ByVal s As Single)
    ⋮
End Sub
```

ByVal and ByRef Arguments

By default, Visual Basic .NET passes arguments using ByVal, not ByRef, as was the case with previous language versions up to and including Visual Basic 6. If you're manually porting a legacy application, you must add the ByRef keyword for all those arguments that don't have the explicit ByVal keyword. For example, the following Visual Basic procedure

```
Sub MyProc(x As Integer, ByVal y As Long)
    ⋮
End Sub
```

must be translated as follows. (Note the change in data type as well.)

```
Sub MyProc(ByRef x As Short, ByVal y As Integer)
    ⋮
End Sub
```

The ByVal keyword is optional, but it's a good practice to specify it, especially if the code will be used by developers who are unfamiliar with new Visual Basic .NET conventions. Even better, while porting code from an older language version, you should reconsider whether the variable should be actually passed by reference. (Visual Basic 6 developers often mindlessly omit the ByVal keyword but don't really mean to pass all the arguments by reference.)

In most cases, an argument that should be passed by value can also be passed by reference without causing any apparent problems. The opposite isn't true, of course; you immediately see when you're mistakenly passing by value an argument that should be passed by reference when the caller receives an unmodified value. However, when you use an implicit ByRef where ByVal should be explicitly used in Visual Basic 6, you're creating a potential source for subtle bugs and also preventing the compiler from doing the best job optimizing the resulting code. If you then migrate the code in Visual Basic .NET—for example, by importing the project in Visual Studio .NET—the inefficiency and the possibility of introducing bugs persists.

Passing Arrays

In a difference from previous Visual Basic versions, you can use the ByVal keyword for array parameters as well. However, Visual Basic .NET array variables are reference types—in other words, they point to the actual memory area in the managed heap where array items are stored. So you're passing a 4-byte pointer whether you're passing the array by value or by reference. In all cases, all changes to array elements inside the called procedure are reflected in the original array:

```
Sub TestArrayByVal()
    Dim anArray() As Integer = {0, 1, 2, 3, 4}
    ' Pass the array by value to a procedure.
    Call ArrayProcByVal(anArray)
    ' Prove that the array element has been modified.
    Console.WriteLine(anArray(3))      ' => 300
End Sub

' A procedure that modifies its array argument's elements
Sub ArrayProcByVal(ByVal arr() As Integer)
    Dim i As Integer
    For i = 0 To UBound(arr)
        arr(i) = arr(i) * 100
    Next
End Sub
```

Passing an array using ByRef or ByVal makes a difference if you use a ReDim statement inside the called procedure. In this case, the original array is affected if you pass it to a ByRef argument, but it isn't modified if you pass it to a ByVal argument. To show how this works, let's build a procedure that takes two array arguments with different passing mechanisms:

```
Sub TestArrayByRef()
    Dim byvalArray(10) As Integer
    Dim byrefArray(10) As Integer
    ' Pass both arrays to the procedure.
    ArrayProcByRef(byvalArray, byrefArray)
    ' Check which array has been affected by the ReDim.
    Console.WriteLine(UBound(byvalArray))   ' => 10 (not modified)
    Console.WriteLine(UBound(byrefArray))   ' => 100 (modified)
End Sub

Sub ArrayProcByRef (ByVal arr() As Integer, ByRef arr2() As Integer)
    ' Change the size of both arrays.
    Redim arr(100)
    Redim arr2(100)
End Sub
```

Array parameters must specify the rank of the incoming array. For example, the following procedure takes a two-dimensional Long array and a three-dimensional String array:

```
Sub MyProc(ByVal arr(,) As Long, ByVal arr2(, ,) As String)
    ⋮
End Sub
```

Optional Arguments

You can define optional arguments by using the Optional keywords, as you did with Visual Basic 6 procedures. However, you must always provide an explicit default value for each optional argument, even though the default value is 0, an empty string, or Nothing:

```
Sub MyProc(Optional ByVal x As Integer = 0, _
    Optional ByVal y As String = "", Optional ByVal p As Person = Nothing)
    ⋮
End Sub
```

The IsMissing function isn't supported under Visual Basic .NET for this simple reason: the IsMissing function returns True only when a Variant argument has been omitted, but the Variant type isn't supported under the current version of Visual Basic. Instead, you provide a special default value for an argument and test it inside the procedure if you want to determine whether it was omitted:

```
Sub MyProc(Optional ByVal x As Short = -1)
    If x = -1 Then
        ' The x argument has been omitted (presumably).
    End If
    ⋮
End Sub
```

You can use 1 as a special value if the argument shouldn't take negative values; or you can use the largest negative or positive number for that numeric type, which correspond to the MinValue and MaxValue properties that all numeric classes expose:

```
Sub MyProc(Optional ByVal x As Long = Long.MinValue)
    If x = Long.MinValue Then
        ' The x argument has been omitted (presumably).
        Console.WriteLine(x)   ' => -9223372036854775808
    End If
    ⋮
End Sub
```

If the optional argument is a Single or a Double, you can also use the special NaN (Not-a-Number) value for its default:

```
Sub MyProc(Optional ByVal x As Double = Double.NaN)
    If Double.IsNaN(x) Then
        ' The x argument has been omitted.
    End If
End Sub
```

The NaN value is assigned to a floating-point number when you perform operations that don't return a real number, as when you pass a negative argument to the Log or Sqrt function. So there's a (very small) chance that you could mistakenly pass it to a procedure, as in the following code:

```
' This statement passes MyProc the NaN value,
' which is mistakenly taken as a missing argument.
MyProc(Math.Sqrt(-1))
```

ParamArray Arguments

You can create procedures that take any number of optional arguments by using the ParamArray keyword. In a welcome improvement on previous language versions, you can define arrays of arguments of any type. (Visual Basic 6 and previous versions support only Variant arrays for ParamArray arguments.)

```
Function Sum(ParamArray ByVal args() As Integer) As Integer
    Dim sumResult As Integer
    Dim index As Integer
    For index = 0 To UBound(args)
        sumResult += args(index)
    Next
    Sum = sumResult
End Function
```

In three other differences from previous language versions, notice first that ParamArray arguments are always passed by value so that any change inside the procedure itself doesn't affect the caller. Second, you can never omit a parameter to a procedure that expects a ParamArray:

```
' *** If Sum takes a ParamArray, this statement compiles
'      in Visual Basic 6 but not under Visual Basic .NET.
Result = Sum(1, , 3)
```

Finally, you can always pass a real array to a method that expects a ParamArray argument, as in this code:

```
Dim arr() As Integer = {1, 2, 3}
Result = Sum(arr)
```

Interestingly, the ParamArray parameter is an array in all aspects, and you can apply to it all the methods defined for arrays in the .NET Framework. Consider the following function, which returns the minimum value among all the arguments passed to it:

```
' Note: this routine raises an error if no argument is passed to it.
Function MinValue(ParamArray ByVal args() As Integer) As Integer
    MinValue = args(0)
    Dim i As Short
    For i = 1 To UBound(args)
        If args(i) < MinValue then MinValue = args(i)
    Next
End Function
```

The .NET Framework offers a Sort method that can sort an array of any type, so you can rewrite the MinValue function in a more concise (though not necessarily faster) way:

```
Function MinValue(ParamArray ByVal args() As Integer) As Integer
    ' Sort the array, and then return its first element.
    System.Array.Sort(args)
    MinValue = args(0)
End Function
```

Returning a Value

Functions can return a value by assigning it to the function's name (as you do in Visual Basic 6) or by using the new Return statement:

```
Function DoubleIt(ByVal x As Long) As Long
    Return x * 2
End Function
```

The Return statement is especially handy when a function has multiple exit points because it saves your having to write an explicit Exit Function statement. A Return keyword without arguments exits a Sub procedure immediately, even though it doesn't offer any advantage over the Exit Sub keyword. You can also use the Return keyword to return arrays, as you can see in this code:

```
' Return an array containing Integers in the range 0 to n-1.
Function InitializeArray(ByVal n As Integer) As Integer()
    Dim res(n), i As Integer
    For i = 0 To n - 1
        res(i) = i
    Next
    Return res
End Function
```

A reason to prefer the new Return statement to the old syntax is that you can then change the function name without also having to modify all the occurrences of the function name inside the procedure. It's a little detail that can save you some time during the refining phase.

As with previous versions, Visual Basic .NET allows you to use a function's name as a local variable inside the procedure, as I've done in the first version of the MinValue function in previous section. In many cases, this tactic spares you the trouble of using a local variable declaration and allows you to write more concise code. Microsoft documentation states that the Return statement can improve performance because the local variable named after the function can prevent the Just-in-Time (JIT) compiler from optimizing your code. I have never observed a substantial difference in performance between the two approaches, at least in small routines used for my benchmarks, but this is yet another reason for using the new Return statement when possible.

Conditional and Loop Statements

Visual Basic .NET supports all the conditional and loop statements supported by its predecessors—that is, the If and Select conditional blocks and the For, Do, and While loop statements. Nevertheless, Visual Basic .NET offers some new features in this area as well, and Visual Basic .NET 2003 adds a new way to declare the controlling variable in For and For Each loops.

Short-Circuit Evaluation with AndAlso and OrElse Operators

Short-circuit evaluation allows you to avoid the unnecessary evaluation of Boolean subexpressions if they wouldn't affect the value of the main expression. Let's see a simple example:

```
If n1 > 0 And Sqr(n2) < n1 ^ 2 Then ok = True
```

If the n1 variable is 0 or negative, the entire expression can only be False, whether the subexpression following the And operator evaluates to True or False. Previous Visual Basic versions always evaluate the entire If expression, so they incur an unnecessary performance hit.

Visual Basic .NET lets you produce smarter code using the new AndAlso and OrElse operators, which enforce short-circuit evaluation:

```
If n1 > 0 AndAlso Sqr(n2) < n1 ^ 2 Then ok = True
```

This expression is equivalent to the following, more verbose, code:

```
' "Manual" short-circuit evaluation
If n1 > 0 Then
    If Sqr(n2) < n1 ^ 2 Then ok = True
End If
```

You can have short-circuit evaluation in situations in which you use the Or operator:

```
If n1 > 0 Or Log(n2) > 2 Then ok = True
```

In this case, if the n1 variable is greater than 0, the entire expression is surely True, so evaluating the second subexpression Log(n2) can be sidestepped. You can enforce this smarter behavior with the new OrElse operator:

```
If n1 > 0 OrElse Log(n2) > 2 Then ok = True
```

These new operators also work inside complex Boolean expressions:

```
Dim n1, n2, n3 As Integer            ' All variables are 0.
' The expression following the OrElse operator isn't evaluated
' because the test on n1 and n2 is sufficient.
If n1 = 0 AndAlso (n2 = 0 OrElse n3 = 0) Then ok = True
```

Short-circuit evaluation helps you avoid many run-time errors without writing much code. For example, you can use the following approach to read an array element only if the index is in the valid range:

```
' This never throws an exception, even if index is out of range.
If i >= 0 AndAlso i <= UBound(arr) AndAlso arr(i) > 0 Then
    ' arr(i) exists and is positive.
End If
```

Here's another example:

```
' AndAlso ensures that a division by zero error never occurs.
If n1 <> 0 AndAlso n2 \ n1 = n3 Then ok = True
```

The AndAlso operator lets you avoid errors when you check the property of an object variable that might be Nothing:

```
' Set ok to True if obj.Value is defined and non-negative.
If Not (obj Is Nothing) AndAlso obj.Value >= 0 Then ok = True
```

Short-circuit evaluation can speed up your applications, but you must account for subtle bugs that might slip into your code. This is especially true when the subexpression contains user-defined functions that can alter the program's behavior. Consider this code:

```
' Is n2 incremented or not?
If n1 = 0 AndAlso Increment(n2) > 10 Then ok = True

Function Increment(ByRef value As Integer) As Integer
    value += 1
    Increment = value
End Function
```

Unless you're familiar with short-circuit evaluation—which might be the case if you're a C/C++ or Java developer—you might not immediately realize that the n2 variable is incremented only if the n1 variable is 0. You can make your code more readable by using nested If statements—in other words, by writing what you might call manual short-circuiting code:

```
' Is n2 incremented or not?
If n1 = 0 Then
    If Increment(n2) > 10 Then ok = True
End If
```

The And and Or operators work as they do in Visual Basic 6 and perform bitwise operations rather than truly Boolean operations. You can use them for bit-manipulation code as you've always done:

```
' Check whether bit 1 is set.
' (You need the CBool function if Option Strict is On.)
If CBool(n1 And 2) Then ...
```

For Next and For Each Loops

Visual Basic .NET supports For, For Each, and Do loops, and they support exactly the same syntax as under previous versions of the language. The most frequently used looping structure in Visual Basic is undoubtedly the For Next loop:

```
For counter = startvalue To endvalue [Step increment]
    ' Statements to be executed in the loop...
Next
```

You need to specify the Step clause only if an increment is different from 1. You can exit the loop using an Exit For statement, but unfortunately Visual Basic doesn't provide a sort of "Continue" command that lets you skip the remaining part of the current iteration. (This command is available in C#.) The best you can do is use (nested) If statements or use a plain Goto keyword that points to the end of the loop. In fact, this occasion is one of the few when a single Goto statement can make your code more readable and maintainable.

Visual Basic .NET 2003 introduces a new syntax that allows you to declare the controlling variable inside the loop:

```
For counter As Integer = 1 To 100
    ' ...
Next
```

This new syntax doesn't add any groundbreaking possibility, but it is preferred because it prevents you from reusing the value in the variable when the loop exits. You can be glad that you can't reuse the value because most of the time you can't make any correct assumptions about the value in the variable at the end of the loop (which might have been exited because of an Exit For or a Goto statement). For this reason, I will use this syntax in the remainder of this book, even though you can easily fix the code so that it runs under the first edition of Visual Basic .NET simply by declaring the controlling variable in a separate Dim statement.

Always use integer variables as the controlling variable of a For...Next loop. They're always faster than Single, Double, or Decimal controlling variables by a factor of 10 times or more (or even 100, in the case of Decimal control variables). In addition, because of rounding errors, you cannot be completely sure that a floating-point variable is incremented correctly when the increment is a fractional quantity, and you might end up with fewer or more iterations than expected:

```
Dim count As Integer
For d As Single = 0 To 1 Step 0.1
    count = count + 1
Next
Console.WriteLine(count)          ' Displays "10" but should be "11"
```

If you need to increment a floating-point quantity, the safest and most efficient technique is shown in the following code snippet:

```
Dim d As Single
' Scale start and end values by a factor of ten,
' so that you can use integers to control the loop.
For count As Integer = 0 To 10
    ' Do what you want with the D variable, then increment it
    ' to be ready for the next iteration of the loop.
    d += 0.1
Next
```

The For Each loop lets you visit all the elements of an array or a collection (more precisely, all the elements of an object that implements the IEnumerable interface, as I explain in Chapter 8). The controlling variable can be of any type:

```
Dim arr() As Integer = {1, 2, 3}
Dim i As Integer
For Each i In arr
    Console.WriteLine(i)
Next
```

If you are working under Visual Basic .NET 2003, you can also declare the controlling variable inside the loop itself:

```
For Each i As Integer In arr
    Console.WriteLine(i)
Next
```

When you're working with arrays, regular For…Next loops are usually faster and preferable to For Each…Next loops, whereas when you are working with collections, the latter type of loop is usually faster. When coupled with the ability to create an array on the fly, the For Each loop allows you to execute a block of statements with different values for a controlling variable, which don't need to be in sequence:

```
' Check whether the value in Number is prime. (Number must be <1000.)
Dim isPrime As Boolean = True
For Each var As Integer In New Integer() {2, 3, 5, 7, 11, 13, 17, 19, 23, 29, 31}
    If (Number Mod var) = 0 Then isPrime = False: Exit For
Next
```

The Do…Loop structure is more flexible than the For…Next loop in that you can place the termination test either at the beginning or at the end of the loop. (In the latter case, the loop is always executed at least once.) You can use either the While clause (repeat while the test condition is true) or the Until clause (repeat while the test condition is false). You can exit a Do loop at any moment by executing an Exit Do statement, but—as with For…Next loops—Visual Basic doesn't offer a Continue keyword that skips over the remaining statements in the loop and immediately restarts the loop:

```
' Example of a Do loop with test condition on its top.
' This loop is never executed if x <= 0.
Do While x > 0
    y = y + 1
    x = x \ 2
Loop


' Example of a Do loop with test condition on its bottom.
' This loop is always executed at least once, even if x <= 0.
Do
    y = y + 1
    x = x \ 2
Loop Until x <= 0

' Endless loop - requires an Exit Do statement to get out.
Do
    ' ...
Loop
```

Commands, Functions, and Constants

As I explained in the section "The Imports Statement" in Chapter 2, new projects typically import a few important namespaces that are vital to the correct working of most Visual

Basic .NET projects. One such namespace is Microsoft.VisualBasic, which exposes most of the language commands, functions, and constants. Another is Microsoft.VisualBasic.Compatibility.VB6, which contains classes that help you port applications to Visual Basic .NET from older versions using the Visual Basic Upgrade Wizard.

Most commands in these namespaces have retained their original syntax, and I assume that you already know how to use them. In this section, I'll focus only on the differences and a few problems you might encounter in the porting process.

String Constants and Functions

Visual Basic 6 string constants, such as vbCrLf and vbTab, are still supported as fields of the Microsoft.VisualBasic.Constants class (together with all the other Visual Basic 6 constants). This class is marked as a global class by using the StandardModule attribute, so you don't have to include the name of the class in your code, as you'd do if it were a regular class:

```
' vbCrLf is a field of the Microsoft.VisualBasic.Constants class.
Dim separator As String = vbCrLf
```

Alternatively, you can use the fields exposed by the Microsoft.VisualBasic.ControlChars class. Because this class isn't declared globally, you must include the name of the class itself (unless you use an Imports statement to import the entire class). The names of constants are the same as in Visual Basic 6 except that they don't include the vb prefix:

```
' A more .NET-oriented syntax
Dim separator As String = ControlChars.CrLf
```

The ControlChars class contains the following constants: Back, Cr, CrLf, FormFeed, NewLine, NullChar, Quote, Tab, and VerticalTab. Note that the vbNullString constant is no longer necessary because you can simply use Nothing in its place, but it is still supported for backward compatibility.

The Microsoft.VisualBasic.Strings class exposes most of the Visual Basic string functions, including Asc, Chr, ChrW, Filter, Format, FormatCurrency, FormatDateTime, FormatNumber, FormatPercent, InStr, InStrRev, Join, LCase, Left, Len, LTrim, Mid, Replace, Right, RTrim, Space, Split, StrComp, StrReverse, Trim, and UCase. Functions that support multiple syntax forms—such as InStr and Mid—have been conveniently overloaded and all the usual forms are supported. (Read Chapter 4 for more details about overloading.) These methods are globally defined, so you don't have to include the complete class name to invoke them, though you do need to specify the complete names of the constants that are related to them:

```
' Compare two strings in case-insensitive mode.
If StrComp(s1, s2, CompareMethod.Text) = 0 Then res = "Equal"
```

Visual Basic .NET doesn't support $ functions, such as Left$ or Space$.

Math Functions

Most math functions you need in your applications are implemented in the System.Math class. Therefore they aren't part of the Visual Basic .NET library, though they closely resemble the functions you had in previous versions of this language. You can classify the math functions in these groups:

- **Arithmetic functions** Abs, Ceiling, Floor, Min, Max, Sqrt, Exp, Log, Log10, Round, Pow, Sign, IEEERemainder

- **Trig and inverse trig functions**   Sin, Cos, Tan, Asin, Acos, Atan, Atan2

- **Hyperbolic trig functions**   Sinh, Cosh, Tanh

- **Constants** E, PI

Unless you import the System.Math class, you must specify the complete class name when calling one of its methods. The calling syntax of functions that were supported under Visual Basic 6—possibly under a different name, such as Sqrt, Sign, and Atan—hasn't changed. The Log function supports one argument (natural logarithms) or two arguments (logarithms in any base):

```
' The natural logarithm of 10
Console.WriteLine(Math.Log(10))            ' => 2.30258509299405
' Two ways to evaluate the decimal logarithm of 1000
Console.WriteLine(Math.Log(1000, 10))      ' => 3
Console.WriteLine(Math.Log10(1000))        ' => 3
```

The Min and Max methods do what their name suggests and are conveniently overloaded to work with any type of value:

```
Console.WriteLine(Math.Min(1.5, 0.7))      ' => 0.7
Console.WriteLine(Math.Max(99, 87))        ' => 99
```

The Floor function returns the integer less than or equal to the argument, whereas Ceiling returns the integer greater than or equal to the argument:

```
Console.WriteLine(Math.Floor(- 1.5))       ' => -2
Console.WriteLine(Math.Ceiling(2.5))       ' => 3
```

Atan2 returns the angle formed by an object of a given height y at a given distance x; it's similar to Atan, but it returns an unambiguous value for all the four quadrants. The IEEERemainder function returns the remainder of a division; it's therefore similar to the Mod operator but works correctly also with floating-point numbers:

```
Console.WriteLine(Math.IEEERemainder(2, 1.5))   ' => 0.5
```

Date and Time Functions

The DateAndTime class includes several date and time functions, among which are DateAdd, DateDiff, DatePart, DateSerial, DateValue, Year, Month, Day, Hour, Minute,

Second, MonthName, Weekday, WeekdayName, TimeSerial, and TimeValue. This class also exposes two read-only properties, Now and Timer. In general, the syntax hasn't changed from Visual Basic 6 except for the DateAdd, DateDiff, and DatePart functions, which now can take an enumerated constant instead of a string constant:

```
' Get the date two weeks from now.
newDate = DateAdd(DateInterval.WeekOfYear, 2, Now())
' The Visual Basic 6 syntax is still supported.
newDate = DateAdd("w", 2, Now())
```

You have two new properties to retrieve and set the current date and time:

```
' Reset system time to midnight.
TimeOfDay = #12:00:00 PM#
' Evaluate days left until December 31 of current year.
days = DateDiff(DateInterval.Day, Today, _
    DateSerial(Year(Today), 12, 31))
```

These properties replace Time and Date respectively. The MonthName and Week-dayName functions support an extra Boolean argument, to retrieve the abbreviated month or day name:

```
Console.WriteLine(MonthName(1, True))        ' => Jan
```

Interaction Commands and Functions

The Microsoft.VisualBasic.Interaction class exposes many useful commands and methods that were available in Visual Basic 6, including AppActivate, Beep, CallByName, Choose, Command, Environ, IIf, InputBox, MsgBox, Partition, Shell, and Switch. These methods are globally defined, so you don't have to include the class name when you use them:

```
MsgBox("Goodbye", MsgBoxStyle.Information)
```

The Shell function expands on the original version and supports an additional argument that enables you to specify whether to wait until the shelled program terminates, with an optional timeout. This solves an old problem known to many Visual Basic developers without your having to resort to Windows API functions:

```
' Run Notepad.exe, and wait until the user terminates it.
Shell("notepad", AppWinStyle.NormalFocus, True)

' Run Notepad, and then wait max 10 seconds.
Dim taskID As Long
taskId = Shell("notepad", AppWinStyle.NormalFocus, True, 10000)
If taskID = 0 Then
    Console.WriteLine("Notepad has been closed within 10 seconds.")
Else
    Console.WriteLine("Notepad is still running after 10 seconds.")
End If
```

Other Commands, Functions, and Objects

The FileSystem class includes all the usual Visual Basic file commands and functions, including ChDir, ChDrive, CurDir, Dir, FileCopy, FileDateTime, FileLen, GetAttr, Kill, MkDir, RmDir, and SetAttr. There are no relevant differences from their counterparts under previous versions of the language, except that the new FileOpen, FileClose, FileGet, FilePut, PrintLine, InputLine, and InputString commands supersede the Open#, Close#, Get#, Put#, Print#, LineInput#, and Input statements (whose nonstandard syntax can't be supported in Visual Basic .NET):

```
' Read a text file.
Dim handle As Integer = FreeFile()
' Open a file for input.
FileOpen(handle, "C:\autoexec.bat", OpenMode.Input, OpenAccess. Read)
' Read the entire file in one operation.
Dim fileText As String = InputString(handle, CInt(LOF(handle)))
' Close the file.
FileClose(handle)
```

In most cases, however, you should avoid these file-related functions in the Microsoft.VisualBasic namespace and use other objects offered by the .NET Framework because you'll write more flexible code that way. See Chapter 9 for more details about .NET file and directory classes.

The Conversion class provides support for functions such as Fix, Hex, Int, Oct, Str, and Val, which have the same syntax and meaning as under Visual Basic 6. This class also includes the ErrorToString function, which converts an error code to a description. The ErrorToString function is similar to Err.Description, but you don't need to have an actual error to retrieve the description associated with an error code:

```
' Display the description associated with error code 9.
Console.WriteLine(ErrorToString(9))   ' => Subscript out of range.
```

The Information class gathers miscellaneous functions, such as Erl, Err, IsArray, IsDate, IsError, IsNothing, IsNumeric, LBound, UBound, and TypeName.

The IsEmpty and IsNull functions aren't supported because they made sense only with Variant arguments, which in turn aren't supported. However, the .NET Framework supports the DBNull data type (which represents a null value coming from a database field), and Visual Basic .NET conveniently exposes an IsDBNull function, which has therefore more or less the same meaning as IsNull.

Error Handling

For years, Visual Basic programmers have trapped errors by using the time-honored but admittedly limited On Error statement in its two variants: On Error GoTo and On Error Resume Next. Visual Basic .NET supports both of them, even though their use is discouraged in favor of the newer Try...Catch...Finally statement.

Throwing Exceptions

The main problem with the traditional way of dealing with errors under Windows is that there's no approach with which everyone agrees. For example, functions in most DLLs (including Windows system DLLs) report errors through a return value and do that in a very confusing way. In some cases, 0 means success and 1 means error, while in other cases the meaning is reversed. COM components return an error code by means of a 32-bit HRESULT value, and Visual Basic applications raise errors using a COM-compliant mechanism behind the scenes. Other languages, such as C++ and Java, can use an error handling mechanism based on exceptions.

To allow cross-language interoperability, the .NET Framework has standardized on a single method of raising and trapping errors based on exceptions. You can think of exceptions as unexpected conditions that occur during execution of your application or while code is running inside the .NET Framework itself. When this situation occurs, the code is said to *throw an exception* that some other code is expected to catch.

An exception can be caught by code in the same procedure in which the error occurs. If it isn't, the exception is thrown to the caller, and it's up to the caller to remedy the error and possibly retry the operation that caused the malfunction. If the caller doesn't catch the exception, the exception is automatically thrown to the caller's caller. The exception "bubbles up" the call chain until it finds a calling procedure that's willing to catch it. (You'll see in a moment what catching an exception means in practice.)

By default, if no procedure in the call chain catches the exception, the end user is notified by means of an error dialog box, such as the one in Figure 3-1. You can change how the common language runtime behaves when an uncaught exception is thrown by modifying the DbgJITDebugLaunchSetting value under the HKEY_LOCAL_MACHINE \Software\Microsoft\.NETFramework Registry key. By default this value is 0, which makes the error dialog appear; setting it to 1 always terminates the application, whereas setting it to 2 always runs the debugger.

The phrase *throwing an exception* is appropriate because an Exception object is actually passed back to the caller when an exception occurs. The code that catches the exception can examine the Exception object's properties, invoke its methods, and take any step it deems necessary— such as informing the user or silently canceling the operation that caused the problem. Alternatively, the code can throw the Exception object again—possibly after adjusting one or more of its properties—or it can throw a completely different Exception object to its own caller. The Exception object being thrown back and forth exposes properties, such as Message (the error's description), Source (a string that tells where the error occurred), and HelpLink (the position of a help page that describes how to recover from the error). The next section describes these properties in greater detail.

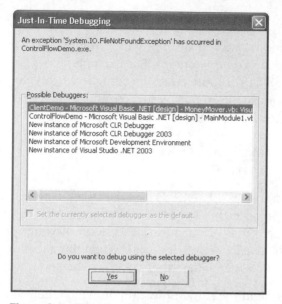

Figure 3-1   The error dialog box that appears when one or more
.NET debuggers are installed on the computer

If you're thinking that all this sounds familiar, you're right. Even though the inner details are different, .NET exceptions work and behave in much the same way Visual Basic's own error handling mechanism does. The Exception object resembles the Err object (with different names for its properties); throwing an exception works surprisingly like raising an error; the "bubbling up" behavior is the one Visual Basic 6 uses when notifying procedures of errors if those procedures don't have an active error handler. This is known ground for Visual Basic developers.

The Exception Object

The Exception object is defined in the .NET Framework, and its complete name is System.Exception. Both .NET classes and your own applications don't usually throw this raw exception object, though. The framework defines two other generic classes, System.SystemException and System.ApplicationException: nearly all the exception objects defined in the .NET Framework inherit from SystemException, whereas custom and application-specific exception objects should inherit from ApplicationException. These two classes don't add any properties or methods to the base Exception class, but they offer an effective way to categorize exceptions. You should become familiar with the exceptions that the .NET Framework exposes, some of which are depicted in Figure 3-2. For example, math operations can throw an ArithmeticException, OverflowException or a DivideByZeroException object, while functions can throw an ArgumentOutOfRangeException object. For a complete list of exception objects, just use the search command in the object browser and look for the Exception substring, or use the Exceptions command from the Debug menu. (See section "Exceptions in Visual Studio .NET," later in this chapter.)

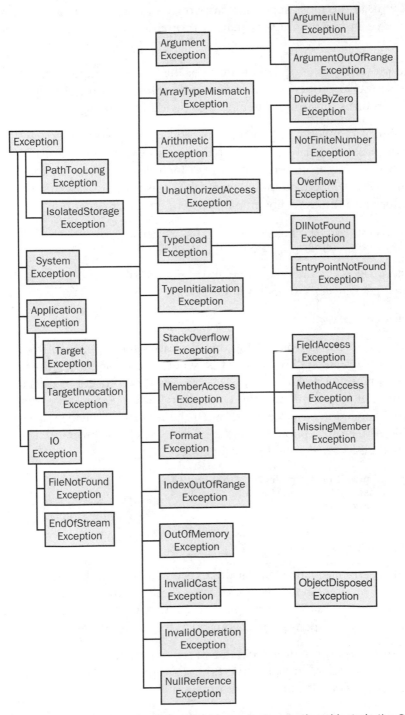

Figure 3-2 The hierarchy of the most important exception objects in the System namespace

Let's have a look at the most important properties and methods that all these exception objects have in common. (Note that all properties are read-only except Source and HelpLink.)

The Message property is the descriptive text for the exception and is therefore similar to the Err.Description property. For example, the Message property of a DivideBy-ZeroException returns the string "Attempted to divide by zero."

The Exception object inherits the ToString method from System.Object, and it returns the same error message that would be displayed to the end user in a dialog box. This is similar to the Message property, but it also includes the name of the module. If debug information is embedded in the executable, this property also returns the name of the procedure and the exact line number where the error occurred:

```
System.DivideByZeroException: Attempted to divide by zero.
at MyApplication.Form1.TestProc in C:\MyApplication\Form1.vb:line 70
```

The TargetSite property returns the name and signature of the procedure in which the exception was first thrown, expressed in C# syntax:

```
Int32 DivideNumber(Int32 x, Int32 y)
```

The StackTrace property returns a string that describes the stack path from the place the exception was originally thrown—that is, where the error occurred—to the place the error was caught. For example, say that your TestProc procedure calls the EvalResult procedure, which in turns calls the DivideNumber function, and assume that the latter two procedures don't catch exceptions. If the innermost DivideNumber function throws a DivideByZeroException, the value of the StackTrace property as read in the TestProc procedure looks like the following code:

```
at MyApplication.Form1.DivideNumber(Int32 x, I nt32 y)
    in C:\MyApplication\Form1.vb:line 91
at MyApplication.Form1.EvalResult() in
    C:\MyApplication\Form1.vb:line 87
at MyApplication.Form1.TestProc() in
    C:\MyApplication\Form1.vb:line 77
```

You get this detailed information only if the executable embeds debug information; if you compiled the program in Release mode, you don't see the name of the source file or the line number. The StackTrace property is your best friend when you're trying to figure out what actually happens when your code throws an exception.

The Source property sets or returns the name of the component in which the exception was thrown and is therefore similar to the Err.Source property. For exceptions thrown in the current application, this property returns a null string.

The HelpLink property sets or returns a Uniform Resource Name (URN) or Uniform Resource Locator (URL) to the help file associated with the Exception object, as you see here:

```
file://C:/MyApplication/manual.html#ErrorNum42
```

The Try...Catch...Finally Statement

So far, you've seen how the exception-throwing mechanism works and what information an exception object carries. Now you're ready to fully appreciate the power and flexibility of the new Try...Catch...Finally block.

The Catch Keyword

Whenever you execute code that might throw an exception, you should enclose it in a Try...End Try block. The portion of code between the Try keyword and the first Catch keyword is guarded against exceptions, and if an exception is thrown, Visual Basic passes the control to the first Catch block, which is also called an exception filter. In the Catch code block, you can examine the properties of the exception object and decide how to react to the error. Here's a simple example:

```
Dim x, y As Integer
Try
    x = x \ y
    ' If y is 0, the following statement is never executed.
    y = CInt(10 ^ x)
Catch ex As Exception
    If ex.Message = "Attempted to divide by zero." Then
        ' Deal with division by zero errors here.
    Else
        ' Deal here with other types of exceptions.
    End If
End Try
```

As soon as an error occurs—or an exception is thrown, to comply with the new terminology—the program jumps to the Catch block, executes that code block, and then jumps to the first statement after the End Try keyword.

Testing the Message string isn't the correct way to deal with exceptions, however. Instead, you should have multiple Catch blocks, each one testing a different exception object:

```
Try
    x = x \ y
    y = CInt(10 ^ x)
Catch ex As DivideByZeroException
    ' Deal here with divide by zero exceptions.
    ⋮
Catch ex As OverflowException
    ' Deal here with overflow exceptions.
    ⋮
Catch ex As Exception
    ' Deal here with all other exceptions.
    ⋮
End Try
```

Visual Basic compares the type of the exception object being thrown with the expressions in Catch clauses in the order in which they appear, and it executes the first one that matches. It's usually a good idea to have a final Catch expression that matches the System.Exception object because this code is guaranteed to execute if no previous Catch expression matches the exception. A Catch clause for the System.Exception object always matches any exception because all exception objects inherit from System.Exception. (This last Catch clause is conceptually similar to the Else clause in a Select Case block.)

Because All Catch expressions are evaluated in the order in which they appear, you should test for the most specific exceptions first, followed by less specific ones. The test for the System.Exception object, if present, should be in the last Catch block because it matches any exception; consequently, no Catch block after it can ever execute. When sorting Catch blocks, though, you should have a look at the exception hierarchy depicted in Figure 3-2, and check that you never catch an exception object after catching its parent exception. For example, the Catch block for a DivideByZeroException object should never follow the Catch block for a less specific ArithmeticException object.

The As expression in the Catch block is optional. You can omit it if you don't need to examine the exception object's properties to make a decision.

```
Try
    ⋮
Catch ex As DivideByZeroException
    ⋮
Catch ex As OverflowException
    ⋮
Catch ex As ArithmeticException
    ' Catch less specific arithmetic exceptions here.
    ⋮
Catch
    Console.WriteLine("An error has occurred." )
End Try
```

You can exit from a Try...End Try structure at any time by calling the Exit Try statement, which can appear inside the Try block or any Catch block.

A closer look at the exception hierarchy reveals that the common language runtime can throw a few exceptions that inherit from ApplicationException or directly from Exception. For example, the PathTooLongException and IsolatedStorageException classes derive directly from Exception; a few exceptions in the System.IO namespace—namely DirectoryNotFoundException, FileNotFoundException, and EndOfStreamException— inherit from IOException, which in turn derives directly from Exception (and not from SystemException). Even worse, some exception classes in the System.Reflection namespace inherit from ApplicationException instead of SystemException. This means that you can't assume that you can trap all system-related exceptions using a Catch filter on SystemException. You also can't assume that a Catch clause on ApplicationException will filter only application-related exceptions.

The .NET runtime defines a few exceptions that occur in really exceptional (and catastrophic) circumstances—namely, StackOverflowException, OutOfMemoryException, and ExecutionEngineException. A common trait among these exceptions is that they can occur at any time because they aren't really caused by your application. Although you can catch them, in practice you should never do anything else but terminate the application with a suitable error message because after these exceptions the application might be in an unstable state.

The When Keyword

The Catch clause supports an optional When expression, which lets you specify an additional condition that must evaluate to True for the Catch block to be selected. This feature lets you define more specific exception filters. Look at this code, for example:

```
Dim x, y, z, res As Integer        ' All variables are 0.
Try
    ' You can see different behaviors by commenting out or changing
    ' the order of the following statements.
    ' ...
    res = y \ x
    ' ...
    res = x \ y
    ' ...
    res = x \ z
Catch ex As DivideByZeroException When (x = 0)
    Console.WriteLine("Division error: x is 0.")
Catch ex As DivideByZeroException When (y = 0)
    Console.WriteLine("Division error: y is 0.")
Catch ex As DivideByZeroException
    Console.WriteLine("Division error: no information on variables")
Catch ex As Exception
    Console.WriteLine("An error has occurred." )
End Try
```

In general, you can achieve the same behavior using an If...ElseIf block inside a Catch block, but the When clause makes for better organization of your error handling code. For example, if no combination of Catch and When clauses matches the current exception, execution flow will go to the last Catch block and you don't have to duplicate any code whatsoever.

The When clause can also reference the exception object's properties, so you can partition your exceptions in subcategories and have a distinct Catch block for each one of them. For example, the following code parses the Message property to extract the name of the file that hasn't been found:

```
Try
    ' Comment out next statement to see the behavior
    ' when another file is missing.
    FileOpen(1, "c:\myapp.ini", OpenMode.Input)
    FileOpen(2, "c:\xxxxx.dat", OpenMode.Input)
Catch ex As System.IO.FileNotFoundException _
    When InStr(ex.Message, """c:\myapp.ini""") > 0
    ' The ini file is missing.
    Console.WriteLine("Can't initialize: MyApp.Ini file not found")
```

```
Catch ex As System.IO.FileNotFoundException
    ' Another file is missing.
    ' Extract the filename from the Message property.
    Dim filename As String = Split(ex.Message, """")(1)
    Console.WriteLine("The following file is missing: " & filename)
End Try
```

An explanation is in order: The Message property of the FileNotFoundException object returns a string in the following format:

```
Could not find file "<filename>".
```

Therefore, you can use the InStr function to test whether a file you're looking for is embedded in this string. Just remember to enclose the searched-for filename in double quotes.

You can take advantage of the When keyword in other ways as well. For example, you might have a local variable that tracks the progress status of the procedure so that you can take different actions depending on where the error occurred. The following code should render the idea:

```
Dim currentStep As Integer      ' You can also use an Enum value.
Try
    CurrentStep = 1             ' Initialize the program.
    ⋮
    currentStep = 2             ' Open the data file.
    ⋮
    currentStep = 3             ' Process the file's contents.
    ⋮
    currentStep = 4             ' ...And so on ...
    ⋮
Catch ex As Exception When currentStep = 1
    Console.WriteLine("An error occurred in the initialization step.")
Catch ex As System.IO.FileNotFoundException When currentStep = 2
    Console.WriteLine("The data file wasn't found.")
Catch ex As Exception When currentStep = 2
    Console.WriteLine("An error occurred while opening the data file.")
Catch ex As Exception When currentStep = 3
    Console.WriteLine("An error occurred while processing data.")
' Add here other Catch blocks.
⋮
End Try
```

Note that it's acceptable to have the first block catch the generic Exception object because the When condition makes the test succeed only if the error occurred in the first (initialization) step of the procedure. When sorting Catch blocks related to the same step, you should catch more specific exception objects first (as when currentStep is 2 in the preceding code).

You can also use the When keyword in a rather unorthodox way to solve one of the recurring problems in error logging and reporting. Let's say that you want to create a log of all the exceptions in your application, including those that are caught in a Catch clause. Apparently, the best solution is to create a generic error log routine and invoke it from inside each and every Catch block in your code, a boring and error-prone task.

Thanks to the When keyword, you can achieve the same effect by adding just one single line of code for each Try block, shown here in boldface:

```
Try
    ' Do something.
    ' ...
Catch ex As Exception When LogException(ex)
Catch ex As FileNotFoundException
    ' ...
Catch ex As DivisionByZeroException
    ' ...
Catch ex As Exception
    ' ...
End Try
```

LogException is a function that is defined elsewhere in the application (for example, in a module); it does the actual logging and always returns False:

```
Function LogException(ByVal ex As Exception) As Boolean
    Debug.WriteLine(ex.Message)
    Return False               ' (Not really necessary)
End Function
```

The first Catch clause begins soon after the Try block matches all exceptions, so Visual Basic always evaluates the When clause to see whether its expression returns True. At this point, the LogException function is invoked, giving you an opportunity to log the exception somewhere. This function returns False; therefore, Visual Basic ignores this Catch block and passes to the ones that follow it, where the exception is actually processed.

The Finally Keyword

In most real-world applications, you often need to execute a cleanup code when an exception is thrown. For example, you want to close a file if an error occurs while the code is processing that file, and you want to release a lock on a database table if an error occurs while the application is processing records in that table. In cases like these, you need a Finally clause. The code between the Finally keyword and the End Try keyword is always guaranteed to run, whether or not the code in the Try block throws an exception. The Finally block runs even if the code in a Catch block throws an exception, the Try...End Try block is exited because of an Exit Try statement, or the method itself is exited because of a Return statement.

Here's an example of a block of code that changes the current directory and ensures that the original directory is restored before exiting the Try...End Try structure:

```
Dim cdir As String
Try
    ' Remember the current directory.
    cdir = Environment.CurrentDirectory
    ' Change to another directory.
    FileSystem.ChDir("c:\xxx")
    :
Catch ex As Exception
```

```
        ' Deal here with errors.

    Finally
        ' In all cases, restore the current directory.
        Environment.CurrentDirectory = cdir
    End Try
```

It's legal to have a Try...Finally...End Try block without a Catch block. Such code might be appropriate when you want the caller to catch and process all the errors in the current procedure, but at the same time you have some cleanup code that must execute no matter what. Such a block might be useful also to provide a common block of cleanup code for a procedure that has multiple Exit Sub, Exit Function, or Return statements scattered in code:

```
Function TestMultipleExitPointFunction() As Integer
    Dim x, y, z As Integer
    Try
        ⋮
        If x > 0 Then Return 1
        ⋮
        If y = 0 Then Return 2
        ⋮
        If z > 0 Then Return 3
        ⋮
        Return 4
    Finally
        ' This code runs whatever exit path the code takes.
        ⋮
        Console.Write ("This function is returning the value ")
        Console.WriteLine(TestMultipleExitPointFunction)
    End Try
End Function
```

The preceding code snippet demonstrates that the code in the Finally block is even able to inspect (and modify) the value being returned by the function to the caller. As the previous code snippet demonstrates, this technique also works if the return value was assigned using a Return statement, as opposed to being assigned to the local variable named after the function.

Finally, note that if the code in the Finally block throws an exception, the Finally block is immediately exited and the exception is thrown to the caller. Therefore, you should always check that no error can occur while the Finally code is being processed; if you can't guarantee this, you should use a nested Try...End Try structure inside the Finally block.

The Throw Keyword

Under Visual Basic 6 and previous versions, you can raise an error using the Err.Raise method. The Err object is still supported under Visual Basic .NET, so any code based on its Raise method will continue to work as before. However, you should throw your exceptions using the new Throw command to comply with the exception mechanism and make your code compatible with components written in other .NET languages.

Throwing an Exception

Unlike Err.Raise, the Throw command takes only one argument, the exception object being thrown. Unless you already have an exception object (which is the case if you are inside a Catch block), you must create such an object and set its properties as required. In most cases, you can create an exception object and throw it in one statement:

```
' This statement broadly corresponds to
'    Err.Raise 53, , "File not found".
Throw New System.IO.FileNotFoundException()
```

When you're creating the exception object, you can specify a more precise message by passing an argument to the exception object's constructor:

```
Dim msg As String = "Initialization File Not Found"
Throw New System.IO.FileNotFoundException(msg)
```

The Throw statement is especially useful when you want to catch a subset of all the possible exceptions and delegate the remaining ones to the caller. This is a common programming pattern: each portion of the code deals with the errors it knows how to fix and leaves the others to the calling code. As I have explained previously, if no Catch expression matches the current exception, the exception is automatically thrown to the caller. But it's a good practice to do the throwing explicitly, so that you make it clear that you aren't just a lazy or distracted programmer:

```
Try
    ' Do some math operations here.
    ⋮
Catch ex As DivideByZeroException
    ⋮
Catch ex As OverflowException
    ⋮
Catch ex As Exception
    ' Explicitly throw this unhandled exception to the caller.
    Throw
 End Try
```

The Throw statement without an argument rethrows the current exception object and must appear in a Catch clause to be valid. The only other significant difference from the version that takes an argument is that the latter also resets the StackTrace property of the exception object (as if a brand-new exception were created), so the version without an argument is preferable for rethrowing the same exception when you want to let the caller routine determine exactly where the exception occurred. On the other hand, you should throw a new exception object if you want to hide this sort of detail.

A good rule of thumb related to expression: don't throw exceptions for relatively common errors, such as end-of-file or timeout; instead, return a special value to the caller. For example, the Math.Sqrt function returns NaN (Not-a-Number) when it receives a negative argument instead of raising an error (as the Sqr function in Visual Basic 6 does).

Coexisting with Old-Style Error Handlers

The Visual Basic .NET Err.Raise method and the Throw command are partially compatible. For example, you can use a Try…End Try block to catch an error raised with the Err.Raise method, and you can use an On Error Resume Next statement and the Err object to neutralize and inspect an exception object created by the Throw command. The old and the new error trapping mechanisms don't always coexist well, though, and there are some limitations. For example, you can't have an On Error Resume Next statement and a Try…End Try block in the same procedure.

To assist you in porting existing applications to Visual Basic .NET, the Err object has been extended with the new GetException method, which returns the Exception object that corresponds to the current error. This feature lets you preserve old-style error handlers in those procedures that don't lend themselves to easy porting to the new syntax. This new method enables such procedures to correctly throw an exception object to their caller, where the exception can be processed using a Try block as usual:

```
Sub TestGetExceptionMethod()
    Try
        Call OldStyleErrorHandlerProc()
    Catch ex As DivideByZeroException
        Console.WriteLine("A DivideByZeroException has been caught.")
    End Try
End Sub


' This procedure traps an error using an old-style On Error Goto
' and returns it to the caller as an exception.

Sub OldStyleErrorHandlerProc()
    On Error Goto ErrorHandler
    Dim x, y As Integer          ' Cause a division by zero error.
    y = 1 \ x
    Exit Sub
ErrorHandler:
    ' Add cleanup code here as necessary.
    ⋮
    ' Then report the error to the caller as an Exception object.
    Throw Err.GetException()
End Sub
```

Keep in mind, however, that backward compatibility with the Visual Basic 6 way of dealing with errors doesn't come free. If you use either On Error Goto or On Error Resume Next, the compiler generates additional IL code after each statement. This additional code can make the procedure run up to five times slower than a procedure without error trapping. By comparison, the Try…Catch…Finally statement adds a fixed overhead (the code that sets up the exception handler), which tends to be negligible for procedures of several statements. For this reason, it is OK to use the On Error statement when efficiency isn't a problem (for example, when working with the user interface), but you shouldn't use it in time-critical routines.

Custom Exception Objects

The old Err.Raise method has one advantage over the Throw command and the more modern exception-based mechanism: it makes it easy to define custom error codes, as in this line of code:

```
Err.Raise 1001, , "Initialization File Not Found"
```

As you saw in the preceding section, by means of the Throw command you can create a new System.Exception object (or an object that inherits from System.Exception) and set its Message property, but you can't do more than that. Sometimes you need to be able to create entirely new exception objects, which, according to .NET guidelines, should inherit from System.ApplicationException (as opposed to .NET runtime exceptions, which derive from System.SystemException).

Let me show how you can create a class that inherits from System.ApplicationException and that overrides the Message property with a custom string:

```
' By convention, the name of all classes that inherit
' from System.Exception must end with "Exception".
Class UnableToLoadIniFileException
    Inherits System.ApplicationException

    Overrides ReadOnly Property Message() As String
        Get
            Return "Unable to load initialization file"
        End Get
    End Property
End Class
```

It's that easy! Because this class inherits from System.Exception, you can use it in a Throw command and in a Catch block:

```
' The caller code
Sub TestCustomException()
    Try
        LoadIniFile
    Catch ex As UnableToLoadIniFileException
        Console.WriteLine(ex.Message)   ' => Unable to load...
    Catch ex As Exception
        ' Deal with other errors here.
    End Try
End Sub

' The routine that opens the ini file
Sub LoadIniFile()
    Try
        ' Try to open the ini file.
        ⋮
    Catch ex As Exception
        ' Whatever caused the error, throw a more specific exception.
        Throw New UnableToLoadIniFileException()
    End Try
End Sub
```

Custom exception objects have many uses other than reporting a custom error message. For example, they can include custom methods that resolve the error condition or at least attempt to do so. For instance, you might devise a DriveNotReadyException class with a method named ShowMessage that displays an error message and asks the user to insert a disk in the drive and retry the operation. Putting this code inside the exception class makes its reuse much easier.

One last note about custom exceptions: if your custom exception object can be thrown across different assemblies, possibly in different processes, you should make the exception class serializable. Read Chapter 10 for more details about serialization.

Exceptions in Visual Studio .NET

The Visual Studio debugger offers complete control of what happens when an application throws an exception or calls a .NET method that throws an exception. You set all the relevant options from inside the Exceptions dialog box (see Figure 3-3), which you open by selecting Exceptions on the Debug menu. This dialog box shows all the exception types defined in the .NET runtime, grouped by their namespace. Depending on which node you select, you can decide the behavior of all the .NET exceptions, only the exceptions in a given namespace, or individual exceptions. The Add button lets you add other exceptions to the list, such as your own custom exception objects.

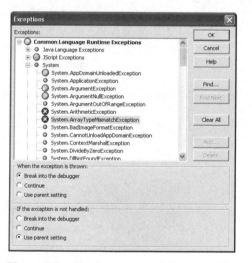

Figure 3-3   The Exceptions dialog box. A larger circular icon marks exceptions that are ignored (the Continue option); a red cross icon marks exceptions that bring up the debugger as soon as they are thrown.

For each selected exception or group of exceptions, you can decide what happens as soon as the exception is thrown—that is, before the application has a chance to deal with it—and what happens if the exception isn't handled somewhere in the application. By default, the debugger comes into play only in the latter case. Activating the debugger for exceptions that the application is going to handle also can be useful in debugging the error handlers in your code or in catching exceptions that would go unnoticed otherwise. For example, you can activate this option if a procedure performs much too slowly and you suspect that the reason is the high number of exceptions it has to deal with.

In most cases, you apply your selections only to the Common Language Runtime Exceptions node, because by default all nodes inherit their parent's setting. If necessary, however, you can establish a distinct behavior for each namespace or individual exception type. Exceptions that are handled in a way other than with the default method are marked with a different icon.

Performance Tips

Throwing exceptions adds overhead to your applications, so you should throw exceptions as sparingly as possible. For example, you should never use exceptions as a mechanism to return special values from a method, and you should reserve them for truly rare cases. Most methods in the .NET runtime adhere to this practice. For example, the Math.Log and Math.Sqrt methods return the special NaN (Not-a-Number) value when you pass them a negative number.

When authoring your own classes, you can provide clients with a read-only property that lets them understand whether a call to a method would result in an exception being thrown. For example, expose an EOF property that returns True when you're at the end of a data file or a bit-coded State property that tells what operations are allowed on the object. (This is the pattern used by the ADO.NET connection object.)

Here's another performance tip that has to do with exceptions. By default, Visual Basic checks the overflow flag after each operation on integers so that it can throw an exception if the result is outside the valid range. If you're sure that this can't happen in your application, you can improve its performance by selecting the Remove Integer Overflow Checks check box on the Optimizations page of the project Property Pages dialog box. In my informal benchmarks, I saw that operations on Integer variables run about 20 percent faster and operations on Long variables run up to 40 percent faster when this option is enabled.

The Trace and Debug Classes

Visual Studio .NET's integrated debugging features are powerful enough for finding and fixing most bugs and logic errors, but in some cases you need to add tracing statements to your code that let you understand why the application is misbehaving. This is especially useful when the problems occur only in compiled applications already deployed at your customer's site. Fortunately, the .NET Framework offers a couple of classes that simplify this task, the Debug and Trace classes, both of which reside in the System.Diagnostics namespace. This namespace is imported at the project level by all Visual Basic projects, so you don't need to specify the complete class names in your code.

The Debug and Trace classes expose methods for sending a message to the Output window in Visual Studio or to another output device. All these methods are shared methods, which means that you don't need to instantiate an instance of these classes to use them. (You will learn more about shared methods in Chapter 4.) For example, both these statements display a string in the Output window in Visual Studio:

```
Debug.WriteLine("Program has started")
Trace.WriteLine("Program has started")
```

The Write method works similarly except that it doesn't append a newline character:

```
Debug.Write("These two strings ")
Debug.WriteLine("appear on the same line.")
```

The Debug and Trace classes are identical and expose the same methods. The only difference between them is that calls to methods of the Debug class are included in the compiled application only if the DEBUG compilation constant is defined, whereas calls to methods of the Trace class are included only if the TRACE compilation constant is defined. By default, the Debug project configuration defines both these compilation constants, while the Release project configuration defines only the TRACE constant. Thus, output from the Trace class is included in all compiled applications, whereas output from the Debug class is discarded in applications compiled in Release mode. So you can include or exclude Debug messages simply by making a different solution configuration active. See Figure 3-4.

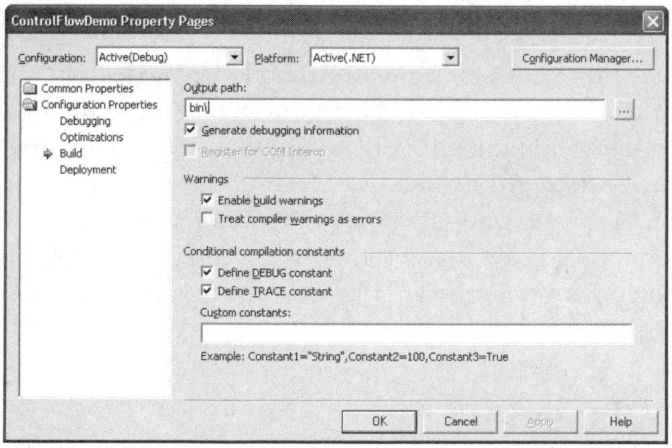

Figure 3-4   The Build page of the project Property Pages dialog box

Unlike the Visual Basic 6 Debug object, which has rather limited functionality, the .NET Debug and Trace classes offer many ways to control how trace messages are sent to the Output window. For example, the WriteIf and WriteLineIf methods emit the trace string only if the expression passed to the first argument is True:

```
Debug.WriteLineIf(x < 0, "Warning: x is negative")
```

The Fail method stops the application and displays a message box that lets the user abort the program, debug it, or just ignore the error. (See Figure 3-5.)

```
' You can specify a message and a detailed message.
Trace.Fail("An error has occurred", "File app.ini not found")
```

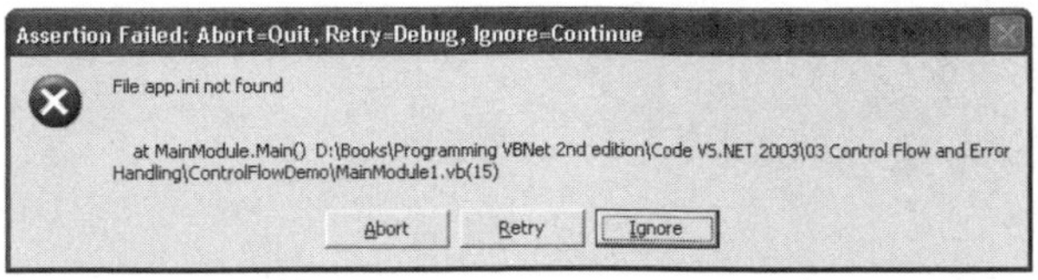

Figure 3-5   The effect of a Trace.Fail method

The Assert method is similar to Fail, with a few key differences. First, it displays the message box only if its first argument is False:

```
' You can omit the detailed message or both messages.
Trace.Assert(Not (obj Is Nothing), "Unable to continue", "Object is Nothing")
```

Second, and more important, you can use a configuration file to control whether the message box is displayed and even specify a text log file that must receive all error messages. I will explain .NET configuration files in detail in Chapter 13; for now let's see how you can disable message boxes coming from Assert methods and redirect them to a text file.

Select the Add New Item command from the Project menu and select the Application Configuration File element from the gallery of available items. This creates an XML file named App.config, which you can modify as follows:

```
<configuration>
   <system.diagnostics>
      <trace autoflush="false" indentsize="4" />
      <assert assertuienabled="false" logfilename=".\ErrorLog.txt"/>
   </system.diagnostics>
</configuration>
```

When you build the current project, Visual Studio .NET correctly copies this configuration file to the directory with the application executable, renames the file to match the name of the EXE file, and adds a .config extension (for example, "myapp.exe.config") so that .NET recognizes it as the configuration file for the application. You can now run the application and you'll see no message boxes on the screen. The autoflush attribute should be false when the application is outputting to a file, so the output isn't flushed to the file at each Assert method. You can also control this feature with the AutoFlush property of the Debug or Trace class.

The Debug and Trace classes expose the Indent and Unindent methods for controlling the indentation level of the output. These methods help you make clear how your routines are nested:

```
Sub MyProc()
    Debug.WriteLine("Entering MyProc")
    Debug.Indent()
    Debug.WriteLine("Inside MyProc")
    Debug.Unindent()
    Debug.WriteLine("Exiting MyProc")
End Sub
```

The preceding debugging code produces this output:

```
Entering MyProc
    Inside MyProc
Exiting MyProc
```

You can control the number of spaces in the indentation by means of the IndentSize property or with the indentsize attribute in the configuration file. The Debug and Trace classes have several other intriguing features, such as the ability to support trace listeners and switches that let you affect trace behavior simply by changing a few entries in the application's configuration file.

This chapter introduced a large number of new language features, although the list is far from complete. In fact, I left out all the object-oriented additions to Visual Basic, which deserve two long chapters of their own. So take a deep breath and start reading about them in the next chapter.

Part II
Object-Oriented Programming

4   Class Fundamentals

Microsoft Visual Basic has always been the Cinderella of object-oriented programming languages (OOPLs), to the point that some purists of object-oriented programming didn't even consider Visual Basic an OOPL at all. And to tell the truth, they were at least partly right because too many features were missing—most notably, constructors and inheritance. Creating truly object-oriented applications with Visual Basic 6 was so difficult that many developers thought it wasn't worth the effort.

Well, those issues are going to vanish. All .NET languages are born equal, and Visual Basic finally offers all the features that you look for in a mature object-oriented language. (Well, you might argue that inheritance from multiple classes isn't supported, but this limitation is common to all other .NET languages because it's imposed by the .NET runtime itself.)

Because of the many new object-oriented features, getting familiar with classes and interfaces under Visual Basic .NET might take longer than with changes in other areas. At any rate, the new syntax is far more rational than under Visual Basic 6, and there are fewer restrictions and exceptions to account for.

Fields

As I explained in Chapter 2, Visual Basic .NET classes are blocks of code enclosed between the Class and End Class statements. You can use these statements in any source file, even if the file contains a Form class. You can also have multiple classes in the same file, which isn't permitted under Visual Basic 6:

```
Class Person
    ' The class implementation goes here.
    ⋮
End Class
```

Classes are visible only from inside the same project if you don't specify a scope qualifier, so their default scope is Friend and you must explicitly add the Public keyword to make them visible to other applications. This is a major change from Visual Basic 6, whose classes have a default public scope. Microsoft guidelines dictate that class names should use names or name combinations and not include a prefix (such as C) or an underscore character. If the class name includes multiple words, you should use Pascal case (as in PartTimeEmployee).

A class can contain both public and private fields, which are nothing but variables declared directly inside the Class block:

```
Class Person
    ' Fields visible from outside the class
    Public FirstName As String
    Public LastName As String
    ' Fields that can be used only from inside the class
    Dim m_BirthDate As Date
    Dim m_LoginDate As Date
    Private EmailUserName As String
    Private EmailEnabled As Boolean = True

    ' The class's properties and methods
    ⋮
End Class
```

Microsoft guidelines dictate that field names use Pascal case when they contain multiple words (for example, FirstName) and never use a prefix to indicate the field's data type (the so-called Hungarian naming convention).

You can use all the syntax variations that you would use with plain variables, including initializers and multiple declarations on the same line (even though the latter practice degrades code readability and is therefore discouraged). Note that the Dim statement defines a Private field inside a Class block, whereas it declares a Public field when it appears in a Structure block. A significant improvement over Visual Basic 6 is that now variables can be declared with a Friend scope, which means that the field is visible from other modules of the same project but not from outside the project:

```
' Inside the Person class
Friend EmailPassword As String
```

From outside the class, Public and Friend fields appear as plain properties and can be used as such:

```
' A block of code that uses the Person class
Dim aPerson As New Person
aPerson.FirstName = "Francesco"
aPerson.LastName = "Balena"
```

Visual Basic .NET is more flexible than its predecessors in that you can also declare an array as a Public field:

```
' You can define up to four addresses for this person,
' from Address(0) to Address(3).
Public Address(3) As String
```

You can access this element as you would access any property with an index:

```
aPerson.Address(0) = "1234 North Street"
```

In another difference from Visual Basic 6, you can declare fields and variables anywhere in a class, not just at its beginning. For example, you can declare a private variable immediately before or after the property that encapsulates it or move all your variables just before the End Class statement. If you're using Visual Studio .NET 2003, and you've enabled the "Show procedure line separators" option (in the VB Specific page of the Basic folder, under the Text Editor folder), a line separator appears immediately before the Property statement.

Another small but significant difference from previous versions is how a field behaves when passed by reference to a procedure that modifies it. I can illustrate this concept using an example:

```
' Raise to the 4th power.
Function Power4(ByRef x As Double) As Double
    ' This is slightly faster than x^4.
    x = x * x
    Power4 = x * x
End Sub

' Here's a VB6 code procedure that passes the Power4 function
' a Public variable defined in a class.
Sub TestByRefPassing()
    Dim obj As New SampleClass
    obj.Number = 3
    Console.Print Power4(obj.Number)   ' => 81
    ' Prove that the property hasn't changed.
    Console.Print obj.Number           ' => 3
End Sub
```

The preceding code contains a logic error because the Power4 function unnecessarily modifies an argument passed to it, but you aren't going to see this error if the Visual Basic 6 program never passes a variable (as opposed to a class field) to the Power4 function. The Number field isn't affected because Visual Basic 6 wraps a pair of hidden Property Get and Property Let procedures around the Number variable, and the Power4 functions can't alter the inner variable.

Visual Basic .NET doesn't wrap hidden procedures around class fields; therefore, a literal translation of the preceding code makes the bug appear, as follows:

```
' A Visual Basic .NET code snippet that passes
' a Public variable defined in a class to the Power4 function
Sub TestByRefPassing()
    Dim obj As New SampleClass
    obj.Number = 3
    Console.WriteLine(Power4(obj.Number))  ' => 81
    ' The Number property has changed as well.
    Console.WriteLine(obj.Number)          ' => 9
End Sub
```

Oddly, you can regard this behavior as a return to the past because Visual Basic 4 worked in the same way as Visual Basic .NET. The behavior of Public class fields changed in Visual Basic 5 and broke existing Visual Basic 4 code. You can expect to encounter a similar problem when you're porting Visual Basic 5 or 6 code to Visual Basic .NET. Incidentally, because there are no hidden wrappers, accessing a field is usually remarkably faster than accessing an equivalent property.

Visual Basic .NET doesn't support the ByVal keyword inside a statement that invokes a method:

```
' This statement works in Visual Basic 6
' but raises a compilation error in Visual Basic .NET.
Dim n As Integer: n = 3
res = Power4(ByVal n)
```

The only way to pass a number by value to a procedure that expects a ByRef argument is by enclosing the argument in parentheses:

```
obj.Number = 3
' This statement passes the obj.Number property by value.
Console.WriteLine(Power4((obj.Number))    ' => 81
' Prove that the Number property hasn't changed.
Console.WriteLine(obj.Number)             ' => 3
```

In a difference from previous language versions, Visual Basic .NET classes can expose Public constants, which are seen outside the class as read-only properties:

```
Public Const DefaultPassword As String = "mypwd"
```

When using a numeric constant in an expression, you can explicitly define its type by appending one of the following characters to the value: I (Integer), L (Long), D (Double), S (Short), or @ (Decimal):

```
Average = sum / 10D     ' Divide by a Double.
```

The old type suffix characters %, &, !, and # are still supported.

Methods

You can implement class methods as Sub and Function procedures, exactly as you do under Visual Basic 6. You must account for the syntax changes already described in Chapter 3—for example, those affecting Optional arguments and argument passing:

```
Function CompleteName(Optional ByVal title As String = "") As String
    ' Use the title if provided.
    If title <> "" Then CompleteName = title & " "
    ' Append first and last name.
    CompleteName &= FirstName & " " & LastName
End Function
```

Microsoft guidelines dictate that you use Pascal case for the names of methods (for example, ClearAll). Parameters should use camel case (for example, mainAddress) and never use a prefix that indicates their data type. Note that, unlike the Visual Basic 6 code editor, Visual Studio .NET can distinguish parameters from variables and doesn't automatically change the casing of a parameter to match the casing of a variable with the same name.

Another interesting suggestion from Microsoft is that you never define a parameter that has as its only purpose "reserved for future use" because newer versions of the class can overload a method (see next section) to support additional arguments without breaking backward compatibility with existing code.

Overloading

Visual Basic .NET lets you overload a method. Method overloading means that you can provide multiple methods with the same name but different parameter signatures—that is, with a different number of parameters or with parameters of a different type. (A method's signature is defined as the list of its parameters and its return value; parameters' names don't affect the signature, but their types and whether they are passed via ByRef or ByVal do.) Before explaining how you implement overloaded methods, I think it makes sense to illustrate why overloading can be useful. Suppose you're creating a collectionlike class and include an Item method that provides access to the collection's elements through either a numeric or a string argument. This is the code that you write under Visual Basic 6 to implement such a method:

```
Function Item(index As Variant) As String
    If VarType(index) = vbLong Or VarType(index) = vbInteger Then
        ' Access an element through its numeric index.
        ⋮
    ElseIf VarType(index) = vbString Then
        ' Access an element through its string key.
        ⋮
    Else
        ' Raise a run-time error otherwise.
        Err.Raise 999, , "Invalid index type"
    End If
End Function
```

The Visual Basic .NET solution is cleaner: you define multiple procedures with the same name and different syntax. You can explicitly state that you're overloading the Item method by prefixing it with the Overloads keyword:

```
' The Visual Basic .NET solution
Overloads Function Item(ByVal index As Integer) As String
    ' Access an element through its numeric index.
    ⋮
End Function

Overloads Function Item(ByVal key As String) As String
    ' Access an element through its string key.
    ⋮
End Function
```

Note that the Overloads keyword is optional, but if you use it for one overloaded method you must use it for all of them. Not only does method overloading make the code less cluttered, it also makes it more efficient. The compiler decides which version of the Item function is called, and no test is necessary at run time:

```
' This statement calls the first overloaded version.
result = myObj.Item(1)
' This statement calls the second overloaded version.
result = myObj.Item("foo")
```

Just as important, the compiler can flag invalid arguments, so you don't have to trap arguments of invalid type:

```
' *** The following code doesn't compile (if Option Strict is On).
Dim value As Double = 1.23
result = myObj.Item(value)
```

Method overloading lets you solve cases that are almost unmanageable under Visual Basic 6. For example, say that you're implementing an InstrWord function, which searches whole words and exposes a syntax similar to that of the standard InStr function. The problem with InStr is that it comes with two syntax forms:

```
result = InStr(text, search)
result = InStr(index, text, search, Optional compareMethod)
```

If you want your InstrWord function to closely mimic the InStr function, your only option under Visual Basic 6 is to declare a single function that takes variants and resolves all the possible cases at run time. The Visual Basic .NET solution is much simpler, also because you can have the simpler form delegate to the most complete one. (Notice that I have omitted the optional Overloads keyword.)

```
Function InstrWord(ByVal source As String, _
    ByVal search As String) As Long
    ' First case is just a special case of the more general case.
    Return InstrWord(1, source, search, CompareMethod.Binary)
End Function

Function InstrWord(ByVal index As Long, _
    ByVal text As String, ByVal search As String, _
    ByVal Optional cmpMethod As CompareMethod = CompareMethod.Binary) As Long
    ' Second case is the more general case.
    ⋮
End Function
```

Again, not only is the code cleaner and easier to maintain, it is also more efficient (because the compiler makes its decisions at compile time) and robust (because invalid calls don't even compile). IntelliSense correctly recognizes overloaded methods and displays a list of all the supported syntax forms. You can visit all of them using the up and down arrow keys:

```
result = InstrWord(
  ▲2 of 2▼  InstrWord (index As Long, text As String, search As String, [cmpMethod As Microsoft.VisualBasic.CompareMethod = CompareMethod.Binary]) As Long
```

Method overloading lets you get rid of optional arguments, even though this decision requires that you create a distinct overloaded version for each possible optional argument. The problem with optional arguments is that a few .NET languages—most notably, C#—don't recognize them. Therefore, C# developers calling a Visual Basic .NET method must pass all the arguments whether they're required or optional. If you plan to expose those methods to languages other than Visual Basic, you should implement overloaded methods rather than methods with optional arguments.

Keep in mind that optional arguments are resolved when you compile the client code, not when you compile the method that defines them. If the client code omits one or more optional arguments, the compiler adds the necessary (hidden) statements that push those arguments' default values onto the stack. This can lead to versioning problems when the client code and the target method belong to different assemblies and therefore are compiled separately. If you then recompile the method and change the default value of the optional argument, you should recompile all its clients as well; otherwise, they'll pass the wrong value. You won't have this problem if you stay clear of optional arguments and replace them with overloaded methods.

Overloading and Coercion

When the argument types don't exactly match the parameter signature of any available method, the compiler attempts to match them through widening coercion exclusively. (Review the section "The Option Strict Statement" in Chapter 2 for the difference between widening and narrowing coercion.) For example, assume that you have two overloaded Sum functions that contain Console.WriteLine statements to help you understand which version is invoked:

```
Function Sum(ByVal n1 As Long, ByVal n2 As Long) As Long
    Sum = n1 + n2
    Console.WriteLine("The integer version has been invoked.")
End Function
Function Sum(ByVal n1 As Single, ByVal n2 As Single) As Single
    Sum = n1 + n2
    Console.WriteLine("The floating-point version has been invoked.")
End Function
```

Now consider what happens when you invoke the Sum function with Integer arguments:

```
Dim intValue As Short = 1234
' This statement invokes the integer version.
Console.WriteLine(Sum(intValue, 1))     ' => 1235
```

In this case, both arguments are 16-bit Integer, but Visual Basic correctly promotes them to Long and calls the first version of the Sum function. Here's another example:

```
' This statement invokes the floating-point version.
' Note that you must specify that the 2nd argument is a Single.
Console.WriteLine(Sum(intValue, 1.25!))     ' => 1235.25
```

In this case, Visual Basic realizes that only the second version can be invoked without losing precision. Finally, consider this third example:

```
Dim dblValue As Double = 1234
' *** The next statement raises a compiler error if Option Strict is On.
Console.WriteLine(Sum(dblValue, 1.25))
```

In this last case, you can't call either Sum function without the risk of losing precision or throwing an out-of-range exception at run time, so Visual Basic refuses to compile this piece of code.

Ambiguous Cases

Visual Basic must be able to resolve a method call at compile time. Therefore, two overloaded procedures of the same method must differ in more respects than in an optional argument. For example, the following third variant of the Sum function can't compile because it differs from the second form only in an optional argument:

```
Function Sum(ByVal n1 As Single, _
    Optional ByVal n2 As Single = 1) As Single
    Sum = n1 + n2
End Function
```

The compiler shows what's wrong with the following message:

```
'Function Sum(n1 As Single, n2 As Single) As Single' and 'Function
Sum(n1 As Single, [n2 As Single = 1]) As Single' differ only by optional
parameters. They cannot override each other.
```

A corollary of this concept is that you can't create overloaded variations of a function that differ only in the type of the returned value. For example, you can't overload a ClearValue function that returns either a null string or a null integer:

```
' *** This code doesn't compile.
Function ClearValue() As String
    ClearValue = ""
End Function
Function ClearValue() As Long
    ClearValue = 0
End Function
```

You can work around this limitation by using Sub procedures instead of functions, with the type of the argument passed to it by reference determining which version of the procedure is actually called:

```
' This code compiles correctly.
Sub ClearValue(ByRef arg As String)
    arg = ""
End Sub
Sub ClearValue(ByRef arg As Long)
    arg = 0
End Sub
' You should add versions for other numeric types.
⋮
```

Finally, remember that you can also overload class properties and that overloading isn't limited to classes; you can overload Sub and Function defined in Module and Structure blocks too.

Properties

Implementing properties under Visual Basic .NET is more straightforward than under Visual Basic 6 once you get accustomed to the new syntax. Instead of having distinct Property Get, Property Let, and Property Set procedures, now you have a single Property...End Property block, which defines the property's name, its type, and its argument signature:

```
Property BirthDate() As Date
    ' Implementation of BirthDate property goes here.
    ⋮
End Property
```

Inside the Property block, you write a Get...End Get block, which defines what value the property returns, and a Set...End Set block, which defines how values are assigned to the property. In most cases, a property simply maps to a Private field, so the code for these two blocks often looks like this:

```
' You can define variables anywhere in a class or module.
Dim m_BirthDate As Date

Property BirthDate() As Date
    Get
        Return m_BirthDate
    End Get
    Set(ByVal Value As Date)
        m_BirthDate = Value
    End Set
End Property
```

At least two points are worth noticing here. First, Let...End Let blocks aren't supported because Visual Basic .NET doesn't support parameterless default properties and there's no need to differentiate between a Let and a Set block. (You might argue that a Let...End Let block would be more appropriate than a Set...End Set block, but this argument is groundless because everything is ultimately an object in the .NET Framework.) Second, the Get...End Get block can return a value either through the new Return keyword or by assigning the value to the property name (as you would do under Visual Basic 6):

```
Property BirthDate() As Date
    Get
        ' Another way to return a value
        BirthDate = m_BirthDate
    End Get
    ⋮
End Property
```

The Set...End Set block always receives a Value argument that stands for the value being assigned to the property itself. This argument must be of the same type as the type defined in the Property statement and must be declared using ByVal. If you happen to have a field named Value, you can distinguish between the field and the Value keyword by prefixing the field with the Me keyword or, more simply, by changing the parameter name to something other than Value:

```
' A class that has a Value field
Class ValueClass
    Private Value As Double

    ' A property that uses the Value field
    Property DoubleValue() As Double
        Get
            Return Me.Value * 2
        End Get
        Set(ByVal newValue As Double)0
            Me.Value = newValue / 2
        End Set
    End Property
End Class
```

Note that Me.Value is a legal syntax, even if the Value field is private. Under Visual Basic 6, only public variables could be accessed through the Me keyword, but this restriction has been lifted in Visual Basic .NET.

Interestingly, you can pass a property to a ByRef parameter of a procedure, and any change to the argument is reflected in the property. The same happens when you increment or decrement a property using the += and -= operators, as this code shows:

```
Sub TestByRefProperty
    Dim vc As New ValueClass
    vc.DoubleValue = 100
    ClearValue(vc.DoubleValue)
    ' Show that the method actually changed the property.
    Console.WriteLine(vc.DoubleValue)              ' => 0

    vc.DoubleValue += 10
    ' Show that the property was actually incremented.
    Console.WriteLine(vc.DoubleValue)              ' => 10
End Sub

Sub ClearValue(ByRef Value As Double)
    Value = 0
End Sub
```

This behavior differs from that of Visual Basic 6, in which a property—implemented as either a Public field or a pair of property procedures—is never modified if passed to a ByRef argument.

Visual Basic .NET property syntax is the same whether the property returns a simple value or an object. After all, everything is an object in the .NET Framework. Therefore, you don't have to worry about the many syntax variations that exist under Visual Basic 6, for which a Variant property can map to three distinct Property procedures. For example, the following Spouse property can return a Person object that represents the wife or husband of the current Person object:

```
    Private m_Spouse As Person

    Property Spouse() As Person
        Get
            Return m_Spouse
        End Get
        Set(ByVal Value As Person)
            m_Spouse = Value
        End Set
    End Property
```

As you see, this syntax is no different from that of a regular property that returns a string or a numeric value.

Read-Only and Write-Only Properties

You define read-only properties by omitting the Set...End Set block, as you do under Visual Basic 6. However, you must use the ReadOnly keyword to explicitly state that you mean to create a read-only property:

```
' The Age property is read-only.
ReadOnly Property Age() As Integer
    Get
        Return Year(Now) - Year(m_BirthDate) ' Simplistic age calculation
    End Get
End Property
```

Similarly, you can create a write-only property by omitting the Get...End Get block and using the WriteOnly keyword in the Property block:

```
' LoginDate is a write-only property.
WriteOnly Property LoginDate() As Date
    Set(ByVal Value As Date)
        m_LoginDate = Value
    End Set
End Property
```

Attempts to write read-only properties, as well as attempts to read write-only properties, are trapped at compile time. The ReadOnly keyword is also allowed for fields, as you see here:

```
Public ReadOnly ID As Long
```

Read-only fields can be written to only from inside constructor methods. (Read "Constructors" later in this chapter.) You can determine whether a property of a .NET class is read/write or read-only by looking at it in the Object Browser. See Figure 4-1.

The only limitation of the Visual Basic .NET way of declaring properties is that you can't use different scope qualifiers for the Get and Set blocks. Thus, you can't create a property that's read/write from inside the current project and read-only from outside it, as you could do in Visual Basic 6. You must instead create two separate properties with different names: one Public read-only property that delegates to another Friend read/write property.

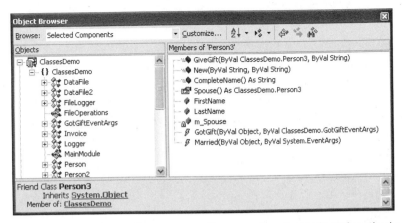

Figure 4-1   The Object Browser uses the same icon for fields and methods, but with different colors (cyan for fields and fuchsia for methods). Those icons are combined with other, smaller icons (an envelope, a padlock, and so on) that indicate the member's scope.

Properties with Arguments

You can define properties that take one or more arguments in a straightforward way:

```
' ...(Add to the Person class)...

Dim m_Notes(10) As String

' The Notes property takes an Integer argument.
Property Notes(ByVal index As Integer) As String
    Get
        Return m_Notes(index)
    End Get
    Set(ByVal Value As String)
        m_Notes(index) = Value
    End Set
End Property
```

As you would expect, you get an IndexOutOfRangeException run-time error if the Index argument is less than 0 or greater than the last valid index of the array. You can provide a more descriptive description by trapping invalid index values and throwing the exception yourself:

```
Property Notes(ByVal index As Integer) As String
    Get
        If index < 0 Or index > UBound(m_Notes) Then
            Throw New IndexOutOfRangeException("Invalid note index.")
        End If
        Return m_Notes(index)
    End Get
    Set(ByVal Value As String)
        If index < 0 Or index > UBound(m_Notes) Then
            Throw New IndexOutOfRangeException("Invalid note index.")
        End If
```

```
        m_Notes(index) = Value
    End Set
End Property
```

Visual Basic .NET lets you expose an array as a Public field directly, which makes properties with arguments somewhat less important than they are under Visual Basic 6. Typically, you'll use properties with arguments when you want to arbitrate access to a more complex structure or when your arguments aren't just indexes into an array. For example, you can build a property that returns a person's age expressed in any time units, not just years:

```
ReadOnly Property Age(Optional ByVal unit As DateInterval _
    = DateInterval.Year) As Integer
    Get
        Return CInt(DateDiff(unit, m_BirthDate, Now))
    End Get
End Property
```

Note that you can overload properties, with or without arguments, as you would overload methods.

Default Properties

As I explained in the "Assigning Object Values" section in Chapter 2, Visual Basic .NET supports default properties only if the property takes one or more arguments because assignments aren't ambiguous in this case. Declaring a property with arguments that also works as the default property requires that you use the Default keyword:

```
Default Property Notes(ByVal index As Integer) As String

End Property
```

Now you can omit the property's name when using it:

```
' Set a note for a person.
Dim aPerson As New Person
aPerson.FirstName = "Joe"
' Prove that Notes is the default property.
aPerson(0) = "Remind Joe to review the proposal"
aPerson(2) = "Joe's birthday is on June 5"

' Display all the notes.
For i As Integer = 0 To 9
    Console.WriteLine(aPerson(i))
Next
```

Constructors

Support for constructors is an important addition to the Visual Basic language. Briefly, a constructor is a method that runs when a new instance of the class is created. In Visual Basic .NET, the constructor method is always named Sub New:

```
Class Person
    Dim CreateTime As Date

    Sub New()
        ' Display a diagnostic message.
        Console.WriteLine("A new instance of Person is being created.")
        ' Remember when this instance was created.
        CreateTime = Now()
        ' Perform other initialization chores.
        ⋮
    End Sub
End Class
```

The New name is appropriate because the client code uses the New keyword to create an instance of the class:

```
Dim aPerson As Person
aPerson = New Person
```

When the constructor runs, all the fields with initializers have been already initialized, so if you access such fields from within the constructor you will find the value assigned to them by the initializer:

```
Class Person
    Public Citizenship As String = "American"

    Sub New
        ' Prove that the field has already been initialized.
        Console.WriteLine(Citizenship)        ' => American
    End Sub
End Class
```

Constructors with Arguments

As an experienced Visual Basic developer, you might associate the constructor concept with the Class_Initialize event, and you would be right—to an extent. The point to grasp is that the constructor method can take arguments. Therefore, you can define which values the calling code *must* pass in order to correctly create an object. For example, you can force the calling code to pass the first and last name when the caller creates a Person2 object:

```
Class Person2
    Public FirstName As String
    Public LastName As String

    Sub New(ByVal firstName As String, ByVal lastName As String)
        ' Note that you can resolve the argument vs. field
        ' ambiguity using the Me keyword.
        Me.FirstName = firstName
        Me.LastName = lastName
    End Sub
End Class
```

This new version of the Person2 class must be instantiated in this way:

```
Dim aPerson As Person2
aPerson = New Person2("Joe", "Doe")
```

You can also use a shortened syntax:

```
Dim aPerson As New Person2("Joe", "Doe")
```

The ability to define parameters for the New method takes Visual Basic .NET constructors far ahead of the old Class_Initialize event—which is no longer supported—and can make your classes more robust. You can be altogether sure that objects are created in a valid state. To achieve this goal, however, you have to ensure that only valid arguments are passed to the constructor:

```
'...(A new version of the Person2 constructor)...
Sub New(ByVal firstName As String, ByVal lastName As String)
    If firstName = "" Or lastName = "" Then
        Throw New ArgumentException()
    End If
    Me.FirstName = firstName
    Me.LastName = lastName
End Sub
```

For a cleaner and more robust design, you should morph all your fields into properties and validate their values in Set...End Set blocks. Once you have this code in place, the constructor method can simply assign the received argument to the corresponding property. If an exception is thrown, it will be reported to the caller as if it were thrown from inside the New procedure.

```
'...(A more robust version of Person2)...
Sub New(ByVal firstName As String, ByVal lastName As String)
    ' Delegate validation to Property procedures.
    Me.FirstName = firstName
    Me.LastName = lastName
End Sub

Private m_FirstName As String
Private m_LastName As String

Property FirstName() As String
    Get
        Return m_FirstName
    End Get
    Set(ByVal Value As String)
        If Value = "" Then
            Throw New ArgumentException("Invalid FirstName property")
        End If
        m_FirstName = Value
    End Set
End Property
```

```
Property LastName() As String
    Get
        Return m_LastName
    End Get
    Set(ByVal Value As String)
        If Value = "" Then
            Throw New ArgumentException("Invalid LastName property")
        End If
        m_LastName = Value
    End Set
End Property
```

This coding pattern, which has all the validation code inside the Property Set block, ensures the best results in terms of robustness and code maintenance. This is the only portion of the class that has to be updated when new validation requirements arise.

Well-designed constructors can improve the usability of your class. For example, you can define optional arguments that let the client code initialize other properties that aren't mandatory:

```
'...(A new version of the constructor that takes an optional argument)...
Sub New(ByVal firstName As String, ByVal lastName As String, _
    Optional ByVal birthDate As Date = #1/1/1800#)
    ' Delegate validation to Property procedures.
    Me.FirstName = firstName
    Me.LastName = lastName
    ' Delegate to the actual Property procedure only if an
    ' argument has been passed.
    If birthDate <> #1/1/1800# Then
        Me.BirthDate = birthDate
    End If
End Sub
```

Overloaded Constructors

Like all methods, the Sub New method can be overloaded. In practice, this means that you can provide users with many ways to instantiate objects, which improves the usability of your class. For example, you might have a Product class that can be instantiated by passing the product name and an optional product numeric code:

```
Class Product
    Dim m_Id As Integer
    Dim m_Name As String

    Sub New(ByVal name As String)
        m_Name = name
    End Sub

    Sub New(ByVal name As String, ByVal id As Integer)
        m_Name = name
        m_Id = id
    End Sub
End Class
```

Note that you can't use the Overloads keyword with constructors. The preceding code can be simplified remarkably if you call the first constructor from inside the second one, or vice versa. In general, I prefer to have simpler constructors call the most complete ones:

```
Sub New(ByVal name As String)
    ' Call the other constructor, pass default value for 2nd argument.
    Me.New(name, 0)
End Sub
```

It is essential that the Me.New call be the first executable statement in the constructor method, otherwise Visual Basic flags it as a compiler error. The advantage of this approach is that all the initialization code is kept in a single procedure and you don't have to worry about subtle bugs caused by multiple constructors performing slightly different initialization chores.

Constructors and Read-Only Fields

A constructor procedure is the only place from inside a class where you can assign a value to read-only fields (not counting assignments made through initializers). For example, the CreateTime field is logically a read-only field and should be declared as such:

```
' This read-only field can be assigned
' only from inside a constructor method.
Public ReadOnly CreateTime As Date

Public Sub New()
    CreateTime = Now
End Sub
```

Remember that you can also initialize a read-only field by using an initializer, so for simpler cases, you don't really need to make the assignment from inside the constructor:

```
Private ReadOnly CreateTime As Date = Now
```

Most of the time, read-only fields have a public scope: you declare a read-only private field only to protect unwanted modifications from code inside the class itself, an infrequent requirement. Private read-only fields can be a good choice with larger classes, especially when different programmers develop distinct portions of the class, but in many cases they are overkill:

```
' Three equivalent ways to define the same read-only field.
Private ReadOnly CreateTime As Date
Dim ReadOnly CreateTime As Date
ReadOnly CreateTime As Date
```

Events

The internal implementations of .NET and COM events are completely different, yet Visual Basic .NET has preserved more or less the same syntax you use in Visual Basic 6, and the changes you have to make when working with events are minimal.

Declaring and Raising an Event

The Event keyword declares that a class can raise a given event and defines the list of arguments passed to the event. The syntax for this statement is exactly the same that Visual Basic 6 supports:

```
Class Logger
    Event LogAction(ByVal actionName As String)
    ⋮
End Class
```

You can raise the event using the RaiseEvent command, again as you do under Visual Basic 6:

```
Class Logger
    Event LogAction(ByVal actionName As String)

    Sub OpenFile()
        RaiseEvent LogAction("OpenFile")
    End Sub

    Sub ReadData()
        RaiseEvent LogAction("ReadData")
    End Sub

    Sub CloseFile()
        RaiseEvent LogAction("CloseFile")
    End Sub
End Class
```

Trapping Events with WithEvents

As in Visual Basic 6, you can trap events using a variable declared with the WithEvents keyword, with two significant improvements. First, the variable can appear inside classes and (unlike previous versions) inside Modules and Structure blocks. Second, you can use the New keyword and the WithEvents keyword in the same statement:

```
Module MainModule
    ' A WithEvents variable declared in a module block with the New keyword
    Dim WithEvents Log As New Logger

    ' This procedure causes some events to be fired.
    Sub TestWithEvents()
        Log.OpenFile()
        Log.ReadData()
        Log.CloseFile()
    End Sub
End Module
```

Trapping events is where Visual Basic .NET differs most from previous versions. In the current version, the name of the event procedure has no effect, and you tell the compiler which procedure is going to trap the event by using the Handles keyword, as you see in this code:

```
' Add inside MainModule.
Sub LogActionEvent(ByVal actionName As String) Handles Log.LogAction
    Console.WriteLine("LogAction event: " & actionName)
End Sub
```

Visual Studio .NET can create the syntax for you. Just select the object in the leftmost combo box near the upper border of the code editor, and then select the specific event in the rightmost combo box—exactly as you do in Visual Basic 6. However, the procedure name doesn't have to abide by the object_eventname name format, so you can rename the procedure however you prefer.

Although the new syntax is slightly more verbose than in previous language versions, it's more versatile because the Handles keyword supports multiple events. For example, you can write one procedure trapping the same event from two different variables, as in the following code:

```
Dim WithEvents Log1 As New Logger
Dim WithEvents Log2 As New Logger

Sub LogActionEvent(ByVal actionName As String) _
    Handles Log1.LogAction, Log2.LogAction
    Console.WriteLine("LogAction event: " & actionName)
End Sub
```

You can also write a procedure that traps events with different names, from the same or distinct variables, provided that the events in question have the same parameter signature. It's evident, though, that mapping multiple events to the same procedure makes sense only if the event handler can discern which object is raising the event. You will learn how this is possible in the "Guidelines for Event Syntax" section, later in this chapter.

Trapping Events with AddHandler

Visual Basic .NET allows you to decide at run time which routine should serve a given event. The key to this feature is the AddHandler keyword, which takes two arguments: the event that you want to handle (in the format object.eventname) and the address of the routine that handles the event (in the format AddressOf routinename). To show how this works in practice, let's rewrite the previous code snippet to use AddHandler instead of two WithEvents variables:

```
Dim Log1 As New Logger
Dim Log2 As New Logger

Sub TestAddHandler()
    AddHandler Log1.LogAction, AddressOf LogActionEvent2
    AddHandler Log2.LogAction, AddressOf LogActionEvent2

    ' Cause some events to be fired.
    Log1.OpenFile()
    Log1.ReadData()
```

```
    Log2.CloseFile()
End Sub

' Note that no Handles clause is used here.
Sub LogActionEvent2(ByVal actionName As String)
    Console.WriteLine("LogAction event: " & actionName)
End Sub
```

Notice that AddHandler is a language keyword, not the name of a method. It doesn't follow the usual syntax rules and doesn't require a pair of parentheses around the argument list.

The counterpart of AddHandler is the RemoveHandler command, which you use to stop a routine from handling a specific event from a given object:

```
    RemoveHandler Log1.LogAction, AddressOf LogActionEvent2
    RemoveHandler Log2.LogAction, AddressOf LogActionEvent2
```

It is a good rule to always remove handlers created by means of the AddHandler keyword, even though sometimes omitting the call to RemoveHandler doesn't cause any problems. This situation is particularly true if the object raising the event and the object serving the event are destroyed at the same time. For example, if you use AddHandler inside a form to handle events raised by a control on that same form, you can safely omit RemoveHandler when the form closes because the event source (the control) and the event handler (the form class) are both destroyed at that time.

In other cases, however, forgetting to remove an event handler can have nasty consequences. For example, say that you use AddHandler in one form (let's call it FormA) to trap events raised by another form (FormB). The problem is that the AddHandler keyword creates a hidden reference inside FormB that points to FormA. If you neglect to call RemoveHandler after FormA closes and before the application sets FormA to Nothing, the hidden reference inside FormB keeps FormA alive, therefore nullifying the effect of setting FormA to Nothing. In this scenario, not only does FormA continue to take memory and resources, it might also affect your application in other ways—for example, if it contains a timer that periodically fires an event.

You should be aware that using WithEvents or AddHandler can make a difference when the object is referenced by two or more variables. In fact, the WithEvents keyword ties an event handler to a specific variable, whereas the AddHandler command ties an event handler to a specific object. It seems a minor detail, but it can affect your code significantly. Consider this code, which traps events from a Logger object declared with WithEvents:

```
Dim WithEvents Log As New Logger

Sub TestWithEvents2()
    ' Create another variable that points to the same object.
    Dim logobj As Logger = Log
```

```
        ' These statements raise three events, even though we access
        ' the object through the new variable.
        logobj.OpenFile()
        logobj.ReadData()
        logobj.CloseFile()

        ' Clear the WithEvents variable.
        Log = Nothing
        ' These statements don't raise any event because the event handler
        ' is tied to the WithEvents variable, not the object.
        logobj.OpenFile()
        logobj.ReadData()
        logobj.CloseFile()
    End Sub

    Sub LogActionEvent(ByVal actionName As String) Handles Log.LogAction
        Console.WriteLine("LogAction event: " & actionName)
    End Sub
```

The next code sample follows the same pattern, except that it creates the event handler using AddHandler instead of WithEvents. As you see, the behavior is different:

```
Dim Log2 As New Logger

Sub TestAddHandler2()
    ' Enable the event handler.
    AddHandler Log2.LogAction, AddressOf LogActionEvent2
    ' Create another variable that points to the same object.
    Dim logobj As Logger = Log2

    ' These statements raise three events, even though we access
    ' the object using the new variable.
    logobj.OpenFile()
    logobj.ReadData()
    logobj.CloseFile()

    ' Clear the original variable.
    Log2 = Nothing
    ' These statements raise three events as well because handlers created
    ' with AddHandler are tied to the object, not a specific variable.
    logobj.OpenFile()
    logobj.ReadData()
    logobj.CloseFile()
End Sub

Sub LogActionEvent2(ByVal actionName As String)
    Console.WriteLine("LogAction event: " & actionName)
End Sub
```

A corollary of this rule is that you might continue to receive events from an object even after all the variables in your class pointing to it are cleared if the object is kept alive by variables defined elsewhere in the current application and you defined its event handlers using the AddHandler command.

In a few special cases, you might receive extra events from an object even after all its clients have set all their variables to Nothing and the object is about to be garbage collected. This situation occurs when the object raises an event from its Finalize method (which is something that you should never do because it violates the rule that code in the Finalize method shouldn't reference other objects). It also occurs, for example, when the object uses a timer to poll a system resource (CPU usage or free space on disk) and raises an event when that resource goes below a given threshold. Such a timer would continue to run even after the object has been logically destroyed, until the next garbage collection.

Module Events

The AddHandler command is useful for handling events raised from inside a Module block. Consider the following module, which exposes a couple of procedures that process a file and raise an event when the operation has completed:

```
Module FileOperations
    Event Notify_CopyFile(ByVal source As String, ByVal destination As String)
    Event Notify_DeleteFile(ByVal filename As String)

    Sub CopyFile(ByVal source As String, ByVal destination As String)
        ' Perform the file copy.
        System.IO.File.Copy(source, destination)
        ' Notify that a copy occurred.
        RaiseEvent Notify_CopyFile(source, destination)
    End Sub

    Sub DeleteFile(ByVal filename As String)
        ' Perform the file deletion.
        System.IO.File.Delete(filename)
        ' Notify that a deletion occurred.
        RaiseEvent Notify_DeleteFile(filename)
    End Sub
End Module
```

A client procedure might use the event mechanism to keep a log of all the file operations that have occurred. You can't use the WithEvents keyword to take advantage of these events because you can't assign a module to a variable. However, the AddHandler command fits the bill nicely:

```
Private Sub TestModuleEvents()
    ' Install the event handlers.
    AddHandler FileOperations.Notify_CopyFile, AddressOf NotifyCopy
    AddHandler FileOperations.Notify_DeleteFile, AddressOf NotifyDelete

    ' Create a copy of Autoexec.bat, and then delete it.
    CopyFile("c:\autoexec.bat", "c:\autoexec.$$$")
    DeleteFile("c:\autoexec.$$$")

    ' Remove the event handlers.
    RemoveHandler FileOperations.Notify_CopyFile, AddressOf NotifyCopy
    RemoveHandler FileOperations.Notify_DeleteFile, AddressOf NotifyDelete
End Sub
```

```
' These procedures log the file operation to the console window.
Sub NotifyCopy(ByVal source As String, ByVal destination As String)
    Console.WriteLine(source & " copied to " & destination)
End Sub

Sub NotifyDelete(ByVal filename As String)
    Console.WriteLine(filename & " deleted")
End Sub
```

Trapping Events from Arrays and Collections

The AddHandler command lets you overcome one of the most serious limitations of the WithEvents keyword: the inability to trap events from an array or a collection of objects.

To support event trapping from an array or a collection of objects, the event should pass the client code a reference pointing to the object that's raising the event. This is precisely what all the events exposed by Windows Forms controls do. In fact, all these events pass the client two values: a sender argument (a reference to the control raising the event) and an e argument (whose properties contain any additional information that might be required by the client). The presence of the sender argument makes it possible to use very concise code to trap a given event from all the controls stored in the form's Controls collection:

```
Private Sub Form1_Load(ByVal sender As Object, ByVal e As EventArgs) _
    Handles MyBase.Load
    For Each ctrl As Control In Me.Controls
        AddHandler ctrl.Click, AddressOf ClickHandler
    Next
End Sub

Private Sub ClickHandler(ByVal sender As Object, ByVal e As EventArgs)
    ' Cast to strong reference.
    Dim ctrl As Control = DirectCast(sender, Control)
    ' Process the click somehow...
    Debug.WriteLine(ctrl.Name & " has been clicked")
End Sub
```

Remember that you should always clean up after yourself, which you can do in the form's Closing event handler:

```
Private Sub Form1_Closing(ByVal sender As Object, ByVal e _
    As System.ComponentModel.CancelEventArgs) Handles MyBase.Closing
    For Each ctrl As Control In Me.Controls
        RemoveHandler ctrl.Click, AddressOf ClickHandler
    Next
End Sub
```

Guidelines for Event Syntax

Without exception, all the events exposed by .NET objects follow a syntax similar to the one I just illustrated for Windows Forms controls and have only two arguments: an Object argument named sender, which represents the object that's raising the event;

and an argument named e, which exposes the event's arguments through its fields or properties. This second argument should be a System.EventArgs object or an object whose class inherits from System.EventArgs. (The name of such a class should end with EventArgs.)

As you've seen, this syntax allows a caller to set up a single event handler that serves multiple objects, or even arrays or collections of objects. If an event procedure can handle events from multiple objects, the sender argument is the only way for a client to learn which specific object raised the event. So it makes sense to define all your events along the same guidelines whether or not you plan to work with arrays of objects in the near future. Abiding by this naming convention requires only a little extra code today, but it might simplify your job a great deal tomorrow. Also, it makes your objects appear similar to native .NET objects, thus simplifying the life of programmers who use your objects.

Let's create a Person3 class to expose two events that follow Microsoft guidelines: Married and GotGift. The Married event fires when the Spouse property is assigned a new value. Because the client can check the Spouse property to learn the spouse's name, there's no point in passing additional arguments in the event, and the e argument can be of type System.EventArgs:

```
Class Person3
    Event Married(ByVal sender As Object, ByVal e As System.EventArgs)

    Dim m_Spouse As Person3

    Property Spouse() As Person3
        Get
            Return m_Spouse
        End Get
        Set(ByVal Value As Person3)
            ' Raise an event only if this is a different object.
            If Not (m_Spouse Is Value) Then
                m_Spouse = Value
                ' Pass an empty EventArgs object.
                RaiseEvent Married(Me, EventArgs.Empty)
            End If
        End Set
    End Property

    ' ...(Plus all the usual properties, methods, and constructors)...
    ⋮
End Class
```

The GotGift event must pass two pieces of information to the caller: the Person who gave the gift and a string that describes the gift itself. To comply with Microsoft guidelines, you must define a new class named GotGiftEventArgs that inherits from System.EventArgs and that defines two new fields. I will explain inheritance in depth in Chapter 5, but the following code should be self-explanatory:

```
Class GotGiftEventArgs
    Inherits System.EventArgs

    ' The additional fields exposed by this class
    Public Giver As Person3
    Public GiftDescription As String

    ' A convenient constructor
    Sub New(ByVal giver As Person3, ByVal giftDescription As String)
        Me.Giver = giver
        Me.GiftDescription = giftDescription
    End Sub
End Class
```

Now you can extend the Person3 class with the support for the GotGift event:

```
' ...(Add anywhere in the Person3 class)...

Event GotGift(ByVal sender As Object, ByVal e As GotGiftEventArgs)

' Client code calls this method to give a gift to this person.
Sub GiveGift(ByVal giver As Person3, ByVal description As String)
    ' (In this demo, we just raise an event.)
    ' Create a GotGiftEventArgs object on the fly.
    RaiseEvent GotGift(Me, New GotGiftEventArgs(giver, description))
End Sub
```

In the procedure that handles the GotGift event, you extract the Giver and GiftDescription fields of the GotGiftEventArgs object you receive in the second argument:

```
Dim WithEvents joe As New Person3("Joe", "Doe")

Sub TestNewEventSyntax()
    ' Create another Person3 object (Joe's wife).
    Dim ann As New Person3("Ann", "Smith")
    ' Test the Married event.
    joe.Spouse = ann
    ' Let Ann give Joe a gift, and test the GotGift event.
    joe.GiveGift(ann, "a book")
End Sub

Sub Married(ByVal sender As Object, ByVal e As System.EventArgs) _
        Handles joe.Married
    ' Get a strongly typed reference to the object that raised the event.
    Dim p As Person3 = DirectCast(sender, Person3)
    Console.WriteLine(p.CompleteName() & " married " & _
        p.Spouse.CompleteName())
End Sub

Sub GotGift(ByVal sender As Object, ByVal e As GotGiftEventArgs) _
        Handles joe.GotGift
    ' Get a strongly typed reference to the object that raised the event
    ' (that is, the Person3 object that got the gift).
    Dim p As Person3 = DirectCast(sender, Person3)
    Console.WriteLine(e.Giver.CompleteName() & " gave " & p.CompleteName() _
        & " the following gift: " & e.GiftDescription)
End Sub
```

Shared Members

Visual Basic .NET classes support shared fields, properties, and methods, a feature missing in Visual Basic 6. Shared members are also known as *static members* in other object-oriented languages.

Shared Fields

Shared fields are variables that can be accessed (that is, shared) by all the instances of a given class. You declare a shared field as you would define any regular field, except that you prefix the variable name with the Shared keyword:

```
Class Invoice
    ' This variable holds the number of instances created so far.
    Shared InstanceCount As Integer

    Sub New()
        ' Increment number of created instances.
        InstanceCount += 1
    End Sub
End Class
```

The default scope for shared fields is Private, but you can create shared members that are visible from outside the class by using the Public or Friend keyword:

```
' This shared variable is visible from inside the current assembly.
Friend Shared InstanceCount As Integer
```

Shared members are useful for many purposes. For example, you can use the Instance-Count shared variable to implement a read-only ID property that returns a unique number for each instance of this particular class during the application's lifetime:

```
Class Invoice
    ' This variable holds the number of instances created so far.
    Shared InstanceCount As Integer

    ' A unique ID for this instance
    Public ReadOnly Id As Long

    Sub New()
        ' Increment number of created instances.
        InstanceCount += 1
        ' Use the current count as the ID for this instance.
        Id = InstanceCount
        ⋮
    End Sub
End Class
```

Shared fields are also useful when all the instances of a class compete for a limited amount of resources. For example, say that you have a SerialPort class whose instances are meant to operate on the serial ports installed on the machine. Whenever you instantiate the SerialPort class, the new object should allocate the first available serial port for itself, and therefore it needs to know which ports aren't taken by other objects. Under Visual Basic 6, you can solve this problem only by using a Public array defined in a BAS module, which would break the encapsulation of the class (because the class would depend on something defined outside it). Visual Basic .NET offers a more elegant and better-encapsulated solution:

```
Class SerialPort
    ' This array is shared by all instances of the class.
    ' (This example assumes that 4 ports are available.)
    Public Shared AllocatedPorts(3) As Boolean
    ' The serial port used by this instance (in the range 0-3)
    ReadOnly Public Port As Short

    Sub New()
        ' Search the first available port.
        For i As Short = 0 To 3
            If AllocatedPorts(i) = False Then
                ' This port is still available.
                Port = i
                ' Mark the port as unavailable.
                AllocatedPorts(i) = True
                Exit Sub
            End If
        Next        ' Throw an exception if all ports are used.
        Throw New Exception()
    End Sub

    ' Mark the port as available when this instance closes it.
    Sub Close()
        AllocatedPorts(Port) = False
    End Sub
End Class
```

You can even have ReadOnly shared fields, which are logically equivalent to class-level Const statements, with an important difference. Constants are assigned at compile time, whereas a ReadOnly shared field is assigned at run time either by means of an initializer or from inside the shared constructor. (Read on to learn more about shared constructors.)

```
Public Shared ReadOnly StartExecutionTime As Date = Now()
```

Shared Methods

You can use the Shared keyword to mark a method as static, which makes the method callable without your needing to instantiate an object of that class. For example, assume that an application wants to determine which serial port an instance of the SerialPort class is going to use, before actually creating the instance. This information logically belongs to the SerialPort class, as opposed to individual SerialPort instances, and should be exposed through a shared GetAvailablePort function. The code in this method can be reused in the class constructor, so the new version of the class is as follows:

```
Class SerialPort

    ' Return the number of the first available serial port.
    Shared Function GetAvailablePort() As Short
        For i As Short = 0 To 3
            If AllocatedPorts(i) = False Then
                ' This port is still available.
                GetAvailablePort = i
                Exit For
            End If
        Next
        ' Return -1 if no port is available.
        GetAvailablePort = -1
    End Function

    Sub New()
        Port = GetAvailablePort()
        ' Throw a (generic) exception if no available port.
        If Port < 0 Then Throw New Exception()
        ' Mark the port as unavailable.
        AllocatedPorts(Port) = True
    End Sub

    ' ...(Remainder of class as before)...
    ⋮
End Class
```

You can access a shared method from outside the class in two ways: through an instance variable (as for all methods) and through the name of the class, as you see here:

```
port = SerialPort.GetAvailablePort()
```

When you type the name of a class and press the dot key, IntelliSense correctly omits instance members and displays only the list of all the shared fields, properties, and methods:

```
port = SerialPort.
```

| AllocatedPorts |
| GetAvailablePort |

Code inside a shared method must abide by special scoping rules. It can access shared members but can't access instance fields, properties, and methods. This is a reasonable limitation in that the code in the shared method wouldn't know which specific object should provide the instance data. (Because shared methods can be invoked before you create an instance of a given class, there might be no running object at all.)

When you're creating a class that works as a library of functions, you can use shared functions if you don't want to force the user to create an object just to access those functions. For example, consider the following Triangle class, which exposes functions for evaluating the perimeter and the area of a triangle given its three sides:

```
Class Triangle
    Shared Function GetPerimeter(ByVal side1 As Double, _
        ByVal side2 As Double, ByVal side3 As Double) As Double
        Return side1 + side2 + side3
    End Function

    Shared Function GetArea(ByVal side1 As Double, _
        ByVal side2 As Double, ByVal side3 As Double) As Double
        ' First evaluate half of the perimeter.
        Dim halfP As Double = (side1 + side2 + side3) / 2
        ' Then apply the Heron formula.
        Return (halfP * (halfP - side1) * (halfP - side2) * _
            (halfP - side3)) ^ 0.5
    End Function
End Class
```

Using this class is straightforward because you don't need to instantiate a Triangle object:

```
Console.WriteLine(Triangle.GetPerimeter(3, 4, 5))    ' => 12
Console.WriteLine(Triangle.GetArea(3, 4, 5))         ' => 6
```

You don't even need to prefix method names with the class name if you use a proper Imports statement, such as this one:

```
' This statement assumes that Triangle is defined in
' the MyProject namespace.
Imports MyProject.Triangle

' Invoke the GetArea shared method without specifying the class name.
Console.WriteLine(GetArea(3, 4, 5))                  ' => 6
```

This Imports statement works correctly even if the Triangle class is defined in the current project.

In general, there are two types of classes that contain shared members exclusively. One is a class that works as a container for library functions, such as the Triangle class seen previously. The other case is when you have a type for which only one instance can exist. An example of the latter type is the Console class, which contains only shared methods and can't be instantiated; the class itself maps to the one and only console window the application manages. Such classes are known as *singletons*. The .NET Framework contains several other examples of singletons, for example, System.GC (the garbage collection), System.Environment (the operating system environment), System.Diagnostics.Debug (the Debug window), and System.Windows.Forms.Application (the running Windows Forms application).

If a class contains only shared methods—be it a function library or a singleton—there's no point in instantiating it. You can make a class noncreatable simply by adding a Private constructor, whose only purpose is to suppress the automatic generation of the Public constructor that the Visual Basic compiler would perform if no constructor were provided:

```
' A class that contains only shared members
Class LibraryFunctions
```

```
         ⋮
      Private Sub New()
         ' This private constructor contains no code. Its only purpose
         ' is to prevent clients from instantiating this class.
      End Sub
End Class
```

A class that contains only shared members is functionally equivalent to a module. As a matter of fact, a Visual Basic .NET module is nothing but a class that can't be instantiated and whose members are implicitly marked with the Shared keyword. As an added convenience, you can omit the name of the module when you access a module's member from a Visual Basic application—be it the same application where the module is defined, or another application. But if the module is public and you access it from any language other than Visual Basic, you must specify the module name when you access its shared members, because only Visual Basic recognizes the special attribute that is used to mark modules.

Along the same lines, when selecting the Sub Main entry point in an application, you can also select any module defined in the application. This action is necessary when you have two or more modules containing the Sub Main procedure.

> **Note**   A class can contain a special shared method named Shared Sub Main. This procedure can be used as the entry point of the entire application. Simply select the class name in the Startup Object combo box on the General page of the project Property Pages dialog box, exactly as you do when the Sub Main procedure is in a module.

A class can also declare shared events, as in this line of code:

```
Shared Event InvalidTriangle(ByVal sender As Object, ByVal e As EventArgs)
```

Typically, you expose a shared event in singleton classes. For example, the Application object in the System.Windows.Forms namespace exposes a few static events. Because there is no object you can assign to a WithEvents variable, you can handle its events only by means of the AddHandler command:

```
AddHandler Application.ApplicationExit, AddressOf ApplicationExitHandler
```

Shared Constructors

If you define a parameterless Shared Sub New method in a class, this procedure is called automatically just before the first instance of that class is instantiated. Typically, you use such a shared constructor to correctly initialize Shared fields. For example, let's say that all the instances of a class must write to a log file. This file must be opened when the first object of this class is created, and it must be kept open until the application terminates. One solution to this problem is to check whether the log file is opened in the standard constructor:

```
Class FileLogger
    Shared FileHandle As Integer

    Sub New()
        ' Open the log file if not done already.
        If FileHandle = 0 Then
            FileHandle = FreeFile
            FileOpen(FileHandle, "C:\data.log", OpenMode.Output)
        End If
    End Sub
End Class
```

Here's a more structured solution, which is also slightly faster because it doesn't check whether the log file has to be created whenever a new object is instantiated:

```
Class FileLogger
    Shared FileHandle As Integer

    ' The shared constructor
    Shared Sub New()
        ' Open the log file before the first object from
        ' this class is instantiated.
        FileHandle = FreeFile
        FileOpen(FileHandle, "C:\data.log", OpenMode.Output)
    End Sub

    Sub New()
        ' Here goes the initialization code for a specific instance.
        :
    End Sub
End Class
```

The Shared Sub New procedure runs before the Sub New procedure for the first object instantiated for the class. Shared constructors are implicitly Private (unlike other shared procedures, which are Public by default) and can't be declared with the Public or Friend scope qualifier. Shared constructors are the only places where you can assign a Shared ReadOnly field:

```
Public Shared ReadOnly InitialDir As String

Shared Sub New()
    ' Assign the directory that's current when the first
    ' instance of this type is created.
    InitialDir = System.IO.Directory.GetCurrentDirectory()
End Sub
```

Note that there isn't such a thing as a shared destructor method.

In this chapter, you've seen many new object-oriented features in Visual Basic .NET, such as constructors and shared members. They prepare the ground for the next chapter, in which I'll describe what undoubtedly is the most important innovation in the Visual Basic language: inheritance.

5 Inheritance

To the majority of developers, the most important new feature of Visual Basic is inheritance. In a nutshell, inheritance is the ability to derive a new class (the derived or inherited class) from a simpler class (the base class). The derived class inherits all the fields, properties, and methods of the base class and can modify the behavior of any of those properties and methods by overriding them. And you can also add new fields, properties, and methods to the inherited class.

Inheritance is especially effective for rendering an is-a relationship between two classes. For example, you can create a Bird class from the Animal class because a bird is an animal and therefore inherits the characteristics and behaviors of the generic animal, such as the ability to move, sleep, feed itself, and so on. You can then extend the Bird class with new properties and methods, such as the Fly and LayEgg methods. Once the Bird class is in place, you can use it as the base class for a new Falcon class, and so on. A more business-oriented example of inheritance is an Employee class that derives from the Person class, an example that we will use often in the following sections.

A few programming languages, such as Microsoft Visual C++, support multiple-class inheritance, by which a class can derive from more than one base class. All .NET languages, however, support at most single-class inheritance.

Inheritance Basics

To see how inheritance works in Visual Basic .NET, let's start by defining a simple Person base class:

```
Class Person
    ' Fields visible from outside the class
    Public FirstName As String
    Public LastName As String
End Class
```

All you need to inherit an Employee class from Person is an Inherits clause immediately after the Class statement:

```
' The Employee class inherits from Person
Class Employee
    Inherits Person
    ⋮
End Class
```

Or you can use the following syntax to convince your C# colleagues that Visual Basic .NET is a first-class language:

```
' A more C++-like syntax
Class Employee: Inherits Person
    ⋮
End Class
```

The great thing about inheritance in Visual Basic .NET is that you can inherit from *any* object, including objects for which you don't have the source code, because all the plumbing code is provided by the .NET Framework. The only exception to this rule occurs when the author of the class you want to derive from has marked the class sealed, which means that no other class can inherit from it. (You'll find more information about sealed classes later in this chapter.)

The derived class inherits all the Public and Friend fields, properties, methods, and events of the base class. Inheriting a field can be a problem, though, because a derived class becomes dependent on that field, and the author of the base class can't change the implementation of that field—for example, to make it a calculated value—without breaking the derived class. For this reason, it's usually preferable that classes meant to work as base classes should include only Private fields. You should always use a property instead of a field to make a piece of data visible outside the class because you can always change the internal implementation of a property without any impact on derived classes. (To save space and code, some of the examples in this section use fields instead of properties: in other words, do as I say, not as I do.)

The derived class also inherits all the shared members of the base class. For this reason, all types expose the Equals and ReferenceEquals shared methods that they inherit from System.Object.

Extending the Derived Class

You can extend the derived class with new fields, properties, and methods simply by adding these new members anywhere in the class block:

```
Class Employee
    Inherits Person

    ' Two new public fields
    Public BaseSalary As Single
    Public HoursWorked As Integer
    ' A new private field
    Private m_HourlySalary As Single

    ' A new property
    Property HourlySalary() As Single
        Get
            Return m_HourlySalary
        End Get
        Set(ByVal Value As Single)
            m_HourlySalary = Value
```

```
        End Set
    End Property

    ' A new method
    Function Salary() As Single
        Return BaseSalary + m_HourlySalary * HoursWorked
    End Function
End Class
```

Using the Derived Class

You can use the new class without even knowing that it derives from another class. However, being aware of the inheritance relationship between two classes helps you write more flexible code. For example, inheritance rules state that you can always assign a derived object to a base class variable. In this case, the rule guarantees that you can always assign an Employee object to a Person variable:

```
Dim e As New Employee
e.FirstName = "Joe"
e.LastName = "Doe"
' This assignment always works.
Dim p As Person = e
' This proves that p points to the Employee object.
Console.WriteLine(p.CompleteName)    '=> Joe Doe
```

The compiler knows that Person is the base class for Employee, and it therefore knows that all the properties and methods that you can invoke through the p variable are exposed by the Employee object as well. As a result, these calls can never fail. This sort of assignment also works when the derived class inherits from the base class indirectly. Indirect inheritance means that there are intermediate classes along the inheritance path, such as when you have a PartTimeEmployee class that derives from Employee, which in turn derives from Person.

A consequence of this rule is that you can assign any object reference to an Object variable because all .NET classes derive from System.Object either directly or indirectly:

```
' This assignment *always* works, regardless of
' the type of sourceObj.
Dim o As Object = sourceObj
```

Assignments in the opposite direction don't always succeed, though. Consider this code:

```
' (This code assumes that Option Strict is Off.)
Dim p As Person
If Math.Rnd < .5 Then
    ' Sometimes P points to an Employee object.
    p = New Employee()
Else
    ' Sometimes P points to a Person object.
    p = New Person()
End If
' This assignment fails with an InvalidCastException if Math.Rnd was >=.5.
Dim e As Employee = p
```

The compiler can't determine whether the reference assigned to the e variable points to an Employee or a Person object, and the assignment fails at runtime in the latter case. For this reason, this assignment is rejected at compile time if Option Strict is on. (As you remember from Chapter 2, you should set Option Strict On for all the files in the project or from inside the Build page of the project Property Pages dialog box.) An assignment that is accepted by the compiler regardless of the Option Strict setting requires that you perform an explicit cast to the destination type, using the CType or the DirectCast operator:

```
' This statement works also when Option Strict is On.
Dim e As Employee = DirectCast(p, Employee)
```

Polymorphic Behavior

Inheriting from a base class implicitly adds a degree of polymorphism to your code. In this context, polymorphism means that you can use the same variable to invoke members of objects of different type:

```
Dim p As Person
If Math.Rnd < .5 Then
    ' Sometimes P points to an Employee object.
    p = New Employee()
Else
    ' Sometimes P points to a Person object.
    p = New Person()
End If
' In either case, this polymorphic code uses early binding.
Console.WriteLine(p.FirstName & " " & p.LastName)
```

A base class variable can't access methods that are defined only in the derived class. For example, the following code doesn't compile:

```
' *** This code doesn't compile because you're trying to access
'     a method defined in the Employee class through a Person variable.
p.BaseSalary = 10000
```

As an exception to this rule, you can access—more precisely, you can try to access—any member in any class via an Object variable and late binding as long as Option Strict is set to Off:

```
' *** This code requires that Option Strict be Off.
  ⋮
Dim o As Object = New Employee()
' The following statement uses late binding.
o.BaseSalary = 10000
```

Overriding Members in the Base Class

The derived class can modify the behavior of one or more properties and methods in the base class. Visual Basic .NET requires that you slightly modify your code in both the base class and the derived class to implement this new behavior. For example, say that you have a CompleteName method in the Person class. You must prefix it with the Overridable keyword to tell the compiler that this method can be overridden:

```
' ...(In the Person (base) class)...
Overridable Function CompleteName() As String
    Return FirstName & " " & LastName
End Function
```

You must use the Overrides keyword to redefine the behavior of this method in the derived class:

```
' ...(In the Employee (derived) class)...
Overrides Function CompleteName() As String
    Return LastName & ", " & FirstName
End Function
```

Another common term for such a method is virtual method. Visual Studio offers a simple and effective way to create the template code for an overridden method: click the down arrow for the Class Name drop-down list, scroll until you find the name of the derived class, and click the Overrides element immediately below it. (See Figure 5-1.) Then click the down arrow for the Method Name drop-down list, and click the method you want to override. You can also use this technique to generate the template for event handlers and for procedures that implement methods of an interface. (I explain interfaces in the next chapter.)

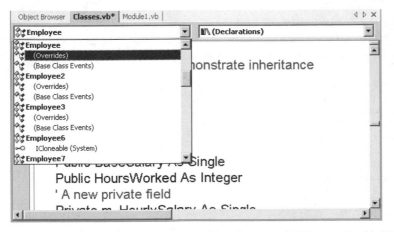

Figure 5-1 Generating the template code for an overridden method in Visual Studio

Visual Basic .NET also supports the NotOverridable keyword, which explicitly states that a method can't be overridden; however, this is the default behavior. In fact, you can use this keyword only in conjunction with the Overrides keyword, as I explain in the following section.

When you override a property in the base class, you can redefine its internal implementation, but you can't alter the read or write attribute. For example, if the base class exposes a ReadOnly property, you can't make it writable by overriding it in the derived class. Similarly, you can't define a read-write property that overrides a WriteOnly property in the base class. Along the same lines, if you're overriding a default member in the base class, the method in the derived class must be the default member in the derived class and requires the Default keyword.

Notice that you can't override fields, constants, or shared members defined in the base class.

Override Variations

By default, a method marked with the Overrides keyword is itself overridable, so you never need both the Overrides and Overridable keywords in the same procedure definition, even though using both is legal. You need the NotOverridable keyword to explicitly tell the compiler that an overridden method isn't overridable in derived classes:

```
' This procedure overrides a procedure in the base class, but this
' procedure can't be overridden in any class that inherits from the current
' class.
NotOverridable Overrides Sub MyProc()
    ⋮
End Sub
```

When adding a member with the same name but a different signature, you need neither the Overrides keyword in the derived class nor the Overridable keyword in the base class. For example, if the Employee class contains a CompleteName method with one argument, it doesn't override the parameterless method with the same name in the Person class. Therefore, no Overridable or Overrides keyword is necessary. Oddly enough, however, the method in the derived class does require the Overloads keyword:

```
' ...(In the Person (base) class)...
' Note: no Overridable keyword
Function CompleteName() As String
    Return FirstName & " " & LastName
End Function

' ...(In the Employee (derived) class)...
' Note: no Overrides keyword, but Overloads is required.
Overloads Function CompleteName(ByVal title As String) As String
    Return title & " " & LastName & ", " & FirstName
End Function
```

The general rule is therefore as follows: you don't need the Overloads keyword when a class defines multiple members with identical names, but you need the Overloads keyword in the derived class when the derived class exposes a new member with the same name but a different signature. If the derived class additionally overrides a base class member with the same signature, you're forced to use both the Overloads and the Overrides keywords for this member. You also must honor the rule (stated in

Chapter 4) that says if you use Overloads for a member in a class, you must use it for all the members with the same name.

The compiler can generate more efficient code when calling nonoverridable methods instead of overridable (virtual) methods, so you might want to avoid using the Overridable keyword if you can. For example, the JIT compiler can inline regular methods but not virtual methods. (Inlining is an optimization technique through which the compiler moves code from the called method into the caller's procedure.) In addition, allocating an object that contains virtual methods takes slightly longer than the allocation of an object that has no virtual methods. An informal benchmark shows that an overridable method can be twice as slow as a nonoverridable one, even though the difference in absolute terms is small and you need a loop with millions of iterations to make it evident.

While we're talking about performance, remember that calling a virtual method on a value type forces the compiler to consider it a reference type, which causes the object to be boxed in the heap and therefore degrades the overall execution speed. For example, this happens when you call the ToString method on a value type such as a Structure, as you can see by looking at the IL code produced by such a call.

The MyBase Keyword

The MyBase keyword is useful when you want to reference a field, property, or method of the base object. If a member hasn't been overridden in the derived class, the expressions *Me.membername* and *MyBase.membername* refer to the same member and execute the same code. However, when *membername* has been redefined in the inherited class, you need the MyBase keyword to access the member as defined in the base class. Consider the following method:

```
' ...(In the Person (base) class)...
Overridable Function CompleteName() As String
    Return FirstName & " " & LastName
End Function
```

Now, let's assume that the Employee class overrides this method to prefix the complete name with the employee's title. Here's a not-so-smart implementation of this method:

```
' ...(In the Employee (derived) class)...
Public Title As String

Overrides Function CompleteName() As String
    If Title <> "" Then CompleteName = Title & " "
    CompleteName &= FirstName & " " & LastName
End Function
```

The preceding solution isn't optimal because it doesn't reuse any code in the base class. In this particular case, the code in the base class is just a string concatenation operation, but in a real class it might be dozens or hundreds of statements. Worse, if you later change or improve the implementation of the CompleteName function in the base class, you must dutifully apply these changes to all the classes that inherit from Person. The MyBase keyword lets you implement a better solution:

```
Overrides Function CompleteName() As String
    If Title <> "" Then CompleteName = Title & " "
    CompleteName &= MyBase.CompleteName
End Function
```

Constructors in Derived Classes

Even though you declare constructor procedures with the Sub keyword, they aren't ordinary methods and aren't inherited from the base class in the way all other methods are. It's up to you to provide the derived class with one or more constructors if you want the derived class to be creatable using the same syntax as the base class.

If the base class has a Sub New procedure that takes no arguments, you don't strictly need to define an explicit constructor for the derived class. The same happens if you have a class with no explicit constructor because in that case the Visual Basic compiler creates a hidden constructor for you behind the scenes. As a matter of fact, all the preceding examples show that you can create an instance of the Employee class without defining a constructor for it:

```
Dim e As Employee = New Employee()
```

Things are different when the base class doesn't include either an explicit or an implicit parameterless constructor. In this case, the derived class must contain a constructor method, and the first executable line of this method must be a call to the base class's constructor. Say that the Person2 class has the following constructor method:

```
Class Person2
    Sub New(ByVal firstName As String, ByVal lastName As String)
        Me.FirstName = firstName
        Me.LastName = lastName
    End Sub
    ' ...(other properties and methods as in Person class) ...
    ⋮
End Class
```

The derived Employee2 class must therefore contain the following code:

```
Class Employee2
    Inherits Person2

    Sub New(ByVal firstName As String, ByVal lastName As String)
        ' The first executable statement *must* be a call
        ' to the constructor in the base class.
        MyBase.New(firstName, lastName)
        ' You can continue with the initialization step here.
        ⋮
    End Sub
End Class
```

The constructor in the derived class can have a different argument signature from the constructor in the base class, but in this case the first executable statement must be a call to the base class's constructor:

```
Public Title As String                    ' A new field

Sub New(ByVal firstName As String, ByVal lastName As String, _
    ByVal title As String)
    MyBase.New(firstName, lastName)
    Me.Title = title
End Sub
```

The MyClass Keyword

You can easily miss a subtle but important detail of inheritance: when a client calls a nonoverridden method of an inherited class, the called method is the one defined in the base class, but it runs in the context of the derived class.

The simplest way to explain this concept is through an example, once again based on the Person-Employee pair. Let's define a Person3 base class exposing a TitledName method that returns the complete name of the person, prefixed with his or her title if one has been specified:

```
Enum Gender
    NotSpecified
    Male
    Female
End Enum

Class Person3
    ' (In a real-world class, these would be properties.)
    Public FirstName As String
    Public LastName As String
    Public Gender As Gender = Gender.NotSpecified
    ' ...(other members omitted for brevity) ...
    :

    Dim m_Title As String
    Overridable Property Title() As String
        Get
            Return m_Title
        End Get
        Set(ByVal Value As String)
            m_Title = Value
        End Set
    End Property

    ' Prefix the name with a title if one has been specified.
    Function TitledName() As String
        If Title <> "" Then
            Return Title & " " & FirstName & " " & LastName
        Else
            Return FirstName & " " & LastName
        End If
```

```
        End Function
End Class
```

The derived Employee3 class doesn't override the TitledName method, but it does override the Title property, so it's never an empty string:

```
Class Employee3
    Inherits Person3

    ' Override Title to provide a title if no one has been assigned.
    Overrides Property Title() As String
        Get
            If MyBase.Title <> "" Then
                Return MyBase.Title
            ElseIf Gender = Gender.Male Then
                Return "Mr."
            ElseIf Gender = Gender.Female Then
                Return "Mrs."
            End If
        End Get
        Set(ByVal Value As String)
            MyBase.Title = Value
        End Set
    End Property
End Class
```

Because the derived class doesn't override the TitledName property, the version in the base class is used. However, that code runs in the context of the derived class. Therefore, it uses the overridden version of the Title property, the one defined in Employee3 instead of the one defined in Person3:

```
Dim e As New Employee3("Joe", "Doe")
e.Gender = Gender.Male
' The TitledName method defined in Person3 uses the overridden
' version of Title property defined in Employee3.
Console.WriteLine(e.TitledName)      ' => Mr. Joe Doe
```

A better way to anticipate the effect of inheritance is to pretend that all the nonoverridden routines in the base class have been pasted inside the derived class. So if they reference another property or method, they call the version of the member that's defined in the derived class—not the original one defined in the base class.

However, sometimes you want a piece of code in the base class to use the nonoverridden version of the properties and methods it references. Let's use another example to clarify this concept. Let's say that a person can vote only if he or she is 18 years old, so the Person3 class contains this code:

```
Class Person3
    ⋮
    Public BirthDate As Date

    ' Age is defined as the number of whole years passed from BirthDate.
    Overridable ReadOnly Property Age() As Integer
        Get
```

```
        Age = Now.Year - BirthDate.Year
        If Now.DayOfYear < BirthDate.DayOfYear Then Age -= 1
    End Get
End Property

ReadOnly Property CanVote() As Boolean
    Get
        Return (Age >= 18)
    End Get
End Property
End Class
```

The Employee3 class uses a looser definition of the age concept and overrides the Age property with a simpler version that returns the difference between the current year and the year when the employee was born:

```
Class Employee3
    ⋮

    ' Age is defined as difference between the current year
    ' and the year the employee was born.
    Overrides ReadOnly Property Age() As Integer
        Get

            Age = Now.Year - BirthDate.Year
        End Get
    End Property
End Class
```

Do you see the problem? The CanVote property of an Employee3 object is inherited as is from the Person3 class but incorrectly uses the Age property defined in the Employee3 class rather than the original version in the base class. To see what kind of bogus result this logical error can cause, run this code:

```
' Create a person and an employee.
Dim p As New Person3("Joe", "Doe")
Dim e As New Employee3("Robert", "Smith")
' They are born on the same day.
p.BirthDate = #12/31/1985#
e.BirthDate = #12/31/1985#
' (Assuming that you run this code in the year 2003...)
' The person can't vote yet (correct).
Console.WriteLine(p.CanVote)          ' => False
' The employee is allowed to vote (incorrect).
Console.WriteLine(e.CanVote)          ' => True
```

Once you understand where the problem is, its solution is simple: you use the MyClass keyword to ensure that a method in a base class always uses the properties and methods in that base class (as opposed to their overridden version in the inherited class). Here's how to fix the problem in our example:

```
    ' ...(In the Person3 class)...
    ReadOnly Property CanVote() As Boolean
        Get
```

```
            ' Ensure that it always uses the nonoverridden
            ' version of the Age property.
            Return (MyClass.Age >= 18)
        End Get
    End Property
```

Member Shadowing

.NET lets you inherit from a class in a compiled DLL for which you neither have nor control the source code. This raises an interesting question: what happens if you extend the base class with a method or a property and then the author of the base class releases a new version that exposes a member with the same name?

Visual Basic copes with this situation in such a way that the application that uses the derived class isn't broken by changes in the base class. If the derived class has a member with the same name as a member in the new version of the base class, you get a compilation warning, but you are still able to compile the two classes. In this case, the member in the derived class is said to be *shadowing* the member with the same name in the base class. Visual Basic offers three different syntax forms of shadowing:

■ A member in the derived class shadows all the members in the base class with the same name, regardless of their parameter signatures. As I've explained, you get a compilation warning that doesn't prevent successful compilation (unless you select the Treat Compiler Warnings As Errors check box on the Build page of the project Property Pages dialog box).

■ A member in the derived class marked with the Shadows keyword hides all the members in the base class with the same name, regardless of their signatures. The effect is exactly the same as in the preceding case. In addition, you don't get any compilation warning, so you should use the Shadows keyword to make it clear that you are intentionally shadowing one or more members in the base class.

■ A member in the derived class marked with the Overloads keyword shadows only the member in the base class that has the same name and argument signature. (Note that you can't apply the Shadows and Overloads keywords to the same member.)

Shadowing can be confusing, so it's best to look at a concrete example:

```
Class AAA
    Sub DoSomething()
        Console.WriteLine("AAA.DoSomething")
    End Sub
    Sub DoSomething(ByVal msg As String)
        Console.WriteLine("AAA.DoSomething({0})", msg)
    End Sub

    Sub DoSomething2()
        Console.WriteLine("AAA.DoSomething2")
    End Sub
    Sub DoSomething2(ByVal msg As String)
        Console.WriteLine("AAA.DoSomething2({0})", msg)
    End Sub
```

```
End Class

Class BBB
    Inherits AAA

    Overloads Sub DoSomething()
        Console.WriteLine("BBB.DoSomething")
    End Sub
    Shadows Sub DoSomething2()
        Console.WriteLine("BBB.DoSomething2")
    End Sub
End Class
```

The following routine calls the methods in the two classes:

```
Dim b As New BBB()
b.DoSomething()          ' => BBB.DoSomething
b.DoSomething("abc")     ' => AAA.DoSomething(abc)
b.DoSomething2()         ' => BBB.DoSomething2
```

As you see, the DoSomething procedure in class BBB shadows the procedure DoSomething with zero arguments in class AAA, but the procedure that takes one argument isn't shadowed and can be accessed as usual. This behavior contrasts with the DoSomething2 procedure in class BBB, which is declared with the Shadows keyword and therefore hides both procedures with the same name in class AAA. For this reason, the following statement raises a compilation error:

```
' *** This statement doesn't compile.
b.DoSomething2("abc")
```

If you drop the Shadows keyword in class BBB, the overall effect is the same, the only difference being that the call to DoSomething2 causes a compilation warning.

You've just seen that you can shadow a property or a method even if the procedure isn't marked with Overridable (or is marked with NotOverridable Overrides) in the base class. This raises an interesting question: what is the point of omitting the Overridable keyword, then?

In practice, member shadowing makes it impossible for a developer to prevent a method from being overridden, at least from a logical point of view. In fact, let's say that by omitting the Overridable keyword, the author of the Person3 class makes the Address property not overridable:

```
Class Person3
    ⋮
    Dim m_Address As String

    Property Address() As String
        Get
            Return m_Address
        End Get
```

```
        Set(ByVal Value As String)
            m_Address = Value
        End Set
    End Property
End Class
```

The author of the Employee3 class can still override the Address property—for example, to reject null string assignments—by using the Shadows keyword (to suppress compilation warnings) and manually delegating to the base class using the MyBase.Address expression:

```
Class Employee3
    Inherits Person3
    ⋮
    Shadows Property Address() As String
        Get
            Return MyBase.Address
        End Get
        Set(ByVal Value As String)
            If Value = "" Then Throw New ArgumentException()
            MyBase.Address = Value
        End Set
    End Property
End Class
```

As you see, you can't prevent a class member from being overridden, at least from a logical point of view. However, you see a different behavior when you access the member through a base class variable, depending on whether you override the member in the standard way or you shadow it implicitly or explicitly using the Shadows keyword. When a member has been overridden with Overrides, you always access the member in the derived class, even if you're referencing it through a base class variable. When a member has been shadowed (with or without the Shadows keyword), no inheritance relationship exists between the two members, and therefore, you access the member in the base class if you're using a base class variable. An example makes this concept clearer:

```
Dim e As New Employee3("Joe", "Doe")
' This statement correctly raises an ArgumentException
' because of the code in the Employee class.
e.Address = ""

' Access the same object through a base class variable.
Dim p As Person3 = e
' This raises no run-time error because the Address property procedure
' in the base class is actually executed.
p.Address = ""
```

If the Address property had been redefined using the Overrides keyword, the last statement would invoke the Address property procedure in the derived class, not in the base class.

Because the redefined method in the derived class has nothing to do with the original method in the base class, the two members can have different scope qualifiers, which isn't allowed if the method in the derived class overrides the method in the base class. For example, you can have a Public method in the derived class that shadows (and possibly delegates to) a Friend method in the base class. However, keep in mind that a Private member in the derived class does not shadow a member in the base class. In other words, the Shadows keyword has no effect on Private members.

One last detail on shadowing: you can't shadow a method that is defined as MustOverride in the base class; in this case, the compiler expects a method marked with the Overrides keyword and flags the derived class as incomplete.

Redefining Shared Members

You can use neither the Overridable nor the Overrides keyword with shared members because shared members can't be overridden. Either they're inherited as they are or they must be shadowed and redefined from scratch in the derived class.

You cannot use the MyBase variable to invoke shared methods defined in the base class if you're redefining them in the derived class because MyBase is forbidden in shared methods. For example, say that you have a Person class with the following shared method:

```
' ...(In the Person (base) class)...
Shared Function AreBrothers(ByVal p1 As Person, ByVal p2 As Person) As Boolean
    Return (p1.Father Is p2.Father) Or (p1.Mother Is p2.Mother)
End Function
```

In addition, you have an Employee class that inherits from Person and redefines the AreBrothers shared method so that two Employee objects can be considered brothers if they have one parent in common and the same family name. The following code builds on the AreBrother shared method in the Person class so that if you later change the definition in the Person class, the Employee class automatically uses the new definition:

```
' In the Employee (derived) class
Shared Shadows Function AreBrothers(ByVal e1 As Employee, _
    ByVal e2 As Employee) As Boolean
    Return Person.AreBrothers(e1, e2) And (e1.LastName = e2.LastName)
End Function
```

Unfortunately, no keyword lets you reference shared members in the base class in a generic way (similar to what the MyBase keyword does with instance members of the base class). You have to hard-code the name of the base class inside the source code of the derived class when calling a shared method of the base class.

Sealed and Virtual Classes

Visual Basic .NET provides a few additional keywords that let you decide whether other developers can or must inherit from your class and whether they have to override some of its members.

The NotInheritable Keyword

For security (or other) reasons, you might want to ensure that no one extends a class you created. You can achieve this by simply marking the class with the NotInheritable keyword:

```
' Ensure that no one can inherit from the Employee class.
NotInheritable Class Employee
    ⋮
End Class
```

Classes that can't be inherited from are called sealed classes. In general, you rarely need to seal a class, but good candidates for the NotInheritable keyword are utility classes that expose only shared members. As you might expect, you can't use the Overridable keyword inside a sealed class.

The MustInherit Keyword

A situation that arises more frequently is that you want to prevent users from using your class as is and instead force them to inherit from it. In this case, the class is called a virtual or abstract class. You can use it only to derive new classes and can't instantiate it directly.

To prevent direct usage of a class, you must flag it with the MustInherit keyword. You typically use this keyword when a class is meant to define a behavior or an archetypal object that never concretely exists. A typical example is the Animal class, which should be defined as virtual because you never instantiate a generic animal; rather, you create a specific animal—a cat, a dog, and so on, which derives some of its properties from the abstract Animal class.

Here's a more business-oriented example: your application deals with different types of documents—invoices, orders, payrolls, and so on—and all of them have some behaviors in common in that they can be stored, printed, displayed, or attached to an e-mail message. It makes sense to gather this common behavior in a Document class, but at the same time you want to be sure that no one mistakenly creates a generic Document object. After all, you never say "I am creating a document." Rather, you say "I am creating an invoice, an order, and so on."

```
MustInherit Class Document
    ' Contents in RTF format
    Private m_RTFText As String

    Overridable Property RTFText() As String
        Get
            Return m_RTFText
        End Get
        Set(ByVal Value As String)
            m_RTFText = Value
        End Set
    End Property
```

```
    ' Save RTF contents to file.
    Overridable Sub SaveToFile(ByVal fileName As String)
        ⋮
    End Sub

    ' Load RTF contents from file.
    Overridable Sub LoadFromFile(ByVal fileName As String)
        ⋮
    End Sub

    ' Print the RTF contents.
    Overridable Sub Print()
        ⋮
    End Sub
End Class
```

Now you can define other classes that inherit their behavior from the Document virtual class:

```
Class PurchaseOrder
    Inherits Document

    ' Redefines how a PO is printed.
    Overrides Sub Print()
        ⋮
    End Sub
End Class
```

Note that you must explicitly use the Overridable keyword in the base class and the Overrides keyword in the inherited class, even if the base class is marked with MustInherit, because the base class can contain nonoverridable members as well.

The MustOverride Keyword

In general, users of a virtual class aren't forced to override its properties and methods. After all, the main benefit in defining a virtual class is that derived classes can reuse the code in the base class. Sometimes, however, you want to force inherited classes to provide a custom version of a given method. For example, consider this Shape virtual class, which defines a few properties and methods that all geometrical shapes have in common:

```
MustInherit Class Shape
    ' Position on the X-Y plane
    Public X, Y As Single

    ' Move the object on the X-Y plane.
    Sub Offset(ByVal deltaX As Single, ByVal deltaY As Single)
        X = X + deltaX
        Y = Y + deltaY
        ' Redraw the shape at the new position.
        Display
    End Sub

    Sub Display()
        ' No implementation here
    End Sub
End Class
```

The Shape virtual class must include the Display method—otherwise, the code in the Offset procedure won't compile—even though that method can't have any implementation because actual drawing statements depend on the specific class that will be inherited from Shape. Alas, the author of the derived class might forget to override the Display method, and no shape will be ever displayed.

In cases like this, you should use the MustOverride keyword to make it clear that the method is virtual and must be overridden in derived classes. When you're using the MustOverride keyword, you specify only the method's signature and must omit the End Property, End Sub, or End Function keyword:

```
MustInherit Class Shape
    ' ... (Other members as in previous example) ...
    ⋮
    MustOverride Sub Display()
End Class
```

If a class has one or more virtual methods, the class itself is virtual and must be marked with the MustInherit keyword. The following Square class inherits from Shape and overrides the Display method:

```
Class Square
    Inherits Shape

    Public Side As Single

    Overrides Sub Display()
        ' Add here the statements that draw the square.
        ⋮
    End Sub
End Class
```

Scope

Visual Basic .NET accepts five scope qualifiers, which are the three qualifiers available to Visual Basic 6 developers (Public, Friend, and Private), plus two new ones (Protected and Protected Friend). These new qualifiers are related to inheritance, which explains why I deferred their description until now. Before diving into a thorough discussion of scope, though, you must learn about one more Visual Basic .NET feature: nested classes.

Nested Classes

Unlike previous versions of the language, Visual Basic .NET lets you nest class definitions:

```
Class Outer
    ⋮
    Class Inner
        ⋮
    End Class
End Class
```

The code inside the Outer class can always create and use instances of the Inner class, regardless of the scope qualifier used for the Inner class. If the nested class is declared using a scope qualifier other than Private, the nested class is also visible to the outside of the Outer class, using the dot syntax:

```
Dim obj As New Outer.Inner
```

Nested classes serve a variety of purposes. First, they're useful for organizing all your classes in groups of related classes and for creating namespaces that help resolve name ambiguity. For example, you might have a Mouse class nested in an Animal class and another Mouse class nested in a Peripheral class:

```
Class Animal
    ⋮
    ' This class can be referred to as Animal.Mouse.
    Class Mouse
        ⋮
    End Class
End Class

Class Peripheral
    ⋮
    ' This class can be referred to as Peripheral.Mouse.
    Class Mouse
        ⋮
    End Class
End Class
```

You saw a similar example in "The Imports Statement" section of Chapter 2, but on that occasion we used classes nested in namespaces instead of other classes. Code in the Animal class can refer to the inner Mouse class without using the dot syntax. It also can refer to the other mouse class using the Peripheral.Mouse syntax. Things become more complex when you have multiple nesting levels, as in the following code:

```
Class Peripheral
    Dim m As Mouse
    Dim kb As Keyboard
    Dim k As Keyboard.Key

    ⋮
    ' This class can be referred to as Peripheral.Mouse.
    Class Mouse
        Dim kb As Keyboard
        Dim k As Keyboard.Key
        ⋮
    End Class

    ' This class can be referred to as Peripheral.Keyboard.
    Class Keyboard
        Dim m As Mouse
        Dim k As Key
        ⋮
```

```
              ' This class can be referred to as Peripheral.Keyboard.Key.
              Class Key
                  Dim m As Mouse
                  Dim kb As Keyboard
                  ⋮
              End Class
          End Class
      End Class
```

Only classes nested immediately inside the outer class can be referenced without the dot syntax from inside the outer class (or its nested classes). For example, you need the dot syntax to refer to the Key class from any class other than Keyboard. However, the rule isn't symmetrical. You can refer to the Mouse class without the dot syntax from inside the Key class.

Another common use for nested classes is to encapsulate one or more auxiliary classes inside the class that uses them and to avoid making them visible to other parts of the application. In this case, the inner class should be marked with the Private scope qualifier. For example, you might create a DoubleLinkedList class that internally uses the ListItem class to store the value of each element, the pointer to previous and next element, etc. The ListItem class isn't meant to be visible from the outside, so it's marked as private. As a consequence, you can't have any nonprivate member in the outer class return a reference to the inner, private class:

```
Class DoubleLinkedList
    ' These members are private, because they refer to private type.
    Private FirstListItem As ListItem
    Private LastListItem As ListItem
    ⋮
    ' This class isn't visible from outside the DoubleLinkedList class.
    Private Class ListItem
        Public Value As Object
        Public NextItem As ListItem
        Public PreviousItem As ListItem
        ⋮
    End Class
End Class
```

Inner classes have one peculiar feature: they can access private members in their container class if they're provided with a reference to an object of that container class:

```
    Private Class ListItem
        Private m_Dll As DoubleLinkedList
        ' The constructor takes a reference to the outer
        ' DoubleLinkedList object.
        Public Sub New(ByVal dll As DoubleLinkedList)
            m_Dll = dll
        End Sub

        ' This method references a private member in the outer class.
        Public Function IsFirstItem() As Boolean
            Return (Me Is m_Dll.FirstListItem)
```

```
    End Function
        :
End Class
```

You don't need an object reference to access a shared member in the outer class.

Public, Private, and Friend Scope Qualifiers

As a Visual Basic 6 developer, you're already familiar with three of the five scope keywords in Visual Basic .NET.

The Public scope qualifier makes a class or one of its members visible outside the current assembly if the project is a library project. The meaning of Public scope is therefore the same as in Visual Basic 6.

The Private scope makes a class or a member usable only inside its container class. You can use the Private keyword with nested classes only, and you get a compilation error if the class isn't nested. A private class is usable only inside the class in which it's defined, and this includes any other nested class defined in the same container. Leaving aside nested classes, the Private keyword has the same meaning as it does in Visual Basic 6.

The Friend scope qualifier makes a class or one of its members visible to the current assembly. So this keyword has the same meaning as under Visual Basic 6, if you replace the word assembly with project. Because most assemblies are made of just one project, for most practical purposes this keyword has retained its meaning in the transition to Visual Basic .NET. You can use the Friend keyword to make a nested class visible from outside its container without making it Public and visible from outside the project. Note that Friend is the default scope for classes, unlike Visual Basic 6 classes, whose default scope is Public. To make a Visual Basic .NET class visible outside the assembly that contains it, you must explicitly flag the class with the Public keyword.

In general, few restrictions apply to using and mixing these scope keywords at the class and at the member level. For example, you can have a Private class that exposes a Public method; however, a Public method in a Public class can't expose a Protected or Private member because Visual Basic .NET wouldn't know how to marshal it outside the current assembly. Similarly, you can't inherit a Friend class from a Private class and you can't have a Public class that inherits from a Friend or Private class. The reason is that all the members in the base class should be visible to clients of the inherited class, so the scope of members in the base class can't be more limited than the scope of members in the derived class.

You can't use scope qualifiers to alter the scope of an overridden method. If a base class contains a Public method, for example, you can't override it with a Private or Friend method in the derived class. This rule ensures that if a base class variable points to an object from the derived class you can still access the variable to invoke all the overridden methods in the derived class.

The Protected Scope Qualifier

Protected is a new scope qualifier that makes a member or a nested class visible inside the current class, as well to all classes derived by the current class. Put another way, Protected members are private members that are also inherited by derived classes. In general, a class author defines one or more members as Protected to provide inheritors with a way to modify the usual behavior of the class, but without letting regular clients do the same. For example, consider this Report class that prints a document with a header and a footer:

```
Class Report
    Public Sub Print()
        ' Print the header.
        ⋮
        ' Print the body of the document.
        ⋮
        ' Print the footer.
        ⋮
    End Sub
End Class
```

This is an example of how you should never write a class that is meant to be inherited from. Here's a better version, which splits the three basic steps into their own Protected methods:

```
Class Report
    Public Sub Print()
        OnPrintHeader()
        OnPrintBody()
        OnPrintFooter()
    End Sub

    Protected Overridable Sub OnPrintHeader()
        ⋮
    End Sub
    Protected Overridable Sub OnPrintBody()
        ⋮
    End Sub
    Protected Overridable Sub OnPrintFooter()
        ⋮
    End Sub
End Class
```

Because you usually provide Protected members so that inheritors can customize the base class behavior, these members are often marked with the Overridable keyword as well. For this reason, you should rarely use the Protected keyword with fields (which can't be overridden).

Thanks to the three protected and overridable members, you can easily create new classes that reuse most of the code in the base Report class. For example, here's a Report2 class that displays no header and adds totals before the standard footer text:

```
Class Report2
    Inherits Report

    Protected Overrides Sub OnPrintHeader()
        ' Print no header.
    End Sub

    Protected Overrides Sub OnPrintFooter()
        ' Print all totals here.
        ⋮
        ' Print the standard footer.
        MyBase.OnPrintFooter()
    End Sub
End Class
```

This pattern based on protected and overridable members is applied extensively anywhere in the .NET Framework. For example, the System.Windows.Forms.Form class exposes tons of Onxxxx methods, so all form classes you define in your program (which derive from the base Form class) can control every minor detail of the form's appearance and behavior.

The Protected Friend Scope Qualifier

The fifth scope qualifier available in Visual Basic .NET is Protected Friend, which combines the features of the Friend and Protected keywords and therefore defines a member or a nested class that's visible to the entire assembly and to all inherited classes. This keyword seems to be redundant—you might think that Friend also comprises inherited classes—until you consider that Visual Basic .NET allows you to inherit classes from other assemblies.

In the Report sample class introduced in the previous section, you might flag the three Onxxxx methods with the Protected Friend Overridable keywords. This change in source code would enable other classes in the same assembly to individually print the header, the body, or the footer of the document, without providing clients outside the assembly with this capability.

Using Scope Qualifiers with Constructors

You might find it interesting to see what happens when you apply a scope qualifier other than Public to a constructor in a Public class. Using a Friend constructor makes the class creatable from inside the assembly but not from outside it, while leaving the class usable outside the current assembly. This is the closest equivalent of PublicNot-Creatable classes in Visual Basic 6:

```
Public Class Widget
    ' This class can be created only from inside the current assembly.
    Friend Sub New()
        ⋮
    End Sub
End Class
```

You can see that clients outside the current assembly must have a way to receive an instance of the Widget class somehow—for example, by calling a Public method of another class. A class whose methods are used to create instances of another class is often called factory class.

You can define a Private Sub New method if you want to prevent clients—inside and outside the assembly—from instancing the class. This approach can be useful when the class contains only shared members, so there's no point in creating an instance of it:

```
Class Triangle
    ' This private constructor prevents clients from
    ' instancing this class.
    Private Sub New()
        ' No implementation code here.
    End Sub

    ' Add here all the shared members for this class.
    Shared Function GetArea( ... ) As Double
        ⋮
    End Function
    ⋮
End Class
```

Another use for Private constructors arises when you want clients to create instances through a shared member rather than with the usual New keyword, as in the following example:

```
Class Square
    Public Side As Double

    ' This private constructor prevents clients from
    ' instancing this class directly.
    Private Sub New(ByVal side As Double)
        Me.Side = side
    End Sub

    ' Clients can create a square only through this shared method.
    Shared Function CreateSquare(ByVal side As Double) As Square
        Return New Square(side)
    End Function
End Class
```

Clients can create a new Square object using this syntax:

```
Dim sq As Square = Square.CreateSquare(2.5)
```

Some classes in the .NET Framework expose this sort of constructor method, also known as factory method, but in general you should stick to standard constructor methods because this alternative technique doesn't offer any clear advantage, except for the ability to run custom code before actually creating the instance. The following CachedFile class offers an example of why this feature can be useful:

```
Class CachedFile
    ' The private constructor initializes the Text property.
    Private Sub New(ByVal filename As String)
        ' Read the file using a StreamReader object (see Chapter 10).
        ' (A real-world application should use a Try block here.)
        Dim sr As New System.IO.StreamReader(filename)
        m_Text = sr.ReadToEnd()
        sr.Close()
    End Sub

    ' The Text property returns the contents of the text file.
    Dim m_Text As String

    Public ReadOnly Property Text() As String
        Get
            Return m_Text
        End Get
    End Property

    ' The cache holding existing instances of this class
    Shared cache As New Hashtable

    ' The factory method
    Public Shared Function Create(ByVal filename As String) As CachedFile
        If cache.Contains(filename) Then
            ' Return a cached version if possible.
            Return CType(cache(filename), CachedFile)
        Else
            ' Else create a new object and cache it.
            Dim item As New CachedFile(filename)
            cache.Add(filename, item)
            Return item
        End If
    End Function
End Class
```

The CachedFile provides easy access to the contents of text files and caches all instances created so far; if a client requests to read a file that has already been read, an existing instance is returned to save both memory and disk activity. For this trick to work, clients are prevented from directly calling the constructor (which is private) and must go through the Create factory method:

```
' Read the contents of the same file twice.
Dim f1 As CachedFile = CachedFile.Create("c:\tryme.txt")
Dim f2 As CachedFile = CachedFile.Create("c:\tryme.txt")
' Prove that the actual instance was returned.
Console.WriteLine(f1 Is f2)       ' => True
```

The scope of the constructor has a far-reaching and somewhat surprising effect on the inheritance mechanism. To begin with, a class that has only Private constructors can't be used as a base class, even if it isn't flagged with the NotInheritable keyword. In fact, the first statement in the constructor of the derived class should invoke the base class constructor, but any attempt to call MyBase.New will fail because the Sub New procedure isn't visible outside the base class.

Along the same lines, a Public class that has one or more Friend Sub New constructors can be used as a base class, but only if the derived class is defined in the same assembly. Any attempt to inherit that class from outside the assembly would fail because the inherited class can't call a constructor with a Friend scope. To let clients outside the current assembly instantiate the base class, you can add a shared public factory method that returns a new instance of the class:

```
' This class is visible from outside the assembly but can't
' be used as a base class for classes outside the assembly.
Public Class Widget
    ' This constructor can be called only from inside
    ' the current assembly.
    Friend Sub New()
        ⋮
    End Sub

    ' A pseudoconstructor method for clients located
    ' outside the current assembly.
    Public Shared Function CreateWidget() As Widget
        Return New Widget()
    End Function
End Class
```

Even if clients outside the current assembly don't use the Widget class, you still have to mark it as Public (rather than Friend or Private) if you use Widget as the base class for other Public classes, as I explained in the preceding section.

If the constructor has Protected scope, the class can be used as a base class because the constructor of the derived class can always access this constructor, but the class can't be instantiated from either inside or outside the current assembly. Finally, if the constructor has Protected Friend scope, the class can be used as a base class but can be instantiated only from inside the assembly it resides in and from inside derived classes.

Understanding from where you can instantiate a class, and from where you can use it as a base class, is complicated by the fact that nested classes can always access Private and Protected constructors. Table 5-1 can help you determine the effect of the scope of the constructor and the class itself.

Table 5-1   The Effect of Class Scope and Constructor Scope on a Class's Ability to Be Instantiated or Used as a Base Class

Class Scope[*]	Constructor Scope	Types That Can Instantiate This Class	Classes That Can Inherit from This Class
Private	Private	Nested types	Nested classes
	Protected	Nested types and inherited classes	Private classes defined in the same container
	Friend, Protected Friend, Public	Types defined in the same container	Private classes defined in the same container

Table 5-1   The Effect of Class Scope and Constructor Scope on a Class's Ability to Be Instantiated or Used as a Base Class

Class Scope*	Constructor Scope	Types That Can Instantiate This Class	Classes That Can Inherit from This Class
Protected	Private	Nested types	Nested classes
	Protected	Nested types and inherited classes	Private/Protected classes defined in the same container
	Friend, Protected Friend, Public	Types defined in the same container and inherited classes	Private/Protected classes defined in the same container
Friend, Protected Friend	Private	Nested types	Nested classes
	Protected	Types defined in the same container and inherited classes	Classes defined in current assembly
	Friend, Protected Friend, Public	Types defined in current assembly	Classes defined in current assembly
Public	Private	Nested types	Nested classes
	Protected	Nested types and inherited classes	All classes, inside or outside current assembly
	Friend	Types defined in current assembly	Classes defined in current assembly
	Protected Friend	Types defined in current assembly and inherited classes	All classes, inside or outside current assembly
	Public	All types, inside or outside current assembly	All classes, inside or outside current assembly

* Note that you can have Private, Protected, and Protected Friend classes only inside a container type.

Redefining Events

You can't override events in the same way you override properties and methods, and in fact, you can't use the Overrides keyword on events. (However, you can use the Shadows keyword on events.)

Occasionally, you might want to redefine what happens when the base class raises an event. For example, the inherited class might need to perform some additional processing when an event is fired from inside the base class, or it might need to suppress some or all of the events that the base class raises. These two tasks require two different approaches.

If the derived class just needs to get a notification that an event is being raised from inside the base class, you just need to add Handles MyBase.eventname to the event handler routine. A common example of this technique is when you trap form events in a class that inherits from System.Windows.Forms.Form:

```
Public Class Form1
    Inherits System.Windows.Forms.Form

    Private Sub Form1_Load(ByVal sender As Object, ByVal e As EventArgs) _
        Handles MyBase.Load
        ' Code for the Form.Load event here.
    End Sub
End Class
```

Visual Studio .NET makes it simple to generate the template for such event handlers. Just select the (BaseClassName Events) item in the left-most combo box above the code editor window, and then select an event in the right-most combo box.

This programming technique doesn't require that you change the base class in any way, but it has a serious shortcoming. The derived class has no control over the event itself, and it can't modify its arguments or prevent it from firing. To solve this problem, you must change the way the base class fires events—in other words, you must build the base class with inheritance in mind. Instead of using the RaiseEvent statement whenever you want to raise an event in the base class, you call an overridable method, which by convention is named OnEventname. Consider these two classes, with the base DataReader class raising a DataAvailable event when new data is available. The derived DataReaderEx class intercepts the event and exposes it to the outside only for the first 10 occurrences of the event itself:

```
Class DataReader
    Event DataAvailable(ByVal sender As Object, ByVal e As EventArgs)

    Sub GetNewData()
        ' Should raise the event, but calls the Onxxxx method instead.
        OnDataAvailable(EventArgs.Empty)
    End Sub

    Protected Overridable Sub OnDataAvailable(ByVal e As EventArgs)
        ' Just raise the event.
        RaiseEvent DataAvailable(Me, e)
    End Sub
End Class

Class DataReaderEx
    Inherits DataReader

    ' A counter that is incremented after each event.
    Public EventCounter As Integer

    Protected Overrides Sub OnDataAvailable(ByVal e As EventArgs)
        ' Increment the counter.
      EventCounter += 1
```

```
        ' Raise only up to 10 events.
        If EventCounter <= 10 Then MyBase.OnDataAvailable(e)
    End Sub
End Class
```

Notice that the derived class can't directly use the RaiseEvent statement to raise one of its own events if the event is defined in the base class. The only way to indirectly raise the event is by calling the OnDataAvailable method in the base class, as shown in the preceding code. For consistency, Onxxxx methods should take an EventArgs-derived argument, even if it is an empty (and useless) EventArgs object as in this case.

Object Lifetime

Visual Basic .NET classes don't have destructor methods. In other words, no method or event in the class fires when the instance is destroyed. This major difference from Visual Basic 6 classes stems from the different approach that the .NET Framework uses to reclaim allocated memory. This is arguably one of the most controversial features of the framework and was discussed for months in forums and newsgroups while the .NET Framework was in beta version.

COM and the Reference Counter

Before exploring the .NET way to deal with object destruction, let's see how Visual Basic 6 objects (and COM objects in general) behave in this respect. All COM objects maintain a memory location known as the reference counter. An object's reference counter is set to 1 when the object is created and a reference to it is assigned to a variable; the object's reference counter is incremented by 1 when a reference to the object is assigned to another variable. Finally, the object's reference counter is decremented when a variable that points to the object is set to Nothing. This mechanism is hidden from Visual Basic developers and is implemented behind the scenes through the AddRef and Release methods of the IUnknown interface, an interface that all COM objects must expose. More specifically, Visual Basic 6 calls the AddRef method for you when you assign an object reference to a variable with the Set keyword. It calls the Release method when you set an object variable to Nothing.

At any given moment, a COM object's reference counter contains the number of variables that are pointing to that specific object. When the Release method is called, the object checks whether the reference counter is going to be decreased from 1 to 0, in which case the object knows it is no longer required and can destroy itself. (If the object is written in Visual Basic 6, a Class_Terminate event fires at this point.) In a sense, a COM object is responsible for its own life. An erroneous implementation of the AddNew or Release method or an unbalanced number of calls to these methods can be responsible for memory and resource leakage, a serious potential shortcoming in COM applications. Besides, managing the reference counter itself and frequently calling the AddRef and Release methods can be a time-consuming process, which has a negative impact on the application's performance.

Even more important, it frequently happens that two objects keep themselves alive, such as when you have two Person objects that point to each other through their Spouse property. Unless you take some special steps to account for this situation, these objects will be released only when the application terminates, even if the application cleared all the variables pointing to them. This is the notorious circular reference problem and is the most frequent cause of memory leakage, even in relatively simple COM applications.

When Microsoft designed the .NET Framework, the designers decided to get rid of reference counting overhead and all the problems associated with it. .NET objects have no reference counter, and there is no counterpart for the AddRef and Release methods. Creating an object requires that a block of memory be allocated from the managed heap, an area in memory that holds all objects. (I introduced the heap in the "Value Types and Reference Types" section of Chapter 2.) Assigning an object reference requires storing a 32-bit address in a variable (under 32-bit Windows platforms, at least), and clearing an object variable requires storing 0 in it. These operations are extremely fast because they involve no method calls. However, this approach raises an issue that doesn't exist under COM: how can the .NET Framework determine when an object isn't used by the application and can be safely destroyed to free the memory that that object uses in the heap?

Garbage Collection

The .NET Framework memory management relies on a sophisticated process known as garbage collection, or GC. When an application tries to allocate memory for a new object and the heap has insufficient free memory, the .NET Framework starts the garbage collection process. The garbage collector visits all the objects in the heap and marks those objects that are pointed to by any variable in the application. (These variables are known as roots because they're at the top of an object graph.) This process is sophisticated in that it also recognizes objects referenced indirectly from other objects, such as when you have a Person object that references another Person object through its Spouse property. After marking all the objects that can be reached from the application's code, the garbage collector can safely release the remaining (unmarked) objects because they're guaranteed to be unreachable by the application. Next the garbage collector compacts the heap and makes the resulting block of free memory available to new objects. Interestingly, this mechanism indirectly resolves the circular reference problem because the garbage collector doesn't mark unreachable objects and therefore correctly releases memory associated with objects pointed to by other objects in a circular reference fashion but not used by the main program.

In most real-world applications, the .NET way to deal with object lifetime is remarkably faster than the COM way—and this is an all-important advantage because everything is an object in the .NET architecture. On the other hand, the garbage collection mechanism introduces a new problem that COM developers don't have: nondeterministic finalization. A COM object always knows when its reference counter goes from 1 to 0, so it knows when the main application doesn't need the object any longer. When that time arrives, a Visual Basic 6 object fires the Class_Terminate event and the code inside the event handler can execute the necessary cleanup chores, such as closing any open file and releasing Win32 resources (brushes, device contexts, and kernel objects). Conversely, a .NET object is actually released *some time* after the last variable pointing to it was set to Nothing. If the application doesn't create many objects, a .NET object is collected only when the program terminates. Because of the way .NET garbage collection works, there's no way to provide a .NET class with a Class_Terminate event, regardless of the language used to implement the class.

If memory is the only resource an object uses, deferred destruction is seldom a problem. After all, if the application requires more memory, a garbage collection eventually fires and a block of new memory is made available. However, if the object allocates other types of resources—files, database connections, serial or parallel ports, internal Windows objects—you want to make such releases as soon as possible so that other applications can use these resources. In some cases, the problem isn't just a shortage of resources. For example, if the object opens a window to display the value of its properties, you surely want that window to be closed as soon as the object is destroyed so that a user doesn't have to look at outdated information. So the problem is, how can you run some code when your .NET object is *logically* destroyed?

This question has no definitive answer. A partial solution comes in the form of two special methods: Finalize and Dispose

The Finalize Method

The Finalize method is a special method that the garbage collector calls before releasing the memory allocated to the object. It works more or less the same way the Class_Terminate event under Visual Basic 6 works except that it can be called several seconds (or even minutes or hours) after the application has *logically* killed the object by setting the last variable pointing to the object to Nothing (or by letting the variable go out of scope, which has the same effect). Because all .NET objects inherit the Finalize method from the System.Object class, this method must be declared using the Overrides and Protected keywords:

```
' ...(Add this to the Person2 class.)...
Protected Overrides Sub Finalize()
    Debug.WriteLine("Person " & Me.FirstName() _
        " " & Me.LastName & " is being destroyed.")
End Sub
```

The following application shows that the Finalize method isn't called immediately when all variables pointing to the object are set to Nothing:

```
Module MainModule
    ' This is the main entry point for the application.
    Sub Main()
        TestFinalize()
        Debug.WriteLine("About to terminate the application.")
    End Sub
```

```
    Sub TestFinalize()
        Debug.WriteLine("About to create a Person object.")
        Dim aPerson As New Person2("Joe", "Doe")
        Debug.WriteLine("Exiting the TestFinalize procedure.")
    End Sub
End Module
```

These are the messages that you'll see in the Debug window:

```
About to create a Person object.
Exiting the TestFinalize procedure.
About to terminate the application.
Person Joe Doe is being destroyed.
```

The sequence of messages makes it apparent that the Person2 object isn't destroyed when the TestFinalize procedure exits—as would happen in Visual Basic 6—but only some time later, when the application itself terminates.

Here's one important .NET programming guideline: *never access any external object from a Finalize procedure*. The object might have been destroyed already. In fact, the object is being collected because it can't be reached from the main application, so a reference to another object isn't going to keep that object alive. The garbage collector can reclaim unreachable objects in any order, so the other object might be finalized before the current one. An object that can be safely accessed from a Finalize method is the base object of the current object, using the MyBase keyword.

In general, it is safe to invoke static methods from inside the Finalize method, except when the application is shutting down. In the latter case, in fact, the .NET Framework might have already destroyed the System.Type object corresponding to the type that exposes the static method. For example, you shouldn't use the Console.WriteLine method because the Console object might be gone. The Debug object is one of the few objects that are guaranteed to stay alive until the very end, however, and that's why the previous code example uses Debug.WriteLine instead of Console.WriteLine. You can discern the two cases by querying the Environment.HasShutdownStarted method:

```
Protected Overrides Sub Finalize()
    If Not Environment.HasShutdownStarted Then
        ' It is safe to access static methods of other types.
        ⋮
    End If
End Sub
```

You can force a garbage collection during the lifetime of an application by creating a sufficiently large number of objects. For example, try this code:

```
Sub Main()
    TestFinalize2
End Sub

Sub TestFinalize2()
    ' NOTE: If no Finalize method is invoked on your system,
    ' increment the loop upper limit.
```

```
    For i As Integer = 1 To 10000
        TestFinalize_Create()
    Next
    Debug.WriteLine("About to terminate the application.")
End Sub

Sub TestFinalize_Create()
    Dim aPerson As New Person2("Joe", "Doe")
End Sub
```

Here's a much simpler way to force a garbage collection: just ask the garbage collector to do it. The garbage collector is just one .NET object defined in the Framework, and it conveniently exposes a Collect method, which fires a garbage collection. You can see how this works by calling this procedure:

```
Sub TestFinalize3()
    Debug.WriteLine("About to create a Person object.")
    Dim aPerson As New Person2("Joe", "Doe")
    aPerson = Nothing
    Debug.WriteLine("About to fire a garbage collection.")
    GC.Collect()
    GC.WaitForPendingFinalizers()
End Sub
```

The WaitForPendingFinalizers method stops the current thread until all objects are correctly finalized; this action is necessary because the garbage collection process might run on a different thread. The sequence of messages in the Debug window is now different:

```
About to create a Person object.
About to fire a garbage collection.
Person object named Joe Doe is being destroyed.
About to create a Person object.
⋮
```

However, calling the GC.Collect method manually is usually a bad idea. The preceding code example, which uses the GC.Collect method only to fire the object's Finalize method, illustrates what you should *never* do in a real .NET application. If you run a garbage collection frequently, you're missing one of the most promising performance optimizations that the new .NET Framework offers. You should invoke the GC.Collect method only when the application is idle—for example, while it waits for user input—and only if you see that unexpected (that is, not explicitly requested) garbage collections are slowing the program noticeably during time-critical operations. For example, unrequested GCs might be an issue when your application is in charge of controlling hardware devices that require a short response time.

Here's another reason for staying clear of the Finalize method: objects that expose such a method aren't immediately reclaimed and usually require at least another garbage collection before they are swept out of the heap. The reason for this behavior is that the code in the Finalize method might assign the current object (using the Me keyword) to a global variable, a technique known as resurrection, which I talk about later in this chapter. If the object were garbage collected at this point, the reference in the global variable would become invalid; the runtime can't detect this special case until the subsequent garbage collection and must wait until then to definitively release the object's memory.

The Dispose Method

Because .NET objects don't have real destructors, well-designed classes should expose a method to let well-behaved clients manually release any resource such as files, database connections, and system objects as soon as they don't need the object any longer—that is, just before setting the reference to Nothing—rather than waiting for the subsequent garbage collection.

Classes that want to provide this feature should implement IDisposable, an interface defined in the .NET Framework. This interface exposes only the Dispose method:

```
Class Widget
    Implements IDisposable

    Sub Dispose() Implements IDisposable.Dispose
        ' Close files and release other resources here.
        ⋮
    End Sub
End Class
```

The Implements keyword is described in Chapter 6. Even if the Dispose method belongs to the IDisposable interface, it's marked as Public and therefore appears in the class interface as well. Thus, you don't need to cast the object to an IDisposable variable to call this special method (as you do in Visual Basic 6):

```
' Using an object that exposes a Dispose method
' Create the object.
Dim obj As New Widget()
' Use the object.
⋮
' Clean up code.
obj.Dispose
```

.NET programming guidelines dictate that the Dispose method of an object should invoke the Dispose method of all the inner objects that the current object owns and that are hidden from the client code, and then it should call the base class's Dispose method (if the base class implements IDisposable). For example, if the Widget object has created a System.Timers.Timer object, the Widget class's Dispose method should call the timer's Dispose method. This suggestion and the fact that an object can be shared by multiple clients might cause a Dispose method to be called multiple times, and in fact a Dispose method shouldn't raise any errors when called more than once, even though all calls after the first one should be ignored. You can easily avoid releasing resources multiple times by using a class-level variable:

```
Private disposed As Boolean

Sub Dispose() Implements IDisposable.Dispose
    If disposed Then Exit Sub
    ' Ensure that further calls are ignored.
    disposed = True
    ' Close files and release other resources here.
    ⋮
End Sub
```

The IDisposable interface gives you the ability to test whether an object exposes the Dispose method and to write generic cleanup routines, such as the following:

```
' Set an object to Nothing and clear its Dispose method if possible.
Sub ClearObject(ByRef obj As Object)
    If TypeOf obj Is IDisposable Then
        ' You need an explicit cast if Option Explicit is On.
        DirectCast(obj, IDisposable).Dispose
    End If
    ' This works because the object is passed by reference.
    obj = Nothing
End Sub
```

If you use an object that implements IDisposable, you should bracket critical statements in a Try...End Try block so that you're sure that the Dispose method is called in the Finally clause:

```
Dim obj As Widget
Try
    ' Create and use the object.
    obj = New Widget
    ⋮
Catch ex As Exception
    ⋮
Finally
    ' Ensure that the Dispose method is always invoked.
    obj.Dispose()
End Try
```

Interestingly, C# offers a using statement that simplifies this kind of code and that automatically invokes the Dispose method of any object exposing the IDisposable interface. No similar statement is present in the current version of Visual Basic .NET.

Combining the Dispose and Finalize Methods

Typically, you can allocate a resource other than memory in one of two ways: by invoking a piece of unmanaged code (for example, a Windows API function) or by creating an instance of a .NET class that wraps the resource. You need to understand this difference because the way you allocate a resource affects the decision of implementing the Dispose or the Finalize method.

You need to implement the IDisposable interface if your object allocates resources other than memory and that resource should be released as soon as possible, regardless of whether it is allocated directly (via a call to unmanaged code) or indirectly (through an object in the .NET Framework). Conversely, you need to implement the Finalize method only if your object allocates an unmanaged resource directly. In general, therefore, you must account for four different cases:

1. Neither the Dispose nor the Finalize method: your object only uses memory or other resources that don't require explicit deallocation. This is by far the most frequent case.

2. The Dispose method only: your object allocates resources other than memory indirectly through other .NET objects, and you want to provide clients with a method to release those resources as soon as possible. This is the second most frequent case.

3. Both the Dispose and the Finalize methods: your object directly allocates a resource (typically by calling a piece of unmanaged code through PInvoke) that requires explicit deallocation or cleanup. You do such explicit deallocation in the Finalize method, but provide the Dispose method as well, to provide clients with the ability to release the resource before your object's finalization.

4. Only the Finalize method: you want to release a resource or perform some other action when your object is finalized. This is the least likely case, and in practice it is useful only in a few uncommon scenarios.

Let's focus on the third case, which is also the most interesting of the group in that we need to find a way to have the Dispose and Finalize methods cooperate with each other. Here's an example of a ClipboardWrapper object that opens and closes the system clipboard:

```
Class ClipboardWrapper
    Implements IDisposable

    Private Declare Function OpenClipboard Lib "user32" _
        Alias "OpenClipboard" (ByVal hwnd As Integer) As Integer
    Private Declare Function CloseClipboard Lib "user32" _
        Alias "CloseClipboard" () As Integer

    ' Remember whether the clipboard is currently open.
    Dim isOpen As Boolean

    ' Open the clipboard and associate it with a window.
    Sub Open(ByVal hWnd As Integer)
        ' OpenClipboard returns 0 if any error.
        If OpenClipboard(hWnd) = 0 Then
            Throw New Exception("Unable to open clipboard")
        End If
        isOpen = True
    End Sub
```

```
' Close the clipboard - ignore the command if not open
Sub Close()
    If isOpen Then CloseClipboard()
    isOpen = False
End Sub

Public Sub Dispose() Implements System.IDisposable.Dispose
    Close()
End Sub

Protected Overrides Sub Finalize()
    Close()
End Sub
End Class
```

What the OpenClipboard and CloseClipboard functions do isn't important in this context because I just selected two of the simplest Windows API procedures that allocate and release a system resource. What really matters is that an application that opens the clipboard and associates it with a window must also release it as soon as possible, because the clipboard is a shared resource and no other window can access the clipboard in the meantime. (A real-world class would surely expose other useful methods to manipulate the clipboard, but I want to keep this example as simple as possible.)

Because the cleanup code is usually the same in all cases, it's a good practice to have both the Dispose and the Finalize methods call the same routine that performs the actual release operation (the Close method, in this example), so that you don't duplicate the code. Such a method can be public, as in this case, or it can be a private helper method. You also need a class-level variable (isOpen in the preceding code) to ensure that cleanup code doesn't run twice, once when the client invokes Dispose and once when the garbage collector calls the Finalize method. The same variable also ensures that nothing happens if clients call the Close or Dispose method multiple times.

A Better Dispose-Finalize Pattern

A problem with the technique just illustrated is that the garbage collector calls the Finalize method even if the client has already called the Dispose or Close method. As I explained previously, the Finalize method affects performance negatively because an additional garbage collection is required to completely destroy the object. Fortunately, you can control whether the Finalize method is invoked via the GC.SuppressFinalize method. Using this method is straightforward. You typically call it from inside the Dispose method so that the garbage collector knows that it shouldn't call the Finalize method during the subsequent garbage collection.

Another problem that you might need to solve in a class that is more sophisticated than the ClipboardWrapper demo seen before is that the cleanup code might access other objects referenced by the current object—for example, a control on a form—but you should never perform such access if the cleanup code runs in the finalization phase, because those other objects might have been finalized already. You can solve this issue by moving the actual cleanup code to an overloaded version of the Dispose method. This method takes a Boolean argument that specifies whether the object is being disposed or finalized and avoids accessing external objects in the latter case. Here's a new version of the ClipboardWrapper class that solves these issues:

```
Class ClipboardWrapper2
    Implements IDisposable
    ⋮
    Public Sub Dispose() Implements System.IDisposable.Dispose
        Dispose(True)
    End Sub

    Protected Overrides Sub Finalize()
        Dispose(False)
    End Sub

    ' Remember whether the object has been already disposed.
    ' (Protected makes it available to derived classes.)
    Protected disposed As Boolean

    Protected Overridable Sub Dispose(ByVal disposing As Boolean)
        ' Exit if the object has been already disposed.
        If disposed Then Exit Sub

        If disposing Then
            ' The object is being disposed, not finalized.
            ' It is safe to access other objects (other than the base
            ' object) only from inside this block.
            ⋮
            ' Remember that the object has been disposed.
            disposed = True
            ' Tell .NET not to call the Finalize method.
            GC.SuppressFinalize(Me)
        End If

        ' Perform cleanup chores that have to be executed in either case.
        Close()
    End Sub
End Class
```

A problem that the preceding code example doesn't address is that public methods other than Dispose should throw an exception if they are called after the object has been disposed. This is a symptom of a programming mistake. The common language runtime defines the special ObjectDisposedException object for this type of error. You can enhance the ClipboardWrapper2 class by adding a helper method and invoking it at the top of all the methods in the class except Dispose:

```
Private Sub CheckIfDisposed()
    If disposed Then
        Throw New ObjectDisposedException("ClipboardWrapper2")
    End If
End Sub
```

Notice that, even in this improved implementation, the .NET runtime unnecessarily invokes the Finalize method if the client opens and then closes the clipboard and if the client instantiates the class but never calls the Open method. You can enhance the ClipboardWrapper2 class by unregistering the Finalize method by calling the GC.SuppressFinalize(Me) method from inside the constructor and the Close method, and the GC.ReRegisterForFinalize(Me) method from inside the Open method. The companion source code includes a more complete version of this class that accounts for these details.

Finalization issues can become even more problematic if you consider that the Finalize method runs also if the object threw an exception in its constructor method. This means that the code in the Finalize method might access members that haven't been initialized correctly; thus, your finalization code should always avoid accessing class members if there is any chance that an error occurred in the constructor. Even better, the constructor method might use a Try…Catch block to trap errors, release any allocated resource, and then call GC.SuppressFinalize(Me) to prevent the standard finalization code from running on uninitialized members.

Finalizers in Derived Classes

As you know, a well-written class that allocates and uses unmanaged resources (ODBC database connections, file and Windows object handles, and so on) should implement both a Finalize method and the IDisposable.IDispose method. If your application inherits from such a class, you should check whether your inherited class allocates any additional unmanaged resources. If not, you don't have to write any extra code because the derived class will inherit the base class implementation of both the Finalize and the Dispose methods. However, if the inherited class does allocate and use additional unmanaged resources, you should override the implementation of these methods, correctly release the unmanaged resources that the inherited class uses, and then call the corresponding base class method. For example, the Finalize method in the derived class should always call the Finalize procedure from the base class:

```
Protected Overrides Sub Finalize()
    ' Release unmanaged resources created by the inherited class.
    ⋮
    ' Ask the base class to release its own unmanaged resources.
    MyBase.Finalize()
End Sub
```

In the previous section, I illustrated a generic technique for correctly implementing these methods in a class, based on an overloaded Dispose method that contains the code for both the IDisposable.Dispose and the Finalize methods. As it happens, this overloaded Dispose method has a Protected scope, so in practice you can correctly implement the Dispose-Finalize pattern in derived classes by simply overriding one method:

```
Class BetterClipboardWrapper
    Inherits ClipboardWrapper2
```

```
' Insert here regular methods, some of which may allocate additional
' unmanaged resources.
    ⋮

' The only method we need to implement the Dispose-Finalize
' pattern for this class.
Protected Overloads Overrides Sub Dispose(ByVal disposing As Boolean)
    ' Exit now if the object has been already disposed.
    ' (The disposed variable is declared as Protected in the base class.)
    If disposed Then Exit Sub

    If disposing Then
        ' The object is being disposed, not finalized.
        ' It is safe to access other objects (other than the base
        ' object) only from inside this block.
            ⋮
    End If

    ' Perform clean up chores that have to be executed in either case.
        ⋮

    ' Call the base class's Dispose method.
    MyBase.Dispose(disposing)
End Sub
End Class
```

> **See Also**   Read the document "Advanced Garbage Collection Topics.doc" on the companion CD to learn about GC generations, multithreading issues, and an advanced programming technique known as *object resurrection* and how you can use it to implement a pool of objects.

Weak Object References

The .NET Framework provides a special type of object reference that doesn't keep an object alive: the so-called weak reference. A weakly referenced object can be reclaimed during a garbage collection and must be re-created afterward if you want to use it again. Typical candidates for this technique are objects that take a lot of memory but whose state can be re-created with relatively little effort. For example, consider a class whose main purpose is to provide an optimized cache for the contents of text files. Traditionally, whenever you cache a large amount of data you must decide how much memory you set aside for the cache, but reserving too much memory for the cache might make the overall performance worse. You don't have this dilemma if you use weak references. You can store as much data in the cache as you wish, because you know that the system will automatically reclaim that memory when it needs it. Here's the complete source code for the CachedFile class:

```
Class CachedFile
    ' The name of the file cached
    Public ReadOnly Filename As String
```

```
    ' A weak reference to the string that contains the text.
    Dim wrText As WeakReference

    ' The constructor takes the name of the file to read.
    Sub New(ByVal filename As String)
        Me.Filename = filename
    End Sub

    ' Read the contents of the file.
    Private Function ReadFile() As String
        Dim sr As New System.IO.StreamReader(Me.Filename)
        ReadFile = sr.ReadToEnd()
        sr.Close()
        ' Create a weak reference to the return value.
        wrText = New WeakReference(ReadFile)
    End Function

    ' Return the textual content of the file.
    Public Function GetText() As String
        Dim text As Object
        ' Retrieve the target of the weak reference.
        If Not (wrText Is Nothing) Then text = wrText.Target
        If Not (text Is Nothing) Then
            ' If non-null, the data is still in the cache.
            Return text.ToString()
        Else
            ' Otherwise, read it and put it in the cache again.
            Return ReadFile()
        End If
    End Function
End Class
```

There are two points of interests in this class. The first one is in the ReadFile procedure, where the value about to be returned to the caller (the text variable) is also passed to the constructor of the WeakReference class. A weak reference to the string is created here. The second point of interest is in the GetText method, where the code queries the WeakReference.Target property. If this property returns a non-Nothing value, it means the weak reference hasn't been broken and still points to the original, cached string. Otherwise, the ReadFile method is invoked so that the file contents are read from disk and cached once again before being returned to the caller.

Using this class is easy:

```
' Read and cache the contents of the "c:\alargefile.txt" file.
Dim cf As New CachedFile("c:\alargefile.txt")
Console.WriteLine(cf.GetText())
 ⋮
' Uncomment next line to force a garbage collection.
' GC.Collect(): GC.WaitForPendingFinalizers()
 ⋮
' Read the contents again some time later
' no disk access is performed, unless a GC has occurred in the meantime.
Console.WriteLine(cf.GetText())
```

By tracing into the CachedFile class, you can easily prove that in most cases the file contents can be retrieved through the weak reference and that the disk isn't accessed again. By uncommenting the statement in the middle of the previous code snippet, you force a garbage collection, in which case the internal WeakReference object won't keep the String object alive and the code in the class will read the file again. The key point in this technique is that the client code doesn't know whether the file is read again. It just uses the CachedFile class as an optimized building block for dealing with large text files.

Remember that you create a weak reference by passing your object to the constructor of a System.WeakReference object. However, if the object is also reference by a regular, non-weak reference, it will survive any intervening garbage collection. In our example, this means that the code using the CachedFile class should not store the return value of the GetText method in a string variable because that would prevent the string from being garbage collected until that variable is explicitly set to Nothing or goes out of scope:

```
' The wrong way of using the CachedFile class.
Dim cf As New CachedFile("c:\alargefile.txt")
Dim text As String = cf.GetText()
' The string will survive any garbage collection.
```

Inheritance is so central to Visual Basic .NET programming that you'll probably come back to this chapter to revisit these concepts more than once. But for now, you're ready to see how you can implement interfaces and take advantage of a completely new feature of the language—delegates, one of the topics of the next chapter.

6 Interfaces, Delegates, and Attributes

This chapter covers three topics that are central to .NET programming. In the first part, you'll learn how to implement an interface and, above all, how to use a few all-important .NET interfaces. Next, you'll read about delegates and how you can put them to good use in your applications. At the end of the chapter, I introduce the new concept of attributes.

Interfaces

As you might remember, an interface is a set of properties and methods that a class exposes. An interface defines only the *signature* of such properties and methods (member name, number and type of each parameter, and type of return value), while a class can implement that interface by providing actual code for those properties and methods as necessary. The code in each property or method can differ from class to class, provided the semantics of each method are preserved. The fact that each class can implement the same property or method in a different way is the basis for polymorphic behavior.

Visual Basic .NET supports the definition of interfaces in a much more streamlined way than its predecessors. Under Visual Basic 6, you can define an interface only indirectly, by using a class module that contains property and method signatures but no implementation code. This lame approach has been replaced in Visual Basic .NET by the Interface...End Interface block:

```
Interface IPluggableAddin
    Readonly Property Id() As Long

    Property State() As Boolean

    Function OnConnection(ByVal environment As String) As Boolean

    Sub OnDisconnection()

End Interface
```

Visual Basic .NET interface blocks can't contain executable code, and you can include only method and property signatures. The ReadOnly and WriteOnly keywords let you define whether a property can be read from and written to without your having to omit the Get and Set procedures, as you would have to do in Visual Basic 6. An interface can't include variables, and properties and methods can't take scope qualifiers because all of them are implicitly Public. The structure and meaning of the interface is clear, and you can't accidentally write executable statements that are never actually executed or Private members that don't actually appear in the interface. In a difference from Visual Basic 6, a Visual Basic .NET interface can contain an event definition, even though including events in an interface isn't recommended.

Interfaces have a scope, whether or not you declare it explicitly. The default scope for interfaces is Friend, so a Public class can't expose a Public member that returns an interface whose declaration doesn't include a scope:

```
Public Class MyComponent
    ' *** Next statement raises a compilation error because a Public
    '     class can't expose a Friend type as a Public member.
    Public addin As IPluggableAddin
End Class
```

The preceding code snippet works only if the IPluggableAddin interface is explicitly declared as Public:

```
Public Interface IPluggableAddin
    ' ...(all members as in the original definition)...
End Interface
```

Interfaces with a scope other than Public or Friend can be declared only inside another type, as is also the case with classes and structures. Surprisingly, you can also define a type—a class, a structure, an enum, or another interface—inside an Interface...End Interface block. However, the nested type doesn't really belong to the interface and placing it inside the interface means only that you need an additional dot to reach it. For example, consider this interface:

```
Interface IGetRange
    Function GetRange() As Range

    Class Range
        Public StartValue, EndValue As Double
    End Class
End Interface
```

In this case, having the Range class defined inside the interface might make sense so that you ensure that there is no name conflict with any other class with the same name. Here's a routine that receives an interface argument and retrieves a Range object:

```
Sub UseTheRangeClass(ByVal igr As IGetRange)
    Dim r As IGetRange.Range
    r = igr.GetRange
    ⋮
End Sub
```

Microsoft guidelines dictate that all interface names start with the *I* character, that they not include the underscore character, and that they use Pascal casing when the name contains multiple words.

Implementing the Interface

You tell Visual Basic that a class exposes an additional interface by means of the Implements keyword:

```
Class MyAddin
    Implements IPluggableAddin
    ⋮
End Class
```

Visual Basic .NET supports the Implements keyword inside Structure blocks as well. The syntax for implementing individual properties and methods reuses the Implements keyword to tell the compiler which procedure in your class implements what member in the interface:

```
Class MyAddin
    Implements IPluggableAddin

    Private ReadOnly Property Id() As Long Implements IPluggableAddin.ID
        Get
            ⋮
        End Get
    End Property

    Private Property State() As Boolean Implements IPluggableAddin.State
        Get
            ⋮
        End Get
        Set(ByVal Value As Boolean)
            ⋮
        End Set
    End Property

    Private Function OnConnection(ByVal environment As String) As Boolean _
        Implements IPluggableAddin.OnConnection
        ⋮
    End Function

    Private Sub OnDisconnection() Implements IPluggableAddin.OnDisconnection
        ⋮
    End Sub
End Class
```

Note that the preceding code uses Private scope for all the procedures so that those procedures can't be invoked directly from clients of the MyAddin class, but working this way isn't a requirement. As a matter of fact, you can omit the Private keyword and make the procedures implicitly Public, specify an explicit scope qualifier, or even use other keywords, such as Overridable:

```
Class MyAddin
    Implements IPluggableAddin

    Protected Overridable Function OnConnection(ByVal Environment As String) _
```

```
          As Boolean Implements IPluggableAddin.OnConnection
        ⋮
      End Function

    ⋮
  End Class
```

Visual Studio .NET gives you an effective way to create templates for these procedures. Just drop down the Class Name list in the code editor and click one of the interfaces implemented by the current class, and then click a specific method in the Method Name list. A Visual Basic .NET file can contain multiple classes, so you have to select the right one. (See Figure 6-1.)

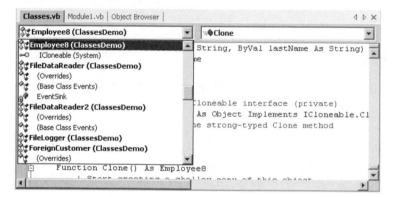

Figure 6-1   Letting Visual Studio .NET create a template for a procedure in an interface

Speaking of scope, notice that Visual Basic enforces no constraint related to the scope of the interface that a class can implement. For example, you can have a Public class that implements a Private interface, a Private class that implements a Public interface, or any other combination of the supported scope qualifiers. However, only clients that have access to the interface's definition can access that interface's members through an interface variable. For example, if a class exposes an interface declared with Friend scope, only clients inside the same assembly can access that interface through an interface variable. Unless the individual procedures that implement the interface's members are declared with Public scope, there is no way for a client outside the current assembly to access the code inside those procedures.

The Implements keyword that marks a method as an interface method supports multiple arguments, so you can have methods from multiple interfaces that map to the same procedure. The following example shows that methods in the interfaces and methods in the class that implements the interface can have different names:

```
' Another interface with just one property
Interface IHostEnvironment
    ReadOnly Property HashCode() As Long
End Interface
```

```
' This new version of the class implements two interfaces.
Class MyAddin
    ' You can have two distinct Implements statements if you prefer.
    Implements IPluggableAddin, IHostEnvironment

    ' The following procedure implements two read-only properties
    ' from distinct interfaces.
    ReadOnly Property Id() As Long _
        Implements IPluggableAddin.ID, IHostEnvironment.HashCode
        Get
            ⋮
        End Get
    End Property

    ' ...(Other implemented methods have been omitted)...
End Class
```

A variant of this technique lets you map multiple methods from one interface to the same procedure in the class. Mapping multiple methods to the same procedures works only if all the methods have the same argument signature and the same data type for the return value.

Accessing the Interface

You access the interface that a class implements by assigning the object to a variable typed after the interface:

```
' An instance of the class
Dim addin As New MyAddin()
' Cast to an interface variable.
Dim iplug As IPluggableAddin = addin
' Now you can access all the methods and properties in the interface.
iplug.State = True
```

If you're calling just one or two methods in the interface, you might find it convenient to do the cast operation on the fly with a CType or a DirectCast operator:

```
' Cast to the interface type and invoke a method in one operation.
' (These two statements are equivalent.)
CType(addin, IPluggableAddin).OnConnection("MyHost")
DirectCast(addin, IPluggableAddin).OnConnection("MyHost")
```

You can also use a With...End With block:

```
' Create a hidden, temporary interface variable.
With CType(addin, IPluggableAddin)
    .OnConnection("MyHost")
    .State = True
End With
```

If a member of an interface is implemented through a Public procedure, you don't need to cast the object to a different type, and you can access the interface's member through a standard variable pointing to the object. For example, classes that implement the IDisposable interface usually expose a Public Sub Dispose method, which can therefore be accessed through the main object variable. (See "The Dispose Method" in Chapter 5.)

As I mentioned in the previous section, even a Structure can implement an interface. However, keep two points in mind when you access an interface implemented in a value type. First, you can't use the DirectCast operator because it requires its first argument to be a reference type. Second, and more important, the value type needs to be boxed before one of its interface members can be accessed, so you pay a performance penalty every time you access an interface method through an interface variable.

Interfaces and Inheritance

An interface can inherit from another interface. An inherited interface contains all the members that it defines, plus all members in the base interface. This feature is especially useful when you're creating a new, extended version of an interface:

```
Public Interface IPluggableAddin2
    Inherits IPluggableAddin
    Property Description() As String
End Interface
```

A derived interface can't redefine any member in the base interface, so you can't use the Overridable or Overrides keyword inside an interface definition. If the derived interface contains a member with the same name as a member in the base interface, the member in the derived interface shadows the member in the base class. In this case, you get a compilation warning that you can suppress by using the Shadows keyword in the derived interface. In all cases, however, the class that implements the interface must implement both the member in the base class and the member in the derived class with the same name, which can become quite confusing. For this reason, you should refrain from defining a derived interface that contains a member with the same name as a member in its base interface, even though Visual Basic .NET allows you to do so.

A derived class automatically inherits all the interfaces (and their implementation) defined in the base class, whether they're implemented through public or private methods. You must not include any Implements statement in the derived class.

```
' This class inherits all the interfaces defined in the MyAddin class.
Class AnotherAddin
    Inherits MyAddin
End Class

' Client code
Dim addin2 As New AnotherAddin
' Prove that the inherited class exposes the IPluggableAddin interface.
CType(addin2, IPluggableAddin).State = True
```

The derived class can even override the implementation of interface methods defined in the base class as long as methods in the base class aren't Private and have been defined using the Overridable keyword. The code in the derived class must not use the Implements keyword in the method declaration.

```
' This class inherits all the interfaces defined in the MyAddin class.
Class AnotherAddin
    Inherits MyAddin

    Protected Overrides Function OnConnection(ByVal Environment As String) _
        As Boolean
        ⋮
    End Function
End Class
```

As I showed in the "Finalizers in Derived Classes" section of Chapter 5, if the base class implements the IDisposable interface, .NET programming guidelines dictate that you override the Dispose method, perform your cleanup chores, and finally call the Dispose method in the base class:

```
' Assuming that the MyAddin base class implements IDisposable...

Class AnotherAddin
    Inherits MyAddin

    Overrides Sub Dispose()
        ' Clean up code for the AnotherAddin class.
        ' ...(omitted)...

        ' Complete the cleanup step by calling the base class's
        ' Dispose method.
        MyBase.Dispose
    End Function
End Class
```

Using .NET Interfaces

The .NET Framework defines and consumes dozens of different interfaces, and expert Visual Basic .NET developers should learn how to take advantage of them. In this section, you'll see how such systemwide interfaces can make your life simpler.

The IComparable Interface

In the "ParamArray Arguments" section of Chapter 3, you saw that the System.Array class exposes the Sort shared method, which lets you sort an array of simple data types, such as numbers or strings. However, the Sort method can't directly sort more complex objects, such as Person, because it doesn't know how two Person objects compare with one another.

Implementing the IComparable interface makes your objects sortable by means of the Sort method exposed by the Array and ArrayList classes. This interface exposes only one method, CompareTo, which receives an object and is expected to return -1, 0, or 1, depending on whether the current object (that is, the object on which CompareTo is called) is less than, equal to, or greater than the object passed as an argument. Let's see how you can define a Person class that's sortable on its ReverseName property:

```
Class Person
    Implements IComparable

    ' Public fields (should be properties in a real-world class)
    Public FirstName As String
    Public LastName As String

    ' A simple constructor
    Sub New(ByVal firstName As String, ByVal lastName As String)
        Me.FirstName = firstName
        Me.LastName = lastName
    End Sub

    ' A property that returns the name in the format "Doe, Joe"
    ReadOnly Property ReverseName() As String
        Get
            Return LastName & ", " & FirstName
        End Get
    End Property

    ' This procedure adds sorting capabilities to the class.
    Private Function CompareTo(ByVal obj As Object) As Integer _
        Implements IComparable.CompareTo
        ' Any non-Nothing object is greater than Nothing.
        If obj Is Nothing Then Return 1
        ' Cast to a specific Person object to avoid late binding.
        Dim other As Person = DirectCast(obj, Person)
        ' Use StrComp to simplify case-insensitive comparisons.
        Return StrComp(Me.ReverseName, other.ReverseName, CompareMethod.Text)
    End Function
End Class
```

Here's the client code that demonstrates how the IComparable interface works:

```
Dim Persons() As Person = { New Person("John", "Smith"), _
    New Person("Robert", "Doe"), New Person("Joe", "Doe") }
Array.Sort(Persons)
' Display all the elements in sorted order.
    For Each p As Person In Persons
    Console.WriteLine(p.ReverseName)
Next
```

Notice that the implementation of CompareTo is less than optimal because it creates a lot of temporary strings (the results of calls to ReverseName), which may significantly slow down your application. Here's an implementation that's less concise and less linear, but faster:

```
Private Function CompareTo(ByVal obj As Object) As Integer _
        Implements IComparable.CompareTo
        ' Any non-Nothing object is greater than Nothing.
        If obj Is Nothing Then Return 1
        ' Cast to a specific Person object to avoid late binding.
        Dim other As Person = CType(obj, Person)
        ' Compare LastName first.
        Dim result As Integer = StrComp(Me.LastName, other.LastName, CompareMethod.Text)
        If result = 0 Then
            ' Compare FirstName only if LastName is the same.
            result = StrComp(Me.FirstName, other.FirstName, CompareMethod.Text)
        End If
        Return result
    End Function
```

The IComparer Interface

The IComparable interface is all you need when your objects can be compared in only one way. Most real-world objects, however, can be compared and sorted on different fields or field combinations; in this case, you can use a variation of the Array.Sort method that takes an IComparer interface as its second argument. The IComparer interface exposes only one method, Compare, which receives two object references and returns -1, 0, or 1 depending on whether the first object is less than, equal to, or greater than the second object.

A class that can be sorted on different field combinations might expose two or more nested classes that implement the IComparer interface, one class for each possible sort method. For example, you might want to sort the Person class on either the (LastName, FirstName) or (FirstName, LastName) field combination; these combinations correspond to the ReverseName and CompleteName read-only properties in the code that follows. Here's a new version of the class that supports these features:

```
Class Person2
    ' (Definition of FirstName, LastName, ReverseName, and constructor omitted)
    ⋮

    ' A property that returns a name in the format "Joe Doe"
    ReadOnly Property CompleteName() As String
        Get
            Return FirstName & " " & LastName
        End Get
    End Property

    ' First auxiliary class, to sort on CompleteName
    Class ComparerByName
        Implements IComparer

        Function Compare(ByVal o1 As Object, ByVal o2 As Object) _
            As Integer Implements IComparer.Compare
            ' Two null objects are equal.
            If (o1 Is Nothing) And (o2 Is Nothing) Then Return 0
            ' Any non-null object is greater than a null object.
```

```
            If (o1 Is Nothing) Then Return 1
            If (o2 Is Nothing) Then Return -1
            ' Cast both objects to Person, and do the comparison.
            ' (Throws an exception if arguments aren't Person objects.)
            Dim p1 As Person2 = DirectCast(o1, Person2)
            Dim p2 As Person2 = DirectCast(o2, Person2)
            Return StrComp(p1.CompleteName, p2.CompleteName, _
                CompareMethod.Text)
        End Function
    End Class


    ' Second auxiliary class, to sort on ReverseName
    Class ComparerByReverseName
        Implements IComparer

        Function Compare(ByVal o1 As Object, ByVal o2 As Object) _
            As Integer Implements IComparer.Compare
            ' Two null objects are equal.
            If (o1 Is Nothing) And (o2 Is Nothing) Then Return 0
            ' Any non-null object is greater than a null object.
            If (o1 Is Nothing) Then Return 1
            If (o2 Is Nothing) Then Return -1
            ' Save code by casting to Person objects on the fly.
            Return StrComp(DirectCast(o1, Person2).ReverseName, _
                DirectCast(o2, Person2).ReverseName, CompareMethod.Text)
        End Function
    End Class
End Class
```

In a real-world class, you should avoid all the temporary strings created by calls to
CompleteName and ReverseName properties and compare the LastName and First-
Name properties individually, as described at the end of "The IComparable Interface"
section in this chapter. Using the two auxiliary classes is straightforward:

```
Dim Persons() As Person2 = { New Person2("John", "Smith"), _
    New Person2("Robert", "Doe"), New Person2("Joe", "Doe") }
' Sort the array on name.
Array.Sort(Persons, New Person2.ComparerByName)
' Sort the array on reversed name.
Array.Sort(Persons, New Person2.ComparerByReverseName)
```

You can also provide two shared functions in the Person class that instantiate the Com-
pareBy*xxxx* classes and return the IComparer interface:

```
Class Person2
    :' (First part of implementation as in previous example)
    :
    ' Shared methods that return an auxiliary object
    Shared Function CompareByName() As IComparer
        Return New ComparerByName()
    End Function

    Shared Function CompareByReverseName() As IComparer
        Return New ComparerByReverseName()
    End Function
End Class
```

The client code becomes

```
' Sort the array on name.
Array.Sort(Persons, Person.CompareByName())
' Sort the array on reversed name.
Array.Sort(Persons, Person.CompareByReverseName())
```

The Array.Sort method works in case-sensitive mode by default, but the System.Collections namespace contains a class, CaseInsensitiveComparer, that implements the IComparer interface and lets you compare strings in case-insensitive mode:

```
' Sort a string using case-insensitive comparisons.
Array.Sort(arr, System.Collections.CaseInsensitivComparer.Default)
```

String comparisons are based on the current locale, or more precisely on the value of Thread.CurrentCulture. Case-insensitive comparisons are different from what Visual Basic 6 developers might expect, however, because they are never based on ASCII values of individual characters. For example, under Visual Basic .NET, all the variations of the character A (uppercase, lowercase, or accented) come before the character B. If you're migrating Visual Basic code that relies on ASCII code sorting for case-insensitive string comparisons, you should define a custom class that works as a custom comparer, as follows:

```
Class CaseInsensitiveComparerVB6
    Implements IComparer

    Function Compare(ByVal o1 As Object, ByVal o2 As Object) As Integer _
        Implements IComparer.Compare
        ' Let the StrComp function do the work for us.
        Return StrComp(o1.ToString, o2.ToString, CompareMethod.Binary)
    End Function
End Class
```

The ICloneable Interface

Everything is an object under Visual Basic .NET. One consequence of this arrangement is that when you assign a variable to another variable, you get two variables pointing to the same object, rather than two distinct copies of the data (unless you're working with value types instead of reference types). Typically, you can get a copy of the data by invoking a special method that the class exposes. In the .NET world, a class should implement the ICloneable interface and expose its only method, Clone, to let the outside world know that it can create a copy of its instances. Several objects in the framework implement this interface, including Array, ArrayList, BitArray, Font, Icon, Queue, and Stack. Most of the time, implementing the ICloneable interface is straightforward:

```
Class Employee
    Implements ICloneable

    Public FirstName As String
    Public LastName As String
    Public Boss As Employee
```

```
      Sub New(ByVal firstName As String, ByVal lastName As String)
          Me.FirstName = firstName
          Me.LastName = lastName
      End Sub

      ' The only method of the ICloneable interface
      Public Function Clone() As Object Implements ICloneable.Clone
          ' Create a new Employee with same property values.
          Dim e As New Employee(FirstName, LastName)
          ' Properties not accepted in the constructors
          ' must be copied manually.
          e.Boss = Me.Boss
          Return e
      End Function
End Class
```

The System.Object class, from which all other classes derive, defines the Memberwise-Clone protected method, which helps you clone an object without your having to manually copy every property. See how we can use this method to simplify the implementation of the Clone method in the Employee class:

```
Public Function Clone() As Object Implements ICloneable.Clone
    Return Me.MemberwiseClone
End Function
```

The ICloneable interface is never called by the .NET runtime, and its only purpose is to provide a standardized way to let other developers know that your class supports cloning by means of a well-established syntax:

```
' Define an employee and his boss.
Dim joe As New Employee("Joe", "Doe")
Dim robert As New Employee("Robert", "Smith")
joe.Boss = robert

' Clone it--The Clone method returns an object,
' so you need CType if Option Strict is On.
Dim joe2 As Employee = DirectCast(joe.Clone, Employee)
' Prove that all properties were copied.
' (Console.WriteLine supports multiple placeholders.)
Console.WriteLine("{0} {1}, whose boss is {2} {3}",
    joe2.FirstName, joe2.LastName, joe2.Boss.FirstName, joe2.Boss.LastName)
    ' => Joe Doe, whose boss is Robert Smith
```

Shallow Copies and Deep Copies

The Clone method can create either a *shallow copy* or a *deep copy* of the object. A *shallow copy* creates only a copy of the object in question. It doesn't make copies of secondary objects referenced by it. In contrast, a *deep copy* operation clones all secondary objects as well. The following code snippet makes this difference clear:

```
' Define an employee and its boss.
Dim joe As New Employee("Joe", "Doe")
Dim robert As New Employee("Robert", "Smith")
joe.Boss = robert
```

```
' Clone it.
Dim joe2 As Employee = DirectCast(joe.Clone, Employee)
' Prove that the Employee object was cloned but his boss wasn't.
Console.WriteLine(joe Is joe2)                    ' => False
Console.WriteLine(joe.Boss Is joe2.Boss)          ' => True
```

When shallow copying isn't enough and you really need to create a clone of the entire *object graph* that has the object at its root, you can't rely on the MemberwiseClone method alone; you must manually copy properties of each object. Here's a new Employee2 class that correctly clones the entire object graph:

```
Class Employee2
    Implements ICloneable

    Public Boss As Employee2
    ' ... (other fields and constructor as in Employee) ...

    Public Function Clone() As Object Implements ICloneable.Clone
        ' Start creating a shallow copy of this object.
        ' (This copies all nonobject properties in one operation.)
        Dim e As Employee2 = DirectCast(Me.MemberwiseClone, Employee2)
        ' Manually copy the Boss property, reusing its Clone method.
        If Not (e.Boss Is Nothing) Then
            e.Boss = DirectCast(Me.Boss.Clone, Employee2)
        End If
        Return e
    End Function
End Class
```

This new version of the Clone method is still concise because it uses the Memberwise-Clone method to copy all nonobject values, and it builds on the Clone method for the secondary objects (only Boss, in this case). This approach also works if the employee's boss has her own boss.

However, most real-world object graphs are more complex than this example, and exposing a Clone method that works correctly isn't a trivial task. For example, if the Employee2 class had a Colleagues property (a collection holding other Employee2 objects), the ensuing circular references would cause the Clone method to enter a recursion that would end with a stack overflow error. Fortunately, the .NET Framework offers a clean solution to this problem, but you won't learn it until Chapter 10.

A Strongly Typed Clone Method

The ICloneable interface is highly generic, so its Clone method returns an Object value. As you've seen in previous examples, this involves a hidden boxing and unboxing sequence and forces you to use a CType function to assign the cloned object to a strongly typed variable. Is there a way to avoid this overhead?

The answer is yes, and the technique is surprisingly simple. You define a public, strongly typed Clone method in the main class interface of your object and have a private ICloneable.Clone method point to it. Here's a new Employee3 class that uses this technique:

```
Class Employee3
    Implements ICloneable
    Public Boss As Employee3
    ' ... (other fields and constructor as in Employee) ...

    ' The only method of the ICloneable interface (private)
    Private Function CloneMe() As Object Implements ICloneable.Clone
        ' Reuses the code in the strongly typed Clone method.
        Return Clone
    End Function

    ' The strongly typed Clone method (public)
    Function Clone() As Employee3
        ' Start creating a shallow copy of this object.
        ' (This copies all nonobject properties in one operation.)
        Clone = DirectCast(Me.MemberwiseClone, Employee3)
        ' Manually copy the Boss property, reusing its Clone method.
        If Not (Clone.Boss Is Nothing) Then
            Clone.Boss = Me.Boss.Clone
        End If
    End Function
End Class
```

The client code isn't cluttered with CType or DirectCast functions or slowed down by hidden unboxing operations:

```
Dim joe2 As Employee3 = joe.Clone
```

Using a strongly typed Clone method makes your code faster and more robust at the same time because the compiler can flag incorrect assignments that would otherwise throw an exception at run time. Note that you can still access the original, weakly typed, Clone method by means of an ICloneable variable or by using a CType or DirectCast operator, as in this line of code:

```
Dim c As Object = DirectCast(joe, ICloneable).Clone
```

In the remainder of the book, you'll become familiar with many other .NET interfaces—for example, IEnumerable and IEnumerator (Chapter 8), and ISerializable (Chapter 10).

Delegates

The use of delegates is new to Visual Basic developers. Broadly speaking, a delegate is similar to a C function pointer in that it lets you call a procedure through a pointer to the procedure itself. However, there are a few important differences between function pointers and delegates:

- Each delegate can invoke only procedures with a given argument signature, which you specify in the delegate declaration. For example, a given delegate can point only to a sub that takes an Integer argument by value. This constraint makes delegates inherently safer than C function pointers because the compiler can check that a delegate doesn't point to an arbitrary procedure or region in memory.

- A delegate can point to either a static procedure, such as a procedure declared in a module or a Shared method in a class, or an instance procedure. By comparison, a C function pointer can call only a static procedure. When you call an instance procedure, it's as if you're calling a particular method or property of an object. So in this respect, a delegate behaves more like the Visual Basic 6 CallByName function, but it's faster (being early-bound), more robust (you can't pass an arbitrary method name at run time), and safer (you can't pass arguments that don't match the called procedure's parameters).

Delegates play a central role in the .NET architecture. For example, .NET events are internally implemented through delegates, as are asynchronous operations and many other features of the .NET base classes. Even if you aren't going to use these .NET Framework features in your applications, delegates can be useful in themselves because they let you implement programming techniques that would be otherwise impossible.

Invoking Static Methods

You must define a delegate before you can use it. The following line declares a delegate named OneArgSub, which points to a procedure that takes a string argument:

```
' In the declaration section of a module or a class
Delegate Sub OneArgSub(ByVal msg As String)
```

The preceding line doesn't declare a single delegate object. Rather, it defines a *class* of delegates. Behind the scenes, in fact, Visual Basic creates a new class named OneArgSub that inherits from the System.MulticastDelegate class. Once you have defined the OneArgSub delegate class, you can declare a variable of the new class:

```
Dim deleg As OneArgSub
```

Now you're ready to create an instance of the OneArgSub delegate class:

```
deleg = New OneArgSub(AddressOf DisplayMsg)
```

where DisplayMsg is a procedure that must have the same argument signature as the OneArgSub delegate:

```
' Display a string in the Debug window.
Sub DisplayMsg(ByVal msgText As String)
    Debug.WriteLine(msgText)
End Sub
```

Finally, you're ready to call the DisplayMsg procedure through the deleg variable, using its Invoke method. (The OneArgSub class has inherited this method from the System.MulticastDelegate class, which in turn has inherited it from the System.Delegate class.)

```
' This statement displays the "FooBar" string in the Output window.
deleg.Invoke("FooBar")
```

It's a long trip to just display a message, so you might wonder why delegates are so important in the .NET architecture and why you should use them. Alas, Visual Basic developers aren't accustomed to function pointers and the degree of flexibility they can introduce in a program. To give you an example, let's define another procedure that follows the OneArgSub syntax:

```
' Display a string in a pop-up message box.
Sub PopupMsg(ByVal msgText As String)
    MsgBox(msgText)
End Sub
```

Now you can decide that all the messages in your program should be displayed in message boxes instead of in the Debug window, and you need only to replace the statement that creates the delegate variable to do so:

```
deleg = New OneArgSub(AddressOf PopupMsg)
```

All the existing deleg.Invoke statements scattered in the source code will work flawlessly but will send their output to the window instead.

You might have noticed the use of the AddressOf operator. This operator has the same syntax that it had in previous language versions, but in general, it can't be applied to the same situations you used it for in Visual Basic 6. The Visual Basic .NET keyword creates a Delegate object pointing to a given procedure, and in fact, you can usually assign the result of AddressOf to a Delegate variable without having to explicitly create a Delegate object of the proper type:

```
deleg = AddressOf PopupMsg
```

When you use this shortened syntax, the compiler checks that the target procedure has an argument signature compatible with the Delegate variable being assigned. In this chapter, I will use the more verbose syntax based on the New operator when I want to emphasize the class of the Delegate object being created, but you should be aware that both syntax forms are legal and that they are equally fast and robust.

Delegates work as described for any static method—that is, Sub and Function procedures in Module and shared procedures in classes. For example, here's a complete example that uses a delegate to invoke a shared Function method in a class:

```
Module MainModule
    ' Declare a delegate class.
    Delegate Function AskYesNoQuestion(ByVal msg As String) As Boolean
```

```
    Sub Main()
        ' A delegate variable that points to a shared function.
        Dim question As New AskYesNoQuestion(AddressOf MessageDisplayer.AskYesNo)

        ' Call the shared method. (Note that Invoke is omitted.)
        If question("Do you want to save?") Then
            ' ... (save whatever needs to be saved here)...
        End If
    End Sub
End Module

Class MessageDisplayer
    ' Show a message box; return True if user clicked Yes.
    Shared Function AskYesNo(ByVal msgText As String) As Boolean
        Dim answer As MsgBoxResult
        ' Display the message.
        answer = MsgBox(msgText, MsgBoxStyle.YesNo Or MsgBoxStyle.Question)
        ' Return True if the user answered yes.
        Return (answer = MsgBoxResult.Yes)
    End Function
End Class
```

When working with delegates, you must pay attention to optional arguments. The procedure pointed to by the delegate can include Optional and ParamArray arguments, and the delegate will correctly pass the expected number of arguments. This holds true even if the target procedure is overloaded, in which case the delegate will invoke the correct overloaded version of that procedure. However, the delegate definition itself cannot include Optional or ParamArray arguments.

Invoke is the default member for the System.Delegate class and all the classes that derive from it; thus, you can omit it when calling it. In the end, invoking a procedure through a delegate variable looks like a call to a method:

```
If question("Do you want to save?") Then
```

Omitting the Invoke method works even if the delegate is pointing to a procedure that takes no arguments, and this is an exception to the general rule that only methods and properties with arguments can become the default member of a class.

Invoking Instance Methods

Using delegates with instance methods and properties is also straightforward. The only remarkable difference is in the argument to the AddressOf operator, which must include a reference to an instance of the class. Here's a complete example that invokes an instance method of the MessageDisplayer class through a delegate:

```
Module MainModule
    Delegate Function AskQuestion(ByVal DefaultAnswer As Boolean) As Boolean

    Sub Main()
        ' Create an instance of the class, and initialize its properties.
        Dim msgdisp As New MessageDisplayer()
```

```
            msgdisp.MsgText = "Do you want to save?"
            msgdisp.MsgTitle = "File has been modified"

            ' Create the delegate to the instance method.
            ' (Note the object reference in the AddressOf clause.)
            Dim question As New AskQuestion(AddressOf msgdisp.YesOrNo)

            ' Call the instance method through the delegate.
            If question(False) Then
                ' ... (save whatever needs to be saved here)...
            End If
        End Sub
    End Module

Class MessageDisplayer
    Public MsgText As String
    Public MsgTitle As String

    ' Display a message box, and return True if the user selects Yes.
    Function YesOrNo(ByVal DefaultAnswer As Boolean) As Boolean
        Dim style As MsgBoxStyle

        ' Select the default button for this msgbox.
        If DefaultAnswer Then
            style = MsgBoxStyle.DefaultButton1     ' Yes button
        Else
            style = MsgBoxStyle.DefaultButton2     ' No button
        End If
        ' This is a yes/no question.
        style = style Or MsgBoxStyle.YesNo Or MsgBoxStyle.Question
        ' Display the msgbox, and return True if the user replied Yes.
        Return (MsgBox(MsgText, style, MsgTitle) = MsgBoxResult.Yes)
    End Function
End Class
```

Other Properties

All delegate classes ultimately derive from System.Delegate; therefore, they inherit all the properties and methods defined in this base class. The two properties you're likely to find useful are Target and Method.

The Target property simply returns a reference to the object that is the target of the delegate. In the previous example, you might access a property of the MessageDisplayer object with the following code:

```
' The Target method returns an Object, so you need an explicit
' cast if Option Strict is On.
Console.WriteLine(CType(question.Target, MessageDisplayer). MsgText)
```

If the delegate is pointing to a shared method, the Target method returns a reference to the System.Type object that represents the class. In this case, you need to use reflection methods to extract information about the class itself.

The other useful delegate property is Method, which returns a System.Reflection.MethodInfo object that describes the method being called, its attributes, and so on. For example, you can learn the name of the target method as follows:

```
Console.WriteLine(log.Method.Name)
```

For more information about reflection, see Chapter 14.

Callback Procedures and Code Reuse

The ability for a procedure to call back its caller can augment your code's reuse potential. For example, many Windows API functions, such as EnumWindows and EnumFonts, use the following technique: you pass them the address of a routine in your application that must be invoked for each window or font being enumerated. Your routine can then display these elements in a list box, store them in an array, or even decide to stop enumeration if your routine finds the window or the font you were interested in. By comparison, Visual Basic 6 allows you to use such a Windows API function, but it isn't powerful enough to let you implement a procedure that can take and use the address of another routine. In other words, you couldn't write the Enum-Windows or EnumFont routines in Visual Basic 6.

Delegates offer a clean, efficient, and safe solution to this problem in Visual Basic .NET. In fact, you can write a routine that takes a delegate as an argument, and the routine can call the caller through the delegate when there's something to report. This technique gives you unparalleled flexibility and the ability to reuse your code often. For example, consider the following routine that displays all the folder names in a directory tree:

```
Sub DisplayDirectoryTree(ByVal path As String)
    For Each dirName As String In System.IO.Directory.GetDirectories(path)
        ' Display name of this directory.
        Console.WriteLine(dirName)
        ' Call this routine recursively to display all subfolders.
        DisplayDirectoryTree(dirName)
    Next
End Sub
```

The problem with this naive implementation is that it can rarely be reused as is in another project. For example, you have to create another, slightly different version of the DisplayDirectoryTree method if you want to display directory names in a list box rather than in the Console window, or if you want to process these names in any other way.

Among their many other benefits, delegates let you create code that can be reused much more easily. All you have to do is to provide the procedure a delegate argument that points to a callback routine that decides what to do with the name of individual folders:

```
' A delegate that defines the syntax of the function whose address
' can be passed to TraverseDirectoryTree.
Delegate Sub TraverseDirectoryTree_CBK(ByVal dirName As String)
```

```
' A reusable routine that visits all the folders in a directory tree
' and callbacks the caller by passing the name of each folder.
Sub TraverseDirectoryTree(ByVal path As String, ByVal callback As _
   TraverseDirectoryTree_CBK)
      For Each dirName As String In System.IO.Directory.GetDirectories(path)
          ' Do the actual job by invoking the callback procedure.
          callback.Invoke(dirName)
          ' Call this routine recursively to process subfolders.
          TraverseDirectoryTree(dirName, callback)
      Next
End Sub
```

Using this procedure is straightforward:

```
Sub TestCallbacks()
    ' Print the name of all the directories under c:\WINDOWS.
    TraverseDirectoryTree("C:\WINDOWS", AddressOf DisplayDirName)
End Sub
```

```
' A function that complies with the TraverseDirectoryTree_CBK syntax
Function DisplayDirName(ByVal path As String) As Boolean
    Console.WriteLine(path)
End Function
```

The companion code includes an improved version, containing a TraverseDirectoryTree procedure that stops enumeration by returning a special value when a specific subfolder is found.

Multicast Delegates

You can get extra flexibility using multicast delegates, which can dispatch a call to more than just one procedure. You can do this by taking two delegates of the same type and combining them to create a new delegate that invokes both the procedures pointed to by the original delegate objects. You can have a multicast delegate point to either a Sub or a Function, but it should be clear that when a delegate performs a chain of calls to functions, only the return value from the last function in the series is returned to the caller.

You combine two delegates into a multicast delegate by using the Combine shared method of the System.Delegate class and then assigning the result to a delegate variable of the same type. This target variable can be one of the two original delegate variables or a third delegate variable of the proper type:

```
' Define two distinct delegates.
Dim cbk As New TraverseDirectoryTree_CBK(AddressOf Console.WriteLine)
Dim cbk2 As New TraverseDirectoryTree_CBK(AddressOf Debug.WriteLine)
' Combine them into a multicast delegate, assign back to first variable.
cbk = System.Delegate.Combine(cbk, cbk)
```

Because shared methods are exposed by object instances, you can also combine two delegates as follows:

```
cbk = cbk.Combine(cbk, cbk2)
```

You can make your code more concise if you create the second delegate on the fly:

```
cbk = cbk.Combine(cbk, _
    New TraverseDirectoryTree_CBK(AddressOf Debug.WriteLine))
```

There's one problem, however. If the Option Strict option is On, Visual Basic prevents you from assigning the result of the Combine method (which returns a generic Delegate) to a variable of a different type. So you must cast explicitly, using the CType or DirectCast function:

```
' We need this statement if Option Strict is On.
cbk = DirectCast(cbk.Combine(cbk, _
    New TraverseDirectoryTree_CBK(AddressOf Debug.WriteLine)), _
    TraverseDirectoryTree_CBK)
```

The following test procedure is a variant of the one you saw previously. In this case, the names of directories being scanned by the TraverseDirectoryTree method appear in the Console window and in the Debug window:

```
Dim cbk As New TraverseDirectoryTree_CBK(AddressOf Console.WriteLine)
cbk = DirectCast(cbk.Combine(cbk, _
    New TraverseDirectoryTree_CBK(AddressOf Debug.WriteLine)), _
    TraverseDirectoryTree_CBK)
TraverseDirectoryTree("C:\WINDOWS", cbk)
```

The preceding code creates two distinct delegate objects and then combines them. Keeping the two delegates in separate variables makes it easier to remove them (using the Remove shared method) from the list that the multicast delegate maintains internally. Because Remove is a shared method, you can invoke it from any instance or by specifying the System.Delegate prefix. The Remove method returns a multicast delegate that points to all the procedures originally in the delegate, minus the one being removed:

```
' Change the log delegate so that it doesn't display to Debug window.
cbk = DirectCast(cbk.Remove(cbk, cbk2), TraverseDirectoryTree_CBK)
' This method only displays a log message on the console.
TraverseDirectoryTree("C:\WINDOWS", cbk)
```

You can list all the individual delegate objects in a multicast delegate using the Get-InvocationList method, which returns an array of System.Delegate objects. For example, the following code prints the name of the target for each delegate that has been combined in a multicast delegate:

```
' Delegate is a reserved word and must be enclosed in square brackets.
' (Alternatively, you can use System.Delegate.)
Dim delegs() As [Delegate]
' Get the list of individual delegates in a multicast delegate.
delegs = cbk.GetInvocationList()

' List the names of all the target methods.
For Each d As [Delegate] In delegs
    Console.WriteLine(d.Method.Name)
Next
```

You can make the preceding code more concise by using the GetInvocationList method directly in the For loop, as follows:

```
For Each d As [Delegate] In cbk.GetInvocationList()
    Console.WriteLine(d.Method.Name)
Next
```

The GetInvocationList method is also useful when you don't maintain references to the individual delegates and you want to remove one of them:

```
' Remove the first delegate in the cbk multicast delegate.
cbk = DirectCast(cbk.Remove(cbk, cbk.GetInvocationList(0)), _
    TraverseDirectoryTree_CBK)
```

Delegates and Events

Multicast delegates have many traits in common with events. For example, the code that raises an event or invokes a delegate never knows how many calls will be actually performed. So it shouldn't surprise you that .NET events are internally implemented through multicast delegates. The two concepts are so close that you can define the syntax of an event in terms of a delegate:

```
' These two event declarations are equivalent.
Event FoundDir(ByVal msg As String)
Event FoundDir As TraverseDirectoryName_CBK
```

As with events, if any called method throws an exception, any subsequent delegate in the chain won't be invoked and the exception is immediately reported to the code that called the delegate's Invoke method.

A relevant difference between the two mechanisms is that you can raise an event even if no listeners have been registered for that event, but you can't use a multicast delegate that doesn't contain at least one valid reference to a method. Also, you can't use a delegate of Function type in the definition of an event because event handlers can't have a return value. A perfectly reasonable limitation of multicast delegates is that all the individual delegates you combine must have the same argument signature. However, nothing prevents you from combining variables from different delegate classes as long as these delegates have the same argument signature.

If you use ILDASM to explore the IL generated by a Visual Basic class that exposes an event, you'll find that the compiler creates a delegate class named *eventname*-EventHandler and a private variable of that delegate type, named *eventname*Event. For example, the declaration of an event named MatchFound generates a delegate class named MatchFoundEventHandler and a variable named MatchFoundEvent. Visual Studio .NET IntelliSense doesn't show the name of this variable; nevertheless, you can reference it in your code. Accessing this hidden delegate variable directly helps you perform a few interesting tricks.

For example, you can check the value of the variable before attempting to raise an event. If the variable is Nothing, there is no point in executing a RaiseEvent statement because no clients have registered for the event. If your code has to do some preparatory work before raising the event—for example, create the EventArgs-derived object you typically use as the second argument to all events that abide by the .NET coding guidelines—you can save some precious CPU cycles by sidestepping that section:

```
' Check whether one or more clients are waiting for the MatchFound event.
If Not MatchFoundEvent Is Nothing Then
    ' Create the object to be used as the event's second argument.
    Dim e As New MatchFoundEventArgs(search, matches)
    ' Raise the event.
    RaiseEvent MatchFound(Me, e)
End If
```

If you access the hidden delegate variable you can replace the standard RaiseEvent keyword with an improved version that manually calls to each delegate in the array returned by the GetInvocationList. This technique lets you sort event handlers according to their priority and, more importantly, you have the option to stop event invocation if any event handler returns a special value in a ByRef argument or in a property of an object argument. Here's an outline of this technique that reuses the CancelEventArgs class defined in the System.ComponentModel namespace (which you must have imported at the top of the source file):

```
Event Progress(ByVal sender As Object, ByVal e As CancelEventArgs)

' A procedure that replaces the built-in RaiseEvent keyword.
Sub RaiseTheEvent(ByVal sender As Object, ByVal e As CancelEventArgs)
    ' Nothing to do if no client has registered for the event.
    If ProgressEvent Is Nothing Then Exit Sub
    ' Initialize the Cancel property to False.
    e.Cancel = False
    For Each d As ProgressEventHandler In ProgressEvent.GetInvocationList()
        ' Call each event handler in turn.
        d.Invoke(Me, e)
        ' Exit the loop if an event handler sets Cancel property to True.
        If e.Cancel Then Exit For
    Next
End Sub
```

Now you know all you need to know to work with delegates in your programs, but this isn't the last time that you'll see code based on delegates in this book.

Attributes

The *attribute* is a new concept in programming and is used virtually everywhere in the .NET Framework. The underlying idea is that—regardless of the language you're using—some aspects of your application can't be expressed with plain executable statements.

For example, each language offers its own way to define project-level properties (such as the application name and version), and languages such as C++ use *pragmas* to affect how the compiler behaves. There isn't any consistency in how this information is associated with code; each language has its own way, and different types of information often require different techniques, even within the same language. Worse, you can't extend these techniques and create custom attributes for your own purposes.

.NET attributes can solve all these problems and offer a streamlined, standardized way to associate additional information with specific pieces of code. In practice, attributes let you extend the metadata associated with an assembly, a class, or a method. Different languages use a slightly different syntax for attributes, but there's a unified mechanism for querying a data type for all the attributes associated with it, based on reflection. Even better, attributes are themselves a data type, and you can create your own custom attribute by simply creating a new class that inherits from System.Attribute. (See Chapter 14.)

Attribute Syntax

You can consider attributes to be annotations that you intersperse throughout your code. You can apply attributes to nearly every programming entity that Visual Basic .NET supports, including classes, modules, structures, properties, methods, and enumeration blocks. Not all attributes can be applied to all entities, but the general syntax you use for inserting an attribute is consistent within each .NET language. For example, all Visual Basic .NET attributes require an identical syntax, which differs from C# syntax.

Under Visual Basic .NET, you enclose an attribute in angle brackets (<>) and insert it immediately before the item to which it refers. For example, you can apply System.ComponentModel.DescriptionAttribute to a class as follows:

```
<System.ComponentModel.DescriptionAttribute("Person")> Class Person
    ⋮
End Class
```

You can simplify attribute syntax in many ways. First, because attributes are .NET classes, you can shorten an attribute name by using a suitable Imports statement. Second, .NET guidelines dictate that the names of all attribute classes end with *Attribute*, but most .NET compilers, including Visual Basic and C#, let you drop *Attribute* from the name. Finally, you can break long lines using the underscore character to make code more readable. After applying these three rules, our initial example becomes:

```
Imports System.ComponentModel

<Description("Person")> _
Class Person
    ⋮
End Class
```

Attributes are rather peculiar .NET classes. They support properties and methods, but you can't reference them in code as you do with regular classes. In fact, you set one or more properties only when you create the attribute, and those properties don't change during the application's lifetime.

The syntax seen in the preceding code snippet is actually a call to the Description attribute's constructor method, which takes the value of the Description property as an argument. Once this property has been set, it isn't changed or queried, at least not by the application that uses the attribute. The properties of specific attributes can be queried, however, by an external application, such as the compiler or the .NET Framework, by using reflection, as you'll see in Chapter 14. Because of their nature, attribute classes rarely have methods other than the constructor method.

An attribute's constructor method takes zero or more arguments. It can also take optional *named* arguments. Named arguments allow you to set additional properties not required in the constructor, and are passed to the attribute constructor in the form *name:=value*. For example, WebMethodAttribute requires optional named arguments because it exposes more properties than those you can set through its constructor:

```
' A method that is exposed as an XML Web Service.
' First argument is required, second and third arguments are optional.
<WebMethod(True, Description:="Add operation", CacheDuration:=60)> _
Function Add(ByVal n1 As Double, ByVal n2 As Double) As Double
    Return n1 + n2
End Function
```

Most attributes are closely related to specific features of the .NET runtime. Thus, it makes more sense to discuss specific attributes only in the chapter where I explain those features. For example, I explain the WebMethod attribute in Chapter 29, where I show how to build Web services.

The Conditional Attribute

Visual Basic has always offered a way to include or exclude pieces of code in the compiled code using #If directives. All the techniques based on compiler directives have a weak point, which is apparent in the following piece of code:

```
#If LOG Then
    Sub LogMsg(ByVal MsgText As String)
        Console.WriteLine(MsgText)
    End Sub
#End If

    Sub Main()
        LogMsg("Program is starting")
        ⋮
        LogMsg("Program is ending")
    End Sub
```

You could exclude the LogMsg procedure from the compiled code by setting the LOG constant to a zero value, but you would get many compile errors if you did so because all the calls to that procedure would be unresolved. The only way to deal with this problem (short of adding one #If statement for each call to LogMsg) is to exclude just the body of the procedure itself:

```
    Sub LogMsg(ByVal MsgText As String)
#If LOG Then
        Console.WriteLine(MsgText)
#End If
    End Sub
```

This solution is unsatisfactory, however, because of the overhead of all the calls to the empty LogMsg procedure. Visual Basic .NET (and other .NET languages, such as C#) offers a much cleaner solution, based on the Conditional attribute:

```
<Conditional("LOG")> _
Sub LogMsg(ByVal MsgText As String)
    Console.WriteLine(MsgText)
End Sub
```

The procedure marked with the Conditional attribute is always included in the compiled application; however, calls to it are included only if the specified compilation constant has been defined and has a nonzero value. Otherwise, these calls are discarded. This practice produces the most efficient code without forcing you to add too many directives to your listing.

You define application-wide compilation constants in the Build page of the project Property Pages dialog box, as shown in Figure 6-2. This dialog box lets you define a couple of often-used compilation constants, named DEBUG and TRACE, with a click of the mouse, as you might remember from "The Trace and Debug Classes" section in Chapter 3. For the task at hand, you might have used the TRACE constant instead of your custom LOG constant.

Because the compiler can drop all the calls to the target method—LogMsg, in the preceding example—the Conditional attribute works only with procedures that don't return a value and is ignored when applied to Function procedures. If you want to use the Conditional attribute with a procedure that should return a value to the caller, you must use a Sub procedure with ByRef arguments.

One more thing about the Conditional attribute: it allows multiple definitions, which means that you can specify a number of Conditional attributes for the same method. In this case, calls to the method are included in the compiled application if *any* of the mentioned compilation constants have a nonzero value:

```
<Conditional("LOG"), Conditional("TRACE")> _
Sub LogMsg(ByVal MsgText As String)
    Console.WriteLine(MsgText)
End Sub
```

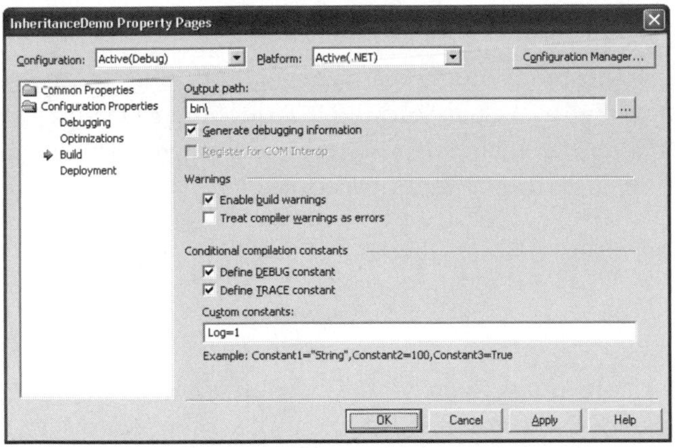

Figure 6-2 The Build page of the project Property Pages dialog box lets you define compilation constants throughout an application.

The Obsolete Attribute

Let's say that you inherited a nontrivial project and your job is to improve its performance by rewriting some of it. Consider the following procedure:

```
Sub BubbleSort(arr() As String)
    ⋮
End Sub
```

BubbleSort isn't very efficient, so you create a new sort routine based on a more efficient sort algorithm (or just use the Array.Sort method) and start replacing all calls to Bubble-Sort. You don't want to perform a straight find-and-replace operation, however, because you want to double-check each call. In the end, the BubbleSort routine will be deleted, but you can't do it right now because some portions of the application won't compile. The framework offers a simple solution to this recurring situation in the form of the Obsolete attribute. The constructor method for this attribute can take no arguments, one argument (the warning message), or two arguments (the message and a Boolean value that indicates whether the message is to be considered a compilation error):

```
' Mark BubbleSort as obsolete.
<Obsolete("Replace BubbleSort with ShellSort")> _
Sub BubbleSort(arr() As String)
    ⋮
End Sub
```

The following variant additionally causes the BubbleSort routine to appear as a compilation error:

```
' Mark BubbleSort as obsolete.
<Obsolete("Replace BubbleSort with ShellSort", True)> _
Sub BubbleSort(arr() As String)
    ⋮
End Sub
```

The DebuggerStepThrough Attribute

You can use the System.Diagnostics.DebuggerStepThrough attribute to mark a routine that should be skipped over by the Visual Studio .NET debugger because it must run as a whole or just because it has been already tested and debugged. The form designer uses this attribute for the InitializeComponent procedure:

```
<System.Diagnostics.DebuggerStepThrough()> _
Private Sub InitializeComponent()
    ⋮
End Sub
```

This chapter concludes our long journey across the Visual Basic .NET language and the new object-oriented extensions. Now you have all the tools you need to start exploring the .NET Framework to see how you can write powerful applications easily with the many classes that it gives to developers.

Part III
Programming the .NET Framework

7 .NET Framework Basic Types

The .NET Framework exposes hundreds of different classes to accomplish such jobs as opening files, parsing XML, and updating databases. As a Visual Basic developer, you're accustomed to working with libraries of objects that perform tasks whose implementation in plain Visual Basic would be impractical—just think of the Data Access Objects (DAO), Remote Data Objects (RDO), ActiveX Data Objects (ADO), and FileSystemObject libraries you've used to work with databases and files.

The .NET Framework is more than just a collection of useful objects. It's a well-structured object tree that also provides objects to *store* values, such as numbers, dates, and strings. Everything in the .NET Framework is a class, and at the top of the object hierarchy sits the System.Object class.

The System.Object Type

All classes inherit—directly or indirectly—from System.Object, which means that you can always assign any object to a System.Object variable and never get a compilation or run-time error when you do so:

```
' Most .NET programs import the System namespace; therefore,
' you can drop the System prefix from the Object class name.
Dim o As Object = New AnyOtherClass()
```

Incidentally, note that interfaces are the only things in the .NET Framework that do *not* derive from System.Object.

Public and Protected Methods

Because .NET classes inherit from System.Object (see Figure 7-1), all of them expose the four instance methods that System.Object exposes, namely

- **Equals** An overridable method that checks whether the current object has the same value as the object passed as an argument. It returns True when two object references point to the same object instance, but many classes override this method to implement a different type of equality. For example, numeric classes override this method so that it returns True if the objects being compared have the same numeric value.

- **GetHashCode** An overridable method that returns a hash code for the object. This method is used when the object is a key for collections and hash tables. Ideally, the hash code should be unique for any given object instance so that you can check that two objects are "equal" by comparing their hash code. However, implementing a hash function that provides unique values is seldom possible, and different objects might return the same hash code. A class can override this method to implement a different hash algorithm to improve performance when its objects are used as keys in collections. A class that overrides the Equals method should always override the GetHashCode method as well, so that two objects considered to be equal also return the same hash code.

- **GetType**   A method that returns a value that identifies the type of the object. The returned value is typically used in reflection operations. (See Chapter 14.)

- **ToString**   An overridable method that returns the complete name of the class, for example, MyNamespace.MyClass. However, most classes redefine this method so that it returns a string that better describes the value of the object. For example, basic types such as Integer, Double, and String override this method to return the object's numeric or string value. The ToString method is implicitly called when you pass an object to the Console.Write and Debug.Write methods. Interestingly, ToString is culturally aware. For example, when applied to a numeric type, it uses a comma as the decimal separator if the current culture requires it.

The System.Object class also exposes two shared methods:

- **Equals**   A shared member that takes two object arguments and returns True if they can be considered to be equal. It is similar to, and often used in lieu of, the instance method with the same name, which would fail if invoked on a variable reference that is Nothing.

- **ReferenceEquals**   A shared method that takes two object arguments and returns True if they reference the same instance; thus, it corresponds to the Is operator in Visual Basic. This method is similar to the Equals method except that derived classes can't override it.

The System.Object class also exposes two protected methods. Because everything in the .NET Framework derives directly or indirectly from System.Object, all the classes you write can invoke the following methods in their base class and override them:

- **MemberwiseClone**   A method that returns a new object of the same type and initializes the new object's fields and properties so that the new object can be considered a copy (a clone) of the current object.

- **Finalize**   An overridable method that the .NET Framework calls when the object is garbage collected. (For more information about this method, see the section "Object Lifetime" in Chapter 5.)

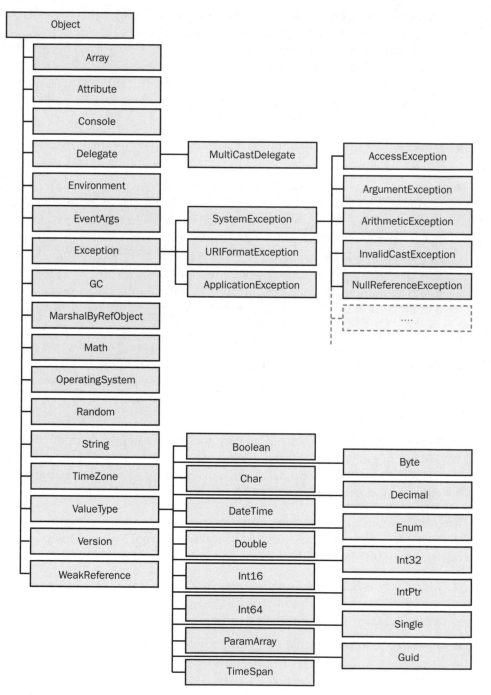

Figure 7-1   The most important classes in the System hierarchy

The System class hierarchy includes all the most common and useful objects in the .NET Framework, including all the basic data types. The most important classes are depicted in Figure 7-1.

Value Types and Reference Types (Revisited)

Most basic data types (numbers, dates, and so on) in the .NET hierarchy inherit from System.ValueType and so have a common behavior. For example, System.ValueType overrides the Equals method and redefines equality so that two object references are considered equal if they have the same value (which is the way we usually compare numbers and dates), rather than if they point to the same instance. In addition, all classes deriving from System.ValueType override the GetHashCode method so that the hash code is created by taking the object's fields into account.

Classes that inherit from System.ValueType are commonly referred to as *value types*, to distinguish them from other classes, which are named *reference types*. All numeric and Enum types are value types, as are types that work with dates. The .NET documentation uses the term *type* to encompass the meaning of value and reference types. I follow that convention in this book and reserve the word *class* for reference types only.

Visual Basic .NET prevents you from explicitly inheriting from System.ValueType. The only way to create a value type is by creating a Structure block:

```
Structure PositionXY
    Dim X As Integer
    Dim Y As Integer
    ' Add here other fields, properties, methods, and interfaces.
    :
End Structure
```

Broadly speaking, value types are more efficient than reference types because their data isn't allocated in the managed heap and therefore isn't subject to garbage collection. For example, a value type declared in a procedure is allocated on the stack; when the procedure is exited, the value is simply discarded without making any extra work for the garbage collector. (The Finalize method is ignored in structures.) This description isn't strictly accurate if the Structure includes a member of a reference type, though. Consider this new version of the PositionXY type:

```
Structure PositionXY
    Dim X As Integer
    Dim Y As Integer
    Dim Description As String      ' A reference type
    :
End Structure
```

The garbage collector has to reclaim the memory used for the Description string member when such a structure is destroyed. In other words, value types are significantly faster than reference types only if they don't expose any members of a reference type.

Other factors might affect your choice of a value type or a reference type. You should use a Structure if your object acts like a primitive type and doesn't need to inherit special behaviors from other types, and other types don't need to derive from it. (Value types are implicitly sealed and marked as NotInheritable.) Also, Structures can't be abstract and can't contain virtual methods.

A detail that might confuse many Visual Basic veterans is that the String class is a reference type, not a value type. (See Figure 7-1.) You can easily demonstrate this by assigning a String variable to another variable and then testing whether both variables point to the same object:

```
Dim s1 As String = "ABCD"
Dim s2 As String = s1
' Prove that both variables point to the same object.
Console.WriteLine(s1 Is s2)    ' => True
```

.NET arrays are reference types too, and assigning an array to an Array variable copies only the object's reference, not the array contents. The Array class exposes the Clone method to let you make a (shallow) copy of its elements. (See the "The ICloneable Interface" section in Chapter 6 for a discussion of shallow and deep copy operations.)

Boxing and Unboxing

Even if performance is your primary concern, you shouldn't *always* opt for value types. Sometimes reference types are faster. For example, an assignment between value types involves the copy of every field in the object, whereas assigning a reference value to a variable requires only the copy of the object's address (4 bytes in 32-bit versions of Windows).

When you pass a value type to a method that expects an Object argument, a different kind of performance hit occurs because the value must be boxed in this case. *Boxing a value* means that the compiler creates a copy of it in the managed heap and assigns the address of this copy to an Object variable or argument so that the type can then be used as a reference type. (See the section "Value Types and Reference Types" in Chapter 2.) A boxed value doesn't maintain a link to the original value, which means you can modify either one without affecting the other.

If this boxed value is later assigned to a variable of the original (value) type, the object is said to be *unboxed* and data is copied from the managed heap into the memory allocated to the variable (for example, on the stack if it's a local variable). Not surprisingly, boxing and unboxing takes CPU time and eventually requires some memory to be reclaimed during a garbage collection. The bottom line: if you carry out many assignments or frequently perform operations that result in a boxing and unboxing sequence, implementing a reference type might be a wiser choice.

Boxing occurs transparently in most cases, whereas you require an explicit CType or DirectCast operator to convert back from an Object to a value type if Option Strict is On. You can determine whether a call causes a boxing operation by looking at the method declaration in the object browser or in the class documentation. If the method takes an argument of the type you're passing, no boxing occurs; if it takes a generic Object argument, your argument will be boxed. When creating your own methods, you might consider including overloaded variations that take arguments of different types as well as a catchall procedure that takes an Object argument.

In general, it doesn't make sense to compare the performance of a method that uses boxing with a similar method that doesn't. However, the companion code includes a simple benchmark named TestBoxing that gives you a broad idea of what kind of overhead boxing and unboxing is going to add to your applications. It shows that a tight loop that calls a function that requires boxing can be up to 30 times slower than a loop that doesn't use boxing. However, you must repeat the loop 10 million times to see a significative difference in absolute terms, so in practice you should worry about boxing only in time-critical code sections.

You might be using boxing sometimes without knowing it. First, you implicitly box a Structure if you call one of the virtual methods that the Structure inherits from System.Object—for example, ToString. Second, you implicitly box a Structure if you call a method of an interface the structure exposes.

As I mentioned, boxing typically occurs transparently. In rare cases, however, you must explicitly tell Visual Basic that you want to box a value, by using the CObj function. This is necessary, for example, when you want to invoke the ToString method (or another method inherited from System.Object) on an interface variable, as in

```
Sub DisposeIt(ByVal idisp As IDisposable)
    ' Dispose the object and display a diagnostic message.
    idisp.Dispose()
    ' Explicitly box the reference to call ToString.
    Console.WriteLine("Disposing " & CObj(idisp).ToString())
End Sub
```

The String Type

You saw in Chapter 2 that Visual Basic .NET supports the String data type, which maps to the System.String class. In earlier chapters, we used this class as a storage medium for string data exclusively and operated on them through string functions, such as Trim and Left, as we've done for years under previous versions of the language. However, the System.String class is much more powerful than what we've seen so far; it exposes methods that allow adoption of a more object-oriented syntax and—in some cases—achieve better performance than old-style string functions.

To begin with, the String class exposes many overloaded constructor methods, so you can create a string in a variety of ways—for example, as a sequence of N same characters. (This technique duplicates the functionality of the String function in Visual Basic 6, which was dropped because String is now a reserved keyword.)

```vb
' A sequence of <N> characters - similar to the VB6 String function
'    (Note the c suffix to make "A" a Char rather than a String.)
Dim s As New String("A"c, 10)                    ' => AAAAAAAAAA

'  Another way to get the same result
s = New String(CChar("A"), 10)                   ' => AAAAAAAAAA
```

Properties and Methods

The only properties of the String class are Length and Chars. The former returns the numbers of characters in the string and therefore corresponds to the Len function; the latter returns the character at a given index and is therefore similar to the Mid function when it extracts one character only:

```vb
Dim s As String = "ABCDEFGHIJ"
Console.WriteLine(s.Length)           ' => 10
' Note that index is always zero-based.
Console.WriteLine(s.Chars(3))         ' => D
```

Sometimes the reference nature of the String type causes behaviors you might not anticipate. For example, consider this simple code:

```vb
Dim s As String
Console.WriteLine(s.Length)
```

You probably expect that the second statement displays the value zero, but this statement actually throws a NullReferenceException because the string object hasn't been initialized. A simple way to avoid this problem is to make a habit of initializing all String variables explicitly, as in this code:

```vb
Dim s As String = ""
```

You can tap the power of the String class by invoking one of its many methods. I listed its main methods in Table 7-1, with a brief description and the corresponding Visual Basic 6 function that returns the same result. I don't provide a code example for every method, but you can easily see that Visual Basic .NET strings are richer in functionality and let you adopt a more object-oriented, concise syntax in your applications. For example, see how much simpler and more readable the operation of inserting a substring has become:

```vb
Dim s As String = "ABCDEFGHIJ"
' The VB6 way of inserting a substring after the third character
s = Left(s, 3) & "1234" & Mid(s, 4)

' The VB.NET object-oriented way to perform the same operation
s = s.Insert(3, "1234")        ' => ABC1234DEFGHIJ
```

Here's another example of the compactness that you can get by using the String methods. Let's say you want to trim all the space and tab characters from the beginning of a string.

You just have to load all the characters to be trimmed in an array of Chars and pass the array to the TrimStart function (and you can use the same pattern with the TrimEnd and Trim functions):

```
Dim cArr() As Char = { " "c, ControlChars.Tab }
s = s.TrimStart(cArr)
```

You can even create the Char array on the fly:

```
s = s.TrimStart(New Char() {" "c, ControlChars.Tab})
```

In many cases, the new methods can deliver better performance because you can state more precisely what you're after. For example, you can determine whether a string begins or ends with a given sequence of characters by a variety of means under Visual Basic 6, but none of the available techniques is especially efficient. Visual Basic .NET strings solve this problem elegantly with the StartsWith or EndsWith method:

```
' Check whether the strings starts with "abc" and ends with "xyz".
If s.StartsWith("abc") And s.EndsWith("xyz") Then ok = True
```

The next example shows how to pad a string to the right with zeros so that the resulting length is 10 characters, by means of the PadRight method:

```
s = s.PadRight(10, "0"c)
```

Although most of the time you can use the newer methods to replace the old-style functions, you should pay attention to the subtle differences that can break your code:

- String indexes are always zero-based in Visual Basic .NET.

- PadLeft and PadRight are similar to the RSet and LSet commands, respectively, but they never trim the current string if it's longer than the requested number of characters.

- CompareTo is similar to the StrComp function but doesn't support case-insensitive comparisons; it considers empty strings greater than null references (Nothing).

- IndexOf and LastIndexOf are similar to the InStr and InStrRev functions, respectively, but don't support case-insensitive searches.

The String class also exposes a GetEnumerator method, which means that it supports enumeration of its own characters in a For Each loop:

```
For Each c As Char In "ABCDE"
    Console.Write(c & ".")        ' => A.B.C.D.E.
Next
```

However, iterating over individual characters of a long string in this way is significantly slower (in the range of two to five times) than extracting individual characters using the Chars property in a standard For loop.

Table 7-1   Instance Methods of the System.String Class

Syntax	Description
Clone	Returns a copy of the current string.
TrimStart ([chars])	Trims all the leading spaces from the string. If an array of characters is passed, it trims all the leading characters that are specified in the array. (Similar to the LTrim function.)
TrimEnd ([chars])	Trims all the trailing spaces from the string. If an array of characters is passed, it trims all the trailing characters that are specified in the array. (Similar to the RTrim function.)
Trim ([chars])	Trims all the leading and trailing spaces from the string. If an array of characters is passed, it trims all the leading and trailing characters that are specified in the array. (Similar to the Trim function.)
StartsWith (prefix)	Returns True if the string passed as an argument is a prefix for the current string. Comparison is case sensitive; passing a null string returns True. (Same as using InStr and comparing the result with 1.)
EndsWith (postfix)	Returns True if the current string ends with the characters in the argument. Comparison is case sensitive. (Similar to using InStrRev and testing the result.)
IndexOf (search[, start[, end]])	Searches a substring inside the current string and returns the index of the first match, or -1 if the substring isn't found. The search can start and end at given indexes. The first argument can be a String, a Char, or an array of Chars. (Similar to InStr but more powerful because it also supports an end index.)
LastIndexOf (search[, start[, end]])	Same as IndexOf but returns the index of the last occurrence of a substring. (Similar to InStrRev but more powerful because it supports both start and end indexes.)
IndexOfAny (chars[, start[, end]])	Searches for any of the characters specified by the Char array passed as the first argument and returns the index of the first occurrence, or -1 if the search failed.
LastIndexOfAny (chars[, start[, end]])	Same as IndexOfAny but returns the index of the last occurrence of any character among those specified in the Char array, or -1 if the search failed.
ToUpper	Converts the current string to uppercase. (Same as UCase.)
ToLower	Converts the current string to lowercase. (Same as LCase.)
Substring (start[, length])	Extracts a substring of the current string, starting at a given index and continuing for the specified number of characters, or to the end of the string if the length is omitted. (Same as Mid function.)

Table 7-1   Instance Methods of the System.String Class

Syntax	Description
Replace (search, replace)	Replaces all the occurrences of a substring with another substring.
Insert (index, substring)	Inserts a substring into the current string at the given index. (Same as using a combination of the & operator and the Left and Mid functions.)
Remove (index, length)	Removes the specified number of characters, starting at the specified index. (Same as concatenating the return value from the Left and Mid functions.)
PadLeft (totallength[, char])	Pads the current string by adding a number of spaces to the left to reach the specified length. If a second argument is passed, it uses that character to do the padding. If the current string is longer than the total length requested, no characters are added and the string isn't trimmed. (Similar to using the RSet command for aligning a value to the right but is more flexible because you can select the padding character.)
PadRight (totallength[, char])	Same as PadLeft but appends characters to the right. (Similar to using the LSet command but more flexible.)
CompareTo (string)	Compares the current string with another string (or any object that can be converted to a string) in a case-sensitive way and returns -1, 0, or 1, depending on whether the current string is less than, equal to, or greater than the argument. (Similar to StrComp but lacks the ability to compare in a case-insensitive way.)
CopyTo (index, chars, destIndex, length)	Copies a substring of the current string into the Char array passed as the second argument. The first argument is the position of the substring, the third argument is the index in the destination Char array, and the last argument is the number of characters to be copied.
Split (chars[, maxcount])	Splits a string into words and returns them as an array of strings. The first argument is a Char array holding all the valid separators. The second argument indicates the maximum number of words; if there are more words than this value, the last item in the result array contains all the unsplit words. (Similar to the Split function, plus it can take multiple single-character separators; however, it can't take a separator longer than one character.)
ToCharArray ([start, length])	Converts the current string (or a portion of it) to a Char array.

String Optimizations

An important detail to keep in mind is that a String object is *immutable*: once you create a string, its contents can never change. In fact, all the methods seen so far don't modify the original String; rather, they return *another* String object that you might or might not assign to the same String variable. Understanding this detail lets you avoid a common programming mistake:

```
Dim s As String = "abcde"
' You *might* believe that next statement changes the string...
s.ToUpper()
' ... but it isn't the case because the result wasn't assigned to s.
Console.WriteLine(s)        ' => abcde
' This is the correct way to invoke string methods.
s = s.ToUpper()
```

If you do assign the result to the original variable, the original String becomes unreachable from the application (unless there are other variables pointing to it) and eventually will be garbage collected. If you think that this is a waste of memory and CPU resources, just remember that this train of events is similar to what happens with a regular string in Visual Basic 6: anytime the string changes its length, a new block of memory is allocated and the old memory is marked as free and will be reclaimed when a garbage collection starts. (Visual Basic 6 can reduce the number of garbage collections and optimize string operations by allocating a buffer that is larger than the initial length of the string.)

Because String values are immutable, the compiler can optimize the resulting code in ways that wouldn't be possible otherwise. For example, consider this code fragment:

```
Dim s1 As String = "1234" & "5678"
Dim s2 As String = "12345678"
Console.WriteLine(s1 Is s2)                      ' => True
```

In this case, the compiler can compute the & operator at compile time and realizes that both variables contain the same characters, so it can allocate only one block of memory for the string and have the two variables pointing to it. Because the string is immutable, a new object is created behind the scenes as soon as you attempt to modify the characters in that string:

```
' ...(Continuing the previous code fragment)...
' Attempt to modify the S1 string using the Mid statement.
Mid(s1, 2, 1) = "x"
' Prove that a new string was created behind the scenes.
Console.WriteLine(s1 Is s2)                      ' => False
```

Because of this behavior, you never really need to invoke the Clone method to explicitly create a copy of the String. Simply use the string as you would normally, and the compiler creates a copy for you if and when necessary. Also note that the Mid statement isn't as fast as it is in Visual Basic because it doesn't prevent the memory manager from allocating a new block of memory for the new string value.

A .NET application can optimize string management by maintaining an internal pool of string values known as an *intern pool*. If the value being assigned to a string variable coincides with one of the strings already in the intern pool, no additional memory is created and the variable receives the address of the string value in the pool. As you saw at the beginning of the current section, the compiler is capable of using the intern pool to optimize string initialization and have two string variables pointing to the same String object in memory. This optimization step isn't performed at run time, though, because the search in the pool takes time and in most cases it would fail, adding overhead to the application without bringing any benefit.

```
' Prove that no optimization is performed at run time.
s1 = "1234"
s1 &= "5678"
s2 = "12345678"
' These two variables point to different String objects.
Console.WriteLine(s1 Is s2)                    ' => False
```

You can optimize string management by using the Intern shared method. This method searches a string value in the intern pool and returns a reference to the pool element that contains the value if the value is already in the pool. If the search fails, the string is added to the pool and a reference to it is returned. Notice how you can "manually" optimize the preceding code snippet by using the String.Intern method:

```
s1 = "ABCD"
s1 &= "EFGH"
' Move S1 to the intern pool.
s1 = String.Intern(s1)
' Assign S2 a string constant (that we know is in the pool).
s2 = String.Intern("ABCDEFGH")
' These two variables point to the same String object.
Console.WriteLine(s1 Is s2)                    ' => True
```

This optimization technique makes sense only if you're working with long strings that appear in multiple portions of the applications. Another good time to use this technique is when you have many instances of a server-side component that contain similar string variables, such as a database connection string. Even if these strings don't change during the program's lifetime, they're usually read from a file, and therefore the compiler can't optimize their memory allocation automatically. Using the Intern method, you can help your application produce a smaller memory footprint. You can also use the IsInterned shared method to check whether a string is in the intern pool (in which case the string itself is returned) or not (in which case the method returns Nothing):

```
' Continuing previous example...
If Not String.IsInterned(s1) Is Nothing Then
    ' This block is executed because s1 is in the intern pool.
End If
```

Here's another simple performance tip: try to gather multiple & operators in the same statement instead of spreading them across separate lines. The Visual Basic compiler can optimize multiple concatenation operations only if they're in the same statement.

Shared Methods

The String class exposes additional shared methods that you can call without first instancing a String object. For example, the Concat method supports an arbitrary number of String arguments (or Object arguments that can be converted to strings) and returns the string that results from the concatenation of all the arguments:

```
Console.Write(String.Concat("ABC ", "DEF ", "GHI"))  ' => ABC DEF GHI
```

In some cases, shared methods are more flexible than the corresponding instance methods in Table 7-1. For example, the Compare method compares two strings and is overloaded to support case-insensitive comparisons:

```
' Compare two strings in case-insensitive mode.
Select Case String.Compare(s1, s2, True)
    Case 0: Console.WriteLine("s1 = s2")
    Case 1: Console.WriteLine("s1 > s2")
    Case -1: Console.WriteLine("s1 < s2")
End Select
```

Even better, when using the shared Compare method you don't have to care whether either string is Nothing, which might be an issue when you're using the CompareTo instance method. Two overloaded variations of this method let you compare a portion of two strings in a case-sensitive or case-insensitive way:

```
' Compare the first four characters in s1 and s2 in a case-sensitive way.
' Second and fourth arguments are the index in the two strings;
' the last argument is the length of the substrings to compare.
If String.Compare(s1, 1, s2, 1, 4) = 0 Then Console.Write("Equal")

' Same as above, but in a case-insensitive way
If String.Compare(s1, 1, s2, 1, 4, True) = 0 Then Console.Write("Equal")
```

All the overloaded versions of the Compare method make the comparison by considering the local national language or culture. Another shared method, CompareOrdinal, compares two strings (or substrings) without considering the local national language:

```
' Compare two strings.
If String.CompareOrdinal(s1, s2) = 0 Then Console.Write("Equal")
' Compare two substrings.
If String.CompareOrdinal(s1, 1, s2, 1, 4) = 0 Then Console.Write("Equal")
```

On average, CompareOrdinal is six to seven times faster than Compare because it works with the numeric code of individual characters. Also, you can get better performance if you use Option Compare Binary so that regular comparison operations such as = and >= work in the same way as CompareOrdinal. Note that Option Compare Binary is the default projectwide setting, but you can change it in the Build page of the Project Properties dialog box or via the Option Compare Text statement at the top of a specific source code module.

Visual Basic .NET also lets you compare strings using any language, not just the end user's language; you just have to pass the proper CultureInfo object to the Compare method.

The CultureInfo Auxiliary Class

The System.Globalization.CultureInfo class defines an object that you can inspect to determine some key properties of any installed languages. The class exposes a shared property that returns the CultureInfo object for the current language:

```
' The following code assumes that the module contains this Imports statement.
Imports System.Globalization

' Get information about the current locale.
Dim ci As CultureInfo = CultureInfo.CurrentCulture

' Assuming that the current language is Italian, we get:
Console.WriteLine(ci.Name)                              ' => it
Console.WriteLine(ci.EnglishName)                       ' => Italian
Console.WriteLine(ci.NativeName)                        ' => italiano
Console.WriteLine(ci.LCID)                              ' => 16
Console.WriteLine(ci.TwoLetterISOLanguageName)          ' => it
Console.WriteLine(ci.ThreeLetterISOLanguageName)        ' => ita
Console.WriteLine(ci.ThreeLetterWindowsLanguageName)    ' => ITA
```

You can get additional information about the locale through the TextInfo object, exposed by the property with the same name:

```
Dim ti As TextInfo = ci.TextInfo
Console.WriteLine(ti.ANSICodePage)          ' => 1252
Console.WriteLine(ti.EBCDICCodePage)        ' => 20280
Console.WriteLine(ti.OEMCodePage)           ' => 850
Console.WriteLine(ti.ListSeparator)         ' => ;
```

The CultureInfo object exposes two properties, NumberFormat and DateTimeFormat, which return information about how numbers and dates are formatted according to a given locale. For example, consider this code:

```
' How do you spell "Sunday" in German?
' First create a CultureInfo object for German/Germany.
' (Note that you must pass a string in the form "locale-COUNTRY" if
' a given language is spoken in multiple countries.)
Dim ciDe As New CultureInfo("de-DE")
' Next get the corresponding DateTimeFormatInfo object.
Dim dtfi As DateTimeFormatInfo = ciDe.DateTimeFormat
' Here's the answer:
Console.WriteLine(dtfi.GetDayName(DayOfWeek.Sunday))    ' => Sonntag
```

You'll find the "locale-COUNTRY" strings in many places of the .NET Framework; for all practical purposes, these strings replace the LCID values you used in COM. The Get-Cultures shared method returns an array of all the installed cultures, so you can inspect all the languages that your operating system supports:

```
' Get info on all the installed cultures.
Dim ciArr() As CultureInfo = CultureInfo.GetCultures(CultureTypes.AllCultures)
' Print abbreviation and English name of each culture.
For Each c As CultureInfo In ciArr
    Console.WriteLine(c.Name & " (" & c.EnglishName & ")")
Next
```

The auxiliary TextInfo object permits you to convert a string to uppercase, lowercase, or title case (for example, "These Are Four Words") for a given language:

```
' Create a CultureInfo object for Canadian French.
Dim ciFr As CultureInfo = New CultureInfo("fr-CA")
' Convert a string to title case using Canadian French rules.
s = ciFr.TextInfo.ToTitleCase(s)
```

Now that you know how you can use the CultureInfo object to retrieve information about installed languages, let's see how you can pass it to the String.Compare shared method so that you can compare strings according to the collation rules defined by a given language. One overloaded version of the Compare method takes four arguments: the two strings to be compared, a Boolean value that indicates whether the comparison is case insensitive, and a CultureInfo object that specifies the language to be used:

```
' Compare these two strings in case-insensitive mode
' according to rules of Italian language.
Dim s1 As String = "cioè"
Dim s2 As String = "CIOÈ"
' You can create a CultureInfo object on the fly.
If String.Compare(s1, s2, True, New CultureInfo("it")) = 0 Then
    Console.WriteLine("s1 = s2")
End If
```

Here also is an overloaded version that compares two substrings:

```
If String.Compare(s1, 1, s2, 1, 4, True, New CultureInfo("it")) = 1 Then
    Console.WriteLine("s1's first four chars are greater than s2's")
End If
```

Interestingly, most Windows and Web Form controls adapt themselves to the local culture.

The Encoding Class

All .NET strings store their characters in Unicode format, so sometimes you might need to convert them to and from other formats—for example, ASCII or the UTF-7 or UTF-8 variants of the Unicode format. You can do this with the Encoding class in the System.Text namespace. All these classes inherit from Encoding and therefore expose the same members.

The first thing to do when converting a .NET Unicode string to or from another format is create the proper encoding object. The Encoding class opportunely exposes the most common encoding objects though the following shared properties: ASCII, Unicode (little-endian byte order), BigEndianUnicode, UTF7, UTF8, and Default (the system's current ANSI code page). Here's an example of how you can convert a Unicode string to a sequence of bytes that represent the same string in ASCII format:

```
Dim text As String = "A Unicode string with accented vowels: àèéìòù"
Dim uni As Encoding = Encoding.Unicode
Dim uniBytes() As Byte = uni.GetBytes(text)
Dim ascii As Encoding = Encoding.ASCII
Dim asciiBytes() As Byte = Encoding.Convert(uni, ascii, uniBytes)

' Convert the ASCII bytes back to a string.
Dim asciiText As String = ascii.GetChars(asciiBytes)
Console.WriteLine(asciiText)   ' => A Unicode string with accented vowels: ?????
```

You can also create other Encoding-derived objects with the GetEncoding shared method, which takes either a code page number or code page name and throws a NotSupportedException if the code page isn't supported:

```
' Get the encoding object for code page 1252
Dim enc As Encoding = Encoding.GetEncoding(1252)
```

The GetChars method expects that the byte array you feed it will contain an integer number of characters. (For example, it must end with the second byte of a two-byte character.) This can be a problem when you read the byte array from a file or from another type of stream, and you're working with a string format that allows one, two, or three bytes per character. In such cases, you should use a Decoder object, which remembers the state between consecutive calls. For more information, read the MSDN documentation.

Formatting Numeric Values

The Format shared method of the String class allows you to format a string and include one or more numeric or date values in it, in a way similar to the C language's printf function or the Console.Write method. The string being formatted can contain placeholders for arguments, in the format {N} where N is an index that starts at 0:

```
' Print the value of a string variable.
Dim xyz As String = "foobar"
Dim msg As String
msg = String.Format("The value of {0} variable is {1}", "XYZ", xyz)
    ' => The value of XYZ variable is foobar
```

If the argument is numeric, you can add a colon after the argument index and then a character that indicates what kind of formatting you're requesting. The available characters are G (General), N (Number), C (Currency), D (Decimal), E (Scientific), F (Fixed-point), P (Percent), R (Round-trip), and X (Hexadecimal):

```
' Format a Currency according to current locale.
msg = String.Format("Total is {0:C}, balance is {1:C}", 123.45, -67)
    ' => Total is $123.45, balance is ($67.00)
```

The number format uses commas—or to put it more precisely, the thousands separator defined by the current locale—to group digits:

```
msg = String.Format("Total is {0:N}", 123456.78)   ' => Total is 123,456.78
```

You can append an integer after the N character to round or extend the number of digits after the decimal point:

```
msg = String.Format("Total is {0:N4}", 123456.785555)    ' => Total is 123,456.7856
```

The decimal format works with integer values only and throws a FormatException if you pass a noninteger argument; you can specify a length that, if longer than the result, causes one or more leading zeros to be added:

```
msg = String.Format("Total is {0:D8}", 123456)           ' => Total is 00123456
```

The fixed-point format is useful with decimal values, and you can indicate how many decimal digits should be displayed (two if you omit the length):

```
msg = String.Format("Total is {0:F3}", 123.45678)        ' => Total is 123.457
```

The scientific (or exponential) format displays numbers as n.nnnnE+eeee, and you can control how many decimal digits are used in the mantissa portion:

```
msg = String.Format("Total is {0:E}", 123456.789)   ' => Total is 1.234568E+005
msg = String.Format("Total is {0:E3}", 123456.789)  ' => Total is 1.235E+005
```

The general format converts to either fixed-point or exponential format, depending on which format delivers the most compact result:

```
msg = String.Format("Total is {0:G}", 123456)   ' => Total is 123456
msg = String.Format("Total is {0:G4}", 123456)  ' => Total is 1235E5
```

The percent format converts a number to a percentage with two decimal digits by default, using the format specified for the current culture:

```
msg = String.Format("Percentage is {0:P}", 0.123)    ' => Total is 12.30%
```

The round-trip format converts a number to a string containing all significant digits so that the string can be converted back to a number later without any loss of precision:

```
' The number of digits you pass after the "R" character is ignored.
msg = String.Format("Value of PI is {0:R}", Math.PI)
    ' => Value of PI is 3.1415926535897931
```

Finally, the hexadecimal format converts numbers to hexadecimal strings. If you specify a length, the number is padded with leading zeros if necessary:

```
msg = String.Format("Total is {0:X8}", 65535)    ' => Total is 0000FFFF
```

You can also build custom format strings by using a few special characters, whose meaning is summarized in Table 7-2. Here are a few examples:

```
msg = String.Format("Total is {0:##,###.00}", 1234.567)    ' => Total is 1,234.57
msg = String.Format("Percentage is {0:##.000%}", .3456)    ' => Percentage is 34.560%

' An example of prescaler
msg = String.Format("Length in {0:###,.00 }", 12344)       ' => Total is 12.34
```

```
' Two examples of exponential format
msg = String.Format("Total is {0:#.#####E+00}", 1234567) ' => Total is 1.23457E+06
msg = String.Format("Total is {0:#.#####E0}", 1234567)   ' => Total is 1.23457E6

' Two examples with separate sections
msg = String.Format("Total is {0:##;<##>}", -123)        ' => Total is <123>
msg = String.Format("Total is {0:#;(#);zero}", 1234567)  ' => Total is 1234567
```

You can also use two or three sections in some cases to avoid If or Select Case logic. For example, you can replace the following code:

```
If n1 > n2 Then
    msg = "n1 is greater than n2"
ElseIf n1 < n2 Then
    msg = "n1 is less than n2"
Else
    msg = "n1 is equal to n2"
End If
```

with the more concise but somewhat more cryptic code:

```
msg = String.Format("n1 is {0:greater than;less than;equal to} n2", n1 - n2)
```

Table 7-2 Special Formatting Characters in Custom Formatting Strings

Format	Description
#	Placeholder for a digit or a space.
0	Placeholder for a digit or a zero.
.	Decimal separator.
,	Thousands separator; if used immediately before the decimal separator, it works as a prescaler. (For each comma in this position, the value is divided by 1,000 before formatting.)
%	Displays the number as a percentage value.
E+000	Displays the number in exponential format, that is, with an E followed by the sign of the exponent, and then a number of exponent digits equal to the number of zeros after the plus sign.
E-000	Like the previous exponent symbol, but the exponent sign is displayed only if negative.
;	Section separator. The format string can contain one, two, or three sections. If there are two sections, the first applies to positive and zero values, and the second applies to negative values. If there are three sections, they are used for positive, negative, and zero values, respectively.
\char	Escape character, to insert characters that otherwise would be taken as special characters (for example, \; to insert a semicolon and \\ to insert a backslash).
'...' "..."	A group of literal characters. You can add a sequence of literal characters by enclosing them in single or double quotes.
other	Any other character is taken literally and inserted in the result string as is.

Formatting Date Values

The String.Format method also supports date and time values with both standard and custom formats. Table 7-3 summarizes all the standard date and time formats and makes it easy to find the format you're looking for at a glance.

```
msg = String.Format("Current Date Time is {0:f}", Now())
    ' => Current Date Time is Sunday, January 06, 2002 3:54 PM
```

If you can't find a standard date and time format that suits your needs, you can create a custom format by putting together the special characters listed in Table 7-4:

```
msg = String.Format("Current year is {0:yyyy}", Now())  ' => Current year is 2002
```

The / and : formatting characters are particularly elusive because they're replaced by the default date and time separator defined for the current locale. In some cases—most notably when formatting dates for an SQL SELECT or INSERT command—you want to be sure that a given separator is used on all occasions. In this case, you must use the backslash escape character to force a specific separator:

```
' Format a date in the format mm/dd/yyyy, regardless of current locale.
msg = String.Format("{0:MM\/dd\/yyyy}", Now())   ' => 01/06/2002
```

Table 7-3   Standard Formats for Date and Time Values

Format	Description	Pattern	Example
d	ShortDatePattern	MM/dd/yyyy	1/6/2002
D	LongDatePattern	dddd, MMMM dd, yyyy	Sunday, January 06, 2002
f	full date and time (long date and short time)	dddd, MMMM dd, yyyy HH:mm	Sunday, January 06, 2002 3:54 PM
F	FullDateTimePattern (long date and long time)	dddd, MMMM dd, yyyy HH:mm:ss	Sunday, January 06, 2003 3:54:20 PM
g	general (short date and short time)	MM/dd/yyyy HH:mm	1/6/2002 3:54 PM
G	General (short date and long time)	MM/dd/yyyy HH:mm:ss	1/6/2002 3:54:20 PM
M,m	MonthDayPattern	MMMM dd	January 06
Y,y	YearMonthPattern	MMMM, yyyy	January, 2002
t	ShortTimePattern	HH:mm	3:54 PM
T	LongTimePattern	HH:mm:ss	3:54:20 PM
s	SortableDateTime Pattern (conforms to ISO 8601) using current culture	yyyy-MM-dd HH:mm:ss	2002-01-06T15:54:20

Table 7-3   Standard Formats for Date and Time Values *(continued)*

Format	Description	Pattern	Example
u*	UniversalSortable DateTime-Pattern (conforms to ISO 8601), unaffected by current culture	yyyy-MM-dd HH:mm:ss	2002-01-06 20:54:20Z
U*	UniversalSortable DateTime-Pattern	dddd, MMMM dd, yyyy HH:mm:ss	Sunday, January 06, 2002 5:54:20 PM
R,r*	RFC1123Pattern	ddd, dd MMM yyyy HH':'mm':'ss 'GMT'	Sun, 06 Jan 2002 15:54:20 GMT

* Notice that formats U, u, R, and r use Universal (Greenwich) Time, regardless of the local time zone, so example values for these formats are 5 hours ahead of example values for other formats (which assume local time to be U.S. Eastern time). The Pattern column specifies the corresponding custom format string made up of the characters listed in Table 7-4.

Table 7-4   Character Sequences That Can Be Used in Custom Date and Time Formats

Format	Description
d	Day of month (one or two digits as required)
dd	Day of month (always two digits, with a leading zero if required)
ddd	Day of week (three-character abbreviation)
dddd	Day of week (full name)
M	Month number (one or two digits as required)
MM	Month number (always two digits, with a leading zero if required)
MMM	Month name (three-character abbreviation)
MMMM	Month name (full name)
y	Year (last one or two digits, no leading zero)
yy	Year (last two digits)
yyyy	Year (four digits)
H	Hour in 24-hour format (one or two digits as required)
HH	Hour in 24-hour format (always two digits, with a leading zero if required)
h	Hour in 12-hour format (one or two digits as required)
hh	Hour in 12-hour format
m	Minutes (one or two digits as required)
mm	Minutes (always two digits, with a leading zero if required)
s	Seconds (one or two digits as required)
ss	Seconds

Table 7-4   Character Sequences That Can Be Used in Custom Date and Time Formats *(continued)*

Format	Description
t	The first character in the AM/PM designator
f	Second fractions, represented in one digit. (ff means second fractions in two digits, fff in three digits, and so on up to 7 fs in a row.)
tt	The AM/PM designator
z	Time zone offset, hour only (one or two digits as required)
zz	Time zone offset, hour only (always two digits, with a leading zero if required)
zzz	Time zone offset, hour and minute (hour and minute values always have two digits, with a leading zero if required)
/	Default date separator
:	Default time separator
\char	Escape character, to include literal characters that would be otherwise considered special characters
%format	Includes a predefined date/time format in the result string.
'...' "..."	A group of literal characters. You can add a sequence of literal characters by enclosing them in single or double quotes.
other	Any other character is taken literally and inserted in the result string as-is.

> **See Also**   Read the document "Improved Custom Formatting.doc" on the companion CD to learn how you can use the IFormattable, IFormatProvider, and ICustomFormatter interfaces to extend your classes with better formatting support.

The Char Type

The Char class represents a single character. There isn't much to say about this data type, other than that it exposes a number of useful shared methods that let you test a single character according to several criteria. All these methods are overloaded and take either a single Char or a String plus an index in the string. For example, you check whether a character is a digit as follows:

```
' Check an individual Char value.
Console.WriteLine(Char.IsDigit("1"c))          ' => True
' Check the nth character in a string.
Console.WriteLine(Char.IsDigit("A123", 0))     ' => False
```

This is the list of the most useful static methods that test single characters: IsControl, IsDigit, IsLetter, IsLetterOrDigit, IsLower, IsNumber, IsPunctuation, IsSeparator, IsSymbol, IsUpper, and IsWhiteSpace.

The Char class doesn't directly expose the methods to convert a character into its Unicode value and back. If you don't want to use the Asc, AscW, Chr, and ChrW methods in a Microsoft.VisualBasic.Strings module, you can resort to a pair of shared methods in the System.Convert type:

```
' Get the Unicode value of a character (same as Asc, AscW).
Dim uni As Short = Convert.ToInt16("A")
' Convert back to a character.
Dim ch As Char = Convert.ToChar(uni)
```

I cover the Convert class in more detail later in this chapter.

The StringBuilder Type

As you might remember, a String object is immutable, and its value never changes after the string has been created. This means that anytime you apply a method that changes its value, you're actually creating a new String object. For example, the following statement:

```
S = S.Insert(3, "1234")
```

doesn't modify the original string in memory. Instead, the Insert method creates a new String object, which is then assigned to the S object variable. The original string object in memory is eventually reclaimed during the next garbage collection unless another variable points to it, as is often the case with strings in the intern pool. The superior memory allocation scheme of .NET ensures that this mechanism adds a relatively low overhead; nevertheless, too many allocate and release operations can degrade your application's performance. The System.Text.StringBuilder object offers a solution to this problem.

You can think of a StringBuilder object as a buffer that can contain a string with the ability to grow from zero characters to the buffer's current capacity. Until you exceed that capacity, the string is assembled in the buffer and no memory is allocated or released. If the string becomes longer than the current capacity, the StringBuilder object transparently creates a larger buffer. The default buffer initially contains 16 characters, but you can change this by assigning a different capacity in the StringBuilder constructor or by assigning a value to the Capacity property:

```
' Create a StringBuilder object with initial capacity of 1000 characters.
Dim sb As New System.Text.StringBuilder(1000)
```

You can process the string held in the StringBuilder object with several methods, most of which have the same name as and work similarly to methods exposed by the String class—for example, the Insert, Remove, and Replace methods. The most common way to build a string inside a StringBuilder object is by means of its Append method, which takes an argument of any type and appends it to the current internal string:

```
' Create a comma-delimited list of the first 100 integers.
For n As Integer = 1 To 100
    ' Note that two Append methods are faster than a single Append,
    ' whose argument is the concatenation of N and ",".
    sb.Append(n)
    sb.Append(",")
Next
' Insert a string at the beginning of the buffer.
sb.Insert(0, "List of numbers: ")
Console.WriteLine(sb)    ' => List of numbers: 1,2,3,4,5,6,...
```

There's also an AppendFormat method, which lets you specify a format string, much like the String.Format method. The Length property returns the current length of the internal string:

```
' Continuing previous example...
Console.WriteLine("Length is " & sb.Length.ToString)    ' => 309
```

The following procedure compares how quickly the String and StringBuilder classes perform a large number of string concatenations:

```
    Dim s As String
    Const TIMES As Integer = 10000

    Dim dt As DateTime = Date.Now
    For i As Integer = 1 To TIMES
        s &= CStr(i) & ","
    Next
    Console.WriteLine("Regular string: {0} secs",  Now.Subtract(dt))

    dt = Date.Now
    Dim sb As New System.Text.StringBuilder(TIMES * 4)
    For i As Integer = 1 To TIMES
        sb.Append(CStr(i))
        sb.Append(",")
    Next
    Console.WriteLine("StringBuilder: {0} secs.", Now.Subtract(dt))
```

The results of this benchmark can be really astonishing as they show that the String-Builder object can be more than 100 times faster than the regular String class. The actual ratio depends on how many iterations you have and how long the strings are.

Numeric Types

I illustrated most of the useful operations you can perform on numbers and dates in Chapter 3. In this section, I'll complete the discussion by showing you a few methods exposed by the basic numeric and date classes, particularly those related to parsing and formatting.

As you know, Short, Integer, and Long types are nothing but .NET Int16, Int32, and Int64 classes with Visual Basic-ish names. By recognizing their class nature, you can exploit these types better; for example, by using their methods and properties. This section applies to all the numeric classes in the .NET Framework, such as Boolean, Byte, Short (Int16), Integer (Int32), Long (Int64), Single, Double, and Decimal.

Properties and Methods

All numeric types—and all .NET classes, for that matter—expose the ToString method, which converts their numeric value to a string. This method is especially useful when you're appending the number value to another string:

```
Dim myValue As Double = 123.45
Dim res As String = "The final value is " & myValue.ToString()
```

The ToString method is culture aware. For example, it uses a comma as a decimal separator if the current culture is Italian or German. Numeric types overload the ToString method to take either a format string or a custom formatter object. (For more detail, refer to the section "Formatting Numeric Values" earlier in this chapter.)

```
' Convert an integer to hexadecimal.
Console.WriteLine(1234.ToString("X"))        ' => 4D2
' Display PI with 6 digits (in all).
Dim d As Double = Math.PI
Console.WriteLine(d.ToString("G6"))          ' => 3.14159
```

As a rule, the ToString method is more efficient than the Format method and should be preferred if its formatting features are sufficient for your purposes.

You can use the CompareTo method to compare a number with another numeric value of the same type. This method returns 1, 0, or -1, depending on whether the current instance is greater than, equal to, or less than the value passed as an argument:

```
Dim sngValue As Single = 1.23
' Compare the Single variable sngValue with 1.
' Note that you must force the argument to Single.
Select Case sngValue.CompareTo(CSng(1))
    Case 1
        Console.WriteLine("sngValue is > 1")
    Case 0
        Console.WriteLine("sngValue is = 1")
    Case -1
        Console.WriteLine("sngValue is < 1")
End Select
```

The argument must be the same type as the value you're applying the CompareTo method to, so you must convert it if necessary. You can use a conversion function, such as the CSng function in the preceding code, or append a conversion character, such as ! for Single, I for Integer, and so on:

```
' ...(Another way to write the previous code snippet)...
Select Case sngValue.CompareTo(1!)
    ⋮
```

All the numeric classes expose the MinValue and MaxValue shared properties, which return the smallest and greatest value that you can express with the corresponding type:

```
' Display the greatest value you can store in a Double variable.
Console.WriteLine(Double.MaxValue)      ' => 1.79769313486232E+308
```

The numeric classes that support floating-point values—namely Single and Double classes—expose a few additional shared read-only properties. The Epsilon property returns the smallest positive (nonzero) number that can be stored in a variable of that type:

```
Console.WriteLine(Single.Epsilon)       ' => 1.401298E-45
Console.WriteLine(Double.Epsilon)       ' => 4.94065645841247E-324
```

The NegativeInfinity and PositiveInfinity properties return a constant that represents an infinite value, whereas the NaN property returns a constant that represents the Not-a-Number value (NaN is the value you obtain, for example, when evaluating the square root of a negative number). In some cases, you can use infinite values in expressions:

```
' Any number divided by infinity gives 0.
Console.WriteLine(1 / Double.PositiveInfinity)      ' => 0
```

The Single and Double classes also expose some shared methods that let you test whether they contain special values, such as IsInfinity, IsNegativeInfinity, IsPositiveInfinity, and IsNaN.

Formatting Numbers

All the numeric classes support an overloaded form of the ToString method that lets you apply a format string:

```
Dim intValue As Integer = 12345
Console.WriteLine(intValue.ToString("##,##0.00", Nothing))  ' => 12,345.00
```

The method uses the current locale to interpret the formatting string. For example, in the preceding code it uses the comma as the thousands separator and the period as the decimal separator if running on a U.S. system, but reverses the two separators on an Italian system.

Another overloaded ToString method takes an IFormatProvider object to format the current value. In this section, I'll show you how you can take advantage of one of the several .NET objects that implement this interface, the NumberFormatInfo object.

The NumberFormatInfo class exposes many properties that determine how a numeric value is formatted, such as NumberDecimalSeparator (the decimal separator character), NumberGroupSeparator (the thousands separator character), NumberDecimalDigits (number of decimal digits), CurrencySymbol (the character used for currency), and many others. The simplest way to create a valid NumberFormatInfo object is by means of the CurrentInfo shared method of the NumberFormatInfo class; the returned value is a read-only NumberFormatInfo object based on the current locale:

```
' All the code samples in this section assume this Imports statement.
Imports System.Globalization
  ⋮
Dim nfi As NumberFormatInfo = NumberFormatInfo.CurrentInfo
```

(You can also use the InvariantInfo property, which returns a default read-only NumberFormatInfo object that is culturally independent.)

The problem with the preceding code is that the returned NumberFormatInfo object is read-only, so you can't modify any of its properties. This object is therefore virtually useless because the ToString method implicitly uses the current locale anyway when formatting a value. The solution is to create a clone of the default NumberFormatInfo object and then modify its properties, as in the following snippet:

```
' Format a number with current locale formatting options, but
' use a comma for the decimal separator and a space for the thousands
' separator. (You need DirectCast because the Clone method returns an Object.)
Dim nfi As NumberFormatInfo = _
    DirectCast(NumberFormatInfo.CurrentInfo.Clone, NumberFormatInfo)
' The nfi object is a read-write object, so you can change its properties.
nfi.NumberDecimalSeparator = ","
nfi.NumberGroupSeparator = " "
' You can now format a value with the custom NumberFormatInfo object.
Dim sngValue As Single = 12345.5
Console.WriteLine(sngValue.ToString("#,##0.00", nfi)) ' => 12 345,50
```

For the complete list of NumberFormatInfo properties and methods, see the MSDN documentation.

Parsing Strings into Numbers

All numeric types support the Parse shared method, which parses the string passed as an argument and returns the corresponding numeric value. The simplest form of the Parse method takes one string argument:

```
' Next line assigns 1234 to the variable.
Dim shoValue As Short = Short.Parse("1234")
```

The second overloaded form of the Parse method takes a NumberStyle enumerated value as its second argument. NumberStyle is a bit-coded value that specifies which portions of the number are allowed in the string being parsed. Valid NumberStyle values are AllowLeadingWhite (1), AllowTrailingWhite (2), AllowLeadingSign (4), AllowTrailingSign (8), AllowParentheses (16), AllowDecimalPoint (32), AllowThousand (64), AllowExponent (128), AllowCurrencySymbol (256), and AllowHexSpecifier (512). You can specify which portions of the strings are valid by using the OR operator on these values, or you can use some other predefined compound values, such as Any (511, allows everything), Integer (7, allows trailing sign and leading/trailing white), Number (111, like Integer but allows thousands separator and decimal point), Float (167, like Integer but allows decimal separator and exponent), and Currency (383, allows everything except exponent).

The following example extracts a Double from a string and recognizes white spaces and all the supported formats:

```
Dim dblValue As Double = Double.Parse(" 1,234.56E6  ", NumberStyles.Any)
    ' dblValue is assigned the value 1234560000.
```

You can be more specific about what is valid and what isn't:

```
Dim style As NumberStyles = NumberStyles.AllowDecimalPoint _
    Or NumberStyles.AllowLeadingSign
' This works and assigns -123.45 to sngValue.
Dim sngValue As Single = Single.Parse("-123.45", style)
' This throws a FormatException because of the thousands separator.
sngValue = Single.Parse("12,345.67", style)
```

The Convert Class

The System.Convert class exposes several shared methods that help in converting to and from the many data types available in .NET. In their simplest form, these methods can convert any base type to another type and are therefore equivalent to the conversion functions that Visual Basic offers:

```
' Convert the string "123.45" to a Double (same as CDbl function).
Dim dblValue As Double = Convert.ToDouble("123.45")
```

The Convert class exposes many To*xxxx* methods, one for each base type: ToBoolean, ToByte, ToChar, ToDateTime, ToDecimal, ToDouble, ToInt16, ToInt32, ToInt64, ToSingle, and ToString (plus a few non-CLS-compliant methods: ToSByte, ToUInt16, ToUInt32, and ToUInt64).

You see the added flexibility of the Convert class when you pass an IFormatProvider object as a second argument to a To*xxxx* method to describe how the value being converted is formatted. You can author a class that works as a formatter, or you can use a .NET object that implements IFormatProvider, such as a NumberFormatInfo or a DateTimeFormatInfo object:

```
Dim nfi As NumberFormatInfo = _
    CType(NumberFormatInfo.CurrentInfo.Clone, NumberFormatInfo)
```

```
' Use a period to group digits, and a comma as a decimal separator.
nfi.NumberGroupSeparator = "."
nfi.NumberDecimalSeparator = ","
' Parse a string using the specified separators.
Dim dblValue As Double = Convert.ToDouble("12.345,56", nfi)
Console.WriteLine(dblValue)     ' => 12345.56
```

The Convert class exposes two methods that make conversions to and from Base64-encoded strings a breeze. (This is the format used for MIME e-mail attachments.) The ToBase64String method takes an array of bytes and encodes it as a Base64 string. The FromBase64String method does the conversion in the opposite direction:

```
' An array of 16 bytes (two identical sequences of 8 bytes)
Dim b() As Byte = {12, 45, 213, 88, 11, 220, 34, 0, _
    12, 45, 213, 88, 11, 220, 34, 0}
' Convert it to a Base64 string.
Dim s64 As String = Convert.ToBase64String(b)
Console.WriteLine(s64)
' Convert it back to an array of bytes, and display it.
Dim b2() As Byte = Convert.FromBase64String(s64)
For i As Integer = 0 To b.GetUpperBound(0)
    Console.Write(b2(i).ToString & " ")
Next
```

In addition, the Convert class exposes the ToBase64CharArray and FromBase64CharArray methods, which convert a Byte array to and from a Char array instead of a String. Finally, the class also exposes a generic ChangeType method that can convert (or at least, attempt to convert) a value to any other type. You must use the Visual Basic GetType operator to create the System.Type object to pass in the method's second argument:

```
' Convert a value to Double.
Console.WriteLine(Convert.ChangeType(value, GetType(Double)))
```

Random Number Generators

Visual Basic .NET still supports the time-honored Randomize statement and Rnd function for backward compatibility, but serious .NET developers should use the System.Random class instead. You can set the seed for random number generation in this class's constructor method:

```
' The argument must be a 32-bit integer.
Dim rand As New Random(12345)
```

When you pass a given seed number, you always get the same random sequence. To get different sequences each time you run the application, you can have the seed depend on the current time. In Visual Basic 6, you use the following statement:

```
Randomize Timer
```

This is the closest Visual Basic .NET statement that delivers the same result:

```
' You need these conversions because the Ticks property
' returns a 64-bit value that must be truncated to a 32-bit integer.
Dim rand As New Random(CInt(Date.Now.Ticks And Integer.MaxValue))
```

Once you have an initialized Random object, you can extract random positive 32-bit integer values each time you query its Next method:

```
For i As Integer = 1 To 10
    Console.WriteLine(rand.Next)
Next
```

You can also pass one or two arguments to keep the return value in the desired range:

```
' Get a value in the range 0 to 1000.
Dim intValue As Integer = rand.Next(1000)
' Get a value in the range 100 to 1000.
intValue = rand.Next(100, 1000)
```

The NextDouble method is similar to the old Rnd function in that it returns a random floating-point number between 0 and 1:

```
Dim dblValue As Double = rand.NextDouble()
```

Finally, you can fill a Byte array with random values with the NextBytes method:

```
' Get an array of 100 random byte values.
Dim buffer(100) As Byte
rand.NextBytes(buffer)
```

The DateTime Type

System.DateTime is the main .NET class for working with date and time values. Not only does it offer a place to store data values, it also exposes many useful methods that virtually replace all the Visual Basic 6 date and time functions. For backward compatibility's sake, Visual Basic .NET lets you use the Date type as a synonym for the System.DateTime type. In this section, I'll use the Date class name, but keep in mind that you can always replace it with System.DateTime or just DateTime (because of the projectwide Imports System statement).

You can initialize a Date value in a number of ways:

```
' Create a Date value by providing year, month, and day values.
Dim dt1 As Date = New Date(2002, 1, 6)          ' January 6, 2002

' Provide also hour, minute, and second values.
Dim dt2 As Date = New Date(2002, 1, 6, 18, 30, 20) ' January 6, 2002 6:30:20 PM

' Add millisecond value (half a second in this example).
Dim dt3 As Date = New Date(2002, 1, 6, 18, 30, 20, 500)
```

```
' Create a time value from ticks (10 million ticks = 1 second).
Dim ticks As Long = 20000000                         ' 2 seconds
' This is considered the time elapsed from Jan. 1, 2001.
Dim dt4 As Date = New Date(ticks)                    ' 1/1/0001 12:00:02 AM
```

Because Date and System.DateTime are perfect synonyms, the first Dim statement in the preceding code could have been written in one of the following ways:

```
Dim dt1 As Date = New DateTime(2002, 1, 6)
Dim dt2 As DateTime = New Date(2002, 1, 6)
Dim dt3 As DateTime = New DateTime(2002, 1, 6)
```

You can use the Now and Today shared properties:

```
' The Now property returns the system date and time.
Dim dt5 As Date = Date.Now        ' For example, January 06, 2002 3:54:20 PM
' The Today property returns the system date only.
Dim dt6 As Date = Date.Today      ' For example, January 06, 2002 12:00:00 AM
```

Once you have an initialized Date value, you can retrieve individual portions by using one of its read-only properties, namely Date (the date portion), TimeOfDay (the time portion), Year, Month, Day, DayOfYear, DayOfWeek, Hour, Minute, Second, Millisecond, and Ticks:

```
' Is today the first day of the current month?
If Date.Today.Day = 1 Then Console.WriteLine("First day of month")
' How many days have passed since January 1?
Console.WriteLine(Date.Today.DayOfYear)
' Get current time - note that ticks are included.
Console.WriteLine(Date.Now.TimeOfDay)      ' => 10:39:28.3063680
```

The TimeOfDay property is peculiar in that it returns a TimeSpan object, which represents a difference between dates. While this class is distinct from the Date class, it shares many of its properties and methods and nearly always works together with Date values, as you'll see shortly.

Adding and Subtracting Dates

The Date class exposes several instance methods that let you add and subtract a number of years, months, days, hours, minutes, or seconds to or from a Date value. The names of these methods leave no doubt about their function: AddYears, AddMonths, AddDays, AddHours, AddMinutes, AddSeconds, AddMilliseconds, AddTicks. You can add an integer value when you're using AddYears and AddMonths and a decimal value in all other cases. In all cases, you can pass a negative argument to subtract rather than add a value:

```
' Tomorrow's date
Console.WriteLine(Date.Today.AddDays(1))
' Yesterday's date
Console.WriteLine(Date.Today.AddDays(-1))
' What time will it be 2 hours and 30 minutes from now?
Console.WriteLine(Date.Now.AddHours(2.5))
```

```
' A CPU-intensive way to pause for 5 seconds.
Dim endTime As Date = Date.Now.AddSeconds(5)
Do: Loop Until Date.Now > endTime
```

A generic Add method takes a TimeSpan object as an argument. Before you can use it, you must learn to create a TimeSpan object, choosing one of its overloaded constructor methods:

```
' One Long value is interpreted as a Ticks value.
Dim ts1 As TimeSpan = New TimeSpan(13500000)          ' 1.35 seconds
' Three Integer values are interpreted as hours, minutes, seconds.
Dim ts2 As TimeSpan = New TimeSpan(0, 32, 20)          ' 32 minutes, 20 seconds
' Four Integer values are interpreted as days, hours, minutes, seconds.
Dim ts3 As TimeSpan = New TimeSpan(1, 12, 0, 0)        ' 1 day and a half
' (Note that arguments aren't checked for out-of-range errors; therefore,
'  the next statement delivers the same result as the previous one.)
Dim ts4 As TimeSpan = New TimeSpan(0, 36, 0, 0)        ' 1 day and a half
' A fifth argument is interpreted as a millisecond value.
Dim ts5 As TimeSpan = New TimeSpan(0, 0, 1, 30, 500) ' 90 seconds and a half
```

Now you're ready to add an arbitrary date or time interval to a Date value:

```
' What will be the time 2 days, 10 hours, and 30 minutes from now?
Console.WriteLine(Date.Now.Add(New TimeSpan(2, 10, 30, 0)))
```

The Date class also exposes a Subtract instance method that works in a similar way:

```
' What was the time 1 day, 12 hours, and 20 minutes ago?
Console.WriteLine(Date.Now.Subtract(New TimeSpan(1, 12, 20, 0)))
```

The Subtract method is overloaded to take another Date object as an argument, in which case it returns the TimeSpan object that represents the difference between the two dates:

```
' How many days, hours, minutes, and seconds have elapsed
' since the beginning of the third millennium?
Dim startDate As New Date(2001, 1, 1)
Dim ts As TimeSpan = Date.Now.Subtract(startDate)
' (I am running this code on July 26, 2001, late morning.)
Console.WriteLine(ts)                ' => 206.11:11:35.4627792
```

The Subtract method offers a simple way to benchmark a piece of code, and I have used this technique elsewhere in this book:

```
Dim startTime As Date = Now()
⋮
' ...(Place here the code to be benchmarked)...
⋮
Console.WriteLine("{0} seconds.", Now.Subtract(startTime))
```

Once you have a TimeSpan object, you can extract the information buried in it by using one of its many properties, whose names are self-explanatory: Days, Hours, Minutes, Seconds, Milliseconds, Ticks, TotalDays, TotalHours, TotalMinutes, TotalSeconds, and TotalMilliseconds. The TimeSpan class also exposes methods such as Add, Subtract, Negate, and CompareTo.

You don't need the Subtract method if you simply have to determine whether a Date value is greater or less than another Date value because the CompareTo method is more appropriate for this job:

```
' Is current date later than October 30, 2001?
Select Case Date.Today.CompareTo(New Date(2001, 10, 30))
    Case 1    ' Later than Oct. 30, 2001
    Case -1   ' Earlier than Oct. 30, 2001
    Case 0    ' Today is Oct. 30, 2001.
End Select
```

Of course you can also use comparison operators if you don't need three-state logic:

```
If Date.Today > New Date(2001, 10, 30) Then ...
```

Finally, the Date class exposes two shared methods that can be handy in many applications:

```
' Test for a leap year.
Console.WriteLine(Date.IsLeapYear(2000))          ' => True
' Retrieve the number of days in a given month.
Console.WriteLine(Date.DaysInMonth(2000, 2))      ' => 29
```

Formatting Dates

The Date type overrides the ToString method to provide a compact representation of the date and time value it contains. (This is the format implicitly used by Console.Write and similar methods.) You can format a Date value in other ways by using some peculiar methods that only this type exposes:

```
' This is January 6, 2002 6:30:20.500 PM - U.S. Eastern Time.
Dim dt As Date = New Date(2002, 1, 6, 18, 30, 20, 500)

Console.WriteLine(dt.ToShortDateString)   ' => 01/06/2002
Console.WriteLine(dt.ToLongDateString)    ' => Sunday, January 06, 2002
Console.WriteLine(dt.ToShortTimeString)   ' => 6:30 PM
Console.WriteLine(dt.ToLongTimeString)    ' => 6:30:20 PM
Console.WriteLine(dt.ToFileTime)          ' => 126548334205000000
Console.WriteLine(dt.ToOADate)            ' => 37262.7710706019
Console.WriteLine(dt.ToUniversalTime)     ' => 1/6/2002 11:30:20 PM
Console.WriteLine(dt.ToLocalTime)         ' => 1/6/2002 1:30:20 PM
```

A few of these formats might require additional explanation:

■ The ToFileTime method returns an unsigned 8-byte value representing the date and time as the number of 100-nanosecond intervals that have elapsed since 1/1/1601 12:00 AM.

■ The ToOADate method converts to an OLE Automation–compatible value. (This is a Double value similar to the Date values used in Visual Basic 6.)

- The ToUniversalTime method considers the Date value a local time and converts it to Coordinated Universal Time (UTC).

- The ToLocalTime method considers the Date value a UTC value and converts it to a local time.

Parsing Dates

The operation complementary to date formatting is date parsing. The Date class provides a Parse shared method for parsing jobs of any degree of complexity:

```
Dim dt As Date = Date.Parse("2002/1/6 12:30:20")
```

The flexibility of this method becomes apparent when you pass an IFormatProvider object as a second argument to it—for example, the DateTimeFormatInfo object. This object is conceptually similar to the NumberFormatInfo object described earlier in this chapter (see the "Formatting Numbers" section). This object, however, holds information about separators and formats allowed in date and time values:

```
' Get a writable copy of the current locale's DateTimeFormatInfo object.
Dim dtfi As DateTimeFormatInfo
dtfi = CType(DateTimeFormatInfo.CurrentInfo.Clone, DateTimeFormatInfo)
' Change date and time separators.
dtfi.DateSeparator = "-"
dtfi.TimeSeparator = "."
' Now we're ready to parse a date formatted in a nonstandard way.
Dim dt2 As Date = Date.Parse("2002-1-6 12.30.20", dtfi)
```

Many non-U.S. developers will appreciate the ability to parse dates in formats other than month/day/year. In this case, you have to assign a correctly formatted pattern to the DateTimeFormatInfo object's ShortDatePattern, LongDatePattern, ShortTimePattern, LongTimePattern, or FullDateTimePattern property before doing the parse:

```
' Prepare to parse (dd/mm/yy) dates, in short or long format.
dtfi.ShortDatePattern = "d/M/yyyy"
dtfi.LongDatePattern = "dddd, dd MMMM, yyyy"

' Both dt3 and dt4 are assigned the date "January 6, 2002".
Dim dt3 As Date = Date.Parse("6-1-2002 12.30.44", dtfi)
Dim dt4 As Date = Date.Parse("Sunday, 6 January, 2002", dtfi)
```

You can use the DateTimeFormatInfo object to retrieve standard or abbreviated names for weekdays and months, according to the current locale or any locale:

```
' Display the abbreviated names of months.
 For Each s As String In DateTimeFormatInfo.CurrentInfo.AbbreviatedMonthNames
    Console.WriteLine(s)
Next
```

Even more interesting, you can set weekday and month names with arbitrary strings if you have a writable DateTimeFormatInfo object, and then you can use the object to parse a date written in any language, including invented ones. (Yes, including Klingon!)

Another way to parse strings in formats other than month/day/year is to use the Parse-Exact shared method. In this case, you pass the format string as the second argument, and you can pass Nothing to the third argument if you don't need a DateTimeFormat-Info object to further qualify the string being parsed:

```
' dt5 is assigned the date "January 6, 2002".
Dim dt5 As Date = Date.ParseExact("6-1-2002", "d-M-yyyy", Nothing)
```

Finally, the Date class exposes two shared methods, FromFileTime and FromOADate, for the less common operations of parsing from a date, formatted as a file time, or from an OLE Automation date value.

Working with Time Zones

The .NET Framework supports time-zone information via the System.TimeZone object, which you can use to retrieve information about the time zone set in Windows regional settings:

```
' Get the TimeZone object for the current time zone.
Dim tz As TimeZone = TimeZone.CurrentTimeZone
' Display name of time zone, without and with daylight saving time.
' (I got these results by running this code in Italy.)
Console.WriteLine(tz.StandardName)   ' => W. Europe Standard Time
Console.WriteLine(tz.DaylightName)   ' => W. Europe Daylight Time
```

The most interesting piece of information here is the offset from Universal time (UTC), which you retrieve by means of the GetUTCOffset method. You must pass a date argument to this method because the offset depends on whether daylight-saving time is in effect. The returned value is in ticks:

```
' Display the time offset of W. Europe time zone in March 2001,
' when no daylight saving time is active.
Console.WriteLine(tz.GetUTCOffset(New Date(2001, 3, 1)))   ' => 01:00:00
' Display the time offset of W. Europe time zone in July,
' when daylight saving time is active.
Console.WriteLine(tz.GetUTCOffset(New Date(2001, 7, 1)))   ' => 02:00:00
```

The IsDaylightSavingTime method returns True if daylight-saving time is in effect:

```
' No daylight-saving time in March
Console.WriteLine(tz.IsDaylightSavingTime(New Date(2001, 3, 1)))
' => False
```

Finally, you can determine when daylight-saving time starts and ends in a given year by retrieving an array of DaylightTime objects with the TimeZone's GetDaylight-Changes method:

```
' Retrieve the DaylightTime object for year 2001.
Dim dlc As System.Globalization.DaylightTime = tz.GetDaylightChanges(2001)
' Note that you might get different start and end dates if you
```

```
' run this code in a country other than the United States.
Console.WriteLine("Starts at " & dlc.Start)
    ' => Starts at 4/1/2001 2:00:00 AM
Console.WriteLine("Ends at " & dlc.End)
    ' => Ends at 10/28/2001 3:00:00 AM
' Delta returns a TimeSpan object.
Console.WriteLine("Delta is {0} minutes", dlc.Delta.TotalMinutes)
    ' => Delta is 60 minutes.
```

The Guid Type

The System.Guid type exposes several shared and instance methods that can help you work with GUIDs, that is, those 128-bit numbers that serve to uniquely identify elements and that are ubiquitous in Windows programming. The NewGuid shared method is useful for generating a new unique identifier:

```
' Create a new GUID.
Dim guid1 As Guid = Guid.NewGuid
' By definition, you'll surely get a different output here.
Console.WriteLine(guid1.ToString)
    '=> 3f5f1d42-2d92-474d-a2a4-1e707c7e2a37
```

If you already have a GUID—for example, a GUID you have read from a database field—you can initialize a Guid variable by passing the GUID representation as a string or as an array of bytes to the type's constructor:

```
' Initialize from a string.
Dim guid2 As New Guid("45FA3B49-3D66-AB33-BB21-1E3B447A6621")
```

There are only two more things you can do with a Guid object: you can convert it to a Byte array with the ToByteArray method, and you can compare two Guid values for equality using the Equals method (inherited from System.Object):

```
' Convert to an array of bytes.
Dim bytes() As Byte = guid1.ToByteArray
For Each b As Byte In bytes
    Console.Write(b.ToString & " ")
        ' => 239 1 161 57 143 200 172 70 185 64 222 29 59 15 190 205
Next

' Compare two GUIDs.
If Not guid1.Equals(guid2) Then
    Console.WriteLine("GUIDs are different.")
End If
```

Enums

I briefly covered enumerated values in Chapter 2. Now I complete the description of Enum blocks by mentioning all the methods you can apply to them.

Any Enum you define in your application derives from System.Enum, which in turn inherits from System.ValueType. Ultimately, therefore, user-defined Enums are value types, but they are special in that you can't define additional properties, methods, or events. All the methods they expose are inherited from System.Enum. (Notice that it's illegal to explicitly inherit a class from System.Enum in Visual Basic.)

All the examples in this section refer to the following Enum block:

```
' This Enum defines the data type accepted for a
' value entered by the end user.
Enum DataEntry As Integer          ' As Integer is optional.
    IntegerNumber
    FloatingNumber
    CharString
    DateTime
End Enum
```

By default, the first enumerated type is assigned the value 0. You can change this initial value if you want, but you aren't encouraged to do so. In fact, it is advisable that 0 be a valid value for any Enum blocks you define; otherwise, a noninitialized Enum variable will contain an invalid value.

The .NET documentation defines a few guidelines for Enum values:

- Use names without the *Enum* suffix; use singular names for regular Enum types and plural for bit-coded Enum types.

- Use Pascal case for the name of both the Enum and its members. (An exception is constants from the Windows API, which are usually all uppercase.)

- Use Integer unless you need a larger range, which normally happens only if you have a bit-coded Enum with more than 32 possible values.

- Don't use Enums for open sets, that is, sets that you might need to expand in the future (for example, operating system versions).

Displaying and Parsing Enum Values

The Enum class overrides the ToString method to return the value as a readable string format. This method is useful when you want to expose a (nonlocalized) string to the end user:

```
Dim de As DataEntry = DataEntry.DateTime
' Display the numeric value.
Console.WriteLine(de)              ' => 3
' Display the symbolic value.
Console.WriteLine(de.ToString)     ' => DateTime
```

Or you can use the capability to pass a format character to an overloaded version of the ToString method—for example, using the "X" formatting option to display the value in hexadecimal format:

```
' Show the value in hexadecimal format, with 4 digits.
Console.WriteLine(de.ToString("X"))    ' => 0003
```

The opposite of ToString is the Parse shared method, which takes a string and converts it to the corresponding enumerated value:

```
de = DataEntry.Parse(GetType(DataEntry), "CharString"))
Console.WriteLine(de)                   ' => CharString
```

There are two things worth noticing in the preceding code. First, the Parse method takes a Type argument, so you must convert DataEntry to a type with the GetType operator. Second, Parse is a shared method and can be invoked through any Enum object, including DataEntry itself. In some cases, however, you don't have a specific variable to use as a prefix for the Parse method, and you are forced to use Enum as the prefix. Enum is a reserved Visual Basic word, so you must either use its complete System.Enum name or enclose its name between square brackets:

```
' These statements are equivalent to the one in the previous fragment.
Console.WriteLine([Enum].Parse(GetType(DataEntry), "CharString"))
Console.WriteLine(System.Enum.Parse(GetType(DataEntry), "CharString"))
```

Being inherited from the generic Enum class, the Parse method returns a generic object, so you have to set Option Strict to Off or use an explicit cast to assign it to a specific enumerated variable:

```
' You can use the GetType method (inherited from System.Object)
' to get the Type object required by the Parse method.
de = CType([Enum].Parse(de.GetType, "CharString"), DataEntry)
```

The Parse method throws an ArgumentException if the name doesn't correspond to a defined enumerated value. Names are compared in a case-sensitive way, but you can pass a True optional argument if you don't want to take the string case into account:

```
' *** This statement throws an exception.
Console.WriteLine([Enum].Parse(de.GetType, "charstring"))
' This works well because case-insensitive comparison is used.
Console.WriteLine([Enum].Parse(de.GetType, "charstring", True))
```

Other Enum Methods

The GetUnderlyingType shared method returns the base type for an enumerated class:

```
Console.WriteLine([Enum].GetUnderlyingType(de.GetType))    ' => System.Int16
```

The IsDefined method lets you check whether a numeric value is acceptable as an enumerated value of a given class:

```
' NOTE: The IsDefined method requires that the value being checked be
'        the same underlying value as the Enum (Short in this case).
If [Enum].IsDefined(GetType(DataEntry), 3S) Then
    ' 3 is a valid value for the DataEntry class.
    de = CType(3, DataEntry)
End If
```

The IsDefined method is useful because the CType operator doesn't check whether the value being converted is in the valid range for the target enumerated type. In other words, the following statement doesn't throw any exception:

```
' This code produces an invalid result, yet it doesn't throw an exception.
de = CType(123, DataEntry)
```

Another way to check whether a numeric value is acceptable for an Enum object is the GetName method, which returns the name of the enumerated value or returns Nothing if the value is invalid:

```
' GetName doesn't require that the value being converted be
' the same type as the Enum.
If [Enum].GetName(GetType(DataEntry), 3) <> "" Then
    de = CType(3, DataEntry)
End If
```

You can quickly list all the values of an enumerated type with the GetNames and GetValues methods. The former returns a String array holding the individual names (sorted by the corresponding values); the latter returns an Object array that holds the numeric values:

```
' List all the values in DataEntry.
Dim names() As String = [Enum].GetNames(GetType(DataEntry))
Dim values As Array = [Enum].GetValues(GetType(DataEntry))
For i As Integer = 0 To names.Length - 1
    Console.WriteLine("{0} = {1}", names(i), CInt(values.GetValue(i)))
Next
```

Here's the output of the preceding code snippet:

```
IntegerNumber = 0
FloatingNumber = 1
CharString = 2
DateTime = 3
```

Bit-Coded Values

The .NET Framework supports a special Flags attribute that you can use to specify that an Enum object represents a bit-coded value. For example, let's create a new class named ValidDataEntry class, which lets the developer specify two or more valid data types for values entered by an end user:

```
<Flags()> Enum ValidDataEntry As Short
    None = 0                   ' Always define an enum value = 0.
    IntegerNumber = 1
    FloatingNumber = 2
    CharString = 4
    DateTime = 8
End Enum
```

The FlagAttribute class doesn't expose any property, and its constructor takes no arguments: the presence of this attribute is sufficient to label this Enum type as bit coded.

Bit-coded enumerated types behave exactly like regular Enum values except that their ToString method recognizes the Flags attribute. When an enumerated type is composed of two or more flag values, this method returns the list of all the corresponding values, separated by commas:

```
Dim vde As ValidDataEntry
vde = ValidDataEntry.IntegerNumber Or ValidDataEntry.DateTime
Console.WriteLine(vde.ToString)          ' => IntegerNumber, DateTime
```

If no bit is set, the ToString method returns the name of the enumerated value corresponding to the zero value:

```
Dim vde2 As ValidDataEntry
Console.WriteLine(vde2.ToString)     ' => None
```

If the value doesn't correspond to a valid combination of bits, the Format method returns the number unchanged:

```
vde = CType(123, ValidDataEntry)
Console.WriteLine(vde.ToString)      ' => 123
```

The Parse method is also affected by the Flags attribute:

```
vde = CType([Enum].Parse( _
    vde.GetType, "IntegerNumber, FloatingNumber"), ValidDataEntry)
Console.WriteLine(CInt(vde))         ' => 3
```

This chapter concludes the description of .NET basic data types. In the next chapter, you'll read about more complex data structures, such as arrays, collections, and hash tables, and you'll learn how to create your own collection and dictionary classes.

8 Arrays, Lists, and Collections

The .NET Framework doesn't merely include classes for managing system objects, such as files, directories, processes, and threads. It also exposes objects, such as complex data structures (queues, stacks, and hash tables), that help developers solve recurring problems.

Many real-world applications use arrays and collections, and the .NET Framework support for arrays and collection-like objects is really outstanding. It can take a while for you to get familiar with the many possibilities that the .NET runtime offers, but this effort pays off nicely at coding time.

The Array Class

The Array class constructor has a Protected scope, so you can't directly use the New keyword with this class. In practice, this is no problem because you create an array using the standard Visual Basic syntax, and, as you saw in Chapter 2, you can even use initializers:

```
' An array initialized with the powers of 2
Dim intArr() As Integer = {1, 2, 4, 8, 16, 32, 64, 128, 256, 512}
' Noninitialized two-dimensional array
Dim lngArr(10, 20) As Long
' An empty array
Dim dblArr() As Double
```

A variation of this syntax lets you create an array and initialize it on the fly, which is sometimes useful for passing an argument or assigning a property that takes an array without having to create a temporary array:

```
' Create a temporary array.
Dim tmp() As Integer = {2, 5, 9, 13}
' The obj.ValueArray property takes an array of Integer.
obj.ValueArray = tmp
' Clear the temporary variable.
tmp = Nothing
```

The ability to create and initialize an array in a single statement makes the code more concise, even though the syntax you need isn't exactly intuitive:

```
obj.ValueArray = New Integer() {2, 5, 9, 13}
```

As in Visual Basic 6, you get an error if you access an empty array, which is an array that has no elements. Because the array is an object, you can test it using a plain Is operator and use ReDim on the array if necessary:

```
If dblArr Is Nothing Then
    ReDim dblArr(100)                   ' Note: no As clause in ReDims
End If
```

You can query an array for its rank (that is, the number of dimensions) by using its Rank property, and you can query the total number of its elements by means of its Length property:

```
' ...(Continuing the first example in this chapter)...
Console.WriteLine(lngArr.Rank)     ' => 2
' lngArr has 11*21 elements.
Console.WriteLine(lngArr.Length)     ' => 231
```

Starting with version 1.1, the .NET Framework supports 64-bit array indexes, so an array index can also be a Long. Additionally, the Array class has been expanded with a LongLength property that returns the number of elements as a Long value.

The GetLength method returns the number of elements along a given dimension, whereas GetLowerBound and GetUpperBound return the lowest and highest index along the specified dimension. Unlike values returned by the LBound and UBound functions, the dimension number is 0-based, not 1-based:

```
' ...(Continuing previous example)...
Console.WriteLine(lngArr.GetLength(0))        ' => 11
Console.WriteLine(lngArr.GetLowerBound(1))     ' => 0
Console.WriteLine(lngArr.GetUpperBound(1))     ' => 20
```

You can visit all the elements of an array using a single For Each loop and a strongly-typed variable. This is an improvement on Visual Basic 6, which forces you to use a Variant when working with numeric or string arrays. This technique also works with multidimensional arrays, so you can process all the elements in a two-dimensional array with just one loop:

```
Dim strArr(,) As String = {{"00", "01", "02"}, {"10", "11", "12"}}
Dim s As String
For Each s In strArr
    Console.Write(s & ",")        ' => 00,01,02,10,11,12
Next
```

For Each loops on multidimensional arrays work in previous language versions as well, but with an important difference. Visual Basic 6 visits array elements in a column-wise order (all the elements in the first column, then all the elements in the second column, and so on), whereas Visual Basic .NET follows the more natural row-wise order.

> **See Also**   Read the document "Nonzero-based Arrays.doc" on the companion CD for information about using the Array.CreateInstance method to create arrays with a lowest index other than zero (and all the good reasons why this technique is discouraged).

The Array class supports the ICloneable interface, so you can create a shallow copy of an array using the Clone instance method. (See "The ICloneable Interface" in Chapter 6 for a discussion about shallow and deep copy operations).

```
' This works if Option Strict is Off.
Dim anotherArray(,) As Integer = arr.Clone

' This is the required syntax if Option Strict is On.
' (You can also use CType instead of DirectCast.)
Dim anotherArray(,) As Integer = DirectCast(arr.Clone, Integer())
```

You can copy a one-dimensional array to another one-dimensional array, and you decide the starting index in the destination array:

```
' Create and initialize an array (10 elements).
Dim sourceArr() As Integer = {1, 2, 3, 5, 7, 11, 13, 17, 19, 23}
' Create the destination array (must be same size or larger).
Dim destArr(20) As Integer
' Copy the source array into the second half of the destination array.
sourceArr.CopyTo(destArr, 10)
```

Sorting Elements

The Array class offers several shared methods for processing arrays quickly and easily. In Chapter 3 you read about the Array.Sort method, and in Chapter 6 you learned that you can sort arrays of objects using an arbitrary group of keys by means of the IComparable and IComparer interfaces. The Sort method is even more flexible than anything you've seen so far. For example, you can sort just a portion of an array:

```
' Sort only elements [10,100] of the targetArray.
' Second argument is starting index; last argument is length of the subarray.
Array.Sort(targetArray, 10, 91)
```

You can also sort an array of values using another array that holds the sorting keys, which lets you sort arrays of structures or objects. To see how this overloaded version of the Sort method works, let's start defining a structure:

```
Structure Employee
    Public FirstName As String
    Public LastName As String
    Public HireDate As Date

    Sub New(ByVal firstName As String, ByVal lastName As String, _
        ByVal hireDate As Date)
        Me.FirstName = firstName
        Me.LastName = lastName
        Me.HireDate = hireDate
```

```
        End Sub

        ' A function to display an element's properties easily
        Function Description() As String
            Return FirstName & " " & LastName & _
                " (hired on " & HireDate.ToShortDateString & ")"
        End Function
End Structure
```

The following code creates a main array of Employee structures, then creates an auxiliary key array that holds the hiring date of each employee, and finally sorts the main array using the auxiliary array:

```
' Create a test array.
Dim employees() As Employee = { _
    New Employee("Joe", "Doe", #3/1/2001#), _
    New Employee("Robert", "Smith", #8/12/2000#), _
    New Employee("Ann", "Douglas", #11/1/1999#)}
' Create a parallel array of hiring dates.
Dim hireDates(UBound(employees)) As Date
For j As Integer = 0 To employees.Length - 1
    hireDates(j) = employees(j).HireDate
Next
' Sort the array of Employees using HireDates to provide the keys.
Array.Sort(hireDates, employees)
' Prove that the array is sorted on the HireDate field.
For j As Integer = 0 To employees.Length - 1
    Console.WriteLine(employees(j).Description)
Next
```

Interestingly, the key array is sorted as well, so you don't need to initialize it again when you add another element to the main array:

```
' Add a fourth employee.
ReDim Preserve employees(3)
employees(3) = New Employee("Chris", "Doe", #5/9/2000#)
' Extend the key array as well - no need to reinitialize it.
ReDim Preserve hireDates(3)
hireDates(3) = employees(3).HireDate
' Re-sort the new, larger array.
Array.Sort(hireDates, employees)
```

An overloaded version of the Sort method lets you sort a portion of an array of values for which you provide an array of keys. This is especially useful when you start with a large array that you fill only partially:

```
' Create a test array with a lot of room.
Dim employees(1000) As Employee
' Initialize only its first four elements.
⋮
' Sort only the portion actually used.
Array.Sort(hireDates, employees, 0, 4)
```

All the versions of the Array.Sort method that you've seen so far can take an additional IComparer object, which dictates how the array elements or keys are to be compared with one another. (See the "The IComparer Interface" section in Chapter 6.)

The Array.Reverse method reverses the order of elements in an array or in a portion of an array, so you can apply it immediately after a Sort method to sort in descending order:

```
' Sort an array of Integers in reverse order.
Array.Sort(intArray)
Array.Reverse(intArray)
```

You pass the initial index and number of elements to reverse only a portion of an array:

```
' Reverse only the first 10 elements in intArray.
Array.Reverse(intArray, 0, 10)
```

You have a special case when you reverse only two elements, which is the same as swapping two consecutive elements, a frequent operation when you're working with arrays:

```
' Swap elements at indexes 5 and 6.
Array.Reverse(intArray, 5, 2)
```

Clearing, Copying, and Moving Elements

You can clear a portion of an array with the Clear method, without a For loop:

```
' Clear elements [10,100] of an array.
Array.Clear(arr, 10, 91)
```

The Array.Copy method lets you copy elements from a one-dimensional array to another. There are two overloaded versions for this method. The first version copies a given number of elements from the source array to the destination array:

```
Dim intArr() As Integer = {1, 2, 3, 4, 5, 6, 7, 8, 9, 10}
Dim intArr2(20) As Integer
' Copy the entire source array into the first half of the target array.
Array.Copy(intArr, intArr2, 10)
For i As Integer = 0 To 20
    Console.Write(CStr(intArr2(i)) & " ")
        ' => 1 2 3 4 5 6 7 8 9 10 0 0 0 0 0 0 0 0 0 0 0
Next
```

The second version lets you decide the starting index in the source array, the starting index in the destination array (that is, the index of the first element that will be over-written), and the number of elements to copy:

```
' Copy elements at indexes 5-9 to the end of destArr.
Array.Copy(intArr, 5, intArr2, 15, 5)
' This is the first element that has been copied.
Console.WriteLine(intArr2(15))                    ' => 6
```

You get an exception of type ArgumentOutOfRangeException if you provide wrong values for the indexes or the destination array isn't large enough, and you get an exception of type RankException if either array has two or more dimensions.

The Copy method works correctly even when source and destination arrays have a different type, in which case it attempts to cast each individual source element to the corresponding element in the destination array. The actual behavior depends on many factors, though, such as whether the source or the destination is a value type or a reference type. For example, you can always copy from any array to an Object array, from an Integer array to a Long array, and from a Single array to a Double array because they are widening conversions and can't fail. Copy throws an exception of type TypeMismatchException when you attempt a narrowing conversion between arrays of value types, even though individual elements in the source array might be successfully converted to the destination type:

```
' This Copy operation succeeds even if array types are different.
Dim intArr3() As Integer = {1, 2, 3, 4, 5, 6, 7, 8, 9, 10}
Dim lngArr3(20) As Long
Array.Copy(intArr3, lngArr3, 10)

' This Copy operation fails with TypeMismatchException.
'    (But you can carry it out with an explicit For loop.)
Dim lngArr4() As Long = {1, 2, 3, 4, 5, 6, 7, 8, 9, 10}
Dim intArr4(20) As Integer
Array.Copy(lngArr4, intArr4, 10)
```

Conversely, if you copy from and to an array of reference type, the Array.Copy method attempts the copy operation for each element; if an InvalidCastException object is thrown for an element, the method copies neither that element nor any of the values after the one that raised the error. For more details about the Array.Copy method, see the MSDN documentation.

The Array.Copy method can even copy a portion of an array over itself. In this case, the Copy method performs a "smart copy," in the sense that elements are copied correctly in ascending order when you're copying to a lower index and in reverse order when you're copying to a higher index. So you can use the Copy method to delete one or more elements and fill the hole that would result by shifting all subsequent elements one or more positions toward lower indexes:

```
Dim lngArr5() As Long = {1, 2, 3, 4, 5, 6, 7, 8, 9, 10}
' Delete element at index 4.
Array.Copy(lngArr5, 5, lngArr5, 4, 5)
' Complete the delete operation by clearing the last element.
Array.Clear(lngArr5, lngArr5.GetUpperBound(0), 1)
' Now the array contains: {1, 2, 3, 4, 6, 7, 8, 9, 10, 0}
```

You can use this code as the basis for a reusable routine that works with any type of array:

```
Sub ArrayDeleteElement(ByVal arr As Array, ByVal index As Integer)
    ' Shift elements from arr(index+1) to arr(index).
    Array.Copy(arr, index + 1, arr, index, UBound(arr) - Index)
    ' Clear the last element.
    arr.Clear(arr, arr.GetUpperBound(0), 1)
End Sub
```

Inserting an element is also easy, and again you can create a generic routine that works with arrays of any type:

```
Sub ArrayInsertElement(ByVal arr As Array, ByVal index As Integer, _
    Optional ByVal newValue As Object = Nothing)
    ' Shift elements from arr(index) to arr(index+1) to make room.
    Array.Copy(arr, index, arr, index + 1, arr.Length - index - 1)
    ' Assign the element using the SetValue method.
    arr.SetValue(newValue, index)
End Sub
```

The Array class exposes the SetValue and GetValue methods to assign and read elements. You don't normally use these methods in regular programming, but they turn out to be useful in generic routines (such as the two preceding routines) that work with any type of array.

You can also use Copy with multidimensional arrays, in which case the array is treated as if it were a one-dimensional array with all the rows laid down in memory one after the other. This method works only if the source and destination arrays have the same rank, even if they can have a different number of rows and columns.

Searching Values

The IndexOf method searches an array for a value and returns the index of the first element that matches or -1 if the search fails:

```
Dim strArray() As String = {"Robert", "Joe", "Ann", "Chris", "Joe"}
Console.WriteLine(Array.IndexOf(strArray, "Ann"))    ' => 2
' Note that string searches are case sensitive.
Console.WriteLine(Array.IndexOf(strArray, "ANN"))    ' => -1
```

You can also specify a starting index and an optional ending index; if an ending index is omitted, the search continues until the end of the array. You can use the following approach to find all the values in the array with a given value:

```
' Search for all the occurrences of the "Joe" string.
Dim index As Integer = Array.IndexOf(strArray, "Joe")
Do Until index < 0
    Console.WriteLine("Found at index {0}", index)
    ' Search next occurrence.
    index = Array.IndexOf(strArray, "Joe", index + 1)
Loop
```

The LastIndexOf method is similar to IndexOf except that it returns the index of the last occurrence of the value. Because the search is backward, you must pass a start index higher than the end index:

```
' A revised version of the search loop, which searches
' from higher indexes toward the beginning of the array.
index = Array.LastIndexOf(strArr, "Joe", strArr.Length - 1)
Do Until index < 0
    Console.WriteLine("Found at index {0}", index)
    index = Array.LastIndexOf(strArr, "Joe", index - 1)
Loop
```

The IndexOf and LastIndexOf methods perform a linear search, so their performance degrades linearly with larger arrays. You deliver much faster code if the array is sorted and you use the BinarySearch method:

```
' Binary search on a sorted array
Dim strArr2() As String = {"Ann", "Chris", "Joe", "Robert", "Sam"}
Console.WriteLine(Array.BinarySearch(strArr2, "Chris"))      ' => 1
```

If the binary search fails, the method returns a negative value that's the bitwise complement of the index of the first element that's larger than the value being searched. This feature lets you determine where the value should be inserted in the sorted array:

```
index = Array.BinarySearch(strArr2, "David")
If index >= 0 Then
    Console.WriteLine("Found at index {0}", index)
Else
    ' Negate the result to get the index for the insertion point.
    index = Not index
    Console.WriteLine("Not Found. Insert at index {0}", index)
        ' => Not found. Insert at index 2
End If
```

You can pass a start index and the length of the portion of the array in which you want to perform the search, which is useful when you're working with an array that's only partially filled:

```
Console.Write(Array.BinarySearch(strArr2, 0, 3, "Chris"))   ' => 1
```

Finally, both syntax forms for the BinarySearch method support an IComparer object at the end of the argument list, which lets you determine how array elements are to be compared. In practice, you can use the same IComparer object that you passed to the Sort method to have the array sorted.

Arrays of Arrays

Visual Basic .NET also supports arrays of arrays, that is, arrays whose elements are arrays. This is a familiar concept to most C++ programmers, but it might be new to many Visual Basic programmers, even though a little-known feature of Visual Basic

5 and 6 lets you create such structures by leveraging the ability to store arrays in Variants. The good news is that Visual Basic .NET supports arrays of arrays natively, so you don't have to resort to any hack. Oddly, this feature isn't mentioned in language documentation.

Arrays of arrays—also known as *jagged arrays*—are especially useful when you have a two-dimensional matrix whose rows don't have the same length. You can render this structure by using a standard two-dimensional array, but you'd have to size it to accommodate the row with the highest number of elements, which would result in a waste of space. The arrays of arrays concept isn't limited to two dimensions only, and you might need three-dimensional or four-dimensional jagged arrays. Here is an example of a "triangular" matrix of strings:

```
"a00"
"a10"  "a11"
"a20"  "a21"  "a22"
"a30"  "a31"  "a32"  "a33"
```

Even though Visual Basic .NET supports arrays of arrays natively, I can't consider their syntax to be intuitive. The next code snippet shows how you can initialize the preceding structure and then process it by expanding its rows:

```
' Initialize an array of arrays.
Dim arr()() As String = {New String() {"a00"}, _
    New String() {"a10", "a11"}, _
    New String() {"a20", "a21", "a22"}, _
    New String() {"a30", "a31", "a32", "a33"}}

' Show how you can reference an element.
Console.WriteLine(arr(3)(1))                    ' => a31
' Assign an entire row.
arr(0) = New String() {"a00", "a01", "a02"}
' Read an element just added.
Console.WriteLine(arr(0)(2))                    ' => a02

' Expand one of the rows.
ReDim Preserve arr(1)(3)
' Assign the new elements. (Currently they are Nothing.)
arr(1)(2) = "a12"
arr(1)(3) = "a13"
' Read back one of them.
Console.WriteLine(arr(1)(2))                    ' => a12
```

An obvious advantage of jagged arrays is that they take less memory than regular multidimensional arrays. Even more interesting, the JIT compiler produces code that is up to 5 or 6 times faster when accessing a jagged array than when accessing a multidimensional array. However, keep in mind that jagged arrays aren't CLS-compliant, so they shouldn't appear as arguments or return values in public methods.

The System.Collections Namespace

The System.Collections namespace exposes many classes that can work as generic data containers, such as collections and dictionaries. You can learn the features of all these objects individually, but a smarter approach is to learn about the underlying interfaces that these classes might implement.

The ICollection, IList, and IDictionary Interfaces

All the collection classes in the .NET Framework implement the ICollection interface, which inherits from IEnumerable and defines an object that supports enumeration through a For Each loop. The ICollection interface exposes a read-only Count property and a CopyTo method, which copies the elements from the collection object to an array.

The ICollection interface defines the minimum features that a collectionlike object should have. The .NET Framework exposes two more interfaces whose methods add power and flexibility to the object: IList and IDictionary.

Many classes in the framework implement the IList interface. This interface inherits from ICollection, and therefore from IEnumerable, and represents a collection of objects that can be individually indexed. All the implementations of the IList interface fall into three categories: read-only (the collection's elements can't be modified or deleted, nor can new elements be inserted), fixed-size (existing items can be modified, but elements can't be added or removed) and variable-size (items can be modified, added, and removed).

Table 8-1 summarizes the main properties and methods of the IList interface. You should be familiar with most of them because they're implemented in many other collectionlike objects you've worked with in the past, most notably Collection and Dictionary objects in Visual Basic 6.

Table 8-1   Members of the IList Interface

Syntax	Description
Count	Returns the number of elements in the collection (inherited from ICollection).
CopyTo(array, index)	Copies elements from the collection to an array, starting at the specified index in the array (inherited from ICollection).
Item(index)	Gets or sets the element at the specified 0-based index. This is the default member.
Clear	Removes all items from the collection.
Add(object)	Appends an element after the last element in the collection and returns the index to where it was inserted.

Table 8-1 Members of the IList Interface

Syntax	Description
Insert(index, object)	Inserts an element at a given index.
Remove(object)	Removes an object from the collection.
RemoveAt(index)	Removes an element at the specified index.
Contains(object)	Returns True if an object is in the collection.
IndexOf(object)	Returns the index of the object in the collection, or -1 if not found.
IsFixedSize	Returns True if no item can be added to the collection.
IsReadOnly	Returns True if items can't be written to.

The IDictionary interface defines a collectionlike object that contains one or more (key, value) pairs for which the key can be any object (not just a string, as in Visual Basic 6 collections). The IDictionary interface inherits from ICollection and extends it using the methods defined in Table 8-2. As for the IList interface, implementations of the IDictionary interface can be read-only, fixed-size, or variable-size.

Table 8-2 Members of the IDictionary Interface

Syntax	Description
Count	Returns the number of elements in the dictionary (inherited from ICollection).
CopyTo(array, index)	Copies elements from the dictionary to an array, starting at the specified index in the array (inherited from ICollection).
Item(key)	Gets or sets the element associated with the specified key. This is the default member.
Clear	Removes all items from the dictionary.
Add(key, value)	Inserts a (key, value) pair into the dictionary; key must not be Nothing.
Remove(key)	Removes the dictionary element associated with a given key.
Contains(key)	Returns True if an element with the specified key is in the dictionary.
Keys	Returns an ICollection object that contains all the keys in the dictionary.
Values	Returns an ICollection object that contains all the values in the dictionary.
IsFixedSize	Returns True if no item can be added to the dictionary.
IsReadOnly	Returns True if items can't be written to.

A class that implements the ICollection, IList, or IDictionary interface isn't required to expose all the interface's properties and methods as Public members. For example, the Array class implements IList, but the Add, Insert, and Remove members don't appear in the Array class interface because the array has a fixed size. You get an exception if you try to access these methods by casting an array to an IList variable.

A trait that all the classes in System.Collections except the BitArray class have in common is that they can store Object values. This means that you can store any type of value inside them and even mix data types inside the same structure. In this sense, they're similar to the Collection object in Visual Basic 6, which used Variants internally and could therefore store numbers, strings, dates, and objects.

The BitArray Class

The BitArray object can hold a large number of Boolean values in a compact format, using a single bit for each element. This class implements IEnumerable (and thus supports For Each), ICollection (and thus supports indexing of individual elements), and ICloneable (and thus supports the Clone method). You can create a BitArray object in many ways:

```
' Provide the number of elements (all initialized to False).
Dim ba As New BitArray(1024)
' Provide the number of elements, and initialize them to a value.
Dim ba2 As New BitArray(1024, True)

' Initialize the BitArray from an array of Boolean, Byte, or Integer.
Dim boolArr(1023) As Boolean
' ...(Initialize the boolArr array)...
Dim ba3 As New BitArray(boolArr)

' Initialize the BitArray from another BitArray object.
Dim ba4 As New BitArray(ba)
```

You can retrieve the number of elements in a BitArray by using either the Count property or the Length property. The Get method reads and the Set method modifies the element at the specified index:

```
' Set element at index 9, and read it back.
ba.Set(9, True)
Console.WriteLine(ba.Get(9))      ' => True
```

The CopyTo method can move all elements back to an array of Booleans, or it can perform a bitwise copy of the BitArray to a 0-based Byte or Integer array:

```
' Bitwise copy to an array of Integers
Dim intArr(31) As Integer         ' 32 elements * 32 bits each = 1024 bits
' Second argument is the index in which the copy begins in target array.
ba.CopyTo(intArr, 0)
' Check that bit 9 of first element in intArr is set.
Console.WriteLine(intArr(0))      ' => 512
```

The Not method complements all the bits in the BitArray object:

```
ba.Not()                               ' No arguments
```

The And, Or, and Xor methods let you perform the corresponding operation on pairs of Boolean values stored in two BitArray objects:

```
' Perform an AND operation of all the bits in the first BitArray
' with the complement of all the bits in the second BitArray.
ba.And(ba2.Not)
```

Finally, you can set or reset all the bits in a BitArray class using the SetAll method:

```
' Set all the bits to True.
ba.SetAll(True)
```

The BitArray class doesn't expose any methods that let you quickly determine how many True (or False) elements are in the array. You can take advantage of the IEnumerator support of this class and use a For Each loop:

```
Dim TrueCount As Integer
For Each b As Boolean In ba
    If b Then TrueCount += 1
Next
Console.Write("Found {0} True values.", TrueCount)
```

The BitVector32 Class

The BitVector32 class (in the System.Collections.Specialized namespace) is similar to the BitArray class, in that it can hold a packed array of Boolean values, one per bit, but it's limited to 32 elements. However, a BitVector32 object can even store a set of small integers that take up to 32 consecutive bits and is therefore useful with bit-coded fields, such as those that you deal with when passing data to and from hardware devices.

```
' This code assumes that you have the following Imports
'    Imports System.Collections.Specialized

Dim bv As New BitVector32()
' Set one element and read it back.
bv(1) = True
Console.WriteLine(bv(1))     ' => True
```

You can also pass a 32-bit integer to the constructor to initialize all the elements in one pass:

```
' Initialize all elements to True.
bv = new BitVector32(-1)
```

To define a BitVector32 that is subdivided in sections that are longer than 1 bit, you must create one or more BitVector32.Section objects and use them when you later read and write individual elements. You define a section by means of the BitVector32.CreateSection shared method, which takes the highest integer you want to store in that section and (for all sections after the first one) the previous section. Here's a complete example:

```
Dim bv As New BitVector32()
' Create three sections, of 4, 5, and 6 bits each.
Dim se1 As BitVector32.Section = BitVector32.CreateSection(15)
Dim se2 As BitVector32.Section = BitVector32.CreateSection(31, se1)
Dim se3 As BitVector32.Section = BitVector32.CreateSection(63, se2)

' Assign a given value to each section.
bv(se1) = 10
bv(se2) = 20
bv(se3) = 40
' Read values back.
Console.WriteLine(bv(se1))
Console.WriteLine(bv(se2))
Console.WriteLine(bv(se3))
```

The Data property sets or returns the internal 32-bit integer; you can use this property to save the bit-coded value into a database field or to pass it to a hardware device:

```
' Read the entire field as a 32-bit value.
Console.WriteLine(bv.Data)                ' => 20810
Console.WriteLine(bv.Data.ToString("X"))  ' => 514A
```

The Stack Class

In Visual Basic 6 you can simulate a last-in-first-out (LIFO) structure by using an array and an Integer variable that works as the pointer to the current element. Under Visual Basic .NET, you can build a stack structure by simply instantiating a System.Collections.Stack object:

```
' Define a stack with initial capacity of 50 elements.
Dim st As New Stack(50)
```

The three basic methods of a Stack object are Push, Pop, and Peek; the Count property returns the number of elements currently in the stack:

```
' Create a stack that can contain 100 elements.
Dim st As New Stack(100)
' Push three values onto the stack.
st.Push(10)
st.Push(20)
st.Push(30)
' Pop the value on top of the stack, and display its value.
Console.WriteLine(st.Pop)       ' => 30
' Read the value on top of the stack without popping it.
Console.WriteLine(st.Peek)      ' => 20
' Now pop it.
Console.WriteLine(st.Pop)       ' => 20
' Determine how many elements are now in the stack.
Console.WriteLine(st.Count)     ' => 1
' Pop the only value still on the stack.
Console.WriteLine(st.Pop)       ' => 10
```

```
' Check that the stack is now empty.
Console.WriteLine(st.Count)     ' => 0
```

The only other method that can prove useful is Contains, which returns True if a given value is currently in the stack:

```
' Is the value 10 somewhere in the stack?
If st.Contains(10) Then Console.Write("Found")
```

The Queue Class

A first-in-first-out (FIFO) structure, also known as a *queue* or *circular buffer*, is often used to solve recurring programming problems. You need a queue structure when a portion of an application inserts elements at one end of a buffer and another piece of code extracts the first available element at the other end. This situation occurs whenever you have a series of elements that you must process sequentially but you can't process immediately.

You can render a queue in Visual Basic .NET by leveraging the System.Collections.Queue object. Queue objects have an initial capacity, but the internal buffer is automatically extended if the need arises. You create a Queue object by specifying its initial capacity and an optional growth factor:

```
' A queue with initial capacity of 200 elements; a growth factor equal to 1.5
' (When new room is needed, the capacity will become 300, then 450, 675, etc.)
Dim qu1 As New Queue(200, 1.5)
' A queue with 100 elements and a default growth factor of 2
Dim qu2 As New Queue(100)
' A queue with 32 initial elements and a default growth factor of 2
Dim qu3 As New Queue()
```

The key methods of a Queue object are Enqueue, Peek, and Dequeue. Check the output of the following code snippet, and compare it with the behavior of the Stack object:

```
Dim qu As New Queue(100)
' Insert three values in the queue.
qu.Enqueue(10)
qu.Enqueue(20)
qu.Enqueue(30)
' Extract the first value, and display it.
Console.WriteLine(qu.Dequeue)    ' => 10
' Read the next value, but don't extract it.
Console.WriteLine(qu.Peek)       ' => 20
' Extract it.
Console.WriteLine(qu.Dequeue)    ' => 20
' Check how many items are still in the queue.
Console.WriteLine(qu.Count)      ' => 1
' Extract the last element, and check that the queue is now empty.
Console.WriteLine(qu.Dequeue)    ' => 30
Console.WriteLine(qu.Count)      ' => 0
```

The Queue object also supports the Contains method, which checks whether an element is in the queue, and the Clear method, which clears the queue's contents.

The ArrayList Class

You can think of the ArrayList class as a hybrid of the Array and Collection objects, in that it lets you work with a set of values as if it were an array and a collection at the same time. For example, you can address elements by their indexes, sort and reverse them, and search a value sequentially or by means of a binary search as you do with an array; you can append elements, insert them in a given position, or remove them as you do with a collection.

The ArrayList object has an initial capacity—in practice, the number of slots in the internal structure that holds the actual values—but you don't need to worry about that because an ArrayList is automatically expanded as needed, as all collections are. However, you can optimize your code by choosing an initial capability that offers a good compromise between used memory and the overhead that occurs whenever the Array-List object has to expand:

```
' Create an ArrayList with default initial capacity of 16 elements.
Dim al As New ArrayList
' Create an ArrayList with initial capacity of 1000 elements.
Dim al2 As New ArrayList(1000)
```

You can modify the capacity at any moment to enlarge the internal array or shrink it, by assigning a value to the Capacity property. However, you can't make it smaller than the current number of elements actually stored in the array (which corresponds to the value returned by the Count property):

```
' Have the ArrayList take just the memory that it strictly needs.
al.Capacity = al.Count
' Another way to achieve the same result
al.TrimToSize()
```

When the current capacity is exceeded, the ArrayList object doubles its capacity automatically. You can't control the growth factor of an ArrayList as you can a Queue object, so you should set the Capacity property to a suitable value in order to avoid time-consuming memory allocations.

Another way to create an ArrayList object is by means of its shared Repeat method, which lets you determine an initial value for the specified number of elements:

```
' Create an ArrayList with 100 elements equal to a null string.
Dim al As ArrayList = ArrayList.Repeat("", 100)
```

The ArrayList class fully implements the IList interface, so you're already familiar with its basic methods. You add elements to an ArrayList object by using the Add method (which appends the new element after the last item) or the Insert method (which inserts at the specified index). You remove a specific object by passing it to the Remove method, remove the element at a given index by using the RemoveAt method, or remove all elements by using the Clear method:

```
' Be sure that you start with an empty ArrayList.
al.Clear
' Append the elements "Joe" and "Ann" at the end of the ArrayList.
al.Add("Joe")
al.Add("Ann")
' Insert "Robert" item at the beginning of the list. (Index is 0-based.)
al.Insert(0, "Robert")
' Remove "Joe" from the list.
al.Remove("Joe")
' Remove the first element of the list ("Robert" in this case).
al.RemoveAt(0)
```

The Remove method removes only the first occurrence of a given object, so you need a loop to remove all the elements with a given value. You can't simply iterate through the loop until you get an error, however, because the Remove method doesn't throw an exception if the element isn't found. Therefore, you must use one of these two approaches:

```
' Using the Contains method is concise but not very efficient.
Do While al.Contains("element to remove")
    al.Remove("element to remove")
Loop


' A more efficient technique: loop until the Count property becomes constant.
Dim saveCount As Integer
Do
    saveCount = al.Count
    al.Remove("element to remove")
Loop While al.Count < saveCount
```

You can read and write any ArrayList element using the Item property. This property is the default property, so you can omit it and deal with this object as if it were a standard 0-based array:

```
al(0) = "first element"
```

Just remember that an element in an ArrayList object is created only when you invoke the Add method, so you can't reference an element whose index is equal to or higher than the ArrayList's Count property. As with collections, the preferred way to iterate over all elements is through the For Each loop:

```
For Each o As Object In al
    Console.WriteLine(o)
Next
```

The ArrayList class exposes methods that allow you to manipulate ranges of elements in one operation. The AddRange method appends to the current ArrayList object all the elements contained in another object that implements the ICollection interface. Many .NET classes other than those described in this chapter implement ICollection, such as the collection of all the items in a ListBox control and the collection of nodes in a TreeView control. The following routine takes two ArrayList objects and returns a third ArrayList that contains all the items from both arguments:

```
Function ArrayListJoin(ByVal al1 As ArrayList, ByVal al2 As ArrayList) _
    As ArrayList
    ' Note how we avoid time-consuming reallocations.
    ArrayListJoin = New ArrayList(al1.Count + al2.count)
    ' Append the items in the two ArrayList arguments.
    ArrayListJoin.AddRange(al1)
    ArrayListJoin.AddRange(al2)
End Function
```

The InsertRange method works in a similar way but lets you insert multiple elements at any index in the current ArrayList object:

```
' Insert all the items of al2 at the beginning of the current ArrayList.
al.InsertRange(0, al2)
```

RemoveRange deletes multiple elements in the current ArrayList object:

```
' Delete the last four elements (assumes there are at least four elements).
al.RemoveRange(al.Count - 4, 4)
```

You can quickly extract all the items in the ArrayList object by using the ToArray method or the CopyTo method. Both of them support one-dimensional target arrays of any compatible type, but the latter also allows you to extract a subset of ArrayList:

```
' Extract elements to an Object array (never raises an error).
Dim objArr() As Object = al.ToArray()
' Extract elements to a String array (might throw an exception
' of type InvalidCastException).
' (Requires CType or DirectCast if Option Strict is On.)
Dim strArr() As String = CType(al.ToArray(GetType(String)), String())

' Same as above but uses the CopyTo method.
' (Note that the target array must be large enough.)
Dim strArr2(al.Count) As String
al.CopyTo(strArr2)
' Copy only items [1,2], starting at element 4 in the target array.
Dim strArr3() As String = {"0", "1", "2", "3", "4", "5", "6", "7", "8", "9"}
' Syntax is: sourceIndex, target, destIndex, count.
al.CopyTo(0, strArr3, 4, 2)
```

The ArrayList class supports other useful methods, such as Sort, SortRange, Binary-Search, IndexOf, LastIndexOf, and Reverse. I described most of these methods in depth in the section devoted to arrays, so I won't repeat their descriptions here.

The last feature of the ArrayList class that's worth mentioning is its Adapter shared method. This method takes an IList-derived object as its only argument and creates an ArrayList wrapper around that object. In other words, instead of creating a copy of the argument, the Adapter method creates an ArrayList object that "contains" the original collection. All the changes you make on the outer ArrayList object are duplicated in the inner collection. The reason you might want to use the Adapter method is that the ArrayList class implements several methods—Reverse, Sort, BinarySearch, ToArray, IndexOf, and LastIndexOf, just to name a few—that are missing in a simpler IList object. The following code sample demonstrates how you can use this technique to reverse (or sort, and so on) all the items in a ListBox control:

```
' Create a wrapper around the Listbox.Items (IList) collection.
Dim lbAdapter As ArrayList = ArrayList.Adapter(ListBox1.Items)
' Reverse their order.
lbAdapter.Reverse()
```

If you don't plan to reuse the ArrayList wrapper further, you can make this code even more concise:

```
ArrayList.Adapter(ListBox1.Items).Reverse()
```

The Hashtable Class

The Hashtable class implements the IDictionary interface, and it behaves much like the Scripting.Dictionary object you might have used from Visual Basic 6 days. (The Dictionary object can be found in the Microsoft Scripting Runtime library.) All objects based on IDictionary manage two internal series of data, values, and keys, and you can use a key to retrieve the corresponding value. The actual implementation of the methods in this interface depends on the specific object. For example, the Hashtable class uses an internal hash table, a well-known data structure that has been studied for decades by computer scientists and has been thoroughly described in countless books on algorithms.

When a (key, value) pair is added to a Hashtable object, the position of an element in the internal array is based on the numeric hash code of the key. When you later search for that key, the key's hash code is used again to locate the associated value as quickly as possible, without sequentially visiting all the elements in the hash table. Collection objects in Visual Basic 6 use a similar mechanism, except that the key's hash code is derived from the characters in the key and the key must necessarily be a string. Conversely, the .NET Hashtable class lets you use *any* object as a key. Behind the scenes, the Hashtable object uses the key object's GetHashCode, a method that all objects inherit from System.Object.

Depending on how the hash code is evaluated, it frequently happens that multiple keys map to the same slot (or *bucket*) in the hash table. In this case, you have a *collision*. The Hashtable object uses double hashing to minimize collisions, but it can't avoid collisions completely. Never fear—collisions are automatically dealt with transparently for the programmer, but you can get optimal performance by selecting an adequate initial capacity for the hash table. A larger table doesn't speed up searches remarkably, but it makes insertions faster.

You can also get better performance by selecting a correct *load factor* when you create a Hashtable object. This number determines the maximum ratio between values and buckets before the hash table is automatically expanded. The smaller this value is, the more memory is allocated to the internal table and the fewer collisions occur when you're inserting or searching for a value. The default load factor is 1.0, which in most cases delivers a good-enough performance, but you can set a smaller load factor when you create the Hashtable if you're willing to trade memory for better performance. You can initialize a Hashtable object in many ways:

```
' Default load factor and initial capacity
Dim ht As New Hashtable
' Default load factor and specified initial capacity
Dim ht2 As New Hashtable(1000)
' Specified initial capacity and custom load factor
Dim ht3 As New Hashtable(1000, 0.8)
```

You can also initialize the Hashtable by loading it with the elements contained in any other object that implements the IDictionary interface (such as another Hashtable or a SortedList object). This technique is especially useful when you want to change the load factor of an existing hash table:

```
' Decrease the load factor of the current Hashtable.
ht = New HashTable(ht, 0.5)
```

Other, more sophisticated, variants of the constructor let you pass an IComparer object to compare keys in a customized fashion or an IHashCodeProvider object to supply a custom algorithm for calculating hash codes of keys.

Once you've created a Hashtable, you can add a key and value pair, read or modify the value associated with a given key through the Item property, and remove an item with the Remove method:

```
' Syntax for Add method is Add(key, value).
ht.Add("Joe", 12000)
ht.Add("Ann", 13000)
' Referencing a new key creates an element.
ht.Item("Robert") = 15000
' Item is the default member, so you can omit its name.
ht("Chris") = 11000
Console.Write(ht("Joe"))       ' => 12000
' The Item property lets you overwrite an existing element.
' (You need CInt or CType if Option Strict is On.)
ht("Ann") = CInt(ht("Ann")) + 1000
' Note that keys are compared in case-insensitive mode,
' so the following statement creates a *new* element.
ht("ann") = 15000
' Reading a nonexistent element doesn't create it.
Console.WriteLine(ht("Lee"))        ' Doesn't display anything.
```

```
' Remove an element given its key.
ht.Remove("Chris")
' How many elements are now in the hashtable?
Console.WriteLine(ht.Count)         ' => 4

' Adding an element that already exists throws an exception.
ht.Add("Joe", 11500)               ' Throws ArgumentException.
```

As I explained earlier, you can use virtually anything as a key, including a numeric value. When you're using numbers as keys, a Hashtable looks deceptively similar to an array:

```
ht(1) = 123
ht(2) = 345
```

But never forget that the expression between parentheses is just a key and not an index; thus, the ht(2) element isn't necessarily stored "after" the ht(1) element. As a matter of fact, the elements in a Hashtable object aren't stored in a particular order, and you should never write code that assumes that they are. This is the main difference between the Hashtable object and the SortedList object (which is described next).

The Hashtable object implements the IEnumerable interface, so you can iterate over all its elements with a For Each loop. Each element of a Hashtable is a DictionaryEntry object, which exposes a Key and a Value property:

```
For Each de As DictionaryEntry In ht
    Console.WriteLine("ht('{0}') = {1}", de.Key, de.Value)
Next
```

The Hashtable's Keys and Values properties return an ICollection-based object that contains all the keys and all the values, respectively, so you can assign them to any object that implements the ICollection interface. Or you can use these properties directly in a For Each loop:

```
' Display all the keys in the Hashtable.
For Each o As Object In ht.Keys     ' Or use ht.Values for all the values.
    Console.WriteLine(o)
Next
```

One last note: by default, keys are compared in a case-sensitive way, so *Joe, JOE,* and *joe* are considered distinct keys. You can create case-insensitive instances of the Hashtable class through one of its many constructors, or you can use the CreateCaseInsensitiveHashtable shared method of the System.Collections.Specialized.CollectionsUtil, as follows:

```
Dim ht2 As Hashtable = _
    Specialized.CollectionsUtil.CreateCaseInsensitiveHashtable()
```

The SortedList Class

The SortedList object is arguably the most versatile collectionlike object in the .NET Framework. It implements the IDictionary interface, like the Hashtable object, and also keeps its elements sorted. Alas, you pay for all this power in terms of performance, so you should use the SortedList object only when your programming logic requires an object with all this flexibility.

The SortedList object manages two internal arrays, one for the values and one for the companion keys. These arrays have an initial capacity, but they automatically grow when the need arises. Entries are kept sorted by their key, and you can even provide an IComparer object to affect how complex values (an object, for example) are compared and sorted. The SortedList class provides several constructor methods:

```
' A SortedList with default capacity (16 entries)
Dim sl As New SortedList()
' A SortedList with specified initial capacity
Dim sl2 As New SortedList(1000)

' A SortedList can be initialized with all the elements in an IDictionary.
Dim ht As New Hashtable()
ht.Add("Robert", 100)
ht.Add("Ann", 200)
ht.Add("Joe", 300)
Dim sl3 As New SortedList(ht)
```

As soon as you add new elements to the SortedList, they're immediately sorted by their key. Like the Hashtable class, a SortedList contains DictionaryEntry elements:

```
For Each de As DictionaryEntry In sl3
    Console.WriteLine("sl3('{0}') = {1}", de.Key, de.Value)
Next
```

Here's the result that appears in the console window:

```
sl3('Ann') = 200
sl3('Joe') = 300
sl3('Robert') = 100
```

Keys are sorted according to the order implied by their IComparable interface, so numbers and strings are always sorted in ascending order. If you want a different order, you must create an object that implements the IComparer interface. For example, you can use the following class to invert the natural string ordering:

```
Class ReverseStringComparer
    Implements IComparer

    Function CompareValues(ByVal x As Object, ByVal y As Object) As Integer _
        Implements IComparer.Compare
```

```
      ' Just change the sign of the String.Compare result.
      Return -String.Compare(x.ToString, y.ToString)
   End Function
End Class
```

You can pass an instance of this object to one of the two overloaded constructors that take an IComparer object:

```
' A SortedList that sorts elements through a custom IComparer
Dim s14 As New SortedList(New ReverseStringComparer)

' Here's a SortedList that loads all the elements in a Hashtable and
' sorts them with a custom IComparer object.
Dim s15 As New SortedList(ht, New ReverseStringComparer)
```

Here are the elements of the resulting SortedList object:

```
s15('Robert') = 100
s15('Joe') = 300
s15('Ann') = 200
```

Table 8-3 summarizes the most important properties and methods of the SortedList class. You have already met most of them, and the new ones are almost self-explanatory, so I won't describe them in detail.

The SortedList class compares keys in case-sensitive mode, with lowercase characters coming before their uppercase versions (for example with *Ann* coming before *ANN*, which in turn comes before *Bob)*. If you want to compare keys without taking case into account, you can create a case-insensitive SortedList object using the auxiliary CollectionsUtil object in the System.Collections.Specialized namespace:

```
Dim s16 As SortedList = _
    Specialized.CollectionsUtil.CreateCaseInsensitiveSortedList()
```

In this case, trying to add two elements whose keys differ only in case throws an ArgumentException object.

As I said before, the SortedList class is the most powerful collectionlike object, but it's also the most demanding in terms of resources and CPU time. To see what kind of overhead you can expect when using a SortedList object, I created a routine that adds 100,000 elements to an ArrayList object, a Hashtable object, and a SortedList object. The results were pretty interesting: The ArrayList object was about 4 times faster than the Hashtable object, which in turn was from 8 to 100 times faster than the SortedList object. Even though you can't take these ratios as reliable in all circumstances, you clearly should never use a more powerful data structure if you don't really need its features.

Table 8-3   Properties and Methods of the SortedList Class

Syntax	Description
Capacity	Sets or returns the capacity of the SortedList object.
Count	Returns the number of elements currently in the SortedList object.
Item(key)	Sets or returns a value given its key (default member).
Keys	Returns all the keys in the SortedList object as an ICollection object.
Values	Returns all the values in SortedList as an ICollection object.
Add(key, value)	Adds a (key, value) pair to SortedList.
Clear	Removes all the elements from SortedList.
Clone	Creates a shallow copy of the SortedList object.
Contains(key)	Returns True if a given key exists.
ContainsKey(key)	Returns True if a given key exists (same as Contains).
ContainsValue(value)	Returns True if a given value exists.
CopyTo(array, index)	Copies all the DictionaryEntries elements to a one-dimensional array, starting at a specified index in the target array.
GetByIndex(index)	Retrieves a value by its index. (Similar to the Item property but works with the index instead of the key.)
GetKey(index)	Retrieves the key associated with the element at the given index.
GetKeyList	Returns all the keys as an IList object. All the changes in SortedList are reflected in this IList object (similar to the Keys property but returns an IList object instead of an ICollection object, and the result continues to be linked to the list of keys).
GetValueList	Returns all the values as an IList object; all the changes in the SortedList are reflected in this IList object (similar to Values property but returns an IList object instead of an ICollection object, and the result continues to be linked to the list of values).
IndexOfKey(key)	Returns the 0-based index of an element with a given key, or -1 if the key isn't in the SortedList object.
IndexOfValue(value)	Returns the 0-based index of the first occurrence of the specified value, or -1 if the value isn't in the SortedList object.
Remove(key)	Removes the element associated with a given key.
RemoveAt(index)	Removes the element at the given index.
SetByIndex(index, value)	Assigns a new value to the element at the specified index. (Similar to the Item property but works with the index instead of the key.)
TrimToSize	Sets the capacity to the current number of elements in the SortedList object.

Custom Collection and Dictionary Classes

The collection classes provided by the .NET Framework are generic and can contain any type of object. In building an object model, however, you often need to implement strongly typed collections that are bound to a specific type exclusively. A classic example of this concept is when you render the one-to-many relationship that exists between an invoice and its invoice lines. A weak implementation of such a relationship would use a generic collection class, such as an ArrayList:

```
' The parent class in the relationship
Class Invoice
    Public Lines As New ArrayList
End Class

' The child class in the relationship
Class InvoiceLine
    Public Product As String, UnitPrice As Double, Qty As Integer

    Sub New(ByVal product As String, ByVal unitPrice As Decimal, ByVal qty As Integer)
        Me.Product = product
        Me.UnitPrice = unitPrice
        Me.Qty = qty
    End Sub
End Class
```

The preceding code shows something you should *never* do in a real-world class because a client might mistakenly add an invalid object to the collection:

```
Dim invoice1 As New Invoice
' An InvoiceLine is what you want to add to the Lines collection.
invoice1.Lines.Add(New InvoiceLine("Monitor", 359, 2))
' You'd like next line to trigger a compiler error, but it doesn't.
invoice1.Lines.Add("a string")
```

To make your code more robust, you must implement a custom collection class, say InvoiceLineCollection, whose Add, Remove, and Item members can only take or return an InvoiceLine object. A strongly-typed collection also makes your code look better because you don't need to cast its elements to a specific type when you read them back:

```
' Retrieve the first line. (No CType or DirectCase is needed)
Dim invLine1 As InvoiceLine = invoice1.Lines(0)
```

In most cases creating a collection class is as simple as inheriting from one of the special abstract classes that the .NET Framework kindly provides. These classes provide much of the functionality you need in a collectionlike object, and you simply have to add the missing pieces. In this section, I'll describe four such objects: the Collection-Base class, for implementing full-featured collection classes; the ReadOnlyCollection-Base class, which is more convenient for collection classes with fixed membership (that is, collections you can't add items to or remove items from); the DictionaryBase class, for implementing dictionary-like objects; and the NameObjectCollectionBase class, for creating collections whose elements can be indexed by either their string key or index.

The CollectionBase Abstract Class

You can create a regular read/write, strongly typed collection by inheriting a class from CollectionBase. This base collection provides all the members that are generic, such as Count, RemoveAt, and Clear, and you can complete the collection by providing only the members that take or return objects of the specific type that the collection is expected to contain. For example, you can build an initial version of the InvoiceLine-Collection class by adding the Add, Insert, and Remove methods, and the Item property:

```
Class InvoiceLineCollection
    Inherits CollectionBase

    ' The type-safe Add method
    Sub Add(ByVal il As InvoiceLine)
        Me.List.Add(il)
    End Sub

    ' Remove the specified InvoiceLine object.
    Sub Remove(ByVal il As InvoiceLine)
        Me.List.Remove(il)
    End Sub

    ' Set or return an element at the specified index.
    Default Property Item(ByVal index As Integer) As InvoiceLine
        Get
            ' This operation requires a cast.
            Return DirectCast(Me.List.Item(index), InvoiceLine)
        End Get
        Set(ByVal Value As InvoiceLine)
            Me.List.Item(index) = Value
        End Set
    End Property
End Class
```

As you see, all members are implemented simply by delegating to the member with the same name as the inner List object. List is a protected property (of type IList) inherited from CollectionBase, and therefore isn't visible to users of your InvoiceLineCollection object. Now you can make the Invoice class more robust simply by changing the type of the Lines public member and making it read-only:

```
Class Invoice
    Public ReadOnly Lines As New InvoiceLineCollection()
End Class
```

After this change, a client can only add InvoiceLine objects to the invoice's Lines collection. You can extend the InvoiceLineCollection class with other methods that a client would expect to find in a full-fledged collection, such as Insert and Contains:

```
' Insert an InvoiceLine element at a given index.
Sub Insert(ByVal index As Integer, ByVal il As InvoiceLine)
    Me.List.Insert(index, il)
End Sub

' Check that a given element is in the collection
Function Contains(ByVal il As InvoiceLine) As Boolean
    Return Me.List.Contains(il)
End Sub
```

Another common addition to collection classes is an overloaded version of the Add method that takes the arguments you'd pass to the constructor of the inner object:

```
Function Add(ByVal product As String, ByVal unitPrice As Decimal, _
    ByVal qty As Integer) As InvoiceLine
    Dim newItem As New InvoiceLine(product, unitPrice, qty)
    ' Delegate to the main Add method.
    Me.Add(newItem)
End Sub
```

Adding new invoice lines is now easier:

```
Dim invLine As InvoiceLine = invoice1.Lines.Add("Monitor", 359, 2)
```

You aren't limited to the members that a generic collection exposes. For example, you might add a GetTotalItems method that returns the total number of pieces in the invoice:

```
Function GetTotalItems() As Integer
    For Each il As InvoiceLine In Me.List
        GetTotalItems += il.Qty
    Next
End Function
```

The CollectionBase class also exposes the InnerList protected member, which returns a reference to the inner ArrayList used to store individual items. This member lets you implement the public methods that a client would expect to find in an ArrayList-like object and that you can't reach through the List protected member (which returns an IList object)—for example, AddRange, Reverse, Sort, BinarySearch, IndexOf, and LastIndexOf:

```
Sub Sort()
    Me.InnerList.Sort()
End Function

Function IndexOf(ByVal il As InvoiceLine) As Integer
    Return Me.InnerList.IndexOf(il)
End Function
```

You can also extend and improve the collection class by overriding a bunch of protected methods defined in the CollectionBase class and invoked whenever the inner ArrayList object is modified.

I'll give an example showing how to override one of these protected methods, and why you should. Say you want to implement a GetTotalPrice method that returns the sum of the value of each individual InvoiceLine object. You can implement such a method by simply iterating over the inner ArrayList object in a way similar to what you did for the GetTotalItems method. However, for illustration purposes I'll further suppose that you want to implement the GetTotalPrice method as a wrapper on a private field that keeps updating the current total price, so that it doesn't have to be re-evaluated at each call:

```
Private m_TotalPrice As Double
Function GetTotalPrice() As Double
    Return m_TotalPrice
End Function
```

It is trivial to update the m_TotalPrice private field when the client code invokes Add and Remove methods, but this approach fails to account for elements removed through the RemoveAt and Clear methods that are inherited from the CollectionBase class. Fortunately, the CollectionBase class provides the hooks you need to intercept calls to these methods, in the form of the On*xxxx* protected methods. (See Table 8-4.) The base class invokes a *xxxx*Complete method when an action has been successfully performed on the inner ArrayList object, making it easy to keep the m_TotalPrice variable up-to-date, regardless of how the inner ArrayList was modified. For example, the OnRemoveComplete method runs after either the Remove or the RemoveAt method is executed. So you can deal with element removal in a single place in your code:

```
Protected Overrides Sub OnInsertComplete(ByVal index As Integer, value As Object)
    Dim invLine As InvoiceLine = DirectCast(value, InvoiceLine)
    m_TotalPrice += invLine.UnitPrice * invLine.Qty
End Sub

Protected Overrides Sub OnRemoveComplete(ByVal index As Integer, value As Object)
    Dim invLine As InvoiceLine = DirectCast(value, InvoiceLine)
    m_TotalPrice -= invLine.UnitPrice * invLine.Qty
End Sub

Protected Overrides Sub OnClearComplete()
m_TotalPrice = 0
End Sub
```

Overriding the OnInsert, OnRemove, and OnClear methods lets you prevent a client from modifying the contents of your custom collection without your approval. For example, you can set a limit to the capacity of a custom collection object:

```
Protected Overrides Sub OnInsert(index As Integer, value As Object)
    If Me.Count >= 100 Then
        Throw New ArgumentException("Too many invoice lines")
    End If
End Sub
```

You get extra robustness when you override the OnInsert method instead of simply putting this code inside the Add method. To understand why, consider this code:

```
' This code should throw an exception, but it doesn't!
Dim ilst As IList = invoice1.Lines
ilst.Add("a string")
```

The problem with the code example is that it throws no exception when an element is added to the collection, even though you'll get an InvalidCastException when you later attempt to cast that element back to an InvoiceLine variable. To make your collection super robust, just override the OnValidate protected method:

```
Protected Overrides Sub OnValidate(ByVal value As Object)
    If Not TypeOf value Is InvoiceLine Then
        Throw New ArgumentException("Incorrect argument type")
    End If
End Sub
```

The public methods you expose in your custom collection, such as Add, Remove, and Item, should never perform validation on the elements being added, removed, or assigned. Instead, you should override the OnAdd, OnRemove, OnSet, and OnValidation methods and put your validation code there. This way the validation code will execute correctly when the collection class is accessed by means of the IList interface. You can even implement a method or property that returns the protected List member of a CollectionBase-derived class to clients without reducing the class's robustness. The On*xxxx* protected methods are correctly called even when clients invoke methods directly on this IList object. However, these protected methods don't fire if an operation is performed directly on the ArrayList member, so you should never expose this member directly to clients.

Table 8-4 Protected Methods of the CollectionBase and DictionaryBase Classes

Syntax	Description
OnClear	The inner collection is about to be cleared.
OnClearComplete	The inner collection has been successfully cleared.
OnInsert	A new element is about to be added to the inner collection.
OnInsertComplete	A new element has been successfully added to the inner collection.
OnRemove	An element is about to be removed from the inner collection.
OnRemoveComplete	An element has been successfully removed from the inner collection.
OnSet	An object is about to be assigned to an existing element of the inner collection.
OnSetComplete	An object has been successfully assigned to an existing element of the inner collection.
OnValidate	An object is about to be added to the inner collection or assigned to an existing element.
OnGet	An element is being read from the inner dictionary. (DictionaryBase only.)

The ReadOnlyCollectionBase Abstract Class

Not all the collection classes you build should let clients add or remove elements. For example, think of a TextLineCollection class that returns the individual lines of a text file in a For Each loop. Implementing such a collection is as easy as inheriting from the ReadOnlyCollectionBase abstract class and implementing a suitable constructor and the Item property:

```
Class TextLineCollection
    Inherits ReadOnlyCollectionBase

    Sub New(ByVal path As String)
        ' Load the inner ArrayList with text lines in the specified file.
        Dim sr As System.IO.StreamReader
        Try
            sr = New System.IO.StreamReader(path)
            Do Until sr.Peek < 0
                Me.InnerList.Add(sr.ReadLine)
            Loop
        Finally
            If Not sr Is Nothing Then sr.Close()
        End Try
    End Sub

    Default ReadOnly Property Item(ByVal index As Integer) As String
        Get
            Return Me.InnerList(index).ToString
        End Get
    End Property
End Class
```

I explain the System.IO.StreamReader object in more details in Chapter 9. Here's how you can use the TextLineCollection class:

```
Dim lines As New TextLineCollection("c:\myfile.txt")
' Display the last line.
Console.WriteLine(lines(lines.Count - 1))
' Display all lines.
For Each s As String In lines
    Console.WriteLine(s)
Next
```

In this specific example, the Item property is marked ReadOnly because a client isn't supposed to change individual lines once the collection has been initialized. But don't confuse this ReadOnly attribute with the fact that the collection inherits from ReadOnlyCollectionBase. When applied to a collection, read-only means that the collection has a fixed size, not that individual elements aren't writable.

The DictionaryBase Abstract Class

Now that you know the mechanism, you should have no problem grasping how you can use the DictionaryBase class to implement a strongly typed, custom dictionary-like object. Again, all you have to do is provide your custom Add and Item members and reference the protected Dictionary object that you inherit from DictionaryBase. The following example creates a PersonDictionary class that can manage Person objects and associate them with a string key. (For brevity's sake, I omitted the code for the Person class.)

```
Class PersonDictionary
    Inherits DictionaryBase

    Sub Add(ByVal key As String, ByVal p As Person)
        Me.Dictionary.Add(key, p)
    End Sub

    Sub Remove(ByVal key As String)
        Me.Dictionary.Remove(key)
    End Sub

    Default Property Item(ByVal key As String) As Person
        Get
            Return DirectCast(Me.Dictionary.Item(key), Person)
        End Get
        Set(ByVal Value As Person)
            Me.Dictionary.Item(key) = Value
        End Set
    End Property

    Function Contains(ByVal key As String) As Boolean
        Return Me.Dictionary.Contains(key)
    End Function
End Class
```

Here's a sample of client code:

```
Dim pd As New PersonDictionary()
pd.Add("Joe", New Person("Joe", "Doe"))
pd.Add("Ann", New Person("Ann", "Smith"))

Console.WriteLine(pd("Joe").CompleteName)    ' => Joe Doe
' Next line throws a NullReferenceException.
Console.WriteLine(pd("Robert").CompleteName)
```

The custom PersonDictionary class should be completed with properties, such as Values and Keys, and a few other methods that aren't implemented in the DictionaryBase class. As with the CollectionBase class, you can intervene when an operation is performed on the inner dictionary object through the protected methods list in Table 8-4.

The protected Dictionary member returns an IDictionary object, but this object doesn't expose all the members a client would expect to find in a complete Hashtable. You can implement such missing members—for example CopyTo and ContainsValue—by referencing the InnerHashtable protected member instead of Dictionary. Be aware, however, that On*xxxx* protected methods don't fire if you directly add elements to or remove elements from InnerHashtable.

The NameObjectCollectionBase Abstract Class

The Visual Basic 6 Collection object lets you retrieve an element by either its index (the position in the collection) or the string key you've associated with it. Oddly, the .NET Framework doesn't include a native class with this feature, but you can remedy this simply by inheriting from NameObjectCollectionBase in the System.Collections.Specialized namespace. This class uses an inner Hashtable object that isn't exposed as a protected member (unlike the Dictionary protected member of the DictionaryBase class). Instead the NameObjectCollectionBase class exposes several Base*xxxx* methods, one for each basic operation you can expose to the outside. For example, you can implement the Add method by delegating to the BaseAdd protected method, and the Item property by delegating to the BaseGet and BaseSet protected methods. As you'd expect, the BaseGet, BaseSet, and BaseRemove methods are overloaded so that they can take either a numeric index or a string key:

```
Imports System.Collections.Specialized

Class PersonCollection
    Inherits NameObjectCollectionBase

    Sub Add(ByVal key As String, ByVal p As Person)
        Me.BaseAdd(key, p)
    End Sub

    Sub Clear()
        Me.BaseClear()
    End Sub

    ' The Remove method that takes a string key
    Sub Remove(ByVal key As String)
        Me.Remove(key)
    End Sub

    ' The Remove method that takes a numeric index
    Sub Remove(ByVal index As Integer)
        Me.Remove(index)
    End Sub

    ' The Item property that takes a string key
    Default Property Item(ByVal key As String) As Person
        Get
            Return DirectCast(Me.BaseGet(key), Person)
        End Get
        Set(ByVal Value As Person)
            Me.BaseSet(key, Value)
        End Set
    End Property

    ' The Item property that takes a numeric index
    Default Property Item(index As Integer) As Person
        Get
            Return DirectCast(Me.BaseGet(index), Person)
        End Get
```

```
        Set(ByVal Value As Person)
            Me.BaseSet(index, Value)
        End Set
    End Property
End Class
```

You have to write a lot of code to create a collection based on NameObjectCollection-Base. This class exposes only the Count and Keys properties—you have to implement all the other members by code. On the other hand, you are in full control of what happens to the inner Hashtable object, and the class doesn't expose any On*xxxx* protected overridable methods. Usually you use the NameObjectCollectionBase class to create a typed collection class, but you also can create a class that takes Object values (that is, anything) to create a perfect imitation of the Visual Basic 6 Collection object.

The IEnumerable and IEnumerator Interfaces

So far, I've illustrated how you can create a collection class by inheriting from the virtual classes that the .NET Framework gives you just for this purpose. All these virtual classes provide a default implementation of IEnumerable, the interface that is implicitly queried for when the collection appears in a For Each loop. However, nothing prevents you from implementing this interface directly, a technique that requires a lot more code but that provides the greatest flexibility.

When Visual Basic .NET compiles a For Each statement, it checks that the object following the In keyword supports the IEnumerable interface. When the For Each statement is executed, Visual Basic invokes the only method in this interface, GetEnumerator. This function must return an object that supports the IEnumerator interface, which in turn exposes the following three members: MoveNext, Current, and Reset. The MoveNext method is called at each For Each iteration and should return True if a new value is available and False if there are no more elements. The Current read-only property returns the value to be used in the current iteration of the loop. The Reset method resets the internal pointer so that the next returned value is the first one in a new series.

To illustrate these interfaces in action with a nontrivial example, I created a Text-FileReader class that lets you iterate over all the lines in a text file within a For Each loop. This result is similar to what I achieved earlier in this chapter with the TextFile-Collection class, which works well but isn't efficient and takes a lot of extra memory when you're reading long files because you need an array to store all the parsed lines. The TextFileReader object uses no additional memory. Instead, text lines are read from the file one at a time:

```
Class TextFileReader
    Implements IEnumerable, IDisposable

    ' The inner StreamReader object
    Dim sr As System.IO.StreamReader
```

```
        Sub New(ByVal path As String)
            sr = New System.IO.StreamReader(path)
        End Sub

        Public Sub Dispose() Implements IDisposable.Dispose
            ' Close the file stream.
            If Not sr Is Nothing Then sr.Close()
        End Sub

        ' The IEnumerable interface
        Private Function GetEnumerator() As IEnumerator _
            Implements IEnumerable.GetEnumerator
            ' Return an instance of the inner enumerator.
            Return New FileReaderEnumerator(Me)
        End Function
End Class
```

Interestingly, most .NET compilers—including Visual Basic .NET and C#—automatically invoke the Dispose method of any IDisposable object used in a For Each loop, when the loop terminates normally or exits because of an Exit For statement. The Text-FileReader class takes advantage of this detail to ensure that the stream is correctly closed as soon as it is no longer necessary.

The GetEnumerator function returns a FileReaderEnumerator object. You can implement this class as a nested type inside FileReader. It has only a constructor and the three methods of the IEnumerator interface:

```
        ' The nested, private enumerator class
        Private Class FileReaderEnumerator
            Implements IEnumerator

            ' A reference to the parent object
            Dim parent As TextFileReader
            ' The text line just read
            Dim currLine As String

            Sub New(ByVal fr As TextFileReader)
                Me.parent = fr
            End Sub

            ' The IEnumerator interface (three methods)

            Public Function MoveNext() As Boolean Implements IEnumerator.MoveNext
                If parent.sr.Peek >= 0 Then
                    ' If not at end of file, read the next line.
                    currLine = parent.sr.ReadLine()
                    Return True
                Else
                    ' Else, close the stream and return False to stop enumeration.
                    parent.Dispose()
                    Return False
                End If
            End Function
```

```
Public ReadOnly Property Current() As Object Implements IEnumerator.Current
    Get
        ' Just return the line read by MoveNext.
        Return currLine
    End Get
End Property

Public Sub Reset() Implements IEnumerator.Reset
    ' This method is never called and can be empty.
End Sub
End Class
```

Using the TextFileReader class is a breeze:

```
For Each s As String In New TextFileReader("c:\myfile.txt")
    Console.WriteLine(s)
Next
```

Note that you might make the code a bit more concise by having TextFileReader implement both the IEnumerable and the IEnumerator interface. In general, however, keeping the enumerator in a distinct class makes for a better design and helps make your code reusable.

The .NET classes that implement the IEnumerable interface expose a Public GetEnumerator method that you can call explicitly. This technique lets you simplify the implementation of an enumerable class by implementing the IEnumerable interface only and having its GetEnumerator method return an instance of an inner object that supports IEnumerable. Here's the example of a class named ReverseIterator that can be used in a For Each loop to iterate over the elements of a collectionlike object—that is, any object that implements the ICollection interface and hence the For Each statement—in reverse order. The class uses an inner ArrayList object that is filled in the constructor method in such a way that the last element in the original collection becomes the first element in the ArrayList:

```
Class ReverseIterator
    Implements IEnumerable

    ' The inner ArrayList
    Dim list As New ArrayList()

    ' The constructor takes an object that can be enumerated.
    Sub New(ByVal col As ICollection)
        ' Insert elements in reverse order.
        For Each o As Object In col
            list.Insert(0, o)
        Next
    End Sub

    ' Return the enumerator of the inner ArrayList.
    Function GetEnumerator() As IEnumerator Implements IEnumerable.GetEnumerator
        Return list.GetEnumerator()
    End Function
End Class
```

Here's the code that uses the ReverseIterator class:

```
Dim arr() As String = {"one", "two", "three", "four", "five"}
For Each s As String In New ReverseIterator(arr)
    Console.WriteLine(s)
Next
```

> **See Also**   Read the document "Invoking IEnumerator Members.doc" on the companion CD to see how your code can get extra flexibility by directly calling the members of the IEnumerator interface (instead of having Visual Basic .NET do it implicitly in a For Each loop).

At this point, you have added many new classes to your data structure arsenal, and you should be more familiar with how things work in the .NET world, such as how you use inheritance to derive new and more powerful data classes. It's now time to start working with other classes in the .NET Framework, such as files and directories.

9 Files, Directories, and Streams

The .NET Framework offers excellent support for working with files and directories via the classes in the System.IO namespace. These are the five classes of interest:

- **Directory** Contains shared methods that let you enumerate and manipulate directories

- **File** Contains shared methods that let you enumerate and manipulate files

- **Path** Contains shared methods to manipulate path information

- **DirectoryInfo** Represents an individual directory and exposes the methods to query its attributes and manipulate them

- **FileInfo** Represents an individual file and exposes the methods to query its attributes and manipulate them

> **Note** To keep code as concise as possible, all the code samples in this section assume that the following Imports statement is used at the file or project level:
>
> ```
> Imports System.IO
> ```

The Directory and File Classes

The Directory and File classes contain only shared methods that set or return information about entries in the file system. Both classes will look familiar to developers who have worked with the FileSystemObject object hierarchy in the Microsoft Scripting Runtime library; even though property and method names are different in some cases, the underlying principles are the same. Table 9-1 recaps all the methods in these classes. In the paragraphs following the table, I'll draw your attention to the most interesting ones.

Table 9-1 Main Shared Methods of the Directory and File Classes

Class	Syntax	Description
Directory and File	Delete(path)	Deletes a file or directory
	Move(source, dest)	Moves a file or directory
	Exists(path)	Returns True if a file or directory exists

Table 9-1   Main Shared Methods of the Directory and File Classes *(continued)*

Class	Syntax	Description
	GetCreationTime(path)	Returns the creation time of a file or directory
	SetCreationTime (path, datetime)	Sets the creation time of a file or directory
	GetLastAccessTime(path)	Returns the last access time of a file or directory
	SetLastAccessTime(path, datetime)	Sets the last access time of a file or directory
	GetLastWriteTime(path)	Returns the last write time of a file or directory
	SetLastWriteTime(path, datetime)	Sets the last write time of a file or directory
Directory only	GetCurrentDirectory	Returns the current directory (string)
	GetParent(path)	Returns the parent directory as a DirectoryInfo object
	GetDirectoryRoot (path)	Returns the root directory for the specified path (string)
	CreateDirectory (path)	Creates the specified directory and all the directories on its path if necessary
	GetLogicalDrives	Returns a String array with all the logical drives in the system
	GetDirectories (path[, filespec])	Returns a String array with all the subdirectories in a directory, optionally filtered by the specified criteria
	GetFiles (path[, filespec])	Returns a String array with all the files in a directory, optionally filtered by the specified criteria
	GetFileSystemEntries(path[, filespec])	Returns a String array with all the files and subdirectories in a directory, optionally filtered by the specified criteria
	Delete(path[, recursive])	Deletes a directory and all its subdirectories if the second argument is True
File only	GetAttributes(file)	Returns the attributes of a file (but works with directories as well)
	SetAttributes(file, attributes)	Sets the attributes of a file

Table 9-1   Main Shared Methods of the Directory and File Classes *(continued)*

Class	Syntax	Description
	Copy(source, dest[, overwrite])	Copies a file to a new destination, also in different drives, and optionally overwrites the destination file if necessary
	Create(file [, buffersize])	Creates and opens the specified file and returns a FileStream object; the optional argument specifies the buffer size
	Open(file [, mode [, access [, share]]])	Opens a file with specified mode, access, and share; returns a FileStream
	CreateText(file)	Creates a text file and returns a StreamWriter
	AppendText(file)	Opens a text file in append mode and returns a StreamWriter
	OpenRead(file)	Opens a file in read mode and returns a FileStream
	OpenWrite(file)	Opens a file in write mode and returns a FileStream
	OpenText(file)	Opens a text file for reading and returns a StreamReader

The SetCurrentDirectory and GetCurrentDirectory methods of the Directory class set and return the current directory and therefore are equivalent to the ChDrive and ChDir commands and the CurDir function in Visual Basic 6:

```
' Save the current directory.
Dim currDir As String = Directory.GetCurrentDirectory
' Change the current directory to something else.
Directory.SetCurrentDirectory("C:\Temp")
⋮
' Restore the current directory.
Directory.SetCurrentDirectory(currDir)
```

The following code uses the GetLogicalDrives shared method to display the root path for all the drives in the system:

```
' Retrieve all the root paths.
Dim strRoots() As String = Directory.GetLogicalDrives
For Each s As String In strRoots
    Console.WriteLine(s)          ' => C:\   D:\
Next
```

Thanks to the GetDirectories and GetFiles methods, you need very little code to iterate over all the directories and files of a directory tree. For example, the following code snippet prints the structure of a directory tree and (optionally) the names of files in each directory:

```
Sub PrintDirTree(ByVal dir As String, ByVal showFiles As Boolean, _
    Optional ByVal level As Integer = 0)
    ' Display the name of this directory with correct indentation.
    Console.WriteLine(New String("-"c, level * 2) & dir)

    Try
        ' Display all files in this directory with correct indentation.
        If showFiles Then
            For Each fname As String In Directory.GetFiles(dir)
                Console.WriteLine(New String(" "c, level * 2 + 2) & fname)
            Next
        End If
        ' A recursive call for all the subdirectories in this directory
        For Each subdir As String In Directory.GetDirectories(dir)
            PrintDirTree(subdir, showFiles, level + 1)
        Next
    Catch
        ' Do nothing if any error (presumably "Drive not ready").
    End Try
End Sub
```

You can pass a directory name to the PrintDirTree procedure or print the directory tree of all the drives in your system by using this code:

```
For Each rootDir As String In Directory.GetLogicalDrives
    PrintDirTree(rootDir, True)
Next
```

The GetFiles and GetDirectories methods can take a second argument containing wildcards to filter the result:

```
' Display all the *.txt files in C:\DOCS.
For Each fname As String In Directory.GetFiles("c:\docs", "*.txt")
    Console.WriteLine(fname)
Next
```

You can use the GetCreationTime, GetLastAccessTime, GetLastWriteTime, and GetAttributes shared methods to display information about a file or a directory or to filter files according to their attributes:

```
For Each fname As String In Directory.GetFiles("c:\docs", "*.txt")
    ' Display only read-only files.
    If CBool(File.GetAttributes(fname) And FileAttributes.ReadOnly) Then
        Console.WriteLine(fname)
    End If
Next
```

Each Get*xxxx*Time and Set*xxxx*Time method that reads or modifies a DateTime value has a matching Get*xxxx*TimeUtc and Set*xxxx*TimeUtc method (not listed in Table 9-1) that works with coordinated universal time (UTC), that is, an absolute DateTime that isn't affected by the current time zone. These methods were added in .NET Framework 1.1 to let you compare files that are scattered over the worldwide Internet. For example, you can use the File.GetLastWriteUtc method to implement a replication program that compares the files at two Internet sites in different time zones and overwrites the older one with the newer version.

The Directory class doesn't expose a GetAttributes method, but the File.GetAttributes method works also for directories, so this limitation isn't a problem. The SetAttributes and GetAttributes methods set or return a bit-coded FileAttributes value, which is a combination of Normal (no attributes), Archive, ReadOnly, Hidden, System, Directory, Compressed, Encrypted, Temporary, NotContentIndexed, and a few other values:

```
' Display system and hidden files in C:\.
For Each fname As String In Directory.GetFiles("C:\")
    Dim attr As FileAttributes = File.GetAttributes(fname)
    ' Display the file if marked as hidden or system (or both).
    If CBool(attr And FileAttributes.Hidden) Or _
        CBool(attr And FileAttributes.System) Then
        Console.WriteLine(fname)
    End If
Next
```

With a little bit-tweaking, you can make the If expression more concise, as follows:

```
If CBool(attr And (FileAttributes.Hidden Or FileAttributes.System)) Then
```

The Directory.CreateDirectory method creates a directory and all the intermediate directories in the path if necessary:

```
' Next line works even if the C:\MyApp directory doesn't exist yet.
Directory.CreateDirectory("C:\MyApp\Data")
```

The SetCreationTime, SetLastWriteTime, and SetLastAccessTime methods let you modify the date attributes of a file or directory:

```
' Change the access date and time of all files in C:\DOCS.
For Each fname As String In Directory.GetFiles("c:\docs")
    File.SetLastAccessTime(fname, Date.Now)
Next
```

The SetCreationTime method can easily create a "touch" utility that modifies the last write time of all the files specified on its command line:

```
' Change the access date and time of all files whose names are
' passed on the command line.
Sub Main(ByVal args() As String)
    For Each fname As String In args
        File.SetCreationTime(fname, Date.Now)
    Next
End Sub
```

The File object serves primarily two purposes. First, you can use it to process *closed* files—for example, to delete, copy, or move them or to retrieve information such as creation date and attributes. Second, you can use it to open a file and create a FileStream object, which you then use to actually read from and write to the open file. You set three values when you call the Open method:

- **FileMode**   Can be Append, Create, CreateNew, Open, OpenOrCreate, or Truncate. Open and Append modes fail if the file doesn't exist; Create and CreateNew fail if the file exists already. Use OpenOrCreate to open a file or to create one if it doesn't exist yet.

- **FileAccess**   Can be Read, Write, or ReadWrite.

- **FileShare**   Tells which operations other FileStreams can perform on the open file. It can be None (all operations are prohibited), ReadWrite (all operations are allowed), Read, Write, or Inheritable (though Inheritable isn't supported directly by Win32).

The File class exposes three variants of the Open method: Create, OpenRead, and OpenWrite. Both the generic Open method and these variants return a FileStream object, and I'll illustrate all of them later in this chapter. There are also three specific methods for working with text files (CreateText, OpenText, and AppendText) that return a StreamReader or StreamWriter object.

The DirectoryInfo and FileInfo Classes

The DirectoryInfo and FileInfo classes represent individual directories and files. Both classes inherit from the FileSystemInfo virtual class and therefore have several properties and methods in common, such as Name, FullName, and Attributes. (See Table 9-2 for the complete list.) You can get a reference to a DirectoryInfo or FileInfo object by using its constructor method, which takes the path of a specific directory or file:

```
' Create a DirectoryInfo object that points to C:\.
Dim rootDi As New DirectoryInfo("C:\")
' Create a FileInfo object that points to C:\Autoexec.bat.
Dim batFi As New FileInfo("C:\Autoexec.bat")
```

Once you have a reference to a DirectoryInfo object, you can use its methods to enumerate its contents and get other DirectoryInfo or FileInfo objects. (You can also apply filter criteria.)

```
' List the directories in C:\.
For Each di As DirectoryInfo In rootDi.GetDirectories
    Console.WriteLine(di.Name)
Next

' List all the *.txt files in C:\.
For Each fi As FileInfo In rootDi.GetFiles("*.txt")
    Console.WriteLine(fi.Name)
Next
```

The DirectoryInfo.GetFileSystemInfos method returns an array of FileSystemInfo objects. Both the DirectoryInfo and FileInfo classes inherit from the FileSystemInfo class, so you can have a single loop that processes both files and subdirectories in a directory, as you can see in the next code snippet:

```
' Note that we can create the DirectoryInfo object on the fly.
For Each fsi As FileSystemInfo In (New DirectoryInfo("C:\")).GetFileSystemInfos
    ' Use the [dir] or [file] prefix.
    If CBool(fsi.Attributes And FileAttributes.Directory) Then
        Console.Write("[dir] ")
    Else
        Console.Write("[file] ")
    End If
    ' Print name and creation date.
    Console.WriteLine(fsi.Name & " - " & fsi.CreationTime)
Next
```

Most of the members of the DirectoryInfo and FileInfo classes perform the same action of shared methods with similar names exposed by the Directory and File types. For example, the FileInfo.CreationTime property lets you read and modify the creation date of a file, just as the File object's GetCreationTime and SetCreationTime methods do. Among the few exceptions is the FileInfo.Length property, which returns the length of a file:

```
' List all empty files in C:\.
For Each fi As FileInfo In rootDi.GetFiles()
    If fi.Length = 0 Then Console.WriteLine(fi.Name)
Next
```

Table 9-2   Main Properties and Methods of the DirectoryInfo and FileInfo Classes

Class	Syntax	Description
DirectoryInfo and FileInfo (inherited from FileSystemInfo)	Name	Returns the name of the file or directory
	FullName	Returns the full name of the file or directory (including its path)
	Extension	Returns the extension of the file or directory
	Exists	Returns True if the file or directory exists
	Attributes	Sets or returns the attributes of the file or directory as a bit-coded FileAttributes value
	CreationTime	Sets or returns the creation time of the file or directory (Date value)
	LastWriteTime	Sets or returns the last write time of the file or directory (Date value)

Table 9-2 **Main Properties and Methods of the DirectoryInfo and FileInfo Classes** *(continued)*

Class	Syntax	Description
	LastAccessTime	Sets or returns the last access time of the file or directory (Date value)
	Refresh	Refreshes the properties of this FileInfo or DirectoryInfo object
	Delete	Deletes the file or directory
DirectoryInfo only	Parent	Returns the DirectoryInfo object for the parent directory
	Root	Returns the DirectoryInfo object for the root directory
	Create	Creates the directory
	MoveTo(destpath)	Moves the current directory to another path
	Delete ([recursive])	Deletes the current directory; Boolean argument specifies whether all the subdirectories should be deleted as well
	CreateSubdirectory (path)	Creates a subdirectory of the current directory and returns the corresponding DirectoryInfo object
	GetDirectories ([filespec])	Returns information about the subdirectories in the current directory as an array of DirectoryInfo objects; can take an optional search criterion, such as "A*"
	GetFiles([filespec])	Returns information about the files in the current directory as an array of FileInfo objects; can take an optional search criterion, such as "*.txt"
	GetFileSystem-Infos([filespec])	Returns information about the files and subdirectories in the current directory as an array of FileSystemInfo objects; can take an optional search criterion, such as "*.txt"
FileInfo only	Length	Returns the length of the file
	Directory	Returns the DirectoryInfo object for the parent directory
	DirectoryName	Returns the name of the parent directory
	Create	Creates the file
	MoveTo(destpath)	Moves the current file to another path
	CopyTo(destfile [,overwrite])	Copies the current file to another path and optionally overwrites an existing file

Table 9-2   Main Properties and Methods of the DirectoryInfo and FileInfo Classes *(continued)*

Class	Syntax	Description
	Open (mode [,access [,share]])	Opens the current file with specified mode, access, and share; returns a FileStream object
	OpenRead	Opens the current file in read mode and returns a FileStream object
	OpenWrite	Opens the current file in write mode and returns a FileStream object
	OpenText	Opens the current file in read mode and returns a StreamReader object
	CreateText	Creates a text file and returns a StreamWriter object
	AppendText	Opens the current text file in append mode and returns a StreamWriter object

The Path Class

The Path class exposes shared fields and methods that can help you process file and directory paths. The five static fields return information about valid drive and filename separators. You might want to query them only to prepare your programs to run on other operating systems if and when the .NET Framework is ported to platforms other than Windows:

```
Console.WriteLine(Path.AltDirectorySeparatorChar)  ' => /
Console.WriteLine(Path.DirectorySeparatorChar)     ' => \
Console.WriteLine(Path.InvalidPathChars)           ' => "<>|
Console.WriteLine(Path.PathSeparator)              ' => ;
Console.WriteLine(Path.VolumeSeparatorChar)        ' => :
```

The GetTempPath and GetTempFileName methods take no arguments and return the location of the temporary directory in Windows and the name of a temporary file, respectively:

```
' Note that paths are in 8.3 MS-DOS format.
Console.WriteLine(Path.GetTempPath)
    ' => C:\DOCUME~1\ADMINI~1\LOCALS~1\Temp\
Console.WriteLine(Path.GetTempFileName)
    ' => C:\DOCUME~1\ADMINI~1\LOCALS~1\Temp\tmp1B2.tmp
```

A number of other methods let you extract information from a file path without your having to worry about whether the file or the directory exists.

```
Dim fil As String = "C:\MyApp\Bin\MyApp.exe"
Console.WriteLine(Path.GetDirectoryName(fil))           ' => C:\MyApp\Bin
```

```
Console.WriteLine(Path.GetFileName(fil))                    ' => MyApp.exe
Console.WriteLine(Path.GetExtension(fil))                   ' => .exe
Console.WriteLine(Path.GetFileNameWithoutExtension(fil))    ' => MyApp
Console.WriteLine(Path.GetPathRoot(fil))                    ' => C:\
Console.WriteLine(Path.HasExtension(fil))                   ' => True
Console.WriteLine(Path.IsPathRooted(fil))                   ' => True
```

The GetFullPath method expands a relative path to an absolute path, taking the current directory into account:

```
' Next line assumes that current directory is C:\MyApp.
Console.WriteLine(Path.GetFullPath("MyApp.Exe"))        ' => C:\MyApp\MyApp.Exe
```

The ChangeExtension method returns a filename with a different extension:

```
Console.WriteLine(Path.ChangeExtension("MyApp.Exe", "Dat"))   ' => MyApp.Dat
```

Finally, the Combine method takes a pathname and a filename and combines them into a valid filename, adding or discarding backslash characters:

```
Console.WriteLine(Path.Combine("C:\MyApp\", "MyApp.Dat"))
   ' => C:\MyApp\MyApp.Dat
```

The Stream Class

The Stream abstract class represents a sequence of bytes going to or coming from a storage medium (such as a file) or a physical or virtual device (such as a parallel port, an interprocess communication pipe, or a TCP/IP socket). Streams allow you to read from and write to a backing *store*, which can correspond to one of several storage mediums. For example, you can have file streams, memory streams, network streams, and tape streams.

Because it's an abstract class, you don't create a Stream object directly, and you rarely use a Stream variable in your code. Rather, you typically work with classes that inherit from it, such as the FileStream class.

Stream Operations

The fundamental operations you can perform on streams are read, write, and seek. Not all types of streams support all these operations—for example, the NetworkStream object doesn't support seeking. You can check which operations are allowed by using the stream's CanRead, CanWrite, and CanSeek properties.

Most stream objects perform data buffering in a transparent way. For example, data isn't immediately written to disk when you write to a file stream; instead, bytes are buffered and are eventually flushed when the stream is closed or when you issue an explicit Flush method. Buffering can improve performance remarkably. File streams are buffered, whereas memory streams aren't because there's no point in buffering a stream that maps to memory. You can use a BufferedStream object to add buffering capability to a stream object that doesn't offer it natively—for example, a Network-Buffer. (See the MSDN documentation for details about the BufferedStream object.)

Most of the properties of the Stream class—and of classes that inherit from Stream—work as you would intuitively expect them to work:

■ The Length property returns the total size of the Stream, whereas the Position property determines the current position in the Stream (that is, the offset of the next byte that will be read or written). You can change the stream's length using the SetLength method and change the position using the Seek method.

■ The Read method reads a number of bytes from the specified position into a Byte array, then advances the stream pointer, and finally returns the number of bytes read. The ReadByte method reads and returns a single byte.

■ The Write method writes a number of bytes from an array into the stream and then advances the stream pointer. The WriteByte method writes a single byte to the stream.

■ The Close method closes the stream and releases all the associated resources. The Flush method empties a buffered stream and ensures that all its contents are written to the underlying store. (It has no effect on nonbuffered streams.)

Specific streams can implement additional methods and properties, such as the following:

■ The FileStream class exposes the Handle property (which returns the operating system file handle) and the Lock and Unlock methods (which lock or unlock a portion of the file). When you're working with FileStream objects, the SetLength method actually trims or extends the underlying file.

■ The MemoryStream class exposes the Capacity property (which returns the number of bytes allocated to the stream), the WriteTo method (which copies the entire contents to another stream), and the GetBuffer method (which returns the array of unsigned bytes from which the stream was created).

■ The NetworkStream class exposes the DataAvailable property (which returns True when data is available on the stream for reading).

Stream Readers and Writers

Because the generic Stream object can read and write only individual bytes or groups of bytes, most of the time you use auxiliary *stream reader* and *stream writer* objects that let you work with more structured data, such as a line of text or a Double value. The .NET Framework offers several stream reader and writer pairs:

■ The BinaryReader and BinaryWriter classes can work with primitive data in binary format, such as a Single value or an encoded string.

- The StreamReader and StreamWriter classes can work with strings of text in ANSI format, such as the text you read from or write to a text file. These classes can work in conjunction with an Encoder object, which determines how characters are encoded in the stream.

- TextReader and TextWriter are abstract classes that define how to work with strings of text in Unicode format. The StringReader and StringWriter classes inherit from TextReader and TextWriter and can read and write characters from a Unicode string in memory.

- The XmlTextReader and XmlTextWriter classes work with XML text. (For more information about these classes, see Chapter 23.)

- The ResourceReader and ResourceWriter classes work with resource files.

Reading and Writing Text Files

You typically use a StreamReader object to read from a text file. You can obtain a reference to such an object in many ways:

```
' With the File.OpenText shared method
Dim sr As StreamReader = File.OpenText("c:\autoexec.bat")

' With the OpenText instance method of a FileInfo object
Dim fi2 As New FileInfo("c:\autoexec.bat")
Dim sr2 As StreamReader = fi2.OpenText

' By passing a FileStream from the Open method of the File class to
' the StreamReader's constructor method
' (This technique lets you specify mode, access, and share mode.)
Dim st3 As Stream = File.Open("C:\autoexec.bat", _
    FileMode.Open, FileAccess.ReadWrite, FileShare.ReadWrite)
Dim sr3 As New StreamReader(st3)

' By opening a FileStream on the file and then passing it
' to the StreamReader's constructor method
Dim fs4 As New FileStream("C:\autoexec.bat", FileMode.Open)
Dim sr4 As New StreamReader(fs4)

' By getting a FileStream from the OpenRead method of the File class
' and passing it to the StreamReader's constructor
Dim sr5 As New StreamReader(File.OpenRead("c:\autoexec.bat"))

' By passing the filename to the StreamReader's constructor
Dim sr6 As New StreamReader("c:\autoexec.bat")

' By passing the filename and encoding
Dim sr7 As New StreamReader("c:\autoexec.bat", System.Text.Encoding.Unicode)
Dim sr8 As New StreamReader("c:\autoexec.bat", System.Text.Encoding.ASCII)
' As before, but we let the system decide the best encoding.
Dim sr9 As New StreamReader("c:\autoexec.bat", True)
```

After you get a reference to a StreamReader object, you can use one of its many methods to read one or more characters or whole text lines. The Peek method returns the code of the next character in the stream without actually extracting it, or it returns the special -1 value if there are no more characters. In practice, this method is used to test an end-of-file condition:

```
' Display all the text lines in the file.
Do Until sr.Peek = -1
    ' The ReadLine method reads whole lines.
    Console.WriteLine(sr.ReadLine)
Loop
' Always close a StreamReader when you're done with it.
sr.Close()
```

You can also read one character at a time using the Read method, or you can read all the remaining characters using the ReadToEnd method:

```
' Read the entire contents of C:\Autoexec.bat in one shot.
sr = New StreamReader("c:\autoexec.bat")
Dim fileContents As String = sr.ReadToEnd()
```

If you opened the StreamReader through a Stream object, you can use the Stream object's Seek method to move the pointer or even just read its current position. If you did *not* open the StreamReader through a Stream object, you can still access the inner Stream object that the .NET runtime creates anyway, through the StreamReader's BaseStream property:

```
' ...(Continuing previous code example)...
' If the file is longer than 100 chars, process it again, one character at a
' time (admittedly a silly thing to do, but it's just a demo).
If fileContents.Length >= 100 Then
    ' Reset the stream's pointer to the beginning.
    sr.BaseStream.Seek(0, SeekOrigin.Begin)
    ' Read individual characters until EOF is reached.
    Do Until sr.Peek() = -1
        ' Read method returns an integer, so convert it to Char.
        Console.Write(sr.Read.ToString)
    Loop
End If
sr.Close
```

You use a StreamWriter object to write to a text file. As with the StreamReader object, you can create a StreamWriter object in many ways:

```
Dim sw1 As StreamWriter = File.CreateText("c:\temp.dat")

' By passing a FileStream from the Open method of the File class to
' the StreamWriter's constructor method
Dim st2 As Stream = File.Open("C:\temp.dat", _
    FileMode.Create, FileAccess.ReadWrite, FileShare.None)
Dim sw2 As New StreamWriter(st2)
```

```
' By opening a FileStream on the file and then passing it
' to the StreamWriter's constructor method
Dim fs3 As New FileStream("C:\autoexec.bat", FileMode.Open)
Dim sw3 As New StreamWriter(fs3)

' By getting a FileStream from the OpenWrite method of the File class
' and passing it to the StreamWriter's constructor
Dim sw4 As New StreamWriter(File.OpenWrite("C:\temp.dat"))

' By passing the filename to the StreamWriter's constructor
Dim sw5 As New StreamWriter("C:\temp.dat")
```

The StreamWriter class exposes the Write and WriteLine methods: the Write method can write the textual representation of any basic data type (Integer, Double, and so on); the WriteLine method works only with strings and automatically appends a newline character. Leave the AutoFlush property set to False (the default value) if you want the StreamWriter to adopt a limited form of caching; you'll probably need to issue a Flush method periodically in this case. Set this property to True for those streams or devices, such as the console window, from which the user expects immediate feedback.

The following code uses a StreamReader object to read from a file and a StreamWriter object to copy the text to another file, after converting the text to uppercase:

```
Dim sr As New StreamReader("C:\Autoexec.bat")
Dim sw As New StreamWriter("C:\Autoexec.new")
Do Until sr.Peek = -1
    ' The ReadLine method returns a string, so we can
    ' convert it to uppercase on the fly.
    sw.WriteLine(sr.ReadLine.ToUpper)
Loop
sr.Close()
sw.Close()        ' This actually writes data to the file and closes it.
```

If you're working with smaller text files, you can also trade some memory for speed and do without a loop:

```
sr = New StreamReader("C:\Autoexec.bat")
sw = New StreamWriter("C:\Autoexec.new")
sw.Write(sr.ReadToEnd.ToUpper)
sr.Close()
sw.Close()
```

You should always close the Stream object after using it. Otherwise, the stream keeps the file open until the next garbage collection calls the Stream's Finalize method. There are at least two reasons why you'd rather close the stream manually. First, if the file is kept open longer than strictly necessary, you can't delete or move it, nor can another application open it for reading and/or writing (depending on the access mode you specified when opening the file). The second reason is performance: the code in the Stream's Close method calls the GC.SuppressFinalize method, so the stream isn't finalized and therefore the resources it uses are released earlier.

Reading and Writing Binary Files

The BinaryReader and BinaryWriter classes are suitable for working with binary streams; one such stream might be associated with a file containing data in native format. In this context, *native format* means the actual bits used to store the value in memory. You can't create a BinaryReader or BinaryWriter object directly from a file-name as you can with the StreamReader and StreamWriter objects. Instead, you must create a Stream object explicitly and pass it to the constructor method of either the BinaryReader or the BinaryWriter class:

```
' Associate a stream with a new file opened with write access.
Dim st As Stream = File.Open("c:\values.dat", FileMode.Create, _
    FileAccess.Write)
' Create a BinaryWriter associated with the output stream.
Dim bw As New BinaryWriter(st)
```

Working with the BinaryWriter object is especially simple because its Write method is overloaded to accept all the primitive .NET types, including signed and unsigned integers; Single, Double, and String values; and so on. The following code snippet writes 10 random Double values to a binary file:

```
' ...(Continuing previous example)...
' Save 10 Double values to the file.
Dim rand As New Random
For i As Integer = 1 To 10
    bw.Write(rand.NextDouble)
Next
' Flush the output data to the file.
bw.Close()
```

The BinaryReader class exposes many Read*xxxx* methods, one for each possible native data type, and a PeekChar method that returns -1 at the end of the stream:

```
' Read back values written in previous example.

' Associate a stream with an existing file, opened with read access.
Dim st2 As Stream = File.Open("c:\values.dat", FileMode.Open, FileAccess.Read)
' Create a BinaryReader associated with the input stream.
Dim br2 As New BinaryReader(st2)

' Loop until data is available.
Do Until br2.PeekChar = -1
    ' Read the next element. (We know it's a Double.)
    Console.WriteLine(br2.ReadDouble)
Loop
br2.Close()
st2.Close()
```

Outputting strings with a BinaryWriter requires some additional care, however. Passing a string to the Write method outputs a length-prefixed string to the stream. If you want to write only the actual characters (as happens when you're working with fixed-length strings), you must pass the Write method an array of Chars. The Write method is over-loaded to take additional arguments that specify which portion of the array should be written.

Reading back strings requires different techniques as well, depending on how the string was written. You use the ReadString method for length-prefixed strings and the ReadChars method for fixed-length strings. You can see an example of these methods in action in the next section.

File streams can be opened for asynchronous read and write operations, which can speed up your code's performance significantly. You'll learn about asynchronous file operations in Chapter 12.

Reading and Writing Memory Streams

Stream readers and writers aren't just for files. For example, you can use them in con-junction with a MemoryStream object to deal with memory as if it were a temporary file (which usually delivers better performance than using an actual file). The following code snippet performs the same operation seen in the preceding section; this time, the code uses a memory stream instead of a file stream:

```
' Create a memory stream with initial capacity of 1 KB.
Dim st As New MemoryStream(1024)
Dim bw As New BinaryWriter(st)
Dim rand As New Random()
' Write 10 random Double values to the stream.
For i As Integer = 1 To 10
    bw.Write(rand.NextDouble)
Next

' Rewind the stream to the beginning.
st.Seek(0, SeekOrigin.Begin)
Dim br As New BinaryReader(st)

Do Until br.PeekChar = -1
    Console.WriteLine(br.ReadDouble)
Loop
br.Close()
st.Close()
```

Of course, in this particular example you might have used an array to store random val-ues and read them back. However, the approach based on streams lets you move from a memory stream to a file-based stream by changing only one statement (the stream constructor). In a real application, you might test how much memory is available on the computer and decide whether to use memory or a temporary file for your interme-diate results. This example writes two strings to a MemoryStream and then reads them back:

```
' Write two strings to a MemoryStream.
Dim st As New MemoryStream(1000)
Dim bw As New BinaryWriter(st)
bw.Write("length-prefixed string")
' We'll use this 1-KB buffer for both reading and writing.
Dim buffer(1024) As Char

Dim s As String = "13 Characters"         ' A fixed-length string
s.CopyTo(0, buffer, 0, 13)                ' Copy into the buffer.
bw.Write(buffer, 0, 13)                   ' Output first 13 chars in buffer.
bw.Write(buffer, 0, 13)                   ' Do it a second time.

' Rewind the stream, and prepare to read from it.
st.Seek(0, SeekOrigin.Begin)
Dim br As New BinaryReader(st)
' Reading the length-prefixed string is simple.
Console.WriteLine(br.ReadString)                 ' => length-prefixed string

' Read the fixed-length string (13 characters) into the buffer.
br.Read(buffer, 0, 13)
s = New String(buffer, 0, 13)             ' Convert to a string.
Console.WriteLine(s)                      ' => 13 Characters

' Another way to read a fixed-length string (13 characters)
' (ReadChars returns a Char array that we can pass to the string constructor.)
s = New String(br.ReadChars(13))
Console.WriteLine(s)                      ' => 13 Characters
```

Reading and Writing Strings in Memory

If the data you want to read is already contained in a string variable, you might want to use a StringReader object to retrieve portions of it. For example, you can load the entire contents of a text file or a multiline textbox control into a string and then extract the individual lines by using the StringReader.ReadLine method:

```
' The veryLongString variable contains the text to parse.
Dim strReader As New StringReader(veryLongString)
' Display individual lines of text.
Do Until strReader.Peek = -1
    Console.WriteLine(strReader.ReadLine)
Loop
```

Of course, you can solve this problem in other, equivalent ways—for example, by using the Split function to get an array with all the individual lines of code—but the solution based on the StringReader object is more resource-friendly because it doesn't duplicate the data in memory. As a matter of fact, the StringReader and StringWriter classes don't even create an internal stream object because they use the string itself as the stream. (This fact explains why these two classes don't expose the BaseStream property.)

You use a StringWriter object to output values to a string. However, you can't associate it with a String object because String objects are immutable. Instead, you have to create a StringBuilder and then associate it with a StringWriter object:

```
' Create a string with the space-separated abbreviated names of weekdays.
' A StringBuilder of 7*4 characters is enough.
Dim sb As New System.Text.StringBuilder(28)
' The StringWriter associated with the StringBuilder
Dim strWriter As New StringWriter(sb)

' Output day names to the string.
For Each d As String In _
    System.Globalization .DateTimeFormatInfo.CurrentInfo.AbbreviatedDayNames
    strWriter.Write(d)
    strWriter.Write(" ")          ' Append a space.
Next
Console.WriteLine(sb)            ' => Sun Mon Tue Wed Thu Fri Sat
```

> **See Also**   Read the document "Custom Readers and Writers.doc" on the companion CD for an example of custom readers and writers that know to serialize and deserialize objects defined in your application.

Now you know all you need to know about directories, files, and stream objects, and you'll probably agree that—once you get accustomed to the new syntax—working with these .NET objects can provide extra flexibility and power. The next chapter covers an important topic in the .NET Framework: object serialization, which builds on the concepts described in this chapter.

10 Object Serialization

Serialization is the term for the act of saving (or serializing) an object onto a storage medium—a file, a database field, a buffer in memory—and later deserializing it from the storage medium to re-create an object instance that can be considered identical to the original one. Serialization is a key feature in the .NET Framework and is transparently used by the runtime for tasks other than simply saving an object to a file—for example, marshaling an object by value to another application. You should make an object serializable if you plan to send it to another application or save it on disk, in a database field, or in an ASP.NET Session object. For example, even exception objects should be made serializable if they can be thrown from another AppDomain.

Serialization and persistence are often used as synonyms, so you can also say that an object is persisted and depersisted. The MSDN documentation makes a distinction, however, and uses persistence to mean that the data is stored in a durable medium, such as a file or a database field, while serialization can be applied to objects stored in nondurable media, such as memory buffers.

Basic Serialization

The .NET Framework knows how to serialize all basic data types, including numbers, strings, and arrays of numbers and strings, so you can save and reload these types to and from a file stream (or any other type of stream) with minimal effort. All you need to serialize and deserialize a basic object is a proper formatter object.

Formally speaking, a formatter is an object that implements the IFormatter interface (defined in the System.Runtime.Serialization namespace). You can create your own formatter by defining a class that implements this interface, but most of the time you can use one of the formatter objects provided by the .NET Framework:

- The BinaryFormatter object, defined in the System.Runtime.Serialization.Formatters.Binary namespace, provides an efficient way to persist an object in a compact binary format. In practice, the actual bits in memory are persisted, so the serialization and deserialization processes are very fast.

- The SoapFormatter object, defined in the System.Runtime.Serialization.Formatters.Soap namespace, persists data in human-readable XML format, following the Simple Object Access Protocol (SOAP) specifications. The serialization and deserialization processes are somewhat slower than with the BinaryFormatter object. On the other hand, data can be sent easily to another application through HTTP and displayed in a human-readable format.

> **Note**   To keep code as concise as possible, all the code samples in this section assume that the following Imports statements are used at the file or project level:
>
> ```
> Imports System.IO
> Imports System.Runtime.Serialization
> Imports System.Runtime.Serialization.Formatters.Binary
> Imports System.Runtime.Serialization.Formatters.Soap
> Imports System.Reflection
> ```

Binary Serialization

The key methods that all formatter objects support are Serialize and Deserialize, whose purpose is rather evident. The Serialize method takes a Stream object as its first argument and the object to be serialized as its second argument:

```
' Create an array of integers.
Dim arr() As Integer = {1, 2, 4, 8, 16, 32, 64, 128, 256}
' Open a file stream for output.
Dim fs As FileStream = New FileStream("c:\powers.dat", FileMode.Create)
' Create a binary formatter for this stream.
Dim bf As New BinaryFormatter()
' Serialize the array to the file stream, and flush the stream.
bf.Serialize(fs, arr)
fs.Close()
```

Reading back the file data and deserializing it into an object require the Deserialize function, which takes the input Stream as its only argument and returns an Object value, which must be cast to a properly typed variable:

```
' Open a file stream for input.
Dim fs As FileStream = New FileStream("c:\powers.dat", FileMode.Open)
' Create a binary formatter for this stream.
Dim bf As New BinaryFormatter()
' Deserialize the contents of the file stream into an Integer array.
' Deserialize returns an object that must be coerced.
Dim arr() As Integer = CType(bf.Deserialize(fs), Integer())
' Display the result.
For Each n As Integer In arr
    Console.Write(n.ToString & " ")
Next
```

You can indicate the reason you're creating a formatter by passing a StreamingContext object to the second argument of its constructor. The streaming context object contains information about the serialization and deserialization process and can be used by the object being serialized. For example, an object might opt for a compression algorithm if it's being serialized to a file. Even if you don't know whether the object you're serializing takes advantage of this additional information, specifying it is a good programming rule. Here's how you define a formatter that's used to serialize an object to a file:

```
Dim sc As New StreamingContext(StreamingContextStates.File)
Dim bf As New BinaryFormatter(Nothing, sc)
```

Interestingly, the assembly containing the type being deserialized doesn't have to be loaded in memory already. By default, the serialized stream contains information about the assembly identity (name, version, culture, and publisher's key if it is a strong-named assembly) and the assembly is searched and loaded as if you were instantiating one of its type with a standard New keyword. In some cases, the fact that the deserialization process preserves type identity can be a problem when the assembly's version changes. In such cases, you might want to use the formatter's AssemblyFormat to the FormatterAssemblyStyle.Simple value (rather than its FormatterAssemblyStyle.Full default value). In this case, only the assembly name is stored in the serialized stream of bytes, and a newer version of the same assembly can deserialize the object. However, strange things can happen if both versions of the assembly are stored on the machine, so use this feature judiciously.

SOAP Serialization

You can change the serialization format to SOAP by simply using another formatter object, the SoapFormatter in the System.Runtime.Serialization.Formatters.Soap namespace. This namespace isn't available in the default Visual Basic console project, so you have to click Add Reference on the Project menu in Visual Studio to add the System.Runtime.Serialization.Formatters.Soap.dll library to the list of libraries that appear in the Object Browser. The following listing contains two reusable routines that let you save and restore any object to a file in SOAP format. Note that the formatter's constructor is passed a StreamingContext object that specifies where the serialization data is stored:

```
' Serialize an object to a file in SOAP format.
Sub SaveSoapData(ByVal path As String, ByVal o As Object)
    ' Open a file stream for output.
    Dim fs As FileStream = New FileStream(path, FileMode.Create)
    ' Create a SOAP formatter for this file stream.
    Dim sf As New SoapFormatter(Nothing, _
        New StreamingContext(StreamingContextStates.File))
    ' Serialize the array to the file stream, and close the stream.
    sf.Serialize(fs, o)
    fs.Close()
End Sub

' Deserialize an object from a file in SOAP format.
Function LoadSoapData(ByVal path As String) As Object
    ' Open a file stream for input.
    Dim fs As FileStream = New FileStream(path, FileMode.Open)
    ' Create a SOAP formatter for this file stream.
    Dim sf As New SoapFormatter(Nothing, _
        New StreamingContext(StreamingContextStates.File))
    ' Deserialize the contents of the stream into an object and close the stream.
    LoadSoapData = sf.Deserialize(fs)
    fs.Close()
End Function
```

Here's a test routine that saves and reloads a Hashtable object, using the routine just defined:

```
' This example uses the preceding routines.
' Create a Hashtable object, and fill it with some data.
Dim ht As New Hashtable()
ht.Add("One", 1)
ht.Add("Two", 2)
ht.Add("Three", 3)
' Save the Hashtable to disk in SOAP format.
SaveSoapData("c:\hashtbl.xml", ht)

' Reload the file contents into another Hashtable object.
Dim ht2 As Hashtable = CType(LoadSoapData("c:\hashtbl.xml"), Hashtable)
' Display values.
For Each de As DictionaryEntry In ht2
    Console.WriteLine("Key={0}  Value={1}", de.Key, de.Value)
Next
```

You can double-click the c:\hashtbl.xml file from inside Windows Explorer to view its contents in an Internet Explorer window.

The Serializable and NonSerialized Attributes

The .NET Framework can inspect any object at run time to discover, read, and assign all the object's fields and properties. This mechanism is made possible by a portion of the .NET Framework called reflection (which I explore in Chapter 14) and is the basis for automatic persistence of any class you write with a minimum of effort on your part.

In practice, the only thing you do to make a class serializable is to flag it with the Serializable attribute, whose constructor takes no arguments:

```
<Serializable()> Class Person
    ⋮
End Class
```

For this attribute to work correctly, the base class must be serializable. This requirement isn't a problem when you inherit from System.Object because the Object class is serializable, but when you derive a class from something else you should ascertain that your base class is serializable. As you might imagine, the Serializable attribute isn't automatically inherited by derived classes and must be applied to them manually. (If it were inherited, all classes would be serializable because they derive directly or indirectly from System.Object.)

The only other attribute you must learn about is NonSerialized, which you use for those fields or properties that you don't want to be persisted when the object is serialized. As a rule, you don't persist variables that cache values that you can easily derive from other properties or properties that aren't going to be valid when the object is being deserialized. Among such variables would be pointers, file handles, and references to transient, nonserialized objects. Here's a version of the Person class, which serializes all of its fields except m_Age:

```
<Serializable()> _
Class Person
    Public FirstName As String
    Public LastName As String
    Private BirthDate As Date
    <NonSerialized()> Private m_Age As Integer

    ' Note that BirthDate can be set only by means of the constructor method.
    Sub New(ByVal FirstName As String, ByVal LastName As String, _
        ByVal BirthDate As Date)
        Me.FirstName = FirstName
        Me.LastName = LastName
        Me.BirthDate = BirthDate
    End Sub

    ' The Age property caches its value in the m_Age private variable.
    ReadOnly Property Age() As Integer
        Get
            ' Evaluate Age if not cached already.
            If m_Age = 0 Then
                m_Age = Now.Year - BirthDate.Year
                If BirthDate.DayOfYear > Now.DayOfYear Then m_Age -= 1
            End If
            Return m_Age
        End Get
    End Property
End Class
```

The presence of the Serializable attribute is all that the Framework needs to make the class persistable. For example, the following piece of code builds on the SaveSoapData and LoadSoapData routines described in the preceding section and shows how you can serialize and deserialize an ArrayList object containing three Person objects:

```
Dim al As New ArrayList()
al.Add(New Person("Joe", "Doe", #1/12/1960#))
al.Add(New Person("John", "Smith", #3/6/1962#))
al.Add(New Person("Ann", "Doe", #10/4/1965#))
' Save the ArrayList to disk in SOAP format.
SaveSoapData("c:\hashtbl.xml", al)

' Reload the file contents into another ArrayList object.
Dim al2 As ArrayList
al2 = CType(LoadSoapData("c:\hashtbl.xml"), ArrayList)
' Display values.
For Each p As Person In al2
    Console.WriteLine("{0} {1} ({2})", p.FirstName, p.LastName, p.Age)
Next
```

This result appears in the console window:

```
Joe Doe (41)
John Smith (39)
Ann Doe (36)
```

The noteworthy detail here is that although the BirthDate field is private, the deserialization mechanism is able to correctly restore it from the input stream. (The evidence is the fact the Age property is evaluated correctly.) In other words, the deserialization mechanism is capable of ignoring scope rules. Keep this in mind when you define a class with a member containing sensitive information, such as password and credit card numbers, because this information is included in the serialized stream and is easily readable by malicious users (even when you use a BinaryFormatter).

Object Graphs

You can persist object graphs as easily as individual objects. An object graph is a set of multiple objects with references to one another. The previous code examples show a simple form of object graph in that an ArrayList holds references to individual Person objects. As a result, serializing an ArrayList object indirectly causes the serialization of all the referenced Person objects. In general, the serialization infrastructure persists all the objects that are directly or indirectly reachable from the root object (the one passed to the Formatter.Serialize method).

In the simplest cases, when there are no circular references between objects, each object is met exactly once during both the serialization and deserialization processes. Real-world object hierarchies are usually more complex than that, but the serialization infrastructure is capable of dealing with these cases too. To demonstrate this, you can add the following field to the Person class:

```
' In the Person class
Public Spouse As Person
```

Then you can serialize and deserialize an entire object graph with this code:

```
' Create three Person objects.
Dim p1 As New Person("Joe", "Doe", #1/12/1960#)
Dim p2 As New Person("John", "Smith", #3/6/1962#)
Dim p3 As New Person("Ann", "Doe", #10/4/1965#)
' Define the relationship between two of them.
p2.Spouse = p3
p3.Spouse = p2

' Load them into an ArrayList object in one operation.
Dim al As New ArrayList()
al.AddRange(New Person() {p1, p2, p3})
' Save the ArrayList to disk in XML format.
SaveSoapData("c:\arraylst.xml", al)

' Reload into another ArrayList object and display.
Dim al2 As ArrayList = CType(LoadSoapData("c:\arraylst.xml"), ArrayList)
For Each p As Person In al2
    Console.WriteLine("{0} {1} ({2})", p.FirstName, p.LastName, p.Age)
    If Not (p.Spouse Is Nothing) Then
        ' Show the spouse's name if there is one.
        Console.WriteLine("   Spouse of " & p.Spouse.FirstName)
    End If
Next
```

This new version contains a circular reference between p2 and p3 objects, so p3 can be reached from both the root object (the ArrayList) and the p2.Spouse property. This might cause an endless loop, but the serialization mechanism is smart enough to understand that both references point to the same object, which is therefore persisted only once. A look at the Output window can easily prove this point:

```
Joe Doe (42)
John Smith (40)
    Spouse of Ann
Ann Doe (37)
    Spouse of John
```

Deep Object Cloning

As you might remember from the "Shallow Copies and Deep Copies" section in Chapter 6, you can use the protected MemberwiseClone member (inherited from System.Object) to easily implement the ICloneable interface and its Clone method in any class you define:

```
Class Person
    Implements ICloneable

    ' ...(Variables and methods as in previous example)...

    Public Function Clone() As Object Implements ICloneable.Clone
        Return Me.MemberwiseClone
    End Function
End Class
```

This approach to object cloning has two limitations. First, you can clone an object only if you can modify its source code because the MemberwiseClone method is protected and accessible only from inside the class itself. Second, and more important in many circumstances, the MemberwiseClone method performs a shallow copy of the object—that is, it creates a copy of the object but not of any object referenced by the object. For example, the Clone method of the preceding Person class would not also clone the Person object pointed to by the Spouse property. In other words:

```
' Define husband and wife.
Dim p1 As New Person("Joe", "Doe", #1/12/1960#)
Dim p2 As New Person("Ann", "Doe", #10/4/1965#)
p1.Spouse = p2
p2.Spouse = p1
' Clone the husband.
Dim q1 As Person = DirectCast(p1.Clone, Person)
' The Spouse person hasn't been cloned because it's a shallow copy.
Console.WriteLine(q1.Spouse Is p1.Spouse)          ' => True
```

Using the ability of object serialization to work with complex object graphs helps you solve both of the problems I mentioned previously. In fact, you can create a generic routine that performs a deep copy of any object passed to it. For the best performance, it uses a memory stream and a binary formatter, and specifies that the object is being serialized for cloning:

```
Function CloneObject(ByVal obj As Object) As Object
    ' Create a memory stream and a formatter.
    Dim ms As New MemoryStream(1000)
    Dim bf As New BinaryFormatter(Nothing, _
        New StreamingContext(StreamingContextStates.Clone))
    ' Serialize the object into the stream.
    bf.Serialize(ms, obj)
    ' Position stream pointer back to first byte.
    ms.Seek(0, SeekOrigin.Begin)
    ' Deserialize into another object.
    CloneObject = bf.Deserialize(ms)
    ' Release memory.
    ms.Close()
End Function
```

Here's the code that drives the CloneObject routine:

```
' ...(p1 and p2 are initialized as in preceding example)...

' Clone the husband.
Dim q1 As Person = DirectCast(CloneObject(p1), Person)
Dim q2 As Person = q1.Spouse
' Prove that properties were copied correctly.
Console.WriteLine(q1.FirstName & " " & q1.LastName)  ' => Joe Doe
Console.WriteLine(q2.FirstName & " " & q2.LastName)  ' => Ann Smith
' Prove that both objects were cloned because it's a deep copy.
Console.WriteLine("p1 is q1 = {0}", p1 Is q1)        ' => False
Console.WriteLine("p2 is q2 = {0}", p2 Is q2)        ' => False
```

Custom Serialization

The .NET Framework provides developers with everything they need to implement custom serialization through the IDeserializationCallback and the ISerializable interfaces. You should resort to custom serialization only when the standard mechanism based on the Serializable attribute isn't flexible enough for your needs. You can have trouble, for example, when you want to dynamically decide which information should be persisted or when you need to execute code when the object is deserialized, possibly to recalculate values that are no longer valid.

The IDeserializationCallback Interface

The simplest case of custom serialization is when you want to perform some custom actions when the object has been completely deserialized. For example, say that your class opens a FileStream in its constructor and all the other methods in the class rely on this FileStream object to do their chores. As you know, the standard constructor doesn't run when the object is being deserialized, so you have a problem. You can solve this problem by implementing the IDeserializationCallback interface; this interface has only one method, OnDeserialization, which the .NET Framework invokes when the current object has been completely deserialized:

```
<Serializable()> Class FileLogger
    Implements IDeserializationCallback

    Dim fs As System.IO.FileStream
    Sub New()
        ' Open the file stream when the object is instantiated.
        fs = New System.IO.FileStream("c:\log.dat", FileMode.Create)
    End Sub

    ' This method is called when the object has been completely deserialized.
    Sub OnDeserialization(ByVal sender As Object) _
        Implements IDeserializationCallback.OnDeserialization
        ' Open the file stream when the object is deserialized.
        fs = New System.IO.FileStream("c:\log.dat", FileMode.Create)
    End Sub
    ⋮
End Class
```

(Notice that the argument passed to the OnDeserialization method isn't used in the current version of the .NET Framework.)

It is important to be aware that the .NET Framework invokes the OnDeserialization method when the entire object graph has been deserialized. In other words, you can rely on the fact that all the child objects of the current object have been correctly initialized when this method runs.

The ISerializable Interface

You can implement the ISerializable interface in your own classes to enhance them with a custom persistence scheme. The ISerializable interface exposes only one method, GetObjectData, which has the following syntax:

```
Sub GetObjectData(ByVal info As SerializationInfo, _
    ByVal context As StreamingContext)
    ⋮
End Sub
```

The GetObjectData method is invoked when the object is passed to the Formatter.Serialize method. Its purpose is to fill the SerializationInfo object with all the information about the object being serialized (Me in Visual Basic). The code inside this method can examine the StreamingContext structure to retrieve additional details about the serialization process.

The presence of the ISerializable interface implies the existence of a special constructor method with the following syntax:

```
Protected Sub New(ByVal info As SerializationInfo, _
    ByVal context As StreamingContext)
    ⋮
End Sub
```

This special constructor is called by the runtime when the object is deserialized. You should use a Protected scope for this constructor so that regular clients can't call it, but classes that inherit from yours can. You won't get a compilation error if you omit this constructor, but you get a run-time error when you try to deserialize the object if this constructor is missing. Note that a serializable class must have at least another constructor with Public scope; otherwise, you won't be able to instantiate it from your code.

The SerializationInfo object acts like a dictionary object, to which you add one or more values using the AddValue method:

```
' Save the FirstName field.
info.AddValue("FirstName", Me.FirstName)
```

You can later retrieve values with the GetValue method, which requires the value name and type, as you see here:

```
' Retrieve the FirstName value.
' (The conversion is necessary if Option Strict is On.)
Me.FirstName = CStr(info.GetValue("FirstValue", GetType(String)))
```

Conveniently, the SerializationInfo object exposes many other Getxxxx methods, such as GetString and GetInt32, that return data in a specific format:

```
' A more concise way to retrieve the FirstName value
Me.FirstName = info.GetString("FirstValue")
```

In all cases, values in the stream are converted to the requested type, or an Invalid-CastException is thrown if the conversion isn't possible.

A Custom Serialization Example

The following example explains how to build the CompactDoubleArray class, which behaves like an array object that contains Double values except that it can serialize itself in a more compact format by discarding all its elements equal to zero. The CompactDoubleArray class inherits most of its functionality from ArrayList, and it implements the ISerializable interface for dealing with the custom serialization and deserialization process. Notice that you must mark the class with the Serializable attribute even if the class exposes the ISerializable interface:

```
<Serializable()> _
Public Class CompactDoubleArray
```

```
        Inherits ArrayList
        Implements ISerializable

        ' We need this default constructor.
        Sub New()
        End Sub

        ' The special constructor implied by ISerializable
        Protected Sub New(ByVal info As SerializationInfo, _
            ByVal context As StreamingContext)

            ' Retrieve number of elements.
            Dim elCount As Integer = info.GetInt32("Count")
            For index As Integer = 0 To elCount - 1
                Dim Value As Double = 0
                Try
                    ' Try to assign the value in the SerializationInfo object.
                    Value = info.GetDouble(Index.ToString)
                Catch
                    ' If not found, use zero.
                End Try
                ' Add the value to the ArrayList.
                Me.Add(Value)
            Next
        End Sub

        ' Serialize this object.
        Public Overridable Sub GetObjectData(ByVal info As SerializationInfo, _
            ByVal context As StreamingContext) _
            Implements ISerializable.GetObjectData

            ' Remember the total number of elements.
            info.AddValue("Count", Me.Count)
            ' Serialize only nonzero elements.
            For index As Integer = 0 To Me.Count - 1
                ' The AddValue method requires a specific type.
                Dim Value As Double = CType(Me(index), Double)
                If Value <> 0 Then
                    info.AddValue(Index.ToString, Value)
                End If
            Next
        End Sub
End Class
```

The following code is the test program that uses the SaveSoapData and LoadSoapData routines defined earlier in this chapter:

```
' Create a compact array of Double.
Dim ca As New CompactDoubleArray()
' Add some elements (including zero values) in one operation.
ca.AddRange(New Integer() {0, 2, 3, 0, 4, 0, 5})
' Serialize the array.
SaveSoapData("c:\compact.xml", ca)

' Read it back and display its elements.
```

```
Dim ca2 As CompactDoubleArray
ca2 = CType(LoadSoapData("c:\compact.xml"), CompactDoubleArray)
For Each o As Object In ca2
    Console.Write(o.ToString & " ")    ' => 0 2 3 0 4 0 5
Next
```

When you inherit from a class that implements ISerializable, you must create your own version of the GetObjectData method and of the special constructor implied by this interface. For example, if you have a CompactDoubleArrayEx class that inherits from CompactDoubleArray and adds a DefaultValue property, this is the code you should write:

```
<Serializable()> Public Class CompactDoubleArrayEx
    Inherits CompactDoubleArray

    Public DefaultValue As Double

    Sub New()
    End Sub

    Protected Sub New(ByVal info As SerializationInfo, _
        ByVal context As StreamingContext)
        MyBase.New(info, context)
        Me.DefaultValue = info.GetDouble("DefaultValue")
    End Sub

    Public Overrides Sub GetObjectData(ByVal info As SerializationInfo, _
        ByVal context As StreamingContext)
        MyBase.GetObjectData(info, context)
        info.AddValue("DefaultValue", Me.DefaultValue)
    End Sub
End Class
```

You must implement the GetObjectData only if the derived class wants to serialize additional members; otherwise, the inherited class can rely on its base class's implementation of the GetObjectData method. Notice that the derived class automatically inherits the ISerializable interface, so we need no Implements keyword in Compact-DoubleArrayEx. However, we need to override the GetObjectData method, which we can do only because we used the Overridable keyword in the base class.

All interface members are virtual (and therefore overridable) by definition, which means that, in theory, you should be able to override an interface member even if it isn't marked with the Overridable keyword. Unfortunately, this is true for C# but it doesn't work for Visual Basic .NET, which doesn't give you any way to override an interface method unless it is explicitly marked as Overridable. The disappointing result is that you can't derive from many classes in the .NET Framework that implement the ISerializable interface. For example, you can't derive from System.Data.DataTable and add new members because you couldn't serialize and deserialize those members.

The FormatterServices Helper Class

The FormatterServices class exposes a few shared methods that help you build code that serializes and deserializes an object. For example, the GetSerializableMembers method returns an array of System.Reflection.MemberInfo elements, one element for each class member that must be serialized (therefore, all fields except those marked with the NotSerialized attribute). The GetObjectData method takes the array returned by the aforementioned method and returns an Object array holding the value of each member. Here's a helper routine that helps you serialize any object:

```
Sub GetObjectDataHelper(ByVal info As SerializationInfo, _
    ByVal context As StreamingContext, ByVal obj As Object)
    ' Get the list of serializable members.
    Dim members() As MemberInfo = _
        FormatterServices.GetSerializableMembers(obj.GetType)
    ' Read the value of each member.
    Dim values() As Object = FormatterServices.GetObjectData(obj, members)
    ' Store in the SerializationInfo object, using the member name.
    For i As Integer = 0 To members.Length - 1
        info.AddValue(members(i).Name, values(i))
    Next
End Sub
```

The PopulateObjectMembers method takes an array of MemberInfo and of Object values, and assigns all the serializable members of a given object. We can use this method in a generic helper routine that initializes a deserialized object:

```
Public Sub ISerializableConstructorHelper(ByVal info As SerializationInfo, _
    ByVal context As StreamingContext, ByVal obj As Object)
    ' Get the list of serializable members for this object.
    Dim members() As MemberInfo = FormatterServices.GetSerializableMembers(obj.GetType
)
    Dim values(members.Length - 1) As Object
    ' Read the value for this member (assuming it's a field).
    For i As Integer = 0 To members.Length - 1
        ' Retrieve the type for this member.
        Dim member As MemberInfo = members(i)
        If member.MemberType = MemberTypes.Field Then
            Dim memberType As Type = CType(member, FieldInfo).FieldType
            values(i) = info.GetValue(member.Name, memberType)
        End If
    Next
    ' Assign all serializable members in one operation
    FormatterServices.PopulateObjectMembers(obj, members, values)
End Sub
```

These two helper routines make implementation of the ISerializable interface a breeze. This is what a serializable class that uses these routines will look like:

```
<Serializable()> _
Class SampleClass
    Implements ISerializable
```

```
    Public Sub GetObjectData(ByVal info As SerializationInfo, _
        ByVal context As StreamingContext) Implements ISerializable.GetObjectData
        GetObjectDataHelper(info, context, Me)
    End Sub

    Protected Sub New(ByVal info As SerializationInfo, _
        ByVal context As StreamingContext)
        ISerializableContructorHelper(info, context, Me)
    End Sub

    ' ...(the remainder of the class)...
    ⋮
End Class
```

Did you think there was so much to say about object serialization? I surely didn't—
before I began studying the intricacies of this topic. But it's time to move on to the next
chapter, in which I'll illustrate another great, and often underrated, feature of the .NET
Framework: regular expressions.

11 Regular Expressions

Regular expressions are a standard way to parse text files as well as to search for and optionally replace occurrences of substrings and text patterns. If you aren't familiar with regular expressions, just think about the wildcard characters you use in MS-DOS to indicate a group of files (as in **.txt*) or the special characters you can use with the LIKE statement in SQL queries:

```
SELECT name, city FROM customers WHERE name LIKE "A%"
```

Many computer scientists have thoroughly researched regular expressions, and a few programming languages—most notably Perl and Awk—are heavily based on regular expressions. In spite of their usefulness in virtually every text-oriented task (including parsing log files and extracting information from HTML files), regular expressions are relatively rarely used by Windows programmers, probably because they are based on a rather obscure syntax.

You can regard regular expressions as a highly specific programming language, and you know that all languages take time to learn and have idiosyncrasies. But when you see how much time regular expressions can save you—and I am talking about both coding time and CPU time—you'll probably agree that the effort you spend learning their contorted syntax is well spent.

Regular Expression Overview

The .NET Framework comes with a very powerful regular expression engine that's accessible from any .NET language, so you can leverage the parsing power of languages such as Perl without having to switch from your favorite language.

> **Note** All the code in this section assumes that you added the following Imports statement at the top of your module:
>
> ```
> Imports System.Text.RegularExpressions
> Imports System.IO
> ```

The Fundamentals

Regex is the most important class in this group, and any regular expression code instantiates at least an object of this class (or uses the class's shared methods). This object represents an immutable, compiled regular expression. You instantiate this object by passing to it the search pattern, written using the special regular expression language, which I'll describe later:

```
' This regular expression defines any group of 2 characters
' consisting of a vowel followed by a digit (\d).
Dim re As New Regex("[aeiou]\d")
```

The Matches method of the Regex object applies the regular expression to the string passed as an argument; it returns a MatchCollection object, a read-only collection that represents all the nonoverlapping matches:

```
Dim re As New Regex("[aeiou]\d")
' This source string contains 3 groups that match the Regex.
Dim source As String = "a1 = a1 & e2"
' Get the collection of matches.
Dim mc As MatchCollection = re.Matches(source)
' How many occurrences did we find?
Console.WriteLine(mc.Count)                    ' => 3
```

You can also pass to the Matches method a second argument, which is interpreted as the index where the search begins.

The MatchCollection object contains individual Match objects, which expose properties such as Value (the matching string that was found), Index (the position of the matching string in the source string), and Length (the length of the matching string, which is useful when the regular expression can match strings of different lengths):

```
' ...(Continuing the previous example)...
For Each m As Match In mc
   ' Display text and position of this match.
   Console.WriteLine("'{0}' at position {1}" , m.Value, m.Index)
Next
```

The preceding code displays these lines in the console window:

```
'a1' at position 0
'a1' at position 5
'e2' at position 10
```

The Regex object is also capable of modifying a source string by searching for a given regular expression and replacing it with something else:

```
Dim source As String = "a1 = a1 & e2"
' Search for the "a" character followed by a digit.
Dim re As New Regex("a\d")
' Drop the digit that follows the "a" character.
Console.WriteLine(re.Replace(source, "a"))        ' => a = a & e2
```

The Regex class also exposes shared versions of the Match, Matches, and Replace methods. You can use these shared methods when you don't want to explicitly instantiate a Regex object:

```
' This code snippet is equivalent to the previous one, but it doesn't
' instantiate a Regex object.
Console.WriteLine(Regex.Replace("a1 = a1 & e2", "a\d", "a"))
```

As you would find for any programming language new to you, the best way to learn regular expressions is, not surprisingly, through practice. To help you in this process, I have created a RegexTester application that lets you test any regular expression against any source string or text file. (See Figure 11-1.) This application has been a precious tool for me in exploring regular expression intricacies, and I routinely use it whenever I have a doubt about how a construct works.

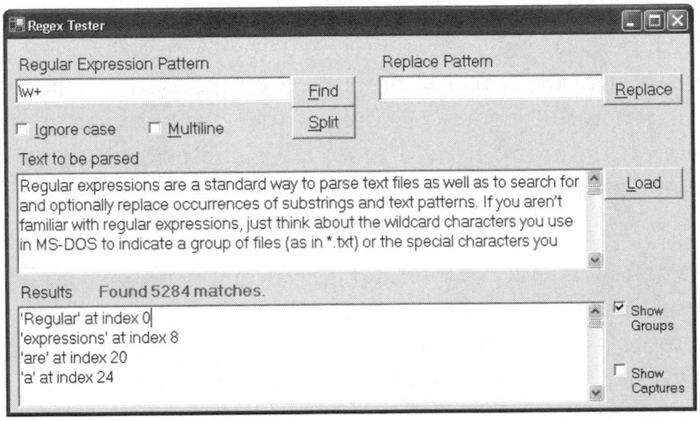

Figure 11-1 The RegexTester application lets you experiment with all the most important methods and options of the Regex object.

The Regular Expression Language

Table 11-1 lists all the constructs that are legal as regular expression patterns, grouped in the following categories:

- **Character escapes** Are used to match single characters. You need them to deal with nonprintable characters (such as the newline and the tab character) and to provide escaped versions for the characters .$^{[(|)*+?\ which have a special meaning inside regular expression patterns.

- **Character classes** Offer a means to match one character from a group that you specify between square brackets, as in [aeiou]. You don't need to escape special characters when they appear in square brackets except in the cases of the dash and the closing square bracket, which are the only characters that have special meaning inside square brackets. For example, [()\[\]{}] matches opening and closing parentheses, square brackets, and curly brackets.

- **Atomic zero–width assertions** Specify where the matching string should be but don't consume characters. For example, the abc$ regular expression matches any *abc* word immediately before the end of a line without also matching the end of the line.

- **Quantifiers**   Add optional quantity data to regular expressions. A particular quantifier applies to the character, character class, or group that immediately precedes it. For example, \w+ matches all the words with one or more characters, whereas \w{3,} matches all the words with at least three characters.

- **Grouping constructors**   Can capture and name groups of subexpressions as well as increase the efficiency of regular expressions with noncapturing look-ahead and look-behind modifiers. For example, (abc)+ matches repeated sequences of the "abc" string; (?<total>\d+) matches a group of one or more consecutive digits and assigns it the name *total*, which can be used later inside the same regular expression pattern or for substitution purposes.

- **Substitutions**   Can be used only inside a replacement pattern and, together with character escapes, are the only constructs that can be used inside replacement patterns. For example, when the sequence ({total}) appears in a replacement pattern, it inserts the value of the group named *total*, after enclosing it in parentheses. Parentheses have no special meanings in replacement patterns, so you don't need to escape them.

- **Backreference constructs**   Let you reference a previous group of characters in the regular expression pattern via its group number or name. You can use these constructs as a simple way to say "match the same thing again." For example, (?<value>\d+)=\k<value> matches identical numbers separated by an = symbol, as in the "123=123" sequence.

- **Alternating constructs**   Provide a way to specify alternatives; for example, the sequence I (am|have) can match both the "I am" and "I have" strings.

- **Miscellaneous constructs**   Include constructs that allow you to modify one or more regular expression options in the middle of the pattern. For example, A(?i)BC matches all the variants of the "ABC" word that begin with uppercase "A" (such as "Abc", "ABc", "AbC", and "ABC"). See Table 11-2 for a description of all the regular expression options.

Table 11-1   The Regular Expression Language[*]

Category	Sequence	Description
Character escapes	any character	Characters other than .$^{[({)}*+?\ are matched to themselves.
	\a	The bell alarm character (same as \x07).
	\b	The backspace (same as \x08), but only when used between square brackets or in a replacement pattern. Otherwise, it matches a word boundary.
	\t	The tab character (same as \x09).
	\r	The carriage return (same as \x0D).
	\v	The vertical tab character (same as \x0B).
	\f	The form-feed character (same as \x0C).

Table 11-1 The Regular Expression Language * *(continued)*

Category	Sequence	Description
	\n	The newline character (same as *\x0A*).
	\e	The escape character (same as *\x1B*).
	\040	An ASCII character expressed in octal notation (must have exactly three octal digits). For example, *\040* is a space.
	\x20	An ASCII character expressed in hexadecimal notation (must have exactly two digits). For example, *\x20* is a space.
	\cC	An ASCII control character. For example, *\cC* is control+C.
	\u0020	A Unicode character in hexadecimal notation (must have exactly four digits). For example, *\u0020* is a space.
	*	When the backslash is followed by a character in a way that doesn't form an escape sequence, it matches the character. For example, * matches the * character.
Character classes	.	The dot character matches any character except the newline character. It matches any character, including newline, if you're using the Singleline option.
	[aeiou]	Any character in the list between the square brackets; [aeiou] matches any vowel.
	[^aeiou]	Any character except those in the list between the square brackets; [^aeiou] matches any nonvowel.
	[a-zA-Z]	The - (dash) character lets you specify ranges of characters: [a-zA-Z] matches any lowercase or uppercase character; [^0-9] matches any nondigit character.
	\w	A word character, which is an alphanumeric character or the underscore character; same as [a-zA-Z_0-9].
	\W	A nonword character; same as [^a-zA-Z_0-9].
	\s	A white-space character, which is a space, a tab, a formfeed, a newline, a carriage return, or a vertical-feed character; same as [\f\n\r\t\v].
	\S	A character other than a white-space character; same as [^ \f\n\r\t\v].
	\d	A decimal digit; same as [0-9].
	\D	A nondigit character; same as [^0-9].
Atomic zero–width assertions	^	The beginning of the string (or the beginning of the line if you're using the Multiline option).
	$	The end of the string (or the end of the line if you're using the Multiline option).
	\A	The beginning of a string (like ^ but ignores the Multiline option).

Table 11-1 The Regular Expression Language[*] *(continued)*

Category	Sequence	Description
	\Z	The end of the string or before the newline character at the end of the string (like $ but ignores the Multiline option).
	\z	Exactly the end of the string, whether or not there's a newline character (ignores the Multiline option).
	\G	The position at which the current search started—usually one character after the point at which the previous search ended.
	\b	The word boundary between \w (alphanumeric) and \W (nonalphanumeric) characters. It indicates the first and last characters of a word delimited by spaces or other punctuation symbols.
	\B	Not on a word boundary.
Quantifiers	*	Zero or more matches; for example, \bA\w* matches a word that begins with "A" and is followed by zero or more alphanumeric characters; same as {0,}.
	+	One or more matches; for example, \b[aeiou]+\b matches a word composed only of vowels; same as {1,}.
	?	Zero or one match; for example, \b[aeiou]\d?\b matches a word that starts with a vowel and is followed by zero or one digits; same as {0,1}.
	{N}	Exactly N matches; for example, [aeiou]{4} matches four consecutive vowels.
	{N,}	At least N matches; for example, \d{3,} matches groups of three or more digits.
	{N,M}	Between N and M matches; for example, \d{3,5} matches groups of three, four, or five digits.
	*?	Lazy *; the first match that consumes as few repeats as possible.
	+?	Lazy +; the first match that consumes as few repeats as possible, but at least one.
	??	Lazy ?; zero repeats if possible, or one.
	{N}?	Lazy {N}; equivalent to {N}.
	{N,}?	Lazy {N,}; as few repeats as possible, but at least N.
	{N,M}?	Lazy {N,M}; as few repeats as possible, but between N and M.
Grouping constructs	(substr)	Captures the matched substring. These captures are numbered automatically, based on the order of the left parenthesis, starting at 1. The zeroth capturing group is the text matched by the whole regular expression pattern.
	(?<name>substr) (?'name'substr)	Captures the substring and assigns it a name. The name must not contain any punctuation symbols.

Table 11-1 **The Regular Expression Language**[*] *(continued)*

Category	Sequence	Description
	(?:substr)	Noncapturing group.
	(imnsx-imnsx: subexpr)	Enables or disables the options specified in the subexpression. For example, (?i-s) uses case-insensitive searches and disables single-line mode (see Table 11-2 for information about regular expression options).
	(?=subexpr)	Zero-width positive look-ahead assertion; continues match only if the subexpression matches at this position on the right. For example, \w+(?=,) matches a word followed by a comma, without matching the comma.
	(?!subexpr)	Zero-width negative look-ahead assertion; continues match only if the subexpression doesn't match at this position on the right. For example, \w+\b(?![,:;]) matches a word that isn't followed by a comma, a colon, or a semicolon.
	(?<=subexpr)	Zero-width positive look-behind assertion; continues match only if the subexpression matches at this position on the left. For example, (?<=[,:])\w+ matches a word that follows a comma or semicolon, without matching the comma or semicolon. This construct doesn't backtrack.
	(?<!subexpr>	Zero-width negative look-behind assertion; continues match only if the subexpression doesn't match at this position on the left. For example, (?<!,)\b\w+ matches a word that doesn't follow a comma.
	(?>subexpr)	Nonbacktracking subexpression; the subexpression is fully matched once, and it doesn't participate in backtracking. The subexpression matches only strings that would be matched by the subexpression alone.
Substitutions	$N	Substitutes the last substring matched by group number N.
	${name}	Substitutes the last substring matched by a (?<name>) group.
Back reference constructs	\N \NN	Back reference to a previous group. For example, (\w)\1 finds doubled word characters, such as *ss* in *expression*. A backslash followed by a single digit is always considered a back reference (and throws a parsing exception if such a numbered reference is missing); a backslash followed by two digits is considered a numbered back reference if there's a corresponding numbered reference; otherwise, it's considered an octal code. In case of ambiguity, use the \k<name> construct.
	\k<name> \k'name'	Named back reference. (?<char>\w)\d\k<char> matches a word character followed by a digit and then by the same word character, as in the "B2B" string.
Alternating constructs	|	Either/or. For example, vb|c#|java. Leftmost successful match wins.

Table 11-1 The Regular Expression Language [*] *(continued)*

Category	Sequence	Description
	(?(expr)yes|no)	Matches the *yes* part if the expression matches at this point; otherwise, matches the *no* part. The expression is turned into a zero-width assertion. If the expression is the name of a named group or a capturing group number, the alternation is interpreted as a capture test (see next case).
	(?(name)yes|no)	Matches the *yes* part if the named capture string has a match; otherwise, matches the *no* part. The *no* part can be omitted. If the given name doesn't correspond to the name or number of a capturing group used in this expression, the alternation is interpreted as an expression test (see previous case).
Miscellaneous constructs	(?imnsx-imnsx)	Enables or disables one or more regular expression options. For example, it allows case sensitivity to be turned on or off in the middle of a pattern. Option changes are effective until the closing parenthesis. (See also the corresponding grouping construct, which is a cleaner form.)
	(?# comment)	Inline comment inserted within a regular expression. The text that follows the # sign and continues until the first closing) character is ignored.
	#	X-mode comment; the text that follows an unescaped # until the end of line is ignored. This construct requires that the x option or the RegexOptions.IgnorePatternWhiteSpace enumerated option be activated.

[*] Only the constructs in the character escapes and substitutions categories can be used in replacement patterns.

Regular Expression Options

The Match, Matches, and Replace shared methods of the Regex object support an optional argument, which lets you specify one or more options to be applied to the regular expression search. (See Table 11-2.) For example, the following code searches for all occurrences of the "abc" word, regardless of its case:

```
Dim source As String = "ABC Abc abc"
Dim mc As MatchCollection = Regex.Matches(source, "abc")
Console.WriteLine(mc.Count)              ' => 1
mc = Regex.Matches(source, "abc", RegexOptions.IgnoreCase)
Console.WriteLine(mc.Count)              ' => 3
```

By default, the Regex class transforms the regular expression into a sequence of opcodes, which are then interpreted when the pattern is applied to a specific source string. If you specify the RegexOptions.Compiled option, however, the regular expression is compiled into explicit Microsoft Intermediate Language (MSIL) rather than regular expression opcodes. This feature enables the Microsoft .NET Framework just-in-time (JIT) compiler to convert the expression to native CPU instructions, which clearly deliver better performance:

```
' Create a compiled regular expression that searches
' words that start with uppercase or lowercase A.
Dim re As New Regex("\Aw+", RegexOptions.IgnoreCase Or RegexOptions.Compiled)
```

This extra compilation step adds some overhead, so you should use this option only if you plan to use the regular expression multiple times. Another factor that you should take into account when using the RegexOptions.Compiled option is that the compiled MSIL code isn't unloaded when the Regex object is released and garbage collected—it continues to take memory until the application terminates. So you should preferably limit the number of compiled regular expressions, especially on systems with scarce memory. Also, consider that the Regex class caches all regular expression opcodes in memory, so a regular expression isn't generally reparsed each time it's used. The caching mechanism also works when you use shared methods and don't create Regex instances.

The RegexOptions.Multiline option enables multiline mode, which is especially useful when you're parsing text files instead of plain strings. This option modifies the meaning and the behavior of the ^ and $ assertions so that they match the start and end of each line of text, respectively, rather than the start or end of the whole string. Thanks to this option, you need only a handful of statements to create a grep-like utility that displays how many occurrences of the regular expression passed in the first argument are found in the files indicated by the second argument:

```
' Compile this application and create FileGrep.Exe executable.

Sub Main(ByVal args() As String)
    ' Show syntax if too few arguments.
    If args.Length <> 2 Then
        Console.WriteLine("Syntax: FILEGREP ""regex"" filespec")
        Exit Sub
    End If

    Dim pattern As String = args(0)
    Dim filespec As String = args(1)
    ' Create the regular expression (throws if pattern is invalid).
    Dim filePattern As New Regex(pattern, RegexOptions.IgnoreCase _
      Or RegexOptions.Multiline)

    ' Apply the regular expression to each file in specified or current directory.
    Dim dirname As String = Path.GetDirectoryName(filespec)
    If dirname.Length = 0 Then dirname = Directory.GetCurrentDirectory
    Dim search As String = Path.GetFileName(filespec)
    For Each fname As String In Directory.GetFiles(dirname, search)
        ' Read file contents and apply the regular expression to it.
        Dim text As String = FileText(fname)
        Dim mc As MatchCollection = filePattern.Matches(text)
        ' Display file name if one or more matches.
        If mc.Count > 0 Then
            Console.WriteLine("{0} [{1} matches]", fname, mc.Count)
        End If
```

```
      Next
   End Sub

   ' Read the contents of a text file. (Throws if file not found.)
   Function FileText(ByVal path As String) As String
      Dim sr As New StreamReader(path)
      FileText = sr.ReadToEnd
      sr.Close
   End Function
```

For example, you can use the FileGrep utility to find all *.VB source files in the current directory that contain the definition of a public ArrayList variable:

```
FileGrep "Public\s+\w+\s+As\s+(New\s+)?ArrayList" *.vb
```

(For simplicity's sake, the regular expression doesn't account for variants of the basic syntax, such as the presence of the ReadOnly keyword or of the complete System.Collections.ArrayList class name.) The companion source code for this book includes a more complete FileGrep utility, that can search entire directory trees and show details of all occurrences.

Another way to specify a regular expression option is by means of the (?imnsx-imnsx) construct, which lets you enable or disable one or more options from the current position to the end of the pattern string. The following code snippet reuses the FileText function and finds all Dim, Private, and Public variable declarations at the beginning of text lines. Note that the regular expression options are specified inside the pattern string instead of as an argument of the Regex.Matches method:

```
Dim source As String = FileText("Module1.vb")
Dim pattern As String = "(?im)^\s+(dim|public|private) \w+ As .+(?=\r\n)"
Dim mc As MatchCollection = Regex.Matches(source, pattern)
```

Table 11-2 Regular Expression Options*

RegexOptions enum Value	Option	Description
None		No option.
IgnoreCase	i	Case insensitivity match.
Multiline	m	Multiline mode; changes the behavior of ^ and $ so that they match the beginning and end of any line, respectively, instead of the whole string.
ExplicitCapture	n	Captures only explicitly named or numbered groups of the form (?<name>) so that naked parentheses act as noncapturing groups without your having to use the (?:) construct.

Table 11-2   Regular Expression Options[*] *(continued)*

RegexOptions enum Value	Option	Description
Compiled	c	Compiles the regular expression and generates MSIL code; this option generates faster code at the expense of longer start-up time.
Singleline	s	Single-line mode; changes the behavior of the . (dot) character so that it matches any character (instead of any character except newline).
IgnorePatternWhitespace	x	Eliminates unescaped white space from the pattern and enables X-mode comments.
RightToLeft	r	Searches from right to left. The regular expression will move to the left of the starting position, so the starting position should be specified at the end of the string instead of its beginning. This option can't be specified in the middle of the pattern. (This restriction avoids endless loops.) The (?<) look-behind construct provides something similar, and it can be used as a subexpression.
ECMAScript		Enables ECMAScript-compliant behavior. This option can be used only in conjunction with the IgnoreCase, Multiline, and Compiled flags; in all other cases, the method throws an exception.

[*]   These regular expression options can be specified when you create the Regex object or from inside a (?) construct. All these options are turned off by default.

Regular Expression Classes

Now that I have illustrated the fundamentals of regular expressions, it's time to dissect all the classes in the System.Text.RegularExpressions namespace.

The Regex Class

As you've seen in the preceding section, the Regex class provides two overloaded constructors—one that takes only the pattern and another that also takes a bit-coded value that specifies the required regular expression options:

```
' This Regex object can search the word "dim" in a case-insensitive way.
Dim re As New Regex("\bdim\b", RegexOptions.IgnoreCase)
```

The Regex class exposes only two properties, both of which are read-only. The Options property returns the second argument passed to the object constructor, while the RightToLeft property returns True if you specified the RightToLeft option. (The regular expression matches from right to left.) No property returns the regular expression pattern, but you can use the ToString method for this purpose.

Searching for Substrings

The Matches method searches the regular expression inside the string provided as an argument and returns a MatchCollection object that contains zero or more Match objects, one for each nonintersecting match. The Matches method is overloaded to take an optional starting index:

```
' Get the collection that contains all the matches.
Dim mc As MatchCollection = re.Matches(source)

' Print all the matches after the 100th character in the source string.
For Each m As Match In re.Matches(source, 100)
    Console.WriteLine(m.ToString)
Next
```

You can change the behavior of the Matches method (as well as the Match method, described later) by using a \G assertion to disable scanning. In this case, the match must be found exactly where the scan begins. This point is either at the index specified as an argument (or the first character if this argument is omitted) or immediately after the point where the previous match terminates. In other words, the \G assertion finds only *consecutive* matches:

```
' Finds consecutive groups of space-delimited numbers.
Dim re As New Regex("\G\s*\d+")
' Note that search stops at the first non-numeric group.
Console.WriteLine(re.Matches("12 34 56 ab 78").Count)       ' => 3
```

Sometimes, you don't really want to list all the occurrences of the pattern when determining whether the pattern is contained in the source string would suffice. If that's your interest, the IsMatch method is more efficient than the Matches method because it stops the scan as soon as the first match is found. You pass to this method the input string and an optional start index:

```
' Check whether the input string is a date in the format mm-dd-yy or
' mm-dd-yyyy. (The source string can use slashes as date separators and
' can contain leading or trailing white spaces.)
Dim re As New Regex("^\s*\d{1,2}(/|-)\d{1,2}\1(\d{4}|\d{2})\s*$")
If re.IsMatch(" 12/10/2001  ") Then
    Console.WriteLine("The date is formatted correctly.")
    ' (We don't check whether month and day values are in valid range.)
End If
```

The regular expression pattern in the preceding code requires an explanation:

1. The ^ and $ characters mean that the source string must contain one date value and nothing else.

2. The \s* subexpression at the beginning and end of the string means that we accept leading and trailing white spaces.

3. The \d{1,2} subexpression means that the month and day numbers can have one or two digits, whereas the (\d{4}|\d{2}) subexpression means that the year

number can have four or two digits. Note that the four-digit case must be tested first; otherwise, only the first two digits are matched.

4. The (/|-) subexpression means that we take either the slash or the dash as the date separator between the month and day numbers. (You don't need to escape the slash character inside a pair of parentheses.)

5. The \1 subexpression means that the separator between day and year numbers must be the same separator used between month and day numbers.

The Matches method is rarely used for parsing very long strings because it returns the control to the caller only when the entire string has been parsed. When parsing long strings, you should use the Match method instead. The Match method returns only the first Match object and lets you iterate over the remaining matches using the Match.NextMatch method, as this example demonstrates:

```
' Search all the dates in a source string.
Dim source As String = " 12-2-1999  10/23/2001 4/5/2001 "
Dim re As New Regex("\s*\d{1,2}(/|-)\d{1,2}\1(\d{4}|\d{2})")

' Find the first match.
Dim m As Match = re.Match(source)
' Enter the following loop only if the search was successful.
Do While m.Success
    ' Display the match, but discard leading and trailing spaces.
    Console.WriteLine(m.ToString.Trim)
    ' Find the next match; exit if not successful.
    m = m.NextMatch
Loop
```

The Split method is similar to the String.Split method except that it defines the delimiter by using a regular expression rather than a single character. For example, the following code prints all the elements in a comma-delimited list of numbers, ignoring leading and trailing white-space characters:

```
Dim source As String = "123, 456,,789"
Dim re As New Regex("\s*,\s*")
For Each s As String In re.Split(source)
    ' Note that the third element is a null string.
    Console.Write(s & "-")      ' => 123-456--789-
Next
```

You can modify the pattern to \s*[,]+\s* to discard empty elements. The Split method supports several overloaded variations, which let you define the maximum count of elements to be extracted and a starting index (if there are more elements than the given limit, the last element contains the remainder of the string):

```
' Split max 5 items.
Dim arr() As String = re.Split(source, 5)
' Split max 5 items, starting at the 100th character.
Dim arr2() As String = re.Split(source, 5, 100)
```

The Replace Method

As I explained earlier in this chapter, the Regex.Replace method lets you selectively replace portions of the source string. The Replace method requires that you create numbered or named groups of characters in the pattern and then use those groups in the replacement pattern. The following code example takes a string that contains one or more dates in the mm-dd-yy format (including variations with a / separator or a four-digit year number) and converts them to the dd-mm-yy format while preserving the original date separator:

```
Dim source As String = "12-2-1999  10/23/2001  4/5/2001 "
Dim pattern As String = _
    "\b(?<mm>\d{1,2})(?<sep>(/|-))(?<dd>\d{1,2})\k<sep>(?<yy>(\d{4}|\d{2}))\b"
Dim re As New Regex(pattern)
Console.WriteLine(re.Replace(source, "${dd}${sep}${mm}${sep}${yy}"))
    ' => 2-12-1999  23/10/2001  5/4/2001
```

The pattern string is similar to the one seen previously, with an important difference: it defines four groups—named *mm*, *dd*, *yy*, and *sep*—that are later rearranged in the replacement string. The \b assertion at the beginning and end of the pattern ensures that the date is a word of its own.

The Replace method supports other overloaded variants. For example, you can pass two additional numeric arguments, which are interpreted as the maximum number of substitutions and the starting index:

```
' Expand all "ms" abbreviations to "Microsoft" (regardless of their case).
Dim source As String = "Welcome to MS Ms ms MS"
Dim re As New Regex("\bMS\b", RegexOptions.IgnoreCase)
' Replace up to three occurrences, starting at the tenth character.
Console.WriteLine(re.Replace(source, "Microsoft", 3, 10))
    ' => Welcome to Microsoft Microsoft Microsoft MS
```

If the replacement operation does something more sophisticated than simply delete or change the order of named groups, you can use another overloaded version of the Replace function, which uses a delegate to call a function that you define in your application. This feature gives you tremendous flexibility, as the following code demonstrates:

```
Sub TestReplaceWithCallback()
    ' This pattern defines two integers separated by a plus sign.
    Dim re As New Regex("\d+\s*\+\s*\d+")
    Dim source As String = "a = 100 + 234: b = 200+345"
    ' Replace all sum operations with their results.
    Console.WriteLine(re.Replace(source, AddressOf DoSum))
        ' => a = 334: b = 545
End Sub

Function DoSum(ByVal m As Match) As String
    ' Parse the two operands.
```

```
        Dim args() As String = m.Value.Split("+"c)
        Dim n1 As Long = CLng(args(0))
        Dim n2 As Long = CLng(args(1))
        ' Return their sum, as a string.
        Return (n1 + n2).ToString
End Function
```

> **See Also**   Read the document "Building an Expression Evalutator.doc" on the companion
> CD to learn how you can expand on the previous example to build a full-fledged expression
> evaluator able to evaluate any math expressoin passed as an argument. The document
> comes with a complete demo application.

The delegate must point to a function that takes a Match object and returns a String object. The code inside this function can query the Match object properties to learn more about the match. For example, you can use the Index property to peek at what immediately precedes or follows in the source string so that you can make a more informed decision.

Shared Methods

All the methods seen so far are also available as shared methods, so most of the time you don't even need to explicitly create a Regex object. You generally pass the regular expression pattern to the shared methods as a second argument after the source string. For example, you can split a string into individual words as follows:

```
' \W means "any nonalphanumeric character."
Dim words() As String = Regex.Split("Split these words", "\W+")
```

The Regex class exposes a few shared methods that have no instance method counterpart. The Escape method takes a string and converts the special characters .$^{[(|)}*+?\ to their equivalent escaped sequence. This method is especially useful when you let the end user enter the search pattern:

```
Console.Write(Regex.Escape("(x)"))       ' => \(x\)

' Check whether the character sequence the end user entered in
' the txtChars TextBox control is contained in the source string.
If Regex.IsMatch(source, Regex.Escape(txtChars.Text))
```

The Unescape shared method converts a string that contains escaped sequences back into its unescaped equivalent. This method can be useful even if you don't use regular expressions; for example, to build strings that contain carriage returns, line feeds, and other nonprintable chapters by using a C#-like syntax and without having to concatenate string constants and subexpressions based on the Chr function:

```
s = Regex.Unescape("First line\r\nSecond line ends with null char\x00"))
```

The CompileToAssembly Method

When you use the RegexOptions.Compiled value in the Regex constructor, you can expect a slight delay for the regular expression to be compiled to IL. In most cases, this delay is negligible, but you can avoid it if you want by using the CompileToAssembly shared method to precompile one or more regular expressions. The result of this precompilation is a separate assembly that contains one Regex-derived type for each regular expression you've precompiled. The following code shows how you can use the CompileToAssembly method to create an assembly that contains two precompiled regular expressions:

```
' The namespace for both compiled regex types in this sample
Dim nsName As String = "CustomRegex"
' The first regular expression compiles to a type named RegexWords.
' (The last argument means that the type is public.)
Dim rci1 As New RegexCompilationInfo("\w+", RegexOptions.Compiled, "RegexWords", ns
   Name, True)
' The second regular expression compiles to a type named RegexIntegers.
Dim rci2 As New RegexCompilationInfo("\d+", RegexOptions.Compiled, "RegexIntegers", ns
   Name, True)
' Create the array that defines all compiled regular expressions.
Dim regexInfo() As RegexCompilationInfo = {rci1, rci2}

' Compile these types to an assembly named "CustomRegularExpressions"
Dim an As New System.Reflection.AssemblyName
an.Name = "CustomRegularExpressions"
Regex.CompileToAssembly(regexInfo, an)
```

The preceding code creates an assembly named CustomRegularExpressions.Dll in the same directory as the current application's executable. You can add a reference to this assembly from any Visual Studio .NET project and use the two RegexWords and Regex-Integers types, or you can load these types via reflection. In the former case, you can use a strongly typed variable:

```
Dim reWords As New CustomRegex.RegexWords
For Each m As Match In reWords.Matches("A string containing five words")
    Console.WriteLine(m.Value)
Next
```

The MatchCollection and Match Classes

The MatchCollection class represents a set of matches. It has no constructor because you can create a MatchCollection object only by using the Regex.Matches method.

The Match class represents a single match. You can obtain an instance of this class either by iterating on a MatchCollection object or directly by means of the Match method of the Regex class. The Match object is immutable and has no public constructor.

The Match class's main properties are Value, Length, and Index, which return the matched string, its length, and the index at which it appears in the source string. The ToString method returns the same string as the Value property does. I already showed you how to use the Match class's IsSuccess property and its NextMatch method to iterate over all the matches in a string.

You must pay special attention when the search pattern matches an empty string, for example, \d* (which matches zero or more digits). When you apply such a pattern to a string, you typically get one or more empty matches, as you can see here:

```
Dim re As New Regex("\d*")
For Each m As Match In re.Matches("1a23bc456de789")
    ' The output from this loop shows that some matches are empty.
    Console.Write(m.Value & ",")   ' => 1,,23,,456,,,789,,
Next
```

As I explained earlier, a search generally starts where the previous search ends. However, the rule is different when the engine finds an empty match because it advances by one character before repeating the search. You would get trapped in an endless loop if the engine didn't behave this way.

If the pattern contains one or more groups, you can access the corresponding Group object by means of the Match object's Groups collection, which you can index by the group number or group name. I'll discuss the Group object in a moment, but you can already see how you can use the Groups collection to extract the variable names and values in a series of assignments:

```
Dim source As String = "a = 123: b=456"
Dim re As New Regex("(\s*)(?<name>\w+)\s*=\s*(?<value>\d+)")
For Each m As Match In re.Matches(source)
    Console.WriteLine("Variable: {0}  Value: {1}", _
        m.Groups("name").Value, m.Groups("value").Value)
Next
```

This is the result displayed in the console window:

```
Variable: a  Value: 123
Variable: b  Value: 456
```

The Result method takes a replace pattern and returns the string that would result if the match were replaced by that pattern:

```
' This code produces exactly the same result as the preceding snippet.
For Each m As Match In re.Matches(source)
    Console.WriteLine(m.Result("Variable: ${name}  Value: ${value}"))
Next
```

The Group Class

The Group class represents a single group in a Match object and exposes a few properties whose meanings should be evident. The properties are Value (the text associated with the group), Index (its position in the source string), Length (the group's length), and Success (True when the group has been matched). This code sample is similar to the preceding example, but it also displays information concerning where each variable appears in the source string:

```
Dim source As String = "a = 123: b=456"
Dim re As New Regex("(\s*)(?<name>\w+)\s*=\s*(?<value>\d+)")
For Each m As Match In re.Matches(source)
    Dim g As Group = m.Groups("name")
    ' Get information on variable name and value.
    Console.Write("Variable '{0}' found at index {1}", g.Value, g.Index)
    Console.WriteLine(", value is {0}", m.Groups("value").Value)
Next
```

This is the result displayed in the console window:

```
Variable 'a' found at index 0, value is 123
Variable 'b' found at index 9, value is 456
```

The following example is more complex but also more useful. It shows how you can parse <A> tags in an HTML file and display the anchor text (that is, the text that appears underlined in an HTML page) and the URL it points to. As you see, it's just a matter of a few lines of code:

```
Dim re As New Regex("<A\s+HREF\s*=\s*""?([^"" >]+)""?>(.+)</A>", _
    RegexOptions.IgnoreCase)
' Load the contents of an HTML file.
Dim source As String = FileText("test.htm")
' Display all occurrences.
Dim m As Match = re.Match(source)
Do While m.Success
    Console.WriteLine("{0} => {1}", m.Groups(2).Value, m.Groups(1).Value)
    m = m.NextMatch()
Loop
```

To understand how the preceding code works, you must keep in mind that the <A> tag is followed by one or more spaces and then by an HREF attribute, which is followed by an equal sign and then the URL, optionally enclosed between double quotation marks. All the text that follows the closing angle bracket up to the ending tag </A> is the anchor text. The regular expression defined in the preceding code defines two unnamed groups—the URL and the anchor text—so displaying details for all the <A> tags in the HTML file is just a matter of looping over all the matches. The regular expression syntax is complicated by the fact that double quotation mark characters must be doubled when they appear in a string constant. Also, note that the URL group is defined by the repetition of any character other than the double quotation marks, spaces, and closing angle brackets.

A few methods in the Regex class can be useful for getting information about the groups that the parser finds in the regular expression. The GetGroupNames method returns an array with the names of all groups; the GroupNameFromNumber returns the name of the group with a given index; and the GroupNumberFromName returns the index of a group with a given name. See the MSDN documentation for more information.

> **See Also**   Read the document "The CaptureCollection and Capture Classes.doc" on the companion CD to learn how you can extract additional information from parsed strings.

Multithreading has always been the Achilles' heel of Visual Basic, and in fact you had to resort to coding in another language to achieve free-threaded applications. Well, this problem will soon be a thing of the past thanks to the multithreading support offered by the .NET Framework, as you'll learn in the next chapter.

12 **Threading**

If you weren't looking closely at the Microsoft Windows architecture, you might think that the operating system allocates CPU time to processes so that they can execute at the same time, even on single-CPU systems. The truth is that CPU time is allocated to threads, not processes. You can think of threads as independent execution paths, which can access resources such as memory. Processes, on the other hand, are passive containers for running threads, even though they have many other interesting features, such as the ability to allocate resources and provide a linear address space where you can store your variables and arrays.

The .NET Framework fully supports multithreaded applications, thanks to a rich set of classes in the base library. To ensure safe multithreaded applications, the language must offer a special synchronization construct, as you'll learn later in this chapter.

> **Note** To keep code as concise as possible, all code samples in this section assume the use of the following Imports statements at the file or project level:
>
> ```
> Imports System.IO
> Imports System.Threading
> ```

Threading Fundamentals

Windows allows *preemptive multitasking,* a fancy term that means a thread can be suspended at almost any time and another thread can be given CPU time. This contrasts with *cooperative multitasking*, allowed by versions of Windows through 3.1, in which each thread has to explicitly ask for suspension. (As you might imagine, cooperative multitasking makes the operating system more fragile because a thread crash affects the entire system.)

When to Use Threads

Each thread maintains a private set of structures that the operating system uses to save information (the *thread context*) when the thread isn't running, including the values of CPU registers at the time when the thread was suspended and the processor was allocated to another thread. A thread also maintains its own exception handlers and a priority level. For example, you can assign higher priority to threads that manage the user interface (so that they're more responsive) and lower priority to threads for less urgent tasks, such as background printing. In all cases, the time slice allocated to each thread is relatively short, so the end user has the perception that all the threads (and all the applications) run concurrently.

Alas, the thread scheduler—that is, the portion of the operating system that schedules existing threads and preempts the running thread when its time slice expires—takes some CPU time for its own chores. Moreover, the operating system consumes some memory to keep the context of each thread, be it active or temporarily suspended. For this reason, if too many threads are active at the same time, this scheduling activity can take a non-negligible amount of time and can degrade the overall performance, leaving less spare time to *worker threads* (the threads that do something useful). So you should never create more threads than strictly necessary, or you should use threads taken from the thread pool, as I explain at the end of this chapter.

You might want to create additional threads to perform operations such as asynchronous file or database I/O, communication with a remote machine or a Web server, or low-priority background jobs. You make the most of multithreading when you allocate distinct threads to tasks that have different priorities or that take a lot of time to complete. Before opting for a multithreading application, you should consider available alternatives, such as using timers for scheduling recurring tasks, as I'll explain later in this chapter.

The main problem with threads is that they can compete for shared resources, where a resource can be as simple as a variable or as complex as a database connection or a hardware device. You must synchronize access to such resources—otherwise, you can get into trouble, for reasons that will be clear shortly. Visual Basic .NET provides the SyncLock construct to help you deal with these problems, and the runtime offers several synchronization objects. The key to effective multithreading is learning how to use these features properly.

Creating Threads

The System.Threading.Thread class offers all the methods and properties you need to create and manage threads. To create a new thread, you simply instantiate a new Thread object and then invoke its Start method. The Thread object's constructor requires one argument, a ThreadStart delegate object that points to the routine that runs when the thread starts. Such a routine must be a Sub without any arguments.

The following Visual Basic application spawns a second thread that prints some messages to the console window:

```
Sub TestThread()
    ' Create a new thread, and define its starting point.
    Dim t As New Thread(New ThreadStart(AddressOf DoTheTask))
    ' Run the new thread.
    t.Start()

    ' Print some messages to the Console window.
    For i As Integer = 1 to 10
        Console.WriteLine("Msg #{0} from main thread", i)
        ' Wait for 0.2 second.
        Thread.Sleep(200)
    Next
End Sub
```

```
Sub DoTheTask()
    For i As Integer = 1 To 10
        Console.WriteLine("Msg #{0} from secondary thread", i)
        ' Wait for 0.2 second.
        Thread.Sleep(200)
    Next
End Sub
```

The console window will contain intermixed messages from both the main and the secondary thread, evidence that they are running independently.

The Start method is asynchronous, in the sense that it might return before the spawned thread has actually started its execution. A thread terminates when its main routine (DoTheTask, in this case) exits or when the thread is programmatically killed by a Thread.Abort method. The application as a whole terminates only when all its threads terminate. You can check how many threads an application has created by using the Process Viewer utility, which comes with Microsoft Visual Studio 6. (See Figure 12-1.) Interestingly, this utility shows that .NET applications might have additional threads— for example, the thread that manages garbage collections and finalizers—over which you apparently have no control.

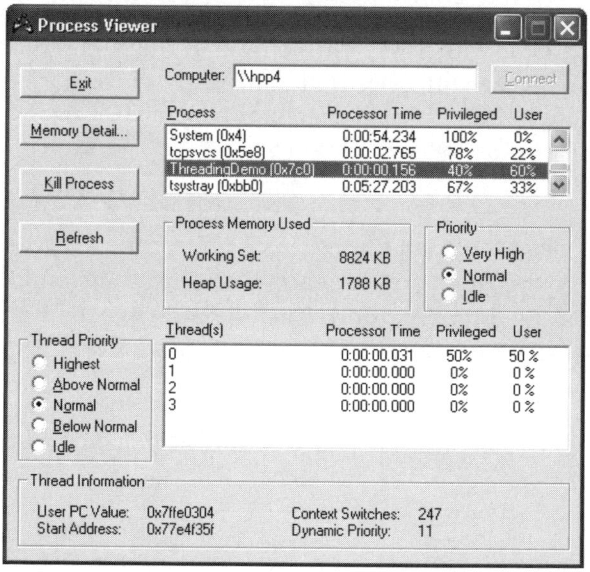

Figure 12-1   The Process Viewer utility displays diagnostic information about processes and their threads.

Working with Threads

To manipulate a Windows thread, you need a reference to the corresponding Thread object. This can be a reference to a new thread or a reference to the current thread— that is, the thread that is running the code—which you get by using the

Thread.CurrentThread shared method. Once you have a reference to a Thread object, you can start, suspend, resume, or abort it using methods of the Thread class.

As I explained earlier, a thread naturally terminates when it reaches the Exit or End statement of its main procedure, but it also can be suspended or aborted by another thread (or by itself) by means of a Suspend or Abort method. Like the Start method, the Suspend and Abort methods are asynchronous in the sense that they don't suspend or abort the thread immediately (unless you call the method for the current thread). In fact, threads can be suspended or aborted only when they reach a safe point. In general, a *safe point* is a point in time when it's safe to perform a garbage collection—for example, when a method call returns.

The runtime has several ways to take control when a thread reaches a safe point for a garbage collection. It can, for example, *hijack* the thread: when the thread is making a call to a class in the framework, the runtime pushes an extra return address (which points to a location in the runtime itself) onto the call stack. Then, when the method call completes, the runtime can take control and decide whether it's time to perform a garbage collection, to suspend the thread, or to abort it if there's a pending Abort method.

There's another reason the Abort method doesn't immediately halt a thread. Instead of killing the thread immediately—as is the case with the ExitThread and TerminateThread Windows API functions—the Abort method causes a ThreadAbortException to be thrown in the target thread. This exception is special in that managed code can't catch it. However, if the target thread is executing inside a Try...End Try block, the code in the Finally clause is guaranteed to be executed and the thread is aborted only at the completion of the Finally clause. A thread might even detect that it's being aborted (by means of the ThreadState property, described in the next section) and might continue to run code in the Finally clause to postpone its death. (Trusted code can also cancel an Abort method using the ResetAbort method—see the MSDN documentation for additional details.)

The Suspend and Resume instance methods let you temporarily suspend and then resume a thread. (A thread can suspend itself, but obviously it can't resume itself from a suspended state.) As for Abort, a thread is actually suspended only when it can be suspended safely, even though the Suspend method never blocks the caller (unless the calling thread is suspending itself, of course). The Suspend method has no effect on threads that are already suspended, and the Resume method has no effect on threads that are running. However, calls to the Suspend and Resume methods must be balanced. In addition, both methods throw a ThreadStateException if the target thread hasn't started yet or is already dead, or they throw a SecurityException if the caller doesn't have the necessary security permissions:

```
' Define and start a new thread.
' (Note that you don't strictly need a New ThreadStart object explicitly
'  because the AddressOf operator returns a delegate.)
Dim t As New Thread(AddressOf DoTheTask)
```

```
t.Start
⋮
' Suspend the thread.
t.Suspend
⋮
' Resume the thread.
t.Resume
⋮
' Abort the thread.
t.Abort
```

A thread can suspend itself temporarily by using the Thread.Sleep shared method, which takes a timeout in milliseconds:

```
' Pause for half a second.
Thread.Sleep(500)
```

The Sleep method works only on the current thread. Using this method is similar to calling the Windows API Sleep function. You can use the special 0 timeout value to terminate the current time slice and relinquish control to the thread scheduler, or you can use the Timeout.Infinite value (-1) to suspend the current thread indefinitely until another thread wakes it up. You can also pass a TimeSpan object to specify the length of the timeout.

It's quite common to wait for a thread to terminate; for example, the main thread can start a worker thread and then continue to execute to the point at which it must ensure that the worker thread has completed its task. You can use the Join method to easily achieve this behavior, as you can see in the following snippet:

```
Dim t As New Thread(AddressOf DoTheTask)
t.Start
' ...(Do something else.)...
⋮
' Wait for the other thread to die.
t.Join
```

The Join method can take an optional timeout, expressed in milliseconds or as a TimeSpan object. The method returns True if the thread died within the specified timeout; it returns False if the method returned because the timeout elapsed:

```
' Wait for the other thread to die, but print a message every second.
Do Until t.Join(1000)
    Console.WriteLine("Waiting for the other thread to die...")
Loop
```

When a thread calls Sleep on itself or Join on another thread, the calling thread enters the WaitSleepJoin state. (See Table 12-1.) A thread exits this state when the timeout expires or when another thread invokes the Interrupt method on it. When the Interrupt method is called, the target thread receives a ThreadInterruptedException, which must be caught or the thread will be killed. So the following is the typical code that you should write for threads that go to sleep and are waiting for another thread to wake them up:

```
Sub DoTheTask2()
    Try
        ' Go to sleep for 10 seconds or until another thread
        ' calls the Interrupt method on this thread.
        Thread.Sleep(10000)
        ' We get here if the timeout elapsed and no exception is thrown.
        ⋮
    Catch e As ThreadInterruptedException
        ' We get here if the thread has been interrupted.
        ⋮
    End Try
End Sub
```

Thread Properties

You can test whether a thread is active—that is, it has started and isn't dead yet—using the IsAlive read-only property. When it's applied to the current thread, this property always returns True, for obvious reasons.

You can also check the state of any thread—including the current one—by using the ThreadState enumerated property, whose values are summarized in Table 12-1. This is a bit-coded value because a thread can be in more than one state at any given time, so you should test individual bits with the And operator:

```
If Thread.CurrentThread.ThreadState And ThreadState.StopRequested Then
    ' The current thread is stopping.
End If
```

The IsBackground property tells whether a thread is a low-priority background thread. Interestingly, you can change the background state of a thread by assigning True or False to this property before the thread starts:

```
' Make a thread a background thread before starting it.
t.IsBackground = True
t.Start
```

An important detail: background threads don't keep an application alive, so if your application has created one or more background threads, it should check the IsAlive property of all of them before exiting the main thread. Otherwise, those threads are mercilessly killed, regardless of what they're doing that moment.

The Priority property offers a different way to affect a thread's priority without making it a background thread. This property sets or returns one of the ThreadPriority enumerated values, which are Normal, AboveNormal, BelowNormal, Highest, or Lowest:

```
' Supercharge the current thread.
Thread.CurrentThread.Priority = ThreadPriority.Highest
```

Windows can adjust the priority of threads automatically—for example, when an application becomes the foreground application—but remember that changing the priority of a thread isn't recommended, so you should do it only for a good reason.

Finally, all threads have a Name property. This property is usually a null string, but you can assign it a value for the threads you create. The Name property doesn't change the behavior of a thread, but it turns useful during the debugging phase, as you'll read in the next section. For example, the thread name is reported in the message that the Visual Studio .NET debugger displays when a thread terminates.

Oddly, the Thread class doesn't expose any property that returns the ID of the underlying Windows physical thread. Under Windows you can retrieve the physical thread ID with a call to the GetCurrentThreadId Windows API function or, even better, by calling the AppDomain.GetCurrentThreadId static property:

```
Dim currThreadId As Integer = AppDomain.GetCurrentThreadId()
```

Table 12-1   The Possible Values for the ThreadState Property

State	Description
Aborted	The thread has been aborted.
AbortRequested	The thread is responding to an Abort request.
Background	The thread is running in the background. (Same as the IsBackground property.)
Running	The thread is running. (Another thread has called the Start method.)
Stopped	The thread has been stopped. (A thread can never leave this state.)
StopRequested	The thread is about to stop.
Suspended	The thread has been suspended.
SuspendRequested	The thread is responding to a Suspend request.
Unstarted	The thread has been created, but the Start method hasn't been called yet.
WaitSleepJoin	The thread has called Monitor.Wait or Thread.Join on another thread.

Debugging Threads

You can see the name of the running thread—as well as other information such as the application name and the stack frame—by activating the Debug Location toolbar inside Visual Studio .NET. This data is especially useful when you want to determine where a thread is executing when you hit a breakpoint. You can display this toolbar by right-clicking on any toolbar and clicking Debug Location on the shortcut menu. (See Figure 12-2.)

The Thread window in Visual Studio .NET lets you list all the running threads, their status, and their priority. You activate this window by pointing to Windows on the Debug menu and clicking Threads. (The current program must be in break mode for you to see this menu command.) The yellow arrow on the left identifies the current thread, and you can switch to another thread by right-clicking on it. (See Figure 12-3.) You can also freeze a thread, which is then displayed with two vertical blue bars, and restart (thaw) it.

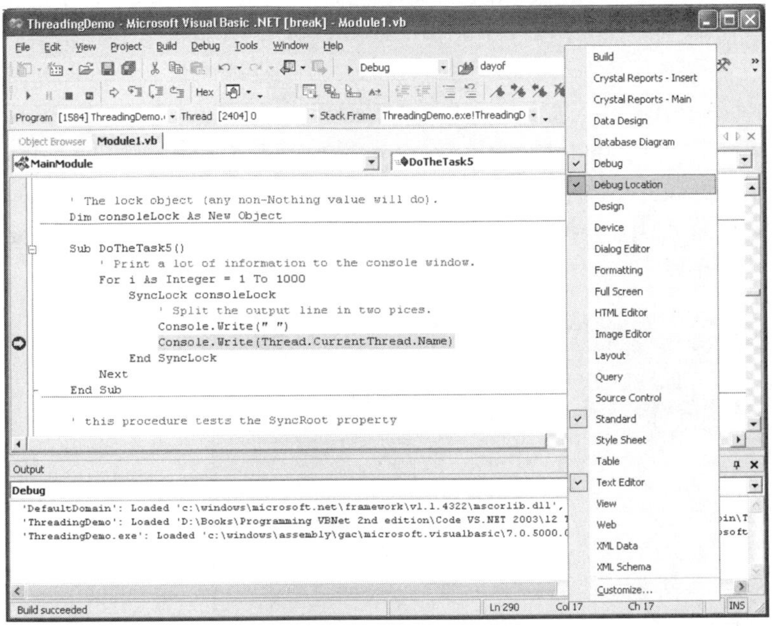

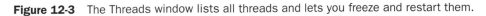

Figure 12-2   The Debug Location toolbar displays the thread name and other information about the running process.

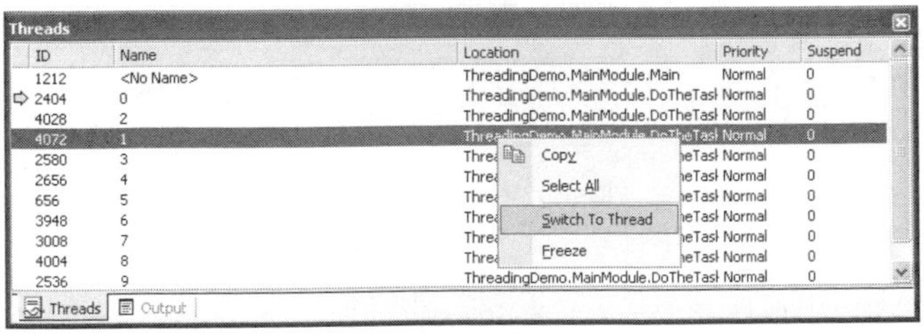

Figure 12-3   The Threads window lists all threads and lets you freeze and restart them.

The Performance utility offers a way to monitor threads and the performance bottle-necks they might create. (See Figure 12-4.) The .NET Framework has a performance object named .NET CLR LocksAndThreads that exposes several counters, the most important of which are

- **# of current logical threads**   The current number of threads in the application known to the common language runtime in a given application.

- **# of current physical threads**   The number of native Windows threads created and owned by the common language runtime.

- **# of current recognized threads**   The number of threads that were created outside the common language runtime (for example, in a COM component) that the runtime has recognized.

- **contention rate/sec**   Rate at which threads in the runtime fail to acquire a managed lock—for example, when reaching a SyncLock block. A high number for this counter is a symptom that the application isn't well designed for multi-thread operations.

- **total # of contentions**   The total number of times threads in the common language runtime have failed to acquire a managed lock.

- **current queue/sec**   The average number of threads waiting to acquire a lock; a high value means that most threads spend most of their time waiting for a lock to become available.

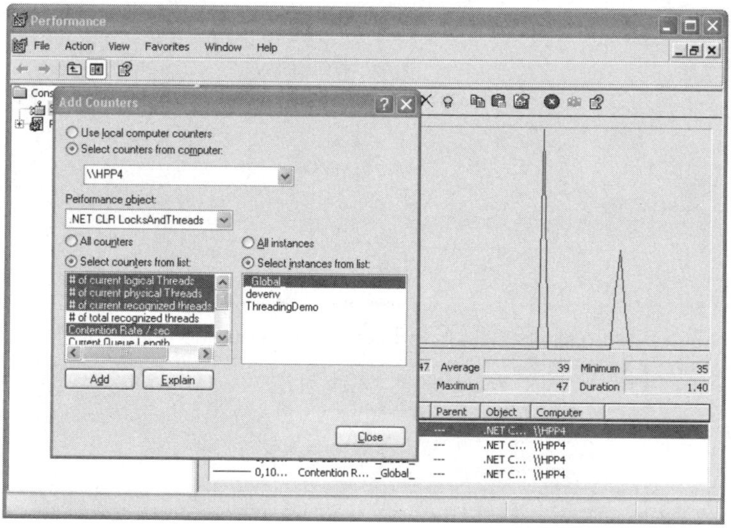

Figure 12-4   The Performance utility lets you visualize several statistics regarding common language runtime threads.

The meaning of some of these counters—most notably, those related to contention and locks—will become evident later in this chapter.

Threads and Unhandled Exceptions

A thread is always terminated when an unhandled exception occurs. However, an exception on a secondary thread—for example, a thread used by the garbage collector to call the Finalize method, a thread created with the Thread class, or a thread taken from the thread pool—isn't fatal for the application (even if it might cause error messages to appear, depending on the type of current application). Only uncaught exceptions thrown by the main thread or an unmanaged thread—for example, a thread running in COM objects called by a .NET assembly—terminate the application.

You can get a notification when an unhandled exception is about to terminate a thread by trapping the UnhandledException event of the AppDomain object pointing to the current AppDomain. The event's second argument receives an UnhandledException-EventArgs object, which exposes two properties, ExceptionObject and IsTerminating. The former is of course the exception being thrown, but it returns an Object value, and you must cast it to an Exception variable before you can read the usual properties such as Message and StackTrace. The second property is True if the exception is fatal and will terminate the application: this is the case when the exception is thrown on the main thread (the thread that was created when the application began its execution) or on an unmanaged thread created outside the .NET runtime. The IsTerminating property is False when the exception is thrown on a thread that you created yourself, a thread borrowed from the thread pool (for example, a thread that serves a timer), or the special thread that executes all Finalize methods. The following example shows how you can trap the UnhandledException event:

```
Dim WithEvents CurrAppDomain As AppDomain

Sub Main()
    ' Prepare to trap AppDomain events.
    CurrAppDomain = AppDomain.CurrentDomain
    ' Cause an exception on a secondary thread.
    ' (It will show a message with IsTerminating = False.)
    Dim t As New Thread(AddressOf ThrowException)
    t.Start()
    Thread.Sleep(500)
    ' Cause a fatal exception on the main thread.
    ' (It will show a message with IsTerminating = True.)
    Throw New IndexOutOfRangeException()
End Sub

Sub ThrowException()
    Throw New DivideByZeroException()
End Sub

Sub CurrAppDomain_UnhandledException(ByVal sender As Object, _
    ByVal e As UnhandledExceptionEventArgs) _
    Handles CurrAppDomain.UnhandledException
    ' Get a reference to the exception.
    Dim ex As Exception = CType(e.ExceptionObject, Exception)
    ' Show information about the current exception.
    Console.WriteLine("{0}  (IsTerminating={1})", ex.Message, e.IsTerminating)
End Sub
```

One important thing about this event: you can trap it correctly only when the application isn't running under the Visual Studio debugger, so you must start the program by choosing Start Without Debugging from the Debug menu or by pressing the Ctrl+F5 key combination. This is the output that the preceding code sends to the Console window:

```
Attempted to divide by zero.  (IsTerminating=False)
Index was outside the bounds of the array.  (IsTerminating=True)
```

All fatal exceptions cause the dialog shown in Figure 12-5 to appear, so you'll have to click No before you can see the second line in the preceding output.

Although the UnhandledException event can be useful, keep in mind that you can't catch and solve every unhandled exception using this technique. In practice, you can only save any unsaved data, log the exception somewhere (for example, in the system event log), and display a dialog box to inform the user that the application is closing. This dialog box might offer the option of sending a bug report to the producer of the application (you) and maybe restart the application on the same data file. (This is what Visual Studio .NET itself does when an unhandled exception occurs.)

> **Note**   In the "Global Error Handlers" section of Chapter 16, you'll learn about the ThreadEx-ception event of the Application object, which provides the ability to trap *and recover* from unhandled exceptions in Windows Forms applications.

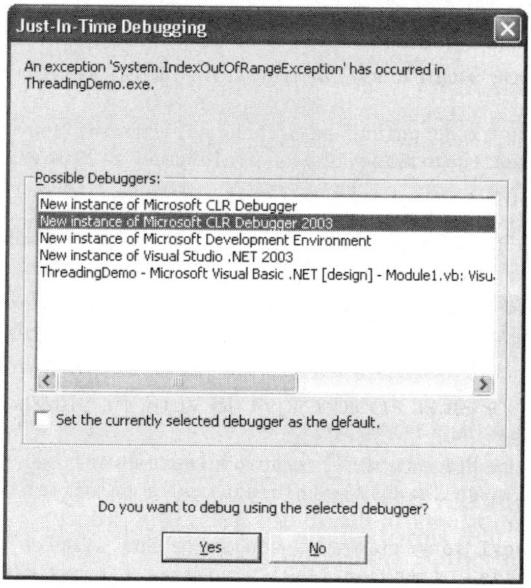

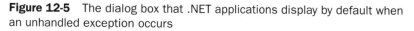

Figure 12-5   The dialog box that .NET applications display by default when an unhandled exception occurs

Storing and Sharing Data

You should realize that whenever you have multiple threads that share data, you also need a way to synchronize access to that data. If two threads can access the same (shared) variables, you might ensure that they don't change them at the same time because the result isn't a pleasant one. Data sharing and synchronization are always two facets of the same issue.

Local, Class, and Static Variables

The scope of a variable determines whether multiple threads can share it. Threads never share local dynamic variables—that is, variables defined inside a procedure and not marked by the Static keyword—even if the threads happen to be executing inside that procedure in the same moment. The reason is simple: local variables are allocated on the stack. Each thread maintains its own private stack and keeps its own copy of all local dynamic variables, which means that you can't share data among threads using local dynamic variables. The good news is that you don't have to worry about synchronizing access to such variables.

By default, threads share all other types of variables—that is, class-level fields and properties, module-level variables, and local Static variables. You can use these variables to make data visible to all the running threads. Unfortunately, you also have to provide a way to synchronize access to this data. Consider this simple code:

```
If globalVar = 0 Then
    Console.WriteLine("About to change globalVar")
    globalVar = globalVar + 1
End If
```

If access to the globalVar variable isn't arbitrated and synchronized in some way, a thread might execute, test the value of globalVar, find that it's 0, and enter the Then code block. The first statement in this block is a call into the runtime, which gives the thread manager a chance to perform a thread switch and activate another thread. What happens if the other thread enters the same block of code? As you might expect, it finds that the globalVar variable is still 0, and the other thread (incorrectly) enters the block. As a result, the variable is incremented twice, which you probably don't want and which might cause an error later in the application. Logic errors of this kind are problematic because they occur in random fashion, are rarely reproducible, and therefore are very difficult to debug.

This code summarizes which variables are shared among threads:

```
Class SampleClass
    Dim Field As Integer              ' Field (shared)

    Sub SampleSub()
        Dim dynamicVar As Integer     ' Dynamic variable (nonshared)
        Static staticVar As Integer   ' Static variable (shared)
        ⋮
    End Sub
End Class
```

Surprisingly, you might have to worry about how variables are shared between threads even if your objects don't create multiple threads but just use objects that create secondary threads and fire their events on these secondary threads. In fact, unlike events raised by components written in Visual Basic 6, the handler of a .NET event always runs in the thread of the object that is the source of the event. This situation is especially problematic if you are calling a multithreaded object from inside a Windows Forms application, because code in form objects must run in the same thread that created the form itself—or the application might crash.

The ThreadStatic Attribute

To understand the kinds of problems you have to watch out for when you're working with multithreaded applications, consider this simple class:

```
Class SampleClass2
    Public Shared ThreadName As String
    ⋮
End Class
```

Suppose that this class can be used by multiple threads but that each thread wants to store and retrieve a distinct value for the ThreadName static field. Unfortunately, being static, the ThreadName variable is shared among all the instances of the class and hence all the threads, so each thread will override the current value with its own ThreadName.

To obviate this problem, the .NET runtime supports the concept of *thread-relative* variables, which are static variables and fields that are shared among all class instances but not among threads. You create a thread-relative Static variable by marking the declaration of a Shared class-level field in a class with the ThreadStatic attribute:

```
' The ThreadName variable isn't shared among threads.
<ThreadStatic()> Public Shared ThreadName As String
```

Because Visual Basic modules are just classes whose members are automatically flagged as Shared, you can also apply the ThreadStatic attribute to any module-level variable in a module.

Even if you decide not to explicitly create new threads in your applications, you might have to worry about arbitrating access to module-level and static class-level variables anyway. In fact, by default the Finalize method of your objects runs on a different thread than your application's main thread; therefore, you should ensure that either you don't access any shared variables from Finalize methods or you protect these variables by using synchronization blocks (which I explain later).

Passing Data to and from a Thread

More often than not, you must pass data to a thread before starting its execution. This isn't a trivial task because you can't pass data as an argument. (The ThreadStart delegate doesn't take arguments.) Nor can you store data in a global variable and let the code in the other thread read it. (Other threads might override this value in the meantime.) You often need to solve the opposite problem as well, which is to retrieve data from a thread that has produced a result.

A general solution, which doesn't pose any limit to the amount of data that can be passed in both directions, is to create a class for the sole purpose of sharing data between the main application and the thread and have this class expose the instance method that works as the entry point for the thread. Here's an example that shows how you can pass data in both directions:

```
Class ThreadData
    Public Id As Integer
    Public Msg As String
    Public Done As Boolean

    ' The entry point for the thread
    Sub DoTheTask()
        For i As Integer = 1 To 10
            ' Show that the thread received the correct values.
            Console.WriteLine("{0} (Thread ID = {1})", msg, id)
            ' Wait for 0.2 second.
            Thread.Sleep(200)
        Next
        ' Let the main thread know that this thread has completed.
        Done = True
    End Sub
End Class
```

Here's a routine that uses the ThreadData class:

```
Sub TestThreadData ()
    Dim dc(9) As ThreadData
    Dim t As Thread
    Dim allDone As Boolean

    ' Create multiple threads.
    For i As Integer = 0 To 9
        ' Create a new data object, and initialize its properties.
        dc(i) = New ThreadData
        dc(i).Id = i + 1
        dc(i).Msg = "A message"
        ' Create a new thread, and define its starting point.
        t = New Thread(AddressOf dc(i).DoTheTask)
        t.Start()
    Next

    ' Poll until all threads have completed.
    ' (Just an example that retrieves values from threads.)
    Do Until allDone
        Console.WriteLine("Waiting...")
        Thread.Sleep(200)
```

```
                    ' Check that all threads have set Done = True.
                    allDone = True
                    For i As Integer = 0 To 9
                        allDone = allDone And dc(i).Done
                    Next
            Loop
    End Sub
```

In the preceding example, the main thread polls the Done property in every data object to learn when all the threads have completed their jobs. This approach isn't completely safe because the main thread might access the Done field at the same time as the thread that "owns" that instance of the class. Later in this chapter, you'll see how to solve this problem by means of a SyncLock statement.

Thread Synchronization

Now that you know how a thread can share data or prevent data from being shared, you're ready to tackle synchronization issues related to concurrent access to variables and objects accessible by multiple threads at the same time.

The SyncLock Statement

As you know, a thread can be preempted at any time, usually at the completion of a call to an object's method. The following example demonstrates what can happen when a piece of code isn't guaranteed to execute atomically:

```
Sub TestSynchronizationProblem()
    ' Create ten secondary threads.
    For i As Integer = 0 To 9
        Dim t As New Thread(AddressOf DoTheTask3)
        ' Let's cheat a little to pass a value to this thread.
        t.Name = i.ToString
        t.Start()
    Next
End Sub

Sub DoTheTask3()
    ' Print a lot of information to the console window.
    For i As Integer = 1 To 1000
        ' Split the output line in two pieces.
        Console.Write(" ")
        Console.Write(Thread.CurrentThread.Name)
    Next
End Sub
```

A glance at the console window shows some interruptions of a thread between the Console.Write statements, which result in scrambled output. (See Figure 12-6.)

Figure 12-6   The console window clearly shows that writing a space plus the thread number isn't an atomic operation.

The runtime offers no means for ensuring that a group of statements behaves as an atomic, uninterruptible operation. This would be too stiff a requirement in an operating system that must guarantee multitasking to all applications. However, most of the time you would be satisfied to have atomicity at the application level (rather than at the system level). In the preceding code, for example, it would be enough to ensure that only one thread in the current application can execute a specific block of statements at a time. You can achieve this by enclosing those statements in a SyncLock...End SyncLock block, a language construct that was obviously missing in Visual Basic 6 (which didn't support free threading at all). The SyncLock block requires a variable as an argument, and this variable must satisfy the following requirements:

- It must be a variable shared by all the threads (typically, a class-level or module-level variable without the ThreadStatic attribute).

- It must be a reference type, for example, a String or an Object variable. (Using a value type causes a compilation error.)

- It must not have a Nothing value. (Using a Nothing value causes a run-time error.)

Here's the code seen before, revised to leverage the SyncLock block (additions are in boldface):

```
' The lock object. (Any non-Nothing reference value will do.)
Dim consoleLock As New Object

Sub DoTheTask3()
    ' Print a lot of information to the console window.
    For i As Integer = 1 To 1000
        SyncLock consoleLock
            ' Split the output line in two pieces.
            Console.Write(" ")
            Console.Write(Thread.CurrentThread.Name)
        End SyncLock
    Next
End Sub
```

The preceding code uses the consoleLock variable to arbitrate access to the Console object, which is the only resource that all threads share in this trivial example and is therefore the only resource for which you need to provide synchronization. Real-world applications might contain many SyncLock blocks; such blocks can share the same object variable or use different variables for finer granularity. As a rule of thumb, you should have a distinct object variable for each shared resource that must be synchronized or for each group of statements that must be executed by one thread at a time.

Each SyncLock block implicitly uses a hidden Try…End Try block because Visual Basic must ensure that the lock is correctly released if an exception is thrown. (A lock release requires a Monitor.Exit method.) For this reason, jumping into a SyncLock block by using a Goto statement is illegal.

One final tip: if the SyncLock block is placed inside an instance method of a class and all threads are running inside a method of that instance, you can pass Me to the SyncLock statement because this object surely satisfies all the requirements. It's accessible by all threads, it's a reference value, and it surely is non-Nothing.

```
Class TestClass
    Sub DoTheTask()
        SyncLock Me
            ' Only one thread at a time can access this code.
            ⋮
        End SyncLock
    End Sub
End Class
```

You can use Me in this fashion only for one SyncLock block in the class. If you have multiple synchronization blocks, you'll typically use different variables as the argument of the SyncLock block.

Synchronized Objects

Another problem related to threading is that not every .NET object can be safely shared among threads. In other words, not all .NET objects are *thread-safe*. When you're writing a multithreaded application, you should always check the documentation to determine whether the objects and the methods you're using are thread-safe. For example, all the shared methods of the Regex, Match, and Group classes are thread-safe, but their instance methods aren't and shouldn't be invoked by different threads at the same time. Some .NET objects—most notably, Windows forms and controls—pose even more severe limitations, in that only the thread that created them can call their methods. (You'll learn how to access Windows forms and controls from other threads in the "Multithreaded Controls" section of Chapter 18.)

Synchronized .NET Classes

Several objects that aren't thread-safe natively—including ArrayList, Hashtable, Queue, SortedList, Stack, TextReader, TextWriter, and regular expression Match and Group classes—expose a Synchronized shared method, which returns a thread-safe object that's equivalent to the one you pass as an argument. Most of these classes also expose the IsSynchronized property, which returns True if you're dealing with a thread-safe instance:

```
' Create an ArrayList object, and add some values to it.
Dim al As New ArrayList()
al.Add(1): al.Add(2): al.Add(3)
' Create a synchronized, thread-safe version of this ArrayList.
Dim syncAl As ArrayList = ArrayList.Synchronized(al)
' Prove that the new object is thread-safe.
Console.WriteLine(al.IsSynchronized)        ' => False
Console.WriteLine(syncAl.IsSynchronized)    ' => True
```

Now that it's thread-safe, you can share the syncAl object among different threads.

The Synchronization Attribute

Using the System.Runtime.Remoting.Contexts.Synchronization attribute is the simplest way to provide synchronized access to an entire object so that only one thread can access its instance fields and methods. That is, any thread can use that instance of the class, but only one thread at a time. If a thread is executing code inside the class, any other thread that attempts to use the fields or methods of that class has to wait. In other words, it's as if there were SyncLock blocks enclosing every method of that class, with all these blocks using the same lock variable.

The following code shows how you can synchronize a class using the Synchronization attribute. Notice also that the class must inherit from ContextBoundObject to be marked as a context-bound object:

```
<System.Runtime.Remoting.Contexts.Synchronization()> _
Class Display
    Inherits ContextBoundObject
    ⋮
End Class
```

The Synchronization attribute automatically synchronizes access to all instance fields, properties, and methods, but it doesn't provide synchronization for shared members. The attribute can take an optional argument, which can be either a True or False (to indicate whether reentrant calls are permitted) or one of the constants exposed by the SynchronizationAttribute class itself: NOT_SUPPORTED, SUPPORTED, REQUIRED, and REQUIRES_NEW. For more information, read the MSDN documentation.

The MethodImpl Attribute

In most cases, synchronizing an entire class is overkill, and protecting just a few of its methods from concurrent accesses is often satisfactory. You can apply this sort of protection by wrapping the body of such methods in a SyncLock block. On the other hand, here's a simpler technique, based on the System.Runtime.CompilerServices.MethodImpl attribute:

```
' This code assumes that the following Imports statement has been used:
'  Imports System.Runtime.CompilerServices

Class MethodImplDemoClass
    ' This method can be executed by one thread at a time.
    <MethodImpl(MethodImplOptions.Synchronized)> _
    Sub SynchronizedMethod()
        ⋮
    End Sub
End Class
```

Applying the MethodImpl attribute for multiple methods in the class provides the same effect as wrapping the body of those methods with SyncLock blocks that use the same lock variable. In other words, a thread calling a method marked with the MethodImpl attribute will block any other thread calling the same or a different method marked with this attribute. Interestingly, you also can use the MethodImpl attribute for static methods. The object variable implicitly used to lock static methods is different from the object variable used for instance methods, so a thread invoking a static method marked with the MethodImpl attribute doesn't block another thread calling an instance method marked with the same attribute.

The Monitor Class

The SyncLock block provides an easy-to-use method for dealing with synchronization issues, but it can be inadequate in many situations. For example, a thread can't just *test* a SyncLock code block and avoid being blocked if another thread is already executing that SyncLock block or another SyncLock block is associated with the same object.

SyncLock blocks are internally implemented via Monitor objects. Interestingly, you can use a Monitor object directly and get more flexibility, although it's at the expense of somewhat more complex code.

You never instantiate individual Monitor objects, and in fact, all the methods I'm going to illustrate are shared methods of the Monitor type. The most important method is Enter, which takes an object as an argument. This object works exactly like the argument you pass to a SyncLock block and undergoes the same constraints—it must be a non-Nothing reference variable that's shared by all the threads. If no other thread owns the lock on that object, the current thread acquires the lock and sets its internal lock counter to 1. If another thread currently owns the lock, the calling thread must wait until the other thread releases the lock and the lock becomes available. If the calling thread already owns the lock, each call to Monitor.Enter increments the internal lock counter.

The Monitor.Exit method takes the lock object as an argument and decrements its internal lock counter. If the counter reaches 0, the lock is released so that other threads can acquire it. Calls to Monitor.Enter and Monitor.Exit must be balanced, or the lock will never be released:

```
' A non-Nothing module-level object variable
Dim objLock As New Object
v
Try
    ' Attempt to enter the critical section;
    ' wait if the lock is currently owned by another thread.
    Monitor.Enter(objLock)
    ' ...(Do something.)...
    ⋮
Finally
    ' Release the lock.
    Monitor.Exit(objLock)
End Try
```

If the statements between Monitor.Enter and Monitor.Exit are likely to raise an exception, you should put all the code in a Try…End Try block because it's imperative that you always release the lock. If a thread calls the Interrupt method on another thread currently waiting inside a Monitor.Enter method, the thread receives a ThreadInterruptedException, which is another good reason for using a Try…End Try block.

The Enter and Exit methods of a Monitor object let you replace a SyncLock block but don't bring you any additional advantages. You see the extra flexibility of the Monitor class when you apply its TryEnter method. This method is similar to Enter, but the method exits and returns False if the lock can't be acquired in the specified timeout. For example, you can attempt to get the monitor lock for 10 milliseconds and then give up, without blocking the current thread indefinitely. The following code rewrites a previous example based on SyncLock, this time using the Monitor object, and also displays the failed attempts to acquire the lock:

```
Try
    Do Until Monitor.TryEnter(consoleLock, 10)
        Debug.WriteLine("Thread {0} failed to acquire the lock", _
            Thread.CurrentThread.Name)
    Loop
    ' Split the output line in pieces.
    Console.Write(" ")
    Console.Write(Thread.CurrentThread.Name)
Finally
    ' Release the lock.
    Monitor.Exit(consoleLock)
End Try
```

The Interlocked Class

The Interlocked class provides a way to perform the simple atomic operations of incrementing and decrementing a shared memory variable. This class exposes only shared methods (not counting members inherited from Object). Consider the following code:

```
' Increment and Decrement methods work with 32-bit integers.
Dim lockCounter As Integer

' The procedure that contains the critical section
Sub DoTheTask6()
    ' Increment the lock counter, and return the new value.
    If Interlocked.Increment(lockCounter) = 1 Then
        ' Enter the critical section only if lockCounter was 0.
        ⋮
        ' ... (The critical section) ...
        ⋮
    End If
    ' Allow other threads to enter the critical section.
    Interlocked.Decrement(lockCounter)
End Sub
```

You can see that only one thread at a time can enter the critical section, so in practice, you get the same effect you'd get with the Monitor.TryEnter method. However, the Interlocked class permits something that the Monitor class doesn't allow: you can set a threshold (higher than 1) for the number of threads that run inside the critical section. To see what I mean, just replace one line in the preceding code:

```
' Let up to four threads run in the critical section.
If Interlocked.Increment(lockCounter) <= 4 Then
```

The Interlocked class exposes two additional shared methods. The Exchange method lets you assign a value of your choosing to an Integer, a Single, or an Object variable and return its previous value, as an atomic operation. The CompareExchange method works similarly, but it does the swap only if the memory location is currently equal to a specific value that you provide as an argument.

The Mutex Class

The Mutex class provides yet another synchronization primitive. The Mutex object is a Windows kernel object that can be owned by one thread at a time and is said to be in a *signaled* state if no thread currently owns it.

A thread requests ownership of a Mutex object by means of the Mutex.WaitOne method (which doesn't return until the ownership has been successfully achieved) and releases it by means of the Mutex.ReleaseMutex method. A thread can request ownership of a Mutex object that it owns already without blocking itself, but in that case, it must call ReleaseMutex an equal number of times. This is how you can implement a synchronized section using a Mutex object:

```
' This Mutex object must be accessible to all threads.
Dim m As New Mutex

Sub DoTheTask7()
    m.WaitOne()
    ' Enter the synchronized section.
    ⋮
    ' Exit the synchronized section.
    m.ReleaseMutex()
End Sub
```

In a real application, you should use a Try block to protect your code from unhandled errors, and place the call to ReleaseMutex in the Finally block. If you pass WaitOne an optional timeout argument, the method returns the control to the thread when the ownership is successfully achieved or the timeout expires. You can tell the difference between the two results by looking at the return value. True means ownership was acquired, False means the timeout expired.

```
' Attempt to enter the critical section, but give up after 0.1 second.
If m.WaitOne(100, False) Then
    ' Enter the critical section.
    ⋮
    ' Exit the critical section, and release the Mutex.
    m.ReleaseMutex()
End If
```

When used in this way, the Mutex object provides a mechanism equivalent to the Monitor.TryEnter method, without offering any additional features. You see the added flexibility of the Mutex object when you consider its WaitAny or WaitAll shared method. The WaitAny method takes an array of Mutex objects and returns when it manages to acquire the ownership of one of the Mutex objects in the list (in which case, that Mutex becomes signaled) or when the optional timeout expires. The return value is the array index of the Mutex object that became signaled or the special value 258 if the timeout expired.

You typically use an array of Mutex objects when you have a limited number of resources, such as communication ports, and you want to allocate each one to a thread as soon as the resource becomes available. In this situation, a signaled Mutex object means that the corresponding resource is available, so you can use the Mutex.WaitAny method for blocking the current thread until *any* of the Mutex objects become signaled. Here's the skeleton of an application that uses this approach:

```
' An array of three Mutex objects
Dim mutexes() As Mutex = { New Mutex(), New Mutex(), New Mutex() }

Sub DoTheTask8()
    ' Wait until a resource becomes available.
    ' (Returns the index of the available resource)
    Dim mutexNdx As Integer = Mutex.WaitAny(mutexes)
```

```
            ' Enter the critical section.
            ' (This code should use only the resource corresponding to mutexNdx.)
            ' ...
            ' Exit the critical section, and release the resource.
            mutexes(mutexNdx).ReleaseMutex()
End Sub
```

The WaitAll shared method takes an array of Mutex objects and returns the control to the application only when *all* of them have become signaled. This method is especially useful when you can't proceed until all the other threads have completed their jobs:

```
' Wait until all resources have been released.
Mutex.WaitAll(resources)
```

Unlike other synchronization objects, Mutex objects can be assigned a name, which brings up one of the most important features of these objects. Mutex objects that have the same name are shared among different processes. You can create an instance of a named Mutex using this syntax:

```
Dim m As New Mutex(False, "mutexname")
```

If a Mutex with that name already exists in the system, the caller gets a reference to it, otherwise a new Mutex object is created. This mechanism lets you share Mutex objects among different applications and therefore have these applications synchronize their access to shared resources.

The ReaderWriterLock Class

Many resources in the real world can be either read from or written to. Often these resources allow either multiple read operations or a single write operation running in a given moment. For example, multiple clients can read a data file or a database table, but if the file or the table is being written to, no other read or write operation can occur on that resource. You can create a lock that implements single-writer, multiple-reader semantics by using a ReaderWriterLock object.

Using this object is straightforward. All the threads intending to use the resource should share the same instance of the ReaderWriterLock class. Before attempting an operation on the resource, a thread should call either the AcquireReaderLock or the AcquireWriterLock method, depending on the operation to be performed. These methods block the current thread until the lock of the requested type can be acquired. (For example, until no other thread is holding the lock if you requested a writer lock.) Finally, the thread should call the ReleaseReaderLock or ReleaseWriterLock method when the read or write operation on the resource has been completed.

The following code example creates 10 threads that perform either a read or a write operation on a shared resource (relevant statements are in boldface):

```
Dim rwl As New ReaderWriterLock()
Dim rnd As New Random()

Sub TestReaderWriterLock()
    For i As Integer = 0 To 9
        Dim t As New Thread(AddressOf DoTheTask9)
        t.Name = i.ToString
        t.Start()
    Next
    ⋮
End Sub

Sub DoTheTask9()
    Dim tname As String = Thread.CurrentThread.Name()
    ' Perform 10 read or write operations. (Reads are more frequent.)
    For i As Integer = 1 To 10
        If rnd.NextDouble < 0.8 Then
            ' Attempt a read operation.
            rwl.AcquireReaderLock(Timeout.Infinite)
            Console.WriteLine("Thread {0} is reading", tname)
            Thread.Sleep(300)
            Console.WriteLine("Thread {0} completed the read operation", tname)
            rwl.ReleaseReaderLock()
        Else
            ' Attempt a write operation.
            rwl.AcquireWriterLock(Timeout.Infinite)
            Console.WriteLine("Thread {0} is writing", tname)
            Thread.Sleep(300)
            Console.WriteLine("Thread {0} completed the write operation", tname)
            rwl.ReleaseWriterLock()
        End If
    Next
End Sub
```

If you run this code, you'll see that multiple threads can be reading at the same time and that a writing thread blocks all the other threads.

The AcquireReaderLock and AcquireWriterLock methods can take a timeout argument, expressed as a number of milliseconds or a TimeSpan value. You can test whether the lock was acquired successfully by means of the IsReaderLockHeld or IsWriterLockHeld read-only property if you passed a value other than Timeout.Infinite:

```
' Attempt to acquire a reader lock for no longer than 1 second.
rwl.AcquireWriterLock(1000)
If rwl.IsWriterLockHeld Then
    ' The thread has a writer lock on the resource.
    ⋮
End If
```

A thread that owns a reader lock can also attempt to upgrade to a writer lock by calling the UpgradeToWriterLock method and later go back to the reader lock by calling DowngradeFromWriterLock.

The great thing about ReaderWriterLock objects is that they are lightweight objects and can be used in large numbers without affecting performance significantly. And since the method takes a timeout, a well-designed application should never suffer from deadlocks. (A deadlock occurs when two threads are waiting for a resource that the other thread won't release until the operation completes.)

The ManualResetEvent and AutoResetEvent Classes

The last synchronization objects I'll illustrate in this chapter are a pair of classes that work in a similar way, ManualResetEvent and AutoResetEvent. They're most useful when you want to temporarily stop one or more threads until another thread says it's OK to proceed. You use these objects to wake up a thread much like an event handler can execute code in an idle thread, but don't be fooled by the "event" in their names. You don't use regular event handlers with these objects.

An instance of these classes can be in either a signaled or an unsignaled state. These terms don't really have any special meaning; just think of them as on or off states. You pass the initial state to their constructor, and any thread that can access the object can change the state to signaled (using the Set method) or unsignaled (using the Reset method). Other threads can use the WaitOne method to wait until the state becomes signaled or until the specified timeout expires.

The only difference between ManualResetEvent and AutoResetEvent objects is that the latter automatically reset themselves (that is, become unsignaled) immediately after a thread blocked on a WaitOne method has been restarted. In practice, AutoResetEvent objects wake up only one of the waiting threads when the object becomes signaled, whereas ManualResetEvent objects wake up all the waiting threads and must be manually reset to unsignaled, as their name suggests.

Like many other synchronization objects, AutoResetEvent and ManualResetEvent objects are especially useful in producer-consumer situations. You might have a single producer thread that evaluates some data—or reads it from disk, a serial port, the Internet, and so on—and then calls the Set method on a shared synchronization object so that one or more consumer threads can be restarted and process the new data. You should use an AutoResetEvent object if only one consumer thread should process such data or a ManualResetEvent object if the same data should be processed by all consumers.

The following example shows how you can have multiple threads (the producer threads) performing file searches on different directories at the same time but a single thread (the consumer thread) collecting their results. This example uses a shared AutoResetEvent object to wake up the consumer thread when new filenames have been added to an ArrayList object, and it also uses the Interlocked class to manage the counter of running threads so that the main thread knows when there's no more data to consume.

```
' This code assumes that System.IO namespace has been imported

' The shared AutoResetEvent object
Public are As New AutoResetEvent(False)
' The ArrayList where matching filenames should be added
Public filesAl As New ArrayList()
' The number of running threads
Public searchingThreads As Integer

Sub TestAutoResetEvent()
    ' Search *.zip files in all the subdirectories of C:
    For Each dirname As String In Directory.GetDirectories("C:\")
        Interlocked.Increment(searchingThreads)
        ' Create a new wrapper class, pointing to a subdirectory.
        Dim sf As New FileFinder()
        sf.StartPath = dirname
        sf.SearchPattern = "*.zip"
        ' Create and run a new thread for that subdirectory only.
        Dim t As New Thread(AddressOf sf.StartSearch)
        t.Start()
    Next

    ' Remember how many results we have so far.
    Dim resCount As Integer = 0
    Do While searchingThreads > 0
        ' Wait until there are new results.
        are.WaitOne()

        ' Note that you should always use the SyncRoot property when using
        ' an ArrayList and other collection-like objects as lock objects.
        SyncLock filesAl.SyncRoot
            ' Display all new results.
            For i As Integer = resCount To filesAl.Count - 1
                Console.WriteLine(filesAl(i))
            Next
            ' Remember that you've displayed these filenames.
            resCount = filesAl.Count
        End SyncLock
    Loop
    Console.WriteLine("")
    Console.WriteLine("Found {0} files", resCount)
End Sub
```

Each producer thread runs inside a different FileFinder object, which must be able to access the public variables defined in the preceding code.

```
Class FileFinder
    Public StartPath As String       ' The starting search path
    Public SearchPattern As String   ' The search pattern

    Sub StartSearch()
        Search(Me.StartPath)
        ' Decrease the number of running threads before exiting.
        Interlocked.Decrement(searchingThreads)
        ' Let the consumer know it should check thread counter.
        are.Set()
    End Sub
```

```
' This recursive procedure does the actual job.
Sub Search(ByVal path As String)
    ' Get all the files that match the search pattern.
    Dim files() As String = Directory.GetFiles(path, SearchPattern)
    ' If there is at least one file, let the main thread know about it.
    If Not files Is Nothing AndAlso files.Length > 0 Then
        ' Get a lock on the ArrayList that holds the result.
        SyncLock filesAl.SyncRoot
            ' Add all found files.
            filesAl.AddRange(files)
            ' Let the consumer thread know about the new filenames.
            are.Set()
        End SyncLock
    End If

    ' Repeat the search on all subdirectories.
    For Each dirname As String In Directory.GetDirectories(path)
        Search(dirname)
    Next
End Sub
End Class
```

Using the Thread Pool

As you know, creating too many threads can easily degrade system performance, especially when the additional threads spend most of their time in a sleeping state and are restarted periodically only to poll a resource or to update the display. You can often improve the performance of your code significantly by resorting to a thread pool, which permits the most efficient use of thread resources. Some objects in the System.Threading namespaces, such as Timers, transparently use the thread pool. (See the following sections for more details about timers.)

The ThreadPool Class

The thread pool is created the first time you invoke the ThreadPool.QueueUserWorkItem method or when a timer or a registered wait operation queues a callback operation. The pool has a default limit of 25 active threads; each thread uses the default stack size and runs at the default priority. The thread pool is available in all Windows versions.

You can borrow a thread from the pool by using the ThreadPool.QueueUserWorkItem method, which requires a WaitCallback delegate and an optional object that holds the data you want to pass to the thread. The WaitCallback delegate must point to a Sub procedure that receives one Object argument (whose value is either the optional object passed to the QueueUserWorkItem method or Nothing). The following code shows how you can use a large number of threads to call an instance method of a class:

```
For i As Integer = 1 To 20
    ' Create a new object for the next lightweight task.
    Dim task As New LightweightTask()
    ' Pass additional information to it. (Not used in this demo.)
```

```
    task.SomeData = "other data"
    ' Run the task with a thread from the pool.
    ' (Pass the counter as an argument.)
    ThreadPool.QueueUserWorkItem(AddressOf task.DoTheTask, i)
Next
```

This next block is the LightweightTask class, which contains the code that actually runs in the thread taken from the pool:

```
Class LightweightTask
    Public SomeData As String

    ' The method that contains the interesting code
    ' (Not really interesting in this example)
    Sub DoTheTask(ByVal state As Object)
        Console.WriteLine("Message from thread #{0}", state)
    End Sub
End Class
```

The running thread can determine whether it has been taken from the thread pool by querying the Thread.CurrentThread.IsThreadPoolThread property. You can retrieve the highest number of threads in the pool by invoking the ThreadPool.GetMaxThreads shared method, and the number of the threads that are currently available by invoking the ThreadPool.GetAvailableThreads shared method.

You might be puzzled sometimes about whether you should create a thread yourself or borrow a thread from the pool. A good heuristic rule: use the Thread class when you want to run the associated task as soon as possible or when you perform a time-consuming task that doesn't run often. In the majority of cases, you should use the thread pool for more scalable server-side tasks.

The Timer Class

The .NET Framework offers several types of timers, each one with its strengths and limitations. For example, you should use the System.Windows.Forms.Timer control inside Windows Forms applications. (See Chapter 16.) If your application doesn't have a user interface, you should use either the System.Threading.Timer class or the System.Timers.Timer class. These two classes are broadly equivalent in their functionality, so I'll describe only the first one.

The Timer class in the System.Threading namespace offers a simple way to create a timer that calls back a given procedure. You can use this class to schedule an action in the future, and this action can be performed with whatever frequency you decide, including just once. The Timer's constructor takes four arguments:

- A TimerCallback delegate that points to the procedure that's called when the timer's timeout elapses. The callback procedure must be a Sub that takes a single Object as an argument.

■ An object that will be passed to the callback procedure. This object can be an individual number or string, an array or collection (or any other object) that holds additional data required by the callback method. (This data might be necessary because one callback procedure can serve multiple timers.) Use Nothing if you don't need to pass additional data to the callback procedure.

■ A TimeSpan value that specifies the *due time*—that is, when the timer must invoke the callback routine for the first time. This argument can be specified as a Long value, in which case the elapsed time is measured in ticks (1 second = 10 million ticks).

■ A TimeSpan value that specifies the timer's period—that is, how often the timer must invoke the callback routine after the first time. If you pass Nothing, the callback routine is invoked only once. This argument can be specified as a Long value, in which case the elapsed time is measured in ticks.

The values that you pass to the Timer's constructor aren't exposed as properties. After the timer is running, you can change these values only by means of a Change method, which takes only two arguments, the due time and the period. The Timer object has no Stop method. You stop the timer by calling its Dispose method. The following example shows how to use the timer with a callback procedure:

```
Sub TestThreadingTimer()
    ' Get the first callback after one second.
    Dim dueTime As New TimeSpan(0, 0, 1)
    ' Get additional callbacks every half second.
    Dim period As New TimeSpan(0, 0, 0, 0, 500)
    ' Create the timer.
    Dim t As New Timer(AddressOf TimerProc, Nothing, dueTime, period)
    ' Wait for five seconds in this demo, then destroy the timer.
    Thread.Sleep(5000)
    t.Dispose()
End Sub

' The callback procedure
Sub TimerProc(ByVal state As Object)
    ' Display current system time in console window.
    Console.WriteLine("Callback proc called at {0}", Date.Now)
End Sub
```

The callback procedure runs on a thread taken from the thread pool, so you should arbitrate access to variables and other resources used by the main thread by using one of the synchronization features that I described in this chapter.

Asynchronous Operations

By now, you should be familiar with the Thread class and all the synchronization issues that you have to address when you're creating multithreading applications. At times, however, you'd like simply to execute a method call without blocking the main thread. For example, you might want to perform a long math calculation on a secondary thread while the application's main thread takes care of the user interface. In this case, what you really want to do is make a single *asynchronous method call*, which runs on another thread while the caller thread continues its normal execution. This programming model is so common that the .NET Framework offers special support for it so that *all methods can be called asynchronously*, without your having to specifically design the target method to support asynchronous calls.

This generic mechanism is based on asynchronous delegates. In addition, the framework offers more asynchronous support in many specific areas, including file I/O, XML Web services, and messages sent over Microsoft Message Queuing (MSMQ). Thanks to this unified approach, you need to learn the asynchronous programming pattern only once, and you can apply it to all these areas.

Asynchronous Delegates

I described how delegates work in Chapter 6, but I intentionally left out a few details that are related to asynchronous use of delegates. In this section, I'll show how you can use advanced features of delegates to call a method asynchronously. Let's start by defining a method that could take a significant amount of time to complete and therefore is a good candidate for an asynchronous call:

```
' This procedure scans a directory tree for a file.
' It takes a path and a file specification and returns an array of
' filenames; it returns the number of directories that have been
' parsed in the third argument.

Function FindFiles(ByVal path As String, ByVal fileSpec As String, _
    ByRef parsedDirs As Integer) As ArrayList

    ' Prepare the result ArrayList.
    FindFiles = New ArrayList()
    ' Get all files in this directory that match the file spec.
    FindFiles.AddRange(Directory.GetFiles(path, fileSpec))
    ' Remember that a directory has been parsed.
    parsedDirs += 1

    ' Scan subdirectories.
    For Each subdir As String In Directory.GetDirectories(path)
        ' Add all the matching files in subdirectories.
        FindFiles.AddRange(FindFiles(subdir, fileSpec, parsedDirs))
    Next
End Function
```

You call the FindFiles routine by passing a starting path, a file specification (which can be a filename or contain wildcards), and an Integer variable. On returning from the function, the Integer variable holds the number of directories that have been parsed, whereas the function itself returns an ArrayList object that contains the names of the files that match the specification:

```
Dim parsedDirs As Integer
' Find *.txt files in the C:\DOCS directory tree.
```

```
Dim files As ArrayList = FindFiles("c:\docs", "*.txt", parsedDirs)
For Each file As String In files
    Console.WriteLine(file)
Next
' Use the output argument.
Console.WriteLine("  {0} directories have been parsed.", parsedDirs)
```

Asynchronous Calls

The first step in implementing an asynchronous call to the FindFiles function is defining a delegate class that points to it:

```
Delegate Function FindFilesDelegate(ByVal path As String, _
    ByVal fileSpec As String, ByRef parsedDirs As Integer) As ArrayList
```

To call the FindFiles procedure asynchronously, you create a delegate that points to the routine and use the delegate's BeginInvoke method to call the routine as you would use the delegate's Invoke method. The BeginInvoke method—which has been created for you by the Visual Basic .NET compiler—takes the same arguments as the procedure the delegate points to, plus two additional arguments that I'll describe later. Unlike the Invoke method, though, BeginInvoke returns an IAsyncResult object. You can then query the IsCompleted read-only property of this IAsyncResult object to determine when the called routine has completed its execution. If this property returns True, you call the delegate's EndInvoke method to retrieve both the return value and the value of any argument that was passed by using ByRef (parsedDirs in the following procedure):

```
' Create a delegate that points to the target procedure.
Dim findFilesDeleg As New FindFilesDelegate(AddressOf FindFiles)
' Start the asynchronous call; get an IAsyncResult object.
Dim parsedDirs As Integer
Dim ar As IAsyncResult = findFilesDeleg.BeginInvoke( _
    "c:\docs", "*.txt", parsedDirs, Nothing, Nothing)

' Wait until the method completes its execution.
Do Until ar.IsCompleted
    Console.WriteLine("The main thread is waiting for FindFiles results.")
    Thread.Sleep(500)
Loop

' Now you can get the results.
Dim files As ArrayList = findFilesDeleg.EndInvoke(parsedDirs, ar)
For Each file As String In files
    Console.WriteLine(file)
Next
Console.WriteLine("  {0} directories have been parsed.", parsedDirs)
```

You should call EndInvoke only after IAsyncResult.IsCompleted returns True; otherwise, the EndInvoke method blocks the calling thread until the called procedure completes. (And you would lose the advantage of making an asynchronous call.)

The code in the preceding procedure polls the IsCompleted property to determine when the asynchronous call has completed. A less CPU-intensive means that achieves the same result uses the IAsyncResult.AsyncWaitHandle property, which returns a Wait-Handle synchronization object. You can then use the WaitOne method of this object to make the main thread wait until the asynchronous call completes:

```
ar.AsyncWaitHandle.WaitOne()
```

The WaitHandle class exposes two other shared methods, WaitAny and WaitAll, which are especially useful when you run multiple asynchronous operations in parallel. Both methods take an array of WaitHandle objects: the WaitAny method blocks the calling thread until any of the asynchronous operations complete, whereas the WaitAll method blocks the calling thread until all the asynchronous operations complete. Unfortunately, you can't call these two methods from a thread running in a single-thread apartment (STA), thus you must create a separate thread using the Thread class, and run the asynchronous operations from this new thread (unless you're already running in a thread outside an STA). The companion code for this book includes an example of this technique.

Asynchronous Callback Procedures

As I've already explained, the BeginInvoke method takes all the arguments in the original method's signature, plus two additional arguments. The second-to-last argument is a delegate pointing to a callback procedure that's called when the asynchronous method completes its execution. This callback procedure offers a viable alternative to your making the main thread use the IsCompleted or AsyncWaitHandle property of the IAsyncResult object to determine when it's safe to gather the return value and any ByRef arguments.

The callback procedure must follow the syntax of the AsyncCallback delegate (defined in the System namespace), which defines a Sub procedure that takes an IAsyncResult object as its only argument. The code inside the callback procedure should call the delegate's EndInvoke method to retrieve the return value and the value of any ByRef arguments. Here's a possible implementation of the callback procedure for the example seen previously:

```
Sub MethodCompleted(ByVal ar As IAsyncResult)
    Dim parsedDirs As Integer
    Dim files As ArrayList = findFilesDeleg.EndInvoke(parsedDirs, ar)
    ' Display found files.
    ' ...(Omitted, same as previous examples)...
End Sub
```

This approach poses two minor problems. First, the callback routine doesn't have any way to know why it has been called, so it's difficult to reuse the same callback routine for multiple asynchronous calls. Second, the delegate variable (findFilesDeleg in this particular example) must be visible to both the routine that makes the asynchronous call and the callback routine; this isn't a serious problem when both routines belong to the same class or module (you can just declare it as a private class-level variable), but it makes the approach rather clumsy when the callback routine is in another class, possibly located in a different assembly.

Both problems can be solved if you take advantage of the last argument of the Begin-Invoke method. This argument can be any object, so you can pass a number or a string that helps the callback routine understand which asynchronous method has just completed. More interestingly, you can pass an array that contains the original delegate object that you used to make the asynchronous call plus any other value required by the callback procedure. This approach helps you solve the second problem as well:

```
' Create a delegate that points to the target procedure.
Dim findFilesDeleg As New FindFilesDelegate(AddressOf FindFiles)
' Create an array holding the delegate and other values
Dim values() As Object = {findFilesDeleg, "TXT files in D:\Docs"}
' Start the async call, pass a delegate to the MethodCompleted
' procedure and get an IAsyncResult object.
Dim parsedDirs As Integer
Dim ar As IasyncResult = findFilesDeleg.BeginInvoke( _
    "D:\docs", "*.txt", parsedDirs, AddressOf MethodCompleted, values)
⋮
```

The callback method must extract data out of the values array, which is passed in the AsyncState property of the IAsyncResult object:

```
Sub MethodCompleted(ByVal ar As IAsyncResult)
    ' Extract data from the values array.
    Dim values() As Object = DirectCast(ar.AsyncState, Object())
    Dim deleg As FindFilesDelegate = DirectCast(values(0), FindFilesDelegate)
    Dim msg As String = values(1).ToString
    ' Call the EndInvoke method, and display result.
    Dim parsedDirs As Integer
    Dim files As ArrayList = deleg.EndInvoke(parsedDirs, ar)
    For Each file As String In files
        Console.WriteLine(file)
    Next
    Console.WriteLine("  {0} directories have been parsed.", parsedDirs)
End Sub
```

More on Asynchronous Method Invocation

A relevant detail I haven't covered yet is how the asynchronous architecture deals with exceptions. It turns out that both the BeginInvoke and EndInvoke methods can throw an exception.

If BeginInvoke throws an exception, you know that the asynchronous call hasn't been queued and you shouldn't call the EndInvoke method. These exceptions might be thrown by the .NET asynchronous infrastructure—for example, when the target of the asynchronous call is a remote object that can't be reached.

EndInvoke can throw an exception too; this happens either when the asynchronous method throws an exception or when the .NET asynchronous infrastructure throws an exception—for example, when the remote object can't be reached any longer. The obvious suggestion is that you should bracket EndInvoke calls inside a Try...End Try block, as you would do for any regular method call that can throw an exception.

Sometimes, however, you don't really care whether the called method actually throws an exception. This might be the case, for example, if the procedure doesn't return a value and doesn't take ByRef arguments. You can inform the .NET runtime that you aren't interested in the outcome of the method, including any exceptions it might throw, by marking the method with the System.Runtime.Remoting.Messaging.OneWay attribute:

```
<System.Runtime.Remoting.Messaging.OneWay()> _
Sub MethodThatMayThrow(ByVal anArgument As Object)
    ⋮
End Sub
```

You get no error if this attribute is applied to a method that includes a ByRef argument or a return value, but such argument or return value isn't returned to the calling application. Here are a few more tips about asynchronous calls:

- The effect of calling EndInvoke twice on the same IAsyncResult object is indefinite, so you should avoid performing this operation.

- Even if BeginInvoke takes a ByRef argument, the .NET asynchronous infrastructure doesn't record the address of this argument anywhere, and therefore, it can't automatically update the variable when the method completes. The only way to retrieve the value of an output argument is by passing it to the EndInvoke method.

- If the called method takes a reference to an object (passed with either ByVal or ByRef), it can assign new values to that object's properties. The caller can see those new values even before the asynchronous method completes. If both the caller and the called method access the same object, however, you might want to provide some form of synchronization of its property procedures.

- The .NET asynchronous infrastructure provides no generic means to cancel an asynchronous method once the BeginInvoke method has been called because in many cases there's no reliable way to cancel a running operation. In general, it's up to the class's author to implement a method that cancels an asynchronous method call.

> **See Also**   Read the document "Asynchronous File Operations.doc" on the companion CD for an in-depth discussion on how the asynchronous delegate model applies to file read and write operations.

This concludes my explanation of multithreading. As you know by now, creating multithreaded applications isn't simple, and you have to face and solve many issues. Even if you decide not to create additional threads, you have to account for matters such as synchronization and access to shared variables if your objects expose a Finalize method that, as you've learned, can run on virtually any thread. Let's put threads aside and focus on .NET assemblies, the topic of the next chapter.

13 Components and Assemblies

All the Visual Basic .NET applications you've seen so far were stand-alone executables, with all the code included in a single .exe file. Most larger programs, however, are usually split in multiple executables—typically one .exe file and one or more DLLs. In this chapter, you'll see how easy creating a class library is and how you can be prepared to deal with versioning issues.

Components

Creating a .NET Component with Visual Studio .NET is embarrassingly simple. In practice, you can prototype your component by writing a class in a standard console or Windows Forms application so that you have only one project to worry about. When the debug step is completed and your class works as expected, you can move the class to a separate DLL while continuing to use the same client code in the main application.

Creating a .NET Class Library

Let's say that you already have a PersonDemo project that contains a Person class in the Person.vb source file and some client code that uses it. To move this class into a separate DLL, you need to perform the following three easy steps:

1. Use the Add Project command from the File menu to create a new project of type Class Library. Name your project as PersonLibrary, if you want to match my description. Delete the default Class1.vb file that Visual Studio .NET created.

2. In the Solution Explorer window, drag the Person.vb file from the PersonDemo project to the newly created PersonLibrary project.

3. Right-click on the References node under the PersonDemo project in the Solution Explorer window and select the Add Reference command. Switch to the Projects tab in the dialog box that appears, double-click on the PersonLibrary item to bring it in the Selected Components list, and click the OK button. (See Figure 13-1.)

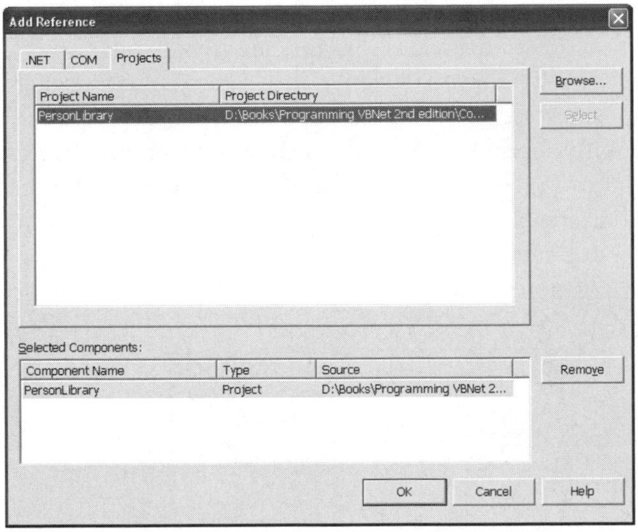

Figure 13-1   The Add Reference dialog box

The reference you just added lets the PersonDemo project reference the Person class with a typed variable and create its instances with the New keyword, exactly as if the Person class was defined in that project. The only change you need to apply to your source code is an Imports statement that lets the client application find the Person class even if it moved to a different namespace:

```
Imports PersonLibrary

Module MainModule
    Sub Main()
        Dim p As New Person("Joe", "Doe")
        Console.WriteLine(p.CompleteName)
    End Sub
End Module
```

Creating Hostable Components

Strictly speaking, compiling a class in a separate DLL doesn't make it a component. From the .NET perspective, a component is a class that inherits from System.ComponentModel.Component. This base class provides an implementation of the IComponent interface, which in turn is what lets you drop an instance of the class onto a designer's surface. The System.Windows.Forms.Timer class is a well-known example of a component. You can drop an instance of this class on a form's surface and set its properties at design time in the Properties window.

You can morph a class into a component by simply adding an Inherits keyword:

```
Public Class Person
    Inherits System.ComponentModel.Component
    ⋮
End Class
```

However, it's advisable that you create a component by selecting the Add Components command from the Project menu so that Visual Studio can create some additional code that makes your component a well-behaved citizen in the .NET world. Visual Studio .NET displays a component by using one of two different editors: the code editor and the designer. (See Figure 13-2.) If your component uses other components (for example, a timer or any object that you can drag from the Server Explorer window), you can drop these components on the designer's surface, much like you do with controls on a form. You don't have to worry about creating and destroying these components because the code that Visual Studio .NET generates does these housekeeping chores for you.

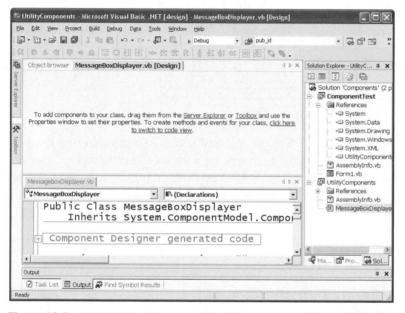

Figure 13-2 A component has a code editor and a designer surface; you can display both at the same time by using the New Horizontal Tab Group command from the Window menu.

The main advantage of a component over a simple class is that the former can be added to the Toolbox and dropped on a designer, and its properties can be assigned at design time in the Properties window. Before you can actually drop a component on a designer, you must compile the project containing the component. Next, right-click on the Toolbox and select the Add/Remove Items command. In the Customize Toolbox window that appears, click on the Browse button and select the component's DLL, and then click OK to add the component (more precisely, all the components in the DLL) to the Toolbox. (See Figure 13-3.)

For illustrational purposes, I have created a MessageBoxDisplayer component that you can drop on the designer surface of a form (or another component) to display a message box. This component is just a wrapper around the MessageBox class in the System.Windows.Forms namespace, but offers a couple of advantages: it lets you set its properties at design time and, above all, it lets you see how the message box looks (without your actually running the program) by clicking on the Preview hyperlink that appears near the bottom of the Properties window. (See Figure 13-4.)

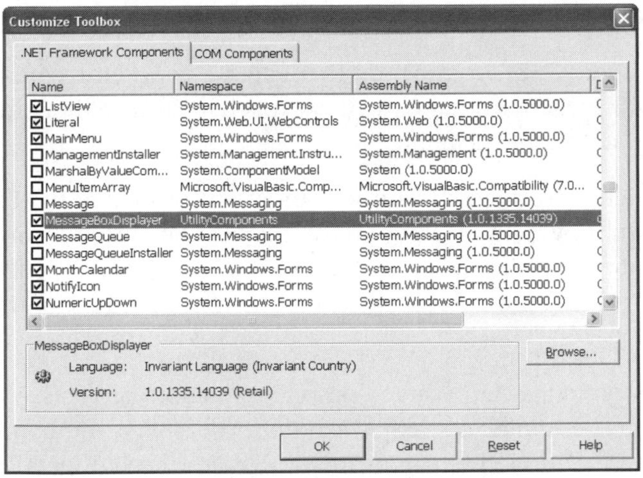

Figure 13-3 The Customize Toolbox dialog box lets you add controls and components to the Toolbox tab that is currently visible. You can sort elements by their Assembly Name to quickly see all the components in a given assembly.

I won't show the complete source code of the MessageBoxDisplayer component here because it uses attributes and features that I'll discuss in Chapter 18. (Components are akin to custom controls, and you can use similar programming techniques for both of them.) Using the component from inside an application, however, couldn't be simpler. Just drop an instance on a form, assign its properties, and invoke its Show method from your code where appropriate:

```
MessageBoxDisplayer1.Show()
```

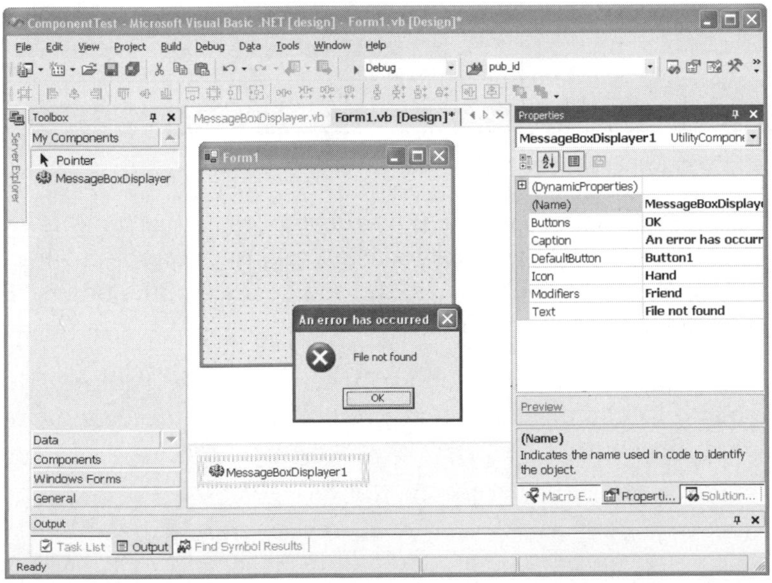

Figure 13-4 The MessageBoxDisplayer component lets you assign all the properties of a message box and preview the result at design time.

Working with Multiple-Project Solutions

There are a few Visual Studio .NET commands that can be important when dealing with multiple projects. All these commands can be reached from either the Project menu or the Solution Explorer context menu.

To begin, you decide which project runs when you press F5 (or invoke the Start command from the Debug menu) by right-clicking on the project item and selecting the Set as StartUp Project command. The startup project appears in boldface. Typically, when you're testing one or more DLLs, the startup project is the client application that references and uses the DLLs

The build order is very important when you're compiling multiple projects. Visual Studio .NET is usually able to determine the correct build order—first the components, then the client application that uses them—but in some cases the IDE gets confused, especially if you remove and re-add projects to the solution. You can check the build order that Visual Studio .NET follows in the Project Dependencies dialog box, which you bring up by right-clicking on any project item and selecting either the Project Dependencies or the Project Build Order command. (See Figure 13-5.)

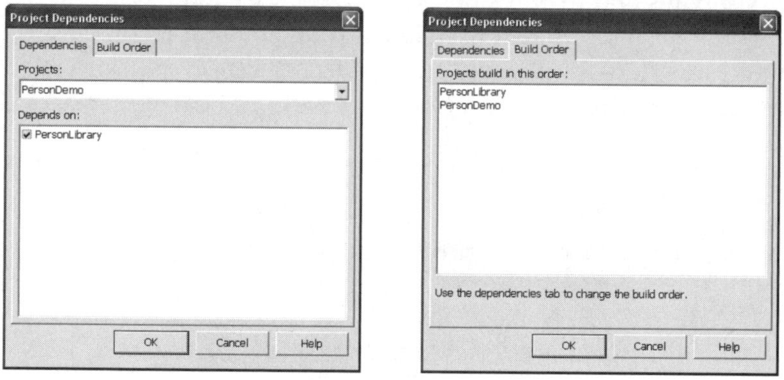

Figure 13-5   The Project Dependencies dialog box

When you compile the solution, Visual Studio recompiles all the projects by default, but this can be a waste of time if you are focusing on just one project—for example, only the component—and you don't change the source code of the others. To reduce compilation time you have a few choices:

- Right-click on a project in the Solution Explorer window and select the Build menu command to compile only that project and the projects on which the selected project depends.

- Select a project in the Solution Explorer window and then select the Unload Project command from the Project top-level menu. This action makes the project temporarily unavailable within the solution, so it won't be compiled during the build process. You can later re-include the project in the solution by selecting the Reload Project command, from either the Project top-level menu or the Solution Explorer's context menu.

- You create a custom solution configuration in which one or more projects aren't part of the build process. (I'll explain solution configurations in the next section.)

Whenever you compile the solution, Visual Studio .NET automatically copies the PersonLibrary.dll file to the PersonDemo\bin directory so that the PersonDemo.exe application can use the most recent version of the component. This happens both when you add a reference to a project in the same solution and when you add a reference directly to a compiled DLL by means of the Browse button in the Add Reference dialog box.

In some cases, you might prefer that a project use the copy of the DLL that happens to be in its local directory, without checking whether a more recent version exists. For example, this choice can be useful if another developer is working on the DLL's source code. You can change Visual Studio .NET's default behavior as follows: select the PersonLibrary element under the References node in the Solution Explorer and press the F4 key to display its properties. All the properties you see now are read-only, except Copy Local. If you set this property to False, Visual Studio won't automatically copy the DLL into the client project's output directory.

The Configuration Manager

When Visual Studio .NET creates a new project, it also creates two project configurations: Debug and Release. As its name suggests, the former is designed for debugging the application. It defines the DEBUG compilation constants and disables optimizations. By contrast, the Release configuration doesn't produce any .pdb files containing information for symbolic debugging.

To change these configuration settings, select the project in the Solution Explorer and click on the Properties icon (or select Properties on the Project menu) to open the project Property Pages dialog box. The Configuration Properties section of this window contains four pages—Debugging, Optimizations, Build, and Deployment—inside which you define compilation constants, required optimization settings, and so on. All the options you select apply to the configuration visible in the Configuration combo box. (See Figure 13-6.) Items in the combo box let you apply your choices to all existing settings or to a well-defined subset of them, so you don't have to select similar settings individually for multiple configurations. (In theory, you might also choose the target platform, but a Visual Basic .NET program can currently target only the .NET platform.)

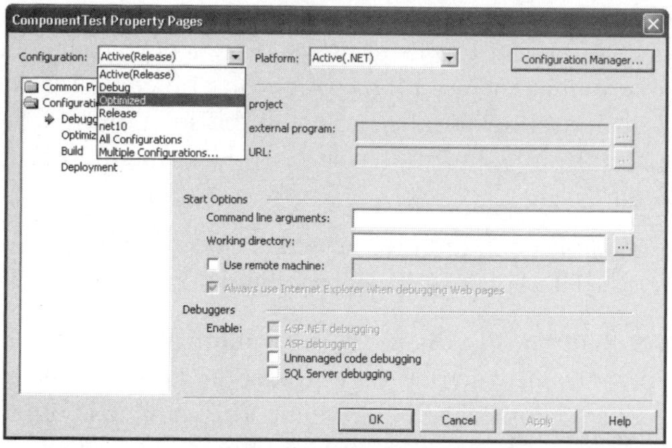

Figure 13-6 The Debugging page in the project Property Pages window. The Configuration combo box includes a custom configuration named Optimized.

You can include or exclude portions of your source code from the compilation process by enclosing them in #If statements that use one of the DEBUG TRACE or CONFIG predefined compilation constants:

```
#If CONFIG = "Release" Then
   ⋮
#ElseIf TRACE Then
   ⋮
#End If
```

In general, when you debug and test the application, you want to compile each project in Debug mode, whereas all projects should be compiled in Release mode before you deploy the application. However, during the debugging and refining phase of the application, you might need to compile constituent projects with different configurations; some in Debug mode, others in Release mode, and yet others in some custom configuration that you've defined for them. Solution configurations let you define whether and how each project is compiled when the solution is rebuilt.

The tool that lets you define new solution configurations is the Configuration Manager, which you can activate from the Build menu on the Solution Explorer's context menu (after you select the topmost solution node), or by clicking Configuration Manager in one of the Configuration Properties pages in the project Property Pages dialog box. In the Configuration Manager, you select a configuration in the Active Solution Configuration combo box and then decide the project configuration to be used for each constituent project—you can even create a new one. By clearing the check box in the Build column, you can exclude a project from the compilation step in a particular solution configuration. (This feature lets you save a lot of time if you've thoroughly tested one of the projects in the solution.) Other options in the Active Solution Configuration combo box let you rename or remove a solution configuration, or create a new one. (See Figure 13-7.)

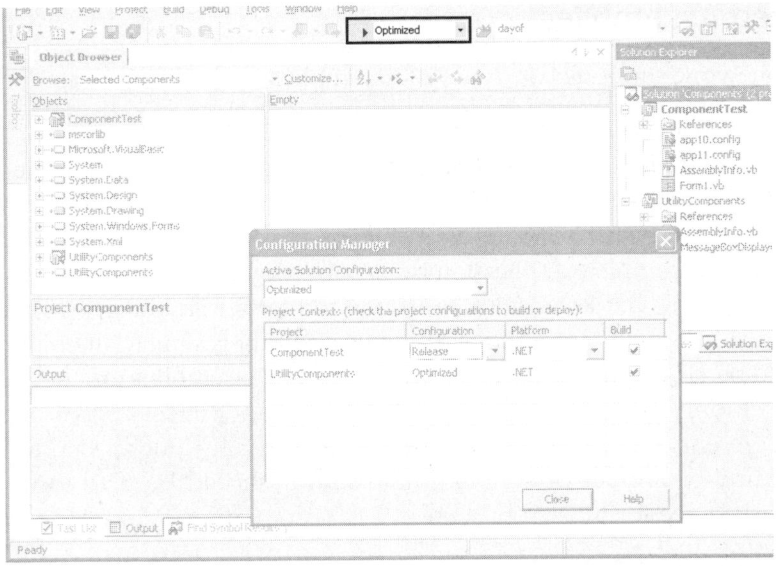

Figure 13-7 The Configuration Manager dialog box lets you define multiple build configurations. The currently showing "Optimized" combo box on the standard toolbar lets you activate a different solution configuration without displaying this window.

You can also select the active solution configuration also by using the combo box on the standard toolbar. You can then rebuild the solution using the configuration that's currently active by selecting the Build Solution command on the Build menu or by pressing the F5 key to run the application.

Assemblies

The assembly has no analogous concept in the pre-.NET programming world, so it might be confusing at first. From a physical point of view, an *assembly* is just a collection of one or more executable and nonexecutable modules. (Examples of nonexecutable modules are resource, image, and html files.) From a logical perspective, an assembly is the smallest unit of reuse, versioning, and deployment for .NET applications. For example, you can't assign different version numbers to the various files that make up an assembly.

When you're deciding which types should go in the same assembly, consider the following points:

- **Code reuse** The assembly is the smallest unit of reuse, so you should keep together types that are normally used together.

- **Versioning** The assembly is also the smallest unit of versioning, and all the modules in an assembly have the same versioning information.

- **Scoping** The assembly scope (enforced by the Friend keyword) lets you define which types are visible from outside the module in which they're defined, but not from the outside world.

Private and Shared Assemblies

The .NET Framework supports two types of assemblies: private and shared.

A private assembly can be stored only in the main application's directory (or one of its subdirectories) and therefore can be used only by that application or another application installed in the same directory. Private assemblies are simpler to build and administer than shared assemblies; they support *XCOPY deployment*, a fancy term that means that you can install a complete application by simply copying all its files and directories to the target computer's hard disk without having to register anything. (Of course, you still have to create shortcuts from the Start menu and other, similar amenities, but the concept should be clear.) In most circumstances, private assemblies are the best choice to make, even though you might end up with multiple identical copies of the same assembly in different directories. Private assemblies can help put an end to so-called DLL hell, and any developer or system administrator should be glad to trade some inexpensive disk space for more robust code.

A shared assembly is usually installed in a well-defined location of the hard disk, under the \Windows\Assembly directory. This location is known as the global assembly cache (GAC). The .NET Framework installs a special shell extension (contained in shfusion.dll) that lets you browse this directory with Windows Explorer and display information about all the shared assemblies installed on the computer, including their version and culture. (See Figure 13-8.) You can also display more extensive version information by right-clicking an item and selecting Properties on the shortcut menu, an action that brings up the Properties dialog box for that shared assembly.

The assembly's public key token is a sort of reduced public key of the software company that published the assembly. The public key token is a 64-bit hash value derived from the publisher's public key (which is 1024 bits long, or 128 bytes); it isn't guaranteed to be universally unique like the public key, but it can be considered unique for most practical purposes.

Note that several assemblies belonging to the framework have been pre-JIT-compiled with the NGEN utility (see Chapter 1), so they start up faster. These assemblies are marked as Native Images in the Type column.

What you see in Windows Explorer doesn't match the actual physical structure of the \Windows\Assembly directory. In fact, the GAC contains several directories—one for each shared assembly; each directory in turn contains individual subdirectories for each version of the assembly. For example, the System.dll assembly belonging to the .NET Framework version 1.1 is found in this directory:

```
C:\WINDOWS\assembly\GAC\System\1.0.5000.0__b77a5c561934e089
```

in which 1.0.5000.0 is the version of the assembly and b77a5c561934e089 is Microsoft's public key token.

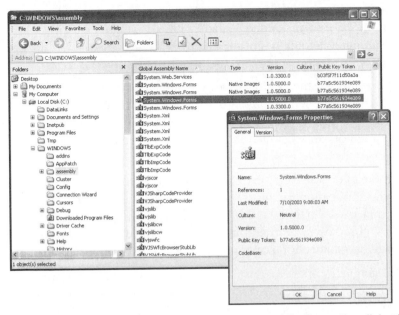

Figure 13-8   The global assembly cache viewer and the Properties dialog box for
the System.Windows.Forms shared assembly

This directory structure allows you to store different versions of the same assembly
without any filename conflicts. You can bypass the Windows shell extension and freely
explore the real structure of the GAC by opening an MS-DOS command prompt window and navigating to the C:\Windows\Assembly\GAC directory.

You can add and delete shared assemblies to and from the GAC only if you have
administrative rights on the system, which makes .NET applications that work with
shared assemblies inherently more robust than those that work with private assemblies.
You can add or remove assemblies to or from the GAC using a utility named GACUTIL,
and you can delete an existing shared assembly by selecting Delete on the shortcut
menu inside Windows Explorer.

There are several key differences between a private and a shared assembly:

- A shared assembly supports version information, and the GAC can keep different
  versions of the same assembly without conflict so that each application can continue to work with the version it was compiled against (unless the administrator
  opts for a different binding policy, a topic that I take up later in this chapter). Private assemblies can be versioned, but version information is for your reference
  only, and the runtime doesn't use it. A private assembly is supposed to be
  deployed with the application itself, so the runtime doesn't enforce any special
  versioning policy.

- A shared assembly in the GAC makes your applications more robust in two ways. First, when the assembly is added to the cache, an integrity check is performed on all the files in the assembly to ensure that they haven't been altered. Second, only the system administrator can delete an assembly from the GAC.

- A shared assembly in the GAC is more efficient than a private assembly because the runtime can locate it faster and it doesn't need to be verified. Moreover, if multiple applications reference the same shared assembly, the runtime loads only one instance in memory in most circumstances (which saves resources and improves load time even more).

- Two (or more) versions of a shared assembly can run in the same process. For example, an application might use version 1.0 of the AAA assembly and a BBB assembly that uses version 1.1 of the AAA assembly. This important feature is called *side-by-side execution*, and it ensures that you won't have a compatibility problem when you mix components together.

- A shared assembly can be signed with an Authenticode digital signature. The signing mechanism uses a public key encryption schema, which guarantees that a particular assembly was created by a given manufacturer and that no one tampered with it.

Shared assemblies are usually stored in the GAC, but this isn't a requirement. For example, you might deploy a shared assembly in a known directory on the hard disk, where two or more applications can find it. However, the advantages in the preceding list apply only to shared assemblies in the GAC. (Shared assemblies deployed in other directories do support side-by-side execution and public key signing, though.)

As a rule, you write code for private and shared assemblies in the same way because you build a shared assembly by adding an attribute to your code. However, the main goal in building shared assemblies is to share them among different applications, so you must take this constraint into account. For example, a shared assembly shouldn't create temporary files with fixed names and paths because calls from different clients might overwrite such files. Moreover, the .NET Framework supports side-by-side execution of shared assemblies in the same process (not just the same machine), so a shared assembly shouldn't depend on processwide resources.

Strong Names

The .NET runtime looks for private assemblies only inside the caller application's directory tree, so the developer is in charge of avoiding naming conflicts for the private assemblies the application references. On the other hand, shared assemblies are typically deployed in the GAC, so it's vital for the runtime to distinguish shared assemblies that have the same name but that come from different publishers.

The .NET Framework ensures that a shared assembly's name is unique at the system level by assigning the assembly a *strong name*. You can think of a strong name as the combination of a textual name, a version number, a culture, and a public key. The security mechanism is based on a public key encryption method, but you don't have to be a cryptography wizard to create assemblies with strong names.

You generate strong name assemblies in a two-step process. First, you run the Strong Name (SN) command-line utility to create an .snk file that contains a random-generated public and private key pair. Second, you tell the compiler that the public key in that .snk file must be burned into the executable file.

You generate a random public and private key pair by using the –k option of the SN utility, which is located in the c:\Program Files\Microsoft Visual Studio .NET 2003\SDK\v1.1\Bin directory:

```
sn -k mykey.snk
```

This command creates the mykey.snk file, which contains the two keys. Store this file in a safe place (and make copies of it if necessary) because from now on you should use it to sign all the shared assemblies produced by you or your client.

After creating an .snk file, you can choose from several ways to produce an assembly with a strong name. If you're compiling from the command prompt, you use the VBC program with the /keyfile option for single-file assemblies, or you use the Assembly Linker utility (AL) with the /keyfile option for assemblies made of multiple files. Another method for creating a signed assembly—which, by the way, is the only one that you can use from inside Visual Studio .NET and therefore the one that is going to be used most frequently—is that of inserting an AssemblyKeyFile attribute in the application's source code (typically in the AssemblyInfo.vb file):

```
<Assembly: AssemblyKeyFile("c:\myapp\mykey.snk")>
```

The filename should be an absolute path so that it can reference the only .snk file that you use for all the strong assemblies you produce.

The AssemblyInfo.vb file that Visual Studio automatically creates contains an AssemblyVersion attribute with an argument equal to 1.0.*, which causes the build and revision number to automatically increment at each build. Shared assemblies should have a fixed version number, though, as in this line of code:

```
<Assembly: AssemblyVersion("1.0.0.0")>
```

Any other assembly that references the shared assembly you've just signed will include the shared assembly's public key in the reference section of its manifest. When the caller assembly invokes one of the types in the shared assembly, the runtime compares the public key token in the caller's manifest with the public key token of the shared assembly so that the caller can be completely sure that the shared assembly hasn't been tampered with. (The runtime uses this 8-byte token instead of the entire public key to save space in the caller assembly manifest.) Notice that any .NET executable can reference a shared assembly, but a shared assembly can reference only other shared assemblies.

Remember that this mechanism can ensure that the shared assembly hasn't been modified, but it doesn't ensure that the shared assembly actually comes from a specific software manufacturer. This latter issue is solved through full Authenticode signatures that can be applied to shared assemblies. These Authenticode signatures add a certificate that establishes trust. You can apply this Authenticode signature to an existing assembly by running the Signcode.exe utility.

Because strong names are a combination of a text name and a public key, they guarantee name uniqueness. If two companies use the same name for their (distinct) assemblies, their public keys are different and therefore the strong names are different as well. Name uniqueness extends to all versions of the same assembly, and the runtime ensures that—when it's opting for a more recent version of an assembly requested by a managed class—only assemblies coming from the same software company will be taken into account.

Installing in the GAC

The preferred way to install shared assemblies is to register them in the GAC. You can use drag-and-drop or the GACUTIL command-line utility. Using drag-and-drop is simple: use Windows Explorer to navigate to the \Windows\Assembly directory, and drop the DLL on the right-hand pane. (See Figure 13-8.) Running the GACUTIL utility is also straightforward:

```
gacutil /i testassembly.dll
```

The advantage of using the latter method is that you can automate the installation process—for example, by running a batch or a script program. Even better, you can add a command to the Tools menu in Visual Studio .NET, by means of the External Tools command.

The /i command overwrites any assembly in the GAC with the same identity, but doesn't remove copies of the same assembly with a different version number. (One of the goals of the GAC is to store multiple versions of the same assembly.) Each new version that you install is added to the GAC, so you should periodically clear intermediate versions of the assembly from the GAC or run GACUTIL using the /u option to remove an outdated version of the assembly before installing a more recent one. You can list all the files in the GAC by means of the /l option.

Adding an assembly to the GAC doesn't make your assembly visible in Visual Studio .NET's Add Reference dialog box. This dialog box never parses the GAC and just displays assemblies located in the following two directories: C:\WINDOWS\Microsoft.NET\Framework\vx.y.zzzz (the main .NET Framework main directory) and C:\Program Files\Microsoft Visual Studio .NET 2003\Common7\IDE\PublicAssemblies. You might save your assemblies to the latter directory to make them quickly selectable from inside Visual Studio .NET.

Even better, you can add a new key under the HKEY_LOCAL_MACHINE\SOFT-WARE\Microsoft\.NETFramework\AssemblyFolders registry key, name it MyAssemblies (or any name you like), and set the default value of this key equal to the directory that contains your assemblies (either private or shared). The next time you launch Visual Studio .NET you'll see all the assemblies in this directory in the list of selectable ones.

Using the DEVPATH Environment Variable

When you're developing and debugging a shared assembly, this installing and uninstalling activity is surely a nuisance. Here's a simple trick to avoid it: create an environment variable named DEVPATH and assign it the name of the directory where you store your shared assemblies in debug mode, for example C:\SharedAssemblies. (Notice that the directory name can't contain spaces.) Next, add these lines to the machine.config file:

```
<configuration>
   <runtime>
      <developmentMode developerInstallation="true"/>
   </runtime>
</configuration>
```

You should use this setting only on your development system. The .NET Framework does no version checking on the assemblies in the directory pointed to by the DEVPATH variable, and just uses the first assembly with a given name. If no assembly with that name is found, the runtime searches the GAC.

As interesting as it sounds, you rarely require this setting when you build your application with Visual Studio .NET because projects under development can reference only DLLs with a specific path and never reference shared assemblies in the GAC.

The Binding Process

When the running application references a different assembly, the runtime must resolve this reference—that is, it must *bind* the assembly of your choice to the caller application. This portion of the runtime is known as the *assembly resolver*. The reference stored in the calling assembly contains the name, version, culture, and public key token of the requested assembly if the assembly is shared. The version is ignored and the public key is missing if the assembly is private. The process that the runtime follows to locate the correct assembly consists of several heuristic steps:

1. Checks version policy in configuration files

2. Uses the assembly if it has been loaded previously

3. Searches the assembly in the GAC

4. Searches the assembly using codebase hints if there are any

5. Probes the application's main directory tree

These five steps apply to a shared assembly. When you're binding a private assembly, the runtime skips step 1 because the runtime ignores version information in private assemblies. Similarly, the runtime skips steps 3 and 4 when binding private assemblies because they can't be stored in the GAC and can't be associated with codebase hints. The following sections describe each step in detail.

Version Policy in Application Configuration Files

You can change the behavior of .NET applications and assemblies by means of configuration files. This mechanism gives both developers and system administrators great flexibility in deciding how managed applications search for the assemblies they must bind to. For example, the many settings in these files let you decide whether requests for version 1.0 of a given assembly should be redirected to version 2.0 of the same assembly. There are three types of configuration files: the application configuration file, the publisher configuration file, and the machine configuration file.

The application configuration file affects the behavior of a single .NET application. This file must reside in the application's directory and have the same name as the application's main executable and the .config extension. For example, the application C:\bins\sampleapp.exe can have a configuration file named C:\bins\sampleapp.exe.config.

The publisher configuration file is tied to a shared assembly and affects all the managed applications that use that assembly. Typically, publishers of .NET components provide a configuration file when they release a new version of the component that fixes a few known bugs. The statements in the publisher's configuration file will therefore redirect all requests for the old version to the new one. A component vendor should provide a publisher configuration file only if the new version is perfectly backward compatible with the assembly being redirected. Each *major.minor* version of an assembly can have its own publisher configuration file. An application can decide to disable this feature for some or all the assemblies that it uses.

Finally, the machine configuration file (also known as the administrator configuration file) affects the behavior of all the managed applications running under a given version of the .NET runtime. This file is named machine.config and is located in the c:\Windows\Microsoft.NET\Framework\v*x.y.zzzz*\Config directory (where *x.y.zzzz* is the .NET Framework version). The settings in this file override the settings in both the application and publisher configuration files and can't themselves be overridden.

All three types of configuration files are standard XML files that can contain several sections. The outermost section is marked by the <configuration> tag and might contain the <runtime> section (among others), which finally contains the information about the assemblies you want to redirect. Here's an example of an application configuration file:

```xml
<?xml version="1.0" encoding="UTF-8" ?>
<configuration>
   <runtime>
      <assemblyBinding xmlns="urn:schemas-microsoft-com:asm.v1">
         <dependentAssembly>
            <assemblyIdentity name="myAsm" culture="en-us"
                              publicKeyToken="378b4bc89e0bb9a3" />
            <bindingRedirect oldVersion="1.0.0.0" newVersion="2.0.0.0" />
            <publisherPolicy apply="no"/>
         </dependentAssembly>
      </assemblyBinding>
   </runtime>
</configuration>
```

Remember that XML tags and attributes are case sensitive, so you must type the tags exactly as reported in the preceding example. Visual Basic developers are accustomed to case-insensitive identifiers and can easily overlook this important detail.

Each <dependentAssembly> section is related to an assembly for which you want to establish a new version policy. This section *must* contain an <assemblyIdentity> subsection that identifies the assembly itself, with the name, culture, and public key token attributes. You can determine the public key token of a shared assembly by browsing the GAC from Windows Explorer or by using the SN command-line utility, as follows:

```
sn -T myasm.dll
```

After the mandatory <assemblyIdentity> subsection, the <dependentAssembly> section can contain the following subsections:

- The <bindingRedirect> section redirects one version of the assembly to another. For example, the preceding configuration file redirects all requests for version 1.0.0.0 of the assembly to version 2.0.0.0. The four numbers specified in the old-Version and newVersion attributes are in the form *major.minor.revision.build*. The oldVersion attribute can specify a range of versions; for example, the following setting specifies that any version from 1.0 to 1.2 should be redirected to version 1.3, regardless of revision and build numbers:

```xml
<bindingRedirect oldVersion="1.0.0.0-1.2.65535.65535"
                 newVersion="1.3.0.0"/>
```

- The <publisherPolicy> section determines whether the publisher configuration file should be applied to this assembly. If you specify a "no" value for the apply attribute, as in the preceding example, the publisher configuration file is ignored and the application is said to work in *safe mode*.

- The <codeBase> section specifies where the assembly is located. This information is especially useful for assemblies downloaded from the Internet. (For more information, read the "Codebase Hints" section coming up shortly.)

By default, the publisher's policy is enabled for all assemblies. You can disable it for a specific assembly by using a <publisherPolicy> tag inside a <dependentAssembly>

section (as seen in the preceding example), or you can disable it for all the assemblies that an application uses by inserting a <publisherPolicy> tag directly inside the <assemblyBinding> section:

```
<assemblyBinding xmlns="urn:schemas-microsoft-com:asm.v1">
   <publisherPolicy apply="no"/>
</assemblyBinding>
```

If you disable the publisher's policy for the entire application, you can't reenable it for individual assemblies. For this reason, the only reasonable setting for the apply attribute is the "no" value, both at the global level and at the individual assembly level.

Previously Loaded Assemblies and GAC Searches

In the second step of the binding process, the runtime checks whether that specific assembly had been requested in previous calls. If this is the case, the runtime redirects the call to the assembly already loaded, and the binding process stops here.

The runtime uses the assembly's strong name to decide whether the assembly is already in memory. This can happen even if the application never requested the assembly previously but another assembly in the same process did so and the requested assembly can be safely shared between multiple clients. As I've already explained, the strong name is a combination of the assembly's name, version, culture, and publisher's public key. The filename isn't part of the identity of the assembly, so you should never assign the same identity to different files.

If the assembly hasn't already been loaded, the binding process continues by searching the GAC for an assembly with that identity. This step applies only to assemblies with strong names because private assemblies can't be stored in the GAC. If the assembly is found in the GAC, the binding process stops here.

Codebase Hints

Once the version of the assembly is known and the assembly isn't in the GAC, the runtime has to locate the assembly file. The runtime usually accomplishes this task by means of a search process known as *probing* (described in the next section), but the developer, the publisher of the component, or the system administrator can disable probing by adding a codebase hint to one of the three configuration files. A codebase hint is a <codeBase> tag that appears in a <dependentAssembly> section.

Codebase hints are especially useful and common in browser-based scenarios for informing the browser of the location from which a given assembly can be downloaded. For example, the following portion of the configuration file tells the runtime that versions from 1.0 through 1.4 of the MathFns assembly can be downloaded from *http://www.vb2themax.com/asms/mathfns.dll* (this is just an example—there is no such assembly at this URL).

```
   ⋮
<assemblyBinding xmlns="urn:schemas-microsoft-com:asm.v1">
   <dependentAssembly>
      <assemblyIdentity name="mathfns" culture="en-us"
                        publicKeyToken="378b4bc89e0bb9a3" />
      <bindingRedirect oldVersion="1.0.0.0" newVersion="2.0.0.0" />
      <publisherPolicy apply="no"/>
      <codeBase version="1.0.0.0-1.4.65535.65535"
         href="http://www.vb2themax.com/ams/mathfns.dll"/>
   </dependentAssembly>
</assemblyBinding>
   ⋮
```

In some cases, you don't even need a codebase hint for every assembly used by an application. For example, if the MathFns assembly references the TrigFns assembly, the runtime automatically reuses the hint for MathFns and assumes that TrigFns can be downloaded from *http://www.vb2themax.com/assemblies/trigfns.dll.*

You can use codebase hints to reference assemblies outside the application's main directory, provided the assembly has a strong name. Either using a codebase hint or installing the assembly in the GAC is the only valid way to reference an assembly located outside the application's main directory, and both methods work only with assemblies with strong names. For example, you might decide to install an assembly in a separate directory if it is going to be used by multiple applications from your client (and you don't want to deploy all these applications in the same directory). In general, however, strong name assemblies deployed to a location other than the GAC don't offer any advantages other than a simpler installation; on the con side, they load more slowly than assemblies in the GAC and aren't protected from accidental deletions.

If a codebase hint is provided but no assembly is found at the specified address, or the assembly is found but its identity doesn't match the identity of the assembly the runtime is looking for, the binding process stops with an error.

Probing

Probing is the process by which the runtime can locate an assembly inside the application's directory or one of its subdirectories. As I explained in the preceding section, the runtime begins probing only if no codebase hint has been provided for the assembly. Probing is a set of heuristic rules based on the following criteria:

- The application's base directory
- The assembly's name
- The assembly's culture
- The application's private binpath

The *binpath* is a list of directories, expressed as relative names that implicitly refer to subdirectories under the application's main directory. (Absolute paths are invalid.) The binpath is specified as a semicolon-delimited list of directories and is assigned to the privatePath attribute of the <probing> tag, inside the <assemblyBinding> section of an application configuration file:

```
⋮
<assemblyBinding xmlns="urn:schemas-microsoft-com:asm.v1">
    <probing privatePath="bin;bin2\subbin;utils"/>
</assemblyBinding>
⋮
```

The sequence of directories searched for during the probing process depends on whether the assembly in question has a culture. For assemblies without a culture, the search is performed in each location in the order listed:

1. The application's base directory

2. The subdirectory named after the assembly

3. Each directory in the binpath list

4. The subdirectory named after the assembly under each directory in the binpath list

The runtime scans these directories first looking for a DLL named after the assembly (for example, myasm.dll). If the search fails, the runtime performs the search again in all these directories, this time looking for an EXE named after the assembly (myasm.exe). However, you can't add a reference to an EXE file from inside Visual Studio .NET.

For example, let's assume that the runtime is searching for an assembly named myasm.dll and the binpath is the one defined in the previous configuration file. Here are the files that the runtime searches for (assuming that the main application directory is C:\myapp):

```
C:\myapp\myasm.dll
C:\myapp\myasm\myasm.dll
C:\myapp\bin\myasm.dll
C:\myapp\bin\subbin\myasm.dll
C:\myapp\utils\myasm.dll
C:\myapp\bin\myasm\myasm.dll
C:\myapp\bin\subbin\myasm\myasm.dll
C:\myapp\utils\myasm\myasm.dll

C:\myapp\myasm.exe
C:\myapp\myasm\myasm.exe
C:\myapp\bin\myasm.exe
C:\myapp\bin\subbin\myasm.exe
C:\myapp\utils\myasm.exe
C:\myapp\bin\myasm\myasm.exe
C:\myapp\bin\subbin\myasm\myasm.exe
C:\myapp\utils\myasm\myasm.exe
```

For assemblies with a culture, the sequence is slightly different:

1. The application's base subdirectory named after the culture

2. The subdirectory named after the assembly under the directory defined in point 1

3. The subdirectory named after the culture under each subdirectory defined in the binpath

4. The subdirectory named after the assembly under each directory defined in point 3

Again, the runtime searches these directories for a DLL named after the assembly and then for an EXE named after the assembly.

For example, let's assume that an application using the preceding configuration file is requesting an assembly named myasm and marked as Italian culture ("it"). These are the places where the runtime would search for this assembly:

```
C:\myapp\it\myasm.dll
C:\myapp\it\myasm\myasm.dll
C:\myapp\bin\it\myasm.dll
C:\myapp\bin\subbin\it\myasm.dll
C:\myapp\utils\it\myasm.dll
C:\myapp\bin\it\myasm\myasm.dll
C:\myapp\bin\subbin\it\myasm\myasm.dll
C:\myapp\utils\it\myasm\myasm.dll

C:\myapp\it\myasm.exe
C:\myapp\it\myasm\myasm.exe
C:\myapp\bin\it\myasm.exe
C:\myapp\bin\subbin\it\myasm.exe
C:\myapp\utils\it\myasm.exe
C:\myapp\bin\it\myasm\myasm.exe
C:\myapp\bin\subbin\it\myasm\myasm.exe
C:\myapp\utils\it\myasm\myasm.exe
```

If even this last step fails, the runtime checks whether the assembly was part of a Windows Installer package; if this is the case, the runtime asks the Windows Installer to install the assembly. (This feature is known as *on-demand installation*.) The Windows Installer 2.0 program has other important features, such as the ability to advertise the application's availability, use the Add/Remove Program option in Control Panel, and easily repair the application if necessary.

The Assembly Binding Log Viewer Utility (FUSLOGVW)

You now know everything you need to know about assembly binding, although in practice you're in the dark when the runtime can't locate one or more assemblies at run time. If you're running the program under Visual Studio .NET 2003 debugger, you can read a log of failed binding operations in the Debug window, data that usually lets you spot and fix the problem quickly and easily.

If you have already deployed the application on the user's machine, however, you just can't use the Visual Studio .NET debugger. In such a situation, the Assembly Binding

Log Viewer can be a real lifesaver. You can run the FUSLOGVW utility from the command line or add it to the Start menu. (See Figure 13-9.) Ensure that the Log Failures check box is enabled when you launch the problematic application.

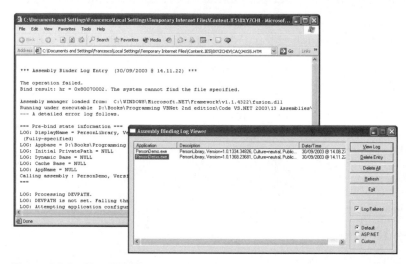

Figure 13-9   The FUSLOGVW utility in action; the window in the background displays the detailed information about a specific entry in the log file.

The .NET runtime maintains three log files: the default log, the ASP.NET log, and a custom log. You select which one to display by clicking one of the three radio buttons near the lower right corner of the FUSLOGVW window. The default log is used for all the failed binding operations of the current user. In other words, each user sees a different log in the FUSLOGVW window. The ASP.NET log is used for all binding operations related to ASP.NET. The Custom log shows only failed binding operations in a directory that you specify in the following registry key:

```
HKEY_LOCAL_MACHINE\Software\Microsoft\Fusion\LogPath
```

You can fine-tune the behavior of FUSLOGVW by setting a couple of other registry keys. As with the preceding key, you must manually add these keys to the registry if necessary. By setting the HKEY_LOCAL_MACHINE\Software\Microsoft\Fusion\Force-Log registry value to 1, you log all the binding operations, not just the unsuccessful ones. As a result, you can exactly detect the location from which an assembly is loaded, which can be useful when you're trying to spot elusive bugs caused by the wrong version of an assembly being bound successfully.

Finally, by setting the HKEY_LOCAL_MACHINE\Software\Microsoft\Fusion\LogResource-Bind registry value to 1, you also get a log of the failed bind operations related to satellite assemblies (which aren't recorded in the log by default).

> **See Also**   Read "A real binding example.doc" on the companion CD for a step-by-step exam-
> ple that shows the kind of problems you might encounter when binding to an assembly and
> how you can solve them.

Configuration Files

You've seen that you can affect the behavior of a specific application or the whole system by means of configuration files. In this section, I'll describe these files in more
depth, though I'll leave out some major topics, such as ASP.NET settings, which will be
covered in later chapters.

Setting the Runtime Version

.NET applications can run on a version of the .NET Framework different from the version under which the application was compiled. This technique is called *redirection,*
and it is implemented via configuration files.

If you compile an application with the first version of Visual Studio .NET, and you want
to run it only under version 1.0 of the .NET Framework, you don't have to provide a
configuration file (unless you need it to specify other settings, of course). Likewise, you
don't need a configuration file if you compile an application with Visual Studio .NET
2003 and you want it to run only under version 1.1 of the .NET Framework. In this section I'll examine how you must modify the configuration file in the remaining cases.

Versions 1.0 and 1.1 of the .NET Framework use different XML tags to enable redirection: version 1.0 uses the <requiredRuntime> tag; version 1.1 ignores the
<requiredRuntime> tag but recognizes multiple <supportedRuntime> tags, the order of
which dictates which runtime version should be used when more than one version is
installed on the end user machine.

The simplest case is when you want to run an application compiled under version 1.0
of the .NET Framework on a machine on which version 1.1 of the .NET Framework is
installed:

```
<?xml version ="1.0"?>
<configuration>
    <startup>
        <supportedRuntime version="v1.0.5000" />
    </startup>
</configuration>
```

Notice that you redirect only the runtime but don't need any <bindingRedirect> tag for
the individual .NET assemblies that the application uses because the runtime of the
.NET Framework 1.1 is able to automatically redirect requests for older assemblies to
the assemblies in the current version. (This feature is called *unification.*)

When you want to run an application compiled under version 1.0 of the .NET Framework on a machine that has either version 1.0 or 1.1 of the .NET Framework (or both), you specify both the <requiredRuntime> tag and a pair of <supportedRuntime> tags, the first of which points to .NET Framework 1.0. (If possible, you should run the assembly under the .NET version under which it was compiled to ensure that no compatibility issues will emerge.) Once again, you don't need to redirect individual assemblies to version 1.1 of the .NET Frameworks, thanks to the unification feature:

```xml
<?xml version="1.0"?>
<configuration>
  <startup>
    <supportedRuntime version="v1.0.3705"/>
    <supportedRuntime version="v1.1.4322"/>
    <requiredRuntime version="v1.0.3705"/>
  </startup>
</configuration>
```

When you run an application compiled under version 1.1 of the .NET Framework on a machine that has either version 1.0 or 1.1 of the .NET Framework (or both), you specify both the <requiredRuntime> tag and a pair of <supportedRuntime> tags, the first of which points to .NET Framework 1.1, which in this case is the preferred version if both versions are available. In this case, however, you must also redirect all the assemblies used by the application to use the DLLs provided with version 1.0 of the .NET Framework:

```xml
<?xml version="1.0"?>
<configuration>
  <startup>
    <supportedRuntime version="v1.1.4322"/>
    <supportedRuntime version="v1.0.3705"/>
    <requiredRuntime version="v1.0.3705"/>
  </startup>
  <runtime>
    <assemblyBinding xmlns="urn:schemas-microsoft-com:asm.v1" appliesTo="v1.0.3705">
      <dependentAssembly>
        <assemblyIdentity name="System.Data"
          publicKeyToken="b77a5c561934e089" culture="neutral"/>
        <bindingRedirect oldVersion="0.0.0.0-65535.65535.65535.65535"
          newVersion="1.0.3300.0"/>
      </dependentAssembly>
      <!-- repeat for all .NET assemblies used by the application -->
        ⋮
    </assemblyBinding>
  </runtime>
</configuration>
```

The appliesTo attribute in the <assemblyBinding> tag has been introduced in .NET Framework 1.1 and specifies that all the redirection tags in that block apply only when the application is running under the specified version of the runtime (1.0.3705 in the previous example). The .NET Framework version 1.0 ignores this attribute and will use the first <assemblyBinding> block that appears in the configuration file. Thanks to the appliesTo attribute, however, this block will be ignored if the application runs under version 1.1 of the .NET Framework. Notice that you need additional

\<assemblyBinding\> blocks that are specific to version 1.1 to redirect assemblies that don't belong to the .NET Framework:

```
<assemblyBinding xmlns="urn:schemas-microsoft-com:asm.v1" appliesTo="v1.0.4322">
  <-- add here desired binding when running under version 1.1 -->
  ⋮
</assemblyBinding>
```

An application compiled under version 1.1 will work under version 1.0 of the .NET Framework only if it never uses a feature (a type, a property, a method, and so on) that was introduced in the newer version. Before you claim that an application built with Visual Studio .NET 2003 will run smoothly under version 1.0 of the .NET Framework, you should thoroughly test it on a machine that only has version 1.0 installed.

As you have seen, there is a lot of work to do and a lot of XML text to write to have an application run on multiple versions of the .NET Framework. Now let me tell you the good news: Visual Studio .NET 2003 can create these configuration files for you. You only have to bring up the Build page of the Project Properties window and click on the Change button. In the dialog box that appears, you can select which version of the .NET Framework the application should run. (See Figure 13-10.) When you close this window, an App.Config file is added to the solution. This file is then automatically renamed appropriately and copied in the output directory when you compile the project.

If you have both versions of the .NET Framework installed on your machine, you can select the option Microsoft .NET Framework v1.0 (advanced) to see how your application behaves on systems that only have the first version of the runtime installed. Now when you run the application you'll see in the Debug window that the runtime is loading version 1.0.3705 of all the .NET assemblies. You can also programmatically test which version of the .NET Framework your code is running under by invoking the GetSystem-Version method of the System.Runtime.InteropServices.RuntimeEnvironment class:

```
If RuntimeEnvironment.GetSystemVersion = "v1.0.3705" Then
    ' Running under version 1.0 of the .NET Framework
    ⋮
End If
```

You can use this method to selectively disable the portions of your application that use features that aren't supported under the version of the .NET Framework in use.

Let me conclude this section with a warning. Even if the .NET Framework gives you the ability to have an application run under different versions of the runtime, this feature comes at a high cost: you must thoroughly debug and test your code under different configurations (and possibly different machines), which takes a lot of time and effort. Version 1.1 is quite different from version 1.0 in many critical ways—for example, security has been greatly increased—so in most cases you can't expect that a program compiled under version 1.0 will run correctly under a newer version. A wiser solution might be investing your time to recompile the source code under the most recent version of the runtime and ensure that your customers have that recent version installed.

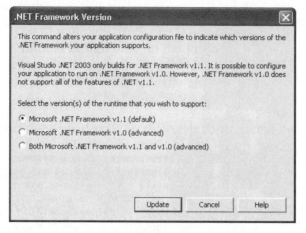

Figure 13-10   You can select which versions of the .NET Framework your application should support.

Dynamic Properties

All real-world applications need to store configuration values somewhere outside their executable code so that their behavior can be modified without your having to recompile them. Database connection strings are a typical example of such configuration values. Over the years, developers have adopted many different solutions to the problem of storing configuration information outside executable files, including using .ini files and the system registry.

In an attempt to put some order in this area, Microsoft has proposed a standardized, simple, flexible way to store values in the application's configuration file. All configuration values, which are formally known as *dynamic properties*, are stored as key/value pairs inside the <appSettings> section, as you see here:

```
<configuration>
    <appSettings>
        <add key="Default User" value="Francesco" />
        <add key="Connection String"
            value="Data Source=P4;User ID=sa;Initial Catalog=pubs" />
        <add key="Timeout" value="50" />
    </appSettings>
</configuration>
```

A Visual Basic program can retrieve all the dynamic properties by using the AppSettings method of the System.Configuration.ConfigurationSettings object and assigning the returned value to a NameValueCollection variable, which you can then use to access each individual value:

```
' Retrieve all values in a NameValueCollection.
Dim colValues As System.Collections.Specialized.NameValueCollection
```

```
colValues = Configuration.ConfigurationSettings.AppSettings()
' Display all key/value pairs.
For Each key As String In colValues.AllKeys
    Console.WriteLine("Key=""{0}""  Value=""{1}""", key, colValues.Get(key))
Next
```

The Get method returns a string, so you might need to convert it to a property data type, such as an Integer, before assigning it to a variable or an object's property:

```
Dim timeout As Integer = CInt(colValues("Timeout"))
```

Once your code invokes the AppSettings method of the Configuration.Configuration-Settings object, dynamic properties are read from the application's file and cached in the NameValueCollection object. If you modify the .config file, the contents of this object aren't updated automatically, so in most cases you have to restart the application. Interestingly, if you modify the configuration file of an ASP.NET application, the runtime restarts the application and automatically enforces the new settings.

The .NET Framework Configuration Tool

Although you should be familiar with the syntax of machine.config and application configuration files, most of the time you can perform your administration chores by using a Microsoft Management Console snap-in. The snap-in offers a simple user interface that lets you browse and modify those files using a visual approach. (See Figure 13-11.) This tool can be used only with Microsoft Windows NT, Windows 2000, Windows XP, and Windows Server 2003. You can launch the Microsoft .NET Framework Configuration from the Administrative Tools submenu of the Start menu.

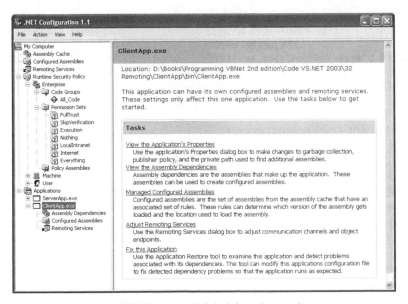

Figure 13-11 The .NET Framework Administration tool

To interactively change the configuration file of an application, you first must add the application to the list of configured applications by right-clicking on the Application element and selecting the Add command. Next, expand the new element, right-click on the Configured Assemblies folder, and select the Add command to add a new assembly to the list of those that this application redirects. (See Figure 13-12.)

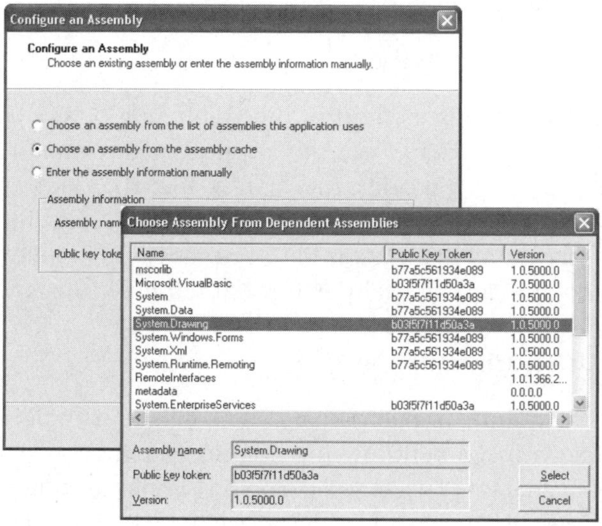

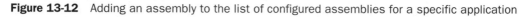

Figure 13-12   Adding an assembly to the list of configured assemblies for a specific application

When you click the Finish button, a window like the one visible in Figure 13-13 appears. Here you specify how versions are redirected and the codebase corresponding to each version of the assembly in question. (These settings correspond to entries in the .config file for the specific assembly.)

One of the most intriguing features of the .NET Framework Configuration tool is the ability to *automatically* remember the five most recent configurations used by any .NET application, including nonconfigured applications. This feature works as follows: each time an application unloads, the .NET runtime checks the version of each of the assemblies the application has loaded. If this configuration is the same as the one used during the preceding execution, nothing happens; if the configuration is different, the runtime stores the details of the new configuration in an .ini file stored in a subdirectory in the C:\Documents and Settings directory tree.

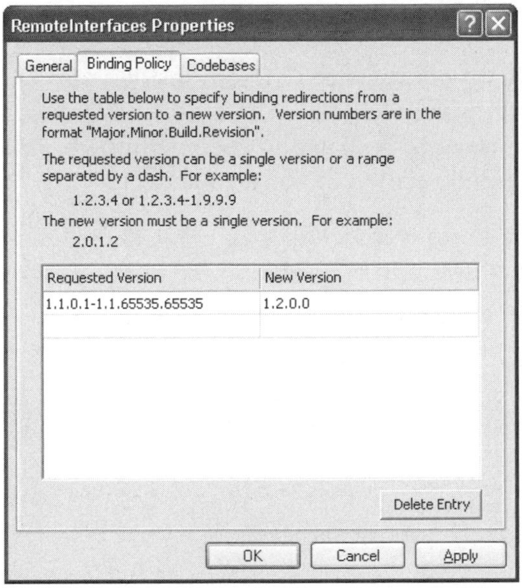

Figure 13-13   The Properties dialog box for a configured assembly

If you later run the application and find that it isn't working properly, you can restore any of the five most recent configurations stored by the runtime. You access this feature by right-clicking the Applications node and clicking Fix An Application on the shortcut menu. (You can also access this feature from the Microsoft .NET Framework Wizards command in the Administrative Tools submenu of the Start menu.) This action brings up a list of all known .NET applications—not just those under the Applications node—so you can select the one you're interested in. The next dialog box (shown in Figure 13-14) lists each stored configuration, identified by the date interval in which it was used. The last entry is always Application SafeMode, which you can use to troubleshoot the application. When you click Apply, the .NET Framework Configuration tool generates the corresponding .config file for the specific application, using remarks to surround the portions that it added or modified.

Figure 13-14   You can select which application you want to fix (left) and then which configuration you want to restore.

Assembly Custom Attributes

You can set many assembly properties directly from inside your source code via the many attribute classes in the System.Reflection namespace. As a matter of fact, new Visual Basic .NET projects include a file named AssemblyInfo.vb, which contains template code for all the attributes described in the next section.

A peculiarity of assembly attributes is that you must explicitly tell the compiler that the custom attribute refers to the assembly by prefixing the attribute name with *Assembly*. For example, the following source code defines a few attributes for the assembly under development:

```
Imports System.Reflection
Imports System.Runtime.InteropServices

<Assembly: AssemblyVersion("1.5.*")>
<Assembly: AssemblyInformationalVersion("1.5")>
<Assembly: AssemblyCopyright("(C) 2001 VB2TheMax")>

' ... (And so on)
```

Table 13-1 lists all the assembly custom attributes that the runtime supports. For more information about the AssemblyVersion and AssemblyKeyFile attributes, read the "Strong Names" section earlier in this chapter.

Table 13-1   The Custom Attributes for Setting Assembly Options in Source Code

Attribute	Description
AssemblyVersion	The assembly version number; can use * for the revision + build or just the build number to let the runtime generate version numbers using a time-based algorithm.
AssemblyFileVersion	The Win32 version number, which doesn't have to be equal to the assembly version.
AssemblyCulture	The supported culture. Passing a nonempty string marks the assembly as a satellite assembly, which is an assembly that contains only resources for a given culture. You shouldn't use a nonempty string for a regular assembly.
AssemblyAlgorithmId	The algorithm used to hash files in a multifile assembly.
AssemblyDelaySign	Marks the assembly for partial or delayed signing. (Takes True or False; requires either AssemblyKeyFile or AssemblyKeyName.)
AssemblyKeyFile	The file that contains the public/private key to make a shared assembly (or only the public key if partial signing).
AssemblyKeyName	The key container that holds the public/private key pair.

Table 13-1   The Custom Attributes for Setting Assembly Options in Source Code

Attribute	Description
AssemblyFlags	Assembly flags, which tell which degree of side-by-side support the assembly offers.
AssemblyInformational-Version	Informational version. A string version to be used in product and marketing literature.
AssemblyProduct	The name of the product.
AssemblyCompany	The company name.
AssemblyCopyright	The copyright string.
AssemblyTrademark	The trademark string.
AssemblyDescription	The product description string.
AssemblyConfiguration	The configuration string.
AssemblyTitle	The title for the assembly.
AssemblyDefaultAlias	A friendly default alias for the assembly manifest.

See Also   You'll find several documents on the companion CD that expand on the concepts I illustrated in this chapter. "Partial Key Signing and Key Containers.doc" explains the additional options you have for signing an assembly; "Command Line Tools.doc" discusses the syntax and the purpose of several command-line utilities that are provided with the .NET Framework; "The AppDomain Class.doc" lists properties, methods, and events of the System.AppDomain class; and "The LoaderOptimization Attribute.doc" shows how you can improve loading time of a shared assembly.

Now that you know how to create an assembly and bind it at run time, you have a more complete picture of what an assembly contains. So you're ready to master the Reflection namespace, which is what the next chapter is all about.

14 Reflection

Reflection is a set of classes that allow you to access and manipulate assemblies and modules and the types and the metadata that they contain. For example, you can use reflection to enumerate loaded assemblies, modules, and classes and the methods, properties, fields, and events that each class exposes. Reflection plays a fundamental role in the .NET Framework and works as a building block for other important portions of the runtime. The runtime uses reflection in many circumstances, such as to enumerate fields when a type is being serialized or is being marshaled to another process or another machine. Visual Basic .NET transparently uses reflection whenever you access an object's method through late binding.

Reflection code typically uses the classes in the System.Reflection namespace; the only class used by reflection outside this namespace is System.Type, which represents a type in a managed module. (Notice that the concept of type is more generic than class, in that the former comprises classes, interfaces, value types, and enumeration types.)

The .NET Framework also contains the System.Reflection.Emit namespace, whose classes let you create an assembly dynamically in memory. The Framework uses the classes in this namespace in many circumstances—for example, to compile a regular expression into IL code when the RegexOptions.Compiled option is specified. Because of its narrow scope, I won't cover the System.Reflection.Emit namespace in this book.

Many code examples in this chapter use the following Person class:

```
Class Person
    Event GotEmail(ByVal msg As String, ByVal priority As Integer)
    ' Some public and private fields
    Public FirstName As String
    Public LastName As String
    Dim m_Age As Short
    Dim m_EmailAddress(4) As String

    Sub New()
    End Sub

    ' A constructor with parameters
    Sub New(ByVal FirstName As String, ByVal LastName As String)
        Me.FirstName = FirstName
        Me.LastName = LastName
    End Sub
```

```
    ' A read-write property
    Property Age() As Short
        Get
            Return m_Age
        End Get
        Set(ByVal Value As Short)
            m_Age = Value
        End Set
    End Property

    ' A property with arguments
    Property EmailAddress(ByVal Index As Short) As String
        Get
            Return m_EmailAddress(Index)
        End Get
        Set(ByVal Value As String)
            m_EmailAddress(index) = Value
        End Set
    End Property

    ' A method that takes optional arguments and that raises an event.
    Sub SendEmail(ByVal msg As String, Optional ByVal Priority As Integer = 1)
        ' ... (No real code in this demo)...
        Console.WriteLine("Message to " & FirstName & " " & LastName)
        Console.WriteLine("Priority = " & Priority.ToString)
        Console.WriteLine(msg)
        RaiseEvent GotEmail(msg, priority)
    End Sub
End Class
```

> **Note** To keep code as concise as possible, all the code samples in this section assume that the following Imports statements are used at the file or project level:
>
> ```
> Imports System.Reflection
> Imports System.Diagnostics
> ```

Working with Assemblies and Modules

The objects in the System.Reflection namespace form a logical hierarchy, at the top of which you find the Assembly class, as you can see in Figure 14-1. In this section, I'll describe the Assembly, AssemblyName, and Module classes.

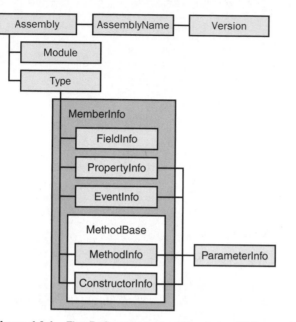

Figure 14-1   The Reflection logical hierarchy. All these classes belong to the System.Reflection namespace, except System.Type.FieldInfo, PropertyInfo, and EventInfo inherit from the MemberInfo abstract class, whereas MethodInfo and ConstructorInfo inherit from the MethodBase abstract class (which in turn derives from MemberInfo).

The Assembly Class

As its name implies, the Assembly class represents a .NET assembly. A minor annoyance is that Assembly is also a reserved word for Visual Basic .NET, so you must either use its complete class name or enclose its name in square brackets:

```
' These three statements are equivalent.
Dim asm As System.Reflection.Assembly
Dim asm As Reflection.Assembly      ' Assumes Imports System.
Dim asm As [Assembly]               ' Assumes Imports System.Reflection.
```

The Assembly class offers no constructor method because you never actually create an assembly, but simply get a reference to an existing assembly. Instead, the Assembly class exposes several shared methods that return a reference to an assembly, either running or not (that is, stored on disk but currently not running):

```
' Get a reference to the assembly this code is running in.
asm = [Assembly].GetExecutingAssembly()

' Get a reference to an assembly given its filename.
asm = [Assembly].LoadFrom("c:\myapp\mylib.dll")

' Get a reference to an assembly given its display name.
' (The argument can be the assembly's full name, which includes
'  version, culture, and public key.)
asm = [Assembly].Load("mscorlib")
```

```
' You can use this method when you don't have the full name.
asm =[Assembly].LoadWithPartialName("System.Xml")

' Get a reference to the assembly that contains a given Type.
' (The argument must be a System.Type value, so we need GetType.)
asm = [Assembly].GetAssembly(GetType(String))
```

Once you have a valid reference to an Assembly object, you can query its properties to learn additional information about it. For example, the FullName property returns a string that holds information about the version and the public key token (this data is the same as the value the ToString method returns).

```
' This is the main .NET Framework assembly.
asm = [Assembly].Load("mscorlib")
Console.WriteLine(asm.FullName)
    ' => mscorlib, Version=1.0.5000.0, Culture=neutral,
    '     PublicKeyToken=b77a5c561934e089
```

The Location and CodeBase read-only properties both return the actual location of the assembly's file, so you can learn where assemblies in the global assembly cache are actually stored (information hidden by the shfusion.dll GAC viewer). For the assemblies that make up the framework, this value points to a directory under c:\Windows\Microsoft.NET \Framework\v*x.y.zzzz* (where *x.y.zzzz* is the framework's version number—for example, 1.1.4322). When you're not working with assemblies downloaded from the Internet, the information these properties return differs only in format:

```
' ...(Continuing previous example)...
Console.WriteLine(asm.Location)
    ' => C:\Windows\Microsoft.NET\Framework\v1.1.4322\mscorlib.dll
Console.WriteLine(asm.CodeBase)
    ' => file:///C:/WINDOWS/Microsoft.NET/Framework/v1.1.4322/mscorlib.dll
' (The actual location can of course be different on your system.)
```

The GlobalAssemblyCache property returns a Boolean value that tells whether the assembly was loaded from the GAC. The EntryPoint property returns a MethodInfo object that describes the entry point method for the assembly, or it returns Nothing if the assembly has no entry point (for example, if it's a DLL class library). MethodInfo objects are described in the "Retrieving Member Information" section later in this chapter.

The Assembly class exposes many instance methods, the majority of which allow you to enumerate all the modules, files, and types in the assembly. For example, the Get-Types method returns an array with all the types (classes, interfaces, and so on) defined in an assembly:

```
' Enumerate all the types defined in an assembly.
For Each ty As Type In asm.GetTypes
    Console.WriteLine(ty.FullName)
Next
```

You can also list only the public types that an assembly exports by using the Get-ExportedTypes method.

The Assembly class overloads the GetType method inherited from System.Object so that it can take a type name and return the specified Type object.

```
' Next statement assumes asm is pointing to MSCORLIB.
Dim ty2 As Type = asm.GetType("System.Int32")
```

If the assembly doesn't contain the specified type, the GetType method returns Nothing. You can have this method throw a TypeLoadException if the specified type isn't found by passing True as its second argument, and you can have the type name compared in a case-insensitive way by passing True as a third argument:

```
' This doesn't raise any exception because type name
' is compared in a case-insensitive way.
Dim ty3 As Type = asm.GetType("system.int32", True, True)
```

Finally, two methods of the Assembly class return an AssemblyName object, which is described in the next section.

The AssemblyName Class

The AssemblyName class represents the objects that .NET uses to hold the identity and to retrieve information about an assembly. A fully specified AssemblyName object has a name, a culture, and a version number, but the runtime can also use partially filled AssemblyName objects when searching for an assembly to be bound to a caller code. Most often, you get a reference to an existing AssemblyName object by using the Get-Name property of the Assembly object:

```
' Get a reference to an assembly and its AssemblyName.
Dim asm As [Assembly] = [Assembly].Load("mscorlib")
Dim an As AssemblyName = asm.GetName
```

You can also get an array of AssemblyName objects using the GetReferencedAssemblies method:

```
' Get information on all the assemblies the current assembly references.
Dim anArr() As AssemblyName
anArr = [Assembly].GetExecutingAssembly.GetReferencedAssemblies()
```

Most of the properties of the AssemblyName object are self-explanatory, and some of them are also properties of the Assembly class (as is the case with FullName and Code-Base properties):

```
' (Note that the version of mscorlib doesn't have to match the version
' of the .NET Framework.)
Console.WriteLine(an.FullName)
   ' => mscorlib, Version=1.0.5000.0, Culture=neutral,
   '    PublicKeyToken=b77a5c561934e089

' These properties come from the version object.
Console.WriteLine(an.Version.Major)        ' => 1
Console.WriteLine(an.Version.Minor)        ' => 0
```

```
Console.WriteLine(an.Version.Build)          ' => 5000
Console.WriteLine(an.Version.Revision)       ' => 0
' You can also get the version as a single number.
Console.WriteLine(an.Version.ToString)       ' => 1.0.5000.0
```

A few methods of the AssemblyName object return a Byte array. For example, you can get the public key and the public key token by using the GetPublicKey and GetPublicKeyToken methods:

```
' Display the public key token of the assembly
For Each b As Byte In an.GetPublicKeyToken()
    Console.Write(b.ToString & ",")
Next
```

The CultureInfo property gets or sets the culture supported by the assembly, or returns Nothing if the assembly is culture-neutral.

The Module Class

The Module class represents one of the modules in an assembly; don't confuse it with a Visual Basic .NET program's Module block, which corresponds to a Type object. You can enumerate all the elements in an assembly by using the Assembly.GetModules method:

```
' Enumerate all the modules in the mscorlib assembly.
Dim asm As [Assembly] = [Assembly].Load("mscorlib")
' (Note that Module is a reserved word in Visual Basic.)
For Each mo As [Module] In asm.GetModules
    Console.WriteLine(mo.Name & " - " & mo.ScopeName)
Next
```

The preceding code produces only one output line:

```
mscorlib.dll - CommonLanguageRuntimeLibrary
```

The Name property returns the name of the actual DLL or EXE, whereas the ScopeName property is a readable string that represents the module. The vast majority of .NET assemblies (and all the assemblies you can build with Visual Studio .NET without using the Assembly Linker tool) contain only one module. For this reason, you rarely need to work with the Module class and I won't cover it in more detail in this book.

Working with Types

The System.Type class is central to all reflection actions. It represents a managed type, which comprises classes, structures, interfaces, enums, and module blocks. The class provides all the means to enumerate a type's fields, properties, methods, and events, as well as set properties and fields and invoke methods dynamically.

An interesting detail: a Type object that represents a managed type is unique in a given AppDomain. This means that when you retrieve the Type object corresponding to a given type (for example, System.String) you always get the same instance, regardless of how you retrieve the object. This feature allows for the automatic synchronization of multiple shared method invocations, among other benefits.

Getting a Type Object

The Type class itself doesn't expose any constructors because you never really create a Type object; rather, you get a reference to an existing one. You can choose from many ways to retrieve a reference to a Type object. In previous sections, you saw that you can enumerate all the types in an Assembly or a Module:

```
For Each ty As Type In asm.GetTypes
    Console.WriteLine(ty.FullName)
Next
```

More often, you get a Type object using the Visual Basic GetType function, which takes the unquoted name of a class:

```
Dim ty2 As Type = GetType(String)
Console.WriteLine(ty2.FullName)       ' => System.String
```

If you already have an instance of the class in question, you can use the GetType method that all objects inherit from System.Object:

```
Dim d As Double = 123.45
Dim ty3 As Type = d.GetType
Console.WriteLine(ty3.FullName)       ' => System.Double
```

The Type.GetType shared method takes a quoted class name, so you can build the name of the class dynamically (something you can't do with the GetType function):

```
' Note that you can't pass Type.GetType a Visual Basic synonym,
' such as Short, Integer, Long, or Date.
Dim ty4 As Type = Type.GetType("System.Int64")
Console.WriteLine(ty4.FullName)       ' => System.Int64
```

The GetType method looks for the specified type in the current assembly and then in the system assembly (mscorlib.dll). Like the assembly's GetType instance method, the Type.GetType shared method returns Nothing if the specified type doesn't exist, but you can also pass True as its second argument to force a TypeLoadException in this case, and you can pass True as its third argument if you want the type name to be compared in a case-insensitive way. If the type you want to reference is neither in the caller's assembly nor in mscorlib.dll, you must append a comma and the assembly name in which the type resides. For example, the following code snippet shows how you get a reference to the System.Data.DataSet class, which resides in the assembly named System.Data. Because the GAC might contain many assemblies with this friendly name, you must pass the complete identity of the assembly after the first comma:

```
Dim ty5 As Type = Type.GetType("System.Data.DataSet, System.Data, " _
    & "Version=1.0.5000.0, Culture=neutral, PublicKeyToken=b77a5c561934e089")
```

Retrieving Type Attributes

All the properties of the Type object are read-only, for one obvious reason: you can't change an attribute (such as name or scope) of a type defined elsewhere in code. The name of most properties is self-explanatory, such as the Name (the type's name), FullName (the complete name, which includes the namespace), and Assembly (the Assembly object that contains the type). The IsClass, IsInterface, IsEnum, and IsValue-Type properties let you classify a given Type object. For example, the following code lists all the types exported by mscorlib.dll, specifying whether each is a class, an enum, a value type, or an interface:

```
Dim asm As [Assembly] = [Assembly].Load("mscorlib")
For Each t As Type In asm.GetExportedTypes()
    If t.IsClass Then
        Console.WriteLine(t.Name & " (Class)")
    ElseIf t.IsEnum Then
        ' Note that an enum is also a value type, so we must
        ' test for IsEnum before IsValueType.
        Console.WriteLine(t.Name & " (Enum)")
    ElseIf t.IsValueType Then
        Console.WriteLine(t.Name & " (Structure)")
    ElseIf t.IsInterface Then
        Console.WriteLine(t.Name & " (Interface)")
    Else
        ' This statement is never reached because a type
        ' can't be something other than one of the above.
    End If
Next
```

The IsPublic and IsNotPublic properties return information about the type's visibility. If the type is nested inside another type, you can use the following IsNested*xxxx* properties to deduce the scope used to declare the type: IsNestedPublic (Public), IsNested-Assembly (Friend), IsNestedFamily (Protected), IsNestedFamORAssembly (Protected Friend), IsNestedPrivate (Private), and IsNestedFamANDAssembly (Protected and visible only from inside the assembly, a scope you can't define with Visual Basic). You can also use the DeclaringType property to get the enclosing type of a nested type.

You can get information about inheritance relationships by means of the BaseType (the base class for a type), IsAbstract (True for MustInherit classes), and IsSealed (True for NotInheritable classes) properties:

```
Dim asm2 As [Assembly] = Reflection.Assembly.Load("mscorlib")
For Each ty As Type In asm2.GetExportedTypes()
    Dim text As String = ty.FullName & " "
    If ty.IsAbstract Then text &= "MustInherit "
    If ty.IsSealed Then text &= "NotInheritable "
    ' We need this test because System.Object has no base class.
    If Not ty.BaseType Is Nothing Then
        text &= "(base: " & ty.BaseType.FullName & ") "
    End If
    Console.WriteLine(text)
Next
```

You can get additional information on a given type by querying a few methods, such as IsSubclassOfType (returns True if the current type is derived from the type passed as an argument), IsAssignableFrom (returns True if the type passed as an argument can be assigned to the current type), and IsInstanceOf (returns True if the object passed as an argument is an instance of the current type). Let me recap a few of the many ways you have to test an object's type:

```
If TypeOf obj Is Person Then
    ' obj can be assigned to a Person variable (the VB way).
End If

If GetType(Person).IsAssignableFrom(obj.GetType) Then
    ' obj can be assigned to a Person variable (the reflection way).
End If

If GetType(Person).IsInstanceOf(obj) Then
    ' obj is a Person object.
End If

If GetType(Person) Is obj.GetType() Then
    ' obj is a Person object (but fails if obj is Nothing).
End If

If obj.GetType().IsSubclassOf(GetType(Person)) Then
    ' obj is an object that inherits from Person.
End If
```

Enumerating Members

The Type class exposes an intimidatingly large number of methods. The following methods let you enumerate type members: GetMembers, GetFields, GetProperties, GetMethods, GetEvents, GetConstructors, GetInterfaces, GetNestedTypes, and GetDefaultMembers. All these methods (note the plural names) return an array of elements that describe the members of the type represented by the current Type object. The most generic method in this group is GetMembers, which returns an array with all the fields, properties, methods, and events that the type exposes. For example, the following code lists all the members of the System.String type:

```
Dim minfos() As MemberInfo = GetType(String).GetMembers()
For Each mi As MemberInfo In minfos
    Console.WriteLine("{0} ({1})", mi.Name, mi.MemberType)
Next
```

The GetMembers function returns an array of MemberInfo elements, a type that represents a field, a property, a method, a constructor, an event, or a delegate. MemberInfo is an abstract type from which more specific types derive—for example, FieldInfo for field members and MethodInfo for method members. The MemberInfo.MemberType enumerated property lets you discern between methods, properties, fields, and so on.

The GetMembers method returns two or more MemberInfo objects with the same name if the class exposes overloaded properties and methods. So, for example, the output from the preceding code snippet includes multiple occurrences of the Format and Concat methods. You also find multiple occurrences of the constructor method, which is always named .ctor. In the next section, I'll show how you can explore the argument signature of these overloaded members. Also note that the GetMembers method returns public, instance, and shared members, as well as methods inherited by other objects, such as the ToString method inherited from System.Object.

The GetMembers method supports an optional BindingFlags enumerated argument. This bit-coded value lets you narrow the enumeration—for example, by listing only public or nonshared members. The BindingFlags type is used in many reflection methods and includes many enumerated values, but in this case only a few are useful:

- The Public and NonPublic enumerated values restrict the enumeration according to the scope of the elements. (You must specify at least one of these flags to get a nonempty result.)

- The Instance and Static enumerated values restrict the enumeration to instance members and shared members, respectively. (You must specify at least one of these flags to get a nonempty result.)

- The DeclaredOnly enumerated value restricts the enumeration to members declared in the current type (as opposed to members inherited from its base class).

- The FlattenHierarchy enumerated value is used to include static members up the hierarchy.

This code lists only the public, nonshared, and noninherited members of the String class:

```
' Get all public, nonshared, noninherited members of String type.
Dim minfo() As MemberInfo = GetType(String).GetMembers( _
    BindingFlags.Public Or BindingFlags.Instance Or BindingFlags.DeclaredOnly)
```

The preceding code snippet produces an array that includes the ToString method, which at first glance shouldn't be in the result because it's inherited from System.Object. It's included because the String class adds an overloaded version of this method, and this overloaded method is the only one that appears in the result array.

To narrow the enumeration to a given member type, you can use a more specific Get*xxxx*s method. When you're using a Get*xxxx*s method other than GetMembers, you can assign the result to an array of a more specific type, namely PropertyInfo, MethodInfo, ConstructorInfo, FieldInfo, or EventInfo. All these specific types derive from MemberInfo, so you can always use an array of MemberInfo when you're assigning the result from the GetProperties, GetMethods, GetConstructors, GetFields, and GetEvents methods, respectively, even though using the more specific type is usually a better idea because it circumvents the need to cast the result to a specific object to access properties not in the base class. For example, this code lists only the methods of the String type:

```
For Each mi As MethodInfo In GetType(String).GetMethods()
    Console.WriteLine(mi.Name)
Next
```

The GetInterfaces or GetNestedTypes methods return an array of Type elements, rather than a MemberInfo array, so the code in the loop is slightly different:

```
For Each ty As Type In GetType(String).GetInterfaces()
    Console.WriteLine(ty.FullName)
Next
```

All the Get*xxxx*s methods—with the exception of GetDefaultMembers and GetInterfaces—can take an optional BindingFlags argument to restrict the enumeration to public or nonpublic, shared or nonshared, and declared or inherited members. For more sophisticated searches, you can use the FindMembers method, which takes a delegate pointing to a function that filters individual members. (See .NET Framework documentation for additional information.)

In many cases, you don't need to enumerate a type's members because you have other ways to find out the name of the field, property, methods, or event you want to get information about. You can use the GetMember or other Get*xxxx* methods (where *xxxx* is a singular word) of the Type class—namely GetMember, GetField, GetProperty, GetMethod, GetEvent, GetInterface, GetConstructor, and GetNestedType—to get the corresponding MemberInfo (or a more specific object):

```
' Get information about the String.Chars property.
Dim mi2 As MemberInfo = GetType(String).GetProperty("Chars")

' You can also cast the result to a more specific variable.
Dim pi2 As PropertyInfo = GetType(String).GetProperty("Chars")
```

If you're querying for an overloaded property or method, you actually get an array of MemberInfo elements. In such a case, you can ask for a specific version of the member by using GetProperty or GetMethod and specifying the exact argument signature by passing an array of Type objects as its second argument:

```
' Get the MethodInfo object for the IndexOf string method with the
' following signature: IndexOf(char, startIndex, endIndex).

' Prepare the signature as an array of Type objects.
Dim types() As Type = {GetType(Char), GetType(Integer), GetType(Integer)}
' Ask for the method with given name and signature.
Dim mi3 As MethodInfo = GetType(String).GetMethod("IndexOf", types)
```

Retrieving Member Information

After you get a reference to a MemberInfo object—or a more specific object, such as FieldInfo or PropertyInfo—you can retrieve information about the corresponding member. Because all these specific *xxxx*Info objects derive from MemberInfo, they have some properties in common, including Name, MemberType, ReflectedType (the type used to retrieve this MemberInfo instance), and DeclaringType (the type where this member is declared). The value returned by the last two properties differ if the member has been inherited. The following loop displays the name of all the members exposed by the String type, together with a description of the member type. To make things more interesting, I'm suppressing constructor methods, multiple definitions for overloaded methods, and methods inherited from the base Object class:

```
' We use this ArrayList to keep track of items already displayed.
Dim al As New ArrayList()
For Each mi As MemberInfo In GetType(String).GetMembers()
    If (mi.MemberType And MemberTypes.Constructor) <> 0 Then
        ' Ignore constructor methods.
    ElseIf Not mi.DeclaringType Is mi.ReflectedType Then
        ' Ignore inherited members.
    ElseIf Not al.Contains(mi.Name) Then
        ' If this element hasn't been listed yet, do it now.
        Console.WriteLine("{0}  ({1})", mi.Name, mi.MemberType)
        ' Add this element to the list of processed items.
        al.Add(mi.Name)
    End If
Next
```

Except for the members inherited from MemberInfo, a FieldInfo object exposes only a few properties, including FieldType (the type of the field), IsLiteral (True if the field is actually a constant), IsInitOnly (True if the field is marked as ReadOnly), IsStatic (True if the field is Shared), and other Boolean properties that reflect the scope of the field, such as IsPublic, IsAssembly (Friend), IsFamily (Protected), IsFamilyOrAssembly (Protected Friend), IsFamilyAndAssembly (Protected but visible only from inside the same assembly, a scope not supported by Visual Basic), and IsPrivate. The following code lists all nonconstant fields with Public and Friend scope in the Person type:

```
For Each fi As FieldInfo In GetType(Person).GetFields()
    If (fi.IsPublic Or fi.IsAssembly) And Not fi.IsLiteral Then
        Console.WriteLine("{0} As {1}", fi.Name, fi.FieldType.Name)
    End If
Next
```

Like FieldInfo, MethodInfo exposes the IsStatic property and all the other scope-related properties you've just seen, plus a few additional Boolean properties: IsVirtual (the method is marked with the Overridable keyword), IsAbstract (MustOverride), and IsFinal (NotOverridable). If the method returns a value (a Function, in Visual Basic parlance), the ReturnType property returns the type of the return value; otherwise, it returns a special type whose name is System.Void. This snippet uses these properties to display information on all the methods a class exposes in a Visual Basic–like syntax:

```
For Each mi As MethodInfo In GetType(DateTime).GetMethods()
    If mi.IsFinal Then
        Console.Write("NotOverridable ")
    ElseIf mi.IsVirtual Then
        Console.Write("Overridable ")
    ElseIf mi.IsAbstract Then
        Console.Write("MustOverride ")
    End If
    Dim retTypeName As String = mi.ReturnType.FullName
    If retTypeName = "System.Void" Then
```

```
        Console.WriteLine("Sub {0}", mi.Name)
    Else
        Console.WriteLine("Function {0} As {1}", mi.Name, retTypeName)
    End If
Next
```

The ConstructorInfo type exposes the same members as the MethodInfo type (not surprisingly, as both these types inherit from the MethodBase abstract class, which in turns derives from MemberInfo), with the exception of ReturnType (constructors don't have a return type).

The PropertyInfo type exposes only three interesting properties besides those inherited from MemberInfo: PropertyType (the type returned by the property), CanRead (False for write-only properties), and CanWrite (False for read-only properties). Oddly, the PropertyInfo type doesn't expose members that indicate the scope of the property or whether it's a static property. You can access this information only indirectly by means of one of the following methods: GetGetMethod (which returns the MethodInfo object corresponding to the Get method), GetSetMethod (the MethodInfo object corresponding to the Set method), or GetAccessors (an array of one or two MethodInfo objects, corresponding to the Get and/or Set accessor methods):

```
For Each pi As PropertyInfo In GetType(Person).GetProperties
    ' Get either the Get or the Set accessor methods
    Dim mi As MethodInfo, modifier As String = ""
    If pi.CanRead Then
        mi = pi.GetGetMethod
        If Not pi.CanWrite Then modifier = "ReadOnly "
    Else
        mi = pi.GetSetMethod()
        modifier = "WriteOnly "
    End If
    ' Display only Public and Protected properties.
    If mi.IsPublic Or mi.IsFamily Then
        Console.WriteLine("{0}{1} As {2}", modifier, pi.Name, _
            pi.PropertyType.FullName)
    End If
Next
```

Getting information about an event is complicated by the fact that the EventInfo type has no property that lets you determine the scope of the event or whether it's static. Instead, you must use the GetAddMethod to return the MethodInfo object corresponding to the hidden method (the method that the AddHandler keyword calls for you behind the scenes) that adds a new client to the list of listeners for this event. Typically, this method is named add_*eventname* and is paired with the remove_*eventname* hidden method (the method silently called by RemoveHandler and whose MethodInfo is returned by the GetRemoveMethod). You can then query this MethodInfo object to discover the event's scope and whether it's static:

```
' Get information on the GotEmail event of the Person object.
Dim ei As EventInfo = GetType(Person).GetEvent("GotEmail")
' Get a reference to the hidden add_GotEmail method.
Dim mi2 As MethodInfo = ei.GetAddMethod()
' Test the method scope and check whether it's static.
:
```

Enumerating Parameters

The one thing left to do is enumerate the parameters that a property or a method expects. Both the GetIndexParameters (of ParameterInfo) and the GetParameters (of MethodInfo) methods return an array of ParameterInfo objects, where each element describes the attributes of the arguments passed to and from the member.

A ParameterInfo object has properties whose names are self-explanatory: Name (the name of the parameter), ParameterType (the type of the parameter), Member (the MemberInfo the parameter belongs to), Position (an integer that describes where the parameter appears in the method signature), IsIn (always True in Visual Basic), IsOut (True if the parameter is passed with ByRef), IsOptional, and DefaultValue (the default value for optional parameters). The following code shows how to display the calling syntax for a given method:

```
' Get the MethodInfo for the String.CopyTo method.
Dim mi As MethodInfo = GetType(String).GetMethod("CopyTo")
Console.Write(mi.Name & "(")
For Each pi As ParameterInfo In mi.GetParameters()
    ' Display a comma if it isn't the first parameter.
    If pi.Position > 0 Then Console.Write(", ")
    Dim direction As String = "ByVal"
    If pi.IsOut Then direction = "ByRef"
    Console.Write("{0} {1} As {2}", direction, pi.Name, pi.ParameterType.FullName)
Next
Console.WriteLine(")")
```

The companion source code includes an example that shows how to display more information about each parameter, including optional arguments and array arguments.

Getting the syntax for an event is more complicated because the EventInfo object doesn't expose the GetParameters method. Instead, you must use the EventHandler-Type property to retrieve the Type object corresponding to the delegate that defines the event. The Invoke method of this delegate, in turn, has the same signature as the event:

```
Dim ei As EventInfo = GetType(Person).GetEvent("GotEmail")
Dim delegType As Type = ei.EventHandlerType
Dim mi2 As MethodInfo = delegType.GetMethod("Invoke")
For Each pi As ParameterInfo In mi2.GetParameters()
    ⋮
Next
```

Invoking Members

All the reflection operations that you've seen so far work on types but not on objects. For example, you saw how you can enumerate the types in an assembly or retrieve information about a type's member. In this section, you'll see how to execute a type's method that you discover through reflection. Clearly, unless you're calling a shared method, this operation makes sense only if you have an object on which that method should be invoked.

The easiest operation you can perform is reading or writing a field by means of the GetValue and SetValue methods of the FieldInfo object:

```
' Create a Person object and reflect on it.
Dim pers As New Person("Joe", "Doe")
Dim persType As Type = pers.GetType()
' Get a reference to its FirstName field.
Dim fi As FieldInfo = persType.GetField("FirstName")
' Display its current value then change it.
Console.WriteLine(fi.GetValue(pers))     ' => Joe
fi.SetValue(pers, "Robert")
' Prove that it changed.
Console.WriteLine(pers.FirstName)         ' => Robert
```

Like FieldInfo, PropertyInfo exposes the GetValue and SetValue methods, but properties can take arguments, so you must pass Nothing in the second argument if you're calling parameterless properties:

```
' Get a reference to the PropertyInfo object.
Dim pi As PropertyInfo = persType.GetProperty("Age")
' Note that the type of value must match exactly.
' (Integer constants must be converted to Short, in this case.)
pi.SetValue(pers, 35S, Nothing)
' Read it back.
Console.WriteLine(pi.GetValue(pers, Nothing))    ' => 35
```

If the property takes one or more arguments, you must pass an Object array containing one element for each argument:

```
' Get a reference to the PropertyInfo object.
Dim pi2 As PropertyInfo = persType.GetProperty("EmailAddress")
' Prepare the array of parameters.
Dim args2() As Object = {1S}
' Set the property.
pi2.SetValue(pers, "321 North Street", args2)
' Read it back.
Console.WriteLine(pi2.GetValue(pers, args2))    ' => 321 North Street
```

A similar thing happens when you're invoking methods, except that you use Invoke instead of GetValue or SetValue:

```
' Get the MethodInfo for this method.
Dim mi As MethodInfo = persType.GetMethod("SendEmail")
' Prepare an array for expected arguments.
Dim args() As Object = {"This is a message", 3}
' Invoke the method.
mi.Invoke(pers, args)
```

Things are more interesting when optional arguments are involved. In this case, you pass the Type.Missing special value, as in this code:

```
' ...(Initial code as above)...
' Don't pass the second argument.
Dim args2() As Object = {"This is a message", Type.Missing}
mi.Invoke(pers, args2)
```

Alternatively, you can query the DefaultValue property of corresponding ParameterInfo to learn the default value for that specific argument:

```
' ...(Initial code as above)...
' Retrieve the DefaultValue from the ParameterInfo object.
Dim args3() As Object = {"This is a message", mi.GetParameters(1).DefaultValue }
mi.Invoke(pers, args3)
```

The Invoke method traps all the exceptions thrown in the called method and converts them into TargetInvocationException; you must check the InnerException property of the caught exception to retrieve the real exception:

```
Try
    mi.Invoke(pers, params)
Catch ex As TargetInvocationException
    Console.WriteLine(ex.InnerException.Message)
Catch ex As Exception
    Console.WriteLine(ex.Message)
End Try
```

In some cases, you might find it easier to dynamically set properties and invoke methods by means of the Type object's InvokeMember method. This method takes the name of the member, a flag that says whether it's a field, property, or method, the object for which the member should be invoked, and an array of Objects for the arguments if there are any. Here are a few examples:

```
' Set the FirstName field.
Dim args() As Object = {"Francesco"}        ' One argument
persType.InvokeMember("FirstName", BindingFlags.SetField, _
    Nothing, pers, args)
' Read the FirstName field.
' (Note that we're passing Nothing for the argument array.)
Dim value As Object = persType.InvokeMember("FirstName", _
    BindingFlags.GetField, Nothing, pers, Nothing)

' Set the Age property.
Dim args2() As Object = {35S}               ' One argument
persType.InvokeMember("Age", BindingFlags.SetProperty, Nothing, pers, args2)

' Call the SendEMail method, create the argument array on the fly.
Dim args3() As Object = {"This is a message", 2}
persType.InvokeMember("SendEmail", BindingFlags.InvokeMethod, Nothing, pers, args3)
```

InvokeMember works correctly also if one or more arguments are passed by reference. For example, if the SendEmail method would take the priority in a ByRef argument, on return from the method call the args3(1) element would contain the new value assigned to that argument.

Creating an Object Dynamically

The last reflection feature left to be examined lets you dynamically create an object on the fly if you have its class name. This feature is the .NET counterpart of the Visual

Basic CreateObject function. You can choose from three ways to create a .NET object via reflection: by using the CreateInstance method of the System.Activator class, by using the InvokeMember method of the Type class, or by invoking one of the type's constructor methods.

If the type has a parameterless constructor, creating an instance is trivial:

```
' Next statement assumes that the Person class is defined in
' an assembly named "ReflectionDemo".
Dim persType = Type.GetType("ReflectionDemo.Person")
Dim o As Object = Activator.CreateInstance(persType)
' Prove that we created a Person.
Console.WriteLine("A {0} object has been created", o.GetType.Name)
```

To call a constructor that takes one or more parameters, you must prepare an array of values:

```
' (We reuse the persType variable from previous code...)
' Use the constructor that takes two arguments.
Dim args2() As Object = {"Joe", "Doe"}
' Call the constructor that matches the parameter signature.
Dim o2 As Object = Activator.CreateInstance(persType, args2)
```

You can use InvokeMember to create an instance of the class and even pass arguments to its constructor, as in the following code:

```
' Prepare the array of parameters.
Dim args3() As Object = {"Joe", "Doe"}
' Constructor methods have no name and take Nothing in last-but-one argument.
Dim o3 As Object = persType.InvokeMember("", BindingFlags.CreateInstance, _
    Nothing, Nothing, args3)
```

Creating an object through its constructor method is a bit more convoluted, but I'll demonstrate the technique here for the sake of completeness:

```
' Prepare the argument signature as an array of types (2 strings).
Dim types() As Type = {GetType(String), GetType(String)}
' Get a reference to the correct constructor.
Dim ci As ConstructorInfo = persType.GetConstructor(types)
' Prepare the parameters.
Dim args4() As Object = {"Joe", "Doe"}
' Invoke the constructor and assign the result to a variable.
Dim o4 As Object = ci.Invoke(args4)
```

Dynamic Registration of Event Handlers

Another programming technique you can implement via reflection is the dynamic registration of an event handler. For example, let's say that you have the following event handler for the Person method's GotEmail event:

```
Module MainModule
    Sub EventHandler(ByVal msg As String, ByVal priority As Integer)
```

```
        Console.WriteLine("GotEmail event fired. Msg='{0}', Priority={1}", msg, priori
ty)
    End Sub
        ⋮
End Module
```

Here's the code that registers the procedure for this event, using reflection exclusively:

```
' pers and persType initialized as in previous examples...
' Get a reference to the GotEmail event.
Dim ei As EventInfo = persType.GetEvent("GotEmail")
' Get a reference to the delegate that defines the event.
Dim handlerType As Type = ei.EventHandlerType
' Create a delegate of this type that points to a method in this module
Dim handler As [Delegate] = [Delegate].CreateDelegate( _
    handlerType, GetType(MainModule), "EventHandler")
' Register this handler dynamically.
ei.AddEventHandler(pers, handler)
' Call the method that fires the event. (Use late-binding.)
persType.InvokeMember("SendEmail", BindingFlags.InvokeMethod, Nothing, pers, _
    New Object() {"Hello", 2})
```

A look at the console window proves that the EventHandler procedure was invoked when the code in the Person.SendEmail method raised the GotEmail event. If the event handler is an instance method, the second argument to the Delegate.CreateDelegate static method must be an instance of the class that defines the method; if the handler is a static method (as in this example), this argument must be a Type object corresponding to the class where the method is defined.

Tracing the Stack Frame

A common question from Visual Basic 6 developers is whether a routine can identify its caller, and the caller of its caller, and so on. This feature might be valuable in case of errors (so that the error handler can display the execution path that led to the code that raised the error), for debugging or profiling reasons, and more. You can achieve this capability in Visual Basic 6 only by augmenting your code with calls to a logging routine or by resorting to very advanced techniques that analyze the symbolic information produced by the compiler.

Finding a routine's caller is almost trivial under Visual Basic .NET, thanks to a class named StackTrace, found in the System.Diagnostics namespace. As its name implies, the StackTrace object keeps track of all the procedures that are pending, waiting for the current one to complete.

You can create the StackTrace object in many ways. In its simplest form, you pass no arguments to its constructor and you get the complete stack image as a collection of StackFrame objects, which you can enumerate by their index:

```
Dim st As New StackTrace()
' Enumerate all the stack frame objects.
' (The frame at index 0 corresponds to the current routine.)
```

```
For i As Integer = 0 To st.FrameCount - 1
    ' Get the ith stack frame and print the method name.
    Dim sf As StackFrame = st.GetFrame(i)
    Console.WriteLine(sf.GetMethod.Name)
Next
```

Another occasion for creating a StackTrace object is when an exception is caught. In this case, you should pass the exception object to the first argument of the StackTrace constructor so that the StackTrace object contains the stack state at the time the exception was thrown, rather than when you create the StackTrace object itself. The following code creates a chain of calling procedures, with the innermost procedure causing an exception that's trapped in the outermost one:

```
Sub TestStackFrameFromException()
    Try
        ' This causes an exception.
        TestStackFrameFromException_1(1)
    Catch e As Exception
        DisplayExceptionInfo(e)
    End Try
End Sub

Sub TestStackFrameFromException_1(ByVal x As Integer)
    TestStackFrameFromException_2("abc")
End Sub

Function TestStackFrameFromException_2(ByVal x As String) As String
    TestStackFrameFromException_3()
End Function

Sub TestStackFrameFromException_3()
    ' Cause an exception (null reference).
    Dim o As Object
    Console.Write(o.ToString)
End Sub

' A reusable routine that displays error information
Sub DisplayExceptionInfo(ByVal e As Exception)
    ' Display the error message.
    Console.WriteLine(e.Message)
    Dim res As String = ""
    Dim st As New StackTrace(e, True)
    For i As Integer = 0 To st.FrameCount - 1
        ' Get the ith stack frame.
        Dim sf As StackFrame = st.GetFrame(i)
        ' Get the corresponding method for that stack frame.
        Dim mi As MemberInfo = sf.GetMethod
        ' Append the type and method name.
        res &= mi.DeclaringType.FullName & "." & mi.Name & " ("
        ' Append information about the position in the source file
        ' (but only if Debug information is available).
        If sf.GetFileName <> "" Then
            res &= String.Format("{0}, Line {1}, Col {2},", _
                sf.GetFileName, sf.GetFileLineNumber, sf.GetFileColumnNumber)
        End If
```

```
      ' Append information about offset in MSIL code, if available.
      If sf.GetILOffset <> StackFrame.OFFSET_UNKNOWN Then
          res &= String.Format("IL offset {0},", sf.GetILOffset)
      End If
      ' Append information about offset in native code and display.
      res &= " native offset " & sf.GetNativeOffset & ")"
      Console.WriteLine(res)
    Next
End Sub
```

The code inside the DisplayExceptionInfo procedure shows how you can use other methods of the StackFrame object, such as GetFileName (the name of the source file), GetFileLineNumber and GetFileColumnNumber (the position in the source file), GetILOffset (offset in MSIL code from the top of the module), and GetNativeOffset (offset in JIT-compiled native code). By using all these pieces of information, the DisplayExceptionInfo routine can provide a more informative error report than you usually get inside the IDE. As a result, you might launch ILDASM and see the individual MSIL opcode that threw the exception. Note that the source code's filename, line, and column are available only if the program was compiled with debugging information. If you compiled the executable for Release configuration, these properties return a null string or 0.

Because the GetMethod method of the StackFrame object returns a MethodInfo object, you can leverage reflection to learn more about that procedure, including its argument signature, which is useful when there are overloaded versions of the same procedure or any custom attribute associated with it.

One last note about visiting the stack with the StackTrace object: some methods might not appear in the list because they've been inlined by the JIT compiler. In other words, the JIT compiler has eliminated the call to the method by moving its code in the calling routines. This kind of optimization can occur only when the project is compiled in Release mode with optimizations turned on, so it's never a problem in the debugging phase. If your program depends on the contents of the StackTrace object, you should disable inlining optimization by marking the method in question with the MethodImpl(MethodImplOptions.NoInlining) attribute.

Attributes and Reflection

As you learned in previous chapters, attributes are pieces of metadata information that you attach to code entities—assemblies, classes, methods, or individual fields—to affect the behavior of the Visual Basic compiler, the JIT compiler, or other portions of the .NET runtime.

Most of the time, you'll use only predefined attributes that are defined in the .NET Framework and documented in the MSDN documentation. Occasionally, however, you might want to define your own custom attributes, and the next section tells you how to do it.

Building a Custom Attribute Class

A custom attribute is nothing but a class that inherits from System.Attribute. Its name must end with Attribute and it contains an AttributeUsage attribute that tells the compiler what program entities this attribute class can be applied to (classes, modules, methods, and so on). A custom attribute class can contain fields, properties, and methods that accept and return values only of the following types: Boolean, Byte, Short, Integer, Long, Char, Single, Double, String, Object, System.Type, and public Enum. It can also receive and return one-dimensional arrays of one of the preceding types. A custom attribute class can have no explicit constructor at all, but it's customary to have one or more constructors that specify the mandatory arguments to be passed to the attribute.

The following example shows a custom attribute class that lets you annotate any class or class member with the name of the author, the source code version when the member was completed, and an optional property that specifies whether the code has been reviewed:

```
' The AttributeTargets.All value means that this attribute
' can be used with any program entity.
<AttributeUsage(AttributeTargets.All)> _
Class VersioningAttribute
    ' All attribute classes inherit from System.Attribute.
    Inherits System.Attribute

    ' These should be Property procedures in a real application,
    ' but fields are OK in this demo.
    Public Author As String
    Public Version As Single
    Public Tested As Boolean

    ' The Attribute constructor takes two required values.
    Sub New(ByVal Author As String, ByVal Version As Single)
        Me.Author = Author
        Me.Version = Version
    End Sub
End Class
```

The argument passed to the AttributeUsage attribute specifies that the VersioningAttribute attribute—or just Versioning because the trailing Attribute portion of the name can be omitted—can be used with any program entity. The argument you pass to the Attribute-Usage constructor is a bit-coded value formed by adding one or more elements in this list: Assembly (1), Module (2), Class (4), Struct (8), Enum (16), Constructor (32), Method (64), Property (128), Field (256), Event (512), Interface (1024), Parameter (2048), Delegate (4096), ReturnValue (8192), or All (16,383, the sum of all preceding values).

The AttributeUsage attribute supports two additional properties, which can be passed as named arguments in the constructor method. The AllowMultiple property specifies whether the attribute being defined—VersioningAttribute in this case—can be used multiple times inside angle brackets. The Inherited attribute tells whether a derived class inherits the attribute. The default value for both properties is False.

The Conditional attribute, which I described in Chapter 6, is an example of an attribute that supports multiple instances and is also an example of an attribute that's inherited by derived classes. If the Conditional attribute class were implemented in Visual Basic, its source code would be more or less as follows:

```
<AttributeUsage(AttributeTargets.Method, AllowMultiple:=True, Inherited:=True)> _
Class ConditionalAttribute
    Inherits System.Attribute

    Private m_ConditionString As String

    ' The constructor method
    Sub New(ByVal ConditionString As String)
        Me.ConditionString = ConditionString
    End Sub

    ' The only property of this attribute class
    Property ConditionString() As String
        Get
            Return m_ConditionString
        End Get
        Set(ByVal Value As String)
            m_ConditionString = Value
        End Set
    End Property
End Class
```

Discovering Attributes at Run Time

Whenever you define a custom attribute, you also typically build a piece of code that uses reflection to discover how the developer applied the attribute to code entities in an assembly. For example, let's suppose that a developer has decorated a class with some Versioning attributes:

```
<Versioning("John", 1.01)> _
Class TestClass
    <Versioning("Robert", 1.01, Tested:=True)> _
    Sub MyProc()
        ⋮
    End Sub

    <Versioning("Ann", 1.02)> _
    Function MyFunction() As Long
        ⋮
    End Function
End Class
```

The following procedure shows how you can use reflection to list the Versioning attributes for the class and its methods. It uses the GetCustomAttributes method that most reflection types—namely, Assembly, Module, Type, ParameterInfo, and all classes that inherit from MemberInfo—expose:

```
Dim att As VersioningAttribute
Dim attType As Type = GetType(VersioningAttribute)
```

```
Dim classType As Type = GetType(TestClass)
Dim attributes() As Object

' Retrieve all Versioning attributes for TestClass.
' (False means we don't want to see inherited attributes.)
attributes = classType.GetCustomAttributes(attType, False)

' Check whether the array contains an element. (It should contain one in our case.)
If attributes.Length > 0 Then
    ' Move to a specific type so that we can use early binding.
    att = DirectCast(attributes(0), VersioningAttribute)
    ' Display versioning information on the class.
    Console.WriteLine("Class {0} => Author={1}, Version={2}, Tested={3}", _
        classType.FullName, att.Author, att.Version, att.Tested)
End If


' Iterate over all the members in TestClass.
For Each mi As MemberInfo In classType.GetMembers
    ' Get Versioning attributes for this member.
    attributes = mi.GetCustomAttributes(attType, False)
    ' If there are custom Versioning attributes
    If attributes.Length > 0 Then
        ' Get a Versioning object to use early binding.
        att = DirectCast(attributes(0), VersioningAttribute)
        ' Display versioning attributes of this member.
        Console.WriteLine("  {0} => Author={1}, Version={2}, Tested={3}", _
            mi.Name, att.Author, att.Version, att.Tested)
    End If
Next
```

Here's the result displayed in the Output window:

```
Class TestClass => Author=John, Version=1.01, Tested=False
  MyProc => Author=Robert, Version=1.01, Tested=True
  MyFunction => Author=Ann, Version=1.02, Tested=False
```

The GetCustomAttributes method isn't the only way of discovering attributes in a .NET assembly, and for sure it isn't the most efficient one. For example, it returns an array of attributes because it must be able to work with attributes that allow multiple instances for each code element—that is, attributes for which AllowMultiple is True, as is the case with the custom VersioningAttribute class. When you deal with attributes that allow only one instance at a time, you can use the simpler and more efficient GetCustomAttribute shared method of the Attribute class, which returns either the found attribute or Nothing. Because the VersioningAttribute class is defined with AllowMultiple equal to False, you can simplify the discovery code as follows:

```
' Retrieve the only custom attribute of type VersioningAttribute.
att = DirectCast(Attribute.GetCustomAttribute(classType, attType), _
    VersioningAttribute)
' Check whether we found an attribute.
If Not (att Is Nothing) Then
    Console.WriteLine("Class {0} => Author={1}, Version={2}, Tested={3}", _
        classType.FullName, att.Author, att.Version, att.Tested)
End If
```

```
For Each mi As MemberInfo In classType.GetMembers
    ' Get the Versioning attribute for this method.
    att = DirectCast(Attribute.GetCustomAttribute( _
        mi, attType), VersioningAttribute)
    ' If there are custom Versioning attributes
    If Not (att Is Nothing) Then
        Console.WriteLine("  {0} => Author={1}, Version={2}, Tested={3}", _
            mi.Name, att.Author, att.Version, att.Tested)
    End If
Next
```

Both the techniques I illustrated here work by instantiating the attribute object—as you can verify by inserting a Debug.WriteLine statement in the attribute's constructor method—so they perform relatively slowly. If you just have to check whether an attribute is present, you can use the IsDefined shared method of the Attribute class, which doesn't instantiate the attribute and is therefore slightly faster:

```
' Check whether VersioningAttribute is defined for the TestClass.
' (Assumes that classType and attType are defined as in preceding
'  code snippets.)
If Attribute.IsDefined(classType, attType) Then
    ⋮
End If
```

One last word about attribute discovery: you can use this technique to detect both custom attributes and attributes defined in the .NET Framework, such as the Conditional and the DebuggerStepThrough attributes. However, to optimize memory and CPU time, the .NET runtime stores the information about a few common attributes—such as the Serializable, NotSerialized, DllImport, StructLayout, and FieldOffset attributes—in the assembly's metadata using a different format, therefore you can't retrieve them by using the technique seen in this section. However, you can access these special attributes by means of other reflection properties, such as the IsSerializable and the IsLayoutSequential properties.

The ability to create custom attributes adds an unparalleled flexibility to programming. As an example of this flexibility, the companion code for this book includes the complete source code of the CsvField custom attribute that you can apply to properties and fields in any class, and a CsvSerializer class that honors those attributes when it reads and writes objects to a text file in Comma Separated Value (CSV) format.

Even if Visual Basic and C# were the first mainstream programming languages that can use attributes, their foundations have been studied by computer scientists who have worked for some time on an entirely new branch of computer science named Aspect Oriented Programming (AOP). This field is evolving quickly, and searching the Internet is the most effective way to learn more about it.

On-the-Fly Compilation

Earlier in this chapter I mentioned the System.Reflection.Emit namespace, whose classes let you create an assembly on the fly. The .NET Framework uses these classes internally in a few cases—for example, when you pass the RegexOptions.Compiled option to the constructor of the Regex object. (See Chapter 11.) Using reflection emit, however, isn't exactly the easiest .NET programming task, and I'm glad I've never had to use it heavily in a real-world application.

Nevertheless, at times the ability to create an assembly out of the thin air can be quite tantalizing because it opens up a number of programming techniques that are otherwise impossible. For example, consider building a routine that takes a math expression entered by the end user (as a string), evaluates it, and returns the result. You might use such a routine for a variety of tasks, for example to do function plotting or to find the roots of a higher-degree equation. (See Figure 14-2.) If the reflection emit classes are ruled out, the only other option is to generate the source code of a Visual Basic .NET program, compile it on the fly, and then instantiate one of its classes.

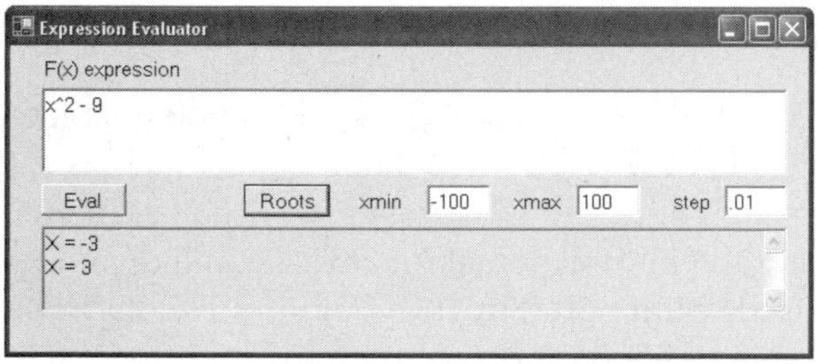

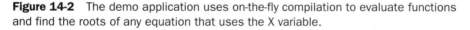

Figure 14-2   The demo application uses on-the-fly compilation to evaluate functions and find the roots of any equation that uses the X variable.

The types that allow us to compile an assembly at run time are in the Microsoft.VisualBasic namespace (or in the Microsoft.CSharp namespace, if you want to compile a C# source code) and in the System.CodeDom.Compiler namespace, so you need to add proper Imports statements to your code to run the code samples that follow. The first thing to do is generate the source code for the program to be compiled dynamically. In our expression evaluator demo application, such source code is obtained by inserting the expression that the end user enters in the txtExpression field in the middle of the Eval method of an Evaluator public class:

```
Dim source As String = String.Format( _
    "Imports Microsoft.VisualBasic{0}" _
    & "Imports System.Math{0}" _
    & "Public Class Evaluator{0}" _
    & "   Public Function Eval(ByVal x As Double) As Double{0}" _
    & "      Return {1}{0}" _
    & "   End Function{0}" _
    & "End Class{0}", _
    ControlChars.CrLf, txtExpression.Text)
```

Next, you create a CompilerParameters object and set its properties; this object broadly corresponds to the options you'd pass to the VBC.EXE command-line compiler:

```
      Dim params As New CompilerParameters
      ' Generate a DLL, not an EXE executable.
      ' (Not really necessary, as False is the default.)
      params.GenerateExecutable = False
#If DEBUG Then
          ' Include debug information.
          params.IncludeDebugInformation = True
          ' Debugging works if we generate an actual DLL and keep temporary files.
          params.TempFiles.KeepFiles = True
          params.GenerateInMemory = False
#Else
          ' Treat warnings as errors, don't keep temporary source files.
          params.TreatWarningsAsErrors = True
          params.TempFiles.KeepFiles = False
          ' Optimize the code for faster execution.
          params.CompilerOptions = "/Optimize+"
          ' Generate the assembly in memory.
          params.GenerateInMemory = True
#End If

      ' Add a reference to necessary strong-named assemblies.
      params.ReferencedAssemblies.Add("Microsoft.VisualBasic.Dll")
      params.ReferencedAssemblies.Add("System.Dll")
```

The preceding code snippet shows the typical actions you perform to prepare a CompilerParameters object, as well as its most important properties. The statements inside the #If block are especially interesting. You can include debug information in a dynamic assembly and debug it from inside Visual Studio .NET by setting the IncludeDebugInformation property to True. To enable debugging, however, you must generate an actual .dll or .exe file (GenerateInMemory must be False) and must not delete temporary files at the end of the compilation process (the KeepFiles property of the TempFiles collection must be True). If debugging is correctly enabled, you can force a break in the generated assembly by inserting the following statement in the code you generate dynamically:

```
System.Diagnostics.Debugger.Break
```

You are now ready to compile the assembly:

```
      ' Create the VB compiler.
      Dim provider As New VBCodeProvider
      Dim comp As ICodeCompiler = provider.CreateCompiler()
      Dim compRes As CompilerResults = comp.CompileAssemblyFromSource(params, source)

      ' Check whether we have errors.
      If compRes.Errors.Count > 0 Then
          ' Gather all error messages and display them.
          Dim msg As String = ""
          For Each compErr As CompilerError In compRes.Errors
              msg &= compErr.ToString & ControlChars.CrLf
          Next
          MessageBox.Show(msg, "Compilation Failed", MessageBoxButtons.OK, _
            MessageBoxIcon.Error)
```

```
Else
    ' Compilation was successful.
    ⋮
End If
```

If the compilation was successful, you use the CompilerResults.CompiledAssembly property to get a reference to the created assembly. Once you have this Assembly reference, you can create an instance of its Evaluator class and invoke its Eval method by using standard reflection techniques:

```
Dim asm As [Assembly] = compRes.CompiledAssembly
Dim evaluator As Object = asm.CreateInstance("Evaluator")
Dim evalMethod As MethodInfo = evaluator.GetType.GetMethod("Eval")
Dim args() As Object = {CDbl(123)}    ' Pass x = 123
Dim result As Object = evalMethod.Invoke(evaluator, args)
```

Notice that you can't reference the Evaluator class by a typed variable because this class (and its container assembly) doesn't exist when you compile the main application. For this reason, you must use reflection both to create an instance of the class and to invoke its members.

Another tricky thing to do when applying this technique is having the dynamic assembly call back the main application—for example, to let the main application update a progress bar during a lengthy routine. If the main application is an .exe program, you can't add a reference to the main application to the list of referenced assemblies held in the CompilerParameters.ReferencedAssemblies collection, and therefore the dynamic assembly can't have a strong-typed reference to a class in the main application. The dynamic assembly can call back a method in a class defined in the main application by means of reflection, however. Alternatively, you can define a public interface in a DLL and must have the class in the main application implement the interface. Being defined in a DLL, the dynamic assembly can create an interface variable and therefore it can call methods in the main application via that interface.

You must be aware of another detail when you apply on-the-fly compilation in a real application: once you load the dynamically created assembly, that assembly will take memory in your process until the main application ends. In most cases, this problem isn't serious and you can just forget about it. But you can't ignore it if you plan to build many assemblies on the fly. The only solution to this problem is to create a separate AppDomain, load the dynamic assembly in that AppDomain, use the classes in the assembly, and finally unload the AppDomain when you don't need the assembly any longer. On the other hand, loading the assembly in another AppDomain means that you can't use reflection to manage its types (reflection only works with types in the same AppDomain as the caller). Please see the demo application on the companion CD for a solution to this complex issue.

This chapter on reflection completes the overview of the most important lower-level classes of the .NET runtime, which provide the building blocks you're likely to use in any application, whether it's client-side or server-side, database-oriented or Internet-oriented. In the remainder of the book, you'll see this knowledge put to use. The next topic I'll cover is Windows Forms, the heir of the Visual Basic 6 form engine that you've learned to use and love (and hate, at times) in recent years.

Part IV
Win32 Applications

15 Windows Forms Applications

In spite of the potential that Visual Basic has now in areas such as component and Internet programming, I expect that many developers will continue to use the language to create standard Win32 applications. The .NET Framework offers a lot of features in this area and lets you create applications with a rich user interface without the annoyances and limitations of previous language versions. To qualify as a Visual Basic 6 user-interface wiz, you had to learn a lot of tricks and advanced techniques, such as tons of Windows API calls and subclassing. Now you need only to correctly use the classes and methods defined in the System.Windows.Forms namespace.

Form Basics

As I explained in Chapter 2, a Visual Basic .NET form is nothing but a class that inherits from the System.Windows.Forms.Form class. It isn't special in comparison with other .NET classes. For example, there's no global variable named after the form class (as happens in Visual Basic 6), so you can't display an instance of a form named Form1 by simply executing Form1.Show. Instead, you have to correctly create an instance of the proper form class, as in this code:

```
Dim frm As New Form1
frm.Show
```

The Form Designer

Visual Studio .NET comes with a designer similar to the one provided with earlier versions of Visual Basic. Behind the scenes, however, things work very differently. The Visual Studio .NET designer is a sophisticated code generator; when you set a control's property in the Properties window, you're just creating one or more Visual Basic statements that assign a value to that property after the form has been created. The designer encloses the generated code in a collapsed #Region so that you can't modify it accidentally:

```
Public Class Form1
    Inherits System.Windows.Forms.Form

#Region " Windows Form Designer generated code "
    Public Sub New()
        MyBase.New()
        'This call is required by the Windows Form Designer.
        InitializeComponent()
        'Add any initialization after the InitializeComponent() call
    End Sub
```

```
'Form overrides dispose to clean up the component list.
Protected Overloads Overrides Sub Dispose(ByVal disposing As Boolean)
    If disposing Then
        If Not (components Is Nothing) Then
            components.Dispose()
        End If
    End If
    MyBase.Dispose(disposing)
End Sub
'Required by the Windows Form Designer
Private components As System.ComponentModel.IContainer

'NOTE: The following procedure is required by the Windows Form Designer
'It can be modified using the Windows Form Designer.
'Do not modify it using the code editor.
Friend WithEvents Label1 As System.Windows.Forms.Label
Friend WithEvents TextBox1 As System.Windows.Forms.TextBox
Friend WithEvents Button1 As System.Windows.Forms.Button
<System.Diagnostics.DebuggerStepThrough()> Private Sub InitializeComponent()
    Me.Label1 = New System.Windows.Forms.Label
    Me.TextBox1 = New System.Windows.Forms.TextBox
    Me.Button1 = New System.Windows.Forms.Button
    Me.SuspendLayout()
    '
    'Label1
    '
    Me.Label1.Location = New System.Drawing.Point(24, 24)
    Me.Label1.Name = "Label1"
    Me.Label1.Size = New System.Drawing.Size(328, 23)
    Me.Label1.TabIndex = 0
    Me.Label1.Text = "Type your value here"
    '
    'TextBox1
    '
    Me.TextBox1.Location = New System.Drawing.Point(24, 56)
    Me.TextBox1.Name = "TextBox1"
    Me.TextBox1.Size = New System.Drawing.Size(312, 20)
    Me.TextBox1.TabIndex = 1
    Me.TextBox1.Text = ""
    '
    'Button1
    '
    Me.Button1.Location = New System.Drawing.Point(352, 56)
    Me.Button1.Name = "Button1"
    Me.Button1.TabIndex = 2
    Me.Button1.Text = "OK"
    '
    'Form1
    '
    Me.AutoScaleBaseSize = New System.Drawing.Size(5, 13)
    Me.ClientSize = New System.Drawing.Size(480, 118)
    Me.Controls.Add(Me.Button1)
    Me.Controls.Add(Me.TextBox1)
    Me.Controls.Add(Me.Label1)
    Me.Name = "Form1"
```

```
        Me.Text = "First Windows Form Sample"
        Me.ResumeLayout(False)
    End Sub
#End Region

End Class
```

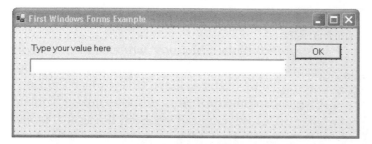

Figure 15-1   A simple form in the Visual Studio form designer

The listing shows a few interesting features of the Form class, starting with the Sub New form constructor—this is where you can put initialization code, after the call to the InitializeComponent procedure that the form designer has created. (You should never add your custom code in the InitializeComponent procedure because it will be overwritten as soon as you use the designer.)

A control on the form is just an object of the proper control class, which the form instantiates in the InitializeComponent procedure and assigns to a WithEvents variable named after the control itself. By default, control variables are Friend members of the form class, but you can change this by assigning a different scope to the control's Modifiers property in the Properties window. Property values are set through regular assignments in code; Visual Basic .NET source code modules don't contain hidden sections that you can't load in the Visual Studio editor.

New Designer Features

The Visual Studio .NET form designer is virtually identical to the designer in Visual Basic 6, with a few interesting new features. For example, controls that are invisible at run time are displayed on the component tray, near the bottom border of the designer. This area isn't normally visible until you drop an invisible control, such as a Timer control, on the designer.

You can save time by arranging the TabIndex property in a visual manner, using the Tab Order command on the View menu. This command displays little numbered labels over each control, and you can create the correct TabIndex sequence by simply clicking on each control in the order you want it to appear in relation to the others. As you see in Figure 15-2, controls that are themselves a container have a TabIndex subsequence. You terminate the Tab Order command by pressing the Esc key.

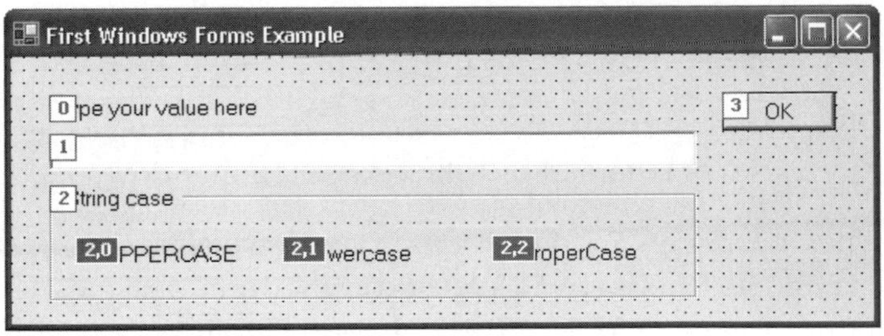

First Windows Forms Example
0 pe your value here
3 OK
1
2 tring case
2,0 PPERCASE
2,1 wercase
2,2 roperCase

Figure 15-2 Arrange the TabIndex property using the Tab Order command.

Another timesaving feature is the ability to resize multiple controls by using the mouse. Just select multiple controls—by clicking on each one while pressing the Ctrl or the Shift key, or by pressing the Ctrl+A key combination to select all the controls on the form—and then use the mouse to resize one of them. All the selected controls will be sized accordingly.

Finally, note that you can lock each individual control (so as not to accidentally move or resize it with the mouse) by setting its Locked property to True in the Properties window. Or you can lock all controls by using the Lock Controls command on the Format menu.

The Windows Forms Class Hierarchy

The classes in the System.Windows.Forms namespace make up a fairly complex hierarchy, at the root of which is the System.Windows.Forms.Control class (see Figure 15-3). The Control class inherits from the System.ComponentModel.Component class, which represents an object that can be placed on a container (see Chapter 13 for more information about components).

Control
ScrollableControl
ContainerControl
Form
UserControl

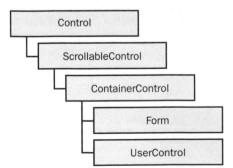

Figure 15-3 A partial view of the Windows Forms class hierarchy

You might be surprised to see that the Form object is a descendant of the Control object; you might have expected a relationship in the opposite direction. Keep in mind that this is an inheritance diagram, not a containment diagram. The Control, ScrollableControl, and ContainerControl classes are generic objects that expose properties that are inherited by more specific controls. These classes aren't abstract classes, and you can actually create an instance of each class, even though there's no point in doing so. (You must do this from code, however, because these classes don't appear in the Toolbox.)

Even if you don't work with these classes in code directly, it's interesting to see the functionality of each class because it's inherited by other classes further down the hierarchy.

The Control class defines a generic Windows Forms control, which is an object that can be hosted in the Visual Studio Toolbox and placed on the form designer's surface. It has methods such as BringToFront and SendToBack (for controlling Z-ordering), properties such as Location and Size (for defining position and dimension), and many others. Many actual controls that don't require advanced functionality—for example, the Label and PictureBox controls—inherit directly from the System.Windows.Forms.Control class. (Notice that the Visual Basic .NET PictureBox control can't work as a container for other controls.) But even a few sophisticated controls inherit directly from Control, including the DataGrid control.

The ScrollableControl class inherits all the members of the Control class, to which it adds the ability to scroll its own contents. It exposes properties such as AutoScrollPosition and methods such as ScrollControlIntoView. The Panel control—which replaces the Visual Basic 6 Frame control—inherits directly from the ScrollableControl class.

The ContainerControl class represents an object that can contain other controls. It exposes properties such as ActiveControl and BindingContext, and the Validate method. The Form class inherits directly from the ContainerControl class.

Windows Forms Controls

The Visual Studio .NET 2003 Toolbox includes 47 controls, many of which are similar to their Visual Basic 6 counterparts and retain the same names (see Figure 15-4). The System.Windows.Forms.dll library includes a few other controls that don't appear on the Toolbox, such as the PropertyGrid control.

The Label, Button, TextBox, CheckBox, RadioButton, PictureBox, ListBox, ComboBox, HScrollBar, VScrollBar, and Timer controls are virtually identical to the intrinsic controls in Visual Basic 6, but they often have additional features and different method syntax. CheckedListBox controls replace ListBox controls with the Style property set to 1-CheckBox. The old Frame control is gone and has been replaced by two new controls: GroupBox and Panel. Both these controls work as containers for other controls, but the Panel control is also scrollable. In a difference from previous Visual Basic versions, you now have two explicit menu controls: MainMenu and ContextMenu.

The majority of Windows Common Controls are available in the default Toolbox. This group includes the following controls (names in parentheses are the old Visual Basic 6 versions): ImageList, ListView, TreeView, ProgressBar, TrackBar (SlideBar), RichTextBox, TabControl (TabStrip), ToolBar, StatusBar, DateTimePicker, and MonthCalendar (MonthView).

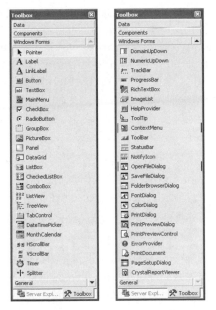

Figure 15-4   All the Windows Forms controls as they appear in the Visual Studio Toolbox

The new NumericUpDown control replaces the combination of a TextBox control and an UpDown control. The new DomainUpDown is like a single-row list box. The DataGrid control has more or less the same functionality as the old control of the same name. The Visual Basic 6 CommonDialog control has been replaced by six more specific controls: OpenFileDialog, SaveFileDialog, FontDialog, ColorDialog, PrintDialog, and PageSetupDialog. Version 1.1 of the .NET Framework added a new common dialog control, the FolderBrowserDialog control.

There are also a few brand-new controls. The LinkLabel control is an enhanced label control that can be used to implement Web-like hyperlinks to other portions of the application or to URLs on the Internet. The Splitter control lets you create resizeable regions on your form. The NotifyIcon control enables your program to create those little icons in the Windows taskbar and to react to mouse actions on them.

The PrintPreviewDialog control works together with the PrintPreviewControl object to provide a WYSIWYG preview of printed documents. You can simplify actual printing operations by using the PrintControl object, and you can create complex reports using the CrystalReportViewer control.

Finally, there are three controls known as *extender provider controls* because they augment the functionality of other controls on the form. The ToolTip control displays a ToolTip message when the mouse hovers over any other control. The HelpProvider control provides help functionality (and therefore replaces the help functionality in the CommonDialog control). The ErrorProvider control can display a red icon beside controls that don't pass input validation.

A few Visual Basic 6 controls are no longer available, including DriveList, DirListBox, FileListBox, OLE container, UpDown, Animation, the two flat scroll bars, MSFlexGrid, and a bunch of others. The Windows Forms library doesn't support windowless controls, which explains why the Line and Shape controls are no longer supported. The Image control is also gone, but its lightweight capabilities have been embedded in the new PictureBox control. All the Data, RDO Data, and ADO Data controls have been dumped.

Common Tasks for Forms and Controls

Before I discuss the Form object in detail, it makes sense to illustrate how you can use many of the properties, methods, and events that forms and controls have in common. Once you're familiar with the philosophy that underlies Windows Forms, learning more advanced features specific to form and control objects is considerably easier.

> **See Also**   Many of the programming techniques that are applicable to Visual Basic 6 forms are still valid and valuable under Visual Basic .NET, even though in most cases you'll have to account for the different names of properties and methods. You can review these techniques in Chapter 9 of the *Programming Microsoft Visual Basic 6* book, on the companion CD.

Working with Text and Colors

Visual Basic 6 makes a distinction between the text that a control displays and the text that the end user can edit in the control. It uses the Caption property for the former type of text and the Text property for the latter. Visual Basic .NET gets rid of this distinction, and all the controls that display a string of characters expose just one property, Text. For example, the following statement (inside a form class) changes the caption of the form itself:

```
Me.Text = "A new caption for this form"
```

The same change applies to other .NET controls that have a Caption property in previous versions of Visual Basic, such as Button, CheckBox, and RadioButton.

Some controls—most notably Label, TextBox, Button, CheckBox, RadioButton, NumericUpDown, and DomainUpDown—support the TextAlign property, which specifies where the string is displayed in the control. You can set the alignment in a visual way by using the Properties window, or by means of code, as in this snippet:

```
' Center the string in the Label control.
Label1.TextAlign = ContentAlignment.MiddleCenter
```

Only the Label, Button, CheckBox, and RadioButton controls support all the nine variations offered by the ContentAlignment enumerated type. The remaining controls support only horizontal text alignment and use the HorizontalAlignment enumeration:

```
' Align the TextBox contents to the right.
TextBox1.TextAlign = HorizontalAlignment.Right
```

All visible controls expose the ForeColor and BackColor properties. As in Visual Basic 6, you can assign a value to these properties from the Properties window, selecting the new color from the Custom palette, the System palette, or the new Web palette (see Figure 15-5). What has changed from previous versions is how you can define a new color in code by using shared methods of the System.Drawing.Color class. First, you can use the FromArgb method if you know the red, green, and blue components of the value you're assigning:

```
' This is the color orange.
TextBox1.BackColor = Color.FromArgb(255, 16, 0)
```

The Color class has several shared properties that return common colors, so you can rewrite the preceding statement as follows:

```
' This is the color orange.
TextBox1.BackColor = Color.Orange
```

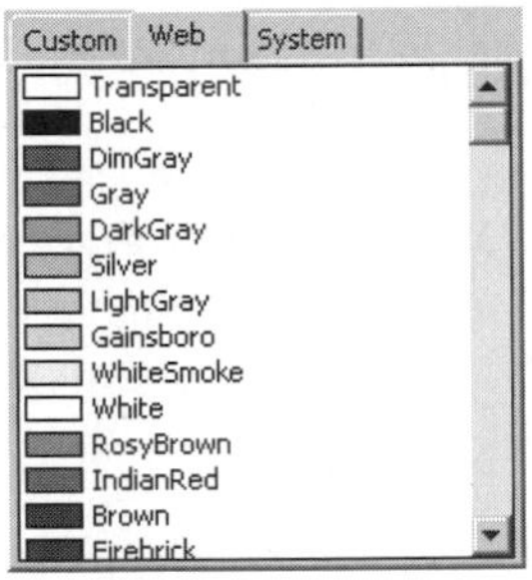

Figure 15-5   The new Web color palette

Most common colors are gathered in the KnownColor enumerated type, so you can easily create a list from which the end user can pick a color—for example, by using a ComboBox control:

```
' No loop is needed if you use the Items collection's AddRange method.
cboColors.Items.AddRange([Enum].GetNames(GetType(KnownColor)))
```

When the user selects a color, you can update your user interface element (such as the background color of a TextBox control) by using the Color.FromName shared method:

```
Private Sub cboColors_SelectedIndexChanged(ByVal sender As Object, _
    ByVal e As System.EventArgs) Handles cboColors.SelectedIndexChanged
    TextBox1.BackColor = Color.FromName(cboColors.Text)
End Sub
```

(This is the approach used in the demo program shown in Figure 15-6.) Once you have a Color value, you can extract its red, green, and blue components by using the R, G, and B methods:

```
' Display the three components' values in a label.
Dim c As Color = TextBox1.BackColor
lblColors.Text = String.Format("Red={0}, Green={1}, Blue={2}", c.R, c.G, c.B)
```

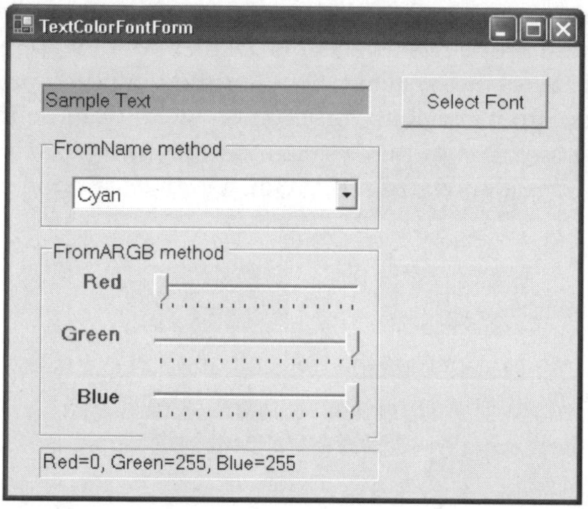

Figure 15-6   The TextColorFontForm dialog box in the demo program

Working with Fonts

Old-style Font*xxxx* properties, such as FontName and FontSize, are no longer available. All Visual Basic .NET controls that can display text expose a Font property, to which you assign a System.Drawing.Font object. You can assign individual font properties at design time after expanding the Font node in the Properties window. (See Figure 15-7.)

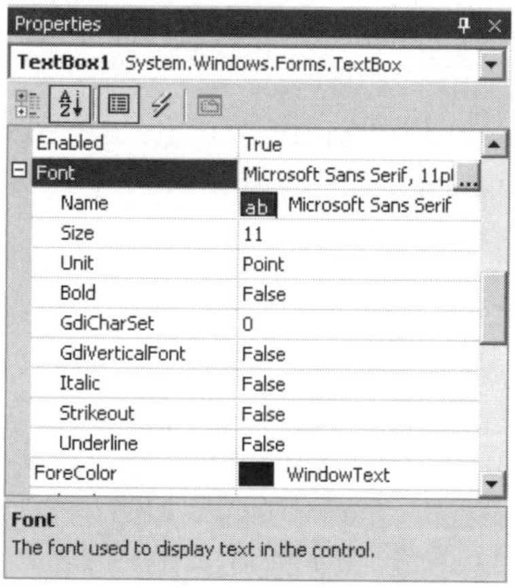

Figure 15-7   Setting Font properties in the Properties window at design time

The Font class exposes all the properties that you would expect, plus a few new ones. The Unit property indicates the unit of measure used for the Size property and can be one of the following GraphicsUnit enumerated values: Point, Pixel, Inch, Millimeter, Display, Document, and World. (See the "Transformations" section in Chapter 17 for additional information about each unit of measure.)

In an important difference from the way you used fonts in Visual Basic 6, you can't modify a font attribute after you create a new font. In fact, properties such as Size, Height, Bold, Italic, Underline, Strikeout, and Style are read-only, and you can assign them only in the constructor method, which is overloaded to provide 13 different syntax forms that let you specify any possible combination of attributes:

```
' Font name, size, and style
TextBox1.Font = New Font("Arial", 12, FontStyle.Bold Or FontStyle.Italic)
' Font name, size, and unit
TextBox1.Font = New Font("Tahoma", 20, GraphicsUnit.Millimeter)
```

The following code shows how you can increase the size of a control's font by 30 percent without affecting any other property:

```
With TextBox1
    .Font = New Font(.Font.Name, .Font.Size * 1.3, .Font.Style, .Font.Unit)
End With
```

You can also use an existing font as a prototype and change only the style:

```
' Change the font to set Bold attribute.
TextBox1.Font = New Font(TextBox1.Font, TextBox1.Font.Style Or FontStyle.Bold)
' Toggle the italic attribute.
TextBox1.Font = New Font(TextBox1.Font, _
    TextBox1.Font.Style Xor FontStyle.Italic)
```

Another important difference from the Visual Basic 6 way of doing things is that all controls point to their parent form's font unless you set a different font for the control. This change means that if you change the form's font—either at design time or through code—all the controls will inherit the new font except the controls for which you set a custom font. If you want to assign a control the same form as its parent form, but you want to change either font without affecting the other, you must use the Clone method:

```
TextBox1.Font = Me.Font.Clone()
```

The easiest way to let the user select a font at run time is by means of the FontDialog control. For example, this code lets the user dynamically change the Font property of the TextBox1 control. As you see, it couldn't be simpler:

```
With FontDialog1
    ' Ensure that current font attributes are displayed.
    .Font = TextBox1.Font
    ' Display the Font dialog.
    If .ShowDialog() = DialogResult.OK Then
        ' If the user didn't cancel the dialog, assign the Font.
        TextBox1.Font = .Font
    End If
End With
```

Other properties of the FontDialog control let you define exactly what appears in the Font dialog, the minimum and maximum font size, whether styles can be modified, and so on. Read Chapter 16 for more information about the FontDialog control.

Working with Size and Position

You specify the size and position of both forms and controls by using objects such as Size and Point instead of scalar properties such as Left, Top, Width, and Height (the old-style properties are still supported, though). Controls also expose the new Bottom and Right properties, which are handy if you want to avoid simple but annoying calculations. By default, size and position are measured in pixels, not twips. The size of all visible controls corresponds to a System.Drawing.Size object, so you can resize a control by making a single assignment:

```
' Make PictureBox1 300 pixels wide and 200 pixels high.
PictureBox1.Size = New Size(300, 200)
' Make PictureBox2 as large as PictureBox1.
PictureBox2.Size = PictureBox1.Size
```

You can't change Width, Height, and other properties of the Size object because they're read-only. The only way to change a control's size is to assign it a brand-new Size object. You can also assign a value to the control's Width or Height property, but this technique doesn't deliver better performance.

You assign a position to a control by assigning a System.Drawing.Point object to the control's Location property. The Point object exposes the X and Y properties, which correspond to the old-style Left and Top properties, respectively:

```
' Move PictureBox1 at coordinates (450, 230).
PictureBox1.Location = New Point(450, 230)
' Move TextBox1 over PictureBox1 so that their upper left corners coincide.
TextBox1.Location = PictureBox1.Location
```

Windows Forms controls (and the Form object itself) expose a SetBounds method, which lets you set both position and size in one operation. This method is virtually identical to the Visual Basic 6 Move method:

```
' Move PictureBox1 to the form's upper left corner, and resize it.
PictureBox1.SetBounds(0, 0, 300, 200)
```

Several other properties relate to size and position. For example, Bounds is a System.Drawing.Rectangle object that represents the external border of the control; ClientRectangle is the Rectangle object that represents the internal area; ClientSize is the Size object that represents the dimension of the internal area. These properties let you perform sophisticated operations with surprisingly little code, as you see here:

```
' Expand PictureBox1 to cover the form's client area.
PictureBox1.Bounds = Me.ClientRectangle

' As before, but leave a 10-pixel margin near the left and right
' edges of the PictureBox control, and an 8-pixel margin near the
' top and bottom edges.
Dim rect As Rectangle = Me.ClientRectangle
```

```
' Arguments are negative because we are deflating the rectangle.
rect.Inflate(-10, -8)
PictureBox1.Bounds = rect
```

ClientSize is assignable, so you assign it a value to resize the form:

```
' Resize the current form so that its client area
' is 500 pixels wide and 300 pixels high.
Me.ClientSize = New Size(500, 300)
```

Working with Docked and Anchored Controls

A frequent difficulty in creating a good user interface is correctly moving and resizing all the controls on a form when the end user resizes the form itself. As a matter of fact, several third-party vendors have proposed smart resizer controls that do this job with minimal code on your part. Windows Forms controls offer a nice solution to this problem in the Dock and Anchor properties that all of them expose.

The Dock property lets you dock a control at its container's border, so it's virtually identical to the Visual Basic 6 Align property, but with this important difference: all Windows Forms controls expose the Dock property, so all controls are dockable. At design time, you can select the border at which the control is docked in the Properties window, as shown in Figure 15-8. You can also click the square in the middle to dock the control to all four borders. In this case, the control always covers the entire client area of its container.

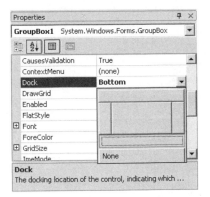

Figure 15-8 Setting the Dock property at design time

Setting the Dock property via code is also very simple:

```
' Have the PictureBox1 control be resized to cover the entire form.
PictureBox1.Dock = DockStyle.Fill
```

Remember that a control is docked to its container's internal border, and this container isn't necessarily the parent form.

The parent form's DockPadding property affects the distance between a docked control and the form's borders. You can assign this property at design time, or at run time via code. This property returns a DockPaddingEdges structure, and you can assign a value to its fields to set the same distance from all borders or a different distance from each border:

```
' All docked controls are 6 pixels from the form's edges.
Me.DockPadding.All = 6

' Controls docked at the bottom edge use a 4-pixel docking border.
Me.DockPadding.Bottom = 4
```

The DockPadding property is exposed also by the Panel control but not by the Group-Box control. So you can dock a control in a GroupBox, even though you can't specify the distance from the contained control and the GroupBox's border.

The Anchor property is the key to automatic control resizing. You set this property at design time by using the special selector shown in Figure 15-9 to select the container's edge to which this control is anchored. You can also choose to anchor a control to all of its container's edges or to none. When the parent form is resized, the distance between the control and the specified edges remains constant.

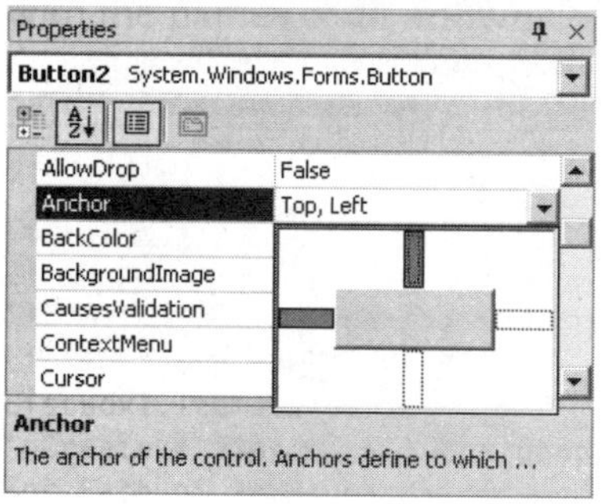

Figure 15-9   Setting the Anchor property at design time

By default, all controls are anchored to the left and top edges of their containers, which means that a control doesn't move or get resized when the container is resized. However, interesting things happen when you select a different combination of the anchored sides:

- If you anchor a control to the top and right edges (like the Save button in Figure 15-10), the control sticks to the right border of the form and moves horizontally when the form becomes wider or narrower.

- If you anchor a control to the right and bottom edges (like the Cancel and OK buttons in Figure 15-10), the control moves to maintain a fixed distance from the lower right corner when the form is resized.

- If you anchor a control to the top, left, and right edges (like the single-line Text-Box control in Figure 15-10), the control changes its width when the form is resized horizontally.

- If you anchor a control to all four edges (like the multiline TextBox control in Figure 15-10), the control is resized when the form is resized.

If the control is anchored to neither the left nor the right edge, the control is resized and moved horizontally so that the ratio between its width and its container's width is constant. (Something similar happens if the control is anchored to neither the top nor the bottom edge.)

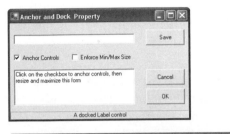

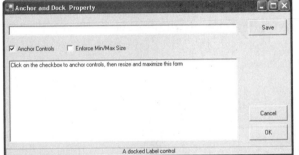

Figure 15-10 Automatic control resizing using the Anchor property

Of course, you can set the Anchor property by using code. For example, this is the code that resizes the form shown in Figure 15-10:

```
TextBox1.Anchor = AnchorStyles.Top Or AnchorStyles.Left Or AnchorStyles.Right
TextBox2.Anchor = AnchorStyles.Left Or AnchorStyles.Right Or _
    AnchorStyles.Top Or AnchorStyles.Bottom
Button1.Anchor = AnchorStyles.Top Or AnchorStyles.Right
Button2.Anchor = AnchorStyles.Bottom Or AnchorStyles.Right
Button3.Anchor = AnchorStyles.Bottom Or AnchorStyles.Right
```

Interestingly, if you set the Dock property in the Properties window, the control is correctly moved or resized at design time as well, which makes it simple to adjust the form layout when you add new controls.

When you're working with resizeable dialog boxes, you often need to set a minimum and maximum size for the form itself to prevent controls from overlapping one another when the form becomes too small. The only way to implement this feature under Visual Basic 6 requires subclassing wizardry (or the purchase of a third-party control).

In Visual Basic .NET, you merely have to assign a proper Size object to the form's MinimumSize and MaximumSize properties:

```
Me.MinimumSize = New Size(300, 240)
Me.MaximumSize = New Size(700, 460)
```

Setting these properties at design time is also simple. Resize the form to its smallest acceptable size, and then switch to the Properties window and copy the current value of the Size property into the MinimumSize property. Next resize the form to its largest acceptable size, and copy the Size property into the MaximumSize property.

Working with the Keyboard

At first glance, it seems that you deal with the keyboard under Visual Basic .NET as you did under Visual Basic 6, using the three events KeyDown, KeyUp, and KeyPress. But as you'll see in a moment, you have to account for a few important differences.

Like all Windows Forms events, the KeyPress event receives two arguments. The sender argument is a reference to the object that raised the event; for this event, the e argument is a KeyPressEventArgs object that exposes only two properties: Handled and KeyChar. As you might guess, KeyChar is the character corresponding to the key pressed, and Handled is a Boolean value that you can set to True to tell the form engine that you've processed the event and that the engine should take no further action regarding the key being pressed. For example, let's say that you have a numeric field and you want to discard all keys except digits and control keys. This task is simple, thanks to the Handled property and a couple of shared methods of the Char class:

```
Private Sub txtNumber_KeyPress(ByVal sender As Object, _
    ByVal e As KeyPressEventArgs) Handles txtNumber.KeyPress
    If Not (Char.IsDigit(e.KeyChar) Or Char.IsControl(e.KeyChar)) Then
        ' If the character is neither a digit nor a control character,
        ' tell the form engine to ignore it.
        e.Handled = True
    End If
End Sub
```

In other cases, you use the KeyPress event to change the character being typed by the user. A typical example is when you want to convert all keys to uppercase. In a difference from Visual Basic 6, however, the character code is read-only, so you can't simply assign it a new value. A solution to this problem, which works with TextBox and ComboBox controls, consists of inserting the (modified) character yourself rather than having the form engine do it. The following code shows an example of a TextBox control that converts all keys to uppercase:

```
Private Sub txtUpperCase_KeyPress(ByVal sender As Object, _
    ByVal e As KeyPressEventArgs) Handles txtUpperCase.KeyPress
    ' Replace the selected text with an uppercase character.
    ' (Inserts at caret position if no text is selected.)
```

```
    txtUpperCase.SelectedText = e.KeyChar.ToString.ToUpper
    ' Cancel standard processing.
    e.Handled = True
End Sub
```

The KeyDown and KeyUp events fire when a key is pressed and released. (KeyDown can fire repeatedly if the key is being pressed, but only one KeyUp event fires in this case.) The second argument passed to this event is a KeyEventArgs object, which exposes the following properties: Alt, Shift, Control (the state of shift keys), Modifiers (the state of shift keys as a bit-coded value), KeyCode (the key being pressed or released, as a Keys-enumerated value), and KeyValue (the numeric code of the key). As in other events, the Handled property is a Boolean value to which you should assign True if you handle the event yourself. This example shows how you can detect a function key:

```
' Insert the current date into a TextBox control
' when the user presses Shift+F2.
Private Sub txtDate_KeyDown(ByVal sender As Object, _
    ByVal e As KeyEventArgs) Handles txtDate.KeyDown
    If e.Shift And (e.KeyCode = Keys.F2) Then
        txtDate.SelectedText = Today.Date.ToString
        e.Handled = True
    End If
End Sub
```

You might find it interesting to know that setting the Handled property to True inside a KeyDown event handler discards arrow keys and function keys but not printable keys (such as letters and digits). You don't need to be inside a keyboard event procedure to determine the current state of shift keys because you can use the Control.ModifierKeys shared method anywhere in a form module.

The HelpRequested event fires when the end user presses the F1 key inside the control:

```
' Display a message box when the user presses the F1 key.
Private Sub txtDate_HelpRequested(ByVal sender As Object, _
    ByVal e As HelpEventArgs) Handles txtDate.HelpRequested
    MessageBox.Show("Insert a date", "Help Requested", _
        MessageBoxButtons.OK, MessageBoxIcon.Information)
End Sub
```

Working with the Mouse

Visual Basic .NET offers far better support for mouse handling than Visual Basic 6. The three standard events MouseDown, MouseMove, and MouseUp are complemented by the new MouseWheel event, which fires when the mouse wheel is rotated. All these events receive rich information about the mouse status in a MouseEventArgs object:

- The Button property is a bit-coded value that tells which mouse buttons are pressed. The MouseButtons enumerated type supports the five-button Microsoft IntelliMouse Explorer mouse under Windows 2000, Windows XP, and Windows Server 2003. (You can get the same information from anywhere in the form module by using the Control.MouseButtons shared property.)

- X and Y are the current mouse coordinates in pixels and relative to the current control's upper left corner. (You can get the same information from anywhere in the form module with the Control.MousePosition shared property.)

- Clicks is the number of clicks since the last event.

- Delta is the number of detents the mouse wheel has been rotated since the last event. A positive value means the wheel was rotated forward, while a negative value means the wheel was rotated backward. (In the current version, this value is always a multiple of 120.)

No information about shift keys is provided directly to mouse events, but you can retrieve this piece of information by using the Control.ModifierKeys shared property. The following code shows how a single routine can serve all the main mouse events for a form, and it displays the mouse state in a Label control:

```
Private Sub Form_MouseEvent(ByVal sender As Object, _
    ByVal e As MouseEventArgs) Handles MyBase.MouseDown, _
    MyBase.MouseUp, MyBase.MouseMove, MyBase.MouseWheel
    lblInfo.Text = _
        String.Format("Mouse: Buttons={0} X={1} Y={2} Clicks={3} Delta={4}", _
        e.Button, e.X, e.Y, e.Clicks, e.Delta)
End Sub
```

All controls support the Click and DoubleClick mouse events, which behave much like the corresponding events under Visual Basic 6. They don't receive any additional information, but you can retrieve mouse position and button state using the MousePosition and MouseButtons shared properties of the Control object. Note that the Click event isn't fired when the user selects an element of a ListBox or ComboBox control with the keyboard. (In this case, a SelectedIndexChanged event is fired instead.)

All Windows Forms controls inherit three more mouse events from the Control class: MouseHover, MouseEnter, and MouseExit. The first event fires when the mouse pointer hovers over a control and is therefore similar to the MouseMove event. The other two events fire when the mouse cursor enters and exits a control's border and are especially useful for making a control react to the mouse hovering over it (as commonly happens with hyperlinks on Web pages) or for displaying a help message related to the control under the mouse. For example, these two routines change the background of one Textbox to yellow when the mouse enters the control's area and restore it to white when the mouse leaves the control:

```
Private Sub MouseEnterEvent(ByVal sender As Object, ByVal e As EventArgs) _
    Handles txtNumber.MouseEnter, txtName.MouseEnter, txtDate.MouseEnter
    ' Must cast to Control to set the BackColor property.
    CType(sender, Control).BackColor = Color.Yellow
End Sub
```

```
Private Sub MouseLeaveEvent(ByVal sender As Object, ByVal e As EventArgs) _
    Handles txtNumber.MouseLeave, txtName.MouseLeave, txtDate.MouseLeave
    ' Must cast to Control to set the BackColor property.
    CType(sender, Control).BackColor = Color.White
End Sub
```

Thanks to the fact that you can link an event to a control at run time by using the AddHandler command, you can create a generic procedure that allows the MouseEnterEvent and MouseLeaveEvent procedures to serve all the controls on the current form or just all the controls of a given type:

```
Private Sub InitializeMouseEvents()
    For Each ctrl As Control In Me.Controls
        If (TypeOf ctrl Is TextBox) Or (TypeOf ctrl Is ComboBox) Then
            AddHandler ctrl.MouseEnter, AddressOf MouseEnterEvent
            AddHandler ctrl.MouseLeave, AddressOf MouseLeaveEvent
        End If
    Next
End Sub
```

The Control class exposes the Capture property, which is therefore inherited by the Form object and all the controls. When you assign True to this property, the control is said to *capture* the mouse. From this point on, the control receives all the mouse notifications and events—including MouseMove, MouseDown, MouseUp, and Mouse-Wheel—even if the cursor moves outside the control's client area. The mouse capture is released when you reset the Capture property to False or when the user clicks one of the mouse buttons.

Working with Input Focus

Little has changed in the way you deal with input focus in controls. For example, the Enabled, TabStop, and TabIndex properties are still supported. In a minor difference from Visual Basic 6, the form engine doesn't require that all controls have different values for their TabIndex property. In fact, this happens regularly if two controls are hosted in different container controls. If two controls in the same container have the same TabIndex value, the one with the higher Z-order—the one "closer" to the user if you prefer—gets the input focus before the other.

You can use the new CanFocus property to determine whether a given control can get the input focus (which happens if its Visible and Enabled properties are both True), and you can use the new Focused property to determine whether the control actually has the focus. You move the focus on a control by using the Focus method. You can use it together with another new method, GetNextControl, which returns the control visited immediately before or after another control in a given container when the user presses the Tab key. For example, the following routine handles the Down and Up arrow keys at the form level so that the end user can use these keys to move among fields in addition to Tab and Shift+Tab key combinations:

```
' This code assumes that Me.KeyPreview = True so that the form
' captures all keys before the currently active control.

Private Sub KeyboardMouseForm_KeyDown(ByVal sender As Object, _
    ByVal e As KeyEventArgs) Handles MyBase.KeyDown

    ' Move focus among controls with the Up/Down arrow keys.
    If Me.Controls.Count = 0 Then
        ' Ignore forms without any control.
    ElseIf e.KeyCode = Keys.Up Or e.KeyCode = Keys.Down Then
        ' Start at the currently selected control.
        Dim ctrl As Control = Me.ActiveControl
        ' Are we moving forward or backward?
        Dim moveForward As Boolean = (e.KeyCode = Keys.Down)
        Do
            ' Get the next control in that direction.
            ' (Returns Nothing if ctrl is the first control.)
            ctrl = Me.GetNextControl(ctrl, moveForward)
            If Not (ctrl Is Nothing) AndAlso ctrl.CanFocus _
                AndAlso ctrl.TabStop Then
                ' If the control can receive the focus, give it.
                ctrl.Focus()
                Exit Do
            End If
        Loop
    End If
End Sub
```

Visual Basic 6 supports only three events related to input focus: GotFocus, LostFocus, and Validate. The first two events are still supported in Visual Basic .NET, but you should use the new Enter and Leave events instead. The Validate event isn't supported any longer and has been replaced by an event pair, Validating and Validated. These are the events that fire whenever the user gives the focus to another control, such as Enter, GotFocus, Leave, Validating, Validated, and LostFocus.

The Validating and Validated events fire only if the CausesValidation property is set to True in both the control that has the focus and the control that's trying to get the focus. In general, you use the Validating event to trap invalid values in a field. If the control's value doesn't pass your validation routine, you simply set the Cancel property of the e argument to True:

```
Private Sub txtNumber_Validating(ByVal sender As Object, _
    ByVal e As System.ComponentModel.CancelEventArgs) _
    Handles txtNumber.Validating
    ' This is a required field, so reject null strings.
    If txtNumber.Text = "" Then e.Cancel = True
End Sub
```

If the validation fails, the focus is returned to the control that had it previously, and the Validated event and the final LostFocus event don't fire.

The new input focus management has resolved a few quirks in the previous version. For example, the LostFocus and Validate events also fire if the user activates the default pushbutton on the form by pressing the Enter key (or the default Cancel button by pressing the Esc key), which isn't the case under Visual Basic 6.

Not all the oddities in Visual Basic 6 have been purged, though. You can easily prove this by creating three TextBox controls named TextBox1, TextBox2, and TextBox3. Set the TextBox2.CausesValidation property to False so that when you press the Tab key on the first box, the TextBox1_Validating event doesn't fire. If you press the Tab key a second time, the focus should move to TextBox3. Because this control's CausesValidation property is True, Visual Basic .NET fires the pending TextBox1_Validating event. If this event cancels the focus shift, the focus will return to TextBox1—a rather disorienting behavior for your end user. You can test this behavior with the demo application, shown in Figure 15-11.

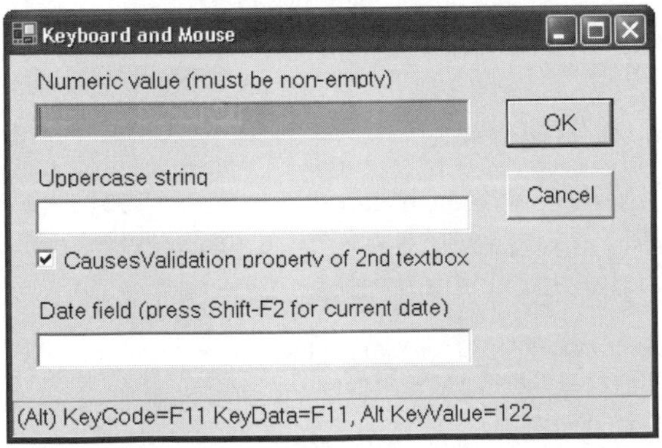

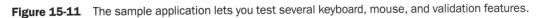

Figure 15-11 The sample application lets you test several keyboard, mouse, and validation features.

Working with Container Controls

A few objects in the Windows Forms portion of the Framework—most notably, the Form object, the Panel control, and the GroupBox control—inherit from the Container-Control class and can therefore work as containers for other objects. The most relevant difference between the Panel control and the GroupBox control is that the former is also scrollable, whereas the latter has a border and a caption. (Notice that the Picture-Box control isn't a container any longer; you should use a Panel control instead.) Containers have a few specific properties and methods, which I'll describe in this section.

All container controls (and the Form object itself) have a Controls collection that you can parse to enumerate contained objects. This collection contains only the top-level objects, not objects owned by the contained objects. Let's make an example to clarify this point. Suppose you have a form with two GroupBox controls, which in turn contain some RadioButton objects, as in the following hierarchy:

```
Form (Me)
    GroupBox1
        RadioButton1
        RadioButton2
    GroupBox2
        RadioButton3
        RadioButton4
        RadioButton5
```

In this case, the form's Controls collection contains only the two GroupBox controls:

```
Debug.WriteLine(Me.Controls.Count)            ' => 2
Debug.WriteLine(GroupBox1.Controls.Count)     ' => 2
Debug.WriteLine(GroupBox2.Controls.Count)     ' => 3
```

Having separate Controls collections means that you don't have to test all the controls on the form to determine which ones are inside a given container, as you have to do under earlier versions of Visual Basic. You don't even have to scan the Controls collection of a container to determine whether it contains a specific control because you can take advantage of the Contains method:

```
Debug.WriteLine(GroupBox1.Contains(RadioButton1))    ' => True
```

The Visual Basic 6 Container property has been renamed Parent (it returns a reference to the container), whereas the old Parent property has been replaced by the FindForm method (it returns a reference to the containing form):

```
Debug.WriteLine(RadioButton1.Parent.Name)     ' => GroupBox1
Debug.WriteLine(RadioButton1.FindForm Is Me)  ' => True
```

You can also retrieve a reference to a child control located at given coordinates inside the container, using the GetChildAtPoint method:

```
' Determine the child control at coordinates (30, 50) inside GroupBox1.
Dim ctrl As Control = GroupBox1.GetChildAtPoint(New Point(30, 50))
If ctrl Is Nothing Then
    Debug.WriteLine("No child control at this position")
Else
    Debug.WriteLine("Child control is " & ctrl.Name)
End If
```

Finally, you can use the Scale method to move and resize one or more controls in a container. This method is inherited from Control and is therefore exposed by all controls, but I discuss it here because it's usually applied to containers. Its effect is to change the size and dimensions of a control by a scaling factor that you specify. You can specify two distinct factors for the X and Y axes, as in this code:

```
' Double both coordinates and size of a control.
RadioButton1.Scale(2, 2)
```

The great feature of this method is that it applies the transformation to all contained controls if there are any. Even better, if one of the contained controls is a container, the scaling applies to the contained control's children, and so on in a recursive fashion. This means that you can resize a form *and* all its controls using just one statement:

```
' Stretch a form by 30 percent horizontally and 20 percent vertically.
Me.Scale(1.3, 1.2)
```

Fortunately, the Scale method resizes a form but doesn't move it. (If an enlarged form also moved, it might fall outside the visible portion of the desktop.)

Working with ActiveX Controls

You aren't limited to using Windows Forms controls in your .NET applications; in fact, you can reuse ActiveX controls as well, even though their performance isn't optimal and their use is discouraged. To import an ActiveX control, select the Toolbox tab where you want to place the control, right-click the Toolbox and click Customize Toolbox, and then select the COM components you want to import.

For example, you might want to import the Microsoft WebBrowser control to let users browse the Internet from inside your .NET applications. Importing an ActiveX control creates a wrapper control named Ax*controlname*. For example, the WebBrowser control is imported as AxWebBrowser. All the properties are accessible from inside the Properties window, even though a few properties are unavailable because they are read-only at run time. These are the properties that don't appear in the Visual Basic 6 Properties window. A few properties—namely those added by the Visual Basic 6 environment, such as DragIcon and DragMode—are missing. On the other hand, you'll find the new properties that .NET adds to all Windows Forms controls, such as Anchor, Dock, Location, and Size. The (Custom) item that you used under Visual Basic 6 to bring up the property pages associated with the ActiveX control is gone, but you can display those property pages by clicking on the ActiveX Properties link that appears at the bottom of the Visual Studio .NET Properties window.

When a property has the same name as a property or a method that the .NET default designer adds to all .NET controls—such as Visible or Refresh—it's prefixed by *Ctl* to avoid name clashing. (So you have the CtlVisible property and the CtlRefresh method.) Except for these minor details, you code against an imported ActiveX control as you would do with a regular .NET control.

You can also create an assembly for any ActiveX control from outside Visual Studio by using the Windows Forms ActiveX Control Importer tool (Aximp.exe). This tool generates a set of assemblies for all the ActiveX controls and all the COM components contained in the specified library. For example, you can run Aximp against the DLL that contains the WebBrowser control:

```
aximp c:\windows\system32\shdocvw.dll
```

The preceding command generates two assemblies: SHDocVw.dll for the component and AxSHDocVw.dll for the ActiveX control. (You shouldn't run Aximp in the same directory as the source DLL because you might accidentally overwrite the DLL. Or use the /out option to select a different output file.)

ActiveX controls can be used in .NET because Visual Studio or Aximp automatically creates a wrapper class for them. Such a wrapper class inherits from System.Windows.Forms.AxHost. You can use the /source option of Aximp to generate the C# source code for the wrapper class:

```
aximp c:\windows\system32\shdocvw.dll /source
```

Should the need arise, you can edit this source code and recompile it. You might need to edit and recompile—for example, if you want to change the control name, add new properties, or hide a few items in the Properties window.

Unfortunately, you can't successfully import any type of ActiveX control. For example, the Windows Forms portion of the Framework doesn't support windowless controls, so you can't use the Line and Shape controls, and any controls in the Windowless Control Library (WinLess.ocx) and the Microsoft Forms 2.0 control library (FM20.Dll). Some ActiveX controls can be imported but don't always work correctly on a Visual Basic .NET form—for example, SSTab, UpDown, and Coolbar. You can replace a horizontal or vertical Line control with a Label control whose Height or Width property is set to one pixel and whose BorderStyle property is set to FixedSingle, but in all other cases you must be prepared for more substantial changes in your code.

The Form Object

The Form object derives from the ContainerControl object, which in turn derives from ScrollableControl and ultimately from Control, so working with forms is similar to working with a control. For example, you can count on properties such as Text, Size, and Location, and you can apply most of the concepts I illustrated earlier in this chapter. Of course, forms are more complicated and richer in functionality than controls and deserve a thorough discussion in a section of their own.

It's interesting to see the life cycle of a form in terms of the events it fires:

1. **New**   The form object is created.

2. **Load**   The form is being loaded but is still invisible.

3. **Paint**   The form is being painted. This event can fire several times in the form's lifetime.

4. **Activated**   The form is receiving the focus. This event replaces the Enter event exposed by the Control object.

5. **Deactivate**   The form is losing the input focus. This event replaces the Leave event exposed by the Control object.

6. **Closing**   The form is being closed. This event corresponds to the Visual Basic 6 Unload event.

7. **Closed**   The form has been closed and is now invisible.

8. **Dispose**   The form object is being destroyed.

Common Form Tasks

Let's see how to put all the form's properties, methods, and events to good use.

Moving and Resizing the Form

You can move and resize a form as you do a control—that is, by assigning a Point object to the Location property, a Size object to the Size property, or a Rectangle object to the Bounds property. (You might want to review the "Working with Size and Position" section earlier in this chapter.) The Form object, however, offers a few additional capabilities in this area.

The DesktopBounds and DesktopLocation properties are similar to the Bounds and Location properties, except that they refer to the working area of the screen, which is the screen area not occupied by an always-visible task bar:

```
' Move the form to the upper left corner of the screen's working area.
Me.DesktopLocation = New Point(0, 0)
```

The Windows.Forms.Screen object represents one of the screens that a Windows system can support, and its Screen.PrimaryScreen shared method returns a reference to the main screen object:

```
' Expand the form to cover the entire screen's working area.
Me.DesktopBounds = Screen.PrimaryScreen.WorkingArea
```

You can get the same results using the SetDesktopLocation and SetDesktopBounds methods, which take multiple individual coordinates and size values:

```
' Move the form to the upper left corner of the screen's working area.
Me.SetDesktopLocation(0, 0)
```

```
' Move and resize the form so that it takes the upper right
' quadrant of the screen's working area.
With Screen.PrimaryScreen.WorkingArea
    Me.SetDesktopBounds(.Width \ 2, 0, .Width \ 2, .Height \ 2)
End With
```

Centering a form doesn't require that you do any math; just use the CenterToScreen or CenterToParent method in code. Or you can set the StartupPosition property to the appropriate value at design time, using the Properties window.

Creating a topmost form—that is, a form that's always in front of other forms belonging to the same application—is a breeze under Visual Basic .NET, thanks to the TopMost property. Like most properties in the Windows Forms namespace, the TopMost property can be assigned in the Properties window or by means of code:

```
' Load another form, and make it the topmost form for the application.
Dim frm As New frmPalette
frm.TopMost = True
frm.Show
```

As I explained in the "Working with Docked and Anchored Controls" section earlier in this chapter, you can limit how small or large a form can be by using the MinimumSize and MaximumSize properties. To make it clear to the end user that a form can be resized, you can make sure that the form's sizing grip in the lower right corner is always visible by setting the SizeGripStyle property to the SizeGripStyle.Show value.

Creating Scrollable Forms

If a form contains many controls, you can choose from a couple of ways to make your user interface less cluttered: tabbed dialog boxes or scrollable forms. Tabbed dialogs are a popular way to concentrate a lot of controls in a reduced screen area, but scrollable forms are probably a better choice in several situations, especially now that users have a habit of scrolling long HTML pages in their browsers.

Creating a scrollable form has become an easy task in Visual Basic .NET. All you have to do is set the form's AutoScroll property to True, either at design time or at run time. When the user (or your code) resizes the form in a way that would make one of its controls partly invisible, the form displays a horizontal or vertical scroll bar, as appropriate. (See Figure 15-12.)

A few other properties and methods are useful when you're working with scrollable forms. The AutoScrollMargin property is a Size object that determines the width and the height of the invisible border drawn around each control on the form. When this border is covered by the form's edges because of a resize operation, the form displays one or both scroll bars. By default, this invisible border is 0 pixels wide and tall, but you can select a different value for this property if you want.

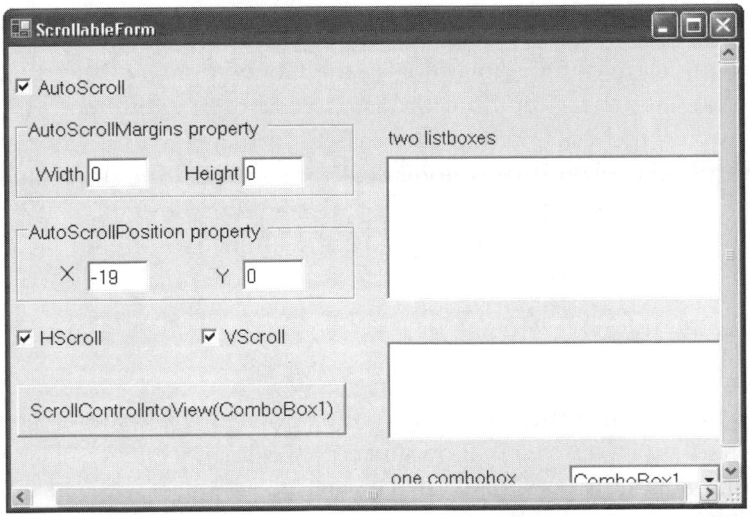

Figure 15-12 Fields and buttons in the ScrollableForm application let you test the properties and methods related to scrollable forms.

The AutoScrollPosition property is a Point object that tells you whether the form has been scrolled and in which direction. The X and Y properties of this Point object always take negative values. For example, if Me.AutoScrollPosition.X is equal to -20, it means that the user scrolled the form 20 pixels to the right. You can also assign a new Point object to this property to scroll the form programmatically, as in this code:

```
' Scroll the form so that the pixel at (100, 40)
' appears at the upper left corner.
Me.AutoScrollPosition = New Point(-100, -40)
```

You can read the HScroll and VScroll Boolean properties to determine whether either scroll bar is currently visible. The only method that has to do with scrolling is Scroll-ControlIntoView, which ensures that a given control is in the visible area of the form and scrolls the form accordingly:

```
Me.ScrollControlIntoView(ComboBox1)
```

No specific event fires when the end user scrolls the form. If you want to perform an action when this happens, you can use the Paint event. The demo application in Figure 15-12 uses this event to update the fields labeled X and Y inside the AutoScrollPosition Property GroupBox control.

Showing Forms

You select the startup form of the application in the General page of the project Property Pages dialog box, much as you do with Visual Basic 6. In a difference from previous versions, however, the .NET startup form has a peculiar feature: when you close the startup form, all other forms are automatically closed and the application terminates. You don't have to select the startup form at design time; instead, you can opt for the Sub Main procedure as the starting object and then use the Application.Run method to run the startup form:

```
Dim frm As New StartupForm
Application.Run(frm)
```

You must bring up all the other forms in your program by using the Show or ShowDialog method after you create an instance of the form itself. Visual Basic .NET doesn't support the default form variable that Visual Basic 6 uses, so you must create a variable of the appropriate type:

```
' Show the form as a modeless window.
Dim frm As New CalleeForm
frm.Show
```

The Show method is inherited from the Control class and doesn't take any arguments, so you can use it only to display modeless forms. The new form doesn't stop the execution flow of the caller code, and the end user can freely switch between the new form and any other form in the application. This arrangement raises a couple of interesting questions. First, how can the caller code determine when the callee form is closed? Second, how can the caller code retrieve values currently held in the callee's controls?

The answer to the first question is simple: all forms raise a Closing event when they're about to be closed, so the caller code can trap this event by declaring a WithEvents variable pointing to the form or by using the AddHandler command to bind a procedure to the Closing event. Here's an example of the latter technique:

```
Sub ShowTheModelessForm()
    ' Declare and create the Form object.
    Dim frm As New CalleeForm()
    ' Set up a handler for the Closing event and show the form.
    AddHandler frm.Closing, AddressOf CalleeForm_Closing
    frm.Show()
End Sub

Sub CalleeForm_Closing(ByVal sender As Object, _
    ByVal e As System.ComponentModel.CancelEventArgs)
    ' Cast the first argument to a specific object.
    Dim frm As CalleeForm = DirectCast(sender, CalleeForm)
    ' Use a label control to display the value of a field in CalleeForm.
    lblMessage.Text = "UserName = " & frm.txtUserName.Text
End Sub
```

So that you can read the contents of controls placed on the callee form's surface, the controls in the callee form must be non-Private. You decide the scope of a control by setting the Modifiers property in the Properties window. This property can be Public, Protected, Friend, or Private. Because the default value for this property is Friend, you have to worry about this detail only if your form is going to be used from another assembly.

However, for a cleaner object-oriented design and better data encapsulation, you might decide to use a narrower scope for your controls—for example, Private. (Or you might use Protected if you plan to use the form as a base class for inherited forms, as I'll explain in the section "Form Inheritance" in this chapter.) Using a narrower scope is usually a wiser decision because you don't expose details of your form class to the outside and you can later change its internal implementation—for example, by replacing a TextBox control with a ComboBox control—without any impact on code that creates and uses instances of the form. Another benefit of not exposing controls to the outside world is that caller code can't accidentally enter invalid values in the controls.

If you use private controls, you must provide the caller code with a way to read their contents. You can do this easily by wrapping the controls in a property procedure, as in this code:

```
' ...(In the CalleeForm code module)...
Property UserName() As String
    Get
        Return txtUserName.Text
    End Get
    Set(ByVal Value As String)
        txtUserName.Text = Value
    End Set
End Property
```

Of course, you can use read-only properties if you want to prevent the caller form from assigning a value to these controls. The code in the CalleeForm_Closing procedure becomes

```
Dim frm As CalleeForm = CType(sender, CalleeForm)
lblMessage.Text = "Name = " & frm.UserName
```

Working with Owned Forms

The Windows operating system supports the concept of *owned forms*. If a form owns another form, the owned form always will be displayed in front of its owner form, no matter which is the active form (see Figure 15-13). This arrangement makes owned forms ideal for implementing tool and palette windows. In another feature of owned forms, all the owned forms are also closed or minimized when the user closes or minimizes the owner form. When minimized, the owner form and all its owned forms count as one icon in the Windows task bar.

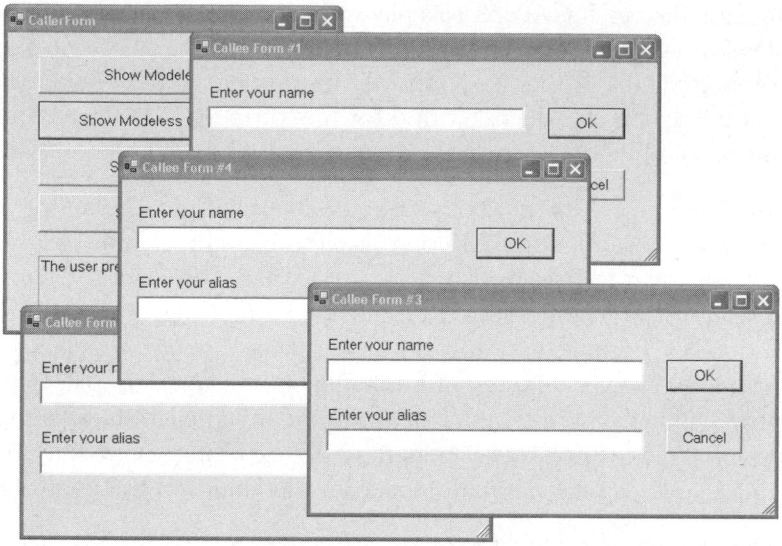

Figure 15-13   A group of owned forms; note that all forms are in front of their owner form (upper left corner), even if the owner form is the active form.

You declare that the callee form is owned by the caller form by invoking the Add-OwnedForm method:

```
' Create a form and add it to the list of owned forms.
Dim frm As New CalleeForm()
Me.AddOwnedForm(frm)
frm.Show()
```

The Owner property allows a form to detect whether it's owned by another form. A form can enumerate its owned forms by iterating over the collection returned by the OwnedForms property:

```
If Me.Owner Is Nothing Then
    Debug.WriteLine ("No owner form for this form")
Else
    Debug.WriteLine("Owned by form " & Me.Owner.Text)
End If

Debug.WriteLine("List of owned forms:")
For Each frm As Form In Me.OwnedForms
    Debug.WriteLine(frm.Text)
Next
```

You can change the ownership status of an owned form by removing it from its owner's OwnedForms collection using the RemoveOwnedForm method.

Displaying Message Boxes and Dialog Boxes

Visual Basic .NET still supports the old-style MsgBox command (defined in the Microsoft.VisualBasic namespace), but you might want to use the newer MessageBox object and its Show method:

```
Dim res As DialogResult
res = MessageBox.Show("File not found", "A MessageBox example", _
    MessageBoxButtons.AbortRetryIgnore, MessageBoxIcon.Error, _
    MessageBoxDefaultButton.Button1, _
    MessageBoxOptions.DefaultDesktopOnly)
lblMessage.Text = "The user clicked " & res.ToString
```

As you can see, the MessageBox.Show method doesn't require that you stuff multiple options in a bit-coded argument, as the original MsgBox command does. This approach makes for a cleaner and more readable (yet more verbose) syntax. All arguments after the first one are optional. The DialogResult enumerated type defines the seven possible return values from a message box.

If a predefined message box isn't enough for your needs, you must create a custom form with precisely the buttons and fields you need, and you must display it modally using the ShowDialog method instead of the Show method. You can pass values to the modal form and retrieve values from it, using the technique demonstrated in the preceding section. You don't have to set up an event handler to detect when the form is closed because the ShowDialog method doesn't return until the modal form is closed:

```
' Display a form modally.
Dim frm As New CalleeForm()
frm.ShowDialog()
' Display the value of a field in CalleeForm.
lblMessage.Text = "Name = " & frm.UserName
```

Most dialog forms, however, have multiple push buttons. Typically they have the OK and Cancel buttons, but you might also need Retry and Cancel buttons and many other combinations. In cases like this, you have to determine which action the end user selected. To make your job easier, the Form class defines a DialogResult public enumerated property, which can take the same values that a message box can return. You typically assign this property from inside the Click event procedure in the callee form:

```
Private Sub btnOK_Click(ByVal sender As Object, ByVal e As EventArgs) _
    Handles btnOK.Click
    Me.DialogResult = DialogResult.OK
    Me.Close
End Sub

Private Sub btnCancel_Click(ByVal sender As Object, ByVal e As EventArgs) _
    Handles btnCancel.Click
    Me.DialogResult = DialogResult.Cancel
    Me.Close
End Sub
```

An interesting detail: if your form is always used as a modal form, you don't need to explicitly close the form with a Me.Close method inside the Click event procedures because assigning a value to the DialogResult property suffices. Even better, if a button's Click procedure does nothing but set the DialogResult property, you don't even need to write the event procedure because you can assign this property to each Button control at design time, in the Property window. If the end user clicks a Button control whose DialogResult property has a value other than DialogResult.None, the form is always closed automatically and the DialogResult value is sent to the caller as the return value of the ShowDialog method.

So the typical code in the caller form becomes

```
' Create a Form object, display it modally, and test the result.
Dim frm As New CalleeForm()
If frm.ShowDialog() = DialogResult.OK Then
    ' The user clicked the OK button.
    lblMessage.Text = "Name = " & frm.UserName
Else
    ' The user canceled the dialog.
    lblMessage.Text = "The end user canceled the action"
End If
```

You can design a form so that it can be invoked in either modal or nonmodal mode. Visual Basic .NET forms expose a Modal property, which you can test to find out whether a form was displayed using a ShowDialog method. Say that you want to make a modal form nonresizeable. All you need are the statements in boldface near the end of the Sub New procedure:

```
Public Sub New()
    MyBase.New()
    ' This call is required by the Windows Form Designer.
    InitializeComponent()
    ' Add any initialization after the InitializeComponent() call.
    ' Different style and behavior, depending on whether the form is modal
    If Me.Modal Then
        Me.FormBorderStyle = FormBorderStyle.FixedDialog
    Else
        Me.FormBorderStyle = FormBorderStyle.Sizable
        Me.SizeGripStyle = SizeGripStyle.Show
    End If
End Sub
```

Two more form properties, AcceptButton and CancelButton, affect dialog boxes. Under previous versions of Visual Basic, you decide which are the default button and the cancel button—that is, the buttons that are activated by pressing the Enter and Esc keys, respectively—by assigning True to the Default or Cancel property of the button in question. The Default and Cancel properties are gone in Visual Basic .NET, but you achieve the same result by assigning to the form's AcceptButton and CancelButton properties a reference to the proper Button control. As usual, you can set these properties in the Properties window at design time or by means of code:

```
Me.AcceptButton = btnOk
Me.CancelButton = btnCancel
```

Adding Controls Dynamically

Visual Basic .NET doesn't support control arrays, but this isn't a serious problem because the Windows Forms portion of the Framework offers everything control arrays offer, and a lot more. Under previous language versions, you typically use control arrays for dynamically creating new controls at run time or for simplifying the code by creating event routines that serve multiple controls. You have already seen that you can create the latter kind of event procedures with Visual Basic .NET by using multiple Handles clauses or by using the AddHandler command. In this section, you'll see how you can create controls dynamically in Visual Basic .NET.

As you already know, the form designer is nothing but a sophisticated code generator, and controls are actually created and placed on the form's surface at run time. So you can see how dynamic control creation works simply by looking at the code that the form designer generates for any control you place on the form.

By doing so, you can see that you create controls as you would create any other kind of objects—that is, by using the New keyword. You later assign all the necessary properties to the control—most notably, its Name, Location, Size, and TabIndex—and finally you add it to the Controls collection of the parent form. For example, the following code generates a Button control:

```
Private Sub CreateButton()
    ' Create the control, assign it a name, and set other properties.
    Dim btnOK As New System.Windows.Forms.Button
    btnOK.Name = "Button-OK"
    btnOK.Location = New System.Drawing.Point(328, 32)
    btnOK.Size = New System.Drawing.Size(72, 32)
    btnOK.TabIndex = 10
    btnOK.Text = "OK"
    ' Add it to the parent form's Controls collection.
    Me.Controls.Add(btnOK)
End Sub
```

You should note that the Name property doesn't have the same role it had under Visual Basic 6. What we usually consider the name of the control is now the name of the variable that points to the control (btnOK in the preceding example), whereas the Name property is a string value that you can use to identify the control itself. (You can use spaces and other symbols in this property.) You can even use the same Name value used for another control on the form if you create the control in code. In this respect, the Name property is similar to the Tag property (which is still supported).

Another thing worth noting in the preceding code snippet is that the btnOK variable is local to the procedure, so it goes out of scope when the End Sub statement is reached. The control isn't destroyed at this time, however, because the form's Controls collection keeps it alive.

In general, you might not know in advance how many controls you're going to create dynamically when you write the code portion of the application. For example, you might want to create all the controls on a form to match the structure of a database table or an SQL query typed by the end user. For this reason, most of the time you can't create the appropriate number of WithEvents variables to trap events from the controls you add dynamically, and you must use the AddHandler command instead.

I've prepared a demo form that asks the user for a number of TextBox controls, creates them dynamically, and traps a few key events from them. (See Figure 15-14.) This is the code behind the Button control:

```
Private Sub btnCreateControls_Click(ByVal sender As Object, _
    ByVal e As EventArgs) Handles btnCreateControls.Click

    Dim answer As String
    answer = InputBox("How many controls?", "Dynamic Control Creation", "5")
    If answer = "" Then Exit Sub

    For index As Integer = 1 To CInt(answer)
        ' Create the Nth text box.
        Dim tb As New TextBox()
        tb.Size = New System.Drawing.Size(400, 30)
        tb.Location = New System.Drawing.Point(50, 40 + index * 40)
        ' We need this to identify the control.
        tb.Name = "TextBox #" & CStr(index)
        ' Add to the Controls collection.
        Me.Controls.Add(tb)
        ' Create event handlers.
        AddHandler tb.KeyPress, AddressOf TextBox_KeyPress
        AddHandler tb.TextChanged, AddressOf TextBox_TextChanged
        AddHandler tb.MouseEnter, AddressOf TextBox_MouseEnter
        AddHandler tb.MouseLeave, AddressOf TextBox_MouseLeave
    Next
End Sub

Private Sub TextBox_TextChanged(ByVal sender As Object, ByVal e As EventArgs)
    ' Show that an event fires by updating a Label control.
    lblStatus.Text = "TextChanged in " & CType(sender, TextBox).Name
End Sub

' ...(Code for other event procedures omitted)...
```

As you see in the TextBox_TextChanged procedure, assigning a value to the Name property makes it easier to detect which specific control raised the event.

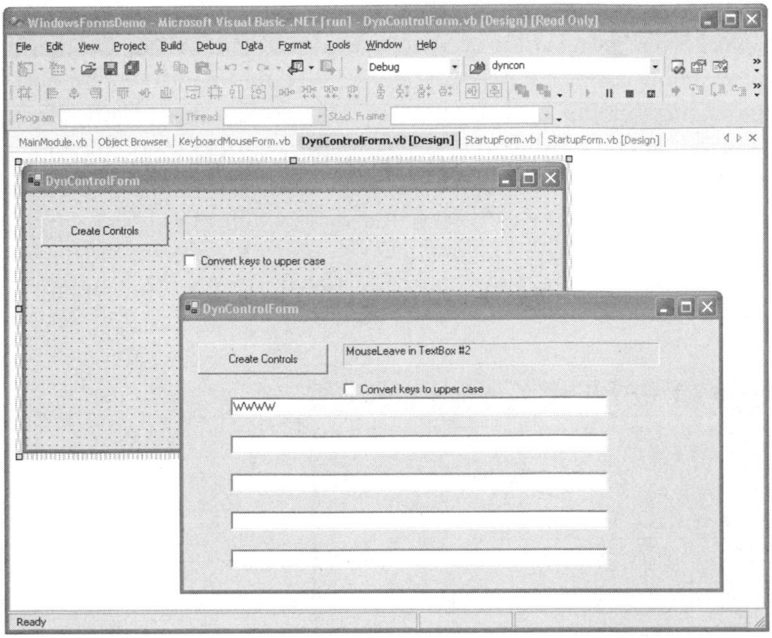

Figure 15-14   A form that creates a group of TextBox controls at run time
and traps events from them

One last note about control creation: you can destroy any control on a form by using
the Remove method of the form's Controls collection. This method can remove any
control, not just those that you've added after the form became visible:

```
Me.Controls.Remove(btnOk)
```

Menus

Personally, I have always disliked the Visual Basic menu editor, and above all I'm both-
ered by the fact that this designer hasn't evolved in six language versions. (And I'm in
good company if the comments I've heard for years at conferences and user group
meetings are any indication.) The good news is that the Windows Form designer now
lets you create the menu structure of your applications using a more streamlined
approach in a WYSIWYG editor. You can even move elements and entire submenus
using drag-and-drop.

Creating a Menu Structure

The first step in creating a menu structure is to drag a MainMenu object from the Toolbox to the form designer. Because this object is invisible at run time, a new element
named MainMenu1 appears in the designer's component tray area. You can change the
name of this control if you want, but usually there's no point in doing so because most
forms have only one menu structure and you don't need multiple MainMenu objects on
a given form.

You can now click the menu bar and type the captions of menu items. (See Figure 15-15.) Depending on where you start typing, you can create new items on the menu bar, new submenus, or new menu items. Each item you create is automatically assigned a name—such as MenuItem1, MenuItem2, and so on—but you can edit these names by right-clicking the menu structure and selecting Edit Names on the shortcut menu (see Figure 15-16). When in Edit Names mode, you can edit the item names but can't modify their captions. The pop-up menu also lets you insert new items and delete existing ones. (You can also delete items by pressing the Delete key.) Regardless of whether you're in Edit Names mode, you can see and modify all the attributes of the current menu item in the Properties window.

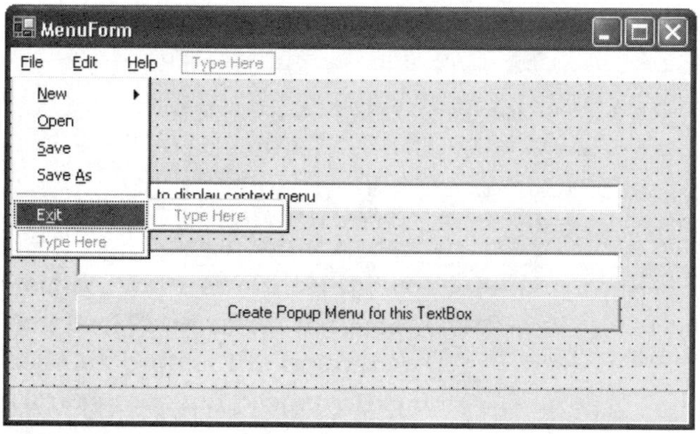

Figure 15-15   The menu designer in normal mode

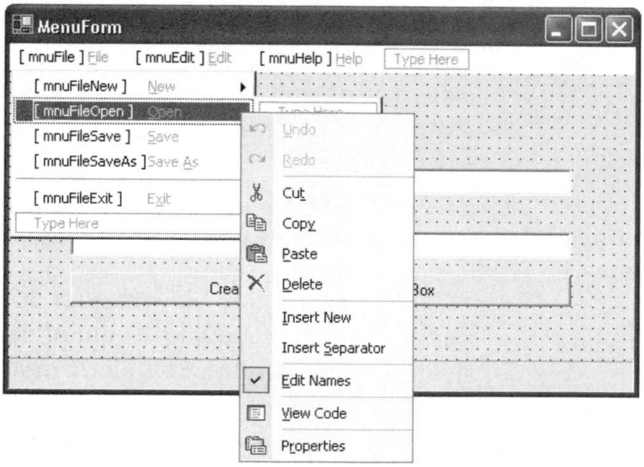

Figure 15-16   The menu designer in Edit Names mode and with the pop-up menu displayed

As in previous versions, menu separators are just MenuItem elements whose Text property is - (hyphen). All other properties of such elements are ignored.

I already mentioned that the menu editor supports drag-and-drop to move submenus around the menu structure. You can also achieve the same result by cutting a top-level menu or a submenu and pasting it elsewhere in the menu hierarchy.

Properties, Methods, and Events

The Windows Forms namespace exposes three objects that are related to menus: Main-Menu, ContextMenu, and MenuItem. I'll talk about the ContextMenu object in a later section, but for now it's important to note that the MainMenu and ContextMenu objects expose a similar programming interface, and both of them work as containers for MenuItem objects. For this reason, it makes sense to describe their properties, methods, and events in one place.

If you're a Visual Basic 6 developer, you should be familiar with most properties of the MenuItem object, such as Text (the caption that appears on the menu item), Visible, Enabled, Checked (if True, a check mark appears to the left of the menu item), and Shortcut (the shortcut key assigned to the menu item). The meaning of many new properties should be evident: RadioCheck (if True, a circular mark instead of a check mark is displayed when Checked is True), Mnemonic (returns the mnemonic character associated with the menu item), and Index (the position of the item in its submenu).

A MenuItem object can also work as a submenu, as the MainMenu and the Context-Menu objects do. Therefore, all these three objects have a few properties in common, which they inherit from the Menu abstract class. The IsParent read-only property returns True if the menu contains menu items; the MenuItems collection is the collection of child menu items; Handle is the Windows handle for the menu (can be useful when acting on the menu by means of a call to the operating system).

Reacting to Menu Events

Windows Forms menu items raise a Click event when the user selects them, so you react to menu choices exactly as you do in Visual Basic 6:

```
Private Sub mnuFileNew_Click(ByVal sender As Object, _
    ByVal e As EventArgs) Handles mnuFilenew.Click
    ' Put the code for the File | New command here.

End Sub
```

You can create an empty Click event handler by double-clicking on a menu item in the designer window. Note that the second argument is a plain EventArgs object that doesn't carry any additional information with it.

The MenuItem class also exposes the Select event, which fires when the user highlights the corresponding menu command with the mouse or the keyboard without selecting it. This event is useful for displaying a short description of the menu command in a Label or a Status bar control, as shown in Figure 15-17:

```
Private Sub mnuFileNew_Select(ByVal sender As Object, _
    ByVal e As EventArgs) Handles mnuFileNew.Select
    lblStatus.Text = "Create a new file"
End Sub
```

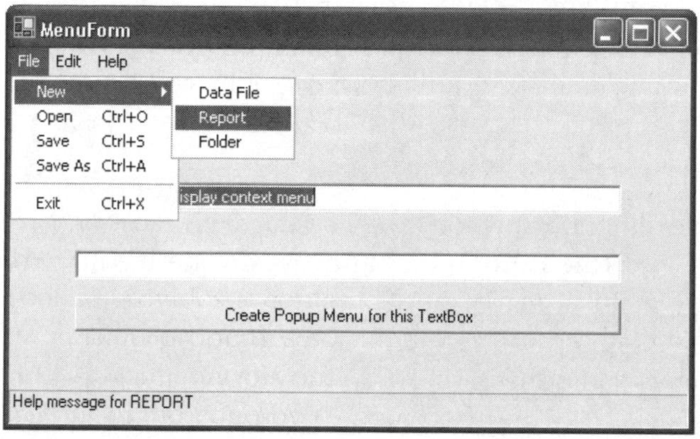

Figure 15-17   The Select event lets you display a short description of the menu command currently selected.

The Form object raises two events that are related to menus: MenuStart and MenuComplete. As their names suggest, MenuStart is raised as soon as the user activates the menu system, whereas MenuComplete fires when the user has closed the menu. (This event fires before the Click event if a menu item has been selected.) For example, you can use MenuStart to show the Label control used to display the description of each menu item and MenuComplete to make the Label control invisible again:

```
Private Sub MenuForm_MenuStart(ByVal sender As Object, _
    ByVal e As EventArgs) Handles MyBase.MenuStart
    lblStatus.Visible = True
End Sub

Private Sub MenuForm_MenuComplete(ByVal sender As Object, _
    ByVal e As EventArgs) Handles MyBase.MenuComplete
    lblStatus.Visible = False
End Sub
```

Creating Menus Using Code

Creating a menu bar via code is just a matter of creating the necessary number of MenuItem objects, setting their properties as needed, and then adding them to the MainMenu.MenuItems collection. You can add each MenuItem individually, or you can add all of them in one operation by using the collection's AddRange method:

```
' Variables for the main menu and top-level menu items
Friend WithEvents MainMenu1 As System.Windows.Forms.MainMenu
Friend WithEvents mnuFile As System.Windows.Forms.MenuItem
Friend WithEvents mnuEdit As System.Windows.Forms.MenuItem
Friend WithEvents mnuHelp As System.Windows.Forms.MenuItem

Private Sub CreateMenuTree()
    ' Create all the menu objects.
    Me.MainMenu1 = New System.Windows.Forms.MainMenu()
    Me.mnuFile = New System.Windows.Forms.MenuItem()
    Me.mnuEdit = New System.Windows.Forms.MenuItem()
    Me.mnuHelp = New System.Windows.Forms.MenuItem()
    ' Set menu items' properties.
    Me.mnuFile.Index = 0
    Me.mnuFile.Text = "&File"
    Me.mnuEdit.Index = 1
    Me.mnuEdit.Text = "&Edit"
    Me.mnuHelp.Index = 2
    Me.mnuHelp.Text = "&Help"
    ' Add to the main menu's MenuItems collection.
    ' (Note how you can create a MenuItem array on the fly and pass it
    '  to the AddRange method in a single statement.)
    Me.MainMenu1.MenuItems.AddRange(New MenuItem() _
        {Me.mnuFile, Me.mnuEdit, Me.mnuHelp})
    ' Assign the MainMenu object to the form's Menu property.
    Me.Menu = Me.MainMenu1
End Sub
```

Adding menu items to the MainMenu1 object doesn't create the menu automatically because this object isn't automatically placed on the form. (The action of putting the component on a designer's surface is called *siting*.) The statement that associates the menu structure you've created with the specific form is the last one in the preceding code, where you assign the MainMenu object to the Me.Menu property. This fact opens up interesting possibilities: for example, a form can display another form and have that other form expose the same menu structure. The code that implements this solution is trivial:

```
Dim frm As New frmOtherForm
frm.Menu = Me.MainMenu1
frm.Show
```

Because both the caller and the callee share the same menu objects, you can place all the event procedures in one form, thus saving a lot of code.

The MenuItem class also exposes the MenuItems collection, so creating items for each submenu follows the same pattern:

```
Friend WithEvents mnuFileNew As System.Windows.Forms.MenuItem
Friend WithEvents mnuFileOpen As System.Windows.Forms.MenuItem
Friend WithEvents mnuFileSave As System.Windows.Forms.MenuItem
Friend WithEvents mnuFileSaveAs As System.Windows.Forms.MenuItem
Friend WithEvents mnuFileSep As System.Windows.Forms.MenuItem
Friend WithEvents mnuFileExit As System.Windows.Forms.MenuItem
```

```
Private Sub CreateFileSubmenu()
    ' Create all the menu objects.
    Me.mnuFileNew = New System.Windows.Forms.MenuItem()
    Me.mnuFileOpen = New System.Windows.Forms.MenuItem()
    Me.mnuFileSave = New System.Windows.Forms.MenuItem()
    Me.mnuFileSaveAs = New System.Windows.Forms.MenuItem()
    Me.mnuFileSep = New System.Windows.Forms.MenuItem()
    Me.mnuFileExit = New System.Windows.Forms.MenuItem()
    ' Add them to the File submenu.
    Me.mnuFile.MenuItems.AddRange(New MenuItem() _
        {Me.mnuFileNew, Me.mnuFileOpen, Me.mnuFileSave, _
        Me.mnuFileSaveAs, Me.mnuFileSep, Me.mnuFileExit})

    ' Set properties of individual menu items.
    Me.mnuFileNew.Index = 0
    Me.mnuFileNew.Shortcut = Shortcut.CtrlN
    Me.mnuFileNew.Text = "&New"
    -
    Me.mnuFileSep.Index = 4
    Me.mnuFileSep.Text = "-"               ' A menu separator

    Me.mnuFileExit.Index = 5
    Me.mnuFileExit.Shortcut = Shortcut.CtrlX
    Me.mnuFileExit.Text = "E&xit"
End Sub
```

Of course, you can apply this technique recursively. For example, you can create a New submenu under the File menu by adding one or more MenuItem objects to the mnuFileNew.MenuItems collection.

The code I've shown you so far is similar to what the menu designer creates. Each menu item corresponds to a MenuItem class-level variable, and each variable is declared with the WithEvents keyword, so you can easily trap events raised from the corresponding Menu-Item object. However, you can also adopt other techniques that offer more flexibility.

For example, you might want to offer your customers the ability to redefine the entire menu structure on a user-by-user basis by storing the menu tree for each user in an XML file that you parse when the application starts. In this case, you can't create an individual MenuItem variable for each menu item (because you don't know how many menu items you're going to create), and you have to add each menu item to its parent submenu's MenuItems collection as you read the XML element that describes that menu item.

Regardless of how you create the menu structure, the hierarchical nature of the menu tree suggests a simple way to create a centralized routine that handles the Click or the Select event for all the menu commands in your application. In some cases, such a centralized routine can be a superior approach. I've prepared a reusable routine that visits all the items in a menu structure to have their Click and Select events point to the specified procedures:

```
' Make the Click and Select event handlers of all the menu items
' in a form point to the same procedures.
' The main application should call this routine with m = Me.Menu.

Sub InitializeMenuEvents(ByVal m As Menu, _
```

```
    ByVal ClickEvent As EventHandler, ByVal SelectEvent As EventHandler)

    If TypeOf m Is MenuItem Then
        ' Cast the argument to a MenuItem object.
        Dim mi As MenuItem = DirectCast(m, MenuItem)
        ' Initialize the Select event for this menu item.
        AddHandler mi.Select, SelectEvent
        ' Initialize the Click event if this isn't a submenu.
        If m.MenuItems.Count = 0 Then
            AddHandler mi.Click, ClickEvent
        End If
    End If

    ' Call recursively for all items in the MenuItems collection.
    For Each mi As MenuItem In m.MenuItems
        InitializeMenuEvents(mi, ClickEvent, SelectEvent)
    Next
End Sub
```

You can call this routine from the Load event procedure of a form or just before exiting the Sub New procedure, passing the Me.Menu property as the first argument and the delegates that point to the Click and Select event procedures in the remaining arguments, as in this code:

```
Private Sub MenuForm_Load(ByVal sender As Object, _
    ByVal e As System.EventArgs) Handles MyBase.Load
    InitializeMenuEvents(Me.Menu, AddressOf MenuItem_Click, _
        AddressOf MenuItem_Select)
End Sub

' Select common routine for all menu items.
Private Sub MenuItem_Select(ByVal sender As Object, ByVal e As EventArgs)
    Dim mi As MenuItem = DirectCast(sender, MenuItem)
    ' Display a generic message in this demo.
    lblStatus.Text = "Help message for " & mi.Text.ToUpper
End Sub

' Click common routine for all menu items.
Private Sub MenuItem_Click(ByVal sender As Object, ByVal e As EventArgs)
    Dim mi As MenuItem = DirectCast(sender, MenuItem)
    ' Display a generic message in this demo.
    lblStatus.Text = mi.Text.ToUpper & " has been selected."
End Sub
```

In this example, the event procedures common to all menu items display a generic message in a status bar. In a real application, the MenuItem_Select procedure might read its messages from a database, an XML file, a resource file, and so on. A Click event procedure common to all menu items lets you group similar menu commands by using a Select Case statement, as in this code:

```
Private Sub MenuItem_Click(ByVal sender As Object, ByVal e As EventArgs)
    Dim mi As MenuItem = DirectCast(sender, MenuItem)
    Select mi.Text.ToUpper
        Case "NEW"        ' Create a new file.
            -
```

```
          Case "OPEN"       ' Open an existing file.
              -
      End Select
End Sub
```

The two approaches—WithEvents variables tied to standard event procedures and dynamic events created for all menu items with the AddHandler keyword—can coexist in the same form. In this case, a menu item raises two Click or Select events.

Multiple-Column Menus

The Break and BarBreak properties of the MenuItem object let you create menus with multiple columns. All you have to do is set either property to True for the MenuItem object that must become the first item of a new menu column. The only difference between these two properties is that BarBreak displays a vertical line between adjacent columns, whereas Break does not. (See Figure 15-18.)

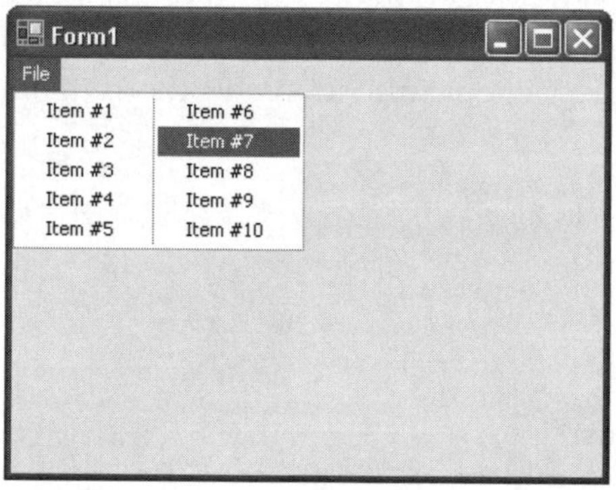

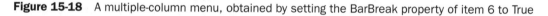

Figure 15-18   A multiple-column menu, obtained by setting the BarBreak property of item 6 to True

A minor annoyance attached to these properties is that they don't appear in the Properties window, so you have to set them via code, as you see here:

```
mnuFileItem6.BarBreak = True
```

You can place this statement at the end of the New method, or in the Form_Load event procedure. Using these two locations ensures that your code isn't overwritten by the form designer when you change another property of the same MenuItem object.

Displaying Context Menus

Creating and displaying a context menu isn't very different from working with a regular menu. You drag a ContextMenu object from the Toolbox to the form designer's component tray area, and then you visually create the structure of the context menu. (See Figure 15-19.) For the design of a context menu, the root of the menu tree is the fictitious node named ContextMenu, and you can create nodes only under this one. Except for this detail, the menu designer works as I described previously.

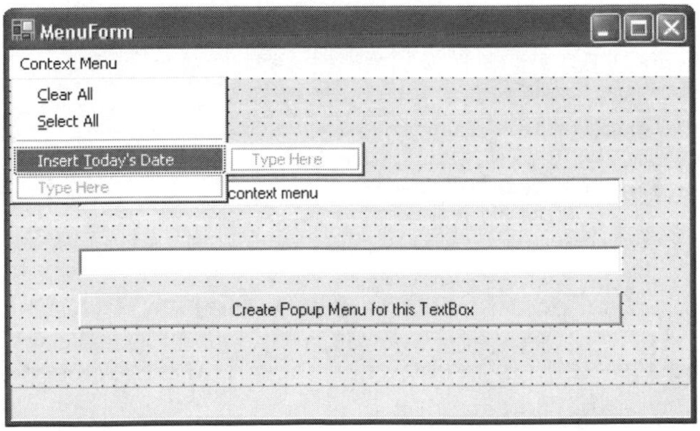

Figure 15-19   The menu designer when you're working on a ContextMenu object

After designing the structure of the context menu object, you must associate it with one or more controls on the form's surface or with the Form object itself. You do this by assigning the ContextMenu1 object to the ContextMenu property of the form or the control, from inside the Properties window or by means of code:

```
TextBox1.ContextMenu = ContextMenu1
```

You can associate a ContextMenu object with multiple controls (which will therefore share the same context menu), or you can associate different ContextMenu objects with different controls. It usually makes sense to create multiple ContextMenu objects on the same form, so it might be convenient to assign each object a name that suggests its function, such as ctxConvertCmds.

A ContextMenu object exposes a MenuItems collection that contains MenuItem objects, so you can create this object in code as you'd create a regular menu. The following code snippet shows how to perform this task in a concise way, without creating distinct WithEvents class-level variables and by using a variant of the MenuItem's constructor that takes the Text property and a delegate to the Click event procedure:

```
Sub CreateContextMenu()
    Dim ctxConvertCmds As New ContextMenu()
    ' Create all MenuItem objects, and add them to the MenuItems collection.
    With ctxConvertCmds.MenuItems
        .Add(New MenuItem("Clear", AddressOf ContextMenu_Click))
        .Add(New MenuItem("Upper Case", AddressOf ContextMenu_Click))
        .Add(New MenuItem("Lower Case", AddressOf ContextMenu_Click))
    End With
    ' Assign the control's ContextMenu property.
    TextBox2.ContextMenu = ctxConvertCmds
End Sub

Private Sub ContextMenu_Click(ByVal sender As Object, ByVal e As EventArgs)
    ' Cast to a MenuItem object.
    Dim mi As MenuItem = DirectCast(sender, MenuItem)
    ' Select the action depending on the menu's caption.
```

```
        Select Case mi.Text
            Case "Clear"
                TextBox2.Text = ""
            Case "Upper Case"
                TextBox2.Text = TextBox2.Text.ToUpper
            Case "Lower Case"
                TextBox2.Text = TextBox2.Text.ToLower
        End Select
    End Sub
```

Items in a ContextMenu object support the Select event as well.

The ContextMenu object raises a Popup event when the menu becomes visible. You can use this event to display further information in a status bar. Unfortunately, there's no menu event that fires when a pop-up menu is being closed without the user making a selection. (You can use the Idle event of the Application object to perform an action when a popup menu is closed, as I explain in the section "The Application Object" in Chapter 16.)

MDI Forms

The Windows Forms namespace doesn't expose a separate class for MDI forms: an MDI form is nothing but a regular Form object whose IsMdiContainer property is set to True. You usually assign this property at design time, but you can also do it using code. The only noteworthy limitation of MDI containers is that they can't also be scrollable. If you attempt to set the IsMdiContainer property to True, the AutoScroll property resets to False, and vice versa.

Here's an important difference from Visual Basic 6: an MDI form can contain any type of control, and these controls appear in front of any child form. By comparison, the Visual Basic 6 MDI forms can host only alignable controls, such as a status bar, a tool-bar, or a PictureBox control.

Showing MDI Child Forms

An MDI child form is a regular form whose MdiParent property points to its MDI container form, so the code that creates and displays a child window is simple:

```
' Display the DocumentForm form as a child of this form.
Dim frm As New DocumentForm()
' Make it a child of this MDI form before showing it.
frm.MdiParent = Me
frm.Show()
```

A form that can be used as either a regular form or an MDI child form might need to determine how it's being used. It can do that by testing its MdiParent property or its read-only IsMdiChild property.

You can list all the child forms of an MDI parent by using the Form array returned by its MdiChildren property:

```
For Each frm As Form In Me.MdiChildren
    Debug.Write(frm.Text)
Next
```

The MDI parent form can activate one of its child forms by using the ActivateMdiChild method:

```
' Activate the first MDI child form.
If Me.MdiChildren.Length > 0 Then
    ActivateMdiChild(Me.MdiChildren(0))
End If
```

The ActiveMdiChild property returns a reference to the active child form or Nothing if there are no active child forms. Such a situation can occur when all child forms have been closed. This property is often used inside the MdiChildActivate event, which fires when a new child form becomes active:

```
' Change the title of the MDI parent form to match the caption
' of the active child form.
Private Sub MDIForm_MdiChildActivate(ByVal sender As Object, _
    ByVal e As EventArgs) Handles MyBase.MdiChildActivate
    If Me.ActiveMdiChild Is Nothing Then
        Me.Text = "MDI Demo Program"
    Else
        Me.Text = Me.ActiveMdiChild.Text & " - MDI Demo Program"
    End If
End Sub
```

MDI forms often contain a Window menu that exposes commands to cascade, tile, arrange, or close all child forms, as shown in Figure 15-20. You can implement these commands easily by using the LayoutMdi method, which replaces the Visual Basic 6 Arrange method:

```
Private Sub mnuWindowCascade_Click(ByVal sender As Object, _
    ByVal e As EventArgs) Handles mnuWindowCascade.Click
    Me.LayoutMdi(MdiLayout.Cascade)
End Sub

Private Sub mnuWindowTileHor_Click(ByVal sender As Object, _
    ByVal e As EventArgs) Handles mnuWindowTileHor.Click
    Me.LayoutMdi(MdiLayout.TileHorizontal)
End Sub

Private Sub mnuWindowTileVer_Click(ByVal sender As Object, _
    ByVal e As EventArgs) Handles mnuWindowTileVer.Click
    Me.LayoutMdi(MdiLayout.TileVertical)
End Sub
```

```
Private Sub mnuWindowArrange_Click(ByVal sender As Object, _
    ByVal e As System.EventArgs) Handles mnuWindowArrange.Click
    Me.LayoutMdi(MdiLayout.ArrangeIcons)
End Sub

Private Sub mnuWindowCloseAll_Click(ByVal sender As Object, _
    ByVal e As EventArgs) Handles mnuWindowCloseAll.Click

    Do While Me.MdiChildren.Length > 0
        Me.MdiChildren(0).Close()
    Loop
End Sub
```

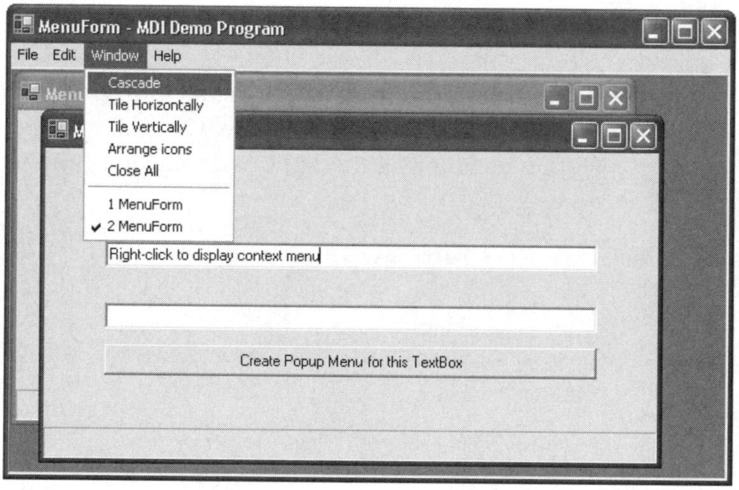

Figure 15-20   A typical MDI application with its Window menu

As you can see in Figure 15-20, the Window menu contains a list of all visible MDI child windows, with a check mark near the one that is currently selected. The end user can use the elements in this menu to activate another child form. You can create this list simply by setting the MdiList property of the Windows MenuItem object to True. (This property replaces the Visual Basic 6 WindowList property.)

Menu Merging

If the currently active MDI child form has a menu, this menu is merged with the MDI container's menu. You can finely control how each submenu, and even each individual menu item in the child form, is merged with a menu in the MDI container form. You exert this control by using two related properties: MergeType is an enumerated value that specifies what happens to menu items (in the parent MDI form and in the MDI child form) when they are merged; the MergeOrder property specifies the relative order of items that are merged in the same submenu. The MergeType property can take four different values:

- **Add** This menu item is added to the menu in the MDI parent form; this is the default value, so the standard behavior is that all menus in the child form are added to the menu in the parent form. The position at which the item is inserted depends on the MergeOrder property.

- **Remove** This menu item never appears in the parent form's menu.

- **Replace** This menu item replaces the menu item with the same MergeOrder value in the other form.

- **MergeItems** This menu item is merged and appears in the resulting menu at the position indicated by the MergeOrder property. If this item is actually a submenu, items of this submenu are merged with items in the submenu with the same MergeOrder value in the other form; in this case, the menu merge mechanism takes into account the MergeType and MergeOrder properties of each individual menu item.

Implementing a correct menu merging is more complicated than you might think, so a practical example is in order. First create an MDI parent form with this menu structure:

```
File                (MergeOrder = 0, MergeType = MergeItems)
    New File        (MergeOrder = 0, MergeType = MergeItems)
    Open File       (MergeOrder = 1, MergeType = Remove)
    Save File       (MergeOrder = 2, MergeType = Remove)
    Exit            (MergeOrder = 9, MergeType = MergeItems)
Window              (MergeOrder = 5, MergeType = Add)
    Close All       (MergeOrder = 0, MergeType = Add)
Help                (MergeOrder = 9, MergeType = MergeItems)
    Contents        (MergeOrder = 0, MergeType = MergeItems)
    About           (MergeOrder = 2, MergeType = MergeItems)
```

Next create a child form with this menu hierarchy:

```
File                (MergeOrder = 0, MergeType = MergeItems)
    New             (MergeOrder = 0, MergeType = Remove)
    Open            (MergeOrder = 1, MergeType = Replace)
    Save            (MergeOrder = 2, MergeType = Replace)
    Close           (MergeOrder = 3, MergeType = Add)
Edit                (MergeOrder = 1, MergeType = Add)
    Undo            (MergeOrder = 0, MergeType = Add)
Help                (MergeOrder = 9, MergeType = MergeItems)
    Index           (MergeOrder = 1, MergeType = Add)
```

This is the resultant menu tree when the child form becomes the active MDI form:

```
File                (merge from both forms)
    New File        (from parent form)
    Open            (from child form)
    Save            (from child form)
    Close           (from child form)
```

```
        Exit              (from parent form)
    Edit                  (from child form)
        Undo              (from child form)
    Window                (from parent form)
        Close All         (from parent form)
    Help                  (merge from both forms)
        Contents          (from parent form)
        Index             (from child form)
        About             (from parent form)
```

Form Inheritance

Because a form is just an object, you shouldn't be surprised to learn that you can inherit a form from another form. Form inheritance isn't different from regular inheritance, and everything you learned in Chapter 5 holds true in this case as well. However, the form is a peculiar object in that it exposes a user interface, and this detail has some interesting implications. Before diving into technical details, let's see what form inheritance is good for.

Advantages of Form Inheritance

Inheriting a new form from a base form means reusing the user interface, the code, and the functionality in the base form. For example, you can create a DialogBaseForm that contains a Label, the OK and Cancel buttons, and some code for the button Click events. If you then inherit a new form from DialogBaseForm, you inherit both the user interface and the behavior of the base form, which means that you can redefine the text of the Label and the behavior of the two buttons. You can resize the form and move the buttons accordingly (if you assigned their Anchor property correctly), and of course you can add new controls.

The great thing about inheritance is that you can later add new functionality or user interface elements to the DialogBaseForm form, for example a Help button and the logo of your company. When you recompile the inherited form, the new button and the logo will be part of all the forms that inherit from DialogBaseForm.

An Example of Form Inheritance

To see in practice how form inheritance works, let's create a dialog box that can work as a base class for other forms. (See Figure 15-21.) The DialogBaseForm form contains three Button controls that are anchored to the top and right borders so that they move correctly when the form is resized. The TextBox and Label controls are anchored to the left, top, and right borders so that they expand and shrink when the form is resized. You'll also see a PictureBox control with an icon in it; add a little imagination, and it could be the logo of your company.

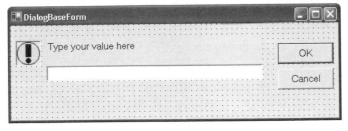

Figure 15-21   The DialogBaseForm form

The OK and Cancel buttons have their DialogResult property set to OK and Cancel so that the dialog closes when the end user clicks on them. The Label control has a generic Text property because it's bound to be overwritten in the inherited form.

As you know, in general you get better encapsulation if you use private controls only and you encapsulate all your controls in public properties. However, when creating a base form class, you should use a Protected scope for your controls. Bear in mind that the Modifiers property of your controls corresponds to the scope of the variable that the form designer creates in the code module. If you use a Private scope for this variable, it isn't visible to the inherited form and you can't modify its properties from inside the derived form (even though the control appears on the inherited form's surface). Therefore, you should set the Modifiers property to Protected for all controls that you want to manipulate in the inherited form but that you don't want the base or the inherited form to expose to the regular client code. Not all controls must have a Friend scope, however. For example, if you don't plan to change your company logo anytime soon, you can use a Private scope for the PictureBox control.

Because a Protected control isn't visible to the outside, the base class must expose the TextBox control's contents as a property, as in this code:

```
Property InputValue() As String
    Get
        Return txtValue.Text
    End Get
    Set(ByVal Value As String)
        txtValue.Text = Value
    End Set
End Property
```

You can create an inherited form by simply defining a class that inherits from an existing form class instead of the generic System.Windows.Forms.Form class:

```
Class DialogInheritedForm
    Inherits DialogBaseForm
    -
End Class
```

In practice, however, you don't have to write this code manually because Visual Studio .NET lets you do it in a visual manner. For this mechanism to work correctly, you must compile the application by using the Build command on the Build menu. You need this step to create a compiled class that Visual Studio can use as a base class for the new form.

Next, choose the Add Inherited Form command on the Project menu. This command displays the familiar Add New Item dialog box. Give the new form a name (use DialogInheritedForm to match the code that follows), and click the Open button. This action brings up the Inheritance Picker dialog box, which lets you select the base form among all the form classes defined in the current project. (You can use the Browse button to view forms in other assemblies.) Pick the DialogBaseForm class, as shown in Figure 15-22, and click OK.

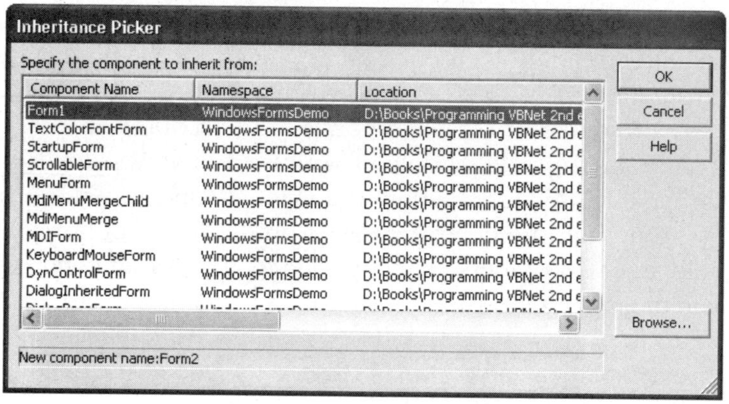

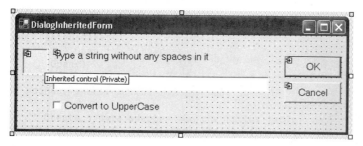

Figure 15-22 The Inheritance Picker dialog box

Visual Studio creates a new form that inherits all the controls that are in the DialogBaseForm class, and you can add new controls and modify the properties of all controls that aren't private to the base class. Figure 15-23 shows the new DialogInheritedForm after I modified the text in the form and the Label control and added a new CheckBox control.

Figure 15-23 The DialogInheritedForm after changing a few properties and adding a CheckBox control

You can select controls that were private in the base form, such as the PictureBox control that holds the computer icon, and you can browse their properties, but you can't modify them. (In fact, they're grayed in the Properties window.) However, you can browse *and* change all the properties of all other controls except the Name and Modifiers properties. This limitation is understandable because a derived class can't change the name or the scope of an inherited variable. You can quickly see the scope of each control in the inherited form by hovering the mouse over it to make a ToolTip appear, as you can see in Figure 15-23.

Trapping and Overriding Events

Because an inherited class can access all the Protected elements in the base class, the DialogInheritedForm form can trap events raised by controls defined in the Dialog-BaseForm class by using standard syntax. For example, the following code in the derived class enables the OK button only if a non-null string has been typed in the txtValue control, and it converts typed characters to uppercase if the chkUpperCase control is checked:

```
' Enable the OK button only after the user enters a string.
Private Sub txtValue_TextChanged(ByVal sender As Object, _
    ByVal e As EventArgs) Handles txtValue.TextChanged
    Me.btnOK.Enabled = (txtValue.Text <> "")
End Sub

' Convert to uppercase if so requested.
Private Sub txtValue_KeyPress(ByVal sender As Object, _
    ByVal e As KeyPressEventArgs) Handles txtValue.KeyPress
    If chkUpperCase.Checked AndAlso Char.IsLower(e.KeyChar) Then
        txtValue.SelectedText = Char.ToUpper(e.KeyChar)
        e.Handled = True
    End If
End Sub
```

Just trapping an event from a control in the base form isn't enough in some cases. For example, let's say that in the inherited form you want to close the dialog and accept the value typed by end users only if the string doesn't contain any spaces. Creating a btnOk_Click event handler doesn't work in this case because the form engines would execute both Click events—in the base class and in the derived class—and the code in the derived class couldn't prevent the code in the Click event in DialogBaseForm from closing the form. It's obvious that in this case you need to *override* the default behavior in the base class.

In the "Redefining Events" section in Chapter 5, I describe a technique that you can use to override events. That technique applies in this situation as well. All events in the base class should delegate their job to an On*xxxx* procedure with Protected scope. For example, the btnOk_Click event procedure should call the OnOkClick procedure, the btnCancel_Click event procedure should likewise call the OnCancelClick procedure, and so on. Even if it isn't strictly necessary in this example, the On*xxxx* procedure takes the last argument passed to the event handler as their only argument:

```
' ...(In the DialogBaseForm class)...

Private Sub btnOK_Click(ByVal sender As Object, _
    ByVal e As EventArgs) Handles btnOK.Click
    OnOkClick(e)
End Sub

Private Sub btnCancel_Click(ByVal sender As Object, _
    ByVal e As EventArgs) Handles btnCancel.Click
    OnCancelClick(e)
End Sub

' Since this form has been designed for being inherited from,
' you put the actual Button code in two Protected procedures.
Protected Overridable Sub OnOkClick(ByVal e As EventArgs)
    ' Close this form; return OK.
    Me.DialogResult = DialogResult.OK
End Sub

Protected Overridable Sub OnCancelClick(ByVal e As EventArgs)
    ' Close this form; return Cancel.
    Me.DialogResult = DialogResult.Cancel
End Sub
```

Because these procedures are marked with Overridable, the inherited form can redefine the default behavior by overriding them. A well-written derived class should delegate actions to the procedure in the base class if possible so that you can later improve the code in the base class and have the derived classes automatically inherit the improved code:

```
' In this inherited form, you reject strings that contain a space.
Protected Overrides Sub OnOkClick(ByVal e As EventArgs)
    If InStr(txtValue.Text, " ") = 0 Then
        ' Call the base procedure only if the string doesn't contain a space.
        MyBase.OnOkClick(e)
    Else
        ' Display an error message, and don't close the form.
        MessageBox.Show("Please remove all spaces from this string", _
            "Error", MessageBoxButtons.OK, MessageBoxIcon.Error)
    End If
End Sub
```

A base form doesn't need to have controls on it, yet creating such a base form might be useful to easily build new forms that inherit a given behavior. For example, you might create a base form that saves its current size and position in the Closing event (for example, to an XML file) and restores them in the Form event. Or a form with a KeyPreview property set to True that lets the user navigate through its fields with the up and down keys, using the technique I illustrated in the section "Working with Input Focus" earlier in this chapter.

Advanced Form Techniques

In this section, I'll describe a few advanced form techniques, such as form subclassing, localization, and customization.

Window Subclassing

Window subclassing is an advanced programming technique that consists of intercepting the messages that the operating system sends to your forms when something relevant happens—for example, when the user clicks the mouse on the form's title bar or clicks on the X button near the upper right corner. In Visual Basic 6 you must resort to subclassing to implement several features that are missing in the language, such as the ability to detect when a form is moved or when a menu item is selected. The objects in the System.Windows.Forms namespace are more powerful than the corresponding Visual Basic 6 objects, so subclassing has become less necessary than in the past. Nevertheless, in some cases you might need to use it even under Visual Basic .NET.

Subclassing Principles

It's a pleasant surprise to see that the Form object lets you implement subclassing in a simple, safe, and reliable way. Subclassing a Form object relies heavily on inheritance. The System.Windows.Forms.Form class exposes the WndProc method, which is invoked for each message sent from Windows to the form. The code for this method in the base Form class processes the incoming message in the standard way—for example, a click on the form's surface activates the form, a click in the lower right corner of a form starts a resize operation, and so on.

The WndProc method is marked as Protected and Overridable, so a derived class can override it. Because all forms derive from the System.Windows.Forms.Form class, you can always redefine the behavior of your forms by overriding this method. This method receives a Message object, whose properties expose the four values that Windows sends to a form's window procedure: Msg (the number of the message), HWnd (the handle of the window), and WParam and LParam (arguments passed to the window procedure, whose meaning depends on the specific message). A fifth property, Result, is the value that will be returned to the operating system.

Subclassing Example

When you override the WndProc procedure, your primary concern should be delegating to the default procedure in the base class so that the usual message processing can take place (except in those rare cases in which you're subclassing the form to suppress the default action). Then you can check the value of the message's Msg property to see whether you want to deal with this specific message. If you're subclassing a form just to get a notification that something has happened, usually these actions are all you need to perform. For example, the following code traps the WM_DISPLAYCHANGE message to learn when the screen resolution changes, and the WM_COMPACTING message to be informed when the system is low on memory:

```
Private Const WM_DISPLAYCHANGE As Integer = &H7E
Private Const WM_COMPACTING As Integer = &H41

Protected Overrides Sub WndProc(ByRef m As Message)
    ' Let the base form process this message.
    MyBase.WndProc(m)
    ' Display an informative message on a Label control
    ' if this is one of the messages we want to subclass.
    Select Case m.Msg
        Case WM_DISPLAYCHANGE
            lblStatus.Text = "Screen resolution has changed"
        Case WM_COMPACTING
            lblStatus.Text = "The system is low on memory"
    End Select
End Sub
```

In some cases, you might need to check the value of WParam or LParam properties to obtain additional information about the message. For example, the WM_APPACTIVATE message comes with a 0 value in WParam if the current application is being deactivated and a nonzero value if it's being activated:

```
' ...(Insert this code in the preceding Select Case block.)...
        Case WM_ACTIVATEAPP
            ' Application has been activated or deactivated.
            If m.WParam.ToInt32 <> 0 Then
                lblStatus.Text = "Application has been activated"
            Else
                lblStatus.Text = "Application has been deactivated"
            End If
```

You can subclass several Windows messages to obtain information about what has happened at the system level, including WM_SYSCOLORCHANGE (one or more system colors have been redefined), WM_PALETTEISCHANGING and WM_PALETTECHANGED (the color palette has changed), WM_FONTCHANGE (one or more fonts have changed), WM_DEVICECHANGE and WM_DEVMODECHANGE (settings of a device have changed), WM_ENDSESSION (the Windows session is closing), and WM_SPOOLERSTATUS (a print job has been added to or removed from the spooler queue). For example, you can subclass WM_ENDSESSION to learn whether the form is closing because the user has closed it or because Windows is shutting down. This information can be useful in some cases, and unfortunately you can't use the QueryUnload event to obtain it because this event is no longer supported. (You can trap a few of these systemwide events by means of the SystemEvents object, as I demonstrate in Chapter 19.)

Returning a Value to Windows

In some situations, you need to return a specific value to Windows. You can do this by setting the Result property of the Message argument, but this operation isn't as straightforward as you might think. In fact, this property doesn't directly contain the value being returned to the operating system. Instead, it contains a System.IntPtr structure, which is defined as a 32-bit pointer (or a 64-bit pointer on 64-bit versions of Windows). Languages that don't support pointers natively, such as Visual Basic .NET, can use this type to get limited functionality with pointers. Many methods in .NET also use this type to store a handle whose size is platform-specific—for example, file handles.

The most common operations you can execute on an IntPtr type are the creation of a pointer equal to the Integer value that you pass to its constructor, and the ToInt32 method, which reads the 32-bit value stored in the pointer. You can also call the Copy method of the System.Runtime.InteropServices.Marshal class to directly read and write the memory area pointed to by an IntPtr value, or use PInvoke to call the Windows API RtlMoveMemory function directly (a function that many programmers know by the name of CopyMemory).

Let's see how to use the IntPtr type to read and modify the value being returned to the operating system. This example subclasses the WM_NCHITTEST message that Windows sends to a form when the mouse cursor hovers on the form. The form is supposed to reply to this message by returning an integer that represents the area on the form hit by the mouse. For example, the HTCLIENT value means that the cursor is on the client area, and HTCAPTION means that the mouse is on the form's title bar.

The following example cheats a little by intercepting this message and returning HTCAPTION if the mouse is on the client area. Remember that this code executes after the base Form class has processed the WM_NCHITTEST message, so the Result property already contains the information about the actual position of the mouse:

```
Case WM_NCHITTEST
    ' If on client area, make Windows believe it's on title bar.
    If m.Result.ToInt32 = HTCLIENT Then
        ' You assign an IntPtr by creating a new object.
        m.Result = New IntPtr(HTCAPTION)
    End If
```

The effect of this code is that users can grab and move the form by clicking on its client area as if they had clicked on the title bar. (See Figure 15-24.) If the form is resizeable, it can be maximized with a double-click anywhere on the client area.

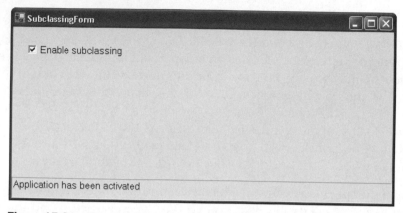

Figure 15-24   The subclassing demo contains a form that you can drag by clicking anywhere on the client area.

Sometimes the data passed together with a message is a structure pointed to by the LParam value. In this case, you can use the GetLParam method to read values in that structure. For example, when the user starts a resize operation on the form, Windows sends a WM_GETMINMAXINFO message whose LParam value points to a MINMAX-INFO structure, defined as follows:

```
Structure POINTAPI
    Dim X As Integer
    Dim Y As Integer
End Structure

Structure MINMAXINFO
    Dim ptReserved As POINTAPI
    Dim ptMaxSize As POINTAPI
    Dim ptMaxPosition As POINTAPI
    Dim ptMinTrackSize As POINTAPI
    Dim ptMaxTrackSize As POINTAPI
End Structure
```

The ptMinTrackSize and ptMaxTrackSize elements define the smallest and largest size that the form can assume. For example, on a 1024-by-768 pixels screen, a form usually can be resized up to 1032 by 776 pixels. (See Figure 15-24.) Here's the code in the demo application that reads this information:

```
Case WM_GETMINMAXINFO
    Dim mmi As MINMAXINFO = CType(m.GetLParam(mmi.GetType), MINMAXINFO)
    lblStatus.Text = String.Format("Max size = ({0}, {1})", _
        mmi.ptMaxSize.X, mmi.ptMaxSize.Y)
```

Unfortunately, you can't modify the values in a memory block pointed to by LParam by using a method in the Message object. However, you can do that by calling the Windows API CopyMemory function:

```
' Get the size of the MINMAXINFO structure in bytes.
Dim length As Integer = System.Runtime.InteropServices.Marshal.SizeOf(mmi)
' Change the minimum size of the form in a resize operation.
mmi.ptMinTrackSize.X = 600
mmi.ptMinTrackSize.Y = 300
CopyMemory(m.LParam, mmi, length)
```

This code works if you declare the API CopyMemory function in such a way that it can take a MINMAXINFO structure as the destination of the copy operation:

```
Declare Sub CopyMemory Lib "kernel32" Alias "RtlMoveMemory" _
    (ByVal dest As IntPtr, ByRef mmi As MINMAXINFO, ByVal bytes As Integer)
```

Visual Effects

The Form object exposes a pair of properties that can add some graphical pizzazz to your applications with minimum effort. Additionally, the Application.EnableVisualStyles method lets you leverage the new Windows XP visual styles with just one line of code.

The TransparencyKey Property

If you assign a color value to the TransparencyKey property, all the pixels of that color are considered transparent and won't be drawn. If the user clicks on one such point, the underlying window is activated instead. You can create oddly shaped forms by simply painting the area that doesn't belong to the form with the color that you assign to the TransparencyKey property.

You get the best effect if you work with a form whose FormBorderStyle is set to None so that you don't have to worry about the title bar. Then you have to select a color to be used as a transparent color, and of course you must be sure that no graphic element in the form contains any pixel of this color. If the form has a regular shape, such as the elliptical form in Figure 15-25, you can draw such pixels using graphic methods of the Graphics object passed to the Paint event. For example, this is the code the demo application uses to create an elliptical form:

```
Private Sub TransparentForm_Paint(ByVal sender As Object, _
    ByVal e As System.Windows.Forms.PaintEventArgs) Handles MyBase.Paint

    ' Make blue the transparent color so that only the ellipse is visible.
    Me.TransparencyKey = Color.Blue
    ' Create a brush of the same color as the form's background color.
    Dim b As New SolidBrush(Me.BackColor)
    ' Draw a blue rectangle over the entire form.
    e.Graphics.FillRectangle(Brushes.Blue, Me.ClientRectangle)
    ' Draw a filled ellipse of the original background color.
    e.Graphics.FillEllipse(b, Me.ClientRectangle)
    ' Create a black border for the ellipse.
    e.Graphics.DrawEllipse(Pens.Black, Me.ClientRectangle)
    ' Destroy the brush.
    b.Dispose()
End Sub
```

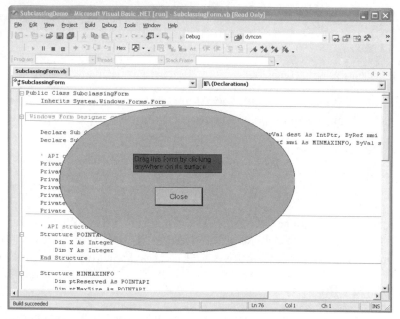

Figure 15-25   An elliptical form

Even if you aren't familiar yet with the graphical possibilities of GDI+, the sense of the preceding code should be clear. If the shape of your form can't be created easily with graphic methods, you might create a bitmap with any graphic application, including Microsoft Paint, and load the image into the form's BackgroundImage property. If the form is resizeable, you should use a DrawImage method to resize the bitmap so that it always covers the entire form's surface.

Regardless of how you define the form's shape, remember that you should provide end users with the ability to move and close the form. The form in the demo application uses the subclassing technique described earlier to let the user move the form by clicking anywhere on its client area.

The Opacity Property

The Opacity property lets you apply a level of transparency to the entire form, including its title bar and borders. It's a Double value in the range 0 to 1, so you can change the opacity level with fine granularity. You can use it for special effects such as fade-ins and fade-outs. You can mix it with the TransparencyKey property, as the sample application provided with the companion code for this book demonstrates. (See Figure 15-26.)

Oddly, both the TransparencyKey and Opacity properties make the form completely transparent to most screen capture programs, and in fact I was in trouble when I had to shoot Figures 15-25 and 15-26. I was so desperate that I almost gave up, but I tried the nearly forgotten PrintScreen key, which worked perfectly and copied the screen image to the Clipboard.

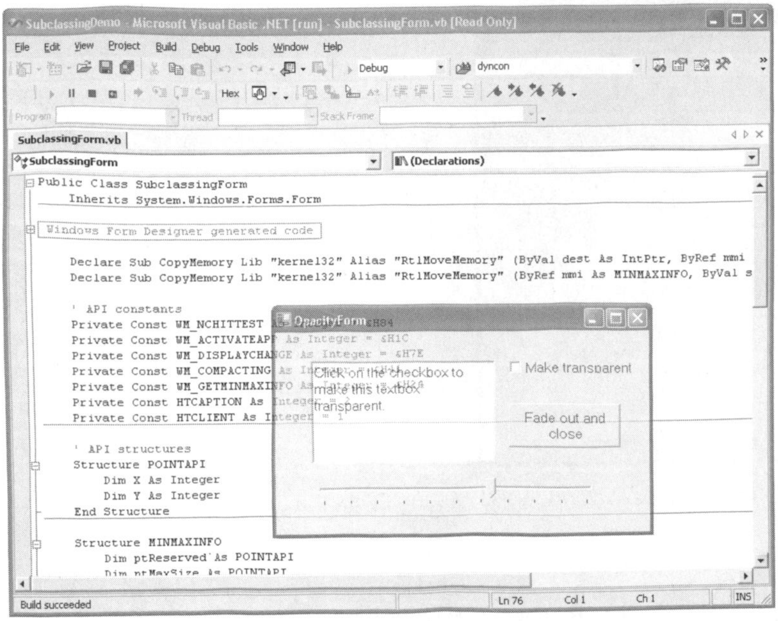

Figure 15-26   Mixing the TransparencyKey and Opacity properties on one form

The Application.EnableVisualStyles Method

Most Windows XP applications use the look and feel introduced with this version of the operating system. Controls using this visual style have rounded corners and change their appearance when the mouse hovers on them. More specifically, the Windows XP visual style changed the way the non-client area of the control is drawn. Enforcing Windows XP visual styles is as simple as invoking the Application.EnableVisualStyles method, which was added in .NET Framework 1.1. You must call this method before the first form is displayed, so an application that leverages this feature should display its startup form from inside the Sub Main procedure:

```
<System.STAThread()> _
Public Sub Main()
    Application.EnableVisualStyles()
    Application.Run(New StartupForm)
End Sub
```

The majority of Windows Forms controls adopt the most recent UI style automatically, for example the TextBox, ListBox, ComboBox, DataGrid, TreeView, ListView, Progress-Bar, TrackBar, DateTimePicker, MonthCalendar, TabControl, and the two scroll bar controls. The four controls that inherit from ButtonBase class—namely Button, Check-Box, RadioButton, and GroupBox—take the new style only if you set their FlatStyl property to System. Finally, a few controls aren't affected at all by the EnableVisu Styles method, including the Label, LinkLabel, NumericUpDown, DomainUpDo and CheckListBox. Figure 15-27 shows a form that uses the new UI style.

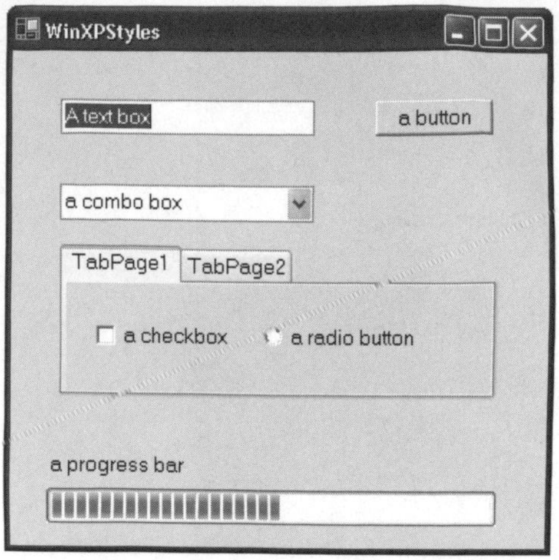

Figure 15-27   A form that uses Windows XP visual styles

Localized Forms

Windows developers traditionally used resource files to create multilanguage applications. The problem with resource files is that they don't lend themselves well to the Rapid Application Development (RAD) approach. For example, in all previous versions of Visual Basic you can use only one language for the user interface. To support additional languages, you have to author a resource file yourself and write the code that extracts each string or image and moves the strings or images into controls. This problem has been solved in the Visual Studio .NET form designer in a simple, elegant, and effective way.

A Simple Localization Example

Let's take the simple form shown in Figure 15-28 as an example. This form contains three strings and one image that should be localized. In general, however, the localization process can involve more than just changing the visible strings in the user interface or strings used from code. For example, you might need to move a control to a different location or make it invisible under some localized versions. At any rate, you should test your form thoroughly before you make it localizable because any change you make to its user interface afterward will require more coding and efforts.

Figure 15-28   A localizable form with captions and one image, as it appears when the Language property is set to (Default)

The first step in localizing a form is to set its Localizable property to True. This is a design-time property that you won't find in the Object Browser. It tells the designer's code generator that the values of the properties of the form and its controls are to be loaded from a .resx resource file instead of hard-coded in the source code.

Next you should set the form's Language property to the alternative locale that you want to support. This property is available only at design time and you can assign any of the locales that .NET supports to it. (See Figure 15-29.) The form designer continues to display the same interface as before, but you can now change all the properties of the form and its controls (including their position, size, visibility, and so on). All the values that you set from now on will be associated with the alternative locale just selected. Figure 15-30 shows how the form might look to an Italian end user. Of course, you can repeat this procedure with any language that you want to support.

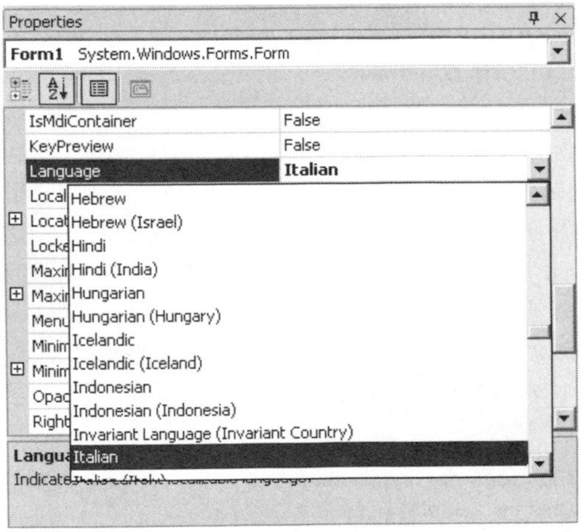

Figure 15-29   Setting the Language property to Italian

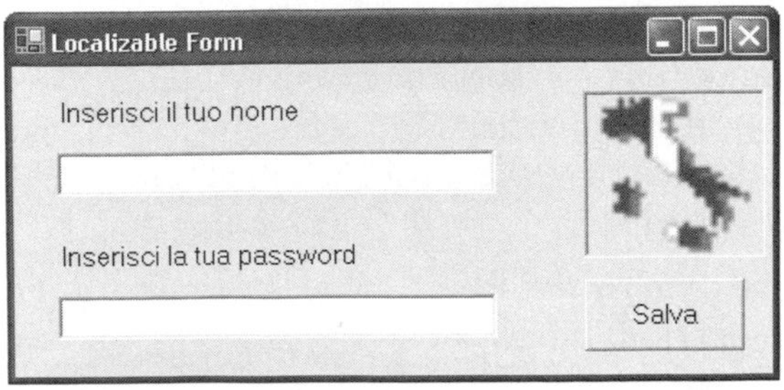

Figure 15-30   The Italian version of the original form

Running and Testing the Localized Application

The great thing about localized forms is that in most cases, you can simply forget about them. You run an application containing localized forms as you'd run a regular application. If the culture of the current user matches one of the languages you have defined, the form and its controls will use the properties you've set for that language; otherwise, the default language will be used.

A minor problem with localized forms is that they require additional testing and debugging. The easiest way to test a localized form is to modify the culture of the UI thread, which you do by assigning a suitable CultureInfo object to the CurrentUICulture property of the Thread.CurrentThread object. This is the property tested by the form engine when it's deciding which set of localized properties should be used. You should put the following routine in a separate module so that you can call it from all the forms in your application:

```
Sub SetUICulture(ByVal culture As String)
    Try
        ' Create a new CultureInfo object and assign it to the current thread.
        System.Threading.Thread.CurrentThread.CurrentUICulture = _
            New System.Globalization.CultureInfo(culture)
    Catch
        MessageBox.Show("Locale '" & culture & "' isn't supported", _
            "Error", MessageBoxButtons.OK, MessageBoxIcon.Error)
    End Try
End Sub
```

It's essential that you call SetUICulture in the form's Sub New procedure before calling InitializeComponent, the routine where form and control properties are assigned:

```
Public Sub New()
    MyBase.New()
    ' Set Italian as the culture for the interactive user.
    SetUICulture("IT")
    ' This call is required by the Windows Form Designer.
    InitializeComponent()
    ' Add any initialization after the InitializeComponent() call.
End Sub
```

Working with Resource Files

As usual, you can leverage a feature better if you know what's going on behind the scenes. When you make a form localizable, Visual Studio creates a .resx file for each specified language, including the default one. You must click the Show All Files button in the Solution Explorer's toolbar to see these .resx files inside the Visual Studio window. (See Figure 15-31.) Each file is named after the locale to which it's bound.

When you compile the project, Visual Studio .NET creates a subdirectory of the Bin directory, names this subdirectory after the locale for which the resource has been created ("It" in this example), and places there a new DLL named *application-name*.resources.dll (CustomizedFormsDemo.resources.dll in this example). You can then XCOPY the Bin directory and all its subdirectories to the end user's machine without having to deploy the .resx file.

Solution Explorer - CustomizedFormsDemo
Solution 'CustomizedFormsDemo' (1 project)
CustomizedFormsDemo
References
bin
obj
AssemblyInfo.vb
Form1.vb
Form1.it.resx
Form1.resx
licenses.licx
Solution Explorer
Class View

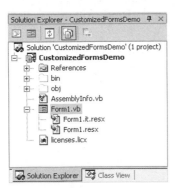

Figure 15-31 The .resx resource files as they appear in the Solution Explorer window after you click the Show All Files button

If you double-click a .resx file in the Solution Explorer, a resource editor window appears. You can edit a resource file as XML or by using a grid, such as the one shown in Figure 15-32. The four columns in the grid are the value of the resource, its key, the corresponding .NET type (such as System.Int32 or System.String), and its MIME type. The last column holds a non-null value only for binary data, such as images.

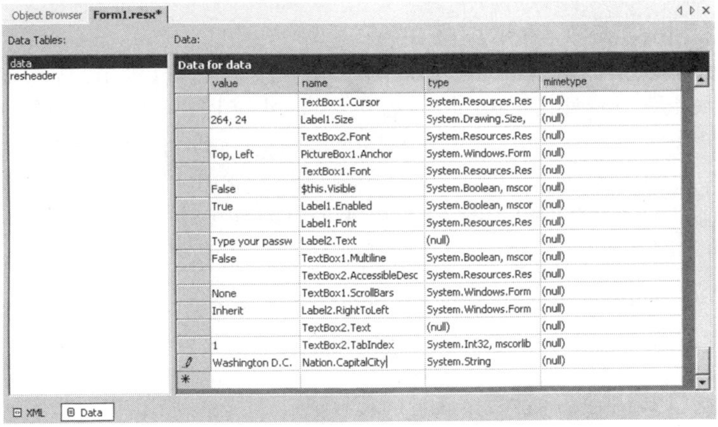

Object Browser
Form1.resx*
Data Tables:
data
resheader
Data:
Data for data
value
name
type
mimetype
TextBox1.Cursor System.Resources.Res (null)
264, 24 Label1.Size System.Drawing.Size, (null)
TextBox2.Font System.Resources.Res (null)
Top, Left PictureBox1.Anchor System.Windows.Form (null)
TextBox1.Font System.Resources.Res (null)
False $this.Visible System.Boolean, mscor (null)
True Label1.Enabled System.Boolean, mscor (null)
Label1.Font System.Resources.Res (null)
Type your passw Label2.Text (null) (null)
False TextBox1.Multiline System.Boolean, mscor (null)
TextBox2.AccessibleDesc System.Resources.Res (null)
None TextBox1.ScrollBars System.Windows.Form (null)
Inherit Label2.RightToLeft System.Windows.Form (null)
TextBox2.Text (null) (null)
1 TextBox2.TabIndex System.Int32, mscorlib (null)
Washington D.C. Nation.CapitalCity System.String (null)
XML
Data

Figure 15-32 You can edit a .resx file using a grid or the XML editor; you can switch between the two approaches by clicking on the tabs near the bottom edge of the editor.

Most of the time, the key associated with each value is the *controlname.propertyname* pair that identifies which property of which control that value will be assigned to. This makes it easy to quickly revise and check the spelling of all the properties without visiting every control.

Working with Embedded Resources

You can also create resource files containing strings that aren't related to a specific form or a specific locale by invoking the Add New Item command in the Project menu and selecting the Assembly Resource File from the gallery of available items. Give the file a meaningful name—for example, UserStrings.resx. By double-clicking on this file, you'll see a grid like the one in Figure 15-32, so you can start adding your strings, numbers, and any other type that can be typed in the value field. For example, add a System.Int32 value named Quantity. (Beware: type names are case-sensitive.)

You can now access this resource file from anywhere in the application by using this code:

```
' This code assumes that you have the following Imports
'     Imports System.Reflection

' Create a resource manager for the UserStrings resource file.
Dim asm As [Assembly] = [Assembly].GetExecutingAssembly
Dim resName As String = asm.GetName.Name & ".UserStrings"
Dim resources As New System.Resources.ResourceManager(resName, asm)
' Read the quantity item.
Dim quantity As Integer = CInt(resources.GetObject("Quantity"))
```

Notice that a resource file of this type can contain resources for multiple cultures and language, but it's up to you to devise a naming schema for discerning which value should be used by each locale. Please see source code on the companion CD for an example of such a technique.

Creating a text or binary file, a bitmap, an icon, a cursor, or virtually any type of file and saving it as an embedded resource in the current assembly is even easier. Drop the file in question from Windows Explorer to the Solution Explorer window or create a new text file, icon, bitmap, or cursor with the Add New Item command in the Project menu. Visual Studio .NET provides reasonably good editors for bitmaps and icons, or you can use your favorite graphic editor to retouch bitmaps and icons if you need to.

By default, all items created in this way or dragged from Windows Explorer are considered as content files that will be deployed on the end user's system together with all the executables that make up the application. However, you can have Visual Studio .NET embed one of such files in the compiled assembly by selecting the file in the Solution Explorer window, pressing the F4 key to access its properties, and changing the Build Action property from Content to Embedded Resource. An embedded resource can be accessed by means of the Assembly.GetManifestResourceStream method. For example, here's how you can load an embedded text file into a TextBox control:

```
' Get the current assembly.
Dim asm2 As [Assembly] = [Assembly].GetExecutingAssembly()
' Resources are named using a fully case-sensitive qualified name.
Dim resName2 As String = "MyRootnamespace.mytextfile.txt"
Dim stream2 As System.IO.Stream = asm2.GetManifestResourceStream(resName2)
' Read the contents of the embedded file and close it.
Dim reader As New System.IO.StreamReader(stream2)
TextBox1.Text = reader.ReadToEnd()
reader.Close()
```

It's essential that the resource name you provide is formed by the assembly's root namespace followed by the filename. This holds true even if the file is stored in a folder of the current project. The folder name is meaningless and it isn't included in the resource name. Because the GetManifestResourceStream returns a stream, you can load files of any type, including bitmaps:

```
Dim asm3 As [Assembly] = [Assembly].GetExecutingAssembly()
Dim resName3 As String = "CustomizedFormsDemo.demoresource.bmp"
Dim stream3 As System.IO.Stream = asm.GetManifestResourceStream(resName3)
PictureBox1.Image = New Bitmap(stream3)
stream3.Close()
```

You can enumerate all the manifest resources with the GetManifestResourceNames method, which returns a String array that contains all the files you've embedded in the assembly, as well as one .resource file for each form in the application.

Dynamic Control Properties

Let's consider the form shown in Figure 15-33, a login dialog box for connecting to Microsoft SQL Server. To help the test phase, I already placed the name of my SQL Server and my user name in the first two fields so that I just have to enter my password. It would be great if the end user had the ability to define these two preset values, but clearly I can't hard code them in the listing because I'd have to recompile the application for each end user. The obvious solution is to store these values in a file so that each user can customize them. In pre-.NET days, you might have used an .ini file for this purpose, but .NET offers a more structured and standard solution in the form of dynamic properties in configuration files.

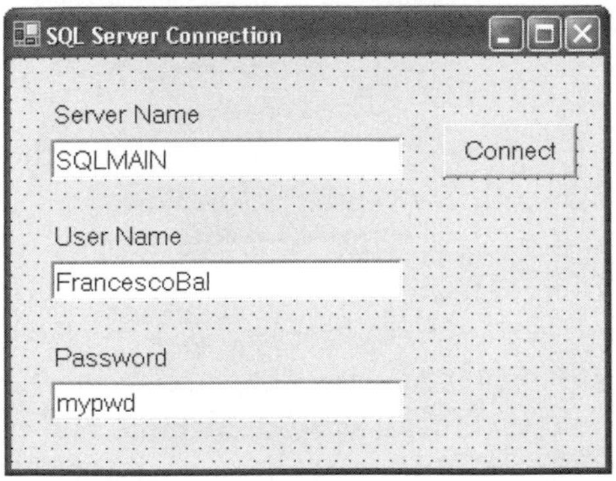

Figure 15-33 A simple form that demonstrates dynamic properties

In the section "Dynamic Properties" of Chapter 13, I explained how you can retrieve strings stored in the <appSettings> section of the application's configuration file. The good news is that you can bind one or more properties of the form or its controls to such dynamic properties and you don't even have to write a single line of code because the form designer's code generator does it automatically for you.

To bind a property in the form designer to a value in the configuration file, you must select the control in question (or the form itself), expand the (DynamicProperties) element in the Properties window, and click the ellipses button for the Advanced item. This action brings up the dialog box visible in Figure 15-34.

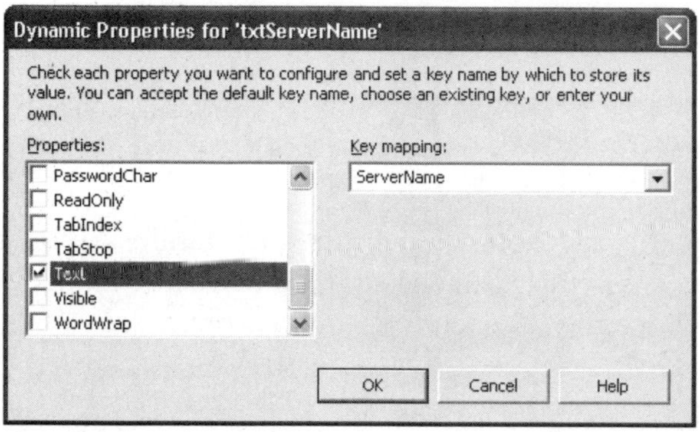

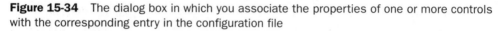

Figure 15-34   The dialog box in which you associate the properties of one or more controls with the corresponding entry in the configuration file

Scroll down the list box until you reach the property you want to make dynamic, select the corresponding check box, and enter in the text box on the right the name of the key in the <appSettings> section that will contain the value of this property. The demo application I provide on the companion CD binds the Text properties of the txtServer and txtUserName controls to the ServerName and UserName dynamic properties, but you can use the same technique for other properties, including ForeColor and Back-Color. An apparent limit of this feature is that you can't bind object properties in this way—for example, Font, Size, and Location. If a property of a control has been bound to a value in the configuration file, a small green icon appears beside its name in the Properties window.

When you create one or more dynamic properties, Visual Studio creates the application's .config file if you haven't created it already for other reasons. You can create this file explicitly by selecting the Add New Item command from the Project menu, and then double-clicking the Application Configuration File element in the template gallery. This creates a file named App.Config in the same directory as all the other source files. You can then edit this XML file directly. When you later compile the project, Visual Studio .NET copies this file in the same directory as the .exe file and renames it applicationname.exe.config. (See Figure 15-35.)

> **Note**   When deciding which properties should be stored in the .config file, keep in mind that their value is stored in clear text. Think twice before storing passwords and other critical pieces of information.

Figure 15-35   The application configuration file with the dynamic properties
you created in the Properties window

Form as Child Controls

The Form object exposes a property named TopLevel, a Boolean value that is usually
True and denotes that the form is a top-level form—that is, a form that has no parent
form or whose parent is the desktop window. I discovered this property almost by
chance; it doesn't appear in Visual Studio's object browser or IntelliSense. However, it
is included in the MSDN documentation, so I can't really consider it as undocumented.

The mention of the "parent form" of a form seems to suggest that you can make a form
a child of another form if you set this property to False. To my surprise, the following
code works without a problem. (See Figure 15-36.)

```
'...(inside the Form1 class)...
' Create an instance of Form2 and make it a child of this form.
Dim childform As New Form2
childform.TopLevel = False      ' Don't rely on IntelliSense to write this line.
childform.Visible = True        ' Make the child form visible.
Me.Controls.Add(childform)      ' Add to this form's collection of controls.
```

ContainerForm

Person Form

First Name | Last Name
Birth Date | Country

Figure 15-36   A form as a child control of another form

Working with a child form is a bit like working with an MDI child form. You can drag
and resize the child form as you do with an MDI child form, with one notable difference: a non-MDI child form hides all other controls under it, whereas an MDI child
form always appears behind any control on the parent form.

Creating a non-MDI child form isn't really exciting at first because such forms don't appear to offer any remarkable advantage over MDI child forms. One of the most interesting features is that you can use borderless child forms, so that they merge perfectly with the parent form's background and the user might use a child form without even realizing it's a form rather than a group of controls placed directly on the parent form's surface. For example, you might carefully build a form that shows, say, all the properties of a Person object and reuse it inside other forms.

However, the fact that you add a child form to the Controls collection of the parent form suggests that you can render a form as a child of any control that can work as a container control. This details leads to an interesting technique that consists of creating multiple instances of the same form and making all of them children of a Panel control whose AutoScroll property has been set to True. Then you can use each child form to display the properties of a different instance of a class or a different record in a database. I created a procedure that uses reflection to achieve the highest degree of reusability:

```
Sub LoadFormsInPanel(ByVal container As Panel, ByVal formType As Type, _
    ByVal dataArray As Array)
    Dim ypos As Integer = 0
    container.Visible = False        ' To reduce flickering...

    For index As Integer = 0 To dataArray.Length - 1
        ' Create an instance of the form via Reflection.
        Dim frm As Form = DirectCast(Activator.CreateInstance(formType), Form)
        ' Drop titlebar and border and make it a non-toplevel form.
        frm.FormBorderStyle = FormBorderStyle.None
        frm.TopLevel = False
        ' Set its position and size.
        frm.Top = ypos
        frm.Width = container.Width - 4

        ' Read the array element.
        Dim item As Object = dataArray.GetValue(index)
        ' Bind all controls whose Tag property isn't null
        For Each ctrl As Control In frm.Controls
            If Not ctrl.Tag Is Nothing AndAlso ctrl.Tag.ToString.Length > 0 Then
                ' Bind this control to the array item.
                ctrl.DataBindings.Add("Text", item, ctrl.Tag.ToString)
            End If
        Next

        ' Add the form to the panel and make it visible.
        container.Controls.Add(frm)
        frm.Visible = True
        ' Prepare position of next form.
        ypos += frm.ClientSize.Height
    Next
    container.Visible = True
End Sub
```

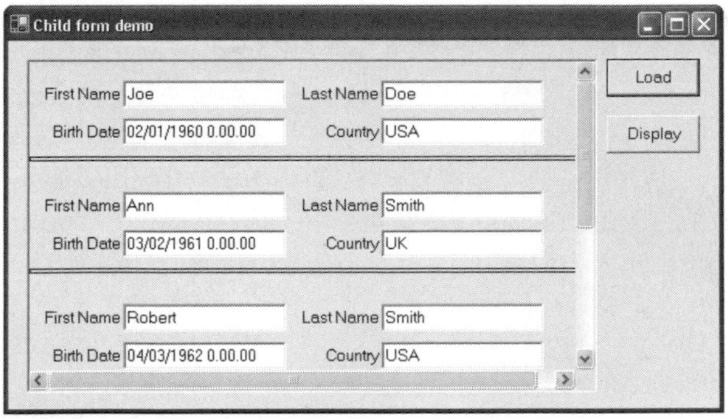

Figure 15-37 A Panel control that contains multiple instances of the PersonForm form, each one bound to a different Person object

The routine uses data binding, but you can figure out how it works even before reading about binding in Chapter 16. Here's the code that creates the form shown in Figure 15-37:

```
Dim persons() As Person
' Fill the persons array.
⋮
LoadFormsInPanel(Panel1, GetType(PersonForm), persons)
```

The second argument is the form that contains the controls that you want to bind to the properties of the source objects (Person objects, in this case) in the array you pass in the third argument. The routine assumes that the Tag property of these bound controls has been assigned the name of the corresponding property in the source object. The routine always binds the source object property to the control's Text property, but you can easily modify its code, for example to account for Boolean properties bound to the Checked property of CheckBox controls.

Thanks to data binding, the end user can edit the control values, and the new values are immediately assigned to the corresponding properties of the source object. You can test this feature in the demo application by clicking on the Display button. (Incidentally, this technique lets you migrate Visual Basic 6 applications based on the DataRepeater control, which isn't supported under the .NET Framework.)

At the end of this long chapter, you know enough to build great and highly functional Windows Forms applications. However, I haven't discussed all the controls you can use and how you can create eye-catching graphic effects with the classes in the GDI+ portion of the Framework. These are the topics of the next two chapters.

16 Windows Forms Controls

To create great Windows Forms applications, you need to learn more about the controls and other classes in the System.Windows.Forms namespace, such as Application and Clipboard.

> **Note** To keep the code as concise as possible, all the code samples in this section assume that the following Imports statements are used at the file or project level:
>
> ```
> Imports System.System.Drawing
> Imports System.Windows.Forms.DataGrid
> Imports System.IO
> ```
>
> These Imports are in addition to those that are defined at the project level for all Windows Forms applications.

Overview of Windows Forms Controls

Unfortunately, I don't have space in this book to dissect all the controls in the Windows Forms package, which expose just too many properties, methods, and events. On the other hand, most of these controls are just improved versions of the Visual Basic controls you've worked with for years, so I'll provide only a brief description of what has changed or has been added.

> **See Also** Several chapters of my *Programming Microsoft Visual Basic 6* book, available on the companion CD, are devoted to forms and controls. The techniques I illustrate there are in most cases valid under Visual Basic .NET, possibly after fixing a few minor issues. You might want to review Chapter 3 (which is about Textbox, ListBox, ComboBox, buttons, menus, and other basic controls), Chapter 10 (ImageList, TreeView, ListView, Toolbar, StatusBar, and ProgressBar), Chapter 11 (DateTimePicker, MonthCalendar, NumericUpDown, and DomainUpDown), and Chapter 12 (RichTextBox and common dialog controls).

The TextBox Control

The TextBox control supports many new properties and methods, and several of the old properties have been renamed:

- The TextChanged event replaces the Change event.

- The ReadOnly property replaces the Locked property. (The Locked property now has a different meaning. It prevents controls from being accidentally moved at design time.)

- You can set the new CharacterCasing property to Upper or Lower to automatically convert characters typed by the end user, pasted from the Clipboard, or assigned from code.

- The SelectedText, SelectionStart, and SelectionLength properties replace SelText, SelStart, and SelLength. You can also select part or all of the contents by using the Select(start, length) and SelectAll methods.

- You can perform copy and paste operations by using the new Clear, Copy, Cut, and Paste methods.

- You can append text to a TextBox by using the new AppendText method, which is much faster than using the & operator with the Text property.

- The new Modified property returns True if the TextBox contents have been modified. If the CanUndo property is True, you can revert to the previous value with the Undo method or clear undo data by using the ClearUndo method.

- The TextAlign property replaces the Alignment property and can be used to align text left (the default), right, or center.

- You can set the AutoSize property to True to have the size of the control automatically reflect the current font size.

- The ScrollToCaret method ensures that the insertion point or selected text is in the visible portion of a TextBox control.

A few properties are significant only for multiline TextBox controls:

- You can decide whether Enter and Tab keys inside a multiline TextBox should insert a character, instead of performing their usual actions of pushing the default button or moving to the next field, by assigning True to the AcceptReturns and AcceptTabs properties.

- By default, multiline TextBox controls work in word-processing mode—that is, with wordwrapping enabled, even if the ScrollBars property is set to Both. You must explicitly set the new WordWrap property to False to make the horizontal scroll bar appear and have the control work like an editor.

- You can use the Lines property to arrange for the contents of multiline TextBox controls to be read and assigned as an array of individual strings.

The Label Control

The Label control can now display an image and has a more flexible way of position-ing the caption (which now corresponds to the Text property, as for all other controls):

- The TextAlignment property replaces Alignment and can be one of nine possible values, such as TopLeft, MiddleCenter, and so on.

- The FlatStyle property replaces Appearance and provides a flat or 3-D appearance.

- The PreferredWidth and PreferredHeight properties return the optimal size for the control, given its current text and font.

- The new Image property can be assigned the image to be displayed in the Label control. Or you can assign an ImageList control to the ImageList property and the index of the image to the ImageIndex property. You control the position of the image in the control by using the ImageAlign property (nine possible values).

You can set all the image properties from the Properties window. To delete an image assigned at design time, right-click on the property name and select the Reset menu command.

The LinkLabel Control

This new control is a Label control that can contain one or more hyperlink areas. You can choose from two ways to define a hyperlink inside a LinkLabel control. In the sim-plest case, you assign a LinkArea object to the property with the same name and define its underline behavior by using the LinkBehavior property:

```
LinkLabel1.Text = "Visit the www.vb2themax.com site"
' Make the URL a hyperlink. (Arguments are start, length.)
LinkLabel1.LinkArea = New LinkArea(10, 17)
' Underline the URL only when the mouse is over it.
LinkLabel1.LinkBehavior = LinkBehavior.HoverUnderline
```

If you have multiple links, you have to add each of them to the Links collection pro-grammatically because you can't do it from the Properties window. After you build the collection, you can further read or modify properties of individual LinkLabel.Link objects by means of their Enabled and Visited properties:

```
LinkLabel1.Text = "Visit our Home Page, or jump to the document"
' Make "Home Page" a link.
LinkLabel1.Links.Add(10, 9, "home")
' Make "document" a link.
LinkLabel1.Links.Add(36, 8, "doc")
' Mark the Home Page document as visited.
LinkLabel1.Links(0).Visited = True
```

The third argument of the Add method can be any string or object that identifies that specific link. This value is then exposed to the LinkClicked event as a property of the LinkLabel.Link object. You typically react to this event by displaying an Internet page inside a WebBrowser control or a new instance of Internet Explorer. The easiest way to do it is by invoking the Process.Start shared method. (I cover the Process object in Chapter 19.)

```
Private Sub LinkLabel1_LinkClicked(ByVal sender As Object, _
    ByVal e As LinkLabelLinkClickedEventArgs) Handles LinkLabel1.LinkClicked
    Select Case e.Link.LinkData
        Case "home"
            Process.Start("http://www.vb2themax.com")
        Case "doc"
            Process.Start("http://www.vb2themax.com/team.asp")
    End Select
    ' Mark the link as visited, and disable it.
    e.Link.Visited = True
    e.Link.Enabled = False
End Sub
```

You can control the colors used for hyperlinks with the ActiveLinkColor, VisitedLink-Color, and DisabledLinkColor properties. The LinkLabel control (see Figure 16-1) inherits all the remaining properties from the Label control, including the ability to align text and display images.

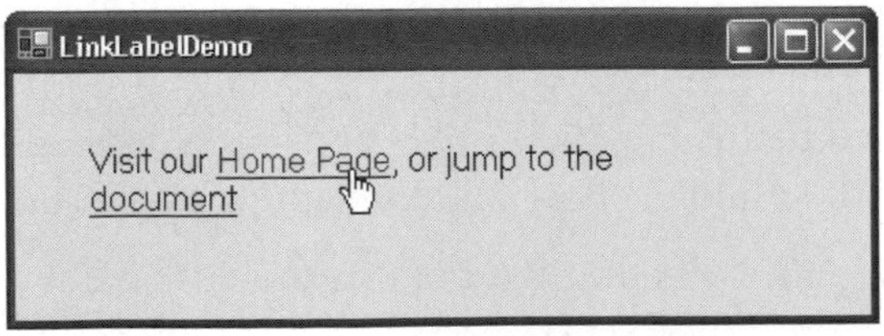

Figure 16-1   The LinkLabel control, with two link areas in it

The CheckBox, RadioButton, and Button Controls

These three controls inherit from the same ButtonBase class, so they have several properties and features in common.

- The Text property replaces Caption. As I mentioned before, you can align the text in nine different ways by using the TextAlign property.

- The FlatStyle property replaces Appearance and provides a flat or 3-D appearance.

- You have full control of ForeColor and BackColor properties, even for Button controls.

- You can display icons by using the Image property, align them with the ImageAlign property, or load them from an ImageList control with the ImageList and ImageIndex properties. You can also assign an image to the BackgroundImage property to create a textured button. (See Figure 16-2.)

- The Appearance property replaces Style and determines whether a CheckBox or a RadioButton control is displayed as a button.

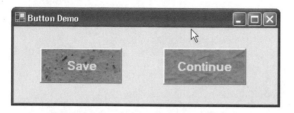

Figure 16-2 You can create a colored or textured background for all controls inherited from the ButtonBase class.

The CheckBox Control

The new CheckBox control works much like it does under Visual Basic 6, with only a few noteworthy differences:

- The AutoCheck property is True (the default) if the control automatically toggles its state when clicked. You can set it to False to get more control over when the end user can change the state of the control.

- The CheckAlign property lets you select among nine possible positions of the check box. You can combine this property with the TextAlign property to create many visual variations. (Notice that if the Style property is set to System, you can move the check box only to the MiddleLeft or MiddleRight positions.)

- The ThreeState property determines whether the control should have two or three states. If the property is False, you should set or read the state of the control with the Checked property; if True, you should use the CheckState property instead. By default, the control has only two states. (The Value property is no longer supported.)

Depending on the value of the ThreeState property, you use three different events to react to user actions: the CheckedChanged, CheckStateChanged, and Click events, which fire in this order. The only case in which only the latter two events fire occurs when AutoCheck and ThreeState are both True and user clicks bring the CheckState property from Checked to Indeterminate without changing the Checked property.

Not all combinations of the new properties make sense. For example, when setting the Appearance property to Button, you should set ThreeState to False and ensure that the FlatStyle property is set to System; otherwise, the button won't appear to rise when it's clicked a second time.

The RadioButton Control

Not counting the properties inherited from ButtonBase, the only relevant new properties of this control are the Checked, CheckAlign, and AutoCheck properties, which have the same meaning that they have for the CheckBox control.

You can detect a change in state by using the CheckedChanged event, whereas the Click event fires only if the user clicks on the control with the mouse. The only new method is PerformClick, which simulates a click.

The Button Control

Except for the new properties inherited from ButtonBase, the Button control is virtually identical to the old CommandButton control you used under Visual Basic 6. As I explained in Chapter 15, the Default and Cancel properties have been replaced by the AcceptButton and CancelButton properties of the parent form. The Value property is gone as well. The only new method for this control is PerformClick, which indirectly fires the Click event.

The ListBox Control

The ListBox control has been completely redesigned in its programmatic interface and is much more powerful.

Adding Elements

For starters, we have the new Items property, which gathers all the elements in the control and lets you manipulate them using the familiar Add, AddRange, Insert, Remove, and Clear methods.

```
With ListBox1.Items
    .Clear()                  ' Start with a clean collection.
    .Add("One")               ' Add two items.
    .Add("Two")
    .Insert(0, "Zero")        ' Insert before element at index 0.
End With
For Each o As Object In ListBox1.Items
    Debug.Write(o & " ")      ' => Zero One Two
Next
```

You can add any object to this collection, not just strings. If an object is loaded in the Items collection, the ListBox control calls the object's ToString method to retrieve the string that must be displayed for that item. Therefore, you just need to override the ToString method in your own class to decide what text appears in the control:

```
Class Person
    Public FirstName As String, LastName As String
```

```
Overrides Function ToString() As String
    Return FirstName & " " & LastName
End Function

ReadOnly Property ReverseName() As String
    Get
        Return LastName & ", " & FirstName
    End Get
End Property
End Class
```

You can change this default behavior by assigning the name of any property to DisplayMember. (You must make this assignment *before* loading values into the ListBox, however.) For example, here's how you tell the ListBox control to display the ReverseName property instead of the value returned by the ToString method:

```
ListBox1.DisplayMember = "ReverseName"
```

The ItemData property isn't supported, but the ability to store objects makes it superfluous. In fact, you just have to convert the items in the control to their native type and then extract any property you need:

```
' Get the ID of the first Person element in the list.
Dim id As Integer = DirectCast(ListBox1.Items(0), Person).ID
```

Working with Selected Items

The way you test whether an item is selected has changed as well. For a single-selection ListBox, you can retrieve the index of the selection by using the new SelectedIndex property, which replaces the ListIndex property. Or you can use the new SelectedItem property, which returns the selected item or Nothing if no element is selected:

```
' Get the LastName of the selected Person element.
lastName = DirectCast(ListBox1.SelectedItem, Person).LastName
```

You create a multiple-selection ListBox by setting its SelectionMode property to MultiSimple or MultiExtended. (This property replaces the MultiSelect property in Visual Basic 6.) You can choose from three ways to detect which items are selected. If you want the actual objects that are selected in the control, you use the SelectedItems collection:

```
' Display the LastName of selected Person elements.
For Each p As Person In ListBox1.SelectedItems
    Debug.WriteLine(p.LastName)
Next
```

If you're interested in just the index of selected items, you can iterate over the SelectedIndices collection. For example, you can remedy the lack of the SelCount property as follows:

```
Dim selectedCount As Integer = ListBox1.SelectedIndices.Count
```

You can also retrieve the selection state of an item by using the GetSelected method, which works like the now-unsupported Selected property:

```
' Check whether the first element in the ListBox is selected.
Dim state As Boolean = ListBox1.GetSelected(0)
```

You can change the selection state of an element by using the SetSelected method, which is the only way to programmatically select or deselect an element because you can't add or remove elements from the SelectedItems and SelectedIndices collections:

```
ListBox1.SetSelected(0, True)      ' Select the first element.
ListBox1.SetSelected(1, False)     ' Deselect the second element.
```

When the SelectedIndex property changes, the control raises a SelectedIndexChanged event. You should react to user action using this event because the Click event now doesn't fire if the user moves the selection by means of arrow keys.

Other Properties and Methods

A ListBox control can display multiple columns, but you don't use the Columns property as you do in Visual Basic 6. Instead, you must set the MultiColumn property to True and then assign a value (in pixels) to the ColumnWidth property. Or you can use the default 0 value for the latter property and let the control find out the most appropriate value. (You can then read ColumnWidth to learn which column width is being used.) The UseTabStops property can be set to True to let the control expand tab characters embedded in the elements.

The ScrollAlwaysVisible property determines whether a vertical scroll bar is always visible. If the property is True, the scroll bar will be visible but disabled if all the elements in the control are visible. You can also display a horizontal scroll bar so that the user can read elements wider than the control's client area. The horizontal scroll bar becomes visible only if there is at least one element wider than the visible area.

The BeginUpdate and EndUpdate methods suspend and reactivate repainting of the control. You can use these methods to reduce flickering and speed execution:

```
ListBox1.BeginUpdate
' Add many elements here.
⋮
ListBox1.EndUpdate
```

The FindString and FindStringExact methods let you quickly find an item in the list:

```
' Find the first element that begins with "Ba".
Dim index As Integer = ListBox1.FindString("Ba")
If index = -1 Then
    Debug.WriteLine("Not found")
Else
    ' Find the "Smith" element (exact search) that follows the previous one.
    index = ListBox1.FindStringExact("Smith", index)
End If
```

You can also perform searches directly on the Items collection by using its Contains and IndexOf methods.

Finally, two methods help you understand which element is under the mouse cursor. IndexFromPoint returns the index of the element under a given point specified in the control's client coordinates, whereas GetItemRectangle returns the rectangle that corresponds to an element with a given index.

Owner-Draw ListBox Controls

The most exciting new feature of the ListBox control—as well as the ComboBox control and the MenuItem object—is the complete control it gives developers over how individual elements are rendered. Exercising that control isn't straightforward, however—that it requires familiarity with GDI+ objects and methods is one complication.

The key to this new feature is the DrawMode property, used together with the Item-Height property and the DrawItem event. To create an owner-draw ListBox, you set its DrawMode property to OwnerDrawFixed, set the ItemHeight property to the height of individual items (in pixels), and fill the control with all your items, as you do with a regular ListBox. For example, the following routine uses reflection methods to fill the control with the names of all known colors (which the Color class exposes as shared properties):

```
' This code assumes that you've imported the System.Reflection namespace.

' Make the ListBox owner-draw.
ListBox1.DrawMode = DrawMode.OwnerDrawFixed
ListBox1.ItemHeight = 24
' Avoid flickering while filling the Listbox.
ListBox1.BeginUpdate()
ListBox1.Items.Clear()
' Create a list of all the properties in the Color class.
For Each pi As PropertyInfo In GetType(Color).GetProperties( _
    BindingFlags.Static Or BindingFlags.Public)
    ' Add the name of the property (that is, the color name).
    ListBox1.Items.Add(pi.Name)
Next
' Now display the result.
ListBox1.EndUpdate()
```

An owner-draw ListBox object fires a DrawItem event just before displaying each element. Your job is to trap this event and draw the element on the ListBox control's surface. You decide how to render the element by checking a few properties of the second argument passed to the event. Index is the index of the element in question; State is a bit-code value that lets you determine the element's state, such as whether the element is selected or disabled. Other properties tell you where the item should be rendered (Bounds) and what its attributes are (Font, ForeColor, BackColor). All the graphic operations must be performed on the Graphics object exposed by the property of the same name. The following procedure completes the preceding example and actually displays all the colors in the ListBox object, as shown in Figure 16-3:

```
Private Sub ListBox1_DrawItem(ByVal sender As Object, _
    ByVal e As DrawItemEventArgs) Handles ListBox1.DrawItem

    ' Get the rectangle to be drawn.
    Dim rect As Rectangle = e.Bounds
    ' Draw the background of the proper color.
    If (e.State And DrawItemState.Selected) Then
        ' Fill the rectangle with the highlight system color.
        e.Graphics.FillRectangle(SystemBrushes.Highlight, rect)
    Else
        ' Else, fill the rectangle with the Window system color.
        e.Graphics.FillRectangle(SystemBrushes.Window, rect)
    End If

    ' Get the color of the item to be drawn.
    Dim colorName As String = ListBox1.Items(e.Index)
    ' Build a brush of that color.
    Dim b As New SolidBrush(Color.FromName(colorName))

    ' Shrink the rectangle by some pixels.
    rect.Inflate(-16, -2)
    ' Draw the rectangle interior with the color.
    e.Graphics.FillRectangle(b, rect)
    ' Draw the rectangle outline with a black pen.
    e.Graphics.DrawRectangle(Pens.Black, rect)

    ' Decide the color of the text (black or white).
    Dim b2 As Brush
    If CInt(b.Color.R) + CInt(b.Color.G) + CInt(b.Color.B) > 128 * 3 Then
        b2 = Brushes.Black
    Else
        b2 = Brushes.White
    End If

    ' Draw the name of the color using the default font.
    e.Graphics.DrawString(colorName, e.Font, b2, rect.X + 4, rect.Y + 2)
    ' Destroy the custom brush.
    ' (Don't dispose of b2 because it is a system brush.)
    b.Dispose()
End Sub
```

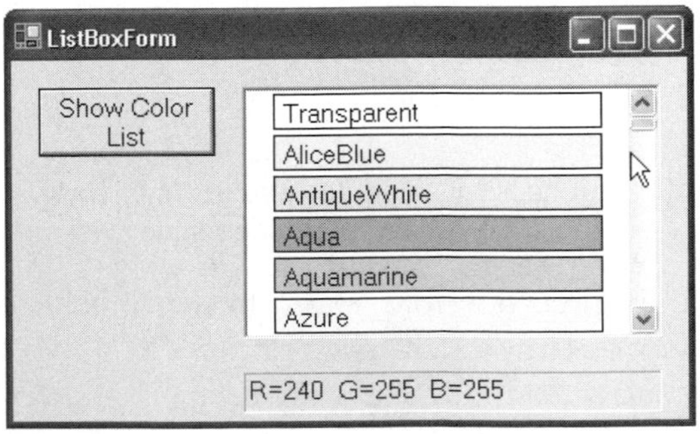

Figure 16-3   An owner-draw ListBox control

The DrawMode property of the ListBox, ComboBox, and MainMenu controls supports the OwnerDrawVariable setting, which lets you create elements with varying height. When such a control is created, it fires one MeasureItem event for each element. You're expected to return the height of each element, given its index.

If you create owner-draw ListBox controls with the HorizontalScrollBar property set to True, you should also assign a suitable value in pixels to the HorizontalExtent property to inform the control about the width of the largest element.

The CheckedListBox Control

The CheckedListBox control is a variant of the ListBox control that displays a check box to the left of each element. (See Figure 16-4.) In Visual Basic 6, you can create this control by setting a ListBox control's Style property to 1-Checkboxes.

The CheckedListBox control inherits from ListBox, so it exposes the same properties, methods, and events. As its name implies, this control lets users check one or more items. However, you use the SelectionMode property only to decide whether one or no elements can be selected, and the SelectedItems and SelectedIndices collections replace the CheckedItems and CheckedIndices collections.

The CheckedListBox control exposes two new properties. ThreeDCheckBoxes can be set to True to display three-dimensional check boxes, whereas CheckOnClick can be set to True to let users check or uncheck elements by means of a single click. The default value for both properties is False.

Figure 16-4   A CheckedListBox with the ThreeDCheckBoxes property set to True. When an element is checked or unchecked, the control fires an ItemCheck event, as it does under Visual Basic 6.

The individual check boxes can be in three possible states, like a CheckBox control whose ThreeState property is set to True. However, a click on the check box can only select or clear it, and the Indeterminate state can be set only by means of code, when you use the SetItemCheckState method. The control also exposes the GetItemCheck-State, GetItemChecked, and SetItemChecked methods to read and write the state of individual check boxes. To iterate over all checked elements, you can use the CheckedItems and CheckedIndices collections, as I mentioned previously.

The ComboBox Control

Both the ComboBox and the ListBox controls derive from the same class, ListControl; this fact explains why these controls have so many properties in common. Moreover, because a ComboBox also has an editable area, it exposes many of the members that you can find in a TextBox control, such as the SelectedText, SelectionStart, Selection-Length, and MaxLength properties; the SelectAll method; and the TextChanged event. Here are a few properties peculiar to the ComboBox control:

- The Visual Basic 6 Style property has been renamed DropDownStyle (can be DropDown, Simple, or DropDownList).

- The MaxDropDownItems property specifies the maximum number of items to be displayed in the drop-down area, whereas the DropDownWidth property specifies the width of the drop-down area. (Values less than the control's width have no effect.)

- The DroppedDown property can be set to True or False to programmatically open or close the drop-down area.

- As with the old Visual Basic 6 control, you get a DropDown event when the drop-down area opens. You get a SelectedIndexChanged event when a new element is selected.

The ComboBox control supports the DrawMode property and the DrawItem event, so you can create a user-draw ComboBox control that displays icons, items in a different color, and so on. For this reason, the ImageCombo control is no longer supported.

Provider Controls

The Windows Forms architecture is quite extensible. For example, you can create so-called *provider controls*, which add new properties to all the controls on the form. The Windows Forms namespace includes three such controls: ToolTip, ErrorProvider, and HelpProvider.

The ToolTip Control

The ToolTip control enables any control on a form to display a ToolTip when the mouse hovers over it.

The ToolTip control isn't visible at run time, so it appears in the designer's component tray area when you drop the control from the Toolbox. This action creates a new control named ToolTip1. If you now select the control, you'll see the few properties that it exposes at design time: InitialDelay, AutoPopDelay, ReshowDelay, and AutomaticDelay. (You can read a short description of each in the Properties window.) In most cases, you can leave them at their default value.

If you next select another control on the form, you'll see that a new property is now visible in the Properties window: ToolTip on ToolTip1. (All the provider controls add properties whose names are in the *propername* on *controlname* format.) You can assign this property at design time the same way you used to assign the ToolTipText property under Visual Basic 6.

In practice, at design time you can deal with extender properties in the same way you do with regular properties, with one most notable exception: if you copy and paste a control on another form, the new control retains the original values of all intrinsic properties, but it loses the values of all extender properties.

You see the difference from previous language versions when you have to assign this property in code. In fact, the new property doesn't truly belong to the control associated with the ToolTip; instead, it's just a string that's stored inside the ToolTip control. In general, all provider controls expose a pair of methods for each of the properties they provide to other controls. The names of these methods are Get*propertyname* and Set*propertyname*, and they follow a similar syntax:

```
' Assign a ToolTip to the TextBox1 control.
ToolTip1.SetToolTip(TextBox1, "Enter the name of the product")
' Read it back.
Debug.WriteLine(ToolTip1.GetToolTip(TextBox1))
```

All provider controls expose the CanExtend method, which lets you test whether a control of a given type can be extended using the new properties (only the ToolTip property in this specific case). This method is useful when you're writing generic routines:

```
' Clear the ToolTip for all the controls on this form.
 For Each ctrl As Control In Me.Controls
    If ToolTip1.CanExtend(ctrl) Then ToolTip1.SetToolTip(ctrl, "")
Next
```

In a welcome improvement from Visual Basic 6, you can now embed carriage returns to create multiline Tooltips, shown in Figure 16-5:

```
ToolTip1.SetToolTip(btnCancel, "Click here" & ControlChars.CrLf & "to close the form")
```

Alas, you can't embed unprintable characters at design time in the Properties window, but there is an easy workaround. Just use the same escape sequences you'd use for regular expression strings (see Chapter 11)—for example, \r for carriage returns. Then execute this code from inside the Form_Load event handler:

```
For Each ctrl As Control In Me.Controls
    If ToolTip1.CanExtend(ctrl) AndAlso ToolTip1.GetToolTip(ctrl) <> "" Then
        ToolTip1.SetToolTip(ctrl, System.Text.RegularExpressions.Regex.Unescape( _
            ToolTip1.GetToolTip(ctrl)))
    End If
Next
```

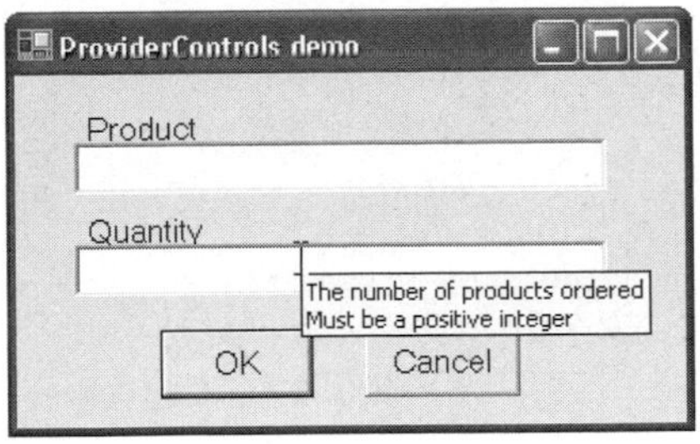

Figure 16-5 You can create multilined ToolTips.

The ErrorProvider Control

The ErrorProvider control lets you implement Windows Forms applications that use a validation method now familiar to all users who spend their time on the Internet. Typical Internet applications validate all the controls on the form when the user clicks the OK or Save button, and they display a red icon (or some other icon) near all the controls that failed the validation. This approach to validation leaves end users free to skip among fields and fill them in the order they prefer. (See Figure 16-6.)

You can drop an ErrorProvider control on a form and then set its few properties in the Properties window. BlinkStyle tells whether the icon should blink; BlinkRate is the blink frequency in milliseconds; Icon is the icon that will be displayed beside each control that contains an invalid value. All the controls use the same icon, but you can use multiple ErrorProvider controls on the same form to provide different icons for different types of errors.

The ErrorProvider control adds two properties to controls on forms. IconAlignment tells where the icon should be displayed, and IconPadding is the distance from the control's edge. In most cases, the default values are OK.

You actually display an error icon beside a control by using the ErrorProvider's SetError method, which takes a reference to the control and an error description that will be used as a ToolTip for the icon itself. You hide the icon by calling SetError again with a null string argument. The following code is behind the simple form you see in Figure 16-6:

```
Private Sub btnOK_Click(ByVal sender As System.Object, _
    ByVal e As System.EventArgs) Handles btnOK.Click

    ' Assume it's OK to close the form.
    Me.DialogResult = DialogResult.OK
    ' Clear all error icons.
    ErrorProvider1.SetError(txtProduct, "")
    ErrorProvider1.SetError(txtQty, "")
    ' Check that first field contains something.
    If txtProduct.Text = "" Then
        ErrorProvider1.SetError(txtProduct, "Must enter a product name")
        Me.DialogResult = DialogResult.None
    End If
```

```
    Try
        ' Attempt to get a valid quantity in second field (might throw).
        Dim qty As Integer = CInt(txtQty.Text)
        ' Throw a generic error if out of range.
        If qty < 1 Or qty > 100 Then Throw New Exception()
    Catch
        ' Regardless of the exception type, use the same error message.
        ErrorProvider1.SetError(txtQty, "Enter a valid number in range 1-100")
        Me.DialogResult = DialogResult.None
    End Try

    ' Close the form only if validation passed.
    ' (This line isn't really required if this is a dialog box.)
    If Me.DialogResult = DialogResult.OK Then Me.Close()
End Sub
```

You can embed carriage returns in the string passed to the SetError method to create multilined error messages.

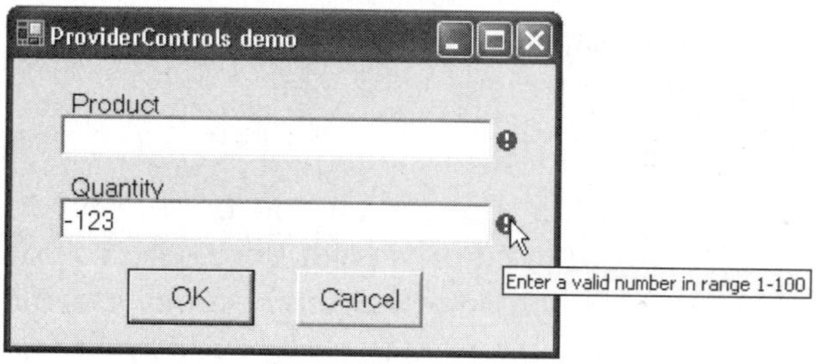

Figure 16-6 The ErrorProvider control in action

The HelpProvider Control

The HelpProvider control works as a bridge between your program and the Help class so that you can display either simple help messages or more complex help pages when the user presses the F1 key and the focus is on a control in your form. (See later in this chapter for more information about the Help class.)

The only property of the HelpProvider control is HelpNamespace, which should be assigned the name of the compiled Help file (.chm) or raw HTML file. The HelpProvider control adds three properties to each control on your form.

- The HelpNavigator property tells what kind of action must be performed when the end user presses the F1 key. It can be one of the following enumerated values: Find, Index, TableOfContents, Topic, KeywordIndex, and AssociateIndex.

- The HelpKeyword property specifies the keyword or the topic to be searched.

- The HelpString property is a short message that is displayed in a ToolTip-like window when the user presses the F1 key. (See Figure 16-7.) This property is used only if HelpKeyword is left blank.

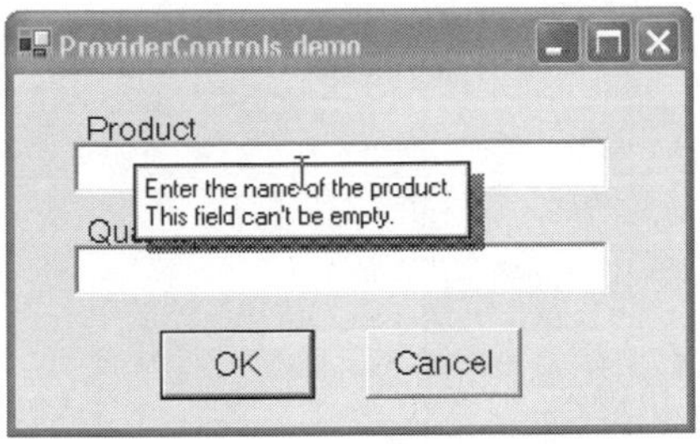

Figure 16-7   The pop-up message produced by the HelpString property of the HelpProvider control

The HelpString property can embed carriage return characters to create multiline help messages. You can't type these characters in the Properties window, but you might use special escape sequences, such as \r, and resolve them from inside the Form_Load event handler by using a technique similar to the one I explained for the ToolTip control.

In most cases, you don't need to assign these properties in code. But if you must, you can do so by using the SetHelpNavigator, SetHelpKeyword, and SetHelpString methods. You can leave the HelpNamespace property blank if you use just the HelpString property and never access an actual help file.

The Splitter Control

The Splitter control makes it incredibly easy to create splitter bars, that is, those dividers that you use to partition the space on a form among different controls.

A minor problem with this control is that it is somewhat tricky to change the layout of a form once you've created it, so you should think long and hard about what controls you want to have on the form and how they should be arranged. Let's take as an example the form visible in Figure 16-8, which contains a ListBox, a TextBox, a PictureBox, and two Splitter controls. The following list shows the right sequence for building the form's layout:

1. Drop the ListBox control on the form, and dock it to the left border.

2. Drop the first Splitter control; since the default value for its Dock property is Left, it will automatically stick to the ListBox.

3. Drop the TextBox control in the unoccupied area of the form, and dock it to the top border; set its Multiline property to True, and make it taller than its default height.

4. Drop the second Splitter control in the available area of the form. It will dock to the left, so you have to change its Dock property to Top so that it sticks to the bottom border of the TextBox.

5. Finally, drop the PictureBox in the empty area on the form, and set its Dock property to Fill.

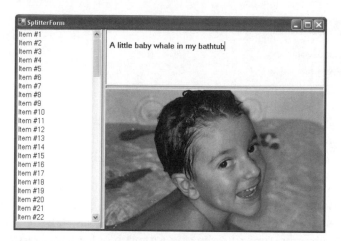

Figure 16-8   A form with two Splitter controls

Now you can run the program and check that the controls resize correctly when you drag the splitter bars.

For more complex layouts, you can drop Panel controls on the form's surface and use them as containers for other controls. You can set the Dock and Anchor properties of controls inside each panel to achieve many different effects.

You can set the minimum and maximum sizes of controls being resized by means of the Splitter's MinSize and MinExtra properties. The former specifies the minimum size of the docked control; the latter, the minimum size of the part of the form that was empty when you dropped the Splitter. For example, in the case of the vertical Splitter in Figure 16-8, MinSize is the minimum width of the ListBox control to its left, whereas MinExtra is the minimum width of the TextBox and PictureBox to its right.

At run time, you can use the Splitter's Move event to determine when the splitter bar has been moved, and you can check the position of the splitter by using the Split-Position property.

Common Dialog Controls

The Windows Forms namespace contains seven controls that replace and extend the functionality of the Visual Basic 6 CommonDialog control. All these controls expose the ShowDialog method, which brings up the dialog box and returns DialogResult.OK if the user confirmed the action, or DialogResult.Cancel if the user canceled it. They also expose the ShowHelp property, which can be set to True to display a Help button, and the HelpRequest event, which fires if the end user asks for help.

The OpenFileDialog Control

This control shows an Open File dialog box. Instead of setting the bit-coded Flags property, as you do under Visual Basic 6, you can count on self-describing Boolean properties, such as CheckFileExists, CheckPathExists, MultiSelect, ShowReadOnly, ReadOnlyChecked, AddExtension, RestoreDirectory, ValidateNames, and DereferenceLinks. Other properties retained their old names, and you now have the FileNames property that returns a String array with all the files that have been selected in a multiple-selection dialog box. The following example asks for a bitmap file and loads it into a PictureBox control:

```
With OpenFileDialog1
    .CheckFileExists = True
    .ShowReadOnly = False
    .Filter = "All Files|*.*|Bitmap Files (*)|*;*.gif;*.jpg"
    .FilterIndex = 2
    If .ShowDialog = DialogResult.OK Then
        ' Load the specified file into a PictureBox control.
        PictureBox1.Image = Image.FromFile(.FileName)
    End If
End With
```

The control also exposes an OpenFile method, which opens the file and returns a Stream object, so you can load the image using this syntax as well:

```
Dim st As System.IO.Stream = OpenFileDialog1.OpenFile
PictureBox1.Image = Image.FromStream(st)
st.Close
```

Interestingly, the control exposes a FileOk event that lets you cancel a click on the Open button:

```
Private Sub OpenFileDialog1_FileOk(ByVal sender As Object, _
    ByVal e As System.ComponentModel.CancelEventArgs) _
    Handles OpenFileDialog1.FileOk

    ' Check the Hidden attribute of the currently selected file.
    If System.IO.File.GetAttributes(OpenFileDialog1.FileName) _
        And IO.FileAttributes.Hidden Then
        ' Reject hidden files.
        MessageBox.Show("You can't select hidden files")
        e.Cancel = True
    End If
End Sub
```

The SaveFileDialog Control

The SaveFileDialog control is similar to OpenFileDialog, with a slightly different set of properties. For example, you can set the CreatePrompt or OverwritePrompt property to True to display a warning when a new file would be created or an existing file would be overwritten. You can use the OpenFile method to create a Stream object, and the FileOk event to cancel the user's selection.

The FolderBrowserDialog Control

This control—added in version 1.1 of the .NET Framework—allows you to display a dialog in which the end user can select an existing directory, and even create a new one if you leave the ShowNewFolderButton property set to True. (See Figure 16-9.) The most important property of this control is SelectedPath, which is the path of the folder that is initially selected when the dialog appears. You read this property when the dialog closes to learn what directory was selected by the user:

```
With FolderBrowserDialog1
    ' Desktop is the root folder in the dialog.
    .RootFolder = Environment.SpecialFolder.Desktop
    ' Select the C:\Windows directory on entry.
    .SelectedPath = "c:\windows"
    ' Prompt the user with a custom message.
    .Description = "Select the source directory"
    If .ShowDialog = DialogResult.OK Then
        ' Display the selected folder if the user clicked on the OK button.
        MsgBox(.SelectedPath)
    End If
End With
```

You can assign an Environment.SpecialFolder constant to the RootFolder property to determine which folder appears at the top of the directory tree shown in the control, for example Desktop, MyComputer, System, or ProgramFiles. Unfortunately, many features of the underlying Windows common dialog—such as the ability to browse printers and networked computers—haven't been encapsulated in this control.

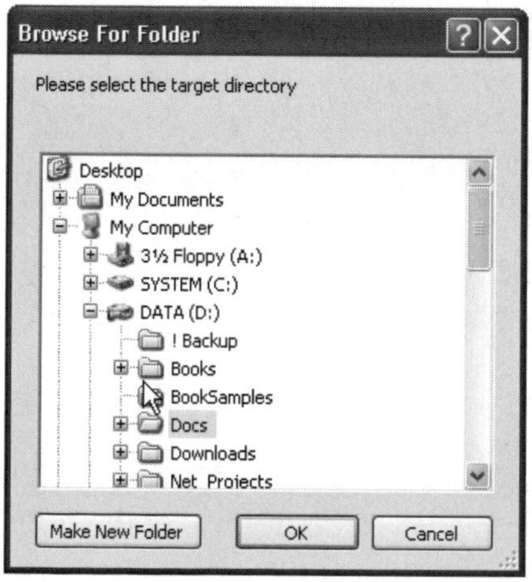

Figure 16-9   The FolderBrowserDialog control

The ColorDialog Control

You can set three Boolean properties before opening a common dialog with the ColorDialog control: AllowFullOpen, SolidColorOnly, and AnyColor. The FullOpen property can be set to True to display an open custom color pane. When the user closes the color dialog box, the Color property returns the selected color, whereas the CustomColors array contains all the custom colors defined by the user:

```
' Let the user select the BackColor of a TextBox control.
With ColorDialog1
    .Color = TextBox1.BackColor
    .SolidColorOnly = True
    If .ShowDialog() = DialogResult.OK Then
        TextBox1.BackColor = .Color
    End If
End With
```

The FontDialog Control

The FontDialog control exposes a set of properties whose meaning should be immediately clear: FontMustExist, ShowColor, ShowEffects, AllowVectorFonts, Fixed-PitchOnly, MinSize, and MaxSize. Of course, there's also a Font property, which sets or returns the selected font:

```
' Let the user select Font and ForeColor for a TextBox control.
With FontDialog1
    ' Enable the selection of effects and color.
    .ShowEffects = True
    .ShowColor = True
    ' Set a limit to font size.
    .MinSize = 8
    .MaxSize = 72
    ' Initialize with font and color from a TextBox control.
    .Font = TextBox1.Font
    .Color = TextBox1.ForeColor
    ' Display the Apply button. (See next code snippet.)
    .ShowApply = True
    If .ShowDialog = DialogResult.OK Then
        ' Apply to TextBox properties.
        TextBox1.Font = .Font
        TextBox1.ForeColor = .Color
    End If
End With
```

The ShowApply property enables a great feature of the FontDialog control, which is the ability to trap clicks on the Apply button and process them while the dialog is open. All you have to do is write some code for the Apply event:

```
Private Sub FontDialog1_Apply(ByVal sender As Object, _
    ByVal e As System.EventArgs) Handles FontDialog1.Apply
    ' Enforce font properties without closing the dialog.
    TextBox1.Font = FontDialog1.Font
    TextBox1.ForeColor = FontDialog1.Color
End Sub
```

The PrintDialog Control

Before you use the PrintDialog control, you need to know a few things about the Print-erSettings object. This object exposes all the settings you see in a Print dialog box as properties, the most important of which are PrinterName, FromPage, ToPage, Copies, PrintToFile, and PrintRange (can be AllPages, SomePages, or Selection). You can also set the MinimumPage and MaximumPage properties to the lowest and highest valid page numbers. The following code snippet should give you an idea of how you can set up a Print dialog box:

```
With PrintDialog1
    ' Set a few basic properties.
    .AllowPrintToFile = True
    .AllowSelection = True
    .AllowSomePages = True

    ' Create the PrinterSettings object, and set its properties.
    .PrinterSettings = New PrinterSettings()
    With .PrinterSettings
        .PrintRange = PrintRange.SomePages
        .FromPage = 1
        .ToPage = 10
        .MinimumPage = 1
        .MaximumPage = 10
    End With

    ' Exit current procedure if the user canceled the operation.
    If .ShowDialog <> DialogResult.OK Then Exit Sub

    ' Get the values entered by the user.
    If .PrinterSettings.PrintRange = PrintRange.SomePages Then
        Dim firstPage As Integer = .PrinterSettings.FromPage
        Dim lastPage As Integer = .PrinterSettings.ToPage
        ' Call the procedure that does the printing. (See next code.)
        PrintDocumentPages(firstPage, lastPage)
    End If
End With
```

At this point, you're just halfway through your task because you still have to print the document or a selected portion of it. Printing under .NET isn't as simple as it was under Visual Basic. You have to create a PrintDocument object, set up a handler for its Print-Page event, and do the actual printing from inside that event. Here's a simple example of how you implement the PrintDocumentPages routine called from the preceding code:

```
Dim WithEvents PrintDoc As PrintDocument
Dim currPage As Integer
Dim lastPage As Integer

Sub PrintDocumentPages(ByVal firstPage As Integer, ByVal lastPage As Integer)
    ' Move arguments into variables for sharing them with other procedures.
```

```
        Me.currPage = firstPage
        Me.lastPage = lastPage
        Me.PrintDoc = New PrintDocument()
        ' Start a print operation.
        Try
            PrintDoc.Print()
        Catch ex As Exception
            MessageBox.Show(ex.Message, "Print error")
        End Try
    End Sub

    Private Sub PrintDoc_PrintPage(ByVal sender As Object, _
        ByVal e As System.Drawing.Printing.PrintPageEventArgs) _
        Handles PrintDoc.PrintPage
        ' This demo prints a rectangle on the printable area of the sheet.
        e.Graphics.DrawRectangle(Pens.Black, e.MarginBounds)
        ' Increment the page number.
        currPage += 1
        ' Let the print engine know whether there are more pages.
        e.HasMorePages = (currPage <= lastPage)
    End Sub
```

You can take advantage of two more events of the PrintDocument object: BeginPrint and EndPrint, which fire before printing the first page and after printing the last page of the document, respectively.

The PageSetupDialog Control

The PageSetupDialog control displays the Page Setup dialog box and lets the user select things such as print orientation (portrait or landscape), paper size, and the four page margins. (See Figure 16-10.) All these values are held in a PageSettings object, which you must initialize before showing the dialog:

```
With PageSetupDialog1
    ' Initialize the PageSettings property.
    .PageSettings = New PageSettings()
    ' Allow the user to select paper size and margins.
    .AllowPaper = True
    .AllowMargins = True
    ' Disable the Printer button.
    .AllowPrinter = False
    ' Set minimum margins (100 units = 1 inch).
    .MinMargins = New Margins(50, 50, 50, 50)

    ' Display the dialog; exit if user canceled the action.
    If .ShowDialog() <> DialogResult.OK Then Exit Sub

    ' Save some of the page settings in variables.
    Dim leftMargin As Single = .PageSettings.Margins.Left
    Dim rightMargin As Single = .PageSettings.Margins.Right
    Dim landscapeOrientation As Boolean = .PageSettings.Landscape
    Dim paperSize As PaperKind = .PageSettings.PaperSize.Kind
    ' Do something with these values.
    ⋮
End With
```

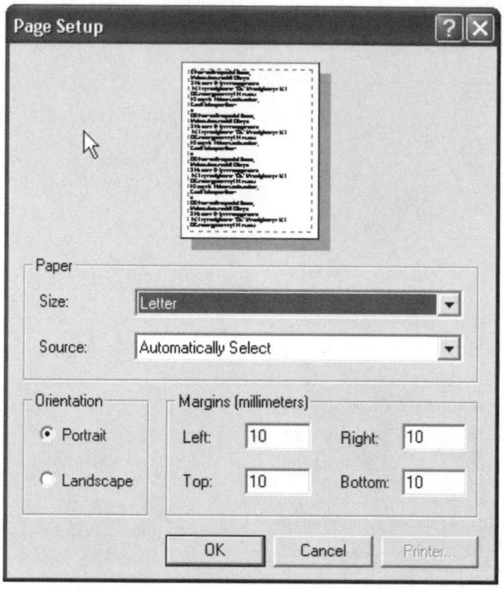

Figure 16-10 The Page Setup common dialog box

If you enable the Printer button, you can also set and read back a PrinterSettings object, as I explained in the section about the PrintDialog control.

The ImageList Control

This control is essentially the same control you have under Visual Basic 6 and works as a repository for images. You can associate an ImageList control with any control that supports the Image property, not just Windows common controls such as TreeView or ListView (as you can in Visual Basic 6). Creating the list of images at design time is simple, thanks to the new Image Collection Editor dialog box. (See Figure 16-11.) In an important difference from previous versions, you can't assign a key to an image, and you can reference an image only by its index.

The new ColorDepth property specifies the number of colors to use when rendering the images (8, 16, 24, or 32 bits). The TransparentColor property defines the transparent color. (This property replaces MaskColor.) The ImageSize property returns a Size object that defines the dimension of the images in the control and therefore replaces the ImageHeight and ImageWidth properties.

At run time, you can access all the images through the Images collection (which replaces the ListImages collection you have under Visual Basic 6). This object inherits from IList, so it exposes the usual members—for example, Count, Item, Add, RemoveAt, and Clear. You can add an image via code this way:

```
ImageList1.Images.Add(Image.FromFile("c:\myimage"))
```

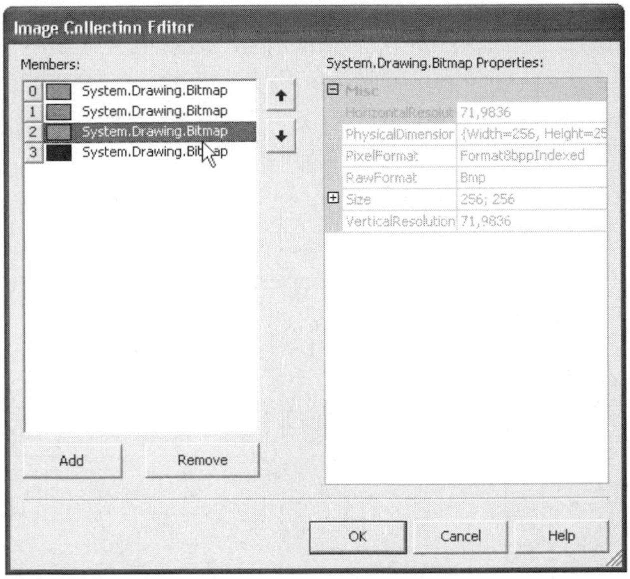

Figure 16-11   The Image Collection Editor lets you add images to an ImageList control at design time.

You can render images on a graphic surface by using the Draw method. This method takes a Graphics object (the destination device context), the target coordinates, and the index of the image to be displayed:

```
Dim gr As System.Drawing.Graphics = Me.CreateGraphics
' Display the first image on the form's surface, at coordinates (100, 200).
ImageList1.Draw(gr, 100, 200, 0)
' Display the second image at coordinates (200, 300) - alternate syntax.
ImageList1.Draw(gr, New Point(200, 300), 1)
' Stretch the third image to fill a rectangle 160 x 160 at upper left corner.
ImageList1.Draw(gr, 0, 0, 160, 160, 2)
```

The TreeView Control

If you have worked with the Visual Basic 6 TreeView control, you'll feel at ease immediately with this new version. The great news is that you can edit the Nodes collection at design time by using the TreeNode Editor dialog box. (See Figure 16-12.) These are the most important new properties:

- The ShowLines, ShowRootLines, and ShowPlusMinus Boolean properties affect the style of connecting lines. They replace the enumerated Style property.

- The Indent property is the indentation width of child nodes. It replaces Indentation.

- The Scrollable property replaces Scroll. If True, the control displays the scroll bars if necessary.

■ The ImageIndex and SelectedImageIndex properties contain the index in the companion ImageList control of the image to be used for unselected nodes and the selected node, respectively. (You can override this default image for individual nodes, though.) The Properties window lets you browse all the images in the ImageList control, so selecting the right one is easy.

■ The new ItemHeight property affects the height of individual nodes.

■ At run time, you can query the VisibleCount read-only property to get the number of visible nodes, and the TopNode read-only property to get a reference to the first visible TreeNode object.

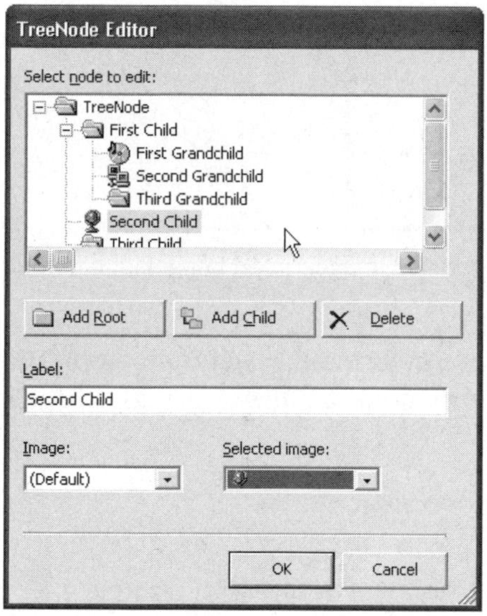

Figure 16-12   You can display the TreeNode Editor dialog box by clicking on the ellipsis button beside the Nodes element in the Properties window.

You can build the Nodes collection by means of code by adding new TreeNode objects to it. The constructor for this object can take the Text for the node, the image index, and the selected image index:

```
' Append two new nodes at the root level.
TreeView1.Nodes.Add(New TreeNode("A new node"))
TreeView1.Nodes.Add(New TreeNode("Another new node"))
' Another way to create a TreeNode.
Dim tn As TreeNode = TreeView1.Nodes.Add("A third node")
' Create a new root-level node after the first root node.
' (The first argument becomes the index of the new node.)
TreeView1.Nodes.Insert(1, New TreeNode("Another root node"))
```

In a significant difference from previous versions of this control, each TreeNode object exposes its own Nodes collection, which greatly simplifies the creation and deletion of nodes at any level in the hierarchy:

```
' Get a reference to the first node.
Dim firstNode as TreeNode = TreeView1.Nodes(0)
' Insert a new node as the first child node.
firstNode.Nodes.Insert(0, New TreeNode("The new first child node"))

' Create a new node, and append it as the last child node.
Dim lastChild As TreeNode = New TreeNode("A new child node")
firstNode.Nodes.Add(lastChild)
' Create a grandchild node.
lastChild.Nodes.Add(New TreeNode("A new grandchild node"))
```

When adding a large number of nodes, you should bracket your code within a Begin-Update and EndUpdate pair of methods to speed up operations and reduce flickering. Thanks to the truly hierarchical structure, you can easily create recursive procedures that perform a given operation over all or a subset of the TreeView nodes. For example, the following procedure calculates and displays (or hides if the second argument is False) the number of child nodes in the Text property of all the nodes in the control:

```
Sub DisplayChildrenCount(ByVal nodes As TreeNodeCollection, _
    ByVal display As Boolean)
    For Each node As TreeNode In nodes
        ' Remove any child count at the end of the Text, if there.
        node.Text = System.Text.RegularExpressions.Regex.Replace( _
            node.Text, " \[.*\]$", "")
        ' Add it again if so requested.
        If display Then
            node.Text &= " [" & CStr(node.Nodes.Count) & "]"
        End If
        ' Recurse over child nodes.
        DisplayChildrenCount(node.Nodes, display)
    Next
End Sub
```

To see this procedure in action, add some nodes to a TreeView control, and then create a Button control and add this code:

```
Private Sub Button1_Click(ByVal sender As System.Object, _
    ByVal e As System.EventArgs) Handles Button1.Click
    ' Toggle current display status.
    Static display As Boolean
    display = Not display
    ' Display or hide children count.
    DisplayChildrenCount(TreeView1.Nodes, display)
End Sub
```

If you have a reference to a TreeNode object, you can navigate the node hierarchy by using the Parent, FirstNode, LastNode, NextNode, PreviousNode, NextVisibleNode, and PrevVisibleNode properties. You can expand or collapse a node by using its Expand, ExpandAll, Collapse, and Toggle methods, and you can test its current state by using the IsExpanded, IsSelected, IsVisible, and IsEditing properties.

You can control the many other attributes of a TreeNode object with the Text, Checked, ForeColor, BackColor, ImageIndex, and SelectedImageIndex properties. Or you can let the user edit the node's label by using the BeginEdit method and terminate the edit operation by using EndEdit.

The TreeView control offers several pairs of events, which fire immediately before and after a node is edited, selected, expanded, collapsed, or checked. In all cases, you can examine the node in question and decide whether to cancel the operation. The following event procedure continues the previous example and ensures that the user can't edit a node's label that contains the count of children nodes. (See the preceding code example.)

```
Private Sub TreeView1_BeforeLabelEdit(ByVal sender As Object, ByVal e _
    As NodeLabelEditEventArgs) Handles TreeView1.BeforeLabelEdit
    ' Refuse to edit a node that has a children count on its Text.
    If System.Text.RegularExpressions.Regex.IsMatch(e.Node.Text, _
        " \[.*\]$") Then
        e.CancelEdit = True
        MessageBox.Show("You can't edit while children count is displayed")
    End If
End Sub
```

The ListView Control

The new ListView control exposes most of the properties and methods that the Visual Basic 6 version does, and you have to account only for a few different names. The Properties window lets you add new ListViewItem objects and one or more subitems (see Figure 16-13), as well as define all the ColumnHeader objects that you want to define. Another great improvement is the ability to resize column width at design time.

The ListView control exposes only a few new properties. This group includes Activation (whether items are activated with one or two clicks), HeaderStyle (whether column headers are clickable), Scrollable (should be set to False to prevent scrolling), LargeImageList (the ImageList control used for the images in large icon mode), and SmallImageList (the ImageList control used for all other modes). The View property defines the display mode, as in Visual Basic 6, but the Report mode has been renamed Details mode. (Details is the mode that displays column headers and subitems.)

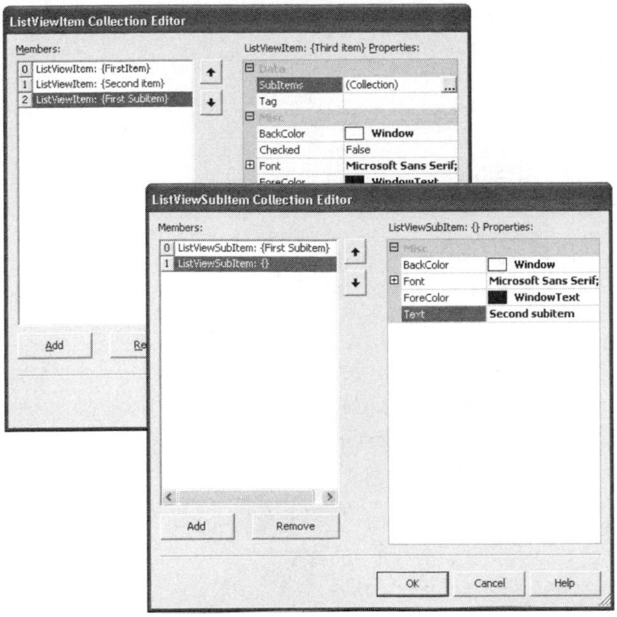

Figure 16-13   At design time, you can edit ListView items using the ListViewItem Collection Editor and subitems using the ListViewSubItem Collection Editor.

You create new ListView items—displayed as rows when in details mode or icons in all other modes—by adding ListViewItem objects to the control's Items collection. The constructor for the ListViewItem object can take a string (the caption of the icon) and an optional integer used as an index for the companion ListImage controls:

```
' Append a new list item; use the first icon in companion ListImage controls.
ListView1.Items.Add(New ListViewItem("A list item", 0))
' Another way to create a ListViewItem object.
Dim lvi As ListViewItem = ListView1.Items.Add("Another item", 0)
' Insert a new item at the beginning of the collection, with no icons.
ListView1.Items.Insert(0, New ListViewItem("A third first item"))
```

The ListViewItem object exposes many of the properties of the Visual Basic 6 ListItem object. The Bounds property returns a Rectangle object that tells where the item is on the screen, and the Focused property returns True if the item has the focus. Unfortunately, a few properties were lost in the transition, such as Key and Ghosted.

You create new subitems by using the Add method of the ListViewItem's SubItems collection:

```
' Create a ListViewItem object, and add it to the ListView.
Dim lvi As ListViewItem = ListView1.Items.Add("A new list item", 0)
' Next add three subitems.
lvi.SubItems.Add("First subitem")
lvi.SubItems.Add("Second subitem")
lvi.SubItems.Add("Third subitem")
```

In a difference from previous versions, individual subitems can have their own Text, Font, ForeColor, and BackColor properties:

```
' ...(Continuing previous code snippet)...
' Add a fourth subitem.
With lvi.SubItems.Add("Fourth subitem")
    ' Change text and background colors.
    .ForeColor = Color.Red
    .BackColor = Color.Yellow
    ' Use standard form font, but make it bold and italic.
    .Font = New Font(Me.Font, FontStyle.Bold Or FontStyle.Italic)
End With
```

(Subitems from the second one onward are visible only in Details mode and only if you have defined sufficient numbers of ColumnHeader objects.) The following routine fills a ListView control with information about files in a given directory, so it mimics the contents of the right pane in Windows Explorer:

```
' Show files in specified directory.
Sub ShowFilesInListView(ByVal lv As ListView, ByVal path As String)
    ' Get the DirectoryInfo object corresponding to the path.
    Dim di As New DirectoryInfo(path)
    lv.BeginUpdate()         ' Suppress refresh.
    lv.Items.Clear()
    ' Get data about all the files.
    For Each fi As FileInfo In di.GetFiles()
        ' Create a new ListViewItem object, and add to the Items collection.
        Dim item As ListViewItem = lv.Items.Add(fi.Name)
        ' Create all subitems.
        item.SubItems.Add(fi.Length)
        item.SubItems.Add(fi.CreationTime)
        item.SubItems.Add(fi.LastWriteTime)
        item.SubItems.Add(fi.LastAccessTime)
    Next
    lv.EndUpdate             ' Reenable refresh.
End Sub
```

This routine paints the rows with alternating background color. (See Figure 16-14.)

```
' Display alternating color for background.
Sub PaintAlternatingBackColor(ByVal lv As ListView, _
    ByVal color1 As Color, ByVal color2 As Color)
    For Each item As ListViewItem In lv.Items
        ' Set the color for this Item object.
        If (item.Index Mod 2) = 0 Then
            item.BackColor = color1
        Else
            item.BackColor = color2
        End If
        ' Assign same color to all subitems.
        For Each subitem As ListViewItem.ListViewSubItem In item.SubItems
            subitem.BackColor = item.BackColor
        Next
    Next
End Sub
```

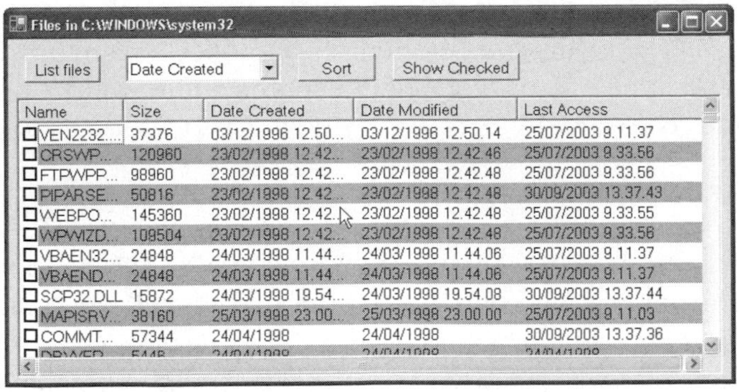

Figure 16-14   The demo application shows how to sort elements in a ListView according to different sort criteria.

The demo program uses the following code to display files in the Windows system directory:

```
ShowFilesInListView(ListView1, System.Environment.SystemDirectory)
PaintAlternatingBackColor(ListView1, Color.White, Color.Cyan)
```

A great feature of this control is the ability to sort its contents according to the sort criterion that you decide. You just have to define a class that implements the IComparer interface, assign an instance of this class to the ListView's ListViewItemSorter property, and then invoke the Sort method. The CompareTo function of this class receives a reference to the two ListViewItem objects being compared, so you can access their properties and the properties of their subitems. Following is the code that sorts the items according to the filename:

```
    ListView1.ListViewItemSorter = New CompareByName()
    ListView1.Sort()
```

This is the complete listing of the CompareByName class. You can browse the companion code for the classes that sort files according to their size, creation date, write date, and last access date:

```
Class CompareByName
    Implements IComparer

    Function Compare(ByVal x As Object, ByVal y As Object) As Integer _
        Implements System.Collections.IComparer.Compare
        ' Cast the two arguments to ListViewItem objects.
        Dim item1 As ListViewItem = CType(x, ListViewItem)
        Dim item2 As ListViewItem = CType(y, ListViewItem)
        ' Compare their text property.
        Return String.Compare(item1.Text, item2.Text)
    End Function
End Class
```

The CheckedItems and CheckedIndices properties return information about all the checked elements. The SelectedItems and SelectedIndices collections return the list of selected items. To use these collections, you should set the value of the CheckBoxes and MultiSelect properties correctly.

The PropertyGrid Control

The PropertyGrid control is the component that the Visual Studio .NET Properties window uses internally. You can use this control to let the end user dynamically change any property of any object defined in your application. For example, you can use it to let users change the colors and the font of your forms, almost without writing code.

The PropertyGrid is included in the System.Windows.Forms.dll library but doesn't appear in the Toolbox by default, so you must either create it through code or right-click on the Toolbox, select the Add/Remove Items menu command, and then select the PropertyGrid entry.

After you add a PropertyGrid to a form you can set its properties as you do with any control, but this control doesn't expose many interesting design-time properties. In practice, you can just set the color of a few of the control's areas. ViewForeColor and ViewBackColor affect the area where properties are edited; HelpForeColor and HelpBackColor affect the bottom area, where properties descriptions appear; PropertySort is an enumerated property that tells whether properties are displayed by category or in alphabetical order; ToolbarVisible can be set to False to hide the little toolbar whose buttons let the user switch from a categorized to an alphabetically sorted view.

The most important property of the PropertyGrid control is SelectedObject, which references the object whose properties are listed in the PropertyGrid control. You can assign this property at design time to have it point to the parent form or another control or component hosted on the form, but in most cases you do this assignment at run time:

```
' Let the PropertyGrid display the properties of a Person object.
Dim p As Person = New Person("Joe", "Doe")
PropertyGrid1.SelectedObject = p
```

The PropertyGrid control honors all the attributes that decorate the class whose values are being displayed, such as Description, DefaultValue, and Category. You'll learn more about these attributes in Chapter 18. Notice that the PropertyGrid displays all the public properties of the selected object, but not its public fields.

To show you a nontrivial example of the PropertyGrid control in action, I created a base form named CustomizableForm. All forms derived from this base form allow end users to edit control properties by pressing the Ctrl+F12 key when the focus is on a control, as well as to create new TextBox or Button controls. (See Figure 16-15.) You'll find the complete source code for the base class and a sample project that uses it in the companion code.

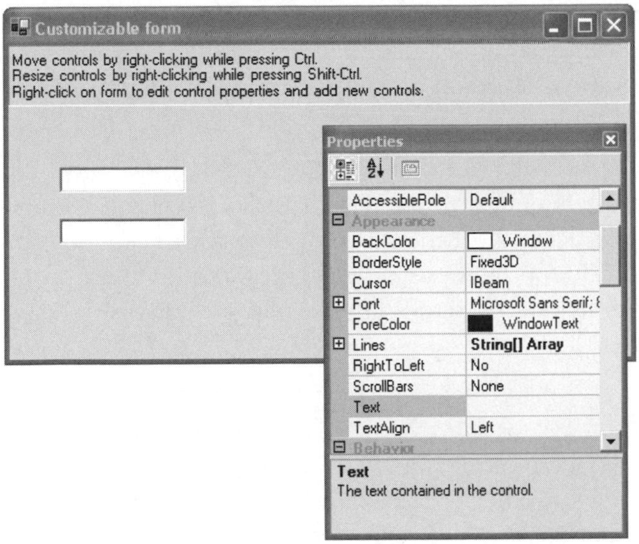

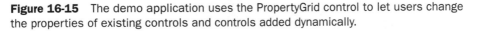

Figure 16-15   The demo application uses the PropertyGrid control to let users change the properties of existing controls and controls added dynamically.

Other Controls

This section summarizes the changes in the controls that I haven't discussed in previous sections, with the exception of the DataGrid control, which I'll cover later in this chapter. In most cases, I won't discuss them in depth because there are only minimal differences from the corresponding Visual Basic 6 control or because I assume that you'll understand how they work by just using my hints. (And because I want to devote the remainder of this chapter to more interesting things.)

The PictureBox Control

The PictureBox control is less powerful and complex than the corresponding Visual Basic 6 control in that you can't use it as a container. The Image property replaces the Picture property, and you can also load an image in the BackgroundImage property. (In the latter case, the image is tiled to cover the entire control.)

You can load images in the following formats: bitmap, icon, metafiles, enhanced metafiles, GIF, JPEG, and PNG. You can center or stretch the image to fit the control or stretch the control to fit the image by using the SizeMode property.

The HScrollBar and VScrollBar Controls

There are no relevant differences from the corresponding Visual Basic 6 controls except that the Change event is no longer supported and you can trap user actions with the Scroll event exclusively. In most cases, however, you'll use the new ValueChanged event, which fires whenever the Value property changes, either programmatically or because of UI interaction. Notice that these controls don't support a flat appearance, so you can't create flat scroll bars in this Windows Forms version.

The Timer Control

The Timer control is virtually identical to the Visual Basic 6 control, with two exceptions. First, the Tick event replaces the Timer event. Second, you can enable or disable the timer using the Start and Stop methods or by setting the Enabled property. (You can't prevent a Timer from ticking by setting its Interval property to 0, as you can in previous language versions.)

The Panel Control

The Panel control is similar to the old Frame control, but it has no caption. The Panel control provides a container for other controls, and it can support AutoScroll and all the related properties so that the end user can scroll its contents. You can also dock one or more controls on its borders, and you can control the distance of contained controls from the edge by using the DockPadding property.

The GroupBox Control

The GroupBox control is identical to the old Frame control. In practice, the only properties that you usually modify after you drop it on a form are Text and FlatStyle. Unlike the Frame control, you can't hide the border. (Use a Panel control if you need to group controls without a visible border.)

The NotifyIcon Control

This new control makes it easy to add an icon to the Windows taskbar tray area, as many recent programs do. It has only a handful of properties: Icon is the icon being used, Text is the ToolTip being displayed when the mouse hovers over the icon, Visible lets you hide the icon, and ContextMenu is a menu that appears when the user clicks the icon. The control fires the Click, DoubleClick, MouseDown, MouseUp, and MouseMove events, so you can control exactly what happens when the user interacts with the icon in the tray area.

The ToolBar Control

The new version of this control comes with a Buttons collection that you can populate at design time. Elements in this collection can be push buttons, toggle buttons, separators, or drop-down buttons with which you can associate a MainMenu object that you defined in the form's component tray area. Each button can have text, ToolTip text, and an image taken from a companion ImageList control. When a button is clicked, the control fires a ButtonClicked event, and you can react to it by writing this kind of code:

```
Private Sub ToolBar1_ButtonClick(ByVal sender As Object, _
    ByVal e As ToolBarButtonClickEventArgs) Handles ToolBar1.ButtonClick
    Select Case e.Button.Text
        Case "Open"
            ' Open the document.
        Case "Save"
            ' Save the document.
        ⋮
    End Select
End Sub
```

The TabControl Control

This control replaces the Visual Basic 6 TabStrip control, as well as the other tab control, named SSTab, provided with previous versions of the language. The new control is remarkably simple to use because you define all the tabs at design time by using properties such as Text, ToolTipText, and ImageIndex (the icon that appears near the tab). Each tab you create is an instance of the TabPage class, which is a scrollable container for other controls.

You rarely need to interact with this control at run time by means of code. You might need to check the control's SelectedIndex property (the index of the active TabPage object) and trap the SelectedIndexChanged event to detect when the user activates another tab, but these would be the only operations you'd need to perform. You can also receive events from individual TabPage objects if necessary—for example, Click and Paint events.

The StatusBar Control

By default, the status bar displays the value assigned to its Text property, and you have to explicitly set the ShowPanels property to True to see the panels. Each Panel object has text, ToolTip text, an icon, and a minimum width; you can add these objects to the Panels collection from the Properties window or with code. The control fires a Panel-Click event when the user clicks on a panel, as under Visual Basic 6, but the PanelDblClick event is no longer supported.

Panels can have an owner-draw style, so you can define their appearance in the Draw-Item event. For example, you might use this feature to display an animated icon or a progress bar inside the StatusBar control.

The NumericUpDown and DomainUpDown Controls

The NumericUpDown control displays a numeric value that the user can edit directly or increment and decrement by using the arrow keys. These two controls have several members in common, such as UpDownAlign (the position of the arrow buttons) and InterceptArrowKeys (True if arrow keys are processed automatically). You can also programmatically click the arrow buttons by using the UpButton and DownButton methods.

The NumericUpDown control lets you set a minimum and maximum value, an increment value, the number of decimal places, and whether thousand separators should be displayed. You extract the numeric contents (as a Decimal) by using the Value property, and you get a ValueChanged event when this property changes.

The DomainUpDown control is conceptually similar to a ListBox control with only one visible element. You can scroll through all the elements of the list by using the arrow keys, and you can cycle through them if the Wrap property is True. This control exposes an Items collection that you can initialize at design time or by means of code. The control fires a SelectedIndexChanged event when the user selects another item in the list.

The RichTextBox Control

This control has several new properties and methods that make it markedly more powerful than the Visual Basic 6 version. For example, the new version of the control has a ZoomFactor property that can apply a zoom level in the range of 0.64 to 64. The DetectURLs property, if True, makes the control automatically recognize and format URLs in text. (You receive a LinkClicked event when one of those URLs is clicked.) If the new AutoWordSelection is True, a mouse click selects entire words. The new Protected event fires when the user attempts to edit text that has been protected.

The MonthCalendar Control

This control is comparable to the MonthView available under Visual Basic 6. It displays a calendarlike series of one or more months and lets you select dates. You decide how many months you display in a MonthCalendar by using its CalendarDimensions property, which dates appear in bold by using the BoldedDates property, and whether today's date should be highlighted by using the ShowToday and ShowTodayCircle properties. The SelectionRange property returns the series of dates that the end user selected.

The DateTimePicker Control

This control is virtually the same as the control that was available under Visual Basic 6. It's basically a text box–like field specialized for date and time input. You select the date format using the Format and CustomFormat properties, display a trailing check box using the ShowCheckBox property, and decide whether the user can display a monthly calendar by clicking on the button on the right using the ShowUpDown property. You can assign and read back the DateTime value in the control using the Value property.

The TrackBar Control

Except for the name, this control is identical to the Visual Basic 6 Slider control. In addition, it exposes the SetRange method (for setting both the Minimum and Maximum properties in one operation) and the ValueChanged event (similar to Scroll but also fires when the Value property is set programmatically).

The ProgressBar Control

This control is very similar to the Visual Basic 6 version. It has just two new methods: PerformStep (which increments the Value property by the quantity defined by the Step property) and Increment (which takes the increment as an argument). Not very exciting, after all.

Data Binding

Data binding allows you to link a control to a data source so that the control automatically displays (and possibly updates) the data without your having to write any specific code. Unlike previous versions, however, Visual Basic .NET doesn't offer a Data control, and you have to create the navigational buttons.

You can classify data binding according to how many items or properties of the bound control are bound to the data source. In *simple data binding*, only one property of the control is bound to a given column of the database (or, more generally, to a single value in the data source). This situation arises, for example, when you have the Text property of a TextBox control bound to a string or a numeric column in a database table. In *complex data binding*, you bind multiple items of a control to the same or different fields in the data source. For example, you have complex data binding when you fill the Items collection of a ListBox or ComboBox control with the values coming from a column in the data source or when you display multiple fields of the data source in a DataGrid control.

The data-binding mechanism lets you bind a control to virtually any potential data source. In fact, the minimum prerequisite for an object to qualify as a data source is that it must expose the IList interface, so you can bind a control to an array and to most of the collectionlike objects described in Chapter 8. And of course you can bind them to ADO.NET sources, including DataTable, DataSet, and DataView objects.

Binding to an Array of Objects

As you might expect, you pay for all this flexibility in the amount of code you have to write to set up the binding mechanism correctly. For starters, four different object types cooperate in a form that contains bound controls, here listed from the simplest to the most complex. (See Figure 16-16.)

The Binding object binds a single property of a control to a single field of the data source. You rarely interact directly with this object unless you want to trap its Format or Parse event. These two events give you the highest flexibility in how individual values are displayed or stored back in the data source.

The ControlBindingCollection object gathers all the Binding objects associated with a given control; in practice, you create a new Binding object by invoking the Add method of this collection. You can access this collection through the DataBindings property, which all Windows Forms controls expose. Thanks to the DataBindings property, you can bind multiple properties to different fields of a given control. For example, a TextBox control might have its Text property bound to the Model field and its BackColor property bound to the Color field of the Cars class.

The BindingManagerBase object gathers all the Binding objects associated with the same data source. When its Position property changes, the BindingManagerBase object notifies all the Binding objects that they should transfer current values of controls into the data source and retrieve the values at the new position. As these changes occur, this object also fires a PositionChanged event, which you can trap to perform additional processing (such as updating a calculated field).

The BindingContext object is returned by the property of the same name exposed by the Form object (and more generally by all classes derived from ContainerControl). This object is necessary because a form or a container control might contain multiple sets of bound controls, with each group associated with a different data source. For example, a form might contain a group of controls bound to the Employees array and another group of controls bound to the Cars array.

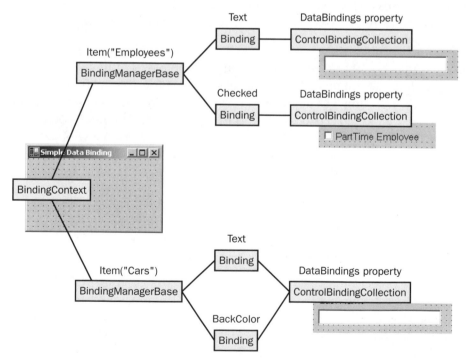

Figure 16-16 Data-binding objects

Simple Data-Bound Form

Let's see a complete example of a form with four controls, in which each control binds to one of the properties of the Employee class: FirstName, LastName, BirthDate, and PartTimeEmployee. (The code of the Employee class is omitted because of its simplicity, but the code on the companion CD contains its complete definition.) The form is shown in Figure 16-17; it also contains all the buttons to navigate in the data source, which in this case is an array of Employee objects.

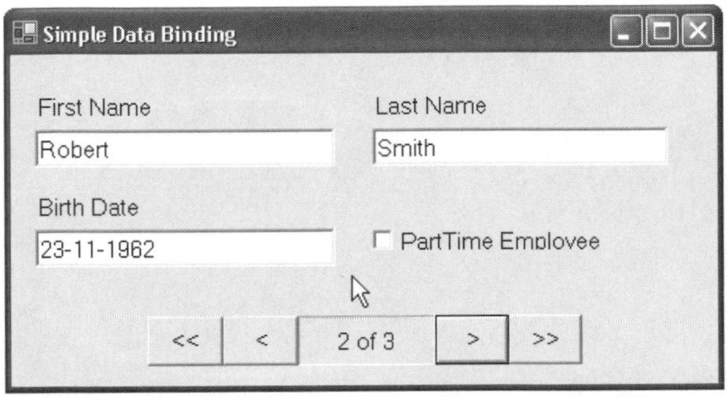

Figure 16-17   The Simple Data Binding demo form

As you see in the following code, you create the individual Binding objects by using the DataBindings.Add method, which takes the name of the bound property, a reference to the data source (the Employees array in this case), and the name of the member in the data source. The last argument is the name of a field when you're binding to a database table or the name of a property when you're binding to an object:

```
' This is the data source.
Dim employees() As Employee = {New Employee("Joe", "Doe", #1/3/1960#), _
    New Employee("Robert", "Smith", #11/23/1962#), _
    New Employee("Ann", "Ross", #2/5/1965#, True)}
' This is the BindingManagerBase object that manages all the bindings.
Dim WithEvents bmb As BindingManagerBase

' Initialize the binding when the form loads.
Private Sub SimpleBindingForm_Load(ByVal sender As Object, _
    ByVal e As EventArgs) Handles MyBase.Load
    InitializeBinding()
End Sub

' Create all the necessary bindings.
Sub InitializeBinding()
    ' Save a reference to the BindingManagerBase object.
    bmb = Me.BindingContext(employees)
    ' Create the Binding object for each bound field.
    txtFirstName.DataBindings.Add("Text", employees, "FirstName")
    txtLastName.DataBindings.Add("Text", employees, "LastName")
    txtBirthDate.DataBindings.Add("Text", employees, "BirthDate")
    chkPartTime.DataBindings.Add("Checked", employees, "PartTimeEmployee")
End Sub
```

The remainder of the code manages the actions performed when someone clicks on the navigational buttons. As you see, this code just changes the value of the Position property of the BindingManagerBase object and traps the PositionChanged event to display the correct record number:

```
Private Sub btnFirst_Click(ByVal sender As Object, _
    ByVal e As EventArgs) Handles btnFirst.Click
    bmb.Position = 0
End Sub

Private Sub btnPrevious_Click(ByVal sender As Object, _
    ByVal e As EventArgs) Handles btnPrevious.Click
    bmb.Position -= 1
End Sub

Private Sub btnNext_Click(ByVal sender As Object, _
    ByVal e As EventArgs) Handles btnNext.Click
    bmb.Position += 1
End Sub

Private Sub btnLast_Click(ByVal sender As Object, _
    ByVal e As EventArgs) Handles btnLast.Click
    bmb.Position = bmb.Count - 1
End Sub

' Display current position in label.
Private Sub bmb_PositionChanged(ByVal sender As Object, _
    ByVal e As EventArgs) Handles bmb.PositionChanged
    lblRecord.Text = String.Format("{0} of {1}", bmb.Position + 1, bmb.Count)
End Sub
```

When you bind to an IList object, you get two-way binding, and any new value the user enters in bound fields is assigned to the underlying data source. You can also support AddNew and Delete operations, even though you must implement them manually—for example, by writing the code that adds or deletes elements in the source array.

Formatting Events

You can enforce much finer control over how values are transferred to and from the data source by using the two events that individual Binding objects fire. The Format event fires when data is transferred from the data source to the bound control, whereas the Parse event fires when data is moved back into the data source. The latter control fires only if the data in the control has been modified after the most recent Format event.

Typically you take advantage of these events to change the display format of one or more values—for example, to display data as uppercase but store it as lowercase. Or you might store currency values in a currency unit (such as U.S. dollars or Euros) and display the values in the unit selected by the end user. The demo application uses these two events to display the BirthDate value in dd-mm-yyyy format instead of the default long-date format. To trap the two events, you must modify the code in the InitializeBinding procedure:

```
Sub InitializeBinding()
    ' Save a reference to the BindingManagerBase object.
    bmb = Me.BindingContext(employees)
    ' We need to suspend and resume the binding to have the DataFormat
    ' event fire when the first record is displayed
    bmb.SuspendBinding()
    ⋮
    ' Get a reference to this binding and bind it to two events.
    Dim bnd As Binding
    bnd = txtBirthDate.DataBindings.Add("Text", employees, "BirthDate")
    AddHandler bnd.Format, AddressOf DataFormat
    AddHandler bnd.Parse, AddressOf DataParse
    bmb.ResumeBinding()
    ⋮
End Sub


' Change format of BirthDate value.
Private Sub DataFormat(ByVal sender As Object, ByVal e As ConvertEventArgs)
    If DirectCast(sender, Binding).Control Is txtBirthDate Then
        e.Value = String.Format("{0:dd-MM-yyyy}", e.Value)
    End If
End Sub

' Convert BirthDate string back to a Date value.
Private Sub DataParse(ByVal sender As Object, ByVal e As ConvertEventArgs)
    If DirectCast(sender, Binding).Control Is txtBirthDate Then
        e.Value = CDate(e.Value)
    End If
End Sub
```

The preceding code uses the AddHandler statement to create event handlers dynamically because this technique gives more flexibility than a WithEvents variable does and lets you have two procedures that serve the Format or Parse event from multiple controls. The code in event handlers shows how you can discern which control is the destination (for Format) or the source (for Parse) of the operation.

Data-Bound ListBox and ComboBox Controls

As I've explained, the complex data-binding mechanism lets you bind a data source to multiple items in a control. Three Windows Forms controls support complex data binding: the ListBox control, the ComboBox control, and the DataGrid control.

Data binding to a ListBox or ComboBox control is especially useful because these controls can be used to display lookup tables. Say that you define a Department class with two properties, Name and ID. You can extend the Employee class with a new property, DepartmentID, which holds the numeric ID value of the department for a given employee. In this case, you can consider the array of Employee objects the main data source and the array of Department objects the lookup data source.

A data entry form could include a ListBox or ComboBox control that lists all the department names so that the operator can see or change the department where each employee works, as shown in Figure 16-18. Binding a ListBox or ComboBox control in this fashion requires that you assign three of its properties:

- The DisplayMember property must be assigned the name of the property in the lookup class that's used to fill the list area of the control. In the example, this is the Name property of the Department class.

- The ValueMember property must be assigned the name of the property in the lookup class whose value is actually stored in the main data source when the end user selects an element from the ListBox or ComboBox control. In the example, this is the ID property of the Department class.

- The DataSource property must be assigned the lookup data source, which can be an IList object or one of the ADO.NET objects that can work as a data source, such as DataTable or DataSet. In the example, this is the array of Department objects.

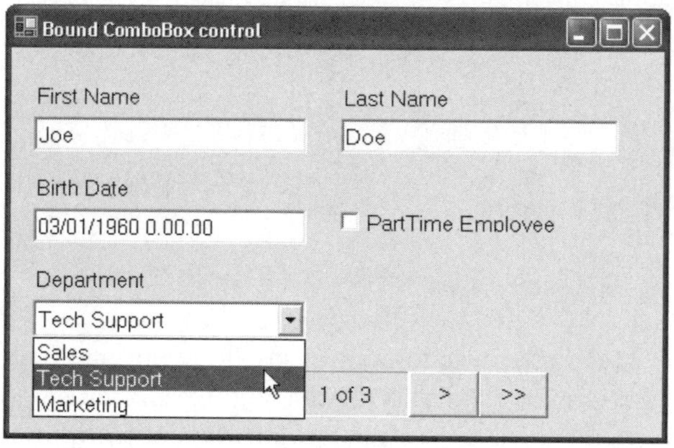

Figure 16-18   The improved version of the data-bound form includes a bound ComboBox control.

Once you've correctly assigned these properties, you can bind the SelectedValue property of the ListBox or ComboBox control to the field in the main data source. In the example, this field is the DepartmentID property of the Employee class. In practice, you can extend the original code to support a lookup ComboBox control by adding just four lines of code in the InitializeBinding procedure:

```
' An array of three Department objects
Dim departments() As Department = {New Department("Sales", 1), _
    New Department("Tech Support", 2), _
    New Department("Marketing", 3)}

Sub InitializeBinding()
    ' Load the Departments array in the ComboBox control's list area.
    cboDepartments.DisplayMember = "Name"
    cboDepartments.ValueMember = "ID"
    cboDepartments.DataSource = departments
    ' Bind the ComboBox control to the main data source.
    cboDepartments.DataBindings.Add("SelectedValue", employees, _
        "DepartmentID")
```

```
' ...(The remainder of the procedure is unchanged)...
    ⋮
End Sub
```

ADO.NET Data Binding

Although binding to an array of objects is useful, most of the time you'll use Windows Forms data binding with ADO.NET objects. You can implement this kind of data binding either by using designable components that you add to the form's component tray or by creating ADO.NET objects and defining the binding mechanism via code.

Using Designable Components

In this section, I'll show you how you can use the features of the Visual Studio IDE to bind controls to fields in a data table using a RAD approach, almost without writing code. Follow this sequence of actions:

1. Open the Server Explorer window, and define a new data connection to a database of your choice; to follow the remainder of this example, you should create a connection to Biblio.mdb, but any Access or SQL Server database can be used. You can then open the data connection node to browse the tables in the selected database. (See Figure 16-19.)

Figure 16-19   The Server Explorer window after you've added a data connection to Biblio.mdb

2. Expand Biblio.mdb and then the Tables nodes in the Server Explorer window, select the Publishers table, and drop it onto the form. This action creates two objects in the component tray, named OleDbConnection1 and OleDbAdapter1. Select the former, and in the Properties window change its name to cnBiblio; repeat the same operation with the latter component to change its name to daPublishers.

3. Right-click on the daPublishers component, and click Generate Dataset on the shortcut menu; this action brings up the Generate Dataset dialog box. Ensure that

the New radio button is selected and that the check box near the Publishers (daPublishers) element is selected, and then click OK. This operation creates a third component named DataSet11, but you should change its name to dsBiblio. At the end of this operation, the component tray should look like the one in Figure 16-20. You can see that a new DataSet1.xsd file has been added to the Solution Explorer window. (You'll learn more about this object in Chapter 23.)

4. Create three TextBox controls on the form; name them txtName, txtCity, and txt-State; and place appropriate labels on top of them. Next create the usual four navigation buttons, and name them btnFirst, btnPrevious, btnNext, and btnLast. (You can arrange them as you see in Figure 16-20.)

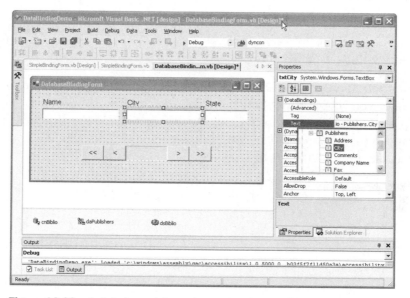

Figure 16-20   A data-bound form that uses ADO.NET components

5. Select the txtName control; in the Properties window, expand the DataBinding node; and click the down arrow button near the Text item to associate this control with the dsBiblio.Publishers.Name field. Repeat this operation to bind the txtCity control to the City field and the txtState control to the State field in the Publishers data table.

To make the binding mechanism fully operational, you have to write the code that fills the dsBiblio DataSet object with data from the database, gets a reference to the BindingManagerBase object associated with the Publishers table, and reacts to clicks on navigational controls.

```
Private Sub Form_Load(ByVal sender As Object, _
    ByVal e As EventArgs) Handles MyBase.Load
    ' Fill the DataSet using the defined DataAdapter.
    Me.daPublishers.Fill(dsBiblio.Publishers)
    ' Get a reference to the BindingManagerBase object.
    bmb = Me.BindingContext(dsBiblio.Publishers)
End Sub
```

```
Dim bmb As BindingManagerBase

' ...(Navigational code as in preceding example)...
⋮
```

Data Binding via Code

If you open the region of source code automatically generated by the form designer, you can see how to set up the binding to an ADO.NET data source by means of code only, without resorting to any components in the component tray. The code-only approach requires more time and attention, but in general it's more flexible and slightly more efficient. Here's the code-only version of the same bound form created in the preceding example:

```
Private Sub Form_Load(ByVal sender As Object, ByVal e As EventArgs) _
    Handles MyBase.Load
    CreateDataSet()
    InitializeBinding()
End Sub

Dim dsBiblio As New DataSet()
Dim bmb As BindingManagerBase

Sub CreateDataSet()
    ' Open a connection to the Biblio.mdb database.
    ' (You might have to provide a different connection string or path.)
    Dim cn As New OleDbConnection("Provider=Microsoft.Jet.OLEDB.4.0;Data " _
        & " Source=C:\Program Files\Microsoft Visual Studio\VB98\BIBLIO.MDB")
    cn.Open()
    ' Create a data adapter for the Publishers table.
    Dim daPublishers As New OleDbDataAdapter("SELECT * FROM Publishers", cn)
    ' Fill the DataSet object with data from the Publishers table.
    da.Fill(dsBiblio, "Publishers")

    ' Close the connection.
    cn.Close()
End Sub

Sub InitializeBinding()
    ' Bind controls to database fields.
    txtName.DataBindings.Add("Text", dsBiblio, "Publishers.Name")
    txtCity.DataBindings.Add("Text", dsBiblio, "Publishers.City")
    txtState.DataBindings.Add("Text", dsBiblio, "Publishers.State")

    ' Get a reference to the BindingManagerBase object.
    bmb = Me.BindingContext(dsBiblio, "Publishers")
    ' Force a refresh.
    bmb.Position = bmb.Count
    bmb.Position = 0
End Sub

' ...(Navigational code as in preceding example)...
⋮
```

Notice that ADO.NET data binding is two-way, in the sense that when you modify a value in a bound field, the new value is stored in the data source. However, don't forget that the data source is the DataSet object, not the database table, so the data in the database isn't automatically updated. (Read Chapter 22 to learn more about how you can update data modified in a disconnected DataSet object.)

Master-Detail Bound Forms

A common type of data-bound form is the one that displays data coming from two tables between which a relationship exists. For example, you can create a form like the one in Figure 16-21, with the DataGrid control displaying all the titles related to the publisher currently shown in the topmost TextBox controls.

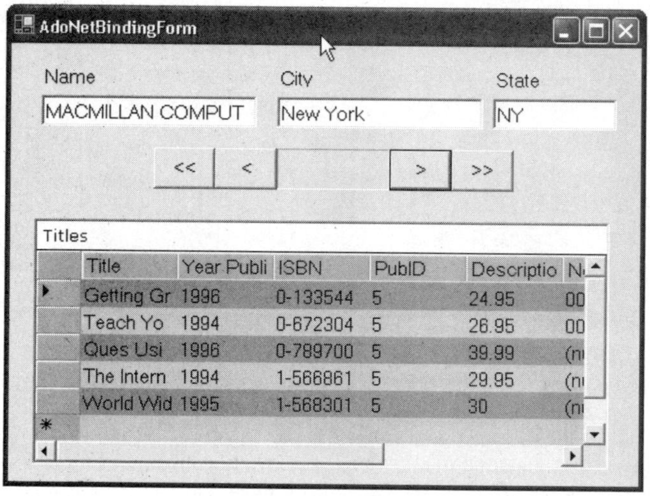

Figure 16-21 A master-detail form

Creating such a master-detail form is a breeze with the great data-binding features of Windows Forms. In fact, you only have to drop a DataGrid control, name it grdTitles on the form, and add a few statements to the CreateDataSet and InitializeBinding procedures (added statements are in boldface):

```
Sub CreateDataSet()
    :     ' Open the connection.
    cn.Open()
    ' Fill the DataSet object with data from the Publishers table.
    daPublishers.Fill(dsBiblio, "Publishers")

    ' Create a data adapter for the Titles table.
    Dim daTitles As New OleDbDataAdapter("SELECT * FROM Titles", cn)
    ' Fill the DataSet object with data from the Titles table.
    daTitles.Fill(dsBiblio, "Titles")
```

```
    ' Create a Relation between the two tables.
    dsBiblio.Relations.Add("PubTitles", _
        dsBiblio.Tables("Publishers").Columns("PubID"), _
        dsBiblio.Tables("Titles").Columns("PubId"))
    ' Close the connection.
    cn.Close()
End Sub

Sub InitializeBinding()
    ' Bind fields to database fields.
    txtName.DataBindings.Add("Text", dsBiblio, "Publishers.Name")
    txtCity.DataBindings.Add("Text", dsBiblio, "Publishers.City")
    txtState.DataBindings.Add("Text", dsBiblio, "Publishers.State")
    ' Bind the DataGrid.
    grdTitles.DataSource = dsBiblio
    grdTitles.DataMember = "Publishers.PubTitles"
    ' Get a reference to the BindingManagerBase object.
    bmb = Me.BindingContext(dsBiblio, "Publishers")
    ' Force a refresh.
    bmb.Position = bmb.Count
    bmb.Position = 0
End Sub
```

The DataMember property of the DataGrid control usually takes the name of the table to which you're binding the grid. However, when you're creating detail grids, the value of the DataMember property becomes the complete name of the relation, in the format *mastertablename.relationname* (Publishers.PubTitles in the preceding example).

The last example of the master-detail form has two DataGrid controls on it: grdPublishers, displaying data from the Publishers table; and grdTitles, displaying data from the Titles table, as shown in Figure 16-22. Because the database data is the same as in the preceding example, you don't have to modify the CreateDataSet procedure and the only changes are inside the InitializeBinding procedure. This procedure is actually simpler than before because you don't have to create a BindingManagerBase object to manage the navigational buttons:

```
Sub InitializeBinding()
    ' Bind the master grid to the Publishers table.
    grdPublishers.DataSource = dsBiblio
    grdPublishers.DataMember = "Publishers"
    ' Don't allow navigation to child tables (optional).
    grdPublishers.AllowNavigation = False
    ' Bind the detail grid to the Titles table.
    grdTitles.DataSource = dsBiblio
    grdTitles.DataMember = "Publishers.PubTitles"
End Sub
```

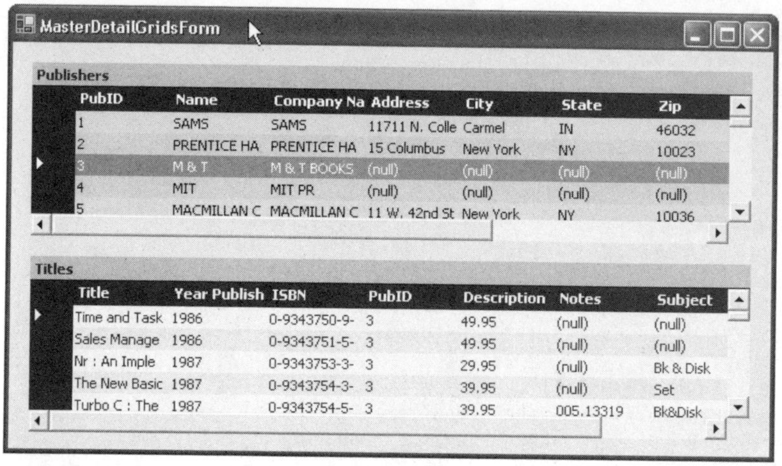

Figure 16-22   Two DataGrid controls in master-detail relationship

The DataGrid Control

The DataGrid control is one of the most powerful and complicated controls in the Windows Forms library. As you've seen, you use the DataGrid in bound mode with a data source, and this is also the only way you have to display data in this control, which explains why I postponed the section on the DataGrid control until this section. You can bind a DataGrid control to any ADO.NET data source—DataTable, DataSet, DataView, and DataViewManager—as well non-ADO.NET sources such as a single dimension array and any component that implements the IList or the IListSource interface.

After you drop a DataGrid control on a form, you can set a myriad of properties, or just click on the Auto Format link you find at the bottom of the Properties window to choose from a list of predefined styles. You have full control on the colors of the grid cells, the grid lines, the column headers, the caption, and the alternating background color for even-numbered rows. And of course you can also set the DataSource and DataMember properties.

The AllowSort property determines whether the user can sort the grid rows by clicking on a column header. There are no properties for allowing the user to edit, add, or delete rows because the availability of these commands depends on the properties of the underlying data source—for example, you can control them with the AllowEdit, AllowNew, and AllowDelete properties of a DataView object. The DataGrid's AllowNavigation tells whether the user can navigate to a child table when the data source is the parent table tied with another table in a master-detail relation.

Table and Column Styles

One of the great features of the DataGrid is that you can decide exactly how a given data source appears in the grid. You do so by creating one or more DataGridTableStyle objects, one for each possible style that you want to apply. For example, you might decide that only the pub_name and city fields appear when the grid is displaying data from the Publishers table, and only the title and price columns appear when the user navigates to the child Titles table. Or you might have multiple styles that can be applied when the DataGrid is bound to the Publishers (or the Titles) table.

You can create a DataGridTableStyle object at design time with Visual Studio .NET by clicking on the TableStyles item in the Properties window (left portion of Figure 16-23). A given table style is applied when the DataGrid's DataMember property is equal to the value of the DataGridTableStyle's MappingName property, so it's essential that this latter property matches the DataMember property exactly, including character casing.

Once you have set the appearance of a table style, you can define what columns should be displayed by clicking on the GridColumnStyles element in the DataGridTableStyles Collection Editor window. In the window that appears, you add a DataGridTextBoxColumn object to the table styles by clicking the Add button, and set the MappingName for this column (that is, the name of the bound field this column must display). You may also want to assign a few other properties, such as Width, ReadOnly (True if the column can't be edited), HeaderText (the caption of the column header), Alignment (the column alignment), NullText (the string to be used for null values), and Format (how the bound value must be formatted; you can use any argument you can pass to the ToString method, as explained in Chapter 7).

In addition to the DataGridTextBoxColumn class, the .NET Framework provides the DataGridBoolColumn class, which renders the bound value as a CheckBox control. This class has all the properties just mentioned for the DataGridTextBoxColumn class, except Format. You can also decide whether you want to support Null values in a DataGridBoolColumn object by setting its AllowNull property.

You decide which column type you want to add when you click on the Add button in the DataGridColumnStyle Collection Editor window. Later in this section, I'll show you how you can create a custom column style that displays a control other than TextBox or CheckBox.

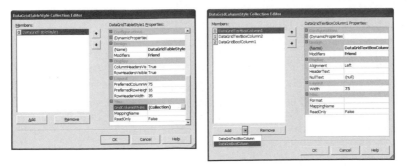

Figure 16-23   The dialog boxes that Visual Studio .NET gives to edit DataGridTableStyle objects (on the left) and DataGridColumnStyle objects (on the right) at design time

Programming the DataGrid Control

The DataGrid control has too many properties, methods, and events for me to cover all of them in these pages. For this reason, I'll only draw your attention to some of its most interesting members.

The Item property lets you read and write any cell in the DataGrid:

```
' Increment the value of top-left cell.
DataGrid1.Item(0, 0) = CInt(DataGrid1.Item(0, 0)) + 1
```

Additionally, you can set the value of a DataGrid cell by assigning the new value to the corresponding element in the underlying data source object, for example:

```
' Change the value of the second cell in the first row.
DataTable1.Rows(0)(1) = "New value"
```

You can learn how many visible rows and columns the DataGrid displays in a given moment by querying the VisibleRowCount and VisibleColumnCount properties, respectively, and using the FirstVisibleColumn property to determine the leftmost visible column.

The CurrentCell property lets you set and get the DataGrid's current cell, which is a DataGridCell object that exposes only two properties: RowNumber and ColumnNumber, both of which are zero-based. You can detect when the user selects a different cell by trapping the CurrentCellChanged event:

```
Private Sub grdValues_CurrentCellChanged(ByVal sender As Object, ByVal e As EventArgs) _
    Handles DataGrid1.CurrentCellChanged
    Dim cell As DataGridCell = DataGrid1.CurrentCell
    ' Display cell coordinates in a Label control.
    lblStatus.Text = String.Format("Current cell at ({0},{1})", _
        cell.RowNumber, cell.ColumnNumber)
End Sub
```

You can programmatically change the selected cell by assigning a different object to the CurrentCell property:

```
' Move the selection to top-left cell.
DataGrid1.CurrentCell = New DataGridCell(0, 0)
```

The DataGrid control doesn't expose any event that fires when the user edits a cell. Instead, you must trap the ColumnChanging event of the underlying DataTable and possibly set an error for the column and/or the cell if the entered value isn't valid:

```
Private Sub Publishers_ColumnChanging(ByVal sender As Object, _
ByVal e As DataColumnChangeEventArgs)
    ' Only check for errors in the ZipCode column.
    If e.Column.ColumnName = "zipcode" Then
        ' Check for invalid zip codes.
        If Not Regex.IsMatch(e.ProposedValue.ToString, "^\d{5}$") Then
```

```
                e.Row.RowError = "The ZipCode must be a 5-digit string."
            End If
        End If
End Sub
```

You can also restore the original value in the data source by reading the value corresponding to the Row and Column properties of the DataColumnChangeEventArgs passed to the event handler. Also, remember that this event fires only if the data-binding mechanism doesn't reject the proposed value in the first place. For example, you don't get this event if the user attempts to enter a non-numeric value in a column defined as numeric because the data binding rejects it before it reaches the DataGrid control.

The HitTest method lets you determine which portion of the DataGrid is under the mouse cursor. It returns a DataGrid.HitTestInfo object, whose Type property is an enumerated value that contains the information you need:

```
Private Sub grdValues_MouseMove(ByVal sender As Object, ByVal e As System.Windows.Form
s.MouseEventArgs) Handles DataGrid1.MouseMove
    Dim hi As HitTestInfo = DataGrid1.HitTest(e.X, e.Y)
    Dim msg As String
    Select Case hi.Type
        Case HitTestType.Cell: msg = "Cell at ({0},{1})"
        Case HitTestType.Caption: msg = "Caption"
        Case HitTestType.ColumnHeader: msg = "Header of column {1}"
        Case HitTestType.ColumnResize: msg = "Header resizer of column {1}"
        Case HitTestType.None: msg = "Background"
        Case HitTestType.ParentRows: msg = "Parent row"
        Case HitTestType.RowHeader: msg = "Header of row {0}"
        Case HitTestType.RowResize: msg = "Row resizer for row {0}"
    End Select
    lblStatus.Text = "Mouse is over " & String.Format(msg, hi.Row, hi.Column)
End Sub
```

If the DataGrid is displaying multiple tables in a master-detail relation, you can programmatically navigate back and forth with the NavigateTo and NavigateBack methods.

Creating Custom Column Styles

The most intriguing feature of the DataGrid control is the ability to define custom control styles, that is, columns that contain any assortment of controls you wish, instead of the standard TextBox and CheckBox controls that you get by default. A custom column style is a class that derives from the DataGridColumnStyle abstract type and that overrides a few protected methods.

There are three problems in creating a custom column style. First, it requires writing a lot of code. Second, the DataGridColumnStyle class is poorly documented in the .NET SDK. Third, you have to forgo the code generation capabilities of Visual Studio .NET when you create a table style that uses custom column styles because Visual Studio isn't aware of the new class you've authored.

I can't do much about the last problem, but I can help you with the first two issues by providing a class named DataGridControlColumn that is able to host any control that you define. I created this class by modifying the only sample I found in the official documentation so that it can work with a generic control. The companion code includes the complete commented source for the DataGridControlColumn class, but here I'll just show you how you can use it in your applications.

Let's say you want to define a table style that maps on the publishers table and that contains standard DataGridTextBoxColumn objects for the pub_name, city, and state fields, and one custom DataGridControlColumn object that displays a ComboBox control for the country field. (See Figure 16-24.) You begin by defining the DataGridTableStyle object and the styles for its first columns:

```
Dim gridStyle As New DataGridTableStyle
gridStyle.MappingName = "publishers"
' Add one column style for each column.
Dim pubNameStyle As New DataGridTextBoxColumn
pubNameStyle.MappingName = "pub_name"
pubNameStyle.HeaderText = "Name"
pubNameStyle.Width = 200
gridStyle.GridColumnStyles.Add(pubNameStyle)
' ...(Similar code for city and state fields)...
⋮
```

The constructor of my generic DataGridControlColumn object takes several arguments: a System.Type that defines the type of the inner control, the name of the bound property, the name of the event that the inner control fires when the bound property changes, the preferred width, the preferred height, and the minimum row height:

```
Dim countryStyle As New DataGridControlColumn( _
    GetType(ComboBox), "Text", "TextChanged", 120, 20, 20)
countryStyle.MappingName = "country"
countryStyle.HeaderText = "Country"
countryStyle.Width = 200
gridStyle.GridColumnStyles.Add(countryStyle)
```

The DataGridControlColumn class exposes the InnerControl read-only property, which lets you access the inner control that is made visible when a cell in the column is being edited. In the current demo, this property is used to fill the list area of the ComboBox control:

```
Dim cbo As ComboBox = CType(countryStyle.InnerControl, ComboBox)
cbo.Items.AddRange(New String() {"France", "Germany", "Italy", "UK", "USA"})
```

For more information, please see the source code provided with this book.

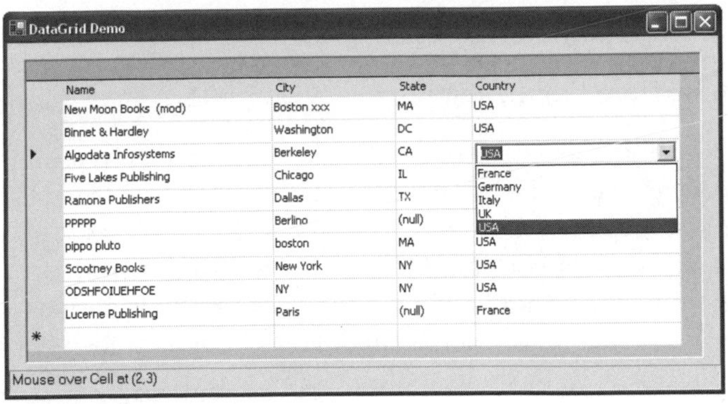

Figure 16-24 A DataGrid that uses a custom column style created with the DataGridControlStyle class provided in the companion code

Other Useful Objects

The System.Windows.Forms namespace contains many other objects that you'll surely need to know about for creating full-featured Win32 applications.

The Clipboard Object

As you can easily guess, the Clipboard object gives you the ability to copy data to the Clipboard and then paste it somewhere else.

Copying Data to the Clipboard

Copying a piece of information to the Clipboard is as easy as calling Clipboard.Set-DataObject. You can pass this method a string, an image, and so on. If you pass it a string that contains text in Rich Text Format (RTF), the Clipboard object detects this format automatically. For example, the following procedure copies the selected portion of a TextBox control (or the entire control's contents if no text is selected) to the Clipboard:

```
Sub CopyFromTextBox(ByVal tb As TextBox)
    ' Copy the TextBox's selected text to the Clipboard.
    Dim text As String = tb.SelectedText
    ' Copy the entire text if no text is selected.
    If text.Length = 0 Then text = tb.Text
    ' Proceed only if there is something to be copied.
    If text.Length > 0 Then
        Clipboard.SetDataObject(text)
    End If
End Sub
```

The SetDataObject method can take a second argument, which you should set to True if you want to make the copied object available after the current program terminates:

```
Clipboard.SetDataObject(text, True)
```

Remember that you can store any object to the Clipboard, including objects that are private to your application and that shouldn't be accessed by other programs. (Only serializable objects can be stored to the Clipboard.)

The Clipboard object supports several formats, each identified by a string constant exposed by the DataFormats class. The list includes common formats, such as Text, Rtf, Html, Bitmap, MetafilePict, EnhancedMetafile, Tiff, and Palette. There is also a CommaSeparatedValue format that lets you import data in CSV format from spreadsheets and many other applications. If a control can export data in multiple formats, it should call the SetDataObject method once for each format. For example, a RichTextBox control should copy the value of both the SelectedRtf and SelectedText properties so that its contents can be pasted in either a TextBox or a RichTextBox control.

While the SetDataObject method can understand a few formats automatically, it doesn't give you full control over the format used to store the data to the Clipboard. For a higher degree of control, you must create a new instance of DataObject, a class that works as a storage medium for data in different formats. Next you should call DataObject's SetData method once for every format you want to support, and you should use the Clipboard.SetDataObject method to store the DataObject object to the Clipboard:

```
Sub CopyFromRichTextBox(ByVal rtf As RichTextBox)
    ' Copy the RichTextBox's selected text to the Clipboard.
    Dim data As New DataObject()
    ' Get the selected RTF text if there is a selection
    ' or the entire text if no text is selected.
    Dim text As String = rtf.SelectedRtf
    If text.Length = 0 Then text = rtf.Rtf
    ' Do the copy only if there is something to be copied.
    If text.Length > 0 Then data.SetData(DataFormats.Rtf, text)

    ' Do it again with the plaintext.
    text = rtf.SelectedText
    If text.Length = 0 Then text = rtf.Text
    ' Proceed only if there is something to be copied.
    If text.Length > 0 Then
        data.SetData(DataFormats.Text, text)
    End If
    ' Move the DataObject into the Clipboard.
    ' (Pass True to make the data available to other applications.)
    Clipboard.SetDataObject(data, True)
End Sub
```

The first argument in the SetData method can be any string, including a user-defined string that defines a custom format. This lets you create private Clipboard formats that only your application can understand.

The DataObject class is usually used in conjunction with the Clipboard, but it doesn't have to be so. For example, you can use it as a temporary repository for your data in multiple formats. It's like having as many private Clipboards as you need.

Pasting Data from the Clipboard

Pasting data from the Clipboard requires more code because you must ascertain whether the Clipboard contains data in one of the formats you're willing to process. First use the Clipboard.GetDataObject method to retrieve an IDataObject object. Next use the Get-DataPresent method of this IDataObject object to determine whether the Clipboard contains data in the format specified by the first argument. If the second argument is True or omitted, the method attempts to force the conversion to the specified format—for example, it might try to force the conversion from RTF text to plaintext. If the GetDataPresent method returns True, you can extract the actual value with the GetData method. The following routine attempts to paste the current contents of the Clipboard to a TextBox control:

```
Sub PasteIntoTextBox(ByVal tb As TextBox)
    ' Get the data currently in the Clipboard.
    Dim data As IDataObject = Clipboard.GetDataObject
    ' Check whether there is any data in text format,
    ' converting it if necessary.
    If data.GetDataPresent(DataFormats.Text, True) Then
        ' If yes, paste into the selection.
        tb.SelectedText = data.GetData(DataFormats.Text, True).ToString
    End If
End Sub
```

Depending on the type of the target controls, you might need to make multiple attempts before you find a matching format. For example, this procedure attempts a paste operation to a RichTextBox control. Notice that you need to start by testing the richest format (RTF in this case) without attempting a conversion and then continue with less rich formats (plaintext in this case):

```
Sub PasteIntoRichTextBox(ByVal rtf As RichTextBox)
    ' Get the data currently in the Clipboard.
    Dim data As IDataObject = Clipboard.GetDataObject
    ' Check whether there is any data in RTF format,
    ' WITHOUT attempting a conversion.
    If data.GetDataPresent(DataFormats.Rtf, False) Then
        ' If available, paste into the RTF selection.
        rtf.SelectedRtf = data.GetData(DataFormats.Rtf).ToString
    ElseIf data.GetDataPresent(DataFormats.Text, True) Then
        ' Else, attempt to get data in plaintext format.
        rtf.SelectedText = data.GetData(DataFormats.Text, True).ToString
    End If
End Sub
```

The GetDataPresent and GetData methods are overloaded to take a System.Type argument; you can use this form to test whether the Clipboard contains an object in any class other than the standard Clipboard formats:

```
Dim data As IDataObject = Clipboard.GetDataObject
If data.GetDataPresent(GetType(Person)) Then
    ' The Clipboard contains a Person object.
    Dim p As Person = CType(data.GetData(GetType(Person)), Person)
End If
```

The IDataObject interface exposes the GetFormats method, which returns the formats of all the pieces of data currently stored in the Clipboard:

```
' Prepare the list of formats currently in the Clipboard.
' (You can pass True to include formats obtained by converting data.)
Dim msg As String = ""
For Each t As String In Clipboard.GetDataObject.GetFormats(False)
    msg &= t & ControlChars.CrLf
Next
MessageBox.Show(msg, "Current Clipboard formats")
```

Once you extract an IDataObject object from the Clipboard, this object has an independent life and doesn't necessarily reflect the *current* contents of the Clipboard.

Implementing Drag-and-Drop

Once you know how to store and retrieve data from the Clipboard, understanding drag-and-drop is a breeze. You can also leverage much of your knowledge about drag-and-drop in Visual Basic 6 because the conceptual differences are minor.

For starters, Visual Basic .NET doesn't support automatic drag-and-drop as Visual Basic 6 does. You must write code that initiates a drag-and-drop operation in the source control, and you must write code for events in the target control. In fact, the only property related to drag-and-drop is AllowDrop, which you must set to True to have a control raise events when it works as a drag-and-drop target.

How you initiate a drag-and-drop operation depends on which control is the target. Typically, you detect the user's intention to start a drag-and-drop operation when the mouse leaves the control while one of its buttons is being pressed. If this is the case, you should create a new DataObject instance and fill it with the data in the source control that might be dropped elsewhere. (This step is identical to what you do when copying data to the Clipboard and includes your having the ability to store data in multiple formats.) Here's the first part of a MouseMove event handler that works equally well with a TextBox control or a RichTextBox control:

```
Private Sub TextBox_MouseMove(ByVal sender As Object, _
    ByVal e As System.Windows.Forms.MouseEventArgs) _
    Handles TextBox1.MouseMove, RichTextBox1.MouseMove
    ' Exit if no button is pressed.
    If e.Button = 0 Then Exit Sub
    ' Get a reference to the control. We leverage the fact that both
    ' the TextBox and the RichTextBox control inherit from TextBoxBase.
    Dim tbase As TextBoxBase = DirectCast(sender, TextBoxBase)
    ' Exit if there is no data to be dragged.
    If tbase.TextLength = 0 Then Exit Sub
    ' Exit if the cursor is inside the control's borders.
    If tbase.Bounds.Contains(e.X, e.Y) Then Exit Sub
    ' The mouse is being dragged outside the control's client area,
    ' so we can start a drag-and-drop operation.
    Dim data As New DataObject()
```

```
' Store the selected text, or all the text if no selection.
If tbase.SelectionLength > 0 Then
    data.SetData(DataFormats.Text, tbase.SelectedText)
Else
    data.SetData(DataFormats.Text, tbase.Text)
End If
' If the control is a RichTextBox, store also the selected Rtftext
' or its entire contents if no selection.
If TypeOf sender Is RichTextBox Then
    Dim rtfbox As RichTextBox = DirectCast(sender, RichTextBox)
    If rtfbox.SelectionLength > 0 Then
        data.SetData(DataFormats.Rtf, rtfbox.SelectedRtf)
    Else
        data.SetData(DataFormats.Rtf, rtfbox.Rtf)
    End If
End If
```

In the next step, you define which drag-and-drop effects you want to support, using a DragDropEffects bit-coded value (supported effects are Copy, Move, Scroll, Link, and All), and you pass this value and the DataObject object to the control's DoDragDrop method, which actually initiates the drag-and-drop operation. The DoDragDrop method is synchronous and doesn't return until the drag-and-drop operation has been completed (or canceled). The return value from the method is another DragDropEffect value that tells which effect was chosen by the user (Copy, Move, or Scroll), or is None if the operation was canceled; if the selected effect is Move, you must delete the selected data in the source control. Here's the second part of the MouseMove event handler that implements the entire process:

```
    ' Start the drag operation - wait until it's completed.
    Dim effect As DragDropEffects = _
        DragDropEffects.Copy Or DragDropEffects.Move
    effect = tbase.DoDragDrop(data, effect)
    ' Delete the text if it was a move operation.
    If effect = DragDropEffects.Move Then
        If tbase.SelectionLength > 0 Then
            tbase.SelectedText = ""
        Else
            tbase.Text = ""
        End If
    End If
End Sub
```

Let's see now what code you must write to have a control act as a drag-and-drop target. A control that works as a drag-and-drop target can receive four events: DragEnter (the mouse is entering the control's client area), DragOver (the mouse is moving inside the control), DragLeave (the mouse is exiting the control), and DragDrop (the mouse button is being released while over the control). Remember that you must set the target control's AllowDrop property to True; otherwise, none of these events will ever fire.

The DragEnter, DragOver, and DragDrop events receive a DragEventArgs object in their second argument. You can learn more about the drag-and-drop operation being performed by querying its read-only properties: AllowedEffect (a bit-coded value that specifies which actions are available), Data (the DataObject instance that contains the data), KeyState (the state of Shift, Ctrl, and Alt keys and mouse buttons), and X and Y (the position of the cursor in client coordinates). The KeyState bit-coded property doesn't correspond to any enumerated value, so you must use numeric constants: 1 (left button), 2 (right button), 4 (Shift key), 8 (Ctrl key), 16 (middle button), and 32 (Alt key).

The only writable property is Effect, to which you assign a value that reflects which operations the target control is willing to accept. In the DragEnter event, you check the format of the data being dragged, the available effects, and the state of keys and mouse buttons. If you want to accept the drag-and-drop, you assign a value other than None to the Effect property. The following procedure shows how to implement a DragEnter event handler that works equally well with a TextBox control or a RichTextBox control:

```
Private Sub TextBox_DragEnter(ByVal sender As Object, _
    ByVal e As System.Windows.Forms.DragEventArgs) _
    Handles TextBox1.DragEnter, RichTextBox1.DragEnter
    ' Check that the user is dragging some text.
    If e.Data.GetDataPresent(DataFormats.Text, True) Then
        If CBool(e.KeyState And 8) Then
            ' If Ctrl key is pressed, this is a copy operation.
            e.Effect = e.AllowedEffect And DragDropEffects.Copy
        Else
            ' Otherwise, it is a move operation.
            e.Effect = e.AllowedEffect And DragDropEffects.Move
        End If
    Else
        ' Reject any other type.
        e.Effect = DragDropEffects.None
    End If
End Sub
```

You can also use the DragEnter event to change the appearance of the target control—for example, by drawing a special border around it or changing its background color. If you do this, you should restore the original appearance in the DragLeave event handler as well as in the DragDrop event handler. When the mouse is moving inside the target control's client area, you receive DragOver events, but you need to trap this event only if you want to provide different drag-and-drop effects (or disable drag-and-drop completely) for different areas of the control.

This leaves the DragDrop event, which is where you write the code that manages the actual data processing. As you see in the following example, getting the data being dropped is similar to a paste operation:

```
Private Sub TextBox_DragDrop(ByVal sender As Object, _
    ByVal e As System.Windows.Forms.DragEventArgs) _
    Handles TextBox1.DragDrop, RichTextBox1.DragDrop
    ' Exit if data isn't in text format.
    If Not e.Data.GetDataPresent(DataFormats.Text, True) Then Exit Sub
```

```
      ' Decide whether this is a copy or a move operation.
      If CBool(e.KeyState And 8) Then
          e.Effect = DragDropEffects.Copy
      Else
          e.Effect = DragDropEffects.Move
      End If

      If (TypeOf sender Is RichTextBox) Then
          ' Do nothing if target is a RichTextBox, because this control manages
          ' drag-and-drop internally and this behavior can't be overridden.
      Else
          ' Otherwise, paste plaintext.
          Dim tbase As TextBoxBase = DirectCast(sender, TextBoxBase)
          tbase.SelectedText = e.Data.GetData(DataFormats.Text).ToString
      End If
End Sub
```

As remarks in the code explain, the RichTextBox control manages drag-and-drop autonomously, so you must not perform any action when it is the target of a drag-and-drop operation.

The only other event that I haven't covered yet is QueryContinueDrag, which is received by the source control while the drag-and-drop operation is in progress. This event receives a QueryContinueDragEventArgs object, which exposes the KeyState, EscapePressed, and Action properties. Your code should check the pressed keys and whether the user pressed the Esc key, and assign one of the following DragAction enumerated values to the Action property: Continue (the default), Drop, or Cancel. Here's the typical implementation of this event:

```
Private Sub TextBox1_QueryContinueDrag(ByVal sender As Object, _
    ByVal e As System.Windows.Forms.QueryContinueDragEventArgs) _
    Handles TextBox1.QueryContinueDrag, RichTextBox1.QueryContinueDrag
    If e.EscapePressed Then e.Action = DragAction.Cancel
End Sub
```

The Application Object

The System.Windows.Forms.Application object exposes a few interesting properties, methods, and events. All the members of this class are shared, and you can't create an instance of the Application object. By and large, this object replaces the App object you have under Visual Basic 6, but is more powerful.

Properties, Methods, and Events

All the properties of the Application objects are read-only, and the name of most of them is self-explanatory: ExecutablePath (the complete filename of the executable), Startup-Path (the path portion of the executable file), ProductName (the name of the running application), ProductVersion (the application's version), CompanyName (who created the application), and CurrentCulture (culture information about the current thread).

Other properties return information about the registry key or the directory that this application can use to store values: CommonAppDataPath (the directory under C:\Documents and Settings that can be used by all users), LocalUserAppDataPath (same as previous, but related to current user), CommonAppDataRegistry (the registry key under HKEY_LOCAL_MACHINE that can be used by all users of the application), and a few others.

I won't give you an example of the value returned by each property because the demo application lets you test the most useful features of this object. (See Figure 16-25.) Notice that the demo application displays the company name, product name, and product version that I have set by using attributes in the AssemblyInfo.vb module:

```
<Assembly: AssemblyCompany("VB2TheMax Software")>
<Assembly: AssemblyProduct("WinForm Objects Demo")>
<Assembly: AssemblyVersion("1.0.2.*")>
```

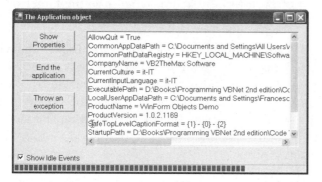

Figure 16-25   The demo program to test the Application object

You can reach this information by using reflection methods, but the properties of the Application object are surely a handy shortcut. (You must use reflection methods for other attributes, such as AssemblyTitle and AssemblyDescription, but you rarely need to read them from inside the application.)

The Application object also exposes methods and events. The Application.Exit method provides a way to terminate a Windows Forms application, whereas Application.Do-Events yields to the operating system and returns only when all the pending messages have been processed. This method is useful if you are inside a loop that the user can terminate by pressing a key, as in this short demo:

```
Sub ALengthyProcess()
    Me.Canceled = False
    For i As Integer = 1 To 1000000
        ⋮
        ' Let Windows process pending messages.
        Application.DoEvents
        ' Exit if end user clicked on the Cancel button.
        If Me.Canceled Then Exit For
    Next
End Sub
```

```
Dim Canceled As Boolean
Private Sub btnCancel_Click(ByVal sender As Object, ByVal e As EventArgs) _
    Handles btnCancel.Click
    Me.Canceled = True
End Sub
```

The Idle event can be useful for performing actions when the UI is idle. This event doesn't fire periodically, but only when the form engine has completed the processing of one or more messages in the message loop. This event is useful if you want to update variables or UI elements after every action performed by the end user. (See the next section, "The Cursor Object," for an example of this technique.)

The ApplicationExit event fires just before the application ends, so you can use it for clean-up chores. The event fires even if the application is ending because of a fatal error. Keep in mind that all windows have been destroyed already when this event fires, so you can display a message to the user only by using a message box, or you can store a message in the system log. Remember that all the Application object's events are shared events, so you must use the AddHandler command to set up an event handler for them.

Global Error Handlers

The ThreadException event lets you leverage a powerful feature of Windows Forms, so it deserves a section of its own. To understand why this feature is so important, let's review what happens when an unhandled error occurs inside an event handler. In normal circumstances, the exception would be passed to the caller code, but an event procedure has no caller, so errors of this kind usually terminate the application.

The Application.ThreadException event fires whenever an unhandled exception is thrown on the current thread, so you can easily write a global error handler that protects all your forms from any unhandled errors. Your global handler can ignore the error, log it to a file, display a message box that asks the end user whether to abort the application, send an e-mail message to the tech support group, and perform any other action you deem desirable. (See Figure 16-26.)

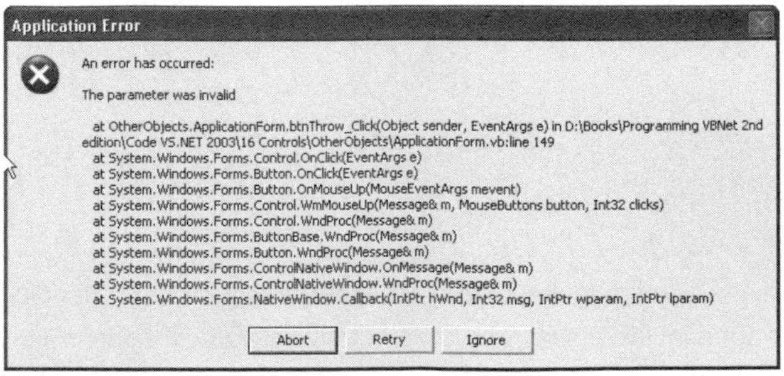

Figure 16-26 The message box shown by the global error handler in the demo application

To implement this feature correctly, you must use a Sub Main procedure as the start-up object of your application and you must mark it with the STAThread attribute to set the threading model of the application to Single Thread Apartment (STA) mode. After you set up the ThreadException event, you can start the main form by using an Application.Run method, as shown in the following code:

```
Module MainModule
    <STAThread()> _
    Sub Main()
        ' Install the event handler.
        AddHandler Application.ThreadException, _
            AddressOf Application_ThreadException
        ' Run the start-up form.
        Application.Run(New ApplicationForm())
    End Sub

    ' This is the global error handler.
    Sub Application_ThreadException(ByVal sender As Object, _
        ByVal e As System.Threading.ThreadExceptionEventArgs)
        Try
            ' Prepare an informative message.
            Dim msg As String = _
                String.Format("An error has occurred:{0}{0}{1}{0}{0}{2}", _
                ControlChars.Cr, e.Exception.Message, e.Exception.StackTrace)
            ' Display it, asking whether the application should terminate.
            Dim result As DialogResult = _
                MessageBox.Show(msg, "Application Error", _
                MessageBoxButtons.AbortRetryIgnore, MessageBoxIcon.Error)
            ' End the application if the end user said so.
            If result = DialogResult.Abort Then
                Application.Exit()
            End If
        Catch
            ' If the message box couldn't be displayed (presumably because
            ' the Exception object wasn't available), try with a simpler
            ' message, and then close the application anyway.
            Try
                MessageBox.Show("The application will be terminated", _
                    "Fatal Error", MessageBoxButtons.OK, MessageBoxIcon.Error)
            Finally
                Application.Exit()
            End Try
        End Try
    End Sub
End Module
```

> **Important** This feature clashes with the Visual Studio debugger, and global error handlers don't work well when the application runs inside Visual Studio. To see this feature in action, you should run the program using the Start Without Debugging command on the Debug menu (which corresponds to the Ctrl+F5 key combination) or run it from Windows Explorer or the command prompt.

The global error handler serves all the unhandled exceptions of your application, including the most critical ones. For this reason, the code inside the handler should account for exceptional conditions—for example, the case when the e.Exception object isn't available or when it isn't possible to display a message box. (In the latter case, you might want to log the error to the system log or to a bug report file.)

The Cursor Object

The Cursor class has a dual purpose. Its static properties and methods allow you to control several features of the mouse cursor. Its constructor method lets you create a new mouse cursor, which you can later assign to the Mouse.Current static property or to the Cursor property of any control.

Static Properties and Methods

The Position property is the Point object that represents the position of the cursor. This property is similar to the form's MousePosition property, but it's expressed in screen coordinates, and more important, it can be written to. For example, the following code moves the mouse cursor to the center of the current form:

```
With Me.ClientRectangle
    ' The PointToScreen method converts from client to screen coordinates.
    Cursor.Position = Me.PointToScreen( _
        New Point(CInt(.Width / 2), CInt(.Height / 2)))
End With
```

The demo application takes advantage of the Application.Idle event to display the current mouse position in client coordinates. (See Figure 16-27.) This approach is extremely efficient because this event fires immediately after the form has processed a mouse move message:

```
Private Sub Application_Idle(ByVal sender As Object, ByVal e As EventArgs)
    lblStatus.Text = Me.PointToClient(Cursor.Position).ToString
End Sub
```

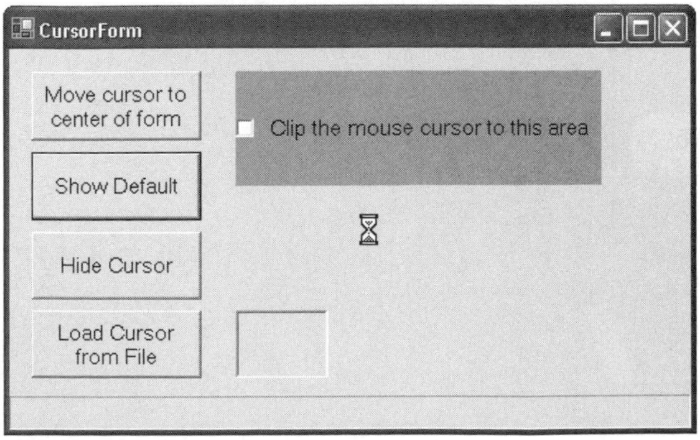

Figure 16-27   The demo application lets you test a few features of the Cursor class.

The Clip property is the rectangle within which the mouse cursor is confined; its value is Nothing if the mouse can move over the entire screen. This rectangle is in screen coordinates, so you must do some conversions if you want to confine the mouse to an object on the form:

```
' Clip the mouse to the TextBox1 control's client area.
Cursor.Clip = TextBox1.RectangleToScreen(TextBox1.ClientRectangle)
  ⋮
' Free the mouse cursor.
Cursor.Clip = Nothing
```

The Current static property is the current cursor used for the mouse at the screen level. You can set this property by using one of the standard cursors exposed by the Cursors type, as in this code:

```
' Show an hourglass cursor during a lengthy operation.
Cursor.Current = Cursors.WaitCursor
```

A problem with the preceding code is that the form restores its default cursor whenever the user moves or clicks the mouse, so setting the Cursor.Current property is rarely a good idea. A better approach is to set the Cursor property of the form or the individual control:

```
Me.Cursor = Cursors.WaitCursor
  ⋮
' Restore the default pointer.
Me.Cursor = Cursors.Default
```

The Cursors type exposes 28 different mouse cursors. You can see all of them by selecting any control and then clicking the down arrow beside the Cursor property in the Properties window. (See Figure 16-28.)

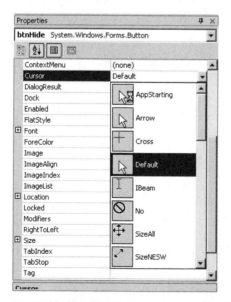

Figure 16-28   The settings for a control Cursor property

The Hide and Show shared methods of the Cursor class let you control the visibility of the mouse cursor. You must call the Show method a number of times equal to the number of calls to the Hide method to make the mouse cursor appear again.

Creating New Cursors

You can also instantiate new Cursor objects—for example, by loading a cursor from a .cur file. (The Cursor class doesn't support animated cursors in .ani files.) You just have to pass the name of the file to the class constructor, as in this line of code:

```
Dim cur As New Cursor("c:\Windows\cursors\3dsmove.cur")
```

You also can use an overloaded variation of the constructor to load the cursor from a stream, which is useful if a file contains multiple cursors.

After you create a cursor, you can assign it to the Cursor.Current property or to the Cursor property of a control. It's important, however, that you destroy the cursor in an orderly fashion when you don't use it any longer—for example, when you restore the default cursor shape for the control:

```
' Create a new cursor from the file and assign it to the form
Dim cur As New Cursor("c:\Windows\cursors\3dsmove.cur")
Me.Cursor = cur
' Perform a lengthy operation.
⋮
' Restore the default cursor and destroy the cursor loaded from file.
Me.Cursor = Cursors.Default
cur.Dispose
```

The SendKeys Class

This class replaces the command of the same name that you use under Visual Basic 6. With its Send shared method, you can send one or more keystrokes to the active application—for example:

```
' Send the V and B keystrokes, followed by the Enter key.
SendKeys.Send("VB~")
' Send the HOME, Shift+END, and DEL keys.
' (If sent to a text field, this sequence deletes the current line.)
SendKeys.Send("{HOME}+{END}{DEL}")
' Insert 40 asterisks, and then move the caret to the first asterisk.
SendKeys.SendWait("{* 40}{LEFT 40}")
```

The SendWait method works in the same fashion except that it waits until the application processes all the keystrokes:

```
' Send the Ctrl+HOME, Ctrl+Shift+END, and DEL keys.
' (Clears the contents of the current text box window.)
SendKeys.SendWait("^{HOME}^+{END}{DEL}")
```

See the .NET Framework SDK for more details about the syntax you can use to specify the keystroke sequence.

The third and last method, Flush, forces the processing of all the Windows messages (keystrokes and mouse actions) currently in the message queue:

```
SendKeys.Flush()
```

The Help Class

This class encapsulates the HTML Help 1.0 engine and lets you display the index, the search page, or a specific topic in an HTML file in HTML Help format, in a compiled help file (.chm) authored with the HTML Help Workshop, or in some third-party tool.

This class exposes two shared methods, and you can't create an instance of this class. The ShowHelpIndex method displays the index of the specified help file, as in this code:

```
' The first argument is a Control object that works as the
' parent for the help dialog box.
Help.ShowHelpIndex(Me, "c:\myhelpfile.chm")
```

(You can also use a URL that uses forward slashes as separators.) The other method, ShowHelp, is overloaded to provide access to different portions of the help document:

```
' Display the contents of the help file.
Help.ShowHelp(Me, "c:\myhelpfile.chm")
' Display the index page of the help file.
Help.ShowHelp(Me, "c:\myhelpfile.chm", HelpNavigator.Index)
' Display the search page of the help file.
Help.ShowHelp(Me, "c:\myhelpfile.chm", HelpNavigator.Find)
' Display the help page for a specific keyword.
Help.ShowHelp(Me, "c:\myhelpfile.chm", "mykeyword")
' Display the help page for the specific topic #123.
Help.ShowHelp(Me, "c:\myhelpfile.chm", HelpNavigator.Topic, 123)
```

The Help class replaces the Help Common Dialog, which is no longer supported. Earlier in this chapter you learned about the HelpProvider control, which encapsulates the Help object to automatically display help when the F1 key is pressed at a time that a control has the input focus.

At the end of our exploration of Windows Forms controls and other classes in the System.Windows.Forms namespace, you know enough to create functional Win32 applications. To create a truly functional and eye-catching user interface, however, you need to leverage the GDI+ portion of the .NET Framework. This is the topic of the next chapter, so keep reading.

17 GDI+

GDI+ is the technology in the .NET Framework with which you produce text and graphic output and deal with bitmaps and other kinds of images. I already used a few GDI+ methods in previous chapters, but without engaging in a thorough description of this important part of the new architecture. Broadly speaking, you can subdivide GDI+ into three parts:

- **2-D vector graphics** This subset of GDI+ includes objects for drawing lines, polygons, ellipses, and arcs, possibly filled with color. GDI+ supports sophisticated features in this area, such as gradient brushes, complex cardinal and Bézier spline curves, scalable regions, persistent paths, and more. Most of the objects for doing 2-D vector graphics are in the System.Drawing and System.Drawing.Drawing2D namespaces.

- **Imaging** This subset gathers objects for displaying and processing image formats such as bitmaps and icons. The .NET capabilities for working with raster images are really outstanding and include image stretching, conversion to and from the most common graphic formats, and support for semitransparent regions by means of alpha blending. The objects that you use for making images are in the System.Drawing.Imaging namespace.

- **Typography** This subset includes all the objects you use to display text in a variety of forms, colors, and styles. You have complete control over how text is displayed, and you can even activate anti-aliasing and special techniques for better text rendering on LCD displays, such as those of PDAs. The objects for typography are in the System.Drawing.Text namespace.

2-D Vector Graphics

The three segments of GDI+ have many objects in common, and above all, they employ a similar programming model. In this section, I'll cover 2-D vector graphics, but most concepts apply to other parts of GDI+ as well.

> **Note** To keep the code as concise as possible, all the code samples in this section assume that the following Imports statements are used at the file or project level:
>
> ```
> Imports System.Drawing
> Imports System.Drawing.Drawing2D
> Imports System.Drawing.Imaging
> Imports System.Drawing.Text
> ```

The Graphics Object

The first operation you must perform to draw a graphic primitive on a drawing surface is get a reference to a Graphics object, which represents the canvas on which you'll draw your lines and other shapes even though it isn't necessarily a visible surface. (The Graphics object broadly corresponds to a device context in "classic" GDI programming.) This object doesn't have a public constructor method, so you can't create it by using the New keyword. Instead, you must use one of these two techniques: get a Graphics object from the argument of an event or get a Graphics object by using the CreateGraphics method that the form and all control objects expose.

Here's an example that uses the first technique to display a circle as large as the form inside the Paint event of a form. The PaintEventArgs object passed to this event has a property that exposes the Graphics object that represents the visible surface of the object being repainted:

```
Private Sub Form1_Paint(ByVal sender As Object, _
    ByVal e As PaintEventArgs) Handles MyBase.Paint
    ' Get the Graphics object that corresponds to the form's surface.
    Dim gr As Graphics = e.Graphics
    ' Clear the background with azure color.
    gr.Clear(Color.Azure)
    ' Draw a red ellipse as large as the form.
    gr.DrawEllipse(Pens.Red, 0, 0, Me.ClientSize.Width, Me.ClientSize.Height)
End Sub
```

Other events let you get a reference to the Graphics object in this way—for example, the DrawItem event that you use for owner-draw controls. But if your code runs inside the handler of an event that doesn't make this object available, you must use the CreateGraphics method of the form or the control to get a valid Graphics object. The main difference with the technique that uses the object received as an argument is that you must destroy the Graphics object before exiting the procedure—otherwise, the corresponding Windows resource (that is, the underlying device context) will be destroyed only at the next garbage collection. The following example shows how you can draw an ellipse as large as the form, which will be automatically redrawn when the form is resized:

```
Private Sub Form1_Resize(ByVal sender As Object, _
    ByVal e As EventArgs) Handles MyBase.Resize
    ' Get the Graphics object corresponding to the form's surface.
    Dim gr As Graphics = Me.CreateGraphics
    ' Clear the background with azure color.
    gr.Clear(Color.Azure)
```

```
        ' Draw a red ellipse as large as the form.
        gr.DrawEllipse(Pens.Red, 0, 0, Me.ClientSize.Width, Me.ClientSize.Height)
        ' Destroy the Graphics object.
        gr.Dispose()
End Sub
```

The Graphics object exposes many properties and methods, and I'll illustrate most of them in the sections that follow.

Lines, Rectangles, Polygons, Ellipses, and Arcs

The Graphics object exposes methods for drawing graphic primitives such as lines, rectangles, and ellipses. Each method is overloaded and therefore several syntax forms are available, but as a rule you pass a Pen object as the first argument and a set of coordinates or a bounding rectangle in the remaining arguments. In a difference from Visual Basic 6, there's no concept of current foreground color, and you must pass the Pen object at each call. Moreover, the Graphics object doesn't remember the last point drawn. Putting it another way, the Graphics object is stateless—although this statement isn't completely accurate because the object does maintain some important values that you can assign to its properties, as I'll explain later.

```
' Create a Graphics object.
Dim gr As Graphics = Me.CreateGraphics
' Draw a red line from (100, 30) to (500, 300).
gr.DrawLine(Pens.Red, 100, 30, 500, 300)
' Draw a white square with left-top corner at (130, 50) and side=300 pixels.
gr.DrawRectangle(Pens.White, New Rectangle(130, 50, 300, 300))
' Draw a green circle with radius=200 and center at (350,250).
Dim r As Integer = 200
gr.DrawEllipse(Pens.Green, 350 - r, 250 - r, r * 2, r * 2)
' Destroy the Graphics object.
gr.Dispose()
```

Drawing an arc of an ellipse using the DrawArc method is similar to drawing an ellipse, but you must supply two additional arguments: the starting angle and the sweep angle, both of which are measured in degrees. The starting angle is measured clockwise from the X axis; the sweep angle is also measured clockwise. For example, the following statement

```
' Draw a quarter of a circle, whose center is at (200, 150)
' with radius equal to 100.
Dim r2 As Integer = 100
gr.DrawArc(Pens.Blue, 200 - r2, 150 - r2, r2 * 2, r2 * 2, 0, 90)
```

draws the following arc:

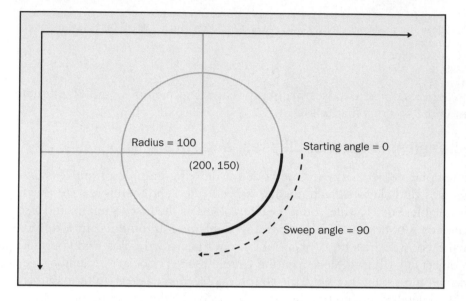

A few methods let you create multiple lines with one call. The DrawLines method draws a series of connected lines; it takes an array of Point or PointF objects:

```
' Draw three straight lines.
Dim points() As Point = {New Point(10, 10), _
    New Point(100, 80), New Point(200, 20), New Point(300, 100)}
gr.DrawLines(Pens.Black, points)
```

(The only difference between these two objects is that PointF expresses the two coordinates as Single numbers.)

If the end point of the last line coincides with the first point of the first line, you're actually drawing a polygon and you can use the DrawPolygon method:

```
' Draw a rhombus. (Note we build the Point array on the fly.)
gr.DrawPolygon(Pens.Red, New Point() {New Point(200, 50), _
    New Point(300, 100), New Point(200, 150), New Point(100, 100)})
```

You can also quickly draw multiple rectangles using the DrawRectangles method:

```
' Draw three rectangles.
Dim rects() As Rectangle = {New Rectangle(50, 30, 200, 100), _
    New Rectangle(70, 40, 220, 110), New Rectangle(90, 50, 240, 120)}
gr.DrawRectangles(Pens.Green, rects)
```

Cardinal and Bézier Splines

GDI+ supports two different forms of a complex curve that can't be represented as an arc of a circle or an ellipse: a cardinal spline and a Bézier spline. A cardinal spline is the curve that you would create by taking a piece of flexible material—such as a thin strip of steel or wood—and making it pass through a given set of fixed points on the X-Y plane. Unless the material you're using is infinitely flexible (as would be a string of rope or rubber), the path drawn by the material would be a curve that doesn't create any sharp angles at the connecting points. Depending on the degree of flexibility (also known as *tension*) of the material used, a given set of points can generate different curves. The default tension is 0.5. The following code snippet draws five cardinal splines, with a tension that goes from 0 (which corresponds to a material with infinite flexibility, which therefore draws straight lines) to 2:

```
Dim points() As Point = {New Point(100, 100), New Point(200, 200), _
    New Point(250, 30), New Point(350, 100)}
 For tension As Single = 0 To 2 Step 0.5
    gr.DrawCurve(Pens.Blue, points, tension)
Next
```

Figure 17-1 shows the resulting cardinal splines. You can also draw a closed cardinal spline by using the DrawClosedCurve method, which takes an array of Point objects.

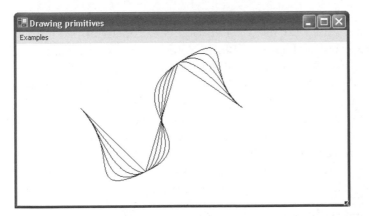

Figure 17-1   Five cardinal splines with tensions from 0 (the straight line) to 2

A Bézier spline is a curve specified by four points: the initial point, the ending point, and two control points. The curve doesn't pass through the control points, but they influence the direction of the curve at the starting and ending points. More precisely, the Bézier spline begins in the direction indicated by the imaginary line that joins the starting point and the first control point and ends in the direction indicated by the imaginary line that joins the second control point and the ending line. Figure 17-2 is an example of a Bézier curve that also shows these two tangent lines. You can draw this kind of curve by using the DrawBezier method, which takes four Point objects (in this order): the starting point, the first control point, the second control point, and the ending point. For example, here's the code that draws the curve shown in the figure:

```
gr.DrawBezier(Pens.Black, New Point(10, 30), New Point(100, 20), _
    New Point(140, 190), New Point(200, 200))
```

You can also draw multiple connected Bézier curves with the DrawBeziers method. This method takes an array of Point objects. The first four objects define the first curve, and then each subsequent group of three objects defines the control points and the ending point for the next curve.

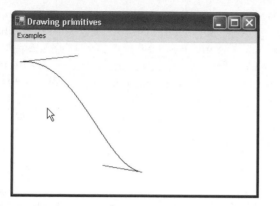

Figure 17-2   A Bézier curve with two tangent lines joining its end points to its control points

The Pen Object

All the examples shown so far used a Pen object taken from predefined objects exposed by the Pens class, such as Pens.Black. You can also use one of the Pen objects that correspond to a system color using the SystemPens class—for example, System-Pens.ActiveCaptionText to use the color defined for the title bar of the active window. In many cases, however, you need to create a custom Pen object yourself if you want to use one of the colors not available in the Pens or SystemPens class, define a width larger than 1 pixel, define a dashed line, or in general have more control over the appearance of the lines or curves being drawn. A key difference between predefined and custom Pen objects is that you must always destroy the latter objects by calling their Dispose method. Here are a couple of examples:

```
' Draw the inner rectangle with a pen of custom color.
Dim p1 As New Pen(Color.FromArgb(128, 0, 60))
gr.DrawRectangle(p1, 50, 50, 100, 50)
' Draw the outer rectangle with a blue pen 4 pixels wide.
Dim p2 As New Pen(Color.Blue, 4)
gr.DrawRectangle(p2, 10, 10, 200, 100)
' Destroy the two Pen objects.
p1.Dispose()
p2.Dispose()
```

When you're working with a Pen object wider than 1 pixel, you also must account for its alignment, which affects how the line is drawn in respect to its beginning and ending points. For example, Figure 17-3 shows two squares with sides of the same length but drawn with pens aligned differently:

```
Dim p As New Pen(Color.Yellow, 12)
Dim rect As New Rectangle(20, 20, 100, 100)
' Draw first square, with alignment = center (default).
gr.DrawRectangle(p, rect)
' Draw also the theoretical line as a reference.
gr.DrawRectangle(Pens.Black, rect)
```

```
' Move the rectangle to the right.
rect.Offset(150, 0)
' Change the alignment to inset, and draw the two squares once again.
p.Alignment = Drawing.Drawing2D.PenAlignment.Inset
gr.DrawRectangle(p, rect)
gr.DrawRectangle(Pens.Black, rect)
' Destroy the custom Pen object.
p.Dispose()
```

Note that the PenAlignment enumeration defines three more settings—Left, Outset, and Right—but they appear to be nonfunctional and deliver the same result as the default setting (Center).

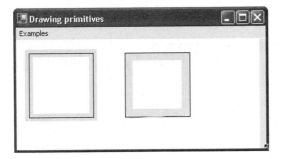

Figure 17-3   Two squares drawn with different pen alignments

You can set other properties of the Pen object to create custom lines. For example, you can use the DashStyle enumerated property to draw dashed lines using a predefined pattern, and you can even create custom dash patterns by assigning an array of Single values to the DashPattern property. The StartCap and EndCap properties can take an enumerated value and let you change the shape of the starting and ending points of the line so that you can easily create arrows or other common shapes. Figure 17-4 shows some of the many line variations that you can achieve using these properties. Here's the source code that creates that output:

```
Dim p1 As New Pen(Color.Black, 3)
p1.DashStyle = Drawing.Drawing2D.DashStyle.Dash
gr.DrawLine(p1, 10, 10, 200, 10)
p1.DashStyle = Drawing.Drawing2D.DashStyle.DashDot
gr.DrawLine(p1, 10, 30, 200, 30)
p1.DashStyle = Drawing.Drawing2D.DashStyle.DashDotDot
gr.DrawLine(p1, 10, 50, 200, 50)
p1.DashStyle = Drawing.Drawing2D.DashStyle.Dot
gr.DrawLine(p1, 10, 70, 200, 70)

' Create a custom dash pattern.
Dim sngArray() As Single = {4, 4, 8, 4, 12, 4}
p1.DashPattern = sngArray
gr.DrawLine(p1, 10, 90, 200, 90)

' Display pens with nondefault caps.
Dim p2 As New Pen(Color.Black, 8)
p2.StartCap = Drawing.Drawing2D.LineCap.DiamondAnchor
```

```
p2.EndCap = Drawing.Drawing2D.LineCap.ArrowAnchor
gr.DrawLine(p2, 280, 30, 500, 30)

p2.StartCap = Drawing.Drawing2D.LineCap.RoundAnchor
p2.EndCap = Drawing.Drawing2D.LineCap.Round
gr.DrawLine(p2, 280, 70, 500, 70)

' Destroy custom Pen objects.
p1.Dispose()
p2.Dispose()
```

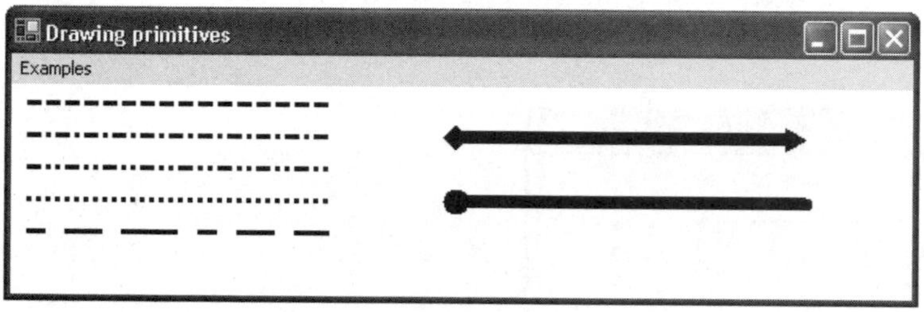

Figure 17-4   Dashed lines and lines with different starting and ending caps

Paths

A GraphicPath object is a collection of graphic primitives that are drawn and manipulated as a single entity. A path can contain lines, arcs, rectangles, ellipses, polygons, and in general any shape that I've described so far. A path also can contain one or more closed figures, but this isn't a requirement. Before you can draw a GraphicPath object, you must create it and define its contents, using one or more Addxxxx methods. The end point of each segment is automatically connected to the start point of the next unless you explicitly invoke the StartFigure method between the two AddLine methods. Here's an example of a path that contains a parallelepiped and a triangle:

```
' Create a new Path object.
Dim pa As New GraphicsPath()
' Start a figure.
pa.StartFigure()
pa.AddRectangle(New Rectangle(20, 20, 200, 150))
pa.AddRectangle(New Rectangle(50, 50, 200, 150))
pa.AddLine(20, 20, 50, 50)
pa.StartFigure()    ' Avoid connecting the two segments.
pa.AddLine(220, 20, 250, 50)
pa.StartFigure()    ' Avoid connecting the two segments.
pa.AddLine(220, 170, 250, 200)
pa.StartFigure()    ' Avoid connecting the two segments.
pa.AddLine(20, 170, 50, 200)

' Start another triangular (closed) figure.
pa.StartFigure()
pa.AddLine(300, 20, 400, 20)
pa.AddLine(400, 20, 400, 120)
pa.CloseFigure()
```

Notice that the CloseFigure method automatically closes the most recently opened polygonal shape. Once you have defined a path, you can draw it with the pen of your choice, using the DrawPath method:

```
' ...(Continuing the preceding code snippet)...
' Draw the path, using a thick red pen.
Dim p As New Pen(Color.Red, 3)
gr.DrawPath(p, pa)
' Destroy both the Path and the Pen object.
pa.Dispose()
p.Dispose()
```

Figure 17-5 shows the effect of the code sample just completed.

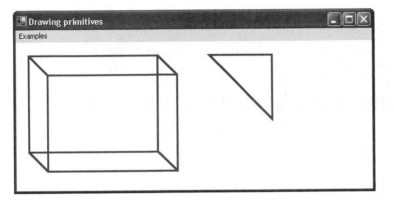

Figure 17-5   A GraphicPath object containing two figures

Filled Shapes

The Graphics object exposes eight methods that create filled geometrical shapes: FillRectangle, FillRectangles, FillEllipse, FillPolygon, FillPie, FillClosedCurve, FillPath, and FillRegion. These methods support several overloaded variations, but all of them take a Brush object as a first argument, which determines how the shape is filled. Several types of brush classes are available—solid brushes, hatch brushes, gradient brushes, and texture brushes—but all of them derive from the System.Drawing.Brush class, so you can use any of these types whenever a generic brush is expected. I'll discuss the several types of brushes in the next section; for now I will use only predefined solid-color brushes:

```
' Draw a green-filled rectangle.
gr.FillRectangle(Brushes.Green, New Rectangle(20, 10, 200, 100))
' Draw a blue-filled ellipse.
gr.FillEllipse(Brushes.Blue, 20, 150, 200, 100)
' Draw a red pie (portion of an ellipse).
gr.FillPie(Brushes.Red, 320, 150, 200, 100, -45, 90)
' Draw the remainder of the ellipse in pink.
gr.FillPie(Brushes.Pink, 320, 150, 200, 100, 45, 270)
' Note that you don't have to dispose of system brushes.
```

You can fill irregular polygonal shapes by using the FillPolygon method, which takes an array of Point objects, each defining a vertex of the polygon. An optional fill mode argument lets you specify how intersecting areas are filled, and you can choose between alternate mode (the default) and winding mode. Figure 17-6 shows the effects of the two modes on a similar polygon. It was produced by the following code:

```
Dim points() As Point = {New Point(200, 100), New Point(300, 300), _
    New Point(50, 170), New Point(350, 170), New Point(100, 300)}
gr.FillPolygon(Brushes.Gray, points, Drawing.Drawing2D.FillMode.Alternate)

Dim points2() As Point = {New Point(600, 100), New Point(700, 300), _
    New Point(450, 170), New Point(750, 170), New Point(500, 300)}
gr.FillPolygon(Brushes.Green, points2, Drawing.Drawing2D.FillMode.Winding)
```

You can fill irregular curves by using the FillClosedCurve method, which takes an array of Point objects, a tension value, and an optional fill mode argument. The FillPath method can be used to paint complex paths, and the FillRegion method paints a Region object. (I'll talk about region objects a little later in this chapter.)

Figure 17-6   You can produce the filled starlike shape on the left by using the alternate fill mode, and the one on the right by using the winding fill mode.

Brush Objects

All the examples I've shown you so far use one of the predefined Brush objects exposed as properties of the Brushes or the SystemBrushes class. You can create a custom brush by using one of the many available classes in the GDI+ subsystem. The most notable difference between custom and predefined brushes is that you must dispose of your custom brushes before you set them to Nothing or let them go out of scope. The simplest type of custom brush is the SolidBrush object, whose constructor takes a color:

```
' Create a solid brush with a custom color, and use it to fill a rectangle.
Dim br As New SolidBrush(Color.FromArgb(128, 30, 100))
gr.FillRectangle(br, New Rectangle(10, 10, 200, 100))
' Destroy the brush.
br.Dispose()
```

The HatchBrush class (in the System.Drawing.Drawing2D namespace) is a simple way to create two-color brushes that use one of the 56 predefined motifs available. The following listing shows the code that generates the upper left hatched rectangle in Figure 17-7:

```
Dim br1 As New HatchBrush(HatchStyle.BackwardDiagonal, _
    Color.White, Color.Blue)
gr.FillRectangle(br1, New Rectangle(10, 10, 200, 100))
br1.Dispose()
```

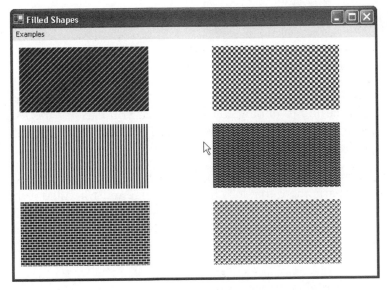

Figure 17-7   Six of the 56 available styles for hatch brushes

The LinearGradientBrush class represents a gradient brush, that is, a brush that contains all the color nuances that vary from a starting color to an ending color, like the typical background screen of many installation procedures or Microsoft PowerPoint slides. The simplest way to create a linear gradient brush is to pass its size (by means of a Rectangle object), the two colors, and a direction to the brush's constructor. You can then use this brush to paint any filled shape:

```
Dim br As New LinearGradientBrush(New Rectangle(0, 0, 200, 100), _
    Color.Blue, Color.Black, LinearGradientMode.ForwardDiagonal)
gr.FillRectangle(br, 0, 0, 200, 100)
gr.FillRectangle(br, 220, 0, 200, 100)
br.Dispose()
```

The constructor that you see in the preceding code lets you indicate four directions for the gradient: horizontal, vertical, forward diagonal, and backward diagonal. If the shape being painted is larger than the brush rectangle, the brush is tiled to cover the shape. If the shape's coordinates aren't exact multiples of the rectangle's size, the color of the shape's upper left corner won't coincide with the brush's first color, as is the case with the rightmost rectangle in Figure 17-8 (which shows the outcome of the preceding code snippet). You can influence how the brush is used to fill the shape by using the WrapMode property, which can be Tile (the default), TileFlipX, TileFlipY, TileFlipXY, or Clamp.

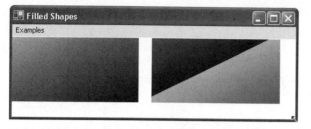

Figure 17-8   Two rectangles painted with linear gradient brushes

By default, this type of brush uses a linear gradient, in which intermediate pixels change linearly from starting to ending color. However, you can use the Blend property to define a nonlinear progression. (See the .NET Platform SDK for more details about nonlinear gradient brushes.)

Yet another type of brush is the TextureBrush class, whose constructor takes an Image object and an optional argument that tells how the image must be tiled if the painted shape is larger than the image. By default, the image is tiled as is, but you can also decide to flip it on the horizontal axis, the vertical axis, or both, as the following code illustrates. (See Figure 17-9.)

```
' These examples use a bitmap loaded in a PictureBox control.
Dim br1 As New TextureBrush(PictureBox1.Image)
gr.FillRectangle(br1, New Rectangle(20, 20, 250, 150))
br1.Dispose()

Dim br2 As New TextureBrush(PictureBox1.Image, WrapMode.TileFlipY)
gr.FillRectangle(br2, New Rectangle(300, 20, 250, 150))
br2.Dispose()

Dim br3 As New TextureBrush(PictureBox1.Image, WrapMode.TileFlipX)
gr.FillRectangle(br3, New Rectangle(20, 220, 250, 150))
br3.Dispose()

Dim br4 As New TextureBrush(PictureBox1.Image, WrapMode.TileFlipXY)
gr.FillRectangle(br4, New Rectangle(300, 220, 250, 150))
br4.Dispose()
```

The final type of brush class to be examined is PathGradientBrush, which patterns a gradient brush after a GraphicsPath object. Unlike other rectangular brushes, which are automatically tiled to cover surfaces of any size and shape, this type of brush doesn't extend over the boundaries of the path object used to define it, and in practice it should be used only to paint a specific path surface. In its simplest form, a PathGradientBrush is defined by a GraphicsPath object, the color of the center point, and the color at the path's borders:

```
' Define an elliptical path.
Dim pa As New GraphicsPath()
pa.AddEllipse(10, 10, 200, 100)
' Create the Brush shaped after the Path.
Dim br As New PathGradientBrush(pa)
br.CenterColor = Color.Yellow
' Define a one-element array of colors.
Dim colors() As Color = {Color.Blue}
br.SurroundColors = colors
' Paint the path.
gr.FillPath(br, pa)
' Destroy the Brush and Path objects.
br.Dispose()
pa.Dispose()
```

The ellipse in Figure 17-10 shows the result of the preceding code.

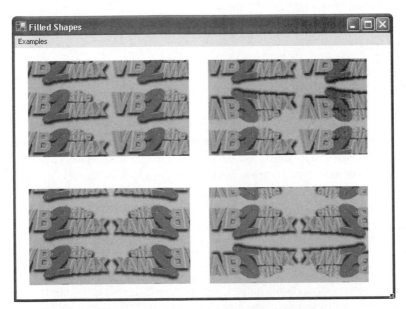

Figure 17-9   Texture brushes that tile a bitmap and flip it on one or both axes

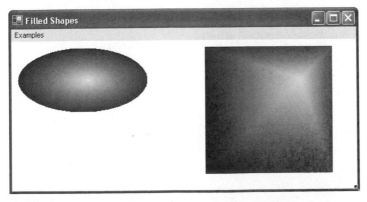

Figure 17-10   Two examples of path gradient brushes

You can create fancier path gradient brushes by specifying multiple colors on the path's border. In practice, you can use a Point array for defining the path's vertices, then define a Color array with an equal number of elements, and then pass the array to the brush's SurroundColors property:

```
Dim pa2 As New GraphicsPath()
' This defines a square path.
Dim points() As Point = {New Point(300, 10), New Point(500, 10), _
    New Point(500, 210), New Point(300, 210)}
pa2.AddLines(points)
pa2.CloseFigure()
' Create a brush patterned after that path.
Dim br2 As New PathGradientBrush(pa2)
' Define color and position of the center.
br2.CenterColor = Color.Yellow
br2.CenterPoint = New PointF(450, 60)
' Define an array of colors, one for each vertex.
Dim colors2() As Color = {Color.Blue, Color.Green, Color.Red, Color.Black}
br2.SurroundColors = colors2
' Paint the path.
gr.FillPath(br2, pa2)
' Destroy the Brush and Path objects.
br2.Dispose()
pa2.Dispose()
```

You can see the effect of the preceding code on the right in Figure 17-10. Path gradient brushes can be customized in many other ways—for example, you can add an intermediate color (so that the color varies from the beginning color to the intermediate color and from the intermediate color to the end color), or you can specify a nonlinear variation between the beginning and end colors (for more information, see the .NET Platform SDK).

Regions

A Region object consists of a combination of other, simpler shapes, such as rectangles and paths. You can combine these shapes using many different methods, such as the following:

- **Union**   The shape is added (ORed) to the current region. The resulting region contains all the points belonging to the original region and all the points belonging to the specified shape.

- **Intersect**   The shape is intersected (ANDed) with the region. The resulting region contains only the points common to both the original region and the specified shape.

- **Exclude**   The shape is subtracted from the region. The resulting region includes only the points in the original region that aren't also in the specified shape.

- **Xor**   The resulting region contains all the points belonging to either the original region or the specified shape, but not to both of them.

- **Complement**   The resulting region contains only the points in the specified shape that don't belong to the original region.

Two more methods affect a region's size: MakeEmpty and MakeInfinite. The former reinitializes the region to an empty region; the latter initializes it to the entire X-Y plane. Once you have defined a Region object, you can paint it with the FillRegion method of the Graphics object using any predefined or custom brush:

```
' Start with a square region.
Dim reg As New Region(New Rectangle(20, 20, 300, 300))
' Create a circular hole in it.
Dim pa As New GraphicsPath()
pa.AddEllipse(120, 120, 100, 100)
reg.Exclude(pa)
' Add another, smaller, square in the center.
reg.Union(New Rectangle(150, 150, 40, 40))
' Paint the region.
gr.FillRegion(Brushes.Green, reg)
' Destroy the Path and Region objects.
pa.Dispose()
reg.Dispose()
```

Regions are most useful for hit testing and clipping. The goal of hit testing is to determine whether a point or another shape is contained by the region. You might want to check whether the mouse cursor is over a given shape, but you can exploit the concept of regions for other purposes as well. The IsVisible method is overloaded to take a Point object, an X-Y pair of coordinates, or a Rectangle object as an argument:

```
' This code assumes that the reg variable references a Region object.
If reg.IsVisible(Me.MousePosition) Then
    ' The mouse cursor is over the region.
    ⋮
End If
```

If you define a clipping region for the Graphics object, all the pixels that would fall outside the region aren't drawn at all. You define a clipping region by using the SetClip method, which takes a Rectangle, a Path, or a Region object as its first argument, and a second argument that tells whether the shape in question must replace the current clipping region or must augment, complement, or intersect with the current clipping region. The following code uses the Region object specified earlier as a clipping region and then draws a series of circles with random colors. (You can see the result in Figure 17-11.)

```
' Use the Region as a clipping region (replaces any current region).
gr.SetClip(reg, CombineMode.Replace)
' Display circles with random colors.
Dim r As New Random()
For x As Integer = 10 To 400 Step 40
```

```
        For y As Integer = 10 To 400 Step 40
            Dim br As New SolidBrush( _
                Color.FromArgb(r.Next(0, 255), r.Next(0, 255), r.Next(0, 255)))
            gr.FillEllipse(br, x, y, 30, 30)
            br.Dispose()
        Next
    Next
    ' Dispose the region, if you are done with it.
    reg.Dispose()
```

Figure 17-11   Using a region for clipping

The Graphics object exposes the VisibleClipBounds property, which returns a RectangleF object that represents the visible area of the corresponding window. You can use this property to optimize your graphic routines by not processing shapes that are completely outside this rectangular area. When used with the printer, this property returns the printable area of the page.

Alpha Blending

One of the great features of GDI+ is *alpha blending*, which is the ability to define semitransparent colors and then use them to draw or paint all kinds of shapes. You define the transparency degree in the first argument of the Color.FromArgb method, passing a number in the range of 255 (opaque) to 0 (completely transparent). Any value less than 255 causes the background to show behind the figure being drawn. For example, the result visible in Figure 17-12 was produced by the following code:

```
' A solid green square
gr.FillRectangle(Brushes.Green, 20, 20, 200, 200)
' A semitransparent red ellipse
Dim br1 As New SolidBrush(Color.FromArgb(128, 255, 0, 0))
gr.FillEllipse(br1, 120, 50, 200, 120)
' An even more transparent blue rectangle
```

```
Dim br2 As New SolidBrush(Color.FromArgb(30, 0, 0, 255))
gr.FillRectangle(br2, 160, 80, 120, 200)
' A semitransparent thick yellow ellipse
Dim p As New Pen(Color.FromArgb(128, 128, 128, 128), 5)
gr.DrawEllipse(p, 100, 100, 200, 200)

' Destroy brushes and pens.
br1.Dispose()
br2.Dispose()
p.Dispose()
```

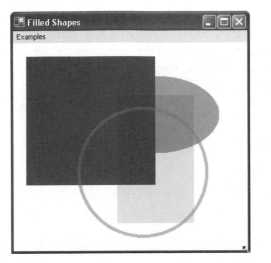

Figure 17-12   Alpha blending with outline and filled shapes

Transformations

All the code samples seen so far assumed that the coordinate origin was the upper left corner of the client area and that all values were in pixels. However, the Graphics object is highly flexible and lets you change these default settings as your needs dictate. To take advantage of this ability, you should understand that three different coordinate systems come into play whenever you draw any graphic object (including bitmaps and text):

- **The world coordinate system**   This is the system that you use to model your "graphic world." All the coordinates that you pass to graphic methods are expressed in this system.

- **The page coordinate system**   This is the system used by the surface on which you're drawing, be it a form, a control, or a printer document. By default, the origin and scale of this system coincide with the world coordinate system, but they don't have to. For example, you can have the origin of the world system at the center of the form, which might be convenient if you're plotting a mathematical function. The conversion between world and page coordinates is called *world transformation*.

- **The device coordinate system**   This is the system used by the physical device on which the drawing operation occurs—that is, the actual window if you're drawing on the screen or the sheet of paper if you're sending output to the printer. You can define precisely the unit of measure of the system (inches, millimeters, and so on), the ratio between the horizontal and vertical axes, and more. The conversion between page and device coordinates is called *page transformation*. Notice that you can't perform translations along the X or Y axis, nor can you reverse the direction along these axes. In other words, you can't flip an image using page transformation.

The Graphics object exposes several methods for affecting how world transformation is performed. The TranslateTransform method lets you change the origin of the coordinate system; so, for example, you can draw the same GraphicsPath object in a different location simply by translating the origin of the X-Y axes:

```
' Create a Path that we can draw multiple times.
Dim pa As New GraphicsPath()
pa.AddRectangle(New Rectangle(20, 20, 200, 100))
pa.AddEllipse(New Rectangle(30, 30, 180, 80))
' Draw the path without any transformation.
gr.DrawPath(Pens.Black, pa)
' Apply a translation, and redraw the object in another position.
gr.TranslateTransform(30, 200)
gr.DrawPath(Pens.Red, pa)
```

The two leftmost shapes in Figure 17-13 show the effect of the preceding code.

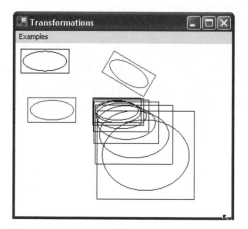

Figure 17-13   Effects of translation, rotation, and scaling world transformation

The RotateTransform method lets you rotate all the shapes you draw on the Graphics object by the angle you specify:

```
' Ensure that we start with default values (that is, no transformations).
gr.ResetTransform()
```

```
' Apply both a translation and a rotation, and redraw the Path.
gr.TranslateTransform(400, 0)
gr.RotateTransform(30)
gr.DrawPath(Pens.Green, pa)
```

See the result in the rotated shape near the upper right corner in Figure 17-13.

You also can vary the scale used to draw along the two axes by using the ScaleTransform method:

```
gr.ResetTransform()
gr.TranslateTransform(300, 200)
' Create multiple shapes that vary in angle and scale.
Dim scaleX As Single = 1
Dim scaleY As Single = 1
For i As Integer = 1 To 6
    gr.ScaleTransform(scaleX, scaleY)
    gr.DrawPath(Pens.Blue, pa)
    scaleX += 0.05
    scaleY += 0.1
Next
```

See the result in the lower right corner of Figure 17-13.

You also can combine multiple transformations in the Transform property, which takes a Matrix object that defines all the translations, rotations, and scaling that you want to apply. Correctly initializing a Matrix object takes some knowledge of the math theory behind scale transformations (you can read more about this object in the .NET Platform SDK), but even without going so in depth, you can use the Transform property to save and restore the current state of world transformation:

```
' Save current world transformation state.
Dim mat As Matrix = gr.Transform
' Apply any xxxxTransform method here.
  ⋮
' Restore original world transformation settings.
gr.Transform = mat
```

You can control how page transformation is carried out by means of the PageUnit and PageScale properties. The PageUnit property takes a GraphicsUnit enumerated value, which can be Pixel (the default for video), Inch, Millimeter, Point ($1/72$ inch), Display ($1/75$ inch), or Document ($1/300$ inch):

```
' Use inches as the unit of measure.
gr.PageUnit = GraphicsUnit.Inch
```

PageScale is a Single value that lets you reduce or magnify the output on the screen or printer by a given factor:

```
' Shrink output to 10 percent of the original size.
gr.PageScale = 0.1
```

Setting a page unit value other than pixels requires special attention because by default Pen objects are 1 unit wide (as measured in device coordinates). So if you use inches as your graphic unit by default, lines and curves are drawn with a pen 1 inch wide. You can address this problem by using the DpiX and DpiY read-only properties to determine the value to pass to the Pen's constructor:

```
' Create a Pen that is 1 pixel wide, regardless of current graphic unit.
Dim p As New Pen(1 / gr.DpiX)
```

Sometimes you might want to see how one or more points would be affected by the current transformation settings, but without actually drawing the points. You can do this by using the TransformPoints method of the Graphics object, which takes two CoordinateSpace enumerated values to specify from which and to which system you're converting, and an array of PointF objects:

```
' Define an array of points (in World system).
Dim points() As PointF = { New PointF(10, 20), New PointF(190, 220)}
' Convert then from World to Device systems.
gr.TransformPoints(CoordinateSpace.World, CoordinateSpace.Device, points)
' The result is now in the points array.
```

Here are a few more tips for coordinate transformations:

- The DrawImage method of the Graphics object is affected by world transformation, but not by page transformation. (See the "Imaging" section, which immediately follows, for more details about this method.)

- Hatched brushes aren't affected by either world or page transformation.

- TextureBrush and LinearGradientBrush classes have their own Translate property and TranslateTransform, RotateTransform, MultiplyTransform, and ResetTransform methods, so you can modify their appearance independently of the Graphics object on which you use them.

Imaging

A portion of GDI+ lets you display and process raster images as well as metafiles. The two most important objects for working with images are the Image class (which offers methods to save and load images from disk) and the Bitmap class (which inherits from Image and lets you access the individual pixels and other features of the image). Both these objects are in the System.Drawing namespace, but the imaging subsystem uses a few other objects in the System.Drawing.Imaging namespace, such as Metafile and ColorPalette.

Loading and Saving Images

The LoadFromFile and LoadFromStream methods of the Image and Bitmap classes allow you to load an image from a file or from an open Stream object (not necessarily a file stream). The following code snippet shows how you can use an OpenFileDialog control to ask the user for an image name and then display it on the surface related to a Graphics object with a DrawImage method:

```
With OpenFileDialog1
    .Filter = "Image files|*;*.jpg;*.jpeg;*.gif;*.png;*.tif"
    If .ShowDialog = DialogResult.OK Then
        ' Load a file into a Bitmap object.
        Dim bmp As Bitmap = Bitmap.FromFile(.FileName)
        ' Create a Graphics object and draw the bitmap on it.
        Dim gr As Graphics = Me.CreateGraphics
        gr.DrawImage(bmp, 0, 0)
        ' Destroy both the Bitmap and the Graphics objects.
        bmp.Dispose()
        gr.Dispose()
    End If
End With
```

An even simpler way to load an image into a Bitmap object is by taking advantage of its constructor:

```
    ' (This line can replace the FromFile call in preceding code.)
    Dim bmp As New Bitmap(.Filename)
```

GDI+ can load images in the following formats: bitmaps (BMP); Graphics Interchange Format (GIF, for compressing images with up to 8 bits per pixel); Joint Photographic Experts Group (JPEG, for compressed images with adjustable compression ratios); Exchangeable Image File (EXIF, an extended JPEG format that can store additional information about the photo, such as date, exposure, and so on); Portable Network Graphics (PNG, a compression format similar to GIF that can store images with 24 or 48 bits per pixel); and Tag Image File Format (TIFF, a compressed format that can carry additional information by means of tags).

You can save an image stored in an Image or Bitmap object using its Save method, which takes the filename and an argument that specifies the target format. The following code shows how you can prompt the user to save the contents of a Bitmap object in several different formats by using a SaveFileDialog control:

```
' This code assumes that you have a bmp Bitmap variable holding an image.
With SaveFileDialog1
    .Title = "Select target image and format"
    .Filter = "Bitmap|*.bmp|GIF|*.gif|TIFF|*.tif"
    .OverwritePrompt = True
    If .ShowDialog = DialogResult.OK Then
        Select Case System.IO.Path.GetExtension(.FileName).ToUpper
            Case ""
                bmp.Save(.FileName, ImageFormat.Bmp)
            Case ".GIF"
                bmp.Save(.FileName, ImageFormat.Gif)
            Case ".TIF"
                bmp.Save(.FileName, ImageFormat.Tiff)
```

```
                  Case Else
                      MessageBox.Show("Unrecognized extension", "Error", _
                          MessageBoxButtons.OK, MessageBoxIcon.Error)
              End Select
          End If
End With
```

You can save an image in any format, but in some cases you might need to specify additional details, such as the compression ratio. (Read the .NET Platform SDK for additional information.)

Displaying an Image

As you saw in the preceding section, you display an image on a Graphics object by using the DrawImage method. In its simplest syntax, this method takes the image to be displayed and the coordinates of the upper left corner of the destination area:

```
' Display an image at coordinates 100,200.
gr.DrawImage(bmp, 100, 200)
```

The DrawImage method supports 30 overloaded variations. One such variation allows you to specify the rectangular portion of the image that must be drawn:

```
' Draw only the left half of the image to coordinates 20,20.
gr.DrawImage(bmp, 20, 20, _
    New RectangleF(0, 0, bmp.Width / 2, bmp.Height), GraphicsUnit.Pixel)
```

Another overloaded variation copies the entire image to the specified destination rectangle. By changing the size of the target rectangle, you can zoom or reduce the image during the copy operation:

```
' Create a destination rectangle 3 times as wide and twice as tall.
Dim rect As New RectangleF(20, 120, bmp.Width * 3, bmp.Height * 2)
' Draw the enlarged bitmap.
gr.DrawImage(bmp, rect)
```

You can also combine the two effects by specifying both the destination rectangle and the source rectangle:

```
Dim destRect As New RectangleF(20, 320, bmp.Width * 1.5, bmp.Height)
' Create a rectangle corresponding to the upper left quarter of the image.
Dim sourceRect As New RectangleF(0, 0, bmp.Width / 2, bmp.Height / 2)
' Draw the portion of bitmap in the destination rectangle.
gr.DrawImage(bmp, destRect, sourceRect, GraphicsUnit.Pixel)
```

Figure 17-14 shows the effect of the last three code snippets. As I mentioned in the previous section about coordinate transformations, the DrawImage method is affected by world transformation, but not by page transformation.

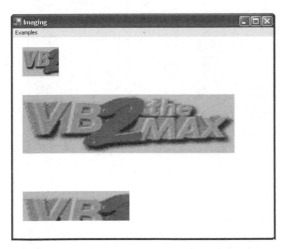

Figure 17-14   Copy all or part of an image with optional stretching of the result

You can draw on an image by getting a Graphics object (with the Graphics.FromImage static method), as in the following code snippet:

```
' This code assumes that the bmp holds a reference to a bitmap.
Dim gr As Graphics = Graphics.FromImage(bmp)
' Draw directly on the Graphics object, and then release it.
gr.FillRectangle(Brushes.Red, 20, 20, 100, 100)
gr.Dispose()
```

You can do more sophisticated processing on a bitmap by using the Bitmap class Lock-Bits method, which returns a BitmapData object. Among other pieces of information, the BitmapData object exposes the memory address of actual pixels. Unfortunately, you can't access the bitmap's memory in Visual Basic because this language doesn't support pointers, so you have to either use C# or call unmanaged code. Bitmaps locked with this method should be unlocked with the UnlockBits method.

Flipping, Rotating, and Skewing an Image

The DrawImage method can also take an array of three Point elements as an argument; these points define a parallelogram on the target Graphics object that will be used as the destination area for the image being painted. More specifically, the three points define where the upper left, upper right, and lower left points in the original image will be copied to on the destination surface. You can flip, rotate, or skew the image by arranging these points appropriately, as shown in the following diagram.

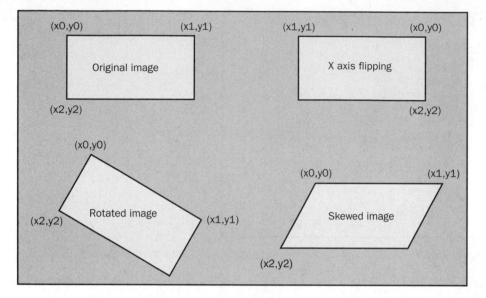

Understanding how you specify these three points to achieve the desired effect isn't immediate. For example, the rotation effect requires some trigonometric calculations. So I prepared three reusable routines that let you flip an image on one or both axes, rotate it by a specified angle (in degrees), and skew it by a given amount along one or both axes:

```
Sub DrawFlipImage(ByVal gr As Graphics, ByVal bmp As Bitmap, _
    ByVal x As Single, ByVal y As Single, _
    ByVal flipX As Boolean, ByVal flipY As Boolean)
    ' Start with values of parallelogram's vertices as if no flipping occurs.
    Dim x0 As Single = x
    Dim y0 As Single = y
    Dim x1 As Single = x + bmp.Width
    Dim y1 As Single = y
    Dim x2 As Single = x
    Dim y2 As Single = y + bmp.Height

    ' Account for horizontal flipping.
    If flipX Then
        x0 = x + bmp.Width
        x1 = x
        x2 = x0
    End If
    ' Account for vertical flipping.
    If flipY Then
        y0 = y + bmp.Height
        y1 = y0
        y2 = y
    End If
```

```
        ' Create the points array.
        Dim points() As Point = _
            {New Point(x0, y0), New Point(x1, y1), New Point(x2, y2)}
        ' Draw the flipped image.
        gr.DrawImage(bmp, points)
    End Sub

    Sub DrawRotateImage(ByVal gr As Graphics, ByVal bmp As Bitmap, _
        ByVal x As Single, ByVal y As Single, ByVal angle As Single)
        ' Convert the angle in degrees.
        angle = angle / (180 / Math.PI)
        ' Find the position of (x1,y1) and (x2,y2).
        Dim x1 As Single = x + bmp.Width * Math.Cos(angle)
        Dim y1 As Single = y + bmp.Width * Math.Sin(angle)
        Dim x2 As Single = x - bmp.Height * Math.Sin(angle)
        Dim y2 As Single = y + bmp.Height * Math.Cos(angle)

        ' Create the points array.
        Dim points() As Point = _
            {New Point(x, y), New Point(x1, y1), New Point(x2, y2)}
        ' Draw the rotated image.
        gr.DrawImage(bmp, points)
    End Sub

    Sub DrawSkewImage(ByVal gr As Graphics, ByVal bmp As Bitmap, _
        ByVal x As Single, ByVal y As Single, _
        ByVal dx As Single, ByVal dy As Single)
        ' Find the position of (x1,y1) and (x2,y2).
        Dim x1 As Single = x + bmp.Width
        Dim y1 As Single = y + dy
        Dim x2 As Single = x + dx
        Dim y2 As Single = y + bmp.Height
        ' Create the points array.
        Dim points() As Point = _
            {New Point(x, y), New Point(x1, y1), New Point(x2, y2)}
        ' Draw the skewed image.
        gr.DrawImage(bmp, points)
    End Sub
```

Using these three routines, drawing a flipped, rotated, or skewed image is a breeze.
For example, the following code produces the effects you can see in Figure 17-15:

```
DrawFlipImage(gr, bmp, 100, 20, False, False)
DrawFlipImage(gr, bmp, 300, 20, True, False)
DrawFlipImage(gr, bmp, 100, 120, False, True)
DrawFlipImage(gr, bmp, 300, 120, True, True)

DrawRotateImage(gr, bmp, 100, 220, 45)
DrawRotateImage(gr, bmp, 300, 220, 90)
DrawRotateImage(gr, bmp, 500, 220, 135)

DrawSkewImage(gr, bmp, 100, 400, -50, 0)
DrawSkewImage(gr, bmp, 300, 400, 0, 50)
DrawSkewImage(gr, bmp, 500, 400, -50, 50)
```

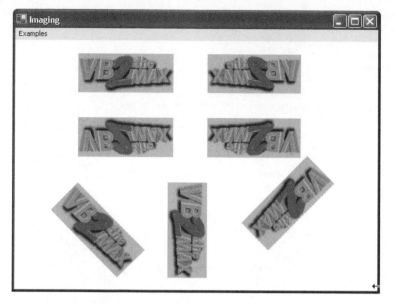

Figure 17-15   Flipped, rotated, and skewed images

When you're stretching or shrinking an image, in some cases one point in the source image maps to multiple points in the destination image or vice versa. So GDI+ must determine the color of the destination pixel by interpolating the colors of more than one pixel. You can control how this interpolation is performed by assigning a value to the Graphics.InterpolationMode property. The available modes are Low, High, Bilinear, Bicubic, NearestNeighbor, HighQualityBilinear, and HighQualityBicubic. (Read the .NET Platform SDK documentation for additional details about these modes.)

When you don't need to transform anything, you can improve the performance of the DrawImage method by explicitly specifying that the destination rectangle have the same size as the source image, thereby preventing any transformation that takes place if the number of dots per inch on the destination Graphics object is different from the number of dots on the device where the image was created. Here's a simple way to ensure that the image is copied as fast as possible:

```
gr.DrawImage(bmp, 20, 50, bmp.Width, bmp.Height)
```

Or you can use the DrawImageUnscaled method, which draws the image in its original size at the location specified by the target Point or X,Y pair of coordinates:

```
gr.DrawImageUnscaled(bmp, 20, 50)
```

You can also specify a Rectangle object, which works as a clipping region for the image:

```
gr.DrawImageUnscaled(bmp, New Rectangle(20, 50, 200, 100))
```

Transparent and Semitransparent Bitmaps

GDI+ gives you three ways to create a transparent or semitransparent bitmap: you can select one of the colors in the bitmap to be transparent; you can select a degree of transparency for the entire bitmap (in much the same way you can select the degree of transparency of a form using its Opacity property); or you can set a different degree of transparency for each individual pixel in the bitmap.

Creating a bitmap with a transparent color is the simplest technique of the three. You just have to invoke the MakeTransparent method, which takes the transparent color as an argument:

```
' Create a clone bitmap, and make it transparent.
Dim bmp As New Bitmap("logo")
bmp.MakeTransparent(Color.FromArgb(140, 195, 247))
gr.DrawImage(bmp, 20, 20)
```

The leftmost image in Figure 17-16 shows the effect of this operation.

Figure 17-16   Transparent and semitransparent bitmaps

Creating a bitmap with a fixed degree of transparency for all its pixels requires that you pass an appropriate ImageAttributes object to the DrawImage method. Before you do so, however, you must assign a 5-by-5-pixel color matrix to the ImageAttributes object by using the SetColorMatrix method. The code that you need to write to perform this operation isn't trivial because the color matrix actually is an array of Single arrays. Here's a code example that draws an image using a transparency level equal to 0.8. (This code produces the images in the middle of Figure 17-16.)

```
Dim bmp As New Bitmap("logo")
' Define the transparency level common to all pixels in the bitmap.
Dim transparency As Single = 0.8
' Create a 5x5 matrix with the transparency value in position (4,4).
Dim values()() As Single = {New Single() {1, 0, 0, 0, 0}, _
    New Single() {0, 1, 0, 0, 0}, _
    New Single() {0, 0, 1, 0, 0}, _
    New Single() {0, 0, 0, transparency, 0}, _
    New Single() {0, 0, 0, 0, 1}}
' Use the matrix to initialize a new colorMatrix object.
Dim colMatrix As New ColorMatrix(values)
' Create an ImageAttributes object, and assign its color matrix.
Dim imageAttr As New ImageAttributes()
```

```
imageAttr.SetColorMatrix(colMatrix, ColorMatrixFlag.Default, _
    ColorAdjustType.Bitmap)
' Draw the bitmap using the specified ImageAttributes object.
gr.DrawImage(bmp, New Rectangle(200, 20, bmp.Width, bmp.Height), _
    0, 0, bmp.Width, bmp.Height, GraphicsUnit.Pixel, imageAttr)
```

The last way to create a semitransparent bitmap is the most flexible of the three because you control the alpha component of each individual pixel in the image. You can access the color of an individual pixel in an image with the GetPixel method and modify the color (and possibly its alpha blend component) with the SetPixel method. As you can probably guess, it's also the slowest method of the group, but on the other hand it lets you achieve truly stunning results, such as the rightmost image in Figure 17-16, which was created by means of the following code:

```
Dim bmp As New Bitmap("logo")
' This loop visits all the pixels in the bitmap.
For x As Single = 0 To bmp.Width - 1
    For y As Single = 0 To bmp.Height - 1
        ' Get the current color.
        Dim oldColor = bmp.GetPixel(x, y)
        ' Enforce a transparency value that goes from 0 (the left border)
        ' to 1 (the rightmost border).
        Dim newColor As Color = Color.FromArgb(x / bmp.Width * 256, oldColor)
        bmp.SetPixel(x, y, newColor)
    Next
Next
gr.DrawImage(bmp, 400, 20)
```

Icons

An icon is like a small bitmap that contains a transparent color and whose size is determined by the system. The System.Drawing namespace contains an Icon class, which is the one you must use to load and draw icons. This class doesn't inherit from Image, so you can't use any of the methods you've seen so far. In fact, the operations you can perform on an Icon object are fairly limited. You load an icon by passing a filename or a Stream object to the icon's constructor:

```
Dim icon As New Icon("W95MBX01.ICO")
```

Another way to get an icon is by using the objects exposed by the SystemIcons class, which exposes properties that return the icons that you can display in a message box and a few others:

```
Dim icon2 As Icon = SystemIcons.Exclamation()
Dim icon3 As Icon = SystemIcons.WinLogo()
```

Once you have an Icon object, you can display it on a Graphics surface by using the DrawIcon method, which can take either a target coordinate pair or the destination rectangle:

```
' Draw the icon in its original size.
gr.DrawIcon(icon, 20, 20)
' Draw the icon with a 400% zoom.
gr.DrawIcon(icon, New Rectangle(100, 20, icon.Width * 4, icon.Height * 4))
' All icons must be destroyed.
icon.Dispose()
```

Most of the time, loading an icon and displaying it is all you need to do. If you want to achieve more sophisticated graphics effects, such as rotating an icon or defining another transparent color, you must convert the icon to a bitmap:

```
Dim icon As New Icon("W95MBX01.ICO")
' Convert the icon to a bitmap.
Dim bmp As Bitmap = icon.ToBitmap
' Make red the second transparent color, and draw the image.
bmp.MakeTransparent(Color.Red)
gr.DrawImage(bmp, 20, 200)
' Destroy both the bitmap and the icon.
icon.Dispose()
bmp.Dispose()
```

The Graphics object also exposes the DrawIconUnstretched method, which takes the icon to be displayed and a Rectangle object. The icon isn't stretched to fit the target rectangle, but it's clipped if it's larger than the rectangle itself.

Metafiles

A metafile is akin to a Path object in that it stores a sequence of drawing actions on a Graphics surface, including imaging and text operations. The main difference between a Metafile object and a Path object is that a Metafile object lets you save and reload this sequence of operations from a disk file. The constructor of the Metafile class offers as many as 39 overloaded variations, but in the most common case you pass the name of the file you want to create and a handle to the device context on which the metafile will be drawn:

```
' Get the Graphics object associated with the current form.
Dim gr As Graphics = Me.CreateGraphics
' Create a new metafile object, with the same features as the form's Graphics.
Dim mf As New Metafile("sample.emf", gr.GetHdc)
```

The next step is to retrieve the inner Graphics object associated with the metafile. This object lets you draw any shape or text on the metafile's invisible graphic surface:

```
' Retrieve the metafile's internal Graphics object.
Dim mfgr As Graphics = Graphics.FromImage(mf)
' Draw some graphics on the metafile's Graphics.
mfgr.DrawLine(Pens.Blue, 20, 20, 200, 200)
mfgr.DrawRectangle(Pens.Red, 50, 50, 200, 120)
mfgr.FillEllipse(Brushes.Green, 70, 20, 200, 120)
' Draw a text string in Arial 20 font.
Dim fnt As New Font("Arial", 20, FontStyle.Bold Or FontStyle.Italic)
mfgr.DrawString("Test String", fnt, Brushes.Yellow, 120, 100)
```

When the Metafile object is destroyed, the associated file is updated. Playing back the drawing instructions in a metafile is simple:

```
' Retrieve the form's Graphics object.
Dim gr As Graphics = Me.CreateGraphics
' Read the metafile from the file.
Dim mf As New Metafile("sample.emf")
' Draw the metafile in two different positions.
gr.DrawImage(mf, 0, 0)
gr.DrawImage(mf, 300, 100)
' Destroy all objects.
mf.Dispose()
gr.Dispose()
```

You can see the result of these operations in Figure 17-17.

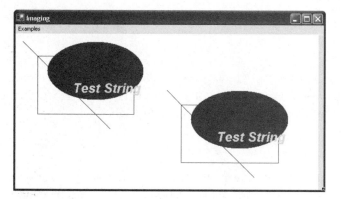

Figure 17-17   Displaying a metafile

One last note about metafiles: when you're playing back a metafile, the properties of the Graphics object used for world transformation, clipping, and so on are those that were active when the metafile was recorded, not those currently active.

Typography

Typography is the portion of the .NET Framework that has to do with displaying or printing text in various fonts or style. You already saw how to create textual output in several code samples earlier in this chapter, but I have yet to explain the operational details.

GDI+ supports only TrueType and OpenType fonts. These fonts are continuously scalable, rotatable, and shareable and can be used on both video and printer without any limitation.

Font Families

In GDI+ parlance, a *font family* is a group of fonts with the same typeface and different styles. For example, the Tahoma font family includes Tahoma Regular, Tahoma Bold, Tahoma Italic, and Tahoma Bold Italic. You can enumerate all the installed font families using the Families property of the InstalledFontCollection object. This property returns an array of FontFamily objects, which you can then enumerate to extract properties of individual font families:

```
' Get the collection of installed Fonts.
Dim fonts As New System.Drawing.Text.InstalledFontCollection()
' Get an array with all installed font families.
Dim fontFamilies() As FontFamily = fonts.Families
' Create a comma-delimited list of font family names.
Dim list As String = ""
For Each fontFam As FontFamily In fontFamilies
    If list <> "" Then list &= ", "
    list &= fontFam.Name
Next
' Display the list of fonts in the Debug window.
Debug.WriteLine(list)
```

Another way to get an array of installed font families is by using the FontFamily.Get-Families shared method. This method takes a Graphics object and returns only the font installed for that device, so you can use it to enumerate only the fonts installed for the screen or for the printer:

```
' Enumerate fonts installed for the screen.
Dim gr As Graphics = Me.CreateGraphics
Dim fontFamilies() As FontFamily = FontFamily.GetFamilies(gr)
gr.Dispose
```

You can get a reference to a standard font family by using three static properties of the FontFamily class: GenericMonospace returns a generic monospace FontFamily object; GenericSansSerif returns a generic sans serif FontFamily; and GenericSerif returns a generic serif FontFamily.

Once you have a FontFamily object, you can determine whether a given style is available by means of a call to the IsStyleAvailable method:

```
If fontFam.IsStyleAvailable(FontStyle.Bold) Then
    ' This font family supports bold style.
    ⋮
End If
```

Note that for some fonts the Regular style might be unavailable. You can determine font metrics information by using other methods of the FontFamily class, such as GetEmHeight, GetCellAscent, GetCellDescent, and GetLineSpacing (read the .NET Platform SDK for more details about these methods).

Drawing Text

You can't use FontFamily objects in printing operations, however, because they don't have a specific size or other attributes, such as underline or strikethrough. You can create a Font object in many ways, as demonstrated by the following code snippet:

```
' Create a font from a family and a size in points.
Dim font1 As New Font("Arial", 12)
' Create a font from a family, a size, and a style.
Dim font2 As New Font("Arial", 14, FontStyle.Bold)
' Create a font from a family, a size, and two combined styles.
Dim font3 As New Font("Arial", 16, FontStyle.Italic Or FontStyle.Underline)
' Create a font from a family and a size in another unit.
Dim font4 As New Font("Arial", 10, FontStyle.Regular, GraphicsUnit.Millimeter)
' Create a font family and then a font of that family.
Dim fontFam As New FontFamily("Courier New")
Dim font5 As New Font(fontFam, 18, FontStyle.Italic)
```

The size argument you pass to the Font's constructor is a metrical size, not a pixel size, and the result for a given size isn't affected by the current page transforms. (Text size is subject to world transformation, however.) You can specify a given GraphicsUnit by passing an extra argument to the constructor, as you see here:

```
Dim font1 As New Font("Arial", 12, GraphicsUnit.Pixel)
Dim font2 As New Font("Arial", 14, FontStyle.Bold, GraphicsUnit.Pixel)
⋮
```

You can't use the GraphicsUnit.Display setting for a font size.

You draw text by using the DrawString method of the Graphics object. In its simplest form, this method takes the string to be printed, a Font object, a Brush object, and the coordinates of the point where the string must be drawn:

```
' ...(Continuing preceding code snippet)...
Dim gr As Graphics = Me.CreateGraphics
gr.DrawString("Arial 12 Regular", font1, Brushes.Black, 20, 20)
gr.DrawString("Arial 14 Bold", font2, Brushes.Black, 20, 60)
gr.DrawString("Arial 16 Italic & Underline", font3, Brushes.Black, 20, 100)
gr.DrawString("Arial 10 millimeters", font4, Brushes.Black, 20, 140)
' Note that the destination point can be a PointF object.
gr.DrawString("Courier 18 Italic", font5, Brushes.Black, New PointF(20, 200))
' Always destroy Font objects when you don't need them any longer.
font1.Dispose()
font2.Dispose()
font3.Dispose()
font4.Dispose()
font5.Dispose()
```

You can see the result of this code in Figure 17-18.

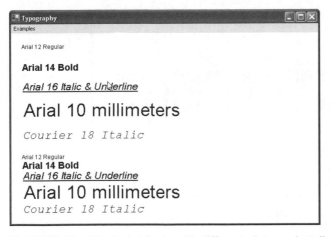

Figure 17-18 Displaying fonts with different sizes and attributes

When displaying strings on consecutive lines, you can take advantage of the font's GetHeight method, which returns the height of the font on the specified Graphics object. For example, this code is similar to the preceding snippet except that it displays individual lines closer to one another:

```
' Redraw the same font output with a more compact line spacing.
Dim y As Integer = 20
gr.DrawString("Arial 12 Regular", font1, Brushes.Black, 20, y)
y += font1.GetHeight(gr)
gr.DrawString("Arial 14 Bold", font2, Brushes.Black, 20, y)
y += font2.GetHeight(gr)
gr.DrawString("Arial 16 Italic & Underline", font3, Brushes.Black, 20, y)
y += font3.GetHeight(gr)
gr.DrawString("Arial 10 millimeters", font4, Brushes.Black, 20, y)
y += font4.GetHeight(gr)
gr.DrawString("Courier 18 Italic", font5, Brushes.Black, New PointF(20, y))
```

Because you draw text using a Brush (and not a Pen) object, you can easily create dazzling effects by using textured, hatched, or gradient brushes, as in the following code. (See the result in Figure 17-19.)

```
' Create a textured brush. (Ensure it references an existing file.)
Dim br As New TextureBrush(Image.FromFile("greenstone"))
' Create a large font.
Dim fnt As New Font("Arial", 50, FontStyle.Bold, GraphicsUnit.Millimeter)
' Paint a string with textured pattern.
gr.DrawString("Textured", fnt, br, 20, 20)
gr.DrawString("Text", fnt, br, 20, 200)
```

Figure 17-19   Drawing text with a textured brush

Aligned Text

The DrawString method can also take a RectangleF object as an argument, in which it draws the text inside the specified rectangle, as you see in this code:

```
Dim msg As String = "This is a long string whose purpose is to show how" _
    & " you can format a message inside a rectangle."
Dim fnt As New Font("Arial", 12)
Dim rectF As RectangleF

' Draw the text inside the rectangle.
rectF = New RectangleF(20, 20, 140, 160)
gr.DrawString(msg, fnt, Brushes.Black, rectF)
' Also display the bounding rectangle.
gr.DrawRectangle(Pens.Red, 20, 20, 140, 160)
```

You can determine both the horizontal and vertical alignment of the text inside the bounding rectangle by initializing a StringFormat object and passing it to the Draw-String method. The Alignment property of the StringFormat object affects the horizontal alignment and can be Near (default), Center, or Far (which corresponds to left, center, right in all languages that write text from left to right). The LineAlignment property affects the vertical alignment and again can be Near (top, the default), Center (middle), or Far (bottom).

```
' ...(Continuing the preceding code snippet)...

' Draw the text again, but align it to the right.
Dim strFormat As New StringFormat()
strFormat.Alignment = StringAlignment.Far
' Draw the text inside the rectangle with the format string.
rectF = New RectangleF(220, 20, 140, 160)
gr.DrawString(msg, fnt, Brushes.Black, rectF, strFormat)
' Also, display the bounding rectangle.
gr.DrawRectangle(Pens.Red, 220, 20, 140, 160)

' Draw the text again, but center it horizontally AND vertically.
strFormat.Alignment = StringAlignment.Center
```

```
strFormat.LineAlignment = StringAlignment.Center
' Draw the text inside the rectangle with the format string.
rectF = New RectangleF(420, 20, 140, 160)
gr.DrawString(msg, fnt, Brushes.Black, rectF, strFormat)
' Also, display the bounding rectangle.
gr.DrawRectangle(Pens.Red, 420, 20, 140, 160)
```

You can see the result of this code sample in Figure 17-20.

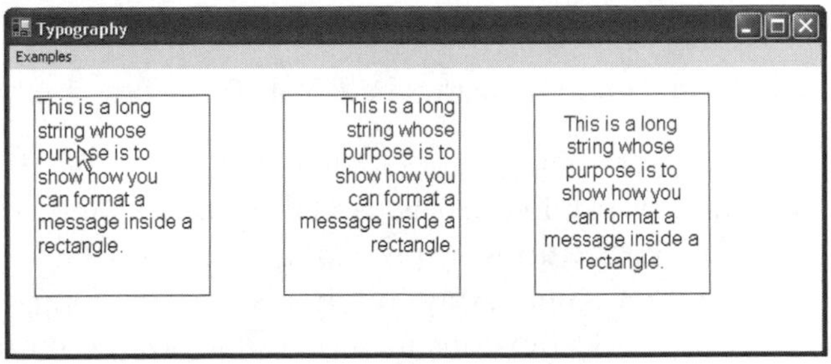

Figure 17-20   Text alignment inside a bounding rectangle

When you're deciding how large the bounding rectangle should be, you can use the MeasureString method of the Graphics object, which at a minimum takes a string and a Font object:

```
' Determine the room necessary to print the text as one long line.
Dim size As SizeF = gr.MeasureString(msg, fnt)
Debug.WriteLine(size.ToString)
```

Most of the time, you want to wrap the text so that it doesn't extend beyond a given width, so you must pass an additional width argument:

```
' Determine how tall the bounding rectangle must be if the
' text can't extend wider than 200 pixels.
Dim size As SizeF = gr.MeasureString(msg, fnt, 200)
Debug.WriteLine(size.ToString)
```

Textual Variations

Other properties of the StringFormat object affect how the text is displayed. For example, the Trimming property tells whether text that is too long to be displayed entirely should be trimmed at the character boundary or at the word boundary, or whether an ellipsis should be inserted at the end of the visible portion of the string:

```
' Text is trimmed at the last whole word.
strFormat.Trimming = StringTrimming.Word
' Text is trimmed at the last visible character,
' and an ellipsis is inserted after it.
strFormat.Trimming = StringTrimming.EllipsisCharacter
' An ellipsis is used in the center of the string.
' (Useful to display long files' paths.)
strFormat.Trimming = StringTrimming.EllipsisPath
```

The FormatFlags property is a bit-coded field that gives you even more control over how text is printed:

```
' Ensure that only whole lines are displayed. (The last line isn't
' displayed if it isn't completely visible in the bounding rectangle.)
strFormat.FormatFlags = StringFormatFlags.LineLimit

' Display the text vertically.
strFormat.FormatFlags = StringFormatFlags.DirectionVertical
gr.DrawString(msg, fnt, Brushes.Black, 20, 20, strFormat)
```

(Note that you can rotate text to any angle by using the RotateTransform method of the Graphics object.)

One more thing you can do when displaying text is use tab stops to align columns of data, as in Figure 17-21. You can make tab stops by preparing a string containing tab and carriage-return characters, preparing a Single array that holds the position of each tab stop, and then passing the array to the SetTabStops method of the StringFormat object:

```
' Prepare a message with tabs and carriage returns.
Dim msg As String = String.Format("{0}Column 1{0}Column 2{0}Column 3{1}" _
    & "Row 1{0}Cell (1,1){0}Cell (1,2){0}Cell (1,3){1}" _
    & "Row 2{0}Cell (2,1){0}Cell (2,2){0}Cell (3,3){1}", _
    ControlChars.Tab, ControlChars.CrLf)

Dim fnt As New Font("Arial", 12)
Dim strFormat As New StringFormat()
' Set the tab stops.
Dim tabStops() As Single = {80, 140, 200}
strFormat.SetTabStops(0, tabStops)
' Draw the text with specified tab stops.
gr.DrawString(msg, fnt, Brushes.Black, 20, 20, strFormat)
' Destroy the Font object.
fnt.Dispose()
```

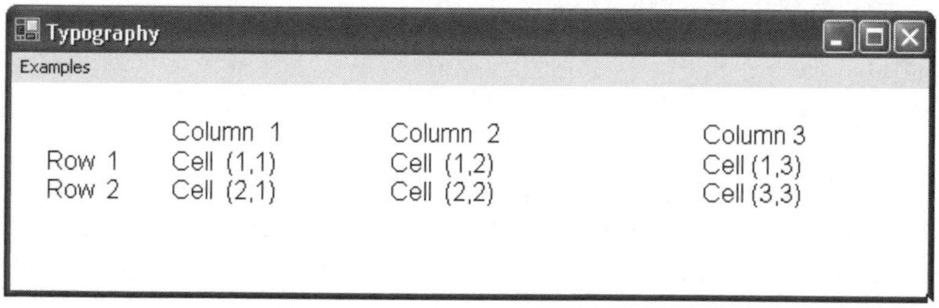

Figure 17-21   Using tab stops

Anti-Aliasing

Anti-aliasing is a technique that allows you to process graphic output so that lines don't appear jagged. You achieve this smoothing effect by using a color halfway between those of the line and the background. For example, if you draw a jagged black line over a white background, you can smooth it by using gray pixels for the points near the boundary.

The small ellipse on the right in Figure 17-22 is the anti-aliased version of the ellipse on the left. It looks better defined, even though you probably can't really say why. But if you enlarge the two ellipses (see bottom part of figure), you see that the anti-aliased version uses gray pixels to smooth its edges.

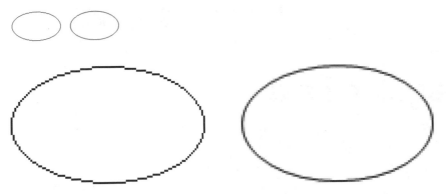

Figure 17-22   Using anti-aliasing on shapes

GDI+ supports anti-aliasing of both text and shapes. You can choose between two types of smoothing modes: anti-aliasing and high quality. The former works well on any type of display, whereas the latter takes advantage of the subpixel resolution of LCD screens. A pixel on an LCD screen is subdivided into three stripes that can be turned on or off individually, so you can achieve even more refined effects. (This is the smoothing mode used by the Microsoft ClearType display technology.) High-quality mode has no effect on regular CRT displays. Because of the required extra processing time, anti-aliasing is slower than regular display, and high-quality rendering is even slower than standard anti-aliasing.

You use two different properties of the Graphics object to activate anti-aliasing, depending on whether you want to smooth lines or text. The SmoothingMode property affects how lines and curves are drawn. For example, this is the code that produces the two ellipses in Figure 17-22:

```
' Draw a first ellipse in regular mode.
gr.DrawEllipse(Pens.Black, 20, 20, 100, 60)
' Draw a second ellipse in anti-aliasing mode.
gr.SmoothingMode = Drawing.Drawing2D.SmoothingMode.AntiAlias
gr.DrawEllipse(Pens.Black, 140, 20, 100, 60)
```

You can further influence graphic anti-aliasing by using the PixelOffsetMode property. (Read the .NET Platform SDK for more details.)

Text anti-aliasing is controlled by the TextRenderingHint property. Here's a code example, which produces the result visible in Figure 17-23:

```
Dim fnt As New Font("Arial", 14)
gr.DrawString("Regular Text", fnt, Brushes.Black, 20, 200)
' Standard anti-aliasing
gr.TextRenderingHint = Drawing.Text.TextRenderingHint.AntiAlias
gr.DrawString("Standard Anti-aliasing", fnt, Brushes.Black, 20, 260)
' ClearType anti-aliasing
gr.TextRenderingHint = Drawing.Text.TextRenderingHint.ClearTypeGridFit
gr.DrawString("ClearType Anti-aliasing", fnt, Brushes.Black, 20, 320)
' Destroy the Font object.
fnt.Dispose()
```

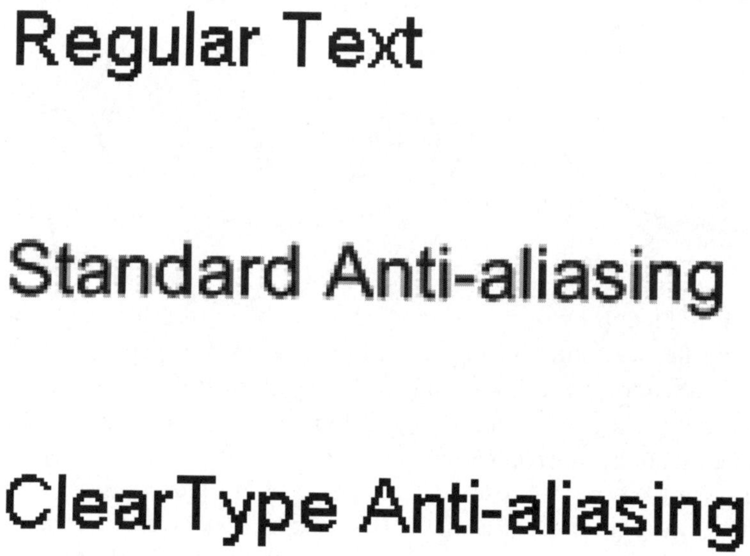

Regular Text

Standard Anti-aliasing

ClearType Anti-aliasing

Figure 17-23   The two flavors of anti-aliasing methods compared with regular text output

Alas, I don't have enough pages to cover all the great features of GDI+, so I have to stop here. For example, I haven't explained transformation matrix objects, graphic containers, or advanced color manipulations. However, I believe that you now know enough to leverage the great potential of this portion of the .NET Framework. Now it's time to explore how you can create custom Windows Forms controls.

18 Custom Windows Forms Controls

As if the controls in the Windows Forms package weren't enough, you can create your own controls. As a matter of fact, Visual Studio makes the creation of new controls a breeze. In this chapter, I'll show how you can create custom controls using one of the following approaches:

- Inheriting from an existing control
- Composing multiple controls
- Creating a control from scratch

You can deploy the control as a private assembly or install it in the GAC. The latter solution is preferable if the control must be used by many applications, but using private assemblies is OK in many cases. The control must not be installed in the GAC if it is being displayed from inside Internet Explorer. (See the section "Hosting Custom Controls in Internet Explorer" at the end of this chapter.)

> **Note** To keep the code as concise as possible, all the code samples in this section assume that the following Imports statements are used at the file or project level:
>
> ```
> Imports System.ComponentModel
> Imports System.ComponentModel.Design
> Imports System.Text.RegularExpressions
> Imports System.Drawing.Drawing2D
> Imports System.Threading
> Imports System.Drawing.Design
> Imports System.Windows.Forms.Design
> ```

Inheriting from an Existing Control

The easiest way to author a new Windows Forms control is by inheriting it from an existing control. This approach is the right one when you want to extend an existing control with new properties, methods, or events but without changing its appearance significantly. For example, you can create a ListBox that supports icons by using the owner-draw mode internally and exposing an Images collection to the outside. Here are other examples: an extended PictureBox control that supports methods for graphic effects and a TreeView-derived control that automatically displays the file and folder hierarchy for a given path.

In the example that follows, I use this technique to create an extended TextBox control named TextBoxEx, with several additional properties that perform advanced validation chores. I chose this example because it's relatively simple without being a toy control and because it's complete and useful enough to be used in a real application.

The TextBoxEx control has a property named IsRequired, which you set to True if the control must be filled before moving to another control, and the ValidateRegex property, which is a regular expression that the field's contents must match. There's also an ErrorMessage property and a Validate method, which returns True or False and can display a message box if the validation failed. The control will take advantage of the Validating event of the standard TextBox control to cancel the focus shift if the current value can't be validated.

Creating the Control Project

Create a new Windows Control Library project named CustomControlDemo. A project of this type is actually a Class Library project (that is, it generates a DLL) and contains a file named UserControl1.vb. Rename the file TextBoxEx.vb, then switch to its code portion, and replace the template created by Visual Studio with what follows:

```
Public Class TextBoxEx
    Inherits System.Windows.Forms.TextBox

End Class
```

This is just the skeleton of our new control, but it already has everything it needs to behave like a TextBox control. Because you want to expand on this control, let's begin by adding the new IsRequired property:

```
Public Class TextBoxEx
    Inherits System.Windows.Forms.TextBox

    Sub New()
        MyBase.New()
    End Sub

    ' The IsRequired property
    Dim m_IsRequired As Boolean

    Property IsRequired() As Boolean
        Get
            Return m_IsRequired
        End Get
        Set(ByVal Value As Boolean)
            m_IsRequired = Value
        End Set
    End Property
End Class
```

Note that you can't use a public field to expose a property in the Properties window, so you must use a Property procedure even if you don't plan to validate the value entered by the user, as in the preceding case.

The Sub New constructor isn't strictly required in this demo, but it doesn't hurt either. In a more complex custom control, you can use this event to initialize a property to a different value—for example, you might set the Text property to a null string so that the developer who uses this control doesn't have to do it manually.

The control doesn't do anything useful yet, but you can compile it by selecting Build on the Build menu. This action produces a DLL executable file. Take note of the path of this file because you'll need it very soon.

Creating the Client Application

On the File menu, point to Add Project and then click New Project to add a Windows Application project named CustomControlsTest to the same solution as the existing control. You can also create this test application using another instance of Visual Studio, but having both projects in the same solution has an important advantage, as I'll explain shortly.

Next make CustomControlsTest the start-up project so that it will start when you press F5. You can do this by right-clicking the project in the Solution Explorer window and clicking Set As Startup Project on the shortcut menu. Visual Studio confirms the new setting by displaying the new start-up project in boldface.

Right-click the Toolbox and click Add Tab on the shortcut menu to create a new tab named My Custom Controls, on which you'll place your custom controls. This step isn't required, but it helps you keep things well ordered.

Right-click the new Toolbox tab (which is empty), and click Add/Remove Items on the shortcut menu. Switch to the .NET Framework Components page in the Customize Toolbox dialog box that appears, click Browse, and select the CustomControlDemo.dll file that you compiled previously. The TextBoxEx control appears now in the Customize Toolbox dialog box, so you can ensure that its check box is selected and that it is ready to be added to the custom tab you've created in the Toolbox. (See Figure 18-1.)

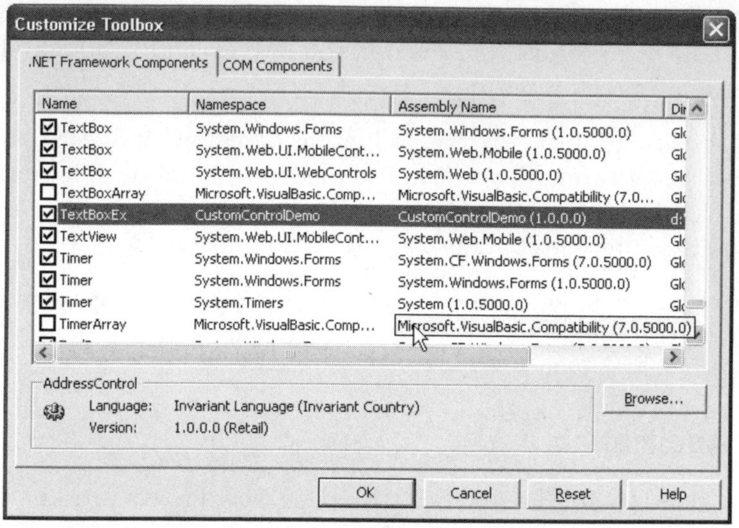

Figure 18-1   Adding a new control to the Toolbox

Drop an instance of the control on the form, and switch to the Properties window. You'll see all the properties of the TextBox control, which should be no surprise because the TextBoxEx control inherits them from its base class. Scroll the Properties window to ensure that the new IsRequired property is also there; the designer has detected that it's a Boolean property, so the designer knows that the property can be set to True or False.

Adding the Validation Logic

Now that you know your control is going to work correctly on a form's surface, you can go back to the TextBoxEx code module and add the remaining two properties. Notice that the code checks that the regular expression assigned to the ValidateRegex property is correct by attempting a search on a dummy string:

```
' The ErrorMessage property
Dim m_ErrorMessage As String

Property ErrorMessage() As String
    Get
        Return m_ErrorMessage
    End Get
    Set(ByVal Value As String)
        m_ErrorMessage = Value
    End Set
End Property

' The ValidateRegex property
Dim m_ValidateRegex As String
```

```
Property ValidateRegex() As String
    Get
        Return m_ValidateRegex
    End Get
    Set(ByVal Value As String)
        ' Check that this is a valid regular expression.
        Try
            If Value <> "" Then
                Dim dummy As Boolean = Regex.IsMatch("abcde", Value)
            End If
            ' If no error, value is OK.
            m_ValidateRegex = Value
        Catch ex As Exception
            MessageBox.Show(ex.Message, "Invalid Property", _
                MessageBoxButtons.OK, MessageBoxIcon.Error)
        End Try
    End Set
End Property
```

You now have all you need to implement the Validate method, which returns False if the current value doesn't pass the validation test. Notice that the code uses the MyBase.Text property to access the control's contents:

```
Function Validate() As Boolean
    ' Assume control passed the validation.
    Validate = True
    ' Apply the IsRequired property.
    If Me.IsRequired And Me.Text = "" Then
        Validate = False
    End If
    ' Apply the ValidateRegex property if specified.
    If Validate = True And Me.ValidateRegex <> "" Then
        Validate = Regex.IsMatch(Me.Text, Me.ValidateRegex)
    End If
End Function
```

The structure of the Validate method permits you to add other validation tests just before the End Function statement. Having a single place in which the validation occurs means that this is the only point to modify when you want to extend the control with new properties.

You still need to write the code that actually validates the current value when the user moves the input focus to a control that has CausesValidation set to True. The inner TextBox control fires a Validating event when this happens, so you can implement the validation by using the following naive approach:

```
Private Sub TextBoxEx_Validating(ByVal sender As Object, _
    ByVal e As CancelEventArgs) Handles MyBase.Validating
    ' If the validation fails, cancel the focus shift.
    If Me.Validate() = False Then e.Cancel = True
End Sub
```

This technique works in the sense that it does prevent the focus from leaving the Text-BoxEx control. The problem, however, is that you can't prevent the Validating event from propagating to your client form. In other words, the developer who uses this control will see a Validating event even if the focus shift is going to be canceled anyway.

A far better technique consists of intercepting the validation action *before* the inner TextBox object fires the event. You can do this by overriding the OnValidating protected method in the base class. You can create the template for the overridden method by clicking Overrides in the Class Name combo box in the code editor and then clicking the method in question in the Method Name combo box. (See Figure 18-2.) The correct code for performing the internal validation follows; it correctly raises the Validating event only if the validation passed:

```
Protected Overrides Sub OnValidating(ByVal e As CancelEventArgs)
    If Me.Validate() Then
        ' If validation is OK, let the base class fire the Validating event.
        MyBase.OnValidating(e)
    Else
        ' Else, cancel the focus shift.
        e.Cancel = True
    End If
End Sub
```

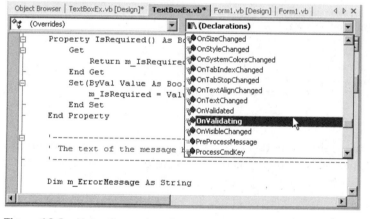

Figure 18-2   Using the code editor and the Class Name and Method Name combo boxes to create an overridden method

The focal point here is the call to MyBase.OnValidating, where the base class fires the Validating event and possibly performs additional actions.

Testing the Control

You can test your control in the client form at last. Create a form in the client application, and drop the following controls on it: a TextBoxEx control, a regular TextBox control, and a Label control that you'll use for displaying messages. Next set the Text-BoxEx properties as follows:

```
' A required field that can contain only digits
TextBoxEx1.IsRequired = True
TextBoxEx1.ValidateRegex = "\d+"
```

Run the program; you'll see that you can't move the focus from the TextBoxEx control to the TextBox control unless you enter one or more digits (or you set the TextBox control's CausesValidation property to False). You can also add a Validating event procedure that proves that the form receives this event only if the internal validation passed:

```
Private Sub TextBoxEx1_Validating(ByVal sender As Object, _
    ByVal e As CancelEventArgs) Handles TextBoxEx1.Validating
    MsgBox("Validating event in form")
End Sub
```

Design-Time Debugging

Whenever you set a control's property from inside the Properties window, Visual Studio .NET invokes the Property Set procedure for that property, so in general design-time property assignments work in much the same way as they work at run time. Sometimes, however, you might see slightly different behaviors at design time and run time and might like to run the control under a debugger to see what's going wrong. Alas, you can't debug a control when Visual Studio .NET is in design time because the debugger can't work on an instance of the DLL that isn't running yet. In this section, I'll show you a simple technique that lets you run the control under the debugger at run time *and* design time.

The trick is quite simple, once you know it. Create a new solution with the control library as its only project, open the Debugging page of the Project Properties dialog, set the Start Action to Start external program, and type the complete path to Visual Studio .NET's executable (C:\Program Files\Microsoft Visual Studio .NET 2003\Common7\IDE\devenv.exe for a standard installation). In the Command line arguments field, type the complete path to the demo project or solution that uses the custom control, enclosing it between double quotation marks if it contains spaces. (See Figure 18-3.) That's all you need!

Set all the breakpoints you want in the custom control's source code, and run the project. Visual Studio .NET will compile the control and run another instance of Visual Studio itself, which in turn will load the sample project that uses the custom control. You can now set properties in the Properties window and execution will stop at your breakpoints. (Of course, these breakpoints will be active also when the control is in runtime mode.)

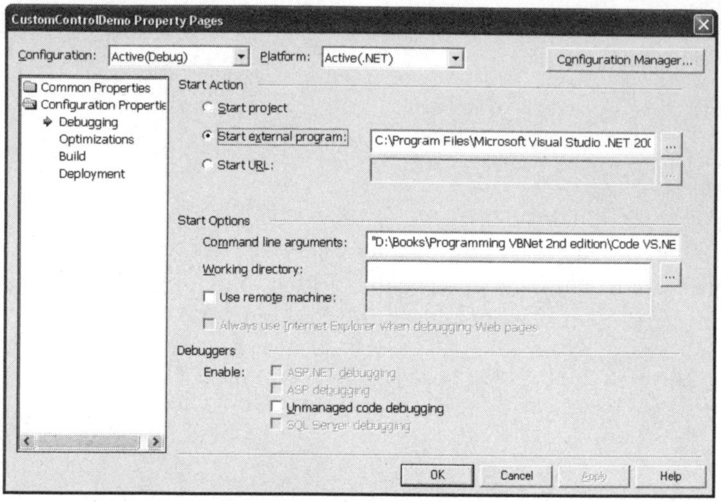

Figure 18-3 Setting project properties for testing a custom control at design time with a different instance of Visual Studio .NET

Improving the Custom Control

You can add many other properties to the TextBoxEx control to increase its usefulness and flexibility. Each property is an occasion to discuss additional advanced capabilities of custom control creation.

Working with Other Types

It is interesting to see how the Properties browser works with properties that aren't plain numbers or strings. For example, you can add a DisplayControl and an ErrorFore-Color property. The former takes a reference to a control that will be used to display the error message, and the latter is the color used for the error message itself. Implementing these properties is straightforward:

```
Dim m_ErrorForeColor As Color = SystemColors.ControlText

Property ErrorForeColor() As Color
    Get
        Return m_ErrorForeColor
    End Get
    Set(ByVal Value As Color)
        m_ErrorForeColor = Value
    End Set
End Property

Dim m_DisplayControl As Control

Property DisplayControl() As Control
    Get
        Return m_DisplayControl
    End Get
```

```
        Set(ByVal Value As Control)
            m_DisplayControl = Value
        End Set
End Property
```

You reference these new properties at the end of the Validate method, after the validation code you wrote previously:

```
    ⋮
    ' If the validation failed but the client defined a display control
    ' and an error message, show the message in the control.
    If Not (DisplayControl Is Nothing) And Me.ErrorMessage <> "" Then
        If Validate() Then
            ' Delete any previous error message.
            DisplayControl.Text = ""
        Else
            ' Display error message, and enforce color.
            DisplayControl.Text = Me.ErrorMessage
            DisplayControl.ForeColor = m_ErrorForeColor
        End If
    End If
End Function
```

Rebuild the solution, select the TextBoxEx control, and switch to the Properties window, where you'll see a couple of interesting things. First, the ErrorForeColor property displays the same color palette that all other color properties expose. Second, the Properties window recognizes the nature of the new DisplayControl property and displays a drop-down list that lets you select one of the controls on the current form. In this particular example, you can set this property to the Label1 control so that all error messages appear there. Also, remember to store a suitable message in the ErrorMessage property. Of course, you can do these operations from code as well, which is necessary if the target control is on another form:

```
TextBoxEx1.ErrorMessage = "This field must contain a positive number"
TextBoxEx1.ErrorForeColor = Color.Red
TextBoxEx1.DisplayControl = Label1
```

You can see another smart behavior of the Properties window if you have an enumerated property. For example, you can create a ValueType property that states the type of variable to which the contents of the field will be assigned:

```
Enum ValidTypes
    AnyType = 0
    ByteType
    ShortType
    IntegerType
    LongType
    TypeSingleType
    DoubleType
    DecimalType
    DateTimeType
End Enum
```

```
Dim m_ValidType As ValidTypes = ValidTypes.AnyType

Property ValidType() As ValidTypes
    Get
        Return m_ValidType
    End Get
    Set(ByVal Value As ValidTypes)
        m_ValidType = Value
    End Set
End Property
```

You can browse the demo application to see how this feature is implemented, but for now just rebuild the solution and go to the Properties window again to check that the ValueType property corresponds to a combo box that lets the user select the valid type among those available.

Adding Attributes

You can further affect how your custom control uses and exposes the new properties by means of attributes. For example, all public properties are displayed in the Properties window by default. This isn't desirable for read-only properties (which are visible but unavailable by default) or for properties that should be assigned only at run time via code. You can control the visibility of elements in the Properties window by using the Browsable attribute. The default value for this attribute is True, so you must set it to False to hide the element. For example, let's say that you want to hide a read-only property that returns True if the control's current value isn't valid:

```
<Browsable(False)> _
ReadOnly Property IsInvalid() As Boolean
    Get
        Return Not Validate()
    End Get
End Property
```

The EditorBrowsable attribute is similar to Browsable, but it affects the visibility of a property, method, or event from inside the code editor, and in practice determines whether you see a given member in the little window that IntelliSense displays. It takes an EditorBrowsableState enumerated value, which can be Never, Always, or Advanced. The Advanced setting makes a member visible only if you clear the Hide advanced members option in the General page under the All languages folder (or the folder named after the language you're using), which in turn is in the Text Editor folder in the Options dialog box that you reach from the Tools menu:

```
<EditorBrowsable(EditorBrowsableState.Advanced)> _
Sub EnterExpertMode()
    ⋮
End Sub
```

Another frequently used attribute is Description, which defines the string displayed near the bottom edge of the Properties window:

```
<Description("The control that will display the error message")> _
Property DisplayControl() As Control
    ⋮
End Property
```

You put a property into a category in the Properties window by using the Category attribute. You can specify one of the existing categories—Layout, Behavior, Appearance—or define a new one. If a property doesn't belong to a specific category, it appears in the Misc category:

```
<Description("The control that will display the error message"), _
    Category("Validation")> _
Property DisplayControl() As Control
    ⋮
End Property
```

By default, properties aren't localizable and the form designer doesn't save their values in a separate source file when the user selects a language other than the default one. You can change this default behavior by using the Localizable attribute:

```
<Localizable(True) > _
Property HeaderCaption() As String
    ⋮
End Property
```

The DefaultProperty attribute tells the environment which property should be selected when the user creates a new instance of the control and then activates the Properties window. Similarly, the DefaultEvent attribute specifies the event handler that's automatically created when you double-click on a control in the designer. (For example, TextChanged is the default event for the TextBox control.) You apply these attributes to the class and pass them the name of the property or the event:

```
<DefaultProperty("IsRequired"), DefaultEvent("InvalidKey")> _
Public Class TextBoxEx
    Inherits System.Windows.Forms.TextBox

    Event InvalidKey(ByVal sender As Object, ByVal e As EventArgs)
    ⋮
End Class
```

The MergableProperty attribute tells whether a property is visible in the Properties window when multiple controls are selected. The default value of this attribute is True, so you must include it explicitly only if you don't want to allow the user to modify this property for all the selected controls. In practice, you use this attribute when a property can't have the same value for multiple controls on a form (as in the case of the TabIndex or Name property):

```
<MergableProperty(False)> _
Property ProcessOrder() As Integer
    ⋮
End Class
```

The RefreshProperties attribute is useful if a new value assigned to a property can affect other properties in the Properties window. The default behavior of the Properties window is that only the value of the property being edited is updated, but you can specify that all properties should be requeried and refreshed by using this attribute:

```
Dim m_MaxValue As Long = Long.MaxValue

<RefreshProperties(RefreshProperties.All)> _
Property MaxValue() As Long
    Get
        Return m_MaxValue
    End Get
    Set(ByVal Value As Long)
        m_MaxValue = Value
        ' This property can affect the Value property.
        If Value > m_MaxValue Then Value = m_MaxValue
    End Set
End Property
```

Working with Icons

Each of your carefully built custom controls should have a brand-new icon assigned to them, to replace the default icon that appears in Visual Studio .NET's control Toolbox. Control icons can be either stand-alone .bmp or .ico files, or bitmaps embedded in a DLL (typically that is the same DLL that contains the custom control, but it can be a different DLL as well). The lower left pixel in the bitmap determines the transparent color for the icon—for example, use a yellow color for this pixel to make all other yellow pixels in the icon transparent (so they will be shown as unavailable if your current color setting uses gray for the control Toolbox).

The procedure to embed the bitmap in the DLL that contains the control isn't exactly intuitive. First, use the Add New Item command from the Project menu to add a bitmap file to your project and name this bitmap after your control (TextBoxEx.bmp in this example). Next, ensure that the bitmap is 16-by-16 pixels by setting its Width and Height properties in the Properties window and draw the bitmap using your artistic abilities and the tools that Visual Studio .NET gives you. (See Figure 18-4.) Then go to the Solution Explorer, select the bitmap file, press F4 to display the Properties window for the file (as opposed to the Properties window for the bitmap that you used to set the image's size), and change the Build Action property to Embedded Resource. If you now recompile the CustomControlDemo.dll assembly, you'll see that the TextBoxEx control uses the new icon you defined. (You must use the Add/Remove Items command twice to see the new icon—once to remove the previous version and once to add the new one.)

Notice that you haven't used any attribute to assign the icon to the TextBoxEx because the association is implicitly made when you assign the bitmap the same name as the control it's related to. This technique works only if the custom control is in the project's default namespace.

You can make the association explicit by using a ToolboxBitmap attribute. For example, you need this attribute when the bitmap or icon file isn't embedded in the DLL:

```
<ToolboxBitmap("C:\CustomControlDemo\TextBoxEx.ico")> _
Public Class TextBoxEx
    ⋮
End Class
```

This attribute is also useful when the bitmap is embedded in a DLL other than the one that contains the custom control. In this case, you pass this attribute the System.Type object that corresponds to any class defined in the DLL containing the resource (Visual Studio .NET uses this Type object only to locate the assembly), and you can pass a second optional argument equal to the name of the bitmap (this is necessary if the bitmap isn't named after the custom control):

```
<ToolboxBitmap(GetType(TextBoxEx), "TextBoxIcon.bmp")> _
Public Class TextBoxEx
    ⋮
End Class
```

Another case for which you need the ToolboxBitmap attribute is when your control belongs to a nested namespace below the project's root namespace. For example, if the TextBoxEx control lives inside the CustomControlDemo.Controls namespace, you must rename the bitmap file as Controls.TextBoxIcon.bmp (even though you must continue to use TextBoxIcon.bmp in the attribute's constructor).

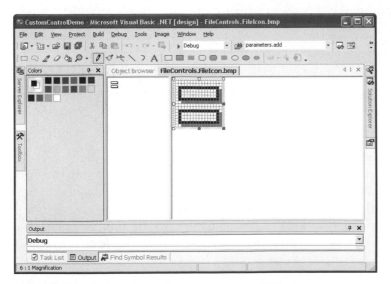

Figure 18-4   The Visual Studio .NET bitmap editor

Working with Default Values

You have surely noticed that the Properties window uses boldface to display values different from the property's default value, so you might have wondered where the default value is defined. As you might guess, you define the default value with yet another attribute, appropriately named DefaultValue. This example is taken from the demo application:

```
Dim m_BeepOnError As Boolean = True

<Description("If True, a beep will be emitted if validation fails"), _
    DefaultValue(True)> _
Property BeepOnError() As Boolean
    Get
        Return m_BeepOnError
    End Get
    Set(ByVal Value As Boolean)
        m_BeepOnError = Value
    End Set
End Property
```

Note that the DefaultValue attribute is just a directive to the Properties window: it doesn't actually initialize the property itself. For that, you must use an initializer or use the necessary code in the Sub New procedure.

Unfortunately, the DefaultValue attribute has a problem: it can take only constant values, and in several cases the default value isn't a constant. For example, the value SystemColors.ControlText, which is the initial value for the ErrorForeColor property, isn't a constant, so you can't pass it to the DefaultValue attribute's constructor. To resolve this difficulty, the author of the custom control can create a special Reset*xxxx* procedure, where *xxxx* is the property name. Here is the code in the TextBoxEx class that the form designer implicitly calls to initialize the two color properties:

```
Sub ResetErrorForeColor()
    ErrorForeColor = SystemColors.ControlText
End Sub
```

If a property is associated with a Reset*xxxx* method, you can reset the property by clicking Reset on the context menu that you bring up by clicking on the property name in the Properties window.

The DefaultValue attribute has another, less obvious, use: if a property is set to its default value—as specified by this attribute—this property isn't persisted, and the designer generates no code for it. This behavior is highly desirable because it avoids the generation of a lot of useless code that would slow down the rendering of the parent form. Alas, you can't specify a nonconstant value, a color, a font, or another complex object in the DefaultValue attribute. In this case, you must implement a method named

ShouldSerialize*xxxx* (where *xxxx* is the name of the property) that returns True if the property must be serialized and False if its current value is equal to its default value:

```
Function ShouldSerializeErrorForeColor() As Boolean
    ' We can't use the = operators on objects, so we use
    ' the Equals method.
    Return Not Me.ErrorForeColor.Equals(SystemColors.ControlText)
End Function
```

Creating Composed Multiple Controls

More complex custom controls require that you combine multiple controls. You can think of several custom controls of this type, such as a control that implements Windows Explorer–like functionality by grouping together a TreeView, a ListView, and a Splitter control; or a control made up of two ListBox controls that lets you move items from one ListBox to the other, using auxiliary buttons or drag-and-drop.

In this section, I build a composite custom control named FileTextBox, which lets the user enter a filename by typing its name in a field or by selecting it in an OpenFile common dialog box.

Creating the UserControl Component

Add a new UserControl module named FileTextBox to the CustomControlDemo project by selecting the project and then selecting Add UserControl on the Project menu. Ensure that you've selected the CustomControlDemo project before you perform this action— otherwise, the custom control will be added to the test application instead.

The UserControl class derives from the ContainerControl class, so it can work as a container for other controls. In this respect, the UserControl object behaves very much like the Form object, and in fact, the programming interface of these classes is very similar, with properties such as Font, ForeColor, AutoScroll, and so on. A few typical form properties are missing because they don't make sense in a control—for example, Main-Menu and TopMost—but by and large, you code against a UserControl as if you were working with a regular form.

You can therefore drop on the UserControl's surface the three child controls you need for the FileTextBox control. These are a TextBox for the filename (named txtFilename, with a blank Text property); an OpenFileDialog control to display the dialog box (named OpenFileDialog1); and a Button control to let the user bring up the common dialog (named btnBrowse, with the Text property set to three dots). You can arrange these controls in the manner of Figure 18-5. Don't pay too much attention to their alignment, however, because you're going to move them on the UserControl's surface by means of code.

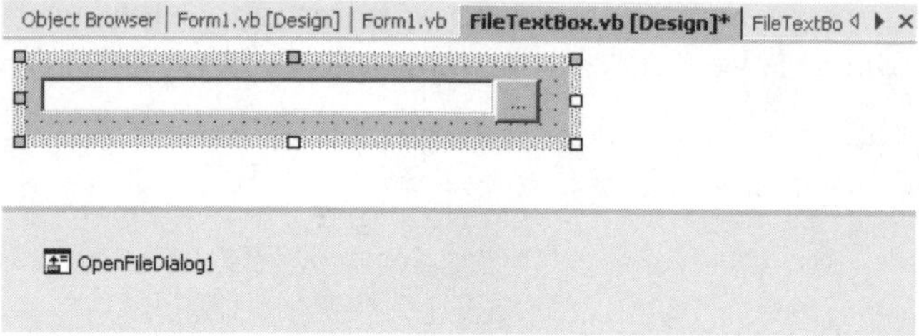

Figure 18-5   The FileTextBox custom control at design time

Before you start adding code, you should compile the CustomControlDemo project to rebuild the DLL and then switch to the client project to invoke the Customize ToolBox command. You'll see that the FileTextBox control doesn't appear yet in the list of available .NET controls in the Toolbox, so you have to click on the Browse button and select CustomControlDemo.dll once again.

If all worked well, the new FileTextBox is in the Toolbox and you can drop it on the test form. You can resize it as usual, but its constituent controls don't resize correctly because you haven't written any code that handles resizing.

Adding Properties, Methods, and Events

The FileTextBox control doesn't expose any useful properties yet, other than those provided by the UserControl class. The three child controls you placed on the UserControl's surface can't be reached at all because by default they have a Friend scope and can't be seen from code in the client project. Your next step is to provide programmatic access to the values in these controls. In most cases, all you need to do is create a property procedure that wraps directly around a child control property—for example, you can implement the Filename and Filter properties, as follows:

```
<Description("The filename as it appears in the Textbox control")> _
Property Filename() As String
    Get
        Return Me.txtFilename.Text
    End Get
    Set(ByVal Value As String)
        Me.txtFilename.Text = Value
    End Set
End Property

<Description("The list of file filters"), _
    DefaultValue("All files (*.*)|*.*")> _
Property Filter() As String
    Get
        Return OpenFileDialog1.Filter
    End Get
    Set(ByVal Value As String)
        OpenFileDialog1.Filter = Value
    End Set
End Property
```

If you wrap your property procedures around child control properties, you must be certain that you properly initialize the child controls so that the initial values of their properties match the values passed to the DefaultValue attribute. In this case, you must ensure that you set the OpenFileDialog1.Filter property correctly.

You don't create wrappers around child control properties only. For example, you can implement a ShowDialog method that wraps around the OpenFileDialog1 control method of the same name:

```
Function ShowDialog() As DialogResult
    ' Show the OpenFile dialog, and return the result.
    ShowDialog = OpenFileDialog1.ShowDialog
    ' If the result is OK, assign the filename to the TextBox.
    If ShowDialog = DialogResult.OK Then
        txtFilename.Text = OpenFileDialog1.FileName
    End If
End Function
```

You can also provide wrappers for events. For example, exposing the FileOk event gives the client code the ability to reject invalid filenames:

```
Event FileOk(ByVal sender As Object, ByVal e As CancelEventArgs)

Private Sub OpenFileDialog1_FileOk(ByVal sender As Object, _
    ByVal e As CancelEventArgs) Handles OpenFileDialog1.FileOk
    RaiseEvent FileOk(Me, e)
End Sub
```

Bear in mind that the client will receive the event from the FileTextBox control, not from the inner OpenFileDialog control, so you must pass Me as the first argument of the RaiseEvent method, as in the preceding code snippet. In some cases, you also need to change the name of the event to meet the client code's expectations—for example, the TextChanged event from the inner txtFilename should be exposed to the outside as FilenameChanged because Filename is the actual property that will appear as modified to clients. In other cases you might need to adjust the properties of the EventArgs-derived object—for example, to convert mouse coordinates so that they refer to the UserControl rather than the constituent control that fired the event.

Not all events should be exposed to the outside, however. The button's Click event, for example, is handled internally to automatically fill the txtFilename field when the user selects a file from the common dialog box:

```
Private Sub btnBrowse_Click(ByVal sender As Object, _
    ByVal e As EventArgs) Handles btnBrowse.Click
    ShowDialog()
End Sub
```

Shadowing and Overriding UserControl Properties

If you modify the Font property of the FileTextBox control, you'll notice that the new settings are immediately applied to the inner txtFilename control, so you don't have to manually implement the Font property. The custom control behaves this way because you never assign a specific value to txtFilename.Font, so it automatically inherits the parent UserControl's settings. This feature can save you a lot of code and time. The group of properties that you shouldn't implement explicitly includes Enabled and TabStop because all the constituent controls inherit these properties from their UserControl container.

You're not always that lucky. For example, TextBox controls don't automatically inherit the ForeColor of their container, and you have to implement this property manually. A minor annoyance is that the UserControl already exposes a property of this name, so you receive a compilation warning. You can get rid of this warning by using the Shadows keyword. Note that you also must use explicit shadowing with the Reset*xxxx* procedure:

```
Shadows Property ForeColor() As Color
    Get
        Return txtFilename.ForeColor
    End Get
    Set(ByVal Value As Color)
        txtFilename.ForeColor = Value
    End Set
End Property

Shadows Sub ResetForeColor()
    Me.ForeColor = SystemColors.ControlText
End Sub

Function ShouldSerializeForeColor() As Boolean
    Return Not Me.ForeColor.Equals(SystemColors.ControlText)
End Function
```

If your custom control exposes a property with the same name, return type, and default value as a property in the base UserControl, you can override it instead of shadowing it—for example, the FileTextBox control overrides the ContextMenu property so that the pop-up menu also appears when the end user right-clicks on constituent controls:

```
Overrides Property ContextMenu() As ContextMenu
    Get
        Return MyBase.ContextMenu
    End Get
    Set(ByVal Value As ContextMenu)
        MyBase.ContextMenu = Value
        ' Propagate the new value to constituent controls.
        ' (This generic code works with any UserControl.)
        For Each ctrl As Control In Me.Controls
            ctrl.ContextMenu = Me.ContextMenu
        Next
    End Set
End Property
```

In many cases, however, you really have to go as far as overriding a property in the base UserControl only if you need to cancel its default behavior. If you just want a notification that a property has changed, you can be satisfied by simply trapping the *xxxx-* Changed event—for example, the following code displays the btnBrowse button control with a flat appearance when the FileTextBox control is disabled:

```
Private Sub FileTextBox_EnabledChanged(ByVal sender As Object, _
    ByVal e As EventArgs) Handles MyBase.EnabledChanged
    If Me.Enabled Then
        btnBrowse.FlatStyle = FlatStyle.Standard
    Else
        btnBrowse.FlatStyle = FlatStyle.Flat
    End If
End Sub
```

Notice that *xxxx*Changed events don't fire at design time, so you can't use this method to react to setting changes in the Properties window.

You often need to shadow properties in the base class for the sole purpose of hiding them in the Properties window. For example, the demo FileTextBox control can't work as a scrollable container, so it shouldn't display the AutoScroll, AutoScrollMargins, AutoScrollPosition, and DockPadding items in the Properties window. You can achieve this by shadowing the property and adding a Browsable(False) attribute:

```
<Browsable(False)> _
Shadows Property AutoScroll() As Boolean
    Get
        ' Don't really need to delegate to inner UserControl.
    End Get
    Set(ByVal Value As Boolean)
        ' Don't really need to delegate to inner UserControl.
    End Set
End Property
```

Although you can easily hide a property in the Properties window, inheritance rules prevent you from completely wiping out a UserControl property from the custom control's programming interface. However, you can throw an exception when this property is accessed at run time programmatically so that the developer using this custom control learns the lesson more quickly. You can discern whether you're in design-time or run-time mode with the DesignMode property, which the UserControl inherits from the System.ComponentModel.Component object:

```
<Browsable(False)> _
Shadows Property AutoScroll() As Boolean
    Get
        If Not Me.DesignMode Then Throw New NotImplementedException()
    End Get
    Set(ByVal Value As Boolean)
        If Not Me.DesignMode Then Throw New NotImplementedException()
    End Set
End Property
```

You must check the DesignMode property before throwing the exception—otherwise, the control doesn't work correctly in design-time mode. You can use this property for many other purposes, such as displaying a slightly different user interface at design time or run time.

Adding Resize Logic

The code inside your UserControl determines how its constituent controls are arranged when the control is resized. In the simplest cases, you don't have to write code to achieve the desired effect because you can simply rely on the Anchor and Dock properties of constituent controls. However, this approach is rarely feasible with more complex custom controls. For example, the btnBrowse button in FileTextBox always should be square, and so its height and width depend on the txtFilename control's height, which in turn depends on the current font. Besides, the height of the FileText-Box control always should be equal to the height of its inner fields. All these constraints require that you write custom resize logic in a private RedrawControls procedure and call this procedure from the UserControl's Resize event:

```
Private Sub FileTextBox_Resize(ByVal sender As Object, _
    ByVal e As System.EventArgs) Handles MyBase.Resize
    RedrawControls()
End Sub

Private Sub RedrawControls()
    ' This is the inner width of the control.
    Dim width As Integer = Me.ClientRectangle.Width
    ' This is the (desired) height of the control.
    Dim btnSide As Integer = txtFilename.Height

    ' Adjust the height of the UserControl if necessary.
    If Me.ClientRectangle.Height <> btnSide Then
        ' Resize the UserControl.
        Me.SetClientSizeCore(Me.ClientRectangle.Width, btnSide)
        ' The above statement fires a nested Resize event, so exit right now.
        Exit Sub
    End If

    ' Resize the constituent controls.
    txtFilename.SetBounds(0, 0, width - btnSide, btnSide)
    btnBrowse.SetBounds(width - btnSide, 0, btnSide, btnSide)
End Sub
```

Don't forget that the custom control's height also should change when its Font property changes, so you must override the OnFontChanged method as well. (You can't simply trap the FontChanged event because it doesn't fire at design time.)

```
Protected Overrides Sub OnFontChanged(ByVal e As EventArgs)
    ' Let the base control update the TextBox control.
    MyBase.OnFontChanged(e)
    ' Now we can redraw controls if necessary.
    RedrawControls()
End Sub
```

Creating a Control from Scratch

The third technique for creating a custom control is building it from scratch by inheriting from the Control class and painting directly on its surface using graphic methods in the GDI+ package. In general, it's a more complex approach than the other two techniques shown so far.

In this section, I'll illustrate a relatively simple example: a custom control named GradientControl that can be used to provide a gradient background for other controls. Figure 18-6 shows this control at design time, but most of the time you'll set its Docked property to Fill so that it spreads over the entire form. This control has only three properties: StartColor, EndColor, and GradientMode. This is the complete source code for this control:

```
Public Class GradientBackground
    Inherits System.Windows.Forms.Control

    ' The StartColor property
    Dim m_StartColor As Color = Color.Blue

    <Description("The start color for the gradient")> _
    Property StartColor() As Color
        Get
            Return m_StartColor
        End Get
        Set(ByVal Value As Color)
            m_StartColor = Value
            ' Redraw the control when this property changes.
            Me.Invalidate()
        End Set
    End Property

    Sub ResetStartColor()
        m_StartColor = Color.Blue
    End Sub

    Function ShouldSerializeStartColor() As Boolean
        Return Not m_StartColor.Equals(Color.Blue)
    End Function

    ' The EndColor property
    Dim m_EndColor As Color = Color.Black

    <Description("The end color for the gradient")> _
    Property EndColor() As Color
        Get
            Return m_EndColor
        End Get
        Set(ByVal Value As Color)
            m_EndColor = Value
            ' Redraw the control when this property changes.
            Me.Invalidate()
        End Set
    End Property
End Class
```

```
    Sub ResetEndColor()
        m_EndColor = Color.Black
    End Sub

    Function ShouldSerializeEndColor() As Boolean
        Return Not m_EndColor.Equals(Color.Black)
    End Function

    ' The GradientMode property
    Dim m_GradientMode As LinearGradientMode = _
        LinearGradientMode.ForwardDiagonal

    <Description("The gradient mode"), _
        DefaultValue(LinearGradientMode.ForwardDiagonal)> _
    Property GradientMode() As LinearGradientMode
        Get
            Return m_GradientMode
        End Get
        Set(ByVal Value As LinearGradientMode)
            m_GradientMode = Value
            ' Redraw the control when this property changes.
            Me.Invalidate()
        End Set
    End Property

    ' Render the control background.

    Protected Overrides Sub OnPaint(ByVal e As PaintEventArgs)
        ' Create a gradient brush as large as the client area, with specified
        ' start/end color and gradient mode.
        Dim br As New LinearGradientBrush(Me.ClientRectangle, _
            m_StartColor, m_EndColor, m_GradientMode)
        ' Paint the background and destroy the brush.
        e.Graphics.FillRectangle(br, Me.ClientRectangle)
        br.Dispose()
        ' Let the base control do its chores (e.g., raising the Paint event).
        MyBase.OnPaint(e)
    End Sub

    Private Sub GradientBackground_Resize(ByVal sender As Object, _
        ByVal e As EventArgs) Handles MyBase.Resize
        Me.Invalidate()
    End Sub
End Class
```

A custom control implemented by inheriting from the Control class must render itself in the overridden OnPaint method. In this particular case, redrawing the control is trivial because the System.Drawing.Drawing2d namespace exposes a LinearGradientBrush object that does all the work for you. In practice, for this particular control you only have to create a gradient brush as large as the control itself and then use this brush to paint the control's client rectangle. The last argument you pass to the brush's constructor is the gradient mode, an enumerated value that lets you create horizontal, vertical, forward diagonal (default), and backward diagonal gradients. The GradientMode property is opportunely defined as type LinearGradientMode so that these four gradients appear in a drop-down list box in the Properties window.

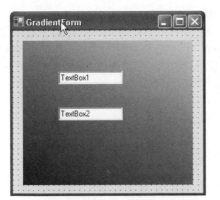

Figure 18-6   You can use the GradientControl to create eye-catching backgrounds by setting just three properties.

The only other detail to take care of is refreshing the control whenever a property changes. The best way to do so is by invalidating the control appearance with its Invalidate method so that the form engine can refresh the control at the first occurrence. This is considered a better practice than invoking the Refresh method directly because the form engine can delay all repaint operations until it's appropriate to perform them.

The ControlPaint Class

You might find the ControlPaint class especially useful when creating the user interface of your custom control. This class, in the System.Windows.Forms namespace, exposes shared methods for performing common graphic chores—for example, you can use the DrawFocusRectangle method for drawing the dotted rectangle around your control when it gets the focus:

```
Private Sub GradientBackground_GotFocus(ByVal sender As Object, _
    ByVal e As EventArgs) _
    Handles MyBase.GotFocus
    Dim gr As Graphics = Me.CreateGraphics
    ControlPaint.DrawFocusRectangle(gr, Me.Bounds)
    gr.Dispose()
End Sub
```

Other methods in the ControlPaint class can draw a border (DrawBorder), a three-dimensional border (DrawBorder3D), a button (DrawButton), a standard check box (DrawCheckBox), a three-state check box (DrawMixedCheckBox), a radio button (DrawRadioButton), a scroll bar button (DrawScrollButton), a combo box button (DrawComboButton), a disabled (grayed) string (DrawStringDisabled), and an image in disabled state (DrawImageDisabled). All these borders and buttons can be rendered in normal, checked, flat, pushed, and inactive states. (See Figure 18-7.)

The DrawReversibleLine method draws a line in such a way that you can make the line disappear if you invoke the method again. The DrawReversibleFrame and FillReversibleRectangle methods do the same, but draw an empty and a filled rectangle, respectively. You can use these methods to implement "rubber band" techniques—for example, to let users draw lines and rectangles with the mouse. (Notice that you can't implement rubber banding with GDI+ methods because GDI+ doesn't support XOR drawing. For drawing any shape other than a line and a rectangle in rubber-banding mode, you must call the native Windows GDI functions though PInvoke.)

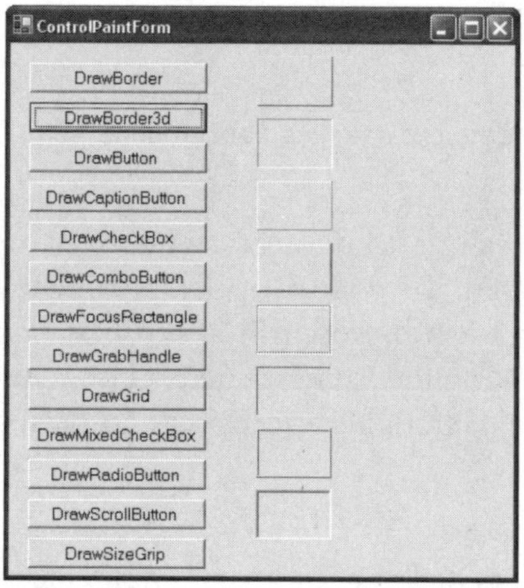

Figure 18-7   The demo application lets you preview the effect you can achieve by invoking some of the methods in the ControlPaint class.

Advanced Topics

Windows Forms control creation is a complex topic, and I don't have enough space to cover every detail. But what you learned in previous chapters and the techniques I'll cover in this section are more than sufficient to enable you to author useful and complex controls with relatively little effort.

The ISupportInitialize Interface

If you create a control or a component that is meant to interact with other controls on the form, you might have the following problem: the control hasn't been sited on the form's surface when its constructor method runs, so you can't reference the Container property from inside that method. And even if you could, your code couldn't see any controls that are added to the form after it.

You can easily solve these and other similar problems simply by having your control or component expose the System.ComponentModel.SupportInitialize interface. When Visual Studio .NET adds your control to the form, it will invoke the ISupportInitialize.BeginInit method before any control is added to the form, and the ISupportInitialize.EndInit method after all controls have been added to the form. Several built-in controls expose this interface, including the DataGrid, Timer, and NumericUpDown controls, and the DataSet, DataTable, and FileSystemWatcher components—for example, look at the code that Visual Studio .NET generates when you drop a DataGrid control on a form's surface:

```
<System.Diagnostics.DebuggerStepThrough()> Private Sub InitializeComponent()
    Me.TextBox1 = New System.Windows.Forms.TextBox
    Me.DataGrid1 = New System.Windows.Forms.DataGrid
    CType(Me.DataGrid1, ISupportInitialize).BeginInit()
    Me.SuspendLayout()
    ' ...(Assign properties of all the controls and the form itself)...
    ⋮
    ' ...(Add controls to the parent form)...
    Me.Controls.Add(Me.TextBox1)
    Me.Controls.Add(Me.DataGrid1)
    CType(Me.DataGrid1, ISupportInitialize).EndInit()
    Me.ResumeLayout(False)
End Sub
```

Here's how this interface looks when implemented in a component:

```
Public Sub BeginInit() Implements ISupportInitialize.BeginInit
    ' Code that runs before any other control is hosted on the form.
End Sub

Public Sub EndInit() Implements ISupportInitialize.EndInit
    ' Code that runs after any other control is hosted on the form.
End Sub
```

Multithreaded Controls

Creating a multithreaded control class isn't different from creating a new thread in a regular application, and you have several options: you can create a new Thread object, use a thread from the thread pool, or just use asynchronous method invocation. (Threading is covered in Chapter 12.) The only potential glitch you should watch for is that the control you create—whether it's inherited from a Control, a UserControl, or another control—must be accessed *exclusively* from the thread that created it. In fact, all the Windows Forms controls rely on the single-threaded apartment (STA) model because windows and controls are based on the Win32 message architecture, which is inherently apartment-threaded. This means that a control (or a form, for that matter) can be created on any thread, but all the methods of the control must be called from the thread that created the control. This constraint can create a serious problem because other .NET portions use the free-threading model, and carelessly mixing the two models isn't a wise idea.

The only methods that you can call on a control object from another thread are Invoke, BeginInvoke, and EndInvoke. You already know from Chapter 12 how to use the latter two methods for calling a method asynchronously, so in this section I'll focus on the Invoke method exclusively. This method takes a delegate pointing to a method (Sub or Function) and can take an Object array as a second argument if the method expects one or more arguments.

To illustrate how to use this method, I've prepared a CountdownLabel control, which continuously displays the number of seconds left until the countdown expires. (See Figure 18-8.) The code that updates the Label runs on another thread. You start the countdown by using the StartCountdown method, and you can stop it before the end by using the StopCountdown method.

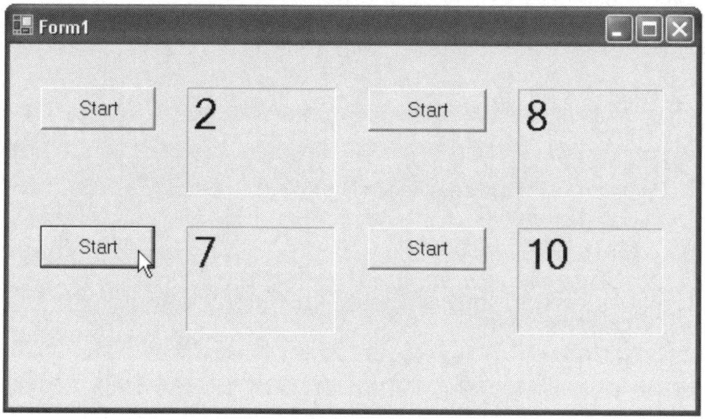

Figure 18-8   A form with four CountdownLabel instances

Here are the steps you must take to correctly implement multithreading in a control:

1. Define a private method that operates on the control or its properties. This method runs in the control's main thread and can therefore access all the control's members. In the sample control, this method is named SetText and takes the string to be displayed in the Label control.

2. Declare a delegate patterned after the method defined in step 1; in the sample control, this is called SetTextDelegate.

3. Declare a delegate variable and make it point to the method defined in step 1; this value is passed to the Invoke method. In the sample control, this variable is named SetTextMarshaler: the name comes from the fact that this delegate actually marshals data from the new thread to the control's main thread.

4. Create a method that spawns the new thread using one of the techniques described in Chapter 12. For simplicity's sake, the sample application uses the Thread object; in the sample control, this task is performed by the StartCountdown method.

Here's the complete listing of the CountdownLabel control:

```
Public Class CountdownLabel
    Inherits System.Windows.Forms.Label

    ' A delegate that points to the SetText procedure
    Delegate Sub SetTextDelegate(ByVal Text As String)
    ' An instance of this delegate that points to the SetText procedure
    Dim SetTextMarshaler As SetTextDelegate = AddressOf Me.SetText
    ' The internal counter for number of seconds left
    Dim secondsLeft As Integer
    ' The end time for countdown
    Dim endTime As Date
    ' The thread object: if Nothing, no other thread is running.
    Dim thr As Thread

    Sub StartCountdown(ByVal seconds As Integer)
        ' Wait until all variables can be accessed safely.
        SyncLock Me
            ' Save values where the other thread can access them.
            secondsLeft = seconds
            endTime = Now.AddSeconds(seconds)

            ' Create a new thread, and run the procedure on that thread
            ' only if the thread isn't running already.
            If (thr Is Nothing) Then
                thr = New Thread(AddressOf CountProc)
                thr.Start()
            End If
        End SyncLock

        ' Display the initial value in the label.
        SetText(CStr(seconds))
    End Sub

    Sub StopCountdown()
        SyncLock Me
            ' This statement implicitly causes CountProc to exit.
            endTime = Now
        End SyncLock
    End Sub

    ' This procedure is just a wrapper for a simple property set and runs
    ' on the control's creation thread. The other thread(s) must call it
    ' through the control's Invoke method.
    Private Sub SetText(ByVal Text As String)
        Me.Text = Text
    End Sub

    ' This procedure runs on another thread.
    Private Sub CountProc()
        Do
            ' Ensure that this is the only thread that is accessing variables.
            SyncLock Me
```

```
                        ' Calculate the number of seconds left.
                        Dim secs As Integer = CInt(endTime.Subtract(Now).TotalSeconds)
                        ' If different from current value, update the Text property.
                        If secs <> secondsLeft Then
                            ' Never display negative numbers.
                            secondsLeft = Math.Max(secs, 0)
                            ' Arguments must be passed in an Object array.
                            Dim args() As Object = {CStr(secondsLeft)}
                            ' Update the Text property with current number of seconds.
                            MyBase.Invoke(SetTextMarshaler, args)

                            ' Terminate the thread if countdown is over.
                            If secondsLeft <= 0 Then
                                ' Signal that no thread is running, and exit.
                                thr = Nothing
                                Exit Do
                            End If
                        End If
                    End SyncLock
                    ' Wait for 100 milliseconds.
                    Thread.Sleep(100)
            Loop
        End Sub
End Class
```

As usual in multithreaded applications, you must pay a lot of attention to how you access variables shared among threads to prevent your control from randomly crashing after hours of testing. Other problems can arise if the user closes the form while the other thread is running because this extra thread attempts to access a control that no longer exists and would prevent the application from shutting down correctly. You can work around this obstacle by killing the other thread when the control is being destroyed, which you do by overriding the OnHandleDestroyed method:

```
' Kill the other thread if the control is being destroyed.
Protected Overrides Sub OnHandleDestroyed(ByVal e As EventArgs)
    SyncLock Me
        If Not (thr Is Nothing) AndAlso thr.IsAlive Then
            thr.Abort()
            thr.Join()
        End If
    End SyncLock
    MyBase.OnHandleDestroyed(e)
End Sub
```

Remember that you can't use the RaiseEvent statement from another thread. To have the CountdownLabel control fire an event when the countdown is complete, you must adopt the same technique described previously. You must create a method that calls RaiseEvent and runs on the main thread, define a delegate that points to it, and use Invoke from the other thread when you want to raise the event.

The techniques described in this section should be used whenever you access a Windows Forms control from another thread and not just when you're creating a custom control. If you are unsure whether you must use the Invoke method on a control (in other words, you don't know whether your code is running in the same thread as the control), just check the InvokeRequired read-only property. If it returns True, you must use the technique described in this section.

Extender Provider Controls

You can create property extender controls similar to those provided with the Windows Forms package, such as ToolTip and HelpProvider. In this section, I'll guide you through the creation of a component named UserPropExtender, which adds a property named UserRole to all the visible controls on the form. The developer can assign a user role to this list, or even a semicolon-separated list of roles, such as Manager;Accountants. At run time, the UserPropExtender control makes invisible those controls that are associated with a user role different from the current role (information that you assign to the UserPropExtender control's CurrentUserRole property). Thanks to the UserPropExtender control, you can provide different control layouts for different user roles without writing any code. Here are the steps you must follow when creating an extender provider control:

1. You define a class for your extender provider, making it inherit from System.Windows.Forms.Control (if the new control has a user interface) or from System.ComponentModel.Component (if the new control isn't visible at run time and should be displayed in the component tray of the form designer).

2. Associate a ProvideProperty attribute with the class you created in the preceding step. The constructor for this attribute takes the name of the property that's added to all the controls on the form and a second System.Type argument that defines which type of objects can be extended by this extender provider. In this example, the new property is named UserList and can be applied to Control objects.

3. All extender providers must implement the IExtenderProvider interface, so you must add a suitable Implements statement. This interface has only one method, CanExtend, which receives an Object and is expected to return True if that object can be extended with the new property. The code in the sample control returns True for all control classes except the Form class.

4. Declare and initialize a class-level Hashtable object that stores the value of the UserName property for all the controls on the form, where the control itself is used as a key in the Hashtable. In the sample project, this collection is named userListValues.

5. Define two methods, Get*xxxx* and Set*xxxx*, where *xxxx* is the name of the property that the extender provider adds to all other controls. (These methods are named GetUserName and SetUserName in the sample control.) These methods can read and write values in the Hashtable defined in the preceding step and modify the control's user interface as necessary. (The Set*xxxx* method is invoked from the code automatically generated by the form designer.)

Armed with this knowledge, you should be able to decode the complete listing for the UserPropExtender component quite easily:

```
' Let the form know that this control will add the UserRole property.
<ProvideProperty("UserRole", GetType(Control))> _
Public Class UserPropExtender
    Inherits Component
    Implements IExtenderProvider

    ' Return True for all controls that can be extended with
    ' the UserRole property.
    Public Function CanExtend(ByVal extendee As Object) As Boolean _
        Implements IExtenderProvider.CanExtend
        ' Extend all controls but not forms.
        If Not (TypeOf extendee Is Form) Then
            Return True
        End If
    End Function

    ' The Hashtable object that associates controls with their UserRole
    Dim userRoleValues As New Hashtable()

    ' These are the Get/Set methods related to the property being added.

    Function GetUserRole(ByVal ctrl As Control) As String
        ' Check whether a property is associated with this control.
        Dim value As Object = userRoleValues(ctrl)
        ' Return the value found or an empty string.
        If value Is Nothing Then value = ""
        Return value.ToString
    End Function

    Sub SetUserRole(ByVal ctrl As Control, ByVal value As String)
        ' In case Nothing is passed
        If Value Is Nothing Then Value = ""
        If Value.Length = 0 And userRoleValues.Contains(ctrl) Then
            ' Remove the control from the hash table.
            userRoleValues.Remove(ctrl)
            ' Remove event handlers, if any (none in this example).
            ⋮
        ElseIf Value.Length > 0 Then
            If Not userRoleValues.Contains(ctrl) Then
                ' Add event handlers here (none in this example).
                ⋮
            End If
            ' Assign the new value, and refresh the control.
            userRoleValues.Item(ctrl) = Value
            SetControlVisibility(ctrl)
        End If
    End Sub

    ' This property is assigned the name of the current user.
    Dim m_CurrentUserRole As String
```

```
Property CurrentUserRole() As String
    Get
        Return m_CurrentUserRole
    End Get
    Set(ByVal Value As String)
        m_CurrentUserRole = Value
        RefreshAllControls()        ' Redraw all controls.
    End Set
End Property

' Hide/show all controls based on their UserRole property.
Sub RefreshAllControls()
    For Each ctrl As Control In userRoleValues.Keys
        SetControlVisibility(ctrl)
    Next
End Sub

' Hide/show a single control based on its UserRole property.
Private Sub SetControlVisibility(ByVal ctrl As Control)
    ' Do nothing if no current role or control isn't in the hash table.
    If CurrentUserRole = "" Then Exit Sub
    If Not userRoleValues.Contains(ctrl) Then Exit Sub

    ' Get the value in the hash table.
    Dim value As String = userRoleValues(ctrl).ToString
    ' Check whether current role is among the role(s) defined
    ' for this control.
    If InStr(";" & value & ";", ";" & CurrentUserRole & ";", _
        CompareMethod.Text) > 0 Then
        ctrl.Visible = True
    Else
        ctrl.Visible = False
    End If
End Sub
End Class
```

The UserPropExtender control is fully functional and uses many of the techniques you should know about when writing extender providers. But because of its simplicity, it doesn't need to trap events coming from other controls on the form, which is often a requirement for extender providers. For example, the ToolTip control intercepts mouse events for all controls that have a nonempty ToolTip property, and the HelpProvider control intercepts the HelpRequested event to display the associated help page or string.

Intercepting events from controls isn't difficult; however, when the control is added to the Hashtable (typically in the Set*xxxx* method), you use the AddHandler command to have one of its events trapped by a local procedure, and you use Remove-Handler to remove the event added dynamically when the control is removed from the Hashtable. Remarks in the preceding listing clearly show where these statements should be inserted.

Custom Property Editors

If you're familiar with custom control authoring under Visual Basic 6, you might have noticed that I haven't mentioned property pages, either when describing built-in controls or in this section devoted to custom control creation. Property pages aren't supported in the .NET architecture and have been replaced by custom property editors.

The most common form of property editor displays a Windows Forms control in a drop-down area inside the Properties window. You can display any control in the drop-down area, such as a TrackBar, a ListBox, or even a complex control such as a TreeView or a DataGrid, but the limitation is that you can display only *one* control. If you want to display more controls, you'll have to create a custom control with multiple child controls for the sole purpose of using it in the drop-down area—for example, the editors used by Anchor and Dock properties work in this way.

The Windows Form designer also supports property editors that display modal forms. Because you're in charge of drawing the appearance of such modal forms, you can display tab pages and multiple controls, and even modify more than one property. For example, you can add OK, Cancel, and Apply buttons and have a Visual Basic 6–like property page. Because these forms are modal, the Property window should be updated only when the user closes them, but you can offer a preview of what the custom control being edited will look like when the property or properties are assigned. As a matter of fact, it's perfectly legal to use your custom control inside the property editor you create for one of its properties, regardless of whether these editors use the drop-down area or a modal form.

Implementing a custom property editor isn't simple. Worse, the MSDN documentation is less than perfect—to use a euphemism—so I had to dig deep in the samples provided with the .NET Framework and use some imagination. The companion source code with this book includes a GradientBackgroundEx control that extends Gradient-Background with a new RotateAngle property, which permits you to rotate the gradient brush. (I have purposely chosen to extend an existing control so that I don't need to lead you through all the steps necessary to create a brand-new custom control.) The new property is associated with a custom property editor that uses a TrackBar control in a drop-down area of the Properties window to let the user select the angle with the mouse. Thanks to inheritance, the code for the GradientBackgroundEx control is concise and includes only the new Property procedure and a redefined OnPaint procedure, which differs from the original OnPaint procedure by one statement only, here shown in boldface:

```
Public Class GradientBackgroundEx
    Inherits GradientBackground

    Dim m_RotateAngle As Single
```

```
<Description("The rotation angle for the brush"), DefaultValue(0)> _
Property RotateAngle() As Single
    Get
        Return m_RotateAngle
    End Get
    Set(ByVal Value As Single)
        m_RotateAngle = Value
        Me.Invalidate()
    End Set
End Property

' Redefine the OnPaint event to account for the new property.
Protected Overrides Sub OnPaint(ByVal e As PaintEventArgs)
    ' Create a gradient brush as large as the client area, with specified
    ' start/end color and gradient mode.
    Dim br As New LinearGradientBrush(Me.ClientRectangle, _
        Me.StartColor, Me.EndColor, Me.GradientMode)
    ' Apply the rotation angle.
    br.RotateTransform(Me.RotateAngle)
    ' Paint the background and destroy the brush.
    e.Graphics.FillRectangle(br, Me.ClientRectangle)
    br.Dispose()
    ' Let the base control do its chores (e.g., raising the Paint event).
    MyBase.OnPaint(e)
End Sub
End Class
```

The first step in defining a custom editor for a given property is to specify the editor itself in the Editor attribute associated with the property procedure itself. The editor we're going to create is named RotateAngleEditor, so the new version of the RotateAngle Property procedure becomes:

```
<Description("The rotation angle for the brush"), DefaultValue(0), _
    Editor(GetType(RotateAngleEditor), GetType(UITypeEditor))> _
Property RotateAngle() As Single
    ⋮
End Property
```

Note that the attribute's constructor takes two System.Type arguments, so you must use the GetType function. The second argument is always GetType(UITypeEditor).

The property editor is a class that you define. If you don't plan to reuse this property editor for other custom controls, you can avoid namespace pollution by making the editor a nested class of the custom control class.

The property editor class inherits from System.Drawing.Design.UITypeEditor and must override two methods in its base class, GetEditStyle and EditValue. The form designer calls the GetEditStyle method when it's filling the Properties window with the values of all the properties of the control currently selected. This method must return an enumerated value that tells the designer whether your property editor is going to display a single control in a drop-down area or a modal form. In the former case, a down-arrow button is displayed near the property name; in the latter case, a button with an ellipsis is used instead.

The form designer calls the EditValue method when the user clicks the button beside the property name. This method is overloaded, but we don't have to override all the overloaded versions of the method. In the most general overloaded version—the only one I override in the demo program—this method receives three arguments:

■ The first argument is an ITypeDescriptorContext type that can provide additional information about the context in which the editing action is being performed—for example, Context.Instance returns a reference to the control whose property is being edited, and Context.Container returns a reference to the control's container.

■ The second argument is an IServiceProvider type. You can query the GetService method of this object to get the editor service object that represents the properties editor; this is an IWindowsFormEditorService object that exposes the three methods that let you open the drop-down area (DropDownControl), close it (Close-DropDown), or display a modal form (ShowDialog).

■ The third argument is the current value of the property being edited. You should use this value to correctly initialize the control about to appear in the drop-down area (or the controls on the modal form). The EditValue method is expected to return the new value of the property being edited.

Here's the complete listing of the RotateAngleEditor class. Its many remarks and the details already given should suffice for you to understand how it works:

```
Class RotateAngleEditor
    Inherits UITypeEditor

    ' Override the GetEditStyle method to tell that this editor supports
    ' the DropDown style.
    Overloads Overrides Function GetEditStyle( _
        ByVal context As ITypeDescriptorContext) As UITypeEditorEditStyle
        If Not (context Is Nothing) AndAlso _
            Not (context.Instance Is Nothing) Then
            ' Return DropDown if you have a context and a control instance.
            Return UITypeEditorEditStyle.DropDown
        Else
            ' Otherwise, return the default behavior, whatever it is.
            Return MyBase.GetEditStyle(context)
        End If
    End Function

    ' This is the TrackBar control that is displayed in the editor.
    Dim WithEvents tb As TrackBar
    ' This the editor service that creates the drop-down area
    ' or shows a dialog.
    Dim wfes As IWindowsFormsEditorService
```

```
' Override the EditValue function,
' and return the new value of the property.
Overloads Overrides Function EditValue( _
    ByVal context As ITypeDescriptorContext, _
    ByVal provider As IServiceProvider, _
    ByVal value As Object) As Object

    ' Exit if no context, instance, or provider is provided.
    If (context Is Nothing) OrElse (context.Instance Is Nothing) _
        OrElse (provider Is Nothing) Then
        Return value
    End If
    ' Get the Editor Service object; exit if not there.
    wfes = CType(provider.GetService( _
        GetType(IWindowsFormsEditorService)), IWindowsFormsEditorService)
    If (wfes Is Nothing) Then Return value

    ' Create the TrackBar control, and set its properties.
    tb = New TrackBar()
    ' Always set Orientation before Size property.
    tb.Orientation = Orientation.Vertical
    tb.Size = New Size(50, 150)
    tb.TickStyle = TickStyle.TopLeft
    tb.TickFrequency = 45
    tb.SetRange(0, 360)
    ' Initalize its Value property.
    tb.Value = CInt(value)

    ' Show the control. (It returns when the drop-down area is closed.)
    wfes.DropDownControl(tb)
    ' The return value must be of the correct type.
    EditValue = CSng(tb.Value)
    ' Destroy the TrackBar control.
    tb.Dispose()
    tb = Nothing
End Function

' Close the drop-down area when the mouse button is released.
Private Sub TB_MouseUp(ByVal sender As Object, _
    ByVal e As MouseEventArgs) Handles tb.MouseUp
    If Not (wfes Is Nothing) Then
        wfes.CloseDropDown()
    End If
End Sub
End Class
```

The RotateAngleEditor class automatically closes the drop-down area when the user releases the mouse button, but this isn't strictly necessary because the Properties window closes the drop-down area when the user clicks somewhere else. I implemented this detail only to show you how you can react to user selections in the drop-down area. Figure 18-9 shows the new property editor in action.

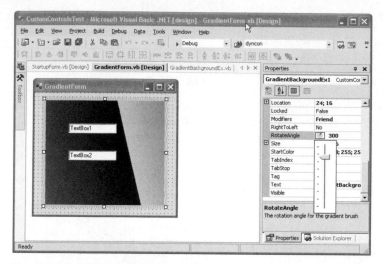

Figure 18-9   The RotateAngle property of a GradientBackgroundEx control is being edited with a custom property editor.

The steps you must take to display a modal form instead of the drop-down area are the same as those you've seen so far, with only two differences:

- The GetEditStyle method must return the UITypeEditorEditStyle.Modal value to let the Property window know that an ellipsis button must be displayed beside the property name.

- Your class library project must contain a form class in which you drop the controls that make up the editor interface. In the EditValue method, you create an instance of this form and pass it to the ShowModal method of the IWindowsFormsEditorService object (instead of the DropDownControl method, as in the preceding code example).

Custom property editors provide support for one more feature: the ability to offer the visual representation of the current value in the Properties window in a small rectangle to the left of the actual numeric or string value. (You can see how the form designer uses such rectangles for the ForeColor, BackColor, and BackgroundImage properties.) In this case, you must override two more methods of the base UITypeEditor class: Get-PaintValueSupported (which should return True if you want to implement this feature) and PaintValue (where you place the code that actually draws inside the small rectangle). The latter method receives a PaintValueEventArgs object, whose properties give you access to the Graphics object on which you can draw, the bounding rectangle, and the value to be printed. The following code extends the RotateAngleEditor class with the ability to display a small yellow circle, plus a black line that shows the current value of the RotateAngle property in a visual manner:

```
' Let the property editor know that we want to paint the value.
Overloads Overrides Function GetPaintValueSupported( _
    ByVal context As ITypeDescriptorContext) As Boolean
```

```
            ' In this demo, we return True regardless of the actual editor.
            Return True
        End Function


        ' Display a yellow circle to the left of the value in the Properties window
        ' with a line forming the same angle as the value of the RotateAngle property.
        Overloads Overrides Sub PaintValue(ByVal e As PaintValueEventArgs)
            ' Get the angle in radians.
            Dim a As Single = CSng(e.Value) * CSng(Math.PI) / 180!
            ' Get the rectangle in which we can draw.
            Dim rect As Rectangle = e.Bounds
            ' Evaluate the radius of the circle.
            Dim r As Single = Math.Min(rect.Width, rect.Height) / 2!
            ' Get the center point.
            Dim p1 As New PointF(rect.Width / 2!, rect.Height / 2!)
            ' Calculate where the line should end.
            Dim p2 As New PointF(CSng(p1.X + Math.Cos(a) * r), _
                CSng(p1.Y + Math.Sin(a) * r))
            ' Draw the yellow-filled circle.
            e.Graphics.FillEllipse(Brushes.Yellow, rect.Width / 2! - r, _
                rect.Height / 2! - r, r * 2, r * 2)
            ' Draw the line.
            e.Graphics.DrawLine(Pens.Black, p1, p2)
        End Sub
```

You can see the effect in Figure 18-9.

Object Properties

A few common properties, such as Font and Location, return objects instead of scalar values. These properties are displayed in the Properties window with a plus sign (+) to the left of each of their names so that you can expand those items to edit the individual properties of the object. If you implement properties that return objects defined in the .NET Framework (such as Font, Point, and Size objects), your control automatically inherits this behavior. However, when your control exposes an object defined in your application, you must implement a custom TypeConverter class to enable this feature.

The companion source code includes an AddressControl custom control, which lets the user enter information such as street, city, postal code, state, and country. (See the form on the left in Figure 18-10.) Instead of exposing this data as five independent properties, this control exposes them as a single Address object, which is defined in the same application:

```
Public Class Address
    ' This event fires when a property is changed.
    Event PropertyChanged(ByVal propertyName As String)

    ' Private members
    Dim m_Street As String
    Dim m_City As String
    Dim m_Zip As String
    Dim m_State As String
    Dim m_Country As String
```

```
    Property Street() As String
        Get
            Return m_Street
        End Get
        Set(ByVal Value As String)
            If m_Street <> Value Then
                m_Street = Value
                RaiseEvent PropertyChanged("Street")
            End If
        End Set
    End Property

    ' ...(Property procedures for City, Zip, State, and Country
    '     omitted because substantially identical to Street property)...
    ⋮

    Overrides Function ToString() As String
        Return "(Address)"
    End Function
End Class
```

Note that property procedures in the Address class are just wrappers for the five private variables and that they raise a PropertyChanged event when any property changes. The ToString method is overridden to provide the text that will appear as a dummy value for the Address property in the Properties window. The AddressControl control has an Address property that returns an Address object:

```
Public Class AddressControl
    Inherits System.Windows.Forms.UserControl

#Region " Windows Form Designer generated code "
    ⋮
#End Region

    Dim WithEvents m_Address As New Address()

    <TypeConverter(GetType(AddressTypeConverter)), _
        DesignerSerializationVisibility(DesignerSerializationVisibility.Content)> _
    Property Address() As Address
        Get
            Return m_Address
        End Get
        Set(ByVal Value As Address)
            m_Address = Value
            RefreshControls()
        End Set
    End Property

    ' Refresh controls when any property changes.
    Private Sub Address_PropertyChanged(ByVal propertyName As String) _
        Handles m_Address.PropertyChanged
        RefreshControls()
    End Sub
```

```
' Display Address properties in the control's fields.
Private Sub RefreshControls()
    txtStreet.Text = m_Address.Street
    txtCity.Text = m_Address.City
    txtZip.Text = m_Address.Zip
    txtState.Text = m_Address.State
    txtCountry.Text = m_Address.Country
End Sub

' Update a member property when user updates a field.
Private Sub Controls_TextChanged(ByVal sender As Object, _
  ByVal e As EventArgs) Handles txtStreet.TextChanged, txtCity.TextChanged, _
    txtZip.TextChanged, txtState.TextChanged, txtCountry.TextChanged
    Dim Text As String = DirectCast(sender, Control).Text
    If sender Is txtStreet Then
        m_Address.Street = Text
    ElseIf sender Is txtCity Then
        m_Address.City = Text
    ElseIf sender Is txtZip Then
        m_Address.Zip = Text
    ElseIf sender Is txtState Then
        m_Address.State = Text
    ElseIf sender Is txtCountry Then
        m_Address.Country = Text
    End If
End Sub
End Class
```

The key statement in the preceding code is the TypeConverter attribute, which tells the form designer that a custom TypeConverter object is associated with the Address property. Or you can associate this attribute with the Address class itself, in which case all the controls that expose a property of type Address will automatically use the AddressTypeConverter class. (The .NET Framework uses this approach for classes such as Point and Font.) The DesignerSerializationVisibility attribute, which is also assigned to the Address property, tells Visual Studio .NET that it must serialize each and every property of the Address object when it generates the source code for initializing this object.

The AddressTypeConverter class derives from TypeConverter and overrides two methods. The GetPropertiesSupported method must return True to let the editor know that a plus symbol must be displayed to the left of the Address property in the Properties window; the GetProperties method must return a PropertyDescriptorCollection object, which describes the items that will appear when the plus symbol is clicked:

```
' The TypeConverter class for the Address property
' (It can be a nested class of AddressControl.)

Public Class AddressTypeConverter
    Inherits TypeConverter

    Overloads Overrides Function GetPropertiesSupported( _
        ByVal context As ITypeDescriptorContext) As Boolean
        ' Tell the editor to display a + symbol near the property name.
```

```
            Return True
        End Function

    Overloads Overrides Function GetProperties( _
        ByVal context As ITypeDescriptorContext, ByVal value As Object, _
        ByVal attributes() As Attribute) As PropertyDescriptorCollection

        ' Use the GetProperties shared method to return a collection of
        ' PropertyDescriptor objects, one for each property of Address.
        Return TypeDescriptor.GetProperties(GetType(Address))
    End Function
End Class
```

You see the effect of this custom TypeConverter class in the right portion of Figure 18-10.

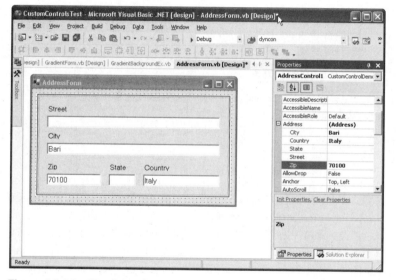

Figure 18-10   The AddressControl control includes a TypeConverter for its
custom property, Address.

To keep code as concise as possible, the AddressTypeConverter class uses the Type-
Descriptor.GetProperties shared method to create a PropertyDescriptorCollection
object that describes all the properties of the Address class. In some cases, you might
need to create this collection manually. You must take this step, for example, when not
all the properties should be made available in the Properties window, or when you
need to define a custom editor for one of them.

A custom TypeConverter object can do more than add support for object properties.
For example, you can use a custom TypeConverter class to validate the string entered
in the Properties window or to convert this string to a value type other than a standard
numeric and date .NET type. For more information about custom TypeConverter
classes, see the MSDN documentation.

Custom Control Designers

You surely noticed that a few Windows Forms controls display one or more hyperlinks near the bottom edge of the Properties window, or additional commands on the context menu that appears when you right-click on them. Implementing this and a few other features is relatively simple, and requires that you create a custom control designer and associate it with your custom control.

A control designer is a class that inherits from System.Windows.Forms.Design.ControlDesigner class, which is defined in the System.Design.dll assembly. (You must add a reference to this assembly because Visual Basic .NET projects don't reference it by default.) Providing one or more commands in the Property window or in the context menu requires that you override the Verbs read-only property. In the demo application, I created a control designer for the AddressControl; my custom designer adds two verbs to the control, InitProperties and ClearProperties:

```
Class AddressControlDesigner
    Inherits System.Windows.Forms.Design.ControlDesigner

    ' Return a collection of verbs for this control
    Public Overrides ReadOnly Property Verbs() As DesignerVerbCollection
        Get
            Dim col As New DesignerVerbCollection
            col.Add(New DesignerVerb("Init Properties", AddressOf InitProperties))
            col.Add(New DesignerVerb("Clear Properties", AddressOf ClearProperties))
            Return col
        End Get
    End Property
    ⋮
End Class
```

When the user clicks on the link in the Properties window or selects the verb from the context menu, Visual Studio .NET invokes the handler pointed to by the corresponding delegate. The ClearProperties routine simply resets the control's Address property, but you must take additional steps to let Visual Studio .NET know that you assigned a new value to a property. I encapsulated these steps in the SetAddressProperty private procedure, so that you can easily adapt my code to other procedures:

```
Sub ClearProperties (ByVal sender As Object, ByVal e As EventArgs)
    SetAddressProperty(New Address)
End Sub

' Assign a new Address property, raise all expected events.
Private Sub SetAddressProperty(ByVal newValue As Address)
    Dim thisCtrl As AddressControl = CType(Me.Control, AddressControl)
    ' Let Visual Studio know we're about to change the Address property.
    Dim pdCol As PropertyDescriptorCollection = _
      TypeDescriptor.GetProperties(thisCtrl)
    Dim pd As PropertyDescriptor = pdCol.Find("Address", True)
    RaiseComponentChanging(pd)
    ' Assign the value, but remember old value.
```

```
            Dim oldValue As Address = thisCtrl.Address
            thisCtrl.Address = newValue
            ' Let Visual Studio know we've done the assignment.
            RaiseComponentChanged(pd, oldValue, thisCtrl.Address)
        End Sub
```

The InitProperties procedure does something more interesting: it creates a form that displays another instance of the AddressControl class so that the programmer can change the Street, City, Zip, State, and Country properties simply by typing in the control:

```
    Sub InitPropertiesHandler(ByVal sender As Object, ByVal e As EventArgs)
        ' Create a new control that points to the same Address object.
        Dim thisCtrl As AddressControl = CType(Me.Control, AddressControl)
        Dim newCtrl As New AddressControl
        newCtrl.Address = thisCtrl.Address
        ' Display a form that displays the new control.
        Dim frm As New Form
        frm.Text = "Set AddressControl's Address members"
        frm.ClientSize = newCtrl.Size
        frm.Controls.Add(newCtrl)
        frm.ShowDialog()
        ' Raise all required events.
        SetAddressProperty(thisCtrl.Address)
    End Sub
```

You complete your job by flagging the AddressControl class with an appropriate Designer attribute:

```
<Designer(GetType(AddressControlDesigner))> _
Public Class AddressControl
    ⋮
End Class
```

Figure 18-11 shows what happens when the programmer clicks on the Init Properties command. Interestingly, the AddressControl reacts to the PropertyChanged events of the Address class; therefore, the underlying control is immediately updated as you type in the foreground form.

A control designer can do more than provide custom commands. For example, you can react to the mouse hovering over the control at design time by overriding the OnMouseEnter and OnMouseLeave protected methods of the ControlDesigner class, or you can limit the way a control can be resized by overriding the SelectionRules property—for example, the AddressControl doesn't know how to resize its constituent controls, so you might make it visible and moveable, but not resizable:

```
    Public Overrides ReadOnly Property SelectionRules() As SelectionRules
        Get
            Return SelectionRules.Moveable Or SelectionRules.Visible
        End Get
    End Property
```

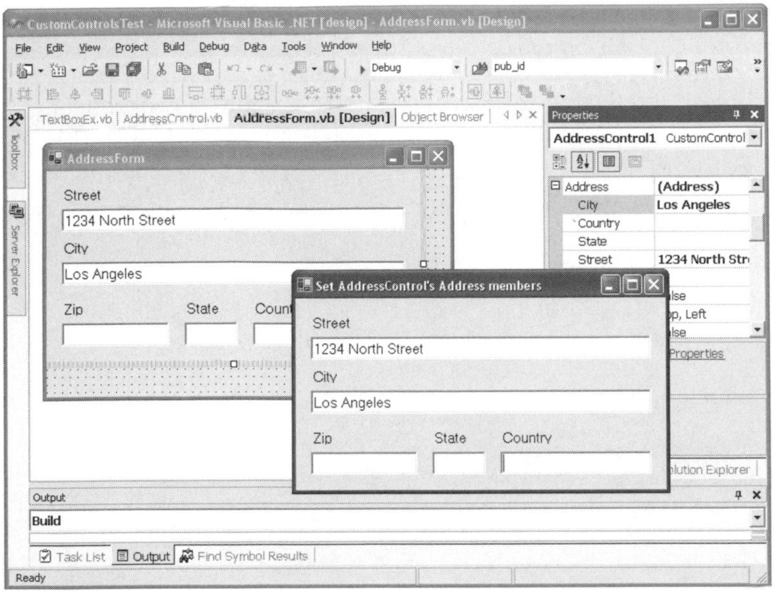

Figure 18-11   You can add verbs to the Properties window and the context menu that appears when you right-click a custom control.

> **Note**   When you create a component rather than a control, you can associate a custom designer to it by creating a class that inherits from ComponentDesigner instead of Control-Designer. For an example of a component that uses a custom designer, see the Message-BoxDisplayer component introduced in Chapter 13.

Data-Binding Support

Chances are that you want to add data-binding support to your custom controls, and the good news is that in most cases you don't need to do anything to support it. In fact, because data binding is offered by the Windows Forms infrastructure, users of your control can bind any public property simply by clicking on the (Advanced) button under (DataBindings) in the Property window, and select which property is bound to which field in any data source defined on the form. (Of course, you have to do the binding via code if you wish to bind to a component that doesn't appear in the parent form's tray area.)

In practice, however, you can expect that your users will want to bind only one or two properties in the control. This is the case of the Text property for TextBox-like controls, or the Checked property for CheckBox-like controls. You can make this task much simpler if you mark this property (or properties) with the Bindable attribute:

```
<Bindable(True)> _
Public Property Caption() As String
    :
End Property
```

When you do this, the property appears under (DataBindings) and users don't have to search for it in the list of all bindable properties.

Things become more interesting (and complicated) if your control must support complex data binding, the type of binding that controls such as ListBox and DataGrid support. To let users bind your control to a DataSet or a DataTable, as they do with built-in controls, you should expose a DataSource property of the IListSource type:

```
Private m_DataSource As IListSource

<Category("Data")> _
Public Property DataSource() As IListSource
    Get
        Return m_DataSource
    End Get
    Set(ByVal Value As IListSource)
        SetDataObject(Value, DataMember)
        m_DataSource = Value
    End Set
End Property
```

You should also expose a DataMember property to fully support the DataSet as a potential data source. DataMember is a string property, but built-in controls let users select it among all the members exposed by the object assigned to the DataSource property. It took some investigation with ILDASM for me to discover what attribute gives the desired effect:

```
Private m_DataMember As String

<Category("Data"), DefaultValue(""), _
Editor("System.Windows.Forms.Design.DataMemberListEditor, System.Design,
    Version=1.0.5000.0, Culture=neutral, PublicKeyToken=b03f5f7f11d50a3a", _
    "System.Drawing.Design.UITypeEditor,System.Drawing,
    Version=1.0.5000.0, Culture=neutral, PublicKeyToken=b03f5f7f11d50a3a")> _
    Public Property DataMember() As String
        Get
            Return m_DataMember
        End Get
        Set(ByVal Value As String)
            SetDataObject(DataSource, Value)
            m_DataMember = Value
        End Set
    End Property
```

It's essential that the two long boldface strings be entered on the same logical line, though they are split here for typographical reasons. Also, keep in mind that these strings are valid only for version 1.1 of the .NET Framework.

The code for both the DataSource and DataMember properties invoke a common SetDataObject private procedure, which is where the control can get a reference to the actual CurrencyManager associated with the data source:

```
Dim WithEvents CurrencyManager As CurrencyManager

Private Sub SetDataObject(ByVal dataSource As IListSource, ByVal dataMember As String)
    ' Do nothing at design-time.
    If Me.DesignMode Then Exit Sub

    Dim cm As CurrencyManager
    ' Find a reference to the CurrencyManager (Throws if invalid).
    If dataSource Is Nothing Or Me.BindingContext Is Nothing Then
        cm = Nothing
    ElseIf Not dataSource.ContainsListCollection Then
        ' Ignore DataMember if data source doesn't contain a collection.
        cm = DirectCast(Me.BindingContext(dataSource), CurrencyManager)
    Else
        ' Nothing to do if DataMember hasn't been set.
        If dataMember = "" Then Exit Sub
        cm = DirectCast(Me.BindingContext(dataSource, dataMember), CurrencyManager)
    End If

    If Not (cm Is Me.CurrencyManager) Then
        ' Only if the CurrencyManager has actually changed.
        Me.CurrencyManager = cm
        ReadDataSchema()
        DisplayData()
    End If
End Sub
```

The control reads all data from the data source and displays them in the ReadDataSchema and DisplayData procedures, respectively. The example included on the companion CD is a data-bound ListView control that displays all the columns in a data source. (See Figure 18-12.) Here's how you can read the schema of the underlying data source and fill the control with data:

```
Sub ReadDataSchema()
    If Me.CurrencyManager Is Nothing Then Exit Sub
    Me.Columns.Clear()
    ' Add one ListView column for each property in data source.
    For Each pd As PropertyDescriptor In Me.CurrencyManager.GetItemProperties
        Me.Columns.Add(pd.Name, 100, HorizontalAlignment.Left)
    Next
End Sub

Private Sub DisplayData()
    If Me.CurrencyManager Is Nothing Then Exit Sub
    ' Get the list of values managed by the CurrencyManager.
    Dim innerList As IList = Me.CurrencyManager.List
    If innerList Is Nothing Then Exit Sub

    ' Iterate over all the rows in the data source.
    For index As Integer = 0 To innerList.Count - 1
        ' Iterate over all columns in the data source.
        Dim currItem As ListViewItem = Nothing
        For Each pd As PropertyDescriptor In Me.CurrencyManager.GetItemProperties
            ' Get the value of this property for Nth row.
```

```
                Dim value As Object = pd.GetValue(innerList(index))
                ' Add as a ListView item or subitem.
                If currItem Is Nothing Then
                    currItem = Me.Items.Add(value.ToString)
                Else
                    currItem.SubItems.Add(value.ToString)
                End If
            Next
        Next
End Sub
```

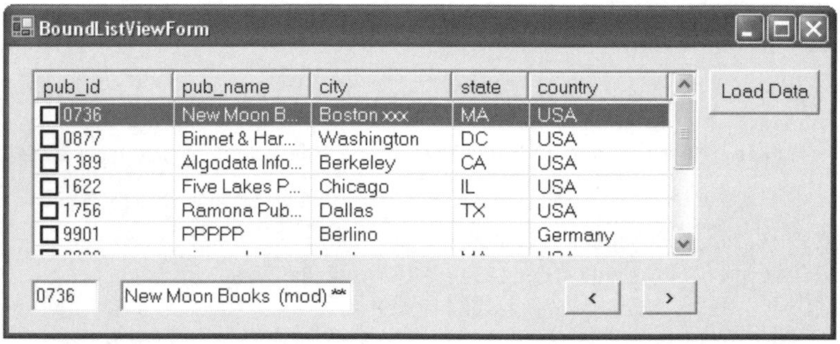

Figure 18-12   The DataBoundListView control is an example of how you can implement complex data binding.

For a fully functional data-bound control you must ensure that the control is always in sync with the CurrencyManager. In other words, a new row in the data source becomes current when the user selects a different row in your control, and a new row in your control becomes selected when the user moves to another row by some other means (for example, via navigational buttons). The DataBoundListView control achieves this synchronization by overriding the OnSelectedIndexChanged protected method and by trapping the CurrencyManager's PositionChanged event. Please see the sample code for more details on how you can complete these tasks and how you can write edited values back in the data source.

Design-Time and Run-Time Licensing

If you plan to sell your custom controls and components, you probably want to implement some type of licensing for them to enforce restrictions on their use. The good news is that the .NET Framework comes with a built-in licensing scheme, but you can override it to create your own licensing method.

To explain how licensing works, I'll show how to create a license provider class named LicWindowsFileLicenseProvided, which checks the design-time license of a control and refuses to load the control in the Visual Studio .NET environment after a given expiration date. This expiration date must be stored in a text file named *controlname*.lic stored in c:\Windows\System32 directory (more in general, the path of your Windows System32 directory). The first line of this file must be in this format:

```
controlname license expires on expirationdate
```

where *controlname* is the full name of the control and *expirationdate* is the date of the end of the license agreement. For example, according to this license schema, a license file for the AddressControl in the CustomControlDemo namespace must be named CustomControlDemo.AddressControl.lic. If the license for this control expires on January 1, 2006, the first line of this file must be

```
CustomControlDemo.AddressControl license expires on 01/01/2006
```

(Character case is significant.) You must do two things to apply a license provider to the class that must be licensed. First, you decorate the class definition with a LicenseProvider attribute. Second, you query the .NET licensing infrastructure from inside the control's constructor method by using the LicenseManager.Validate shared method, which throws an exception if the .lic file can't be found or its contents aren't correct. If successful, the method returns a License object, which you later dispose of when the object is destroyed. Here's a revised version of the AddressControl class that employs the licensing mechanism based on the LicWindowsFileLicenseProvider custom license provider. (Added lines are in boldface.)

```
<LicenseProvider(GetType(LicWindowsFileLicenseProvider))> _
Public Class AddressControl
    Inherits System.Windows.Forms.UserControl

    ' The License object
    Private lic As License

    Public Sub New()
        MyBase.New()
        ' Validate the License.
        lic = LicenseManager.Validate(GetType(AddressControl), Me)
        ' This call is required by the Windows Form Designer.
        InitializeComponent()
    End Sub

    ' Destroy the License object without waiting for the garbage collection.
    Protected Overloads Overrides Sub Dispose(ByVal disposing As Boolean)
        If disposing Then
            ' Destroy the license.
            If Not (lic Is Nothing) Then
                lic.Dispose()
                lic = Nothing
            End If
        End If
        MyBase.Dispose(disposing)
    End Sub
    ⋮
End Class
```

Alternatively, you can use the LicenseManager.IsValid shared method to check a license object without throwing an exception if the license isn't valid.

Obviously, this licensing mechanism is easy to violate, in that a user might change the expiration date in the .lic file to postpone the license expiration, but you can use this example to create a more robust schema. For example, you might encrypt the license text and store it in a nonobvious location (including the registry).

A custom license provider is a class that derives from the abstract LicenseProvider class and overrides the virtual GetLicense method. This method is indirectly called by the LicenseManager.Validate method (in the custom control's constructor method) and receives several arguments that let you determine the name of the control or component in question, whether you're at design time or run time, and other pieces of information. The Windows Forms infrastructure expects the GetLicense method to return a license object if it's OK to use the custom control or component; otherwise, it returns Nothing or throws a LicenseException object. (You decide whether the method should return Nothing or throw the exception by inspecting the allowException argument passed to the GetLicense method.) Here's the implementation of the LicWindowsFileLicenseProvided class:

```
Class LicWindowsFileLicenseProvider
    Inherits LicenseProvider

    Public Overrides Function GetLicense(ByVal context As LicenseContext, _
        ByVal typ As System.Type, ByVal instance As Object, _
        ByVal allowExceptions As Boolean) As License

        ' This is the name of the control.
        Dim ctrlName As String = typ.FullName

        If context.UsageMode = LicenseUsageMode.Designtime Then
            ' We are in design mode.
            ' Check that there is a .lic file in Windows system directory.
            ' Build the full path of the .lic file.
            Dim filename As String = Environment.SystemDirectory() _
                & "\" & ctrlName & ".lic"
            ' This is the text that we expect at the beginning of file.
            Dim licenseText As String = ctrlName & " license expires on "
            Dim fs As System.IO.StreamReader
            Try
                ' Open and read the license file (throws exception if not found).
                fs = New System.IO.StreamReader(filename)
                ' Read its first line.
                Dim text As String = fs.ReadLine
                ' Throw if it doesn't match the expected text.
                If Not text.StartsWith(licenseText) Then Throw New Exception
                ' Parse the expiration date (which follows the expected text).
                Dim expireDate As Date = _
                    Date.Parse(text.Substring(licenseText.Length))
                ' Throw if license has expired.
                If Now > expireDate Then Throw New Exception
            Catch ex As Exception
```

```
                    ' Throws a LicenseException or just returns Nothing.
                    If allowExceptions Then
                        Throw New LicenseException(typ, instance, _
                            "Can't find design-time license for " & ctrlName)
                    Else
                        Return Nothing
                    End If
                Finally
                    ' In all cases, close the StreamReader.
                    If Not (fs Is Nothing) Then fs.Close()
                End Try

                ' If we get here, we can return a RuntimeLicense object.
                Return New DesignTimeLicense(Me, typ)
            Else
                ' We enforce no licensing at run time,
                ' so we always return a RunTimeLicense.
                Return New RuntimeLicense(Me, typ)
            End If
        End Function
End Class
```

In general, you should return two different license objects, depending on whether you're at design time or run time. (Otherwise, a malicious and clever user might use the run-time license at design time.) A license object is an instance of a class that derives from System.ComponentModel.License and overrides its LicenseKey and Dispose virtual methods. Here's a simple implementation of the DesignTimeLicense and RuntimeLicense classes referenced by the preceding code snippet. (These classes can be nested inside the LicWindowsFileLicenseProvider class.)

```
Class LicWindowsFileLicenseProvider
    ⋮
    ' Nested class for design-time license

    Public Class DesignTimeLicense
        Inherits License

        Private owner As LicWindowsFileLicenseProvider
        Private typ As Type

        Sub New(ByVal owner As LicWindowsFileLicenseProvider, ByVal typ As Type)
            Me.owner = owner
            Me.typ = typ
        End Sub

        Overrides ReadOnly Property LicenseKey() As String
            Get
                ' Just return the type name in this demo.
                Return typ.FullName
            End Get
        End Property
```

```
            Overrides Sub Dispose()
                ' There is nothing to do here.
            End Sub
    End Class


    ' Nested class for run-time license

    Public Class RuntimeLicense
        Inherits License

        Private owner As LicWindowsFileLicenseProvider
        Private typ As Type

        Sub New(ByVal owner As LicWindowsFileLicenseProvider, ByVal typ As Type)
            Me.owner = owner
            Me.typ = typ
        End Sub

        Overrides ReadOnly Property LicenseKey() As String
            Get
                ' Just return the type name in this demo.
                Return typ.FullName
            End Get
        End Property

        Overrides Sub Dispose()
            ' There is nothing to do here.
        End Sub
    End Class
End Class
```

Read the remarks in the demo project to see how to test the LicWindowsFileLicenseProvider class with the AddressControl custom control. Figure 18-13 shows the
kind of error message you see in Visual Studio if you attempt to load a form that contains a control for which you don't have a design-time license.

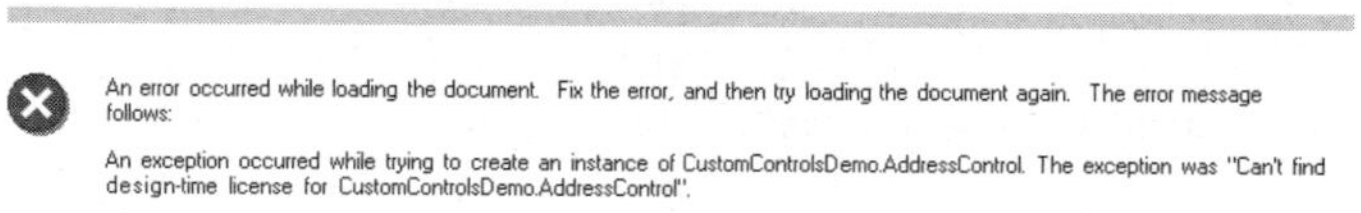

Figure 18-13   The error message that Visual Studio displays when you load a form containing
a control for which you don't have a design-time license

Hosting Custom Controls in Internet Explorer

Windows Forms controls have one more intriguing feature that I have yet to discuss:
you can host a Windows Forms control in Internet Explorer in much the same way that
you can use an ActiveX control, with an important improvement over ActiveX controls—Windows Forms controls don't require any registration on the client machine.
However, the .NET Framework must be installed on the client, so in practice you can
adopt this technique only for intranet installations.

You specify a Windows Forms control in an HTML page using a special <OBJECT> tag that contains a CLASSID parameter pointing to the DLL containing the control. For example, the following HTML page hosts an instance of the TextBoxEx control. You can see the effect in Figure 18-14.

```
<HTML><BODY>
<H2>Loading the TextBoxEx custom control in IE</H2>

Enter a 5-digit value:<BR>
<OBJECT ID="TextBoxEx1"
    CLASSID="/CustomControlDemo.dll#CustomControlDemo.TextBoxEx"
    HEIGHT=80 WIDTH="300" VIEWASTEXT>
        <PARAM NAME="Text" VALUE="12345">
</OBJECT>
<P><INPUT type="button" value="Clear Text" onClick="ClearText()">

<SCRIPT>
function ClearText() {
        TextBoxEx1.Text = "";
}
</SCRIPT>
</BODY></HTML>
```

The boldface portions show how you insert the control in the page, initialize its properties using the <PARAM> tag, and access its properties programmatically from a JScript function. The value of the CLASSID attribute is the path of the DLL hosting the control, followed by a pound sign (#) and the complete name of the control in question. In the preceding example, the DLL is in the root virtual directory, but it can be located anywhere in the virtual directory tree of Internet Information Services (IIS). When testing the preceding code, remember that you must deploy the HTML file in an IIS directory and access it from Internet Explorer using HTTP. Nothing happens if you display it by double-clicking the file from inside Windows Explorer.

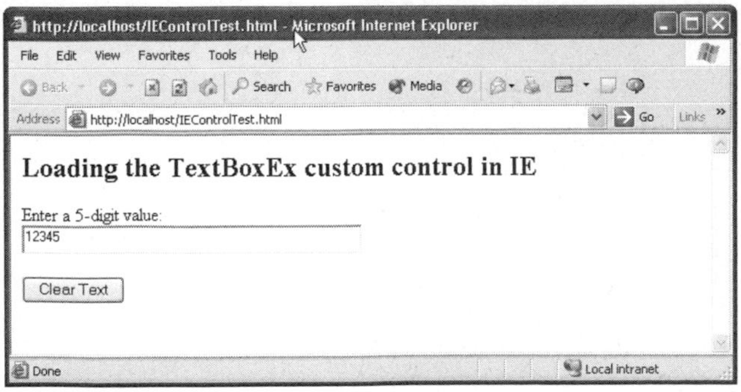

Figure 18-14   Hosting the TextBoxEx control in Internet Explorer 6

Using a control hosted in Internet Explorer has other limitations. For example, you can't use a control stored in the local machine's GAC and you can't use a CAB file to host multiple assemblies because Internet Explorer 6 is able to deal only with CAB files containing only one assembly. There are limitations also when accessing the control programmatically. For one, you can't access object properties (such as the Address property of the AddressControl sample described in this chapter) because the runtime creates a COM Callable Wrapper (CCW) to make the control visible to the script, but it doesn't create a CCW for dependent properties. (Read Chapter 30 for more details about the CCW.)

Finally, the IIS virtual directory containing the control must have its security set to Scripts only. Any other value, including Scripts and Executables, will prevent the control from loading. The code running in the control appears to the runtime as having been downloaded from the Internet; therefore, many operations won't be allowed unless you grant this assembly broader privileges. (You can learn more about these security-related limitations in Chapter 33.)

> **Note**   An ASP.NET page can check whether the client browser supports the .NET runtime by querying the HTTPRequest.Browser.ClrVersion property. A well-behaved ASP.NET application might use ActiveX controls, DHTML, or plain HTML if the browser isn't able to host Windows Forms controls.

At the end of our exploration of built-in controls, GDI+, and custom Windows Forms controls, you should be able to create truly functional and eye-catching Win32 applications. In the next chapter, you'll see how you can create even more powerful Win32 programs by coding against a few .NET components that have no user interface.

19 Advanced Win32 Techniques

Creating a Windows application involves more than just making a nice user interface with Windows Forms controls. The .NET Framework offers many nonvisual objects that you can use to empower your Win32 applications. In this chapter, we'll have a look at some of these objects, including

- The System.Environment class, to read information about the Windows operating system

- The Registry and RegistryKey classes, to read and write registry keys and values

- The SystemEvents class, to detect when a systemwide setting changes, such as the screen resolution or the system time

- The FileSystemWatcher component, to get a notification when a file or a directory is created, deleted, or modified

- The Process, ProcessModule, and ProcessThread components, to get information about running processes, their modules, and their threads

- The PerformanceCounter component, to read and write performance counters and list all the performance counters installed on a local or remote machine

- The EventLog component, to read existing entries in an event log on a local or remote machine

> **Note** To keep code as concise as possible, all the code samples in this chapter assume that the following Imports statements are used at the file or project level:
>
> ```
> Imports Microsoft.Win32
> Imports System.IO
> Imports System.Diagnostics
> ```

The Environment Class

The System.Environment class exposes several properties and methods that formerly were part of the Visual Basic language and that give you access to information related to the operating system—for example, the current directory:

```
' Display the current directory, then change it.
Console.WriteLine(Environment.CurrentDirectory)
Environment.CurrentDirectory = "c:\"
```

(You can also perform these tasks through the System.IO.Directory class.)

You can read environment variables (but not modify them) in three ways:

```
' Get the value of a single variable.
Console.WriteLine("Username=" & _
    Environment.GetEnvironmentVariable("USERNAME"))

' Expand a string that contains %variables%.
Dim msg As String = "CPU is %PROCESSOR_LEVEL%, " _
    & "revision is %PROCESSOR_REVISION%"
Console.WriteLine(environment.ExpandEnvironmentVariables(msg))

' Get a list of all environment variables and their values.
For Each de As DictionaryEntry In Environment.GetEnvironmentVariables
    Console.WriteLine("{0} = {1}", de.Key, de.Value)
Next
```

Several properties return information that wasn't available in Visual Basic 6, short of calling one or more Windows API functions, such as the system directory and the amount of memory allocated to the current process:

```
' Windows system directory
Console.WriteLine(Environment.SystemDirectory)
' Physical memory allocated to the current process
Console.WriteLine(Environment.WorkingSet)
```

The OSVersion property returns an OperatingSystem object, which in turn exposes properties such as Platform and Version:

```
Console.WriteLine(Environment.OSVersion.Platform)    ' => 2
    ' Platform = 2 means Windows NT/2000.
Console.WriteLine(Environment.OSVersion.Version)     ' => 5.0.2195.0
    ' Major version number = 5 means Windows 2000.
```

The Version property returns the version of the common language runtime under which the application is running:

```
' I run this code under .NET Framework 1.1 version.
Console.WriteLine("common language runtime version = {0}", Environment.Version)
    ' => 1.1.4322.573
```

Other properties return the name of the user who started the current thread, the network domain name associated with the current user, and the NETBios name of the current computer:

```
' Display information about the current user.
Console.WriteLine("UserName = {0}", Environment.UserName)
Console.WriteLine("UserDomain = {0}", Environment.UserDomainName)
Console.WriteLine("MachineName = {0}", Environ ment.MachineName)
```

The Exit method lets you exit the current application and return an error code to the operating system. This method is especially useful in console programs that are meant to be invoked from the command line and from batch files:

```
' Return error code 1 to the operating system.
Environment.Exit(1)
```

Finally, the GetCommandLineArgs method returns all the arguments passed to the application from the command line. This is the same array that you can receive in the Sub Main procedure. (See Chapter 2.)

The Registry and RegistryKey Classes

The Registry and RegistryKey classes belong to the Microsoft.Win32 namespace rather than to the System namespace because they're platform-specific classes that would be very difficult to port to non-Windows operating systems. As their name suggests, these classes provide an easy, object-oriented way to access the system registry. If you've ever played with the limited registry commands that Visual Basic 6 offers or the rather complex functions exposed by the Windows API, you'll surely appreciate the power and simplicity of the Registry and RegistryKey classes. However, keep in mind that these classes are provided only for interoperability with existing applications or for the gradual porting of legacy code—for example, to read what a legacy application wrote in the registry or to write data that a legacy application expects to find in the registry. Developers of applications for the .NET platform should avoid using the registry as a repository for their own data.

Reading Registry Keys

The only purpose of the Registry class is to expose seven read-only shared properties, each returning a RegistryKey object that represents one of the main registry subtrees (also known as hives).

```
' Define the RegistryKey objects for the registry hives.
Dim regClasses As RegistryKey = Registry.ClassesRoot
Dim regCurrConfig As RegistryKey = Registry.CurrentConfig
Dim regCurrUser As RegistryKey = Registry.CurrentUser
Dim regDynData As RegistryKey = Registry.DynData
Dim regLocalMachine As RegistryKey = Registry.LocalMachine
Dim regPerfData As RegistryKey = Registry.PerformanceData
Dim regUsers As RegistryKey = Registry.Users
```

Each RegistryKey object has three instance properties, whose names are entirely self-explanatory: Name, SubKeyCount, and ValueCount. If SubKeyCount is higher than 0, you can use the GetSubKeyNames method to return an array of strings that contains the names of all the subkeys, and then you can use the OpenSubKey method to retrieve the RegistryKey object corresponding to each subkey. If the key doesn't exist, this method returns Nothing without throwing an exception:

```
' Check whether Microsoft Word is installed on this computer
' by searching the HKEY_CLASSES_ROOT\Word.Application key.
Dim regWord As RegistryKey = regClasses.OpenSubKey("Word.Application")
```

```
If regWord Is Nothing Then
    Console.WriteLine("Microsoft Word isn't installed")
Else
    Console.WriteLine("Microsoft Word is installed")
End If
' Always close registry keys after using them.
regWord.Close
```

If the ValueCount property is greater than 0, you can use the GetValueNames method to retrieve an array of all the value names under the current key, and then you can use the GetValue method to retrieve the data associated with a given value. The following reusable routine peeks in the registry to retrieve the CLSID associated with the specified COM component:

```
' Return the CLSID of a COM component, or "" if not found.
Function GetCLSID(ByVal ProgId As String) As String
    ' Open the key associated with the ProgID.
    Dim regProgID As RegistryKey = Registry.ClassesRoot.OpenSubKey(ProgId)
    If Not (regProgID Is Nothing) Then
        ' If found, open the CLSID subkey.
        Dim regClsid As RegistryKey = regProgID.OpenSubKey("CLSID")
        If Not (regClsid Is Nothing) Then
            ' If found, get its default value. 2nd optional argument is the
            ' string to be returned if the specified value doesn't exist.
            ' (Returns an Object that we must convert to a string.)
            GetCLSID = CStr(regClsid.GetValue(""))
            regClsid.Close()
        End If
        regProgId.Close()
    End If
End Function

' A usage example: get the CLSID of the ADODB.Recordset object.
Console.WriteLine(GetCLSID("ADODB.Recordset"))
    ' => {00000514-0000-0010-8000-00AA006D2EA4}
```

Remember always to close any RegistryKey object that you opened using the OpenSubKey method or CreateSubKey (which I'll discuss shortly). You don't have to close the registry keys corresponding to the upper-level hives returned by shared methods of the Registry class.

The GetValue method returns an Object, which can contain a number, a string, an array of bytes, or Nothing if the value doesn't exist. If you want to tell a nonexistent value from a value whose associated data is a null string, you can pass a second argument, which is the data returned if the value hasn't been found:

```
' Return the data, or "<not found>" if the value isn't there.
Console.Write(regClsid.GetValue("", "<not found>"))
```

The following snippet demonstrates how these classes let you implement routines that extract information from the registry with few lines of code:

```
' Display information on all the COM components installed on this computer.
Sub DisplayCOMComponents()
    ' Iterate over the subkeys of the HKEY_CLASSES_ROOT\CLSID key.
    Dim regClsid As RegistryKey = Registry.ClassesRoot.OpenSubKey("CLSID")
    For Each clsid As String In regClsid.GetSubKeyNames
        ' Open the subkey.
        Dim regClsidKey As RegistryKey = regClsid.OpenSubKey(clsid)
        ' Get the ProgID. (This is the default value for this key.)
        Dim ProgID As String = CStr(regClsidKey.GetValue(""))
        ' Get the InProcServer32 key, which holds the DLL path.
        Dim regPath As RegistryKey = regClsidKey.OpenSubKey("InprocServer32")
        If regPath Is Nothing Then
            ' If not found, it isn't an in-process DLL server;
            ' let's see if it's an out-of-process EXE server.
            regPath = regClsidKey.OpenSubKey("LocalServer32")
        End If
        If Not (regPath Is Nothing) Then
            ' If either key has been found, retrieve its default value.
            Dim filePath As String = CStr(regPath.GetValue(""))
            ' Display all the relevant info gathered so far.
            Console.WriteLine(ProgId & " " & clsid & " -> " & filePath)
            regPath.Close()
        End If
        regClsidKey.Close()
    Next
End Sub
```

Figure 19-1 shows the output produced by a similar routine in the demo application, which displays the result in a TextBox control instead of in the console window.

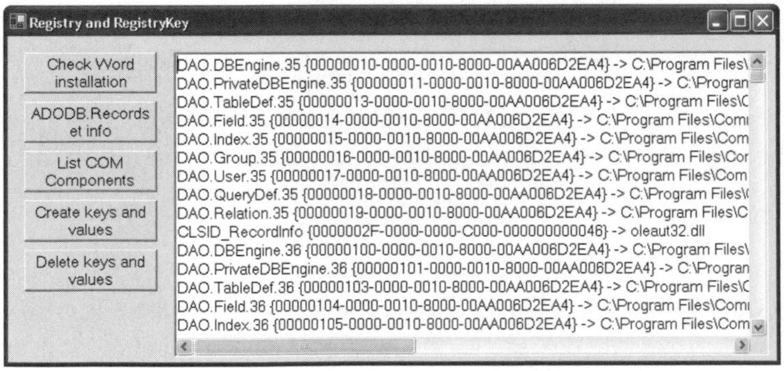

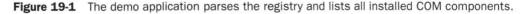

Figure 19-1   The demo application parses the registry and lists all installed COM components.

The RegistryKey class also lets you modify the registry—for example, by creating or deleting subkeys and values. When you plan to write data under a key, you must open it for writing, which you do by passing True as the second argument to the OpenSub-Key method:

```
' The following code snippets, taken together, add company/product
' keys under the HKEY_LOCALMACHINE\SOFTWARE key, as many Windows apps do.
```

```
' Open the HKEY_LOCALMACHINE\SOFTWARE key.
Dim regSoftware As RegistryKey = _
    Registry.LocalMachine.OpenSubKey("SOFTWARE", True)
```

The CreateSubKey method creates a registry key or opens an existing key. You don't need to specify that you're opening in writing mode:

```
' Add a key for the company name (or open it if it exists already).
Dim regCompany As RegistryKey = regSoftware.CreateSubKey("VB2TheMax")
' Add another key for the product name (or open it if it exists already).
Dim regProduct As RegistryKey = regCompany.CreateSubKey("VBMaximizer")
```

The SetValue method creates a new value and associates data with it. The second argument can be any data type that can be stored in the registry:

```
' Create three Values under the Product key.
regProduct.SetValue("Path", "C:\VBMaximizer\Bin")    ' A string value
regProduct.SetValue("MajorVersion", 2)               ' A number
regProduct.SetValue("MinorVersion", 1)               ' A number
```

You can delete values by using the DeleteValue method and delete keys by using the DeleteSubKey method:

```
' Delete the three values just added.
regProduct.DeleteValue("Path")
regProduct.DeleteValue("MajorVersion")
regProduct.DeleteValue("MinorVersion")
' Delete the Product and Company keys after closing them.
regProduct.Close()
regCompany.DeleteSubKey("VBMaximizer")
regCompany.Close()
regSoftware.DeleteSubKey("VB2TheMax")
```

The RegistryKey object also exposes the DeleteSubTreeKey, which deletes an entire registry subtree. So the previous code snippet could be replaced by the following one-liner:

```
regSoftware.DeleteSubKeyTree("VB2TheMax")
```

> **Warning**   Writing to the registry is a dangerous activity, and you must know very well what you're doing. Otherwise, you might damage sensitive data and be forced to reinstall one or more applications or the complete operating system. At a minimum, you should back up your registry before proceeding.

The SystemEvents Class

The Microsoft.Win32.SystemEvents class enables you to trap a few important systemwide events—such as the changing of display settings or the ending of the current user session—with a minimum amount of code on your part, especially when compared with the sophisticated window subclassing code you have to write under Visual Basic 6.

You never instantiate a SystemEvents object, and this class exposes only shared methods and events. Most of the events have self-explanatory names and receive a standard EventArgs object in their second argument: DisplaySettingChanged (screen resolution has changed), PaletteChanged (the color palette has changed), Installed-FontsChanged (user has added or removed fonts), TimeChanged (system time has changed), and LowMemory (the system is low on memory). As you know from Chapter 4, you can trap shared events by means of the AddHandler keyword:

```
AddHandler SystemEvents.DisplaySettingsChanged, AddressOf DisplaySettingsChanged
⋮
Private Sub DisplaySettingsChanged(ByVal sender As Object, ByVal e As EventArgs)
    Debug.WriteLine("Display settings have changed")
End Sub
```

The PowerModeChanged event fires when the user suspends or resumes the system, or when the power mode status of the operating system changes—for example, when battery is low or in the transition from AC to battery or vice versa. You can detect why the event was fired by inspecting the Mode property of the object passed to the second argument of your event handler:

```
Private Sub PowerModeChanged(ByVal sender As Object, ByVal e As PowerModeChangedEventArgs)
    Select Case e.Mode
        Case PowerModes.Suspend
            ' System is being suspended.
        Case PowerModes.Resume
            ' System is being resumed
        Case PowerModes.StatusChange
            ' Battery is low, or switching to/from AC.
    End Select
End Sub
```

When the current user's session is closing, you receive two events: SessionEnding and SessionEnded. The object passed to both events has a Reason property that lets you determine why the session is ending and can be Logoff or SystemShutdown. The object passed to SessionEnding also has a Cancel property that, if set to True, cancels the action of ending the session:

```
Private Sub SessionEnding(ByVal sender As Object, ByVal e As SessionEndingEventArgs)
    ' Reject system shutdown.
    If e.Reason = SessionEndReasons.SystemShutdown Then
        e.Cancel = True
    End If
End Sub
```

When one user preference is about to change, you receive two events: UserPreferenceChanging and UserPreferenceChanged. The objects passed to these events expose one property, Category, which is an enumerated value that reflects the type of the change—for example, General, Color, Mouse, or Power. There is no way to reject a change in user preferences, though.

When you're using the SystemEvents object, keep in mind that all its events are served by a system thread that is different from your application's main thread. This fact can have some important implications—for example, the fact that code in event handlers shouldn't access controls and forms.

The FileSystemWatcher Component

The System.IO.FileSystemWatcher component lets you monitor a directory or a directory tree and get a notification when something happens inside it—for example, when a file or a subdirectory is created, deleted, or renamed or when its attributes are changed. This component can be useful in many circumstances. For example, say that you're creating an application that automatically encrypts all the files stored in a given directory. Without this component, you should poll the directory at regular time intervals (typically using a Timer), but the FileSystemWatcher component makes this task easy. Unfortunately, this component works only on Microsoft Windows Me, Windows NT, Windows 2000, Windows XP, and Windows 2003 Server. Another good example of how this component can be useful is when you cache a text or an XML file in memory to access its contents quickly, but need to reload it when another application modifies the data.

Initializing a FileSystemWatcher Component

You can create a FileSystemWatcher component in either of two ways: by means of code or by dragging it from the Components tab of the Toolbox to the form's component tray area. There's no noticeable difference in performance or flexibility, so any method is fine. The demo application uses a component in the form's component tray area, which I have renamed *fsw* (see Figure 19-2), but creating it through code is equally simple:

```
' Use WithEvents to be able to trap events from this object.
Dim WithEvents fsw As New FileSystemWatcher()
```

Before you use this component, you must initialize at least its Path, IncludeSubdirectories, Filter, and NotifyFilter properties. The Path property is the name of the directory that you want to watch; notice that you're notified of changes occurring inside this directory, but not of changes to this directory's attributes (such as its Hidden or ReadOnly attribute).

The IncludeSubdirectories property should be set to False if you want to be notified of any change inside the specified directory only, or to True if you want to watch for changes in the entire directory tree whose root is the directory specified by the Path property.

The Filter property lets you specify which files you're interested in; for example, use *.* to get notifications about all the files in the directory or *.txt to watch only files with the .txt extension. The default value for this property is a null string, which means all files (same as *.*).

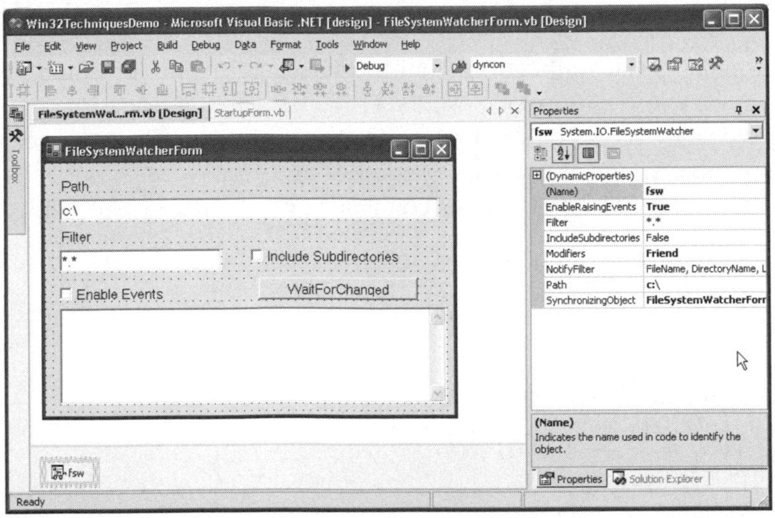

Figure 19-2 The demo application lets you experiment with the FileSystemWatcher component.

The NotifyFilter property is a bit-coded value that specifies which kind of modifications are announced by means of the component's Changed event. This property can be a combination of one or more NotifyFilters enumerated values: Attributes, CreationTime, DirectoryName, FileName, LastAccess, LastWrite, Security, and Size. The initial value of this property is LastWrite Or FileName Or DirectoryName, so by default you don't get notifications when an attribute is changed.

Here's an example of how you can set up a FileSystemWatcher component to watch for events in the C:\Windows directory and its subdirectories:

```
Dim WithEvents fsw As New FileSystemWatcher()
⋮
fsw.Path = "c:\Windows"
fsw.IncludeSubdirectories = True    ' Watch sudirectories.
fsw.Filter = "*.dll"                ' Watch only DLL files.
' Add attribute changes to the list of changes that can fire events.
fsw.NotifyFilter = fsw.NotifyFilter Or NotifyFilters.Attributes
' Enable event notification.
fsw.EnableRaisingEvents = True
```

Getting Notifications

Once you've set up the component correctly, you can get a notification when something happens. You can achieve this by writing event handlers or using the Wait-ForChanged method.

Events

The simplest way to get a notification from the FileSystemWatcher component is by writing handlers for the component's events. However, events don't fire until you set EnableRaisingEvents to True. The Created, Deleted, and Changed events receive a FileSystemEventArgs object, which exposes two important properties: Name (the name of the file that has been created, deleted, or changed) and FullPath (its complete path):

```
Private Sub fsw_Created(ByVal sender As Object, _
    ByVal e As FileSystemEventArgs) Handles fsw.Created
    LogMessage("File created: " & e.FullPath)
End Sub

Private Sub fsw_Deleted(ByVal sender As Object, _
    ByVal e As FileSystemEventArgs) Handles fsw.Deleted
    LogMessage("File deleted: " & e.FullPath)
End Sub

Private Sub fsw_Changed(ByVal sender As Object, _
    ByVal e As FileSystemEventArgs) Handles fsw.Changed
    LogMessage("File changed: " & e.FullPath)
End Sub

' Add a string to the txtLog TextBox control.
Sub LogMessage(ByVal msg As String)
    txtLog.AppendText(msg & ControlChars.CrLf)
End Sub
```

The FileSystemEventArgs object also exposes a ChangeType enumerated property, which tells whether the event is a create, delete, or change event. You can use this property to use a single handler to manage all three events, as in this code:

```
Private Sub fsw_All(ByVal sender As Object, _
    ByVal e As FileSystemEventArgs) _
    Handles fsw.Changed, fsw.Created, fsw.Deleted
    LogMessage(String.Format("File changed: {0} ({1})", _
        e.FullPath, e.ChangeType))
End Sub
```

Notice that the Changed event receives no information about the type of change that fired the event (such as a change in the file's LastWrite date or attributes). Finally, the Renamed event receives a RenamedEventArgs object, which exposes two additional properties: OldName (the name of the file before being renamed) and OldFullPath (its complete path):

```
Private Sub fsw_Renamed(ByVal sender As Object, _
    ByVal e As RenamedEventArgs) Handles fsw.Renamed
    LogMessage("File renamed: " & e.OldFullPath & " => " & e.FullPath)
End Sub
```

You can also have multiple FileSystemWatcher components forward their events to the same event handler. In this case, you can use the first argument to detect which specific component raised the event.

The FileSystemWatcher component raises one event for each file and for each action on the file. For example, if you delete 10 files, you receive 10 distinct Deleted events. If you move 10 files from one directory to another, you receive 10 Deleted events from the source directories and 10 Created events from the destination directory.

The WaitForChanged Method

If your application doesn't perform any operation other than waiting for changes in the specified path, you can write simpler and more efficient code by using the Wait-ForChanged method. This method is synchronous in the sense that it doesn't return until a file change is detected or the (optional) timeout expires. This method returns a WaitForChangedResult structure, whose fields let you determine whether the timeout elapsed, the type of the event that occurred, and the name of the involved file:

```
' Create a *new* FileSystemWatcher component with values from
' the txtPath and txtFilter controls.
Dim tmpFsw As New FileSystemWatcher(txtPath.Text, txtFilter.Text)
' Wait max 10 seconds for any file event.
Dim res As WaitForChangedResult
res = tmpFsw.WaitForChanged(WatcherChangeTypes.All, 10000)

' Check whether the operation timed out.
If res.TimedOut Then
    LogMessage("10 seconds have elapsed without an event")
Else
    LogMessage("Event: " & res.Name & " (" & res.ChangeType.ToString & ")")
End If
```

The WaitForChanged method traps changes only in the directory pointed to by the Path property and ignores the IncludeSubdirectories property. For this reason, the WaitForChangedResult structure includes a Name field but not a FullPath field. The first argument you pass to the WaitForChanged method lets you further restrict the kind of file operation you want to intercept:

```
' Pause the application until the c:\temp\temp.dat file is deleted.
Dim tmpFsw2 As New FileSystemWatcher("c:\temp", "temp.dat")
tmpFsw2.WaitForChanged(WatcherChangeTypes.Deleted)
```

Buffer Overflows

You should be aware of potential problems when too many events fire in a short time. The FileSystemWatcher component uses an internal buffer to keep track of file system actions so that events can be raised for each one of them even if the application can't serve them fast enough. By default, this internal buffer is 8 KB long and can store about 160 events. Each event takes 16 bytes, plus 2 bytes for each character in the filename. (Filenames are stored as Unicode characters.) If you anticipate a lot of file activity, you should increase the size of the buffer by setting the InternalBufferSize to a larger value. The size should be an integer multiple of the operating system's page size (4 KB under Windows 2000 and later versions). Alternatively, you can use the NotifyFilter property to limit the number of change operations that fire the Changed event or set IncludeSub-directories to False if you don't really need to monitor an entire directory tree. (Use multiple FileSystemWatcher components to monitor individual subdirectories if you aren't interested in monitoring all the subdirectories under a given path.)

You can't use the Filter property to prevent the internal buffer's overflow because this property filters out files only after they've been added to the buffer. When the internal buffer overflows, you get an Error event:

```
Private Sub fsw_Error(ByVal sender As Object, _
    ByVal e As ErrorEventArgs) Handles fsw.Error
    LogMessage("FileSystemWatcher error")
End Sub
```

Troubleshooting

By default, the Created, Deleted, Renamed, and Changed events run in a thread taken from the system thread pool. (See Chapter 12 for more information about the thread pool.) Because Windows Forms controls aren't thread safe, you should avoid accessing any control or the form itself from inside the FileSystemWatcher component's event handlers. If you find this limitation unacceptable, you should assign a Windows Form control to the component's SynchronizingObject property, as in this code:

```
' Use the Form object as the synchronizing object.
fsw.SynchronizingObject = Me
```

The preceding code ensures that all event handlers run in the same thread that serves the form itself. When you create a FileSystemWatcher component using the Visual Studio .NET designer, this property is automatically assigned the hosting form object.

Here are a few more tips about the FileSystemWatcher component and the problems you might find when using it:

■ The FileSystemWatcher component starts raising events when the Path property is nonempty and the EnableRaisingEvents property is True. You can also prevent the component from raising unwanted events during the initialization phase by bracketing your setup statements between a call to the BeginInit method and a call to the EndInit method. (This is the approach used by the Visual Studio designer.)

■ As I mentioned before, this component works only on Windows Me, Windows NT, Windows 2000, Windows XP, and Windows 2003 Server. It raises an error when it points to a path on machines running earlier versions of the operating system. Remote machines must have one of these operating systems to work properly, but you can't monitor a remote Windows NT system from another Windows NT machine. You can use UNC-based directory names only on Windows 2000 or later systems. The FileSystemWatcher component doesn't work on CD-ROM and DVD drives because their contents can't change.

- In some cases, you might get multiple Created events, depending on how a file is created and on the application that creates it. For example, when you create a new file with Notepad, you see the following sequence of events: Created, Deleted, Created, and Changed. (The first event pair fires because Notepad checks whether the file exists by attempting to create it.)

- A change in a file can generate an extra event in its parent directory as well because the directory maintains information about the files it contains (their size, last write date, and so on).

- If the directory pointed to by the Path property is renamed, the FileSystemWatcher component continues to work correctly. However, in this case, the Path property returns the old directory name, so you might get an error if you use it. (This happens because the component references the directory by its handle, which doesn't change if the directory is renamed.)

- If you create a directory inside the path being watched and the IncludeSubdirectories property is True, the new subdirectory is watched as well.

- When a large file is created in the directory, you might not be able to read the entire file immediately because it's still owned by the process that's writing data to it. You should protect any access to the original file with a Try block and, if an exception is thrown, attempt the operation again some milliseconds later.

- When the user deletes a file in a directory, a new file is created in the Recycle Bin directory.

The Process Component

The System.Diagnostics.Process component lets you start and stop processes on the local computer and query a running process for information (such as the names of its modules and the number of its threads) on either the local or a remote computer. You can use the Process component on any Windows platform, but you must have sufficient rights to stop a process or query it for information.

Running and Stopping a Process

You can create a Process component by dragging the corresponding item on the Components tab of the Toolbox or by instantiating it by means of code. In the following code samples, I'll follow the latter approach because it's the most frequently used in real-world applications.

Starting a Process

Creating a new Process component doesn't create or start a new process on the local computer. You should think of this component as a means through which your application can start a new process or retrieve information from a running process.

Before you start a new process, you must set the StartInfo property. This property is itself an object (of the ProcessStartInfo class) and exposes members such as Filename (the name of the executable file), WorkingDirectory (the initial directory), and Arguments (a string passed to the executable). Once all the necessary information is in place, you can actually run the other application by using the Start method:

```
Dim proc As New Process()
' Prepare to run Notepad and load C:\Autoexec.bat in it.
proc.StartInfo.FileName = "Notepad.exe"
' (Change the following statement to match your system.)
proc.StartInfo.WorkingDirectory = "c:\windows"
proc.StartInfo.Arguments = "c:\autoexec.bat"
' Run it.
proc.Start()
```

A great feature of the Process component is its ability to run the application associated with a data file so that you can simulate the action that occurs when the end user double-clicks on a file in Windows Explorer. In this case, you specify a document file in the FileName member of the StartInfo property and ensure that the UseShellExecute property is True:

```
' Use an OpenFileDialog control to ask the user for a data file,
' and load it in the application associated with that extension.
OpenFileDialog1.CheckFileExists = True
OpenFileDialog1.Filter = "All Files|*.*"
If OpenFileDialog1.ShowDialog = DialogResult.OK Then
    proc = New Process()
    proc.StartInfo.FileName = OpenFileDialog1.FileName
    proc.StartInfo.UseShellExecute = True
    ' In case no application is associated with this extension
    Try
        proc.Start()
    Catch ex As Exception
        MessageBox.Show(ex.Message, "Error")
    End Try
End If
```

You can also start a process by using the Process.Start shared method, which takes only two arguments (the name of the file and the command-line arguments) and returns the Process object associated with the application being launched:

```
Dim proc As Process = Process.Start("Notepad.exe", "c:\autoexec.bat")
```

Another, less obvious way to use the Start method is for displaying a Web page inside the browser:

```
Dim proc As Process = Process.Start("Notepad.exe", "http://www.vb2themax.com")
```

If the process you've started has a graphical user interface, you can use the WaitForInputIdle method to pause the current application until the launched process enters the idle state and is therefore able to process other messages. For example, you should use the WaitForInputIdle method before sending keystrokes to the other application:

```
' Run Notepad on an empty file.
proc = Process.Start("Notepad.exe")
' Wait until its main window is ready to receive keystrokes.
proc.WaitForInputIdle()
SendKeys.Send("Hello from VB.NET")
```

Setting Other Startup Properties

You can decide whether you want Windows to display its standard error dialog box if the executable pointed to by FileName can't be found or can't run for some other reason. If you're loading a document and no application has been registered for that extension, the standard error dialog box is replaced by the Open With dialog box, which lets the user select the application that should open the data file. You enable this feature by setting the ErrorDialog property to True and ErrorDialogParentHandle to the handle of the parent form, and by ensuring that the UseShellExecute property is True:

```
proc.StartInfo.ErrorDialog = True
proc.StartInfo.ErrorDialogParentHandle = Me.Handle
proc.StartInfo.UseShellExecute = True
Try
    proc.Start()
Catch ex As Exception
    ' No need to display an error message in case of error.
End Try
```

The ProcessStartInfo class exposes many other interesting properties. For example, you can enumerate all the environment variables that the child process is going to inherit from the current process (and even create new ones) by means of the Environment-Variables property:

```
For Each de As DictionaryEntry In proc.StartInfo.EnvironmentVariables
    Debug.WriteLine(de.Key.ToString & "=" & de.Value.ToString)
Next
```

The WindowStyle enumerated property determines the state of the child process's main window and can be Normal, Minimized, Maximized, or Hidden.

Stopping a Process

You can terminate the application associated with a Process component in two ways: by calling the CloseMainWindow method or by invoking the Kill method. The former method is the better way because it simulates the user's action of closing the application main window and so gives the application a chance to save data and release resources in an orderly fashion:

```
proc.CloseMainWindow()
```

The latter method abruptly terminates an application, so it might cause data loss; however, it's the only way to stop an application without a graphical user interface that isn't responding. You can determine whether an application isn't responding by using the Responding property, so you might use Kill only when strictly necessary, as the following code snippet shows:

```
If proc.Responding Then
    ' The application is responding: CloseMainWindow should be OK.
    proc.CloseMainWindow()
Else
    proc.Kill()
End If
```

In a real application, however, you should always enclose a call to the CloseMainWindow or Kill method in a Try block because they aren't guaranteed to work and might throw an exception.

You can learn whether a process has exited by querying the HasExited read-only property. If a process has terminated, you can determine when it ended by querying the ExitTime property:

```
If proc.HasExited Then
    lblStatus.Text = "Process terminated at " & proc.ExitTime
End If
```

Redirecting the Input, Output, and Error Channels

As I mentioned earlier, the UseShellExecute property determines whether you should start the process by using the Windows shell. This property must be True (the default value) to start the application associated with a document or to display the standard error message if the application can't run. By setting this property to False, however, you can redirect the standard input, output, and error channels of the child process, which is useful when you launch command-line system commands or utilities. Depending on which channels you want to redirect, you must also set the RedirectStandardInput, RedirectStandardOutput, or RedirectStandardError member of the StartInfo property to True, and you must set the CreateNoWindow member to True to suppress the creation of a console window:

```
' Search all the lines in C:\AUTOEXEC.BAT that contain an "x" character.
proc.StartInfo.FileName = "find ""x"""
proc.StartInfo.Arguments = "c:\autoexec.bat"
' UseShellExecute must be False.
proc.StartInfo.UseShellExecute = False
' Redirect the standard output channel.
proc.StartInfo.RedirectStandardOutput = True
' Suppress the creation of the console window.
proc.StartInfo.CreateNoWindow = True
proc.Start()
```

When the process terminates, you can read the output it sent to its standard output channel by using the Process component's StandardOutput property, which returns a StreamReader object that you can use to read the output data:

```
' Get the StreamReader that points to output data.
Dim sr As StreamReader = proc.StandardOutput
' Display the output data in a TextBox control.
txtOutput.Text = sr.ReadToEnd
' Close the stream.
sr.Close()
```

Similarly, the StandardError property returns a StreamReader object that lets you read any error message, whereas the StandardInput property returns a StreamWriter object that lets you write data to the standard input channel of the child process.

Querying a Process for Information

The Process class exposes a few shared methods that enable you to get a reference to a process that is already running on the local or a remote computer. Once you have a reference to the other process, you can stop it or query for its properties.

Getting a Reference to a Running Process

The simplest way to get a reference to a running process is by using the Process.GetCurrentProcess shared method, which returns the Process object that represents the current application:

```
Dim currProc As Process = Process.GetCurrentProcess
```

You can easily list all the processes running on the local computer by using the Process.GetProcesses shared method, which returns an array of Process objects. For example, the following code fills a ListBox control with all the Process objects and displays the name of each process:

```
 ' Display ProcessName property in the list area.
lstProcesses.DisplayMember = "ProcessName"
' Load info on all running processes in the ListBox control.
lstProcesses.Items.Clear()
For Each p As Process In Process.GetProcesses
    lstProcesses.Items.Add(p)
Next
```

The GetProcessById shared method returns the Process object associated with the process with a given ID. (The process ID uniquely identifies a process on a given system.) The Process.GetProcessByName shared method returns an array of Process objects associated with the processes with the specified name. (The process name is the name of the executable file without its path and extension.) Because you can have multiple processes with a given name, the Process.GetProcessByName method returns an array.

You can use this method to kill the current application if there is another instance of the same application already running:

```
Dim currProc As Process = Process.GetCurrentProcess
Dim processes() As Process = Process.GetProcessesByName(currProc.ProcessName)
For Each proc As Process In processes
    If proc.Id <> currProc.Id Then
        AppActivate(proc.Id)
        Application.Exit()
    End If
Next
```

In a variation of this technique, before exiting you might pass the previously running instance the string that the current instance has received on the command line, by using one of the inter-communication technologies available (.NET remoting, for example). The GetProcesses, GetProcessById, and GetProcessByName methods are overloaded and can take an extra String argument, which is taken as the name of the remote computer on which the processes that interest you are running.

Getting Information About Processes

The Process class exposes many instance properties that make it easy to collect information about a running process, once you've retrieved a reference to a running process using one of the methods outlined in the preceding section. The meaning of most properties should be clear, for example ProcessName, ID, Handle (the process handle), MachineName, MainWindowTitle, and MainWindowHandle.

The StartTime property returns the time when the process was started. If the process has ended, the HasExited property returns True and you can query the ExitTime and the ExitCode properties. The UserProcessorTime and PrivilegedProcessorTime properties return a TimeSpan value that indicates the amount of CPU time spent by the process running the application code and the operating system code, respectively. The TotalProcessorTime property returns the sum of the last two properties.

Three properties are related to the process' priority. BasePriority is the base priority assigned by Windows—that is, the starting priority of the process threads, and can be one of the following values: 4 (idle), 8 (normal), 13 (high), or 24 (real-time). You can change the priority by assigning a value to the PriorityClass enumerated value, which can be Idle, BelowNormal, Normal, AboveNormal, High, or RealTime. You can also boost the process' priority when its main window gets the input focus by setting the PriorityBoostEnabled property to True.

Finally, a group of properties return information on how the process uses memory and the working set: VirtualMemorySize, PrivateMemorySize, PagedMemorySize, PagedSystemMemorySize, NonpagedSystemMemorySize, PeakVirtualMemorySize, PeakPagedMemorySize, WorkingSet, and PeakWorkingSet. The MinWorkingSet and MaxWorkingSet properties can be assigned to set a limit on the size of the application's working set. (Read the MSDN documentation for more information about these properties.)

When querying a process for information, you should bear in mind that dynamic data—such as WorkingSct, VirtualMemorySize, and the list of threads and processes—is loaded the first time you read any property and is then cached in the Process object. The information that you read might therefore be stale and you might want to issue a Refresh method before reading process data. Also, you should use a Try…Catch block to work around exceptions that some properties might raise in certain circumstances. For example, the BasePriority, PriorityClass, HandleCount, and Responding properties aren't available under Windows 95 and Windows 98 if the process wasn't started from the Windows shell.

Getting Information About Threads

The Threads property returns a collection of ProcessThread objects, each one representing a thread of the specified process. The ProcessThread class exposes several properties that are useful for diagnostic purposes.

The Id property returns an integer value that uniquely identifies the thread in the system; because the system reuses thread IDs, however, the uniqueness is guaranteed only during the thread's lifetime. The ThreadState read-only property tells which state the thread currently is in; it can be Initialized (not yet running), Ready, Running, StandBy, Wait, Terminated, Transition (switching between states), or Unknown.

If a thread is in a wait state, you can query its WaitReason property to determine what the thread is waiting for. The most common wait states are Suspended, Executive (waiting for the scheduler), UserRequest (waiting for a user request), PageIn (waiting for a virtual memory page to arrive in memory), and PageOut (waiting for a virtual memory page to be written to disk).

Most other properties of the ProcessThread class are similar to properties of the same name as the Process class. For example, you can check the processor time spent by a thread by means of the UserProcessorTime, PrivilegedProcessorTime, and TotalProcessorTime properties. You can check the thread priority by using the BasePriority and CurrentPriority properties and even change it by using the PriorityLevel and PriorityBoostEnabled properties. Finally, you can learn when a thread started its execution by means of its StartTime property, and you can get the address of its startup function by using the StartAddress property.

Getting Information About Modules

The Modules property returns a collection of all the modules loaded in the address spaces of a process. This list includes the main module (typically the .exe file that started the process, represented by the value returned by the Process.MainModule property) and all the DLLs that the process has loaded. Each element in this collection is a ProcessModule object, which exposes properties such as ModuleName (the name of the module), BaseAddress (an IntPtr value that tells where in memory the module is loaded), ModuleMemorySize (the amount of bytes of memory allocated for the module), and EntryPointAddress (an IntPtr value that specifies the address of the function that runs when the system loads the module).

The FileVersionInfo property returns a FileVersionInfo object that exposes detailed information about the module's file:

- The FileVersionNumber property returns the complete version number as a string. You can also check individual portions of the version number by using the FileMajorPart, FileMinorPart, FileBuildPart, and FilePrivatePart properties. The Language property returns the default language string for the version information block.

- The ProductName property returns the name of the product distributed with a file. You can learn more about this product by querying the ProductVersion, Product-MajorPart, ProductMinorPart, ProductBuildPart, and ProductPrivatePart properties.

- The CompanyName property returns the name of the company that produced this file. You can also query the LegalCopyright and LegalTrademarks properties for additional information about who legally owns this file.

- The IsDebug property returns True if an executable file has been compiled with debug information. The IsPatched property returns True if the file has been modified and isn't identical to the original shipping file.

- You can get additional information about the file by means of the OriginalFilename, Comments, and FileDescription properties.

The FileVersionInfo class has no instance methods (other than those inherited by System.Object) and has one shared method, GetVersionInfo, that lets you retrieve version information on any file, not just process module files.

```
Dim fvi As FileVersionInfo
fvi = FileVersionInfo.GetVersionInfo("c:\myapp.exe")
Console.WriteLine("Version {0}.{1}", fvi.FileMajorPart, fvi.FileMinorPart)
```

The companion code for this book includes an advanced reporting utility that scans the local system and displays detailed information about running processes, their threads, and their modules. (See Figure 19-3.)

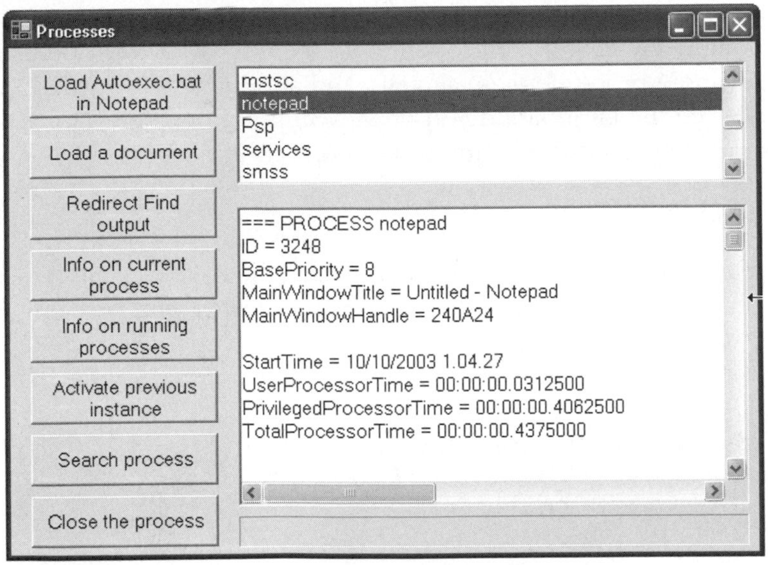

Figure 19-3 Displaying detailed information about all running processes, their threads, and their modules

Waiting for a Process to End

You can wait for a process to terminate with just one call to the WaitForExit method of the Process class, or you can wait until the associated Process object raises an Exited event.

Using the WaitForExit Method

Using the WaitForExit method is a breeze, as this code snippet demonstrates:

```
' Run Notepad and load a file in it.
Dim proc As Process = Process.Start("notepad.exe", "c:\autoexec.bat")
' Wait until Notepad exits and display its exit code.
proc.WaitForExit()
MessageBox.Show("Notepad exited. Exit code is " & proc.ExitCode.ToString)
```

You can also pass an optional timeout in milliseconds. In this case, the method returns True if the process exited and False if it's still running. This overloaded variation is useful when you don't want to block the calling thread until the other process terminates:

```
Do Until proc.WaitForExit(1000)
    ' Do something every 1 second while waiting.
    ⋮
Loop
```

When a process exits, you can query its ExitCode and ExitTime properties. Because the process isn't running any longer, all properties—except these two properties and the HasExited and Handle properties—are invalid and shouldn't be queried. Better yet, after you've collected the information you need, you should call the Close method to release the resources associated with the Process object.

Using the Exited Event

Instead of polling for process termination, you can trap the Exited event. However, you must explicitly enable this event by setting the EnableRaisingEvent property to True:

```
Dim WithEvents proc As Process

Sub StartNotepad()
    proc = Process.Start("notepad.exe", "c:\autoexec.bat")
    proc.EnableRaisingEvents = True
End Sub

Private Sub proc_Exited(ByVal sender As Object, ByVal e As EventArgs) _
    Handles proc.Exited
    MessageBox.Show("Notepad has exited. Exit code = " _
        & proc.ExitCode.ToString)
End Sub
```

You can trap events from both the processes that you started and from Process objects that represent running processes. In the latter case, you probably want to use dynamic event handlers because you don't know in advance how many processes you're going to monitor:

```
Sub ListProcesses()
    ' This is necessary because some processes might prevent your
    ' setting the EnableRaisingEvents property to True.
    On Error Resume Next

    ' Load info on all running process in the ListBox control.
    lstProcesses.DisplayMember = "ProcessName"
    lstProcesses.Items.Clear()
    For Each p As Process In Process.GetProcesses
        lstProcesses.Items.Add(p)
        ' Bind each element to the event handler.
        AddHandler p.Exited, AddressOf Process_Exited
        p.EnableRaisingEvents = True
    Next
End Sub

Private Sub Process_Exited(ByVal sender As Object, ByVal e As EventArgs)
    ' Get a reference to the process.
    Dim proc As Process = DirectCast(sender, Process)
    MessageBox.Show(String.Format( _
        "Process {0} has exited - Exit code is {1}", proc.Id, proc.ExitCode)
End Sub
```

When you attach multiple Process objects to the same event handler, you don't have an immediate way to determine which process has exited because when the Exited event fires, only a few properties can be queried—namely, Id, ExitCode, and ExitTime. To get more informative data, such as the name of the process that terminated, you should maintain all the (ID, name) pairs of values in an Hashtable object so that you can easily retrieve the name of a process from its Id property.

The PerformanceCounter Component

Performance counters are values that the operating system or individual applications set whenever something relevant occurs. (Performance counters are supported under the Windows NT, Windows 2000, Windows XP, and Windows 2003 Server platforms.) Examples of common performance counters are the number of processes running in the system, the number of file write operations per second, and the number of lock requests per second in SQL Server. You can even read performance counters on a remote machine if you're granted sufficient permissions to do so.

Introduction to Performance Counters

Classes in the .NET Framework let you read the value of existing performance counters and create your own counters as well. If your application creates and updates one or more performance counters, you can then use standard tools—such as the Performance utility (see Figure 19-4)—to monitor the performance of your code. Or you can create another .NET application to periodically check the performance counters of your main application, create logs, and maybe automatically fine-tune one or more critical settings while the application is running on the end user's machine.

Categories, Counters, and Instances

A performance counter is completely identified by its category, name, and instance. A performance counter category is useful for gathering related counters—for example, the Memory category includes all the counters related to memory management, such as Page Reads/sec, Committed Bytes, and Page Faults/sec. Windows comes with several built-in categories, such as Cache, Memory, Physical Disk, Processor, System, and Thread. Many applications, especially applications that run as services, add one or more categories—for example, the Active Server Pages category, the MSMQ Queue category, and the SQL Server: SQL Statistics category. (SQL Server and a few other applications add many categories.)

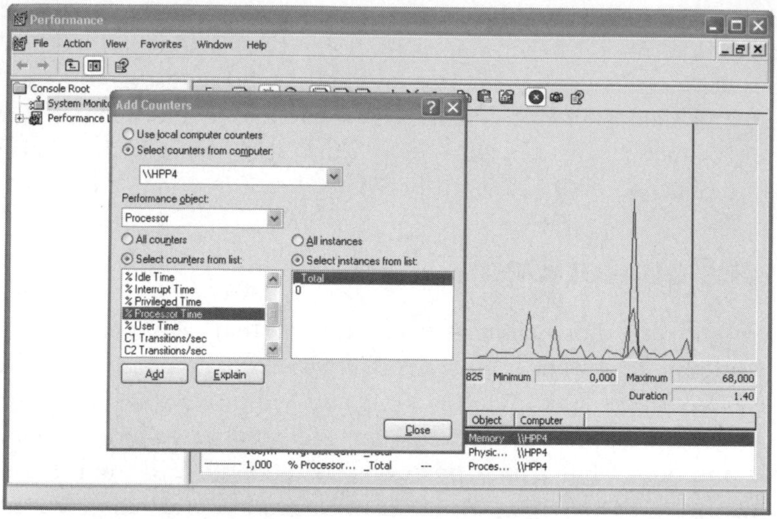

Figure 19-4 The Performance utility

A category might expose multiple instances for each performance counter. For example, the counters in the Processor category have multiple instances, each one associated with an individual CPU. These instances enable you to check values and statistics for each distinct processor, such as % Processor Time, % User Time, and Interrupts/sec. (The Processor category also exposes a _Total_ instance, which lets you read values averaged on all the installed CPUs.) Similarly, the counters in the Process category have multiple instances, one for each running process, plus a _Total_ instance that averages all processes.

Other categories don't expose instances because it doesn't make any sense to do so. This is the case with categories such as Cache, Indexing Service, Memory, Server, and most SQL Server categories.

You can browse the properties of all installed performance counters by expanding the Performance Counters sub-tree in the Server Explorer window, right-clicking on a specific category, and selecting the View Category menu command.

You can create a PerformanceCounter object at design time, either by dragging a specific performance counter from the Server Explorer window or by dragging a Performance-Counter element from the Components tab in the Toolbox. In both cases, you end up with an object in the component tray area and you can read or modify its CategoryName, CounterName, InstanceName, and MachineName properties in the Properties window. In the examples that follow, however, I'll create the counter via code at run time.

.NET Performance Counters

The .NET Framework creates and manages several categories and counters, the most interesting of which are summarized in Table 19-1. (This table doesn't include ASP.NET counters, which are described in the "ASP.NET Performance Counters" section of Chapter 27.) For a detailed description of these counters and for the complete list of all the available .NET counters, see the .NET Platform SDK.

Table 19-1   Partial List of .NET CLR Performance Counters

Category	Counter	Description
.NET CLR Exceptions	# of Exceps Thrown	Total number of exceptions being thrown. Exceptions should occur only in rare situations, not in the normal control flow of the program.
	# of Exceps Thrown/sec	Rate at which exceptions are being thrown.
.NET CLR Interop	# of CCWs	Current number of existing COM–Callable Wrappers (CCWs). A CCW wraps a CLR class and allows it to be called from COM.
	# of marshalling	Number of times marshaling is done for arguments and return values. Custom marshaling is not counted.
.NET CLR Jit	# of Methods Jitted	Number of methods JIT-compiled.
	% Time in Jit	Percentage of total time spent in the JIT compiler since the last sample.
	Total # of IL Bytes Jitted	Total number of IL bytes JIT-compiled since the beginning of the application.
.NET CLR Loading	% Time Loading	Percentage of execution time spent loading assemblies, application domains, classes, etc.
	Current appdomains	Current appdomains loaded in this application.
	Current assemblies	Current assemblies loaded in this application.
	Current Classes Loaded	Current classes loaded in all appdomains.
	Total # of Load Failures	Total number of classes that failed to load since the beginning of the application's execution.
.NET CLR LocksAnd Threads	# of current logical Threads	Total number of existing logical threads created by the runtime. Some of these might not have a physical thread associated.
	# of current physical Threads	Total number of native OS threads created by the runtime.
	Contention Rate/sec	Rate at which threads in the runtime unsuccessfully attempt to acquire a lock.

Table 19-1   Partial List of .NET CLR Performance Counters *(continued)*

Category	Counter	Description
	Current Queue Length	Average number of threads currently waiting to acquire a lock.
	Queue Length Peak	Average peak number of threads that waited to acquire a lock.
.NET CLR Memory	# Bytes in all Heaps	Total bytes in heaps for generation 0, 1, and 2 and from the large object heap. This indicates how much memory the garbage collector is using to store allocated objects.
	# Gen 0 Collections	Number of collections of generation 0 (youngest) objects.
	# Gen 1 Collections	Number of collections of generation 1 objects.
	# Gen 2 Collections	Number of collections of generation 2 (oldest) objects.
	% Time in GC	Percentage of elapsed time that was spent in doing a Garbage Collection since the last Garbage Collection cycle.
	Get 0 heap size	Size of generation 0 (youngest) heap in bytes.
	Get 1 heap size	Size of generation 1 heap in bytes.
	Get 2 heap size	Size of generation 2 (oldest) heap in bytes.
	Large Object Heap size	Size of the Large Object Heap in bytes.
.NET CLR Remoting	Channels	Current number of remoting channels.
	Contexts	Current number of remoting contexts.
	Remote Calls/ sec	Rate of remote calls being made. Remote calls are calls between processes, between appdomains, or between machines.
	Total Remote Calls	Total number of remote calls since the start of the application.
.NET CLR Security	Total Runtime Checks	Number of runtime security checks performed.

Reading Performance Counter Values

The System.Diagnostics namespace includes several classes that let you read the value of any performance counter defined on the local or remote system. The namespace also contains classes to list all the categories, counters, and instances defined on a given machine.

Reading Raw Values

If you know exactly which performance counter you're interested in, reading its value is just a matter of instantiating a PerformanceCounter object that points to the specific category and counter (and instance name if that category exposes multiple instances) and then reading the object's RawValue property. For example, the following code reads a few counters from the System and Server categories:

```
' Create a few performance counters.
Dim pcProcesses As New PerformanceCounter("System", "Processes")
Dim pcThreads As New PerformanceCounter("System", "Threads")
Dim pcFilesOpen As New PerformanceCounter("Server", "Files Opened Total")
' Display their values.
Console.WriteLine("Processes = {0}", pcProcesses.RawValue)
Console.WriteLine("Threads = {0}", pcThreads.RawValue)
Console.WriteLine("Files Open Total = {0}", pcFilesOpen.RawValue)
```

If the category exposes multiple categories, you must pass a third argument to the PerformanceCounter object's constructor:

```
' Display handle count of Devenv process (that is, Visual Studio).
Dim pcHandles As New PerformanceCounter("Process", "Handle Count", "devenv")
Console.WriteLine("Devenv Handle Count = {0}", pcHandles.RawValue)
```

You can also pass a fourth argument to specify the name of the machine from which the counter must be retrieved. (Use "." for the local machine.) You don't have to create a different object for each distinct instance exposed by its category because you can simply assign a new value to the InstanceName property and read the new value, as in the following code:

```
' ...(continuing the preceding code sample)...
pcHandles.InstanceName = "WINWORD"
Console.WriteLine("WinWord Handle Count = {0}", pcHandles.RawValue)
```

Similarly, you can have the PerformanceCounter object point to a different category or counter by assigning a new value to the object's CategoryName or CounterName.

Reading Calculated Values

Although the RawValue property is appropriate when the value of the performance counter is a simple integer value—such as the number of processes, threads, and open files—for many cases, the value this property returns should be processed in some way—as when you're evaluating quantities such as percentages or rates of operations per second. In these instances, you need to use either the NextValue or the NextSample property.

The NextValue property returns the current value of a calculated value. The first time you retrieve this property, you might get the value 0, but after the first time, you start receiving meaningful values:

```
Dim pcCpu As New PerformanceCounter("Process", "% Processor Time", "myapp")
Console.WriteLine("Devenv % Processor Time = {0}", pcCpu.NextValue)
```

The problem with the NextValue property is that you might receive unusually high or low values, depending on when you invoke it. In these cases, you should use the Next-Sample property instead, which returns a CounterSample object. This object exposes several properties, including RawValue (the value just read) and TimeStamp (when the value was sampled). You can use these objects in your application by storing a first sample object and then comparing it with another sample taken later. The actual (averaged) value of the performance counter is returned by the Calculate method of the CounterSample class:

```
Dim pcSwitches As New _
    PerformanceCounter("Thread", "Context Switches/sec", "_Total")
' Read the first sample.
Dim cs1 As CounterSample = pcSwitches.NextSample
' Wait for one second, then read a second sample.
System.Threading.Thread.Sleep(1000)
Dim cs2 As CounterSample = pcSwitches.NextSample
' Evaluate the result.
Dim result As Single = CounterSample.Calculate(cs1, cs2)
Console.WriteLine("Thread switches/sec = {0}", result)
```

Because you decide when to read the samples, the value that you actually calculate is averaged over the period of time that you decide. For example, you might want to display both the average in the most recent second and the average since the program started:

```
' ...(continuing preceding code snippet)...
 For i As Integer = 1 To 10
    ' Get a new sample after one second.
    System.Threading.Thread.Sleep(1000)
    Dim cs3 As CounterSample = pcSwitches.NextSample
    ' Evaluate "instantaneous" (moving) average.
    result = CounterSample.Calculate(cs2, cs3)
    Console.WriteLine("Thread switches/sec = {0}", result)
    ' Evaluate average value since the first sample.
    result = CounterSample.Calculate(cs1, cs3)
    Console.WriteLine("Average Thread switches/sec = {0}", result)
    ' Use most recent sample as the basis for next moving average.
    cs2 = cs3
Next
```

Enumerating Existing Counters

The techniques shown so far assume that you know the category name, counter name, and instance name of the performance counter you want to monitor. When this information isn't available or when you want to let the end user select one or more performance counters among the available ones, you must enumerate all the existing categories and the counters and instances inside each category. Getting the list of all the performance counter categories on a computer requires a call to the Performance-CounterCategory.GetCategories shared method. The following code is taken from the demo application (see Figure 19-5) and loads the names of all categories in a ComboBox control:

```
Private Sub btnGetCategories_Click(ByVal sender As Object, _
    ByVal e As EventArgs) Handles btnGetCategories.Click
    ' Store categories in the ComboBox control, but display their names.
    cboCategories.DisplayMember = "CategoryName"
    cboCategories.Items.Clear()
    For Each pcc As PerformanceCounterCategory In PerformanceCounterCategory.GetCatego
ries
        cboCategories.Items.Add(pcc)
    Next
End Sub
```

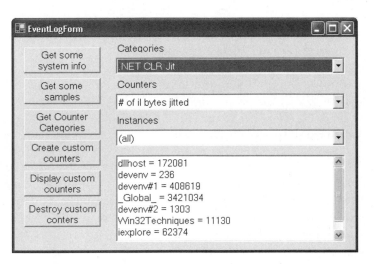

Figure 19-5 The demo application lists all the performance counter categories, counters, and instances.

Retrieving the list of counters and instances in each category requires a call to the ReadCategory and GetInstanceNames methods, respectively. The following code runs when the user selects a category in the cboCategories control (filled by the preceding snippet) and loads the names of all the counters and instances in the selected category in two ComboBox controls:

```
' Populate the other two ComboBox controls when a category is selected.
Private Sub cboCategories_SelectedIndexChanged(ByVal sender As Object, _
    ByVal e As EventArgs) Handles cboCategories.SelectedIndexChanged
    ' Get a reference to the selected category.
    Dim pcCat As PerformanceCounterCategory
    pcCat = DirectCast(cboCategories.SelectedItem, PerformanceCounterCategory)
    ' Fill cboCounters with the list of counters for this category.
    cboCounters.Items.Clear()
    Dim idcc As InstanceDataCollectionCollection = pcCat.ReadCategory
    ' Each element of this collection is associated with a counter.
    For Each cntName As String In idcc.Keys
        cboCounters.Items.Add(cntName)
    Next
```

```
    ' Fill cboInstances with the list of instances.
    cboInstances.Items.Clear()
    Try
        ' Not all categories have multiple instances.
        For Each instName As String In pcCat.GetInstanceNames
            cboInstances.Items.Add(instName)
        Next
    Catch ex As Exception
        ' There's nothing to do in this case.
    End Try
End Sub
```

The PerfomanceCounterCategory class also exposes the GetCounters method, which returns all the PerformanceCounter objects associated with a given instance name. However, you must know in advance whether the category has one or more instances, which makes this method less usable than the ReadCategory method, as seen in the preceding code snippet.

Working with Custom Performance Counters

Your .NET applications can create new performance counter objects and write data to them so that you or the end user can check these values by using the standard Performance utility or a custom application that you've written. For example, you might write a service that continuously monitors these counters and does something when they go below or above a given threshold. (For example, it might adjust your application's settings or send an e-mail to the tech support folks.)

Creating Custom Performance Counters

You can't create new performance counters in an existing category, even if you created the category yourself—all the counters in a category must be created when the category itself is created. To create a category and its counters, you begin by creating a CounterCreationDataCollection object. This collection will hold one or more Counter-CreationData objects, where each object describes an individual counter associated with the category. When you've filled this collection with data related to all the counters that you want, you can pass it to the Create shared method of the PerformanceCounterCategory class. The following sample code shows how you can create a new category named MyApp, which contains two counters:

```
Sub CreateCounters()
    ' Exit if the category exists already.
    If PerformanceCounterCategory.Exists("MyApp") Then Exit Sub

    ' Create the collection of all counters in this category.
    Dim counters As New CounterCreationDataCollection()

    ' Define the first counter, and then add it to the collection.
    Dim ccd As CounterCreationData = New CounterCreationData( _
        "Flush operations", "Total number of flush operations", _
```

```
            PerformanceCounterType.NumberOfItems32)
        counters.Add(ccd)

        ' Define the second counter, and then add it to the collection.
        ccd = New CounterCreationData("Flush operations / sec", _
            "Number of flush operations per second", _
            PerformanceCounterType.RateOfCountsPerSecond32)
        counters.Add(ccd)

        ' Create the category and its counters in one operation.
        PerformanceCounterCategory.Create("MyApp", _
            "Counters for MyApp program", counters)
End Sub
```

The second argument of the CounterCreationData object's constructor is the help string associated with the new counter, whereas the second argument of the Performance-CounterCategory.Create method is the help string of the new category. These help strings appear when you browse available counters with the Performance utility.

The last argument you pass to the CounterCreationData object's constructor is the type of the new counter, expressed as an enumerated PerformanceCounterType value. The most frequent types are NumberOfItems32 (a 32-bit count value), NumberOfItems64 (a 64-bit count value), RateOfCountsPerSecond32 (the amount per second stored as a 32-bit number), RateOfCountsPerSecond64 (the amount per second stored as a 64-bit number), and AverageTimer32 (the average time to perform an operation). For the complete list of types, see the .NET Platform SDK.

Notice that new counter categories that you create through code don't appear in the Performance utility until you close and restart the utility. But they do appear in the list of categories that you retrieve via the PerformanceCounterCategory.GetCategories shared method.

Writing Values

Writing values to a custom performance counter you've created is easy, thanks to a few methods of the PerformanceCounter class. The Increment and Decrement methods increase and decrease the current value by 1; the IncrementBy method increases the counter by the specified value (or decreases it if the argument is negative); the RawValue property assigns a new value to the counter. Before you can apply any of these methods, though, you must create a writable instance of the PerformanceCounter object:

```
' Create a writable instance of the two counters created previously.
' (The last argument is the ReadOnly mode. If omitted, it's True.)
Dim pc1 As New PerformanceCounter("MyApp", "Flush operations", False)
Dim pc2 As New PerformanceCounter("MyApp", "Flush operations / sec", False)
' Assign a starting value to both counters.
' (Not really needed in this case since this value is 0.)
pc1.RawValue = 0
pc2.RawValue = 0
' Store an initial sample for the latter counter.
Dim cs1 As CounterSample = pc2.NextSample
```

(You must evaluate an initial CounterSample object for the latter counter because it represents a rate-per-second value.) Now you can use the Increment, Decrease, and IncrementBy methods to update the counters. In this specific example, the two counters are just two different ways of seeing the same data, so you must always assign and increment them at the same time:

```
' Wait some time, and increment values.
System.Threading.Thread.Sleep(200)
pc1.IncrementBy(15)
pc2.IncrementBy(15)
' Display current values.
Dim res As Single = CounterSample.Calculate(cs1, pc2.NextSample)
Console.WriteLine("Flush operations = {0}", pc1.RawValue)
Console.WriteLine("Flush operations / sec = {0}", res)

' Wait some time, and increment values.
System.Threading.Thread.Sleep(200)
pc1.IncrementBy(25)
pc2.IncrementBy(25)
' Display current values.
res = CounterSample.Calculate(cs1, pc2.NextSample)
Console.WriteLine("Flush operations = {0}", pc1.RawValue)
Console.WriteLine("Flush operations / sec = {0}", res)
```

In the preceding demo code, the same application increments the two performance counters and then queries their values. Most real-world applications, however, perform only the first kind of operation, leaving the task of sampling the counters to the Performance utility or another application.

You don't have to explicitly create instances of a given counter. Just assigning the Raw-Value property of a PerformanceCounter object that points to a given instance creates that instance if necessary, as this code demonstrates:

```
Dim pc1 As New PerformanceCounter("MyApp", "Flush operations", False)
' Create a first instance.
pc1.InstanceName = "First"
pc1.RawValue = 10
' Create a second instance.
pc1.InstanceName = "Second"
pc1.RawValue = 20

' Display the value of the two instances.
pc1.InstanceName = "First"
Console.WriteLine("First Instance = {0}", pc1.RawValue)
pc1.InstanceName = "Second"
Console.WriteLine("Second Instance = {0}", pc1.RawValue)
```

Deleting Instances and Counters

You can remove an instance by assigning its name to the InstanceName property and then invoking the RemoveInstance method:

```
pc1.InstanceName = "Second"
pc1.RemoveInstance()
```

You can delete a category and all the counters it contains by using the Performance-CounterCategory.Delete shared method:

```
' Check whether the category exists.
If PerformanceCounterCategory.Exists("MyApp") Then
    PerformanceCounterCategory.Delete("MyApp")
End If
```

Installing a Custom Performance Counter

The .NET Framework offers a simplified way to install a custom performance counter on a target machine, based on the PerformanceCounterInstaller class, so that you don't have to write all the code that creates a category and all its counters. Visual Studio .NET makes this process even easier, as you'll see in a moment.

Start by adding a form or a component file—in general, any type of file that provides a designer surface—to your project. Then switch to the Components tab of the Toolbox and drop an instance of the PerformanceCounter class to the tray area. Next, go to the Properties window to give the new PerformanceCounter object a suitable name, and assign its essential properties: CategoryName, CounterName, and (optionally) Instance-Name. For this example, you might just set CategoryName equal to MyApplication and CounterName equal to MyCounter. You also should set its ReadOnly property to False so that you can assign values to the new counter. In most cases, you can leave the MachineName property at its default value of "." (the local computer).

Click the Add Installer link in the bottom portion of the Properties window (see Figure 19-6) to add a new file named ProjectInstaller1.vb to the current project. This file contains a class named ProjectInstaller that inherits from System.Configuration.Install.Installer and that contains an instance of the System.Diagnostics.PerformanceCounterInstaller component. Select this component and check that its CategoryName property matches the CategoryName of the performance counter ("MyApplication") and its Counters collection contains MyCounter. (This is a collection property because in a real-world application you'll probably install multiple performance counters.) You also can set a help message for the MyApplication category by assigning it to the CategoryHelp property. Finally, compile the application to an EXE file—say, PerformanceCounterDemo.exe.

All the classes that inherit from System.Configuration.Install.Installer can interact with a .NET command-line tool named InstallUtil. (You can find it in the c:\Windows\Microsoft.NET\Framework*vx.y.zzzz* directory, where *x.y.zzzz* is the version of the installed Framework.) In this specific case, passing the executable file name to the InstallUtil utility can activate the code inside the PerformanceCounterInstaller class:

```
InstallUtil PerformanceCounterDemo.exe
```

This command installs all the performance counters you've defined, and you can see them in the Performance system tool. Likewise, you can uninstall these counters simply by running InstallUtil with the /U option:

```
InstallUtil /U PerformanceCounterDemo.exe
```

The installation procedure is a transaction, in that if any of the action performed during the installation fails for any reason, all the actions already undertaken are rolled back in an orderly fashion.

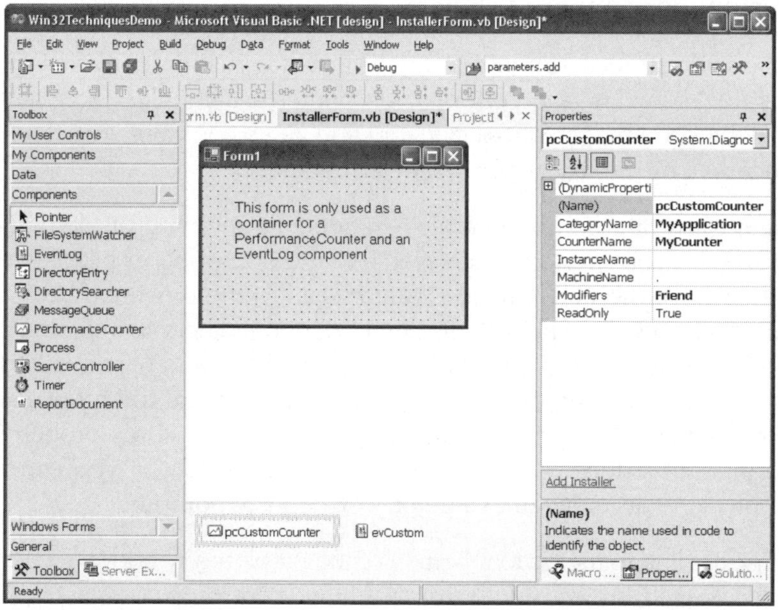

Figure 19-6   A PerformanceCounter component exposes an Add Installer option in the Properties window.

The EventLog Component

The .NET Framework gives you the classes to read and write from one of the event logs installed on a local or remote machine, and even to create new logs. This feature overcomes one of the limitations of Visual Basic 6 and offers a standard way for applications to record the success or failure of key operations.

Introduction to Event Logging

When something relevant happens in an application—particularly in applications that don't have a user interface, such as components, ASP.NET server applications, and Windows services—your code should record an event in one of the system logs so that the user or the administrator can check whether something went wrong. For example, an application might write to the event log when it can't start correctly, when it can't complete a critical operation, or when a low-memory situation is degrading performance.

Event logs are available only on Windows NT, Windows 2000, Windows XP, and Windows 2003 Server machines. By default, three event logs are available: the System log (which records events occurring on system components, such as drivers), the Security log (which records security changes and attempted violations of security permissions), and the Application log (which records events coming from registered applications). Applications can create their own logs, as is the case with the Active Directory and the DNS Server programs, but in most cases they write their events to the Application log. Five different types of events are available:

- **Information**   A significant successful operation—for example, when a service starts or when a complex backup operation completes. This is the default type if you don't specify otherwise.

- **Warning**   A problem has occurred, but the application can recover from it without having to shut down. A typical warning records a low-resource situation, which might cause later problems, such as loss of performance.

- **Error**   A significant problem has occurred, such as loss of data or functionality; for example, Windows writes an error event when it can't load a service.

- **Success audit**   A security event that occurs when an access attempt is successful, such as when a user successfully logs on to the machine.

- **Failure audit**   A security event that occurs when an access attempt fails, such as when a user can't log on or when a file can't be opened because the user has insufficient security permissions.

The main tool for browsing the current state of all event logs is the Event Viewer, a Microsoft Management Console (MMC) snap-in that's installed with the operating system. (See Figure 19-7.) In most cases, you want to filter events by their source—that is, the program that wrote them. You can achieve this filtering by using the Filter command in the View menu.

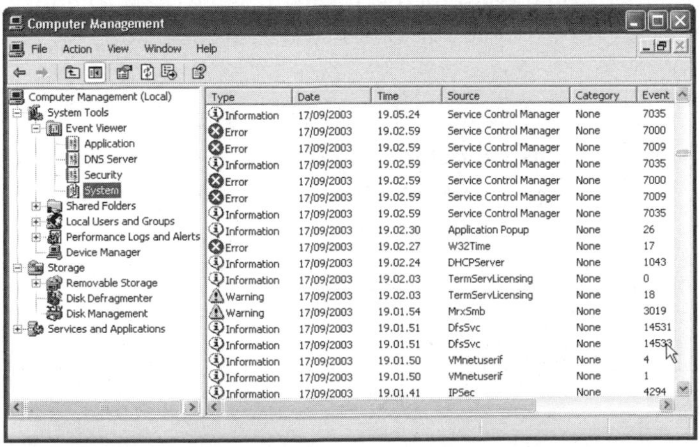

Figure 19-7   The Event Viewer MMC snap-in

You also can manage the event logs from the Visual Studio .NET Server Explorer window, which lets you browse existing entries grouped by their source application, as you can see in Figure 19-8.

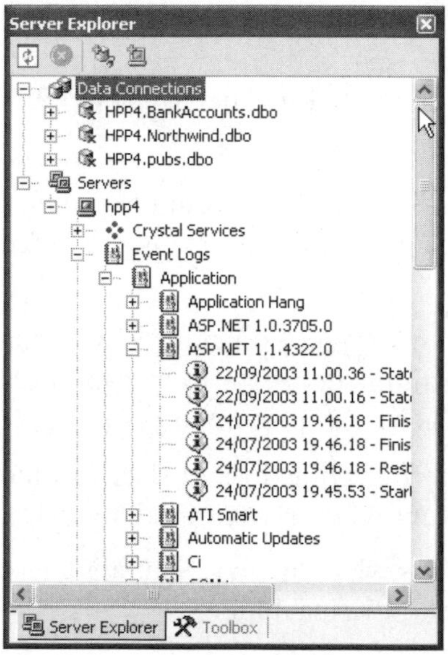

Figure 19-8   The Server Explorer window in Visual Studio .NET

Reading Event Log Entries

You can read event log entries by defining a System.Diagnostics.EventLog object that points to a specific event log—for example, the Application log or the System log. You can create such an object in three ways: by dragging an element from the Server Explorer window to the form's component tray area, by dragging an item from the Component tab of the Toolbox to a form or component's tray area, or entirely through code. In this section, I'll focus on the last method, which also works from inside classes and modules, but the concepts apply to the other two cases as well.

Listing Existing Logs

If you aren't sure which event logs are defined on the local or a remote machine, you can use the EventLog.GetEventLogs shared method, which returns one EventLog object for each existing log:

```
For Each evlog As EventLog In EventLog.GetEventLogs
    Console.WriteLine(evlog.Log)
Next
```

The GetEventLogs method takes the machine name as an optional argument, so you can also list event logs on any remote machine. (Use "." to point to the local machine.) You can also check whether a log exists on the local or remote machine with the Exists shared method:

```
If EventLog.Exists("CustomLog", "DomainServer") Then
    Console.Write("The CustomLog log exists on the DomainServer machine.")
End If
```

The name of the log is case insensitive.

Reading Existing Event Log Entries

Most of the time, you already know which log you're interested in, so you can just create an instance of the EventLog class and use it to read existing entries by using its Entries property. This property returns an array of EventLogEntry objects, each one representing an individual entry in the log. These objects expose properties whose names are self-explanatory, such as EntryType, TimeGenerated, TimeWritten, Source, Category, EventID, UserName, MachineName, Message, and Data. The following code snippet is adapted from the demo application (Figure 19-9) and lists all the entries in the Application log on the local machine:

```
Private Sub ListApplicationEntries()
    ' Get a reference to the Application event log.
    Dim elApp As New EventLog("Application")
    For Each entry As EventLogEntry In elApp.Entries
        Console.WriteLine(GetEntryInfo(entry))
    Next
End Sub

' Return readable information about an event log entry.
Private Function GetEntryInfo(ByVal entry As EventLogEntry) As String
    Return String.Format("{0}  {1}  {2}  {3}  {4}  {5}  {6}", _
        entry.EntryType, entry.TimeGenerated, entry.Source, _
        entry.Category, entry.EventID, entry.UserName, entry.Message)
End Function
```

Even if you can specify a source when you instantiate the EventLog object, the Entries property always returns all the items in that log. In other words, you must filter events according to their source (or any other property) manually, as in this code:

```
' Display information about SQL Server events only.
For Each entry As EventLogEntry In elApp.Entries
    If entry.Source = "MSSQLServer" Then
        Console.WriteLine(GetEntryInfo(entry))
    End If
Next
```

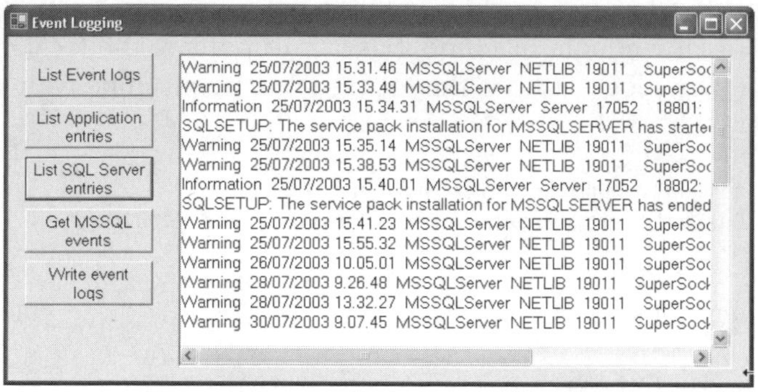

Figure 19-9   The demo application lets you list all the entries in the Application log or just the ones coming from Microsoft SQL Server.

Handling EntryWritten Events

The ability to read existing log entries is fine when you want to build a log viewer application—for example, a custom version of the Event Viewer system utility. In many cases, however, you really need to get a notification when an entry is written to the event log by a specific source. You can achieve this functionality in a relatively simple way, thanks to the EntryWritten event of the EventLog component. An important limitation: you can receive notifications only from event logs on the local machine, not from remote machines.

You first need to check that the application you're interested in is registered as an event source on the machine; to do this, use the SourceExists shared method. Next, by using the LogNameFromSourceName shared method, you retrieve the name of the log that contains entries written by that specific event source. At this point, you're ready to create an EventLog object that points to the log in question, and you can use the AddHandler command or a WithEvents variable to bind the EntryWritten event to a specific event handler in your application. To actually receive events, however, you must set the EnableRaisingEvents property to True:

```
Private Sub StartLogging()
    ' We're interested in SQL Server events on the local machine only.
    Dim source As String = "MSSQLServer"
    ' Exit if the source isn't registered.
    If Not EventLog.SourceExists(source) Then Exit Sub
    ' Get the name of the log that contains entries from SQL Server.
    ' (Notice that you must specify the computer name.)
    Dim logName As String = EventLog.LogNameFromSourceName(source, ".")
    ' Get the corresponding EventLog object.
    Dim evLog As New EventLog(logName)
    ' Associate it with an event handler.
    AddHandler evLog.EntryWritten, AddressOf EntryWritten
    ' This statement is very important.
    evLog.EnableRaisingEvents = True
End Sub
```

```
Private Sub EntryWritten(ByVal sender As Object, _
    ByVal e As System.Diagnostics.EntryWrittenEventArgs)
    ' Filter out events from sources we aren't interested in.
    If e.Entry.Source = "MSSQLServer" Then
        ' (GetEntryInfo has been defined previously.)
        Console.WriteLine(GetEntryInfo(e.Entry))
    End If
End Sub
```

As the preceding code shows, the EntryWritten event fires when *any* source writes to the specified log, regardless of the source argument you might have specified in the constructor of the EventLog component. For this reason, you have to manually filter out events from sources you aren't interested in.

Writing Event Log Entries

The EventLog class makes it simple to write to an event log as well, even though an application can write to an event log only if it's registered as a valid event source.

Registering Your Application as an Event Source

You can register your application as a valid event source by means of the CreateEvent-Source shared method of the EventLog class. This method takes the source name (the string that will identify messages from this application in the log) and the name of the log your application will write to (typically the Application log):

```
' Register your demo app as an event source.
EventLog.CreateEventSource("DemoApp", "Application")
```

If you skip this registration step, however, your application will be registered on the fly when you write the first entry to the log. The DeleteEventSource shared method unregisters an event source. Notice that you don't have to specify the name of the log because the system can deduce it from the name of the source:

```
' Delete this event source.
EventLog.DeleteEventSource("DemoApp")
```

The DeleteEventSource method can be useful when you want to change the destination log for events written by your application. Deleting an event source doesn't remove the existing log entries associated with that source.

Creating a Custom Log

Creating a custom log is much simpler than you probably think it is, and you might argue that it's a bit *too* simple. In fact, if the log name that you pass to the second argument of the CreateEventSource method or to the EventLog's constructor doesn't correspond to an existing log, a new log is automatically created for you. This means that you might accidentally create new logs just because you misspelled the name of the log in one of these calls:

```
' Create a new custom log named MyLog.
EventLog.CreateEventSource("MyDemoApp", "MyLog")
```

Only the first eight characters of the log name are significant; if the first eight characters in your custom log's name match the name of an existing log (as in ApplicationNew), you won't create a new log. You can create a custom log on a remote machine by passing a third argument to the CreateEventSource method, provided you have sufficient administrative rights on the remote system.

You delete a custom log using the EventLog.Delete shared method. Pay attention when using this method because it deletes all the event entries and all the event sources associated with the deleted log. Also notice that you might accidentally delete one of the predefined system logs, in which case you might have to reinstall the operating system:

```
' Delete the custom log.
EventLog.Delete("MyLog")
```

A less radical operation consists of removing all the entries from a given log, which you can do by invoking the Clear method:

```
Dim evLog As New EventLog("MyLog", ".")
evLog.Clear()
```

Clearing an event log periodically—possibly after saving its current contents to a file from inside the Event Viewer utility—helps you avoid problems when the event log becomes full. (The default behavior when this happens is to start overwriting the oldest entries with the newest entries.) By default, the Application, System, and Security logs can grow up to 4992 KB, whereas custom logs have a default maximum size of 512 KB. You can change these default values and modify the default behavior from inside the Event Viewer utility.

Writing to the Event Log

Once your application is a registered event source, you only have to instantiate an EventLog object that points to the correct log on the target machine. The constructor for this class takes a third argument, which is the name of the source and must match the event source argument you specified in the CreateEventSource method. Now you can invoke the WriteEntry method, which at the very least takes the message associated with the event you're writing:

```
' Create an EventLog object connected to that event log.
Dim evLog As New EventLog("Application", ".", "DemoApp")
' Write two entries to the Application log.
evLog.WriteEntry("First message")
evLog.WriteEntry("Second message")
```

(The message you write can't be longer than 16 KB.) If you're using the Event Viewer utility, you have to refresh the display to see the new entries added by your application.

The WriteEntry method is overloaded to take additional arguments, such as an event type, an application-defined event identifier, an application-defined category identifier, and a Byte array containing binary data to be associated with the event:

```
' Write an error message.
evLog.WriteEntry("Third message", EventLogEntryType.Error)
' Write a warning error with an application-defined event ID.
evLog.WriteEntry("Fourth message", EventLogEntryType.Warning, 123)
' Write a warning error with an application-defined event ID and category ID.
evLog.WriteEntry("Fifth message", EventLogEntryType.Warning, 123, CShort(456))
' Write a warning error with an application-defined event ID and category ID,
' plus associated binary data.
Dim bytes() As Byte = {0, 2, 4, 6, 8, 10, 12}
evLog.WriteEntry("Fifth message", EventLogEntryType.Warning, 123, 456, bytes)
```

Installing an EventLog Component

The .NET Framework and Visual Studio .NET let you install an EventLog object using a RAD approach, which is similar to the one I explained earlier in this chapter in the section "Installing a Custom Performance Counter."

First drop an EventLog component from the Components tab of the Toolbox and set its main properties—namely, Source, Log, and MachineName. Then click on the Add Installer link near the bottom of the Properties window to create a ProjectInstaller.vb file that contains an instance of the EventLogInstaller class. (If you have multiple installer objects in the project, all of them appear in the ProjectInstaller.vb file.) The properties of this installer object are already set correctly for you, so in general you don't need to modify them.

You can now install the new EventLog object (and make your application a permanent event source) by passing the name of the executable as an argument to the InstallUtil command-line utility that comes with the .NET Framework:

```
InstallUtil yourapplication.exe
```

You should run InstallUtil with the /U option when uninstalling your application.

Dealing with Security Issues

Because event logs are such a critical part of the system, not all applications are allowed to read, write, or clear them. The operations actually permitted depend on the identity under which the code is running and are summarized in Table 19-2. The Local-System account is the account under which most services run, and it's the most powerful account in terms of the operations it can perform on system logs.

Table 19-2   Operations Allowed on System Logs from Different Accounts

Account	Application Log	System Log	Security Log
LocalSystem	Read, Write, Clear	Read, Write, Clear	Read, Write, Clear
Administrator	Read, Write, Clear	Read, Write, Clear	Read, Write
ServerOperator	Read, Write, Clear	Read	(none)
World	Read, Write	Read, Clear	(none)

In addition to the rights listed in Table 19-2, users have the right to read and clear the Security log if they have been granted the Manage Auditing And Security Log user right or the SE_AUDIT_NAME privilege. (See the Windows SDK for additional information.)

In this chapter, you've seen that the .NET Framework exposes many objects for leveraging Win32 applications, but I haven't illustrated another, really intriguing, feature: the ability to create, run, stop, and list Windows services. This capability is the topic of the next chapter.

20 Windows Services

Service applications are programs that are designed to run unattended. They typically start as soon as the operating system completes the bootstrap phase and run even if no interactive user has logged in, even though you can configure them to be started manually. Windows services are available only on Windows NT, Windows 2000, Windows XP, and Windows Server 2003. They are used for many server-side tasks, such as running Microsoft Internet Information Services (IIS), Microsoft SQL Server, the Microsoft Search engine, and so on.

In this chapter, you'll learn how to create and control Windows services by means of the classes in the System.ServiceProcess namespace. Notice that this namespace isn't included among the available references in most project types and you must manually add a reference to the System.ServiceProcess.dll component.

> **Note** To keep the code as concise as possible, all the code samples in this section assume the use of the following Imports statement at the file or project level:
>
> ```
> Imports System.ServiceProcess
> Imports System.IO
> ```

Windows Service Fundamentals

From the perspective of .NET developers, a Windows service application is just a class that inherits from the System.ServiceProcess.ServiceBase abstract class. In practice, all you have to do to implement a service is create a class that derives from this abstract class, set its properties, and override a few of its methods so that your code can react appropriately when the service is started or stopped.

Creating the Project

Our demo application will be a service named Encryptor, which monitors a directory on the hard disk and automatically encrypts all the files that the user copies to it. The encryption algorithm is a simple one; it won't resist the cracking attempts of a determined hacker, but is sufficient for most ordinary situations. Once you understand the underlying principles, it's easy to replace the provided encryption routine with one of the encryption routines illustrated in the "Cryptography" section of Chapter 33.

Start by creating a new project of type Windows Service. Assign a suitable name to the project. (Use EncryptorService to parallel the code in the demo application provided on the companion Web site.) Then click OK. This action creates a new project with two files: Service1.vb and the ubiquitous AssemblyInfo.vb. You can rename the former as Encryptor.vb.

If you select the now-renamed Encryptor file, you'll see that it has a designer surface. This is where you can drop any component this service uses. For example, you can add the FileSystemWatcher component that you'll use to detect any files added to the watched directory. In most cases, however, you'll work mostly with the code module behind this designer.

Setting Service Properties

Before you start working with code, you should assign a few key properties of the service component you've just created. To do so, right-click on the designer's surface and click Properties on the shortcut menu, which will bring you to the Properties window (shown in Figure 20-1), where you should modify the following properties:

1. Set the Name property equal to Encryptor. This is the name of the class that the designer generates.

2. Set the ServiceName property equal to Encryptor. This is the name of the service that will be created; it's usually the same as the name of the class, but nothing prevents you from using a different name.

3. Ensure that the CanStop property is True. This property determines whether the service can be stopped once started.

4. Set the CanPauseAndContinue property to True. This property determines whether the service can be paused and resumed.

5. Ensure that the AutoLog property is True. When this property is True, the service automatically writes entries in the Application event log when it starts and stops successfully, when it's paused and resumed, and when any command fails to complete correctly. The messages sent to the event log are rather generic—for example, "Service started successfully"—and you have no control over their contents, but they're OK in most cases and very useful, especially during the debug phase.

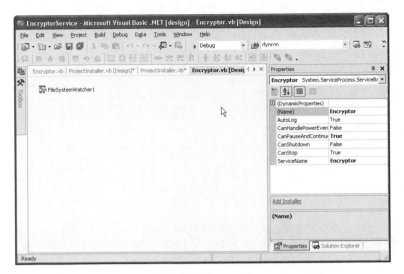

Figure 20-1   The designer window of a service component

Browsing and Fixing the Code

After you set these properties, you can switch to the code editor. Here's an abridged version of the code the designer generates for you:

```vb
Public Class Encryptor
    Inherits System.ServiceProcess.ServiceBase

#Region " Component Designer generated code "
    Public Sub New()
        MyBase.New()
        ' This call is required by the Component Designer.
        InitializeComponent()
        ' Add any initialization after the InitializeComponent() call.
    End Sub

    ' The main entry point for the process
    Shared Sub Main()
        Dim ServicesToRun() As System.ServiceProcess.ServiceBase

        ' More than one NT Service may run within the same process. To add
        ' another service to this process, change the following line to
        ' create a second service object. For example,
        '
        '    ServicesToRun = New System.ServiceProcess.ServiceBase () _
        '          {New Service1, New MySecondUserService}
        '
        ServicesToRun = New System.ServiceProcess.ServiceBase() _
            {New Service1()}
        System.ServiceProcess.ServiceBase.Run(ServicesToRun)
    End Sub
```

```
           'Required by the Component Designer
           Private components As System.ComponentModel.Container

           ' NOTE: The following procedure is required by the Component Designer.
           ' It can be modified using the Component Designer.
           ' Do not modify it using the code editor.
           <System.Diagnostics.DebuggerStepThrough()> _
               Private Sub InitializeComponent()
                   '
               'Encryptor
                   '
               Me.CanPauseAndContinue = True
               Me.ServiceName = "Encryptor"
           End Sub
#End Region

           Protected Overrides Sub OnStart(ByVal args() As String)
               ' Add code here to start your service. This method should set things
               ' in motion so your service can do its work.
           End Sub

           Protected Overrides Sub OnStop()
               ' Add code here to perform any tear-down necessary to stop
               ' your service.
           End Sub
End Class
```

The preceding code reveals how your service class actually works. The code in the Shared Sub Main procedure creates an array of all the service classes that share the same process space and then passes this array to the ServiceBase.Run shared method:

```
           System.ServiceProcess.ServiceBase.Run(ServicesToRun)
```

Thanks to this approach, your project can include multiple service classes that run in the same process (and therefore save system resources), yet can be stopped, paused, and resumed independently of one another.

A careful examination of the preceding code shows a minor bug in the code generated by the designer. Although the name of the class correctly reflects the Name property you set in the Properties window, the name of the class instantiated in the Shared Sub Main procedure is still Service1 (the statement in boldface in the preceding listing), so you must change it manually as follows:

```
           ServicesToRun = New System.ServiceProcess.ServiceBase() _
               {New Encryptor()}
```

Overriding ServiceBase Methods

A nontrivial service application typically must execute code when the service starts and stops, as well as when the service is paused and resumed (if you set the CanPauseAndContinue property to True). When these events occur, the .NET runtime invokes one of the public methods of the ServiceBase class, so you have to override these methods to execute your custom code instead.

The Encryptor service uses a FileSystemWatcher component to be notified when a new file is created in a given directory on the hard disk. As you saw in Chapter 19, you can create this component by means of code or by dropping it from the Components tab of the Toolbox. In our demo Encryptor service, we'll use the latter approach.

After you drop an instance of the FileSystemWatcher component on the designer surface, you should set its EnableRaisingEvents property to False so that the component won't raise events before the service starts. You can leave all the other properties at their default value. Next you can switch to the code editor and add the following code inside the OnStart and OnStop methods:

```
' The path of the watched directory
Dim Path As String = "C:\Encrypt"

Protected Overrides Sub OnStart(ByVal args() As String)
    ' Ensure that the directory exists.
    If Not Directory.Exists(Path) Then
        Directory.CreateDirectory(Path)
    End If
    ' Start receiving file events.
    FileSystemWatcher1.Path = Path
    FileSystemWatcher1.EnableRaisingEvents = True
End Sub

Protected Overrides Sub OnStop()
    ' Stop receiving file events.
    FileSystemWatcher1.EnableRaisingEvents = False
End Sub
```

Because this service also can be paused and resumed, you should override the OnPause and OnContinue methods as well:

```
Protected Overrides Sub OnPause()
    ' Stop receiving file events.
    FileSystemWatcher1.EnableRaisingEvents = False
End Sub

Protected Overrides Sub OnContinue()
    ' Start receiving file events.
    FileSystemWatcher1.EnableRaisingEvents = True
End Sub
```

Implementing the Encryption Algorithm

The Encryptor service sleeps until the FileSystemWatcher component detects that a new file has been created in the directory and fires a Created event. When this happens, the service invokes the EncryptFile custom routine, which reads the contents of the file (in blocks of 8 KB each) and creates a temporary encrypted file with a .$$$ extension. When the encryption is completed, the service deletes the original file and renames the temporary file as the original file. The encryption routine simply uses an XOR operation on each byte in the original file with a byte specified in a password:

```
' This is the binary password.
Dim pwBytes() As Byte = {123, 234, 12, 9, 78, 89, 212}
' This is the extension used for temporary files.
Dim tempExt As String = ".$$$"

Private Sub FileSystemWatcher1_Created(ByVal sender As Object, _
    ByVal e As FileSystemEventArgs) Handles FileSystemWatcher1.Created
    ' Ignore temporary files created by the encryption process.
    If System.IO.Path.GetExtension(e.FullPath) = tempExt Then Exit Sub
    ' Encrypt the file being created.
    EncryptFile(e.FullPath, pwBytes)
End Sub

' This is the encryption/decryption routine.
Private Sub EncryptFile(ByVal Filename As String, ByVal pwBytes() As Byte)
    ' This is the size of each input block.
    ' (Files must be decrypted using the same block size.)
    Const BLOCKSIZE = 8192

    ' Determine the name of the temporary file.
    Dim tempFile As String = Filename & tempExt
    ' Open the source file as a binary input stream.
    Dim inStream As New FileStream(Filename, IO.FileMode.Open)
    ' Open the temporary output file as a binary input stream.
    Dim outStream As New FileStream(tempFile, IO.FileMode.Create)
    ' Determine the number of bytes to read.
    Dim bytesLeft As Long = inStream.Length
    ' Prepare an input buffer.
    Dim buffer(BLOCKSIZE - 1) As Byte

    ' Loop until there are bytes to read.
    Do While bytesLeft > 0
        ' Read max 8 KB at a time.
        Dim bytesToRead As Long = Math.Min(BLOCKSIZE, bytesLeft)
        ' Read into the input buffer.
        inStream.Read(buffer, 0, bytesToRead)
        ' Encrypt this buffer.
        EncryptArray(buffer, pwBytes)
        ' Output to the temporary file.
        outStream.Write(buffer, 0, bytesToRead)
        ' We have fewer bytes to read now.
        bytesLeft -= bytesToRead
    Loop

    ' Close the two streams.
    inStream.Close()
    outStream.Close()
    ' Delete the source file.
    File.Delete(Filename)
    ' Rename the temporary file as the original file.
    File.Move(tempFile, Filename)
End Sub
```

```
' This routine encrypts an array of bytes.
Sub EncryptArray(ByVal buffer() As Byte, ByVal pwBytes() As Byte)
    ' This index points to the password array.
    Dim i As Integer
    ' The max value for i
    Dim maxval As Integer = pwBytes.Length

    For index As Integer = 0 To buffer.Length - 1
        ' XOR each element with the corresponding element in the password.
        buffer(index) = buffer(index) Xor pwBytes(i)
        ' Ensure that the index is always in the valid range.
        i = (i + 1) Mod maxval
    Next
End Sub
```

Installing the Service

Windows services can't be launched or debugged as regular Windows applications. You must first install the service on the computer on which it will run, and then you must start the process by using the Services MMC snap-in or the NET START command from the command prompt.

The first step in making a service installable is to add an installer class. You can choose from two ways of doing this: by using an automatic tool that Visual Studio provides or by manually creating the installer class in code.

The former method is the easier one and versatile enough in most cases. Switch to the designer of the Encryptor component, and ensure that the Properties window is visible. Near the bottom of this window, you'll see an Add Installer hyperlink. Click on this link, and Visual Studio adds a new component named ProjectInstaller.vb to the current project. The designer of this component hosts two more objects, named ServiceProcessInstaller1 and ServiceInstaller1. (See Figure 20-2.) You don't need to change the names of these objects.

Setting the Service's Main Properties

By setting the properties of the ServiceInstaller object appropriately, you define how your service behaves. The key properties of this object are the following:

- **ServiceName** This property *must* match the ServiceName property of the service class that you have defined in the project (Encryptor, in our case). Visual Studio correctly initializes this property, so in most cases you don't have to worry about it.

- **DisplayName** This property is the descriptive string that appears in the Services MMC snap-in and is retrieved by means of the DisplayName property of the ServiceController class.

- **StartType** This property tells whether the service is started automatically or manually or is disabled; the default value is Manual.

- **ServicesDependedOn** This property is a String array in which each array element contains the name of a service that must be running for this service to be successfully started. (Go to the section titled "The ServiceController Component" to read more about this property.)

For our Encryptor service, you can assign the string Simple Encrypting Service for the DisplayName property and ensure that StartType is set to Manual. Because the Encryptor service doesn't depend on any other service, you don't have to modify the ServicesDependedOn property. Figure 20-2 shows what the Properties window looks like after you set these properties.

If your project contains multiple services, you should create multiple ServiceInstaller objects, one for each service to be installed.

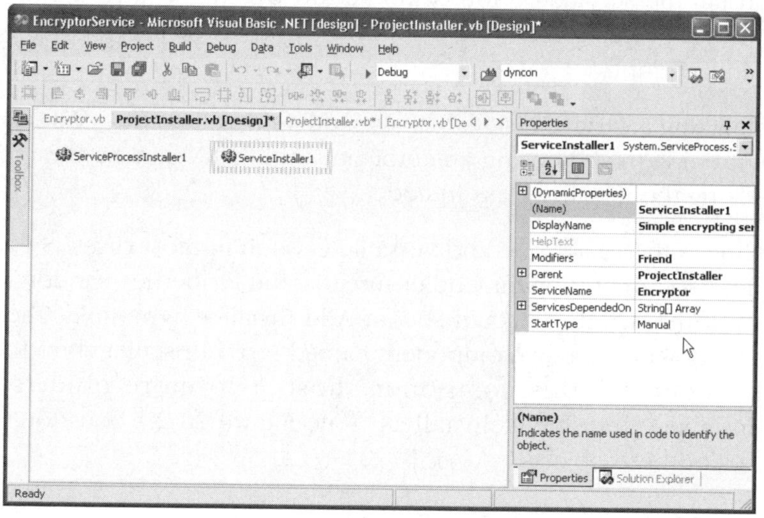

Figure 20-2 Setting the properties of a ServiceInstaller component

Setting the Service's Security Context

The ServiceProcessInstaller object determines the identity under which the service runs. It exposes only three noteworthy properties:

- **Account** This property specifies the type of the account used by the service and can be User (default), LocalSystem, LocalService, or NetworkService. Note that your service won't be able to display a message box or a user interface, even if you specify a user account. In most cases, using the LocalSystem account is the wiser choice.

■ **Username and Password** These properties specify the user account and password to be used if the service runs under a user account; otherwise, they're ignored. The username can refer to a registered user in the local machine or a registered user in the domain, provided that account has sufficient privileges on the machine on which the service is installed. These two properties don't appear in the Properties window and must be set via code in the InitializeComponent procedure.

If the service runs under a user account and you leave the username or the password empty, they are requested during the installation.

Running InstallUtil

When you've set all the properties of the ServiceInstaller and ServiceProcessInstaller components correctly, you can finally build the project. In the case of our demo service, this action creates an executable file named EncryptorService.exe in the Bin subdirectory under the project's main directory. At this point, you're ready to install this service by using the InstallUtil utility provided with the .NET Framework. Before proceeding, ensure that this directory is on the system path.

Open a command prompt window, navigate to the Bin directory, and issue this command to install the service:

```
InstallUtil EncryptorService.exe
```

If everything goes well, you'll see a message that says that the service has been installed correctly. The InstallUtil runs a transacted installation, so if something goes wrong, the utility will clean up any partial actions that couldn't be completed because of an error, such as writes to the registry. If an error occurs, a detailed message is displayed and a log file is created.

You can uninstall the service using the /U option of the InstallUtil program:

```
InstallUtil EncryptorService.exe /u
```

The service must be stopped for the uninstall operation to be successful.

Starting and Stopping the Service

If the installation went well, you can now start the service and check that it behaves as expected. You can start and stop a service in two ways: by using the Services system utility (actually an MMC snap-in under Windows 2000 or later) or by using the NET command from the system prompt. Here's how you start:

```
NET START Encryptor
```

Stopping the service is also easy:

```
NET STOP Encryptor
```

Similarly, you can use the NET PAUSE and NET CONTINUE commands to pause and continue a service from the command prompt. All these commands display a message that tells you the operation was successful or explains why it failed.

Using the Services MMC snap-in is even simpler. (See Figure 20-3.) You can start, stop, pause, and resume any service by right-clicking on the corresponding item, and you can even change all the service's settings by double-clicking on the service. You can also start and stop a service from inside Visual Studio .NET's Server Explorer window.

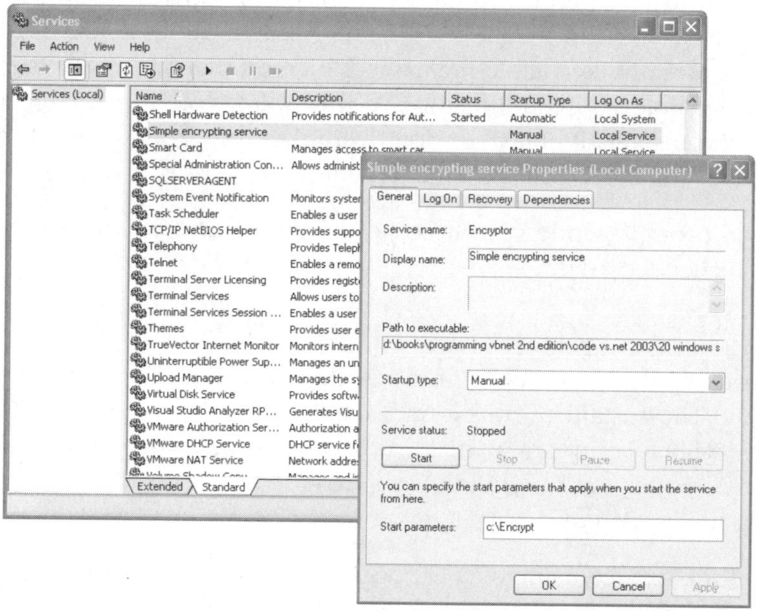

Figure 20-3   You can change the settings of any service with the Services MMC snap-in.

Once the service is running, you can test its functionality by copying one or more files in the C:\Encrypt directory and then trying to read them back. You'll see that the copy of the file in that directory has been automatically encrypted. You can then send it as an e-mail attachment to your friends who have installed the Encryptor service. When they receive the attachment, they'll have to copy the file into their C:\Encrypt directory to have the file automatically decrypted. (This technique works because the encryption mechanism is symmetrical.) To test how the encryption mechanism works without having two distinct machines, you can copy a file to the C:\Encrypt directory to encrypt it, then copy the encrypted file to another directory, and finally copy it back to the C:\Encrypt directory. The file that you obtain at the end of this sequence should be the same as the original file.

More Service Programming Techniques

In this section, I'll give you a few tips that you might find useful when you're writing and debugging Windows service applications.

Custom Event Log Messages

As I explained earlier, if you set the AutoLog property to True, your service class automatically records important events in the Application log, such as when the service is started and stopped or when a problem occurs.

To suppress the standard start/stop log messages or to produce more informative messages, you should set the AutoLog property to False and send custom messages yourself. This is an easy thing to do, thanks to the ServiceBase class's EventLog property. This property returns an EventLog object that lets you send a message to the Application log:

```
' From inside the service class...
Me.EventLog.WriteEntry("Message from the Encryptor service")
```

Here's a caveat, however: don't attempt to send a message to a log before setting your service's ServiceName property in code because this is the moment in time when the service registers itself as an event source.

To send messages to a log other than the Application log, you must register an event source manually, as I explained in the section titled "The EventLog Component" in Chapter 19.

Reacting to Shutdown and Power Events

Most service applications contain cleanup code in their OnStop and (sometimes) OnPause methods so that the service doesn't take resources while it isn't running. In some cases, you also should run special code when the system shuts down, when the system enters suspend mode, or when another power-related event occurs—for example, when batteries are low.

You can execute a custom routine when the system shuts down by setting the CanShutdown property to True and then overriding the OnShutdown protected method. Similarly, you can run a routine when a power event occurs by setting the CanHandlePowerEvent property to True and overriding the OnPowerEvent method. This method receives an enumerated value that explains what specific event happened. The following routine shows how you can take advantage of these methods:

```
' This method is called only if the CanShutdown property is True.
Protected Overrides Sub OnShutdown()
    ' Add the code that executes when the system shuts down here.
End Sub
```

```
' This method is called only if the CanHandlePowerEvent property is True.
Protected Overrides Function OnPowerEvent( _
    ByVal powerStatus As PowerBroadcastStatus) As Boolean
    Select Case powerStatus
        Case PowerBroadcastStatus.Suspend
            ' Add the code to execute when the system enters suspend mode.
        Case PowerBroadcastStatus.ResumeSuspend
            ' Add the code to execute when the system exits suspend mode.
        Case PowerBroadcastStatus.BatteryLow
            ' Add the code to execute when batteries are low.
    End Select
    ' This method must return True.
    Return True
End Function
```

Managing Custom Commands

You also can send a custom command to a service. (A custom command is just an Integer value whose value is defined by the application.) Some system services react to custom commands, but you can implement a similar mechanism in your services by overriding the OnCustomCommand protected method, which fires when another application sends a custom command to your service:

```
' This method is called when a custom command is sent to the service.
Protected Overrides Sub OnCustomCommand(ByVal command As Integer)
    Select Case command
        Case 128
            ' React to custom command #128.
        Case 129
            ' React to custom command #129.
        ⋮
    End Select
End Sub
```

Again, the meaning and the effect of each custom command depends on the specific service exclusively. For example, the Encryptor service might use a custom command to select a different encryption algorithm. You should use command numbers in the range 128 to 256. Read the section on the ServiceController component, later in this chapter, to see how you can send a command to a service.

Passing and Receiving Arguments

A great feature of Windows services is their ability to receive arguments. You specify one or more arguments for your service in the General tab of the Properties dialog box in the Services MMC snap-in. For example, the final version of the Encryptor service provided in the companion code receives the name of the directory in which files are automatically encrypted in this way. (See Figure 20-3.)

The arguments that you specify are converted to a String array and passed as an argument to the OnStart method. So you need only one statement to implement this feature in the Encryptor service. (Added lines are in boldface.)

```
Protected Overrides Sub OnStart(ByVal args() As String)
    ' If an argument has been specified, use it as the path
    ' of the directory being watched.
    If args.Length > 0 Then Path = args(0)
    ⋮
End Sub
```

Debugging a Windows Service

The easiest way to debug a Windows service is to attach the Visual Studio debugger to it. To use this technique, compile the service project in Debug mode, start the process as usual, and switch back to Visual Studio. Next, run the Processes command from the Debug menu, select the Show system processes option, and double-click on the EncryptorService element in the list of running processes. This action brings up the Attach To Process dialog box, which lets you confirm that you want to debug the service application (at this point, the screen looks like Figure 20-4). Click OK to close this dialog box.

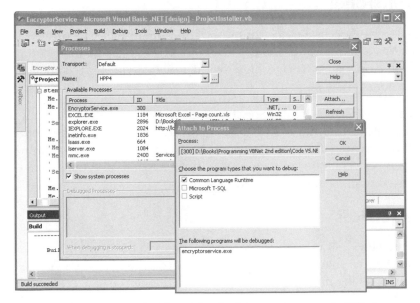

Figure 20-4 Attaching the Visual Studio debugger to a running Windows service application

In the Processes dialog box, you can decide what happens when the debugging is stopped. You can choose the Detach From This Process option (in which case, the service will continue to run when the debugger stops) and the Terminate This Process option (in which case, the service will terminate). Finally, click Close to start debugging the service application.

You can now set one or more breakpoints, as you would in a regular application. For example, you might set a breakpoint at the beginning of the FileSystemWatcher1_Created procedure to trace code in the service application and see what happens when a new file is created in the directory being monitored.

When debugging a service in this fashion, you should keep one limitation in mind: you can attach a debugger only to a service that's already running. For this reason, you can't debug the code in the Main or OnStart procedure. In theory, you might add a pause in the OnStart method to give you the time necessary to set up the debugger immediately after the service is started—however, Windows imposes a 30-second timeout on all attempts to start a service. If your debugging chores take longer than that, the system assumes that the service can't run.

One way to debug the code in the OnStart method is to add another "dummy" service to your service project. You can therefore start the dummy process so that its process appears in the list of processes that can be debugged in Visual Studio. At this point, you can attach the debugger to that process and trace through all its initialization code. Even in this case, however, you're subject to the 30-second timeout mentioned in the preceding paragraph.

The ServiceController Component

The System.ServiceProcess.ServiceController component lets you programmatically control any service on a local or remote machine. You can list all the existing services as well as start, stop, pause, and resume them (provided you have sufficient administrative permissions on the system).

You can create an instance of the ServiceController class in three distinct ways: by dragging an element from the Server Explorer window to the form's component tray area, by dropping an item from the Component tab of the Toolbox, or simply by means of code. The three techniques are equivalent, but I'll focus on the last one because it also can be used from inside classes and modules.

Listing Installed Services

Listing installed services on local or remote machines is trivial if you use the GetServices and GetDevices shared methods of the ServiceController class. These methods return an array of all the nondevice services and all the device services installed on the specified machine, respectively, or the local machine if the argument is omitted:

```
' List all nondevice services on local machines.
Console.WriteLine("--- NON-DEVICE SERVICES:")
For Each sc As ServiceController In ServiceController.GetServices
    Console.WriteLine("{0} ({1})", sc.ServiceName, sc.DisplayName)
Next

' List all device services on local machines.
Console.WriteLine ("--- DEVICE SERVICES:")
For Each sc As ServiceController In ServiceController.GetDevices
    Console.WriteLine("{0} ({1})", sc.ServiceName, sc.DisplayName)
Next
```

The demo application contains a routine that displays the list of installed services. (See Figure 20-5.)

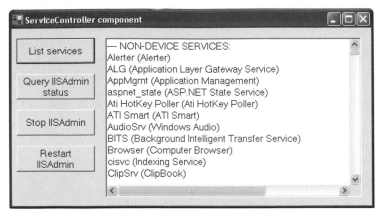

Figure 20-5   The demo application lists all installed services.

Querying a ServiceController Object

Once you have a reference to a ServiceController object, you can query its many properties to learn more about the related service:

- The ServiceName property is the short name of the service, whereas the DisplayName property returns the longer, descriptive name of the service. For example, the service name of the Internet Information Services service is IISADMIN, whereas its display name is IIS Admin Service.

- The MachineName property is the name of the machine on which the service is running.

- The Status property is an enumerated value that indicates the state the service is in. It can be one of the following values: Running, Paused, Stopped, StartPending, PausePending, ContinuePending, or StopPending. A service is in one of the *xxx*-Pending states when a command has been issued but not yet completed.

- The CanStop property is True if the service can be stopped; the CanPauseAndContinue property is True if the service can be paused and resumed; the CanShutdown property is True if the service should be notified when the service shuts down.

- The ServiceType property is a bit-coded value that lets you determine other features of the service. It can be a combination of the following values: Adapter (a service for a hardware device that requires its own driver); FileSystemDriver (a file system driver, which is also a kernel device driver); InteractiveProcess (a service that can communicate with the desktop); KernelDriver (a kernel device driver such as a hard disk or other low-level hardware device driver); RecognizerDriver (a file system driver used during startup to determine the file systems present on the system); Win32OwnProcess (a Win32 program that can be started by the Service Controller, obeys the service control protocol, and is a type of Win32 service that runs in a process by itself); and Win32ShareProcess (a Win32 service that can share a process with other Win32 services).

■ The ServicesDependedOn property returns an array of ServiceController objects, each one identifying a service that must be running for the related service to run. If any of these services isn't running, you won't be able to start the related service.

The following code snippet creates a ServiceController object that points to the IISADMIN service and displays information about it:

```
' Get a reference to the IISADMIN service on the local machine.
Dim scIISAdmin As New ServiceController("IISADMIN", ".")

Console.WriteLine("ServiceName = " & scIISAdmin.ServiceName)
Console.WriteLine("DisplayName = " & scIISAdmin.DisplayName)
Console.WriteLine("MachineName = " & scIISAdmin.MachineName)
Console.WriteLine("Status = " & scIISAdmin.Status.ToString)
Console.WriteLine("CanStop = " & scIISAdmin.CanStop)
Console.WriteLine("CanPauseAndContinue = " & scIISAdmin.CanPauseAndContinue)
Console.WriteLine("CanShutDown = " & scIISAdmin.CanShutdown)
Console.WriteLine("ServiceType = " & scIISAdmin.ServiceType.ToString)

' List services IISADMIN depends on.
Console.WriteLine ("Services this service depends on:")
For Each sc As ServiceController In scIISAdmin.ServicesDependedOn
    Console.WriteLine(" {0} ({1})", sc.ServiceName, sc.DisplayName)
Next

' List services that depend on IISADMIN.
Console.WriteLine("Services that depend on this service:")
For Each sc As ServiceController In scIISAdmin.DependentServices
    Console.WriteLine(" {0} ({1})", sc.ServiceName, sc.DisplayName)
Next
```

Managing a Service

The ServiceController class exposes a few methods that let you manage Windows services:

■ The Start method starts the service. When you invoke this method, the status of the service changes into StartPending and then into Running; you can't stop a service until it reaches the running status. The Start method is overloaded to take an optional String array for services that take arguments.

■ The Stop method stops the service and all the services that depend on this service. You should test the CanStop property before invoking this method. (If CanStop returns False, the Stop method throws an exception.)

■ The Pause method pauses the service. When you invoke this method, the status of the service changes into StartPending and then into Paused. You can't resume a service until it has reached the paused status.

■ The Continue method restarts the paused service. When you invoke this method, the status of the service changes into ContinuePending and then into Running.

■ The ExecuteCommand method executes an application-defined command. This method takes an Integer argument and passes it to the service but doesn't change the status of the service. See the documentation of each service about supported custom commands. (Also read the "Managing Custom Commands" section earlier in this chapter to see how you can write a service that reacts to custom commands.)

■ The Refresh method reads again all the properties of the ServiceController object.

The following code shows how you can stop and restart the IISADMIN service on the local machine. Note that you should ensure that all the services on which the IISADMIN service depends are running before you attempt to invoke the Start method:

```
Sub StopService()
    Dim scIISAdmin As New ServiceController("IISADMIN", ".")
    ' Check that the service can be stopped.
    If scIISAdmin.CanStop Then
        scIISAdmin.Stop()
    Else
        Console.WriteLine("Unable to stop the service at this time")
    End If
End Sub

Sub RestartService()
    Dim scIISAdmin As New ServiceController("IISADMIN", ".")
    ' Ensure that all the services this service depends on are running.
    For Each sc As ServiceController In scIISAdmin.ServicesDependedOn
        If sc.Status <> ServiceControllerStatus.Running Then
            sc.Start()
        End If
    Next
    ' Now you can start this service.
    scIISAdmin.Start()
End Sub
```

The only other method that the ServiceController class exposes is WaitForStatus, which waits until the service reaches a given status:

```
scIISAdmin.Stop()
' Wait until the service has stopped.
scIISAdmin.WaitForStatus(ServiceControllerStatus.Stopped)
Console.WriteLine("The service has stopped")
```

You can also use a timeout so that your application isn't blocked if the service can't reach the specified status. The WaitForStatus method doesn't return any value, so you must manually check the state of the service when the application regains control:

```
' Start this service.
scIISAdmin.Start()
' Wait until the service is running (timeout = 5 seconds)
scIISAdmin.WaitForStatus(ServiceControllerStatus.Running, _
    New TimeSpan(0, 0, 5))
If scIISAdmin.Status = ServiceControllerStatus.Running Then
    Console.WriteLine("The service is running")
Else
    Console.WriteLine("Unable to start the service")
End If
```

Here are two additional notes on the ServiceController component:

■ The component passes the start, stop, pause, and continue commands to the Service Control Manager, not to the service itself. The method returns after the request has been acknowledged, without waiting for the Service Control Manager to pass the request to the service. For this reason, you don't need to catch exceptions inside the code that uses the ServiceController component, but at the same time, you can't assume that the operation was successful.

■ Don't use this component to manipulate a service contained in the same project. The code in a project that creates a service can't control the service itself. The service must be controlled from another context.

All the code samples so far have focused on language features, the user interface, or some other functionality of Windows programs. However, the majority of real-world applications deal with databases, and the .NET Framework has much to offer in that field as well. Read on to learn more about how you read and update databases using the new ADO.NET classes.

Part V
Database Applications

21 ADO.NET in Connected Mode

It's time to get your hands dirty with database programming. If you're a .NET developer, this means writing code against a few classes in System.Data and its child namespaces, which are collectively known as ADO.NET. These classes and their methods let you retrieve data from Microsoft SQL Server, Oracle, or a more generic OLE DB or ODBC data source, process it, and update the original database tables.

ADO.NET is a vast topic, so I'll address it in two chapters to keep it manageable. This chapter introduces ADO.NET and illustrates how to use it in a connected mode scenario—that is, while keeping the database connection open—whereas in Chapter 22, I'll focus on using ADO.NET in disconnected mode. In addition, some sections in Chapter 23 explore the ADO.NET features that are related to XML and how you can simplify your ADO.NET coding with Visual Studio .NET.

> **Note** To keep the code as concise as possible, all the code samples in this chapter assume the use of the following Imports statements at the file or project level:
>
> ```
> Imports System.Data
> Imports System.Data.OleDb
> Imports System.Data.SqlClient
> Imports System.Data.Odbc
> Imports System.IO
> ```

The Transition to ADO.NET

Generally speaking, ADO.NET is remarkably simpler than ActiveX Data Objects (ADO), both because its object model is more straightforward and because it has a narrower field of application. ADO.NET doesn't support server-side cursors, so Visual Basic .NET developers don't have to worry about table locks, or at least not as much as Visual Basic 6 programmers using ADO have to. At first glance, the lack of server-side cursors might be perceived as a defect, but in the next chapter you'll discover that the ADO.NET way of doing things is superior to the ADO way in terms of performance and scalability.

> **See Also** You can review the fundamental concepts of database programming with ADO in *Programming Microsoft Visual Basic 6*, provided in the companion material. Most of the material in that book is still useful when you're working with Visual Basic .NET. For example, Chapter 8 includes a crash course on the SQL language; Chapter 13 touches on details on transactions and cursors; Chapter 14 shows how to build an ADO connection string (which in most cases can be used as is or with few modifications with ADO.NET as well) and the basic principles of disconnected Recordsets (which are the precursors of ADO.NET DataSet objects).

Introducing ADO.NET

ADO.NET is revolutionary by many measures. Nevertheless, if you're familiar with ADO, it won't take much effort or time to learn ADO.NET and become as productive with it as you are using Visual Basic 6.

Major Changes from ADO

From an architectural perspective, the most important change from "classic" ADO is that ADO.NET doesn't rely on OLE DB providers and uses .NET managed providers instead. A .NET Data Provider works as a bridge between your application and the data source, so you see that it can be considered an evolution of the OLE DB provider concept. However, the inner implementation details are very different. ADO.NET and .NET managed data providers don't use COM at all, so a .NET application can access data without undergoing any performance penalty deriving from the switch between managed and unmanaged code. This is completely true, however, only if you are using the OLE DB Provider, which uses COM behind the scenes.

From a programmer's perspective, the most important difference between ADO.NET and ADO is that dynamic and keyset server-side cursors are no longer supported. ADO.NET supports only forward-only, read-only resultsets (known as firehose cursors, even though they aren't really a type of cursor) and disconnected resultsets. Server-side cursors were dumped because they consume resources on the server and create a large number of locks on database tables. Taken together, these two factors can hinder application scalability more than anything else.

Retrieving Data

Many of the concepts you learned in ADO have survived the .NET revolution and are still valid today, even though classes and their methods often have different names and syntax.

For example, ADO.NET exposes a Connection object that's conceptually identical to the ADO Connection object. Before you can perform any operation on a data source, you *must* open a Connection object that points to that data source, and you must close the Connection object when you don't need it any longer. Fortunately, Microsoft didn't change the syntax of the connection string, so you can reuse all the arguments you used with ADO under Visual Basic 6. Likewise, the ODBC Connection object accepts the same ODBC connection string you can use when connecting to an ODBC source from pre-.NET applications. Creating a correct connection string was probably the hardest part of establishing a connection, so this instance of backward compatibility will make most programmers happy. (For sure, it made *me* happy.)

Of the two ways that ADO.NET provides for dealing with data, forward-only, read-only resultsets give you the best performance, as all experienced ADO developers know. In ADO.NET, you create this type of resultset by creating a Command object for the connection in question, defining the SELECT query to be executed, and finally performing an ExecuteReader method.

The second way to retrieve data from a data source is conceptually similar to the way you work with disconnected ADO recordsets: you open a connection, retrieve a block of data and store it on the client, and then close the connection to release the server-side resources associated with it. After you have downloaded the data to the client, you can perform all types of processing on it, including modifying values, adding new rows, and deleting existing rows. You can then reopen the connection and reconcile your local data with the actual data source.

To deal with these disconnected resultsets, ADO.NET introduces a new object, the DataSet, whose specific purpose is to store and process client-side data. You can think of a DataSet as a recordset on steroids. It can hold multiple resultsets coming from a single database table, it can create relationships between resultsets, and it can export and import data from multiple data sources. A better way to think of the DataSet is to consider it a scaled-down relational database that you keep in the client's memory and that contains a local (and partial) copy of data read from one or more data sources (not necessarily databases).

An important feature of the DataSet object is that it's *completely* disconnected from any particular data source, both physically and logically. For example, you might fill a single DataSet with a resultset coming from SQL Server, a resultset coming from Microsoft Access, a third resultset coming from an XML stream, and maybe a table of data that you build in code. Then you can create relations among these different resultsets, navigate through them with ease, and maybe use the DataSet to update an Oracle table. The independence from a specific data source is achieved by means of the Data-Adapter object, the component that actually reads data into a DataSet and is capable of updating a data source with the data that the client application has added or modified.

Something has been lost in the transition from ADO disconnected recordsets to the more powerful DataSet object, however. First, ADO.NET doesn't support the notion of hierarchical resultsets as ADO does, although this isn't a serious problem because ADO hierarchical recordsets were difficult to use and not flexible enough for most real-world applications (even though they looked so nice in demonstrations). In my opinion, the relational capabilities of the DataSet object will keep you from pining for ADO hierarchical recordsets. The second noteworthy limitation is that ADO.NET offers less built-in support for updates than ADO does, so you have to write more code to reconcile a modified DataSet with the data source. Nevertheless, the ADO.NET approach is superior in terms of flexibility and performance because you're in control of virtually every detail of the synchronization process.

New XML Features

As I mentioned earlier, ADO.NET offers superb support for XML sources. As a matter of fact, you can consider XML as the native format for ADO.NET data, even though data is stored in memory in a different format to maximize throughput. You can define the schema of the imported or exported XML stream by using XSD schemas, a feature that simplifies interoperability with other platforms and data sources. For example, you can have a .NET application read and update a data source residing on a non-Windows system by using XML as a common denominator between the two worlds. The tight integration with XML means that when it is more convenient to do so you can process your data according to the familiar relational model by using the DataSet object or according to the hierarchical model promoted by XML.

Being able to exchange data in XML format also allows you to overcome problems that occur when sending information over the Internet. In theory, you can send an ADO resultset through the Internet using the Remote Data Services programming model. In practice, however, sending binary data over the Internet is easier said than done if there's a firewall in the middle. With ADO.NET, you can send plain XML data as text by means of the HTTP protocol, so exchanging data over a firewall is no longer a problem. You can send an entire DataSet object and all the data it contains as XML and rebuild it on the target machine.

ADO.NET also supports strongly typed datasets, which simplify how your code refers to tables and fields in a resultset. You see the convenience of strongly typed DataSet objects when you compare the usual way of referring to a column in a given table,

```
id = myDataSet.Tables("Authors").Fields("au_id").Value
```

with the more concise (though not faster) code you can write against a strongly typed DataSet that exposes all the tables as nested classes and all the fields as properties:

```
id = myDataSet.Authors.au_id
```

.NET Data Providers

.NET data providers play the same role that OLE DB providers play under ADO: they enable your application to read and write data stored in a data source. Microsoft currently supplies five ADO.NET providers:

- **The OLE DB .NET Data Provider**   This provider lets you access a data source for which an OLE DB provider exists, although at the expense of a switch from managed to unmanaged code and the performance degradation that ensues.

- **The SQL Server .NET Data Provider**   This provider has been specifically written to access SQL Server version 7.0 or later using Tabular Data Stream (TDS) as the communication medium. TDS is SQL Server's native protocol, so you can expect this provider to give you better performance than the OLE DB Data Provider. Additionally, the SQL Server .NET Data Provider exposes SQL Server–specific features, such as named transactions and support for the FOR XML clause in SELECT queries.

- **The ODBC .NET Data Provider**   This provider works as a bridge toward an ODBC source, so in theory you can use it to access any source for which an ODBC driver exists. As of this writing, this provider officially supports only the Access, SQL Server, and Oracle ODBC drivers, so there's no clear advantage in using it instead of the OLE DB .NET Data Provider. The convenience of this provider will be more evident when more ODBC drivers are added to the list of those officially supported.

- **The .NET Data Provider for Oracle**   This provider can access an Oracle data source version 8.1.7 or later. It automatically uses connection pooling to increase performance if possible, and supports most of the features of the Microsoft OLE DB Provider for Oracle, even though these two accessing techniques can differ in a few details—for example, the .NET Data Provider for Oracle doesn't support the TABLE data type and ODBC escape sequences.

- **The SQLXML Library**   This DLL, which you can download from the Microsoft Web site, includes a few managed types that let you query and update a Microsoft SQL Server 2000 data source over HTTP. It supports XML templates, XPath queries, and can expose stored procedures and XML templates as Web services.

The ODBC and Oracle providers are included in .NET Framework 1.1 but were missing in the first version of the .NET Framework. If you work with .NET Framework 1.0, you can download these providers from the Microsoft Web site. The downloadable versions of these providers differ from the versions that come with .NET Framework 1.1, mainly in the namespaces they use: Microsoft.Data.Odbc and Microsoft.Data.Oracle instead of System.Data.Odbc and System.Data.Oracle.

The decision about which provider you should use depends on which database you work with, and in some cases its version number. If you work with SQL Server 7.0 or 2000, you should use the SQL Server .NET Data Provider, and you should fall back to the OLE DB .NET Data Provider if you work with SQL Server version 6.5 or earlier. If you work with Oracle version 8.1.7 or later, use the Oracle .NET Data Provider, or use the OLE DB .NET Data Provider if you absolutely need features that the Oracle provider doesn't support. If you work with Access, the OLE DB .NET Data Provider is the only option.

If you work with a database other than SQL Server, Oracle, or Access, you can try using either the OLE DB .NET Data Provider or the ODBC .NET Data Provider, or both, depending on whether you have an OLE DB provider or an ODBC driver capable of reaching your database. Microsoft guarantees the managed providers for OLE DB and ODBC only with the three aforementioned databases, but other databases often can be used with these managed providers. Keep in mind that the OLEDB managed provider doesn't support OLE DB 2.5 interfaces, so it's incompatible with OLE DB providers that require these interfaces—for example, the Microsoft OLE DB Provider for Microsoft Exchange and the Microsoft OLE DB Provider for Internet Publishing.

Using ADO via COM Interop

Before we dive into ADO.NET and its object model, I want to briefly mention using classic ADO objects through the COM Interop layer. You might need to do this to accomplish the few things that aren't yet possible in ADO.NET, such as the following:

- Working with server-side keysets and dynamic cursors

- Accessing an OLE DB provider that the OLE DB .NET Data Provider doesn't support

- Using the Data Definition Language (DDL) and security features of the ADO Extensions for DDL and Security (ADOX) library, none of which is supported in ADO.NET

As you know, server-side cursors generally should be avoided, but in some cases it's OK to use them—for example, you might have an administrative utility (or an ASP.NET page that's accessible only to the site administrator) that the user runs once in a while. Using a server-side cursor can save you coding time without having an impact on overall scalability and performance.

Using ADO objects is actually simple because this library is installed in the global assembly cache (GAC) already, together with the .NET Framework, so it's just a matter of adding a reference to it. You can add a reference to the library by invoking the Add Reference command on the Project menu and selecting the adodb component on the .NET tab (and not the COM tab) of the Add Reference dialog box. The following code shows how to use the ADO Connection and Recordset objects to create a server-side keyset cursor and use it to modify a database table using optimistic locking:

```
' Open an ADO Connection.
Dim adoCn As New ADODB.Connection()
adoCn.Open("Provider=SQLOLEDB.1;Integrated Security=SSPI;" _
    & "Persist Security Info=False;Initial Catalog=pubs;Data Source=(local)")

' Open an ADO Recordset.
Dim adoRs As New ADODB.Recordset()
adoRs.Open("SELECT * FROM Publishers", adoCn, _
    ADODB.CursorTypeEnum.adOpenKeyset, ADODB.LockTypeEnum.adLockOptimistic)

' Convert Publisher names to uppercase.
Do Until adoRs.EOF
    adoRs("pub_name").Value = UCase(adoRs("pub_name").Value)
    adoRs.MoveNext()
Loop
' Close objects to release resources.
adoRs.Close()
adoCn.Close()
```

Even though it looks as if it's using the original COM objects, the preceding code is actually referencing .NET wrappers around the original ADO Connection and Recordset objects, so you must manually close them to release the associated resources as soon as possible. If you omit the last two statements, the connection will be kept open until the next garbage collection, which is something you should avoid.

You can't use the adodb library installed in the GAC to exploit the DDL and security features of ADOX. Instead, you must add a reference to the Microsoft ADO Ext. 2.7 For DDL And Security library from the COM tab of the Add Reference dialog box. The following code uses the ADOX library to list all the tables in a SQL Server database:

```
' Open an ADO connection to SQL Server.
Dim adoCn As New ADODB.Connection()
adoCn.Open("Provider=SQLOLEDB.1;Integrated Security=SSPI;" _
    & "Persist Security Info=False;Initial Catalog=pubs;Data Source=(local)")
' Create an ADOX Catalog on that connection.
Dim cat As New ADOX.Catalog()
cat.ActiveConnection = adoCn
' Enumerate all the database tables and their columns.
For Each tbl As ADOX.Table In cat.Tables
    Debug.WriteLine(tbl.Name)
    For Each col As ADOX.Column In tbl.Columns
        Debug.WriteLine("    " & col.Name)
    Next
Next
' Close the connection, and release resources.
adoCn.Close()
```

The ADO.NET Object Model

It's time to have a closer look at the individual objects that make up the ADO.NET architecture illustrated in Figure 21-1. You'll see that objects are divided into two groups: the objects included in the .NET Data Provider, and those that belong to the ADO.NET disconnected architecture. (In practice, the second group includes only the DataSet and its secondary objects.)

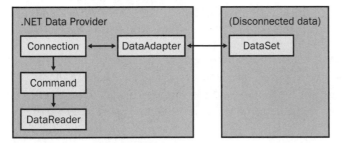

Figure 21-1   The relationships among the main ADO.NET objects

ADO.NET Objects at a Glance

The Connection object has the same function it has under ADO: establishing a connection to the data source. Like its ADO counterpart, it has the ConnectionString property, the Open and Close methods, and the ability to begin a transaction using the BeginTransaction method. The ADO Execute method isn't supported, and the ADO.NET Connection object lacks the ability to send a command to the database.

The Command object lets you query the database, send a command to it, or invoke one of its stored procedures. You can perform these actions by using one of the object's Execute*xxxx* methods. More specifically, you use the ExecuteNonQuery method to send an action query to the database—for example, an INSERT or DELETE SQL statement—an ExecuteReader method to perform a SELECT query that returns a resultset, or an ExecuteScalar method to perform a SELECT query that returns a single value. Other properties let you set the command timeout and prepare the parameters for a call to a stored procedure. You must manually associate a Command object with the Connection object previously connected to the data source.

The DataReader object is the object returned by the ExecuteReader method of the Command object and represents a forward-only, read-only resultset. A new row of results becomes available each time you invoke the DataReader's Read method, after which you can query each individual field using the GetValue method or one of the strongly typed Get*xxxx* methods, such as GetString or GetFloat. Remember that you can't update the database by means of a DataReader object.

The DataSet object is the main object in the ADO.NET disconnected architecture. It works as a sort of small relational database that resides on the client and is completely unrelated to any specific database. It consists of a collection of DataTable objects, with each DataTable object holding a distinct resultset (typically the result of a query to a different database table). A DataTable object contains a collection of DataRow objects, each one holding data coming from a different row in the result. A DataSet also contains a collection of DataRelation objects, in which each item corresponds to a relationship between different DataTable objects, much like the relationships you have between the tables of a relational database. These relations let your code navigate among tables in the same DataSet using a simple and effective syntax.

The DataAdapter object works as a bridge between the Connection object and the DataSet object. Its Fill method moves data from the database to the client-side DataSet, whereas its Update method moves data in the opposite direction and updates the database with the rows that your application has added, modified, or deleted from the DataSet.

ADO.NET Namespaces

I must clarify one point: most of the names described in the preceding section—more precisely, the names of the objects in the .NET Data Provider portion of the figure—are generic names that you never use as is in your code. Not only do different .NET data providers use different namespaces, they also use different names for these objects:

- The System.Data namespace gathers the ADO.NET objects that don't belong to a specific data provider. For example, this namespace contains the DataSet object and all its secondary objects, such as DataTable, DataRow, and DataRelation. The System.Data namespace also contains several ADO.NET interfaces.

- The System.Data.Common namespace contains the DataAdapter type and other virtual classes. These types are used as base classes for several objects in the namespaces that follow. You rarely have to reference items from this namespace in your code.

- The System.Data.OleDb namespace contains the objects associated with the OLE DB .NET Data Provider, such as OleDbConnection, OleDbCommand, OleDbDataReader, and OleDbDataAdapter.

- The System.Data.SqlClient namespace contains the objects associated with the SQL Server .NET Data Provider, such as SqlConnection, SqlCommand, SqlDataReader, and SqlDataAdapter.

- The System.Data.Odbc namespace contains the objects associated with the ODBC .NET Data Provider, such as OdbcConnection, OdbcCommand, OdbcDataReader, and OdbcDataAdapter.

- The System.Data.OracleClient namespace contains the objects associated with the Oracle .NET Data Provider, such as OracleConnection, OracleCommand, OracleDataReader, and OracleDataAdapter.

All the types from the first four preceding namespaces are defined in the System.Data.Dll assembly, whereas the types for working with Oracle databases are defined in the System.Data.OracleClient.Dll assembly. You must explicitly add a reference to this DLL if you want to work with the Oracle .NET Data Provider.

Even if you never explicitly use the DataAdapter object in your code, it's convenient to think in terms of the abstract DataAdapter class because all the concrete xxxxDataAdapter objects inherit from it and therefore expose the same methods and exhibit the same behavior.

Similar objects in different providers share a common interface rather than inherit from the same class. For example, all xxxxConnection objects implement the IDBConnection interface. Similarly, xxxCommand objects implement the IDBCommand interface, and the IDBDataReader interface is the common trait among all the xxxxDataReader objects. These common interfaces let you build provider-agnostic ADO.NET code. See the note at the end of Chapter 22.

The Connection Object

Whether you work in connected or in disconnected mode, the first action you need to perform when working with a data source is to open a connection to it. In ADO.NET terms, this means that you create a Connection object that connects to the specific database.

The Connection object is similar to the ADO object of the same name, so you'll feel immediately at ease with the new ADO.NET object if you have any experience with ADO programming.

Setting the ConnectionString Property

The key property of the Connection class is ConnectionString, a string that defines the type of the database you're connecting to, its location, and other semicolon-delimited attributes. When you work with the OleDbConnection object, the connection string matches the connection string that you use with the ADO Connection object. Such a string typically contains the following information:

- The Provider attribute, which specifies the name of the underlying OLE DB Provider used to connect to the data. The only values that Microsoft guarantees as valid are SQLOLEDB (the OLE DB provider for Microsoft SQL Server), Microsoft.Jet.OLEDB.4.0 (the OLE DB provider for Microsoft Access), and MSDAORA (the OLE DB provider for Oracle).

- The Data Source attribute, which specifies where the database is. It can be the path to an Access database or the name of the machine on which the SQL Server or the Oracle database is located.

■ The User ID and Password attributes, which specify the user name and the password of a valid account for the database.

■ The Initial Catalog attribute, which specifies the name of the database when you're connecting to a SQL Server or an Oracle data source.

Once you've set the ConnectionString property correctly, you can open the connection by invoking the Open method:

```
Dim BiblioConnString As String = "Provider=Microsoft.Jet.OLEDB.4.0;" _
    & "Data Source=C:\Program Files\Microsoft Visual Studio\VB98\BIBLIO.MDB;"
' Open the Biblio.mdb database.
Dim cn As New OledbConnection()
cn.ConnectionString = BiblioConnString
cn.Open()
```

(Notice that ConnectionString is the only writeable property in the Connection object.)

You can make your code more concise by passing the connection string to the Connection object's constructor method:

```
' Another, more concise, way to open the Biblio.mdb database.
Dim cn As New OledbConnection(BiblioConnString)
cn.Open()
```

The same description applies as well to the SqlConnection object, with just one difference: you must omit the Provider attribute from the connection string. In fact, you don't need this attribute in this case because you can connect only to a SQL Server database if you use the SQL Server .NET Data Provider. Also notice that you can specify **(local)** as the Data Source attribute if you're connecting to the SQL Server on the local machine:

```
Dim SqlPubsConnString As String = "Data Source=(local); User ID=sa;" _
    & "Initial Catalog=pubs"
Dim cn As New SqlConnection(SqlPubsConnString)
cn.Open()
```

The connection string can include other attributes. For example, the Connection Timeout attribute sets the number of seconds after which the attempt to open the connection fails with an error. (The default value is 15 seconds.) After you open the connection, you can query the current value of this timeout with the ConnectionTimeout property:

```
' Specify a longer timeout when connecting to Pubs.
Dim cn As New SqlConnection("Data Source=(local); User ID=sa;" _
    & "Initial Catalog=pubs;Connection Timeout=30")
cn.Open()
Debug.WriteLine(cn.ConnectionTimeout)      ' => 30
```

After you open the connection, you can query individual portions of the connection string by means of the DataSource, Database, Provider, ServerVersion, and ConnectionTimeout read-only properties.

Other values that you pass in the connection string depend on the specific OLE DB provider to which you're connecting. For example, the provider Microsoft.Jet.OLEDB.4.0 supports attributes for setting the database password or specifying the system database that contains information about groups and users.

When you're working with the SQL Server .NET Data Provider, you can specify two additional attributes in the connection string: Packet Size and Workstation ID. The former value sets the size of the network packet used to communicate with SQL Server; the latter is a string that can be later used to identify the client. The Packet Size attribute is sometimes useful for optimizing the flux of data to and from SQL Server. For example, you might increase it if your application deals with large BLOB fields (such as images) or decrease it if you often query the server for a small amount of data.

```
' Optimize the connection for large BLOB fields.
Dim cn As New SqlConnection("Data Source=(local); User ID=sa;" _
    & "Initial Catalog=pubs;Packet Size=32767")
cn.Open()
Debug.WriteLine(cn.PacketSize)        ' => 32767
```

The SqlConnection object exposes two additional read-only properties—PacketSize and WorkstationId—that return the values of these attributes as specified in the connection string.

As you might guess, the OdbcConnection object takes a connection string in ODBC format:

```
Dim cn As New OdbcConnection("Driver={SQL Server};" _
    & "Server=localhost;Trusted Connection=yes;Database=pubs")
```

After you have set the connection string, you can read the information it contains by means of the Driver, DataSource, Database, and ServerVersion properties. Additionally, the OdbcConnection object supports the writeable ConnectionTimeout property, by means of which you can decide after how many seconds your application waits when establishing a connection. (This property is writeable because you can't assign a timeout in the ODBC connection string.)

The connection string for an OracleConnection object is designed to look like the connection string you'd pass to the OLE DB .NET Data Provider when it's used with an Oracle database:

```
Dim cn As OracleConnection = New OracleConnection( _
    "Data Source=MyServer;Integrated Security=yes;")
cn.Open()
```

I won't cover the Oracle .NET Data Provider in much depth in this book. For additional information about this provider, please read the section about the System.Data.OracleClient namespace in the .NET platform SDK.

> **Note**   All the code routines in this chapter open a connection to the Biblio.mdb database using the OLE DB .NET Data Provider (which comes with Visual Studio 6 and Access and is also provided on the companion CD), or the Pubs database using the SQL Server .NET Data Provider (which is installed with any version of SQL Server), or the ODBC .NET Data Provider. To keep code as concise as possible, the demo application defines these three connection strings at the module level:
>
> ```
> ' For Biblio.mdb using the OLE DB .NET Data Provider
> Public BiblioConnString As String = "Provider=" _
>     & "Microsoft.Jet.OLEDB.4.0;Data Source=" & _
>     "C:\Program Files\Microsoft Visual Studio\VB98\Biblio.mdb"
>
> ' For SQL Server's Pubs using the OLE DB .NET Data Provider
> Public OleDbPubsConnString As String = "Provider=" _
>     & "SQLOLEDB.1;Data Source=.;" _
>     & "Integrated Security=SSPI;Initial Catalog=Pubs"
>
> ' For Pubs using the SQL Server .NET Data Provider
> Public SqlPubsConnString As String = "Data Source=.;" _
>     & "Integrated Security=SSPI;Initial Catalog=Pubs"
>
> ' For Pubs using the ODBC .NET Data Provider
> Public OdbcPubsConnString As String = "Driver={SQL Server};" _
>     & "Server=localhost;Trusted Connection=yes;Database=pubs"
> ```
>
> You should edit these connection strings to match your system's configuration. For example, you should change the Data Source value in BiblioConnString to assign it the actual path of Biblio.mdb. These connection strings are used also in sample code in later chapters.

Opening and Closing the Connection

You've seen that the Open method takes no arguments, unlike the Open method of the ADO Connection object:

```
Dim cn As New OledbConnection(BiblioConnString)
cn.Open()
```

The State Property and the StateChange Event

The State property is a bit-coded field that indicates the current state of the database connection. It can be the combination of one or more of the following ConnectionState enumerated values: Closed, Connecting, Open, Executing, Fetching, and Broken. You typically check the State property to ensure that you're opening a closed connection or closing an open connection, as in this snippet:

```
' Close the connection only if it was opened.
If (cn.State And ConnectionState.Open) <> 0 Then
    cn.Close()
End If
```

Whenever the State property changes from Open to Close or vice versa, the Connection object fires a StateChange event:

```
Dim WithEvents cn As SqlConnection

Private Sub cn_StateChange(ByVal sender As Object, _
    ByVal e As System.Data.StateChangeEventArgs) Handles cn.StateChange
    ' Show the status of the connection in a Label control.
    If (e.CurrentState And ConnectionState.Open) <> 0 Then
        lblStatus.Text = "The connection has been opened"
    ElseIf e.CurrentState = ConnectionState.Closed Then
        lblStatus.Text = "The connection has been closed"
    End If
End Sub
```

ConnectionState.Closed is equal to 0, so you can't use the And bitwise operator to test this state, unlike all the other values. Be careful not to throw an exception from inside this event handler because it would be returned to the code that issued the Open or Close method.

Although it's a good habit to test the state of the database before performing any operation on it, in some cases ADO.NET is much more forgiving than classic ADO. For example, you can execute the Close method of the Connection object (or any other ADO.NET object that exposes this method) without throwing any exception if the object is already closed:

```
' This statement never throws an exception.
cn.Close()
```

Dealing with Errors

As in ADO, you should protect your code from unexpected errors when attempting a connection to a database as well as while processing data coming from the database itself. However, when working with ADO.NET you have an added responsibility: because of the garbage collection mechanism intrinsic in .NET, the connection isn't automatically closed when the Connection object goes out of scope. In this case, in fact, the connection is closed in the Finalize protected method of the Connection object, and you know that the garbage collector might call this method several minutes after the object goes out of scope. Because an error can occur virtually anywhere you're working in a database, you should protect your code with a Try block and ensure that you close the connection in the Finally section in an orderly way:

```
Dim cn As New OleDbConnectionnString)
Try
    cn.Open()
    ' Process the data here.

Catch ex As Exception
    MessageBox.Show(ex.Message)
```

```
Finally
    ' Ensure that the connection is closed.
    ' (It doesn't throw an exception even if the Open method failed.)
    cn.Close()
End Try
```

Most of the exceptions that you catch when working with the OLE DB .NET Data Provider are of the OleDbException class. In addition to all the members it has in common with other exception classes, this class exposes the Errors collection that contains one or more OleDbError objects, each one describing how the original error in the database (for example, a violation of the referential integrity rules) has been reported to the many software layers that sit between the database and the application. The following code shows how you can explore the OleDbException.Errors collection to show details about the caught exception:

```
' Run a query that references a table that doesn't exist.
Dim cmd As New OleDbCommand("UPDATE xyz SET id=1", cn)
Try
    cmd.ExecuteNonQuery()
Catch ex As OleDbException
    ' An OleDbException has occurred - display details.
    Dim msg As String = ""
    For i As Integer = 0 To ex.errors.Count - 1
        Dim er As OleDbError = ex.Errors(i)
        msg &= String.Format("Message = {1}{0}Source = {2}{0}" & _
            "NativeError = {3}{0}SQLState = {4}{0}", ControlChars.CrLf,_
            er.Message, er.Source, er.NativeError, er.SQLState)
    Next
    MessageBox.Show(msg)
Catch ex As Exception
    MessageBox.Show(ex.Message)          ' A generic exception
Finally
    cn.Close()                           ' Close the connection.
End Try
```

The SqlException object also exposes an Errors collection containing one or more SqlError objects. The SqlError object doesn't support the NativeError and SQLState properties but exposes a few members that aren't in OleDbError: Server (the name of the SQL Server that generated the error), Procedure (the name of the stored procedure or remote procedure call that generated the error), LineNumber (the line number within the T-SQL batch or stored procedure where the error occurred), Number (a number that identifies the type of error), and Class (the severity level of the error, in the range 1 through 25).

Severity level values in the range 1 through 10 are informational and indicate problems deriving from mistakes in the information the user entered. Values in the range 11 through 16 are caused by the user and can be corrected by the user. Severity levels 17 and higher indicate serious software or hardware errors. In general, errors with severity levels of 20 or higher automatically close the connection. For this reason, you should always test the State property when an exception is thrown, regardless of the data provider you're working with.

Opening a Database Asynchronously

One of the great innovations of ADO was its ability to perform a few methods—most notably, the opening of a connection and the querying of data—in an asynchronous fashion; that is, without blocking the current application. Though difficult to set up correctly, asynchronous operations were a great tool in the hands of experienced programmers.

Don't look for asynchronous options in ADO.NET because you won't find any. Does this mean that ADO.NET is less capable than good old ADO? Of course not. It only means that asynchronous operation support is offered at the .NET Framework level through asynchronous delegates. (See Chapter 12.) Moving the support for asynchronous operations out of ADO.NET makes the object model cleaner and simpler, and even more flexible when dealing with asynchronous operations. In fact, you can perform *any* ADO.NET operation, not just a few methods, while the main program does something else.

The following code snippet shows how you can open a connection asynchronously. You can use the same code pattern for any other database operation involving the Connection object or any other ADO.NET object:

```
Delegate Sub OpenMethod()

Sub OpenAsyncConnection()
    Dim cn As New OleDbConnection(BiblioConnString)
    ' Create a delegate that points to the Open method.
    Dim asyncOpen As New OpenMethod(AddressOf cn.Open)
    ' Call it asynchronously - pass the delegate as the cookie.
    Dim ar As IAsyncResult = _
        asyncOpen.BeginInvoke(AddressOf OpenComplete, asyncOpen)
    ' Do something else here.

End Sub

Sub OpenComplete(ByVal ar As IAsyncResult)
    ' Retrieve a reference to the delegate, passed in the cookie.
    Dim asyncOpen As OpenMethod = CType(ar.AsyncState, OpenMethod)
    Try
        ' Complete the operation and let the user know it.
        asyncOpen.EndInvoke(ar)
        MessageBox.Show("The connection has been opened")
    Catch ex As Exception
        MessageBox.Show(ex.Message)
    End Try
End Sub
```

Retrieving Schema Information

Unlike classic ADO, which lets you retrieve detailed information about a database and its tables by using the rich object hierarchy available in its ADOX library (as you saw in the section "Using ADO via COM Interop" earlier in this chapter), ADO.NET gives you a seemingly more primitive way to access database schema information in the form of the GetOleDbSchemaTable method of the OleDbConnection object. Depending on the GUID value you pass to its first argument, this method returns information on databases, tables, columns, indexes, views, foreign keys, procedure arguments, and virtually anything you need to know about a database. This information is returned as a DataTable, so it's easy to display it by binding the DataTable to a DataGrid control:

```
' Return information on all the columns in the Pubs database.
Dim cn As New OleDbConnection(OleDbPubsConnString)
cn.Open()
Dim dt As DataTable = cn.GetOleDbSchemaTable(OleDbSchemaGuid.Columns, Nothing)
DataGrid1.DataSource = dt
```

In this particular example, each row in the returned DataTable (and hence the bound DataGrid) corresponds to a field in the Pubs database, and each column in the DataTable corresponds to an attribute of that field, for example TABLE_NAME, COLUMN_NAME, IS_NULLABLE, or DATA_TYPE. However, the exact sequence of fields in the DataTable depends on the GUID you passed in the first argument. Keep in mind that in a real application the call to the GetOleDbSchemaTable should be wrapped in a Try...Catch block because a database might not support all possible GUIDs.

The second argument passed to the GetOleDbSchemaTable method can be an Object array whose arguments let you reduce the amount of information returned. If the first element in the array is non-Nothing, only the rows with that value in the first column are returned; likewise, if the second element in the array is non-Nothing, only the rows with that value in the second column are returned, and so on. For example, this code returns a DataTable holding information only on the columns in the authors database table.

```
' Return information on columns in the Authors table.
Dim cn As New OleDbConnection(OleDbPubsConnString)
cn.Open()
' TABLE_NAME is the third column in the resultset.
Dim restrict() As Object = {Nothing, Nothing, "authors"}
Dim dt As DataTable = cn.GetOleDbSchemaTable(OleDbSchemaGuid.Columns, restrict)
```

I have prepared a demo application that lets you test all the possible GUIDs against the Pubs database and apply restrictions to the returned information. (See Figure 21-2.)

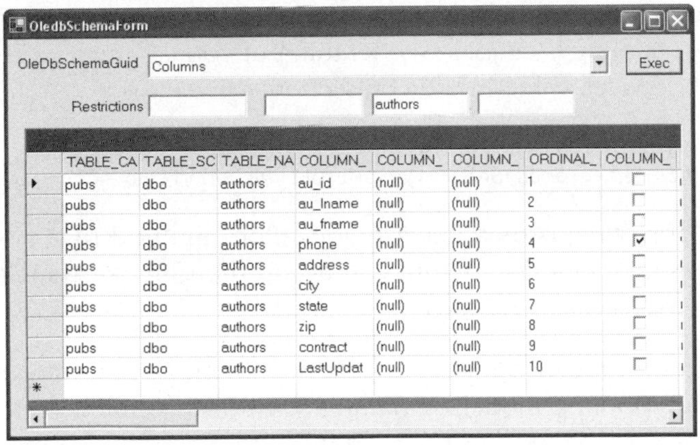

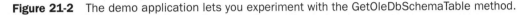

Figure 21-2   The demo application lets you experiment with the GetOleDbSchemaTable method.

Leveraging Connection Pooling

Connection pooling is a great feature of ADO.NET. It lets you transparently reuse a database connection when an application doesn't need it any longer. The mechanism works this way: when the first connection to the database is opened, a pool of identical connections is created, so subsequent requests don't have to wait to get a valid connection. When an application completes its database chores, it should explicitly close the Connection object so that it can be returned to the pool and made available for other applications. (Notice that you must explicitly close the connection to return it to the pool.)

ADO.NET creates a number of connection pools equal to the number of distinct connection strings that your program uses, so the necessary condition for exploiting the connection pool is that you open all your database connections using *exactly* the same connection string. Even an extra space or semicolon makes a connection string different, so pay attention.

This requirement means that you can't take advantage of connection pooling if you specify a different user name and password in the connection string. You're better off, therefore, using Windows integrated security instead of database security whenever it's feasible to do so:

```
Dim cn As New SqlConnection("Data Source=MyServer;" _
    & "Integrated Security=SSPI;Initial Catalog=pubs")
```

Another viable approach to reliable connection pooling is to encapsulate all the database access in a .NET component that logs in to the database using a special account and therefore uses the same connection string for all its open connections.

The OLE DB .NET Data Provider creates a connection pool based on the OLE DB session pooling. Connection pooling is enabled by default, but you can turn it off by specifying a special OLE DB Services value in the connection string:

```
Dim cn As New OleDbConnection("Provider=SQLOLEDB;" _
    & "Data Source=MyServer;Integrated Security=SSPI;OLE DB Services=-4")
```

The OleDbConnection object exposes a ReleaseObjectPool method that discards all unused connections from the pool. You might call it and then invoke the GC.Collect method to free as many resources as possible.

The SQL Server .NET Data Provider offers connection pooling based on Component Services, using an implicit pooling model by default. This arrangement means that if the current thread has already opened a transaction using this provider, any new transaction opened will match the same transactional context. When the thread requests a connection, the pool is searched for a matching connection object. To be eligible for reuse, a connection in the pool must have exactly the same connection string, must have a matching transaction context (or not be associated with any transaction context), and must have a valid link to the specified server.

You can control the behavior of connection pooling under the SQL Server .NET Data Provider by using several values in the connection string. For example, you can disable automatic enlistment in the pooling by setting the Pooling attribute to False:

```
Dim cn As New SqlConnection("Data Source=MyServer;" _
    & "Integrated Security=SSPI;Initial Catalog=pubs;Pooling=false")
```

If you open the connection from inside a class that inherits from ServicedComponent, the connection is automatically enrolled in the current distributed transaction, as I explain in Chapter 31. You can avoid this default behavior by setting the Enlist attribute to False:

```
Dim cn As New SqlConnection("Data Source=MyServer;" _
    & "Integrated Security=SSPI;Initial Catalog=pubs;Enlist=False")
```

You can set the minimum and maximum size of the pool by using the Min Pool Size and Max Pool Size attributes, whose default values are 0 and 100 respectively:

```
' If this is the first connection with this connection string, a
' pool with 10 identical connections is prepared.
Dim cn As New SqlConnection("Data Source=MyServer;" _
    & "Integrated Security=SSPI;Initial Catalog=pubs;" _
    & "Min Pool Size=10;Max Pool Size=120")
```

If the pool has reached its maximum size and all the connections are currently active and serving other applications, a request for an available connection is queued until another application releases one of the connections. If no connection is made available within the connection timeout period, an exception is thrown.

The Connection Lifetime attribute is useful in a clustered environment for taking advantage of any new server activated after the connection pool has been created. As you know, all the connections in the pool link to the server on which they were originally opened. So by default, they never attempt to use any new server brought up after the pool has reached its maximum size. The Connection Lifetime sets the lifetime of a connection in the pool (in seconds). After this period, the connection is destroyed automatically. Presumably, it will be replaced in the pool by a new connection that points to the server activated in the meantime.

```
' Destroy a connection in the pool after 2 minutes.
Dim cn As New SqlConnection("Data Source=MyServer;" _
    & "Integrated Security=SSPI;Initial Catalog=pubs;" _
    & "Connection Lifetime=120")
```

You can activate connection pooling also for ODBC connections, in the Connection Pooling tab of the ODBC Data Source Administrator utility (in Control Panel). The settings you specify in this tab affect all the applications that use the specified connection, and you can't change them though code. For more information, read the ODBC Programmer's Reference at *http://msdn.microsoft.com/library*.

Connection pooling is a mixed blessing. On the one hand, it can dramatically improve the performance and scalability of your applications; on the other, it can give you headaches if you don't use it correctly. When you see a database-intensive piece of code performing with suspicious sluggishness, you should double-check to see that it's using connection pooling correctly. To help you in this task, ADO.NET defines a few performance counters that you might want to monitor while searching for unexpected behaviors in the SQL Server .NET Data Provider. All the counters belong to the .NET CLR Data Performance object:

- **SqlClient: Current # connection pools**   Number of pools associated with the process

- **SqlClient: Current # pooled and nonpooled connections**   Number of connections, pooled or not

- **SqlClient: Current # pooled connections**   Number of connections in pools associated with the process

- **SqlClient: Peak # pooled connections**   Highest number of connections in all pools since the application started

- **SqlClient: Total # failed connects**   Number of connection attempts that failed for any reason

The .NET CLR Data Performance object exposes a sixth counter that isn't directly related to connection pooling, but is useful in many other circumstances:

- **SqlClient: Total # failed commands**   Number of commands that failed for any reason

You can monitor these counters using the Performance utility or by reading them via code using the technique described in the "Reading Performance Counter Values" section of Chapter 19.

Working with Transactions

The way you work with transactions has changed in the transition from ADO to ADO.NET. The ADO Connection class exposes the BeginTrans, CommitTrans, and RollbackTrans methods, which let you start, commit, or abort a transaction. The isolation level of the transaction is determined by the current value of the IsolationLevel property.

Creating a Transaction Object

The ADO.NET Connection object exposes only the BeginTransaction method, which takes an optional argument that specifies the isolation level of the transaction being started. As in ADO, the isolation level is an enumerated value that tells how locks are created and honored during the transaction. In a difference from ADO, the BeginTransaction method is a function that returns a Transaction object: more precisely, it returns an OleDbTransaction, a SqlTransaction, an OdbcTransaction, or an OracleTransaction object, depending on the .NET provider you're using:

```
' Open a transaction with the OLE DB .NET Data Provider.
Dim cn As New OleDbConnection(BiblioConnString)
Dim tr As OleDbTransaction = cn.BeginTransaction(IsolationLevel.Serializable)

' Open a transaction with the SQL Server .NET Data Provider.
Dim cn2 As New SqlConnection(SqlPubsConnString)
Dim tr2 As SqlTransaction = cn2.BeginTransaction(IsolationLevel.Serializable)
```

You then use the Transaction object to control the outcome of the transaction: you invoke the Commit method to confirm all the changes in the transaction and the Rollback method to cancel them:

```
Dim tr As OleDbTransaction
Try
    ' Start a transaction.
    tr = cn.BeginTransaction(IsolationLevel.Serializable)
    ' Insert here database processing code.
    ⋮
    ' If we get here, we can confirm all changes.
    tr.Commit()
Catch ex As Exception
    ' Display an error message, and roll back all changes.
    tr.Rollback()
    MessageBox.Show(ex.Message)
End Try
```

Selecting the Isolation Level

The IsolationLevel property returns an enumerated value that specifies the level of the current transaction and that's equal to the value passed to the BeginTransaction method, as you can see in the preceding code example. Here's a brief description of the isolation levels that ADO.NET supports:

- **Chaos** The pending changes from the more highly isolated transactions can't be overridden. SQL Server doesn't support this isolation level.

- **ReadUncommitted** No shared (read) locks are issued, and no exclusive (write) locks are honored, which means that an application can read data that has been written from inside a transaction but not committed yet. If the transaction is then rolled back, the data that was read doesn't correspond to the data now in the database, a phenomenon known as *dirty reads*.

- **ReadCommitted (default)** Shared (read) locks are issued, and exclusive (write) locks are honored; this isolation level avoids dirty reads, but an application isn't guaranteed to retrieve a given row if the same query is reexecuted (a problem known as *nonrepeatable reads*). Moreover, a reexecuted query might find additional rows because in the meantime the code running in another transaction has inserted one or more records (*phantom rows*).

- **RepeatableRead** Exclusive locks are placed on all the rows being read so that code running in a transaction can't even read the data being read from inside another transaction. This isolation level degrades the scalability of the application but prevents the nonrepeatable reads problem. Phantom rows are still possible, however.

- **Serializable** This level is similar to the RepeatableRead level, but an exclusive lock is issued on the entire range, and therefore code running in another transaction can't even add a new record in the same range. This isolation level is the least efficient one, but it also solves the phantom row problem: each transaction truly runs in complete isolation.

For more information about the implications of each isolation level, you should read a good database book. If you work primarily with SQL Server, I highly recommend *Inside SQL Server 2000* by Kalen Delaney (Microsoft Press).

It should be noted that transactions offer a way to implement pessimistic concurrency in ADO.NET, even though ADO.NET doesn't directly support this type of concurrency. While a transaction is held open, no other user can read the data you have modified (if the transaction level is ReadCommitted) or only read (if the transaction is RepeatableRead or Serializable). Transactions are often the only way you have to ensure that the read and write operations work in a consistent way, but misused transactions can quickly degrade the overall performance and scalability of entire applications. So it's your responsibility to commit or roll back the transaction as soon as possible.

Nesting Transactions

The OleDbTransaction object exposes a Begin method, which lets you start a transaction that's nested in the current transaction. The Begin method takes an optional isolation level and returns another OleDbTransaction object:

```
' Open an OLE DB connection.
Dim cn As New OleDbConnection(BiblioConnString)
cn.Open()
' Open the first (outer) transaction.
Dim tr As OleDbTransaction = cn.BeginTransaction(IsolationLevel.ReadCommitted)
' Do some work here.

' Open a nested (inner) transaction.
Dim tr2 As OleDbTransaction = tr.Begin(IsolationLevel.ReadUncommitted)

' Roll back the inner transaction.
tr2.Rollback()

' Commit the outer transaction and close the connection.
tr.Commit()
cn.Close()
```

Not all databases support nested transactions. For example, Access supports them, but SQL Server doesn't. In fact, if you run the preceding code on a connection opened using the SQLOLEDB provider, you get the following error:

```
Cannot start more transactions on this session.
```

Working with Named Transactions

SQL Server doesn't support true nested transactions—that is, transactions that can be rolled back or committed independently of outer (pending) transactions—and for this reason, the SqlTransaction object doesn't expose the Begin method. However, SQL Server supports named transactions. A *named transaction* is a sort of bookmark that remembers the state of the database at a given moment so that you can restore that state by using a named rollback command. You can create as many bookmarks as you need with the SQL Server SAVE TRAN command. Here's a fragment of a T-SQL routine that shows how to work with named transactions:

```
BEGIN TRAN MainTran
-- Insert, delete, or modify rows here.

SAVE TRAN EndOfFirstPart
-- Do some more work here.

-- Restore the database contents as they were before the second SAVE TRAN.
ROLLBACK TRAN EndOfFirstPart

-- Commit all changes.
COMMIT TRAN
```

To support named transactions, the BeginTransaction method of the SqlConnection object takes an optional transaction name. In addition, the SqlTransaction object exposes a Save method: both this method and the Rollback method can take an optional transaction name. Here's a Visual Basic .NET snippet that performs the same task as the preceding T-SQL fragment:

```
Dim cn As New SqlConnection(SqlPubsConnString)
cn.Open()
' Open a transaction named MainTran.
Dim tr As SqlTransaction = _
    cn.BeginTransaction(IsolationLevel.ReadCommitted, "MainTran")
' Insert, delete, or modify rows here.


' Create a named save point.
tr.Save("EndOfFirstPart")
' Do some more work here.


' Restore the database contents as they were before the second SAVE TRAN.
tr.Rollback("EndOfFirstPart")


' Commit all changes.
tr.Commit()
```

The Command Object

After you've opened a connection, you can decide whether you want to work in connected or disconnected mode. In the former case, you typically create a Command
object that contains a select query (to read data from the database) or an action query
(to update data) and then run one of its Execute*xxxx* methods, for which the exact
name depends on the type of query.

Creating a Command Object

The key properties of the Command object are CommandText (the SQL text of the
action or select query) and Connection (the connection on which the query should
run). You can set these properties individually, as in the following code snippet:

```
' Open a connection.
Dim cn As New OleDbConnection(BiblioConnString)
cn.Open()
' Define the command to insert a new record in the Authors table.
Dim sql As String = _
    "INSERT INTO Authors (Author, [Year Born]) VALUES ('Joe Doe', 1955)"
' Create an action command on that connection.
Dim cmd As New OleDbCommand()
cmd.Connection = cn
cmd.CommandText = sql


' Run the query; get the number of affected records.
Dim records As Integer = cmd.ExecuteNonQuery()
Debug.WriteLine(records)                        ' => 1
' Close the connection.
cn.Close()
```

Or you can pass these two values to the Command object's constructor, which makes
for more concise code:

```
Dim cmd As New OleDbCommand(sql, cn)
```

You can set number of seconds after which the query times out by means of the CommandTimeout property. The default value is 30 seconds; 0 means infinite timeout and should be avoided:

```
cmd.CommandTimeout = 10          ' A 10-second timeout
```

If you've opened a transaction on the connection, you must enlist the command in the transaction by assigning the Transaction object to the property with the same name or you must pass this object to the Command's constructor:

```
' (This code assumes that you've opened a connection and defined a query.)
' Begin a transaction.
Dim tr As OleDbTransaction = cn.BeginTransaction
' Create an action command, and enlist it in the transaction.
Dim cmd As New OleDbCommand(sql, cn, tr)
' Run the query; get the number of affected records.
Dim records As Integer = cmd.ExecuteNonQuery()
' Commit (or roll back) the transaction.
tr.Commit()
```

You get an error if you don't enlist the Command object in the existing transaction (more precisely, the most nested transaction being opened on that connection). Therefore, you can't help passing the Transaction object to the constructor method or to the Transaction property. (See "The Connection.EnlistDistributedTransaction Method" section in Chapter 31 to learn how you can enlist an ADO.NET connection in an existing distributed transaction.)

Issuing Database Commands

As shown in the preceding code snippets, you can perform insert, update, and delete operations through a Command object by means of the ExecuteNonQuery method, which returns the number of records that were affected by the statement:

```
Dim sql As String = _
    "INSERT INTO Authors (Author, [Year Born]) VALUES ('Joe Doe', 1955)"
Dim cmd As New OleDbCommand(sql, cn)
' Run the query; get the number of affected records.
Dim records As Integer = cmd.ExecuteNonQuery()
```

Of course, you can update existing records by using the UPDATE SQL statement and delete existing records with the DELETE statement. There isn't much else to say about this method except that—as with all database operations—you should protect it with a Try block, and ensure that you dispose of the Command object and close the connection in the Finally block:

```
Try
    ' Run the query; get the number of affected records.
    Dim records As Integer = cmd.ExecuteNonQuery()
Catch ex As Exception
    ' Process the error here.
```

```
Finally
    cmd.Dispose()
    cn.Close()
End Try
```

Reading Data

You can read data from a data source in three ways: by using the ExecuteReader method and the DataReader object to read complete resultsets; by using the ExecuteScalar method to read individual values; or by using the ExecuteXmlReader method and the XmlReader object to read the results of a FOR XML query on a SQL Server 2000 data source. (The ExecuteXmlReader method is exposed only by the SqlConnection object.)

Using the ExecuteReader Method

The most common way to query the database in connected mode is through the ExecuteReader method of the Command object. This method returns a DataReader object, which you then use to read the resultset one row at a time, as you'd do with a forward-only, read-only recordset under classic ADO. There are actually different versions of this object: OleDbDataReader, SqlDataReader, OdbcDataReader, and OracleDataReader.

```
' Create a query command on the connection.
Dim cmd As New OleDbCommand("SELECT * FROM Publishers", cn)
' Run the query; get the DataReader object.
Dim dr As OleDbDataReader = cmd.ExecuteReader()
' Read the names of all the publishers in the resultsets.
Do While dr.Read()
    Debug.WriteLine(dr.Item("Name"))
Loop
' Close the DataReader and dispose of the Command.
dr.Close()
cmd.Dispose()
```

I'll discuss the DataReader object and its methods in greater detail in the section "The DataReader Object" later in this chapter. For now, I'll focus on how you can affect the query by passing an optional CommandBehavior bit-coded value to the ExecuteReader method. The available values for this argument are

- **CloseConnection** The connection should be closed immediately after the DataReader object is closed.

- **SingleRow** The SQL statement is expected to return a single row of data. The OLE DB .NET Data Provider uses this information to optimize the data retrieval operation.

- **SingleResult** The SQL statement is expected to return a single resultset. This value ensures that only a resultset is returned, even if the SQL query contains multiple SELECT statements.

- **KeyInfo** The query returns column and primary key information and is executed without locking the selected rows. In this case, the SQL Server .NET Data Provider appends a FOR BROWSE clause to the SQL statement, which requires that the table have a time-stamp field and a unique index. (See SQL Server Books Online for additional information.)

- **SequentialAccess** The query results are read sequentially at the column level instead of being returned as a whole block to the caller. You should use this option when the table contains very large text and binary fields that you read in chunks using the GetChars and GetBytes methods of the DataReader object, as I'll explain in the "Working with BLOB Columns" section, later in this chapter.

- **SchemaOnly** The query returns column information only and doesn't affect the database state.

The CloseConnection value is especially useful when you create a function that opens a connection and returns a DataReader object. Because the caller doesn't have a reference to the Connection object, it can't close it, but the CloseConnection argument ensures that the connection is closed automatically when the caller closes the DataReader:

```
Function GetReader(ByVal connString As String, ByVal sql As String) _
    As OleDbDataReader
    Dim cn As New OleDbConnection(connString)
    cn.Open()
    Dim cmd As New OleDbCommand(sql, cn)
    GetReader =  cmd.ExecuteReader(CommandBehavior.CloseConnection)
    cmd.Dispose()
End Function
```

The SingleRow option is useful when you're absolutely sure that the resultset contains only one row. This is often the case when the WHERE clause of the query filters a single record by its primary key, as in this example:

```
' Read a single line from the Publishers table.
Dim sql As String = "SELECT * FROM Publishers WHERE PubID=1"
Dim cmd As New OleDbCommand(sql, cn)
' Open a DataReader that contains one single row.
Dim dr As OleDbDataReader = cmd.ExecuteReader(CommandBehavior.SingleRow)
' Show name and city of this publisher.
dr.Read()
Debug.WriteLine(dr("Name") & " - " & dr ("City"))
dr.Close()
```

The argument is bit-coded, so you can combine multiple values using the Or operator:

```
Dim dr As OleDbDataReader = cmd.ExecuteReader(CommandBehavior.SingleRow _
    Or CommandBehavior.CloseConnection)
```

As for any other ADO.NET object, the Command object doesn't directly expose any method for asynchronous queries, but you can achieve such a behavior by invoking the ExecuteReader method (or any other method) from another thread. The Command object permits you to cancel a lengthy query by means of its Cancel method, which of course must be called from a thread different from the thread that has invoked the ExecuteReader method.

Using the ExecuteScalar Method

The ExecuteScalar method lets you perform a database query that returns a single scalar value in a more efficient way because it doesn't go through the overhead to build a resultset:

```
' Define the command to read a single scalar value
Dim sql As String = "SELECT Name FROM Publishers WHERE PubID=1"
' Create a command on that connection.
Dim cmd As New OleDbCommand(sql, cn)
' Read the value.
Dim pubName As String = cmd.ExecuteScalar().ToString
```

Another good occasion to use the ExecuteScalar method is for reading the result of aggregate functions, as in this code snippet:

```
' Read the number of records in the Publishers table.
Dim cmd As New OleDbCommand("SELECT COUNT(*) FROM Publishers", cn)
Dim recCount As Integer = CInt(cmd.ExecuteScalar())
```

Remember that the ExecuteScalar method works with *any* SQL query, and in all cases it returns the first field of the first row without raising an error if the query returns multiple columns or multiple rows. If the query returns no rows, the ExecuteScalar method returns Nothing.

Using the ExecuteXmlReader Method

SQL Server 2000 is able to process FOR XML queries and return data in XML format. If you connect to the database by using the SQL Server .NET Data Provider, you can leverage this capability with the ExecuteXmlReader of the SqlCommand object, which returns a System.Xml.XmlReader object that lets you walk through the resultset. Here's a code example that uses this feature:

```
' Open a connection to SQL Server 2000.
Dim cn As New SqlConnection(SqlPubsConnString)
cn.Open()
' Prepare a FOR XML command.
Dim sql As String = "SELECT pub_name FROM Publishers FOR XML AUTO, ELEMENTS"
Dim cmd As New SqlCommand(sql, cn)
' Create the XmlReader.
Dim reader As System.Xml.XmlReader = cmd.ExecuteXmlReader()
' Display XML data in a TextBox control.
Do While reader.Read
    txtOut.AppendText(reader.Value & ControlChars.CrLf)
Loop
' Close the XmlReader and the connection.
reader.Close()
cn.Close()
```

The XmlReader works similarly to the DataReader object, with a Read method that returns True if there are more elements and False when the code arrives at the end of the resultset. I describe the XmlReader and XmlTextReader objects in Chapter 22.

Working with Parameters and Stored Procedures

The SQL command that you pass to a Command object can contain parameters, an especially useful feature when you're working with stored procedures. The exact syntax you can use in the SQL command depends on which data provider you're working with, so we'll examine the two providers separately.

Parameterized Commands

A common misconception is that parameters are useful only when you're working with stored procedures. But in fact, you can define a parameterized SQL command that contains one or more question marks as placeholders, as in this line of code:

```
SELECT * FROM Titles WHERE PubId=? AND [Year Published]=?
```

When you use this syntax—which is valid only with the OLE DB .NET and ODBC .NET Data Providers—you must manually create one or more Parameter objects and add them to the Command object's Parameters collection in the exact order in which the parameter appears in the SQL command. You can choose from three ways of creating a Parameter object: you can use the Parameter's constructor, use the Command's CreateParameter method, or invoke the Add method of the Parameters collection:

```
' First method: the Parameter's constructor
Dim par As New OleDbParameter("PubId", OleDbType.Integer)
par.Value = 156                  ' Set the parameter's value.
cmd.Parameters.Add(par)          ' Add to the collection of parameters.
Dim par2 As New OleDbParameter("YearPub", OleDbType.SmallInt)
par2.Value = 1992
cmd.Parameters.Add(par2)

' Second method: the Command's CreateParameter method
Dim par3 As OleDbParameter = cmd.CreateParameter()
' Note that setting the name and the type isn't mandatory.
par3.Value = 156
cmd.Parameters.Add(par3)
par3 = cmd.CreateParameter()        ' Reuse the same variable.
par3.Value = 1992
cmd.Parameters.Add(par3)

' Third method: passing name and value to the Parameters.Add method
cmd.Parameters.Add("PubId", 156)
cmd.Parameters.Add("YearPub", 1992)
```

The code for a parameterized OdbcCommand is similar, except you use an OdbcParameter variable and an OdbcType enumerated value when specifying the type of the parameter. The Parameters collection implements the IList interface, so it exposes all the usual methods for adding, inserting, and removing elements.

The syntax with the SQL Server .NET Data Provider is different, in that it doesn't support question marks in queries and requires you to use @ parameters, as in this line of code:

```
SELECT * FROM Titles WHERE title_id=@TitleId
```

The code for creating the Parameters collection must use a SqlParameter object and a SqlDbType enumerated value to specify the type of the parameter:

```
Dim par As New SqlParameter("@TitleId", SqlDbType.VarChar)
par.Value = "BU1032"            ' Set the parameter's value.
cmd.Parameters.Add(par)         ' Add to the collection of parameters.
```

After the Parameters collection is set up, you can call the ExecuteReader method to retrieve the resultset as usual, or the ExecuteNonQuery method if it is an action query that doesn't return data rows. Parameterized commands are useful when you must perform the same type of query more than once, each time with different parameter values. The following example shows how you can extract different rows from the same table without having to create a different Command object:

```
' Create a SQL command with one parameter.
Dim sql As String = "SELECT * FROM Publishers WHERE pub_id=@p1"
Dim cmd As New SqlCommand(sql, cn)
' Define the first (and only) parameter, and assign its value.
cmd.Parameters.Add("@p1", "0736")
' Read the result.
Dim dr As SqlDataReader = cmd.ExecuteReader()
' No need to loop because we know there is only one row.
dr.Read()
Debug.WriteLine(dr("pub_name"))
dr.Close()

' Change the parameter's value, and reexecute the query.
cmd.Parameters(0).Value = "0877"
dr = cmd.ExecuteReader()
dr.Read()
Debug.WriteLine(dr("pub_name"))
dr.Close()
```

Stored Procedures

The substantial difference between executing a simple parameterized SQL command and calling a stored procedure is that in the latter case, you specify the name of the stored procedure in the command text and set the CommandType property to StoredProcedure:

```
' Run the byroyalty stored procedure in SQL Server's Pubs database.
Dim cmd As New SqlCommand("byroyalty", cn)
cmd.CommandType = CommandType.StoredProcedure
' Create the first parameter, and assign it the value 100.
' (Note that the parameter name must match the name used in the procedure.)
cmd.Parameters.Add("@percentage", 100)
' Read the result.
Dim dr As SqlDataReader = cmd.ExecuteReader()
```

The ODBC .NET Data Provider requires that you use the full ODBC syntax for calling stored procedures:

```
Dim cmd As New OdbcCommand("{ CALL byroyalty(?) }", cn)
cmd.CommandType = CommandType.StoredProcedure
' Notice that parameter name can be any.
cmd.Parameters.Add("percent", 100)
Dim dr As OdbcDataReader = cmd.ExecuteReader()
```

You can execute a SQL Server stored procedure by using the OLE DB .NET Data Provider, the ODBC .NET Data Provider, or the SQL Server .NET Data Provider. The only difference is that the first two providers don't require that the name you use for a parameter match the parameter's name as defined in the stored procedure itself. (See the previous code snippet.)

In another difference from parameterized commands, when you're working with stored procedures you must account for the type and the direction of each parameter. In general, the type of each parameter must match the type of the argument that the stored procedure accepts; if this doesn't happen, you might have problems passing and retrieving a value from that stored procedure. You can pass the type as the second argument to the Parameter's constructor by using an enumerated OleDbType, SqlDbType, or OdbcType value:

```
' Create a Parameter of type Single.
Dim param1 As New OleDbParameter("param1", OleDbType.Single)
```

When working with strings, you can also specify a size:

```
Dim param2 As New OleDbParameter("param2", OleDbType.VarChar, 100)
```

The names of the values exposed by the OleDbType, SqlDbType, and OdbcType are similar but not perfectly equal. For example, a parameter of type Double is defined by specifying an OleDbType.Double, an OdbcType.Double, or a SqlDbType.Float enumerated value, depending on the provider you're using.

By default, all parameters are created as input parameters. If you're calling a stored procedure that returns a value through an argument, you must set the Direction property to either InputOutput or Output. If the stored procedure returns a value, you must define an additional parameter: the name of this parameter doesn't matter as long as it's the first parameter appended to the Parameters collection and its Direction property is set to ReturnValue. In addition, when you're using the ODBC .NET Data Provider, you must specify that you expect a return value right in the string you pass to the Odbc-Command's constructor or assign to the CommandText property:

```
Dim cmd As New OdbcCommand(" { ? = mystoredproc(?, ?) }", cn)
```

To test how to work with output parameters and return values, you can define a new byroyalty2 stored procedure in the Pubs database by running this script in SQL Server's Query Analyzer:

```
CREATE PROCEDURE byroyalty2 @percentage int, @avgprice float output
AS
-- Return the average price for all titles in the second argument.
SELECT @avgprice= AVG(Price) FROM Titles
-- Return a resultset.
SELECT au_id FROM titleauthor
    WHERE titleauthor.royaltyper = @percentage
-- Return the number of titles in the second argument.
DECLARE @numtitles Int
SELECT @numtitles=COUNT(*) FROM titles
RETURN @numtitles
```

Here's the source code for a routine that invokes the byroyalty2 stored procedure and displays its results in a multiline TextBox control:

```
Dim cmd As New SqlCommand("byroyalty2", cn)
cmd.CommandType = CommandType.StoredProcedure

' Define the return value parameter.
cmd.Parameters.Add("@numtitles", OleDbType.Integer)
cmd.Parameters(0).Direction = ParameterDirection.ReturnValue
' Define the first (input) parameter, and assign its value.
cmd.Parameters.Add("@percentage", 100)
' Define the second (output) parameter (alternative way).
With cmd.Parameters.Add("@avgprice", SqlDbType.Float)
    .Direction = ParameterDirection.Output
End With

' Read the result.
Dim dr As SqlDataReader = cmd.ExecuteReader()
Do While dr.Read
    txtOut.AppendText(dr(0).ToString & ControlChars.CrLf)
Loop
dr.Close()

' You can read the return value and output argument only after
' closing the DataReader object.
txtOut.AppendText("Number of titles = " & _
    cmd.Parameters("@numtitles").Value.ToString & ControlChars.CrLf)
txtOut.AppendText("Average price = " & _
    cmd.Parameters("@avgprice").Value.ToString & ControlChars.CrLf)
```

As a remark in the preceding code snippet explains, you can read output arguments and return values only after you've closed the DataReader object.

When invoking a SQL Server stored procedure that doesn't have output parameters or a return value, you can take the following shortcut: just create an EXEC statement that contains the name of the stored procedure followed by all of its input parameters, as in this code snippet:

```
Dim sql As String = "EXEC byroyalty 100"
Dim cmd As New SqlCommand(sql, cn)
cmd.CommandType = CommandType.Text
```

Notice that in this case you don't have to set the CommandType property to StoredProcedure because from the perspective of ADO.NET, you're executing a regular SQL command.

Automatic Population of the Parameters Collection

When working with stored procedures, you can save some time by having ADO.NET populate the Parameters collection of the Command object automatically by means of the DeriveParameters shared method of the OleDbCommandBuilder, SqlCommandBuilder, or OdbcCommandBuilder class:

```
' Get the parameters for the byroyalty stored procedure in Pubs.
Dim cmd As New SqlCommand("byroyalty", cn)
cmd.CommandType = CommandType.StoredProcedure
' Let the CommandBuilder object populate the Parameters collection.
SqlCommandBuilder.DeriveParameters(cmd)

' Show number and names of parameters.
Debug.WriteLine(cmd.Parameters.Count & " parameters")    ' => 2 parameters
Debug.WriteLine(cmd.Parameters(0).ParameterName)          ' => @RETURN_VALUE
Debug.WriteLine(cmd.Parameters(1).ParameterName)          ' => @percentage
```

Keep in mind that the DeriveParameters method requires a roundtrip to the SQL Server database to acquire the metadata needed to fill the Parameters collection. Because the signature of a stored procedure rarely changes after the application is deployed, it makes sense that you burn the names and the type of the parameters in code to speed up execution.

Even if you don't count performance problems, filling the Parameters collection automatically isn't usually a good idea. For example, the preceding code snippet shows that the DeriveParameters method incorrectly detects a return value parameter, even when the stored procedure doesn't really have a return value. In some circumstances, this method isn't smart enough to read the exact type and direction of parameters. For example, if you run the DeriveParameters method on the byroyalty2 stored procedure that was defined in the preceding section, you'll see that the @avgprice output parameter is incorrectly retrieved as an input/output parameter. You can remedy this problem either by manually adjusting the Direction property to Output or by assigning a dummy value to the @avgprice parameter before calling the stored procedure, even if this value will never be used. If you fail to take either of these steps, the ExecuteReader method will throw an exception.

Despite its defects, the DeriveParameters method fits the bill during the prototyping phase, but be prepared to replace it with code that populates the Parameters collection manually before you ship the application. Here's a tip: you should always reference your parameters by their names rather than by their indexes in the Parameters collection so that you don't have to change your code if you switch from automatic to manual creation of the Parameters collection. And don't include the return value parameter (if the stored procedure doesn't have one):

```
' This statement works regardless of how you fill the Parameters collection.
cmd.Parameters("@percentage").Value = 100
```

Editing and Debugging a Stored Procedure

Visual Studio .NET provides a superb environment for both creating and debugging SQL Server's stored procedures. You'll find all the commands you might need in the Data Connections subtree of the Server Explorer window. These commands are replicated under the SQL Servers node in the Servers branch, which also gives you access to common administrative and management tasks, such as registering a new SQL Server, creating a database, or changing a login. You can customize what you see in the Server Explorer window and what you can do with the database from the Database Tools page in the Options dialog box that you reach from the Tools menu.

You edit a stored procedure by double-clicking on the corresponding element under the Stored Procedures node in the Server Explorer window. Other commands in the context menu or in the Database top-level menu let you create script for elements in the database as well as create a new table, diagram, stored procedure, inline function, scalar function, or table-valued function.

Visual Studio .NET offers many helpful tools for editing a stored procedure or a function, and all of them are available from the context menu that appears with a right-click of the mouse. For example, you can insert a piece of SQL that you design with the Query Builder, or run the selected SQL statement and see the result in the Output window. (See Figure 21-3.) When you save the stored procedure or the function, Visual Studio .NET checks its syntax and rejects malformed SQL statements.

Debugging a stored procedure is also quite simple. For starters, you can set breakpoints inside a stored procedure as you'd do with regular Visual Basic code, and you can even create conditional breakpoints with the Breakpoint Properties command that appears if you right-click on the red bullet that marks the breakpoint or from the Breakpoints window that you reach from the Windows submenu of the Debug top-level menu.

Right-click on the procedure node and select either the Run Stored Procedure or the Step Into Stored Procedure command to execute a stored procedure. If the procedure takes arguments, a dialog box will allow you to enter them. While a stored procedure is being debugged you can hover the mouse on scalar variables to display their values in a Tooltip.

By default, breakpoints in a stored procedure are enabled only if you execute the stored procedure in stand-alone mode—that is, by means of the Run Stored Procedure or the Step Into Stored Procedure commands just described. In most cases, however, you want to debug the stored procedure in the context of the running applications. To do so, you must select the option SQL Server debugging in the Debugging page of the Project Properties dialog box.

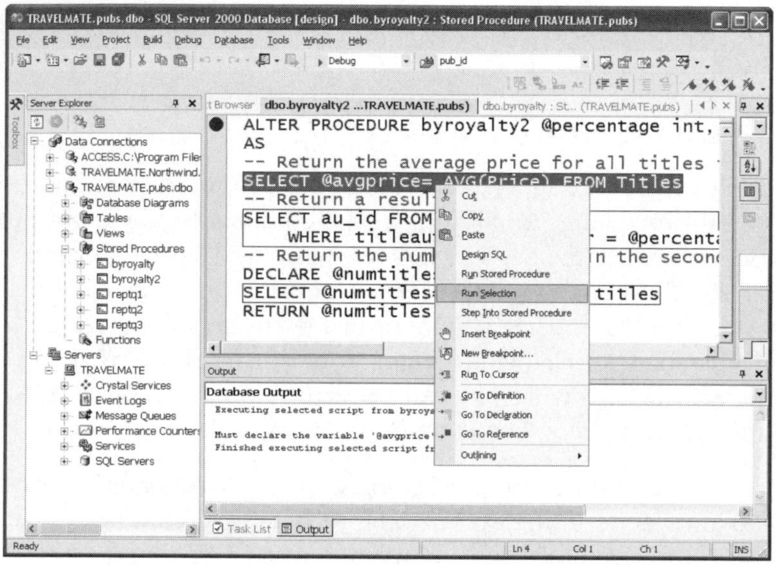

Figure 21-3   You can edit and debug a SQL Server stored procedure with Visual Studio .NET.

The DataReader Object

In this section, I'll explore the DataReader object in more detail and explain how you can perform common and less common tasks—for example, retrieving large text or binary fields from a database.

Iterating Over Individual Rows

Using the DataReader object couldn't be simpler: you invoke its Read method to advance to the next row in the resultset and check its return value to see whether you have more results (if True) or are at the end of the resultset (if False). Because of this double function, you can create tight loops based on the DataReader object:

```
Do While dr.Read()
    ' Process the current row here.
    ⋮
Loop
dr.Close()
```

You can use the HasRows read-only property (added in version 1.1 of the .NET Framework) to check whether the DataReader contains at least one row. More in general, this property lets you check that there are more rows to read without having to call the Read method:

```
If Not dr.HasRows Then
    MsgBox("No rows match this condition")
Else
    ' Process the resultset.
    ⋮
End If
```

It's important that you close the DataReader object when there are no more rows to process. This releases resources on both the client and the server and makes the connection available again for other commands. In fact, you can't issue any other command on a connection while a DataReader object is active on that connection. The only command you can perform on a connection actively serving a DataReader is the Close method. You can check whether a DataReader has been closed by means of its IsClosed property.

Reading Column Values

The DataReader object provides many properties and methods that let you read the value of the columns in the resultset. For starters, the Item read-only property gives you a means to access any field by either its name or its (zero-based) column index in a way that resembles the kind of access you perform with the Fields collection of the ADO Recordset:

```
' Display the Name and City fields for each record.
Do While dr.Read()
    Dim res As String = String.Format("{0} - {1}", _
        dr.Item("Name"), dr.Item("City"))
    Debug.WriteLine(res)
Loop
```

Item is the default member, so you can make your code more concise by omitting it:

```
    Dim res As String = String.Format("{0} - {1}", dr("Name"), dr("City"))
```

You can iterate over all the columns in the resultset by using an index that goes from 0 to FieldCount -1; then you can use the GetName method to retrieve the name of the field and the GetValue method (or the Item property) to read the field's value. If you're dealing with nullable fields, however, you should protect your code from exceptions by checking a field with the IsDBNull method:

```
' Display the value of all fields in current DataReader.
Do While dr.Read
    ' Prepare the buffer for the values of this row.
    Dim res As String = ""
    For i As Integer = 0 To dr.FieldCount - 1
        ' Insert a comma after the first field.
        If res.Length > 0 Then res &= ", "
        ' Append field name and value.
        res &= dr.GetName(i) & "="
        ' Protect the code from null values.
```

```
            If dr.IsDBNull(i) Then
                    res &= "<NULL>"
            Else
                    res &= dr.GetValue(i).ToString
            End If
        Next
        Debug.WriteLine(res)
Loop
```

When you read all the fields in the current row, you can optimize your code by using the GetValues method, which returns all the fields' values in an Object array. The following code snippet uses this method and makes the code even faster by retrieving the names of all fields once and for all outside the main loop and by using a StringBuilder object instead of a regular String. After the value has been moved to an element of the Object array, you must test it using the IsDBNull function instead of the DataReader's IsDBNull method:

```
' Build the array of all field names.
Dim fldNames(dr.FieldCount - 1) As String
For i As Integer = 0 To dr.FieldCount - 1
    fldNames(i) = dr.GetName(i)
Next

' Display all fields.
Dim res As New System.Text.StringBuilder()
Do While dr.Read
    ' Get all the values in one shot.
    Dim values(dr.FieldCount - 1) As Object
    dr.GetValues(values)

    ' Iterate over all fields.
    For i As Integer = 0 To dr.FieldCount - 1
        ' Insert a comma after first field.
        If res.Length > 0 Then res.Append(", ")
        ' Append field name and equal sign.
        res.Append(fldNames(i))
        res.Append("=")
        ' Append the field value, or <NULL>.
        If IsDBNull(values(i)) Then
            res.Append("<NULL>")
        Else
            res.Append(values(i).ToString)
        End If
    Next
    res.Append(ControlChars.CrLf)
Loop
Debug.WriteLine(res.ToString)
```

All .NET Data Providers offer several Get*xxxx* methods to retrieve field values in their native format, including GetBoolean, GetByte, GetChar, GetDateTime, GetDecimal, GetDouble, GetFloat, GetGuid, GetInt16, GetInt32, GetInt64, GetString, and GetTimeSpan. (The last isn't available with the ODBC provider: use the GetTime method instead.) These methods save you the overhead of going through a more generic

Object variable. Compare how you can retrieve an integer value with the generic GetValue method and the more specific GetInt32 method:

```
' The generic GetValue method requires type casting.
Dim res As Integer = CInt(dr.GetValue(0))
' The specific GetInt32 method does not.
Dim res2 As Integer = dr.GetInt32(0)
```

When creating generic routines to retrieve data from a database, you can take advantage of the GetFieldType(n) method (which returns the System.Type object that corresponds to the Nth field in the DataReader) and the GetDataTypeName(n) method (which returns the name of the source data type for the Nth field in the DataReader).

The SQL Server .NET Data Provider provides the same Get*xxxx* methods as the OLE DB and ODBC providers, with one glaring exception: it doesn't support the GetTimeSpan method. On the other hand, the SQL Server provider supports more specific GetSql*xxxx* methods—for example, GetSqlDateTime and GetSqlMoney. These methods behave much like their Get*xxxx* counterparts except that they return specific SQL Server types defined in the System.Data.SqlTypes namespace:

```
' This code assumes that dr is a SqlDataReader object.
Dim res As Integer = dr.GetSqlInt32(0)
```

When you're working with the SQL Server .NET Data Provider, you should always use these more specific types because they prevent conversion errors caused by loss of precision and provide faster code as well. This advice is especially important to follow with the SqlDecimal data type, which provides a precision of 38 digits instead of the 28 digits that the .NET Decimal type provides.

Retrieving Column Information

When creating a generic routine that can query any table in any database, you often need to retrieve precise information about each of the columns returned by the query. For this purpose, the DataReader object exposes the GetSchemaTable method, which returns a DataTable object. Each row of this DataTable corresponds to a field in the DataReader resultset, and each column of the DataTable corresponds to an attribute of the resultset field. Here's a code snippet that retrieves information about the fields returned by a query against the Publishers table:

```
' cn is an open connection.
Dim cmd As New OleDbCommand("SELECT * FROM Publishers", cn)
Dim dr As OleDbDataReader = cmd.ExecuteReader(CommandBehavior.KeyInfo)
Dim dt As DataTable = dr.GetSchemaTable()
' Display name, data type, size, and unique attribute for all columns.
For Each row As DataRow In dt.Rows
    Console.WriteLine("{0}, {1}, {2}, {3}", row("ColumnName"), _
        row("DataType"), row("ColumnSize"), row("IsUnique"))
Next
```

This is the complete list of columns in the DataTable that the GetSchemaTable method returns: ColumnName, ColumnOrdinal, ColumnSize, NumericPrecision, NumericScale, DataType, ProviderType, IsLong, AllowDBNull, IsReadOnly, IsRowVersion, IsUnique, IsKey, IsAutoIncrement, BaseSchema, BaseCatalog, BaseTable, and BaseColumn. (If the query contained aliased columns, the value of the BaseColumn can be different from the column name seen by your program.) You can use the demo program I prepared to experiment with this method. (See Figure 21-4.)

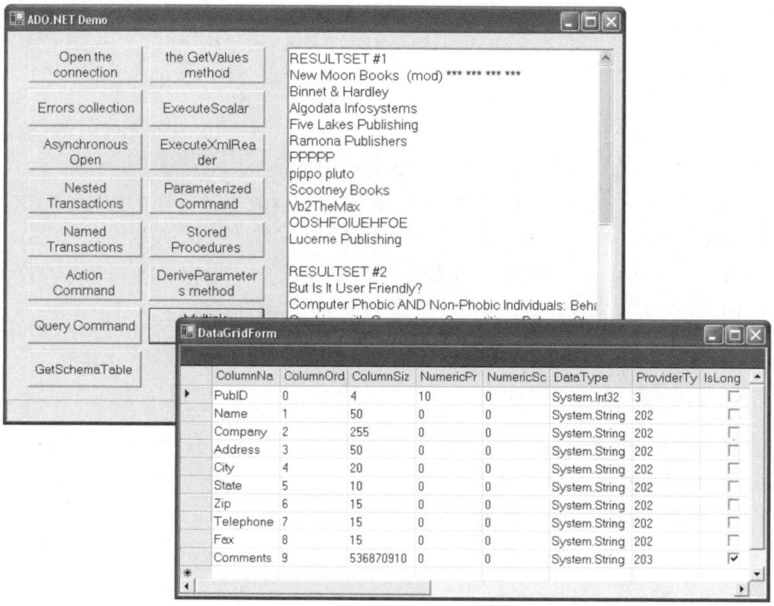

Figure 21-4   The demo program lets you test several features of the DataReader object, including the ability to read multiple resultsets (above) and GetSchemaTable method (below).

Working with BLOB Columns

In simple scenarios, you don't need any special care for large text and binary fields, so you can read them in one shot by means of the GetString and GetValue method, respectively:

```
Dim cn As New SqlConnection(SqlPubsConnString)
cn.Open()
' Pub's pub_info table contains a large text field and a BLOB field.
Dim cmd As New SqlCommand("SELECT pub_id,pr_info,logo FROM pub_info", cn)
Dim dr As SqlDataReader = cmd.ExecuteReader()
' Read data from the the first record only.
dr.Read()
Dim prInfo As String = dr.GetString(1)
Dim buffer() As Byte = DirectCast(dr.GetValue(2), Byte())
dr.Close()
```

Once you have the actual bytes of a binary field, you can process them or display them as appropriate. In this case, the logo field contains a bitmap, so you can display it as follows:

```
' Create a memory stream and load the bitmap from there.
Dim stream As New MemoryStream(buffer)
Dim bmp As New Bitmap(stream)
stream.Close()
' Display the bitmap in a PictureBox control.
Me.PictureBox1.Image = bmp
```

The problem with this approach is that the resultset can grow quite large, which in turn takes a lot of bandwidth and a lot of memory on the client. In some cases you can reduce these problems by reading the BLOB fields only if strictly required. For example, you might omit them in the SELECT query and retrieve them one by one by means of an ExecuteScalar method:

```
Dim cmd As New SqlCommand("SELECT logo FROM pub_info WHERE pub_id='0877'", cn)
Dim buffer() As Byte = DirectCast(cmd.ExecuteScalar, Byte())
```

This approach can reduce network traffic if you aren't going to display a binary field for all the records in a table, but the application still slows down if the BLOB is too large for the client's memory. A better way of handling BLOB fields is based on the CommandBehavior.SequentialAccess option in the ExecuteReader method:

```
Dim cmd As New SqlCommand("SELECT pub_id,pr_info,logo FROM pub_info", cn)
Dim dr As SqlDataReader = cmd.ExecuteReader(CommandBehavior.SequentialAccess)
' Read data from the first record only.
dr.Read()
Dim pub_id As String = dr.GetString(0)
```

The CommandBehavior.SequentialAccess option forces the DataReader to retrieve data from the database one field at a time, in the order in which the fields appear in the SELECT query. Once a field has been read with a Get*xxxx* method, you can't read it again, nor can you read any field that appears before it in the SELECT query. (For example, in the previous code snippet you can't read the pr_info field once you've read the logo field.)

If you expect that the query return fields are too large for the client's memory, you must read and process them in chunks by means of the GetBytes method (for large binary fields) or the GetChars method (for large text fields). The GetBytes method fills a Byte array that you pass as an argument and takes the following syntax:

```
Length = dr.GetBytes(columnIndex, start, buffer, bufferIndex, count)
```

In this case, start is the index in the first byte in the field that must be returned, buffer is the Byte array, bufferIndex is the index of the first element in the array that must be filled, and count is the number of bytes to return. The return value is the number of bytes read. (The GetChars method has a similar syntax, but fills a Char array instead.) In most cases, you'll want to extract a BLOB field and save it to a file, so I prepared a reusable procedure that does it for you:

```
' This routine works with any ADO.NET provider.
Sub BlobToFile(ByVal dr As IDataReader, ByVal fldIndex As Integer, ByVal filename _
   As String)
    Const CHUNK_SIZE As Integer = 1024        ' Change as you wish.
    Dim buffer(CHUNK_SIZE - 1) As Byte
    Dim stream As New FileStream(filename, FileMode.Create)
    Dim index As Long = 0
    Try
        Do
            ' Get the next chunk, exit if no more bytes.
            Dim length As Integer = CInt(dr.GetBytes(fldIndex, index, buffer, 0, _
               CHUNK_SIZE))
            If length = 0 Then Exit Do
            ' Write to file and increment index in field data.
            stream.Write(buffer, 0, length)
            index += length
        Loop
    Finally
        stream.Close()
    End Try
End Sub
```

If you read BLOB values from a database, you'll probably want to write them too. You can define a parameterized UPDATE or INSERT command and pass a Byte array as a parameter, as in this code:

```
' Read a bitmap from a file.
Dim stream As New FileStream("c:\mylogo.bmp", FileMode.Open)
Dim buffer(CInt(stream.Length) - 1) As Byte
stream.Read(buffer, 0, buffer.Length - 1)
stream.Close()
' Use the bitmap to update the logo of a publisher
cmd = New SqlCommand("UPDATE pub_info SET logo=@logo WHERE pub_id=@id", cn)
cmd.Parameters.Add("@logo", buffer)
cmd.Parameters.Add("@id", "0877")
cmd.ExecuteNonQuery()
```

Unfortunately, ADO.NET doesn't provide a native method to write a BLOB in chunks. However, there's still hope because SQL Server's T-SQL supports the UPDATETEXT statement, which can stuff data into a long text or binary field. Using the UPDATETEXT statement isn't exactly simple, though, so I wrapped all the code you need in a reusable procedure:

```
Sub FileToBlob(ByVal cn As SqlConnection, ByVal tableName As String, _
    ByVal blobField As String, ByVal keyField As String, _
    ByVal keyValue As Object, ByVal filename As String)
    ' Get the value of the pointer to the BLOB field.
    Dim sql As String = String.Format("SELECT TEXTPTR({0}) FROM {1} WHERE {2}=@id", _
```

```
            blobField, tableName, keyField)
        Dim cmd As New SqlCommand(sql, cn)
        cmd.Parameters.Add("@id", keyValue)
        ' The pointer is actually a byte array, but we don't really care here.
        Dim pointer As Object = cmd.ExecuteScalar()
        cmd.Dispose()

        ' Open the file, throw if not found.
        Dim stream As New FileStream(filename, FileMode.Open, FileAccess.Read)
        ' Prepare the receiving buffer.
        Const CHUNK_SIZE As Integer = 200
        Dim buffer(CHUNK_SIZE - 1) As Byte

        ' Prepare the UPDATETEXT command.
        sql = String.Format("UPDATETEXT {0}.{1} @pointer @offset 0 @bytes", tableName, _
            blobField)
        cmd = New SqlCommand(sql, cn)
        cmd.Parameters.Add("@pointer", pointer)
        Dim offsetPar As SqlParameter = cmd.Parameters.Add("@offset", SqlDbType.Int)
        Dim bufferPar As SqlParameter = cmd.Parameters.Add("@bytes", SqlDbType.Image, _
            CHUNK_SIZE)

        Dim offset As Integer = 0
        Try
            Do
                ' Read a bunch of bytes from the stream.
                Dim count As Integer = stream.Read(buffer, 0, buffer.Length)
                If count = 0 Then Exit Do
                ' Execute the UPDATETEXT command with this offset and these bytes.
                offsetPar.Value = offset
                bufferPar.Value = buffer
                cmd.ExecuteNonQuery()
                offset += count
            Loop
        Finally
            stream.Close()
        End Try
    End Sub
```

Notice that the FileToBlob procedure works only with database tables whose primary key consists of a single column. Here's how you use it to read the c:\mylogo.bmp file and store its contents in the logo field of the pub_info table, for the record whose pub_id primary key is equal to "0877":

```
FileToBlob(cn, "pub_info", "logo", "pub_id", "0877", "c:\mylogo.bmp")
```

Reading Multiple Resultsets

Some databases support multiple statements in a single query. For example, you can send multiple commands to SQL Server, using the semicolon as a separator:

```
SELECT Name FROM Publishers WHERE PubId=10;
SELECT Name FROM Publishers WHERE PubId=12
```

Multiple queries let you create batch commands, which minimize the number of round trips to the server and network traffic. (One batch command uses a single network packet to carry multiple queries that would otherwise require multiple packets.) The DataReader object supports multiple resultsets by means of the NextResult method, which returns True if there is one more resultset and False otherwise. The following code snippet shows how to use this method with any number of resultsets:

```
' Open a connection to the Pubs database on SQL Server.
Dim cn As New SqlConnection(SqlPubsConnString)
cn.Open()
' Define a SQL statement with multiple queries.
Dim sql As String = "SELECT pub_name FROM Publishers;SELECT Title FROM titles"
Dim cmd As New SqlCommand(sql, cn)
Dim dr As SqlDataReader = cmd.ExecuteReader()

Dim resCount As Integer = 0
Do
    ' Process the next resultset.
    resCount += 1
    Debug.WriteLine("RESULTSET #" & resCount.ToString)
    ' Process all the rows in the current resultset.
    Do While dr.Read
        Debug.WriteLine(dr(0).ToString)
    Loop
    Debug.WriteLine("")
Loop While dr.NextResult
' Close the DataReader and the connection.
dr.Close()
cn.Close()
```

If the SQL statement contains action queries—such as an INSERT, a DELETE, or an UPDATE statement—they're correctly ignored by the NextResult method because they don't return any resultsets. Notice that you cannot use the CommandBehavior.SingleResult option when invoking the ExecuteReader method on a query that contains multiple SELECT statements; otherwise, all queries after the first one will be ignored.

That concludes the first part of my ADO.NET discussion, which covered using the Connection, Command, and DataReader objects. Even though the name and syntax of these objects and their methods differ from classic ADO, you'll probably agree that few things have changed. Using ADO.NET in connected mode is much like using ADO (except that you can't count on keysets and dynamic cursors). However, a disconnected scenario is a different matter, as I'll explain in the following chapter.

22 ADO.NET in Disconnected Mode

In the preceding chapter, you saw how to work with ADO.NET in connected mode, processing data coming from an active connection and sending SQL commands to one. ADO.NET in connected mode behaves much like classic ADO, even though the names of the involved properties and methods (and their syntax) are often different.

You'll see how ADO.NET differs from its predecessor when you start working in disconnected mode. ADO 2.*x* permits you to work in disconnected mode using client-side static recordsets opened in optimistic batch update mode. This was one of the great new features of ADO that proved to be a winner in client/server applications of any size. As a matter of fact, working in disconnected mode is the most scalable technique you can adopt because it takes resources on the client (instead of on the server) and, above all, it doesn't enforce any locks on database tables (except for the short-lived locks that are created during the update operation).

In this chapter, I'll cover most of the features of ADO.NET in disconnected mode, except those that are related to XML—for example, strongly typed DataSet classes and the XmlDataDocument class—which I'll discuss in the next chapter. Also, because my main goal is to teach what each ADO.NET object does, all the samples in this chapter are based on handwritten code. At the end of the next chapter, once you're familiar with the basic concepts, I'll show you how you can rely on Visual Studio .NET and data binding to create functional database applications in minutes.

> **Note** To keep the code as concise as possible, all the code samples in this chapter assume that the following Imports statements are used at the file or project level:
>
> ```
> Imports System.Data
> Imports System.Data.Common
> Imports System.Data.OleDb
> Imports System.Data.SqlClient
> Imports System.Data.Odbc
> Imports System.IO
> Imports System.Text.RegularExpressions
> ```

The DataSet Object

Because ADO.NET (and .NET in general) is all about scalability and performance, the disconnected mode is the preferred way to code client/server applications. Instead of a simple disconnected recordset, ADO.NET gives you the DataSet object, which is much like a small relational database held in memory on the client. As such, it provides you with the ability to create multiple tables, fill them with data coming from different sources, enforce relationships between pairs of tables, and more.

Exploring the DataSet Object Model

The DataSet is the root and the most important object in the object hierarchy that includes almost all the objects in the System.Data namespace. Figure 22-1 shows the most important classes in this hierarchy, with the name of the property that returns each object.

A DataSet object consists of one or more DataTable objects, each one containing data rows and columns. A DataTable is typically filled with data coming from a database query or from a data file, but it might also be produced by code. You can access all the DataTable objects in a DataSet by means of the Tables collection.

An important feature of the DataSet class is its ability to define relationships between its DataTable objects, much like in a real database. For example, you can create a relationship between the Publishers and the Titles DataTable objects by using the PubId DataColumn that they have in common. After you define a DataRelation object, you can navigate from one table to another, using the DataTable's ChildRelations and ParentRelations properties. You can enumerate all the DataRelation objects in a DataSet via the DataSet's Relations collection. Each DataRelation object can reference its parent and child DataTable objects (by means of the ParentTable and ChildTable properties), and the key columns in the parent and child tables (by means of the ParentColumns and ChildColumns properties). Notice that two tables can be tied by a DataRelation only if they belong to the same DataSet.

A DataTable object resembles a database table and has a collection of DataColumn instances (the fields) and DataRow instances (the records), exposed by the Rows and Columns collections, respectively. It can also have a primary key based on one or more columns (the PrimaryKey property) and a collection of Constraint objects, which are useful for enforcing the uniqueness of the values in a column. A DataTable object can also exist outside a DataSet, the main limitation being that it can't participate in any relationships.

The DataRow class represents an individual row (or record) in a DataTable. Each DataRow contains one or more fields, which can be accessed through its Item property. (Because it's the default member, the name of this property can be omitted.) You can also get and set all columns in a single operation, by means of the ItemArray property.

The DataColumn class represents a single column (field) in a DataRow or DataTable. Each instance of this class has a name (ColumnName property), a type (DataType property), a default value (DefaultValue property), a maximum length (MaxLength property), a flag that tells whether the column can take null values (AllowDBNull property), and a flag that tells whether values in this column should be unique (Unique property). ADO.NET supports calculated columns (by means of the Expression property) and auto-incremented columns (via the AutoIncrement, AutoIncrementSeed, and AutoIncrementStep properties).

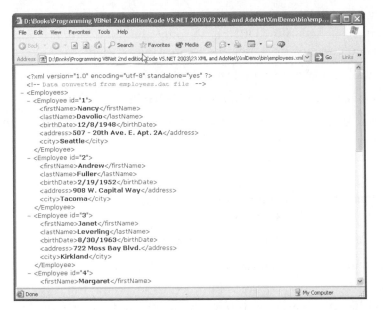

Figure 22-1 The DataSet object hierarchy

The DataView class represents a view over a DataTable object, a concept that doesn't really match any ADO object you might already know. For example, you can filter the data in a table or sort it without affecting the values in the original DataTable object, by means of the DataView's Sort and RowFilter properties. Or you can create a view on a table that does (or doesn't) allow insertions, deletions, or updates by setting the AllowEdit, AllowDelete, and AllowNew properties opportunely. A DataView object is especially useful when you bind it to a Windows Forms or Web Forms DataGrid control.

Building a DataSet

Most applications fill a DataSet with data coming from a database query. However, you can use a DataSet in stand-alone mode as well. In this case, you define its structure, set the relationships between its DataTable objects, and fill it with data exclusively through code. Even though this way of working with a DataSet is less frequently used in real-world applications, I'll describe it first because it reveals many inner details of the DataSet class. (Filling a DataSet with data coming from a database will be described in the "Reading Data from a Database" section later in this chapter.)

Here's the sequence that you typically follow when you're creating a DataSet:

1. Create a DataSet object.

2. Create a new DataTable object with the desired name. You can set its CaseSensitive property to decide how strings are compared inside the table.

3. Create a new DataColumn object with a given name and type, and optionally set other properties such as AllowDBNull, DefaultValue, and Unique; you can also create calculated columns by setting the Expression property.

4. Add the DataColumn object to the DataTable's Columns collection.

5. Repeat steps 3 and 4 for all the columns in the table.

6. Assign an array of DataColumn objects to the PrimaryKey property of the Data-Table. This step is optional but often necessary to leverage the full potential of a DataTable with a primary key.

7. Create one or more constraints for the table, which you do by creating either a UniqueConstraint or a ForeignKeyConstraint object, setting its properties, and then adding it to the DataTable's Constraints collection.

8. Add the DataTable object to the DataSet's Tables collection.

9. Repeat steps 2 through 8 for all the tables in the DataSet.

10. Create all the necessary relationships between tables in the DataSet; you can create a relationship by passing its properties to the Add method of the DataSet's Relations collection or by explicitly creating a DataRelation object, setting its properties, and then adding it to the Relations collection.

Sometimes you can omit some of the steps in the preceding list—for example, when you don't need table constraints or relationships. You can also make your code more concise by creating a DataTable and adding it to the parent DataSet's Tables collection in a single step or by adding a column to the parent DataTable's Columns collection without explicitly creating a DataColumn object. In the following sections, I'll provide examples for each of these techniques.

You create a DataSet by calling its constructor method, which can take the DataSet name. This name is used only in a few cases—for example, when you're outputting data to XML. If the name is omitted, your new DataSet's name defaults to NewDataSet:

```
Dim ds As New DataSet("MyDataSet")
```

As a rule, your application creates and manages only one DataSet object at a time because you can create relationships between tables only if they belong to the same DataSet. In some circumstances, however, working with multiple DataSet objects can be convenient—for example, when you want to render as XML only some of the DataTable objects you're working with or when you want to create a clone of the main DataSet at a given moment in time so that you can restore it later.

Creating a DataTable Object

The code that follows creates a DataSet object that contains an Employees table:

```
Dim ds As New DataSet()
' Create a table; set its initial capacity.
Dim dtEmp As New DataTable("Employees")
dtEmp.MinimumCapacity = 200

' Create all columns.
' You can create a DataColumn and then add it to the Columns collection.
Dim dcFName As New DataColumn("FirstName", GetType(String))
dtEmp.Columns.Add(dcFName)
' Or you can create an implicit DataColumn with the Columns.Add method.
dtEmp.Columns.Add("LastName", GetType(String))
dtEmp.Columns.Add("BirthDate", GetType(Date))

' When you have to set additional properties, you can use an explicit
' DataColumn object, or you can use a With block.
With dtEmp.Columns.Add("HomeAddress", GetType(String))
    .MaxLength = 100
End With
' (When you must set only one property, you can be more concise,
'  even though the result isn't very readable.)
dtEmp.Columns.Add("City", GetType(String)).MaxLength = 20

' Create a calculated column by setting the Expression
' property or passing it as the third argument to the Add method.
dtEmp.Columns.Add("CompleteName", GetType(String), _
    "FirstName + ' ' + LastName")

' Create an identity, auto-incremented column.
Dim dcEmpId As New DataColumn("EmpId", GetType(Integer))
dcEmpId.AutoIncrement = True          ' Make it auto-increment.
dcEmpId.AutoIncrementSeed = 1
dcEmpId.AllowDBNull = False           ' Default is True.
dcEmpId.Unique = True                 ' All key columns should be unique.
dtEmp.Columns.Add(dcEmpId)            ' Add to Columns collection.
' Make it the primary key. (Create the array on-the-fly.)
dtEmp.PrimaryKey = New DataColumn() {dcEmpId}

' This is a foreign key, but we haven't created the other table yet.
dtEmp.Columns.Add("DeptId", GetType(Integer))

' Add the DataTable to the DataSet.
ds.Tables.Add(dtEmp)
```

The MinimumCapacity property offers an opportunity to optimize the performance of the application. The first rows that you create—up to the number defined by this property—won't require any additional memory allocation and therefore will be added more quickly.

As you see in the listing, you define the type of a DataColumn by using a System.Type object. So most of the time you'll use the Visual Basic GetType function for common data types such as String, Integer, and Date. The many remarks explain the several syntax variations you can adopt when you're adding a new column to the table's schema.

Some columns might require that you set additional properties. For example, you should set the AllowDBNull property to False to reject null values, set the Unique property to True to ensure that all values in the column are unique, or set the MaxLength property for String columns. You can create auto-incrementing columns (which are often used as key columns) by setting the AutoIncrement property to True and optionally setting the AutoIncrementSeed and AutoIncrementStep properties, as with the EmpId column in the previous example.

You can set the primary key by assigning a DataColumn array to the PrimaryKey property of the DataTable object. In most cases, this array contains just one element, but you can create compound keys made up of multiple columns if necessary:

```
' Create a primary key on the FirstName and LastName columns.
dtEmp.PrimaryKey = New DataColumn() _
    {dtEmp.Columns("FirstName"), dtEmp.Columns("LastName")}
```

The DataTable built in the CreateEmployeesTable procedure also contains a calculated column, CompleteName, evaluated as the concatenation of the FirstName and Last-Name columns. You can assign this expression to the Expression property or pass it as the third argument of the Add method. The "Working with Expressions" section later in this chapter describes which operators and functions you can use in an expression.

Interestingly, you can store any type of object in a DataSet, including forms, controls, and your custom objects. When using a column to store an object, you should specify the column type with GetType(Object). If the object is serializable, it will be restored correctly when you write the DataSet to a file and read it back. (If the object isn't serializable, you get an error when you attempt to serialize the DataSet.) Notice that the object state isn't rendered correctly as XML when you issue the WriteXml method, however. (See the "Writing XML Data" section in Chapter 23 for more information about this method.)

Adding Rows

The only significant operation that you can perform on an empty DataTable is the addition of one or more DataRow objects. The sequence to add a new row is as follows:

1. Use the DataTable's NewRow method to create a DataRow object with the same column schema as the table.

2. Assign values to all the fields in the DataRow (at least, to all fields that aren't nullable and that don't support a default value).

3. Pass the DataRow to the Add method of the table's Rows collection.

You should ensure that the new row doesn't violate the constraints defined for the table. For example, you must provide a value for all non-nullable columns and set a unique value for the primary key and for all the keys whose Unique property is True. Here's an example that adds a row to the Employees table defined previously. (Notice that it doesn't set the primary key because you've defined an auto-incrementing column.)

```
' Get a reference to the Employees table.
Dim dtEmp As DataTable = ds.Tables("Employees")
' Create a new row with the same schema.
Dim dr As DataRow = dtEmp.NewRow()

' Set all the columns.
dr("FirstName") = "Joe"
dr("LastName") = "Doe"
dr("BirthDate") = #1/15/1955#
dr("HomeAddress") = "1234 A Street"
dr("City") = "Los Angeles"
dr("DeptId") = 1
' Add to the Rows collection.
dtEmp.Rows.Add(dr)
```

When adding a large number of rows, you can optimize the performance of your code by using the LoadDataRow method (which takes an array of the values to be assigned) and bracketing your code in the DataTable's BeginLoadData and EndLoadData methods. (These methods temporarily disable and then reenable notifications, index maintenance, and constraints while loading data.) For example, suppose you want to import data into the Employees table from a semicolon-delimited file structured as follows:

```
"Andrew";"Fuller";2/19/1952;"908 W. Capital Way";"Tacoma"
"Janet";"Leverling";8/30/1963;"722 Moss Bay Blvd.";"Kirkland"
```

(Notice that the third field should follow the data format in use in your system.) Here's how you can solve the problem with a concise routine that's also as efficient as possible:

```
' Open the file, and read its contents.
Dim sr As New StreamReader("employees.dat")
Dim fileText As String = sr.ReadToEnd()
sr.Close()

' This regular expression defines a row of named elements.
Dim re As New Regex( _
    """(?<fname>[^""]+)"";""(?<lname>[^""]+)"";(?<bdate>[^;]+);" _
    & """(?<addr>[^""]+)"";""(?<city>[^""]+)""")

' Turn off index maintenance and constraints.
dtEmp.BeginLoadData()
' Repeat for each match (that is, each line in the file).
For Each ma As Match In re.Matches(fileText)
    ' Load all fields in one operation.
    Dim values() As Object = {ma.Groups("fname").Value, _
        ma.Groups("lname").Value, ma.Groups("bdate").Value, _
        ma.Groups("addr").Value, ma.Groups("city").Value}
    dtEmp.LoadDataRow(values, True)
```

```
Next
' Turn on index maintenance and constraints.
dtEmp.EndLoadData()
```

The syntax of the regular expression used to parse the file is maybe the most complex part of this code, but it's simpler than you might imagine. The purpose of this regular expression is to define the structure of each line in the data file and assign a distinct name to each group of characters delimited by semicolons and (in some cases) enclosed in double quotation marks. The meaning of the pattern becomes clearer if you get rid of the repeated double quotation marks that you see inside the string itself and split the expression according to each of the fields referenced:

```
"(?<fname>[^"]+)";
"(?<lname>[^"]+)";
 (?<bdate>[^;]+);
"(?<addr>[^"]+)";
"(?<city>[^"]+)"
```

Thanks to the groups defined in the regular expression, you can then reference each field by its name when you create the array of values.

Be aware that the LoadDataRow method adds a new row only if the key field isn't already in the table. If you're passing the primary key as a value and the table already contains a record with that key, the LoadDataRow method replaces the existing row with the new values. (This is the same behavior that you have when filling the Data-Table with data coming from a database via a DataAdapter.) For this reason, it's important that you correctly set the DataTable's primary key to avoid duplicate keys.

The BeginLoadData and EndLoadData methods are also useful for performing changes in a DataTable that would result in a temporary violation of the referential integrity rules or other constraints such as the uniqueness of a column—for example, when you have to exchange the primary keys of two rows in a table.

Updating and Deleting Rows

One important difference between an ADO disconnected Recordset and a DataTable is that the latter doesn't support the concept of navigation through its rows. This happens because a DataTable is a collection of DataRow objects and you can access any element by its index. For example, the following loop converts the FirstName and Last-Name columns to uppercase in the first 10 records of the Employees table:

```
For i As Integer = 0 To 9
    Dim dr As DataRow = dtEmp.Rows(i)
    dr("FirstName") = dr("FirstName").ToString.ToUpper
    dr("LastName") = dr("LastName").ToString.ToUpper
Next
```

You can also avoid the temporary DataRow object, as in this code snippet:

```
' Clear the name fields of all the records in the DataTable.
For i As Integer = 0 To dtEmp.Rows.Count - 1
    dtEmp.Rows(i)("FirstName") = ""
    dtEmp.Rows(i)("LastName") = ""
Next
```

You can also use a For Each loop when looping over all the DataRow items in a DataTable:

```
For Each dr As DataRow In dtEmp.Rows
    dr("FirstName") = ""
    dr("LastName") = ""
Next
```

Deleting a row is as easy as issuing a Delete method on the corresponding DataRow object:

```
' Delete the last DataRow in the table. (Can be undeleted.)
dtEmp.Rows(dtEmp.Rows.Count - 1).Delete
```

Deleted rows aren't physically deleted from the DataSet. In fact, the only effect of the Delete method is to mark the row as deleted—the row is still in the DataTable, even though you can perform only a small number of operations on it. You can detect whether a row is deleted by means of the RowState property, which is described in the following section.

The Rows collection supports the Remove method, which removes the DataRow from the collection. Unlike the DataRow's Delete method, the row is immediately removed from the DataSet and not just marked for deletion:

```
' Remove the last DataRow in the table. (Can't be undeleted.)
dtEmp.Rows.Remove(dtEmp.Rows.Count - 1)
```

Accepting and Rejecting Changes

Because the DataSet is just a client-side repository of data and is physically disconnected from any data source, operations you perform on the DataSet, its tables, and its rows aren't reflected in the data source you used to fill it, at least not automatically, as happens with ADO keysets and dynamic recordsets. (I'll discuss how to update a database from a DataSet later in this chapter.)

I mentioned in the preceding section that when you delete a row, you're actually marking it for deletion, but the row is still in the DataTable. You can test the current state of a DataRow object by querying its RowState property, which can return one of the following values: Detached (the row has been created but hasn't been added to a DataTable), Added (the row has been added to a DataTable), Modified (the row has been updated), Deleted (the row has been deleted), and Unchanged (the row hasn't been modified).

Depending on their current state, you can use the DataTable's Select method to filter the rows in a table, as I'll explain in the "Filtering, Searching, and Sorting" section later in this chapter.

The RowState property is read-only, but the DataRow class exposes two methods that affect this property. You invoke the AcceptChanges method to confirm your changes on the current row and the RejectChanges method to cancel them. (Once again, these methods don't really update any data source outside the DataSet.) The effect of the AcceptChanges method is to physically delete rows marked for deletion and then set the RowState property of all the remaining rows to Unchanged. The RejectChanges method drops all the rows that have been added since the DataTable was loaded and then sets the RowState property of all the remaining rows to Unchanged.

To see in greater detail how these methods affect the state of a row, consider the following code:

```
Dim dr As DataRow = dtEmp.NewRow
Debug.WriteLine(dr.RowState)            ' => Detached
dr("FirstName") = "Joe"
dr("LastName") = "Doe"
dtEmp.Rows.Add(dr)
Debug.WriteLine(dr.RowState)            ' => Added

' AcceptChanges marks all records as unchanged.
dr.AcceptChanges()
Debug.WriteLine(dr.RowState)            ' => Unchanged
dr(0) = ""
Debug.WriteLine(dr.RowState)            ' => Modified
dr.Delete()
Debug.WriteLine(dr.RowState)            ' => Deleted

' RejectChanges undeletes the row and restores its unchanged status.
dr.RejectChanges()
Debug.WriteLine(dr.RowState)            ' => Unchanged
dr.Delete()
Debug.WriteLine(dr.RowState)            ' => Deleted

' AcceptChanges definitively deletes the row,
' which now appears to be detached.
dr.AcceptChanges()
Debug.WriteLine(dr.RowState)            ' => Detached
```

Also, the DataTable and the DataSet classes expose the AcceptChanges and RejectChanges methods, so you can easily accept or undo changes that you've made in all the rows in a table and all the tables in a DataSet. Notice that the second argument of the LoadDataRow method specifies whether the method should execute an implicit AcceptChanges.

Validating Values in Rows and Columns

All robust applications should validate data entered by the end user. Doing this is easy when you add data programmatically—you just avoid entering invalid values. But validation is less easy when the end user enters or modifies records through the user interface—for example, by means of a bound DataGrid control. Fortunately, validating data entered by this route is also relatively simple thanks to the events that the Data-Table object exposes. These events are of two types depending on whether they occur before or after the action in question. ColumnChanging, RowChanging, and RowDeleting events occur before a column is changed, a row is changed, or a row is deleted. Column-Changed, RowChanged, and RowDeleted events occur after the column has changed, the row has changed, or the row has been deleted.

The demo application displays the Employees table in the lowest grid and then assigns the Employees table to a DataTable variable marked with the WithEvents keyword so that any editing action on the table underlying the DataGrid control can be handled through code. Validating a new value in a column is as easy as trapping the Column-Changing event, checking the new value (which can be found in the ProposedValue property of the object passed in the second argument to the event handler), and throwing an exception if it can't be accepted. For example, the following code rejects future dates assigned to the BirthDate column:

```
Dim WithEvents DataTable As DataTable

Private Sub DataTable_ColumnChanging(ByVal sender As Object, _
    ByVal e As DataColumnChangeEventArgs) Handles DataTable.ColumnChanging
    If e.Column.ColumnName = "BirthDate" Then
        If CDate(e.ProposedValue) > Date.Now Then
            Throw New ArgumentException("Invalid birth date value")
        End If
    End If
End Sub
```

If the user attempts to enter an invalid birth date in the DataGrid, the old value is automatically restored when the caret leaves the grid cell. Notice that the DataGrid absorbs the exception and no error message is shown to the user. Interestingly, you can check the value and throw the exception even in the ColumnChanged event handler. In this case, the value is rejected only when the caret leaves the row (not the column).

Often you can't validate columns individually and must consider two or more columns at a time. The typical case is when the value in a column must be greater or lower than the value in another column. In this case, you must validate both columns in the RowChanging event handler. This event fires when a row is changed or added to the table. You can determine the action being performed by checking the Action property of the second argument passed to the event handler. For example, you can use the following code to ensure that State and Country columns can't both be null strings:

```
Private Sub DataTable_RowChanging(ByVal sender As Object, _
    ByVal e As DataRowChangeEventArgs) Handles DataTable.RowChanging
    If CStr(e.Row("State")) = "" And CStr(e.Row("Country")) = "" Then
        Throw New ArgumentException("State and Country can't both be empty")
    End If
End Sub
```

In this case, the DataGrid catches the exception when the user moves the caret to another row, displays the error message you've passed to the ArgumentException's constructor, and restores the original values in the row's fields.

The *xxx*Changed events aren't just for validation chores, and you can use them in a variety of other situations as well. For example, you might use them to update a calculated column that depends on one or more other columns but whose value can't be expressed using the operators allowed by ADO.NET for calculated columns. (See the "Working with Expressions" section later in this chapter.)

Setting, Retrieving, and Fixing Errors

Instead of throwing exceptions when a column or a row doesn't contain valid values, you can opt for a different error handling strategy and just mark the column or the row with an error message. This approach lets you show end users a list of all the existing errors so that they can decide to fix the invalid values or cancel the update operation as a whole. (This alternative strategy is more feasible when you're importing data from a file or when the user has submitted all changes together, as is the case when he or she fills out a form in the browser and then clicks the Submit button.)

If you opt for this strategy, you can still use the *xxx*Changing and *xxx*Changed events as before; what changes is the way to react to an invalid value. When you detect an invalid column value, you use the DataRow's SetColumnError method to associate an error message with that column. When you detect an invalid row, you assign an error message to the DataRow's RowError property:

```
Private Sub DataTable_ColumnChanging(ByVal sender As Object, _
    ByVal e As DataColumnChangeEventArgs) Handles DataTable.ColumnChanging
    If e.Column.ColumnName = "BirthDate" Then
        If CDate(e.ProposedValue) > Date.Now Then
            e.Row.SetColumnError(e.Column.ColumnName, _
                "Invalid birth date value")
        End If
    End If
End Sub

Private Sub DataTable_RowChanging(ByVal sender As Object, _
    ByVal e As DataRowChangeEventArgs) Handles DataTable.RowChanging
    If CStr(e.Row("State")) = "" And CStr(e.Row("Country")) = "" Then
        e.Row.RowError = "State and Country can't both be null"
    End If
End Sub
```

It's interesting to see that the DataGrid control reacts to columns and rows marked with an error by displaying an error icon in the column's cell or in the row indicator, respectively, but without automatically restoring the original values. You can then move the mouse cursor over the icon to read the error message you set via code. (See Figure 22-2.)

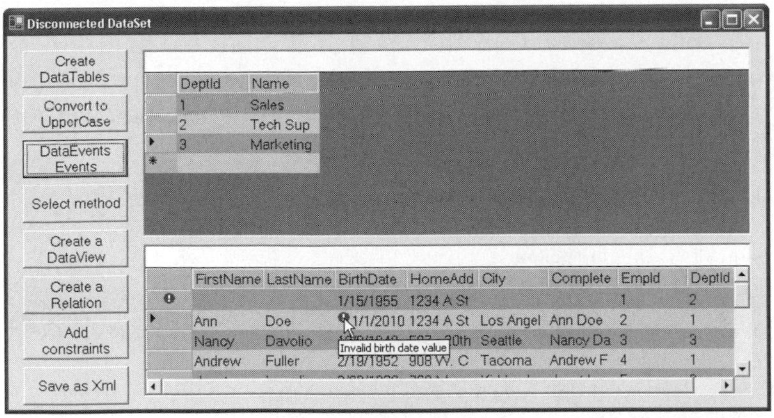

Figure 22-2 The DataGrid control displays error icons near invalid columns and rows.

You can check via code whether a DataRow, a DataTable, or a DataSet contains any error through its HasErrors read-only property, without having to go through each column of each row of each table in the DataSet. For example, you can use the following loop to evaluate the number of rows that contain one or more errors:

```
Dim numErrors As Integer
If ds.HasErrors Then
    ' There is at least one DataTable with an invalid row.
    For Each dt As DataTable In ds.Tables
        If dt.HasErrors Then
            ' There is at least one DataRow with an invalid column.
            For Each dr As DataRow In dt.Rows
                If dr.HasErrors Then numErrors += 1
            Next
        End If
    Next
End If
' Now numErrors contains the number of rows with errors.
```

You can retrieve the actual error message associated with a column by means of the DataRow's GetColumnError method. And you can clear all the error messages associated with a row by using the ClearErrors method. You can get the array of all the columns that have an error with GetColumnsInError:

```
' Gather all the error messages associated with individual columns.
' (dr is the DataRow under examination.)
Dim messages As String
For Each dc As DataColumn In dr.GetColumnsInError()
    Messages &= dr.GetColumnError(dc) & ControlChars.CrLf
Next
```

Your application might even attempt to resolve some errors without the assistance of end users. For example, you might keep a numeric or date value within its valid range, and you can use the spelling checker and automatically correct the name of a state or country. When you attempt to fix the errors each row contains, you can take advantage of the DataRow's ability to preserve both the original value and the current version of the value in each column. After checking with the HasVersion method that the row supports the versioned value you're looking for, you can access these versioned values by passing a DataRowVersion argument to the Item property:

```
' This code attempts to resolve errors in the BirthDate column
' by restoring the original value if there is one.
For Each dr As DataRow In dtEmp.Rows
    If dr.GetColumnError("BirthDate") <> "" Then
        If dr.HasVersion(DataRowVersion.Original) Then
            dr("BirthDate") = dr("BirthDate", DataRowVersion.Original)
            ' This statement hides the error icon in the DataGrid.
            dr.SetColumnError("BirthDate", "")
        End If
    End If
Next
```

When you issue the DataRow's AcceptChanges method, the proposed value becomes the current value and the original value persists. Conversely, when you issue the DataTable's AcceptChanges method, the original value is lost and both the DataRow-Version.Original and DataRowVersion.Current values for the second argument return the same result. The reasons for this behavior will become apparent in the "Updating the Database" section later in this chapter.

If you enclose your edit operations between BeginEdit and EndEdit (or CancelEdit) methods, you can query the value being assigned but not yet committed using the DataRowVersion.Proposed value for the argument. When you issue the EndEdit method, the proposed value becomes the current value. A BeginEdit method temporarily suspends the enforcement of referential rules and other constraints until the EndEdit or CancelEdit method is invoked, so you might use these methods when modifying one or more DataRow objects, from the same or a different table.

Filtering, Searching, and Sorting

You can choose from two different techniques for filtering, searching, and sorting the rows of a DataTable: you can use its Select method, or you can define a DataView object. The Select method takes up to three arguments: a filter expression, a sort criterion, and a DataViewRowState enumerated argument that lets you filter rows on their current state and decide which value you see in the columns of modified rows. In its simplest form, the Select method takes a filter expression and returns an array of matching DataRow elements:

```
' Retrieve all employees whose first name is Joe.
Dim drows() as DataRow = dtEmp.Select("FirstName = 'Joe'")
```

The second (optional) argument is the list of fields on which the result array should be sorted:

```
' Retrieve all employees born in 1960 or later, and
' sort the result on their (LastName, FirstName) fields.
drows = dtEmp.Select("BirthDate >= #1/1/1960#", "LastName, FirstName")
```

You can also sort in descending mode using the DESC qualifier, as in this code snippet:

```
' Retrieve all employees born in 1960 or later, and
' sort the result on their birth date. (Younger employees come first.)
drows = dtEmp.Select("BirthDate >= #1/1/1960#", "BirthDate DESC")
```

Finally, you can filter rows depending on their state by passing a DataViewRowState value that specifies whether you're interested in changed, unchanged, added, or deleted rows:

```
' Retrieve all deleted rows, sorted by (FirstName, LastName) values.
drows = dtEmp.Select("", "FirstName, LastName", DataViewRowState.Deleted)
```

The third argument can take any of the following values: Unchanged (only unchanged rows), Added (only inserted rows), Deleted (only deleted rows), ModifiedCurrent (only changed rows; columns contain current values), ModifiedOriginal (only changed rows; columns contain original values), CurrentRows (unchanged, changed, and new rows; columns contain current values), OriginalRows (unchanged, changed, and deleted rows; columns contain original values), and None (no rows are returned).

If you omit this argument, you see rows with their current values and deleted rows aren't returned. The Select method is therefore able to access the values that were in the Data-Table after the most recent AcceptChanges or RejectChanges method or after reading them from a data source by using a DataAdapter object (as I explain in a later section).

The following code uses the Select method to extract a subset of rows from the Employees table and loads them into another table with the same column structure by means of ImportRow, a method that imports a DataRow object into a table without resetting the row's original and current values and its RowState property:

```
' Copy only the structure of the Employees table in the new table.
Dim newDt As DataTable = dtEmp.Clone()
newDt.TableName = "YoungEmployees"

' Select a subset of all employees, sorted on their names;
' extract only modified rows, with their current values.
Dim drows() As DataRow = dtEmp.Select("BirthDate >= #1/1/1960#", _
    "LastName, FirstName", DataViewRowState.ModifiedCurrent)
' Import the array of DataRows into the new table.
For Each dr As DataRow In drows
    newDt.ImportRow(dr)
Next
```

Using the DataView Object

Another way for you to filter or sort the rows in a DataTable is to use an auxiliary Data-View object. As its name suggests, this object works as a view over an existing DataTable. You can decide which records are visible by means of the DataView's RowFilter property, sort its rows with the Sort property, and decide which column values are displayed by assigning a DataViewRowState enumerated value to the DataView's RowStateFilter property. These properties give you the same filtering and sorting capabilities as the Select method:

```
' Display a subset of all employees, sorted on their names;
' show only modified rows, with their current values.

' Create a DataView on this table, set its filter and sort properties.
Dim dv As New DataView(dtEmp)
dv.RowFilter = "BirthDate >= #1/1/1960#"
dv.Sort = "LastName, FirstName"
dv.RowStateFilter = DataViewRowState.ModifiedCurrent
```

You can add, delete, and modify rows in a DataView by using the same methods you'd use with a regular DataTable, and your edit operation will affect the underlying table. You can also use the Find method to retrieve a DataRow given its primary key value.

The DataView object is especially useful when you bind it to a Windows Forms control or Web Forms control. For example, you might have two DataGrid controls displaying data from two DataView objects, each one containing a different view of the same table—for example, the original and the edited rows or two different sorted views of the same data. You bind a DataView to a Windows Forms DataGrid by assigning it to the control's DataSource:

```
DataGrid1.DataSource = dv
```

Even when you have an unfiltered and unsorted set of data, binding a DataView instead of a DataTable is usually a better idea because you can finely control what operations the end user can perform on data by means of the DataView's AllowDelete, AllowEdit, and AllowNew properties.

Creating Relationships

A great feature of the DataSet is its ability to create relationships between its Data-Table objects. Like real relational databases, a DataSet allows a relationship between two tables if they have a field in common. For example, you can establish a relationship between the Publishers and Titles tables if they have the PubId field in common. In this case, there would be a one-to-many relationship from the Publishers table (the parent or master table) to the Titles table (the child or detail table). Lookup tables often use relationships, such as when you use the DeptId field in the Employees table to retrieve the name of the department in the Departments table. This is the case shown in the following diagram:

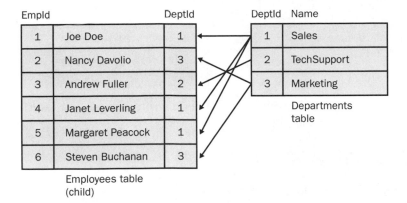

Employees table
(child)

Departments
table

Let's see how to build such a relationship. First of all, let's create the Departments table and add some rows to it:

```
' Create the Departments table.
Dim dtDept As New DataTable("Departments")

' The DeptId field must be marked as unique.
Dim dcDeptId As DataColumn = dtDept.Columns.Add("DeptId", GetType(Integer))
dcDeptId.Unique = True
' The department name must be unique as well.
Dim dcName As DataColumn = dtDept.Columns.Add("Name", GetType(String))
dcName.MaxLength = 50
dcName.Unique = True
' Make DeptId the primary key of the table.
dtDept.PrimaryKey = New DataColumn() {dcDeptId}
' Add this table to the DataSet.
ds.Tables.Add(dtDept)

' Add a few rows.
dtDept.LoadDataRow(New Object() {1, "Sales"}, True)
dtDept.LoadDataRow(New Object() {2, "Tech Support"}, True)
dtDept.LoadDataRow(New Object() {3, "Marketing"}, True)
```

Next, let's ensure that the DeptId field in the Employees table points to an existing row in the Departments table:

```
' Ensure that all Employees are associated with a Department.
For i As Integer = 0 To dtEmp.Rows.Count - 1
    ' Assign a DeptId value in the range 1-3.
    dtEmp.Rows(i).Item("DeptId") = CInt((i Mod 3) + 1)
Next
dtEmp.AcceptChanges()
```

Now we can create the relationship between the Departments and Employees tables. You can choose from a couple of ways to create a relationship: you can create a

DataRelation object explicitly and then add it to the DataSet's Relations collection, or you can create a relationship directly with the Add method of the Relations collection. The following code snippet uses the first approach:

```
' The DataRelation constructor takes the name of the relationship and
' a reference to the DataColumn in the parent and in the child table.
Dim relDeptEmp As New DataRelation("DeptEmp", _
    dtDept.Columns("DeptId"), dtEmp.Columns("DeptId"))
ds.Relations.Add(relDeptEmp)
```

The upper grid in Figure 22-3 shows how a DataGrid control displays a DataTable that works as a parent table in a relationship.

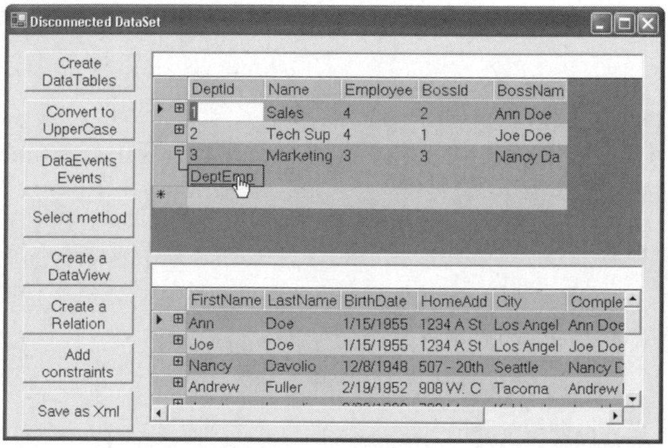

Figure 22-3   The DataGrid control lets you navigate through DataTable objects linked by relationships.

Once you have created a relationship, you can easily navigate from one table to the other using the GetParentRow and GetChildRows methods of the DataRow class. You use the former method to get the row in the parent table that corresponds to the current row in the child table. For example, you can retrieve the name of the department associated with the first row in the Employees table as follows:

```
' Retrieve the name of the department of the first employee.
Dim drDepartment As DataRow = dtEmp.Rows(0).GetParentRow("DeptEmp")
Dim deptName As String = CStr(drDepartment("Name"))
```

You use the GetChildRows method when navigating from a row in the parent table to the corresponding rows in the child table. Because this is a one-to-many relationship, the GetChildRows method returns an array of rows taken from the child table:

```
' Display the names of the employees in the first department.
Dim drEmployees() As DataRow = dtDept.Rows(0).GetChildRows("DeptEmp")
For Each drEmp As DataRow in drEmployees
    Debug.WriteLine(drEmp("LastName"))
Next
```

```
' Display the number of employees in each department.
For Each dr As DataRow In dtDept.Rows
    Debug.WriteLine(dr("Name").ToString & ", " & _
        CStr(dr.GetChildRows("DeptEmp").Length))
Next
```

A DataSet can contain multiple relationships and can even contain more than one relationship between the same pair of tables. For example, the Departments table might have a BossId field that contains the ID of the row in Employees corresponding to the head of the department. Here's how you can set the corresponding relationship:

```
' Add a new BossId column to the Departments table, and fill it with the
' ID of the first 3 employees.
dtDept.Columns.Add("BossId", GetType(Integer))
For i As Integer = 0 To dtDept.Rows.Count - 1
    dtDept.Rows(i)("BossId") = dtEmp.Rows(i)("EmpId")
Next
dtDept.AcceptChanges()

' Create another relationship between the Departments and Employees tables.
ds.Relations.Add("DeptBoss", dtEmp.Columns("EmpId"), dtDept.Columns("BossId"))
```

Here's the code that leverages the new relationship to print the list of departments and the boss for each:

```
' List the name of each department and the name of its boss.
For Each dr As DataRow In dtDept.Rows
    Debug.WriteLine(dr("Name").ToString & ", " & _
        dr.GetParentRow("DeptBoss")("LastName").ToString)
Next
```

The GetChildRows method supports a second DataRowVersion argument that lets you decide whether you want to extract the original or current versions of the child rows. In the next section, you'll learn how to create calculated columns that take advantage of the relationships existing in the DataSet.

You can remove an existing relationship by using the Remove or RemoveAt method of the DataSet's Relations collection. However, these methods throw an exception if the DataRelation object can't be removed from the collection. To avoid this exception, you should test whether the relationship can be removed by means of the CanRemove method:

```
' ds is the DataSet that holds the relationship.
Dim relDeptEmp As DataRelation = ds.Relations("DeptEmp")
If ds.Relations.CanRemove(relDeptEmp) Then
    ' Remove the relationship only if it is safe to do so.
    ds.Relations.Remove(relDeptEmp)
End If
```

Working with Expressions

Many ADO.NET properties and methods support user-defined expressions. For example, you can assign an expression to the Expression property of a calculated DataColumn or pass an expression to the Filter method of a DataTable to extract a subset of all the rows. In all cases, the syntax of the expression you create must obey the few simple rules summarized in this section.

The expression can contain numeric, string, and date constants. String constants must be enclosed in single quotes, and date constants must be enclosed in # characters. You can reference another column in the same table by using its ColumnName property. If a column name contains special punctuation characters, you should enclose the name between square brackets.

The four math operations are supported, as well as the modulo operation (use the % symbol) and the string concatenation operator (use the + sign). All the comparison operators are supported. When applied to strings, they perform case-sensitive or case-insensitive comparisons depending on the CaseSensitive property of the DataTable object. Here are a few examples of valid expressions:

```
FirstName + ' ' + LastName
[Unit Price] * 0.80
BirthDate > #1/4/1980#
```

The LIKE operator is similar to the SQL operator of the same name; you can use either the % or the * character as a wildcard, and they can appear anywhere in the second operand. For example, both of the following expressions filter all employees whose last name starts with "A":

```
LastName LIKE 'A*'
LastName LIKE 'A%'
```

The IN operator is also similar to the SQL operator of the same name and lets you check that a column's value is among those specified. For example, you can filter only those employees whose DeptId is equal to 2, 3, or 4:

```
DeptId IN (2, 3, 4)
```

The expression evaluator also supports a few functions: Len, Trim, Substring, IIf, IsNull, and Convert. For example, suppose you want to create a calculated column named Discount, whose value is equal to Total * .90 when Total is less than or equal to 1000 and Total *.85 if Total is higher than 1000. The IIF function is what you need:

```
dt.Columns.Add("Discount", GetType(Double), _
    "IIF(Total <= 1000, Total * 0.9, Total * 0.85)")
```

The Len and Trim functions work like their Visual Basic counterparts. The Substring function is similar to the Mid function (including the fact that character indexes are 1-based). The IsNull function is useful to provide a textual representation of DBNull values:

```
IfNull(City, '<unknown>')
```

Finally, the Convert function takes the value to convert and a string that corresponds to the full name of the target type, as in:

```
'$' + Convert(Quantity, 'System.String')
```

An expression can also refer to a field in another table if a relationship exists between the current table and the other table. When working with relationships, you can use two different syntaxes, depending on whether the other table is the parent table or the child table in the relationship. For example, if there is a relationship named DeptEmp between the Departments and the Employees tables in the DeptId column that they have in common, you can add a calculated column to the Employees table that returns the name of the department, as follows:

```
' Extend the Employees table with a calculated column that
' returns the name of the department for that employee.
dtEmp.Columns.Add("Department", GetType(String), "Parent(DeptEmp).Name)")
```

The following example uses the DeptBoss relationship to extend the Departments table with a calculated field equal to the name of the department's boss:

```
dtDept.Columns.Add("BossName", GetType(String), _
    "Parent(DeptBoss).CompleteName")
```

If the current table is the parent table of the relationship and you want to reference a field in the child table, you use Child(relname).fieldname syntax. However, because most relationships are of the one-to-many kind when seen from the perspective of the parent table, in most cases what you really want is to evaluate an aggregate function on the matching rows in the child table. The expression engine supports all the usual aggregation functions, including Count, Sum, Min, Max, Avg (average), StDev (standard deviation), and Var (variance). For example, you can leverage the DeptEmp relationship to extend the Departments table with a calculated column that returns the count of employees in each department:

```
' Add a calculated column to the Departments table
' that returns the number of employees for each department.
dtDept.Columns.Add("EmployeesCount", GetType(Integer), _
    "Count(Child(DeptEmp).EmpID)")
```

Assuming that the Employees table has a Salary column, you can add other calculated fields in the Departments table that evaluate to the minimum, maximum, and average salary for the employees in each department:

```
dtDept.Columns.Add("MinSalary", GetType(Double), _
    "Min(Child(DeptEmp).Salary)")
dtDept.Columns.Add("MaxSalary", GetType(Double), _
    "Max(Child(DeptEmp).Salary)")
dtDept.Columns.Add("AvgSalary", GetType(Double), _
    "Avg(Child(DeptEmp).Salary)")
```

You often use aggregate functions together with the DataTable's Compute method, which offers a simple method to extract data from all or a subset of the rows in a DataTable object. This method takes an expression and a filter that specifies the rows that are used to compute the expression:

```
' Evaluate the average salary of all employees.
Debug.WriteLine(dtEmp.Compute("Avg(Salary)", Nothing))
' Evaluate the average salary for employees in a given department.
Debug.WriteLine(dtEmp.Compute("Avg(Salary)", "DeptId = 2"))
```

Enforcing Constraints

The DataTable object supports the creation of constraints, where a constraint is a condition that must be met when you add or modify a row in the table. Two different types of constraints are supported: unique constraints and foreign-key constraints.

A unique constraint mandates that all the values in a column or a collection of columns must be unique—in other words, you can't have two rows that contain the same value for the column or combination of columns specified in the constraint. In the majority of cases, the constraint affects only one column. This is the case with the EmpId field in the Employees table. You can enforce this type of constraint by simply setting the column's Unique property to True when you create the column:

```
' The DeptId field must be unique.
Dim dcDeptId As DataColumn = dtDept.Columns.Add("DeptId", GetType(Integer))
dcDeptId.Unique = True
```

In more complex cases, you have multiple columns whose combination must be unique. For example, let's say that the combination of FirstName and LastName columns must be unique. (In other words, you can't have two people with the same name.) To enforce this type of constraint, you must create a UniqueConstraint object, pass an array of columns to its constructor, and add the constraint to the table's Constraints collection:

```
' Prepare the array of involved DataColumn objects.
Dim cols() As DataColumn = { dtEmp.Columns("LastName"), _
    dtEmp.Columns("FirstName") }
' Create the UniqueConstraint object, assigning it a name.
Dim uc As New UniqueConstraint("UniqueName", cols)
' Add it to the table's Constraints collection.
dtEmp.Constraints.Add(uc)
```

Or you can do everything with a single (but less readable) statement:

```
dtEmp.Constraints.Add(New UniqueConstraint(New DataColumn() _
    {dtEmp.Columns("LastName"), dtEmp.Columns("FirstName")}))
```

Now you get an error if you attempt to add a new employee with the same first and last name as an employee already in the table:

```
Dim dr As DataRow = dtEmp.NewRow
dr("FirstName") = dtEmp.Rows(0)("FirstName")
dr("LastName") = dtEmp.Rows(0)("LastName")
dtEmp.Rows.Add(dr)                  ' This statement causes an error.
```

Constraints are active only if the DataSet's EnforceConstraints property is True (the default value).

You have a foreign-key constraint when the values in a column of a table must match one of the existing values in a column in another table. For example, you can decide that the user won't be able to add an employee whose DeptId field is null or if the field doesn't point to an existing row in the Departments table. You would create such a constraint this way:

```
' Create a foreign-key constraint.
Dim fkrelDeptEmp As New ForeignKeyConstraint("FKDeptEmp", _
    dtDept.Columns("DeptId"), dtEmp.Columns("DeptId"))
' Add it to the child table's Constraints collection.
dtEmp.Constraints.Add(fkrelDeptEmp)
```

Most of the time, however, you don't have to explicitly create a ForeignKeyConstraint object because you can use the foreign-key constraint that's implicitly defined by a relationship between tables and that's available through the ChildKeyConstraint property. (A relationship also creates a unique constraint on the parent table and makes it available through the ParentKeyConstraint property.) The following line of code retrieves a reference to the ForeignKeyConstraint object implied by the relationship between Departments and Employees:

```
Dim fkrel As ForeignKeyConstraint = ds.Relations("DeptEmp").ChildKeyConstraint
```

If you have defined a relationship between two tables, the attempt to set another foreign-key constraint over the same columns throws an exception. Creating the foreign-key constraint first and then the relationship on the same columns doesn't raise an error because the relationship reuses the existing constraints. (You can prove it by checking that the relationship's ChildKeyConstraint property returns the original Data-Constraint object.)

A foreign-key constraint lets you exert more control over what happens when the end user deletes a row or updates the key field of a row in the parent table. Three properties of the ForeignKeyConstraint object come into play in this case:

- **DeleteRule**   This property determines what happens to the rows in the child table when a row in the parent table is deleted. The valid values for this property are Cascade (default, child rows are deleted); None (no action is taken); SetDefault (child column is set to its default value); and SetNull (child column is set to DBNull).

- **UpdateRule** This property specifies what happens to rows in the child table when the key field of a row in the parent table is modified. The valid values for this property are Cascade (default, child column is modified to reflect the new key value); None (no action is taken); SetDefault (child column is set to its default value); and SetNull (child column is set to DBNull).

- **AcceptRejectRule** This property tells how changes in the child table are rolled back when an update operation in the parent table fails because of an error or because the application calls the RejectChanges method. This property can take only one of two values: None (no action occurs) or Cascade (changes are cascaded across the relationship).

Constraints associated with relationships are temporarily suspended during an edit operation until changes are confirmed with the AcceptChanges method. When this happens, constraints are reenabled and an error can occur if the new data doesn't comply with existing constraints. The AcceptRejectRule property determines what happens to child rows when such an error occurs.

You must observe some limitations to the settings that you can assign to the DeleteRule and UpdateRule properties. For example, you can't really use the None value. In fact, after the delete or edit operation, the child row would point to a nonexistent row in the parent table, and this condition would violate the foreign-key constraint itself. In addition, if the child table contains calculated properties that use the relationship, you can't use the SetNull value for most cases.

Let's see how you can set up a foreign-key constraint that automatically updates child rows when the parent row is changed and sets the foreign key in child rows to DBNull if the parent row is deleted:

```
' Note: this code throws an exception if there is already a relationship
'       between the Department.DeptId and Employees.DeptId fields.
Dim fkrelDeptEmp As New ForeignKeyConstraint("FKDeptEmp", _
    dtDept.Columns("DeptId"), dtEmp.Columns("DeptId"))
dtEmp.Constraints.Add(fkrelDeptEmp)
fkrelDeptEmp.DeleteRule = Rule.SetNull
fkrelDeptEmp.UpdateRule = Rule.Cascade
fkrelDeptEmp.AcceptRejectRule = AcceptRejectRule.None
```

Figure 22-4 shows what happens when the user deletes a row in the parent table while the DeleteRule property is set as in the preceding code snippet.

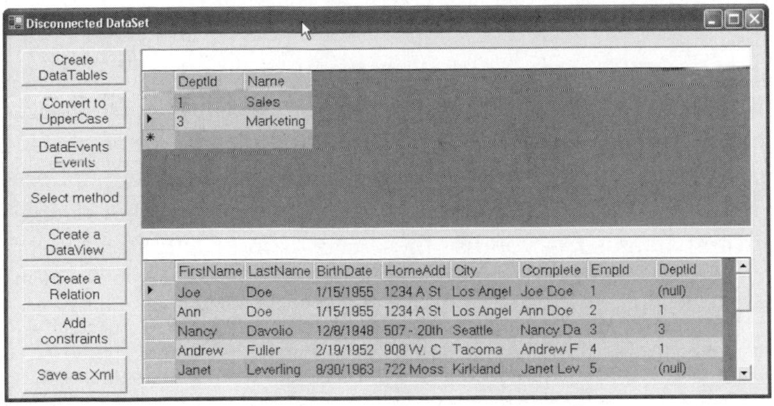

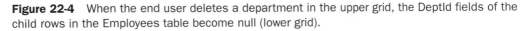

Figure 22-4   When the end user deletes a department in the upper grid, the DeptId fields of the child rows in the Employees table become null (lower grid).

The DataAdapter Class

In the first portion of this chapter, I showed you how to create a DataSet object, load it with data produced by your application (or read from a text file), create constraints and relationships, and define calculated fields. In other words, I showed you how to use the DataSet as a sort of scaled-down client-side database that your code defines and fills with data. While this functionality can be useful in many scenarios, the majority of .NET applications have to process data coming from a real database, such as Access, SQL Server, or Oracle.

The key to using the DataSet in this way is the DataAdapter object, which works as a connector between the DataSet and the actual data source. The DataAdapter is in charge of filling one or more DataTable objects with data taken from the database so that the application can then close the connection and work in a completely disconnected mode. After the end user has performed all his or her editing chores, the application can reopen the connection and reuse the same DataAdapter object to send changes to the database.

Admittedly, the disconnected nature of the DataSet complicates matters for developers, but it greatly improves its versatility. You can now fill a DataTable with data taken from any data source—whether it's SQL Server, a text file, or a mainframe—and process it with the same routines, regardless of where the data comes from. The decoupled architecture based on the DataSet and the DataAdapter makes it possible to read data from one source and send updates to another source when necessary. You have a lot more freedom working with ADO.NET, but also many more responsibilities.

> **Note**   The code samples that follow assume a proper connection string was defined previously and stored in a global variable, as described in "Setting the ConnectionString Property" section in Chapter 21.

Introducing the DataAdapter

The first thing you need to know about the DataAdapter is that there's actually one DataAdapter class for each .NET data provider, so you have an OleDbDataAdapter, an SqlDataAdapter, an OdbcDataAdapter, and an OracleDataAdapter class. All these classes expose the same set of properties and methods because they inherit from the DbDataAdapter abstract type. Except for their names and a few other details—such as how they deal with parameters—you use these classes in exactly the same way.

Reading Data from a Database

The DataAdapter's constructor is overloaded to take zero, one, or two arguments. In its most complete form, you pass to it a SQL SELECT statement (or an ADO.NET Command object containing a SQL SELECT statement) and a Connection object, as in this code snippet:

```
Dim cn As New OleDbConnection(BiblioConnString)
cn.Open()
' Create a DataAdapter that reads and writes the Publishers table.
Dim sql As String = "SELECT * FROM Publishers"
Dim da As New OleDbDataAdapter(sql, cn)
```

Or you can create a DataAdapter and then assign an ADO.NET Command object to its SelectCommand property:

```
da = New OleDbDataAdapter()
da.SelectCommand = New OleDbCommand(sql, cn)
```

Filling a DataTable

Once you've created a DataAdapter object and defined its SELECT command, you can use the object to fill an existing or new DataTable of a DataSet with the Fill method, which takes the name of the target DataTable in its second argument:

```
' Read the Publishers database table into a local DataTable.
Dim ds As New DataSet()
da.Fill(ds, "Publishers")
cn.Close()
```

Because of the disconnected nature of the DataSet, the action of opening a connection only for the short time necessary to read data from a single database table is so frequent that Microsoft engineers provided the DataAdapter object with the ability to open the connection automatically and close it immediately at the completion of the Fill method. For this reason, the preceding code can be written in a more concise way, as you see here:

```
' Define the connection; no need to open it.
Dim cn As New OleDbConnection(BiblioConnString)
```

```
Dim da As New OleDbDataAdapter("SELECT * FROM Publishers", cn)
Dim ds As New DataSet()
' Read the Publishers table; no need to open or close the connection.
da.Fill(ds, "Publishers")
```

(Of course, you shouldn't use this technique when reading data from multiple tables. Instead, you should open the connection manually once and close it afterward.) The Fill method is overloaded to take a variety of arguments, including a reference to an existing DataTable object. You can also omit the name of the target table, in which case a DataTable object named Table is created by default. However, I strongly advise against doing this because it makes your code less readable to other programmers who aren't aware of this detail.

In most real-world applications, you should avoid reading resultsets containing more than a few hundred rows. You can do this by using an overloaded form of the Fill method that takes the starting record and the maximum number of rows to read. To determine how many rows were actually read, you can check the method's return value:

```
' Read only the first 100 rows of the Publishers table.
Dim numRows As Integer = da.Fill(ds, 0, 100, "Publishers")
```

You can then provide the user with the ability to navigate through pages of the result-set, possibly by using the usual Previous, Next, First, and Last buttons:

```
' Read Nth page; return number of rows on the page.
' (Assuming that the da and ds variables have been correctly initialized)
Function ReadPage(ByVal n As Integer) As Integer
    ReadPage = da.Fill(ds, (n - 1) * 100, 100, "Publishers")
End Sub
```

A better way to limit the amount of information read from the database is by using parameters in the WHERE clause of the SQL command. In this case, you can create a parameterized Command object by using the guidelines I described in the "Parameterized Commands" section in Chapter 21, and you can pass it to the constructor or the SelectCommand property of the DataAdapter, as in the following example:

```
' Create a Command object with parameters.
Dim sql As String = "SELECT * FROM Publishers WHERE Name LIKE ?"
Dim cmd As New OleDbCommand(sql, cn)
' Create the parameter with an initial value.
cmd.Parameters.Add("PubNameLike", "S%")

' Create the DataAdapter based on the parameterized command.
Dim da As New OleDbDataAdapter(cmd)
' Get publishers whose name begins with "S".
da.Fill(ds, "Publishers")
' Add publishers whose name begins with "M".
cmd.Parameters(0).Value = "M%"
da.Fill(ds, "Publishers")
```

The Fill method of the OleDbDataAdapter object can even take an ADO Recordset object as an argument. This lets your .NET application use a method in an existing COM component that reads data from the database and returns it as an ADO Recordset. Keep in mind, however, that this is a one-way operation. You can read the contents of an ADO Recordset object, but you can't update it. The following code fills a DataSet by using an ADO Recordset created with the adodb library and COM Interop. You'll never do this in a real .NET application, but the example shows how you can proceed when you have a middle-tier component that returns a query result as an ADO Recordset:

```
' Open an ADO DB connection toward SQL Server's Pubs database.
Dim adoCn As New ADODB.Connection()
adoCn.Open(OledbPubsConnString)
' Read the Publishers table using a firehose cursor.
Dim adoRs As New ADODB.Recordset()
adoRs.Open("SELECT * FROM Publishers", adoCn)

' Use the Recordset to fill a DataSet table.
Dim ds As New DataSet()
Dim da As New OleDbDataAdapter()
' (The following line automatically closes the Recordset.)
da.Fill(ds, adoRs, "Publishers")
adoCn.Close()
```

A great feature of the Fill method is its ability to support SQL batch commands that return multiple resultsets if the back-end database supports them. For example, you can retrieve multiple tables of data from SQL Server (regardless of the .NET data provider you're using) as follows:

```
' Access SQL Server using the OLE DB .NET Data Provider.
Dim cn As New OleDbConnection(OledbPubsConnString)
' Create a DataAdapter that reads three tables.
Dim sql As String = "SELECT * FROM Publishers;SELECT * FROM Titles;" _
    & "SELECT * FROM Authors"
Dim da As New OleDbDataAdapter(sql, cn)

' Create and fill the DataSet's tables.
Dim ds As New DataSet
da.Fill(ds, "Publishers")
' Change the names of the generated tables.
ds.Tables(1).TableName = "Titles"
ds.Tables(2).TableName = "Authors"
```

In the preceding code, the Fill method creates three tables named Publishers, Publishers1, and Publishers2, so you need to change the last two names manually. If you're retrieving data from SQL Server, you should use this technique because it minimizes the number of round trips to the server.

Dealing with Filling Errors

Most of the time, the Fill method shouldn't raise any error, especially if the structure of the DataSet perfectly mirrors the metadata in the data source. In some cases, however, this method can throw an exception, such as when the row being read violates the constraints of a DataColumn or the data being read can't be converted to a .NET data type without losing precision. When such a problem occurs, ADO.NET throws an InvalidCastException exception. You can handle this exception the way you would any other exception, but you can get even better control of the read operation if you write a handler for the FillError event.

The second argument passed to this event is a FillErrorEventArgs object, which exposes the following information: DataTable (the table being filled), Errors (the error that occurred), Values (an Object array that contains values for all the columns in the row being updated), and Continue (a Boolean value that you can set to True to continue the fill operation despite the error). Here's an example that sets up a FillError handler to deal with overflow errors gracefully:

```
Dim ds As New DataSet

Sub FillData()
    Dim cn As New OleDbConnection(OledbPubsConnString)
    Dim da As New OleDbDataAdapter("SELECT * FROM Publishers", cn)
    ' Create a handler for the FillError event.
    AddHandler da.FillError, AddressOf FillError
    ' Create and fill the DataSet's table.
    da.Fill(ds, "Publishers")
End Sub

Sub FillError(ByVal sender As Object, ByVal args As FillErrorEventArgs)
    If TypeOf args.Errors Is System.OverflowException Then
        ' Add here the code that handles overflow errors.
        ⋮
        ' Continue to fill the DataSet.
        args.Continue = True
    End If
End Sub
```

Notice that the FillError event fires only for errors that occur when filling the DataSet. No event fires if the error occurs at the database level.

Mapping DataBase Tables

By default, the DataAdapter's Fill method creates a DataTable whose columns have the same name and type as the columns in the source database table. However, there are occasions when you need more control over how columns are imported—for example, when you want to change the names of the source columns to make them more readable or when you need to assign a name to calculated expressions that don't have an AS clause in the original SQL SELECT statement (as in SELECT @@IDENTITY FROM MyTable).

You can perform all of these tasks, and a few others, by means of the DataAdapter's TableMappings collection. This collection contains zero or more DataTableMapping objects, each one defining the name of the source database table (the SourceTable property) and the name of the corresponding DataTable (the DataSetTable property).

Each DataTableMapping object also exposes a collection of DataColumnMapping objects, which store the mapping between columns in the database table (the Source-Column property) and columns in the DataTable (the DataSetColumn property). Figure 22-5 illustrates the relationships among these objects and their properties. All these objects are in the System.Data.Common namespace.

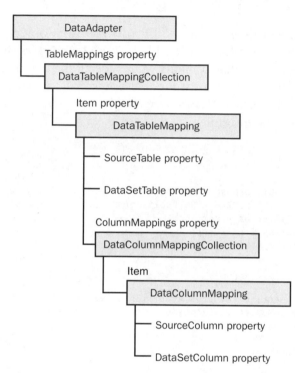

Figure 22-5 The TableMappings collection and its dependent classes

If the meaning of these objects is clear, creating a mapping between a database and a DataSet is simple and ultimately resolves to calling the Add method of the right collection. For example, let's see how you can map the Publishers table in SQL Server's Pubs database to a client-side DataTable named PublishersData and change the names of a few columns in the process:

```
Dim ds As New DataSet
Dim cn As New SqlConnection(SqlPubsConnString)
Dim da As New SqlDataAdapter("SELECT * FROM Publishers", cn)

' Adds an element to the TableMappings collection.
' (Returns a DataTableMapping object.)
With da.TableMappings.Add("Publishers", "DataPublishers")
    ' Add two elements to the ColumnMappings collection.
    .ColumnMappings.Add("pub_id", "ID")
    .ColumnMappings.Add("pub_name", "Name")
End With
```

```
' Fill the DataSet, using the prepared mappings.
' (Note that the second argument is the source database table's name.)
da.Fill(ds, "Publishers")
```

(By default, any column that isn't explicitly mapped is imported with its original name.) Two more properties of the DataAdapter object define what happens if the mapping isn't complete or correct:

- The MissingMappingAction property determines what happens if a table or a column defined in the mapping is missing from the database. It can take three values: Passthrough (the behavior depends on the MissingSchemaAction property); Ignore (missing columns are ignored); and Error (an exception is thrown).

- The MissingSchemaAction property determines what happens if the DataSet doesn't match incoming data. The valid values are Add (adds the necessary columns to complete the schema); AddWithKey (adds the necessary columns and primary key to complete the schema); Ignore (ignores extra columns); and Error (throws an exception).

The default values are Passthrough for MissingMappingAction and Add for Missing-SchemaAction, which means that the DataAdapter extends the DataSet with all the necessary columns. Another common combination of values is Ignore for both properties, which means that a column is imported only if it already exists in the DataSet. For example, consider the following code:

```
Dim cn As New SqlConnection(SqlPubsConnString)
Dim da As New SqlDataAdapter("SELECT * FROM Publishers", cn)

' Adds an element to the TableMappings collection.
With da.TableMappings.Add("Publishers", "DataPublishers")
    .ColumnMappings.Add("pub_id", "ID")
    .ColumnMappings.Add("pub_name", "Name")
End With

' Define the structure of the DataPublishers table in advance.
' (Note that column names must match target names defined by the mapping.)
With ds.Tables.Add("DataPublishers")
    .Columns.Add("ID", GetType(String))
    .Columns.Add("Name", GetType(String))
End With
' Ignore any other column.
da.MissingSchemaAction = MissingSchemaAction.Ignore

' Fill the DataSet, using the prepared mappings.
da.Fill(ds, "Publishers")
```

The effect of the preceding routine is to fill only the ID and Name columns of the Data-Publishers table, ignoring all other columns implied by the SELECT command. Remember that you need to include the key column in the list of fields being retrieved only if you plan to update the data source later or to issue another Fill method to refresh the contents of the DataTable object. (If key columns aren't included in the DataTable, any subsequent Fill method *adds* the rows being read instead of using them to replace the rows already in the DataTable.)

Preloading the Database Structure

You might often want to fill the DataSet with the structure of the database without getting any data—for example,when the end user wants to enter new records but isn't interested in the records already in the database. The ADO.NET DataAdapter object exposes the FillSchema method for handling this case. This method takes the target DataSet; an argument that specifies whether the original table names are used (SchemaType.Source, the default value) or the current table mappings are honored (SchemaType.Mapped); and the name of the DataTable that must be created. Here are two examples:

```
' Fill the Publishers DataTable with the schema of the Publishers
' database table, using original column names.
da.FillSchema(ds, SchemaType.Mapped, "Publishers")

' Fill the DataPublishers DataTable with the schema of the Publishers
' database table, using mapped column names.
With da.TableMappings.Add("Publishers", "DataPublishers")
    ' Add two elements to the ColumnMappings collection.
    .ColumnMappings.Add("pub_id", "ID")
    .ColumnMappings.Add("pub_name", "Name")
End With
da.FillSchema(ds, SchemaType.Mapped, "Publishers")
```

The FillSchema method correctly sets the name, type, MaxLength, AllowDBNull, Read-Only, Unique, and AutoIncrement properties of each column. (You must set the Auto-IncrementSeed and AutoIncrementStep properties manually, however.) The method also retrieves existing table constraints and sets the PrimaryKey and Constraints properties accordingly, but you have to manually set up relations between tables.

Preloading the database schema is important because it ensures that primary key fields are always retrieved and stored in the DataSet. When subsequent Fill methods are issued, new rows are matched with existing rows on their primary key and new rows replace old rows accordingly. If the DataSet holds no primary key information, new rows are appended to existing ones and duplicate rows result. If you don't preload a DataSet with the database structure, you should ensure that all your SELECT commands include the primary key column or a column whose Unique property is True. If in doubt, you should set the MissingSchemaAction property to AddWithKey to ensure that primary key information is automatically retrieved if necessary.

Updating the Database

Most applications that work with databases need to update data in the original tables sooner or later. With ADO.NET, you have two choices when it's time to update a database:

- You can use ADO.NET Command objects with appropriate INSERT, DELETE, and UPDATE SQL statements. This is what you usually do when you work in connected mode and read data by means of a DataReader object.

- You can use the Update method of the DataAdapter object to send changed rows in a DataSet to a database. In this case, you usually use the same DataAdapter object that you created to read data into the DataSet, even though this isn't a requirement. (For example, you might have filled the DataSet manually via code without using a DataAdapter object.)

The real issue when working in disconnected mode is that you have to detect and resolve update conflicts. You have a conflict when another user has modified or deleted the same record that you want to update or delete, or has inserted a new record that has the same primary key as a record that you have inserted. How your application reacts to a conflict depends on the application's own logic—for example, you might follow the simple strategy by which the first update wins and subsequent updates are ignored; or you might decide that the last update wins. I'll explain these conflict-resolution strategies later in this chapter; for now, let's focus on the basics of update operations under the simplistic assumption that there are no update conflicts, an assumption that's realistic only when you're working with single-user applications.

> **Warning**   The code in the following sections modifies the Biblio.mdb demo database or the Pubs database. Before running this code, you might want to make a copy of the database so that you can restore it later. Also notice that you might need to restore the database before running the same sample again—for example, if you want to compare the outcomes of different update strategies.

Getting Familiar with Update Concepts

You can update data in a DataSet by means of the DataAdapter's Update method, which takes one of the following sets of arguments: a reference to a DataTable object; a DataSet and the name of a DataTable it contains; an array of DataRow objects. You usually use one of the first two syntax forms, and pass a DataRow array only when you want more control on the order in which changed rows are submitted to the database.

In all cases, the Update method returns the number of rows that have been successfully updated. The key to performing batch updates with ADO.NET is a group of three properties of the DataAdapter object: InsertCommand, UpdateCommand, and Delete-Command. Here's how the update mechanism works.

When an Update command is issued, the DataAdapter checks the RowState property of each row specified as a source for the update operation. If the state is Added, the Data-Adapter issues the SQL command specified in the InsertCommand property. If the state is Modified, the DataAdapter uses the SQL command in the UpdateCommand property. If the state is Deleted, the command in the DeleteCommand property is used instead. (See Figure 22-6.)

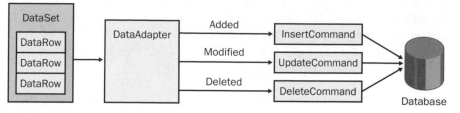

Figure 22-6   How the DataAdapter's Update method works

The InsertCommand, UpdateCommand, and DeleteCommand properties must be assigned actual ADO.NET Command objects with parameters. You can create these commands yourself or generate them more easily by using an auxiliary Command-Builder object. The main drawbacks of the latter technique are that the auxiliary CommandBuilder object must execute the SELECT command to retrieve the metadata, so it requires an additional round trip to the server and adds overhead to your application. Because of its simplicity, however, I'll explain the technique based on the CommandBuilder object first. (There is also a third technique based on Visual Studio .NET code generation features, as you'll see in Chapter 23.)

Each .NET data provider comes with its own CommandBuilder class, so you'll work with either the OleDbCommandBuilder, the SqlCommandBuilder, the OdbcCommand-Builder, or the OracleCommandBuilder object. The following code snippet creates a DataAdapter from a simple SELECT statement and then uses the CommandBuilder object to generate the three *xxx*Command properties:

```
' Connect to Pubs using the OLE DB .NET Data Provider.
Dim cn As New OleDbConnection(OledbPubsConnString)
cn.Open()
Dim da As New OleDbDataAdapter("SELECT * FROM Publishers", cn)
' Ensure that the primary key is set correctly, then fill the DataTable.
Dim ds As New DataSet()
da.FillSchema(ds, SchemaType.Source, "Publishers")
da.Fill(ds, "Publishers")

' Create an auxiliary CommandBuilder object for this DataAdapter.
Dim cmdBuilder As New OleDbCommandBuilder(da)
```

Now you can modify the local DataSet and send the updated rows to the database:

```
With ds.Tables("Publishers")
    ' Modify the first record (just append 3 asterisks to the pub_name field).
    .Rows(0)("pub_name") = .Rows(0)("pub_name").ToString & " ***"
    ' Add a new record.
    Dim dr As DataRow = .NewRow
    dr("pub_id") = "9988"
    dr("pub_name") = "VB2TheMax"
    dr("city") = "Bari"
```

```
    dr("country") = "Italy"
    .Rows.Add(dr)
End With

' Send changes to the database, and disconnect.
da.Update(ds, "Publishers")
cn.Close()
```

If you now browse the Publishers table in Pubs, you'll see that the first record has been changed and a new record has been added near the end.

> **Warning** The code should *not* invoke the AcceptChanges method on the DataSet. This is a very important detail: this method resets the RowState property of all rows to Unchanged, thus making the rows appear as if they have never been modified by the application.

The preceding code snippet keeps the connection open while the application adds, modifies, and deletes rows. This approach makes sense when the editing operations are performed through code, but it works against the overall scalability if editing operations are performed by end users (who seem to have a habit of taking a coffee break in the middle of an editing session). Most of the time, it makes sense to close the connection immediately after the Fill method and reopen it immediately before the Update method. You don't even need to explicitly open and close the connection if you're reading and updating a single table because these two methods can do it for you. In the end, your typical code in a disconnected environment becomes:

```
Dim cn As New OleDbConnection(OledbPubsConnString)
Dim da As New OleDbDataAdapter("SELECT * FROM Publishers", cn)
' Fill the DataSet table.
' (No need to explicitly open and close the connection.)
da.Fill(ds, "Publishers")

' Add, modify, or remove rows here, or let the user do it.
   ⋮
' Send changes to the database.
' (Again, no need to explicitly open and close the connection.)
da.Update(ds, "Publishers")
```

Remember, however, that this code works well only if you're reading and updating a single table. When multiple tables are used, you should open the connection before the read operation and close it immediately afterward to avoid an unnecessary close and reopen operation:

```
Dim cn As New OleDbConnection(OledbPubsConnString)
Dim da As New OleDbDataAdapter("SELECT * FROM Publishers", cn)
Dim da2 As New OleDbDataAdapter("SELECT * FROM Authors", cn)
' Fill the DataSet table.
cn.Open()                          ' Open the connection explicitly.
da.Fill(ds, "Publishers")
da2.Fill(ds, "Authors")
cn.Close()                         ' Close the connection explicitly.
```

```
' Add, modify, or remove rows here, or let the user do it.
   ⋮
' Send changes to the database.
cn.Open()                       ' Open the connection explicitly.
da.Update(ds, "Publishers")
da2.Update(ds, "Authors")
cn.Close()                      ' Close the connection explicitly.
```

A last tip: you can query the DataSet's HasChanges property to detect whether it contains one or more DataTable objects with modified rows. If this property returns True, you can use the GetChanges method to build a second DataSet that contains only the rows that are actually modified and then update only those tables whose Rows collection contains elements:

```
If ds.HasChanges Then
    ' Build another DataSet that contains only modified rows.
    Dim ds2 As DataSet = ds.GetChanges()
    ' Update each data table individually.
    For Each dt As DataTable In ds2.Tables
        If dt.Rows.Count > 0 Then
            ' This table contains modified rows.
            Debug.WriteLine("Updating table " & dt.TableName)
            ' Proceed with the update operation.
               ⋮
        End If
    Next
End If
```

You can achieve the same result in other ways as well. For example, you can use the DataTable's GetChanges method to retrieve the modified rows in a table. You can also pass an argument to both the DataSet's GetChanges method and the DataTable's GetChanges method to retrieve only the rows that have been added, deleted, or modified:

```
' Check whether there are deleted rows in the Publishers table.
Dim dt2 As DataTable = _
    ds.Tables("Publishers").GetChanges(DataRowState.Deleted)
' GetChanges returns Nothing if no row is modified.
If Not (dt2 Is Nothing) AndAlso dt2.Rows.Count > 0 Then
    ' Process deleted rows in the Publishers table.
       ⋮
End If
```

Understanding the CommandBuilder Object

The CommandBuilder object works in a rather odd way. It doesn't modify the DataAdapter object, but it registers itself as a listener for the DataAdapter's RowUpdating event (which I'll discuss later in this chapter), so that it can build the proper command to be sent to the database for each row in the DataTable. You can use the CommandBuilder's Get*xxxx*Command methods to explicitly assign the InsertCommand, DeleteCommand, and UpdateCommand properties of the DataAdapter object:

```
Dim cmdBuilder As New OleDbCommandBuilder(da)
da.InsertCommand = cmdBuilder.GetInsertCommand()
da.DeleteCommand = cmdBuilder.GetDeleteCommand()
da.UpdateCommand = cmdBuilder.GetUpdateCommand()
```

To understand the benefits and disadvantages of using the CommandBuilder object, you need to take a closer look at these SQL commands. Let's start with the INSERT command that the OleDbCommandBuilder object created to manage insertions in the Publishers table:

```
INSERT INTO [Publishers]( [pub_id] , [pub_name] , [city] , [state] , [country] )
  VALUES ( ? , ? , ? , ? , ? )
```

As you see, this command is straightforward. It just inserts a new record and fills its fields with the arguments that will be passed to the InsertCommand object. The CommandBuilder object has conveniently created and initialized the Parameters collection, with each parameter pointing to the current value that the corresponding column has in the DataTable.

The DELETE command is also relatively simple, but its WHERE clause has to account for the fact that some fields (other than the primary key pub_id) might be null when the record is read from the database. So you can't simply use the equality operator, which by default the T-SQL language evaluates to Null instead of True when both operands are Null:

```
DELETE FROM [Publishers] WHERE ( ([pub_id] = ?)
    AND ((? = 1 AND [pub_name] IS NULL) OR ([pub_name] = ?))
    AND ((? = 1 AND [city] IS NULL) OR ([city] = ?))
    AND ((? = 1 AND [state] IS NULL) OR ([state] = ?))
    AND ((? = 1 AND [country] IS NULL) OR ([country] = ?)) )
```

The need to account for null values makes the syntax of the SQL command overly complex.

The meaning of the WHERE clause can be summarized as follows: Delete the row whose pub_id field (the primary key) is equal to the value provided by the first parameter, provided that the current value in the database for all other columns is the same as it was when the DataTable was filled with data from the database. Oddly, the CommandBuilder generates this sort of code for all database fields, including those that aren't nullable. When a field isn't nullable, this precaution is unnecessary, but it doesn't have a noticeable impact on performance either.

The UPDATE command is the most complicated of the lot because its WHERE clause uses the current values for all fields in the SET clause and the original values in the WHERE clause to locate the record that must be updated:

```
UPDATE [Publishers] SET [pub_id] = ? , [pub_name] = ? ,
    [city] = ? , [state] = ? , [country] = ?
```

```
WHERE ( ([pub_id] = ?)
   AND ((? = 1 AND [pub_name] IS NULL) OR ([pub_name] = ?))
   AND ((? = 1 AND [city] IS NULL) OR ([city] = ?))
   AND ((? = 1 AND [state] IS NULL) OR ([state] = ?))
   AND ((? = 1 AND [country] IS NULL) OR ([country] = ?)) )
```

The SQL commands that the CommandBuilder object produces depend on the .NET data provider that you're using. You see the difference when you access the same database table using the native SQL Server .NET Data Provider, which must use parameter names prefixed with @, for example:

```
INSERT INTO Publishers ( pub_id, pub_name, city, state, country )
   VALUES ( @p1 , @p2, @p3, @p4, @p5 )
```

You need to understand the difference between using original column values and current column values. You can determine which version of the column value is used by browsing the Parameters collection and checking the SourceColumn and SourceVersion properties of each parameter. This is the generic routine that I use for my explorations and that works with any .NET Data Provider:

```
Sub DumpCommand(ByVal cmd As IDbCommand)
    Debug.WriteLine(cmd.CommandText)
    For Each p As IDbDataParameter In cmd.Parameters
        Debug.WriteLine(String.Format("   {0} {1} ({2} {3})", _
            p.ParameterName, p.DbType, p.SourceVersion, p.SourceColumn))
    Next
End Sub
```

This is the output in the Debug window that the DumpCommand routine produces when applied to the UPDATE command produced by the SqlCommandBuilder object:

```
UPDATE Publishers SET pub_id = @p1 , pub_name = @p2 , city = @p3 ,
state = @p4 , country = @p5 WHERE ( (pub_id = @p6)
AND ((@p7 = 1 AND pub_name IS NULL) OR (pub_name = @p8))
AND ((@p9 = 1 AND city IS NULL) OR (city = @p10))
AND ((@p11 = 1 AND state IS NULL) OR (state = @p12))
AND ((@p13 = 1 AND country IS NULL) OR (country = @p14)) )
    @p1 AnsiStringFixedLength (Current pub_id)
    @p2 AnsiString (Current pub_name)
    @p3 AnsiString (Current city)
    @p4 AnsiStringFixedLength (Current state)
    @p5 AnsiString (Current country)
    @p6 AnsiStringFixedLength (Original pub_id)
    @p7 Int32 (Current )
    @p8 AnsiString (Original pub_name)
    @p9 Int32 (Current )
    @p10 AnsiString (Original city)
    @p11 Int32 (Current )
    @p12 AnsiStringFixedLength (Original state)
    @p13 Int32 (Current )
    @p14 AnsiString (Original country)
```

Here are a few more details about the CommandBuilder object and some of its limitations:

- The original SELECT command assigned to the DataAdapter (which is also exposed by the SelectCommand property) can reference only one table.

- The source table must include a primary key or at least a column with a unique constraint, and the result returned by the SELECT statement must include that column. Primary keys consisting of multiple columns are supported.

- The InsertCommand object inserts only the columns that are updatable and correctly omits identity, timestamp, and calculated columns and in general all columns that are generated by the database engine.

- The UpdateCommand object uses the values of all the original columns in the WHERE clauses, including the primary key, but correctly omits timestamp and calculated columns from the SET clause.

- The DeleteCommand object uses the values of all the original columns in the WHERE clause to locate the row that has to be deleted.

- The SqlCommandBuilder and OdbcCommandBuilder generate invalid commands when the name of a table or a column contains a space or a special character. (This isn't a problem with the OleDbCommandBuilder object.)

You can easily solve the last problem by forcing the SqlCommandBuilder or OdbcCommandBuilder to use a prefix and a suffix for all the table and column names used in the generated command. You can do this by assigning a string to the QuotePrefix and QuoteSuffix properties so that the resulting SQL text conforms to the syntax expected by the target database:

```
cmdBuilder.QuotePrefix = "["
cmdBuilder.QuoteSuffix = "]"
```

Keep in mind that the CommandBuilder executes the SQL command assigned to the SelectCommand's CommandText property to generate the other three commands, so if you later change the SELECT command, the read and update commands will be out of sync. For this reason, you should always invoke the CommandBuilder's RefreshSchema method anytime you modify the SelectCommand property.

Customizing Insert, Update, and Delete Commands

After you understand how the InsertCommand, UpdateCommand, and DeleteCommand properties work, it's relatively easy to create your custom commands. This technique requires that you write more code than you have to when using the CommandBuilder object, but it lets you generate faster and more scalable code, both because you avoid one round trip to the server and because a well-written command can reduce the number of update conflicts. In general, the InsertCommand object produced by the CommandBuilder is OK for most purposes. So in the following discussion, I'll focus only on the UpdateCommand and DeleteCommand objects.

The DELETE command generated by the CommandBuilder uses the original values of all the columns in its WHERE clause to locate the record that has to be deleted. This approach implements the so-called optimistic lock strategy, which is the safest one because it ensures that no record is deleted if another user has changed one or more columns in the meantime.

In some applications, however, it might make sense to adopt a different strategy for deletions and decide to delete the record even if another user has modified any of its fields (other than the primary key). According to this strategy, sometimes dubbed as the-last-one-wins strategy, the most recent edit operation always wins and successfully updates the record (unless another user has deleted the record or changed its primary key field). You can enforce this strategy simply by using only the primary key field in the WHERE clause. This technique is faster and more scalable, but you should ensure that it doesn't invalidate the business logic of your application.

For example, you might decide that it's legal for a user to delete the record of an author in the Biblio database even though another user has modified the same author's data in the meantime. You can enforce this strategy by manufacturing the DeleteCommand yourself:

```
' Create a delete command that filters records by their Au_ID field only.
Dim cmdDelete As New OleDbCommand("DELETE FROM Authors WHERE Au_ID = ?", cn)
' Create a parameter, and set its properties.
With cmdDelete.Parameters.Add("@p1", OleDbType.Integer)
    ' This is the name of the column in the DataTable.
    .SourceColumn = "Au_ID"
    ' We want to use the original value in each DataRow.
    .SourceVersion = DataRowVersion.Original
End With
' Assign command to the DeleteCommand property of the DataAdapter.
da.DeleteCommand = cmdDelete
```

You can enforce a similar strategy for the UpdateCommand object as well by deciding that changes by the current user always overwrite changes by other users who have modified the same record after the current user imported the record into the DataSet. The following code uses a more compact syntax for the Parameters.Add method and relies on the fact that the default value for the SourceVersion property is DataRow-Version.Current:

```
' Create a custom update command.
Dim cmdUpdate As New OleDbCommand( _
    "UPDATE Authors SET Author = ?, [Year Born] = ? WHERE Au_ID = ?", cn)
' Add arguments for the SET clause. (They use current field values)
cmdUpdate.Parameters.Add("@p1", OleDbType.VarChar, 50, "Author")
cmdUpdate.Parameters.Add("@p2", OleDbType.Integer, 4, "Year Born")
 ' Add the argument in the WHERE clause. (It uses the original field value.)
cmdUpdate.Parameters.Add("@p3", OleDbType.Integer, 4, "Au_ID").SourceVersion _
    = DataRowVersion.Original
 ' Assign the command to the DataAdapter's UpdateCommand property.
da.UpdateCommand = cmdUpdate
```

The knowledge of how your application works often lets you simplify the structure of the UPDATE command. For example, you might have an application that displays all the columns in the records but prevents users from modifying a few columns (typically, the primary key or other keys that might work as foreign keys in other tables). As a result, you can omit such fields in the SET clause of the UPDATE command.

If the database table contains a timestamp field, you have an opportunity to improve the performance of both delete and update operations in a safe way because in this case you can detect whether another user has modified the record in question without verifying that all columns still contain their original values. In fact, a timestamp field is guaranteed to change whenever a database record is changed, so you can shrink the WHERE clause to include only the primary key (which serves to locate the record) and the timestamp field (which serves to ensure that no user has modified the record after it was imported into the DataSet). To see how this technique works in practice, extend the Authors table in the Pubs database with a timestamp field named LastUpdate, and then run this code:

```
Dim cmdDelete As New OleDbCommand("DELETE FROM Authors WHERE au_id = ? And LastUpdate=
?", cn)
cmdDelete.Parameters.Add("@p1", OleDbType.VarWChar, 11, "au_id")
' Timestamp are of VarBinary type (they map to a Byte array).
cmdDelete.Parameters.Add("@p2", OleDbType.VarBinary, 8, "LastUpdate")
da.DeleteCommand = cmdDelete

Dim cmdUpdate As New OleDbCommand("UPDATE Authors " _
    & " SET au_fname = ? , au_lname = ? WHERE au_id = ? AND LastUpdate = ?", cn)
' Add arguments for the SET clause, that use the current field value.
cmdUpdate.Parameters.Add("@p1", OleDbType.VarChar, 20, "au_fname")
cmdUpdate.Parameters.Add("@p2", OleDbType.VarChar, 40, "au_lname")
' Add the arguments in the WHERE clause that use the original field value.
cmdUpdate.Parameters.Add("@p3", OleDbType.VarChar, 11, "au_id").SourceVersion _
    = DataRowVersion.Original
cmdUpdate.Parameters.Add("@p4", OleDbType.VarBinary, 8, "LastUpdate").SourceVersion _
    = DataRowVersion.Original
da.UpdateCommand = cmdUpdate
```

Yet another reason for customizing the InsertCommand, UpdateCommand, and Delete-Command properties is to take advantage of any stored procedure in the database specifically designed to insert, modify, and delete records. By delegating these editing operations to a stored procedure and preventing users and applications from directly accessing the database tables, you can enforce greater control over data consistency. Inserting, updating, and deleting records through a stored procedure isn't conceptually different from what I have described so far. Please refer to the "Stored Procedures" section in Chapter 21 to review how to create parameters for Command objects that call stored procedures.

Changing the Order of Insert, Update, and Delete Operations

By default, all the rows in each table are processed according to their primary key order. Most of the time, the order in which commands are sent to the database doesn't affect the outcome of the operation, but this isn't always the case. For example, suppose you change the primary key of a row from 10 to 20 and then add a new row whose primary key is 10. Because this new row is processed before the old one, the Update method will attempt to insert a record with a primary key of 10 before the key of the existing database record is changed. This attempt raises an error.

You can avoid this problem by sending all the delete operations first, then all the update operations, and finally all the insert operations. This strategy is possible because the Update method takes an array of DataRow objects as an argument, so you can pass the result of a Select method whose third argument is an appropriate Data-ViewRowState value:

```
Dim dt As DataTable = ds.Tables("Authors")
' First process deletes.
da.Update(dt.Select(Nothing, Nothing, DataViewRowState.Deleted))
' Next process updates.
da.Update(dt.Select(Nothing, Nothing, DataViewRowState.ModifiedCurrent))
' Finally process inserts.
da.Update(dt.Select(Nothing, Nothing, DataViewRowState.Added))
```

Another good time to send delete, update, and insert operations separately is when you're updating tables in a parent-child relationship. You must insert a record in the parent table *before* adding the corresponding records in the child table; however, you must delete a record in the parent table *after* deleting the corresponding records in the child table. Here's a piece of code that takes these constraints into account and shows how you can update the Publishers (parent) and Titles (child) tables correctly:

```
' Fill both tables.
Dim daPub As New OleDbDataAdapter("SELECT * FROM Publishers", cn)
Dim daTit As New OleDbDataAdapter("SELECT * FROM Titles", cn)
daPub.Fill(ds, "Publishers")
daTit.Fill(ds, "Titles")

' Insert, update, and delete records in both tables.
  ⋮
' Send updates to both tables without any referential integrity error.
Dim dtPub As DataTable = ds.Tables("Publishers")
Dim dtTit As DataTable = ds.Tables("Titles")

' First process deleted rows in the child table.
daTit.Update(dtTit.Select(Nothing, Nothing, DataViewRowState.Deleted))
' Next process deleted rows in the parent table.
daPub.Update(dtPub.Select(Nothing, Nothing, DataViewRowState.Deleted))

' Next process inserted rows in the parent table and then in the child table.
daPub.Update(dtPub.Select(Nothing, Nothing, DataViewRowState.Added))
daTit.Update(dtTit.Select(Nothing, Nothing, DataViewRowState.Added))
```

```
' Finally process updates in the two tables.
daPub.Update(dtPub.Select(Nothing, Nothing, DataViewRowState.ModifiedCurrent))
daTit.Update(dtTit.Select(Nothing, Nothing, DataViewRowState.ModifiedCurrent))
```

Merging Changes in Another DataSet

The examples shown so far were based on the assumption that the code that modifies the DataSet is the same that updates the actual data source. This holds true in most traditional client/server applications, but multitier systems can adopt a different pattern. For example, consider an application consisting of a middle-tier component (for example, a Web service) that sits between the database and the user interface layer (a Windows Forms program):

In this arrangement, the Web service reads data from the database using a DataAdapter object, manufactures a DataSet object, and sends it as XML to the Windows Forms client, which therefore gets a perfect copy of the DataSet originally held in the Web service. The client code can now update, insert, and delete one or more rows and can send the modified DataSet back to the Web service, which can finally update the data source using the same DataAdapter that was used to read data into the DataSet.

Most of the time, however, the client application doesn't really need to send back the entire DataSet because the middle-tier component needs to know only which tables and which rows were changed after the DataSet was sent to the client user interface layer. You can reduce the amount of data sent over the wire by using the GetChanges method of the DataSet or the DataTable object. This method returns another DataSet or DataTable object that contains only the modified rows:

```
' Produce a DataSet with only the modified tables and rows.
Dim modDs As DataSet = ds.GetChanges()
```

When this new DataSet is sent to the Web service in the middle tier, two things can happen:

- The Web service rebuilds the DataAdapter object (or objects) that was created to extract data from the database, initializes its UpdateCommand, InsertCommand, and DeleteCommand properties, and applies the DataAdapter to the DataSet containing only the modified rows. This behavior is the most scalable one, but it can be adopted only when the changes coming from the client don't need any additional processing.

■ The Web service merges the modified DataSet just received with the original DataSet, processes the resulting DataSet as required, and then invokes the Data-Adapter's Update method to update the data source. This technique requires that the Web service save the original DataSet somewhere while the client is processing the data. Of course, you get the best performance if the original DataSet is kept in memory, but this arrangement reduces the fault tolerance of the entire system and raises affinity issues when you're working with a cluster of servers (because only one server can reply to a given client's request).

To merge the original DataSet with the modified DataSet received by the user-interface layer, the Web service can use the Merge method:

```
' ds is the original DataSet.
' modDs is the modified DataSet received by the Windows Forms client.
ds.Merge(modDs)
```

The Merge method can take two additional arguments: a Boolean that tells whether current changes in the original DataSet should be maintained and a MissingSchemaAction enumerated value that specifies what happens if the schema of the two DataSet objects aren't identical:

```
' Preserve changes in the original DataSet (ds), and
' add any new column found in the modified DataSet (modDs).
ds.Merge(modDs, True, MissingSchemaAction.Add)
```

Before merging data, the Merge method attempts to merge the schema of the two DataSet objects, and it modifies the schema of the original DataSet with any new column found in the DataSet being merged if the third argument is MissingSchemaAction.Add.

While data is being merged, all constraints are disabled. If a constraint can't be reinforced at the end of the merge operation, a ConstraintException object is thrown. In this case, the merged data is preserved, but the EnforceConstraints property is left as False. The middle-tier component should programmatically resolve all conflicts before setting EnforceConstraints back to True and performing the actual update on the data source.

Resolving Update Conflicts

All the update samples you've seen so far were based on the simplistic assumption that the current user was the only one updating the database and that no other user was allowed to modify the records in the database after the application had read data into the DataSet. At last, it's time to see how you can resolve the unavoidable conflicts that occur in all multiuser systems.

By default, if an Update command finds a conflict and can't process a row, it throws an exception, skipping all the remaining rows. This means that you should always protect an Update command with a Try...End Try block:

```
Try
    da.Update(ds, "Authors")
Catch ex As Exception
    MessageBox.Show(ex.Message)
End Try
```

This default behavior makes little sense because you might end up with some rows (all those preceding the conflicting one) sent to the database correctly and others (those that follow the conflicting one) that aren't sent, even if they wouldn't raise any conflict.

In most cases, you want to try the update operation on all the rows in the DataTable instead of stopping the operation at the first row that fails to update. You can do this by simply setting the DataAdapter's ContinueUpdateOnError property to True. In this case, you can test whether one or more rows failed to update by checking the DataSet's HasChanges property:

```
da.ContinueUpdateOnError = True
da.Update(ds, "Authors")
If ds.HasChanges() Then
    ' One or more rows failed to update.
End If
```

You can get more granular control over what happens when an update is attempted by trapping the RowUpdated event. This event lets you detect the conflict and decide to continue the update operation with the remaining rows if possible.

Handling the RowUpdated Event

When an Update command is issued, the DataAdapter object fires a pair of events for each inserted, modified, or deleted row in the table being updated. The RowUpdating event fires before sending the command to the database, whereas the RowUpdated event fires immediately after the database has processed the command. The object passed as the second argument to the RowUpdated event exposes the following properties: StatementType (an enumerated type that specifies the type of command: insert, delete, or update); Command (the ADO.NET Command object sent to the database); Row (the DataRow being updated); TableMapping (the DataTableMapping object used for the update operation); RecordsAffected (the number of records affected by the update operation); Errors (the collection of errors generated by the .NET Data Provider during the update operation); and Status (an enumerated value that specified how to handle the current row; can be Continue, ErrorsOccurred, SkipCurrentRow, or SkipAll-RemainingRows). The object passed as the second argument to the RowUpdating exposes the same properties, except RecordsAffected and Errors.

The key value to test from inside the handler of the RowUpdated event is the Records-Affected property. Any value less than 1 in this property means that the command failed and that there is an update conflict. This is the usual sequence of operations you perform inside a RowUpdated event handler:

1. If the Status property is equal to Continue and the value of the RecordsAffected property is 1, the update operation was successful. In most cases, you have little else to do, and you can exit the event handler.

2. If the Status property is equal to ErrorsOccurred, you can check the Errors property to understand what went wrong. Frequent causes of errors are violations of database constraints or referential integrity rules, such as a duplicated value in a primary key or a unique column or a foreign key that doesn't point to any row in the parent table.

3. If you get a System.Data.DBConcurrencyException exception, it means that the WHERE clause in the SQL command failed to locate the row in the data source. What you do next depends on your application's business logic. Typically, you test the StatementType property to determine whether it was an insert, delete, or update operation; in the last two cases, the conflict is likely caused by another user who deleted or modified the record you're trying to delete or update.

4. You can issue a SELECT query against the database to determine what columns caused the conflict, in an attempt to resynchronize the DataSet with the data source and reconcile the conflicting row. For example, if you have a conflict in an update operation (the most frequent case), you can issue a SELECT command to again read the values now in the database table. If you have a conflict in a delete operation, you can issue a SELECT command to check whether the DELETE command failed because the record was deleted or because another user changed one of the fields listed in your WHERE clause.

5. In all cases, you must decide whether the update operation should continue. You can set the Status property to Continue or SkipCurrentRow to ignore the conflict for now, or SkipAllRemainingRows to end the update operation without raising an error in the application. You can also leave the value set to ErrorsOccurred, in which case the Update method is terminated right away and an exception is thrown to the main application.

You don't have to perform all the preceding operations from inside a RowUpdate event handler, however, and you don't even need to write this event handler in some cases. For example, you can postpone the resychronization step until after the Update method has completed, and you might even decide not to resynchronize at all. The sections that follow illustrate three possible resynchronization strategies that you can adopt when dealing with update conflicts:

■ You don't reconcile at all and just display a warning to the user, mentioning which rows failed to be updated correctly. In this case, you just set the ContinueUpdate-OnError property to True and don't have to intercept the RowUpdated event.

■ You reconcile with the data source after the Update method, using a SELECT command that reads again all the rows that failed to update. In this case, you set the

ContinueUpdateOnError property to True to avoid an exception when a conflict-ing row is found and place the resync code in the main application after the Update method.

■ You reconcile with the data source on a row-by-row basis for each row that failed to update correctly. In this case, you place the resync code right inside the RowUpdated event handler and set the Status property of its argument to Con-tinue. (Otherwise, the Update method will fail when the first conflict is found.)

Displaying Conflicting Rows

In the first strategy for managing conflicts, you don't even try to reconcile them and limit your actions to just displaying the records that failed the update operation. This strategy can be implemented quite simply, as this code demonstrates:

```
' A class-level DataAdapter that has been correctly initialized
Dim da As OleDbDataAdapter

Sub UpdateRecords()
    ' Ensure that conflicting rows don't throw an exception.
    da.ContinueUpdateOnError = True
    ' Send changes to the database, exit if no update conflicts.
    da.Update(ds, "Publishers")
    If Not ds.HasChanges Then Exit Sub

    ' If we get here, there's at least one conflicting row.
    Dim dt As DataTable = ds.Tables("Publishers")
    ' Here's a simple way to evaluate the number of conflicting rows.
    Dim rowCount As Integer = dt.GetChanges().Rows.Count
    Debug.WriteLine(rowCount & " rows failed to update correctly")

    ' Mark all conflicting rows with the proper error message.
    For Each dr As DataRow In dt.Rows
        If dr.RowState = DataRowState.Added Then
            dr.RowError = "Failed INSERT operation"
        ElseIf dr.RowState = DataRowState.Modified Then
            dr.RowError = "Failed UPDATE operation"
        ElseIf dr.RowState = DataRowState.Deleted Then
            dr.RowError = "Failed DELETE operation"
            ' Undelete this record, else it wouldn't show in the table.
            dr.RejectChanges()
        End If
    Next
End Sub
```

This code works because the Update method automatically invokes AcceptChanges on all the rows that were updated correctly without any conflict but leaves the con-flicting rows in the state they were before the update. As a result, you can use the DataSet's HasChanges property to quickly determine whether at least one row is still marked as modified, and then you can iterate over all the rows in the DataTable to mark each row with a proper error message, which shows up in the DataGrid control. (See Figure 22-7.) The only precaution you have to take is to reject changes on deleted rows. Otherwise, these deleted rows won't be included in the DataTable object and won't be displayed in the DataGrid control. Alternatively, you can bind the DataGrid control to a DataView whose RowStateFilter property is set to DataViewRowState.Deleted.

By default, the DataAdapter's Fill method leaves all the inserted rows in the Unchanged state, therefore only the rows that the user has changed appear to be modified. This happens because the default value of the DataAdapter's AcceptChangesDuringFill property is True. If you set this property to False before invoking the Fill method, read rows appear to be added. This setting can be useful in a few cases—for example, when you fill a DataTable from one or more database tables and use it to update another table (possibly in a different database).

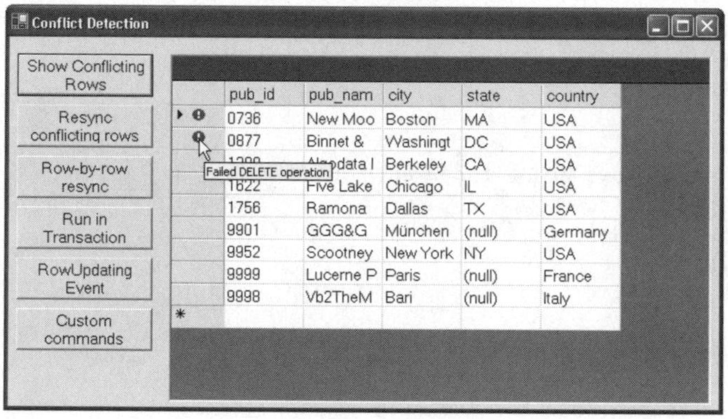

Figure 22-7 Marking conflicting rows with an error message

Resynchronizing After the Update Method

In most cases, you can (and should) try to understand why each update operation failed, instead of just showing the user the list of conflicting rows. You typically do this by rereading rows from the data source and comparing the values found in the database with those read when you filled the DataTable. If you find different values, you're likely to have found the cause of the conflict because the default WHERE clause in the DELETE and UPDATE commands searches for a record that contains the original column values, as I explained in "Understanding the CommandBuilder Object" earlier in this chapter. (If you used custom update commands, you have to retouch the code in this section.)

When synchronizing the DataTable with the data source, you might keep things simple by reapplying the same DataAdapter to fill another DataTable and then comparing this new DataTable with the original one. (Notice that you can't fill the same DataTable again because you would reset the status of all inserted and updated rows to Unchanged.) However, this simple technique requires the transfer of a lot of rows from the server, even though only a small fraction of such rows—that is, the conflicting ones—are actually needed for your purposes.

A much better approach is to read only those rows that caused an update conflict. You can do this by repeatedly calling a parameterized SELECT command or by manufacturing a single SELECT that returns all and only the rows in question. In most cases, you should adopt the latter approach because of its greater efficiency and scalability, even though it requires more code on your part. The code I'll show here isn't exactly trivial, but it's well commented and was designed with ease of reuse in mind:

```
Sub UpdateRecords()
    ' Ensure that conflicting rows don't throw an exception.
    da.ContinueUpdateOnError = True
    ' Send changes to the database, exit if no conflicts.
    da.Update(ds, "Publishers")
    If Not ds.HasChanges Then Exit Sub

    ' Not all rows were updated successfully.
    Dim dt As DataTable = ds.Tables("Publishers")
    ' Keeping key column name in a variable helps make this code reusable.
    Dim keyName As String = "pub_id"

    ' Build the list of the key values for all these rows.
    Dim values As New System.Text.StringBuilder(1000)
    Dim keyValue As String

    For Each dr As DataRow In dt.Rows
        ' Consider only modified rows.
        If dr.RowState <> DataRowState.Unchanged Then
            ' The key to be used depends on the row state.
            If dr.RowState = DataRowState.Added Then
                ' Use the current key value for inserted rows.
                keyValue = dr(keyName, DataRowVersion.Current).ToString
            Else
                ' Use the original key value for deleted and modified rows.
                keyValue = dr(keyName, DataRowVersion.Original).ToString
            End If
            ' Append to the list of key values. (Assume it's a string field.)
            If values.Length > 0 Then values.Append(",")
            values.Append("'")
            values.Append(keyValue)
            values.Append("'")
        End If
    Next

    ' Create a new SELECT that reads only these records,
    ' using the DataAdapter's SELECT command as a template.
    Dim sql2 As String = da.SelectCommand.CommandText
    ' Delete the WHERE clause if there is one.
    Dim k As Integer = sql2.ToUpper.IndexOf(" WHERE ")
    If k > 0 Then sql2 = sql2.Substring(0, k - 1)
    ' Add the WHERE clause that contains the list of all key values.
    sql2 &= " WHERE " & keyName & " IN (" & values.ToString & ")"

    ' Read only the conflicting rows.
    ' (Assume that cn holds a reference to a valid OleDbConnection object.)
```

```
Dim da2 As New OleDbDataAdapter(sql2, cn)
' Fill a new DataTable. (It doesn't have to belong to the DataSet.)
Dim dt2 As New DataTable()
da2.Fill(dt2)
```

The remainder of the UpdateRecords routine compares rows in the original DataTable with those that have just been read from the data source and marks both the conflicting rows and modified columns with a suitable error message:

```
' Loop on all the rows that failed to update.
For Each dr As DataRow In dt.Rows
    If dr.RowState <> DataRowState.Unchanged Then
        ' Mark the row with a proper error message,
        ' and retrieve the key value to be used for searching in DT2.
        If dr.RowState = DataRowState.Added Then
            dr.RowError = "Failed INSERT command"
            keyValue = dr(keyName, DataRowVersion.Current).ToString
        ElseIf dr.RowState = DataRowState.Deleted Then
            dr.RowError = "Failed DELETE command"
            keyValue = dr(keyName, DataRowVersion.Original).ToString
        ElseIf dr.RowState = DataRowState.Modified Then
            dr.RowError = "Failed UPDATE command"
            keyValue = dr(keyName, DataRowVersion.Original).ToString
        End If

        ' Find the matching row in the new table.
        Dim rows() As DataRow
        rows = dt2.Select(keyName & "='" & keyValue & "'")

        If (rows Is Nothing) OrElse rows.Length = 0 Then
            ' We can't find the conflicting row in the database.
            dr.RowError &= " - Unable to resync with data source"
            ' Check whether the user changed the primary key.
            If dr.RowState <> DataRowState.Added AndAlso _
                dr(keyName, DataRowVersion.Current).ToString <> _
                dr(keyName, DataRowVersion.Original).ToString Then
                ' This is a probable source of the conflict.
                dr.SetColumnError(keyName, "Modified primary key")
            End If

        Else
            ' We have found the conflicting row in the database, so
            ' we can compare current values in each column.
            Dim dr2 As DataRow = rows(0)
            For i As Integer = 0 To dr.Table.Columns.Count - 1
                ' The type of comparison we do depends on the row state.
                If dr.RowState = DataRowState.Added Then
                    ' For inserted rows, we compare the current value
                    ' with the database value.
                    If dr(i).ToString <> dr2(i).ToString Then
                        ' Show the value now in the database.
                        dr.SetColumnError(i, "Value in database = " _
                            & dr2(i).ToString)
                    End If
```

```
                Else
                    ' For deleted and modified rows, we compare the
                    ' original value with the database value.
                    If dr(i, DataRowVersion.Original).ToString <> _
                        dr2(i).ToString Then
                        Dim msg As String = ""
                        If dr(i, DataRowVersion.Original).ToString <> _
                            dr(i).ToString Then
                            msg = "Original value = " & dr(i).ToString
                            msg &= ", "
                        End If
                        msg &= "Value in database = " & dr2(i).ToString
                        dr.SetColumnError(i, msg)
                    End If
                End If
            Next
        End If
    End If

    ' If a deleted row, reject changes to make it visible in the table.
    If dr.RowState = DataRowState.Deleted Then
        dr.RejectChanges()
    End If
    Next
End Sub
```

Figure 22-8 shows how row and column error messages are displayed in a DataGrid control.

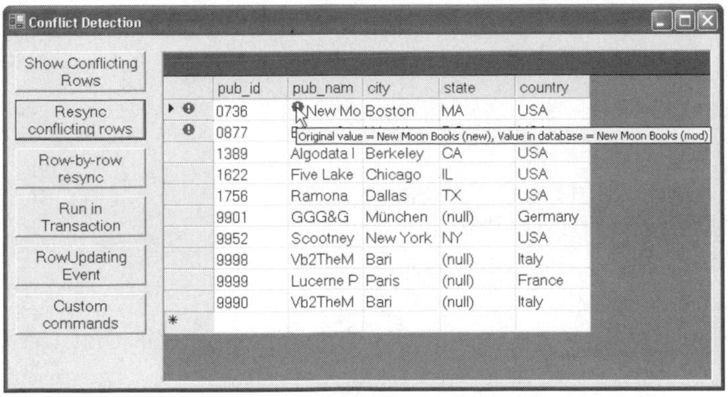

Figure 22-8   Resynchronization with the data source lets you display which columns caused the conflict.

Rolling Back Multiple Updates

As you know, the Update method sends an individual INSERT, DELETE, or UPDATE command to the data source for each modified row in the DataTable. However, an exception is thrown and no more commands are sent if there is an update conflict and you neither set the ContinueUpdateOnError property to True nor set the Status property to Continue inside the RowUpdated event. If an exception is thrown, you must be prepared to catch it in a Try…End Try block.

When the exception is thrown and the Update method returns the execution flow to the main code, some rows might have been already updated in the database. In the majority of cases, this effect is undesirable because usually you want to update either all the rows (at least those that don't cause any conflict) or no row at all. For example, if you get an exception after inserting an Order record but before adding the first OrderDetail row, you'll end up with a database in an inconsistent state, in that it includes an order without any detail.

In the preceding sections, I showed how you can continue to perform updates when a conflict arises, so what's left to learn is how to use transactions to completely roll back any update operation on the database to before the first conflict occurred. Protecting your application from partial updates is actually simple: you just have to open a transaction on the connection and commit it if the Update method completes successfully, or roll it back if an exception is thrown. To do so, you must explicitly assign the Transaction object to all the Command objects in the DataAdapter's UpdateCommand, InsertCommand, and DeleteCommand properties. Here's an example of this technique:

```
' Run the Update method inside a transaction. (Assumes connection is open.)
Dim tr As OleDbTransaction
' Comment next line to see how updates behave without a transaction.
tr = cn.BeginTransaction()

' Enroll all the DataAdapter's commands in the same transaction.
da.UpdateCommand.Transaction = tr
da.DeleteCommand.Transaction = tr
da.InsertCommand.Transaction = tr

' Send changes to the database.
Try
    da.Update(ds, "Publishers")
    tr.Commit()
Catch ex As Exception
    ' Roll back the transaction if there is one.
    If Not (tr Is Nothing) Then tr.Rollback()
    MessageBox.Show(ex.Message)
End Try
```

A subtle issue that the previous code snippet doesn't handle is that the Rollback method restores the database state as it was before you attempted the update operation, but it doesn't restore the DataTable state. All the rows that were successfully updated inside the transaction now appear to be unchanged, and they won't be resubmitted if you attempt another update operation. You can work around this problem by performing the Update method on a copy of the original DataTable:

```
Try
    Dim tmpTable As DataTable = ds.Tables("Publishers").Copy()
    da.Update(tmpTable)
    ' Commit the transaction and accept changes in the real table.
    tr.Commit()
    ds.Tables("Publishers").AcceptChanges()
Catch ex As Exception
```

```
' Don't change the state of rows in the real table.
  ⋮
```

Transactions can be useful even if you protect your code from exceptions by setting the ContinueUpdateOnError property to True or by setting the Status property to Continue from inside the RowUpdated event. For example, you might show the user all the conflicts that you have detected and possibly resolved via code and then ask for approval to commit all changes or roll them back as a whole.

Advanced Techniques

What I described so far covers the fundamentals of update operations in a disconnected fashion, but there's much more to know. In fact, I dare say that each application poses its special challenges, and it's up to you to find the best solution in each specific circumstance. Fortunately, the more I work with ADO.NET, the more I realize that it's far more flexible than I first suspected. In this section, I'll present a few sophisticated techniques that can improve your application's performance and scalability even further.

Working with Identity Columns

A common problem you must solve when you use ADO.NET in real applications is how you deal with identity columns, calculated fields, or, more generally, columns whose value is assigned by the database engine when you add a new row to a table (for example, by means of a trigger). If you are working with a single database table, you might not need to care about identity fields because the end user rarely needs to see them anyway. If you're working with multiple tables in a master-detail relationship, however, you must find a way to retrieve such values generated on the server when you add a new row to the master table because this value must be used in the foreign key in the child table.

The trick that solves this problem is simple: you append a SELECT command to the INSERT (or UPDATE) command that returns the value of all the fields that the database has assigned, and you execute the command with an ExecuteReader method instead of an ExecuteNonQuery method. If you need to read only one field, you can also use the ExecuteScalar method:

```
' An INSERT+SELECT statement
Dim sql As String =
"INSERT INTO jobs (job_desc,min_lvl,max_lvl) VALUES ('A new job', 25, 100);" _
    & "SELECT job_id FROM jobs WHERE job_id = @@IDENTITY"
Dim cmd As New SqlCommand(sql, cn)
' Insert the new row and read back the IDENTITY field.
Dim jobId As Integer = CInt(cmd.ExecuteScalar)
```

Things become more interesting if you're updating a database table from a DataTable object by means of a DataAdapter and its parameterized InsertCommand and Update-Command properties. In this case, you should manually read back the value of an identity field (in general, a database-generated value) and store it in the proper row and column of the DataTable, so that the new value can be displayed to the user (if the DataTable is bound to a control) or used in relations or calculated fields inside the DataSet.

Fortunately, you can have the DataAdapter take this step automatically, without any intervention on your part, thanks to a property of the Command object that I haven't covered yet: the UpdateRowSource property. This property is an enumerated value that can be one of the following: None, OutputParameters, FirstReturnedRecord, or Both. When you use the FirstReturnedRecord value the Command object updates the underlying DataTable with the values from the first row returned by the SELECT command. When you use the OutputParameters value the Command object updates the DataTable with the value of all output parameters from a stored procedure. When you use Both (the default value), the Command object updates the DataTable using both the values in the first row returned by the SELECT command and the output parameters. Let's see how we can use this feature:

```
' The "jobs" DataTable holds these fields: job_id, job_desc, min_lvl, max_lvl.
Dim jobsTable As DataTable = ds.Tables("jobs")
' Add a row in this demo. Don't assign job_id, as it's an identity field.
Dim drow As DataRow = jobsTable.NewRow()
drow("job_desc") = "A new job"
drow("min_lvl") = 25
drow("max_lvl") = 100
dt.Rows.Add(drow)

' Prepare the parameterized INSERT command.
Dim sql As String = _

"INSERT INTO jobs (job_desc,min_lvl,max_lvl) VALUES (@job_desc, @min_lvl, @max_lvl);" _

    & "SELECT job_id, job_desc, min_lvl, max_lvl FROM jobs WHERE job_id = @@IDENTITY"
Dim updCmd As New SqlCommand(sql, cn)
' Add parameters and set their SourceColumn in one statement.
updCmd.Parameters.Add("@job_desc", SqlDbType.VarChar, 50, "job_desc")
updCmd.Parameters.Add("@min_lvl", SqlDbType.TinyInt, 1, "min_lvl")
updCmd.Parameters.Add("@max_lvl", SqlDbType.TinyInt, 1, "max_lvl")
' Set the UpdateRowSource property (Not strictly necessary, as default is OK).
updCmd.UpdatedRowSource = UpdateRowSource.FirstReturnedRecord

' Do the update via a DataAdapter. (Only the InsertCommand is set.)
Dim da As New SqlDataAdapter
da.InsertCommand = updCmd
da.Update(jobsTable)
' Check that the job_id field has been assigned correctly.
Debug.WriteLine(drow("job_id"))
```

You can use a similar code if you insert and update rows by means of stored procedures. In that case, you must only ensure that you set the Direction property of the Command's parameters to ParameterDirection.Output and you assign the value UpdateRowSource.OutputParameters to the UpdateRowSource property. (The latter step is optional because the default value of UpdateRowSource.Both is also OK when working with stored procedures.)

The great thing of this technique is that the new value of the identity field is automatically propagated to any child table whose foreign key points to this identity field, provided that the UpdateRule property of the corresponding ForeignKeyConstraint object has been set to the Rule.Cascade value.

Another, radically different technique you might want to adopt in disconnected scenarios is using client-generated GUID fields (corresponding to uniqueidentifier fields in SQL Server jargon) rather than identity fields that are generated on the server. A client application can easily create GUID values with the Guid.NewGuid shared method and use them as the primary key for any row created in disconnected mode. GUID fields tend to slow database queries and JOINs slightly, but their guaranteed uniqueness has many advantages. For example, you can easily consolidate multiple databases in one, bigger database without worrying about duplicate fields.

Reducing Conflicts with Custom Update Commands

Depending on your application's requirements, you can often reduce update conflicts by means of custom commands assigned to the DataAdapter's UpdateCommand property. For example, consider two users who update a given record with the same values and the conflict that occurs when the second user attempts to send the same record to the database. On the companion CD, you can find a file, "Resolving Conflicts on a Row-by-Row Basis," in which I discuss how you can use the RowUpdated event to solve this unnecessary conflict, but you can achieve the same effect by modifying the UpdateCommand property:

```
UPDATE Publishers SET pub_id=@newPub_id, pub_name=@newPub_name,
    city=@newCity, state@=newState, country=@newCountry
WHERE pub_id=@pub_id
    AND ( (pub_name IS NULL AND (@pub_name IS NULL OR @newPub_name Is NULL))
        OR (pub_name=@pub_name OR pub_name=@newPub_name) )
    AND ( (city IS NULL AND (@city IS NULL OR @newCity Is NULL))
        OR (city=@city OR city=@newCity) )
    AND ( (state IS NULL AND (@state IS NULL OR @newState Is NULL))
        OR (state=@state OR state=@newState) )
    AND ( (country IS NULL AND (@country IS NULL OR @newCountry Is NULL))
        OR (country=@country OR country=@newCountry) )
```

The UPDATE statement must account for the fact that all fields except pub_id are nullable, which makes tests for equality more verbose. I'll omit here the source code that creates a parameterized command based on this SQL statement, but you can find it in the demo program that comes on the companion CD.

Custom Update comments can be useful if you have a data entry form that lets you modify a subset of the columns in a record. For example, let's say that a form in your application lets you modify only the price, advance, and royalty columns of the Titles table in the Pubs database. The custom command that you need must consider only the three fields in the SET clause and the primary key pub_id plus these three columns in the WHERE clause:

```
UPDATE Titles SET price=@newPrice, advance=@newAdvance,
    royalty=@newRoyalty
WHERE title_id=@title_id
    AND ( ((price IS NULL AND @price IS NULL) OR price=@price)
        OR ((@newPrice IS NULL AND @price IS NULL) OR @newPrice=@price) )
    AND ( ((advance IS NULL AND @advance IS NULL) OR advance=@advance)
        OR ((@newAdvance IS NULL AND @advance IS NULL) OR @newAdvance=@advance) )
    AND ( ((royalty IS NULL AND @royalty IS NULL) OR royalty=@royalty)
        OR ((@newRoyalty IS NULL AND @royalty IS NULL) OR @newRoyalty=@royalty) )
```

> **See Also**   "Reducing Conflicts with the RowUpdating Events.doc" on the companion CD describes a technique that allows you to use the RowUpdating event to build a custom command with which you can prevent conflicts whenever two users update two different groups of columns in the same application.

Improving Performance with JOIN Queries

All the examples shown so far are based on rather simple queries. Possibly they retrieved all the records in a database table or perhaps they attempted to reduce the network traffic and database activity by selecting a subset of rows with a WHERE clause or a subset of columns, as in these two examples:

```
-- Only the titles published on or after 10/1/1992.
SELECT title_id, title, pub_id, pubdate FROM Titles WHERE pubdate>'10/1/1992'
-- Only the publishers from the U.S.A.
SELECT pub_id, pub_name, city FROM Publishers WHERE country='USA'
```

Alas, in the real world few queries are that simple, as all database programmers know. For example, consider a query that must return all (and only) the titles published after October 1, 1991, from all (and only) the publishers based in the United States. No problem, you might say: just fill two DataTable objects using the preceding two SELECT queries, and then create a relationship between them. Well, this can work with tables with a few hundred rows, but you aren't going to use this naive technique with tables of 100,000 rows, are you? The point is, you would read a lot of records that you don't really want—such as titles published by publishers not in the United States and U.S. publishers who haven't published any books since October 1991.

Obviously, you must filter rows before the resultset leaves the server if you want to reduce both network traffic and the load on the database engine. The ideal solution would be to issue a JOIN command like this:

```
-- QUERY A: Retrieve data on titles and publishers satisfying
-- the query criteria in one resultset, sorted by Publishers.
SELECT pub_name, city, Publishers.pub_id, title_id, title, pubdate
    FROM Publishers INNER JOIN Titles ON Publishers.pub_id = Titles.pub_id
    WHERE country = 'USA' AND pubdate > '10/1/1991'
    ORDER BY Publishers.pub_id
```

In fact, this is the statement that you would have used in the good old ADO days. Unfortunately, the DataSet update model requires a one-to-one mapping between DataTable objects on the client and a database table on the server. For example, the CommandBuilder can work only if the DataAdapter's SELECT command references only one table.

Even if you can't use a single JOIN like the preceding one, certainly you can use *two* JOIN commands to fill the two DataTable objects without reading more rows than strictly necessary:

```
-- QUERY B: Only the titles published in or after Oct 1991 by a U.S. publisher
SELECT Titles.pub_id, title_id, title, pubdate FROM Titles
    INNER JOIN Publishers ON Publishers.pub_id = Titles.pub_id
    WHERE country = 'USA' AND pubdate > '10/1/1991'
-- QUERY C: Only the publishers from the USA that published a book since 1992
-- (The GROUP BY clause is necessary to drop duplicate rows.)
SELECT pub_name, city, Publishers.pub_id FROM Publishers
    INNER JOIN Titles ON Publishers.pub_id = Titles.pub_id
    WHERE country='USA' AND pubdate > '10/1/1991'
    GROUP BY Publishers.pub_id, pub_name, city
```

This solution is *much* better than the first one, but it still suffers from a couple of problems that negatively affect the resulting scalability. First, you're asking the database engine to perform basically the same filtering operation twice—in fact, the two WHERE clauses are identical—so you can expect that these two JOINs take longer than the single JOIN seen before (though not twice as long). The second problem is subtler: to be *absolutely* certain that the two returned resultsets are consistent with each other, you must run the two SELECT queries inside a transaction with the level set to Serializable, thus holding a lock on both tables until you complete the read operation and commit the transaction.

To see why you need to wrap these commands in a transaction, imagine what would happen if another user deletes a publisher (and its titles) immediately after your first SELECT query and before your second SELECT query. The deleted publisher wouldn't be returned by your second SELECT, and a row in the Titles DataTable would point to a parent row that doesn't exist in the Publishers DataTable. This condition would raise an error when you attempt to establish a relationship between these two DataTable objects, and you'd have a title in your DataSet for which you can't retrieve the corresponding publisher. Reversing the order of the two queries wouldn't help much because you'd get a similar error if a new U.S. publisher and its titles were added to the database after the SELECT on the Publishers table and before the query on the Titles table. Again, the only way to avoid this inconsistency is to run the two SELECT queries inside a serializable transaction, which degrades overall scalability.

Now that the problem is clear, let's see whether we can find a better solution. Have a look at Figure 22-9. At the top, it shows the result of the JOIN statement that returns fields from both tables (labeled as query A in previous code snippets); at the bottom, you see the results from the two JOINs that return fields from a single table (queries B and C). Now it's apparent that you can duplicate the effect of query C by dropping a few columns from the result of query A, which you can do simply by invoking the Remove or RemoveAt method of the Columns collection.

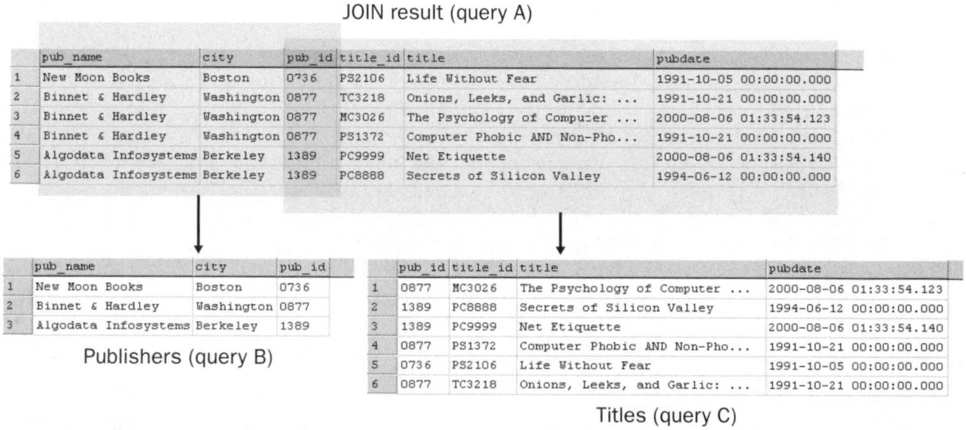

JOIN result (query A)

	pub_name	city	pub_id	title_id	title	pubdate
1	New Moon Books	Boston	0736	PS2106	Life Without Fear	1991-10-05 00:00:00.000
2	Binnet & Hardley	Washington	0877	TC3218	Onions, Leeks, and Garlic: ...	1991-10-21 00:00:00.000
3	Binnet & Hardley	Washington	0877	MC3026	The Psychology of Computer ...	2000-08-06 01:33:54.123
4	Binnet & Hardley	Washington	0877	PS1372	Computer Phobic AND Non-Pho...	1991-10-21 00:00:00.000
5	Algodata Infosystems	Berkeley	1389	PC9999	Net Etiquette	2000-08-06 01:33:54.140
6	Algodata Infosystems	Berkeley	1389	PC8888	Secrets of Silicon Valley	1994-06-12 00:00:00.000

	pub_name	city	pub_id
1	New Moon Books	Boston	0736
2	Binnet & Hardley	Washington	0877
3	Algodata Infosystems	Berkeley	1389

Publishers (query B)

	pub_id	title_id	title	pubdate
1	0877	MC3026	The Psychology of Computer ...	2000-08-06 01:33:54.123
2	1389	PC8888	Secrets of Silicon Valley	1994-06-12 00:00:00.000
3	1389	PC9999	Net Etiquette	2000-08-06 01:33:54.140
4	0877	PS1372	Computer Phobic AND Non-Pho...	1991-10-21 00:00:00.000
5	0736	PS2106	Life Without Fear	1991-10-05 00:00:00.000
6	0877	TC3218	Onions, Leeks, and Garlic: ...	1991-10-21 00:00:00.000

Titles (query C)

Figure 22-9   Splitting the result of a JOIN into two DataTable objects

Deriving the results of query B from query A is slightly more difficult because you must loop through all the rows in a large resultset to filter out duplicate values. However, the ORDER BY clause in query A ensures that the same values are consecutive, so it's easy to filter out all rows with duplicate values in the primary key column. The following code shows how to perform the splitting in an optimized way:

```
' Define all the involved SQL commands.
' NOTE: the code below assumes that the first column in the child
'       table is its foreign key.
Dim titSql As String = "SELECT pub_id, title_id, title, pubdate FROM Titles"
Dim pubSql As String = "SELECT pub_id, pub_name, city FROM Publishers"
Dim joinSql As String = "SELECT Publishers.pub_id, pub_name, city, " _
    & "title_id, title, pubdate FROM Publishers " _
    & "INNER JOIN Titles ON Publishers.pub_id=Titles.pub_id " _
    & "WHERE country = 'USA' AND pubdate > '10/1/1991'" _
    & "ORDER BY Publishers.pub_id"

' Create the connection and all the involved DataAdapter objects.
Dim cn As New SqlConnection(SqlPubsConnString)
Dim titDa As New SqlDataAdapter(titSql, cn)
Dim pubDa As New SqlDataAdapter(pubSql, cn)
Dim joinDa As New SqlDataAdapter(joinSql, cn)

' Open the connection.
cn.Open()
' Manually create the parent and child tables in the DataSet.
```

```
Dim ds As New DataSet
Dim pubDt As DataTable = ds.Tables.Add("Publishers")
Dim titDt As DataTable = ds.Tables.Add("Titles")
' Fill the schema of the master table.
pubDa.FillSchema(pubDt, SchemaType.Mapped)

' Execute the JOIN, using the child DataTable as a target.
' (It creates additional columns that belong to the parent table.)
joinDa.Fill(titDt)
' This variable holds the last value found in the master table.
Dim keyValue As String

' Extract rows belonging to the parent table, and discard duplicate values.
For Each dr As DataRow In titDt.Rows
    ' If we haven't seen this value yet, create a record in the parent table.
    If dr(0).ToString <> keyValue Then
        ' Remember the new key value.
        keyValue = dr(0).ToString
        ' Add a new record.
        Dim pubRow As DataRow = pubDt.NewRow
        ' Copy only the fields belonging to the parent table.
        For i As Integer = 0 To pubDt.Columns.Count - 1
            pubRow(i) = dr(i)
        Next
        pubDt.Rows.Add(pubRow)
    End If
Next

' Remove columns belonging to the master table,
' but leave the foreign key (assumed to be in the zeroth column).
For i As Integer = pubDt.Columns.Count - 1 To 1 Step -1
    titDt.Columns.RemoveAt(i)
Next

' Now we can fill the schema of the child table and close the connection.
titDa.FillSchema(titDt, SchemaType.Mapped)
cn.Close()

' Add the relationship manually. Note that this statement is based on the
' assumption that the foreign key is in the zeroth column in the child table.
ds.Relations.Add("PubTitles", pubDt.Columns(0), titDt.Columns(0))

' Bind to the DataGrid controls.
DataGrid1.DataSource = pubDt
DataGrid2.DataSource = titDt
```

Figure 22-10 shows the result of the preceding code. This solution solves all the problems mentioned previously because SQL Server evaluates only one statement and you don't have to use an explicit transaction to ensure consistent results. (Individual statements run inside an implicit transaction.) The only minor defect of this technique is that it retrieves some duplicated data for the parent table (the rows that you discard in the For Each loop in the previous code), which causes slightly more network traffic. If you're retrieving many columns from the parent table and each parent row has many child records, this extra traffic becomes noticeable, and you might find it preferable to fall back on the solution based on the two JOIN statements running inside a transaction. Only a benchmark based on the actual tables and the actual network configuration can tell which technique is more efficient or scalable.

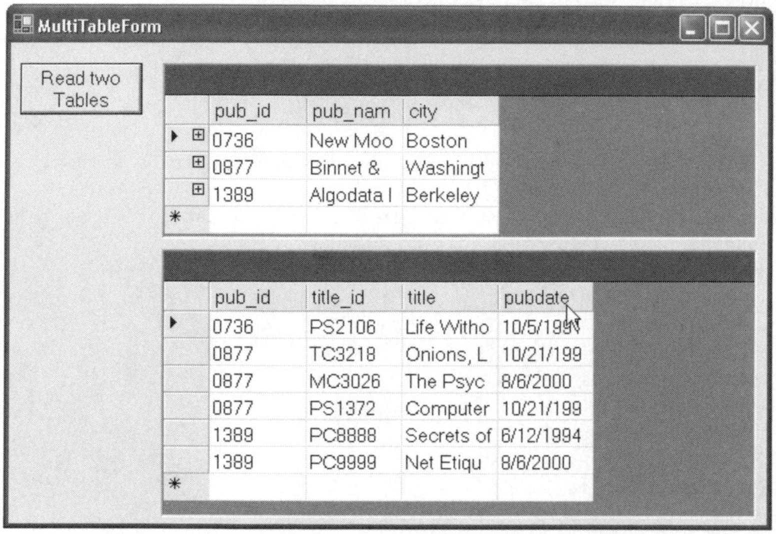

Figure 22-10   The two DataGrid controls contain only the data really needed.

A final note: the preceding code defines two DataAdapter objects, one for each table, and uses them only to retrieve the database table's schema. Even if the DataTable objects weren't filled using these DataAdapters, you could still pass them to a CommandBuilder object to generate the usual INSERT, DELETE, and UPDATE statements that you then use to update either table.

Paginating Results

Even though a DataTable object can contain up to slightly more than 16 million rows, you shouldn't even try loading more than a few hundred rows in it, for two good reasons. First, you'd move just too much information through the wire; second, the user won't browse all those rows anyway. So you should attempt to reduce the number of records read—for example, by refining the WHERE clause of your query. If this remedy isn't possible, you should offer a pagination mechanism that displays results only one page at a time, without reading more rows than strictly needed each time.

Implementing a good paging mechanism isn't trivial. For example, you can easily implement a mediocre paging mechanism by passing a starting record and a number of records as arguments to the DataAdapter's Fill method, as in this code snippet:

```
' Read page N into Publishers table. (Each page contains 10 rows.)
da.Fill(ds, (N - 1) * 10, 10, "Publishers")
```

(I explained this syntax in the "Filling a DataTable" section earlier in this chapter.) What actually happens is that the DataAdapter reads all the records before the ones you're really interested in, and then it discards them. So this approach is OK for small result-sets, but you should never use it for tables containing more than a few hundred rows. You have to roll up your sleeves and start writing some smart SQL code to implement a better paging mechanism.

Let's start by having a look at the following graph, which depicts a small Publishers table of just 12 records, divided into three pages of four rows each. The resultset is sorted on the PubId numeric key.

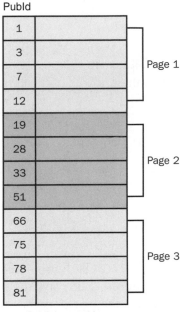

Publishers table

Getting the first page is easy, thanks to the TOP clause offered by both Access's SQL and T-SQL dialects:

```
SELECT TOP 4 * FROM Publishers ORDER BY PubId
```

Moving to the next page is also simple. Say that you're currently positioned on a page in the middle of the table, such as the one that appears in dark gray in the preceding diagram, and you want to read the next four rows. These rows are the first four records whose key value is higher than the value of the key at the last record in the current page:

```
-- 51 is the value of the key at the last row in the current page.
SELECT TOP 4 * FROM Publishers WHERE Pubs > 51 ORDER BY PubId
```

Getting the last page is also simple: we just need to retrieve rows in *reverse* order and select the first four rows of the result. To keep things simple, let's assume that the resultset contains an integer multiple of the page size:

```
SELECT TOP 4 * FROM Publishers ORDER BY PubId DESC
```

The problem here is that we get the result in reverse order and therefore must reverse the rows. We might do this after we load the rows into the DataTable, but it's better to have the database engine do the job for us so that we can bind the resultset directly to a DataGrid control. So we need to run the preceding query as a subquery of another SELECT command that puts all rows in the correct order:

```
SELECT * FROM Publishers WHERE PubId IN
   (SELECT TOP 4 PubId FROM Publishers ORDER BY PubId DESC)
   ORDER BY PubId
```

Implementing the Previous button is slightly more complex because we want the four records that come immediately before the key value in the first row of the current page, as in this code snippet:

```
-- 19 is the value of the key at the first row in the current page.
SELECT TOP 4 * FROM Publishers WHERE PubId < 19 ORDER BY PubId DESC
```

Again, this query returns a resultset whose rows are in reverse order, so we need to run the query as a subquery of another SELECT that puts everything right again:

```
SELECT * FROM Publishers WHERE PubId IN
   (SELECT TOP 4 PubId FROM Publishers WHERE PubId < 19 ORDER BY PubId DESC)
   ORDER BY ISBN
```

We're now able to implement the First, Previous, Next, and Last buttons in our Windows Form or Web Form. We can also add a Goto button that displays the *N*th page. For example, showing the fifth page would mean reading the first 20 rows and extracting the last four rows of the result:

```
SELECT TOP 4 * FROM Publishers WHERE PubId IN
   (SELECT TOP 20 PubId FROM Publishers ORDER BY PubId)
   ORDER BY PubId DESC
```

This query returns the rows in reverse order, so we must run it as a subquery of another query that re-sorts the result in the correct order:

```
SELECT * FROM Publishers WHERE PubId IN
   (SELECT TOP 4 PubId FROM Publishers WHERE PubId IN
      (SELECT TOP 20 PubId FROM Publishers ORDER BY PubId)
      ORDER BY PubId DESC)
   ORDER BY PubId
```

I told you that implementing paging isn't a trivial task, remember? Anyway, at this point creating the application has become just a matter of running the right queries against the database. Here's an abridged version of the demo program you'll find in the companion code for this book. (See Figure 22-11.)

```vb
Dim cn As New OleDbConnection(BiblioConnString)
Dim cmd As New OleDbCommand(sql, cn)
Dim da As OleDbDataAdapter

Dim pageSize As Integer = 10        ' Page size (change as you wish)
Dim recCount As Integer             ' Number of records
Dim pageCount As Integer            ' Number of pages
Dim currPage As Integer             ' Current page number

Dim ds As New DataSet()
Dim dt As DataTable = ds.Tables.Add("Titles")
Dim sql As String

Private Sub PagingForm_Load(ByVal sender As System.Object, _
    ByVal e As System.EventArgs) Handles MyBase.Load
    GetPageNumber()                 ' Evaluate number of pages.
    DataGrid1.DataSource = dt       ' Bind the Titles table.
    btnFirst.PerformClick()         ' Show the first page of results.
End Sub

' Evaluate number of pages in the results.
Sub GetPageNumber()
    Dim closeOnExit As Boolean
    ' Open the connection if necessary.
    If cn.State = ConnectionState.Closed Then
        cn.Open()
        closeOnExit = True
    End If

    ' Evaluate number of records.
    cmd.CommandText = "SELECT COUNT(*) FROM Titles"
    recCount = CInt(cmd.ExecuteScalar())
    ' Close the connection if it was closed.
    If closeOnExit Then cn.Close()

    ' Evaluate number of pages, and display the count.
    pageCount = (recCount + pageSize - 1) \ pageSize
    lblRecords.Text = " of " & pageCount.ToString
End Sub

' Run the specified query, and display the Nth page of results.
Sub DisplayPage(ByVal n As Integer, ByVal sql As String)
    cn.Open
    Dim da As New OleDbDataAdapter(sql, cn)
    dt.Clear()
    da.Fill(dt)
    ' Uncomment next statement to update page count each time
    ' a new page is displayed.
    ' GetPageNumber()
    cn.Close()

    ' Remember current page number, and display it.
    currPage = n
```

```
        lblCurrPage.Text = n.ToString
        ' Enable or disable buttons.
        btnFirst.Enabled = (n > 1)
        btnPrevious.Enabled = (n > 1)
        btnNext.Enabled = (n < pageCount)
        btnLast.Enabled = (n < pageCount)
    End Sub


    ' Manage the four navigational buttons.

    Private Sub btnFirst_Click(ByVal sender As System.Object, _
        ByVal e As System.EventArgs) Handles btnFirst.Click
        sql = String.Format("SELECT TOP {0} * FROM Titles ORDER BY ISBN", _
            pageSize)
        DisplayPage(1, sql)
    End Sub


    Private Sub btnPrevious_Click(ByVal sender As System.Object, _
        ByVal e As System.EventArgs) Handles btnPrevious.Click
        sql = String.Format("SELECT * FROM Titles WHERE ISBN IN " _
            & "(SELECT TOP {0} ISBN FROM Titles WHERE ISBN < '{1}' " _
            & "ORDER BY ISBN DESC) ORDER BY ISBN", pageSize, dt.Rows(0)("ISBN"))
        DisplayPage(currPage - 1, sql)
    End Sub


    Private Sub btnNext_Click(ByVal sender As System.Object, _
        ByVal e As System.EventArgs) Handles btnNext.Click
        sql = String.Format("SELECT TOP {0} * FROM Titles WHERE ISBN > '{1}' " _
            & "ORDER BY ISBN", pageSize, dt.Rows(dt.Rows.Count - 1)("ISBN"))
        DisplayPage(currPage + 1, sql)
    End Sub


    Private Sub btnLast_Click(ByVal sender As System.Object, _
        ByVal e As System.EventArgs) Handles btnLast.Click
        ' Evaluate number of records on last page.
        Dim num As Integer = recCount - pageSize * (pageCount - 1)
        sql = String.Format("SELECT * FROM Titles WHERE ISBN IN (SELECT TOP " _
            & " {0} ISBN FROM Titles ORDER BY ISBN DESC) ORDER BY ISBN", num)
        DisplayPage(pageCount, sql)
    End Sub


    ' Go to Nth page.
    Private Sub btnGoto_Click(ByVal sender As System.Object, _
        ByVal e As System.EventArgs) Handles btnGoto.Click
        Try
            ' txtPageNum contains the page number we want to jump to.
            Dim pageNum As Integer = CInt(txtPageNum.Text)
            sql = String.Format("SELECT * FROM Titles WHERE ISBN IN " _
                & "(SELECT TOP {0} ISBN FROM Titles WHERE ISBN IN " _
                & "(SELECT TOP {1} ISBN FROM Titles ORDER BY ISBN) ORDER BY " _
                & " ISBN DESC) ORDER BY ISBN", pageSize, pageSize * pageNum)
            DisplayPage(pageNum, sql)
        Catch ex As Exception
            MessageBox.Show("Page # must be in the range [1," & _
                pageCount.ToString & "]")
        End Try
    End Sub
```

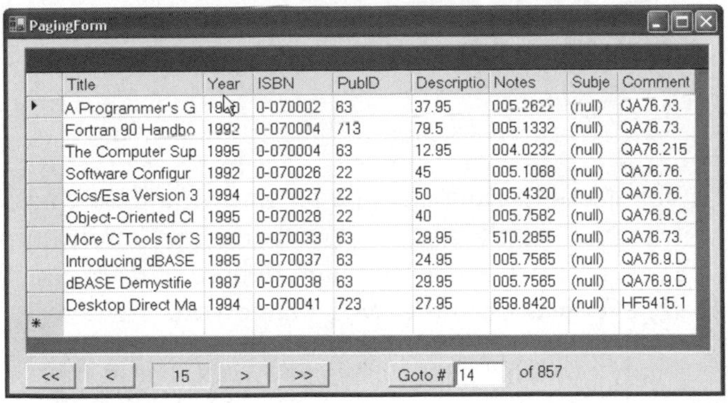

Figure 22-11   The demo program shows how to navigate among pages of the Titles table in Biblio.mdb (more than 8000 records).

The program evaluates the number of pages when the form is loaded, but a more robust implementation should execute the GetPageNumber procedure each time a new page is displayed. (See remarks in the DisplayPage routine.) Updating a DataTable that contains paged results doesn't require any special technique—just define a Data-Adapter based on a generic SELECT statement:

```
Dim titDa As New OleDbDataAdapter("SELECT * FROM Titles", cn)
```

And then use a CommandBuilder object to generate the INSERT, DELETE, and UPDATE commands. Or create your custom update commands, as described earlier in this chapter.

See Also   You can read the "Resolving Conflicts on a Row-by-Row Basis.doc" file on the companion CD to learn how to use the RowUpdated event to solve a conflict immediately after it has occurred.

The document "Writing Provider-Agnostic Code.doc," which you can also find on the companion CD, shows a few advanced techniques based on interfaces and reflection for building code that works with any ADO.NET Data provider.

At this point, you know enough to build great database-centric applications. Yet there are a few more ADO.NET features still to cover. I'll discuss them at the end of the next chapter, after I introduce the new XML-related classes in the .NET Framework.

23 XML and ADO.NET

In recent years, the Extensible Markup Language, better known as XML, has emerged as a leading technology for storing complex data and exchanging it among applications or even different operating systems. Because of the high degree of interoperability that it allows, XML is used nearly everywhere in the .NET Framework.

Paradoxically, XML is so deeply buried in the .NET Framework that in most cases you don't even see it, and you don't have to process it directly. Web services are the perfect example of this concept: you send requests and receive results from a Web service using SOAP (and therefore XML) without having to learn anything about .NET XML classes.

However, you'll come across situations in which you must work with XML directly, so in this chapter I'll cover the most important .NET classes and namespaces related to XML. I'll also cover all the XML-related features of ADO.NET—for example, the support for strongly typed DataSet objects and how you can leverage Visual Studio .NET to create database-intensive applications.

A disclaimer is in order, though: this chapter is about XML in the .NET Framework, not about general XML concepts. Space constraints prevent me from covering basic XML concepts, such as tags, attributes, the Document Object Model (DOM), and XPath. If you are new to XML, you should consider buying an XML-focused book or use your favorite search engine to locate one or more XML tutorial articles on the Internet.

> **Note** To keep the code as concise as possible, all code samples in this chapter assume the use of the following Imports statements at the file or project level:
>
> ```
> Imports System.Xml
> Imports System.Xml.Xsl
> Imports System.Text.RegularExpressions
> ```

Reading and Writing XML Files

The .NET Framework supports different techniques for working with XML data. When you need to simply parse an XML file to process its contents as you read it, you can achieve the best performance with the XmlTextReader class. Similarly, you should use the XmlTextWriter class if you write XML data as you produce it. For more complex tasks, such as loading entire XML files into memory and processing them, you should use the XmlDocument class, which implements the XML Document Object Model (DOM). The XmlDocument class is described later in this chapter.

The XmlTextReader Class

The XmlTextReader class offers a fast way for reading XML data into memory. This object works a bit like the forward-only DataReader object in that the XML stream is consumed as it's being read and parsed, and you cannot backtrack to reread any preceding node. As is the case with a DataReader object, the XML data retrieved by an XmlTextReader object is read-only, so you never affect the original XML file. This object is clearly less powerful than a full-featured XML DOM parser—which can traverse the XML data in both directions and change its structure—but in many situations, using the XmlTextReader is the best choice you can make, especially with very large documents that would seriously tax the memory.

You pass the name of the XML file to be parsed to the XmlTextReader constructor:

```
Dim xtr As New XmlTextReader("mydata.xml")
```

(Other overloaded versions of the constructor can take a Stream-derived object or a TextReader object.) Next, you enter a loop that checks the return value from the Read method, similar to what you do with a DataReader object—inside the loop, you usually test the NodeType property of the current element and proceed appropriately:

```
Do While xtr.Read
    Select Case xtr.NodeType
        Case XmlNodeType.Document
            ' The root element in the XML data
        Case XmlNodeType.Element
            ' An XML element
        Case XmlNodeType.EndElement
            ' A closing XML tag
        Case XmlNodeType.Text
            ' Text value
        Case XmlNodeType.CDATA
            ' A CDATA section
    End Select
Loop
' Close the XML stream.
xtr.Close()
```

All the possible values of the NodeType property are listed in Table 23-1. This table also will be useful when we explore the XML DOM using the XmlDocument class.

Table 23-1   XmlNodeType Enumerated Values and Corresponding XML Class

XmlNodeType Value	XML Class	Description	Can Be a Child Of	Can Have These Nodes as Children	Example
Attribute	XmlAttribute	An attribute	None (It isn't considered the child of an element.)	Text, EntityReference	id='123'
CDATA	Xml-CD ataSection	A CDATA section	DocumentFragment, EntityReference, Element	None	<![CDATA [mydata]]>
Comment	XmlComment	A comment	Document, Document-Fragment, Entity-Reference, Element	None	<!-- mycomment -->
Document	XmlDocument	A document root object	None (It works as the root node of the document.)	XmlDeclaration, Element, Processing-Instruction, Comment, DocumentType	
Document-Fragment	XmlDocument-Fragment	A document fragment used to process a node subtree	None	Element, Processing-Instruction, Comment, Text, CDATA, Entity-Reference	
DocumentType	XmlDocument-Type	The document type declaration indicated by the DOCTYPE tag	Document	Notation, Entity	<!DOCTYPE ...>
Element	XmlElement	An XML element	Document, Document-Fragment, Entity-Reference, Element	Element, Text, Comment, Processing-Instruction, CDATA, EntityReference	<myelement> ⋮ </myelement>
EndElement	n/a	An end element tag; it's returned when an XmlReader gets to the end of an element	n/a	n/a	</myelement>
EndEntity	n/a	The end of an entity declaration; it's returned by the Xml-Reader	n/a	n/a	
Entity	XmlEntity	An entity declaration	DocumentType	Text, EntityReference, or any node that represents an expanded entity	<!ENTITY ...>
EntityReference	XmlEntity-Reference	A reference to an entity	Attribute, Document-Fragment, Element, EntityReference	Element, Processing-Instruction, Comment, Text, CDATA, EntityReference	&ref
None	n/a	It's returned by Xml-Reader if the Read method hasn't been called yet	n/a	n/a	
Notation	XmlNotation	A notation in the document type declaration	DocumentType	None	<!NOTATION ...>

Table 23-1 XmlNodeType Enumerated Values and Corresponding XML Class *(continued)*

XmlNodeType Value	XML Class	Description	Can Be a Child Of	Can Have These Nodes as Children	Example
Processing-Instruction	XmlProcessing-Instruction	A processing instruction	Document, Document-Fragment, Element, EntityReference	None	`<?instr data?>`
Significant-Whitespace	XmlSignificant-Whitespace	White space between markup in mixed content model or within the xml:space = 'preserve' scope	None	None	

Text	XmlText	The text content of a node	Attribute, Document-Fragment, Element, EntityReference	None	`<myelement>`
					mytext
					`</myelement>`

Whitespace	XmlWhitespace	Whitespace between markup	n/a	n/a	
XmlDeclaration	XmlDeclaration	The XML declaration	Document (Must be the first node in the document.)	None (But it has attributes that provide version and encoding information.)	`<?xml version='1.0' ?>`

The following program displays the names of all the publishers in the pubs.xml file (which I obtained by saving a DataSet filled with data from the Publishers table in SQL Server's Pubs database):

```
Dim xtr As New XmlTextReader("pubs.xml")
Do While xtr.Read
    If xtr.NodeType = XmlNodeType.Element Then
        ' Publisher names are inserted as text immediately
        ' after an element named pub_name.
        If xtr.Name = "pub_name" Then
            ' Move to the next element, and display its value.
            xtr.Read()
            Console.WriteLine(xtr.Value)
        End If
    End If
Loop
xtr.Close()
```

By default, attributes are skipped over when XML data is parsed, but you can use the HasAttributes property (or the AttributeCount property) to check whether the current element has any attributes and then iterate over them with the MoveToNextAttribute method, which returns True if attributes are found and False otherwise. When the XmlTextReader is positioned over an attribute, you can use its Value property to read the attribute's value and the QuoteChar property to read the quotation mark character used to enclose the value:

```
' Display elements and attributes in an XML file.
Dim xtr As New XmlTextReader("mydata.xml")
Do While xtr.Read
```

```
        If xtr.NodeType = XmlNodeType.Element Then
            ' Display the name of the current node.
            Console.Write("<" & xtr.Name)
            ' Display name and value of attributes, if any.
            If xtr.HasAttributes Then
                Do While xtr.MoveToNextAttribute()
                    Console.Write(" {0}={1}{2}{1}", xtr.Name, xtr.QuoteChar, xtr.Value)
                Loop
            End If
            ' Go back to the main element.
            xtr.MoveToElement()
            ' Print the ending slash if this is an empty element.
            If xtr.IsEmptyElement Then Console.Write("/")
            ' Close the tag.
            Console.WriteLine(">")
        End If
Loop
xtr.Close()
```

The XmlTextReader class exposes several properties related to the current node in addition to those I explained already: LocalName (the name, without the namespace), BaseURI (the base Uniform Resource Identifier), NamespaceURI (the namespace URI), IsEmptyElement (True, if the node is in the form <ELEM/>), HasValue (True, if the node has a value) and Value (the node's value). Only these node types have a value: Attribute, Text, CDATA, Comment, DocumentType, XmlDeclaration, ProcessingInstruction, Whitespace, and SignificantWhitespace.

Other properties return information about the state of the XmlTextReader: EOF (True at the end of the XML data), LineNumber (row number in XML data), LinePosition (column number in XML data), and ReadState (the current state of the reader). The value of the last property can be Initial (the Read method hasn't been called), Interactive (the Read method has been called), EndOfFile, Error, or Closed.

The only writeable properties of the XmlTextReader class are those that you can assign before you start the parsing: Encoding (the encoding attribute of the XML document), WhitespaceHandling (an enumerated value that specifies how whitespace is handled: All, None, or Significant), Namespaces (whether the parser should provide namespace support; the default is True), and Normalization (True, if whitespace and attribute values should be normalized).

Most of the methods of this class return information about the current node or its attributes: ReadInnerXml (the node's content, including markup), ReadOuterXml (the content for this node and its children, including markup), ReadString (the content of an element or a text node), IsStartElement (True, if current element is a start element), ReadStartElement (checks that current element is a start element and advances to the next element), Read-EndElement (checks that the current element is an end element and advances to the next element), GetAttribute (reads the value of the attribute specified by the argument, which can be a name or an index), and GetRemainder (reads all the XML data not read yet).

The XmlTextWriter Class

The XmlTextWriter class is the writing counterpart of the XmlTextReader class in the sense that it lets you write to an XML file using a forward-only mechanism. Of course, you can output XML text yourself to any stream, but this class offers some advantages, such as ensuring that the output is well-formed XML, that special characters are correctly stored as character entities, and that element names comply with XML specifications.

You create an XmlTextWriter object by passing a filename to its constructor (but you can also pass a Stream-derived object or a TextWriter object). The second argument is an Encoding value that specifies how data is encoded:

```
Dim xtw As New XmlTextWriter("mydata.xml", System.Text.Encoding.UTF8)
```

Before you start outputting data, you can set a few properties that determine whether tags are indented (Formatting), the indent length (Indentation), and the character used to enclose attribute values (QuoteChar):

```
' Indent tags by 2 characters.
xtw.Formatting = Formatting.Indented
xtw.Indentation = 2
' Enclose attributes' values in double quotes.
xtw.QuoteChar = """"c
```

The first method you must call is WriteStartDocument, which outputs the XML declaration for the document. Its argument specifies whether the standalone attribute is set to "yes":

```
' Create the following XML declaration for this XML document:
'    <?xml version="1.0" standalone="yes" ?>
xtw.WriteStartDocument(True)
```

You can now write elements and attributes by using the many methods that the Xml-TextWriter class exposes. The most useful methods are WriteStartElement, which writes the start tag of an XML element; and WriteEndElement, which writes the end tag of the most recently opened XML element. Interestingly, the latter method doesn't require the element name (because the XmlTextWriter object keeps a stack of pending XML elements) and is able to use the short form for the end tag if the element doesn't contain anything else, as in the following line of code:

```
<Invoice id="1" />
```

If you don't need this behavior, you should use the WriteFullEndElement method, which closes the current element and pops the corresponding namespace scope; it never uses the short end tag, so it's useful for adding </SCRIPT> tags and other tags that can't be shortened.

Another method that you'll use often is WriteAttributeString, which outputs the name and the value of an attribute using the correct quote delimiters. You can also write other types of XML elements by using one of the following methods, whose names clearly indicate which type of XML element they produce: WriteComment, WriteCData, WriteProcessingInstruction, WriteCharEntity, and WriteEntityRef.

Finally, a group of methods let you output raw text, while ensuring that it abides by the XML rules (for example, they correctly translate special characters to the corresponding character entities): WriteName, WriteQualifiedName, WriteString, WriteChars, Write-Whitespace, WriteBinHex, and WriteBase64. The WriteRaw method outputs text without converting special characters.

The following code shows how you can read a comma-delimited file and convert it to an XML document. I illustrated how to use regular expressions to parse a comma-delimited file in the section "Adding Rows" in Chapter 22, so I won't explain it again here. The remarks in code should make clear how the XmlTextWriter class works.

```
' Open the file, and read its contents.
Dim sr As New System.IO.StreamReader("employees.dat")
Dim fileText As String = sr.ReadToEnd
sr.Close()

' Create the output XML file.
Dim xtw As New XmlTextWriter("employees.xml", System.Text.Encoding.UTF8)
' Indent tags by 2 spaces.
xtw.Formatting = Formatting.Indented
xtw.Indentation = 2
' Enclose attributes' values in double quotes.
xtw.QuoteChar = """"c
' Create the following XML declaration for this XML document:
'     <?xml version="1.0" standalone="yes" ?>
xtw.WriteStartDocument(True)
' Add a comment.
xtw.WriteComment("Data converted from employees.dat file")
' The root element is <Employees>.
xtw.WriteStartElement("Employees")

' This regular expression defines a row of elements and assigns a name
' to each group (that is, a field in the text row). It expects that bdate
' DateTime field be formatted according to current regional settings.
Dim re As New Regex( _
    """(?<fname>[^""]+)"";""(?<lname>[^""]+)"";(?<bdate>[^;]+);" _
    & """(?<addr>[^""]+)"";""(?<city>[^""]+)""")
' This variable will provide a unique ID for each employee.
Dim id As Integer = 0

For Each ma As Match In re.Matches(fileText)
    ' A new line has been found, increment employee ID.
    id += 1
    ' Write a new <Employee id="nnn"> element.
    xtw.WriteStartElement("Employee")
    xtw.WriteAttributeString("id", id.ToString)
    ' Write fields as nested elements containing text.
    xtw.WriteElementString("firstName", ma.Groups("fname").Value)
    xtw.WriteElementString("lastName", ma.Groups("lname").Value)
    xtw.WriteElementString("birthDate", ma.Groups("bdate").Value)
    xtw.WriteElementString("address", ma.Groups("addr").Value)
```

```
      xtw.WriteElementString("city", ma.Groups("city").Value)
      ' Close the <Employee> element.
      xtw.WriteEndElement()
Next
' Close the root element (and all pending elements, if any).
xtw.WriteEndDocument()
' Close the underlying stream (never forget this).
xtw.Close()
```

Figure 23-1 shows the resulting XML file loaded in Microsoft Internet Explorer.

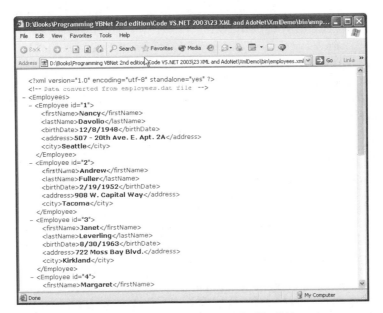

Figure 23-1   An XML file produced by the XmlTextWriter class

Working with the XML DOM

The XmlTextReader and XmlTextWriter classes are OK for parsing or writing XML files, but they can't be used to manipulate the structure of an XML document—for example, to add or remove nodes, search for nested nodes, extract node subtrees, and the like. In cases like these, you must instantiate a full-fledged XmlDocument object and use it to access the XML Document Object Model (DOM).

An XmlDocument object can contain several child objects, each one representing a different node in the DOM. The names of these secondary classes are quite self-explanatory: XmlElement, XmlAttribute, XmlComment, XmlDeclaration, XmlEntityReference, XmlProcessingInstruction, XmlCDataSection, XmlCharacterData, XmlText, and a few others. (See Table 23-1.) But before having a look at these classes, you should get acquainted with the XmlNode class.

The XmlNode Class

XmlNode is a virtual class that works as the base class for several classes in the System.Xml namespace, including the XmlDocument class itself and most of its secondary classes. The XmlNode class represents a generic node in the DOM and exposes several properties and methods that are inherited by other DOM classes—thus, studying this class first means simplifying the exploration of other classes described in later sections.

You can group all the properties of this class in three categories: properties that return information about the node's identity, such as NodeType, Name, LocalName, Prefix, BaseURI, and NamespaceURI; properties that return information about the node's value, such as Value, InnerXml, InnerText, and OuterXml; properties that let you navigate from the current node to elsewhere in the document—for example, OwnerDocument, ParentNode, FirstChild, LastChild, FirstSibling, LastSibling, ChildNodes, and Attributes. Most of these properties are read-only, with Value and InnerXml being the most notable exceptions.

The most important property of this class is NodeType, which you use to determine the type of a given node. The NodeType property returns an XmlNodeType enumerated value, which can be one of the values listed in Table 23-1.

The XmlNode class also exposes several methods, the most important of which let you insert and remove child nodes, such as AppendChild, InsertBefore, InsertAfter, PrependChild, ReplaceChild, RemoveChild, and RemoveAll. Another important group of methods have to do with searching, and I'll cover them later in this chapter.

XmlNode is a virtual class that can't be instantiated, so I will defer showing you a complete code example until I introduce the XmlDocument class in the next section.

The XmlDocument Class

You can't do much with the XmlNode class alone because you need to create a DOM in memory before you can create and manipulate its nodes. You create the DOM by instantiating the XmlDocument class, which also inherits from XmlNode:

```
Dim xmldoc as New XmlDocument()
```

What you do next depends on whether you want to process an existing XML data source or create a new document from scratch. In the first case, you typically use the Load method to load XML data from a file, a Stream, a TextReader, or an XmlReader object:

```
' In a real application, this should be protected in a Try block.
xmldoc.Load("employees.xml")
```

If you already have the XML text in a string, you can use the LoadXml method:

```
' This code assumes that the txtXml TextBox control contains XML data.
xmldoc.LoadXml(txtXml.Text)
```

Table 23-2 lists the main properties, methods, and events of the XmlDocument class (other than those inherited from XmlNode); the sections following the table illustrate how you can use a few of these members.

Table 23-2 Main Members of the XmlDocument Class

Category	Syntax	Description
Properties	DocumentElement	The root XmlElement object for this document.
	DocumentType	The XmlDocumentType object containing the DOCTYPE declaration.
	NameTable	Returns the XmlNameTable associated with this implementation. This is a list of all the atomized strings used in the document and makes it possible to perform fast string comparisons.
	PreserveWhitespace	A Boolean value that says whether whitespace should be preserved (read/write).
	XmlResolver	The XmlResolver object used to resolve external references.
Create methods	CreateAttribute(name)	Creates an attribute and returns an XmlAttribute object. It takes optional arguments for prefix and namespace values.
	CreateCDataSection(text)	Creates a CDATA section and returns an XmlCDataSection object.
	CreateComment(text)	Creates a comment and returns an XmlComment object.
	CreateDocumentFragment	Creates an empty document fragment and returns an XmlDocumentFragment object.
	CreateDocumentType(name, publicId, systemId, internalSubset)	Creates a DOCTYPE section and returns an XmlDocumentType object.
	CreateElement(name)	Creates an element and returns an XmlElement object. It takes optional arguments for prefix and namespace values.
	CreateEntityReference(name)	Creates an entity reference and returns an XmlEntityReference object.

Table 23-2 Main Members of the XmlDocument Class *(continued)*

Category	Syntax	Description
	CreateNode(nodetype, name, namespace)	Creates a node with the specified node type, name, and namespace URI and returns an XmlNode object; the first argument can be an XmlNodeType value or string.
	CreateProcessingInstruction (target, data)	Creates a processing instruction and returns an XmlProcessingInstruction object.
	CreateSignificant-Whitespace(spaces)	Creates significant whitespace and returns an XmlSignificantNamespace object; the argument can contain only space, tab, carriage return, and line feed characters.
	CreateTextNode(text)	Creates a text node and returns an XmlText object.
	CreateWhitespace(spaces)	Creates whitespace and returns an XmlNamespace object; the argument can contain only space, tab, carriage return, and line feed characters.
	CreateXmlDeclaration(version, encoding, standalone)	Creates a declaration and returns an XmlDeclaration object; if the XML document is saved to an XmlTextWriter, this declaration is discarded and the XmlTextWriter's declaration is used instead.
	ImportNode(node, deep)	Imports a node from another document to the current document; a deep copy is performed if the second argument is True.
Search methods	GetElementById(id)	Returns the XmlElement with the specified attribute ID, or Nothing if the search fails.
	GetElementsByTagName(name)	Returns an XmlNodeList collection holding all the descendant elements with the specified name.
File methods	Load(filename)	Loads the specified XML from a file, a Stream, a TextReader, or an XmlReader object.
	LoadXml(string)	Loads the XML contained in the string argument.

Table 23-2   Main Members of the XmlDocument Class *(continued)*

Category	Syntax	Description
	Save(filename)	Saves the XML to a file, a Stream, a Text-Writer, or an XmlWriter object; the file is overwritten if it exists already.
	ReadNode(xmlreader)	Creates an XmlNode object based on the information at the current position in an XmlReader object (which must be positioned on a node or an attribute).
Events	NodeInserting	A node belonging to this document is about to be inserted into another node. The second argument of this and all following events exposes these properties: Action, Node, NewParent, and OldParent.
	NodeInserted	A node belonging to this document has been inserted into another node.
	NodeChanging	A node belonging to this document is about to be changed.
	NodeChanged	A node belonging to this document has been changed.
	NodeRemoving	A node belonging to this document is about to be removed.
	NodeRemoved	A node belonging to this document has been removed.

Exploring the DOM

After you've loaded XML data into an XmlDocument object, you might want to explore all the nodes it contains. The two main entry points for exploring the DOM hierarchy are the Children collection of the XmlDocument itself, which lets you discover any XML declaration, processing instruction, and comment at the top level of the document; and the XmlDocument's DocumentElement property, which jumps directly to the main XML element that contains the real data:

```
' Access the root XML element in the DOM.
Dim xmlEl As XmlElement = xmldoc.DocumentElement
```

The following code shows how you can load an XML file into an XmlDocument object and then traverse the DOM hierarchy and display the data in a TreeView control. (See Figure 23-2.) Not surprisingly, the core routine is a recursive procedure that adds an element to the Nodes collection of the TreeView and then calls itself over all the child nodes of the current XmlNode object. You can iterate over all the child nodes of an XmlNode object in either of two ways: by indexing the ChildNodes collection or by using the FirstChild and NextSibling properties. The second technique is slightly faster and is the one used by the following routine:

```vb
Sub DisplayXmlTree()
    ' Load an XML file into an XmlDocument object.
    Dim xmldoc As New XmlDocument()
    xmldoc.Load("employees.xml")
    ' Add it to the Nodes collection of the TreeView1 control.
    DisplayXmlNode(xmldoc, TreeView1.Nodes)
End Sub


' A recursive procedure that displays an XmlNode object in a TreeView
' control and then calls itself for each child node
Sub DisplayXmlNode(ByVal xmlnode As XmlNode, _
    ByVal nodes As TreeNodeCollection)

    ' Add a TreeView node for this XmlNode.
    ' (Using the node's Name is OK for most XmlNode types.)
    Dim tvNode As TreeNode = nodes.Add(xmlnode.Name)

    ' Specific code for different node types
    Select Case xmlnode.NodeType
        Case XmlNodeType.Element
            ' This is an element: check whether there are attributes.
            If xmlnode.Attributes.Count > 0 Then
                ' Create an ATTRIBUTES node.
                Dim attrNode As TreeNode = tvNode.Nodes.Add("(ATTRIBUTES)")
                ' Add all the attributes as children of the new node.
                For Each xmlAttr As XmlAttribute In xmlnode.Attributes
                    ' Each node shows name and value.
                    attrNode.Nodes.Add(xmlAttr.Name & " = '" & _
                        xmlAttr.Value & "'")
                Next
            End If
        Case XmlNodeType.Text, XmlNodeType.CDATA
            ' For these node types, we display the value.
            tvNode.Text = xmlnode.Value
        Case XmlNodeType.Comment
            tvNode.Text = "<!--" & xmlnode.Value & "-->"
        Case XmlNodeType.ProcessingInstruction, XmlNodeType.XmlDeclaration
            tvNode.Text = "<?" & xmlnode.Name & " " & xmlnode.Value & "?>"
        Case Else
            ' Ignore other node types.
    End Select

    ' Call this routine recursively for each child node.
    Dim xmlChild As XmlNode = xmlnode.FirstChild
    Do Until xmlChild Is Nothing
        DisplayXmlNode(xmlChild, tvNode.Nodes)
        ' Continue with the next child node.
        xmlChild = xmlChild.NextSibling
    Loop
End Sub
```

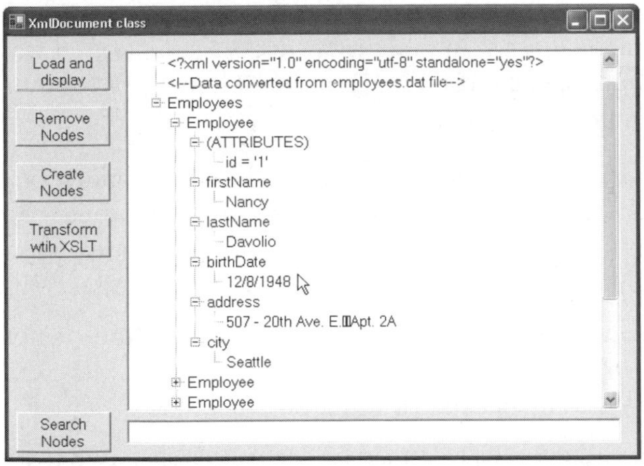

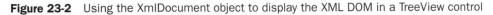

Figure 23-2   Using the XmlDocument object to display the XML DOM in a TreeView control

Adding and Removing Nodes

Usually you don't use the XmlDocument object just to read and display the structure of a piece of XML data, as the real power of this object (and the DOM in general) is its ability to modify the structure of an XML document by adding and removing nodes and then saving the result back to a file (or whatever data source you read it from).

To remove a node, you simply use the RemoveChild method of its parent element node. This method takes the element to be deleted as an argument, so you must find it first by iterating over the ChildNodes collection, by using either the SelectSingleNode method of the generic XmlNode class or the GetElementsByTagName method of the XmlElement class (which is the technique adopted by the code to follow). Likewise, to remove an attribute, you can use the Remove method of the XmlNode's Attributes collection or simply use the RemoveAttribute method of the XmlElement class. The following code snippet loads the XML file, shown in Figure 23-1, in memory and deletes the id attribute and the birthDate subelement under all Employee elements:

```
' Load the XML document.
Dim xmldoc As New XmlDocument()
xmldoc.Load("employees.xml")

' Remove the id attribute and the birthDate subelement from all
' Employee elements.
For Each xmlEl As XmlElement In xmldoc.DocumentElement.ChildNodes
    ' Remove the attribute with a given name.
    xmlEl.RemoveAttribute("id")
    ' Get a reference to the birthDate subelement.
    Dim xmlList As XmlNodeList = xmlEl.GetElementsByTagName("birthDate")
    ' The GetElementsByTagName method returns a collection, so we must take
    ' the result's first element.
    If xmlList.Count > 0 Then
        xmlEl.RemoveChild(xmlList(0))
    End If
Next
```

In theory, you can manipulate the DOM using only the properties and methods exposed by the generic XmlNode class. In practice, however, you'll often want to cast the XmlNode object to a more specific class (such as XmlElement or XmlAttribute) to leverage the additional members it exposes:

■ The XmlElement class exposes several additional methods for working on attributes (other than those inherited from XmlNode); you can create attributes with SetAttribute or SetAttributeNode, and delete them by their name or index with RemoveAttribute, RemoveAttributeAt, RemoveAttributeNode, or RemoveAllAttributes.

■ The XmlAttribute class exposes the OwnerElement property (the owner XmlElement object) and the Specified property (True, if the attribute was explicitly set; False if the attribute exists only because it has a default value).

■ The XmlText class exposes the SplitText method, which creates two text elements by splitting the string at the specified offset.

■ The XmlProcessingInstruction class exposes the Target and Data properties, which get or set the target and the data of the processing instruction.

Adding a node is a three-step process:

1. Call one of the Createxxxx methods of the XmlDocument object to generate an XmlNode-derived object, such as XmlElement or XmlText.

2. Set any additional properties of the object just created if necessary.

3. Add the new node in the correct place in the DOM using the AppendChild, InsertAfter, InsertBefore, or PrependChild method, which all DOM objects expose.

The following code sample shows how you can add a new Employee element (and all its attributes and subelements) to the employees.xml file. The remarks in the listing explain several coding techniques you can adopt to make your code more concise:

```
' Load the XML document.
Dim xmldoc As New XmlDocument()
xmldoc.Load("employees.xml")

' Create a new Employee element.
Dim xmlEl As XmlElement = xmldoc.CreateElement("Employee")
' Append it to the children collection of the DOM root element.
xmldoc.DocumentElement.AppendChild(xmlEl)

' Set the id attribute of the new element.
xmlEl.SetAttribute("id", "100")
' Create all its subelements.
' (Each subelement is created with a different technique.)
Dim xmlChildEl As XmlElement

' This is the firstName subelement.
xmlChildEl = xmldoc.CreateElement("firstName")
' Create a child XmlText element for the firstName element.
```

```
Dim xmlText As XmlText = xmldoc.CreateTextNode("Joe")
xmlChildEl.AppendChild(xmlText)
' Append the firstName element to the new Employee element.
xmlEl.AppendChild(xmlChildEl)

' This is the lastName subelement.
xmlChildEl = xmldoc.CreateElement("lastName")
' Create a child XmlText element, and append it in one operation.
xmlChildEl.AppendChild(xmldoc.CreateTextNode("Doe"))
' Append the lastName subelement to the new Employee element.
xmlEl.AppendChild(xmlChildEl)

' This is the address subelement.
xmlChildEl = xmldoc.CreateElement("address")
' This time we use the InnerText property (a Microsoft extension of WC3 DOM).
xmlChildEl.InnerText = "1234 North Street"
' Append the address subelement to the new Employee element.
xmlEl.AppendChild(xmlChildEl)

' This is the city subelement.
xmlChildEl = xmldoc.CreateElement("city")
xmlChildEl.InnerText = "Boston"
xmlEl.AppendChild(xmlChildEl)

' Save to a different XML file.
xmldoc.Save("employees2.xml")
```

To make your code even more concise, you can prepare a helper routine for creating subelements and their inner text and append them to a parent element as one operation:

```
'   Create an XmlElement object with inner text, and make it
'   a child of another XmlNode.
Function CreateAppendElement(ByVal parentNode As XmlNode, _
    ByVal name As String, Optional ByVal innerText As String = Nothing) _
    As XmlElement
    ' Create a new XmlElement object, and set the return value.
    Dim xmlEl As XmlElement = parentNode.OwnerDocument.CreateElement(name)
    ' Set its inner text if provided.
    If Not (innerText Is Nothing) Then xmlEl.InnerText = innerText
    ' Make it a child of its parent node.
    parentNode.AppendChild(xmlEl)
    ' Return the new node to the caller.
    Return xmlEl
End Function
```

The CreateAppendElement routine makes the job of adding a new Employee element much easier:

```
' Create a new Employee element.
Dim xmlEl As XmlElement
xmlEl = CreateAppendElement(xmldoc.DocumentElement, "Employee")
' Set the id attribute of the new element.
xmlEl.SetAttribute("id", "100")
```

```
' Create all its subelements.
CreateAppendElement(xmlEl, "firstName", "Joe")
CreateAppendElement(xmlEl, "lastName", "Doe")
CreateAppendElement(xmlEl, "address", "1234 North Street")
CreateAppendElement(xmlEl, "city", "Boston")
```

You can create similar helper routines for adding other types of XML nodes, such as comments, processing instructions, and CDATA sections.

Searching Nodes

The XmlNode class exposes two search methods that take an XPath expression. Use the SelectNodes method if the XPath expression can return more than one match or the SelectSingleNode method if it can return only one node (or you're only interested in its first matching node). Since this isn't an XML textbook, I won't go into many details about XPath, but I'll provide a few XPath examples based on the employees.xml file we've been using most recently.

Select all the <Employee> descendant nodes:

```
//Employee
```

Select all the <lastName> child nodes of any Employee descendant node:

```
//Employee/lastName
```

Select the <Employee> descendant node whose id attribute is equal to 3:

```
//Employee[@id='3']
```

Select the <lastName> child node of the first <Employee> element:

```
//Employee[position() = 1]/lastName
```

Select the text child node of the <lastName> child node of the last <Employee> element:

```
//Employee[position() = last()]/lastName/text()
```

Select the <firstName> child node of the <Employee> element whose <lastName> child element is equal to Davolio:

```
//Employee[lastName='Davolio']/firstName
```

Although writing down a search expression can be difficult if you aren't familiar with the XPath syntax, using the expression to select one or more nodes in an XmlDocument is easy:

```
' Select a single node.
Dim xpath As String = "//Employee[lastName='Davolio']/firstName"
Dim xn As XmlNode = xmldoc.SelectSingleNode(xpath)
' Display its text content.
Debug.WriteLine(xn.innerText)               ' => Nancy
```

```
' Select all elements whose id attribute is <= 4.
Dim xnl As XmlNodeList = xmldoc.SelectNodes("//Employee[@id <= 4]")
' Display number of matches.
Debug.WriteLine(xnl.Count)                  ' => 4
For Each node As XmlNode In xnl
    ' Cast result to an XmlElement object.
    Dim xmlEl As XmlElement = DirectCast(node, XmlElement)
    ' Display the innerText property of the <lastName> child element.
    ' (We know that there is only one <lastName> child node.)
    Debug.WriteLine(xmlEl.GetElementsByTagName("lastName")(0).InnerText())
Next
```

The XslTransform Class

The XslTransform class is the key for working with Extensible Stylesheet Language Transformations (XSLT), which allow you to transform an XML document into another XML document. Typically, you use an XSLT to change the layout of existing XML data—for example, to change the order of XML elements, to transform XML elements into attributes, or to produce a browsable file in XHTML format (the XML-compliant version of HTML).

To see how this class works, let's start by creating an XSLT file named Employees.xslt, which transforms the Employee.xml file into an .html file that you can then view inside a browser. You can create an .xslt file using Notepad or by pointing to New on the File menu in Visual Studio .NET, then selecting File, and finally clicking the General category in the New File dialog box and double-clicking XSLT File. Unlike source code files, XSLT documents are created in memory, and you'll be asked for their path only when you save them.

```
<?xml version="1.0" encoding="UTF-8" ?>
<xsl:stylesheet version="1.0"
    xmlns:xsl="http://www.w3.org/1999/XSL/Transform">
  <xsl:template match="/">
    <HTML>
    <TITLE>Employees Table</TITLE>
    <TABLE BORDER='1'>
      <THEAD>
        <TH>First Name</TH>
        <TH>Last Name</TH>
        <TH>Birth Date</TH>
        <TH>Address</TH>
        <TH>City</TH>
      </THEAD>
      <xsl:for-each select="//Employee">
        <TR>
          <TD><xsl:value-of select="firstName" /></TD>
          <TD><xsl:value-of select="lastName" /></TD>
          <TD><xsl:value-of select="birthDate" /></TD>
          <TD><xsl:value-of select="address" /></TD>
          <TD><xsl:value-of select="city" /></TD>
        </TR>
      </xsl:for-each>
```

```
    </TABLE>
    </HTML>
  </xsl:template>
</xsl:stylesheet>
```

Once you have an .xslt file, applying an XSLT transform is easy. You create an Xsl-Transform object, load the .xslt file into it with its Load method, and finally invoke the Transform method, passing the input XML file and the output XML file as arguments:

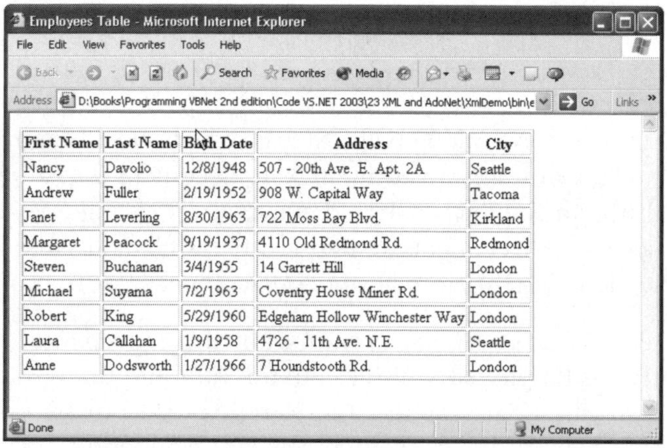

Figure 23-3   An .html file produced by the XslTransform class

Figure 23-3 shows how the resultant employees.html file appears when loaded into Internet Explorer.

```
' Load the XSLT into an XslTransform.
Dim xslTran As New XslTransform()
' Load the .xslt file into it.
xslTran.Load("Employees.xslt")
' Convert the XML file to another XML file. Last argument can be an
' XmlResolver object that resolves URIs to external XML resources.
xslTran.Transform("employees.xml", "employees.html", Nothing)
```

If the input XML data is held in an XmlDocument object rather than in a file, you can use an overloaded version of the Transform method that takes a System.Xml.XPath.XPathNavigator object to indicate the input data and an XmlTextWriter object to indicate where the result must be written. You create the XPathNavigator object using the CreateNavigator method of the XmlDocument class:

```
' Load the XML document.
Dim xmldoc As New XmlDocument()
xmldoc.Load("employees.xml")
' Process the XML data as needed.
⋮
' Create the XslTransform object, and load the .xslt file into it.
Dim xslTran As New XslTransform()
xslTran.Load("Employees.xslt")
```

```
' Open the resultant XML file with an XmlTextWriter object.
Dim xtw As New XmlTextWriter("employees.html", System.Text.Encoding.UTF8)
' Pass the XPathNavigator and XmlTextWriter objects to the Transform method.
' (Last argument can take an XmlResolver object.)
xslTran.Transform(xmldoc.CreateNavigator, Nothing, xtw, Nothing)
xtw.Close()
```

Another overloaded version of the Transform method transforms the DOM contained in an XmlDocument into another XmlDocument; this version takes an XPathNavigator and returns an XmlReader object, which you can pass to the resultant XmlDocument object's Load method:

```
' Load the XML document.
Dim xmldoc As New XmlDocument()
xmldoc.Load("employees.xml")
' Process the XML data as needed.
⋮
' Create the XslTransform object, and load the .xslt file into it.
Dim xslTran As New XslTransform()
xslTran.Load("Employees.xslt")
' Transform the data in the XmlDocument, and get an XmlReader.
Dim xr As XmlReader = xslTran.Transform(xmldoc.CreateNavigator, Nothing)
' Create another XmlDocument that will hold the result.
Dim xmldoc2 As New XmlDocument()
' Load the resultant XML in this XmlDocument using the XmlReader object.
xmldoc2.Load(xr)
xr.Close
' Display the resultant XML in the TreeView object.
DisplayXmlNode(xmldoc2, TreeView1.Nodes)
```

You can use other classes in the System.Xml.Xsl namespace, such as the XmlResolver class, to resolve external references. (XmlResolver objects can be passed to the Transform method of the XmlTransform class, for example.) For more information, read the MSDN documentation.

XML Features in ADO.NET

In this portion of the chapter, I'll describe the XML features supported by ADO.NET and, more specifically, by the DataSet class and its dependent classes. As you'll see in a moment, the contents of a DataSet can be easily saved to and reloaded from an XML file or, more generally, an XML stream. Additionally, you can save the structure of the DataSet to an XML schema.

> **Note**   To keep the code as concise as possible, the following code samples assume the use of the following Imports statements at the file or project level:
>
> ```
> Imports System.Data
> Imports System.Data.OleDb
> Imports System.Data.SqlClient
> Imports System.IO
> ```

Writing XML Data

The main DataSet method for writing XML data is WriteXml. Like most of the methods described in this section, WriteXml is overloaded to take different types of arguments, including a Stream object (and therefore any object that inherits from this class, such as a FileStream), a TextWriter, and an XmlWriter (and therefore any object that inherits from this class, such as an XmlTextWriter):

```
' Save the current contents of the DataSet to C:\Dataset.xml.
' (ds is a DataSet defined and initialized elsewhere.)
ds.WriteXml("C:\dataset.xml")
```

The preceding command saves all the tables in the DataSet in the order in which they appear in the Tables collection. The metadata of the DataSet—that is, the structure of its tables, its relations, and its constraints—isn't saved. For example, consider this code:

```
' Fill a data set with data from two tables.
' (See Chapter 21 for the definition of this and other connection strings.)
Dim cn As New OleDbConnection(OledbPubsConnString)
cn.Open()
Dim daPub As New OleDbDataAdapter("SELECT * FROM Publishers", cn)
Dim daTit As New OleDbDataAdapter("SELECT * FROM Titles", cn)
Dim ds As New DataSet
daPub.Fill(ds, "Publishers")
daTit.Fill(ds, "Titles")
cn.Close()
' Create a relationship between the tables.
ds.Relations.Add("PubTitles", ds.Tables("Publishers").Columns("pub_id"), _
    ds.Tables("Titles").Columns("pub_id"))
ds.WriteXml("ds.xml")
```

This is an abridged version of the ds.xml file that the WriteXml method produces. As you see, the contents of the two tables are listed one after the other, and no schema information is supplied:

```
<?xml version="1.0" standalone="yes"?>
<NewDataSet>
  <Publishers>
    <pub_id>0736</pub_id>
    <pub_name>New Book Books (mod)</pub_name>
    <city>Boston</city>
    <state>MA</state>
    <country>USA</country>
  </Publishers>
    ⋮
  <Publishers>
    <pub_id>9999</pub_id>
    <pub_name>Lucerne P</pub_name>
    <city>Paris</city>
    <country>France</country>
  </Publishers>
  <Titles>
    <title_id>BU1032</title_id>
```

```
   <title>The Busy Executive's Database Guide</title>
   <type>business    </type>
   <pub_id>1389</pub_id>
   <price>19.99</price>
   <advance>5000</advance>
   <royalty>10</royalty>
   <ytd_sales>4095</ytd_sales>
   <notes>An overview of available database systems with emphasis on
       common business applications. Illustrated.</notes>
   <pubdate>1991-06-12T00:00:00.0000000+02:00</pubdate>
  </Titles>
  ⋮
  <Titles>
   <title_id>TC7777</title_id>
   <title>Sushi, Anyone?</title>
   <type>trad_cook    </type>
   <pub_id>0877</pub_id>
   <price>14.99</price>
   <advance>8000</advance>
   <royalty>10</royalty>
   <ytd_sales>4095</ytd_sales>
   <notes>Detailed instructions on how to make authentic
       Japanese sushi in your spare time.</notes>
   <pubdate>1991-06-12T00:00:00.0000000+02:00</pubdate>
  </Titles>
</NewDataSet>
```

Notice that the main node in this output is the name of the DataSet. (NewDataSet is the default value for the DataSetName property.) You can affect the output in several ways—for example, by assigning a value to the Namespace and Prefix properties of the DataSet, DataTable, and DataColumn objects. Or you can create a treelike structure by setting the Nested property of existing relationships to True:

```
ds.Relations("PubTitles").Nested = True
ds.WriteXml("ds.xml")
```

This is the kind of result you obtain with nested relationships:

```
<?xml version="1.0" standalone="yes"?>
<NewDataSet>
  <Publishers>
    <pub_id>0736</pub_id>
    <pub_name>New Book Books (mod)</pub_name>
    <city>Boston</city>
    <state>MA</state>
    <country>USA</country>

    <Titles>
      <title_id>BU2075</title_id>
      <title>You Can Combat Computer Stress!</title>
      ⋮
    </Titles>
    ⋮
  </Publishers>
  <Publishers>
```

```
      <pub_id>0877</pub_id>
      <pub_name>Binnet &amp;</pub_name>
      <city>Washington</city>
      <state>DC</state>
      <country>USA</country>
      <Titles>
        <title_id>MC2222</title_id>
        <title>Silicon Valley Gastronomic Treats</title>
          ⋮
      </Titles>
        ⋮
    </Publishers>
    <Publishers>
      ⋮
    </Publishers>
</NewDataSet>
```

The ColumnMapping property of the DataColumn class lets you customize the output even more. This property is a MappingType enumerated value that can be Element (the default), Attribute (the column is mapped to an XmlAttribute node), SimpleContent (the column is mapped to an XmlText node), or Hidden (the column doesn't appear in the XML output). For example, consider this code:

```
' Set the ColumnMapping property for some columns.
With ds.Tables("Publishers")
    .Columns("pub_id").ColumnMapping = MappingType.Attribute
    .Columns("country").ColumnMapping = MappingType.Hidden
End With
```

This is the XML text produced for a row in the Publishers table:

```
<Publishers pub_id="0736">
    <pub_name>New Book Books</pub_name>
    <city>Boston</city>
    <state>MA</state>
</Publishers>
```

The GetXml method returns the XML that you would write to disk with the WriteXml method:

```
Dim xml As String = ds.GetXml()
```

The only relevant difference in the output produced by the WriteXml method is that GetXml doesn't produce the <?xml> processing instruction at the beginning of the XML text.

Writing the Schema and the DiffGram

Unlike the GetXml method, all the overloaded versions of WriteXml take an additional (optional) XmlWriteMode argument, which can be one of the following values: IgnoreSchema (default, doesn't write the schema), WriteSchema (writes the schema and the table data), or DiffGram (writes the current contents of the DataSet but preserves information about rows that were modified since the most recent AcceptChanges method).

For example, the following statement produces an XML file that contains both the DataSet data and its schema:

```
ds.WriteXml("ds.xml", XmlWriteMode.WriteSchema)
```

This is a condensed version of the resultant file. (I added a blank line between the schema and the data section.)

```
<?xml version="1.0" standalone="yes"?>
<NewDataSet>
  <xs:schema id="NewDataSet" xmlns=""
      xmlns:xs="http://www.w3.org/2001/XMLSchema"
      xmlns:msdata="urn:schemas-microsoft-com:xml-msdata">
    <xs:element name="NewDataSet" msdata:IsDataSet="true">
      <xs:complexType>
        <xs:choice maxOccurs="unbounded">
          <xs:element name="Publishers">
            <xs:complexType>
              <xs:sequence>
                <xs:element name="pub_id" type="xs:string" minOccurs="0" />
                <xs:element name="pub_name" type="xs:string" minOccurs="0" />
                <xs:element name="city" type="xs:string" minOccurs="0" />
                <xs:element name="state" type="xs:string" minOccurs="0" />
                <xs:element name="country" type="xs:string" minOccurs="0" />
              </xs:sequence>
            </xs:complexType>
          </xs:element>
          <xs:element name="Titles">
            <xs:complexType>
              <xs:sequence>
                <xs:element name="title_id" type="xs:string" minOccurs="0" />
                <xs:element name="title" type="xs:string" minOccurs="0" />
                <xs:element name="type" type="xs:string" minOccurs="0" />
                <xs:element name="pub_id" type="xs:string" minOccurs="0" />
                <xs:element name="price" type="xs:decimal" minOccurs="0" />
                <xs:element name="advance" type="xs:decimal" minOccurs="0" />
                <xs:element name="royalty" type="xs:int" minOccurs="0" />
                <xs:element name="ytd_sales" type="xs:int" minOccurs="0" />
                <xs:element name="notes" type="xs:string" minOccurs="0" />
                <xs:element name="pubdate" type="xs:dateTime" minOccurs="0" />
              </xs:sequence>
            </xs:complexType>
          </xs:element>
        </xs:choice>
      </xs:complexType>
      <xs:unique name="Constraint1">
        <xs:selector xpath=".//Publishers" />
        <xs:field xpath="pub_id" />
      </xs:unique>
      <xs:keyref name="PubTitles" refer="Constraint1">
        <xs:selector xpath=".//Titles" />
        <xs:field xpath="pub_id" />
      </xs:keyref>
    </xs:element>
  </xs:schema>
```

```
    <Publishers>
    ⋮
    </Publishers>
    <Titles>
    ⋮
    </Titles>
</NewDataSet>
```

You can also write only the schema (without the data) by using the WriteXmlSchema method. Like WriteXml, the WriteXmlSchema method can take a filename, a Stream, a TextWriter, or an XmlWriter object:

```
ds.WriteXmlSchema("ds.xml")
```

You can retrieve only the schema with the GetXmlSchema method:

```
Dim xml As String = ds.GetXmlSchema
```

A DiffGram is a piece of XML that describes changes in a DataSet. Consider the following code:

```
' Make some changes to the Titles table.
With ds.Tables("Titles")
    ' Delete the first row.
    .Rows(0).Delete()
    ' Modify two fields in the second row.
    .Rows(1)("price") = 49.99
    .Rows(1)("advance") = 12300
    ' Insert a new row.
    Dim dr As DataRow = .NewRow
    dr("title") = "Programming VB .NET"
    dr("type") = "technical"
    dr("price") = 59.99
End With
' Write only the changed rows to disk.
ds.WriteXml("ds.xml", XmlWriteMode.DiffGram)
```

This is the resultant XML DiffGram. (The most important differences are in boldface.)

```
<?xml version="1.0" standalone="yes"?>
<diffgr:diffgram xmlns:msdata="urn:schemas-microsoft-com:xml-msdata"
    xmlns:diffgr="urn:schemas-microsoft-com:xml-diffgram-v1">
  <NewDataSet>
    <Publishers diffgr:id="Publishers1" msdata:rowOrder="0">
      <pub_id>0736</pub_id>
      <pub_name>New Book Books (mod)</pub_name>
      <city>Boston</city>
      <state>MA</state>
      <country>USA</country>
    </Publishers>
    <Publishers diffgr:id="Publishers2" msdata:rowOrder="1">
      ⋮
    </Publishers>
    ⋮
```

```
    </Publishers>
    <Titles diffgr:id="Titles2" msdata:rowOrder="1"
            diffgr:hasChanges="modified">
      <title_id>BU1111</title_id>
      <title>Cooking with Computers: Surreptitious Balance Sheets</title>
      <type>business    </type>
      <pub_id>1389</pub_id>
      <price>49.99</price>
      <advance>12300</advance>
      <royalty>10</royalty>
      <ytd_sales>3876</ytd_sales>
      <notes>Helpful hints on how to use your electronic resources
          to the best advantage.</notes>
      <pubdate>1991-06-09T00:00:00.0000000+02:00</pubdate>
    </Titles>
    <Titles diffgr:id="Titles3" msdata:rowOrder="2">
      ⋮
    </Titles>
    ⋮
    <Titles diffgr:id="Titles19" msdata:rowOrder="18"
          diffgr:hasChanges="inserted">
      <title>Programming VB .NET</title>
      <type>technical</type>
      <price>59.99</price>
    </Titles>
  </NewDataSet>

  <diffgr:before>
    <Titles diffgr:id="Titles1" msdata:rowOrder="0">
      <title_id>BU1032</title_id>
      <title>The Busy Executive's Database Guide***</title>
      <type>business    </type>
      <pub_id>1389</pub_id>
      <price>19.99</price>
      <advance>5000</advance>
      <royalty>10</royalty>
      <ytd_sales>4095</ytd_sales>
      <notes>An overview of available database systems with
          emphasis on common business applications. Illustrated.</notes>
      <pubdate>1991-06-12T00:00:00.0000000+02:00</pubdate>
    </Titles>
    <Titles diffgr:id="Titles2" msdata:rowOrder="1">
      <title_id>BU1111</title_id>
      <title>Cooking with Computers: Surreptitious Balance Sheets</title>
      <type>business    </type>
      <pub_id>1389</pub_id>
      <price>11.95</price>
      <advance>5000</advance>
      <royalty>10</royalty>
      <ytd_sales>3876</ytd_sales>
      <notes>Helpful hints on how to use your electronic resources
          to the best advantage.</notes>
      <pubdate>1991-06-09T00:00:00.0000000+02:00</pubdate>
    </Titles>
  </diffgr:before>
</diffgr:diffgram>
```

When you write a DiffGram, all rows are marked with a unique ID so that it's possible to compare the current state of the DataSet (which is found near the beginning of the XML file) and its state before any change was applied (as described in the <diffgr:before> section). Here's how the modified rows have been reflected in the DiffGram:

1. The first row in the Titles table appears in the <diffgr:before> section but doesn't appear in the first section because it has been deleted.

2. The second row is marked in the first section with the diffgr:hasChanges attribute set to the "modified" value. The original version of this row can be found in the <diffgr:before> section; the correspondence between the two versions is provided by the msdata:rowOrder attribute.

3. The new row appears in the current section with a diffgr:hasChanged attribute set to the "inserted" value.

If you want only the DiffGram related to changed rows and you aren't interested in records that haven't changed, you can use the DataSet's GetChanges method before saving it to file:

```
Dim ds2 As DataSet = ds.GetChanges()
ds2.WriteXmlSchema("ds.xml")
```

Reading XML Data and Schema

The ReadXml method can read XML data into a DataSet. It can take a filename, a Stream, a TextReader, or an XmlReader object (or any object that inherits from it, such as an XmlTextReader object). Each of these overloaded versions can take a second, optional, XmlReadMode argument that can be one of the following values:

- **DiffGram**   Reads a DiffGram and applies all the changes to the DataSet, behaving as the Merge method. If the schema of the data being read is different from the DataSet's schema, an exception is thrown.

- **IgnoreSchema**   Ignores any schema embedded in the XML and reads only the data. If the data being read doesn't match the DataSet's schema (including data from different namespaces), the data in excess is discarded. If the XML being read is a DiffGram, this option behaves as the preceding one does.

- **ReadSchema**   Reads any inline schema and then loads the data. New tables can be added to the DataSet, but an exception is thrown if the schema defines a table already in the DataSet.

- **InferSchema**   Ignores any inline schema, deduces the schema from the data, and loads the data into the DataSet. The DataSet can be extended with new tables or new columns, but an exception is thrown if the new columns conflict with the existing ones or if the inferred new table exists already in another namespace.

- **Fragment**   Reads XML documents such as those produced by a SQL Server's FOR XML query.

- **Auto**   The ReadXml method understands the structure of the data being read and behaves as if the DiffGram, ReadSchema, or InferSchema value was specified. (This is the default behavior.)

Here are a few examples:

```
' Write a DataSet as XML, and load it into another DataSet.
ds.WriteXml("ds.xml")
Dim ds2 As New DataSet
ds2.ReadXml("ds.xml")

' Create a new DataSet that has the same schema as the current one.
ds.WriteXmlSchema("ds.xml")
Dim ds3 As New DataSet
ds3.ReadXml("ds.xml", XmlReadMode.ReadSchema)
```

The ability to read the schema of a DataSet from an XML file can be useful for reducing the number of round trips to the server. For example, say that you're creating a data-entry application that lets end users add new rows to a database table using a DataGrid control bound to a DataSet. You can initialize the DataSet by using the ReadXml method with the ReadSchema option to read the schema from a local XML file without using a DataAdapter's FillSchema method (which requires an open connection).

Strongly Typed DataSets

ADO.NET allows you to create a strongly typed DataSet object that exposes its tables as properties instead of members of the Tables collection. Similarly, a field in a DataRow can be accessed as a member with a given name rather than by the passing of a numeric index or a string to the Item property. To understand the difference this can make to your coding style, consider the code that you typically write to access a column in a DataSet table:

```
value = ds.Tables("Publishers").Rows(0).Item("pub_id")
```

Now see how you can rewrite the same assignment if you're working with a strongly typed DataSet:

```
value = ds.Publishers(0).pub_id
```

Strongly typed DataSet objects offer several advantages. First and foremost, you can write more concise and robust code because it will never fail over a typo in the name of a table or a field. Second, you can write code faster thanks to the support from IntelliSense when inside Visual Studio .NET. Third, you have more control over how the DataSet is saved as XML by adding custom attributes, as I'll explain in the section "XML Serialization" later in this chapter. Fourth, you can drop a strongly typed DataSet on a form and bind a control to a specific field in one of its tables at design time.

You can create a strongly typed DataSet from inside Visual Studio .NET (as I'll explain later in this chapter) or manually using the XSD utility that comes with the .NET Framework SDK. (You can find this utility in the C:\Program Files\Microsoft Visual Studio .NET 2003\SDK\v1.1\Bin folder.) To see how the manual approach works, after changing the DataSetName property to the name of the class that you want to create, create the schema for the DataSet using the WriteXmlSchema method:

```
ds.DataSetName = "PubsDataSet"
ds.WriteXmlSchema("pubs.xsd")
```

Next, run the XSD utility on the .xsd file just produced, using the following syntax:

```
XSD /d /l:VB pubs.xsd
```

The XSD utility creates a pubs.vb file in the current directory, so you can now add this file to the current project and browse it. The pubs.vb file is too long for all of its contents to be published here, so I'll just display the more interesting sections:

```
Public Class PubsDataSet
    Inherits DataSet

    Private tablePublishers As PublishersDataTable
    Private tableTitles As TitlesDataTable
    Private relationPubTitles As DataRelation

    Public ReadOnly Property Publishers As PublishersDataTable
        Get
            Return Me.tablePublishers
        End Get
    End Property

    Public ReadOnly Property Titles As TitlesDataTable
        Get
            Return Me.tableTitles
        End Get
    End Property
    :
    Public Class PublishersDataTable
        Inherits DataTable
        Implements System.Collections.IEnumerable

        Private columnpub_id As DataColumn
        Private columnpub_name As DataColumn
        Private columncity As DataColumn
        Private columnstate As DataColumn
        Private columncountry As DataColumn
        :
    End Class
    :
End Class
```

As you can see, a strongly typed DataSet is nothing more than a class that inherits from System.Data.DataSet and that includes several nested classes. (You can use the Class

View window to explore the structure of this class.) Now you can code against this class using its strongly typed nature:

```
Dim pubsDs As New PubsDataSet()
' Add a new row to the Publishers table.
Dim pubsRow As PubsDataSet.PublishersRow = pubsDs.Publishers.NewPublishersRow
pubsRow.pub_id = "1234"
pubsRow.pub_name = "VB2TheMax"
pubsRow.city = "Bari"
pubsRow.country = "Italy"
pubsDs.Publishers.AddPublishersRow(pubsRow)
```

The strongly typed DataSet defines one Is*xxx*Null function and one Set*xxx*Null method for each column. The former tests whether a field is DBNull; the latter stores a DBNull value in a column:

```
' If the city column is null, set the country column to null as well.
If pubsDs.Publishers(0).IscityNull Then
    pubsDs.Publishers(0).SetcountryNull()
End If
```

The XmlDataDocument Class

The DataSet and the XmlDocument classes are two different ways to store data. The DataSet is the better choice for relational structures, whereas the XmlDocument class (and the XML DOM in general) excels at describing hierarchical data. The relational and XML-like hierarchical worlds have always been completely distinct; traditionally, you had to decide the structure that fits your needs better in the early stages of development. However, the .NET Framework gives you a degree of freedom that was previously inconceivable in that you can process a relational set of data stored in a DataSet using a hierarchical approach when necessary.

This little magic is made possible by the XmlDataDocument class. This class derives from XmlDocument, so it inherits all the properties and methods that you're already familiar with. Usually you create an XmlDataDocument object by passing a DataSet to its constructor method, as in this code snippet:

```
Dim cn As New OleDbConnection(OledbPubsConnString)
Dim daPubs As New OleDbDataAdapter("SELECT * FROM Publishers", cn)
Dim daTitles As New OleDbDataAdapter("SELECT * FROM Titles", cn)
Dim ds As New DataSet

' Fill the DataSet with data from two tables.
cn.Open()
daPubs.Fill(ds, "Publishers")
daTitles.Fill(ds, "Titles")
cn.Close()

' Create a (nested) relationship between the two tables.
Dim rel As New DataRelation("PubsTitles", _
```

```
        ds.Tables("Publishers").Columns("pub_id"), _
        ds.Tables("Titles").Columns("pub_id"))
ds.Relations.Add(rel)
rel.Nested = True

' Associate an XmlDataDocument with the DataSet.
Dim xdd As New XmlDataDocument(ds)
```

After the association has been created, any change in the DataSet is reflected in the XmlDataDocument object, and vice versa. (See Figure 23-4.) For example, you can indirectly insert a new row into a DataTable by adding an appropriate set of nodes to the XmlDataDocument. The only (obvious) requirement is that you add only XML elements that fit in the DataSet schema and that don't violate any null, unique, or relational constraint. Since you add one element at a time, the only way to avoid an exception when adding a row is by temporarily setting EnforceConstraints to False. This code uses the CreateAppendElement helper routine (defined earlier in this chapter) to add a row to the Publishers table:

```
' Before proceeding, you must set EnforceConstraints to False.
ds.EnforceConstraints = False
' It is advisable to normalize before any XML operation.
xdd.Normalize()
' Add a new node to the XmlDataElement.
Dim xmlEl As XmlElement
xmlEl = CreateAppendElement(xdd.DocumentElement, "Publishers")
CreateAppendElement(xmlEl, "pub_id", "9997")
CreateAppendElement(xmlEl, "pub_name", "Sci-Fi Publications")
CreateAppendElement(xmlEl, "city", "Boston")
CreateAppendElement(xmlEl, "state", "MA")
CreateAppendElement(xmlEl, "country", "USA")
' Reenable constraints.
ds.EnforceConstraints = True
```

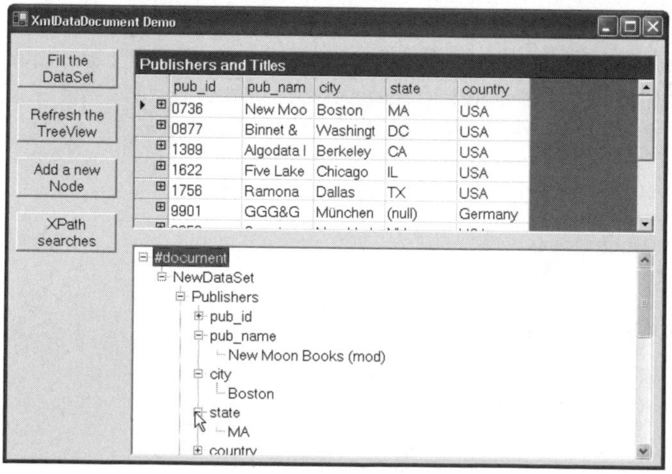

Figure 23-4   An XmlDataDocument is a synchronized hierarchical view of a DataSet.

You see the great benefits in accessing the DataSet using a hierarchical structure when performing complex queries. For example, this code uses the SelectNodes method to display the list of all the titles published by publishers based in Boston:

```
' This is the XPath search expression.
' (Note that node name matches are case sensitive.)
Dim xpath As String = "//Publishers[city = 'Boston']/Titles/title/text()"
Dim xnl As XmlNodeList = xdd.SelectNodes(xpath)
For Each xt As XmlText In xnl
    Debug.WriteLine(xt.Value)
Next
```

The XmlDataDocument object adds only three members to those defined in the base XmlDocument class, namely:

- The DataSet read-only property, which returns a reference to the associated DataSet instance.

- The GetElementFromRow method, which takes a DataRow object and returns the corresponding XmlElement object in the DOM.

- The GetRowFromElement method, which takes an XmlElement object and returns the corresponding DataRow in the DataSet.

For example, the following code snippet applies the GetRowFromElement method to the result of a SelectSingleNode method:

```
' This XPath expression searches for the Publishers XML element
' that has a title descendant whose text is 'Net Etiquette.'
Dim xpath As String = "//Publishers[Titles/title/text() = 'Net Etiquette']"
' Get the only XmlNode that matches the expression, and cast it to XmlElement.
Dim xmlEl As XmlElement = DirectCast(xdd.SelectSingleNode(xpath), XmlElement)
' Retrieve the corresponding DataRow.
Dim dr As DataRow = xdd.GetRowFromElement(xmlEl)
' Display the name and the city of this publisher.
Debug.WriteLine("Name = " & dr("pub_name"))
Debug.WriteLine("City = " & dr("city"))
```

ADO.NET and Visual Studio .NET

In Chapter 22, I explained all the features of ADO.NET in disconnected mode, and in this chapter I introduced strongly typed DataSets. By now you should be convinced that ADO.NET is quite powerful and flexible, even though you pay for this flexibility by writing a lot of code. The good news is that Visual Studio .NET is able to write most of this code on your behalf.

Creating Connections and DataAdapters

Many of the database capabilities of Visual Studio .NET revolve around the Server Explorer window and require that you define a connection to a database, by clicking on the Connect to Database button on the Server Explorer's toolbar. The following description refines a few concepts introduced in the section "ADO.NET Data Binding" in Chapter 16.

Create a connection to the Pubs database, and then open the Tables node and drag the Publishers table onto a form's designer. This operation creates two objects in the component tray: SqlConnection1 and SqlDataAdapter1. (The same operation would create an OleDbConnection and an OleDbDataAdapter if performed on a table belonging to a Microsoft Access database.) To improve readability of the code that Visual Studio produces, change the names of the components to cnPubs and daPublishers. Add a Data-Grid control and two push buttons that the end user can click to load and save records in the Publishers table. (See Figure 23-5.)

Next, create a strongly typed DataSet that contains a Publisher table, by selecting the daPublishers object and then clicking on the Generate Dataset link near the bottom of the Properties window. This command is available also in the Data menu and in the DataAdapter's context menu.

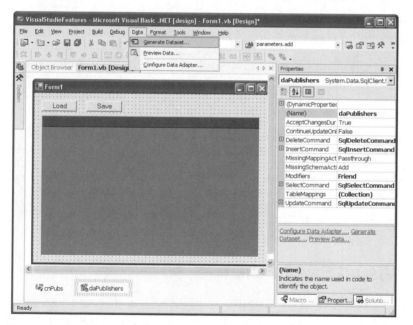

Figure 23-5 Dropping a DataAdapter and its Connection object onto a form's surface

The Generate Dataset window is where you assign a name to the strongly typed DataSet you're about to create. (See Figure 23-6.) Type **dsPubs** in the New field and click OK. Visual Studio .NET adds a new file named dsPubs.xds to the current solution and adds an instance of the dsPubs class (named DsPubs1) to the form's component tray.

Now you can bind the DataGrid control to the Publishers table. Select the DataGrid, switch to the Properties window, and select DsPubs1 as the value of the DataSource property and Publishers as the value of the DataMember property. (You must assign these two properties in this order.) The final step is to write one statement for the btnLoad and btnSave push buttons:

```
Private Sub btnLoad_Click(ByVal sender As Object, ByVal e As EventArgs)
    Handles btnLoad.Click
      daPublishers.Fill(DsPubs1.publishers)
End Sub

Private Sub btnSave_Click(ByVal sender As Object, ByVal e As EventArgs)
    Handles btnSave.Click
      daPublishers.Update(DsPubs1.publishers)
End Sub
```

With just two handwritten statements, you create a form that lets users read and update a database table!

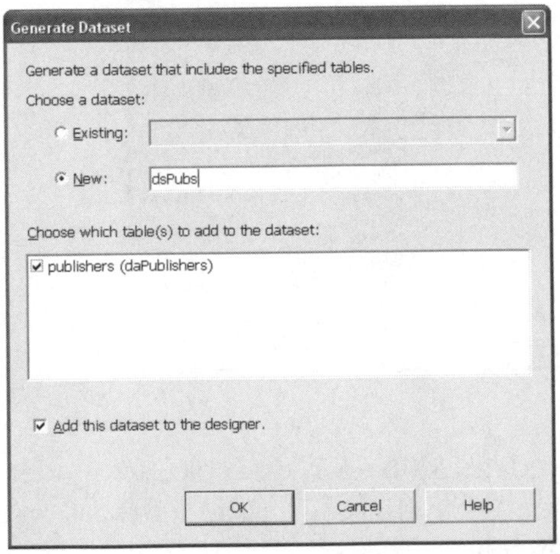

Figure 23-6 The Generate Dataset dialog box

Designing Strongly Typed DataSet Classes

You can create a strongly typed DataSet without starting with a DataAdapter, by invoking the Add New Item command from the Project menu and selecting DataSet from the template gallery. Regardless of how you create the DataSet, you end up with a new .xsd file in the project. If you switch to the Solution Explorer and double-click on this file, you can edit the schema of the DataSet in a graphic fashion, as shown in Figure 23-7. This diagram view lets you perform many interesting operations on the XML schema using a RAD approach—for example, you can:

■ Add a new table patterned after an existing database table by dragging the latter from the Server Explorer window to the DataSet's designer. (I used this technique to create the Titles table in Figure 23-7.)

■ Add a new table and define its elements manually with the New Element command from the Add submenu in the Schema top-level menu. (This command is also available in the context menu of the DataSet designer.)

■ Add new elements to a table in the DataSet by pointing to Add on the Schema menu and clicking New Element. Figure 23-7 shows a new element, DiscountedPrice, added to the Titles table. Notice that DiscountedPrice is a calculated column (as you can see from the corresponding Expression element in the Properties window).

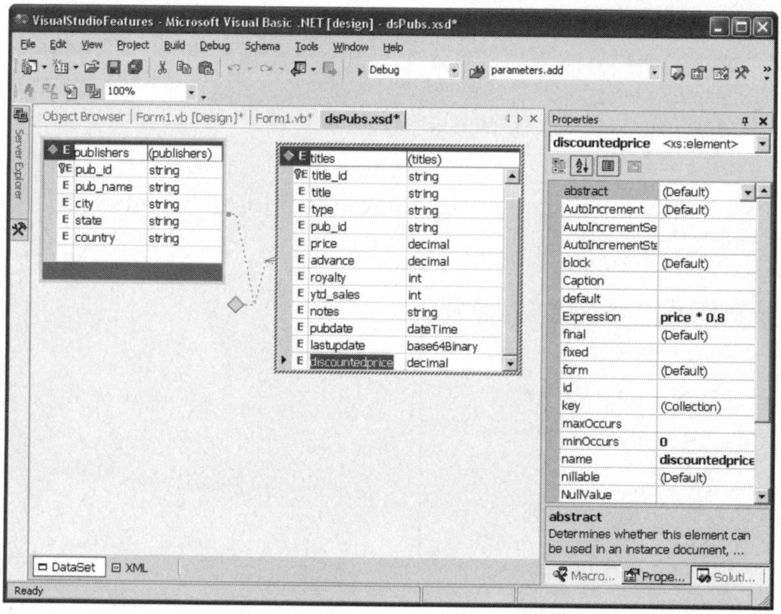

Figure 23-7   The DataSet designer

■ Change the way a field is rendered in XML—for example, to render it as an attribute instead of an XML element—by clicking in the leftmost column and selecting an item from the drop-down list.

■ Create a relationship between two tables by selecting the two tables, pointing to Add on the Schemu menu, and then clicking Add Relation. (You can also reach this command from the shortcut menu of a table in the schema.) This command brings up the Edit Relation dialog box. Ensure that the relationship is between the primary key in the parent table and the foreign key in the child table and determine the behavior to be applied when a row in the parent table is modified or deleted. Enter all these values as shown in Figure 23-8, and click OK to enforce the relationship. The two tables will appear connected in the schema.

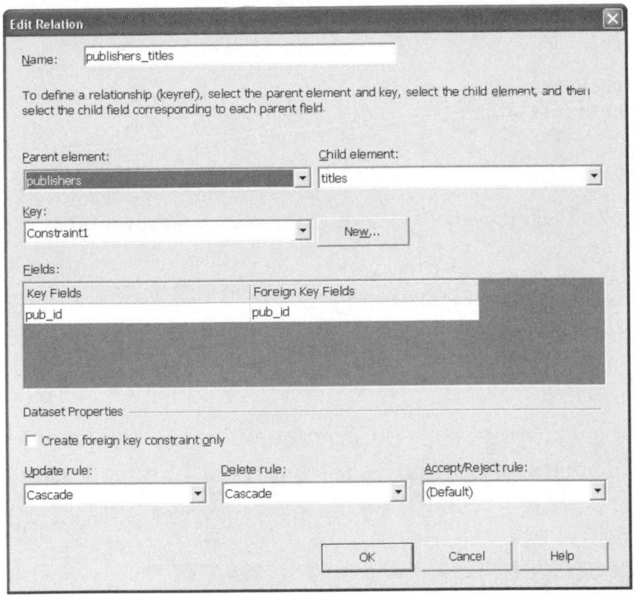

Figure 23-8   Creating a relationship between two tables in the DataSet schema

■ Alternate between the DataSet view and the XML view by clicking buttons near the bottom of the XSD designer. For example, you can use the XML view of the schema to alter the order of the columns in each DataTable, which affects the order in which fields are shown in a DataGrid control.

Remember to save the .xsd file to have Visual Studio .NET regenerate the source code of the dsPubs class.

Working with Table Relations

Now let's see how you can take advantage of the publishers_title relation in the dsPubs class. Go back to the main form, and set the DataGrid's AllowNavigation property to False. Next, create a second DataGrid control below the first one, bind it to the DsPubs1 component, and set its DataMember property equal to publishers.publishers_titles. (It is essential that the DataMember property points to this relation, not to the Titles table.) Finally, drag the Titles table from the Server Explorer window to the form's designer, and rename the resulting DataAdapter as daTitles.

Now you're working with two tables instead of one, so it's more convenient to open and close the connection manually:

```
Private Sub btnLoad_Click(ByVal sender As Object, ByVal e As EventArgs)
    Handles btnLoad.Click
    cnPubs.Open()
    daPublishers.Fill(DsPubs1.publishers)
    daTitles.Fill(DsPubs1.titles)
    cnPubs.Close()
End Sub

Private Sub btnSave_Click(ByVal sender As Object, ByVal e As EventArgs)
    Handles btnSave.Click
    cnPubs.Open()
    daPublishers.Update(DsPubs1.publishers)
    daTitles.Update(DsPubs1.titles)
    cnPubs.Close()
End Sub
```

The result is shown in Figure 23-9. If you now click on the Publishers DataGrid, the Titles DataGrid is automatically updated to display all and only the titles for the selected publisher.

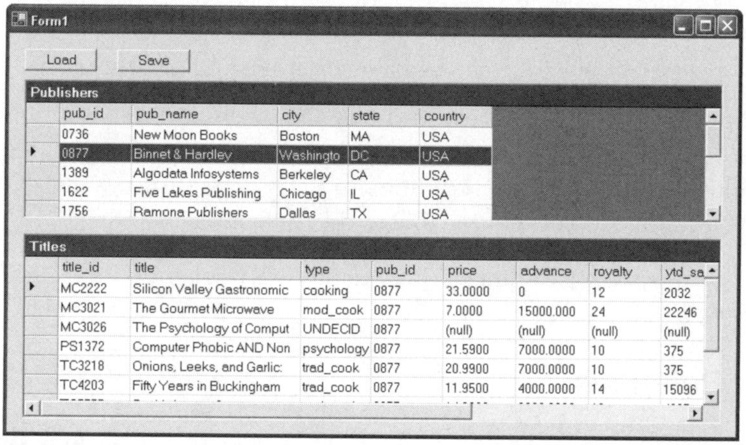

Figure 23-9   Two DataGrid controls in a master-detail relationship

Configuring a DataAdapter

You configure a DataAdapter from inside the Properties window or, more frequently, by clicking on the Configure Data Adapter link near the bottom edge of that window to start the Data Adapter Configuration Wizard. After the welcome page, you select which connection the DataAdapter will use in the wizard's second page.

The third page in this wizard is where you decide whether you want to interact with the database table by means of plain SQL statements, new stored procedures, or existing stored procedures. (See Figure 23-10.) In the following page, you can edit the basic SELECT that is used to retrieve the records, and you can also click on the Query Builder button to define the query in a graphical fashion. (See Figure 23-11, left.) The window that you bring up by clicking on the Advanced Options button is probably the least understood dialog box in Visual Studio .NET. (See Figure 23-11, right.)

If you clear the Generate Insert, Update, and Delete statements option, the wizard will configure only the DataAdapter's SelectCommand property, and the remaining options on this page are disabled. If you clear the Use Optimistic Concurrency statements option, Visual Studio generates UPDATE and DELETE statements whose WHERE clause contains only the primary key value, as in:

```
DELETE titles WHERE title_id=@title_id
```

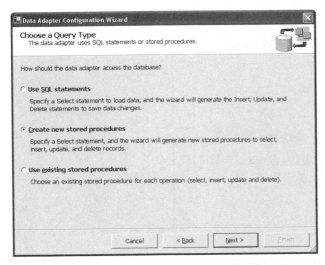

Figure 23-10   The Data Adapter Configuration Wizard

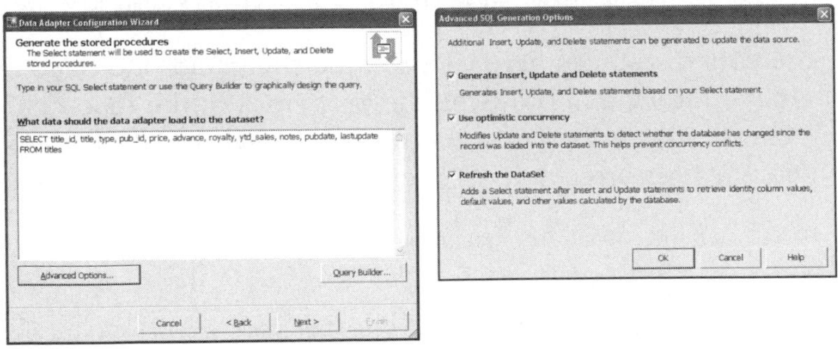

Figure 23-11   The wizard lets you edit the SELECT query (left) and select a few advanced options (right).

As you know from previous chapters, a statement like this enforces the last-one-wins update strategy, and updates don't fail if another user has modified the record in the meantime.

The last option in this window, Refresh the DataSet, causes a SELECT to be appended to the UPDATE and INSERT commands, so that your application can read the value of fields that are assigned by the database engine—for example, identity and calculated fields. The neat result is what you learned to do in the section "Working with Identity Columns" in Chapter 22, but without writing all the necessary code manually.

If you decide to use stored procedures instead of plain SQL statements, the wizard displays one more page, shown in Figure 23-12. Here, you assign a name to the four stored procedures corresponding to the SelectCommand, DeleteCommand, Update-Command, and InsertCommand properties, and you can have them created automatically by Visual Studio .NET. This is an incredible time saver.

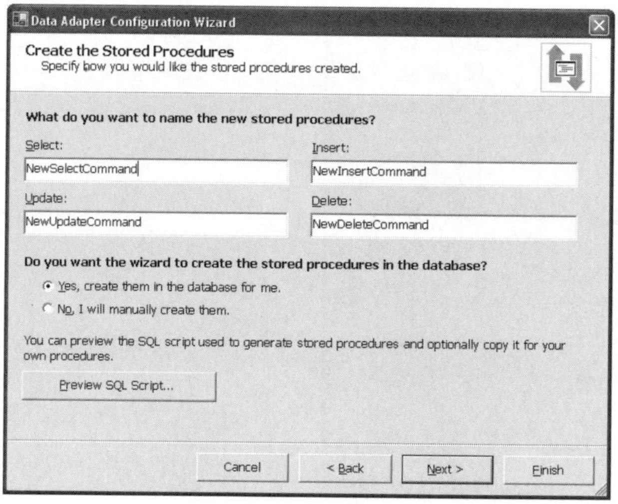

Figure 23-12   You can assign a name to the stored procedures that Visual Studio .NET creates for you.

After you close the wizard, you can have a look at the commands it created by switching to the Properties window and browsing the properties of the four xxxCommand properties. For example, this is the UpdateCommand created for the Publishers table, with the Use Optimistic Concurrency and Refresh the DataSet options selected:

```
UPDATE publishers SET pub_id = @pub_id, pub_name = @pub_name,
    city = @city, state = @state, country = @country
WHERE (pub_id = @Original_pub_id)
    AND (city = @Original_city OR @Original_city IS NULL AND city IS NULL)
    AND (country = @Original_country OR @Original_country IS NULL AND country IS NULL)

    AND (pub_name = @Original_pub_name OR
    @Original_pub_name IS NULL AND pub_name IS NULL)
    AND (state = @Original_state OR @Original_state IS NULL AND state IS NULL);
SELECT pub_id, pub_name, city, state, country FROM publishers
    WHERE (pub_id = @pub_id)
```

More Design-Time Components

Dropping a Connection or a DataAdapter object from the Server Explorer window isn't the only way to create an ADO.NET component at design time; you can also use the objects on the Data tab in the Toolbox. (See Figure 23-13.) This is necessary, for example, to create a connection to SQL Server using an OleDbConnection or an OdbcConnection. (Dragging from a SQL Server table in the Server Explorer window always creates a SqlConnection object.)

The Data tab contains two objects that you can't drop from the Server Explorer window: the untyped DataSet and the DataView. The former isn't very interesting, as you can't define data binding at design time against an untyped DataSet, so let me focus on DataView objects.

You typically drop a DataView on a form if the form already contains a typed DataSet. In this case, you can assign the DataView's Table property so that it points to a specific table in the DataSet, as shown in Figure 23-13. You typically use a DataView instead of a DataTable when you want to filter data or apply a sort criterion. For example, you might set the RowStateFilter property to Deleted to see all the rows that were deleted in the main DataTable, a setting that might be useful to display which deleted records caused an update conflict. You can also set the AllowDelete, AllowEdit, and AllowNew properties to limit what the end user can do in a DataGrid control bound to this DataView.

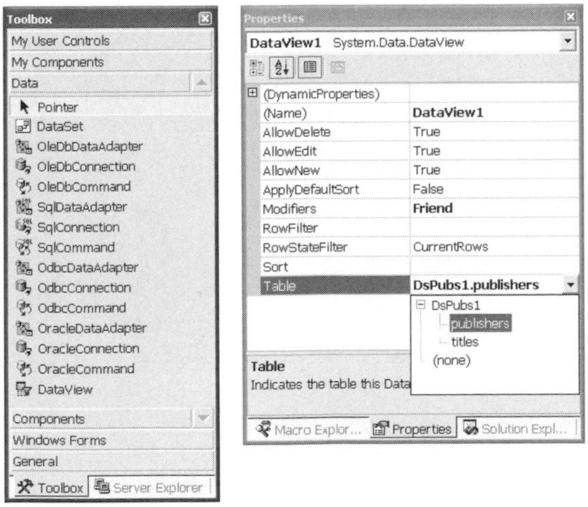

Figure 23-13   You can drop a DataView component from the Data tab in the Toolbox (left) and connect it to a DataTable at design time (right).

> **See Also**   The .NET Framework gives you the ability to serialize an object to XML while remaining in control of how each property is rendered. The "XML Serialization.doc" file on the companion CD explains how to take advantage of this feature and how to use the xsd.exe tool to share data easily among applications from different vendors (including applications running on different platforms).

This chapter concludes the part of the book devoted to database and XML techniques. You've seen that the Visual Basic .NET way of handling data in disconnected mode is different from anything you learned in the past, so you'll probably have to redesign most of your existing applications when moving them to the .NET Framework, especially if you made heavy use of server-side cursors. Although you can still use classic ADO through the COM Interop layer, switching to ADO.NET gives you much better integration with other .NET features—for example, data binding. This is especially true when working with Web Forms and Web services, which I'll cover in the next portion of this book.

Part VI
Internet Applications

24 Web Forms and Controls

ASP.NET is the portion of the .NET Framework that lets you create Internet applications. It was the first part of the Framework to be completed, and to many developers it's still the most innovative part of the .NET initiative. ASP.NET comprises two different but closely related technologies:

- Web Forms, for creating Internet applications with user interfaces that can be accessed via a browser. These are the heirs to Active Server Pages (ASP) applications.

- Web services, for creating nonbrowsable Internet applications that can be accessed only programmatically.

In this and in the next four chapters, I'll explain Web Forms applications; I'll cover Web services in Chapter 29. Version 1.1 of the .NET Framework introduced support for mobile controls and ASP.NET applications browsable from handheld devices, but I won't cover those new features in this book.

You must have Windows 2000 or later with Internet Information Services (IIS) installed to develop ASP.NET applications. It's advisable that IIS be installed before installing the .NET Framework for ASP.NET to work correctly. In some cases you can fix a malfunctioning ASP.NET installation by running the aspnet_iisreg.exe utility. (You can read more about this utility in the "Managing Multiple ASP.NET Versions" section in Chapter 27.)

> **Note** To keep the code as concise as possible, all the code samples in this chapter assume the use of the following Imports statements at the file or project level:
>
> ```
> Imports System.Diagnostics
> Imports System.Data
> Imports System.Data.OleDb
> ```

Basic Web Forms Concepts

At installation time, the .NET Framework registers several new file extensions with Internet Information Services (IIS). One of these extensions is .aspx, which identifies a Web Forms page. When a client browser requests a file with this extension, the aspnet_isapi.dll component is loaded in memory (if not already loaded) and processes the request. Because they use a different file extension, Web Forms applications (and ASP.NET applications in general) can coexist on the same IIS with older ASP sites.

As with all types of .NET applications, the .NET Framework comes with all the tools you need to create Web Forms applications, so in theory you can get along with just an editor as simple as Notepad. In practice, however, you'll want to use Visual Studio .NET and its integrated tools for most real applications, as you'll see countless times while reading this chapter.

Your First Web Forms Project

Load Visual Studio .NET, point to New on the File menu, and choose Project; this series of actions brings up the familiar New Project dialog box. (See Figure 24-1.) When you select the ASP.NET Web Application icon, however, the Name field is grayed and the Location field contains something like *http://localhost/WebApplication1*, where WebApplication1 is the name of a subdirectory under the main directory for IIS projects (c:\inetpub\wwwroot for a default installation). You can specify the name of any virtual IIS directory in the default IIS Web site or in another Web site hosted on the local machine. For your first Web Forms application, you can change this location to *http://localhost/FirstWebForm*. When you click OK, Visual Studio creates a new project in the directory you specified. The project contains several new types of files:

- The WebForm1.aspx file is an empty ASP.NET Web Forms page on which you can drop controls and components. (The components go to the component tray area, as with Windows Forms.)

- AssemblyInfo.vb is the usual source code file that contains all the assembly attributes.

- Global.asax is the first file loaded when the application starts. It contains event handlers that are executed when a new client connects to the application and any time a new request is posted. (It has the same function as the Global.asa file in classic ASP applications.)

- Styles.css is the stylesheet used by default for all the pages in this application. By editing this file, you can modify how common HTML tags are rendered on the client browser. For example, you can select the default color and font used for headings; the colors used for regular, active, and visited links; and the margin left around images.

- The Web.config file is the configuration file for this ASP.NET application. This XML file is functionally similar to the .config files that I described in Chapter 13, even though it contains different entries.

I'll cover the Global.asax and Web.config files in detail in Chapters 26 and 27. For now, let's focus on the WebForm1.aspx file. Web Forms files come with a designer and a code portion, much like Windows Forms files. A Web Forms designer can work in two modes: design and HTML. In design mode, you drop controls taken from the HTML or Web Forms tabs of the Toolbox, as well as from other tabs that contain items that go to the component tray, such as Data or Components. In HTML mode, you can write plain HTML code as you do with any HTML editor; you often need to switch to this mode to add HTML elements that don't correspond to an item on any Toolbox tab.

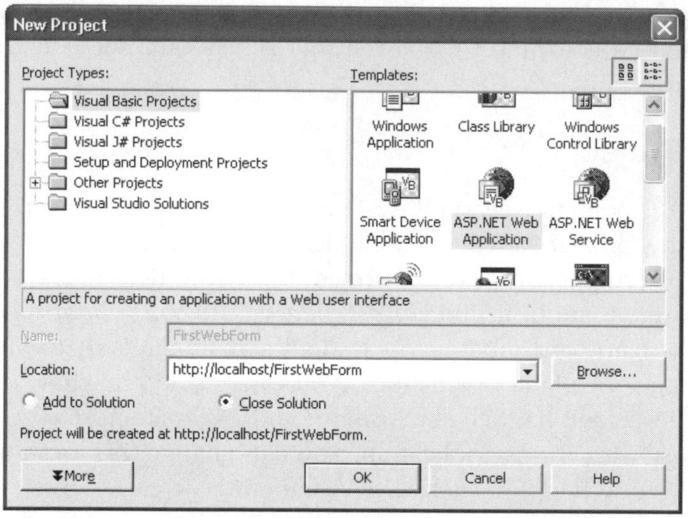

Figure 24-1   Creating a new ASP.NET Web application

Setting Main Page Properties

You should set the pageLayout, targetSchema, and defaultClientScript properties of the page document immediately after creating the form because they affect how your application sends output to the various browsers. Changing these properties in the middle of the development stage usually requires that you recheck how the form behaves, possibly testing it with different browsers. You can also set these properties in the project's Property Pages dialog box to have all new Web Forms inherit them automatically. (See Figure 24-2.)

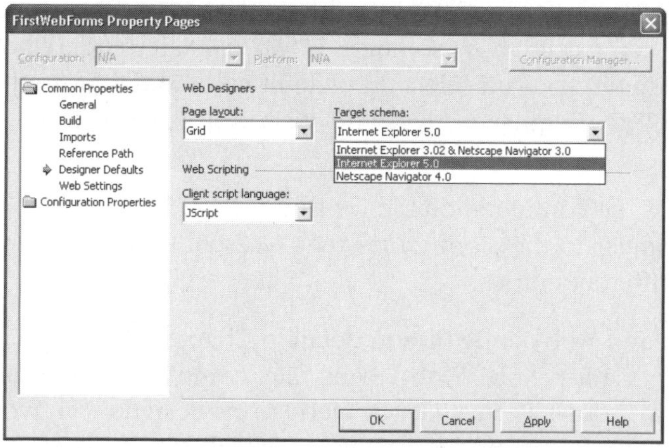

Figure 24-2   The Designer Defaults page of the project Property Pages dialog box

The pageLayout property can be set to FlowLayout or GridLayout. The first value renders HTML elements in a flowing manner, a bit like words in a word processor: if the user resizes the browser's window, the layout of the HTML contents automatically changes to accommodate the new window's dimensions. The GridLayout value sets absolute coordinates for all HTML elements; in this mode, the designer works like the Windows Forms designer.

The targetSchema property tells which HTML flavor to use. It can be Microsoft Internet Explorer 3.02, Netscape Navigator 3.0, Navigator 4.0, Internet Explorer 5.0, or one of the mobile device templates. Needless to say, you get extended functionality when you select a more recent version of Internet Explorer or Navigator, but you lose compatibility with previous versions. In practice, you should use the Internet Explorer 3.02/Navigator 3.0 setting when you create an Internet site, and use one of the other settings only for intranets. For example, when pageLayout is set to GridLayout and you select the Internet Explorer 5.0 target schema, the ASP.NET code that Visual Studio produces sets the position of HTML elements by using a style attribute. If you select the Explorer 3.02/Navigator 3.0 target schema, the ASP.NET code arranges controls on the page using HTML tables. HTML tables require that more HTML text is sent over the wire and is rendered slowly in the browser.

The defaultClientScript property determines which script language is used to activate client-side functionality, such as script code that supports validation controls. By default, this property is set to JScript (which is compatible with all browsers), but you can change it to VBScript if you're sure all your clients use Internet Explorer.

Other page properties are less critical, and most of the time you can leave them at their default values, or you can change them later without a serious impact on the application's testing and debugging. For example, the language property is the language used to compile inline code blocks in the page. It's automatically set to VB because you created this Web Forms page in a Visual Basic .NET project; other valid values are C#, VJ#, and JScript.

Dropping Controls onto the Page

Your first Web Forms application is a simple calculator that takes two numbers and displays their sum in another field. This sample program requires very little code but provides a good opportunity to understand a few basic principles of Web Forms.

Ensure that the form's pageLayout property is set to FlowLayout, open the Web Forms tab on the Toolbox, and drop three TextBox controls, two Label controls, and one Button control, as shown in the upper portion of Figure 24-3. The two Label controls are used for the title at the top of the page and the plus symbol between the two TextBox controls. You can see their captions by setting their Text properties as you would do with a Label control in a Windows Forms application. You can change the size of the first Label by setting its Font.Bold property to True and its Font.Size property to X-Large. (Font sizes for Web controls aren't measured in points.) Unlike Windows Forms, however, if the HTML designer is in FlowLayout mode, you can just type text whenever you want, exactly as you do with a word processor.

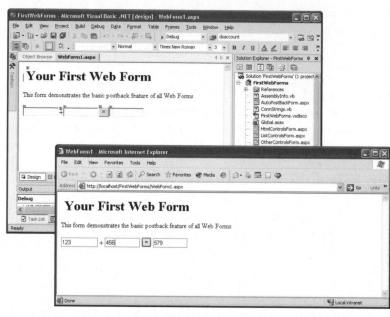

Figure 24-3   Your first Web Forms application in design mode (top) and inside Internet Explorer (bottom)

Next, change the names of the three TextBox controls to txtOne, txtTwo, and txtResult. You use these names when referencing these controls in code. You must set them by using the (ID) property because Web controls don't expose a Name property. Similarly, set the ID property of the button to btnAdd and its Text property to the equal sign.

Finally, you can double-click the Button control to bring up the code editor and enter the following code:

```
Private Sub btnAdd_Click(ByVal sender As Object, _
    ByVal e As EventArgs) Handles btnAdd.Click
    Dim res As Double = CDbl(txtOne.Text) + CDbl(txtTwo.Text)
    txtResult.Text = res.ToString
End Sub
```

As you see, you're using plain Visual Basic .NET code to define what happens when the user clicks the button. The interesting thing—which is also one of the fundamental concepts in ASP.NET programming—is that this code runs on the server, not on the client, so the client machine doesn't need to be running the .NET Framework. More precisely, the client machine doesn't even need to be a Windows computer because the communication with the server is done through plain HTML and HTTP exclusively.

To see this program in action, press the F5 key to run the application. Visual Studio .NET automatically runs Internet Explorer, which in turn asks IIS for the page you've written, and displays it. Enter two numbers in the first two fields, and click on the button. A progress bar in the status bar of the browser shows that a request is posted back to IIS, which returns the same form with the result in the third field.

Server-Side and Client-Side HTML Code

To better understand how Web Forms work, let's see the HTML code that the designer created for us:

```
<%@ Page Language="vb" AutoEventWireup="false" Codebehind="WebForm1.aspx.vb"
  Inherits="FirstWebForm.WebForm1"%>
<!DOCTYPE HTML PUBLIC "-//W3C//DTD HTML 4.0 Transitional//EN">
<HTML>
  <HEAD>
    <title>WebForm1</title>
    ⋮
  </HEAD>
  <body>
    <form id="Form1" method="post" runat="server"><P>
      <asp:Label id="Label1" runat="server" Font-Bold="True"
        Font-Size="X-Large">Your First Web Form</asp:Label></P>
      <P>
      <asp:TextBox id="txtOne" runat="server" Width="88px"></asp:TextBox>
      <asp:Label id="Label2" runat="server"> + </asp:Label>
      <asp:TextBox id="txtTwo" runat="server" Width="84px"></asp:TextBox>
      <asp:Button id="btnAdd" runat="server" Text=" = "></asp:Button>
      <asp:TextBox id="txtResult" runat="server" Width="84px">
        </asp:TextBox></P>
    </form>
  </body>
</HTML>
```

As you see, all the components we dropped onto the designer's surface have been translated to <asp:*xxxx*> tags inside a <form> block. Both the form and the individual controls contain a runat="server" attribute, which makes it clear that the corresponding element is processed on the server, not on the client. Each control has an id attribute that corresponds to the name you've assigned to it. Finally, at the top of the page you'll see an @Page directive that contains information on the page being processed.

No browser is able to interpret this HTML code, and in fact, this isn't plain HTML. More precisely, it's an XML block that's processed before being sent to the browser in a way that depends on the targetSchema and other properties. For example, this is the HTML code that Internet Explorer 5.0 or later versions receive when IIS processes the request for the WebForm1.aspx resource:

```
<!DOCTYPE HTML PUBLIC "-//W3C//DTD HTML 4.0 Transitional//EN">
<HTML>
  <HEAD>
    <title>WebForm1</title>
    ⋮
  </HEAD>
  <body>
    <form name="Form1" method="post" action="WebForm1.aspx" id="Form1">
    <input type="hidden" name="__VIEWSTATE" value="dDwxNDE4MjA3OTY2Ozs+" />
    <P>
    <span id="Label1" style="font-size:X-Large;font-weight:bold;">
      Your First Web Form</span></P>
    <P>
```

```
        <input name="txtOne" type="text" id="txtOne" style="width:88px;" />
        <span id="Label2"> + </span>
        <input name="txtTwo" type="text" id="txtTwo" style="width:84px;" />
        <input type="submit" name="btnAdd" value=" = " id="btnAdd" />
        <input name="txtResult" type="text" id="txtResult" style="width:84px;" />
      </P>
      </form>
   </body>
</HTML>
```

A few points are worth noting here:

- All <asp:*xxxx*> elements have been morphed into plain HTML tags. TextBox controls have been translated to <input type="text"> elements, Label controls have been rendered as <span> elements, and the Button control has been translated to an <input type="submit"> element.

- An action attribute has been added to the <form> element. This attribute causes the submit button to repost the form contents to the same .aspx page, which processes the values in the two text boxes and sends the modified page back again to the client. Forms that behave this way are called *self-posting forms*. As you'll learn shortly, the code in the form can detect whether it's running because of a postback operation.

- A hidden field named __VIEWSTATE has been added to the form. This field contains the values of all the controls if the form has been sent to the client in an encoded format.

The __VIEWSTATE hidden field is central to the ASP.NET architecture. When the form is posted back to the server, ASP.NET compares the current value of each control with its original value (which is encoded in the hidden field), and raises the corresponding event on the server. For example, if the end user has modified the value of a TextBox control, a TextChanged event is fired on the server. In contrast to what happens in Windows Forms applications, this event isn't fired immediately and is postponed until the form is posted back to the server.

Notice that, unlike standard HTML and classic ASP pages, an ASP.NET page can contain only one <form> tag. (More precisely, the page can contain only one <form> tag whose runat attribute is set to server.)

Setting the Main Directory for ASP.NET Projects

You might have noticed that Visual Studio .NET scatters the files that make up an ASP.NET project into two different physical directories. The solution files with .sln and .suo extensions go in the default Visual Studio projects location, which is the C:\Documents and Settings\Administrator\My Documents\Visual Studio Projects folder (unless you've changed it in the Projects and Solutions page of the Options dialog box that you reach from the Tools menu); .aspx, .vb, .vbproj, and other source code files go in a directory under C:\Inetpub\wwwroot so that remote clients can browse them by using a URL such as this one:

```
htpp://www.contoso.com/yourprojectname/mainpage.aspx
```

You can get more control of which folders are used for your source files and keep the solution files in the same directory as the other files by manually creating a virtual directory for IIS before creating the project. Here's how to proceed:

Create a blank solution from the New submenu of the File menu—for example, a solution named AspNetDemoProject in the C:\root directory. Next, right-click on the new C:\AspNetDemoProject folder from inside Windows Explorer, select the Sharing command from the context menu, and then switch to the Web Sharing tab. (See the left portion of Figure 24-4.) Click on the Share This Folder radio button, which displays the Edit Alias dialog box. (See the right portion of Figure 24-4.) If you want the virtual folder and the physical directory to have the same name, click the OK button once to close this window and a second time to close the Properties window.

Go back to Visual Studio .NET and create a new Web Form project in this folder by typing the name of the virtual directory in the New Project dialog box:

```
http://localhost/AspNetDemoProject
```

All the files of the project will be created in this folder.

The only noteworthy limitation of this technique is that you can't reach the solution with the project from Web command in the Open submenu. This command can only see physical folders inside the c:\Inetpub\wwwroot directory.

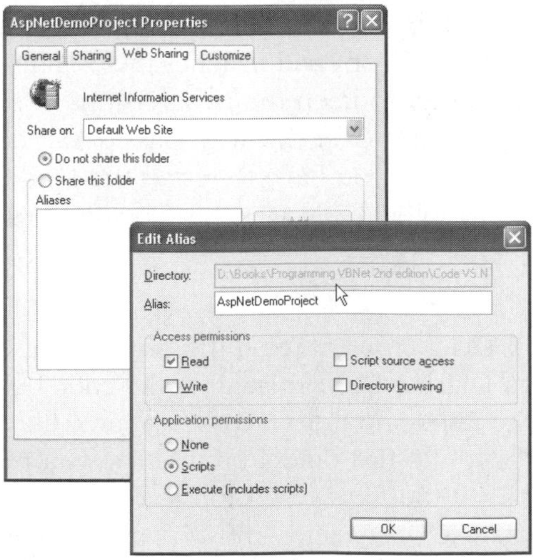

Figure 24-4 Creating a virtual directory for Internet Information Services

Web Forms Dynamics

Let's consider in more detail what happens when a client browser interacts with a Web Forms application. You need this information to understand what you can do with Web Forms, as well as which actions are to be performed on the server and which ones on the client.

Code-Behind Classes

One of the major defects of classic ASP is the inability to separate the user interface (the HTML text) from the script code that does the actual page processing. This obstacle prevents a clear separation between the job of the graphic designer and the job of the programmer, and most ASP developers become experts in user interface issues as well as programming, with overall results that are less than exciting in most cases. (That was the case with *my* results anyway.) Web Forms take a completely new approach that, while not perfect, is a big step in the right direction.

When a browser posts a request to an .aspx file, the ASP.NET DLL intercepts the request, loads the file, and parses its @Page directive looking for the Inherits attribute. This attribute's value is the name of the class that contains the code associated with server-side events for that page—for example, the event handlers that execute when a button is clicked. This class must be in a DLL that's stored in the /Bin subdirectory under the application's root directory. The association between event handlers and user interface elements is based on the id attributes of the interface elements.

Interestingly, ASP.NET doesn't really load the original DLL. Instead, it copies the DLL to another location and then loads this copy, which is called the *shadow copy*. This operation slows the processing of the first request but has a great advantage: you can overwrite the original DLL without getting an error because IIS isn't locking it. When another request comes, ASP.NET checks that the shadow copy still matches the original DLL and performs the copy operation again if necessary to keep the two versions in sync. This shadow copying feature is a great improvement over the way classic ASP deals with compiled DLLs. As many ASP developers know, you have to restart the IIS application (and at times the entire IIS) to replace a compiled COM DLL that's being used by IIS.

On-Demand Compilation

Visual Studio .NET builds the compiled DLL before running the browser on the .aspx page, but ASP.NET works well even if no DLL has been created for the code-behind portion of the form. You can deploy only the .aspx and the .vb (or .cs) source file, in which case the latter file is automatically compiled the first time a browser posts a request for the companion .aspx file. ASP.NET looks at the file's extension to decide which compiler—Visual Basic, C#, or any other valid .NET language—must be used to compile the source file, so it's crucial that you use the .vb extension for your Visual Basic .NET files.

The association between the .aspx file and its code-behind source module is held in the Src attribute of the @Page directive:

```
<%@ Page Src="WebForm1.aspx.vb" Inherits="FirstWebForm.WebForm1"%>
```

The on-demand compilation model has no advantage over the Visual Studio .NET approach, except the ability to create Web Forms pages using a tool as simple as Notepad, and it has a couple of drawbacks. First, the compilation step adds a short delay the first time a page is requested. Second, and more important, you must deploy the source code file to have it compiled on the fly, so you might not be able to protect your intellectual property if you aren't in full control of the server computer.

ASP.NET also supports a third code model, in which the .aspx file contains both the HTML text and the server-side code. In this model, server-side code is enclosed in <script> blocks with a runat="server" attribute, exactly as you find in classic ASP:

```
<%@ Page Language="VB" %>
⋮
<SCRIPT RUNAT="server">
Private Sub btnAdd_Click(ByVal sender As System.Object, _
    ByVal e As System.EventArgs) Handles btnAdd.Click
    Dim res As Double = CDbl(txtOne.Text) + CDbl(txtTwo.Text)
    txtResult.Text = res.ToString
End Sub
</SCRIPT>
```

This code model is often adopted in MSDN documentation and in many ASP.NET books and articles because it shows the HTML and the language code in a single place. But because this book is about using Visual Studio .NET, all my code samples use separate listings for the HTML and Visual Basic portions.

The Page Life Cycle

The great innovation of Web Forms is that they let you adopt the same event-driven programming model that made Visual Basic the most popular programming language under Windows. By and large, Web Forms controls expose the same events as their Windows Forms counterparts: Button controls expose a Click event, TextBox controls expose a TextChanged event, ListBox controls expose the SelectedIndexChanged event, and so on. The Page class is the ASP.NET equivalent of the form and exposes events such as Load and Unload.

Even if the event-driven model is similar, you'll find an important difference between the Windows Forms and the Web Forms worlds. Events in Windows Forms applications fire as soon as end users operate on the user interface element—that is, when they click on buttons, type something in a TextBox, or select another element in a ListBox control. On the other hand, Web Forms events fire on the server, not inside the browser, so their handlers run only when the form is posted back to the server. This usually occurs when the user clicks on the submit button, even though other controls can fire a postback.

This is what happens when a form is posted back to the server:

1. ASP.NET loads the code-behind class and fires the Page_Init event. At this time, your code can't determine whether this is the first time the form has been requested, nor can it retrieve the values the user typed in the form's controls.

2. After the page object and all its controls have been initialized, the Page_Load event fires. At this time, your code can determine whether the page is executing because of a postback operation (by checking the IsPostBack property) and can access current values in controls. Typically, you use this event to initialize controls and bind them to data sources. In other words, you use it for the kind of operations you perform in a Windows Forms Load event.

3. If this is a postback, all the events related to controls fire at this time. For example, TextChanged events for TextBox controls that have been modified by the end user fire now, as well as CheckedChanged events for CheckBox and RadioButton controls that have been clicked.

4. The last control event that fires is the one that caused the postback action, usually the Click event of a Button or ImageButton control.

5. Finally, the Page object fires an Unload event when your code is expected to release all resources, close files and database connections, and so on. After this event all class-level variables are destroyed and are gone forever, unless you save their values somewhere (for example, in a session variable).

The order in which control events fire isn't necessarily the order in which the end user operated on the corresponding controls. The Web Forms object fires these events by analyzing the current state of all the controls on the form posted back to the server and comparing it with the control's state at the time the form was sent to the browser. (This information is stored in the hidden __VIEWSTATE field.) For example, a TextBox's TextChanged event fires if the control contains a string other than its original value. Of course, you receive a single TextChanged event even if the end user modified the control's value several times before posting the form back to the server.

Web Forms controls fire fewer events than their Windows Forms counterparts. For example, Web Forms controls don't expose events such as MouseEnter, MouseExit, GotFocus, and LostFocus because these events are typically used to provide instantaneous feedback to the end user. It makes little sense to cache them and fire them when the form is posted back to the server.

The EnableViewState Property

From the description I gave in the preceding section, it might appear that the Page_Load event fires both in response to the first request for the page and as a result of a postback. Unless you're jumping to another page, however, you typically want to restore the values that the user typed in each control before sending the page back to the browser.

This simple task is overly difficult in classic ASP, but requires no action on your part under ASP.NET because ASP.NET automatically saves the value of all controls.

As a matter of fact, you must explicitly do something only if you do *not* want these values to be saved. More precisely, you can disable the persistence mechanism for a given control by setting its EnableViewState property to False:

```
' Don't save the value of ListBox1 between postbacks.
' (You can set this property also in the Property window at design time.)
ListBox1.EnableViewState = False
```

If you don't need to save the value of any control on the form, you can disable the ViewState mechanism completely by setting the Page object's EnableViewState property to False:

```
' Don't save the value of any control between postbacks.
Me.EnableViewState = False
```

The value of controls whose EnableViewState property is False isn't included in the hidden __VIEWSTATE field, which results in fewer bytes sent to the client browser and then back to the server. For this reason, you should disable the ViewState mechanism for all the controls that don't really need to be saved between postbacks.

Regardless of the value of the EnableViewState property, ASP.NET always restores the state of a few controls—such as TextBox and CheckBox controls—because their value is included in the form that is posted back to the server. To clear these controls, you must explicitly assign a value to them before the page is sent back to the client.

The IsPostBack Property

Consider the following code, which loads a DropDownList control with the list of all the states for which there is at least one publisher:

```
Private Sub Page_Load(ByVal sender As Object, ByVal e As EventArgs) _
    Handles MyBase.Load
    InitializeStateList()
End Sub


' BiblioConnString is the connection string that points to Biblio.mdb.
Dim cn As New OleDbConnection(BiblioConnString)


' Display unique state strings in the ddlStates DropDownList control.
Sub InitializeStateList()
    cn.Open()
    Dim cmd As New OleDbCommand("SELECT DISTINCT State FROM Publishers", cn)
    Dim dr As OleDbDataReader = cmd.ExecuteReader()
    ddlStates.DataSource = dr
    ' The State field is used for filling the list of the DropDownList control.
    ddlStates.DataTextField = "State"
    ' Bind the control to the data source.
```

```
        ddlStates.DataBind()
        dr.Close
        cn.Close
    End Sub
```

(I'll explain data binding in the next chapter.) In the preceding code snippet, the InitializeStateList routine runs each time the page is requested. However, running this code for any request after the first one is useless because the contents of the ddlStates control are embedded in the hidden __VIEWSTATE field and are restored automatically when the page is reloaded after a postback. You can choose from two ways to avoid this overhead:

- Set the EnableStateView property of the ddlStates control to False so that its contents aren't added to the __VIEWSTATE hidden field.

- Run the InitializeStateList routine only the first time the browser requests the page and skip it during a postback operation.

Choosing between these two approaches isn't an easy decision. Sometimes recalculating the contents of a control (or reloading it from a database query) is faster than bloating each page with a large __VIEWSTATE field, especially if the client is connecting to the server through a slow dial-up connection. In the majority of cases, however, the best approach is to load the data once and store it in the __VIEWSTATE field.

To load the data only once, you must distinguish the first page request from postbacks, which you do by means of the page's IsPostBack read-only property. Here's an improved version of the Page_Load event handler that takes advantage of this property:

```
Private Sub Page_Load(ByVal sender As Object, ByVal e As EventArgs) _
    Handles MyBase.Load
    If Not Page.IsPostBack Then
        InitializeStateList()
    End If
End Sub

' ...(The remainder of the code is unchanged)...
```

The AutoPostBack Property

By default, only a few controls can start a postback operation—namely, the Button control and its ImageButton and LinkButton variations. This behavior is OK most of the time because the user is usually expected to fill in all the fields in a form and then click the submit button.

Occasionally, however, you might want to offer immediate feedback when the user selects an item from a list or clicks a check box or a radio button. You can achieve this behavior by setting the AutoPostBack property to True for the controls that can initiate a postback operation. This property is exposed by the following controls: TextBox, CheckBox, RadioButton, CheckBoxList, RadioButtonList, DropDownList, and ListBox.

To see the AutoPostBack property in action, create a new Web Forms component (from the Project menu) and name it AutoPostBackForm. Add a DropDownList and a DataGrid control plus a couple of Label controls on the new form, as shown in the upper portion of Figure 24-5. Rename the DropDownList control ddlStates and the DataGrid control dgrPublishers, and set the DropDownList control's AutoPostBack property to True. Your code-behind module becomes

```
' Page_Load handler and InitializeStateList routines as before
⋮
Private Sub ddlStates_SelectedIndexChanged(ByVal sender As Object, _
    ByVal e As EventArgs) Handles ddlStates.SelectedIndexChanged
    ' Create the query string.
    Dim sql As String = "SELECT Name, Address, City, State FROM Publishers"
    If ddlStates.SelectedIndex >= 0 Then
        sql &= " WHERE State = '" & ddlStates.SelectedItem.Text & "'"
    End If

    ' Display publishers in the DataGrid.
    cn.Open()
    Dim cmd As New OleDbCommand(sql, cn)
    Dim dr As OleDbDataReader = cmd.ExecuteReader()
    ' Bind the control to the data source.
    dgrPublishers.DataSource = dr
    dgrPublishers.DataBind()
    dr.Close()
    cn.Close()
End Sub
```

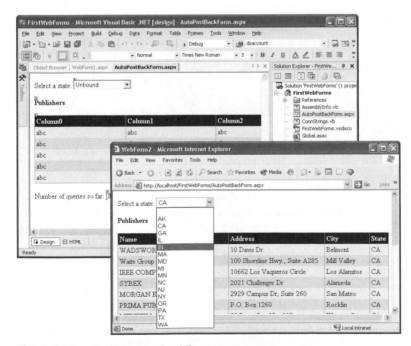

Figure 24-5   The AutoPostBackForm.aspx page

> **Note**   Here's an important point about connection strings in ASP.NET. As you'll learn in Chapter 27, by default an ASP.NET application runs under the identity of a user named ASPNET or under the Network Service identity, depending on the IIS version and whether you're using IIS 6 isolation mode under Windows Server 2003. If you want to use integrated security when you access SQL Server, you must make this account a valid user account for SQL Server. If you don't, you can establish a valid SQL Server connection only by providing a specific User ID and Password in the connection string, as in this line of code:
>
> ```
> Data Source=.;User ID=sa;Password=sapwd;Initial Catalog=pubs
> ```
>
> Similar security issues might arise when you're working with other databases.

To test this Web Forms page from inside Visual Studio, you must modify the start page—that is, the .aspx page shown in Internet Explorer when you run the application. You can do this in the Debugging page of the project Property Pages dialog box. (See Figure 24-6.)

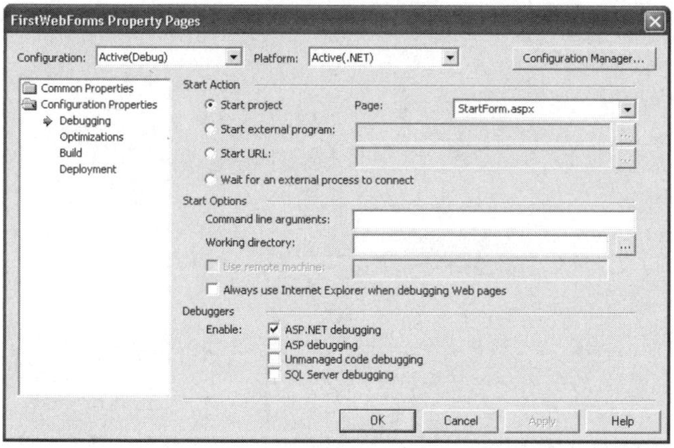

Figure 24-6   The Debugging page of the project Property Pages dialog box

It's interesting to see that the AutoPostBack property is implemented by means of a short client-side JavaScript routine and a couple of hidden fields. When the user selects a new item in the combo box, the routine loads the name of the control that fired the postback in the first control, loads an additional argument in the second hidden field (an empty string in this specific case), and then finally submits the form. Here's the abridged version of the HTML form sent to the browser:

```
<form name="Form1" method="post" action="AutoPostBackForm.aspx" id="Form1">
<input type="hidden" name="__EVENTTARGET" value="" />
<input type="hidden" name="__EVENTARGUMENT" value="" />
<input type="hidden" name="__VIEWSTATE"
  value="dDwtMTc3Nzk0Nzg4NDt0PDtsPGk8MT47PjtsPHQ8O2w8TwxPjtpPDU+Oz47bDx0PHQ8c
  DxwPGw8RGF0YVRl1eHRGaWVsZDs+O2w8U3RhdGU7Pj47Pjt0PGk8MTc+O0A8XGU7QUs7Q0E7R0E7S
  Uw7SU47TUEg001E001J0010005D005K005Z009SO1BB01RY01dB0z47QDxcZTtBSztDQTtHQTtJT
  DtJTjtNQSA7TUQ7TUk7TU47TkM7Tko7Tlk7T1I7UEE7VFg7V0E7Pj47Pjs7Pjt0PEAwPDs7Ozs70
```

```
    zs70zs+0zs+0z4+0z4+0z4=" />

<script language="javascript">
<!--
    function __doPostBack(eventTarget, eventArgument) {
        var theform;
        if (window.navigator.appName.toLowerCase().indexOf("netscape") > -1) {
            theform = document.forms["Form1"];
        }
        else {
            theform = document.Form1;
        }
        theform.__EVENTTARGET.value = eventTarget.split("$").join(":");
        theform.__EVENTARGUMENT.value = eventArgument;
        theform.submit();
    }
// -->
</script>
<P>Select a state:
<select name="ddlStates" id="ddlStates"
    onchange="__doPostBack('ddlStates','')"
    language="javascript" style="width:130px;">
    <option value="AK">AK</option>
    <option value="CA">CA</option>
    ⋮
</select></P>
⋮
</form>
```

Notice that the JavaScript routine accounts for the slightly different syntax forms that Internet Explorer and Netscape Navigator support.

> **Note**   For the AutoPostBack property to work correctly, the user's browser must allow script-ing. This is the default setting for all browsers, but users might turn this feature off for secu-rity reasons. In that case, the AutoPostBack property doesn't work. If in doubt, include a submit button on the form to cover these cases. (Or at least add a warning to your users that they must enable scripting to navigate your site.)

The Page Class

The Page class represents the Web Forms page itself, and its members affect how the .aspx page is displayed in the browser. For this reason, you should become familiar with its properties, methods, and events. I already discussed a few of them, such as EnableViewState and IsPostBack. In the following sections I'll cover the SmartNaviga-tion property and the ViewState dictionary.

Smart Navigation

During a postback, the page is redrawn and users see a brief but annoying flickering. Worse, the scroll position isn't preserved during postbacks (the page scrolls to its top) and the first control on the page takes the input focus. This behavior contrasts with the experience users have with regular Windows applications and tends to be confusing. If you're working with Internet Explorer 5.0 or a later version, you can overcome all these shortcomings by setting the SmartNavigation property to True, which performs the following tasks:

- Eliminates the flashing that occurs when a page is reloaded.

- Preserves the scroll position on longer pages.

- Maintains the input focus between postbacks.

- Retains only the last page state in the browser's history.

This property is especially useful for forms that do a lot of postbacks but whose contents don't change much between postbacks. Remember that it works only with Internet Explorer 5.0 or later versions, even though you can safely set the SmartNavigation property to True in all cases because ASP.NET checks the browser version and ignores this property for down-level browsers, such as earlier versions of Internet Explorer or Navigator.

You can set the SmartNavigation property from the Properties window or by using an @Page directive. You can also set it for the entire application by adding a line to the web.config file:

```
<configuration>
    <system.web>
        <pages smartNavigation="true" />
    </system.web>
</configuration>
```

Smart navigation is implemented by means of a set of client-side scripts, and activated by sending the client the following line:

```
<script language="JScript" src="/aspnet_client/system_web/1_1_4322/SmartNav.js">
</script>
```

If you're curious, just open the SmartNav.js file that you'll find in the C:\Inet-pub\wwwroot\aspnet_client\system_web\1_1_4322 folder to see how the magic works.

As powerful as it is, smart navigation has some problems as well, the most serious of which is its habit of interfering with other client-side scripts in the page. In some cases I had to disable smart navigation to have my Web Forms applications behave correctly.

The ViewState Dictionary Object

In classic ASP, the only way to preserve information—for example, the value of a variable—between consecutive client requests is by means of Session variables, cookies, or other awkward techniques, such as arguments on the query string or values in hidden fields.

ASP.NET gives you yet another method in the form of the ViewState property of the Page object. This property represents the contents of the __VIEWSTATE hidden field and works as a StateBag dictionary of key-value pairs. The following example uses the ViewState property to preserve the number of requests to the current page:

```
Private Sub Page_Load(ByVal sender As Object, ByVal e As EventArgs) _
    Handles MyBase.Load

    ' Number of requests to this page posted so far
    Dim count As Integer = 0
    If Not Me.ViewState("count") Is Nothing Then
        count = CInt(Me.ViewState("count")) + 1
    End If
    ' Store the value back in the ViewState dictionary.
    Me.ViewState("count") = count
    ' Display in a Label control.
    lblCount.Text = count.ToString
End Sub
```

Keep in mind that this property works only if you left the EnableViewState property set to True.

The MapPath and ResolveUrl methods

The Page class exposes only a few interesting methods. The HasControls method returns True if the page contains controls, and the DataBind method binds all the child controls to their data source. The MapPath method converts a virtual path into a physical path, so it's useful for passing arguments to object methods that don't work with virtual paths:

```
Dim sr As New System.IO.StreamReader(Me.MapPath("/data/values.dat"))
```

You can also use MapPath to retrieve information about the current ASP.NET application, as you see in this snippet:

```
' The current directory (same as TemplateSourceDirectory property)
Dim currDir As String = Me.MapPath(".")
' The parent directory
Dim parentDir As String = Me.MapPath("..")
' The root directory
Dim rootDir As String = Me.MapPath("/")
```

The ResolveUrl method converts a relative virtual path into an absolute virtual path, so it's useful for building URLs to be passed to the client (for example, as hyperlinks). Notice that the domain name isn't returned by this function, so you must add it explicitly if necessary:

```
' Provide the complete URL to a file.
' (Assumes that the domain URL is www.vb2themax.com.)
Dim url As String = "www.vb2themax.com" & Me.ResolveUrl("/data/values.dat")
```

You'll learn how to use the remaining methods in the following chapters.

The Error Event

The Page class inherits several events from the Control and TemplateControl classes. All these events receive a plain EventArgs object in their second argument, so in practice, no additional information is passed to the event.

I already covered a few of these events in the section "The Page Life Cycle" earlier in this chapter. The only other event worth mentioning is Error, which fires when an unhandled exception is thrown by code in the page. This event lets you clear the error and redirect the execution flow to another page if you want:

```
Private Sub Page_Error(ByVal sender As Object, ByVal e As EventArgs) _
    Handles MyBase.Error
    ' Clear the server error (optional).
    Server.ClearError()
    ' Redirect to another page.
    Server.Transfer("Instructions.aspx")
End Sub
```

The @Page Directive

Many of the properties that you set inside the Properties window in Visual Studio are converted into attributes of the @Page directive at the top of the .aspx file. Some of these values also appear as properties of the Page object and also can be set in code. In a few cases, however, they can be set only in the @Page directive.

There can be only one @Page directive in an .aspx file, and it's placed at the top of the file. Table 24-1 lists all the valid attributes for this directive.

If you create pages with Visual Studio, the Inherits attribute is added automatically and you never have to use any other attribute in the Dynamic compilation category. I already showed you page properties that map to attributes in the @Page directive—for example, EnableViewState and SmartNavigation. A few other attributes, including Buffer and ContentType, should be clear if you're familiar with classic ASP programming.

The ErrorPage attribute is interesting in that it lets you redirect any unhandled exception to a custom page rather than to the default page supplied by ASP.NET. This attribute gives you much greater flexibility than ASP, in which you have to set the error page's URL using an IIS dialog box. Here's an example of the @Page directive that sets this and a few other attributes:

```
<%@ Page Language="vb" AutoEventWireup="false"
    Codebehind="AutoPostBackForm.aspx.vb" Inherits="FirstWebForm.WebForm2"
    smartNavigation="True" errorPage="/ErrorPage.asp" %>
```

The ValidateRequest attribute is new in .NET Framework 1.1. If you set this attribute to True, ASP.NET checks the data submitted by the browser looking for a match with a hard-coded (and unmodifiable) list of potentially dangerous values, and throws an HttpRequestValidationException if a match is found. This feature is meant to offer a front-line defense against a category of attacks that includes scripting injection and SQL Server injection. While it's a good thing that this feature is turned on by default, it's no substitute for other defensive programming techniques, such as verifying that all data coming from the browser is carefully validated. Visit *http://www.asp.net/faq/Request-Validation.aspx* to learn more about this feature.

Notice that ASP.NET considers any <%@ that lacks an explicit name to be an @Page directive (or an @Control directive if inside a user control, which I'll cover in Chapter 28), so the following syntax is legal:

```
<%@ Language="vb" AutoEventWireup="false"
    Codebehind="AutoPostBackForm.aspx.vb" Inherits="FirstWebForm.WebForm2"
       smartNavigation="True" errorPage="/ErrorPage.asp" %>
```

Table 24-1   Attributes for the @Page Directive

Category	Syntax	Description
Behavior	EnableSessionState=value	Determines the kind of access this page has to the Session object. The value can be True (default), False, or ReadOnly.
	EnableViewState=bool	Enables or disables ViewState for all the controls on the page. (Default is True.)
	EnableViewStateMac=bool	If True, ASP.NET runs a machine authentication check (MAC) on the page's ViewState to ensure that the state hasn't been tampered with. (Default is False.)
	SmartNavigation=bool	Enables or disables smart navigation for this page. (Default is False.)
	ErrorPage=url	The URL of the page that's displayed when an unhandled exception is thrown.
	ValidateRequest=bool	If True, ASP.NET checks input data against a list of potentially dangerous values, and throws an exception if a match is found.
Page rendering	Buffer=bool	Enables or disables HTTP buffering; same as the Response.Buffer property in ASP. (Default is True.)
	ContentType=mimetype	The HTTP content type of the response, as a MIME type; same as the Response.ContentType in ASP.
	ResponseEncoding=encoding	The response encoding for this page.

Table 24-1   Attributes for the @Page Directive   *(continued)*

Category	Syntax	Description
	CodePage=code	The code page value for the response. You set this attribute only if you're creating a page that uses a code page different from the default code page of the Web server.
	LCID=locale	The locale identifier for this page.
	Culture=string	The culture setting for this page. It takes the same values as the Culture-Info class. (See the section "The CultureInfo Auxiliary Class" in Chapter 7.)
	UICulture=id	The user interface culture setting for this page.
COM and COM+ compatibility	AspCompat=bool	If True, the page runs in a single-threaded apartment (STA) and can use STA components, such as those authored with Visual Basic 6. You also must set it to True for calling COM+ 1.0 components that access the unmanaged ASP objects through the Object-Context object. (Default is False.)
	Transaction=mode	Indicates whether transactions are supported for this page. The value can be Disabled (default), NotSupported, Supported, Required, or RequiresNew.
Debug and trace	Debug=bool	Enables or disables the generation of debug symbols for this page. (Default is False.)
	Trace=bool	Enables or disables tracing for this page. (Default is False.)
	TraceMode=value	Determines how trace messages are displayed. The value can be SortBy-Time (default) or SortByCategory.
Dynamic compilation	ClassName=name	The name of the class that is compiled automatically the first time the page is requested. The name must not contain spaces.
	Inherits=classname	The code-behind class for the page; can be any class derived from the Page class.
	Language=langname	The language used for inline code enclosed by <% and %> delimiters.

Table 24-1 Attributes for the @Page Directive *(continued)*

Category	Syntax	Description
	Src=path	The source filename for the code-behind class.
	CompilerOptions=string	A string containing valid options for the Visual Basic compiler; these options are used when dynamically compiling the page the first time a browser requests it.
	WarningLevel=level	The compiler warning level used when compiling this page dynamically. The level is an integer between 0 and 4.
	Explicit=bool	The Option Explicit setting for dynamically compiled .aspx files authored in Visual Basic .NET. This attribute is set to True in the machine.config file.
	Strict=bool	The Option Strict setting for dynamically compiled .aspx files authored in Visual Basic .NET. (Default is False.)
Miscellaneous	AutoEventWireup=bool	If True, event handlers are automatically associated with the page or the control based on the ObjectName_ EventName naming convention, as in Visual Basic 6. (Default is False.)
	ClientTarget=useragentname	The User Agent name for which server-side controls should render their contents; same as the ClientTarget property.
	Description=text	A description for this page; this value is ignored by the ASP.NET parser.

The .aspx file can host other types of directives, namely @Import, @Assembly, @Reference, @Implements, @Control, @OutputCache, and @Register. With the exception of the last two (which I'll cover in Chapter 26 and Chapter 28, respectively), you rarely need any of these directives when you work with Visual Studio .NET.

Web Forms Controls

All the controls in the Web Forms portion of the Framework can be subdivided into the following six groups:

■ **HTML Server controls** These 18 controls are the ASP.NET, server-side versions of the standard HTML controls.

- **Web Forms controls**   These are the native ASP.NET controls, most of which duplicate and extend the functionality of an HTML server control.

- **Validation controls**   This is a group of six controls used to validate the contents of other controls (typically text fields).

- **List controls**   This group includes all the list box–like ASP.NET controls, namely the DropDownList, ListBox, CheckBoxList, and RadioButtonList controls.

- **Template controls**   This group includes the DataList, DataGrid, and Repeater controls. You can customize their appearance and behavior by using templates.

- **Other controls**   These controls don't fall into any of the preceding categories: Calendar, AdRotator, and Xml.

All the controls in these groups are server-side controls, which means that they can be initialized and processed by code running on the server. However, a Web Forms page can include plain HTML controls too, which are called client-side controls to distinguish them from the controls in the preceding groups.

You can drop any item from the HTML tab of Visual Studio's Toolbox onto a Web Forms page to create a client-side HTML control. After you've dropped a client-side HTML control onto the form, you can set its properties in the Property window but you can't write code against it, as you'll realize if you double-click on it. A client-side HTML control is rendered on the browser as a plain HTML tag, as you can see here:

```
<INPUT type="text">
<INPUT type="button" value="Button">
```

You might wonder why you should use client-side HTML controls if you can use their more powerful server-side versions. The answer is simple: performance. Client-side controls aren't processed by ASP.NET and are rendered more efficiently. There are several cases for which you don't really need the full power of HTML Server controls—for example, when you have a hyperlink that points to a different page or a button whose only purpose is to run a client-side script.

> **Note**   I'll cover all the control categories in the remainder of this chapter, except the template controls, which I'll cover in the next chapter.

HTML Server Controls

All HTML Server controls are defined in the System.Web.UI.HtmlControls namespace. This group of controls includes the ASP.NET version of the most common HTML controls, and in fact it has been included in the Web Forms portion of the framework to ease the migration from HTML forms. Strictly speaking, you don't need to use HTML Server controls because most HTML Server controls have a corresponding Web Forms control with extended functionality (with the notable exception of the HtmlInputFile control). HTML Server controls expose a limited set of properties whose names match the attributes of the corresponding HTML tag, so they'll look familiar to all HTML and ASP developers.

HTML Server controls are available on the HTML tab of the Toolbox (see Figure 24-7), but when you drop one of these items onto the form you don't get an HTML Server control. As I explained previously, this action creates a plain client-side control. To transform a client-side HTML control into its corresponding server-side version, you must add a runat="server" attribute. You can do that by editing the actual HTML code in the designer or more simply by right-clicking on the control and clicking Run As Server Control on the shortcut menu.

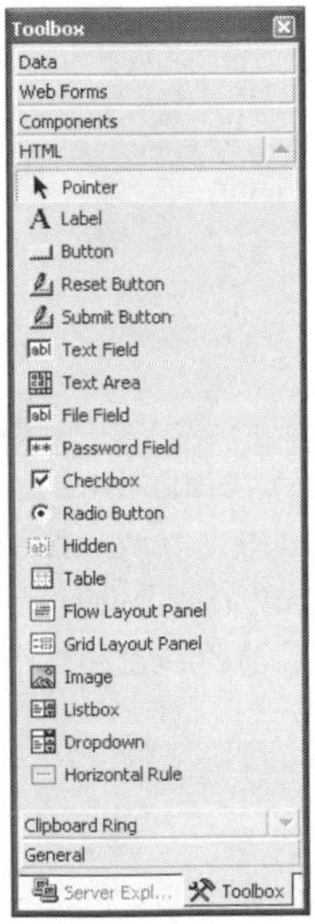

Figure 24-7   The HTML tab of the Toolbox

The HtmlControl and HtmlContainerControl Base Classes

All the controls in the System.Web.UI.HtmlControls namespace derive from the Html-Control class. This base class offers basic functionality that's shared by all the HTML Server controls. A few controls—more specifically, those that always have a closing tag, such as <select> and <table>—derive from the HtmlContainerControl (which in turn inherits from the HtmlControl class).

The HtmlControl class exposes several properties you are already familiar with, such as ID (the programmatic identifier assigned to the control), ClientID (the server control identifier generated by ASP.NET), EnableViewState (True if the value of this control is saved in the parent page's ViewState), Parent (the parent control), Controls (the collection of child controls), Page (the parent Page object), Attributes (the collection of attributes of this control), TagName (the name of the HTML tag used to render this control), Style (a collection of Cascading Style Sheet, or CSS, properties applied to the control), Disabled (True if the control is disabled), and Visible. The HtmlContainerControl class exposes all these properties, plus InnerHtml and InnerText, which set or get the HTML and the text, respectively, between the opening and closing tags for this control.

A couple of collection properties require a more complete description. The Attributes collection gathers all the attributes associated with the HTML Server control. You can use it to iterate over existing attributes, as this code does:

```
Dim res As String = ""
' Iterate over the Attributes collection of the Text1 control.
For Each key As String In Text1.Attributes.Keys
    If res.Length > 0 Then res &= ", "
    res &= key & "=" & Text1.Attributes.Item(key)
Next
' Show the result in a Label control.
lblResult.InnerText = res
```

The Add method lets you add new items to the Attributes collection:

```
' Add a size attribute and set it equal to 30.
Text1.Attributes.Add("size", "30")
```

Browsers ignore HTML attributes that they don't recognize. This behavior lets you use the Attributes collection as a sort of grab bag for values that are related to the control and that you want to persist between postbacks but don't want to store in the page's ViewState. Say that you want to store the first nonempty value that the user types in the Text1 control so that you can compare it with the value found in subsequent postbacks:

```
Private Sub Page_Load(ByVal sender As Object, ByVal e As EventArgs) _
    Handles MyBase.Load

    ' Check whether the InitialValue attribute is still empty.
    If Text1.Attributes("InitialValue") = "" Then
       ' If the control's value isn't an empty string
       If Text1.Value.Length > 0 Then
          ' Store the initial value in the Attributes collection.
          Text1.Attributes.Add("InitialValue", Text1.Value)
       End If
    End If
End Sub
```

The Style property returns a collection of style attributes; you can iterate over this collection or add new items to it, as you do with the Attributes collection:

```
' Change the background color of the Text1 control.
Text1.Style.Add("background-color", "Aqua")
```

You don't have to use the Add method because the default Item property will do this:

```
Text1.Style("font-family") = "Tahoma"
Text1.Style("font-size") = "20px"
Text1.Style("color") = "red"
```

Main Properties and Events

Table 24-2 lists all the HTML Server controls, the corresponding HTML tags, and their main properties and events. The last three classes in the table don't correspond to any element in the HTML tab of the Toolbox, so these controls can be created only programmatically or by inserting HTML text directly. A few properties are common to several controls:

■ The Type property returns the value of the type attribute, such as text or password.

■ The Size property determines the width of single-line text and input file fields, whereas the MaxLength property tells how many characters the user can type in these controls.

■ The CausesValidation property determines whether a click on the control activates the form validation.

Check boxes and radio buttons don't expose a Text property, unlike their Windows Forms and Web Forms counterparts. To provide such a control with a caption, you must add a label or type some text to its right. Also, no HTML Server control exposes the AutoPostBack property; only the HTML submit button can cause a postback.

You typically code against an HTML Server control by handling one of these two events: ServerChange (for controls that contain a textual value) or ServerClick (for buttonlike controls). Their use is straightforward:

```
Private Sub Password1_ServerChange(ByVal sender As Object, _
    ByVal e As EventArgs) Handles Password1.ServerChange
    ' Save the current password value.
    myPwd = Password1.Value
End Sub
```

Table 24-2   HTML Controls and Their Main Properties and Events

Class	HTML Tag	Properties	Events
HtmlInputText	<input type="text"> <input type="password">	Name, Type, Size, Max-Length, Value	Server-Change
HtmlInputCheckBox	<input type="checkbox">	Name, Type, Checked, Value	Server-Change
HtmlInputRadioButton	<input type="radio">	Name, Type, Checked, Value	Server-Change
HtmlInputButton	<input type="button"> <input type="submit"> <input type="reset">	Name, Type, Value, CausesValidation	ServerClick
HtmlInputHidden	<input type="hidden">	Name, Type, Value	Server-Change
HtmlInputFile	<input type="file">	Name, Type, Value, Size, MaxLength, Value, Accept, PostedFile	(none)

Table 24-2   HTML Controls and Their Main Properties and Events   *(continued)*

Class	HTML Tag	Properties	Events
HtmlTextArea	\<textarea>...\</textarea>	Name, Type, Cols, Rows, Value	Server-Change
HtmlSelect	\<select>...\</select>	Name, Size, Multiple, Value, SelectedIndex, Items, DataSource, Data-Member, DataTextField, DataValueField	Server-Change
HtmlImage	\<img>	Src, Align, Border, Width, Height, Alt	(none)
HtmlTable	\<table>...\</table>	Width, Height, Align, BgColor, Border, Border-Color, CellPadding, Cell-Spacing, Rows	(none)
HtmlTableRow	\<tr>...\</tr>	Height, Align, VAlign, BgColor, BorderColor, Cells	(none)
HtmlTableCell	\<td>...\</td> \<th>...\</th>	Width, Height, Align, VAlign, BgColor, Border-Color, RowSpan, Col-Span, NoWrap	(none)
HtmlAnchor	\<a>...\</a>	Name, HRef, Target, Title	ServerClick
HtmlGenericControl	(any)	TagName	(none)
HtmlInputImage	\<input type="image">	Name, Type, Src, Align, Border, CausesValidation	ServerClick

The HtmlGeneric control is a generic object used to render any HTML tag that isn't included in the table. Its peculiarity is that its TagName property is writable. For more information, read the .NET Framework SDK.

The HTML tab of the Toolbox contains three controls that don't appear in Table 24-2 and that map to the \<div> tag. The Label control offers a simple way to enter aligned or data-bound text. The Flow Layout Panel and the Grid Layout Panel controls define an area in the form in which controls are laid out as if the pageLayout property is set to FlowLayout or GridLayout, respectively.

I won't devote many pages to HTML Server controls because, as I mentioned previously, they're provided mainly to ease the migration from classic ASP forms. For new ASP.NET applications, you should use Web Forms controls exclusively. For this reason and the self-describing nature of most properties of these controls, I'll focus exclusively on the features that are less obvious.

The HtmlSelect Class

You can assign most properties of an HtmlSelect control from the Properties window—for example, you set its Size property equal to the number of desired rows, or to 0 to create a drop-down list. (In fact, this property is what makes the difference between a list box and a drop-down list box HTML control.)

You can add elements programmatically by using the Add method of the Items collection. This method takes either a string or a ListItem element. If you pass a string, it works as both the caption of the element and its value. If instead you pass a ListItem element, you can specify different strings for the caption and its value:

```
' Add three elements - caption and value are the same string.
' (Tip: Always clear the Items collection first.)
Select1.Items.Clear
Select1.Items.Add("Computer")
Select1.Items.Add("Monitor")
Select1.Items.Add("Keyboard")

' Fill the control with the list of month names.
Select2.Items.Clear()
 For i As Integer = 1 To 12
    ' Create a ListItem object on the fly.
    Select2.Items.Add(New ListItem(MonthName(i), CStr(i)))
Next
```

At run time, you can determine which element has been selected by checking the SelectedIndex property or the Value property, which returns the value attribute of the selected element. If you want to see the selected element's caption, you must query the Text property of the selected ListItem element:

```
With Select1.Items(Select1.SelectedIndex)
    Debug.WriteLine(.Text)        ' The caption
    Debug.WriteLine(.Value)       ' The value
End With
```

You can create multiple-selection list box controls by setting the Multiple property to True. In this case, you retrieve the caption and value of selected items by checking the Selected property of each element in the Items collection:

```
For Each li As ListItem In Select2.Items
    If li.Selected Then
        Debug.WriteLine(li.Text & " (" & li.Value & ")")
    End If
Next
```

The HtmlTable, HtmlTableRow, and HtmlTableCell Classes

An HTML table consists of an HtmlTable object, which exposes a Rows collection. Each element of this collection is an HtmlTableRow object, which in turn exposes a Cells collection of HtmlTableCell elements. The properties that these classes expose let you finely control the appearance of the table and its cells:

■ The Width and Height properties affect the size of the table or an individual cell. The HtmlTableRow class doesn't expose these properties because a row is as wide as the table and as tall as its tallest cell.

■ The BgColor property affects the background color of the table, its rows, or its individual cells. This property can be assigned a value in the format #RRGGBB (the red, green, and blue components in hex format) or a predefined color name in the following list: Black, Blue, Cyan, Gray, Green, Lime, Magenta, Maroon, Navy, Olive, Purple, Red, Silver, Teal, White, or Yellow.

■ You can control the appearance of the border by using the Border property (border width in pixels) and the BorderColor property.

■ The Align property can be Left, Center, or Right and affects the horizontal alignment of the table, its rows, and its individual cells. The VAlign property can be Top, Middle, or Bottom and is used with table rows and cells to control their vertical alignment.

■ The CellPadding property sets the distance in pixels between a table cell and the table border. The CellSpacing property sets the distance between adjacent cells in the table.

■ The ColSpan property determines how many table columns a given cell takes. The RowSpan property determines how many table rows a cell takes.

You create a table programmatically by adding HtmlTableCell objects to an HtmlTable-Row, and then adding the HtmlTableRow object to the table. Here's a code snippet that creates three rows of four cells each and adds them to the control named Table1. (See Figure 24-8.)

```
For row As Integer = 0 To 2
    Dim tr As New HtmlTableRow()        ' Create a new row.
    For col As Integer = 0 To 3
        Dim tc As New HtmlTableCell()   ' Create a new cell.
        tc.InnerText = String.Format("({0},{1})", row, col)
        tr.Cells.Add(tc)                ' Add the cell to the row.
    Next
    Table1.Rows.Add(tr)                 ' Add the row to the table.
Next
```

You set the text inside each cell by means of the InnerText or InnerHtml property. You can also affect its background color with the BgColor property, and the alignment of the text with the Align and VAlign properties.

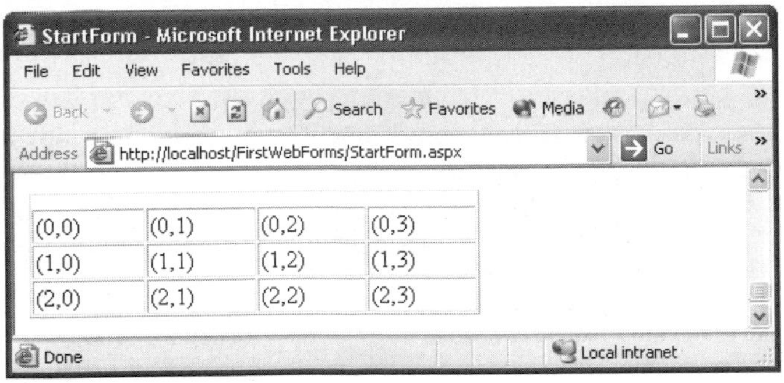

Figure 24-8   An HtmlTable control rendered in Internet Explorer

The HtmlInputFile Class

The HtmlInputFile control is a combination of a text box field and a button. (See Figure 24-9.) It lets the user upload a file to the Web server so that your ASP.NET code can grab it and save it locally for further processing. This control works on Internet Explorer 3.02 or later, and compatible browsers.

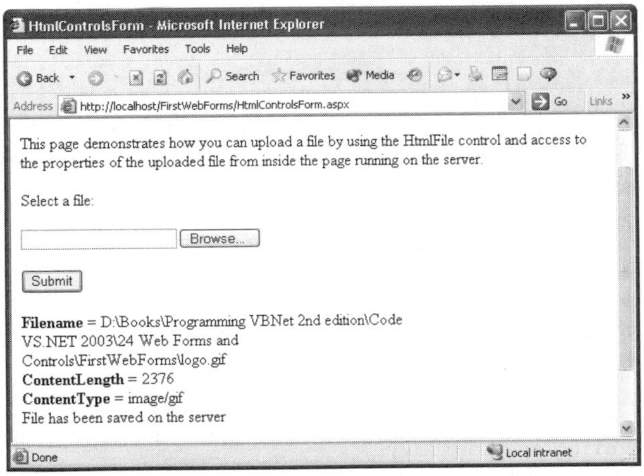

Figure 24-9   The HtmlInputFile control in action

The HtmlInputFile control requires that the Enctype property of the form be set to multipart/form-data. You can't set this property in the Properties window if you're in design mode, so you must switch to HTML mode and click on the <form> tag. At this point, all the form properties appear in the Properties window and you can assign the property. The <form> tag should now look like this:

```
<form id="Form1" method="post" runat="server" enctype="multipart/form-data">
```

The HtmlInputFile control doesn't raise any server-side events, so you must add at least a submit button to process it. You can determine name, size, and type of the file being posted by means of the control's PostedFile property, which also exposes a SaveAs method to save the file on the server. Here's some demo code that shows how to work with this control:

```
' Button1 is the submit button on the form.
Private Sub Button1_ServerClick(ByVal sender As Object, _
    ByVal e As EventArgs) Handles Button1.ServerClick
    Dim msg As String
    If Not File1.PostedFile Is Nothing Then
        ' Determine properties of the posted file.
        msg = "Filename = " & File1.PostedFile.FileName & "<br>"
        msg &= "ContentLength = " & File1.PostedFile.ContentLength & "<br>"
        msg &= "ContentType = " & File1.PostedFile.ContentType & "<br>"
        ' Save it on the server.
        File1.PostedFile.SaveAs("C:\file.dat")
        msg &= "File has been saved on the server"
    Else
        ' No file has been posted.
        msg = "No file has been posted"
    End If
    ' Show the message in a Label control.
    DIV1.InnerHtml = msg
End Sub
```

You can set the control's Accept property to limit the type of files that can be posted to the server. This property is a comma-delimited list of valid MIME types—for example, image/* for accepting all image types or application/octet-stream to accept .exe files. Remember that security must be configured so that the ASP.NET worker process can write to the destination directory. (You can read more about ASP.NET security in Chapter 27.)

Web Forms Controls

All the Web Forms controls are located on the Web Forms tab of the Visual Studio Toolbox and belong to the System.Web.UI.WebControls namespace. However, in this section I'll describe only the simplest controls in this group, namely those that extend the functionality of basic HTML controls. Template controls aren't in this group and are discussed in the next chapter. Figure 24-10 shows how these controls appear in the Visual Studio .NET designer.

Whereas HTML Server controls are rendered in the Visual Studio HTML editor as plain HTML tags, Web Forms controls create special XML tags in the <asp:*classname*> format. For example, this is how the controls in Figure 24-10 appear in the HTML editor after I trim some portions to make the text more concise:

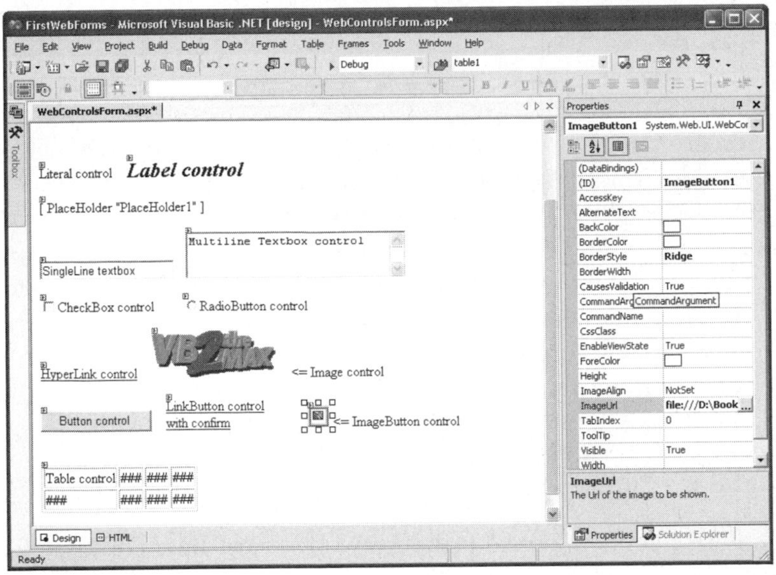

Figure 24-10   The Web Forms controls at design time

```
<form id="Form1" method="post" runat="server">
  <asp:Literal id="Literal1" runat="server"
    Text="Literal control"></asp:Literal>
  <asp:Label id="Label1" runat="server" Font-Bold="True"
    Font-Italic="True" Font-Size="Large">Label control</asp:Label>
  <asp:Panel id="Panel1" runat="server" Width="160px"
    Height="47px">Panel</asp:Panel>
  <asp:PlaceHolder id="PlaceHolder1" runat="server"></asp:PlaceHolder>
  <asp:TextBox id="TextBox1" runat="server">SingleLine textbox</asp:TextBox>
  <asp:TextBox id="TextBox2" runat="server" TextMode="MultiLine"
    Rows="3">Multiline Textbox control</asp:TextBox>
  <asp:CheckBox id="CheckBox1" runat="server"
    Text="CheckBox control"></asp:CheckBox>
  <asp:RadioButton id="RadioButton1" runat="server"
    Text="RadioButton control"></asp:RadioButton>
  <asp:HyperLink id="HyperLink1" runat="server">
    HyperLink control</asp:HyperLink>   
  <asp:Image id="Image1" runat="server" ImageUrl="\logo.gif"></asp:Image>
  <asp:Button id="Button1" runat="server" Text="Button control"></asp:Button>
  <asp:LinkButton id="LinkButton1" runat="server">
    LinkButton control </asp:LinkButton>
  <asp:ImageButton id="ImageButton1" runat="server" BorderStyle="Ridge"
    ImageUrl="print.gif"></asp:ImageButton>

  <asp:Table id="Table1" runat="server" BorderWidth="1px" GridLines="Both">
    <asp:TableRow>
      <asp:TableCell Text="Table control"></asp:TableCell>
      <asp:TableCell></asp:TableCell>
       <asp:TableCell></asp:TableCell>
      <asp:TableCell></asp:TableCell>
```

```
    </asp:TableRow>
      ⋮
  </asp:Table></P>
</form>
```

Unlike HTML Server controls, Web Forms controls expose a consistent set of properties, whose names don't necessarily reflect the name of the HTML attribute to which they map. For example, all the Web Forms controls expose a Text property that determines the string displayed in the control. Even HTML controls that don't display a caption—for example, check boxes and radio buttons—expose the Text property (which in this case is opportunely translated into plain text adjacent to the control). Another example: all controls expose the BorderStyle and BorderColor properties for controlling the border drawn around the control. If the control doesn't have a native border, it's embedded in a <span> tag with an appropriate style attribute.

The WebControl Base Class

All visible Web Forms controls derive from the WebControl class and therefore inherit its properties, methods, and events. So it makes sense to have a look at this abstract class before I describe more specific controls.

You're already familiar with most of the properties exposed by the WebControl class because they're inherited from the Control class (which is also the base class for the Page object). Most of these properties are self-explanatory—such as ForeColor, Back-Color, BorderColor, BorderStyle, BorderWidth, Font, TabIndex, and ToolTip—or have been described previously, such as ID, ClientID, Parent, Page, EnableViewState, Style, and Attributes. All controls expose the DataBind method (which binds the control to its data source), and the DataBinding event (which fires when the control binds to its data source).

You might have problems working with the Width, Height, and BorderWidth properties because they must be assigned a Unit object. This auxiliary class exposes shared methods to convert from pixels, points ($1/_{72}$ inch), and from a percentage value (relative to the container's width):

```
MyControl.Width = Unit.Pixel(100)      ' 100 pixels
MyControl.Width = Unit.Point(144)      ' 144 points (2 inches)
MyControl.Width = Unit.Percentage(50) ' 50% of the parent's width
```

You can also use the Parse method to convert from a string, as in this code snippet:

```
MyControl.Width = Unit.Parse("170px") ' 170 pixels
MyControl.Width = Unit.Parse("60%")   ' 60% of the parent's width
```

Main Properties and Events

Table 24-3 lists the basic Web Forms controls, the corresponding HTML tags, and their main properties and events. (These Web Forms controls don't expose any methods other than those inherited by the WebControl class.) You already know how to use many of these properties, either because I already described them—as is the case with the AutoPostBack and MaxLength properties—or because their names and meanings are the same as in the Windows Forms package—for example, the Text, Checked, Wrap, TextAlign, and Tooltip properties.

Table 24-3 Web Forms Controls and Their Main Properties and Events

Class	Generated HTML	Properties	Events
Literal	plain text	Text	(none)
Label	...	Text	(none)
Panel	<div>...</div>	BackImageUrl, HorizontalAlign, Wrap	(none)
PlaceHolder	(none)	(none)	(none)
TextBox	<input type="text"> <input type="password"> <textarea>...</textarea>	AutoPostBack, TextMode, ReadOnly, MaxLength, Rows, Columns, Wrap, Text	Text-Changed
CheckBox	<input type="checkbox">	AutoPostBack, Checked, Text, TextAlign	Checked-Changed
RadioButton	<input type="radio">	AutoPostBack, Checked, Text, TextAlign, GroupName	Checked-Changed
Image	<img>	ImageUrl, ImageAlign, AlternateText	(none)
HyperLink	<a>...</a>	ImageUrl, Text, NavigateUrl, Target	(none)
Button	<input type="submit"> <input type="button">	Text, CausesValidation, Command-Name, CommandArgument	Click, Command
LinkButton	<a>...</a>	Text, CausesValidation, Command-Name, CommandArgument	Click, Command
ImageButton	<a><img ...></a>	ImageUrl, ImageAlign, AlternateText, CausesValidation, CommandName, CommandArgument	Click, Command
Table	<table>...</table>	BackImageUrl, GridLines, Horizontal-Align, CellPadding, CellSpacing, Rows	(none)
TableRow	<tr>...</tr>	HorizontalAlign, VerticalAlign, Cells	(none)
TableCell	<td>...</td>	Text, HorizontalAlign, VerticalAlign, Wrap, ColumnSpan, RowSpan	(none)

The Literal, Label, Panel, and PlaceHolder Controls

The Literal control is undoubtedly the simplest Web Forms control because it exposes only one property and no events (other than those inherited from the Control class).

You can use it to insert any HTML text you want by using its Text property. Your insertion can be an HTML tag or just text:

```
Literal1.Text = "Just plain text"
Literal2.Text = "<I><B>Bold Italic Text</I></B>"
```

Not counting the properties inherited from the WebControls class, the Label control exposes only the Text property, which it renders inside a <span> and </span> pair of tags. Unlike the Literal control (which derives from Control), the Label control inherits many style properties from its WebControl base class, so you can display a message with a foreground and background color, your preferred font, and so on.

The Panel can be used to define an HTML region enclosed between <div> and </div> tags. The BackImageUrl property lets you specify a background image that's automatically tiled to fill the screen portion assigned to the Panel, and you can decide how the contents are aligned by using the HorizontalAlign and Wrap properties.

The PlaceHolder control doesn't generate any HTML text. Rather, it simply provides a way for you to dynamically insert new controls in a specific position on the form at run time by using its Controls collection:

```
' Use a Literal control to display static text.
PlaceHolder1.Controls.Add(New LiteralControl("Enter the name of the user"))
' Create a TextBox control, and set its main properties.
Dim tb As New TextBox()
tb.Width = Unit.Pixel(100)
tb.ID = "txtUser"
' Show it on the form using the PlaceHolder control.
PlaceHolder1.Controls.Add(tb)
```

The HyperLink, Image, Button, LinkButton, and ImageButton Controls

These controls offer similar functionality and it's easy to get confused, so I'll describe them together and compare their properties.

The Image control is the simplest of the group because it maps to the <img> HTML tag. It exposes only three properties and no events in addition to those inherited from the WebControl class. ImageUrl is the URL of the image. ImageAlign is an enumerated value that tells how the image must be aligned. AlternateText is the text displayed if the browser has disabled graphics rendering. When you're assigning the ImageUrl property from the Properties window, you can select an image by using the Select Image dialog box. (See Figure 24-11.)

The HyperLink control maps to the <a> HTML tag. As a nice touch, you can specify either a string (with the Text property) or an image (with the ImageUrl property) for the visible portion of the hyperlink. You can assign both the ImageUrl and the NavigateUrl property using a dialog box. The Target property indicates the target frame in the page pointed to by the NavigateUrl property. Like the Image control, the

HyperLink control never does a postback: when the user clicks on it, the browser jumps to the new URL without raising any server-side events.

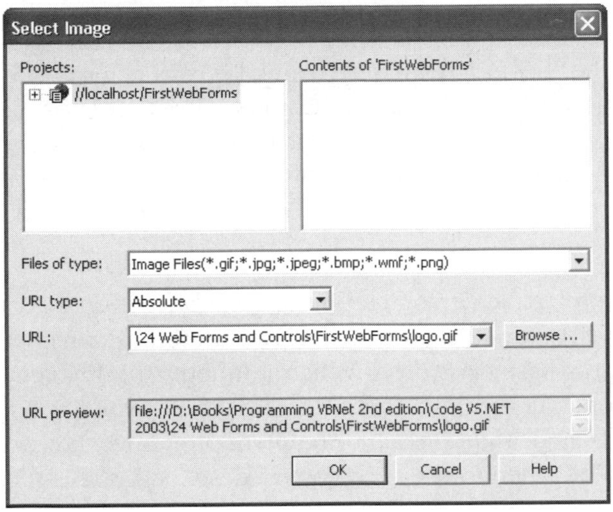

Figure 24-11   The Select Image dialog box

The Button control implements the standard submit button, with a few additional capabilities. You can place multiple buttons on the form, each one with a different Command-Name property (for example, Edit, Sort, GroupBy) and possibly a different CommandArgument property as well (for example, Ascending or Descending to specify the direction of the sort operation). These properties are especially useful when the button is used inside a template control such as DataList, but they simplify programming even when the button is placed directly on the form's surface.

You can trap clicks on a Button control by means of either its Click or Command event. A click fires both events in all cases, but the latter event lets you access the values of the CommandName or CommandArgument properties to determine the action that the user requested:

```
' This routine handles the Command event from three Button controls.
Private Sub Button_Command(ByVal sender As Object, _
    ByVal e As CommandEventArgs) _
    Handles btnEdit.Command, btnSortAsc.Command, btnSortDesc.Command

    Select Case e.CommandName
        Case "Edit"
            ' Start an edit operation.
            ⋮
        Case "Sort"
            If e.CommandArgument = "Ascending" Then
                ' Perform an ascending sort.
                ⋮
            ElseIf e.CommandArgument = "Descending" Then
                ' Perform a descending sort.
                ⋮
```

```
            Else
                ' (This should never happen.)
            End If
    End Select
End Sub
```

The LinkButton appears to the user as a textual hyperlink but works more like a Button control in that it supports the CommandName and CommandArgument properties and raises both a Click and a Command server-side event. It doesn't support the Navigate-Url and the Target properties, and if you want to redirect the browser to another page you must do it manually using a Response.Redirect or a Server.Transfer method from inside the server-side event.

Finally, the ImageButton control implements a graphical, clickable button that raises both the Click and the Command server-side events. You can therefore consider it a mix between the Image control (its base class, from which it inherits the ImageUrl, Image-Align, and AlternateText properties) and the Button control (from which it borrows the CausesValidation, CommandName, and CommandArgument properties, but not the Text property). Here's a summary of when to use each control described in this section:

- Use an Image control to display an image that doesn't react to clicks.

- Use a HyperLink control to display a link to another page that doesn't require any server-side processing.

- Use a Button control for the usual push-button control that must fire a server-side event when clicked.

- Use a LinkButton control for a hyperlink element that must fire a server-side event when clicked.

- Use an ImageButton control for a clickable image that must fire a server-side event.

If a button performs a potentially dangerous operation, such as deleting a record, you might want to ask the user to confirm the operation. You can do that by attaching a piece of JavaScript code to the button's onclick event. The simplest way to do this is via code in the Form_Load event handler:

```
Dim code As String = "javascript:return confirm('Do you confirm?');"
LinkButton1.Attributes.Add("onclick", code)
```

When the user clicks on the button, a message box appears. If the user clicks on the Cancel button, the button won't perform its default operation (typically a postback).

Other Web Forms Controls

The TextBox control exposes the TextMode property, an enumerated value that can be SingleLine, MultiLine, or Password. If it's a multiline TextBox, you can use the Rows and Columns properties to affect its size and the Wrap property to enable or disable wordwrapping.

The RadioButton control exposes a GroupName property. All the RadioButton controls on a form with the same value for this property comprise a group of options that are mutually exclusive. You must assign a nonempty string to this property even if there's only one group of radio buttons on the form; otherwise each control will be considered a group by itself and won't work as expected.

The Table, TableRow, and TableCell controls work exactly like their HTML Server control counterparts, including the ability to add new rows and columns using the Rows and Columns collection. You can, however, assign the contents of a table cell using the Text property (instead of the InnerText or InnerHtml properties for HTML controls). Another important difference is how the Visual Studio designer deals with the Table control: using the dialog boxes shown in Figure 24-12 and without writing any code at all, you can add rows and cells at design time by clicking on the Rows item in the Properties window.

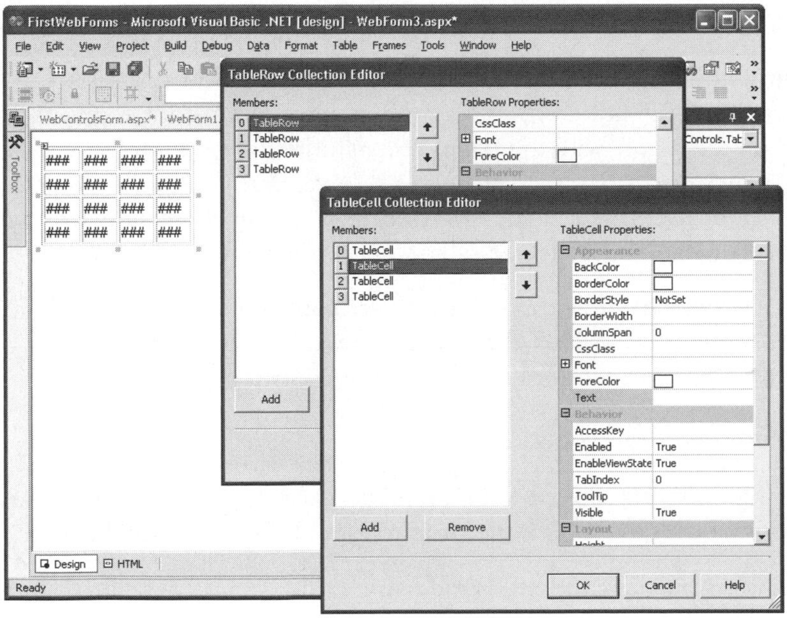

Figure 24-12   Creating TableRow and TableCell elements at design time

Validation Controls

The Web Forms portion of the framework supports six validation controls whose purpose is to perform the most common types of validation on other controls on the form, typically TextBox controls:

- The RequiredFieldValidator control checks that a given input control isn't empty.

- The RangeValidator control checks that the value of an input control is within a specified range of valid values.

- The CompareValidator control checks that the value of an input control is equal to, lower than, or higher than another value, which can be a constant or the contents of another control.

- The RegularExpressionValidator control checks that the value in an input control matches a given regular expression.

- The CustomValidator control defines a client-side or server-side function (or both) that validates the contents of an input control.

- The ValidationSummary control gathers the error messages from all the validation controls on the same form and displays them in a region of the form or in a message box.

An important note: all the validation controls except RequiredFieldValidator check the value of the companion input field only if it isn't empty; if the field is empty, the validation succeeds. For this reason, you must use an additional RequiredFieldValidator control if you want to check that the input field contains a nonempty value.

The great thing about a validation control is that the validation is performed both inside the client browser (if the browser supports scripts and script support hasn't been disabled) and on the server with the page's ClientTarget property or the validation control's EnableClientScript property. The server-side validation is performed in all cases because a malicious user might save the HTML, filter out all client-side scripts, and post the page to the server. (This is a type of spoofing attack.)

The first five validation controls can send their error message to the ValidationSummary control on the same page or can display their own message. In the latter case, you should place the validation control near the input control it validates.

Properties, Methods, and Events

All the validation controls except ValidationSummary derive from the BaseValidator base class, from which they inherit the properties and methods they have in common:

- The ControlToValidate property is the name of the input control to be validated.

- The EnableClientScript property is a Boolean value that determines whether validation can be performed via client-side scripts. (The default is True.)

- The Enabled property is a Boolean value that tells whether the validation must be performed. (The default is True.)

- The ErrorMessage property is the string displayed in the validation control or in the ValidationSummary control if the validation fails.

- The Display property is an enumerated value that specifies whether and how the error message is displayed in the validation control. It can be Static (the default, space for the message is allocated on the form), Dynamic (the validation control takes screen space only when it displays the error message), or None (the error message is never displayed in the validation control).

- The IsValid property is a Boolean that tells whether the validation failed and the error message should be displayed. It can be set programmatically to suppress unwanted error messages.

- The Validate method performs the validation on the associated input control and updates the IsValid property.

The Display property tells whether the error message appears in the validation control. When you use the Static setting (the default), the validation control is resized to contain the error message, but the message itself is initially hidden. This setting ensures that the form layout doesn't suddenly change when the error message is actually displayed. (Validation controls display the error message as soon as the user moves the focus from the input control containing the value that fails the validation.) The error message is made visible by the client-side script code that performs the validation. If client-side scripts are disabled, the Static setting is ignored because the page must be rebuilt anyway on the server, and the validation control behaves as if the Dynamic setting had been specified.

The BaseValidator class derives from the Label control and therefore inherits all the usual display properties, such as BackColor, BorderStyle, BorderColor, and Font. By default, the ForeColor property of validation controls is set to red, but you can change it to match your form's color scheme.

The Text property behaves in a peculiar way with validation controls, however. Even if you specify a nonempty string for this property, it becomes visible only when the associated input control fails to validate (and only if the Display property isn't None). If you leave the Text property empty, the ErrorMessage value is shown instead. However, the string shown inside the ValidationSummary control is always taken from the ErrorString property, not the Text property. Therefore, you can implement several different behaviors:

- You can display the same message near the input field and in the ValidationSummary control by assigning the message to the ErrorMessage property and leaving the Text property empty.

- You can display a message near the input field and a different message in the ValidationSummary control by assigning these messages to the Text and ErrorMessage properties, respectively. For example, you might assign an asterisk to the Text property so that the user can immediately see which fields failed the validation and read a more descriptive error message in the ValidationSummary control.

- You can display just a message near the input field by storing it in the Text property and assigning an empty string to the ErrorMessage property.

- You can display just a message in the ValidationSummary control by assigning the message to the ErrorMessage property and setting the Display property to None.

In addition to the common members inherited from BaseValidator, each validation control exposes its own specific properties and events, which I'll explain in the following sections.

I've prepared a form that contains one example of each validation control, plus a ValidationSummary control at the top of the page. (See Figure 24-13.) As you'll see, in all cases except the CustomValidator control you don't have to write any code to perform validation chores.

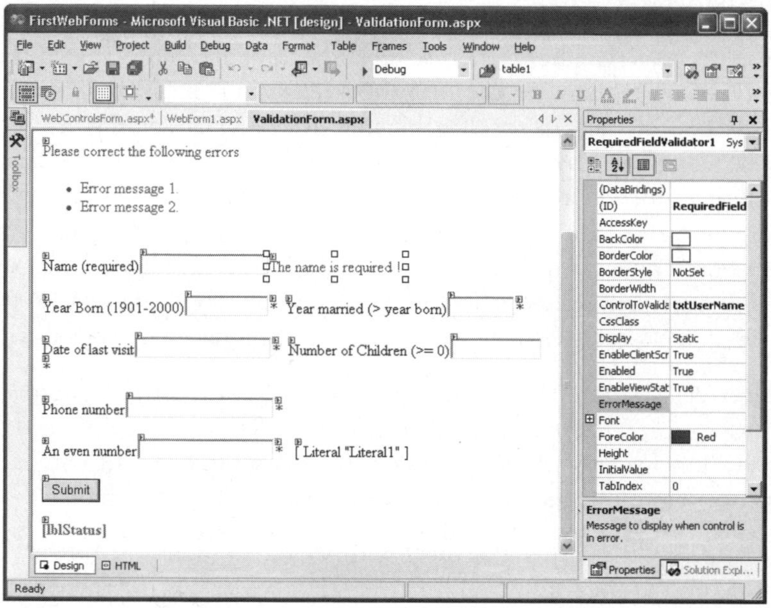

Figure 24-13   A demo form for testing all the validation controls at design time and run time

The RequiredFieldValidator Control

The RequiredFieldValidator control is the simplest of the group; you just assign the name of the control that must contain a value to its ControlToValidate property and set a suitable error message:

```
' Check that the txtUserName control contains a nonempty string.
RequiredFieldValidator1.ControlToValidate = "txtUserName"
RequiredFieldValidator1.ErrorMessage = "User name is a required field"
```

The RequiredFieldValidator control checks that the value of the input control differs from the value of its InitialValue property (which is a null string by default), so you can still use this validation control if the initial value of the input field isn't a null string. This feature is useful if a TextBox control is initialized with a message such as "(Enter your email address)".

```
RequiredFieldValidator1.ControlToValidate = "txtEMailAddress"
RequiredFieldValidator1.InitialValue = "(Enter your email address)"
```

The RangeValidator Control

The RangeValidator control exposes three properties: MinimumValue, MaximumValue, and Type. The third property determines the type of the value and affects how the values are compared. It can be String (the default), Integer, Double, Date, and Currency. (Notice that this control doesn't work with Long values.) This code uses a RangeValidator control to check whether a txtYearBorn field contains a value in the range 1901 to 2000 (inclusive):

```
RangeValidator1.ControlToValidate = "txtYearBorn"
RangeValidator1.MinimumValue = "1901"
RangeValidator1.MaximumValue = "2000"
RangeValidator1.Type = ValidationDataType.Integer
RangeValidator1.ErrorMessage = "Year Born must be in the range [1901,2000]"
```

The CompareValidator Control

The CompareValidator control can compare the contents of the associated input control with another value, either the constant value specified by the ValueToCompare property or the contents of another control specified by the ControlToCompare property. The Type property tells the type of both values and the Operator property is an enumerated value that specifies the comparison operator to be applied to the two values (can be Equal, NotEqual, GreaterThan, GreaterThanEqual, LessThan, LessThanEqual, or Data-TypeCheck). The following code checks that the txtYearMarried control contains an integer value that's greater than the value of the txtYearBorn control:

```
CompareValidator1.ControlToValidate = "txtYearMarried"
CompareValidator1.ControlToCompare = "txtYearBorn"
CompareValidator1.Type = ValidationDataType.Integer
CompareValidator1.Operator = ValidationCompareOperator.GreaterThan
```

You can assign DataTypeCheck to the Operator property if you just want to verify that the contents of the input field can be safely converted to the data type specified by the Type property. In this case, the ControlToCompare and ValueToCompare properties are ignored:

```
' Check that txtLastVisit contains a valid date.
CompareValidator2.ControlToValidate = "txtLastVisit"
CompareValidator2.Type = ValidationDataType.Date
CompareValidator2.Operator = ValidationCompareOperator.DataTypeCheck
CompareValidator2.ErrorMessage = "Last visit isn't a valid date."
```

When comparing the contents of your control to a constant value, you must use the ValueToCompare property:

```
CompareValidator3.ControlToValidate = "txtChildren"
CompareValidator3.ValueToCompare = "0"
CompareValidator3.Type = ValidationDataType.Integer
CompareValidator3.Operator = ValidationCompareOperator.GreaterThanEqual
CompareValidator3.ErrorMessage = "Number of children must >= 0"
```

The following are potential problems you might encounter when using the Compare-Validator control:

■ No validation is performed if the input control is empty, so you should use a RequiredFieldValidator control to ensure that an empty field displays an error message.

- If the value in the input control can be converted to the data type specified by the Type property but the value in the control specified by the ControlToCompare property can't be converted, the input control passes the validation. For this reason, you might need an additional RangeValidator or CompareValidator control to check that the other control contains a valid value.

- If the value specified in the ValueToCompare property can't be converted to the data type specified by the Type property, an exception is thrown.

- In general, you should never specify both the ControlToCompare and ValueToCompare properties. If you do, the ControlToCompare property has the priority.

The RegularExpressionValidator Control

If you're familiar with regular expressions—which I covered in Chapter 11—using the RegularExpressionValidator control is a breeze. You just have to set the ControlToValidate and the ValidationExpression properties:

```
' Ensure that a field contains a phone number in the (###)###-#### format.
RegularExpressionValidator1.ControlToValidate = "txtPhoneNumber"
RegularExpressionValidator1.ValidationExpression = "\(\d{3}\)\d{3}-\d{4}"
RegularExpressionValidator1.ErrorMessage = _
    "Please enter the phone number in (###)###-#### format"
```

In many cases, you don't even have to be a regular expression wizard to use this validation control effectively. In fact, Visual Studio .NET lets you pick the regular expressions for the most common field types, such as phone numbers, postal codes, URLs, e-mail addresses, and social security numbers. (See Figure 24-14.) Here are other useful regular expressions:

```
' (rev1 is a RegularExpressionValidator control.)
' A one-character Yes/No/True/False field
rev1.ValidationExpression = "[YyNnTtFf]"

' 16-digit credit card number, with or without spaces
rev1.ValidationExpression = "(\d{4}( \d{4}){3}|\d{16})"

' A month/year expiration date in the format mm/yy
rev1.ValidationExpression = "(0[1-9]|1[0-2])/\d\d"

' An alphanumeric password of at least 8 characters
rev1.ValidationExpression = "[A-Za-z0-9]{8,}"
```

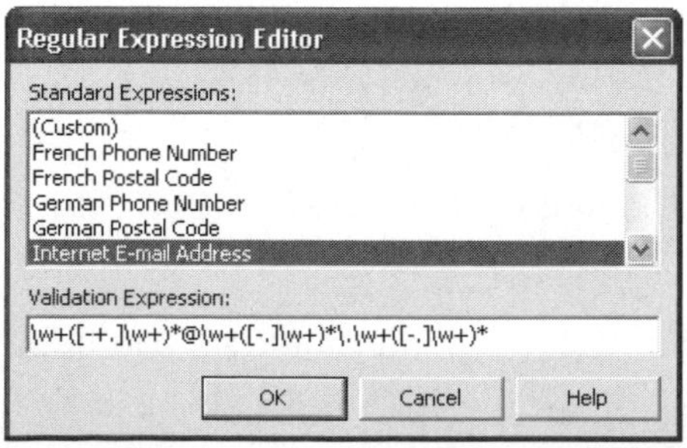

Figure 24-14   Visual Studio lets you select the most common regular expressions from a dialog box.

Keep these particulars in mind when working with the RegularExpressionValidator:

- If the input control is empty, the validation always succeeds. Therefore, you might need to add a RequiredFieldValidation to display an error message if the end user didn't type anything in the field.

- The regular expression is applied either on the client side (using the JScript regular expression engine) or on the server side (using the .NET regular expression engine) if client-side scripts are disabled. The JScript syntax is a subset of the .NET syntax, so in general the same regular expression works well in both cases. But you should either avoid .NET syntax forms that aren't supported by JScript—for example, the (?i) option for case-insensitive comparison—or disable client-side scripting with the EnableClientScript property.

The CustomValidator Control

If none of the validator controls shown you so far fulfills your validation needs, you can write your own validation routine and enforce it with the CustomValidator control. This control supports both client-side validation functions (through the ClientValidationFunction property) and server-side validation functions (through the ServerValidate event). The client-side validation function must be written in any script language supported by the browser—typically JScript, but it also can be VBScript if you're sure all your clients use Internet Explorer.

Both the client-side validation routine and the ServerValidate event receive two arguments: an Object value that contains a reference to the validation control and a ServerValidateEventArgs object that exposes two properties. Value is the value in the input control to be validated, and IsValid is a property that you must set to True to accept the value or False to reject it. For example, consider this JScript function, which checks whether a number is even:

```
<script language="JScript">
<!--
function CheckEvenNumber(source, args) {
    var theNumber = args.Value;
    if (theNumber % 2 == 0)
        args.IsValid = true;
    else
        args.IsValid = false;
}
//-->
</script>
```

You can enter this code right in the HTML editor, or you can dynamically assign it to the Text property of a Literal control on the form:

```
Literal1.Text = "<script language=""JScript""><!-- " & ControlChars.CrLf _
    & "function CheckEvenNumber(source, args) {" & ControlChars.CrLf _
    & " var theNumber = args.Value;" & ControlChars.CrLf _
    & " if (theNumber % 2 == 0) " & ControlChars.CrLf _
    & "   args.IsValid = true;" & ControlChars.CrLf _
```

```
        & "   else " & ControlChars.CrLf _
        & "      args.IsValid = false;" & ControlChars.CrLf _
        & "} " & ControlChars.CrLf _
        & "//--> " & ControlChars.CrLf _
        & "</script>" & ControlChars.CrLf
```

You can (and should) perform the same validation task in a ServerValidate event as well. As you see, the code is the same except for the language used and the fact that you can use early binding on the server:

```
Private Sub CustomValidator1_ServerValidate(ByVal source As Object, _
    ByVal args As System.Web.UI.WebControls.ServerValidateEventArgs) _
    Handles CustomValidator1.ServerValidate

    Dim theNumber As Integer = CInt(args.Value)
    If (theNumber Mod 2) = 0 Then
        args.IsValid = True
    Else
        args.IsValid = False
    End If
End Sub
```

Both the client-side and the server-side functions should implement exactly the same validation strategy—otherwise, your application might perform differently, depending on whether client-side scripting is supported. Also, you should always implement the server-side validation routine to prevent spoofing.

To enable a CustomValidator control, you must assign the ControlToValidate and the ClientValidationFunction properties:

```
CustomValidator1.ControlToValidate = "txtEvenNumber"
CustomValidator1.ClientValidationFunction = "CheckEvenNumber"
CustomValidator1.ErrorMessage = "Enter an even number in this field"
```

If the control referenced by the ControlToValidate property is empty, no validation occurs, so you might need a RequiredFieldValidator control to cover that case as well. Also, it's legal to leave the ControlToValidate property blank, in which case the validation function will be called when the user submits the form. This practice can be useful for performing validation tasks that involve multiple controls. (In this case, the args.Value property always receives a null string.)

The ValidationSummary Control

You use this control to gather the error message strings for all the other controls on the form and display them to the end user:

- If the ShowSummary property is True (the default), the error messages are displayed within the ValidationSummary control itself.

- If the ShowMessageBox property is True, the error messages are displayed in a message box. (The default value for this property is False.) To display the message box, the EnableClientScript property must be True as well.

- The HeaderText property is a string displayed just before the first error message, both on the page and in the message box; you typically assign it a string like "Please correct the following errors."

- The DisplayMode property is an enumerated value that specifies how the individual error messages are arranged on the control or the message box. Available options are BulletList (default), List, and SingleParagraph; if you select the single-paragraph mode, you should append a suitable punctuation symbol at the end of each error message.

The result shown in Figure 24-15 was produced by setting these properties:

```
ValidationSummary1.ShowMessageBox = True
ValidationSummary1.ShowSummary = True           ' (the default)
ValidationSummary1.DisplayMode = ValidationSummaryDisplayMode.BulletList
ValidationSummary1.HeaderText = "Please correct the following errors"
```

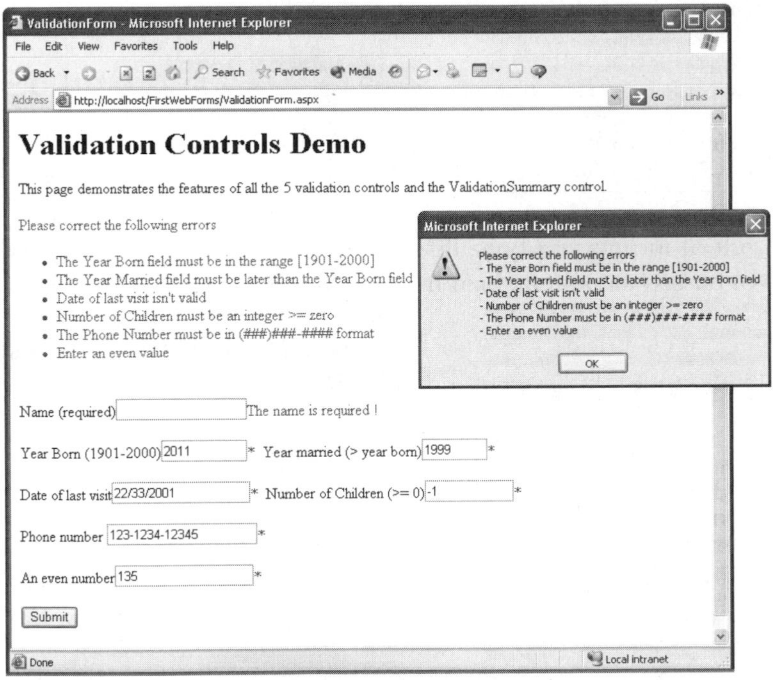

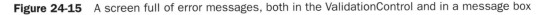

Figure 24-15   A screen full of error messages, both in the ValidationControl and in a message box

Notice that the ErrorMessage property of the first validation control in the demo program—the RequiredFieldValidator associated with the txtUserName control—is set to an empty string, and for this reason it doesn't appear in the ValidationSummary control or in the message box.

Server-Side Validation

Regardless of whether client-side scripts are enabled, all the validation controls validate their companion controls when the page is submitted to the server, without any intervention on you part. Nevertheless, you usually explicitly perform server-side validation in a specific location in code—such as in the Page_Load event or in the Click event of the button that fires the postback—so that your application can take any step that is appropriate.

You can force the validation of all controls by invoking the Validate method. Then you can check the page's IsValid property and, if False, iterate over all the validation controls to detect which fields contain invalid values:

```
Private Sub Button1_Click(ByVal sender As Object, ByVal e As EventArgs) _
    Handles Button1.Click
    ' Force the validation of all controls.
    Me.Validate()

    If Not Me.IsValid Then
        Dim errorCount As Integer
        ' Count how many errors were found.
        For Each ctrl As BaseValidator In Me.Validators
            If Not ctrl.IsValid Then errorCount += 1
        Next
        ' Display a suitable error message.
        lblStatus.Text = "There are " & errorCount.ToString & " errors."
    End If
End Sub
```

Notice that the message prepared by the preceding code is displayed only if the client-side scripts have been disabled in the browser or the client-side validation has been turned off. In fact, if client-side validation is enabled, the form can't be posted back to the server until all input fields contain a valid value.

List Controls

All the controls in this group—DropDownList, ListBox, RadioButtonList, CheckBox-List—inherit from the ListControl class and therefore have several members in common in addition to those inherited from the WebControl base class. Like their Windows Forms counterparts, all these controls expose the Items, SelectedIndex, SelectedItem, and SelectedValue properties (this last property was added in version 1.1 of the .NET Framework), and the SelectedIndexChanged event. They also expose a few properties related to data binding that I'll cover later in the next chapter, namely the DataSource, DataMember, DataTextField, DataValueField, and DataTextFormatString properties.

Filling the Items Collection

The Items property returns a collection of ListItem objects, each one exposing four properties: Text, Selected, Value, and Attributes. The Text property is the string displayed in the control for that item. The Value property is the item's value attribute. The Selected property is a Boolean that tells whether the element is selected or not. (It's useful with the ListBox and CheckBoxList controls, the only controls that support multiple selections.) The Attributes property is, of course, the collection of attributes for that item, which you can use as a repository for additional values associated with the element. You can fill the Items collection in three ways:

- At design time, by clicking on the Items element of the Properties window and adding elements in the ListItem Collection Editor dialog box.

- Through code, by using the Add method of the Items collection; this method takes either a string or a ListItem object.

- By using data binding to fill the controls with the values in a DataReader, a DataTable, a DataView, or any data structure that exposes the IEnumerable interface, such as an ArrayList or a Hashtable object.

The code needed to fill a list control is similar to the code I showed you for the HtmlSelect control. For example, this code creates an array of seven radio buttons displaying the weekday names:

```
Private Sub Page_Load(ByVal sender As Object, ByVal e As EventArgs) _
    Handles MyBase.Load
    If Not Page.IsPostBack Then
        ' Creating the collection of radio buttons via code.
        For i As Integer = 1 To 7
            Dim li As New ListItem(WeekdayName(i), i.ToString)
            RadioButtonList1.Items.Add(li)
        Next
    End If
End Sub
```

Regardless of the technique you adopt to fill the Items collection, you should perform this action only the first time the page is requested—hence the use of the IsPostBack function in the preceding code snippet—because the EnableStateView property is set to True by default. Therefore, the content of a control is automatically preserved in subsequent postbacks. In some cases, you can optimize your application's performance by disabling the ViewState feature for specific controls and filling the control anytime the page is loaded.

Figure 24-16 shows the demo program at design time and inside the browser. All the controls except RadioButtonList were filled using data binding, as I'll explain in the "Data Binding with List Controls" section in Chapter 25.

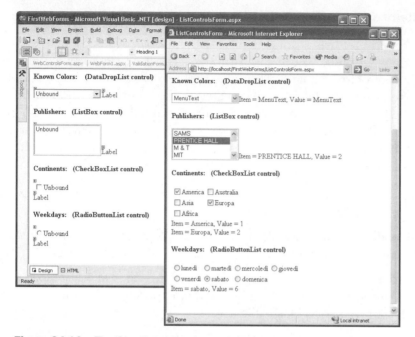

Figure 24-16   The four list controls as they appear in Visual Studio at design time and inside Internet Explorer at run time

The ListBox and DropDownList Controls

From the programmer's perspective, these two controls are very similar. The only difference between a DropDownList control and a ListBox control is that the latter exposes two additional properties: Rows (the number of visible elements in the list area) and SelectionMode (which can be Single or Multiple and serves to enable multiple selections). Both controls expose the BorderStyle, BorderWidth, BorderColor, and all the other members inherited from the ListControl base class.

When the page is posted back to the server, a SelectedIndexChanged event fires if the end user has selected a new element in the control. Inside this event's handler, you can retrieve the selected item by using the SelectedItem property:

```
Private Sub lstPublishers_SelectedIndexChanged(ByVal sender As Object, _
    ByVal e As EventArgs) Handles lstPublishers.SelectedIndexChanged
    ' Update a Label control with information on the selected item.
    Dim li As ListItem = lstPublishers.SelectedItem
    Label1.Text = String.Format("Text={0}, Value={1}", li.Text, li.Value)
End Sub
```

If the SelectionMode property of a ListBox control is set to Multiple, you must iterate over the Items collection and test the Selected property of each ListItem element:

```
Private Sub lstPublishers_SelectedIndexChanged(ByVal sender As Object, _
    ByVal e As System.EventArgs) Handles lstPublishers.SelectedIndexChanged
    Dim msg As String
```

```
    ' Display information on all the selected elements.
    For Each li As ListItem In lstPublishers.Items
        If li.Selected Then
            msg &= String.Format("Text={0}, Value={1}<br>", li.Text, li.Value)
        End If
    Next
    Label1.Text = msg
End Sub
```

The RadioButtonList and CheckBoxList Controls

A RadioButtonList control is functionally similar to a DropDownList or a ListBox control whose SelectionMode property is set to Single, in the sense that it allows the user to select only one of the items in the control. A CheckBoxList control is similar to a List-Box control whose SelectionMode property is set to Multiple.

Even if these two controls don't look like a DropDownList or a ListBox control, you fill their Items collection exactly as you do with the other controls in this group. Likewise, you check which elements are selected by using the SelectedIndex and SelectedItem properties of the control, or the Selected property of individual ListItem objects in the case of the CheckBoxList control. The properties that these two controls have in addition to the ListControl base control affect how they're laid out on the form:

- The TextAlign property tells whether the text is aligned to the right (the default) or the left of the check box or radio button.

- The RepeatLayout property is an enumerated value that specifies whether the elements are displayed in a table (RepeatedLayout.Table value, the default) or not (RepeatedLayout.Flow value).

- The RepeatColumns property specifies how many columns are displayed. By default, elements are displayed in a single column.

- The RepeatDirection property is an enumerated value that specifies whether elements are displayed horizontally (the default) or vertically. If elements are displayed in a single column, this property has no effect.

- The CellPadding and CellSpacing properties specify the distance in pixels between the cells and the border and between individual cells, respectively.

For example, the CheckBoxList control in Figure 24-16 has the RepeatColumns property set to 2 and the RepeatDirection property set to Vertical, whereas the RadioButton-List control has the RepeatColumns property set to 4 and the RepeatDirection property set to Horizontal.

Other Controls

Not counting the template controls, which will be described in the next chapter, the only three controls that I haven't discussed yet are the Calendar control, the AdRotator control, and the Xml control.

The Calendar Control

If you consider the number of properties and events it exposes, the Calendar control is among the most complex controls in ASP.NET, perhaps second only to the DataGrid control. This isn't surprising when you realize that the Calendar control lets you customize the appearance of any visual element; select individual days, weeks, or months; add text or images to individual day cells; finely control whether a day can be selected; and more.

You can precisely determine how the calendar looks by setting the properties in the Style category: DayStyle (style for days in current month); TodayDayStyle (style for today's date); WeekendDayStyle (style for weekend days); SelectedDayStyle (style for selected days); OtherMonthDayStyle (style for days in previous or next months); DayHeaderStyle (style for the header where weekday names appear); TitleStyle (style for the title bar where month name and year number appear); NextPrevStyle (style for navigational Link-Button controls); and SelectorStyle (style for the leftmost column of the selector, which is visible only if week and month selectors are enabled). All these properties are actually TableItemStyle style objects, which derive from the Style class and expose properties such as ForeColor, BackColor, Font, BorderColor, BorderWidth, HorizontalAlign, VerticalAlign, and Wrap. For example, this code changes a few properties of the title bar:

```
' Use a big white title on a red background.
With Calendar1.TitleStyle
    .BackColor = System.Drawing.Color.Red
    .ForeColor = System.Drawing.Color.White
    .Font.Size = New FontUnit(FontSize.XLarge)
End With
' Display only the month name.
Calendar1.TitleFormat = TitleFormat.Month
```

Some properties in the Appearance category affect how the calendar looks: ShowDay-Header, ShowGridLines, ShowNextPrevMonth, ShowTitle, CellPadding (the distance between cells and the control's border), and CellSpacing (the distance between individual cells). A few enumerated properties let you control which day is displayed on the leftmost column (FirstDayOfWeek property), the format of weekday names (DayNameFormat property; can be FirstLetter, FirstTwoLetters, Short, or Full), the title (TitleFormat property; can be MonthYear or Month), and the navigational buttons (NextPrevFormat property; can be ShortMonth, FullMonth, or CustomText). If the Next-PrevFormat property is set to CustomText, you can use the PrevMonthText and Next-MonthText properties to select the caption of the navigational buttons.

The SelectionMode enumerated property determines what the user can select in the calendar. It can be None (selection is disabled), Day (single day), DayWeek (single day or week), or DayWeekMonth (single day, week, or month). In the last case, you can assign the text used for the selector element in the selector column by means of the SelectMonthText property, whose default value is >> (which is rendered as >>). Because this property is taken literally and isn't encoded to HTML, you can also specify an HTML tag—for example, *<img>* to use an image as a selector.

Fortunately, you don't have to assign these properties individually, at least not if you're satisfied with the predefined styles that Visual Studio .NET displays when you click on the Auto Format command in the Properties window or in the control's shortcut menu. (See Figure 24-17.)

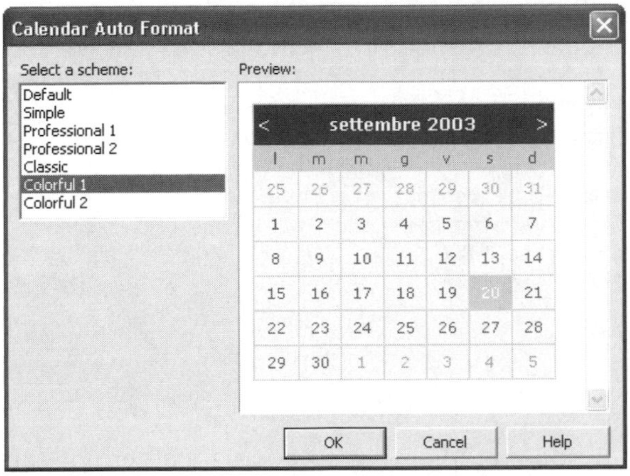

Figure 24-17   Visual Studio .NET predefined calendar styles. Please note that the calendar automatically adapts to the user's locale (Italian, in this case).

You can customize how each individual day cell is rendered by trapping the DayRender event. The second argument for this event exposes two properties:

- Day is the CalendarDay object that describes the day being rendered, and exposes properties such as Date, DayNumberText (the text used to render the day), IsToday, IsWeekend, IsOtherMonth, IsSelected, and IsSelectable. You can set the IsSelectable property to False to prevent the user from selecting this date. All other properties are read-only.

- Cell is the TableCell object that affects the appearance of the cell. This object derives from WebControl and therefore exposes all the usual properties, such as ForeColor, BackColor, and the like, plus a few additional properties, such as HorizontalAlign and VerticalAlign.

For example, see how you can use the DayRender event to change the background color of the days in the range 12/24 to 12/26 and make them nonselectable:

```
Private Sub Calendar1_DayRender(ByVal sender As Object, _
    ByVal e As DayRenderEventArgs) Handles Calendar1.DayRender
    ' Ensures that days 12/24 to 12/26 are displayed with yellow background.
    If Not e.Day.IsOtherMonth Then
        ' Consider only days in the current month.
        If e.Day.Date.Month = 12 AndAlso e.Day.Date.Day >= 24 _
            AndAlso e.Day.Date.Day <= 26 Then
            ' Change the cell background color.
            e.Cell.BackColor = System.Drawing.Color.Yellow
            ' Prevent the user from selecting this day.
```

```
                    e.Day.IsSelectable = False
                End If
            End If
    End Sub
```

You can even display images and load other controls inside each individual cell by leveraging the cell's Controls collection. For example, this code replaces the usual text with a custom image for all the cells corresponding to the first day of the month:

```
Private Sub Calendar1_DayRender(ByVal sender As Object, _
    ByVal e As DayRenderEventArgs) Handles Calendar1.DayRender
    If e.Day.Date.Day = 1 Then
        Dim imgCtrl As New System.Web.UI.WebControls.Image()
        imgCtrl.ImageUrl = "/images/warning.gif"
        imgCtrl.Width = Unit.Percentage(100)
        imgCtrl.Height = Unit.Percentage(100)
        e.Cell.Text = ""
        e.Cell.Controls.Add(imgCtrl)
    End If
End Sub
```

Figure 24-18 shows a calendar based on the preceding code, together with an instance of the AdRotator and the Xml control, which I'll describe shortly. Compared to the DayRender event, the other two events that the Calendar exposes are pretty simple. The event you'll use more frequently is SelectionChanged, which occurs when the user clicks on a day hyperlink:

```
Private Sub Calendar1_SelectionChanged(ByVal sender As Object, _
    ByVal e As EventArgs) Handles Calendar1.SelectionChanged
    ' Display the selected date in a Label control.
    Label1.Text = "Current Selected Date is " & _
        Calendar1.SelectedDate.ToLongDateString()
End Sub
```

Other properties affect date selection and display: TodayDate is the date to be highlighted as the current date; VisibleDate is a date that affects which month is visible in the calendar; SelectedDates is a collection of dates that appear as selected in the calendar. (Use the Add method to add a new selected date or Clear to clear the selection.)

The Calendar control doesn't support data binding, so you must manually assign the SelectedDate property in the Page_Load event and update the data source in the SelectionChanged event handler.

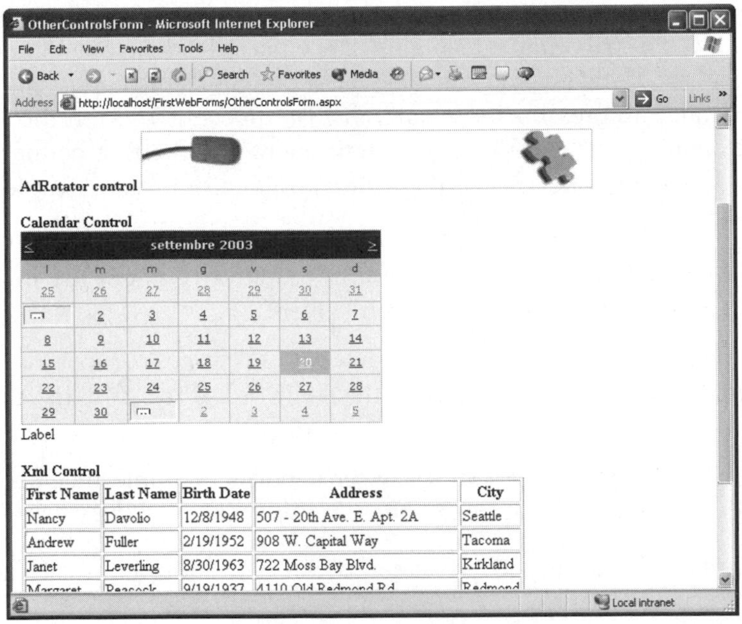

Figure 24-18 A page containing an AdRotator, a Calendar, and an Xml control

The AdRotator Control

The AdRotator control offers the same functionality as the component of the same name included in ASP—that is, the ability to display advertisement banners in a random manner. The most important difference from the ASP component is that the file that contains information about the banners is now in XML format. Here's an example of such a data file:

```xml
<?xml version="1.0" encoding="utf-8" ?>
<Advertisements
    xmlns="http://schemas.microsoft.com/AspNet/AdRotator-Schedule-File">
  <Ad>
    <ImageUrl>/foo_banner.gif </ImageUrl>
    <NavigateUrl>www.foo.com</NavigateUrl>
    <AlternateText>Visit www.foo.com</AlternateText>
    <Keyword>shopping</Keyword>
    <Impressions>20</Impressions>
  </Ad>
  <Ad>
    <ImageUrl>bar_banner.gif</ImageUrl>
    <NavigateUrl>www.bar.com</NavigateUrl>
    <AlternateText>Visit www.bar.com</AlternateText>
    <Keyword>travels</Keyword>
    <Impressions>10</Impressions>
  </Ad>
    ⋮
</Advertisements>
```

Most elements in this file are self-explanatory. ImageUrl is the URL of the image; NavigateUrl is the URL of the page that's displayed if the user clicks on the banner; AlternateText is the text used if the image is unavailable; Keyword is the (optional) category assigned to this banner; Impressions is a number that affects how often the banner is displayed. (For example, in the preceding advertisement file, the first banner appears twice as often as the second one.) Using the AdRotator control is quite simple because it exposes only three properties:

■ The AdvertisementFile property is the path to the advertisement file in XML format. This file must reside on the same Web server.

■ The KeywordFilter property specifies a keyword and forces the control to select only the banners that are associated with this keyword. If the XML file defines no banners with this keyword, the control doesn't display anything.

■ The Target property sets or gets the browser window or frame that displays the content of the Web page that appears when the banner is clicked.

For example, here's how you can filter banners so that only shopping-related ones are displayed:

```
AdRotator1.AdvertisementFile = "/advertisement.xml"
AdRotator1.KeywordFilter = "shopping"
```

Notice that you can specify only one keyword in both the XML file and the KeywordFilter property. The control exposes the AdCreated event, which fires each time a new banner is displayed. You might trap this event to keep a log of which banners were actually displayed.

The AdRotator control doesn't offer any support for detecting when the user clicks a banner and jumps to the site pointed to by the NavigateUrl property. Implementing this feature is simple, however: instead of pointing directly to the site's URL, you can have the NavigateUrl property point to a page on your site that reads the target URL on the query string, updates a log file, and finally redirects the browser to the real destination. Here's an example of how you might retouch the XML file to redirect clicks to your redirector.aspx page:

```
<Ad>
  <NavigateUrl>/redirector.aspx?url=www.foo.com</NavigateUrl>
    ⋮
</Ad>
```

The Xml Control

The Xml control is simply a component that lets you implement XSL transformation using a declarative code style instead of explicitly creating an XmlDocument and an XslTransform object (as we did in Chapter 23). To use this control, you typically need to set the source XML document that contains the data to be displayed and the XSL document that contains the XSL style sheet that specifies how data must be rendered.

You can specify the XML source document in three ways: by assigning an XmlDocument object to the Document property, by assigning a file path to the DocumentSource property, or by storing the raw XML data in the DocumentContent property. Likewise, you can specify the XSL style sheet by assigning an XslTransform object to the Transform property or a file path to the TransformSource property. The only other property, TransformArgumentList, serves to pass arguments to the style sheet.

Here's a simple example that uses the employees.xslt XSL file to render the data in the employees.xml data file:

```
Xml1.DocumentSource = "employees.xml"
Xml1.TransformSource = "employees.xslt"
```

> **Note** After releasing version 1.0 of the .NET Framework, Microsoft created an additional set of ASP.NET server controls known as Internet Explorer Web Controls. This set includes the TreeView, Toolbar, MultiPage, and TabString controls. These controls work well on all browsers but they really shine in Internet Explorer 5.5 and later. (For example, in this version no postback occurs when the user expands a node of the TreeView control.) As of this writing, these controls could be downloaded from the following URL: *http://asp.net/IEWebControls/Download.aspx*.

Formatting and Outlining in Visual Studio .NET

Before we move to more advanced topics, I want to draw your attention to the formatting and outlining capabilities of the HTML editor in Visual Studio .NET.

If you don't need any server-side functionality, you can just drop HTML elements on the page's surface, as you'd do with any HTML editor. In fact, when you're in design mode, four new top-level menus appear in Visual Studio .NET:

- The Format menu lets you apply standard formatting to selected text, justify text, align controls, and so on. (See Figure 24-19.)

- The Insert menu lets you insert <DIV>, <SPAN>, and <FORM> elements, images, and <A> elements (bookmarks). It also lets you transform a portion of text into a hyperlink.

- The Table menu lets you create a new table, add and delete rows, columns, cells, and so on. (See Figure 24-20.)

- The Frames menu lets you add and delete frames.

Instead of applying separate format operations to an HTML element, you can select it and choose Style Builder from the Format menu or in the shortcut menu to display the Style Builder dialog box shown in Figure 24-21. (You can also reach this dialog from the Style element in the Properties window.) The dialog box is a sophisticated builder for the HTML style attribute of an element, and it lets you create font properties, foreground and background colors, text alignment, flow or absolute position, edges, and bulleted lists.

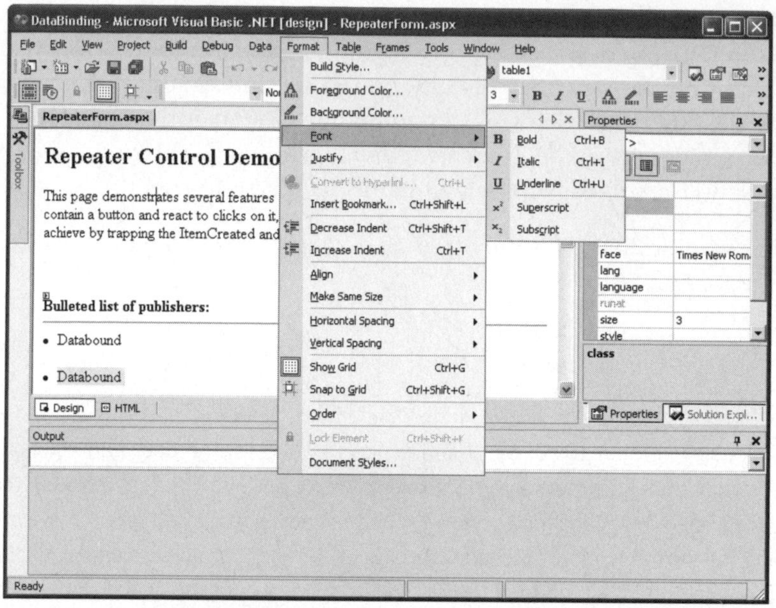

Figure 24-19   Visual Studio offers four additional top-level menus (Format, Table, Insert, and Frames) when the HTML editor is active.

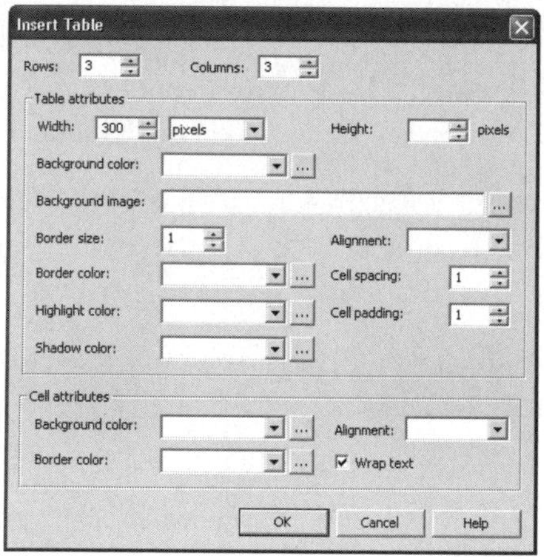

Figure 24-20   The Insert Table dialog box

When you're working with complex page layouts—for example, when you have controls nested in tables or in one of the template controls that I'll discuss in the next chapter—Visual Studio's Document Outline window is your best friend. You display this window from inside the Other Windows command in the View menu, or by pressing the Ctrl+Alt+T key combination. The Document Outline window shows the hierarchical structure of any HTML page, .config file, or XML file, and you can quickly jump to a tag in the HTML or XML editor by double-clicking on the corresponding tree-view node. (Visual Studio's Document Online window is your best friend. (See Figure 24-22.)

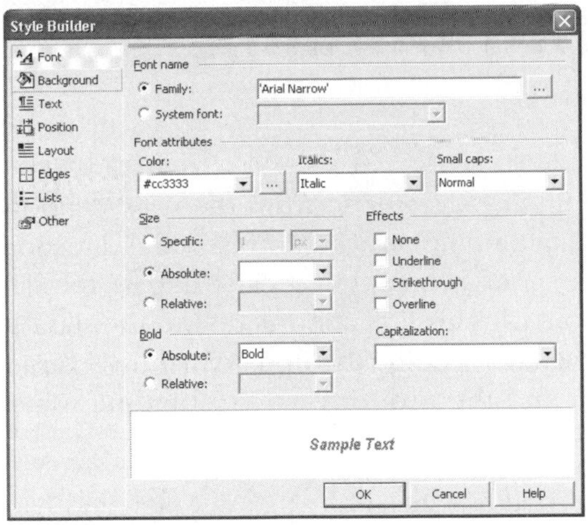

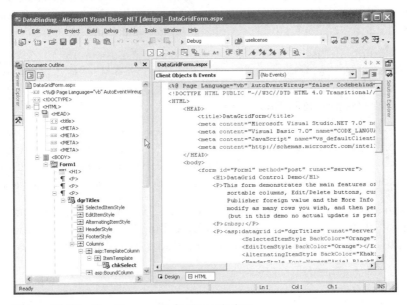

Figure 24-21   The Style Builder dialog box

Figure 24-22   The Document Outline window

We covered a lot of ground in this first chapter on ASP.NET and Web Forms, starting with the Page object and drilling down to individual Web controls. Yet we just scratched the surface of the power that Web Forms provide. To write real-world applications, you must become familiar with ASP.NET data binding, which is what the next chapter is all about.

25 Web Forms Data Binding

Web Forms controls support data binding differently from the way Windows Forms controls implement it. For starters, data binding on Web Forms is one-directional; it can fill a control with data coming from a data source, but it can't update the data source with what the user types inside a control. This limitation is due to the stateless nature of Web Forms and you must circumvent it by doing the update manually through code. Depending on the type of control and the property you're binding, data binding requires different syntax forms:

- If you're binding a single-value property—such as Text, ForeColor, and BackColor—you must use the <%#...%> syntax to embed a binding expression in the HTML code. This is the only binding mode supported by simple controls, such as TextBox, Label, Literal, CheckBox, and RadioButton, but it can be used with single-value properties of any control (for example, the ForeColor property of a DataGrid control).

- If you're binding the list area of a list control, you must assign the DataSource and the DataTextField properties (and optionally the DataValueField property). You can use this binding technique to fill the Items collection of a ListBox, DropDownList, CheckBoxList, or RadioButtonList control.

- If you're binding the content area of a template control—namely the DataGrid, DataList, or Repeater control—you must assign the DataSource property and provide one <%#...%> expression for each bound column. The DataGrid control is also able to automatically create one bound column for each field in the data source.

Regardless of the technique you use to do the binding, you must explicitly activate the data binding for all the controls on the form by calling the DataBind method of the Page object. This method is also exposed by individual bindable controls:

```
' Activate data binding for the TextBox1 control.
TextBox1.DataBind()
' Activate data binding for all the controls on the form.
Me.DataBind()
```

> **Note** To keep the code as concise as possible, all the code samples in this chapter assume the use of the following Imports statements at the file or project level:
>
> ```
> Imports System.IO
> Imports System.Data
> Imports System.Data.Common
> Imports System.Data.OleDb
> Imports System.Data.SqlClient
> ```

Binding Single-Value Properties

Binding single-value properties requires that you switch to the HTML view in the form editor, locate the attribute that you want to bind to a data source, and replace its value with an expression enclosed between <%# and %> delimiters. For example, this HTML code binds the Text property of the TextBox1 control to the UserName field or property of the page object:

```
<asp:TextBox id="TextBox1" runat="server" Text="<%# UserName %>" />
```

The expression between delimiters is any valid expression that can be evaluated correctly in the context of the current page object—for example, if GetValue is a method that takes an integer value, you can use this syntax:

```
<asp:TextBox id="TextBox1" runat="server" Text="<%# GetValue(0) %>" />
```

If the code-behind class exposes a DataTable object as a public variable, you can access its rows and fields as well:

```
<asp:TextBox id="TextBox1" runat="server"
    Text="<%# myDataTable.Rows(0)("Name").ToString %>" />
```

As mentioned previously, you can bind any property using this syntax—for example, the BackColor property can be bound to a field in a DataTable as follows:

```
<asp:TextBox id="TextBox1" runat="server"
    BackColor="<%# myDataTable.Rows(0)("Color").ToString %>" />
```

Another example: you can bind the width of an Image control as a cheap way to display a horizontal histogram that reflects the value in the data source.

If you work with Visual Studio .NET, you don't have to edit the HTML code by hand; just click on the ellipsis button to the right of the (DataBindings) element in the Properties window to bring up the DataBindings dialog box, shown in Figure 25-1, where you can type the binding expression in the Custom binding expression field. All bound properties are marked with a small yellow database icon, both in this dialog and in the Properties window. This dialog also supports binding to designable components dropped onto the form's component tray area, such as a DataSet or a DataAdapter object.

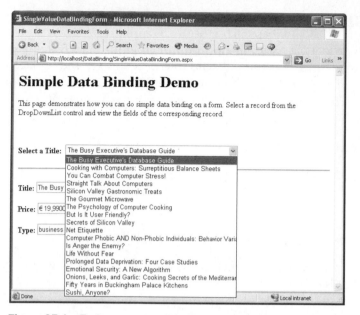

Figure 25-1   Typing a custom binding expression in Visual Studio .NET

If you don't want to use any designable components on the form, you must write some code in the Page_Load event handler to prepare the public variable that bound controls can reference in their bound attributes. The following code example loads a DataTable from the Titles table in the Pubs database, fills a DropDownList control with the list of all available titles, and then prepares a public DataRow variable named Titles, which contains the row that is currently selected in the DropDownList control:

```
' Define a public DataRow variable that is visible from <%# %> expressions.
Public Titles As DataRow

Private Sub Page_Load(ByVal sender As Object, ByVal e As EventArgs) _
    Handles MyBase.Load
    If Not Page.IsPostBack Then
        ' Fill the data table and then close the connection.
        ' (SqlPubsConnString points to the SQL Server's Pubs database.)
        Dim cn As New SqlConnection(SqlPubsConnString)
        Dim da As New SqlDataAdapter("SELECT * FROM Titles", cn)
        Dim dt As New DataTable()
        da.Fill(dt)
        ' Store the DataTable in a Session variable.
        Session("TitlesDataTable") = dt

        ' Manually fill the Items collection of the ddlTitles control.
        ' (You could use data binding for this job as well.)
        For Each dr As DataRow In dt.Rows
            ddlTitles.Items.Add(dr("title").ToString)
        Next
        ddlTitles.SelectedIndex = 0
```

```
          ' Prepare the Titles variable for binding.
          Titles = dt.Rows(0)
          ' Bind all controls on the form.
          Me.DataBind()
      End If
End Sub
```

This code stores the DataTable object in a Session variable, from which it can be retrieved when the user causes a postback by selecting a new element in the Drop-DownList control (whose AutoPostBack property has been opportunely set to True):

```
Private Sub ddlTitles_SelectedIndexChanged(ByVal sender As Object, _
    ByVal e As EventArgs) Handles ddlTitles.SelectedIndexChanged
    ' Retrieve the DataTable object from the session variable.
    Dim dt As DataTable = DirectCast(Session("TitlesDataTable"), DataTable)
    ' Prepare the Titles variable and activate the data binding.
    Titles = dt.Rows(ddlTitles.SelectedIndex)
    Me.DataBind()
End Sub
```

The form contains three databound TextBox controls, whose binding expressions reference the Titles variable:

```
<asp:textbox id="txtTitle" runat="server" Text='<%# Titles("title") %>' />
<asp:textbox id="txtPrice" runat="server" Text='<%# Titles("price") %>' />
<asp:textbox id="txtType" runat="server"  Text='<%# Titles("type") %>' />
```

Figure 25-2 shows the result in the browser.

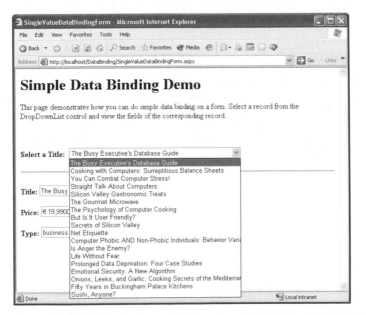

Figure 25-2   A simple form with three bound controls; data binding is one-directional and the data source isn't updated.

Binding expressions can use the Eval method of the DataBinder object for even more flexibility. This method takes two arguments—a reference to a public object and the name of one of its properties—plus an optional argument that affects how the value is formatted before being assigned to the bound control. For example, the following binding expression displays the price field as a currency value with four decimals:

```
<asp:textbox id="txtPrice" runat="server"
    Text='<%# DataBinder.Eval(Titles, "(""price"")", "{0:C4}") %>' />
```

See the "Formatting Numeric Values" and "Formatting Date Values" sections in Chapter 7 for a list of valid format symbols.

Data Binding with List Controls

When you use data binding with a list control, at minimum you must assign the data source object to the DataSource property and the name of the field to be displayed in the control to the DataTextField property. You also must assign the DataValueField property if you want to associate a value with each element. For example, this code uses data binding to display continent names stored in a Hashtable object:

```
Private Sub Page_Load(ByVal sender As Object, ByVal e As EventArgs) _
    Handles MyBase.Load
    If Not Page.IsPostBack Then
        ' Create a Hashtable with continent names.
        Dim continents As New Hashtable(5)
        continents.Add("The Americas", 1)
        continents.Add("Europe", 2)
        continents.Add("Asia", 3)
        continents.Add("Africa", 4)
        continents.Add("Australia", 5)
        ' Bind it to the cblContinents CheckBoxList control.
        cblContinents.DataSource = continents
        ' Each element in the Hashtable has a Key and a Value property.
        cblContinents.DataTextField = "Key"
        cblContinents.DataValueField = "Value"
        ⋮
        ' Bind all the controls on this page.
        Me.DataBind()
    End If
End Sub
```

If you're binding to an array of strings, you don't even need to set the DataTextField property:

```
' Fill a string array with the names of all known colors.
Dim colors() As String = [Enum].GetNames(GetType(System.Drawing.KnownColor))
' Bind it to the ddlColors DropDownList control.
ddlColors.DataSource = colors
```

Finally, you can fill a list control by assigning an ADO.NET object, such as a Data-Reader, a DataTable, a DataView, or a DataSet object, to the control's DataSource property. (You also must assign the DataMember property if you're binding to a DataSet object.) This code shows how you can display a list of publishers' names in a ListBox control and associate each element with the corresponding PubID value:

```
' Open a connection to Biblio.mdb and create a DataReader.
Dim cn As New OleDbConnection(BiblioConnString)
Dim cmd As New OleDbCommand("SELECT PubId,Name FROM Publishers", cn)
cn.Open()
Dim dr As OleDbDataReader = cmd.ExecuteReader(CommandBehavior.CloseConnection)
' Bind the DataReader to the ListBox control.
lstPublishers.DataSource = dr
lstPublishers.DataTextField = "Name"
lstPublishers.DataValueField = "PubId"
' Bind the ListBox and close the DataReader (and the Connection).
lstPublishers.DataBind()
dr.Close()
```

If you can, you should bind an ASP.NET control to a DataReader object, which takes less memory than a DataTable or DataView object. Using a DataTable or DataView object is necessary when you're binding multiple controls because you read the data from the database once and reuse it for all the controls. You can store a DataTable or DataView object in a Session variable between consecutive postbacks; I don't recommend this technique, however, because it creates server affinity and doesn't work on Web farms (unless you use out-of-process sessions, which I'll describe in the "Session State" section of Chapter 26) and because it isn't appropriate when you're working with more than a few hundred rows.

Remember that you aren't limited to displaying a single database field in a list control—for example, you could tweak the SELECT command to display the first and last names of all authors in Pubs by using this code:

```
Dim cn As New OleDbConnection(OledbPubsConnString)
Dim cmd As New OleDbCommand( _
    "SELECT au_id, au_lname+', '+au_fname As Name FROM Authors", cn)
cn.Open()
Dim dr As OleDbDataReader = cmd.ExecuteReader(CommandBehavior.CloseConnection)
' Bind the DataReader to the ListBox control.
lstAuthors.DataSource = dr
lstAuthors.DataTextField = "Name"
lstAuthors.DataValueField = "Au_id"
```

The DataTextFormatString property lets you exert some control over how bound elements are displayed in the control and is especially useful with numeric and date fields. You can assign this property any format string accepted by the String.Format property:

```
' Display a date using a LongDatePattern.
lstDeadlineDates.DataTextField = "deadline_date"
lstDeadlineDates.DataTextFormatString = "{0:D}"
```

One final tip: If you're binding two or more controls and you work with SQL Server or another database that supports multiple queries in one SQL statement, you can reduce the number of round trips to the server by stuffing all the queries you need into one Command object, as in this code:

```
Dim cmd As New SqlCommand("SELECT * FROM Publishers;" _
    & "SELECT * FROM titles", cn)
Dim dr As SqlDataReader = cmd.ExecuteReader()
' Display Publishers in the first DataGrid control.
DataGrid1.DataSource = dr
DataGrid1.DataBind()
' Display Titles in the second DataGrid control.
dr.NextResult()
DataGrid2.DataSource = dr
DataGrid2.DataBind()
```

Simulating Two-Way Data Binding

As you've seen, ASP.NET data binding for simple controls and list controls is less powerful than Windows Forms data binding because ASP.NET data binding is one-directional and offers no automatic way to store modified values back into the data source. In this section, I'll show how you can extend the previous code sample to implement bidirectional data binding. (See Figure 25-3.)

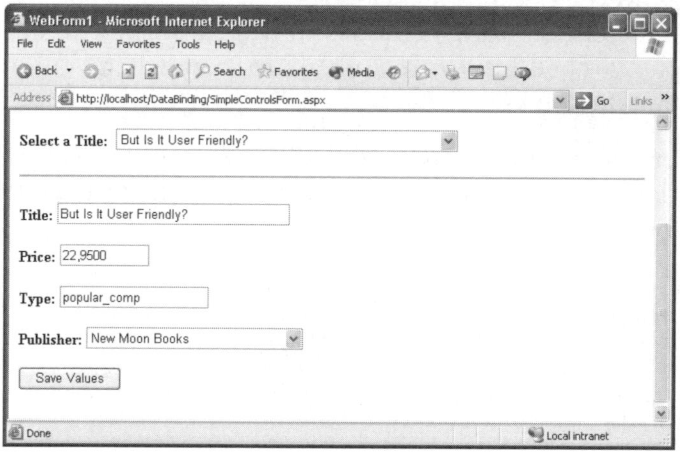

Figure 25-3   An ASP.NET page that implements (simulated) bidirectional data binding

In the sample to follow, data binding for most controls is only simulated via code. More precisely, I use data binding to fill the list portion of the two DropDownList controls, but not to associate values in controls to the corresponding field in the Titles table. I'll also demonstrate how you can have the ddlPublishers DropDownList control look up a value in another table. The code behind this form isn't exactly trivial:

```
' Define a connection object that points to Pubs.
Dim cn As New SqlConnection(SqlPubsConnString)

Private Sub Page_Load(ByVal sender As Object, ByVal e As EventArgs) _
    Handles MyBase.Load
    If Not IsPostBack Then
```

```vbnet
                    ' Fill the two DropDownList (lookup) controls.
                    FillListControl(ddlTitles, cn, "Titles", "title", "title_id")
                    FillListControl(ddlPublishers, cn, "Publishers", "pub_name", "pub_id")
                    ' Display the first record.
                    ShowTitleInfo(ddlTitles.Items(0).Value)
            End If
    End Sub

    ' Bind a List control to a table in a database (provider-agnostic code).
    Sub FillListControl(ByVal ctrl As ListControl, ByVal cn As IDbConnection, _
            ByVal tableName As String, ByVal textField As String, _
            ByVal valueField As String)
            ' Open the connection if necessary.
            If cn.State = ConnectionState.Closed Then cn.Open()
            ' Read the text and the value field.
            Dim cmd As IDbCommand = cn.CreateCommand
            cmd.CommandText = String.Format("SELECT {0},{1} FROM {2}", _
                    textField, valueField, tableName)
            Dim dr As IDataReader = cmd.ExecuteReader

            ' Bind the control.
            ctrl.DataSource = dr
            ctrl.DataTextField = textField
            ctrl.DataValueField = valueField
            ctrl.DataBind()
            ' Close the DataReader.
            dr.Close()
    End Sub

    ' Simulate binding by reading field values of "current" record.
    Sub ShowTitleInfo(ByVal titleId As String)
            ' Open the connection if necessary.
            If cn.State = ConnectionState.Closed Then cn.Open()
            Dim cmd As New SqlCommand("SELECT * FROM Titles WHERE title_id='" _
                    & titleId & "'", cn)
            Dim dr As SqlDataReader = cmd.ExecuteReader(CommandBehavior.SingleRow)
            ' Read field values into controls on the form.
            dr.Read()
            txtTitle.Text = dr("title").ToString
            txtPrice.Text = dr("price").ToString
            txtType.Text = dr("type").ToString
            SelectItemFromValue(ddlPublishers, dr("pub_id").ToString)
            ' Close the DataReader.
            dr.Close()
    End Sub

    ' Select the ListControl element with a given value.
    Sub SelectItemFromValue(ByVal lst As ListControl, ByVal value As String)
            For i As Integer = 0 To lst.Items.Count - 1
                    If lst.Items(i).Value = value Then
                            ' You've found the element - select it and exit.
                            lst.SelectedIndex = i
                            Exit Sub
                    End If
            Next
    End Sub
```

```vb
Private Sub ddlTitles_SelectedIndexChanged(ByVal sender As Object, _
    ByVal e As EventArgs) Handles ddlTitles.SelectedIndexChanged
    ' Display the value of current row.
    ShowTitleInfo(ddlTitles.SelectedItem.Value)
End Sub

Private Sub btnSave_Click(ByVal sender As Object, ByVal e As EventArgs) _
    Handles btnSave.Click
    ' Retrieve title_id and pub_id of visible record.
    Dim titleId As String = ddlTitles.SelectedItem.Value
    Dim pubId As String = ddlPublishers.SelectedItem.Value
    ' Update this record.
    UpdateTitle(titleId, txtTitle.Text, txtPrice.Text, txtType.Text, pubId)
    ' Ensure that the title in the DropDownList control matches the new title.
    ddlTitles.SelectedItem.Text = txtTitle.Text
End Sub


' Update a record in the Titles table.
Sub UpdateTitle(ByVal title_id As String, ByVal title As String, _
    ByVal price As String, ByVal type As String, ByVal pub_id As String)
    ' Prepare the Update command.
    Dim sql As String = "UPDATE Titles SET title=@title, price=@price, " _
        & " type=@type, pub_id=@pub_id WHERE title_id=@title_id"
    Dim cmd As New SqlCommand(sql, cn)
    cmd.Parameters.Add("@title", title)
    cmd.Parameters.Add("@price", CDec(price))
    cmd.Parameters.Add("@type", type)
    cmd.Parameters.Add("@pub_id", pub_id)
    cmd.Parameters.Add("@title_id", title_id)
    ' Open the connection if necessary, and execute the Update command.
    If cn.State = ConnectionState.Closed Then cn.Open()
    cmd.ExecuteNonQuery()
End Sub

Private Sub Page_Unload(ByVal sender As Object, ByVal e As EventArgs) _
    Handles MyBase.Unload
    ' Close the connection if still open.
    If cn.State <> ConnectionState.Closed Then cn.Close()
End Sub
```

While the one-directional binding sample shown previously uses a DataTable object stored in a Session variable to store the individual records, the preceding code reopens the connection each time and reads the data from the database using a DataReader object. This technique offers two important benefits: it's faster and more scalable with large tables, and it can be used with Web farms because no Session variables are used. All the information that the code needs, such as the key value of the record that must be updated, is stored in the form itself.

The code contains a couple of routines that you can reuse in your applications. The FillListControl routine uses binding to fill a list control with data coming from a database table. The demo program uses this routine to fill both the ddlTitles control (which lets the user navigate among available records) and the ddlPublishers control (which works as a lookup control in the Publisher foreign table). Notice that the routine can work with any .NET data provider.

The other reusable routine is SelectItemFromValue, which takes a value stored in a list control and selects the first element with that value. You use this routine when you need to display a publisher's name in the ddlPublisher control, given the pub_id value read from the Titles table.

A final detail worth noting in the preceding listing is that each routine opens the connection if it isn't open already, but never closes it. The connection is closed in the Page_Unload event handler, if necessary, when all other routines have completed. This technique ensures that the connection is opened as late as possible, that it's never opened twice during the page processing, and that it's correctly released when the page has been completely processed.

Template Controls

The only built-in Web Forms controls remaining to be covered are the Repeater, Data-List, and DataGrid controls. The main feature these controls have in common is their support for templates, which provide a simple way to affect the appearance and behavior of the elements they contain, their header and footer, and so on. Another point in common among these controls is that you can fill their contents only by using data binding.

The Repeater control is a simple way to display multiple elements taken from a data source. It provides no default appearance, and you're in complete control of the HTML tags generated for each element. Visual Studio doesn't offer any tools to help you edit the elements of a Repeater control in a WYSIWYG manner. You can decide whether elements are laid out vertically, horizontally, all in one line, or in any other format you like; you can specify the format for the header, the footer, the generic item, the alternate row item, and the separator between items. The control doesn't offer support for selecting or editing elements, or for paging through them.

The DataList control displays elements taken from a data source using a default table appearance that you can customize using templates. As with the Repeater control, you can specify the format for the header, the footer, the regular and the alternate row element, and the separator between items. The DataList control also supports a custom appearance for items that are in selected or edit mode, and Visual Studio .NET offers a WYSIWYG tool to edit how each element is displayed. This control doesn't support paging.

The DataGrid control is the most powerful control of the lot. It renders its contents as an HTML grid that you can customize by using templates for the header, the footer, regular and alternating row items, and selected and edited items. This control can do everything the DataList control can do, and it also supports sorting and paging. You can opt for automatic generation of columns (based on fields of the data source), or be in full control of how each column appears in regular, selected, and edit mode by using column templates.

Templates

To tap the power of the controls in this group, you must become familiar with the concept of templates. Each template is a container for HTML code and affects how a given portion of the control appears. There are eight different types of templates, whose names are self-explanatory. (See Figure 25-4.) All the templates except ItemTemplate are optional. If omitted, the control's corresponding visual element isn't displayed—for example, if you omit the AlternatingItemTemplate, all rows have the appearance defined by the ItemTemplate.

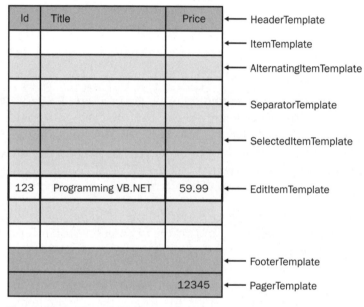

Figure 25-4   The eight types of templates

The SelectedItemTemplate and EditItemTemplate are applied when an element is in selected or edit mode, respectively. Typically, a selected item has a different background color or a visible row selector in the leftmost column, whereas an item in edit mode contains TextBox and CheckBox controls for all the fields that can be edited. In theory, you can select an item while another item is being edited, but in practice you'll never want to do so because it would disorient the end user.

The DataList control supports all types of templates except PagerTemplate. The Repeater control doesn't support SelectedItemTemplate, EditItemTemplate, or Pager-Template, and you can't apply the SeparatorTemplate to the DataGrid control. The Separator-Template is applied between items, but not before the first line or after the last line; if you want to display a separator in these positions, you must include it in the HeaderTemplate and FooterTemplate.

A template can really contain any type of ASP.NET control—including buttons, check boxes, images, and hyperlinks—so there are few limits to how you can customize the appearance and behavior of a Repeater, DataList, or DataGrid control.

The Repeater Control

The Repeater control is the simplest template control. It doesn't expose any custom properties and therefore works well to demonstrate the potential of templates. On the other hand, Visual Studio doesn't support visual editing of Repeater templates, so its templates must be manually typed in the HTML code editor.

Inserting Templates in HTML Text

Each template is a <templatename> block inside the main <asp:Repeater> block. For example, the following HTML code creates a Repeater control that shows a list of publishers as bulleted items, with a <br> tag as a separator between elements, a header on top of the control, and a closing horizontal line. To make things more interesting and to show how to use all the five templates that the Repeater supports, I added an AlternatingItemTemplate element that displays every other row with a yellow background. (See Figure 25-5.)

```
<asp:repeater id="Repeater1" runat="server">
  <HeaderTemplate>
    <b>Bulleted list of publishers: </b><br /><hr />
  </HeaderTemplate>
  <ItemTemplate>
    <li><%# Container.DataItem("Name") %></li>
  </ItemTemplate>
  <AlternatingItemTemplate>
    <span style="BACKGROUND-COLOR: #ffff99">
      <li><%# Container.DataItem("Name") %></li>
    </span>
  </AlternatingItemTemplate>
  <SeparatorTemplate><br /></SeparatorTemplate>
  <FooterTemplate><hr /></FooterTemplate>
</asp:repeater>
```

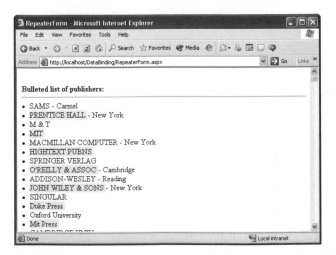

Figure 25-5   A Repeater control that displays a bulleted list of items with alternating background colors

The key point here is that you must bind the content of each item to the data source using a Container.DataItem("fieldname") expression in a <%#...#> block. Notice that the Repeater control doesn't expose the DataField property, so you must use this syntax to access any field exposed by the data source. You can also use the Data-Binder.Eval method, as in this code snippet:

```
<ItemTemplate>
  <li><%# DataBinder.Eval(Container, "DataItem(""Name""))") %></li>
</ItemTemplate>
```

Of course, you must bind the control to a proper data source—such as the Publishers table in Biblio.mdb—to have this code work properly:

```
Private Sub Page_Load(ByVal sender As Object, ByVal e As EventArgs) _
    Handles MyBase.Load
    If Not Page.IsPostBack Then
        ' Open the connection to Biblio.mdb.
        Dim cn As New OleDbConnection(BiblioConnString)
        cn.Open()
        ' Read the Name column into a DataReader.
        Dim cmd As New OleDbCommand("SELECT * FROM Publishers", cn)
        Dim dr As OleDbDataReader = cmd.ExecuteReader()
        ' Bind the control, close the DataReader and the connection.
        Repeater1.DataSource = dr
        Repeater1.DataBind()
        dr.Close()
        cn.Close()
    End If
End Sub
```

You aren't limited to displaying a single data field in each item—for example, you could display the publisher's name and city by using this syntax:

```
<ItemTemplate>
  <li><%# Container.DataItem("Name")+" - "+Container.DataItem("City") %></li>
</ItemTemplate>
```

Or this syntax:

```
<ItemTemplate>
  <li><%# Container.DataItem("Name") %> -
      <%# Container.DataItem("City") %></li>
</ItemTemplate>
```

The preceding expression displays a trailing hyphen if the City field is Null for a given publisher. You'll see how to solve this problem by using the ItemDataBound event, which I'll discuss in its own section shortly. Also, remember that there's no need to retrieve all the fields from the database table if you're going to use only a subset of them. For example, if you're displaying only the publisher's name and city, you should use the following SELECT command to reduce the amount of data travelling over the wire:

```
SELECT name, city FROM Publishers
```

You can use a Repeater control's Items collection to iterate over its elements. This collection holds a series of RepeaterItem objects, and each object exposes the following properties: ItemIndex (the index of the item in the control), ItemType (an enumerated value that can be Item, AlternatingItem, Header, Footer, or Separator), and DataItem (an object that represents the item itself), plus all the members of the Control base class. The most important of these members is the Controls collection, which gathers all the elements contained in the RepeaterItem. I'll show how to use this collection in the following section.

The ItemCreated Event

The ItemCreated event fires when an item in the Repeater control is created. The second argument of this event has an Item property pointing to the RepeaterItem object being created. You can trap this event to modify the style or the contents of items as they're created. For example, the following code counts items being displayed and then shows the total number in the footer element. Notice that you can't display a string in the footer simply by assigning it to the Text property because this property isn't exposed. Instead, you must add a Literal control to the RepeaterItem's Controls collection:

```
Dim itemCount As Integer

Private Sub Repeater1_ItemCreated(ByVal sender As Object, _
    e As RepeaterItemEventArgs) Handles Repeater1.ItemCreated
    Select Case e.Item.ItemType
        Case ListItemType.Item, ListItemType.AlternatingItem
            ' Count repeater items carrying publisher's data.
            itemCount += 1
        Case ListItemType.Footer
            ' Create a Literal control and add it to the current item.
            Dim lc As New Literal()
            lc.Text = itemCount & " publishers."
            e.Item.Controls.Add(lc)
    End Select
End Sub
```

The ItemDataBound Event

The ItemDataBound event fires each time an item of the Repeater control is bound to a field of the data source. The second argument passed to this event has an Item property that returns a reference to the RepeaterItem object being bound, so you can query its properties and manipulate it as you need.

The DataItem property of the RepeaterItem exposes the object that's providing the bound data. This property has a generic Object type because it can really be anything, depending on what the data source is (a Hashtable, an ArrayList, a DataReader, and so on). For example, the DataItem property returns a System.Data.Common.DbDataRecord object when you're binding to a DataReader, and it returns a DataRowView object when you're binding to a DataTable or a DataView object. The following code leverages the ItemDataBound event to display the city in which a publisher resides, but only if the City field isn't Null:

```
Private Sub Repeater1_ItemDataBound(ByVal sender As Object, _
    ByVal e As RepeaterItemEventArgs) Handles Repeater1.ItemDataBound
    Select Case e.Item.ItemType
        Case ListItemType.Item, ListItemType.AlternatingItem
            ' Get the DbDataRecord that is providing the bound data.
            Dim dbr As DbDataRecord = DirectCast(e.Item.DataItem, DbDataRecord)
            ' Retrieve the city field.
            Dim city As String = dbr("city").ToString
            If city.Length > 0 Then
                ' If the city isn't null or an empty string, show it in
                ' a Literal control added to the current item.
                Dim lc As New Literal()
                lc.Text = " - " & city
                e.Item.Controls.Add(lc)
            End If
    End Select
End Sub
```

The ItemCommand Event

Each row in the Repeater can contain one or more button controls, which let the user perform actions on the element displayed in that row. For example, you can display a More Info button to the left of each publisher's name so that the user can jump to another page that displays more detailed information about that publisher. (See Figure 25-6.) Because Visual Studio doesn't support WYSIWYG editing of the Repeater templates, you can add a new control only in the HTML editor:

```
<asp:repeater id="Repeater2" runat="server">
  <HeaderTemplate>List of publishers with MoreInfo button</HeaderTemplate>
  <ItemTemplate>
    <asp:Button runat=server Text='more info' CommandName='moreinf o'
      CommandArgument='<%# Container.DataItem("PubId") %>' />
    <%# Container.DataItem("Name") %>
  </ItemTemplate>
  <SeparatorTemplate><br /></SeparatorTemplate>
  <FooterTemplate><hr /></FooterTemplate>
</asp:repeater>
```

You must set the CommandName attribute to later detect which button was clicked, and you must store a unique value in the CommandArgument attribute so that you can later understand which publisher you must apply the command to. (In this specific example, there's just one button in each row and you could omit the CommandName attribute, but specifying it is a good programming rule.) Keep in mind that if the Repeater control has an AlternatingItemTemplate element, you must add the button to it as well.

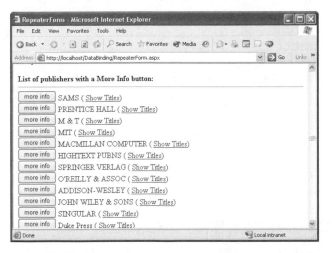

Figure 25-6   A Repeater control can display one or more buttons for each element.

A click on the button causes a postback, and an ItemCommand event is fired on the server. The second argument passed to this event receives an object that exposes all the properties you need to react correctly to the user's action. The Item property is the RepeaterItem that contains the button, CommandSource is the clicked button, and CommandName and CommandArgument are the button's attributes:

```
Private Sub Repeater2_ItemCommand(ByVal source As Object, _
    ByVal e As RepeaterCommandEventArgs) Handles Repeater2.ItemCommand
    Select Case e.CommandName
        Case "moreinfo"
            ' Show additional info about the selected publisher.
            Dim pubId As String = e.CommandArgument
            ' Use the PubId key value to retrieve additional information.
            ' ...(omitted for brevity)...
        Case "showtitles"
            ' Add the code that reacts to other buttons here.
            ⋮
    End Select
End Sub
```

You don't need to set the CommandArgument attribute if you're binding to an ArrayList or a Hashtable object because you can use the e.Item.ItemIndex property to retrieve the index of the element whose button has been clicked.

You can think of other mechanisms to associate one or more commands with elements of a Repeater control. For example, you can use a hyperlink control that carries information about the clicked element on its query string:

```
<ItemTemplate>
  <%# Container.DataItem("Name") %>
  (<asp:HyperLink Runat=server NavigateUrl='ShowTitles.aspx?pubid=
      <%# Container.DataItem("PubId") %>' >Show Titles</asp:HyperLink>)
</ItemTemplate>
```

In this example, the ShowTitle.aspx page is executed when the user clicks on the hyperlink. This page should retrieve the ID of the publisher in question using the following statement in its Page_Load event handler:

```
Dim pubId as String = Me.Request.QueryString("pubid")
```

The DataList Control

The DataList control supports all the available templates except PagerTemplate. The DataList control usually displays data in an HTML table, but you can change its default appearance if you want. Unlike the Repeater control, the DataList templates are editable in a visual manner inside Visual Studio .NET. (See Figure 25-7.)

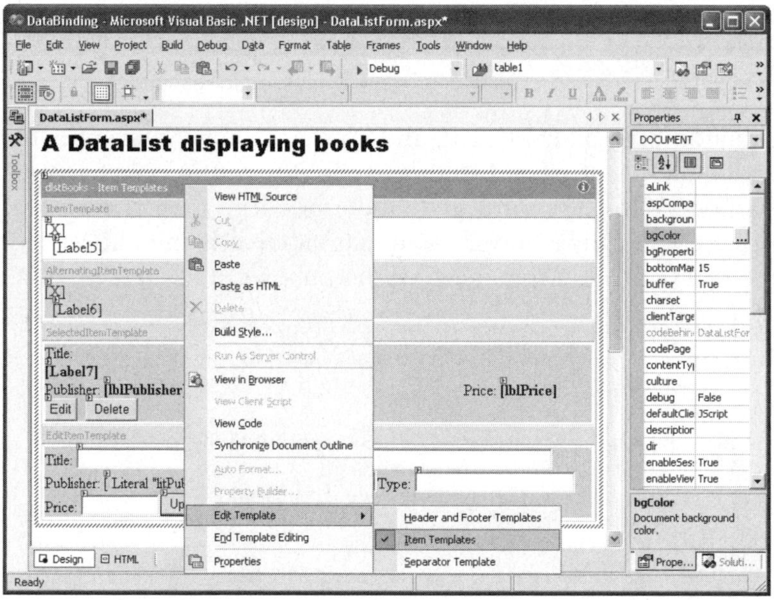

Figure 25-7   Visual Studio .NET lets you edit DataList templates in a WYSIWYG editor.

Each of the seven templates that the DataList control supports corresponds to both an *xxxx*Template property and an *xxxx*Style property. You usually don't have to manipulate these properties in code because it's simpler to set them at design time: just right-click a template and click Build Style on the shortcut menu. You can also assign a visual style quickly by using the Auto Format command on the DataList's shortcut menu.

In addition to the *xxxx*Style properties I already discussed, the DataList control exposes many properties that affect its appearance. ShowHeader and ShowFooter are True (their default value) if the control's header and footer are visibile, respectively. The RepeatLayout property determines whether elements are displayed in flow or table mode; RepeatColumns is the number of columns displayed (the default value is 0, which causes all the elements to be displayed as a single row or a single column); RepeatDirection determines whether elements are displayed horizontally or vertically;

GridLines is the grid line style used when the RepeatedLayout property is set to Table (can be None, Horizontal, Vertical, or Both).

Data Binding with the DataList Control

The DataList control supports two new properties related to data binding. The DataKeyField is the name of the key column in the data source. The DataKeys collection contains the key value for each element in the DataList after you've bound the control. These properties let you retrieve the key of each row without having to display it in a control in the DataList:

```
Dim cmd As New OleDbCommand("SELECT title_id,title FROM Titles", cn)
Dim dr As OleDbDataReader = cmd.ExecuteReader
' Bind the DataReader to the DataList control.
dlstBooks.DataSource = dr
dlstBooks.DataKeyField = "title_id"        ' Name of key field
dlstBooks.DataBind()
```

Now you can access key values in the DataKeys collection:

```
' The key value for the first visible element in the DataList
Dim key As String = dlstBooks.DataKeys(0).ToString
```

Labels, images, and other controls in the ItemTemplate and AlternatingItemTemplate can be bound to the data source if you use the same syntax that I showed you for the Repeater control, and you can do the binding right in the Visual Studio editor. For example, this is the HTML code that defines the DataList control visible in Figure 25-8. (Data binding expressions are in boldface.)

```
<asp:datalist id="dlstBooks" runat="server" Width="538px">
  <HeaderTemplate>
    <DIV style="COLOR: white; FONT-FAMILY: 'Arial Black';
      BACKGROUND-COLOR: navy">
      Click on [X] to select and edit a book</DIV>
  </HeaderTemplate>
  <ItemTemplate>
    <asp:LinkButton id="Linkbutton3" runat="server" CommandName="select">
      [X]</asp:LinkButton> 
    <asp:Label id=Label5 runat="server" Width="559px"
      Text='<%# Container.DataItem("Title") %>' />
  </ItemTemplate>
  <AlternatingItemTemplate>
    <DIV style="BACKGROUND-COLOR: yellow">
    <asp:LinkButton id="Linkbutton4" runat="server" CommandName="select">
      [X]</asp:LinkButton> 
    <asp:Label id=Label6 runat="server" Width="561px"
      Text='<%# Container.DataItem("Title") %>' />
    </DIV>
  </AlternatingItemTemplate>
  <FooterTemplate>
    <DIV style="COLOR: white; FONT-FAMILY: 'Arial Black';
      BACKGROUND-COLOR: navy">
      End of list</DIV>
  </FooterTemplate>
</asp:datalist>
```

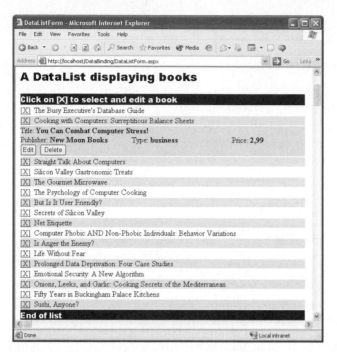

Figure 25-8 A DataList control with alternating styles for rows and a selected element

The Select and Edit Templates

DataList controls support templates for selected and edited elements. A selected row might display additional information about the element and perhaps include buttons for additional commands (such as the control displayed in Figure 25-8), whereas the EditTemplate should include editable controls, such as TextBox, CheckBox, and Drop-DownList controls. (See Figure 25-9.) Here are the two templates that implement the selection and edit states:

```
<asp:datalist id="dlstBooks" runat="server" Width="538px">
  ⋮
  <SelectedItemTemplate>
    <DIV style="BACKGROUND-COLOR: paleturquoise">Title:
    <asp:Label id=Label7 runat="server" Width="547px" Font-Bold="True"
      Text='<%# Container.DataItem("Title") %>' /><BR>
    Publisher:
    <asp:Label id=Label4 runat="server" Width="170px" Font-Bold="True"
      Text='<%# Container.DataItem("pub_name") %>' />
    Type:
    <asp:Label id=Label8 runat="server" Width="168px" Font-Bold="True"
      Text='<%# Container.DataItem("Type") %>' />
    Price:
    <asp:Label id=Label9 runat="server" Width="83px" Font-Bold="True"
      Text='<%# Container.DataItem("Price") %>' />
    <asp:Button id="Button2" runat="server" Text="Edit"
      CommandName="Edit" /> 
    <asp:Button id="Button4" runat="server" Text="Delete"
```

```
      CommandName="delete" /> 
   </DIV>
 </SelectedItemTemplate>

 <EditItemTemplate>
   <DIV style="BACKGROUND-COLOR: paleturquoise">Title:
   <asp:TextBox id="txtTitle" runat="server" Width="500px"
     Text='<%# Container.DataItem("Title") %>' /><BR>
   Publisher:
   <asp:Literal id=PubId runat=server Visible=False
     Text='<%# Container.DataItem("pub_id") %>' />
   <asp:DropDownList id="ddlPublishers" runat="server" Width="170px"
     DataTextField='pub_name' DataValueField='pub_id' />
   <asp:TextBox id="txtType" runat="server" Width="168px"
     Text='<%# Container.DataItem("Type") %>' />
   Price:
   <asp:TextBox id="txtPrice" runat="server" Width="83px"
     Text='<%# Container.DataItem("Price") %>' />
   <asp:Button id="Button1" runat="server" Text="Update"
     CommandName="update" /> 
   <asp:Button id="Button3" runat="server" Text="Cancel"
     CommandName="cancel" /> 
   </DIV>
 </EditItemTemplate>
</asp:datalist>
```

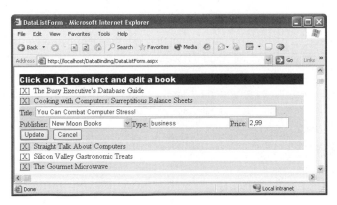

Figure 25-9   A DataList control in edit mode

Notice that the EditItemTemplate contains a Literal control whose Visible attribute is set to False. I'll explain the role of this control in the "Managing the Select and Edit States" section later in this chapter.

The DataList control doesn't offer any support for switching into select or edit mode, so you must provide one or more Button or LinkButton controls on each row to enter these modes. The demo application in the companion CD uses an [X] label in ItemTemplate to select an element and an Edit button in SelectedItemTemplate to enter the edit mode. (Of course, you're free to enter edit mode directly without passing through select mode.) The EditItemTemplate should include buttons to save the modified values in the data source and to cancel the edit operation.

At any moment, you can have zero or one selected element and zero or one edited element. Most of the time, you shouldn't have a selected element if another element is being edited because it could confuse the end user, but there are exceptions to this rule. (See the next note.) You decide which element is in select state by assigning the SelectedIndex property:

```
' Select the first element in the DataList.
dlstBooks.SelectedIndex = 0
```

Similarly, you decide which element is in edit state by assigning the EditItemIndex property. When you do so, you might want to reset SelectedIndex to - 1 to ensure that only one element is highlighted with a style different from the standard one:

```
' Enter the edit mode for the second element.
dlstBooks.EditItemIndex = 1
' Ensure that no other element is selected.
dlstBooks.SelectedIndex = -1
```

You exit the edit mode for an element by assigning the value - 1 to the EditItemIndex property:

```
' Cancel edit mode.
dlstBooks.EditItemIndex = -1
```

> **Note**   The terms *select mode* and *edit mode* are completely arbitrary. For example, the element in *edit* mode might be an element that should have a visual appearance different from the default one. Say you're using the DataList control to display the elements in an array and you want to provide the end user with a command for swapping two elements. You could apply SelectedItemTemplate to the first element and EditItemTemplate to the second element about to be swapped, to highlight each with a different style. (This technique lets you work around the limitation that you can't have two elements in the selected state.)

Command Buttons and Command Events

The Button, LinkButton, or ImageButton controls that you place inside a DataList control should have an appropriate CommandName attribute so that you can trap a click on them from inside an ItemCommand event, as you did with the Repeater control. The DataList control automatically recognizes a button whose CommandName is set to *select* and fires a SelectedIndexChanged event when that button is clicked:

```
Private Sub dlstBooks_SelectedIndexChanged(ByVal sender As Object, _
    ByVal e As EventArgs) Handles dlstBooks.SelectedIndexChanged
    ' End the edit operation, if any is active.
    dlstBooks.EditItemIndex = -1
    ' Rebind the DataList control.
    BindBookList()
End Sub
```

(The BindBookList routine binds the DataList control to its data source; I'll describe this routine in the next section.) Notice that you don't need to explicitly assign the Selected-Index property because it already points to the selected element—that is, the element that contains the button that fired the event. However, you still need to trap this event because you must rebind the DataList control to ensure that it correctly renders the element just selected.

The DataList control recognizes four more special CommandName values: edit, cancel, update, and delete. A click on a button assigned one of these CommandName values automatically translates to an EditCommand, CancelCommand, UpdateCommand, or Delete-Command event. The second argument for each of these events is an object that exposes properties related to the button being clicked. The Item property returns a reference to the DataListItem where the button resides. CommandSource is a reference to the button. CommandName and CommandArgument are each button's same-name properties.

The handler for the EditCommand event typically sets the EditItemIndex property and rebinds the control. It uses the e.Item.ItemIndex property to determine which element should enter the edit state:

```
Private Sub dlstBooks_EditCommand(ByVal source As Object, _
    ByVal e As DataListCommandEventArgs) Handles dlstBooks.EditCommand
    ' Hide any selected item, if any.
    dlstBooks.SelectedIndex = -1
    ' Have the current element enter the edit state.
    dlstBooks.EditItemIndex = e.Item.ItemIndex
    ' Rebind the DataList control.
    BindBookList()
End Sub
```

The code in the CancelCommand event handler is simple: it sets the EditItemIndex property to - 1 to exit edit mode and then rebinds the control:

```
Private Sub dlstBooks_CancelCommand(ByVal source As Object, _
    ByVal e As DataListCommandEventArgs) Handles dlstBooks.CancelCommand
    ' End any edit operation and rebind the control.
    dlstBooks.EditItemIndex = -1
    BindBookList()
End Sub
```

The code you write in the DeleteCommand event handler should delete the element from the data source. Implementing this command is easy because you can retrieve the key value for the selected element from the DataKeys collection:

```
Private Sub dlstBooks_DeleteCommand(ByVal source As Object, _
    ByVal e As DataListCommandEventArgs) Handles dlstBooks.DeleteCommand
    ' Retrieve the ID of the record to be deleted.
    Dim id As String = dlstBooks.DataKeys(e.Item.ItemIndex).ToString
    ' Open the connection if necessary.
    If cn.State = ConnectionState.Closed Then cn.Open()
    ' Delete this row.
```

```
        Dim cmd As New OleDbCommand("DELETE Titles WHERE title_id='" _
            & id & "'", cn)
        cmd.ExecuteNonQuery()
        ' Rebind the control.
        BindBookList()
    End Sub
```

The code that you write in the UpdateCommand event handler should update the current element with the values that the user typed in the controls. We'll look at it in the next section.

> **Note**   The ItemCommand event fires even for buttons whose CommandName property is set to select, edit, cancel, delete, or update. If you don't keep track of these details, you might process a command twice—for example, once in the DeleteCommand and once in the Item-Command event handler.

Managing the Select and Edit States

The demo program that comes with the companion code for this book uses select mode to display additional information about the title that the user has selected and uses edit mode to let the user modify these fields. Displaying data in select mode is simple, and in many cases you can get along with simple data binding expressions in Selected-ItemTemplate. However, in our specific example one of the fields (the publisher's name) comes from another table, so you must specify a JOIN query instead of a single-table SELECT query. Here's the first version of the code that does the data binding and optimizes the SQL query, depending on whether you're in select or edit mode:

```
' The connection to the Pubs database
Dim cn As New OleDbConnection(OledbPubsConnString)

Private Sub Page_Load(ByVal sender As Object, ByVal e As EventArgs) _
    Handles MyBase.Load
    If Not Me.IsPostBack Then
        BindBookList()
    End If
End Sub

Private Sub Page_Unload(ByVal sender As Object, ByVal e As EventArgs) _
    Handles MyBase.Unload
    ' Close the connection if still open.
    If cn.State = ConnectionState.Open Then cn.Close()
End Sub

Sub BindBookList()
    ' Open a connection to Pubs, if necessary.
    If cn.State = ConnectionState.Closed Then cn.Open()

    ' Read title name and key from the Titles table.
    Dim sql As String = "SELECT title_id, title FROM Titles"
```

```
' If you are in select or edit mode, you must read more data.
If dlstBooks.SelectedIndex >= 0 Or dlstBooks.EditItemIndex >= 0 Then
    sql = "SELECT Titles.*, Publishers.pub_name FROM Titles " _
        & "INNER JOIN Publishers ON Titles.pub_id=Publishers.pub_id"
End If

' Bind the DataReader to the DataList control.
Dim cmd As New OleDbCommand(sql, cn)
Dim dr As OleDbDataReader = cmd.ExecuteReader
dlstBooks.DataSource = dr
dlstBooks.DataKeyField = "title_id"
dlstBooks.DataBind()
dr.Close()

If dlstBooks.EditItemIndex >= 0 Then
    ' Get a reference to the DataListItem.
    Dim dli As DataListItem = dlstBooks.Items(dlstBooks.EditItemIndex)
    ' Get a reference to the ddlPublishers DropDownList control.
    Dim ddlPublishers As DropDownList = _
        DirectCast(dli.FindControl("ddlPublishers"), DropDownList)
    ' Get a reference to the PubId hidden Literal control.
    Dim litPubId As Literal = _
        DirectCast(dli.FindControl("litPubId"), Literal)

    ' Fill the list of publishers.
    cmd = New OleDbCommand("SELECT pub_id, pub_name FROM Publishers", cn)
    dr = cmd.ExecuteReader
    ddlPublishers.DataSource = dr
    ddlPublishers.DataTextField = "pub_name"
    ddlPublishers.DataValueField = "pub_id"
    ddlPublishers.DataBind()
    dr.Close()
    ' Highlight the element corresponding to the title's publisher.
    SelectItemFromValue(ddlPublishers, litPubId.Text)
    End If
End Sub
```

You must solve a couple of additional problems when you enter edit mode. First, you must fill the ddlPublishers control with the names of all the publishers. The problem emerges from the fact that you can't reference the ddlPublishers control directly because it isn't a child control of the page. Worse, it isn't even a child control of the DataList control. In fact, all the controls you place on a DataList control are actually children of the many DataListItem objects contained in the DataList. Therefore, you must first use the Items collection to get a reference to the DataListItem object and then use the FindControl method to obtain a reference to the actual control:

```
' Get a reference to the selected DataListItem.
Dim dli As DataListItem = dlstBooks.Items(dlstBooks.EditItemIndex)
' Get a reference to the ddlPublishers DropDownList control.
Dim ddlPublishers As DropDownList = _
    DirectCast(dli.FindControl("ddlPublishers"), DropDownList)
```

The second problem to solve is selecting the ddlPublishers element that corresponds to the publisher of the titles being edited. To do so, you need the value of the pub_id column for the title being edited, but unfortunately this value isn't available in any field in this row. You can choose from several ways to solve this problem. For example, you could bind to a DataTable or a DataView object (instead of a DataReader, as in this example) and retrieve the value of the pub_id column of the row whose index is equal to the EditItemIndex value. However, DataTable or DataView objects consume more memory and are less scalable than a DataReader, so I suggest that you stay clear of these objects if possible.

The demo program solves this problem by creating an invisible Literal control inside EditItemTemplate and binding it to the pub_id field:

```
<asp:Literal id="litPubId" Runat="server" Visible="False"
    Text='<%# Container.DataItem("pub_id")' %> />
```

Now you can retrieve the pub_id field for the current element simply by querying the Text property of this Literal control. Because the control is buried inside the DataList control, you must use the FindControl method to get a reference to it, as you did for the ddlPublishers control. Once you have the value of the pub_id foreign key, you call the SelectItemFromValue routine to highlight the name of the corresponding publisher:

```
' Get a reference to the PubId hidden Literal control.
Dim litPubId As Literal = _
    DirectCast(dli.FindControl("litPubId"), Literal)
' Highlight the element corresponding to the title's publisher.
SelectItemFromValue(ddlPublishers, litPubId.Text)
```

Because the Control class exposes the Controls collection, you can easily implement a generic function that returns a reference to the first control in a form or control with the specified ID. You can use this routine when you don't know which DataListItem contains the control you're looking for:

```
' Find a control in a hierarchy of controls.
Function FindControlRecursive(ByVal ctrl As Control, id As String) As Control
    ' Exit if this is the control you're looking for.
    If ctrl.ID = id Then Return ctrl
    ' Else, look in the control hierarchy.
    For Each childCtrl As Control In ctrl.Controls
        Dim resCtrl As Control = FindControlRecursive(childCtrl, id)
        ' Exit if you've found the result.
        If Not resCtrl Is Nothing Then Return resCtrl
    Next
End Function
```

You need to implement the Update command to complete the sample application. This command reads the string in the txtTitle, txtType, and txtPrice controls, and the value associated with the current element in the ddlPublishers control. Once again, you can solve this problem by using the FindControl method of the DataListItem object:

```
Private Sub dlstBooks_UpdateCommand(ByVal source As Object, _
    ByVal e As DataListCommandEventArgs) Handles dlstBooks.UpdateCommand
    ' Get the ID of the record to be deleted.
    Dim title_id As String = dlstBooks.DataKeys(e.Item.ItemIndex).ToString

    ' This is the DataListItem being edited.
    Dim dli As DataListItem = e.Item
    ' Get the values of the txtTitle child control.
    Dim tb As TextBox = DirectCast(dli.FindControl("txtTitle"), TextBox)
    Dim title As String = tb.Text
    ' Do the same with txtType & txtPrice controls, but use a shorter syntax.
    Dim type As String = DirectCast(dli.FindControl("txtType"), TextBox).Text
    Dim price As Decimal = CDec(DirectCast(dli.FindControl("txtPrice"), _
        TextBox).Text)
    ' Get the value of the selected element in ddlPublishers.
    Dim ddlPublishers As DropDownList = _
        DirectCast(dli.FindControl("ddlPublishers"), DropDownList)
    Dim pub_id As String = ddlPublishers.SelectedValue

    ' Prepare to update this record.
    Dim cmd As New OleDbCommand("UPDATE Titles SET title=?, pub_id=?, " _
        & "type=?, price=? WHERE title_id=?", cn)
    cmd.Parameters.Add("@title", title)
    cmd.Parameters.Add("@pub_id", pub_id)
    cmd.Parameters.Add("@type", type)
    cmd.Parameters.Add("@price", price)
    cmd.Parameters.Add("@title_id", title_id)
    ' Open the connection if necessary, and execute the command.
    If cn.State = ConnectionState.Closed Then cn.Open()
    cmd.ExecuteNonQuery()

    ' End the edit mode and rebind the control.
    dlstBooks.EditItemIndex = -1
    dlstBooks.SelectedIndex = -1
    BindBookList()
End Sub
```

A final note: the demo application deletes and updates the data source without worrying about update conflicts based on editing actions performed by other users. To take these conflicts into account, you *must* read the database table in a DataTable or a DataView object and store it in a Session variable. Then you must use one of the update techniques I explained in Chapter 22. Again, storing DataTable or DataView objects in Session variables kills scalability and can introduce server affinity (unless you use out-of-process sessions, which I'll describe in the next chapter), so you must weigh your decision carefully.

Multiple Columns in DataList Controls

The only feature of the DataList control not yet covered is its ability to display data in multiple columns, using either a vertical or horizontal layout. You can control this feature by means of the RepeatColumns, RepeatDirection, and RepeatLayout properties. Figure 25-10 shows a DataList control that hosts an Image and a CheckBox control in its ItemTemplate and displays all the graphic files in the directory specified by the user in the txtPath TextBox control. This code does the binding when the user clicks the Display button:

```
Private Sub btnDisplay_Click(ByVal sender As Object, _
    ByVal e As EventArgs) Handles btnDisplay.Click
    ' This is the directory you want to browse.
    ' IMPORTANT: you get an exception if ASP.NET account isn't authorized
    ' to access the directory.
    Dim path As String = txtPath.Text
    ' This is the ArrayList that works as the data source.
    Dim arrFiles As New ArrayList()

    ' Fill the ArrayList with complete filenames.
    For Each file As String In Directory.GetFiles(path)
        ' Filter files on their extension.
        Select Case Path.GetExtension(file).ToLower
            Case ".gif", ".ico", ".bmp", ".jpg", ".jpeg"
                arrFiles.Add(file)
        End Select
    Next

    ' Bind the ArrayList to the DataList.
    dlstFiles.DataSource = arrFiles
    dlstFiles.DataBind()
End Sub
```

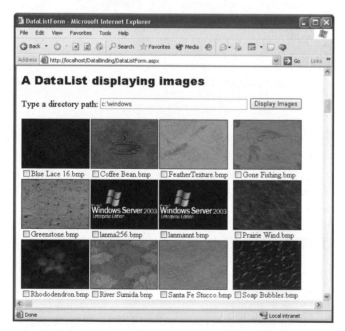

Figure 25-10   A DataList control displaying images in multiple columns

The ImageUrl property of the Image control has to be bound to complete file paths, but you want to display only the filename in the CheckBox control. Here's how to define the binding expression to solve the problem:

```
<asp:DataList id="dlstFiles" runat="server"
    RepeatDirection="Horizontal" RepeatColumns="4">
  <ItemTemplate>
    <asp:Image id=imgFile runat="server" Width="140px"
       ImageUrl="<%# Container.DataItem %>"
       BorderWidth="1" Height="100px" /><BR>
    <asp:CheckBox id=Checkbox1 runat="server"
       Text='<%# System.Io.Path.GetFileName(Container.DataItem) %>' />
  </ItemTemplate>
</asp:DataList>
```

As the preceding code shows, you must reference the current item by using the Container.DataItem expression when you bind to an ArrayList object. Similarly, you can reference the properties of the current item by using Container.DataItem.Key and Container.DataItem.Value when you bind to a Hashtable object.

The demo program doesn't process the selected images—that is, the images whose companion CheckBox control has been flagged—but it's a simple thing to do now that you know how to use the FindControl method to get a reference to controls contained in a DataList control. Here's a routine that returns an ArrayList containing the complete path of all selected images:

```
' Return the list of selected files.
Function GetSelectedFiles() As ArrayList
    Dim arr As New ArrayList()

    For Each dli As DataListItem In dlstFiles.Items
        ' Get a reference to the CheckBox control.
        Dim chkFile As CheckBox = _
            DirectCast(dli.FindControl("chkFile"), CheckBox)
        If chkFile.Checked Then
            ' If check box is checked, get a reference to the Image control.
            With DirectCast(dli.FindControl("imgFile"), WebControls.Image)
                ' Add the filename to the list of results.
                arr.Add(.ImageUrl)
            End With
        End If
    Next
    ' Return the result array.
    Return arr
End Function
```

The DataGrid Control

The DataGrid control is by far the most complex Web Forms control. It supports several templates, automatic edit mode, and sorting and paging capabilities. Yet it shares many of its properties and events with the DataList control, so you already know how to use most of its features. There are also a few new properties, such as BackImageUrl (the URL of the image displayed in the background of the DataGrid), Columns (the collection of columns, which doesn't include the columns created automatically), and a few properties related to paging (AllowPaging, PageSize, PageCount, and CurrentPage-Index). You'll see how to use these and other properties in the following sections.

As for the DataList and most complex controls, Visual Studio provides both an Auto Format command that lets you select the control's appearance from a gallery of available styles (see Figure 25-11) and a Property Builder command that lets you access a paged dialog box where you can set virtually any property of the control. (See Figure 25-12.) Both commands are available on the control's shortcut menu and in the bottom portion of the Properties window.

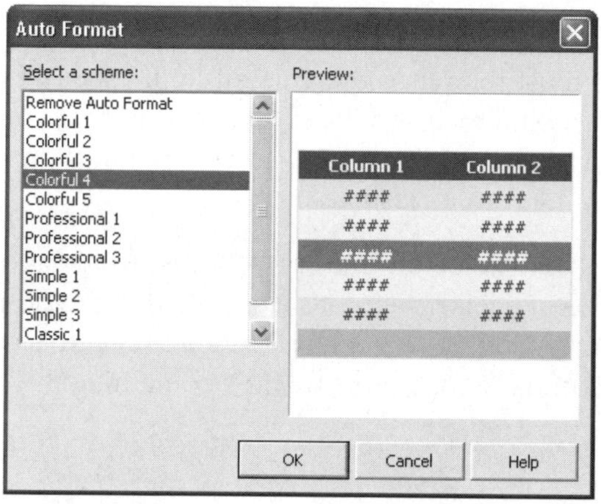

Figure 25-11   The Auto Format dialog box of the DataGrid control

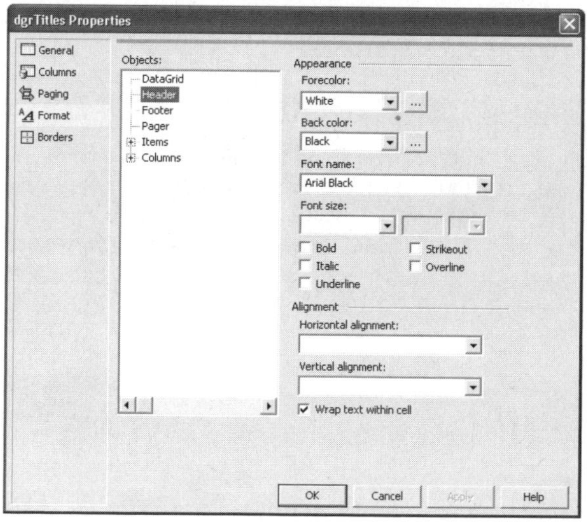

Figure 25-12   The Format page of the Properties dialog box of the DataGrid control

Columns and Templates

You can display a DataGrid control simply by binding it to a data source and leaving its AutoGenerateColumns property set to True (the default value). In this case, the control generates one bound column for each field in the data source:

```
DataGrid1.DataSource = ds.Tables("Titles")
DataGrid1.DataBind()
```

Even if you don't customize the contents of each grid cell, you still have a lot of control over the appearance of the control by means of *xxxx*Style properties. The DataGrid control supports different styles for seven different visual elements. You can set them using Visual Studio's dialog boxes or by inserting them right in the HTML code:

```
<asp:datagrid id="dgrTitles" runat="server" Width="679px" Height="183px" >
  <HeaderStyle Font-Names="Arial Black" ForeColor="White" _
    BackColor="Black" />
  <ItemStyle BackColor="White" />
  <AlternatingItemStyle BackColor="Khaki" />
  <SelectedItemStyle BackColor="Orange" />
  <EditItemStyle BackColor="Orange" />
  <FooterStyle ForeColor="Blue" />
  <PagerStyle BackColor="Gray" />
  <Columns>
     ⋮
  </Columns>
</asp.datagrid>
```

The items in the <Columns> block define the columns in the DataGrid. You need to specify these columns only if the AutoGenerateColumns property is False. The Data-Grid control supports five different types of columns:

- **Bound columns** These columns are bound to the data source's field specified by their DataField property. They automatically display a TextBox control for rows in edit mode.

- **Hyperlink columns** These columns are rendered as hyperlinks that display either a constant caption or a string taken from a data source's field. The target of the hyperlink can be a fixed URL or, more often, a URL based on a data source's field.

- **Button columns** These columns are rendered as Button or LinkButton controls. The button's Text property can be constant or be taken from the data source. When the button is clicked, an ItemCommand event fires on the server and your code can detect which button was clicked by looking at the CommandName and the e.Item.ItemIndex properties. If CommandName is Select, a click on the button fires a server-side SelectedIndexChanged event and activates the edit mode for the current row. If CommandName is Delete, it fires a server-side DeleteCommand event.

- **Edit, Update, and Cancel columns** These columns are rendered with a Button whose caption is Edit. When clicked, this button fires a server-side EditCommand event. Your code inside this event should set the EditItemIndex property to activate the edit mode for the current row; when you do so, the Edit button is replaced by a pair of buttons labeled Update and Cancel. (You can opt for different captions for the Edit, Update, and Cancel buttons, and you can also use Link-Button controls instead of push buttons.)

■ **Template columns**   You are in full control of template controls, and in fact you must specify templates for normal items, alternate items, selected items, and edited items. Each template can contain literal HTML text and one or more controls that can be bound to the data source. For example, you can use a template column to render a Boolean field by means of a CheckBox control, a lookup field with a DropDownList control, an enumerated value with a set of RadioButton controls, an Image control for a field that contains a picture, and so on.

Figure 25-13 shows the DataGrid control created by the demo application. This is the column collection used to generate its columns:

```
<asp:datagrid id="dgrTitles" runat="server" AutoGenerateColumns="False">
   ⋮
  <Columns>
    <asp:TemplateColumn HeaderText="[ ]">
      <ItemTemplate>
        <asp:CheckBox id="chkSelect" runat="server" />
      </ItemTemplate>
    </asp:TemplateColumn>
    <asp:BoundColumn DataField="title" HeaderText="Title" />
    <asp:TemplateColumn HeaderText="Publisher">
      <ItemTemplate>
        <asp:Label id=lblPublisher runat="server" Text=
        '<%# Container.DataItem.Row.GetParentRow("PubsTitles")("pub_name") %>'
          />
      </ItemTemplate>
      <EditItemTemplate>
        <asp:DropDownList id="ddlPublishers" runat="server"
          DataTextField="pub_name" DataValueField="pub_id" />
      </EditItemTemplate>
    </asp:TemplateColumn>
    <asp:BoundColumn DataField="type" HeaderText="Type">
        <HeaderStyle Width="80px" />
    </asp:BoundColumn>
    <asp:BoundColumn DataField="price" HeaderText="Price">
      <HeaderStyle Width="50px" />
    <asp:EditCommandColumn ButtonType="PushButton" UpdateText="Update"
      HeaderText="Edit" CancelText="Cancel" EditText="Edit" />
    <asp:ButtonColumn Text="Delete" ButtonType="PushButton"
      HeaderText="Delete" CommandName="Delete" />
    <asp:HyperLinkColumn Text="Publisher" DataNavigateUrlField="pub_id"
      DataNavigateUrlFormatString="/showpubs.aspx?pub_id={0}"
      HeaderText="More info" />
  </Columns>
</asp:datagrid>
```

The Publisher column is a template column because you want to use a DropDownList control to let the user select a publisher when the element is being edited. The first column is also a template column, which you use to display a CheckBox control. The user can select one or more titles and then click the leftmost button at the bottom to evaluate the sum of the prices of selected titles.

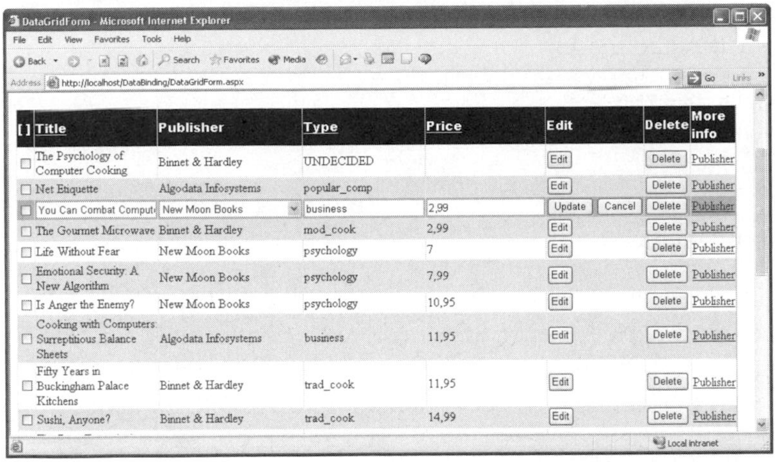

Figure 25-13   The DataGrid created by the demo application

The easiest way to set column properties is by right-clicking the DataGrid, clicking Property Builder on the shortcut menu, and using the Columns page of the Properties dialog box. (See Figure 25-14.) After you create one or more template columns, you can right-click the DataGrid control, point to Edit Template, and click the column on the shortcut menu to edit the template in a visual way, as you did with the DataList control.

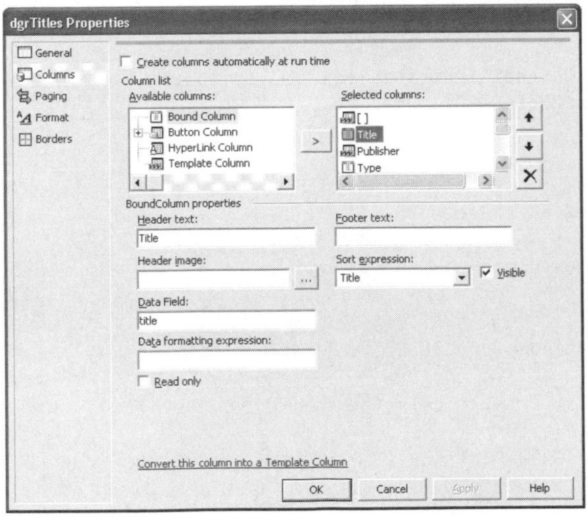

Figure 25-14   The Columns page of the Properties dialog box

The last column is a hyperlink column. It's interesting to see how the hyperlink is generated for each row in the DataGrid. The value of the DataNavigateUrlFormatString attribute is a .NET formatting string; it contains a {0} element, which is replaced by the value provided by the field pointed to by DataNavigateUrlField. For example, this column generates URLs like these:

```
/showpubs.aspx?pub_id=0736
/showpubs.aspx?pub_id=0877
/showpubs.aspx?pub_id=1389
⋮
```

Command Event Handlers

To simplify the code behind Edit, Update, and Delete, the code reads both the Titles and Publishers table in a DataSet object and then stores it in a Session variable. (Of course, all my warnings against storing a DataSet or a DataTable in a Session variable are still valid, but I needed to simplify the code to keep it manageable enough for this demo.)

```
' The DataSet that contains the data.
Dim ds As New DataSet()

Private Sub Page_Load(ByVal sender As Object, ByVal e As EventArgs) _
    Handles MyBase.Load
    If Not Me.IsPostBack Then
        ' If this is the first time the form is displayed, read the DataSet
        ' and store it in a Session variable.
        FillDataSet()
        Session("DataSet") = ds
        ' Bind the DataGrid control.
        BindDataGrid()
    Else
        ' Or just retrieve the DataSet from the Session variable.
        ds = DirectCast(Session("DataSet"), DataSet)
    End If
End Sub

' Fill the DataSet from the Pubs database.
Sub FillDataSet()
    Dim cn As New OleDbConnection(OledbPubsConnString)
    cn.Open()
    ' Fill the Titles DataTable.
    Dim daTitles As New OleDbDataAdapter("SELECT * FROM Titles", cn)
    daTitles.Fill(ds, "Titles")
    ' Fill the Publishers DataTable (with only the fields you need).
    Dim daPubs As New OleDbDataAdapter( _
        "SELECT pub_id,pub_name FROM Publishers", cn)
    daPubs.Fill(ds, "Publishers")
    ' Close the connection.
    cn.Close()
    ' Create the relation between the two tables.
    ds.Relations.Add("PubsTitles", _
        ds.Tables("Publishers").Columns("pub_id"), _
        ds.Tables("Titles").Columns("pub_id"))
End Sub
```

Thanks to the relation between the Titles and the Publishers table, you can display the name of the publisher in each row by using the following data binding expression for the Label control in the third column:

```
<asp:Label id=lblPublisher runat="server"
  Text='<%# Container.DataItem.Row.GetParentRow("PubsTitles")("pub_name") %>'
/>
```

An explanation is in order: the Container.DataItem operand returns a DataRowView object, which doesn't allow you to traverse relationships. However, it exposes the Row property, which returns the corresponding DataRow object and makes it possible for you to use the GetParentRow method to choose the publisher name by using the Pubs-Titles relationship.

Inside the BindDataGrid procedure, the program actually binds the dgrTitles control. If the DataGrid is in edit mode, it also binds the ddlPublishers DropDownList control and fills it with the list of available publishers:

```
' Bind the DataGrid control.
Sub BindDataGrid()
    ' Bind the data source to the DataGrid.
    dgrTitles.DataSource = ds.Tables("Titles")
    dgrTitles.DataKeyField = "title_id"
    dgrTitles.DataBind()

    ' If you are in edit mode, also bind the ddlPublishers control.
    If dgrTitles.EditItemIndex >= 0 Then
        ' Get a reference to the ddlPublishers control.
        Dim dgi As DataGridItem = dgrTitles.Items(dgrTitles.EditItemIndex)
        Dim ddlPublishers As DropDownList = _
            DirectCast(dgi.FindControl("ddlPublishers"), DropDownList)
        ' Bind it to the Publishers DataTable.
        ddlPublishers.DataSource = ds.Tables("Publishers")
        ddlPublishers.DataTextField = "pub_name"
        ddlPublishers.DataValueField = "pub_id"
        ddlPublishers.DataBind()

        ' Highlight the publisher of the current title.
        Dim dr As DataRow
        dr = GetDataRow(dgrTitles.DataKeys(dgrTitles.EditItemIndex).ToString)
        SelectItemFromValue(ddlPublishers, dr("pub_id").ToString)
    End If
End Sub
```

The preceding code is similar to the BindBookList routine shown in the section devoted to the DataList control; the main difference is a call to the GetDataRow function to retrieve the DataRow object from the Titles DataTable with a given key value. This detail is important: you might be tempted to use the EditItemIndex value as an index into the DataTable to extract the DataRow corresponding to a given DataGrid element, but this technique fails if the end user has deleted one or more rows. Such deleted rows don't appear in the DataGrid any longer but are still in the DataTable, so the index of a Data-Grid element can be less than the index of the corresponding row in the DataTable. The only safe way to retrieve the correct DataRow is by using its key value:

```
' Return the DataRow with a given key value.
Function GetDataRow(ByVal id As String) As DataRow
    ' Select the DataTable rows with this key value.
```

```
        Dim drows() As DataRow
        drows = ds.Tables("Titles").Select("title_id='" & id & "'")
        ' Return the DataRow if found.
        If drows.Length > 0 Then Return drows(0)
    End Function
```

The following code for the Edit and Cancel buttons is similar to the code for the Data-List control:

```
Private Sub dgrTitles_EditCommand(ByVal source As Object, _
    ByVal e As DataGridCommandEventArgs) Handles dgrTitles.EditCommand
    ' Enter the edit mode and rebind the control.
    dgrTitles.EditItemIndex = e.Item.ItemIndex
    BindDataGrid()
End Sub

Private Sub dgrTitles_CancelCommand(ByVal source As Object, _
    ByVal e As DataGridCommandEventArgs) Handles dgrTitles.CancelCommand
    ' Exit edit mode and rebind the control.
    dgrTitles.EditItemIndex = -1
    BindDataGrid()
End Sub
```

The code for the Update command is not so simple because it has to retrieve the value stored in the bound controls, and therefore it needs a reference to these controls. You can get a reference to a child control in a template column by using the FindControl method of the DataGridItem object, using a technique similar to the one used with child controls in the DataList control. But this technique doesn't work with child controls in bound columns because in that case you don't know what name to pass to the FindControl method. To access controls in bound columns, you must first use the Cells collection of the DataGridItem object to retrieve a reference to the table cell that contains the control you're interested in, and then use Controls(0) to get a reference to the first (and only) control contained in that cell. Here's the code that implements this technique:

```
Private Sub dgrTitles_UpdateCommand(ByVal source As Object, _
    ByVal e As DataGridCommandEventArgs) Handles dgrTitles.UpdateCommand
    ' Get a reference to the DataGridItem being edited.
    Dim dgi As DataGridItem = e.Item
    ' Get the DataRow with the corresponding key value.
    Dim dr As DataRow = _
        GetDataRow(dgrTitles.DataKeys(e.Item.ItemIndex).ToString)

    ' Update DataRow columns.
    ' The title value is the only control in the 2nd cell in this row.
    dr("title") = DirectCast(dgi.Cells(1).Controls(0), TextBox).Text
    ' The pub_id field is the current value of the ddlPublishers control.
    Dim ddlPublishers As DropDownList = _
        DirectCast(dgi.FindControl("ddlPublishers"), DropDownList)
    dr("pub_id") = ddlPublishers.SelectedItem.Value
    ' The type field is the only control in the 4th cell in this row.
    dr("type") = DirectCast(dgi.Cells(3).Controls(0), TextBox).Text
    ' The price field is the only control in the 5th cell in this row.
    dr("price") = CDec(DirectCast(dgi.Cells(4).Controls(0), TextBox).Text)
```

```
' Exit edit mode and rebind the DataGrid.
dgrTitles.EditItemIndex = -1
BindDataGrid()
End Sub
```

The handler for the DeleteCommand event calls the GetDataRow function to retrieve a reference to the current DataRow and then invokes the Delete method on it:

```
Private Sub dgrTitles_DeleteCommand(ByVal source As Object, _
    ByVal e As DataGridCommandEventArgs) Handles dgrTitles.DeleteCommand
    ' Get the DataRow with the key value of current row.
    Dim dr As DataRow = _
        GetDataRow(dgrTitles.DataKeys(e.Item.ItemIndex).ToString)
    ' Delete it and rebind the control.
    dr.Delete()
    BindDataGrid()
End Sub
```

The code behind the btnEval button scans the Items collection of the DataGrid control and sums the price value for all the titles whose CheckBox controls in the first column have been flagged. Here's an example of what you can do with this technique:

```
Private Sub btnEval_Click(ByVal sender As System.Object, _
    ByVal e As EventArgs) Handles btnEval.Click
    ' Sum the price of all titles that have a selected checkbox.
    Dim totalPrice As Decimal, count As Integer

    For Each dgi As DataGridItem In dgrTitles.Items
        ' Get a reference to the CheckBox control in this item.
        Dim cb As CheckBox = _
            DirectCast(dgi.FindControl("chkSelect"), CheckBox)
        ' If checked, count this element.
        If cb.Checked Then
            ' Get the title_id key value for this row.
            Dim id As String = dgrTitles.DataKeys(dgi.ItemIndex).ToString
            ' Select the DataTable row with this key value.
            Dim dr As DataRow = GetDataRow(id)
            If Not dr.IsNull("price") Then
                ' Add the price to the running total.
                totalPrice += CDec(dr("price"))
                count += 1
            End If
        End If
    Next

    ' Display the total.
    lblTotal.Text = String.Format( _
        "Total price for {0} selected book(s) is ${1}", count, totalPrice)
End Sub
```

For simplicity's sake, the demo program doesn't contain the code that updates the Pubs database from the modified DataSet. But it's easy to implement this code by adopting one of the update techniques outlined in Chapter 22.

Sorting Rows

The DataGrid provides support for sorting its rows. To enable this feature, you must set the AllowSorting property to True and then set the SortExpression property for one or more columns to a suitable string (most often, the name of the field that works as the sort key). You can initialize the latter property in the Columns page of the Property Builder dialog box. (See Figure 25-14.)

When these two properties are properly set, the text in the column's header becomes a hyperlink that the user can click to sort the DataGrid's contents on that field. (For example, the DataGrid in Figure 25-13 can be sorted on the Title, Type, and Price fields.) A click on these hyperlinks fires a server-side SortCommand event that receives the column's sort expression in the SortExpression property of the second argument. You must trap this event, sort the rows as requested, and rebind the control. Typically, you implement sorting by binding the DataGrid control to a DataView object (instead of a DataTable) and setting its Sort property appropriately.

To make things more interesting, the demo application supports sorting in both ascending and descending directions. A first click on a column sorts in ascending order, and a second click on the same column reverses the direction. This technique requires that you preserve the current sort expression between postbacks. You can store this value in the page's ViewState or as a custom attribute of the DataGrid. The demo program adopts the latter technique, which lets you set the attribute at design time by editing the HTML code. For example, the following HTML code sorts titles from the priciest to the least expensive:

```
<asp:datagrid id="dgrTitles" SortExpr="price DESC" runat="server"
    AutoGenerateColumns="False" AllowSorting="True">
  ⋮
</asp:datagrid>
```

To implement sorting, you must trap the SortCommand event and set the SortExpr attribute correctly:

```
Private Sub dgrTitles_SortCommand(ByVal source As Object, _
    ByVal e As DataGridSortCommandEventArgs) Handles dgrTitles.SortCommand
    ' Extract current sort expression and set the new one.
    Dim currSortExpr As String = dgrTitles.Attributes("SortExpr")
    Dim newSortExpr As String = e.SortExpression

    ' If the expression is the same, just reverse the direction.
    If Not (currSortExpr Is Nothing) AndAlso _
        currSortExpr.ToString = e.SortExpression Then
            newSortExpr &= " DESC"
    End If

    ' Remember the new sort expression and rebind.
    dgrTitles.Attributes("SortExpr") = newSortExpr
    BindDataGrid()
End Sub
```

To complete the implementation of the sort command, you must check the SortExpr attribute just before binding the control and use a sorted DataView object if the attribute isn't a null string. The following listing shows the statements (in boldface) that you must add to the BindDataGrid procedure:

```
Sub BindDataGrid()
    ' Bind the data source to the DataGrid.
    dgrTitles.DataSource = ds.Tables("Titles")
    dgrTitles.DataKeyField = "title_id"

    ' Retrieve the SortExpression.
    Dim sortExpr As String = dgrTitles.Attributes("SortExpr")
    If Not (sortExpr Is Nothing) AndAlso sortExpr.ToString <> "" Then
        ' You must bind to a sorted DataView object instead.
        Dim dv As DataView = ds.Tables("Titles").DefaultView
        dv.Sort = sortExpr.ToString
        dgrTitles.DataSource = dv
    End If
    ' Do the binding.
    dgrTitles.DataBind()

    ' ...(The remainder of the routine is as before)...
    ⋮
End Sub
```

Because you're binding to a DataView object instead of a DataTable, you can implement several other features. For example, you can use the RowFilter and RowStateFilter properties to display only a subset of all the rows, find rows with the Find and FindRows methods, and so on.

Default and Custom Paging

We've arrived at the only DataGrid feature not yet covered. The DataGrid control allows the user to navigate through pages of results, which is essential when a table displays more than a few dozen rows. The DataGrid control supports three paging techniques:

- **Default paging with default navigation buttons** The DataGrid displays a set of hyperlink buttons that let you navigate through its pages. You can display either Previous and Next buttons (with any caption you wish) or page numbers.

- **Default paging with custom navigation buttons** You provide the navigation buttons and trap their server-side Click event to move to the page the user requested.

- **Custom paging** You're in complete control of how data is loaded in the DataGrid control, as well as how navigation buttons are displayed.

Not surprisingly, the first technique is the simplest one. You just set the AllowPaging property to True and set the PageSize property to a suitable value (for example, 10 rows). You can quickly set these and other properties related to paging in the

DataGrid's Properties dialog box. (See Figure 25-15.) Ensure that the Show Navigation Buttons check box is selected, decide where you want to display the buttons (top, bottom, or top and bottom), and whether you want to display Previous and Next buttons or page-number buttons. If you want Previous and Next buttons, you can set the button captions (default is < and >). If you want page-number buttons, you can decide how many buttons are visible. (Default is 10.)

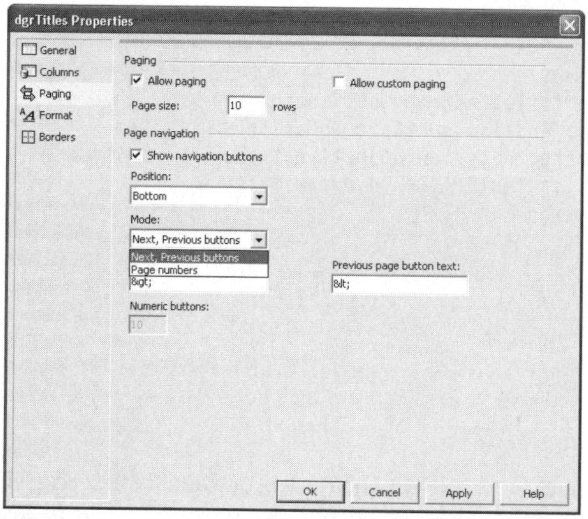

Figure 25-15 The Paging section of the DataGrid's Properties dialog box

When a navigation button is clicked, a PageIndexChanged event is fired on the server. Inside this event's handler, you must assign a new value to the DataGrid's CurrentPage-Index property and rebind the control:

```
Private Sub dgrTitles_PageIndexChanged(ByVal source As Object, _
    ByVal e As DataGridPageChangedEventArgs) _
    Handles dgrTitles.PageIndexChanged
    ' Navigate to another page and rebind the DataGrid.
    dgrTitles.CurrentPageIndex = e.NewPageIndex
    BindDataGrid()
End Sub
```

Implementing the second technique, default paging with custom navigation controls, is only a little more complex. Because you're providing the navigation buttons, you must clear the Show Navigation Buttons check box in the Properties dialog box and place suitable navigation buttons elsewhere on the form. The demo application displays the usual four navigation buttons, plus a Go button that lets you jump to any page. The text box in the center always displays the current page, and buttons are correctly disabled if their use wouldn't move to another page. (See Figure 25-16.)

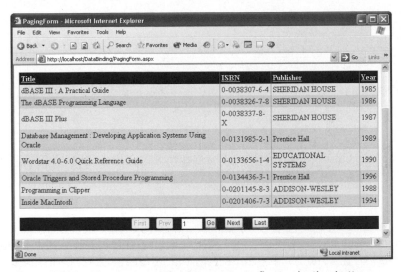

Figure 25-16   The demo application supports five navigation buttons

Here's the code that traps the buttons' server-side Click event, modifies the DataGrid's CurrentPageIndex property as required, and rebinds the control. Each control has been assigned a different CommandName property, so detecting the navigation command being invoked is simple:

```vb
Private Sub ButtonClick(ByVal sender As Object, ByVal e As EventArgs) _
    Handles btnFirst.Click, btnPrevious.Click, btnNext.Click, _
    btnLast.Click, btnGo.Click
    ' The current page number
    Dim pageNum As Integer = dgrTitles.CurrentPageIndex

    Select Case DirectCast(sender, Button).CommandName.ToLower
        Case "first"
            pageNum = 0
        Case "prev"
            pageNum -= 1
        Case "next"
            pageNum += 1
        Case "last"
            pageNum = dgrTitles.PageCount - 1
        Case "go"
            Try
                ' Visible page number is 1-based.
                pageNum = CInt(txtPage.Text) - 1
            Catch
                Exit Sub
            End Try
    End Select

    ' Show the page.
    ShowPage(pageNum)
End Sub
```

```
' Display a page.
Sub ShowPage(ByVal pageNum As Integer)
    ' Keep the page number in valid range.
    pageNum = Math.Max(0, Math.Min(pageNum, dgrTitles.PageCount - 1))
    ' Enforce the new page number and bind the control.
    dgrTitles.CurrentPageIndex = pageNum
    BindDataGrid()
    ' Update button state.
    btnFirst.Enabled = (pageNum > 0)
    btnPrevious.Enabled = (pageNum > 0)
    btnNext.Enabled = (pageNum < dgrTitles.PageCount - 1)
    btnLast.Enabled = (pageNum < dgrTitles.PageCount - 1)
    ' Display the current page number (1-based).
    txtPage.Text = (pageNum + 1).ToString
End Sub
```

When you're doing default paging—using either default or custom navigation buttons—you must bind the DataGrid control to a DataView or DataTable object, as you'd do if paging were disabled so that the control can use the CurrentPageIndex property to display only the requested page. The demo application reduces database activity by creating the DataSet object the first time the page is requested and storing it in a Session variable. Here's the code that does the binding and provides support for column sorting as well:

```
' Bind the DataGrid control.
Sub BindDataGrid()
    ' Retrieve the DataSet from the session variable.
    Dim ds As DataSet = DirectCast(Session("DataSet"), DataSet)

    ' Read data from database if this is the first time you do it.
    If ds Is Nothing Then
        Dim cn As New OleDbConnection(BiblioConnString)
        cn.Open()
        ' Read data from Titles table, plus the publisher's name.
        Dim sql As String
        sql = "SELECT Titles.*, Publishers.Name As PubName FROM Titles " _
            & " INNER JOIN Publishers ON Titles.PubId=Publishers.PubId"
        Dim da As New OleDbDataAdapter(sql, cn)
        ds = New DataSet()
        da.Fill(ds, "Titles")
        cn.Close()
        ' Store the DataSet in a Session variable.
        Session("DataSet") = ds
    End If

    ' Get a DataView object sorted on the required sort expression.
    Dim dv As DataView = ds.Tables("Titles").DefaultView
    dv.Sort = dgrTitles.Attributes("SortExpr")
    dgrTitles.DataSource = dv
    ' Do the data binding.
    dgrTitles.DataBind()
End Sub

Private Sub dgrTitles_SortCommand(ByVal source As Object, _
    ByVal e As DataGridSortCommandEventArgs) Handles dgrTitles.SortCommand
```

```
' Extract current sort column and order.
Dim currSortExpr As String = dgrTitles.Attributes("SortExpr")
Dim newSortExpr As String = e.SortExpression

' If the sort field is the same, just reverse the direction.
If Not (currSortExpr Is Nothing) AndAlso _
    currSortExpr.ToString = e.SortExpression Then
    newSortExpr &= " DESC"
End If

' Remember the new sort expression and show the first page.
dgrTitles.Attributes("SortExpr") = newSortExpr
ShowPage(0)
End Sub
```

Default paging has a great shortcoming: you must load *all* the data in a DataTable or DataView object to let the DataGrid control select only the rows that belong to the current page. This approach might be OK when the data source contains a few hundred rows, but it won't work in real-world applications that manage thousands (or even millions) of rows. In cases like these, custom paging is the only reasonable solution.

You activate custom paging by setting both the AllowPaging and the AllowCustomPaging properties to True. You then assign the total number of rows to the VirtualItemCount property so that the control can correctly evaluate the PageCount value. You can use default buttons or provide your own.

Unlike all the samples shown previously, when in custom paging mode you bind the DataGrid control to a data source that contains *only* the data you want to display in the current page. Fortunately, you already know how to page through a large resultset by using the DataAdapter's Fill method. Thanks to the high modularity of the code written so far, implementing custom paging is just a matter of replacing the BindDataGrid procedure with a new version that takes the CurrentPageIndex and PageSize properties into account. The following code also takes the current sort order into account: Notice that when doing custom paging, you implement sorting by means of an ORDER BY clause in the SQL query so that you can then extract the correct page from the sorted resultset:

```
Sub BindDataGrid()
    ' Open the connection.
    Dim cn As New OleDbConnection(BiblioConnString)
    cn.Open()

    ' If necessary, initialize VirtualItemCount with number of records.
    If Not Me.IsPostBack Then
        Dim cmd As New OleDbCommand("SELECT COUNT(*) FROM Titles", cn)
        dgrTitles.VirtualItemCount = CInt(cmd.ExecuteScalar)
    End If

    ' Prepare to read from Titles table plus Name of publisher.
    Dim sql As String = "SELECT Titles.*, Publishers.Name As PubName FROM " _
        & "Titles INNER JOIN Publishers ON Titles.PubId=Publishers.PubId"
    ' Append sort expression, if there is one.
```

```
        Dim sortExpr As String = dgrTitles.Attributes("SortExpr")
        If Not (sortExpr Is Nothing) AndAlso sortExpr.ToString <> "" Then
            sql &= " ORDER BY " & sortExpr
        End If
        ' Fill a DataSet only with data for the current page.
        Dim ds As New DataSet()
        Dim da As New OleDbDataAdapter(sql, cn)
        da.Fill(ds, dgrTitles.CurrentPageIndex * dgrTitles.PageSize, _
            dgrTitles.PageSize, "Titles")
        cn.Close()

        ' Do the binding.
        dgrTitles.DataSource = ds.Tables("Titles")
        dgrTitles.DataBind()
    End Sub
```

If you really want to squeeze the best performance out of your code, you should use the technique described in the "Paginating Results" section of Chapter 22. This technique performs better than the Fill method with large resultsets.

Nested DataGrids

Although the ASP.NET DataGrid isn't as easy to use as its Windows Forms counterpart, it does offer one feature that's difficult to achieve with a standard Windows Forms DataGrid control: the ability to nest any control inside a DataGrid, for example one DataGrid inside another DataGrid control. This feature is quite useful when you want to display two database tables in a master-detail relationship.

I prepared an example that implements this technique and displays all the records of the Publishers table in the Pubs database; if you select a publisher, the last column in the main grid displays a child grid that lets you browse and even edit the titles for that publisher. (See Figure 25-17.) You can adapt this example to other tables and you can modify this technique to nest a DataGrid inside other template controls, for example a DataList control.

Create a new Web Forms page and add a Connection component, two DataAdapter components, and a typed DataSet named DsPubs1, which contains the publishers and the titles DataTable objects. The code fills the DataSet the very first time the end user navigates to the page and stores it in a Session variable between postbacks. The Save to Database button (at the bottom of the page) uses the DataAdapter's Update method to send all changes back to the database. You should also add a DataView component (from the Data tab in the Toolbox), name it dvTitles, and set its Table property equal to DsPubs1.Titles. Next, create the parent DataGrid control (named grdPublishers in the sample application) and bind it to the publishers DataTable in the dsPubs1 DataSet.

Nesting a DataGrid control inside another DataGrid isn't difficult if you're using Visual Studio .NET: you add a template column to the parent DataGrid, and then you enter template edit mode and add the child DataGrid in the ItemTemplate section. (See Figure 25-18.) Name this child DataGrid as grdTitles and bind it to the dvTitles DataView object.

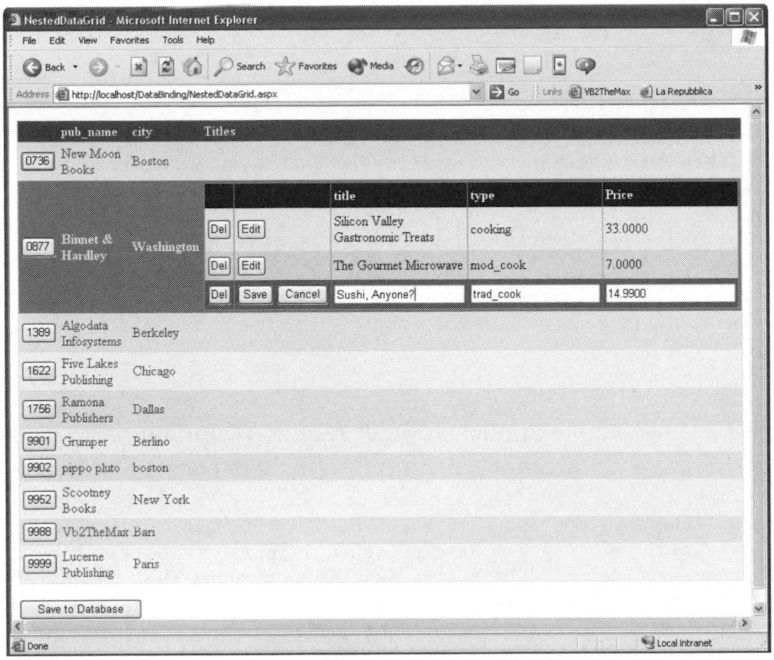

Figure 25-17 The nested DataGrid sample application running inside Internet Explorer

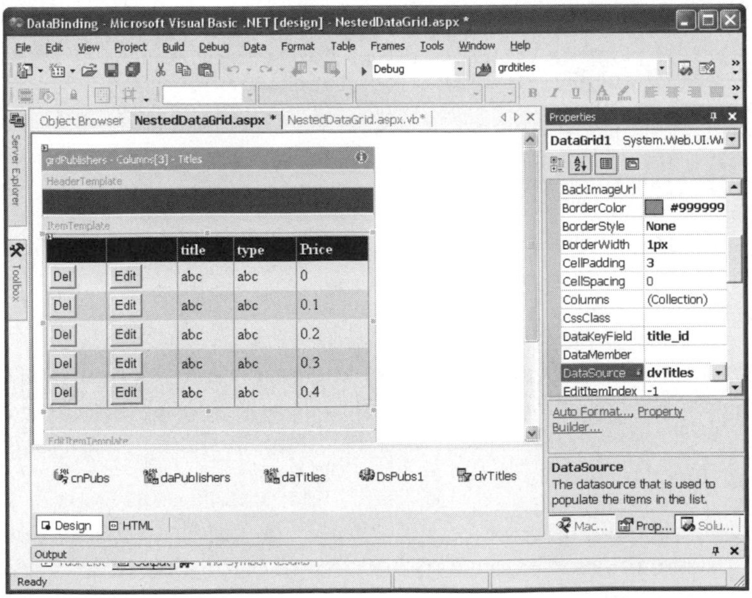

Figure 25-18 The nested DataGrid sample application at design time

The main problem you face is that you can't directly intercept events coming from the grdTitles DataGrid as you do with the main grdPublishers DataGrid, because the child grid isn't on the form surface. Never fear, however, because you just need to get a reference to the grdTitles control in the Page_Load event and use the AddHandler keyword to dynamically register the event handlers for this control:

```
' (In the Page_Load event handler)
For Each dgi As DataGridItem In grdPublishers.Items
    ' Get a reference to the child table, if there is one.
    Dim grdTitles As DataGrid = CType(dgi.Cells(3).Controls(1), DataGrid)
    If Not grdTitles Is Nothing Then
        AddHandler grdTitles.EditCommand, AddressOf grdTitles_EditCommand
        AddHandler grdTitles.UpdateCommand, AddressOf grdTitles_UpdateCommand
        AddHandler grdTitles.CancelCommand, AddressOf grdTitles_CancelCommand
        AddHandler grdTitles.DeleteCommand, AddressOf grdTitles_DeleteCommand
    End If
Next
```

The other section in the sample application that requires your attention is the handler for the ItemDataBound event from the main grdPublishers DataGrid control:

```
Private Sub grdPublishers_ItemDataBound(ByVal sender As Object, _
    ByVal e As DataGridItemEventArgs) Handles grdPublishers.ItemDataBound
    ' Get a reference to the child DataGrid, exit if not found (not an edit type).
    Dim grdTitles As DataGrid = CType(dgi.Cells(3).Controls(1), DataGrid)
    If grdTitles Is Nothing Then Exit Sub
    ' If this item isn't selected, make the grid invisible and exit
    If e.Item.ItemType <> ListItemType.SelectedItem Then
        grdTitles.Visible = False
        Exit Sub
    End If
    ' Have the DataView point to child title rows for this publisher.
    Dim pubID As String = CType(e.Item.DataItem, DataRowView). _
        Item("pub_id").ToString
    dvTitles.RowFilter = "pub_id='" & pubID & "'"
    grdTitles.DataBind()
End Sub
```

For more details, please see the complete source code of the sample application.

Dynamic Templates

All the templates in this chapter are static templates: they are defined in HTML code buried inside the .aspx page and can't be changed at run time. For the highest degree of flexibility, ASP.NET supports the ability to load templates at run time, using one of the following two mechanisms:

■ You can use the LoadTemplate method of the Page object to load a template file (which must have an .ascx extension) and assign it to one of the *xxxx*Template properties that the Repeater, DataList, and DataGrid controls expose.

- You can define a template class in code, and then instantiate it at run time and assign it to an *xxxx*Template property. A template class is a class that implements the ITemplate interface.

Loading a Template File

A template file is simply an .ascx file that contains the text that you would place inside an <*xxxx*Template> block. (.ascx files are usually related to User Controls, as you'll learn in Chapter 28.) For example, you could save the following text in a file named blue_on_orange.ascx and later apply it to display a DataList item with blue foreground color and orange background color, which displays the title and price fields from its data source:

```
<div style="COLOR: Blue; BACKGROUND-COLOR: Orange">
  <b>
  <%# DataBinder.Eval(CType(Container, DataListItem).DataItem, "title") %>
  </b> -
  <%# DataBinder.Eval(CType(Container, DataListItem).DataItem, "price") %>
</div>
```

An important note: you must use the DataBinder.Eval syntax and early binding when you create a dynamic template; hence you need the CType operator to convert from the generic Container reference to a more specific DataListItem or DataGridItem object to invoke the DataItem property. Unfortunately, this requirement means that a single template file containing bound expressions can't serve different types of controls.

Loading an .ascx file at run time into a template control is trivial. For example, this code applies different templates to regular and alternate items in a DataList control:

```
DataList1.ItemTemplate = Me.LoadTemplate("blue_on_orange.ascx")
DataList1.AlternatingItemTemplate = Me.LoadTemplate("blue_on_white.ascx")
DataList1.DataBind()
```

I prepared a demo application that lets you experiment with dynamic template loading. (See Figure 25-19.) The two DropDownList controls are loaded with four template names, and you can select separate templates for the regular and the alternate item. You can use this code as a boilerplate for building applications that users can customize with the templates you provide. The template must belong to the same ASP.NET application as the page that loads it.

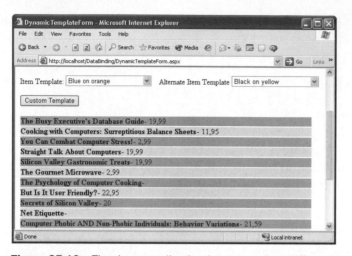

Figure 25-19   The demo application lets you select different custom templates for regular and alternate items.

Template Classes

For maximum flexibility, you can write a template class and assign one of its instances to the *xxxx*Template properties that the Repeater, DataList, and DataGrid controls expose. A template class is just a class that implements the ITemplate interface, which in turn exposes just one method: InstantiateIn. This method is called once for each item in the control and receives a reference to the RepeaterItem, DataListItem, or DataGridItem object. You typically react to this method by creating a child control inside the item:

```
Class MyTemplate
    Implements ITemplate

    Dim WithEvents pan As Panel

    Public Sub InstantiateIn(ByVal container As Control) _
        Implements ITemplate.InstantiateIn

        ' Get a strongly typed reference to the containing item.
        Dim dli As DataListItem = DirectCast(container, DataListItem)
        ' Create a new Panel control.
        pan = New Panel()
        ⋮
        ' Add the Panel control to the DataListItem control.
        dli.Controls.Add(pan)
    End Sub
End Class
```

You must be able to trap events from the control being added (the Panel control in the preceding code) because you must process its DataBinding event, which fires once for every item in the template control:

```
Private Sub pan_DataBinding(ByVal sender As Object, _
    ByVal e As EventArgs) Handles pan.DataBinding
    ⋮
End Sub
```

The demo application uses a custom template class to perform a few tasks that wouldn't be possible with a standard template. First, the template paints items with three different colors. Next, it replaces Null values in the data source with a custom string. Finally it changes the style of a data-bound element, depending on its contents. (See Figure 25-20.) Here's the complete source code of the template class:

```
Class MyCustomTemplate
    Implements ITemplate

    Public ForeColor, BackColor As Color
    Public AltBackColor, AltBackColor2 As Color

    Sub New(ByVal foreColor As Color, ByVal backColor As Color, _
        ByVal altBackColor As Color, ByVal altBackColor2 As Color)
        Me.ForeColor = foreColor
        Me.BackColor = backColor
        Me.AltBackColor = altBackColor
        Me.AltBackColor2 = altBackColor2
    End Sub

    ' You must trap the DataBinding event for this control.
    Dim WithEvents pan As Panel

    Public Sub InstantiateIn(ByVal container As Control) _
        Implements ITemplate.InstantiateIn
        ' Get a strongly typed reference to the containing item.
        Dim dli As DataListItem = DirectCast(container, DataListItem)
        ' Create a panel with specified colors.
        pan = New Panel()
        pan.ForeColor = Me.ForeColor
        ' Use alternate colors for background.
        Select Case dli.ItemIndex Mod 3
            Case 0 : pan.BackColor = Me.BackColor
            Case 1 : pan.BackColor = Me.AltBackColor
            Case 2 : pan.BackColor = Me.AltBackColor2
        End Select
        ' Adapt to the container's size.
        pan.Width = dli.Width
        pan.Height = dli.Height
```

```
                   ' Add child controls to this panel.
                   pan.Controls.Add(New LiteralControl("<b>"))
                   pan.Controls.Add(New Label())            ' The title field
                   pan.Controls.Add(New LiteralControl("</b> - "))
                   pan.Controls.Add(New Label())            ' The price field
                   ' Add the Panel control to the DataListItem control.
                   dli.Controls.Add(pan)
              End Sub

              Private Sub pan_DataBinding(ByVal sender As Object, _
                   ByVal e As EventArgs) Handles pan.DataBinding
                   ' Get a reference to the item container.
                   ' (Note: cast to a DataGridItem if working with a DataGrid.)
                   Dim dli As DataListItem = _
                       DirectCast(pan.NamingContainer, DataListItem)
                   ' Get a reference to the data source row.
                   ' (Note: cast to a DataRowView if binding to a DataTable/DataView.)
                   Dim dbr As System.Data.Common.DbDataRecord = _
                       DirectCast(dli.DataItem, System.Data.Common.DbDataRecord)

                   ' Get the values of all the fields you're interested in,
                   ' and display them in the Panel child controls.
                   Dim lblTitle As Label = DirectCast(pan.Controls(1), Label)
                   lblTitle.Text = dbr("title").ToString
                   ' This is the price Label control.
                   Dim lblPrice As Label = DirectCast(pan.Controls(3), Label)

                   If dbr("price").ToString.Length > 0 Then
                       ' Display price if this field isn't Null.
                       lblPrice.Text = "$" & dbr("price").ToString
                       ' Use special attributes for expensive titles.
                       If CDec(dbr("price")) > 20 Then
                           lblPrice.ForeColor = Color.Red
                           lblPrice.Font.Bold = True
                       End If
                   Else
                       ' Display special message for Null values.
                       lblPrice.Text = "(unknown price)"
                       lblPrice.Font.Italic = True
                   End If
              End Sub
         End Class
```

This is the code behind the button's Click event that activates the custom template:

```
Private Sub btnCustom_Click(ByVal sender As System.Object, _
     ByVal e As EventArgs) Handles btnCustom.Click
     ' Set the alternate item template to Nothing so that the control
     ' uses the custom template for all its elements.
     DataList1.AlternatingItemTemplate = Nothing
     ' Create a custom template and assign it to the ItemTemplate property.
     DataList1.ItemTemplate = New MyCustomTemplate(Color.Blue, Color.White, _
         Color.Cyan, Color.LightGreen)
     BindDataList()
End Sub
```

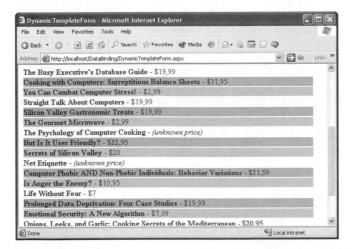

Figure 25-20   The MyCustomTemplate class paints items with alternate background colors, displays high prices in red, and replaces Null values with a custom string.

In this and the previous chapter, you saw how to create a rich and functional user interface for your Web Forms applications. However, ASP.NET isn't just about a pretty interface, and you still have to learn several important details about caching, error handling, configuration, and debugging. I'll discuss those topics in the next two chapters.

26 ASP.NET Applications

Knowing the ins and outs of Web Forms and controls is a good starting point for creating great Internet applications, but you have to learn more to leverage the full potential of ASP.NET. This chapter covers such missing details as these and unveils the essentials of ASP.NET caching, error handling, debugging, and tracing.

> **See Also**   This chapter assumes that you are familiar with Active Server Pages (ASP) programming and intrinsic Request, Response, Server, Session, and Application objects. You can review this information in Chapter 20 of *Programming Microsoft Visual Basic 6*, which is provided on the companion CD.

Configuration files play an essential role in any ASP.NET application. These are XML files that hold critical information about the ASP.NET runtime or individual ASP.NET applications—for example, how state sessions are implemented and which users are granted access to the application. There are three types of configuration files:

- machine.config is the main configuration file and contains the settings related to ASP.NET as a whole. All the ASP.NET applications inherit these settings, but they can override them. This file resides in the c:\WindowsMicrosoft.Net\Framework\vx.y.zzzz\Config directory. There's one machine.config file for each installed version of the .NET Framework.

- web.config is the configuration file that you place in an ASP.NET application's root directory. It often overrides machine.config settings related to session state, page directives, security, and tracing. Visual Studio .NET automatically generates this file when you create a new Web Forms project.

- secondary web.config files can reside in any subdirectory belonging to the application. Each additional configuration file can override values in the application's main web.config file and can assign different settings to files that are located in that subdirectory.

All the web.config files in an application form a hierarchy—each directory inherits all the settings from its parent directory, but it can override them by using a local web.config file. This hierarchical structure makes possible the so-called XCOPY deployment and sharply contrasts with the way you install complex ASP applications, which requires that you manually set Microsoft Internet Information Services (IIS) settings on a directory-by-directory basis (or create a script that does it on your behalf). A few settings can't be overridden by secondary configuration files—for example, those related to state sessions and a few security settings. Regardless of their position, all configuration files have the same basic structure:

```
<?xml version="1.0" encoding="utf-8" ?>
<configuration>
  <system.web>
    ⋮
  </system.web>
</configuration>
```

I'll cover configuration files in detail in the next chapter, but I need to make this introduction so that you'll fully understand the topics I discuss in this chapter.

> **Note**   To keep the code as concise as possible, all the code samples in this section assume the following Imports statements at the file or project level:
>
> ```
> Imports System.IO
> Imports System.Data.OleDb
> Imports System.Runtime.Serialization.Formatters.Soap
> Imports System.Web.SessionState
> Imports System.Web.Cache
> ```

ASP.NET Intrinsic Objects

The five "classic" Active Server Pages objects—namely, Request, Response, Server, Session, and Application—are now properties of the Page object. Because your code runs in the page's context, you can access these objects under ASP.NET exactly as you did under ASP. For example, you can still send raw output to the browser by using the Response.Write method, and you can read arguments passed to the page by using the Request.QueryString collection.

```
' These two statements are equivalent.
Response.Write("<h1>Welcome to ASP.NET</h1>")
Me.Response.Write("<h1>Welcome to ASP.NET</h1>")
```

Here's the source code of a simple ASP.NET page that redirects the browser to another page whose URL is passed as an argument and keeps a running total of redirections performed so far:

```
Public Class RedirectPage
    Inherits System.Web.UI.Page

    Private Sub Page_Load(ByVal sender As Object, ByVal e As EventArgs) _
        Handles MyBase.Load
        ' Read the target URL on the query string.
        Dim url As String = Request.QueryString("url")

        ' Increment the number of redirections so far.
        Dim appVarName As String = "redirections_count"
        Application.Lock()
```

```
            If Application(appVarName) Is Nothing Then
                Application(appVarName) = 1
            Else
                Application(appVarName) = CInt(Application(appVarName)) + 1
            End If
            Application.UnLock()

            ' Redirect to the specified URL (on this Web server).
            Server.Transfer(url)
        End Sub
End Class
```

You can use the RedirectPage.aspx page as follows:

```
http://www.tailspintoys.com/RedirectPage.aspx?url=/productinfo.aspx
```

Although on the surface the preceding code looks similar to old ASP scripts, these five objects are greatly enhanced in ASP.NET. Let's see how.

The HttpRequest Class

The page's Request property returns an instance of the System.Web.HttpRequest class. The main difference from the old ASP Request object is the addition of many properties that were previously exposed as members of the ServerVariables collection. (See Table 26-1.) For example, we can enhance the previous redirection example to store a different counter for each referrer URL; all we need to do is replace the line of code that defines which application variable holds the number of redirections:

```
Dim appVarName As String = "redirections_from_" & Request.UrlReferrer
```

In classic ASP, you can pass a string as an argument to the Request object as a quick way to look for a value in the QueryString, Form, ServerVariables, and Cookies collections:

```
itemValue = Request("itemname")
```

This syntax isn't supported in ASP.NET. You can port your legacy code quite easily, however, thanks to the new Params collection:

```
itemValue = Request.Params("itemname")
```

The HttpRequest class inherits the BinaryRead method from ASP and adds a few new ones. The MapPath method is similar to Server.MapPath in classic ASP, but it can take a base virtual directory and can work across ASP.NET applications:

```
' The physical location corresponding to the /default.aspx virtual
' path belonging to the /MyAspNetApp application.
' (Last argument must be true to support cross-app references.)
Dim path As String = Request.MapPath("/default.aspx", "/MyAspNetApp", True)
```

Table 26-1   Properties of the HttpRequest Class

Syntax	Description
AcceptTypes	A string array that contains all the MIME types accepted by the browser.
ApplicationPath	The application's virtual root path on the server.
Browser	The HttpBrowserCapabilities object that describes the client browser capabilities.
ClientCertificate	The current request's client security certificate.
ContentEncoding	The character set of the encoding body.
ContentLength	The size of the client request (in bytes).
ContentType	The MIME content type of the client request.
Cookies	The collection of cookies sent by the client.
CurrentExecutionFilePath	The virtual path of the current executing page. This can be different from FilePath if the page has been invoked using a Transfer or Execute method.
FilePath	The virtual path of the current page.
Files	An HttpFileCollection object representing all the files uploaded by the client (for Multipart MIME format).
Filter	Gets or sets the Stream used to filter the current input stream.
Form	The collection of form variables.
Headers	The collection of HTTP headers as a NameValueCollection object.
HttpMethod	A string that specifies the HTTP method (GET, POST, or HEAD).
InputStream	A Stream that represents the contents of the incoming HTTP content body.
IsAuthenticated	True if the user has been authenticated.
IsSecureConnection	True if the connection is using secure sockets (HTTPS).
Params	A collection that combines the values in QueryString, Form, ServerVariables, and Cookies. (This was the default member in ASP.)
Path	The virtual path of the current request.
PathInfo	Additional path information for a resource containing a URL extension.
PhysicalApplicationPath	The physical file system path of the application's root directory.
PhysicalPath	The physical file system path of the current page.
QueryString	The collection of query string arguments.

Table 26-1   Properties of the HttpRequest Class *(continued)*

Syntax	Description
RawUrl	The portion of the URL string that follows the domain name.
RequestType	Gets or sets the HTTP method used by the client (GET or POST).
ServerVariables	The collection of server variables.
TotalBytes	The number of bytes in the current input stream.
Url	The System.Uri object containing information about the URL of the current request.
UrlReferrer	The System.Uri object containing information about the URL of the client's previous request that linked to the current request.
UserAgent	The raw user agent string of the client browser.
UserHostAddress	The IP address of the remote user.
UserHostName	The DNS name of the remote user.
UserLanguages	The sorted string array of client language preferences.

Working with URLs

The Url and UrlReferrer properties return a System.Uri object. You can query the properties of this object to learn more about the address in question, so you don't have to parse the string yourself:

```
' Get information on the referrer for this request.
Dim url As System.Uri = Request.UrlReferrer
Debug.WriteLine(url.AbsoluteUri)    ' => http://www.tailspintoys.com/default.aspx
Debug.WriteLine(url.AbsolutePath)   ' => /default.aspx
Debug.WriteLine(url.Host)           ' => http:/www.tailspintoys.com
Debug.WriteLine(url.Port)           ' => 80
Debug.WriteLine(url.IsLoopback)     ' => False
```

You can also use a Uri object to parse a URL string that the user typed in a field or that you received in an argument:

```
Dim url As New System.Uri("http://www.tailspintoys.com/index.aspx?id=123")
Dim path As String = url.AbsolutePath     ' => /index.aspx
Dim queryString As String = url.Query     ' => id=123
```

Saving HTTP Requests

The new SaveAs method saves the current HTTP request to a file, which can be useful for logging and debugging reasons. You should pass True to its second argument if you want to save HTTP headers as well:

```
Request.SaveAs("lastrequest.txt", True)
```

The saved file contains something like this:

```
GET /AspObjects/RequestForm.aspx HTTP/1.1
Connection: Keep-Alive
Accept: */*
Accept-Encoding: gzip, deflate
Accept-Language: en-us
Cookie: LastVisitDate=12%2F6%2F2001+5%3A02%3A46+PM;
    ASP.NET_SessionId=ee4mi0ugensntgvkfjt0v4nd
Host: localhost
User-Agent: Mozilla/4.0 (compatible; MSIE 6.0; Windows NT 5.0; .NET CLR 1.0.3512)
```

Testing Browser Capabilities

The Browser property returns an HttpBrowserCapabilities object that lets you check whether the client browser supports a given functionality. This class exposes 25 properties, including Browser (the user agent string), MajorVersion and MinorVersion (the browser's version), Platform (the client operating system), JavaApplets, JavaScript, VBScript, ActiveXControls, BackgroundSounds, and Frames:

```
' Check whether the request comes from a search engine robot.
If Request.Browser.Crawler Then
    ' Adapt the response to the search engine.
    ⋮
End If

' Check whether the client supports VBScript.
If Request.Browser.VBScript Then
    ' Send VBScript code to the browser.
    ⋮
End If
```

Reading Uploaded Files

The Files collection gives you access to all uploaded files in a multipart/form-data page. Each element in this collection is an HttpPostedFile object that exposes properties such as FileName, ContentType, and ContentLength. You can read the file's contents using the InputStream property or by calling the SaveAs method:

```
Dim counter As Integer
For Each file As HttpPostedFile In Request.Files
    ' Display the original filename.
    Debug.WriteLine(file.FileName)
    ' Save on the server with a unique file.
    counter += 1
    file.SaveAs("PostedFile" & counter.ToString & ".dat")
Next
```

For more information about file uploading, see the section "The HtmlInputFile Class" in Chapter 24.

The HttpResponse Class

The page's Response property returns an instance of the System.Web.HttpResponse class. This class has several new properties that are missing in the corresponding ASP object. (See Table 26-2.) Some properties and methods—namely Buffer, CacheControl, Expires, ExpiresAbsolute, AddHeader, and Clear—are maintained for backward compatibility but have been deprecated in favor of new ones. Other members have survived the transition from ASP without any noticeable change—as in the case of CharSet, Cookies, IsClientConnected, Status, AppendToLog, Close, End, Flush, and Redirect.

The main method in this class is still Write, which has been overloaded to work with any object and with an array of Chars. However, the ASP.NET Response object has been greatly expanded in its ability to send output to the client browser. For example, the WriteFile method can send the contents of any text, HTML, or XML file to the browser. In classic ASP, you have to load the file in memory and then pass its contents to a Write method to achieve the same effect. For example, you can use this method to apply a common frame and style, typically a menu bar or footer, to any .txt file:

```
' Get the name of the requested document (passed on the query string).
Dim path As String = Request.QueryString("doctitle") & ".txt"
' Convert to a physical path.
path = Request.MapPath(path)
If File.Exists(path) Then
    ' If the file exists, send it to the browser as HTML.
    Response.Write("<HTML><BODY>")
    Response.Write("<H1>Here's the document you requested</H1>")
    Response.WriteFile(path)
    Response.Write("</BODY></HTML>")
Else
    ' Else display an error message.
    Response.Write("Sorry, no document with this name.")
End If
```

The IsClientConnected read-only property is quite useful if your page is performing a long query or a complex calculation. You should periodically check this property and invoke the Response.End method if the property returns False (which means that the client has closed the browser or moved to another page).

Table 26-2   Properties of the HttpResponse Class

Syntax	Description
Buffer	True (default) if output is buffered and sent when the page has been completely processed. This ASP property is now deprecated in favor of BufferOutput.
BufferOuput	True (default) if output is buffered and sent when the page has been completely processed.
Cache	An HttpCachePolicy object that describes the current caching policy.

Table 26-2   Properties of the HttpResponse Class *(continued)*

Syntax	Description
CacheControl	A string that affects the Cache-Control HTTP header. Can be Public or Private; this property has been deprecated in favor of the Http-CachePolicy class.
CharSet	Gets or sets the character set of the output stream.
ContentEncoding	Gets or sets the Encoding object that describes the characters sent to the browser.
ContentType	Gets or sets the string that represents the MIME type of the output stream (for example, "text/html" or "text/xml").
Cookies	The collection of cookies being sent to the client browser.
Expires	Gets or sets the number of minutes after which a cached page expires; this property has been deprecated in favor of the Http-CachePolicy class.
ExpiresAbsolute	Gets or sets the absolute date and time when a cached page expires; this property has been deprecated in favor of the HttpCachePolicy class.
Filter	Gets or sets the Stream object that filters all the data being sent to the browser.
IsClientConnected	Returns True if the client is still connected to the server and waiting for an answer.
Output	Returns the TextStream object that sends text output to the client browser.
OutputStream	Returns the Stream object that sends binary output to the client.
Status	The string representing the status line being returned to the client; the default is "200 OK".
StatusCode	Gets or sets the status code being returned to the client; the default is 200.
StatusDescription	The string representing the status description being returned to the client; the default is "OK".
SuppressContent	If True, no content will be sent to the client.

Working with Cookies

The importance of cookies has decreased under ASP.NET because now you can choose from so many other ways to store information between consecutive requests—for example, by using the page's ViewState property. However, there are still many cases when you want to send a cookie to the browser, especially if you mean for the cookie to persist on the client's system to be read back in future visits that the client makes to a site. You can use cookies in this fashion to store user names, passwords, color schemas, and other preferences, or partially filled shopping carts for orders that can be completed in subsequent sessions.

As in ASP, both the Request and the Response objects expose a Cookies collection, but the way you interact with these collections is slightly different in ASP.NET. The Request.Cookies collection is the collection of HttpCookie objects that the browser is submitting with the current request. This collection is read-only and you can choose to only enumerate its contents or read the value of a specific cookie:

```
' Display name and value of all cookies.
Dim msg As String
For Each cookieName As String In Request.Cookies.AllKeys
    ' Get the cookie with a given name.
    Dim cookie As HttpCookie = Request.Cookies(cookieName)
    ' Add information on this cookie.
    msg &= String.Format("<b>{0}</b> = {1}<br>", cookieName, _
            cookie.Value)
Next
' Display the result in a Literal control.
litCookieValues.Text = msg
```

You create a new cookie and send it to the client browser by creating an HttpCookie object and adding it to the Response.Cookies collection. Here's a code snippet that creates a cookie that expires in two weeks:

```
' Create a cookie with a given name and value.
Dim cookie As New HttpCookie("color", "red")
' Set its expiration date (2 weeks from now).
cookie.Expires = Now.AddDays(14)
' Send it to the client.
Response.Cookies.Add(cookie)
```

The easiest way to remove a cookie from the collection is to add a new cookie with the same name and an expiration date earlier than the current date:

```
' Remove the "color" cookie.
Dim cookie2 As New HttpCookie("color")
' Set its expiration date to yesterday
cookie2.Expires = Now.AddDays(-1)
' Send it to the client.
Response.Cookies.Add(cookie2)
```

The HttpCookie class exposes a few other properties, such as Domain and Path (the domain and path associated with the cookie); HasKeys (a read-only property that returns True if the cookie is multikey); Values (a collection of values for multikey cookies); and Secure (True if the cookie should be transmitted only over HTTPS). Except for HasKeys, you set these properties when you create the cookie.

Generating Graphics Dynamically

The OutputStream property is a Stream object that you can use to send binary output to the client browser. This feature is especially powerful when used together with graphic images generated dynamically on the server. Typically, you create an in-memory Bitmap object of the size and color depth that you want. Then you draw your image in it using GDI+ methods. (See Chapter 17.) Finally you use the Bitmap's Save method to serialize the image in your choice of format to the Stream object returned by Response.Output-Stream. Here's the code that produces the image shown in Figure 26-1:

```
Private Sub Page_Load(ByVal sender As Object, ByVal e As EventArgs) _
    Handles MyBase.Load
    If Request.QueryString("imgtitle") <> "" Then
        ShowImage(Request.QueryString("imgtitle"))
    End If
End Sub

Sub ShowImage(ByVal imgTitle As String)
    ' Create a bitmap with given width, height, and color depth.
    Dim bmp As New Bitmap(400, 200, Imaging.PixelFormat.Format16bppRgb565)
    ' Get the underlying Graphics object and clear its background.
    Dim gr As Graphics = Graphics.FromImage(bmp)
    gr.Clear(Color.Red)
    ' Create a font.
    Dim fnt As New Font("Arial", 16, FontStyle.Regular, GraphicsUnit.Point)

    ' Draw a series of rotated strings.
    For angle As Single = 0 To 360 Step 30
        ' Reset coordinate transforms.
        gr.ResetTransform()
        ' Translate and rotate the coordinate system.
        gr.TranslateTransform(200, 100)
        gr.RotateTransform(angle)
        ' Draw the (rotated) string.
        gr.DrawString(imgTitle, fnt, Brushes.Black, 0, 0)
    Next

    ' Clear current content and set returned content type.
    Response.Clear()
    Response.ContentType = "image/jpeg"
    ' Save to the Response.OutputStream object.
    bmp.Save(Response.OutputStream, Imaging.ImageFormat.Jpeg)

    ' Release resources.
    fnt.Dispose()
    gr.Dispose()
    bmp.Dispose()
    ' Don't process anything else on this page.
    Response.End()
End Sub
```

It's essential that the Response.ContentType property matches the type of the graphic contents that you're sending to the client browser (image/jpeg in this case). Just as important, the routine must stop processing the page by using a Response.End method immediately after sending the graphic data. The code reads the query string to retrieve the text to be displayed in the image, so you can see an image if you navigate to the page using an address like this:

```
http://localhost/AspObjects/ResponseForm.aspx?imgtitle=sample text
```

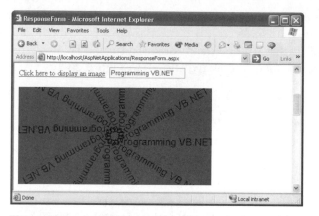

Figure 26-1   An image generated dynamically with ASP.NET

However, a page like this isn't meant to work as the target of browser navigation; more likely you'll use this page as the SRC attribute of an <IMG> tag, or the ImageUrl property of an Image or ImageButton control. This is exactly how the page in Figure 26-1 works, and this is the server-side code behind the Click event for the hyperlink:

```
Private Sub btnImage_Click(ByVal sender As Object, _
    ByVal e As EventArgs) Handles btnImage.Click
    ' Change the ImageUrl of the Image control, so that it makes
    ' a request to this same page.
    Image1.ImageUrl = Request.Url.AbsolutePath & "?imgtitle=sample text"
End Sub
```

Note that the Request.Url.AbsolutePath property returns the URL of the running page. In other words, this page has a dual function. When the user navigates to it, the page returns only the HTML code for the two hyperlinks and the Image control, but the SRC attribute in the Image control causes a second request to be posted to the page, this time with an img-title argument on the query string. The code in the Page_Load event detects that this time the image is requested and returns only the bitmap that's dynamically generated, which is why you must end the page processing and prevent other code in the page from executing.

This (admittedly contorted) technique lets you keep both the controls and the image generation code in the same page and lets you accomplish a lot of intriguing things. You could take data from a database and display it in a graph—for example, a histogram or a pie. Or you could store and retrieve bitmaps stored in database BLOB fields, such as photos, and process them on the fly to adjust their size, color depth, transparency, and so on. Best of all, you can adapt this technique to data formats other than images and generate other types of documents—for example, Microsoft Word or Microsoft Excel documents—based on data stored in a database or returned by a Web service.

Filtering Response Output

The last feature of the Response object I'll cover is the ability it gives you to filter its output. To implement this feature, you must define a class that inherits from Stream and assign an object of this class to the Response's Filter property before any response is sent to the client browser:

```
Private Sub Page_Load(ByVal sender As Object, ByVal e As EventArgs) _
    Handles MyBase.Load
    ' Filter all output.
    Response.Filter = New ConvertTagFilter(Response.Filter)
End Sub
```

Your class must store a reference to the original filter stream and must override the Write method to intercept all the HTML text data sent to the client (although it can be any type of content, such as XML or binary). The demo application uses a ConvertTag-Filter class to convert all <b> and </b> tags into <strong> and </strong>. As you see, the code in the Write method converts from a Byte array to a Char array, then to a string, and then to a Byte array again:

```
Class ConvertTagFilter
    Inherits Stream

    Private m_stream As Stream
    Private m_position As Long

    ' Store the original filter Stream in a private variable.
    Public Sub New(ByVal stream As Stream)
        m_stream = stream
    End Sub

    ' This is the method that actually does the filtering.
    Public Overrides Sub Write(ByVal bytes() As Byte, _
        ByVal offset As Integer, ByVal count As Integer)

        ' Copy the Byte array into an array of chars.
        Dim chars(count - 1) As Char
        For i As Integer = 0 To count - 1
            chars(i) = Convert.ToChar(bytes(i + offset))
        Next

        ' Create a string from the Char array.
        Dim output As New String(chars)
        ' Replace all <BR> with <P>, in case-insensitive mode.
        output = Replace(output, "<b>", "<strong>", , , CompareMethod.Text)
        output = Replace(output, "</b>", "</strong>", , , CompareMethod.Text)

        ' Copy the string back into an array of chars.
        chars = output.ToCharArray
        Dim newBytes(chars.Length - 1) As Byte
        ' Copy the array of chars into another array of bytes.
        For i As Integer = 0 To chars.Length - 1
            newBytes(i) = Convert.ToByte(chars(i))
        Next
        ' Output the bytes.
        m_stream.Write(newBytes, 0, newBytes.Length)
    End Sub

    ' ...(Other overridden methods are omitted.)...
End Class
```

The ConvertTagFilter class must also override all the methods that are marked as Must-Override in the Stream base class—namely, CanRead, CanWrite, Seek, Length, and a few others. The implementation of these methods is really easy because most of the time you just return a True value or delegate the method to the inner Stream object stored in the m_stream variable. See the demo application for the complete source code.

This technique isn't simple, but it allows rather intriguing results. You can use it to implement several advanced features, including content encryption, tag substitution, XML rendering, and dynamic modifications of the URLs embedded in HREF and SRC attributes.

The HttpServerUtility Class

The page's Server property returns an object of the System.Web.HttpServerUtility class. This object is similar to the ASP Server object, with just a few minor differences and improvements.

The HttpServerUtility class exposes only two properties: ScriptTimeout (the timeout in seconds for a request) and the new MachineName property, which returns the name of the server computer. You can use the latter property to understand whether the ASP.NET application is running on the development box or on the production server. This information is useful if you want to adopt slightly different parameters (for example, the connection string to the database).

Class methods haven't changed much in the transition from ASP to ASP.NET, so you can still use Execute, Transfer, MapPath, HtmlEncode, UrlEncode, and UrlPathEncode. The CreateObject method has been overloaded to support a System.Type argument, and you also have a CreateObjectFromClsid method that instantiates a COM object with a given CLSID. The new HtmlDecode method decodes a string that has been encoded, so it reverses the effect of the HtmlEncode method:

```
Dim text As String = "A <tag>"
Dim encoded As String = Server.HtmlEncode(text)   ' => A &lt;tag&gt;
Dim decoded As String = Server.HtmlDecode(encoded) ' => A <tag>
```

Similarly, the new UrlDecode method reverses the action of the UrlEncode method. The only other new method of this object is ClearError, which clears the most recently thrown exception. You typically use it after trapping an exception in a Page_Error event handler, as you saw in "The Error Event" section of Chapter 24.

Because ASP.NET forms are self-posting, you'll find yourself using the Server.Transfer method whenever you want to send back a different form to the user:

```
' The target page must be another .aspx page.
Me.Server.Transfer("resultpage.aspx", True)
```

If the second argument is True, the receiving page can access the Form and the QueryString properties of the Request object to access information submitted to the original page.

The HttpSessionState Class

The Session property of the Page object returns an instance of the System.Web.Session-State.HttpSessionState class. You use this object for storing values that are logically related to a specific user (as opposed to values shared by all users of the application), in much the same way you used the Session object under ASP:

```
Session("username") = "Francesco"
```

If you reference a session variable that doesn't exist, no exception is thrown and Nothing is returned. You must often account for this detail by writing code like this:

```
' Increment the counter session variable, starting at 1.
Dim objCounter As Object = Session("counter")
If objCounter Is Nothing Then objCounter = 0
Session("counter") = CInt(objCounter) + 1
```

You can also create a new session variable by using the Add method:

```
' This statement overwrites the previous value of counter, if there is one.
Session.Add("counter", 0)
```

The Remove and RemoveAt methods remove a single session variable. You can also delete all the session variables by using either the RemoveAll or the Clear method. The Count property returns the number of session variables.

As with ASP, you can read the session identifier by means of the SessionID read-only property, and set or return the session timeout (in minutes) via the Timeout property. The IsNewSession property returns True if the session was created with the current request. The CodePage and LCID writeable properties let you decide the code page identifier and the locale identifier for the current session. The Keys property returns the collection of the names of all session variables:

```
' Display the list of all session variables.
For Each key As String In Session.Keys
    Response.Write(String.Format("<b>{0}</b> = {1}<br>", key, Session(key)))
Next
```

I'll explain the meaning of other new properties—such as IsCookieless, IsReadOnly, and Mode—in the "Session State" section, later in this chapter.

The HttpApplicationState Class

The Page's Application property returns an instance of the HttpApplicationState class. This object is created when the first request is posted to an ASP.NET application and an Application_Start event fires in Global.asax. A single HttpApplicationState object is created for all the clients of an ASP.NET application on a Web server, but it isn't shared across a Web garden (an application hosted in multiple worker processes on the same multi-CPU machine) or a Web farm (an application hosted in multiple computers on the same network).

You use this object in the same way that you use the Session object, except that application variables are shared between all clients of the application. You should use these variables only for data that doesn't change often after the application has been created. In a difference from the way you use session variables, you must lock the Application object before accessing its variables, and you must unlock the object when you're done with them:

```
Application.Lock()
Application("items") = CInt(Application("items")) + CInt(Application("newitems"))
Application.Unlock()
```

After a piece of code has locked the Application object, no other ASP.NET pages can access its variables until the Application object is unlocked. So working with application variables can easily become a bottleneck. Fortunately, if you don't unlock the Application explicitly, the Unlock method is called automatically when the current request has been completed, when it times out, or when an unhandled exception occurs. The Application object also supports the Add method:

```
Application.Add("connectionstring", BiblioConnString)
```

In this case, the variable is created even if there's already another variable with this name and you'd see both variables in the Keys collection. The Application object exposes a subset of the properties and methods of the Session object, including Contents, StaticObjects, Add, Clear, Remove, RemoveAt, and RemoveAll.

Application variables are somewhat less important in ASP.NET than they were under ASP, because the .NET Framework supports the more capable Cache object to store application-level state, as I explain in "The Cache Class" section, later in this chapter.

Don't forget that application variables are lost when the ASP.NET process is stopped or recycled. If you want to preserve the application's state when this happens, you should write code for the Application_OnEnd event in Global.asax to save it to a persistent medium and restore it in the Application_Start event handler.

Application recycling is a great feature that lets you configure an application so that ASP.NET automatically shuts it down and restarts it after a given period or a given number of client requests, or when it consumes more memory than the specified threshold. This feature is a lifesaver if the application progressively degrades its performance because of memory leaks—which can happen if the application uses unmanaged resources. You control application recycling by means of one or more settings in the <processModel> tag in web.config. For example, this setting recycles the ASP.NET application every hour:

```
<configuration>
  <system.web>
    <processModel timeout="60" />
  </system.web>
</configuration>
```

For more information about application recycling, read the section about the <process-Model> tag, in Chapter 27.

State Management and Caching

ASP.NET developers have several options for places they can store values used by applications. In fact, unlike Windows Form applications, ASP or ASP.NET programming is stateless, which means that variables aren't preserved between consecutive requests to the same (or a different) page of the same application. Let me quickly review the advantages and shortcomings of the techniques available to ASP developers for storing state between consecutive requests:

- **Client-side cookies**   Because data travels back and forth at each request to a page of the application, you can use this technique only for small amounts of data. Of course, it doesn't work at all if the end user has disabled cookie support in the browser. A great advantage of this technique is that values can be persisted between consecutive visits to the same site.

- **Session variables**   You can use session variables for larger amounts of data than cookies, but each variable takes memory on the server, so this technique impedes scalability. Worse, ASP sessions don't work on Web gardens or Web farms, so your application can't easily scale out to multiple processes or multiple servers. Finally, sessions are implemented by means of cookies, so they aren't available when cookies are disabled (even though the IIS SDK contains a utility that helps you work around this problem by storing the user ID in the URL instead of a client-side cookie).

- **Application variables**   You can use this technique only for data shared by all the clients that are connected to the application, so its usefulness is limited, in practice, to caching read-only data such as a database connection string or the table of product codes and prices. Finally, Application values aren't shared among Web gardens and farms.

- **Hidden fields or the query string**   This approach doesn't require cookie support but can't be implemented easily and usually requires rather contorted coding techniques. Moreover, unlike cookies and session variables, values stored in hidden fields or the query string are lost when the user hits the Back button to return to a page visited previously.

- **Database records plus a cookie or a session variable that holds the key associated with each user**   This technique is the only one that scales well even with large amounts of data and that (if you use a cookie) can scale out to Web farms. It has some drawbacks, however: it requires extra coding, is slower than all other techniques, and still requires client-side cookie support.

Although all these ASP techniques are still available under ASP.NET, you'll rarely use some of them directly because ASP.NET offers some great alternatives. For example, the Page's ViewState property works exactly like hidden fields, but it's remarkably simpler to use. As you'll see shortly, ASP.NET supports additional session modes that work across Web farms, can use a database to store user data, and can even function without cookie support. Almost unbelievably, you can switch from regular sessions to these enhanced session modes by simply changing a configuration setting without editing a single line in code.

Another important facet of ASP.NET programming is using its caching features correctly. As you'll learn later in this chapter, ASP.NET supports different types of cache techniques. You can cache the output generated by a page and you can cache large data structures in the Cache object. In both cases, you can enforce sophisticated expiration policies. And you can still use other forms of caching as well—for example, application and session variables.

Session State

As I mentioned in the previous section, ASP.NET extends session state management with two new features:

- **Cookieless sessions**   When you enable this feature, the session ID token is burned into the URL instead of being stored in a cookie. This setting slows execution a little but ensures that your application works flawlessly even if the end user disabled cookie support in the browser.

- **Out-of-process sessions**   ASP.NET can store session data in its process's memory (the default behavior, the same as in ASP), in a separate process running as a Windows service, or in a SQL Server database. The last two options let you share session data among all the components of a Web garden or a Web farm, at the cost of slower execution.

You can combine these new features, if necessary, by having cookieless sessions whose data is stored in a Windows service or a SQL Server database. As in classic ASP, you can even disable sessions completely, either for individual pages or the entire application, to reduce memory consumption on the server machine. In addition, ASP.NET supports a new read-only mode at the page level, which enables you to improve the performance of individual pages that read but don't need to modify session variables.

You enable most of the new session state features by setting one or more attributes in machine.config or in the web.config file stored in the application's root directory:

```
<configuration>
  <system.web>
    <sessionState
        mode="InProc"
        stateConnectionString="tcpip=127.0.0.1:42424"
        sqlConnectionString="data source=127.0.0.1;user id=sa;password="
        cookieless="false"
        timeout="20"
    />
    :
```

```
    </system.web>
</configuration>
```

You can edit the web.config file right inside Visual Studio .NET. This file is automatically created with each new ASP.NET application, and it contains several sections with default settings and many remarks that explain how you can change them.

Cookieless Sessions

Enabling cookieless sessions is as simple as setting the cookieless attribute to true:

```
cookieless="true"
```

If you now run the application, you'll notice that the session ID is embedded in the URL and enclosed in parentheses. (See Figure 26-2.) Of course, all the hyperlinks embedded in the page take this extra item into account, as you see here:

```
<a href="/AspObjects/(3s5e3p55lhk0mn55znkurpmv)/AnotherPage.aspx>
Click here to display a file</a>
```

Most of the time, you don't have to do anything else to leverage this feature. An exception to this laissez-faire practice is when you want to pass a URL to another application—for example, an external component. In this case, you should build the URL properly to ensure that the correct session ID is found when the other component accesses the application. You can test whether you're in a cookieless session by using the IsCookieless property and calling the Response.ApplyAppPathModifier method to produce the correct URL:

```
Dim url As String = "/AnotherPage.aspx"
If Session.IsCookieless Then
    url = Response.ApplyAppPathModifier(url)
End If
' You can now safely pass the URL to another component.
```

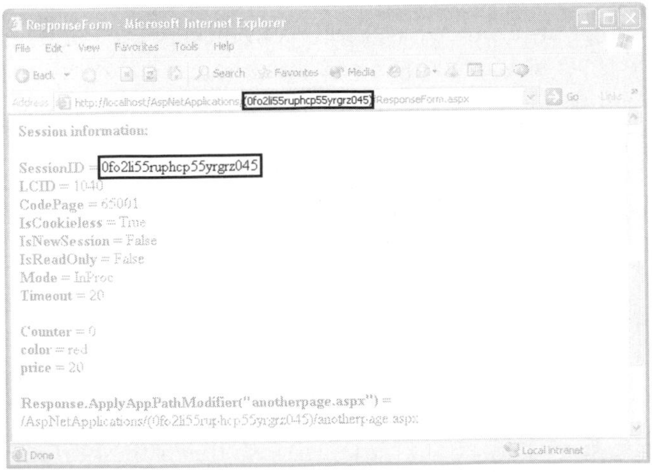

Figure 26-2 Cookieless sessions in Microsoft Internet Explorer

Out-of-Process Sessions Based on a Windows Service

To activate out-of-process sessions based on a Windows service, you must do two things. First, you must start the Windows service named aspnet_state, which is installed with ASP.NET. You can use the NET START command from the command prompt to begin aspnet_state:

```
net start aspnet_state
```

In production sites, however, you'll probably want to run this service automatically when the server reboots. You can do this by setting the start-up–type setting for this service to Automatic in the Properties window of the Services snap-in for Microsoft Management Console. (See Figure 26-3.)

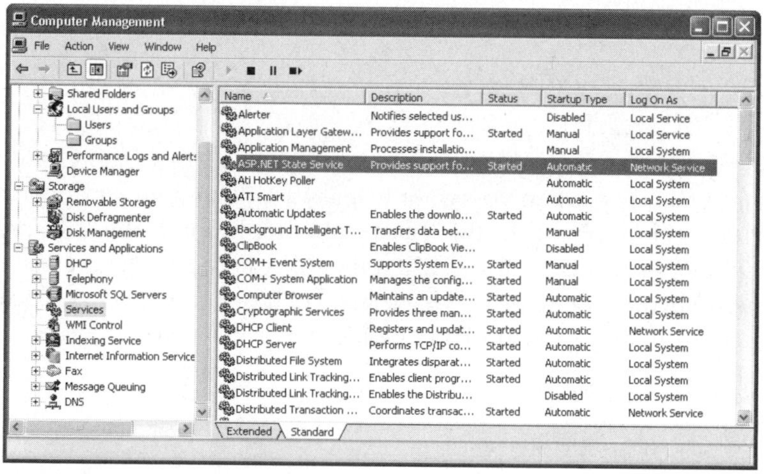

Figure 26-3   The start-up mode for the aspnet_state Windows service should be set to Automatic in production sites.

The second step in activating out-of-process sessions is to modify the configuration file so that the mode attribute is set to the StateServer value and the stateConnectionString attribute points to the IP address and port of the machine on which the service is running. If the service is running on the local machine, you can use the loop-back address 127.0.0.1, but in real life this attribute will point to the one computer in the LAN that stores the session variables for all the other machines in the Web farm:

```
<sessionState
    mode="StateServer"
    stateConnectionString="tcpip=192.168.0.4:42424"
    cookieless="false"
    timeout="20"
/>
```

By default, the aspnet_state service listens to port 42424, so this is the port number you specify in the stateConnectionString attribute. (And you can omit it if you want.) You can configure the service to use a different port by editing the Port value under the

HKEY_LOCAL_MACHINE\SYSTEM\CurrentControlSet\Services\aspnet_state\Parameters key in the registry. You shouldn't change the default port unless you have a good reason to do it, such as if the default port is already being used by another application.

Using out-of-process sessions is the best setting for Web gardens, and it also provides a viable setting for Web farms. If the machine that runs the aspnet_state service isn't one of the machines that are part of the farm, this technique offers increased robustness because the session state will survive restarts of the IIS machines.

One important note: all the machines in a Web farm should have the same machine key settings in their machine.config files or in the web.config files of individual applications. These settings are used to encrypt and validate both the ViewState and values sent through cookies, including the session ID cookie. By default, machine key settings are autogenerated, so each computer uses a different key. To have multiple servers take part in a Web farm, however, all of them should have the same machine key—otherwise, one computer couldn't decipher the session cookie generated by another computer in the farm:

```
<configuration>
   <system.web>
      <machineKey
      validationKey="0123456789abcdef0123456789abcdef0123456789ab cdef"
      decryptionKey="fedcba9876543210fedcba9876543210fedcba987654 3210"
      validation="SHA1" />
        ⋮
   </system.web>
</configuration>
```

The validation attribute can be SHA1, MD5, or 3DES. If you use the special value "autogenerate" for either the validationKey or the decryptionKey attribute, these keys will be generated automatically when ASP.NET is installed.

Out-of-Process Sessions Based on SQL Server

Before you can use ASP.NET sessions based on SQL Server, you must run either the InstallSqlState.sql or the InstallPersistSqlState.sql script in the c:\Windows\Microsoft.Net\Framework\v*x.x.xxxx* directory. The simplest way to run one of these scripts is by dragging them inside the SQL Query Analyzer program or running them from the command prompt using the OSQL utility.

The InstallPersistSqlState.sql script performs the same sequence of actions, except store session variables are persisted in the ASPState database, and therefore they live even after the computer is restarted. ASP.NET also comes with the UninstallSqlState.sql script, should you wish to remove this database. The InstallSqlState.sql script creates a new database named ASPState, containing all the stored procedures that ASP.NET requires. (See Figure 26-4.) It also installs a start-up procedure named ASPState_Startup, which ensures that all the necessary TempDB tables used for storing session data are correctly re-created when SQL Server restarts. Because TempDB is used, write operations are slightly faster but session data won't survive a reboot.

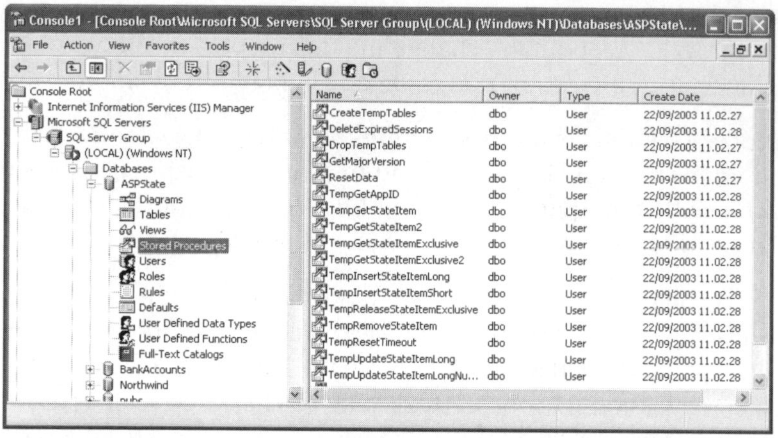

Figure 26-4   The SQL Server database created by the InstallSqlState.sql script

To actually configure ASP.NET to use a SQL Server–based session, you must change the web.config file so that the mode attribute is set to SQLServer and the sqlConnection-String attribute contains all the parameters required to connect to SQL Server:

```
<sessionState
    mode="SQLServer"
    sqlConnectionString="data source=127.0.0.1;user id=sa;password=m ypwd"
    cookieless="false"
    timeout="20"
/>
```

Of course, all the machines in a Web farm should have the sqlConnectionString attribute point to the same SQL Server so that they can share session values.

In general, you can write your ASP.NET code without worrying about which session mode your application is using, even though you can experience a performance hit when using out-of-process sessions. The only exception to this general rule is when you store an object in an out-of-process session variable; the object must be serializable—otherwise, it can't be stored in the database. (See Chapter 10 for a review of serializable objects.)

Disabled or Read-Only Sessions

Because sessions take memory and other resources, you should disable them if you can live without them. You can disable sessions for the entire application or just for selected pages. In the former case, you set the mode attribute to Off in the web.config file:

```
<sessionState mode="Off" />
```

You can disable sessions for individual pages by setting the EnableSessionState attribute in the @Page directive to False, either by editing the HTML file or by setting a property of the page in the Visual Studio .NET Properties window:

```
<%@ Page Language="vb" EnableSessionState="False" %>
```

ASP.NET also supports read-only sessions, which weren't available under classic ASP:

```
<%@ Page Language="vb" EnableSessionState="ReadOnly" %>
```

Read-only sessions can slightly improve the performance of your code because ASP.NET doesn't have to store the collection of session variables back in memory (or in the aspnet_state service or in SQL Server) when the page completes its execution. If you attempt to write a read-only session variable, no exception is thrown but a new session ID is generated. This undocumented behavior is confusing and can create subtle bugs in your code. For this reason, you might want to check the IsReadOnly property before assigning a session variable:

```
If Not Session.IsReadOnly Then
    Session("price") = 345
End If
```

Page Caching

Even though the main goal of ASP.NET is the generation of dynamic pages, the actual HTML text being sent to the client browser doesn't change often for many sites. A typical online newspaper is updated only once a day, and even highly dynamic sites—for example, those providing stock quotes—aren't usually updated more often than every minute or two. In these circumstances, you might want to cache the page content and serve it again to other clients until the data in the cache is out-of-date. This technique can save frequent trips to the database and improve both performance and scalability.

Unlike classic ASP—which supported page caching only through third-party, often quite expensive, tools—ASP.NET supports a flexible page-caching mechanism on a page-by-page basis. Not only can you decide when the cached content expires, you can also create different cached versions that depend on the value of one or more arguments passed on the query string, the value of an HTTP header, or the type of the client browser.

The @OutputCache Directive

The key to page caching is the @OutputCache directive, which can take several attributes:

```
<%@ OutputCache Duration="#ofseconds"
    Location="Any|Client|Downstream|Server|None"
    VaryByControl="controlname"
    VaryByCustom="browser|customstring"
    VaryByHeaders="headerlist|*"
    VaryByParam="paramlist|*|none"     %>
```

You often want to cache a page for a given number of seconds, which you do by setting the Duration attribute to the desired timeout and the VaryByParam attribute to none. This directive caches the current page for 10 seconds:

```
<%@ OutputCache Duration="10" VaryByParam="none" %>
```

You can check that caching works as expected by creating a page with a Label and a Submit control and then adding this code:

```
Private Sub Page_Load(ByVal sender As Object, ByVal e As EventArgs) _
    Handles MyBase.Load
    ' Append current time to the current contents of the Label control.
    lblTime.Text &= "Current time is " & Date.Now.ToLongTimeString & "<br>"
End Sub
```

If the page weren't cached, you'd see the time value of the Label control increase each time you clicked the submit button. Because caching is enabled, however, you'll see that most of your clicks return an unmodified page. (See Figure 26-5.) Notice that no event fires on the server when a cached page is sent back to the browser.

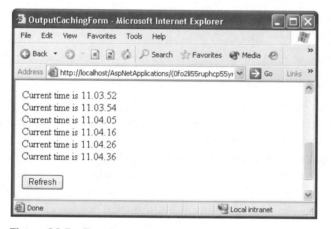

Figure 26-5   The demo application proves that page caching actually works.

The VaryByParam attribute lets you specify a semicolon-separated list of arguments, which can be either query string arguments or arguments passed by means of the POST method. This argument list lets you create different cached versions of the same page, each version associated with a different value for that argument. For example, consider this directive:

```
<%@ OutputCache Duration="10" VaryByParam="id" %>
```

and suppose the users send these requests in sequence:

```
http://www.tailspintoys.com/mypage.aspx?id=1
http://www.tailspintoys.com/mypage.aspx?id=1
http://www.tailspintoys.com/mypage.aspx?id=2
http://www.tailspintoys.com/mypage.aspx?id=1
http://www.tailspintoys.com/mypage.aspx?id=2
```

The effect is that the page is cached twice, at the first and the third request, and all other requests use a cached version of it (unless the cached version has expired in the meantime, of course). Interestingly, because ASP.NET sends control values as POST arguments, in practice you can vary the cached version by the name of a control. For example, the following directive creates a different cached version for each different value that users type in either txtValue or txtDate controls:

```
<%@ OutputCache Duration="10" VaryByParam="txtValue;txtDate" %>
```

You can also vary the cached page according to the value of any parameter, using an asterisk:

```
<%@ OutputCache Duration="10" VaryByParam="*" %>
```

The most frequent value of the VaryByCustom attribute is *browser,* which causes a different cached version of the page to be created for each different brand and version of the browser that requests the page:

```
<%@ OutputCache VaryByParam="none" VaryByCustom="browser" %>
```

(Note that the VaryByParam attribute is required in all cases.) For example, there would be a cached page for Internet Explorer 5, another for Internet Explorer 6, yet another for Netscape Navigator 6, and so on. This setting is useful when your ASP.NET code uses the Request.Browser property to query browser capabilities and return different HTML depending on the browser version.

The VaryByHeader attribute can take a semicolon-delimited list of HTTP headers and create a different cached page for each different value of any of these headers. For example, the following directive creates a different cached page, depending on the value of the Accept-Language HTTP header:

```
<%@ OutputCache VaryByParam="none" VaryByHeader="Accept-Language" %>
```

You typically use this attribute when the code in your page delivers different HTML code depending on the value of a header found in the Request.ServerVariables collection. In the case of the Accept-Language header, you'll probably output text in different languages (English if the header is en-us, French if it is fr-fr, and so on). You can also specify an asterisk to generate a cached page when the value of any header changes, but this setting usually doesn't make sense because you'd end up with too many items in the page cache.

The Location attribute specifies where the page will be cached. The default setting is Any, which allows ASP.NET to cache the page in the most convenient place. Other valid settings are Client (the page is cached on the client); Server (the page is cached on the server that's serving the request); Downstream (the page is cached on a machine other than the server that's serving the request, which can be a proxy server or the client that made the request):

```
<%@ OutputCache Duration="60" Location="Downstream"
    VaryByParam="none" VaryByCustom="browser"   %>
```

The @OutputCache directive is also supported in ASP.NET user controls and permits you to implement caching for portions of the page. When this directive appears in user controls, the VaryByHeader and Location attributes aren't supported. For more information, see the "Caching with the @OutputCache Directive" section in Chapter 28.

The HttpCachePolicy Class

Although the @OutputCache directive is easy to use, in some circumstances it isn't as flexible as your requirements dictate. For example, it doesn't support absolute expiration time (use the cached page until midnight) and you can't specify complex conditions on argument or control values (recache the page when both the txtName and txtDate controls have a new value). In these cases, you must control the page-caching feature via code. The key to programmatic control of page caching is the Http-CachePolicy object, which is exposed by the Response.Cache property. This object exposes many methods, but I'll cover only the most useful ones.

If the page contains an @OutputCache directive, you can query the VaryByParams and VaryByHeaders properties, which return a dictionary of all the headers or parameters specified in the directive. In most cases, however, you want to use the HttpCachePolicy methods to enforce your custom cache policy. The first step in doing so is to invoke the SetCacheability method, which takes one of the following values: Private, Public, Server, or NoCache. (Any value other than the last one activates the caching.) Next, you can set an absolute expiration time by using the SetExpires method (which therefore corresponds to the Duration attribute of the @OutputCache directive):

```
Private Sub Page_Load(ByVal sender As Object, ByVal e As EventArgs) _
    Handles MyBase.Load
    ' Use the cached page for the next 20 seconds.
    Response.Cache.SetCacheability(HttpCacheability.Server)
    Response.Cache.SetExpires(Now.AddSeconds(20))
End Sub
```

You'll often cache the page until a given time:

```
    ' Refresh the cached page until 10 PM today.
    Response.Cache.SetExpires(Date.Parse("10:00:00PM"))
```

The HttpCachePolicy exposes many other features. See the MSDN documentation for the complete list of its properties and methods.

The Cache Class

Another frequently used technique for improving performance is to cache large amounts of data in memory to avoid an expensive read operation from a file or a database each time you need it. For example, you might want to read an XML file into an XmlDocument object once and share it among all the pages that use the data. This approach is surely better than reloading the file in each page because it skips both the read operation and the overhead that is necessary to re-create the DOM in memory.

When you cache data, you must decide *where* in memory to store it. ASP developers have only a couple of choices: application variables for data shared among all users or session variables for data unique to each user. In all cases, you're trading memory for speed, and you get the best results from this trade-off if you're caching data shared by all users. A shortcoming of the Application object is that it's up to you, the programmer, to correctly refresh its contents when the original data—the file, the database table—changes.

Sometimes refreshing the data isn't simple. For example, assume that you'd like to cache currency exchange rates read from a third-party Web service and you want these values to be read every 30 minutes. This scenario requires that every time you're about to access the cached data, you compare the current time with the time of the most recent call to the Web service. (This information should be stored in another application variable.) And then you call the Web service again if necessary. Wouldn't it be great if you could refresh the cached data automatically, without needing to check each time you use it?

The ASP.NET answers to all these problems come in the form of the new System.Web.Caching.Cache object. As with the Application object, all the users share the same instance of the Cache object. In a difference from the way you use the Application object, however, you can enforce sophisticated expiration policies for the Cache object to have it automatically refreshed when a timeout expires, the original file is updated, or another object in the cache expires.

Inserting Items in the Cache

There's only one instance of the Cache object for each AppDomain. When you're inside an ASP.NET page, you can reach this instance through the Cache property of the Page object. When you're inside Global.asax, no Page object is available and you must use the Cache property of the Context object.

In the simplest scenario, you use the Cache object as you'd use the Application object: you check whether an object is already in the cache and load it if necessary. The following code shows how you can use the Cache object to store an XmlDocument object that stores the DOM of a given XML file; the code uses a second Cache variable to keep track of when the XML data was read:

```
Private Sub Page_Load(ByVal sender As Object, ByVal e As EventArgs) _
    Handles MyBase.Load
    ' Check whether XML data is cached already.
    If Cache("Employees") Is Nothing Then
        CacheEmployeesData()
    End If
    ' Get the cached data.
    Dim xmldoc As System.Xml.XmlDocument = _
        DirectCast(Cache("Employees"), System.Xml.XmlDocument)
End Sub
```

```
Sub CacheEmployeesData()
    ' Read an XML document.
    Dim filename As String = MapPath("Employees.xml")
    Dim xmldoc As New System.Xml.XmlDocument()
    xmldoc.Load(filename)
    ' Store it in the Cache object and remember caching time as well.
    Cache("Employees") = xmldoc
    Cache("EmployeesCacheTime") = Date.Now
End Sub
```

When used in this fashion, the Cache object offers no clear advantages over the Application object. Each item in the cache is a DictionaryEntry object, so you can enumerate all the cached items by using this loop:

```
Dim msg As String
For Each de As DictionaryEntry In Cache
    msg &= String.Format("<b>{0}</b> = {1}<br>", de.Key, de.Value)
Next
' Display the result in a Label control.
lblMessage.Text = msg
```

ASP.NET uses the Cache object for its own purposes as well—for example, page caching—but cached elements not explictly set in code aren't displayed in ASP.NET version 1.1. (This is an improvement over the previous version.)

The Cache object does internal synchronization, and for this reason it doesn't expose any Lock and Unlock methods. Even so, you still have to synchronize access to this object when you're performing multistep operations that should be considered atomic, as in this code snippet, where counterLock is a non-Nothing object variable defined in a module to make it visible to all threads and pages.

Of course, you can also use all the synchronized objects that I discussed in Chapter 12, as the circumstances dictate. For example, you can use a ReaderWriterLock object to allow multiple read operations to be performed at the same time.

```
SyncLock counterLock
    If CInt(Cache("counter")) > 1 Then
        Cache("counter") = CInt(Cache("counter"))-1
    End If
End SyncLock
```

Enforcing File and Key Dependencies

You see the higher flexibility of the Cache object when you use its Insert method, which takes a CacheDependency object in its third argument. Depending on how you create this dependency object, you can have a cache item expire when a given file is updated or when the value of another cache item changes (or is removed). For example, the following code makes the Employees cached item expire when the Employees.xml file is updated:

```
' ...(Inside CacheEmployeesData) ...
' Add XML data to the cache, making it dependent on the specified filename.
Dim xmldocDep As New System.Web.Caching.CacheDependency(filename)
Cache.Insert("Employees", xmldoc, xmldocDep)
```

The constructor of the CacheDependency object is overloaded to let you specify more than one file, in which case the element is removed from the cache when any of these files are updated:

```
' Remove an element from the cache when any of these files are updated.
Dim filenames() As String = { MapPath("Employees.xml"), _
    MapPath("Employees.xsl"), MapPath("Orders.xml") }
Dim xmldocDep As New System.Web.Caching.CacheDependency(filenames)
Cache.Insert("Employees", xmldoc, xmldocDep)
```

Because the EmployeesCacheTime element is expected to expire when the Employees element is removed from the cache, you should create a CacheDependency object that makes this dependency explicit:

```
' Create an array of cache keys (only one in this case).
Dim cacheKeys() As String = {"Employees"}
' Pass Nothing in the first argument of the constructor because
' there's no file dependency in this case.
Dim timeDep As New System.Web.Caching.CacheDependency(Nothing, cacheKeys)
' Add the current time to the cache.
Cache.Insert("EmployeesCacheTime", Date.Now, timeDep)
```

You see the real power of key-based dependencies when you work with calculated elements that are based on other numeric or string values, as in this code snippet:

```
' The size of a rectangle.
Cache("rect_width") = 123
Cache("rect_height") = 45
' Cache the area value, and make it dependent on size values.
Dim keys() As String = { "rect_width", "rect_height" }
' Create the CacheDependency on the fly.
Cache.Insert("rect_area", 123 * 45, _
    New System.Web.Caching.CacheDependency(Nothing, keys))
```

Whenever either the rect_width or rect_height value is modified (not just removed), the rect_area element is removed from the cache. When you combine this feature with callback routines (which I'll explain in a moment), you can ensure that a calculated value dependent on other values in the cache is always up-to-date.

The CacheDependency object has only one property, HasChanged, which you can query when you want to know whether the dependency condition has been met.

Enforcing Time Dependencies

The fourth and fifth arguments in the Insert method let you remove an element from the cache when a timeout expires. You can choose from two ways of removing the element. In the first case, you specify an absolute expiration date in the fourth argument and the Cache.NoSlidingExpiration constant in the fifth argument:

```
' Remove this element from the cache after 10 minutes.
Cache.Insert("Employees", xmldoc, Nothing, _
    Now.AddMinutes(10), Cache.NoSlidingExpiration)
```

In the second case, you require that the element be removed from the cache if it hasn't been requested for the amount of time specified by the fifth argument (which can't be negative or higher than one year). You typically use this mode to release memory when an object isn't used frequently:

```
' Make this item expire after 5 minutes of inactivity.
Cache.Insert("Employees", xmldoc, Nothing, _
    Cache.NoAbsoluteExpiration, New TimeSpan(0, 5, 0))
```

You must specify either Cache.NoAbsoluteExpiration for the fourth argument or Cache.NoSlidingExpiration for the fifth argument—otherwise an exception is thrown.

Keep in mind that items might be removed from the cache when ASP.NET runs short of memory, regardless of the expiration policy you enforce. You have some control over which items are removed first by setting their priority in the sixth argument of the Insert method. For example, if rereading a cached element isn't expensive, you can set a low priority for it:

```
' Note that you must pass a seventh argument in this case.
Cache.Insert("Employees", xmldoc, Nothing, _
    Cache.NoAbsoluteExpiration, New TimeSpan(0, 5, 0), _
    Caching.CacheItemPriority.Low, Nothing)
```

The available values for the priority argument are (from lower to higher priorities) Low, BelowNormal, Normal or Default, AboveNormal, High, and NotRemovable. You should use NotRemovable exclusively for items that never expire and that your code can access only once.

The Cache class also exposes an Add method that's similar to Insert, with only two differences. First, it supports only the seven-argument syntax; second, if the item specified in the first argument already exists in the cache, the Add method is ignored. (The Insert method always overwrites an item of the same name.)

```
' Add this element only if it has expired or was removed in the meantime.
Cache.Add("Employees", xmldoc, Nothing, _
    Cache.NoAbsoluteExpiration, New TimeSpan(0, 0, 10), _
    Caching.CacheItemPriority.Low, Nothing)
```

You can also explicitly remove an element from the cache by using the Remove method:

```
Cache.Remove("Employees")
```

Setting Up a Remove Callback

In all the examples I've shown you so far, the application's code had to manually check that the cached element was already in the cache and hadn't been removed in the meantime; the code then had to read the cached element again if necessary:

```
If Cache("Employees") Is Nothing Then
    CacheEmployeesData()
End If
' Get the cached data.
Dim xmldoc As System.Xml.XmlDocument = _
    DirectCast(Cache("Employees"), System.Xml.XmlDocument)
```

This coding style is clumsy and adds a slight overhead each time you access an object. Fortunately, you can solve both problems by specifying a delegate to a callback procedure in the last argument of the Insert and Add methods. This procedure is invoked by ASP.NET immediately after removing the element from the cache. Here's a prototype of the callback procedure that's invoked when the element is removed. As you see, its last argument lets you understand what exactly happened:

```
Sub OnRemoveItem(ByVal key As String, ByVal value As Object, _
    ByVal reason As Caching.CacheItemRemovedReason)
    Select Case reason
        Case Caching.CacheItemRemovedReason.Expired
            ' The element expired.
        Case Caching.CacheItemRemovedReason.DependencyChanged
            ' The element depends on files/keys that have changed.
        Case Caching.CacheItemRemovedReason.Removed
            ' The element has been removed by a Remove method, or by an
            ' Insert method on the same key.
        Case Caching.CacheItemRemovedReason.Underused
            ' The element has been removed because of memory shortage.
    End Select
End Sub
```

The following code shows how you can update the sample application to use this feature. Note that I moved both functions into a module and accessed the Cache object by using the HttpRuntime.Cache property because I'm outside a Page class:

```
Module CacheFunctions
    ' Save a reference to the Cache object.
    Dim Cache As System.Web.Caching.Cache = HttpRuntime.Cache

    Sub CacheEmployeesData()
        ' Read an XML document.
        Dim filename As String = MapPath("employees.xml")
        Dim xmldoc As New System.Xml.XmlDocument()
        xmldoc.Load(filename)

        ' Make this item expire when the file is modified, and
        ' call a callback procedure when this happens.
        Dim xmldocDep As New System.Web.Caching.CacheDependency(filename)
```

```
            Cache.Insert("Employees", xmldoc, xmldocDep, Nothing, Nothing, _
                Caching.CacheItemPriority.Default, AddressOf OnRemoveItem)
    End Sub

    Sub OnRemoveItem(ByVal key As String, ByVal value As Object, _
        ByVal reason As Caching.CacheItemRemovedReason)
        ' Always refresh the XML file when the cached item expires.
        CacheEmployeesData()
    End Sub
End Module
```

The technique based on callbacks is most effective when the data is cached the first time inside the Application_Start event in Global.asax. Because the code is in a module (and not in a Page class), you can access these routines from Global.asax:

```
' Global.asax partial listing

Public Class Global
    Inherits System.Web.HttpApplication

    Sub Application_Start(ByVal sender As Object, ByVal e As EventArgs)
        ' Cache the XML file when the application starts.
        CacheEmployeesData()
    End Sub
    ⋮
End Class
```

You can now reference the cached element from anywhere in your ASP.NET application without testing it for Nothing first because the XML file is automatically recached when it's modified:

```
' You can place this statement in any .aspx page.
Public xmldoc As System.Xml.XmlDocument = _
    DirectCast(Cache("Employees"), System.Xml.XmlDocument)
```

Static Variables

ASP.NET offers another means for storing application-wide values that isn't available under ASP and can work as a viable alternative to standard application variables. Because your code is compiled and runs inside an ASP.NET working process (aspnet_wp.exe under Windows 2000 and XP, w3wp.exe under Windows Server 2003) until the process is shut down or recycled, any static variable in your project will preserve its value between client requests. Consider this simple Module block:

```
Module GlobalVars
    Public PageViewCount As Integer
    Public Counter As Integer
End Module
```

You can then access the fields from any page in the application as a regular variable:

```
Private Sub Page_Load(ByVal sender As Object, ByVal e As EventArgs) _
    Handles MyBase.Load
    PageViewCount += 1          ' Increment page view counter.
End Sub
```

In other words, you created an application-wide variable, akin to the items in the Application object. Why should you use these module variables instead of a standard application variable? Well, the answer is simple: performance. In fact, these variables don't require a lookup in the application collection of variables and, just as important, they're strongly typed, so you don't need to convert their contents as you do with application variables (or unbox the contents of a variable if it's a value type). An informal benchmark shows that incrementing the PageViewCount variable is about 500 times faster than the following statement:

```
' Increment a counter in an application variable.
Application("counter") = CInt(Application("counter")) + 1
```

Of course, you aren't limited to shared fields and you can also implement shared properties and methods. Unlike application variables, which can be locked and unlocked only as a whole, shared variables allow you to implement a much finer granular locking strategy.

Passing Data Between Pages

When developing an ASP.NET application, you frequently need to pass one or more values from one page to another, typically when you display another page by means of a Server.Transfer method. You can pass these values using any of the techniques seen so far—for example, cookies, session variables, or static variables. However, if you only want to pass data from one page to the other, all these techniques require that you take the data out of the variable after the new page has read the values, so as not to consume memory unnecessarily.

A simpler way to pass a single value from one page to another is by storing it in the Items collection of the HttpContext object, as follows:

```
' In the "sender" page...
Me.Context.Items("quantity") = 12
Server.Transfer("ReceivingPage.aspx")

' In the "receiver" page...
Dim quantity As Integer = CInt(Me.Context.Items("quantity"))
```

In addition, you can leverage the fact that the Context.Handler property returns a reference to the "sender" page. ASP.NET Web pages are objects; therefore, the "receiver" page can read any public variable or property in the first page. So your "sender" page might look like this:

```
' In the StartupForm.aspx code-behind class
Private Sub Transfer_Click(ByVal sender As Object, ByVal e As EventArgs) _
    Handles btnTransfer.Click
    Server.Transfer("ReceivingPage.aspx")
End Sub

' The property that wraps the value of a control
ReadOnly Property TextValue() As String
    Get
        Return txtValue.Text
    End Get
End Property
```

The "receiver" page can grab a reference to the "sender" page by means of the Context.Handler property:

```
' In the ReceivingPage.aspx code-behind class
Private Sub Page_Load(ByVal sender As Object, ByVal e As EventArgs) _
    Handles MyBase.Load
    If Not Me.IsPostBack Then
        If TypeOf context.Handler Is StartupForm Then
            Dim sf As StartupForm = DirectCast(context.Handler, StartupForm)
            Dim Value As String = sf.TextValue
            Me.Response.Write("The passed value is " & Value)
        End If
    End If
End Sub
```

The HttpContext class exposes several other interesting properties, such as TimeStamp (the initial DateTime value for the current HTTP request) and AllErrors (the arrays of errors accumulated while processing an HTTP request). Read the MSDN documentation for more information.

The Global.asax File

The Global.asax file is the ASP.NET counterpart of Global.asa in ASP and is used to host the handlers of the Application object's events. As you'll see, however, the contents of this file are quite different in ASP.NET. For example, this is a simple Global.asax file (created in Visual Studio) that keeps a counter of how many client sessions are in memory:

```
Imports System.Web
Imports System.Web.SessionState

Public Class Global
    Inherits System.Web.HttpApplication

    Sub Application_Start(ByVal sender As Object, ByVal e As EventArgs)
        ' We start with zero sessions.
        Application("SessionCount") = 0
    End Sub
```

```
    Sub Session_Start(ByVal sender As Object, ByVal e As EventArgs)
        ' A new session is being created.
        Application.Lock
        Application("SessionCount") = CInt(Application("SessionCount")) + 1
        Application.Unlock
    End Sub

    Sub Session_Start(ByVal sender As Object, ByVal e As EventArgs)
        ' A session is being destroyed.
        Application.Lock
        Application("SessionCount") = CInt(Application("SessionCount")) - 1
        Application.Unlock
    End Sub
End Class
```

A couple of things are worth noticing here. First, the events take the usual two arguments and are named Start and End, not OnStart and OnEnd as they are under classic ASP (though the old names are still recognized correctly). Second, they're contained in a class named Global, which inherits from the HttpApplication class. The original ASP Application class has been split into two classes under ASP.NET: HttpApplicationState provides support for application-wide variables, whereas HttpApplication is the class instantiated when the ASP.NET application starts.

You can create an empty handler for all these events using the Method Name combo box at the top of the Visual Studio .NET editor, as you do with control events. At first, it's rather confusing that the event templates provided with the default Global.asax are in the form Application_*eventname*. The ASP.NET Application object exposes many new events that were missing in the ASP object. The majority of these new events normally fire once at *every* request posted to the server, not just when the application starts or ends. The exception to this frequent firing is the Error event (which one would *hope* doesn't fire for all requests). All the Application events in Table 26-3 are listed in their firing order.

```
Sub Application_BeginRequest(ByVal sender As Object, ByVal e As EventArgs)
    ' Fires at the beginning of each request
    ⋮
End Sub
```

whereas the event templates created with the combo box in the editor are in the form Global_eventname and have a Handles clause:

```
Sub Global_BeginRequest(ByVal sender As Object, ByVal e As EventArgs) _
    Handles MyBase.BeginRequest
    ⋮
End Sub
```

Even though they look different, these event handlers work in exactly the same way. In fact, both of them fire if they're contained in the same Global.asax file, an arrangement that you'll probably want to avoid in real applications because it adds overhead to each page request and can introduce bugs. An exception to this rule: the Start and End events (as well as their OnStart and OnEnd aliases) can be trapped only if you use the Application_eventname syntax. These events, in fact, aren't exposed by the Http-Application object and therefore don't correspond to any valid Handles clause.

I won't discuss every Application event, mainly because most of them exist only to let ASP.NET implement some of their advanced features, such as distributed sessions and page caching. In most applications, you never need to play with these events (except, as mentioned, for the Error event), so I'll cover only the most interesting ones in this section.

Table 26-3   Events of the HttpApplication Class[*]

Syntax	Description
Start	Fires when the ASP.NET application starts—that is, when the first request for an .aspx file is posted to the server. (Same as the OnStart event.)
BeginRequest	Fires as the first event when ASP.NET receives a request from a client; the event provides the developer with the opportunity to process the request before the page does it.
AuthenticateRequest	Fires when ASP.NET has established the identity of the user but before authorization is enforced; it gives you the means to implement a custom authentication and authorization mechanism.
AuthorizeRequest	Fires when ASP.NET has verified user authorization.
ResolveRequestCache	Fires when ASP.NET determines whether the request should be served using a page stored in the cache. (The page caching mechanism uses this event, for example.)
AcquireRequestState	Fires after ASP.NET acquires the current state associated with the current request; if this is the first request from a client, the Session_Start event fires just before the Acquire-RequestState event. ASP.NET traps this event to implement distributed sessions.
PreRequestHandlerExecute	Fires one instant before executing the code in the page or the Web service (more generally, the registered handler for the requested resource).
PostRequestHandlerExecute	Fires after the page or the Web service has completed its processing. At this point, the Response object contains the text being sent to the client.
ReleaseRequestState	Fires when ASP.NET completes the execution of all request handlers and is ready to store the session state. ASP.NET traps this event to implement distributed sessions.
UpdateRequestCache	Fires when caching handlers are able to store data being sent to the client in the page output cache.
EndRequest	Fires when the page has been completely processed. This event is the last in the chain if buffering has been disabled.

Table 26-3   Events of the HttpApplication Class[*] *(continued)*

Syntax	Description
PreSendRequestHeaders	Fires when ASP.NET is about to send HTTP headers to the client. If buffering is enabled, this and the following event are raised after the EndRequest event.
PreSendRequestContent	Fires when ASP.NET is about to send content to the client. This event can fire multiple times during the same request.
End	Fires when ASP.NET is about to shut down. (Same as the OnEnd event.)
Disposed	Fires when the ASP.NET application is being disposed of.
Error	Fires when an unhandled exception is thrown.

[*] All events except Error are in the order in which they fire.

Global Error Handlers

Of all the application events, the majority of ASP.NET applications need to trap only the Error event. This event lets you implement a global error handler that fires when an unhandled exception fires in any page of the current application. In other words, you can enforce a common error resolution strategy by using the same code you'd insert in the Page_Error event but without having to modify each and every .aspx file in the application.

The code inside the application's Error event can use the Server.GetLastError property to access the exception object thrown most recently. However, this property always returns an HttpUnhandledException object, and you must query the InnerException property of this object to retrieve the actual exception that was thrown. The code inside the Error event handler can access all the usual properties in the Request object to understand what went wrong and the methods of the Response object to send an alternative error message. For example, the following error handler displays the custom error message shown in Figure 26-6:

```
Private Sub Global_Error(ByVal sender As Object, ByVal e As EventArgs) _
    Handles MyBase.Error
    ' Prepare an error report.
    Response.Clear()
    Response.Write("<H1>An exception has occurred:</H1>")
    ' Display information on the page being processed.
    Response.Write("<b>URL = </b>" & Request.Path & "<br />")
    Response.Write("<b>QueryString = </b>" & Request.QueryString.ToString _
        & "<p>")
    Response.Write("<b>Error details</b><p>")

    ' Get a reference to the (real) error that occurred.
    Dim ex As Exception = Server.GetLastError.InnerException
    ' Convert the string in a format that is suitable for HTML output.
    Dim errMsg As String = Server.HtmlEncode(ex.ToString)
    errMsg = errMsg.Replace(ControlChars.CrLf, "<BR />")
```

```
        Response.Write(errMsg)
        Response.End()
End Sub
```

Or you can redirect the execution to another .aspx page by using a Response.Redirect method. In general, the standard error page that ASP.NET displays when an unhandled exception is thrown contains a lot of detailed information, so as a rule you shouldn't override it while testing and debugging an application. However, the Error event can be a precious resource in a production site for logging error information to a file or the system log.

You might also use a global error handler to send an e-mail to alert the administrator by using the SmtpMail object. (See Chapter 34.)

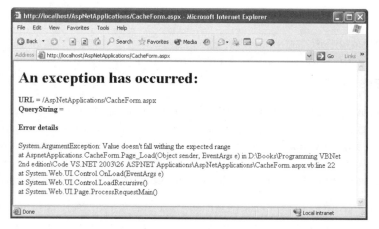

Figure 26-6   An example of a custom error page

Application-Wide Response Filter

In the "Filtering Response Output" section earlier in this chapter, you saw how an ASP.NET page can assign a custom filter to the Response.Filter property to postprocess HTML code being sent to the client browser:

```
Private Sub Page_Load(ByVal sender As Object, ByVal e As EventArgs) _
    Response.Filter = New ConvertTagFilter(Response.Filter)
End Sub
```

Of course, inserting the preceding lines of code in each and every .aspx file is a nuisance, and fortunately you don't have to do that. In fact, the PreRequestHandlerExecute application event fires after the Response object has been created and immediately before the code in a page has a chance to execute, so you just have to assign the Filter property in this event to create a filter for all the pages in an ASP.NET application:

```
' Inside Global.asax file
Private Sub Application_PreRequestHandlerExecute(ByVal sender As Object, _
    ByVal e As EventArgs)
    Response.Filter = New ConvertTagFilter(Response.Filter)
End Sub
```

This technique is very powerful and lets you implement advanced features with relatively little code.

Persistent Session Variables

You learned earlier in this chapter that ASP.NET greatly improves session state management and supports both cookieless sessions and out-of-process sessions. However, there's still one thing that ASP.NET doesn't offer: persistent sessions. For example, it would be great if you could decide whether session values should be persisted between client visits to the site. Imagine an e-commerce site that lets its users keep items in their shopping carts for, say, a week so that users can choose their purchases without feeling hurried.

As you'll see in a moment, implementing persistent sessions isn't trivial, but it isn't overly difficult either. The technique I am about to illustrate makes use of the Aquire-RequestState and ReleaseRequestState events. The former fires immediately after loading data from memory into the "regular" session variables, the latter fires before saving session variables in memory. The code in the AcquireRequestState event handler attempts to read a special client-side cookie named PermSessionID. The value of this cookie is the name of an XML file (on the server machine) that contains the values of session variables as stored at the end of the previous request. The code can read this file and populate the session collection before the page sees the new values. If this cookie doesn't exist yet, you're seeing the first request from this client. So the code creates the cookie and stores a random, unique string in it. (For simplicity's sake, it uses the Session.SessionID value, but you can help ensure its uniqueness by appending the current date or the value of a count that increments each time.)

```
' NOTE: this code requires a reference to the
' System.Runtime.Serialization.Formatters.Soap.dll assembly.

Const SESSIONDATAPATH = "C:\SessionData\"

Private Sub Application_AcquireRequestState(ByVal sender As Object, _
    ByVal e As EventArgs)
    Dim fs As FileStream
    Dim sf As New SoapFormatter()

    Try
        ' Get the special cookie, or exit if not found.
        Dim cookie As HttpCookie = Request.Cookies("PermSessionID")
        If (cookie Is Nothing) Then
            ' If not found, generate it now (use pseudo-random SessionID).
            cookie = New HttpCookie("PermSessionID", Session.SessionID)
            ' Let this cookie expire after one week.
            cookie.Expires = Now.AddDays(7)
            ' Send it to the client browser and exit.
            Response.Cookies.Add(cookie)
            Exit Try
        End If
```

```
                ' The filename is equal to the value of this cookie.
                Dim permSessionId As String = cookie.Value
                ' Build the name of the data file.
                Dim filename As String = SESSIONDATAPATH & permSessionID.ToString & ".xml"
                ' Open the file, or exit if error.
                fs = New FileStream(filename, FileMode.Open)
                ' Deserialize the Hashtable that contains values.
                Dim ht As Hashtable = DirectCast(sf.Deserialize(fs), Hashtable)

                ' Move data into the Session collection.
                Session.Clear()              ' Clear regular Session values.
                For Each key As String In ht.Keys
                    Session(key) = ht(key)
                Next
            Catch ex As Exception
                ' Ignore any exceptions.
            Finally
                If Not (fs Is Nothing) Then fs.Close()
            End Try
        End Sub
```

When the request has been served, the code in the ReleaseRequestState event handler creates a server-side XML file whose name is taken from the PermSessionID cookie that was read or created previously. It then serializes all session variables to the XML file and clears the Session collection to minimize the server's memory usage:

```
Private Sub Application_ReleaseRequestState(ByVal sender As Object, _
    ByVal e As EventArgs)

    ' Get the special cookie.
    Dim cookie As HttpCookie = Request.Cookies("PermSessionID")
    ' The value of the cookie is the name of the .xml file.
    Dim permSessionID As String = cookie.Value

    ' Move data from the Session collection into a Hashtable.
    Dim ht As New Hashtable(Session.Count)
    For Each key As String In Session.Keys
        ht(key) = Session(key)
    Next
    ' Clear the regular session collection, to save memory.
    Session.Clear()

    Dim fs As FileStream
    Dim sf As New SoapFormatter()
    Try
        ' Build the name of the data file.
        Dim filename As String = _
            SESSIONDATAPATH & permSessionID.ToString & ".xml"
        ' Open the file for output, or exit if error.
        fs = New FileStream(filename, FileMode.Create)
        ' Serialize the Hashtable that contains values.
        sf.Serialize(fs, ht)
    Catch ex As Exception
        ' Ignore any exceptions.
```

```
        Finally
            If Not (fs Is Nothing) Then fs.Close()
        End Try
End Sub
```

Notice that the c:\SessionData directory shouldn't be accessible from the outside world, for obvious security reasons, so it isn't under the Inetpub\wwwroot directory tree. Moreover, this directory will be accessed by the ASP.NET process, so it must be located on a non-NTFS partition or it must have been configured to allow access to the account that ASP.NET runs under. By default, this account is the Network Service account (on Windows Server 2003 when Internet Information Services is running in IIS 6 isolation mode) or the ASPNET account (in all other cases).

Next, create a simple test page that increments a session variable:

```
Private Sub Page_Load(ByVal sender As System.Object, ByVal e As EventArgs) _
    Handles MyBase.Load
    If Session("counter") Is Nothing Then
        Session("counter") = 0
    Else
        Session("counter") = CInt(Session("counter")) + 1
    End If
    ' Display current value of the variable.
    lblCounter.Text = "Counter = " & Session("counter").ToString
End Sub
```

Each time you refresh the page, the counter is incremented. However, if you now close the browser and restart the application, you'll see that the counting doesn't restart at 0 because the session state is restored from the XML file on the server!

This technique has another great advantage: if XML data files are stored on a network shared directory, you can implement session variables distributed over a Web farm without using SQL Server (which might be an issue if your site uses another database server) and without the single-point-of-failure problem that you have if you manage distributed sessions with the aspnet_state Windows service. The performance of the preceding code is in the same range as that achieved with SQL Server, and you can make it faster if you persist session values as binary data instead of XML.

As provided, the code doesn't address a minor problem. When the client-side code expires (for example, after one week), you should delete the corresponding data file on the server to reclaim disk memory and make file searches faster. You can solve this problem by creating a Windows service that periodically checks the date of the last access to XML files and deletes those that are older than one week. This isn't a critical issue, however, because session data files that aren't deleted as soon as they expire don't take any server resource except disk space, so a site administrator could even perform these cleanup chores manually once every few days.

Tracing

Tracing plays an important role in debugging and fine-tuning any application, and ASP.NET applications are no exception. Unlike classic ASP, whose tracing capabilities are limited to cluttering the script code with Response.Write statements to display the value of variables and properties, ASP.NET comes with powerful tracing features built in.

The Trace Property

The great thing about ASP.NET tracing is that you can activate it just by adding a new attribute in the @Page directive:

```
<%@ Page Language="vb" trace="True" %>
```

If you're working in Visual Studio .NET, you don't even need to edit this directive manually because you can just set the Trace property of the Page object to True from inside the Properties window.

When tracing is enabled, ASP.NET appends a lot of additional information to the regular content of the page. (See Figure 26-7.) This information includes request details (such as session ID), time spent in page processing steps, information about each control on the form (including size of HTML produced and bytes used in ViewState), session and application variables, cookies, headers, and the collection of server variables.

This information is especially precious when you're debugging a page that doesn't behave as it should—for example, I used tracing extensively when I was working with a DataGrid control containing templates to understand the relationships among parent and child controls.

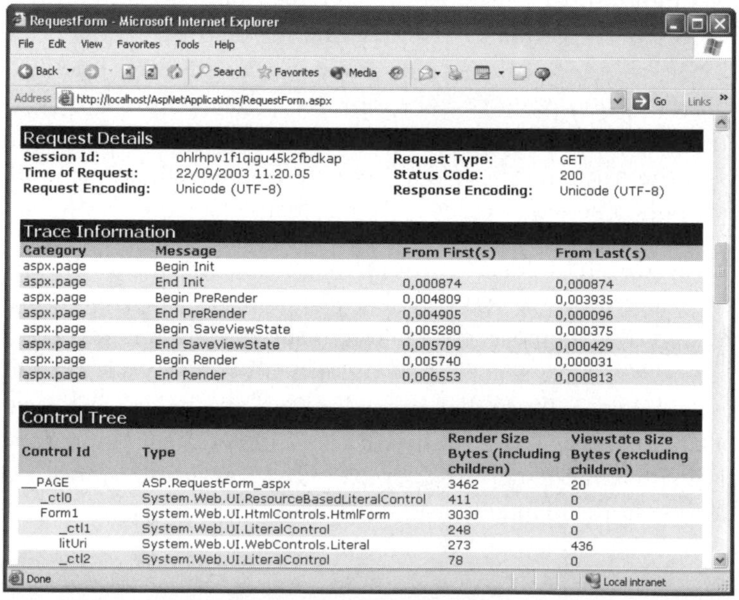

Figure 26-7   Tracing information appended to the regular page content

Application-Level Tracing

You can enable tracing for all the pages in your application by setting a few values in the web.config file, either in the application root directory (if you want to trace all pages) or in a specific directory (to trace only the pages in that directory):

```
<configuration>
  <system.web>
    <trace enabled="false"
        requestLimit="10" pageOutput="false"
        traceMode="SortByTime" localOnly="true" />
    ⋮
  </system.web>
</configuration>
```

You enable application-level tracing by setting the enabled attribute to true. When you do that, however, tracing information isn't appended to the page's regular contents, as you saw in the preceding section. Instead, you must point your browser to a special page named trace.axd. ASP.NET intercepts the request for this .axd page (regardless of the directory in which you look for it) and displays a result like the one shown in Figure 26-8, with the 10 most recent requests processed by the application. You can display details about each request by clicking on the View Details link on the right. Or you can enforce output in each page by setting the pageOutput attribute to true.

The remaining attributes of the trace section in web.config let you control other tracing details. The requestLimit attribute is the number of requests whose details are cached by ASP.NET when not in page mode. (Default is 10.) By default, localOnly is set to true to prevent users on remote machines from viewing trace information, but you can set it to false if you're tracing the application from another computer. The traceMode attribute can be SortByTime (default) or SortByCategory, and affects how trace information is produced. You can set this attribute on an individual page by setting it from inside the Properties window or by including it in the @Page directive:

```
<%@ Page Language="vb" trace="true" traceMode="SortByCategory" %>
```

You see the effect of this attribute only if the page contains custom trace output, as I'll explain in the following section.

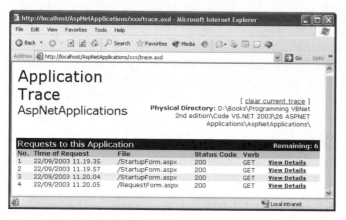

Figure 26-8   The Application Trace page; you must press F5 to refresh the page and see more recent requests.

The TraceContext Class

The TraceContext class has only two properties and two methods. The IsEnabled property gets or sets the current page mode, so you can activate tracing programmatically if you wish; the TraceMode property gets or sets the attribute with the same name. You can output trace information by using either the Write or Warn method, the only difference between them being that the latter displays its message in red instead of black. These methods are overloaded to support three different syntax forms: the Page class exposes the Trace property, which returns a System.Web.TraceContext object and lets you send custom strings to the trace page. Don't confuse this object with the System.Diagnostics.Trace class that you use in Windows Forms programs (and that's still available in ASP.NET applications to display values in the Visual Studio output window). The TraceContext object is also accessible from anywhere in an ASP.NET application, not just from a page, when you use the HttpContext.Current.Trace syntax.

```
Trace.Write(message)
Trace.Write(category, message)
Trace.Write(category, message, exception)
```

Here's an example that uses these methods:

```
Sub DoSomething(ByVal arg As String)
    Trace.Write("FLOW", "Entering Sub DoSomething")
    Trace.Write("arg = " & arg)
    Try
        ⋮
    Catch ex As Exception
        Trace.Warn("ERRORS", "A fatal error has occurred", ex)
        Response.End
    Finally
        Trace.Write("FLOW", "Exiting Sub DoSomething")
    End Try
End Sub
```

Figure 26-9 shows how these trace messages appear in the trace output when trace-Mode is set to SortByTime (the default).

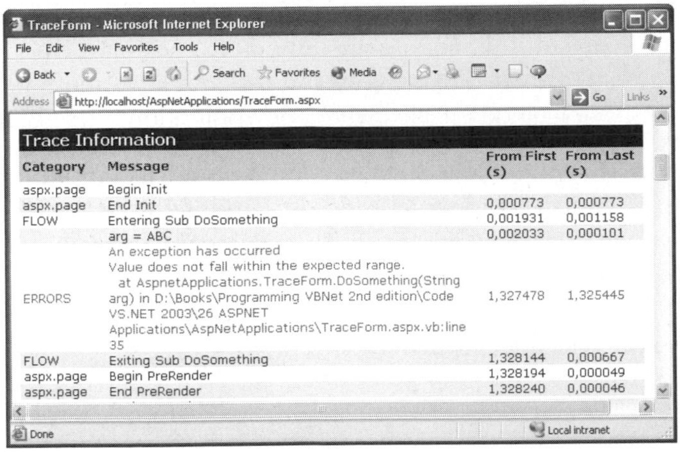

Figure 26-9   Custom message in the trace page; the output from the Warn method is in red.

HTTP Modules and Handlers

The beauty of ASP.NET is that its architecture is extensible. This claim is true also for classic ASP, but you had to be a C++ wizard to create ISAPI filters for IIS. Things are one or two orders of magnitude simpler with ASP.NET, and you can implement all these features in your good old Visual Basic!

For starters, let's compare the two extension mechanisms that ASP.NET provides:

- HTTP handlers are components that handle requests for a given resource type. For example, ASP.NET uses a handler to manage requests for plain .aspx files and another handler to redirect requests for the special trace.axd resource. (Notice that we must use the term *resource* here because trace.axd isn't a physical file; handlers can trap requests for resources before ASP.NET checks that these resources actually exist.)

- HTTP modules are filters that are notified when a request is posted to the ASP.NET application; they loosely correspond to ISAPI filters in IIS. A module can trap a request only if it has been already accepted by ASP.NET, so there must be a registered handler for it. A module can trap the request both before and after the handler associated with it has processed it. ASP.NET uses modules to implement authentication and session state services.

I'll begin with a discussion of the simpler of the two modules. As a matter of fact, implementing HTTP modules is a breeze if you carefully read "The Global.asax File" section, earlier in this chapter.

HTTP Modules

An HTTP module is a .NET class that implements the IHttpModule interface. This interface exposes only two methods, Init and Dispose, which are invoked by the ASP.NET runtime and therefore appear as events to the module implementor. The Init method is called when the ASP.NET application is loaded in memory and receives a reference to the HttpApplication object; the Dispose method is called when the application is being shut down.

Your job in regard to an HTTP module is simple: you take the HttpApplication object passed to the Init method and store it in a variable declared with the WithEvents keyword. From now on, your HTTP module class will listen to all the application events listed in Table 26-3 and can therefore perform all the actions you could perform by writing code right in Global.asax. For example, this simple HTTP module traps all unhandled exceptions and stores details about them in an ArrayList:

```
Public Class ErrorLoggerModule
    Implements IHttpModule

    ' The Application object
    Dim WithEvents Application As HttpApplication
    ' This is where all error messages are stored.
    Public Shared ErrorMessages As New ArrayList()

    Public Sub Init(ByVal context As System.Web.HttpApplication) _
        Implements System.Web.IHttpModule.Init
        ' Store the Application object in a local variable.
        Application = context
    End Sub

    Private Sub Application_Error(ByVal sender As Object, _
        ByVal e As EventArgs) Handles Application.Error
        Dim msg As String
        msg &= "<B>An exception occurred at</B> " & Now.ToString & "<BR />"
        msg &= "<B>URL</B> =" & Application.Request.Path & "<BR />"
        msg &= "<B>QueryString</B> = " & _
            Application.Request.QueryString.ToString & "<BR /><BR />"

        ' Append details about the error, but convert CR-LF pairs.
        msg &= Application.Server.GetLastError.ToString.Replace( _
            ControlChars.CrLf, "<BR />")

        ' Prepend to the collection of error messages.
        SyncLock ErrorMessages.SyncRoot
            ErrorMessages.Insert(0, msg)
        End SyncLock
    End Sub

    Public Sub Dispose() Implements System.Web.IHttpModule.Dispose
        ' The application is being shut down.
        Application = Nothing
    End Sub
End Class
```

Because all the messages are in a global ArrayList object in reverse order, it's easy to display them in a separate page by using a bound DataList control:

```
' The ErrorMessages ArrayList can be reached from anywhere in the application.
DataList1.DataSource = ErrorLoggerModule.ErrorMessages
DataList1.DataBind()
```

An administrator can navigate to such a page and browse all the unhandled exceptions that occurred recently. (You should also provide a button or some other means to clear the ErrorMessages ArrayList.)

An HTTP module must be listed in the web.config file to be instantiated when the application starts:

```
<configuration>
  <system.web>
    ⋮
    <httpModules>
      <add name="ErrorLogger"
          type="AspnetApplications.ErrorLoggerModule,AspnetApplications" />
    </httpModules>
  </system.web>
</configuration>
```

Note that the type argument has a value in the format *classname,assemblyname*. If you're using a private assembly, it should be stored in the \bin directory under the application's root directory.

Thanks to the hierarchical structure of configuration files, you can have a module that filters all the requests to the application by adding it to the web.config file in the application's root, or you can have a module that filters just the requests for the files in a given directory. If you add an HTTP handler in machine.config, it filters all requests for all the installed ASP.NET applications on the local computer. In fact, by peeking at the <httpModules> section in machine.config, you can get an idea of which ASP.NET features are implemented through HTTP modules. (Some of these features are related to security, which I'll discuss in the next chapter.)

HTTP Handlers

HTTP handlers are .NET components that are instantiated when a client requests the resource associated with it. For example, an HTTP handler associated with .xyz files is instantiated whenever a client requests a file with this extension. As I mentioned previously, ASP.NET itself uses HTTP handlers to process .aspx files (Web Forms) and .asmx files (Web services), the special trace.axd request, and a few other resource types. Again, you should reason in terms of resources, not files; there's no trace.axd file anywhere on your system, but ASP.NET uses a component of the class System.Web.Handlers.TraceHandler to handle requests for this resource.

Mapping File Extensions in IIS

You might want to create a handler for files that are already associated with ASP.NET—namely, .aspx, .asmx, .ascx, .asax, .axd, and a few others—or you can create a handler for a file extension not yet handled by ASP.NET, such as .xyz. In the latter case, however, you have to inform IIS that requests for .xyz resources must be passed to the aspnet_isapi.dll component. Otherwise, ASP.NET will never have a chance to pass the request to your handler. The association of a file extension with the aspnet_isapi.dll component is a manual operation that you must perform by using the MMC snap-in for Internet Information Services. (See Figure 26-10.)

1. In the Internet Information Services window, expand the computer node, right-click Web Sites in the console tree, and click Properties in the shortcut menu; the Properties dialog box appears. You can also use the Properties dialog box of a specific Web site, if you don't want to affect all the sites on the server.

2. Click the Home Directory tab and click the Configuration button. This action opens the Application Configuration dialog box, where you can see all the file extensions associated with ASP and ASP.NET.

3. Click the Add button to display the Add/Edit Application Extension Mapping dialog box, in which you can associate the .xyz extension with the aspnet_isapi.dll executable file. (This file is in the C:\Windows\Microsoft.NET\Framework\vx.y.*zzzz* directory.) If your handler processes only files that exist, you should select the Check That File Exists option, or Verify That File Exists under IIS 6. (Leave it deselected for this example, however.)

4. Click OK. You'll see that the .xyz extension has been included in the list of Application Mappings. Click OK twice to close the open dialog boxes.

To help you avoid the nuisance of registering a file extension in IIS for the sole purpose of writing a handler against it, ASP.NET registers the .ashx extension in IIS but leaves it available to your handlers. If you write a handler for this extension, you just have to add an entry in the web.config file, as I explain in the following section.

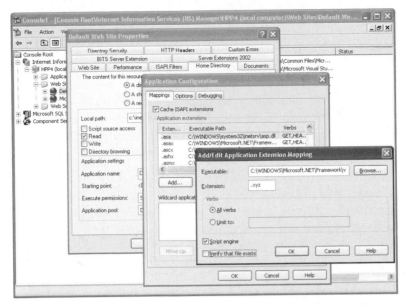

Figure 26-10   All the dialog boxes you need to traverse to map a file extension in IIS

Adding the HTTP Handler to Configuration Files

The second step that you must take is to modify the web.config file (or the machine.config file, if your handler must be used by all the ASP.NET applications on the local computer) so that ASP.NET knows that requests for a given resource type—files with the .xyz extension in this example—must be passed along to your handler. All HTTP handlers are listed in the <httpHandlers> section. For example, here's what this section of machine.config looks like:

```
<configuration>
  <system.web>
    ⋮
    <httpHandlers>
      <add verb="*" path="trace.axd" type="System.Web.Handlers.TraceHandler"/>
      <add verb="*" path="*.aspx" type="System.Web.UI.PageHandlerFactory" />
      <add verb="*" path="*.asmx"
       type="System.Web.Services.Protocols.WebServiceHandlerFactory,
             System.Web.Services, Version=1.0.5000.0, Culture=neutral,
             PublicKeyToken=b03f5f7f11d50a3a" validate="false" />
      <add verb="*" path="*.asax" type="System.Web.HttpForbiddenHandler" />
      <add verb="*" path="*.ascx" type="System.Web.HttpForbiddenHandler" />
      <add verb="*" path="*.config" type="System.Web.HttpForbiddenHandler" />
      <add verb="*" path="*.cs" type="System.Web.HttpForbiddenHandler" />
      <add verb="*" path="*.vb" type="System.Web.HttpForbiddenHandler" />
      ⋮
    </httpHandlers>
  </system.web>
</configuration>
```

Let's see what each attribute in the \<add> block stands for:

- The verb attribute is the HTTP verb that the handler can process. It can be a single verb (Get), a semicolon-delimited list of verbs (Get;Post;Head), or an asterisk for all verbs.

- The path attribute tells which files must be passed to the HTTP handler. It's usually a wildcard expression (*.aspx), but it can also be a filename (trace.axd) or a directory name plus a wildcard expression (/MyApp/MySubDir/*.aspx) if you want your handler to process only files with a given extension in the specified directory.

- The type attribute is the name of your class, in the format *classname,assemblyname*, where the name of the assembly can be a fully qualified or a partial name. All ASP.NET standard handlers are in the GAC, but you can use private assemblies in the \bin subdirectory for handlers that are used by only one application.

The name of the class associated with each extension provides some clues for what ASP.NET does with each file type. For example, .aspx files are managed by the Page-HandlerFactory class (which creates a Page object that handles the request), and .asmx files are passed to the WebServiceHandlerFactory class, which replies by instantiating a Web service. Interestingly, requests for .asax, .ascx, .vb, and .cs files (and a few others) are processed by a class named HttpForbiddenHandler, which correctly prevents remote users from downloading source files.

Now that you know the meaning of the attributes for the \<add> tag, it's easy to come up with the correct \<httpHandlers> section for the sample application's web.config file:

```
<httpHandlers>
   <add verb="*" path="*.xyz"
      type="AspnetApplications.XyzHandler,AspnetApplications" />
</httpHandlers>
```

If you have multiple \<add> tags for the same path or extension, the last one takes precedence. You can slightly improve performance by setting the optional validate attribute to false for handlers that are used infrequently. This setting speeds up start-up time by loading the handler only when a request for the specified resource comes:

```
<add verb="*" path="*.xyz" validate="false"
    type="AspnetApplications.XyzHandler,AspnetApplications" />
```

You can also insert \<remove> tags to disable a handler that was defined in machine.config, or in the web.config file stored in the root directory of the current application. In this case, you use the verb and path attributes only:

```
<httpHandlers>
   <remove verb="*" path="*.xyz" />
</httpHandlers>
```

Writing the HTTP Handler Class

An HTTP Handler is a class that implements the IHttpHandler interface, which consists of just two members. The IsReusable read-only property should return True if another request can use the same instance of the handler class. The ProcessRequest method is invoked when a client requests a resource for which your handler has been registered. This method receives an HttpContext object as an argument, which lets your code access all the ASP.NET intrinsic objects such as Request, Response, and so on.

To show you the power of HTTP handlers, I prepared a class that processes requests for .xyz resources and maps them to a Biblio.mdb table named after the requested page. For example, a request for the Publishers page returns a table with all the records in the Publishers table:

```
http://www.tailspintoys.com/anypath/publishers.xyz
```

Whatever is passed on the query string is considered to be a WHERE clause to restrict the database query, so here's how you can display all the publishers in a given U.S. state:

```
http://www.tailspintoys.com/anypath/publishers.xyz?state='MA'
```

The result of this query is shown in Figure 26-11.

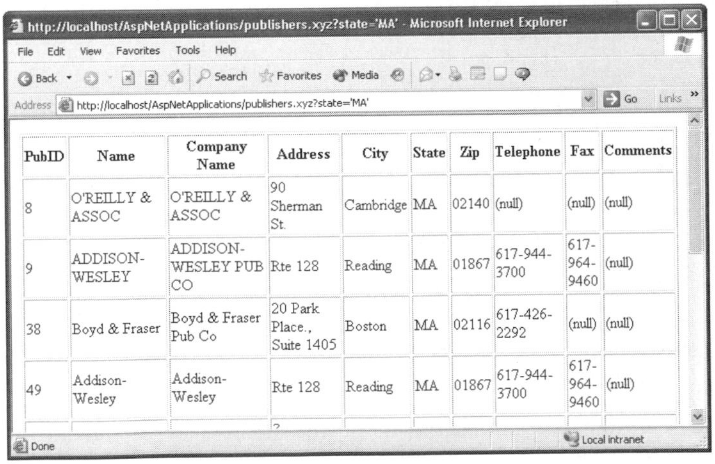

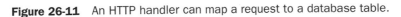

Figure 26-11   An HTTP handler can map a request to a database table.

Here's the complete source code of the XyzHandler class. As you see, its heart is in the ProcessRequest method, which extracts the table name and the WHERE clause from the URL string.

The bulk of the work is done in the MakeHtmlTable function. This routine takes a reference to the HTTP context, which it uses to encode the HTML being sent to the client.

(Otherwise, any special character in fields, like < or &, would be mistakenly interpreted as HTML.)

```vb
Public Class XyzHandler
    Implements IHttpHandler

    ' This method is called for every request for .xyz resources.
    Public Sub ProcessRequest(ByVal context As HttpContext) _
        Implements IHttpHandler.ProcessRequest

        ' The name of the page is the table's name.
        Dim tableName As String = context.Request.Path
        ' Drop directory name, if any, and the extension.
        tableName = Path.GetFileNameWithoutExtension(tableName)
        ' The query string is an optional WHERE clause.
        Dim whereClause As String = context.Request.QueryString.ToString
        ' Build the SQL query.
        Dim sql As String = "SELECT * FROM " & tableName
        If whereClause.Length > 0 Then sql &= " WHERE " & whereClause

        ' Send the table to the client.
        context.Response.Write("<HTML><BODY>")
        context.Response.Write(MakeHtmlTable(sql, context))
        context.Response.Write("</BODY></HTML>")
    End Sub

    ' This property is queried before this handler is reused.
    Public ReadOnly Property IsReusable() As Boolean _
        Implements System.Web.IHttpHandler.IsReusable
        Get
            Return True                    ' Just return True in this demo.
        End Get
    End Property

    ' Perform an SQL query, and return the result as an HTML table.
    Function MakeHtmlTable(ByVal sql As String, _
        ByVal context As HttpContext) As String

        Dim cn As New OleDbConnection(BiblioConnString)
        Dim cmd As New OleDbCommand(sql, cn)
        Dim dr As OleDbDataReader
        ' Use a StringBuilder to create the output.
        Dim sb As New System.Text.StringBuilder(10240)

        Try
            ' Open a connection to Biblio and process the query.
            cn.Open()
            dr = cmd.ExecuteReader

            ' Create an HTML table with correct header row.
            sb.Append("<TABLE Border='1'><THEAD>")
            For i As Integer = 0 To dr.FieldCount - 1
                sb.Append("<TH>")
                sb.Append(dr.GetName(i))
                sb.Append("</TH>")
            Next
            sb.Append("</THEAD>")
```

```
            ' Output data for each record.
            Do While dr.Read
                sb.Append("<TR>")                       ' Row start delimiter
                For i As Integer = 0 To dr.FieldCount - 1
                    sb.Append("<TD>")                   ' Cell start delimiter
                    If Not dr.IsDBNull(i) Then
                        ' A single field value (must be encoded for html)
                        sb.Append(context.Server.HtmlEncode(dr(i).ToString))
                    Else
                        ' Special treatment for Null values
                        sb.Append("(null)")
                    End If
                    sb.Append("</TD>")                  ' Cell end delimiter
                Next
                sb.Append("</TR>")                      ' Row end delimiter
            Loop
            ' Close the table.
            sb.Append("</TABLE>")

        Catch ex As Exception
            sb.Append("<h1>Unable to process the request</h1>")
        Finally
            If Not (dr Is Nothing) Then dr.Close()
            cn.Close()
        End Try

        ' Return the HTML text to the caller.
        Return sb.ToString
    End Function
End Class
```

It's easy to expand on this example to create a fully hierarchical system that appears to remote users as a complex tree of directories but that in reality takes all its data from database tables or XML files. As usual with ASP.NET, the possibilities are virtually endless.

In this chapter, you learned that ASP.NET is a lot more than a tool to create pretty user interfaces. It's a powerful and complete environment for Internet applications of any complexity. In the next chapter, you'll learn that ASP.NET is also able to deliver safe applications, thanks to its first-class security features.

27 ASP.NET Security and Configuration

Any nontrivial ASP.NET application must authenticate its users and implement some form of security. In the first half of this chapter, I'll cover the many facets of ASP.NET security; in the second half, I'll recap the many configuration options that ASP.NET provides.

ASP.NET Security

ASP.NET security is a complex topic because it's actually the convergence of three different security models: Windows security, Internet Information Services (IIS) security, and ASP.NET's own security. Not surprisingly, therefore, you need to know the rudiments of how security works in Windows and IIS to fully comprehend ASP.NET security issues.

> **Note** To keep the code as concise as possible, all the code samples in this chapter assume the following Imports statements at the file or project level:
>
> ```
> Imports System.Web.Security
> Imports System.Data.OleDb
> ```

Basic Concepts

Before we begin our security tour, let's make it clear that we're going to discuss two different but closely related topics: authentication and authorization.

Authentication is the process through which a Web application detects the identity of a user posting a request and associates the request with the user's Windows account, if the user has one. At most Internet sites, users don't have a Windows account on the server, so IIS is configured to accept anonymous requests. In the case of an anonymous posting, the request is considered to be coming from a user named IUSR_machinename, a fictitious identity created when IIS is installed. If anonymous requests aren't enabled and the user can't provide a valid Windows account, the request fails and the user sees an error page with a message such as "You are not authorized to view this page" in the browser.

The authentication process ends after the identity of the user posting the request has been ascertained. If the request was for one of the resources associated with ASP.NET, IIS passes the request to the ASP.NET process.

Authorization is the process during which Windows, IIS, or ASP.NET makes sure that the user identity associated with the request (or the identity associated with anonymous requests) has enough privileges to access the requested resource. In this context, a *resource* is usually an .aspx file, but it can be any other file on the server—for example, a GIF image pointed to by an <img> tag. If the user identity has enough privileges on the .aspx file, the ASP.NET code is given a chance to run. Otherwise, an error message is sent back to the user.

The authorization process doesn't complete when the .aspx file is read and executed because its code might attempt to access other resources on the Web server—for example, an XML data file. Or it might attempt to connect to a SQL Server database using the current user identity. Again, if the identity under which the current request is executing doesn't have enough privileges on the resource, an exception is thrown and an error is returned to the client. The exact identity under which the request runs inside ASP.NET depends on several factors, including the authentication settings in IIS and whether impersonation is enabled.

IIS Authorization

As soon as the request arrives at the server, IIS performs its own authorization chores. IIS supports two different levels of authorizations. Neither of them takes user identity into account, so they can be carried out before the authentication process starts.

First, IIS lets you prevent access to the Web server from unauthorized or unknown users by means of IP address and domain name restrictions. For example, you can reject requests from any IP address other than those associated with recognized users or sites. Domain restrictions are applied before the authentication process begins; you enable them by clicking the button in the middle section of the Directory Security tab in the IIS Properties dialog box. For example, the settings shown in Figure 27-1 allow access to a resource only from the local computer (127.0.0.1) and all the computers in a group (192.168.0.*nnn*). You can apply this type of authorization to the entire site, selected directories, or individual files.

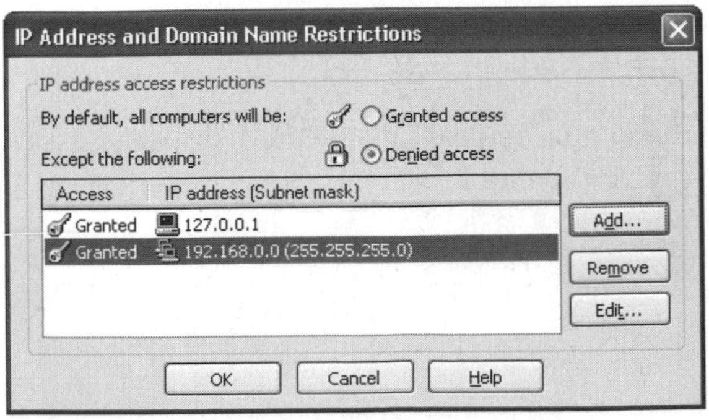

Figure 27-1   IP address and domain name restrictions in IIS

The second type of IIS authorization checks that only permissible operations are performed on the site, a directory, or a file. By default, files can only be read, and you need to change these authorization settings if you want to let users write files, allow them to browse the contents of a directory, or prevent them from accessing the directory or the file. You typically apply this type of authorization to individual files or directories because you'll rarely want to make the entire Web site writable (not to mention nonreadable). For example, IIS uses this type of authorization to hide its own private directories under wwwroot. (See Figure 27-2.) Any attempt to read a resource protected in this way results in an error page entitled "The page cannot be displayed" being sent to the browser.

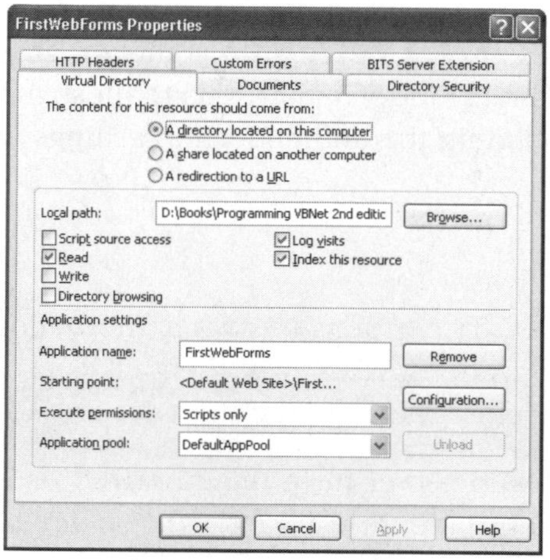

Figure 27-2 Preventing read, write, or directory browsing access to a private directory

IIS Authentication

After you've enforced satisfactory IIS authentication settings, you must decide what kind of authentication IIS can perform on incoming requests. You set these settings inside the Authentication Methods dialog box (Figure 27-3, center), which you reach by clicking the Edit button on the Directory Security tab of the Web Site Properties dialog box (to the left in the same figure). You can apply these settings to the entire site, its directories, or individual files. Here's a brief description of available modes.

- **Anonymous access** Any incoming request is accepted, and it's associated with the identity you specify in the Anonymous User Account dialog box (Figure 27-3, right). By default, this account is IUSR_machinename, and you shouldn't change it if you don't have a good reason to do so.

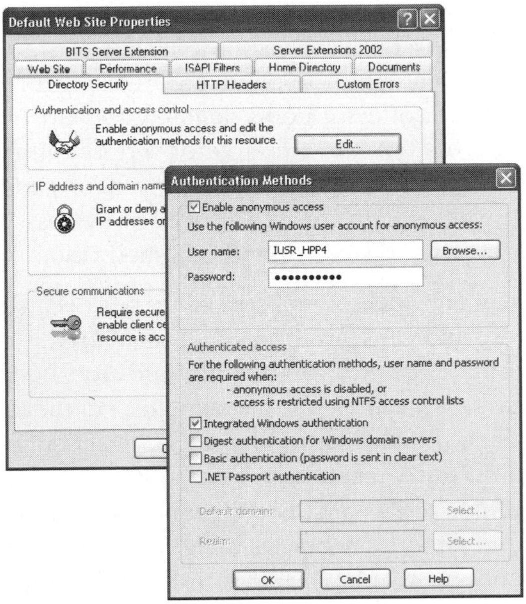

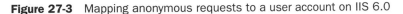

Figure 27-3   Mapping anonymous requests to a user account on IIS 6.0

■ **Basic authentication**   The browser displays the Enter Network Password dialog box that asks the user for a name and password. (See Figure 27-4.) This information is then sent to IIS, which attempts a Windows login for a user with this name and password. This authentication method is compatible with all browsers and works across firewalls and proxy servers, but the user name and password aren't encrypted and can be spoofed relatively easily. For this reason, Basic authentication should be used only when security issues aren't critical or for resources that can be accessed only through an encrypted channel such as HTTPS.

Figure 27-4   The dialog box that the browser displays when accessing a resource for which anonymous access is disabled

- **Digest authentication**   In this case also, a remote user enters a user name and password in a dialog box that the browser displays. Unlike Basic authentication, however, Digest authentication encrypts the password by using a hash value sent by the Web server and therefore offers a good degree of security. It works well with firewalls and proxy servers but has a couple of serious shortcomings—for example, it works only with Internet Explorer 5 or later versions and requires that passwords be stored in clear text on the server. (For security reasons, most Windows servers hash the password and store only the hashed value.)

- **Windows authentication**   This method is very secure because user credentials are never passed on the wire and can't be spoofed. This method is also known as NTLM authentication or Challenge/Response authentication because IIS challenges the browser to provide a hash value that depends on the user name and password. The browser sends IIS information based on the identity specified by the user when she logged on to the client machine, and it displays a dialog box only if this identity isn't authorized to access the requested resource. Unlike the previous two authentication methods, Windows authentication is a Microsoft proprietary standard, works only on Windows and with Internet Explorer (version 2 or later), and doesn't work over firewalls. For these reasons, this authentication method is more suitable for intranet sites and is not recommended as the only authentication method used on Internet sites.

- **.NET Passport authentication**   This method relies on the .NET Passport central server to authenticate users and doesn't require that each site mantains its own authentication mechanism. Sites using this authentication method (which is available only with IIS 6 under Windows Server 2003) can allow users to create a single sign-in name and password that is valid for all other .NET Passport–enabled Web sites.

Any authentication method other than anonymous access requires that, in one way or another, remote users prove they have a valid account on the Windows server. This requirement makes sense when you're running an intranet site, but is unrealistic for large Internet sites that anyone can visit. This doesn't mean that you can't mix authorization methods, however. For example, you might have a public portion of a corporate site that uses anonymous access and a restricted portion that only company employees can access from inside the local network and that is protected with Windows authentication.

I suggest that you create a test user account, such as the JoeDoe user in Figure 27-5, to try out security settings in IIS and ASP.NET. The highlighted user accounts in the figure are crucial when working with IIS and ASP.NET security, as I'll explain in the next section:

- IUSR_machinename is the user account that IIS associates with anonymous requests.

- ASPNET is the default user account for the ASP.NET worker process on Windows Server 2003 (if using IIS 5 isolation mode), Windows 2000, and Windows XP.

Under Windows Server 2003 the identity used for ASP.NET depends on the IIS isolation mode in use. If you've configured Internet Information Services to run in IIS 6.0 isolation mode, no aspnet_wp.exe process is created and the aspnet_isapi.dll ISAPI extension that deals with requests for ASP.NET resources is loaded directly in the w3wp.exe process, which runs under the Network Service account. This account has few privileges, so it is often necessary that you change this default to another, possibly fictitious, identity with more privileges.

There's another account related to IIS security, IWAM_machinename. This account is assigned to IIS applications that run out-of-process, and I won't describe it here.

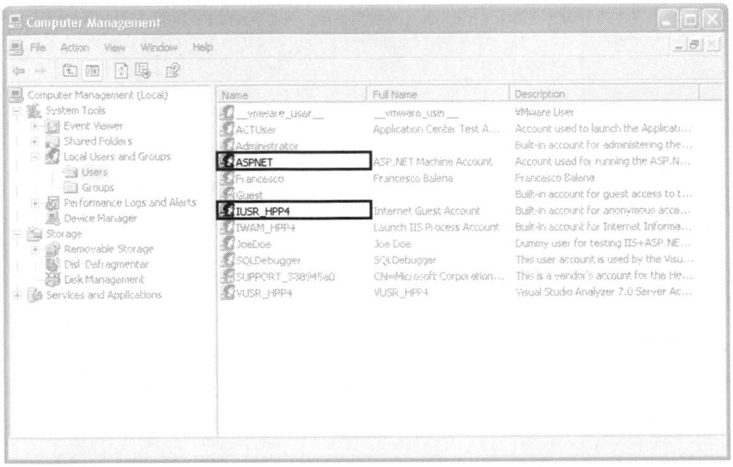

Figure 27-5   Setting users in Windows Server 2003

Windows Authorization

If the authentication process finishes successfully, the remote user has been associated with a Windows account, whether it's a real user's account or the IUSR_machinename built-in account used for anonymous accesses. At this point, the Windows authorization process can begin.

During the Windows authorization process, the operating system checks that the user is allowed to access the resource. This step is performed only if the resource resides on an NTFS drive and has been protected with an access control list (ACL), which specifies which operations (read, write, and so on) a specific user can perform on the resource. To edit an ACL, right-click a file or a directory inside Windows Explorer, click Properties to open the Properties dialog box, and click the Security tab. (See Figure 27-6.)

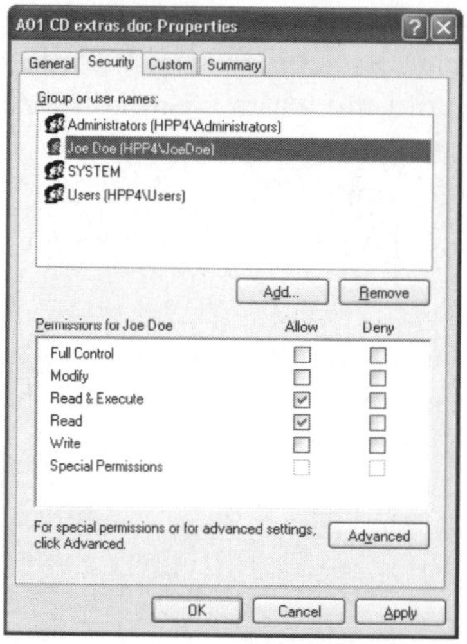

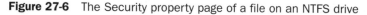

Figure 27-6   The Security property page of a file on an NTFS drive

ASP.NET Impersonation

When the authentication process finishes, IIS checks whether there's an ISAPI filter that's willing to process the request. For example, requests for .asp files are passed to ASP (asp.dll) and requests for .aspx files are passed to ASP.NET. If no ISAPI filter is associated with the extension of the requested file, IIS processes the request by itself and sends the file's content to the client; this is the normal process for .html, .gif, .jpg, and .txt files.

Let's say that the request is for an .aspx file and is therefore passed to the aspnet_isapi.dll filter. In turn, this DLL passes the request to the ASP.NET worker process (aspnet_wp.exe on Windows 2000 and XP, w3wp.exe on Windows Server 2003), launching it from disk if it's not running already. Now the question is under which identity does the worker process run? The answer to this question is important because this is the identity that will be considered during the authorization process. For example, if ASP.NET runs under an account that doesn't have write privileges for the \Temp directory, your code will fail when attempting to create a temporary file there. The process will run under one of three identities, depending on the value of these two tags in the configuration file:

```
<configuration>
  <system.web>
    <identity impersonate="false"/>
    <processModel userName="ASPNET" password="AutoGenerate" />
  </system.web>
</configuration>
```

If impersonation isn't enabled (the default setting), the ASP.NET worker process runs under the identity indicated by the userName attribute in the <processModel> block in machine.config. By default, on Windows Server 2003, this identity is Network Service, whereas on Windows 2000 and XP this identity is ASPNET, an account that was created when ASP.NET was installed. (See Figure 27-5.) These accounts have more privileges than IUSR_machinename, and ASP.NET leverages them to perform dynamic compilations of .aspx files, among other things.

If impersonation is enabled, the ASP.NET worker process runs under the identity of the remote authenticated user. This can be the user's Windows account if she was authenticated through Basic, Digest, or Integrated Windows authentication methods, or it can be IUSR_machinename if anonymous access was used. In impersonation mode, your ASP.NET code is allowed to do what the remote user could do if she were logged on locally. You'll typically use impersonation together with ACLs to deny access to sensitive information.

It's also possible to enable impersonation but opt for a user account other than the authenticated user's account. You can make this choice by specifying a user name and a password in the <identity> block:

```
<identity impersonate="true"
   userName="MyComputer\JoeDoe" password="jdpwd" />
```

As you'll see shortly, in practice impersonation should be enabled only when you use Windows mode for ASP.NET authentication.

Putting Things Together

All these security settings can be confusing, so let me summarize what conditions must be met for a generic HTTP request to pass IIS and Windows authentication and authorization tests:

1. The request comes from an IP address or domain that's granted access.

2. The requested resource is readable in IIS.

3. IIS allows anonymous access to the resource, or the user can provide a user name and password for a valid Windows account on the server by using one of the enabled IIS authentication methods (Basic, Digest, Integrated Windows).

4. If the resource is on an NTFS drive, its ACL specifies that the user has read access to the file.

If the request is for a resource associated with ASP.NET, two more tests are performed:

1. The resource's ACL grants read permissions to the identity under which the ASP.NET worker process runs. This identity depends on whether impersonation is enabled and on other settings in the configuration files.

2. If the resource is an .aspx file, any other file or resource the page uses is accessible from the identity under which the ASP.NET worker process runs.

I prepared a diagram that shows what happens when a request is posted to IIS and the points where the request might be rejected, in which case the client browser is redirected to an error page. (See Figure 27-7.) The last steps in the diagram are related to ASP.NET authentication and authorization, the topic of the following sections.

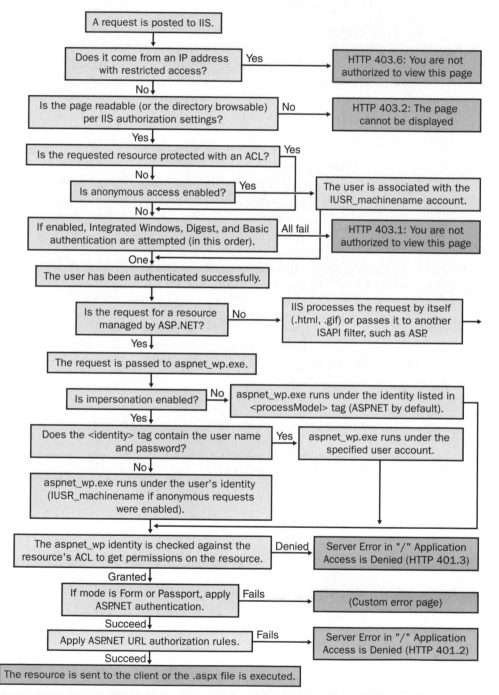

Figure 27-7   The path of requests sent to IIS

ASP.NET Authentication Modes

With IIS and Windows authentication and authorization methods out of the way, we can finally focus on ASP.NET's own security model. Unlike classic ASP, ASP.NET can use configuration files to specify which users can access a given resource or directory and what happens if the user isn't granted access.

ASP.NET supports four authentication modes, and each one corresponds to different authorization techniques. For this reason, I'll cover ASP.NET authentication and authorization together. You decide which mode to enforce by setting the mode attribute of the <authentication> tag in the machine.config or web.config file:

```
<configuration>
  <system.web>
    <authentication mode="Authmode">
       ⋮
    </authentication>
  </system.web>
</configuration>
```

Authmode can be None, Windows, Forms, or Passport. Let's briefly see what each option is all about:

- **None**   ASP.NET doesn't perform any authentication and authorization steps other than those that IIS has already carried out. All resources are accessed by means of the identity assigned to the ASP.NET worker process.

- **Windows**   ASP.NET uses the user identity (as authenticated by IIS) to decide whether the resource is accessible. Settings in web.config let you authorize individuals or groups of users to access the entire application or portions of it, without having to write any code whatsoever. The drawback of this mode is that each user must map to a Windows account, so it works especially well only in intranets. This is the default mode in ASP.NET, but you can change it by editing the machine.config file.

- **Forms**   ASP.NET redirects the first request from unauthenticated users to a custom .aspx login page that asks remote users for their user name and password. You author this login page, so it can have the same look and feel as other pages in the site. The code in the login page then compares the user's name and password against a list of user credentials kept in web.config or another repository (most likely a database). If your code authenticates the user, ASP.NET issues a cookie that will travel with each subsequent request so that the login form isn't shown again.

- **Passport**   ASP.NET uses the centralized Passport service that Microsoft provides and that's able to authenticate users across all the sites that subscribe to this service. A user can log in to one site and browse any other Passport-enabled site, without having to log in to each one. Passport is a secure authentication method—because user credentials can travel on encrypted channels—and makes for a great user experience.

I won't discuss Passport authentication in this book. Those who are interested can find more information and download the Passport SDK at *http://www.passport.com*.

ASP.NET Windows Authentication

Let's restrict our focus to Windows and Forms authentication modes. In this section, I'll describe the first mode and postpone the discussion about ASP.NET Forms authentication to later in this chapter.

Configuration Settings for Windows Authentication

You activate Windows authentication by adding this line in machine.config or web.config:

```
<configuration>
  <system.web>
    <authentication mode="Windows" />
  </system.web>
</configuration>
```

No other tag is used in the authentication block when you're using Windows authentication mode. In Windows authentication mode, it usually makes sense to have ASP.NET impersonate the remote user. If impersonation is enabled, ASP.NET accesses files and other resources on the server under the remote user's account, and all usual ACL constraints must be satisfied. If impersonation is disabled, a remote user might have access to fewer (or more) resources than when he logs in locally, and you'll probably want to avoid this discrepancy. As I already showed you, you enable impersonation by means of the <identity> tag in the configuration file:

```
<configuration>
  <system.web>
    <authentication mode="Windows" />
    <identity impersonate="true"/>
  </system.web>
</configuration>
```

You can also have ASP.NET impersonate a given user if you add the username and password attributes to the <identity> tag, but this rarely makes sense because the main goal of impersonation is to enable different behavior depending on the identity of the remote user.

Once the user has been recognized by means of Windows authentication, you can finally apply ASP.NET authorization rules to allow or deny the user access to specific areas on the site. You can make such distinctions by means of URL authorization rules.

URL Authorizations

Each .config file can include a section named <authorization>, which lists the users who are allowed or denied access to the portion of the site that the .config file is related to. This section can contain a series of <allow> and <deny> elements, each one specifying which users or groups are or aren't granted access:

```
<configuration>
  <system.web>
    <authorization>
       <allow users="userlist" roles="grouplist" verb="verblist" />
       <deny users="userlist" roles="grouplist" verb="verblist" />
    </authorization>
  </system.web>
</configuration>
```

In the sample,

- userlist is a comma-separated list of users, in the format *domainname\username* or *machinename\username*. A question mark (?) stands for anonymous users and an asterisk (*) means all users.

- grouplist is a comma-separated list of Windows account groups, in the format *domainname\rolename* or *machinename\rolename*. An asterisk (*) means all roles.

- verblist is a comma-separated list of HTTP verbs. Verbs registered to ASP.NET are GET, POST, HEAD, and DEBUG. An asterisk (*) means all verbs. The verb attribute is optional; if omitted, all verbs are considered.

<allow> and <deny> tags must contain at least one user's or role's attribute. Notice that user and role names must include either a domain name or the name of the local machine, which means that you must edit the configuration file when you move the application to another machine or another domain. The default settings in machine.config grant access to all users:

```
<authorization>
  <allow users="*" />
</authorization>
```

Of course, you can override these settings in web.config files. For example, these settings grant access to administrators and managers only, and deny access to everybody else:

```
<authorization>
  <allow roles="MyDomain\administrators,MyDomain\managers" verb="*" />
  <deny users="*" />
</authorization>
```

The following example denies access only to anonymous users:

```
<authorization>
  <deny users="?" />
  <allow users="*" />
</authorization>
```

Here's an example that employs user names instead of group names:

```
<authorization>
  <allow users="MyComputer\FrancescoB,MyComputer\JoeDoe" />
  <deny users="*" />
</authorization>
```

The <allow> and <deny> tags are processed in order until one element in the list of users or roles matches the identity of the user. Therefore, the order of entries is significant—for example, if you reverse the order of the two elements in the <authorization> block in the preceding sample, no user is allowed to access any resource controlled by this web.config file (or any ASP.NET resource, if these entries are in machine.config).

ASP.NET processes a web.config file in the directory where the requested resource is, then proceeds toward the application's root directory, and stops as soon as it finds a user or group list that matches the user's identity. This means that you can have a \Documents directory visible only to authors and managers, and a \Documents\Public directory that can be accessed by anyone, including anonymous users:

```
<!-- settings in \Documents\web.config -->
  <allow roles="MyDomain\Authors,MyDomain\Managers" />
  <deny users="*" />

<!-- settings in \Documents\Public\web.config -->
  <allow users="*" />
```

If the current user isn't granted access to the requested page or resource, ASP.NET sends an error page to the client browser, mentioning HTTP error code 401.2.

Forms Authentication Mode

ASP.NET Windows authentication mode is fine and provides a fairly understandable authentication model that's also easily coupled with URL authorizations. However, Windows authentication isn't a practical solution when you're building an Internet site that must authenticate thousands of remote users. When selecting the authentication model for such a site, you must ask yourself *why* you want to authenticate your users. If you authenticate users to carry out secure transactions or arbitrate access to highly confidential information, you must resort to advanced techniques, such as client certificates and communications over Secure Sockets Layer (SSL), which I don't cover in this book. In the vast majority of cases, you authenticate users only to customize your site appearance, without too severe security constraints. In these circumstances, ASP.NET Forms authentication mode fits the bill nicely.

Forms authentication works as follows: if the remote user requests a protected resource managed by ASP.NET—typically, an .aspx page—the ASP.NET infrastructure checks whether the request carries a special authentication cookie, also known as an authentication ticket. If yes, the user has been authenticated and ASP.NET can display the page. If the cookie isn't there, ASP.NET redirects the request to a custom login page, an

.aspx page that you've prepared and that typically asks the user for a user name and password and compares them with the list of registered users. (This list can be kept in web.config or, more frequently, in a database.) If your code successfully authenticates the user, it must issue an authentication cookie so that from that point on the user can visit any other page in the site without being redirected to the login page. You decide whether the authentication ticket is a session cookie (which expires when the user closes the browser or a timeout elapses) or a persistent cookie stored on disk. An easy tip: always give users the ability to choose whether the cookie is persistent; otherwise, no one will ever want to log in to your site from a public computer.

Forms authentication lets you protect only resources directly managed by ASP.NET, such as .aspx files. You can't use Forms authentication for, say, preventing the download of .gif or .jpeg files. If protecting these files is a requirement, you should associate these extensions with the aspnet_isapi.dll. You do this by showing the Properties window of the site or the virtual directory, switch to the Home Directory tab, click the Configuration button, and then the Add button to map the extension to aspnet_isapi.dll.

If changing the site mappings isn't practical—for example, if there are too many extensions to account for—you should opt for another protection mechanism, such as using Windows authentication and protecting those resources with ACLs. Another easy technique is storing all the files in a directory that can be accessed only from the ASP.NET worker process (but not directly from remote users) and using a special .aspx page that reads the file and returns it to the client, for example, by using the Response.WriteFile method:

```
http://www.tailspintoys.com/gettext.aspx?file=instructions.txt
```

Configuration Settings for Forms Authentication

You enforce Forms authentication by setting the mode attribute and adding a <forms> section inside the <authentication> section, as follows:

```
<configuration>
  <system.web>
    <authentication mode="Forms">
      <forms loginUrl="/LoginPage.aspx" name="MySiteName"
          path="/" protection="All"  timeout="10">
        <credentials passwordFormat="Clear" >
          <user name="JoeDoe" password="jdpwd" />
          <user name="AnnSmith" password="aspwd" />
        </credentials>
      </forms>
    </authentication>

    <authorization>
        <deny users="?" />
    </authorization>
  </system.web>
</configuration>
```

The <deny> tag is very important: you must explicitly deny access to anonymous users. If you omit this step, Forms authentication won't work. Let's see what each attribute in the <forms> section stands for:

- loginUrl is the URL of the custom login page you've prepared for the user to enter a user name and password. Its default value is login.aspx.

- name is the name of the authentication cookie. Most of the time, you can omit it and use its .ASPXAUTH default value.

- path is the path of your site where the cookie is valid; its default value is /, which makes the cookie visible to the entire site. You can specify a more specific path, such as /Reserved, if only a portion of your site is protected. This setting prevents the browser from sending the cookie when a user is requesting pages that aren't protected.

- protection is the protection level to be used for the cookie. It can be Validation (the cookie is validated against tampering but not encrypted), Encryption (the cookie is encrypted using Triple-DES or DES but not validated), All (the default; the cookie is both encrypted and validated), or None.

- timeout is the number of minutes of inactivity after which the session cookie expires. (Default is 30 minutes.) If a request is posted to the Web site within this interval, the authentication cookie is automatically renewed.

The default values for all these attributes are those defined in machine.config, so you can change them if you want.

The <forms> section can contain a <credentials> subsection that stores names and passwords of all recognized users. Many real-world ASP.NET applications don't use this section, however, and instead store user data in a database where the data can be processed more easily and can be associated with additional information (such as e-mail addresses and whether users subscribe to the site's newsletter). If you omit this section and accept the default value for most of the attributes in the <forms> section, this is all you really need to activate Forms authentication:

```
<authentication mode="Forms">
    <forms loginUrl="/LoginPage.aspx" />
</authentication>
```

You must be aware of a few potential problems with <forms> settings in web.config. First, setting a path for the cookie other than "/" requires that *all* the links to pages in the reserved section—for example, the NavigateUrl property in Hyperlink controls or HREF attributes in <a> tags—are in the correct case because a few browsers compare paths in case-sensitive mode and don't send the cookie when they access a URL in the wrong case.

A second potential problem is that you must pay attention to authentication cookies if you are in a Web farm. As I explained in the "Out-of-Process Sessions Based on a Windows Service" section in Chapter 26, each server validates and encrypts cookies with two keys whose value is stored in the <machineKey> section of the machine.config file or of the main web.config file of individual applications. By default, these keys are auto-generated and each computer uses a different key, so a server on the Web farm won't recognize an authentication cookie issued by another server. To avoid this problem, ensure that all the computers on the farm use the same validation and decryption key:

```
<configuration>
    <system.web>
      <machineKey
        validationKey="0123456789abcdef0123456789abcdef0123456789abcdef"
        decryptionKey="fedcba9876543210fedcba9876543210fedcba9876543210"
        validation="SHA1" />
  </system.web>
</configuration>
```

Or you can set the protection level for the authentication cookie to None, but that would mean sending the authentication cookie in clear text.

A different problem can occur when you're working with version 1.1 of the .NET Framework. The default machine.config for this version includes the IsolateApps modifier for the validationKey and decryptionKey attributes, as in this code:

```
<machineKey
    validationKey="AutoGenerate,IsolateApps"
    decryptionKey="AutoGenerate,IsolateApps"
    validation="SHA1" />
```

The IsolateApp modifier makes ASP.NET use both the provided value and the application identity to generate the actual validation and decryption key used for each application. This makes it simpler to configure isolated applications on shared servers, but at the same time it makes it impossible to share ViewState or use Forms authentication across different applications on the same machine. If you need to share ViewState or authentication cookies among different applications on the same (or different) machines, use specific keys in individual Web.config files.

> **See Also**   Read the "Storing User Credentials in Configuration Files.doc" file on the companion CD for more information about storing user names and passwords in encrypted formats in ASP.NET configuration files.

The Login Page

To complete the Forms authentication implementation, you must prepare the login page to which unauthenticated users are redirected before they can access any protected resource on the site. The appearance of this login page can vary, but essentially it should look like the one in Figure 27-8 and contain a field for the user name, a field for the password, and a check box to make the authorization cookie persistent. You also have to provide a Login (or Submit) button and a link to a page where new users can register themselves. You should also add a Label control for displaying error messages.

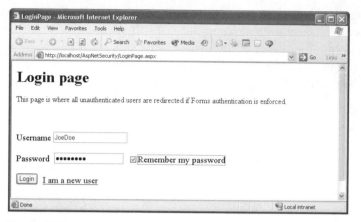

Figure 27-8   A typical login form

The code you write for the Login button's Click event depends on where you've stored the list of user names and passwords. In the simplest case, the user list is stored in the web.config file (with passwords in clear text or encrypted format), and you simply need to check whether the provided name and password are valid. You can do this by using the Authenticate shared method of the FormsAuthentication class:

```
Private Sub btnLogin_Click(ByVal sender As Object, ByVal e As EventArgs) _
    Handles btnLogin.Click
    If FormsAuthentication.Authenticate(txtUsername.Text, txtPassword.Text) Then
        FormsAuthentication.RedirectFromLoginPage(txtUsername.Text, _
            chkRemember.Checked)
    Else
        lblMessage.Text = "Invalid user name or password"
    End If
End Sub
```

If the Authenticate method returns True, you usually call the RedirectFromLoginPage method, passing the user name and a Boolean that specifies whether the authentication cookie is persistent. In the demo program, the user decides whether the cookie is persistent by selecting a CheckBox control, so the preceding code simply passes the Checked property of this control in the second argument to the method.

A persistent cookie is valid for 50 years, so the user will be automatically authenticated whenever she visits the same site again from the same computer. Notice that modern browsers keep a separate list of cookies for each Windows user, in which case the authentication cookie isn't found if the user logs in to the operating system under a different identity.

The user name you pass to the RedirectFromLoginPage method is then used to perform URL authorization against the resource being requested. If the requested resource is denied to the authenticated user, the RedirectFromLoginPage method works partially:

it does authenticate the user, but the redirection fails and the user will be looking again at the login form—without a clue about what happened because no error message is shown in this case.

Custom Forms Authentication

The great thing about Forms authorization is the degree of customization it allows. For example, you can easily change the standard behavior to store user data in a place other than web.config; or you can change the expiration date for a persistent cookie if 50 years sounds like too long a period for you. The FormsAuthentication class exposes all the methods you need to perform these tasks.

The most common reason to switch to custom Forms authorization is when you store user data in a database. In that case, you replace the call FormsAuthentication.Authenticate with a call to a custom function that you provide:

```
If AuthenticateUser(txtUsername.Text, txtPassword.Text) Then
    FormsAuthentication.RedirectFromLoginPage(txtUsername.Text, _
        chkRemember.Checked)
End If
```

Here's an example of how you might implement the custom authenticate function:

```
Function AuthenticateUser(ByVal username As String, _
    ByVal password As String) As Boolean
    ' Open the connection to the database holding user names and passwords.
    Dim cn As New OleDbConnection(PasswordDBConnString)
    cn.Open()
    ' Read the record for this user.
    Dim cmd As New OleDbCommand("SELECT * FROM Users WHERE UserName=?", cn)
    cmd.Parameters.Add("username", username)
    Dim dr As OleDbDataReader = cmd.ExecuteReader(CommandBehavior.SingleRow)

    If dr.Read AndAlso dr("Password") = password Then
        ' Authenticate user if there's a record and the password is correct.
        AuthenticateUser = True
    End If
    ' Close the DataReader and the connection.
    dr.Close()
    cn.Close()
End Function
```

Notice that the preceding code reads all the fields in the Users table, even though it uses just the Password field. This slight inefficiency makes the procedure ready for situations when you offer customization features. For example, you can read the preferred color scheme and store this data in Session variables before closing the DataReader:

```
Session("ForeColor") = CInt(dr("ForeColor"))
Session("BackColor") = CInt(dr("BackColor"))
```

Another reason to override the Forms authorization's standard behavior is for precisely specifying the authentication cookie's lifetime. In fact, the standard method lets you choose only between temporary (session) cookies and persistent cookies. If you want to create a cookie that expires in, say, one month, you must replace the RedirectFrom-LoginPage method with a custom routine:

```
' A custom routine that works like FormsAuthentication.RedirectFromLoginPage
' but lets you control the authentication cookie's expiration date.

Function RedirectFromLoginPageEx(ByVal username As String, _
    ByVal persistentCookie As Boolean, _
    Optional ByVal expirationDays As Integer = -1) As Boolean

    ' Get the URL of the requested resource.
    Dim url As String = _
        FormsAuthentication.GetRedirectUrl(username, persistentCookie)
    ' Create the authentication cookie.
    FormsAuthentication.SetAuthCookie(username, persistentCookie)

    If persistentCookie And expirationDays > 0 Then
        ' Get a reference to the cookie just created.
        Dim cookie As HttpCookie = _
            Response.Cookies(FormsAuthentication.FormsCookieName)
        ' Set its expiration date.
        cookie.Expires = Now.AddDays(expirationDays)
    End If
    ' Redirect to the resource that was requested originally.
    Response.Redirect(url)
End Function
```

Another reason for creating authentication cookies programmatically is to ensure that these cookies can travel only through encrypted channels, a trick that makes Forms authentication infinitely more secure. To implement this technique, you place the login form in a directory that can be accessed only through HTTPS:

```
<forms loginUrl="https://www.tailspintoys.com/protected/login.aspx />
```

You can improve this technique by having the cookie transmitted only when the user navigates to a page of the /Protected subdirectory. You do so by passing a third argument to the SetAuthCookie method:

```
FormsAuthentication.SetAuthCookie(username, persistentCookie, "/Protected")
```

Finally, you ensure that the cookie can travel only over secure lines by setting its Secure property to True:

```
' Add this statement to the RedirectFromLoginPageEx routine.
cookie.Secure = True
```

The FormsAuthentication class exposes other shared members that are useful for customizing the authentication process:

- The FormsCookieName and FormsCookiePath properties return the name and path of the authentication cookie as defined in configuration files.

- The GetAuthCookie method returns the HttpCookie object without adding it to the Response.Cookies collection.

- The SignOut method removes the authentication cookie. You can provide a Sign Out hyperlink in your pages to let users of public computers safely exit your site without having to close the browser to remove the temporary cookie.

- You can find more information about ASP.NET security and how you can interact with it via code in the "Role-Based Security" section of Chapter 33.

ASP.NET Configuration

Configuration files are a key aspect of ASP.NET programming and are a huge improvement over classic ASP. Thanks to configuration files, you can set virtually all features of an ASP.NET application without interacting with IIS and its dialog boxes, except when you're creating the application in IIS and setting its security features. The only other task for which you need to assign values in IIS dialog boxes is associating a new file extension to the ASP.NET ISAPI filter, an infrequent operation that you perform only when you create HTTP handlers or when you want to protect other types of files with ASP.NET security (as I explained in the "Forms Authentication Mode" section earlier in this chapter).

Except for the aforementioned tasks, you can deploy an ASP.NET application or replicate it on another machine by using a simple XCOPY command. This procedure works despite the fact that a few configuration settings might require fixing after this operation—for example, the machine or domain name in the list of users granted access to the application or the connection string for SQL Server–based sessions.

You can change a configuration file even while the application is running, in which case the new settings are immediately used for each new request arriving on the server. This is possible because ASP.NET listens to modifications to these files and can detect when a .config file is created or updated. ASP.NET then creates a new AppDomain and launches another worker process based on the new settings. The existing application continues to process the requests already accepted and shuts down as soon as the last of such requests has been served. This is an important difference from classic ASP, which forces the administrator to stop and restart the application to enforce any new setting.

You should be aware that ASP.NET configuration files, like all XML files, are extremely sensitive to character casing. All element names, attribute names, and attribute values should be typed exactly as described here or in the MSDN documentation. In some cases, a mistyped element can prevent the Web site from working properly.

Configuration Basics

As I explained at the beginning of Chapter 26, ASP.NET relies on three types of configuration files: the machine.config main configuration file, which affects all ASP.NET applications on a local machine; the web.config configuration file that you place in an ASP.NET application's root directory; and secondary web.config files that reside in a subdirectory of an ASP.NET application.

Configuration Sections

As you know, all configuration files have a top-level tag named <configuration>. The data inside this tag can be roughly subdivided into two halves:

- The <configSections> portion defines all the sections and section groups that you can find in the second half of the configuration file and indicates the handler class for each section.

- Section groups and individual sections contain the actual configuration data. Each section group or individual section must correspond to an entry in <configSections>, otherwise the .NET runtime doesn't know how to process data in the section.

This organization is confusing at first, so an example is in order. Here's a condensed listing from machine.config that shows just one individual section and one section group, preceded by the <configSections> entries that define the handler class for the individual section and section group:

```
<?xml version="1.0" encoding="UTF-8"?>
<configuration>
  <configSections>
    <section name="appSettings"
       type="System.Configuration.NameValueFileSectionHandler, System,
            Version=1.0.5000.0, Culture=neutral,
            PublicKeyToken=b77a5c561934e089" />
    <sectionGroup name="system.web">
      <section name="trace"
            type="System.Web.Configuration.TraceConfigurationHandler,
                System.Web, Version=1.0.5000.0, Culture=neutral,
                PublicKeyToken=b03f5f7f11d50a3a" />
      ⋮
    </sectionGroup>
  </configSections>

  <appSettings>
    <add key="XML File Name" value="myXmlFileName.xml" />
  </appSettings>
  <system.web>
    <trace enabled="false" localOnly="true" pageOutput="false"
          requestLimit="10" traceMode="SortByTime" />
    ⋮
  </system.web>
</configuration>
```

Configuration Inheritance

You need to understand how value overriding works with configuration files. Let's say that we have an ASP.NET application in the C:\MyApp directory and that it contains a subdirectory named Public. Consider these settings:

```
<!-- in machine.config -->
<authentication mode="Windows">
<authorization>
    <allow users="*" />
</authorization>

<!-- in c:\MyApp\web.config -->
<authorization>
    <allow roles="MyDomain\Administrator" />
    <deny users="*" />
</authorization>

<!-- in c:\MyApp\Public\web.config -->
<authorization>
    <allow users="?" />
</authorization>
```

Because neither web.config file redefines the <authentication> tag, the entire application uses Windows authentication mode. The main application directory grants access only to domain administrators, and the Public subdirectory is visible to both anonymous users and administrators.

Centralized Configuration Files

Although ASP.NET lets you distribute web.config files over all the application's subdirectories, it surely doesn't force you to do so. You can keep all the application settings in its main web.config file, while enforcing different settings on a directory-by-directory basis, if you want. The key to this useful feature is the <location> tag. For example, let's see how an application's configuration file can specify different authorization settings for its different subdirectories. This web.config file enforces the same settings as the example seen in the preceding section:

```
<configuration>
  <system.web>
    <authorization>
      <allow roles="MyDomain\Administrator" />
      <deny users="*" />
    </authorization>
  </system.web>

  <location path="/Public">
    <system.web>
      <authorization>
        <allow users="?" />
      </authorization>
    </system.web>
  </location>
</configuration>
```

You can also use a <location> tag in machine.config to affect settings in individual ASP.NET applications and their subdirectories. In this case, the path attribute must begin with the IIS site name, as read in the MMC snap-in. For example, here's how you can enable tracing for the .aspx files in the /MyApp virtual directory of the default Web site:

```
<location path="Default Web Site/MyApp">
  <system.web>
    <trace enabled="true" localOnly="true" pageOutput="true" />
  </system.web>
</location>
```

Some ASP.NET settings are so critical that the system administrator should prevent them from being changed by individual applications. This ability is especially crucial for servers that host multiple applications written by different developers. In this case, the administrator can prevent undesired changes by adding an allowOverride attribute to the <location> tag and setting it to false:

```
<location path="Default Web Site/MyApp" allowOverride="false">
  <system.web>
    <authorization>
      <allow roles="MyDomain\Administrator" />
      <deny users="*" />
    </authorization>
  </system.web>
</location>
```

Another way to prevent a set of values from being redefined is by adding an allowDefinition attribute to a <section> tag in the <configSections> portion of the configuration file. For example, the following entry in machine.config effectively prevents the <processModel> key from appearing in the application's web.config files:

```
<section name="processModel"
    type="System.Web.Configuration.ProcessModelConfigurationHandler,
        System.Web, Version=1.0.5000.0, Culture=neutral,
        PublicKeyToken=b03f5f7f11d50a3a"
    allowDefinition="MachineOnly" />
```

The allowDefinition attribute can take three values: MachineOnly for settings that can appear only in machine.config; MachineToApplication for settings that can appear in machine.config and the application's main web.config file, but not in secondary web.config files; and Everywhere for settings that can appear in any .config file. (This is the default behavior if the allowDefinition attribute is omitted.)

ASP.NET Configuration Settings

In this and previous chapters, I already covered some of the settings you can find in the <system.web> section—for example, <authentication>, <authorization>, <httpHandlers>, <httpModules>, <identity>, <machineKey>, and <sessionState>. Here, I'll focus on the remaining <system.web> settings, in alphabetical order.

\<browserCaps\>

This tag controls the settings of the browser capabilities component. When a request arrives, ASP.NET compares the HTTP_USER_AGENT or another server variable with the entries in this tag, using regular expressions to find the best match:

```
<browserCaps>
   <result type="class" />
   <use var="HTTP_USER_AGENT" />
       browser=Unknown  version=n.m  majorver=n  minorver=m
       frames=false tables=false
       <!-- other browser settings -->
       …
   <filter>
     <case match="Windows 98|Win98">platform=Win98</case>
     <case match="Windows NT|WinNT">platform=WinNT</case>
   </filter>
   <!-- other filters and cases -->
   ⋮
</browserCaps>
```

The syntax of this part of the configuration file is convoluted. Because these settings aren't modified for most cases, I won't cover them in more detail. Those who are more curious can learn more from the MSDN documentation.

\<clientTarget\>

This tag adds or removes one or more aliases for specific user agents to or from the collection of aliases known to ASP.NET:

```
<clientTarget>
   <add alias="aliasname" userAgent="useragentstring" />
   <remove alias="aliasname" />
   <clear />
</clientTarget>
```

For example, this section of machine.config adds an alias named ie4 to the collection of ASP.NET aliases:

```
<clientTarget>
 <add alias="ie4"
   userAgent="Mozilla/4.0 (compatible; MSIE 4.0; Windows NT 4.0)" />
</clientTarget>
```

You typically assign browser aliases to the ClientTarget property of the Page object to override automatic detection of browser capabilities and to specify for which browser a page should render its ouput:

```
' (Inside a Page class)
' Output HTML for Internet Explorer 4.0.
Me.ClientTarget = "ie4"
```

\<compilation>

This tag configures all the compilation settings for ASP.NET. When you create a project with Visual Studio .NET, the environment creates a web.config file that overrides these settings, so most of the time you don't have to worry about settings in this section. The only attribute worth mentioning here is debug, which you should set to true during the development stage:

```
<compilation defaultLanguage="vb" debug="true" />
```

\<customErrors>

This tag affects how error pages are managed in an ASP.NET application and whether developers can redirect users to their custom error pages when an exception is thrown.

```
<customErrors mode="On|Off|RemoteOnly" defaultRedirect="url">
   <error statusCode="statuscode" redirect="url"/>
</customErrors>
```

As you've learned, ASP.NET produces an error page like the one shown in Figure 27-9 when an application throws an unhandled exception or when you deploy an .aspx file whose source contains a syntax error without compiling it inside Visual Studio .NET first. Most of the time, you don't want this page to be visible to your site's visitors because the source code might contain confidential information, such as the password to access a database. A simple way to avoid sending source code to the user is by setting the debug attribute to false in the \<compilation> tag. An even better method is to redirect the browser to a custom error page on which you instruct users about error causes and possible remedies.

The mode attribute is required and can be one of the following values: Off (ASP.NET always displays its own error pages), On (ASP.NET never displays its own error pages, and developers can define their own custom error pages), or RemoteOnly (ASP.NET displays its error pages only for requests from the local computer and allows custom error pages for requests from remote users).

RemoteOnly is the default setting in machine.config and allows you to perform debugging chores while remote users are accessing the site. Unless the mode attribute is Off, you should provide a defaultRedirect attribute pointing to your custom error page. You can also indicate different URLs for specific HTTP status codes by using one or more \<error> subtags, as in this example:

```
<customErrors> mode="RemoteOnly" defaultRedirect="ErrorPage.aspx" >
   <error statusCode="500" redirect="InternalError.htm"/>
</customErrors>
```

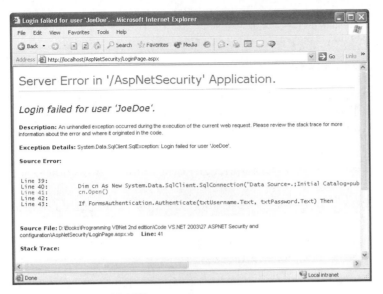

Figure 27-9   An ASP.NET error page

<globalization>

This tag configures the default globalization settings of an application or a portion thereof:

```
<globalization requestEncoding="encodestring"
               responseEncoding="encodestring"
               fileEncoding="encodestring"
               culture="culturestring"
               uiCulture="culturestring" />
```

The values of the requestEncoding and responseEncoding attributes specify how the request data and the response data are expected to be encoded; they can be a string such as UTF-8 or Unicode and are overridden by an Accept-Charset attribute contained in the request header. The fileEncoding attribute is the default encoding method for .aspx, .asax, and .asmx files.

The culture and uiCulture attributes specify the default culture for processing incoming requests and server-side resource searches and can be any valid argument for the constructor of the System.Globalization.CultureInfo class—for example, en-US or fr-FR. The former attribute affects the output of format functions for dates and numbers.

<httpRuntime>

This tag affects important configuration settings of the ASP.NET runtime:

```
<httpRuntime executionTimeout="seconds"
             maxRequestLength="kbytes"
             minFreeThreads="numberOfThreads"
```

```
minLocalRequestFreeThreads="numberOfThreads"
appRequestQueueLimit="numberOfRequests"
useFullyQualifiedRedirectUrl="true|false"  />
```

Here's a brief description of each attribute:

- executionTimeout is the maximum time an .aspx page can run before timing out. The default is 90 seconds, but you should extend this value for pages that perform long database queries or remote calls to a Web service. This attribute corresponds to the Server.ScriptTimeout property.

- maxRequestLength is the maximum length of a request. All requests longer than this value are rejected. The default value is 4096 KB, so it should suffice for most practical purposes, but you have to increase this value for pages that accept posted files larger than 4 megabytes. Or you can reduce this value to prevent denial-of-service attacks caused by posting very large files to the server for all the pages that don't accept uploaded files.

- minFreeThreads is the minimum number of threads that must be free for ASP.NET to accept a request. The default value is 8, so ASP.NET normally rejects a request if there are seven or fewer free threads. This setting lets you prevent stalls when your site accepts a request that creates additional threads.

- minLocalRequestFreeThreads is like the minFreeThreads attribute, but it's applied to local requests, which often issue child requests.

- appRequestQueueLimit is the maximum number of requests that ASP.NET can queue for the application when there aren't enough free threads to serve it. Any request that arrives when the queue is full is rejected with a 503—Server Too Busy error.

- useFullyQualifiedRedirectUrl specifies whether a Request.Redirect method is processed to use a fully qualified URL that also contains the server name. Fully qualified URLs are required by some mobile controls. The default setting is False.

<pages>

This tag specifies default values for page configuration settings:

```
<pages buffer="true|false"
       enableSessionState="true|false|ReadOnly"
       enableViewState="true|false"
       enableViewStateMac="true|false"
       autoEventWireup="true|false"
       smartNavigation="true|false"
       pageBaseType="typename, assembly"
       userControlBaseType="typename" />
```

The values of the buffer, enableSessionState, enableViewState, enableViewStateMac, autoEventWireup, or smartNavigation attribute affect the page properties or directive of the same name. The last two attributes define the code-behind class that pages and user controls inherit by default. These are the default values as defined in machine.config:

```
<pages buffer="true" enableSessionState="true" enableViewState="true"
        enableViewStateMac="false" autoEventWireup="true" />
```

The enableSessionState also can be set to read-only, but it makes sense to do so only inside secondary web.config files. The autoEventWireup attribute is reset to false inside the @Page directive of all .aspx pages created inside Visual Studio .NET.

\<processModel\>

This tag configures the ASP.NET worker process (aspnet_wp.exe on Windows 2000 and XP, w3wp.exe on Windows Server 2003):

```
<processModel enable="true|false" idleTimeout="mins"
              timeout="mins"   shutdownTimeout="hrs:mins:secs"
              requestLimit="num"
              requestQueueLimit="Infinite|num"
              restartQueueLimit="Infinite|num"
              memoryLimit="percent"
              cpuMask="num"  webGarden="true|false"
              userName="username"  password="password"
              logLevel="All|None|Errors"
              clientConnectedCheck="HH:MM:SS"
              comAuthenticationLevel=
                  "Default|None|Connect|Call|Pkt|PktIntegrity|PktPrivacy"
              comImpersonationLevel=
                  "Default|Anonymous|Identify|Impersonate|Delegate"
              maxWorkerThreads="num"
              maxIoThreads="num" />
```

The most intriguing feature that you can control with these settings is process recycling, which lets you automatically launch another worker process after a timeout, after processing a given number of requests, or when free memory goes below the specified threshold. (I briefly mentioned application recycling in the section "The HttpApplicationState Class" in Chapter 26.)

Table 27-1 contains a brief explanation of the attributes in this tag. I covered the username and password attributes in the "ASP.NET Impersonation" section. Unlike other settings in configuration files, settings in this section aren't applied until IIS restarts.

Table 27-1 Main Attributes of the processModel Configuration Tag

Category	Name	Description
General	enable	Tells whether ASP.NET runs outside IIS (true, the default) or inside IIS (false). If you change this setting, you're going to miss many of the advantages of the process model mechanism.
	username	The Windows account under which the worker process runs. The default is ASPNET under Windows 2000 and XP, machine under Windows Server 2003.
	password	The password for the identity adopted for the worker process. The special System and Machine accounts don't require a password.
Process shutdown	idleTimeout	The period of inactivity after which the worker process is shut down. The default value is infinite.
	shutdownTimeout	The timeout after which ASP.NET forces the shutdown of the working process that refuses to shut down gracefully. The default value is 5 seconds.
Process recycling	timeout	The number of minutes after which the worker process is automatically shut down and restarted.
	requestLimit	The number of requests processed before the worker process is automatically shut down and restarted. The default value is infinite.
	memoryLimit	The percentage of the total system memory that the worker process can consume before being automatically recycled. The default is 60 percent.
	response-DeadlockInterval	The interval after which the process is restarted if there hasn't been a response even though there are requests in the queue. The default value is 3 minutes.
	responseRestart-DeadlockInterval	How much time must elapse after the last restart to cure a deadlock before the process is restarted to cure a deadlock again. This setting prevents problems with processes that require a long start-up time. Its value can be infinite or a timeout in the format hh:mm:ss.
	pingFrequency	How often ASP.NET pings the worker process to check whether it's active and restart it if it isn't. The default is 30 seconds.

Table 27-1   Main Attributes of the processModel Configuration Tag

Category	Name	Description
	pingTimeout	How long an ASP.NET ping waits for an unresponsive worker process before restarting it. The default is 5 seconds.
Threads	maxWorkerThreads	The maximum number of worker threads that each CPU can run; it must be in the range 5 to 100. The default is 25.
	maxIoThreads	The maximum number of IO threads that each CPU can run. It must be in the range 5 to 100. Default is 25.
Multi-CPU systems	webGarden	If true, the application works as a Web garden, and the operating system schedules CPU usage. If false, the cpuMask affects CPU usage.
	cpuMask	A bit-coded value that specifies which CPUs on a Multi-CPU system can run a copy of the worker process.
COM interaction	comAuthentication-Level	The authentication level for COM security; can be None, Connect (default), Call, Pkt, PktIntegrity, PktPrivacy, or Default.
	comImpersonation-Level	The COM impersonation level; can be Anonymous, Identify, Impersonate, Delegate, or Default.
Miscellaneous	clientConnected-Check	The period after which ASP.NET checks that the client for a queue request is still connected. An ASP.NET page can check whether the client is connected by using the Request.IsClientConnected property.
	requestQueueLimit	The number of requests allowed in the queue before ASP.NET returns a 503—Server Too Busy error. Default is 5000.
	serverErrorMessage-File	The file path to use instead of the default "Server Unavailable" message in the event of a fatal error; the file location is relative to the machine.config file or is an absolute path.
	logLevel	Specifies which application events must be recorded to the event log. It can be All, Errors (the default), or None.

Explicitly setting the userName attribute in the <processModel> tag helps you fix a problem that manifests itself when you install ASP.NET on a domain controller. The problem occurs because the operating system can't find a local account named machinename\ASPNET. In such circumstances, you should provide a specific user account for the ASP.NET worker process or use the System account. (The latter technique isn't recommended for security reasons, though.) For additional information, see Knowledge Base article Q315158 at *www.msdn.microsoft.com.*

For increased security, ASP.NET version 1.1 lets you store the actual user name and password in the registry in an encrypted form, and have the userName and password attributes point to the registry keys of your choice. For more information about this technique, see Knowledge Base article Q329290.

An ASP.NET application can use the ProcessModelInfo.GetCurrentProcessInfo shared method to get a reference to the ProcessInfo object that contains information about the running worker process:

```
' Get a reference to the current worker process.
Dim pi As ProcessInfo = ProcessModelInfo.GetCurrentProcessInfo
' Get information from the process.
Dim msg As String = "ProcessID = " & pi.ProcessID.ToString & "<br />"
msg &= "Status = " & pi.Status.ToString & "<br />"
msg &= "StartTime = " & pi.StartTime & "<br />"
msg &= "Age = " & pi.Age.ToString & "<br />"
msg &= "RequestCount = " & pi.RequestCount & "<br />"
msg &= "PeakMemoryUsed = " & pi.PeakMemoryUsed.ToString & "<br />"
' Display them in a Label control.
lblProcessInfo.Text = msg
```

You can also get a reference to a ProcessInfo object by means of the ProcessModelInfo.GetHistory method, which lets you access information for up to 100 of the last processes launched. For testing and debugging, you can even replace internal variables with your own values by means of the SetAll method. See the MSDN documentation for additional details.

If you're running ASP.NET over IIS 6.0 running in worker process isolation mode, ASP.NET applications honor only the maxWorkerThreads, maxIoThreads, and responseDeadlockInterval attributes. All other values are ignored, and the values specified in the IIS MMC snap-in for the application pool to which ASP.NET belongs are used instead. (See Figure 27-10.) The worker process isolation mode is the default setting for IIS 6, but you can revert to IIS 5 isolation mode for better backward compatibility from the Services tab of the Properties window that you display by right-clicking on the Web Sites folder in the MMC snap-in.

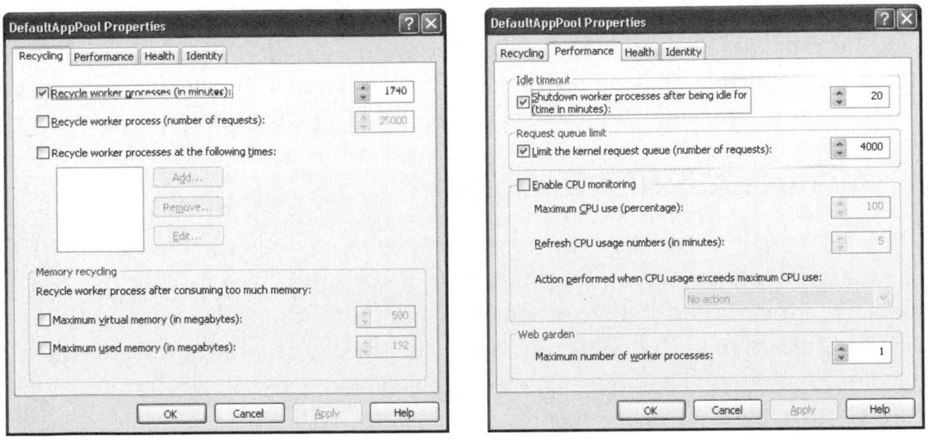

Figure 27-10 The Recycling and Performance tabs of the Properties window of an application pool in IIS 6.0

<securityPolicy>

This tag defines the mapping between named security levels and policy files:

```
<securityPolicy>
    <trustLevel name="value" policyFile="configfilename" />
</securityPolicy>
```

The machine.config file defines five security levels, which are named Full, High, Medium, Low, and Minimal. Each level corresponds to a security configuration file in the C:\Windows\Microsoft.Net\Framework\vx.y.zzzz\Config directory:

```
<securityPolicy>
  <trustLevel name="Full" policyFile="internal" />
  <trustLevel name="High" policyFile="web_hightrust.config" />
  <trustLevel name="Medium" policyFile="web_mediumtrust.config"/>
  <trustLevel name="Low" policyFile="web_lowtrust.config" />
  <trustLevel name="Minimal" policyFile="web_minimaltrust.config"/>
</securityPolicy>
```

This tag is used in conjunction with the <trust> tag, which is up next.

<trust>

This tag configures the code access security level applied to an ASP.NET application; it can appear in all types of configuration files:

```
<trust level="Full|High|Medium|Low|Minimal" originUrl="url" />
```

The level attribute defines the security zone under which the application runs and is one of the named security policies defined in the <securityPolicies> tag. The default is Full, which specifies that ASP.NET doesn't restrict security policy. You can learn more about this setting in the "Policy Level in ASP.NET Applications" section of Chapter 33.

Managing Multiple ASP.NET Versions

When you install ASP.NET on a system that has a previous version of ASP.NET installed, all existing applications are modified to run with the newer version. (This automatic update isn't performed if an application is bound to a more recent version or a version with a different major version number.) This means that all applications will use the machine.config file that comes with the new version; existing applications won't see any manual changes you made to a previous version's machine.config file, and you have to copy those changed sections to the newer version's configuration file manually.

It is possible to maintain different versions of ASP.NET on the same machine and bind each application to a specific version, a step that might be necessary if you find that a newer version breaks your existing code. The version used by each application corresponds to the aspnet_isapi.dll that handles requests for .aspx and other ASP.NET-related files in a given virtual directory of IIS. For example, HTTP requests for files in an application bound to version 1.1 of ASP.NET are handled by the aspnet_isapi.dll file in the C:\Windows\Microsoft.NET\Framework\v1.1.4322 folder. You can view these settings in the App Mappings page of the Application Configuration dialog box, which you can reach by clicking on the Configuration button of the Home Directory page in the Properties window of an IIS application.

By manually changing these settings, you can effectively decide which ASP.NET version an application is bound to, but this is a tedious and error-prone process. Fortunately, there is a simpler way. All ASP.NET installations come with a utility named aspnet_regiis.exe, which you can find in the C:\Windows\Microsoft.NET\Framework\vx.y.zzzz folder. To bind an application named MyApplication (and all applications in its subfolders) to version 1.0 of ASP.NET after you've installed version 1.1, locate the aspnet_regiis.exe utility in folder C:\Windows\Microsoft.NET\Framework\v1.0.3705 and run this command from the system prompt:

```
aspnet_regiis.exe /s W3SVC/1/ROOT/MyApplication
```

You can use the /sn option so as not to affect applications in nested folders. The aspnet_regiis utility is also useful to quickly reinstall ASP.NET if some of its files have been corrupted—for example, if you accidentally modify or delete the files in the C:\Inetpub\wwwroot\aspnet_client directory, which contains JavaScript scripts used to implement smart navigation and client-side validation:

```
aspnet_regiis.exe /i
```

This step is also required if you install IIS after the .NET Framework. (In Windows Server 2003, you can install ASP.NET from the Add or Remove Programs applet of the Control Panel.) You can quickly determine which versions are currently installed with the /lv option:

```
aspnet_regiis.exe /lv
```

For a complete list of all supported options, use the /? option or read the MSDN documentation.

Regardless of how many ASP.NET versions you've installed, all existing applications will use the StateServer service (for service-based sessions), the ASPState SQL Server database, and the ASP.NET user account installed by the latest version installed. If you later remove this version, the most recent version among those remaining on the computer is registered and used in its place.

> **See Also**   The document "ASP.NET Performance Counters.doc" on the companion CD contains a list of all the performance counters that ASP.NET applications and the ASP.NET runtime itself manage and that you can monitor to spot bottlenecks in your code.

This chapter completes the discussion of ASP.NET applications and their advanced features, such as session state, caching, and security. But I have yet to cover one ASP.NET-related topic: user controls. This is what the next chapter is all about.

28 User Controls and Custom Controls

The information in Chapter 24 through Chapter 27 is sufficient to help you create sophisticated Web Form applications, which use advanced features such as out-of-process sessions, caching, HTTP modules, and handlers. ASP.NET lets you trim development time and effort even more by letting you encapsulate and reuse pieces of UI functionality as well as business logic in user-defined controls. There are two types of reusable ASP.NET controls: *user* controls and *custom* controls:

- **User controls** are portions of HTML and script code stored in .ascx files. User controls are similar to .aspx files, and in fact you can easily convert a functioning .aspx page into a user control. ASP.NET compiles .ascx files on the fly the first time they're referenced from inside a page, which is similar to what happens to .aspx pages the first time they're requested by the client browser. User controls are also useful for implementing so-called *partial* or *fragment caching*, in which only the output from a portion of an .aspx page is cached.

- **Custom controls** are compiled components that can encapsulate complex functionality and contain simpler controls. Custom controls use inheritance to gain the functionality of a simpler class, such as Control, WebControl, or an existing Web control, such as the TextBox. Authoring custom controls is more complex than writing user controls, but custom controls let you precisely define what the browser receives.

Having two different types of user-defined controls to choose from can be confusing, and the fact that they have similar names surely doesn't help. As a general guideline, you should think of user controls as rather like subforms that contain multiple controls that you want to reuse in multiple pages or that produce HTML text that you want to cache separately from the remainder of the page that hosts them. Custom controls, on the other hand, are conceptually more similar to the custom controls that you can create for Windows Forms applications.

The ways that you deploy user controls and custom controls are very different. User controls are .ascx files (with an optional code-behind class in source or compiled format) that are part of the same ASP.NET application. Custom controls are usually deployed as compiled DLLs and can be installed in the global assembly cache (GAC) so that every ASP.NET application on the computer can use them.

> **Note** To keep the code as concise as possible, all the code samples in this chapter assume the use of the following Imports statements at the file or project level:
>
> ```
> Imports System.Collections.Specialized
> Imports System.Drawing
> Imports System.ComponentModel
> Imports System.Web.UI
> Imports System.Web.UI.WebControls
> ```

User Controls

Declarative user controls are the simplest user-defined controls that you can build for ASP.NET. User controls are similar to pages deployed in .aspx files in that they can contain a block of HTML text and controls, with the following differences:

- User controls are contained in .ascx files.

- User controls can't contain <html>, <body>, or <form> HTML tags because these tags are provided by the page that hosts the control.

- User controls can't contain the @Page directive. Instead they can contain the @Control directive, which takes a subset of the attributes of the @Page directive.

In a sense, user controls are the ASP.NET counterpart of classic ASP include files, except that they can encapsulate only user interface elements. No code element or procedure in a user control is accessible from the client .aspx page.

Your First User Control

To see how simple creating a User control is, let's author an .aspx page that has a group of controls on it, which we'll then convert to a user control.

Converting an .aspx Page to a User Control

For the example, I'll use the group of one Literal and four Button controls shown in Figure 28-1. These controls can be used to navigate through all the pages of a database query result. (You saw an example of paging techniques in the "Default and Custom Paging" section of Chapter 25.) Adding code behind the buttons is easy, but for now let's focus on the user interface.

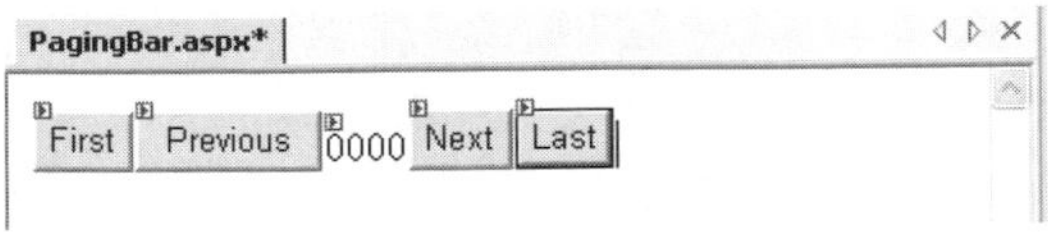

Figure 28-1 An .aspx page with five controls on it

This is the HTML code behind this .aspx page:

```
<%@ Page Language="vb" %>
<HTML>
  <HEAD><title>WebForm1</title></HEAD>
  <body>
    <form id="Form1" method="post" runat="server">
      <asp:Button id="btnFirst" runat="server" Text="First" />
      <asp:Button id="btnPrevious" runat="server" Text="Previous" />
      <asp:Literal id="litNumber" runat="server" Text="0000" />
      <asp:Button id="btnNext" runat="server" Text="Next" />
      <asp:Button id="btnLast" runat="server" Text="Last" />
    </form>
  </body>
</HTML>
```

To convert this page to a user control, you must convert the @Page directive into an @Control directive and delete everything except the controls inside the form. Here's the result of these transformations:

```
<%@ Control Language="vb" %>
<asp:Button id="btnFirst" runat="server" Text="First" />
<asp:Button id="btnPrevious" runat="server" Text="Previous" />
<asp:Literal id="litNumber" runat="server" Text="0000" />
<asp:Button id="btnNext" runat="server" Text="Next" />
<asp:Button id="btnLast" runat="server" Text="Last" />
```

Save this text in the PagingBar.ascx file, and you're done. You've written your first user control!

The .ascx file must be located in the same ASP.NET application as the .aspx pages that use it.

Writing a Test Page

You now need to reuse the control inside a page. Use Notepad to create the following text and save it in a file named TestPagingBar.aspx:

```
<%@ Page Language="vb" %>
<%@ Register TagPrefix="ProgVB" TagName="PagingBar" src="PagingBar.ascx" %>
<HTML>
  <body>
    <form id="Form1" method="post" runat="server">
      <ProgVB:PagingBar name="PagingBar1" runat="server" />
    </form>
  </body>
</HTML>
```

The @Register directive lets the page know that it contains a user control. The meaning of its three attributes is simple:

- The TagPrefix attribute specifies the prefix for the complete name of the user control. This prefix corresponds to the asp prefix in all ASP.NET control names, as in <asp:Label>, and should be a unique string that makes your control (or group of controls) different from any other user control you're likely to use on the same page. (For example, it can be your company name.)

- The TagName attribute specifies the second part of the complete name of the control, which is therefore in the form tagprefix:tagname.

- The Src attribute is the virtual path to the .ascx file that contains the user control.

Once you've registered the user control, you can use it anywhere in the page, exactly as you would any built-in ASP.NET control. If you navigate to this page, you'll see the PagingBar control in the browser. (See Figure 28-2.)

Notice that you can author .aspx and .ascx files with Notepad (or a regular HTML editor) and then import them into a Visual Studio .NET project. When you do so, Visual Studio detects that the new file has no class file associated with the .aspx or .ascx file and asks whether you want to create the new class. Click yes if you want to extend the user control with properties, methods, and event handlers.

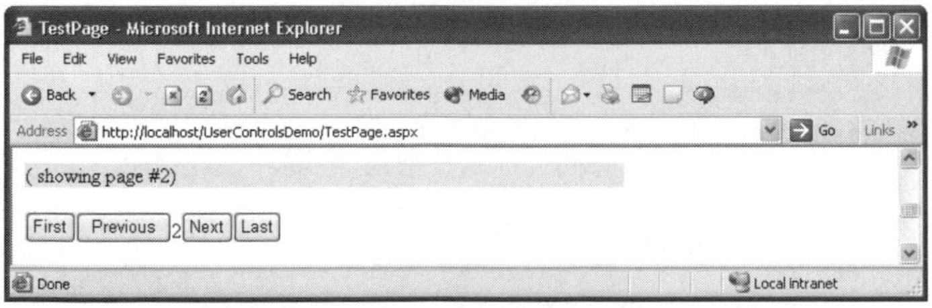

Figure 28-2   An .aspx page that hosts the PagingBar user control

Of course you can create multiple instances of the PagingBar control in the same page by inserting additional <ProgVB:PagingBar> elements. Even if you include multiple instances of the control, you still need a single @Register directive.

This first version of the user control can't do more than display itself because it doesn't expose any property to the outside and doesn't process clicks on the navigational buttons. You could implement all these features using a script inside the .ascx file, but I won't waste your time showing you how to do it because in real development you'd use Visual Studio .NET and its code-behind programming model. This is exactly what I'm showing you next.

User Controls in Visual Studio .NET

Creating a user control inside Visual Studio .NET requires that you abandon the simple approach that I showed you in the preceding section and adopt the code-behind programming model that you already use for .aspx forms.

Adding a Web User Control File

Create a new ASP.NET Web Forms application project, name it UserControlsDemo, and then choose Add Web User Control on the Project menu. Name the new file Paging-Bar.ascx, and click the Open button. Using the editor in design mode, re-create the controls shown in Figure 28-1 and assign them the following IDs (from left to right): btnFirst, btnPrevious, litPageNumber, btnNext, and btnLast. The UI portion of the user control is complete.

Next, create a Web Form file named TestPage.aspx—or just rename the default WebForm1.aspx file created with the project—and make sure that it's the start page for the project. You can create an instance of the user control on this form by simply dragging the PagingBar item from the Solution Explorer window. Unfortunately, the Visual Studio HTML editor isn't able to show you the actual appearance of the .ascx file, so it displays a gray rectangle labeled UserControl-PagingBar1. If you switch to the Properties window, you can change the PagingBar1 ID to something else and set its Visible and EnableViewState properties.

If you switch from Design to HTML view in the editor, you see that Visual Studio has added both the @Register directive and the actual control tag inside the form. This is an abridged version of the resulting HTML text:

```
<%@ Page Language="vb" AutoEventWireup="false" Codebehind="TestPage.aspx.vb"
    Inherits="UserControlsDemo.TestPage"%>
<%@ Register TagPrefix="uc1" TagName="PagingBar" src="PagingBar.ascx" %>
<HTML>
  <body>
    <form id="Form1" method="post" runat="server">
      <uc1:pagingbar id="PagingBar1" runat="server"></uc1:pagingbar>
    </form>
  </body>
</HTML>
```

If you don't like the uc1 tag prefix, you can change it to something else in the @Register directive—for example, ProgVB, provided that you also change the prefix in the start and end <uc1:pagingbar> tags. You need to change the prefix only once because all the other PagingBar controls added to the page from now on will use the new prefix.

To ensure that everything works as expected, run the project and make certain that the user control is correctly displayed in the TestPage.aspx page. This achieves the same result you got by working with Notepad, but now you can continue and add code to the user control's code-behind module.

Adding Code

Click anywhere on the PagingBar.ascx component, and choose Code on the View menu (or just press the F7 key) to display the PagingBar.ascx.vb code-behind module. This is an abridged version of the code you'll find in the editor:

```
Public MustInherit Class PagingBar
    Inherits System.Web.UI.UserControl

    Protected WithEvents btnLast As System.Web.UI.WebControls.Button
    Protected WithEvents btnNext As System.Web.UI.WebControls.Button
    Protected WithEvents btnPrevious As System.Web.UI.WebControls.Button
    Protected WithEvents litNumber As System.Web.UI.WebControls.Literal
    Protected WithEvents btnFirst As System.Web.UI.WebControls.Button

    Private Sub Page_Load(ByVal sender As Object, ByVal e As EventArgs) _
        Handles MyBase.Load
        ' Put user code to initialize the page here.
    End Sub
End Class
```

The code-behind class for a user control is similar to the code-behind class for a Web form, with one important difference: it inherits from UserControl instead of Page. Except for this detail, however, you write code in this class as you do in an .aspx page. For example, you can add a public property named PageNumber, manage the Click event handlers for the four buttons, and use them to change the Text property of the Literal control:

```
Const PageCount As Integer = 100

' The PageNumber property
Private m_PageNumber As Integer = 1

Public Property PageNumber() As Integer
    Get
        Return CInt(litNumber.Text)
    End Get
    Set(ByVal Value As Integer)
        ' Ensure that new value is in valid range.
        If Value >= 1 And Value <= PageCount Then
            litNumber.Text = Value.ToString
        End If
    End Set
End Property

Private Sub btnFirst_Click(ByVal sender As Object, ByVal e As EventArgs) _
    Handles btnFirst.Click
    PageNumber = 1
End Sub

Private Sub btnLast_Click(ByVal sender As Object, ByVal e As EventArgs) _
    Handles btnLast.Click
    PageNumber = PageCount
End Sub

Private Sub btnPrevious_Click(ByVal sender As Object, ByVal e As EventArgs) _
    Handles btnPrevious.Click
    PageNumber -= 1
End Sub

Private Sub btnNext_Click(ByVal sender As Object, ByVal e As EventArgs) _
    Handles btnNext.Click
    PageNumber += 1
End Sub
```

If you now run the application, you'll see that clicking on one of the four buttons actually causes a postback and that the number in the Literal control is updated correctly. The mechanism works because the user control receives the Click event for the button that was actually clicked. Notice that you *must* handle events from constituent controls inside the user control's code-behind class; you can't trap them from inside the host page.

A user control might need to cause a postback when a control other than a Button is clicked. For example, a user control containing a ListBox and a CheckBox control might cause a postback when the end user selects a new element in the ListBox or clicks on the CheckBox control. You can achieve this behavior by simply setting the AutoPostBack property for these constituent controls to True.

Saving Variables and Properties

The first version of the PagingBar user control needs to save only one piece of information between postbacks—that is, the value of the PageNumber property. In the preceding code snippet, I used a trick to have this information moved to the client and then back to the server: I stored it in the Text property of the litPageNumber control. This solution works, but it isn't elegant or efficient (because you have to convert a number to the string and back), and above all it doesn't work with properties that don't correspond to any user interface elements.

To see how to work around this issue, let's improve the user control by morphing the PageCount constant into a property of the same name. The value of this property—which doesn't correspond to any UI element—would be lost between postbacks, so I used the page's ViewState to preserve it.

```
' The PageCount property
Private m_PageCount As Integer = -1      ' An invalid value

Public Property PageCount() As Integer
    Get
        If m_PageCount < 0 Then
            ' Restore variables from the page's ViewState only
            ' the first time this property is read.
            Dim objValue As Object = Me.ViewState("PageCount")
            If Not (objValue Is Nothing) Then
                m_PageCount = CInt(objValue)
            Else
                m_PageCount = 100       ' Use a default value.
            End If
        End If
        Return m_PageCount
    End Get
    Set(ByVal Value As Integer)
        If Value >= 1 Then
            m_PageCount = Value
            ' Save in the page's ViewState as well.
            Me.ViewState("PageCount") = Value
        End If
    End Set
End Property
```

Of course, you can also leverage any other available technique for remembering values between postbacks. For example, session variables are a wise choice when you have to store a large amount of data and don't want to send it back and forth in the View-State dictionary. The problem with using session variables or cookies is that you must devise a naming mechanism that ensures that the names you select are unique for each instance of the control on the form.

Accessing the User Control from the Client Page

In a real application, the PageCount property must be initialized from inside the host page, but when you switch to the code module behind the TestPage.aspx page, you have an unpleasant surprise: you can't reference the PagingBar1 control as if it were a regular ASP.NET control such as a TextBox or a Button control.

You can easily observe another difference between user controls and regular controls. Drop any Web control on the TestPage.aspx—for example, a TextBox control—and then switch to the code module and expand the #Region block. You see that a variable pointing to the TextBox control has been automatically created for you:

```
Protected WithEvents TextBox1 As System.Web.UI.WebControls.TextBox
```

However, no similar variable exists for the PagingBar1 user control that you dropped from the Solution Explorer window. To reach the control programmatically, you must declare the variable yourself and initialize it by using a FindControl method. You can do this initialization from inside the Page_Load or the Page_Init event:

```
Protected WithEvents pbar As PagingBar

Private Sub Page_Load(ByVal sender As Object, ByVal e As EventArgs) _
    Handles MyBase.Load
    ' Get a reference to the PagingBar1 user control.
    pbar = DirectCast(FindControl("PagingBar1"), PagingBar)
    ' Now that you have a reference, you can access its members.
    If Not Me.IsPostBack Then
        pbar.PageCount = 50
    End If
End Sub
```

Creating the User Control Dynamically

A page can also load a user control dynamically by means of the LoadControl method of the Page object. A control added in this way becomes visible only when you add it to the Controls collection of the Page itself or of another control container. In practice, you often drop a PlaceHolder control on the page on which you want to insert the new control and add the user control to the PlaceHolder's Controls collection:

```
Protected WithEvents pbar2 As PagingBar

Private Sub Page_Load(ByVal sender As Object, ByVal e As EventArgs) _
    Handles MyBase.Load
    ⋮
```

```
          ' Add a new PagingBar control dynamically.
          pbar2 = DirectCast(LoadControl("PagingBar.ascx"), PagingBar)
          pbar2.PageCount = 25
          ' Insert it where the PlaceHolder control is now.
          PlaceHolder1.Controls.Add(pbar2)
End Sub
```

Keep in mind that controls added with LoadControl aren't automatically persisted in the page between postbacks. In other words, if you don't take precautions, those controls disappear when the page is posted back. For this reason, user controls are usually added dynamically from inside the Page_Load event handler, possibly after you've checked the state of other variables or controls. For example, you might have a Check-Box control on the page that determines whether one or more additional controls are to be loaded:

```
If chkShowAdditionalControls.Checked Then
    ' Add a new PagingBar control dynamically.
    pbar2 = DirectCast(LoadControl("PagingBar.ascx"), PagingBar)
    ' Insert it where the PlaceHolder control is now.
    PlaceHolder1.Controls.Add(pbar2)
End If
```

Raising Events in the Page

A user control can expose properties, methods, and events. You already saw how to implement properties (such as PageNumber and PageCount), and I won't discuss methods because you implement methods in user controls just as you do any other type of component. This leaves only the task of understanding how a user control can raise events.

In simpler cases, you implement events in a user control the same way that you implement them in other components. For example, the PagingBar control might expose a PageChanged event that the client page can trap to update its content when the user navigates to another page. You need only a handful of additional statements to implement this new feature: an Event statement and a RaiseEvent call when the value of the PageNumber property actually changes:

```
' ...(inside the .ascx file)...

Public Event PageChanged(ByVal sender As Object, ByVal e As EventArgs)

Public Property PageNumber() As Integer
    Get
        Return CInt(litNumber.Text.TrimStart)
    End Get
    Set(ByVal Value As Integer)
        If Value >= 1 And Value <= PageCount AndAlso Value <> PageNumber Then
            ' Update the state of the Literal and Button controls.
            litNumber.Text = Value.ToString
            UpdateButtonState()
            ' Let the parent form know that the page has changed.
```

```
            RaiseEvent PageChanged(Me, EventArgs.Empty)
        End If
    End Set
End Property

' Update buttons' state.
Sub UpdateButtonState()
    btnFirst.Enabled = (PageNumber > 1)
    btnPrevious.Enabled = (PageNumber > 1)
    btnNext.Enabled = (PageNumber < PageCount)
    btnLast.Enabled = (PageNumber < PageCount)
End Sub
```

In this case, you don't need to pass any additional information in the second argument, so you can declare it as an EventArgs object and pass the special EventArgs.Empty shared field in the call to RaiseEvent. Thanks to the WithEvents keyword in the variable declaration, the client page can trap the event exactly like any event from a regular Web control:

```
' ...(Inside the .aspx file)...

Private Sub pbar_PageChanged(ByVal sender As Object, _
    ByVal e As EventArgs) Handles pbar.PageChanged
    ' Display a new page of results.
    ' (Just update a Label control in this demo.)
    lblPageData.Text = "( showing page #" & pbar.PageNumber.ToString & " )"
End Sub
```

Run the demo application and check for yourself that the PageChanged event is fired when you click on a navigation button and that the lblPageData control on the page is correctly updated with the new page number.

In this particular case, using this simple way of raising events is acceptable because the PageChanged event is fired when the PageNumber property is modified, and this can happen only from inside the Click event of a navigation button. Because it's the event that causes the postback, the Click event is guaranteed to fire last after all other controls on the page have fired their own events and have been updated accordingly. When the property isn't updated from a postback event, however, you can't guarantee that this condition is met, and you would incur subtle bugs caused by the user control firing an event before all other controls have been updated. You'll learn how to avoid this problem in the "Raising Server-Side Events" section later in this chapter.

Fragment Caching

User controls let you leverage a great feature of ASP.NET: *partial* or *fragment caching*. This feature is the natural complement to page caching and the @OutputCache directive (which you read about in the "Page Caching" section in Chapter 26) in that it allows you to cache only selected portions of the page—that is, the HTML generated by the user control.

Caching with the @OutputCache Directive

To see when partial caching can be useful, consider the home page of a portal that displays weather information, local news, and stock quotes. Weather information is updated every hour, local news every five minutes, and stock quotes every two minutes. If you want to take advantage of page caching, you must have an @OutputCache directive with a Duration attribute set to two minutes (the lowest value of the three) or just one minute to avoid any delay in displaying local news (which otherwise would be updated after six minutes in some cases). This approach forces you to re-create several portions of the page even if no new content is available for that section.

Fragment caching enables you to solve this issue quite nicely: just encapsulate the different sections of the page in three user controls: one for weather information, another for local news, and a third for stock quotes. Each user control should contain an @OutputCache directive with a different value for its Duration attribute. For example, this is the directive for the weather.ascx file:

```
<%@ OutputCache Duration="3600" VaryByParam="*" %>
```

Everything I explained about the @OutputCache directives with pages applies when this directive is used inside an .ascx file, except that Location and VaryByHeader attributes aren't supported in user controls.

The @OutputCache directive in user controls supports a new attribute that isn't supported in pages: VaryByControl. This attribute can be assigned a semicolon-delimited list of the user control's properties, and the cached content is invalidated when any of the list properties takes a different value. The VaryByControl attribute is required if you omit the VaryByParam attribute:

```
<%@ OutputCache Duration="3600" VaryByControl="Name;Value" %>
```

Caching with the PartialCaching Attribute

You can also enable fragment caching by applying the PartialCaching attribute to the code-behind class of the user control. The constructor for this attribute takes either the value for the Duration attribute or the duration followed by the value for the VaryByParam, VaryByCustom, and VaryByControls properties:

```
' Cache the output of this user control for 1 minute.
<PartialCaching(60)> _
Public MustInherit Class MyUserControl
    Inherits System.Web.UI.UserControl
    ⋮
End Class

' Cache for 1 minute or until the Name or Value properties change.
<PartialCaching(60, "none", "Name;Value", "")> _
Public MustInherit Class MyUserControl2
    Inherits System.Web.UI.UserControl
    ⋮
End Class
```

Notice that the attribute's property is named VaryByControls (plural), whereas the corresponding directive attribute is named VaryByControl (singular).

Regardless of whether you use the @OutputCache directive or the PartialCaching attribute, you should pay a lot of attention when you use fragment caching in an application. For example, the user control's appearance isn't updated if the cached version is used, even if one or more properties have been assigned by code in the client page.

Custom Controls

User controls are fine when you can deploy your control as an .ascx and its code-behind class or when you want to reuse the HTML and the code in an .aspx page. For more powerful Web controls, you must switch to custom controls, which come in at least three flavors:

- Custom controls that extend an existing Web control with new properties, methods, events, or just a different behavior. In this case, you create a control class that inherits directly from the control to be extended.

- Custom controls that don't extend any existing Web control. In this case, you create a control class that inherits from either the Control or WebControl classes. (The latter class should be used for custom controls that expose a user interface and style attributes.)

- Custom controls that are made of two or more constituent controls, such as one TextBox and one ListBox control. In this case, you create a class that inherits from the Control class and creates all the constituent controls programmatically. Custom controls of this type are called composite controls.

Custom controls are harder to create than user controls but deliver more power and flexibility and are especially suited for highly dynamic output. For example, you need to deploy just one copy of the compiled custom control in the GAC to make it usable by all the ASP.NET applications running on the computer. (By comparison, you must deploy an .ascx file with each application that uses it.) Additionally, Visual Studio .NET offers better design-time support for custom controls. You can add a custom control to Visual Studio's Toolbox and actually see how the control is rendered on an .aspx page at design time—two things that you can't do with user controls.

Your First Custom Control

Visual Studio .NET makes creating a custom control an easy task. Just carefully follow this sequence of actions:

1. Create a new project of type Web Control Library. To match the code that follows, you should name the project CustomControlLibrary. (See Figure 28-3.)

2. Delete the WebCustomControl1.vb module that Visual Studio created.

3. Choose Add New Item on the Project menu. In the Add New Item dialog box, select Web Custom Control in the Templates list; name the new module FirstControl.vb, and click Open. (After you become familiar with custom controls, you'll be able to customize the default WebCustomControl1 module instead of creating a new one.)

The module just created in the Solution Explorer implements a functioning custom control that mimics a Label control. In following sections, you'll learn how to make it more interesting and useful, but for now let's see how you can add this control to the Toolbox and then drop it on an .aspx page.

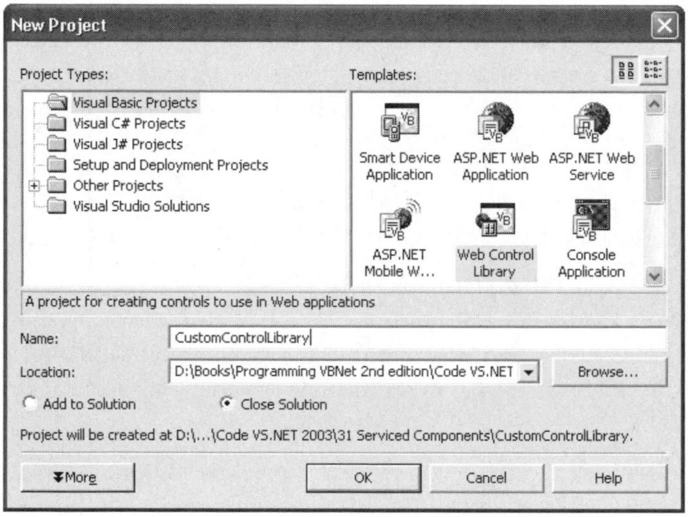

Figure 28-3   Creating a Web Control Library project

4. Compile the CustomControlLibrary project by selecting Build Solution on the Build menu. This action creates the CustomControlLibrary.dll file in the \bin directory under the main project directory.

5. Point to Add Project on the File menu, and click New Project. Create an ASP.NET Web Forms Application project named CustomControlsDemo in the same solution. Right-click the project in the Solution Explorer window, and click Set As StartUp Project on the shortcut menu.

6. Right-click the Toolbox, and click Add Tab on the shortcut menu to create a new tab for all the custom controls you're going to create. Name this new tab Custom Controls or whatever you like.

7. Right-click in the new tab in the Toolbox, and click Add/Remove Items on the shortcut menu. In the Customize Toolbox dialog box, click the .NET Framework Components tab, click Browse, and select the CustomControlLibrary.dll file that you compiled earlier; this action imports all the controls contained in the DLL—only FirstControl, in this example—into the list of components. (See Figure 28-4.) Click OK to add the FirstControl to the Toolbox.

8. Drag the FirstControl item from the Toolbox to the WebForm1.aspx page in the CustomControlsDemo project, as you'd do with a built-in Web control. The First-Control appears on the page as a Label. Switch to the Properties window to assign a string to its Text property and see how the new string is immediately rendered on the .aspx page.

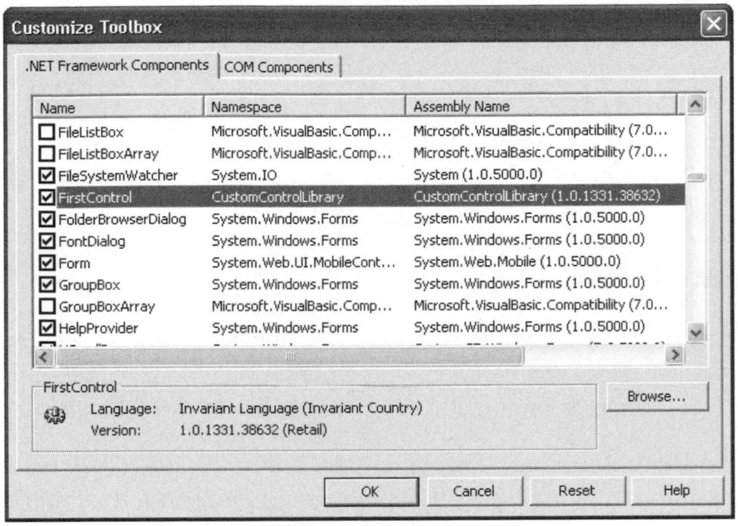

Figure 28-4   Adding the FirstControl custom control to the Toolbox

The Render Method

Let's have a look at the source code that Visual Studio created for the FirstControl class:

```
<DefaultProperty("Text"), _
    ToolboxData("<{0}:FirstControl runat=server></{0}:FirstControl>")> _
Public Class FirstControl
    Inherits System.Web.UI.WebControls.WebControl

    Dim _text As String

    <Bindable(True), Category("Appearance"), DefaultValue("")> _
    Property [Text]() As String
        Get
            Return _text
        End Get
        Set(ByVal Value As String)
            _text = Value
        End Set
    End Property

    Protected Overrides Sub Render(ByVal output As HtmlTextWriter)
        output.Write([Text])
    End Sub
End Class
```

The Render method is the means by which the control generates its own appearance. This method is inherited from the WebControl base class and is invoked by the ASP.NET infrastructure when the control must render itself as HTML text. By overriding this method, you're actually in control of exactly how the control appears on the client page. For example, let's have the FirstControl render itself as a button with a given caption:

```
Protected Overrides Sub Render(ByVal output As HtmlTextWriter)
    ' Pay attention to (repeated) double quotes in the string below.
    output.Write("<input type=""button"" Value=""" & [Text] & """>")
End Sub
```

Now that you have a broad idea of how a custom control works, let's focus on the main classes and interfaces you'll have to become familiar with to get the most out of custom controls.

The HtmlTextWriter Class

The argument passed to the Render method is an HtmlTextWriter object. As its name suggests, it's an auxiliary class that can help you write formatted HTML text. In practice, however, the support it offers is minimal; it does very little that you wouldn't do manually.

Its main methods are Write and WriteLine, which output raw HTML text to the stream. You can write an open tag with WriteBeginTag and close it with WriteEndTag, as in:

```
output.WriteBeginTag("textarea")
output.Write("Type a comment in this box")
output.WriteEndTag("textarea")
```

The HtmlTextWriter class offers better support when you have to write nested tags. In that case, you output the open tag using the RenderBeginTag method and close it with the RenderEndTag method. The latter method doesn't take an argument because the HtmlTextWriter remembers the most recent open tag. The following code is taken from the TableControl demo included on the companion CD:

```
' Output an HTML table.
Public Rows As Integer = 3
Public Columns As Integer = 4

Protected Overrides Sub Render(ByVal output As HtmlTextWriter)
    output.RenderBeginTag("table")
    For r As Integer = 1 To Rows
        output.RenderBeginTag("tr")
        For c As Integer = 1 To Columns
            output.RenderBeginTag("td")
            output.Write(r.ToString & "," & c.ToString)
            output.RenderEndTag()        ' </td>
        Next
        output.RenderEndTag()            ' </tr>
    Next
    output.RenderEndTag()                ' </table>
End Sub
```

The AddAttribute method outputs the name and value of an attribute. Its peculiarity is that you must invoke it *before* the RenderBeginTag method that outputs the main tag:

```
' These statements output this html: <table border="1">
output.AddAttribute("border", "1")
output.RenderBeginTag("table")
```

The HtmlTextWriter doesn't indent its result automatically, but it offers an Indent property that specifies how many tab characters are added at the beginning of any new line. These tab characters are added only after a WriteLine method. Let's see how to revise the code snippet seen previously to create the indented text for an HTML table. Added statements are in boldface:

```
Protected Overrides Sub Render(ByVal output As HtmlTextWriter)
    output.AddAttribute("border", "1")
    output.RenderBeginTag("table")
    output.WriteLine()
    output.Indent += 1
    For r As Integer = 1 To Rows
        output.RenderBeginTag("tr")
        output.WriteLine()
        output.Indent += 1
        For c As Integer = 1 To Columns
            output.RenderBeginTag("td")
            output.Write(r.ToString & "," & c.ToString)
            output.RenderEndTag()
            output.WriteLine()
        Next
        output.Indent -= 1
        output.RenderEndTag()
        output.WriteLine()
    Next
    output.Indent -= 1
    output.RenderEndTag()
End Sub
```

Figure 28-5 shows how the table appears to the end user. The following is the HTML source code received by the browser:

```
<table border="1">
    <tr>
        <td>1,1</td>
        <td>1,2</td>
        ⋮
    </tr>
    <tr>
        <td>2,1</td>
        <td>2,2</td>
        ⋮
</table>
```

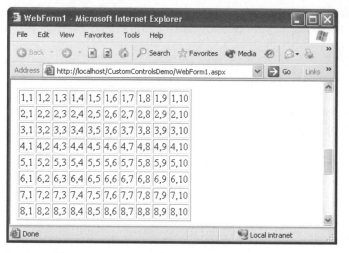

Figure 28-5   A custom control that produces an HTML table

The Control and WebControl Classes

As explained previously, a custom control can inherit from the System.Web.UI.Control class when it exposes a simple user interface or no UI at all. You should be familiar with most of the members of this class, such as Visible, ViewState, EnableViewState, and the Controls collection. There are three properties that affect the identifier used for the control: ID is the (writeable) identifier assigned to the control, and must be set to enable server-side access to the control; UniqueID is the unique, hierarchically qualified identifier assigned to this control; ClientID is the read-only ID assigned to the control by ASP.NET and can be used to reference the control in client-side scripts.

Most of the time, however, you'll inherit your custom control from the System.Web.UI.WebControls.WebControl base class, which offers more support to controls that have a rich user interface. The WebControl class inherits from Control and adds UI-related properties, such as ForeColor, BackColor, Font, Width, Height, BorderStyle, BorderWidth, BorderColor, Style, Enabled, and Attributes. It also adds a few methods, whose meaning will become clear in the following sections.

Improving the Custom Control

You can create functioning controls by applying what you've learned so far, but of course there's a lot more to know. For example, you need to know how your control can participate in postback events and how it can expose events to its client page.

Adding Properties

You can add properties to a custom control as you do with any other class—that is, by implementing a Property procedure. You typically prefix the Property procedure with a Description attribute, which sets the text that appears in Visual Studio's Properties window:

```
Dim m_Rows As Integer = 3

<Description("The number of rows")> _
Property Rows() As Integer
    Get
        Return m_Rows
    End Get
    Set(ByVal Value As Integer)
        If Value > 0 Then
            m_Rows = Value
        End If
    End Set
End Property
```

Other common attributes are DefaultValue (the initial value of the property), Category (the category it belongs to in the Properties window), and Bindable (True, if the property can be bound to a data source):

```
<Bindable(True), Category("Appearance"), DefaultValue(3), _
  Description("The number of rows")> _
Property Rows() As Integer
    ⋮
End Property
```

Remember that Visual Studio uses the DefaultValue attribute only to decide whether the property value should be marked as modified (in bold) in the Properties window, but it's up to you to correctly initialize the property to the given value.

By default, all the properties you inherit from Control and WebControl classes appear in the Properties window, but sometimes you won't like this behavior. For example, let's say that your control has a fixed white background color and you don't want to allow users to change it. You can't remove the BackColor property from the class interface of your control, but at least you can override it to apply a Browsable attribute that hides it in the Properties window and to nullify any assignment to it done programmatically:

```
<Browsable(False)> _
Overrides Property BackColor() As Color
    Get
        ' Always return white.
        Return Color.White
    End Get
    Set(ByVal Value As Color)
        ' Ignore this assignment.
    End Set
End Property
```

The properties that you set for an ASP.NET control in the Properties window are actually translated to attributes inside the .aspx file. For example, the TableControl demo stores the values of the Rows and Columns properties in the .aspx file, as follows:

```
<ccl:TableControl id="TableControl1" runat="server"
    Width="72px" Height="33px" Columns="10" Rows="8">
</ccl:TableControl>
```

Because all your custom properties are ultimately translated to text, you should know more about how this translation is carried out. In general, properties that return a primitive type (Boolean, numeric, date, and String) are translated to text as you'd expect and never create any problems.

ASP.NET works well also with enumerated properties. It stores their textual value in the page if you set the property from the Properties window, but it's also able to parse a new value that you enter directly in the HTML editor. For example, let's add a property that returns a BorderStyle enumerated value:

```
Dim m_CellBorderStyle As BorderStyle

<Description("The border style of table cells")> _
Property CellBorderStyle() As BorderStyle
    Get
        Return m_CellBorderStyle
    End Get
    Set(ByVal Value As BorderStyle)
        m_CellBorderStyle = Value
    End Set
End Property
```

This is how this property is rendered in the .aspx page:

```
<ccl:TableControl id="TableControl1" runat="server" Width="72px" Height="33px"
    Columns="10" Rows="8" CellBorderStyle="Dotted">
</ccl:TableControl>
```

You can now modify the CellBorderStyle attribute and enter another valid enumeration value—for example, Double or Inset—and it's correctly recognized when you switch the editor back to Design mode. If you type a value that doesn't correspond to any element in the enum type, you get a parsing error.

ASP.NET also supports a special syntax for object properties in the format *propertyname-membername*. For example, you can set the Bold and Size members of the Font property as follows:

```
<ccl:TableControl id="TableControl1" runat="server"
    Font-Bold="True" Font-Size="Larger">
</ccl:TableControl>
```

This behavior is applied to your custom object properties as well. For example, let's say that you define the following class:

```
Public Class CellStyle
    Dim m_ForeColor As Color
    Dim m_BackColor As Color

    Property ForeColor() As Color
        Get
            Return m_ForeColor
        End Get
        Set(ByVal Value As Color)
            m_ForeColor = Value
        End Set
    End Property

    Property BackColor() As Color
        Get
            Return m_BackColor
        End Get
        Set(ByVal Value As Color)
            m_BackColor = Value
        End Set
    End Property
End Class
```

The custom control can implement a CellStyle property that returns an instance of the preceding class:

```
    ' ...(inside the TableControl.vb module)...

    Dim m_CellStyle As New CellStyle()

    Property CellStyle() As CellStyle
        Get
            Return m_CellStyle
        End Get
        Set(ByVal Value As CellStyle)
            m_CellStyle = Value
        End Set
    End Property
```

Thanks to ASP.NET support for object properties, you can now set the CellStyle property in the HTML editor as follows:

```
<ccl:TableControl id="TableControl1" runat="server"
    CellStyle-ForeColor="black" CellStyle-BackColor="yellow">
</ccl:TableControl>
```

Notice, however, that you can't edit the CellStyle property in the Properties window because Visual Studio doesn't know how to display an object property unless it's associated with a TypeConverter object. Many .NET Framework objects—for example, Size and FontInfo—are associated with a TypeConverter and that's why they can be edited in the Properties window. (You can learn more about type converters in Chapter 18.) Interestingly, if you define a custom property that returns one of these standard .NET objects, your property can also be set from inside the Properties window. For example, consider a property that returns a FontInfo object:

```
' The CellFont property
Dim m_CellFont As FontInfo = MyBase.Font

Property CellFont() As FontInfo
    Get
        Return m_CellFont
    End Get
    Set(ByVal Value As FontInfo)
        m_CellFont = Value
    End Set
End Property
```

Because this property returns a FontInfo object, it's correctly rendered in the Properties window. (See Figure 28-6.) You can read the "Object Properties" section in Chapter 18 to learn how you can implement a TypeConverter for properties that return a user-defined class.

Figure 28-6 The CellFont property is displayed correctly in the Properties window, but the CellStyle property isn't because it has no associated TypeConverter.

Occasionally, you might want to display a special editor for your properties, even if they don't return an object. The ImageUrl property of the Image control is a good example of this concept. It's a plain String property, but it lets you select the target file using a special editor. (See Figure 28-7.) Although implementing a custom property editor isn't a breeze, you can often "borrow" one that's already defined in the .NET Framework and applied using the Editor attribute, as in this code:

```
' The full name of the assembly depends on the installed .NET version.
<EditorAttribute("System.Web.UI.Design.ImageUrlEditor, System.Design, " _
    & "Version=1.0.5000.0, Culture=neutral, " _
    & "PublicKeyToken=b03f5f7f11d50a3a", _
    GetType(System.Drawing.Design.UITypeEditor))> _
Property ImageUrl As String
    ⋮
End Property
```

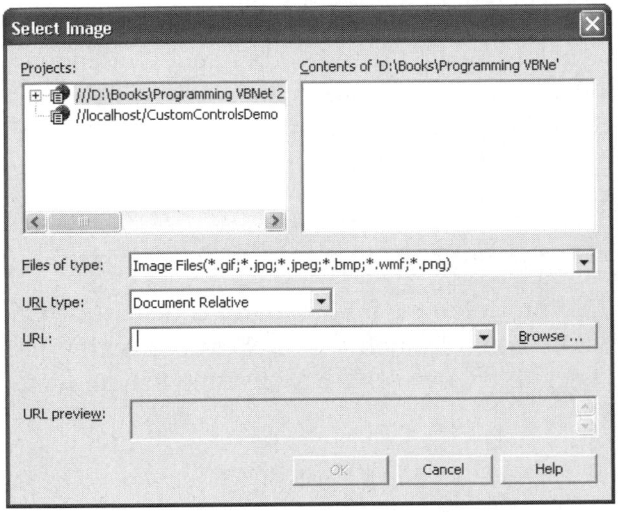

Figure 28-7   You can easily associate your properties with existing custom editors.

It's unfortunate that the object browser that comes with Visual Studio .NET 2003 doesn't display attributes associated with types and members. However, you can retrieve this information with ILDASM (even if the output format isn't always easily readable) or a third-party object browser. Or just leave the previous version of Visual Studio .NET on your hard disk.

You can associate many other common properties with existing editors. A great example is the Items property of the ListBox and DropDownList controls, which returns a ListItemCollection object:

```
<Editor("System.Web.UI.Design.WebControls.ListItemsCollectionEditor, " _
    & "System.Design, Version=1.0.5000.0, Culture=neutral, " _
    & "PublicKeyToken=b03f5f7f11d50a3a", _
    & "GetTypeSystem.Drawing.Design.UITypeEditor,System.Drawing)> _
Property Items() As ListItemsCollection
    ⋮
End Property
```

> **Note**   In general, you can apply to ASP.NET custom controls most of the attributes and design-time techniques I explored for Windows Forms control in Chapter 18.

Rendering Style Attributes

If your control inherits from WebControl, it exposes several properties related to the user interface, such as Font, ForeColor, and BackColor. In the Render method you should output these values as attributes of the main tag in an orderly fashion, with multiple calls to the AddAttribute or AddStyleAttribute methods of the HtmlTextWriter object. To keep the HTML sent to the client as slim as possible, you should output those properties only if they're different from their default value.

The WebControl class offers a helper method called AddAttributesToRender, which lets you render all the attributes that have a nondefault value with a single call. To show this method in action, I prepared a ComboBoxEx custom control, which is similar to a DropDownList control but exposes an ItemList property that takes a comma-delimited list of elements in the control:

```
ComboBoxEx1.ItemList = "First,Second,Third"
```

(See the demo program on the companion CD for the source code of the ItemList property.) Because the ComboBoxEx control inherits from WebControl, the user can set properties such as Width or BackColor. Let's have a look at the Render method of this custom control:

```
Protected Overrides Sub Render(ByVal output As HtmlTextWriter)
    ' Output the <select> tag and its attributes.
    output.AddAttribute("name", Me.ID)
    Me.AddAttributesToRender(output)
    output.RenderBeginTag("select")

    ' Split the elements in an array.
    Dim items() As String = ItemList.Split(","c)
    For index As Integer = 0 To items.Length - 1
        ' Prepare the Value attribute, equal to the element index.
        output.AddAttribute("value", index.ToString)
        ' If this is the selected element, add "selected" attribute.
        If index = SelectedIndex Then
            output.AddAttribute("selected", "selected")
        End If
        ' Output the <option> tag.
        output.RenderBeginTag("option")
        output.Write(items(0))
        output.RenderEndTag()
    Next
    output.RenderEndTag()          ' Close the </select> tag.
End Sub
```

(Notice that the name attribute must be added separately and should be taken from the UniqueID property.) This is the HTML rendered to the browser when the user selects a nondefault value for the BackColor property:

```
<select name="cboItems" id="cboItems"
        style="background-color:#C0FFFF;width:217px;">
  <option value="1">First</option>
```

```
    <option value="2">Second</option>
    <option value="3">Third</option>
</select>
```

Handling Postback Data

The ComboBoxEx custom control displays its contents with the correct style attributes but still lacks an important feature: it doesn't remember the SelectedIndex property between postbacks. To see what I mean, place a ComboBoxEx and a Button control on the form, run the program, select the second element in the ComboBoxEx control, and click on the push control. This action causes a postback, but in the page now returned to the browser the ComboBoxEx control displays the first (default) item.

To correctly implement the behavior of the control during postbacks, you must do two things:

■ Preserve property values between callbacks, which you do by storing them in the ViewState collection.

■ Implement the IPostBackDataHandler interface to receive a notification when a postback occurs.

You already know how to store control properties between postbacks, so this code shouldn't look new to you:

```
' The SelectedIndex property
Property SelectedIndex() As Integer
    Get
        ' If not a postback, the value isn't in the ViewState collection.
        Dim objValue As Object = Me.ViewState("SelectedIndex")
        If objValue Is Nothing Then
            Return 0              ' The default value
        Else
            Return CInt(objValue)
        End If
    End Get
    Set(ByVal Value As Integer)
        If Value >= 0 Then
            Me.ViewState("SelectedIndex") = Value
        End If
    End Set
End Property
```

The IPostBackDataHandler interface exposes only two methods, LoadPostData and RaisePostDataChangedEvent. For now let's focus on LoadPostData, the more important of the two. ASP.NET calls this method when a postback occurs and passes it the post collection that the form posted to itself:

```
Public Function LoadPostData(ByVal postDataKey As String, _
    ByVal postCollection As NameValueCollection) As Boolean _
    Implements IPostBackDataHandler.LoadPostData
    :
End Function
```

Understanding how the postCollection argument is built is crucial. All ASP.NET forms use the POST action method and send the values of all the controls on the form in the request header. The postCollection argument passed to the LoadPostData method contains the name and value pairs posted with the form, and the postDataKey argument is the key of the element in this collection that contains the new value of your custom control. (This argument is equal to the control's ID.)

The value being posted back in the collection for the ComboBoxEx custom control is the value associated with the element that's currently selected in the combo box. Because each element in our custom combo box has a value equal to its index in the list, we can take this value from the collection and assign it to the SelectedIndex property:

```
Public Function LoadPostData(ByVal postDataKey As String, _
    ByVal postCollection As NameValueCollection) As Boolean _
    Implements IPostBackDataHandler.LoadPostData
    ' The posted value is equal to the index of the selected element.
    SelectedIndex = CInt(postCollection(postDataKey))
End Function

Public Sub RaisePostDataChangedEvent() _
    Implements IPostBackDataHandler.RaisePostDataChangedEvent
    ' Nothing to do for now.
End Sub
```

If you now rebuild the ComboBoxEx control and run the demo application (or just run the complete project in the companion code), you'll see that the SelectedIndex property is correctly preserved between postbacks and that the ComboBoxEx control works as expected. You might have noticed that the RaisePostDataChangedEvent method of the IPostBackDataHandler interface is left empty. The purpose of this method will become clear in the next section.

Raising Server-Side Events

The ComboBoxEx control still lacks a SelectedIndexChanged event. You already know how to declare an event in a class:

```
Event SelectedIndexChanged(ByVal sender As Object, ByVal e As EventArgs)
```

The next step is to raise the event when the SelectedIndex property changes. You might be tempted to do this from inside the Set block in the SelectedIndex property procedure or from the LoadPostData event if you detect that a new value is being assigned to the SelectedIndex property. However, as I explained in the "Raising Events in the Page" section earlier in this chapter, this technique can create subtle bugs because the client page can receive the event before all controls on the page have been completely updated after the postback. For example, the code in the event handler might use the SelectedIndex property of another ComboBoxEx control and would get the wrong value if that control hadn't processed its own LoadPostData method yet.

The purpose of the second method in the IPostBackDataHandler interface is to avoid this kind of problem. Here's how it works:

When the page is posted back, ASP.NET calls the LoadPostData method of all the controls that have a value in the post collection and remembers the Boolean value that this method returns. When this first round of calls is completed, ASP.NET calls the Raise-PostDataChangedEvent method of those controls whose LoadPostData method returned True. The code in the LoadPostData method should compare the new value of the property (as taken from the post collection) with the previous value of the same property (as retrieved from the ViewState collection) and return True if the two values differ. Here's a new implementation of the LoadPostData method that follows these guidelines:

```
Public Function LoadPostData(ByVal postDataKey As String, _
    ByVal postCollection As NameValueCollection) As Boolean _
    Implements IPostBackDataHandler.LoadPostData
    ' The posted value is equal to the index of the selected element.
    Dim newSelectedIndex As Integer = CInt(postCollection(postDataKey))
    If SelectedIndex <> newSelectedIndex Then
        ' If the new value is different, store it in the property.
        SelectedIndex = newSelectedIndex
        ' Tell ASP.NET to call the RaisePostDataChangedEvent method.
        Return True
    End If
End Function
```

The code in the RaisePostDataChangedEvent method could contain the RaiseEvent statement. However, if you want to allow other developers to derive from your ComboBoxEx control, you should delegate that action to an On*xxxx* method, as in the following example:

```
Public Sub RaisePostDataChangedEvent() _
    Implements IPostBackDataHandler.RaisePostDataChangedEvent
    OnSelectedIndexChanged(EventArgs.Empty)
End Sub

Protected Overridable Sub OnSelectedIndexChanged(ByVal e As EventArgs)
    RaiseEvent SelectedIndexChanged(Me, e)
End Sub
```

Now you can finally trap the SelectedIndexChanged event in the client page as you'd do for a standard DropDownList control:

```
' ...(Inside the client .aspx page)...

Private Sub cboItems_SelectedIndexChanged(ByVal sender As Object, _
    ByVal e As EventArgs) Handles cboItems.SelectedIndexChanged
    ' Update a Label with the new value of the SelectedIndex property.
    lblMessage.Text = "Element index = " & cboItems.SelectedIndex.ToString
End Sub
```

Generating Postback Events

The ComboBoxEx control is getting closer to a standard DropDownList control, but it still lacks the ability to perform postback events as the standard control does when you set its AutoPostBack property to True. Adding this property to a custom control is relatively simple, but before looking at the actual implementation, let's see how the Auto-PostBack property is implemented in a standard DropDownList control.

Try this simple experiment: create a Web form, drop a DropDownList control on it, add a couple of elements to its Items collection, set the control's AutoPostBack property to True, run the project, and see what source code the browser receives (here in a concise version):

```
<form name="Form1" method="post" action="WebForm1.aspx" id="Form1">
<input type="hidden" name="__EVENTTARGET" value="" />
<input type="hidden" name="__EVENTARGUMENT" value="" />
<input type="hidden" name="__VIEWSTATE" value="dDw5NTg1OTIyODQ7OZ4=" />

<script language="javascript">
<!--
    function __doPostBack(eventTarget, eventArgument) {
        var theform;
        if (window.navigator.appName.toLowerCase().indexOf("netscape") > -1) {
            theform = document.forms["Form1"];
        }
        else {
            theform = document.Form1;
        }
        theform.__EVENTTARGET.value = eventTarget.split("$").join(":");
        theform.__EVENTARGUMENT.value = eventArgument;
        theform.submit();
    }
// -->
</script>

<select name="DropDownList1" id="DropDownList1" style="width:105px;"
    onchange="__doPostBack('DropDownList1','')" language="javascript" >
    <option value="one">one</option>
    <option value="two">two</option>
</select>
</form>
```

A few things should draw your attention in the preceding code. The form contains two new hidden fields named __EVENTTARGET and __EVENTARGUMENT as well as Java-Script function named __doPostBack, which saves its two arguments in the hidden fields and programmatically causes a postback. In addition, the <select> tag (which renders the original DropDownList controls) contains an onchange attribute that points to the __doPostBack routine and passes it a reference to itself (the DropDownList1 name) and an empty argument.

Even if you aren't an expert in client-side JavaScript programming, it should be clear how the AutoPostBack feature works: when the user selects a new element in the

DropDownList control, the onchange attribute causes the __doPostBack routine to run. This routine loads the control name into the __EVENTTARGET field, loads the second argument (a null string in this case) in the __EVENTARGUMENT field, and submits the form via code. When the request gets to the server, the ASP.NET infrastructure can check the value of the __EVENTTARGET field and, if the field isn't empty, ASP.NET can determine which control caused the postback.

Of all the additional elements on the page—the hidden fields, the JavaScript routine, and the attribute in the HTML tag—you only have to care about the onchange attribute in the <select> tag. ASP.NET adds the hidden fields and the JavaScript routine automatically if it recognizes that one or more controls on the form rely on the AutoPostBack feature. The only necessary condition for this to happen is that you use the Page.GetPostBackEvent-Reference method when you build the HTML attribute, as I'll explain in a moment.

Let's start by correctly implementing the AutoPostBack property. This step is simple because this code does nothing but save and restore the value of the property from the ViewState collection:

```
' The AutoPostBack property
Property AutoPostBack() As Boolean
    Get
        Dim objValue As Object = Me.ViewState("AutoPostBack")
        If objValue Is Nothing Then
            Return False
        Else
            Return CBool(objValue)
        End If
    End Get
    Set(ByVal Value As Boolean)
        Me.ViewState("AutoPostBack") = Value
    End Set
End Property
```

We can now focus on the code that emits the onchange attribute from inside the Render method. You need to add only four lines of code to implement this feature:

```
Protected Overrides Sub Render(ByVal output As HtmlTextWriter)
    ' Output the <select> tag and its attributes.
    output.AddAttribute("name", Me.UniqueID)
    Me.AddAttributesToRender(output)
    ' Split the elements in an array.
    Dim items() As String = ItemList.Split(","c)

    ' If this control requires AutoPostBack
    If Me.AutoPostBack Then
        output.AddAttribute("onchange", Page.GetPostBackEventReference(Me))
        output.AddAttribute("language", "javascript")
    End If

    ' ...(The remainder of the routine is unchanged.)...
End Sub
```

This code works as expected because it uses the GetPostBackEventReference method of the Page object. This method does two things. The first and the most evident is that it returns a string in the format expected by the onchange attribute, as in

```
onchange="__doPostBack('clientsidename','')"
```

where *clientsidename* is the client-side ID of the control. (It corresponds to the ClientID property.) In addition to returning this string, the GetPostBackEventReference method remembers that it has been called by a control in the page so that ASP.NET can output the two hidden fields and the JavaScript code of the __doPostBack routine when it sends the page back to the client browser. This method ensures that only one routine and one pair of hidden fields are created, regardless of how many controls on the page have their AutoPostBack property set to True.

The GetPostBackEventReference method takes a control reference in its first argument and a string in its second (optional) argument. The second argument is the string stored in the __EVENTARGUMENT field when the postback occurs. For simpler controls, you can leave this argument blank, but sometimes you need this additional argument to figure out which operation should be performed on callback. I'll show an example of a custom control that uses this feature in the next section.

Handling Postback Events

In many cases, controls that expose the AutoPostBack property should also implement the IPostBackEventHandler interface. This interface contains only one method, Raise-PostBackEvent, which ASP.NET invokes when the postback actually occurs. There are two main reasons why you should implement this interface:

- Your control must raise a particular server-side event—say, Click—when it causes a postback.

- Your control must access the value contained in the __EVENTARGUMENT field— that is, the second argument passed to the __doPostBack function.

Extending the ComboBoxEx control to fire a Click event when it causes a postback is simple. You only have to define the event, raise the event from inside an overridable OnClick procedure, and call this OnClick routine from inside the IPostBack-EventHandler.RaisePostBackEvent method:

```
Public Class ComboBoxEx
    Inherits System.Web.UI.WebControls.WebControl
    Implements IPostBackDataHandler, IPostBackEventHandler
    :
    Public Event Click As EventHandler

    Public Sub RaisePostBackEvent(ByVal eventArgument As String) _
        Implements IPostBackEventHandler.RaisePostBackEvent
        ' Invoke the (overridable) procedure that fires the event
```

```
        ' when this control causes a postback.
        OnClick(EventArgs.Empty)
    End Sub

    Protected Overridable Sub OnClick(ByVal e As EventArgs)
        ' Raise the server-side Click event.
        RaiseEvent Click(Me, e)
    End Sub
End Class
```

In the next example, I'll show you a custom control that uses both arguments of the __doPostBack procedure and therefore needs to implement the IPostBack-EventHandler interface. This new custom control, named NavigateRibbon, is similar to the PagingBar user control that you saw earlier in this chapter, but it uses hyperlinks instead of buttons. (See Figure 28-8.)

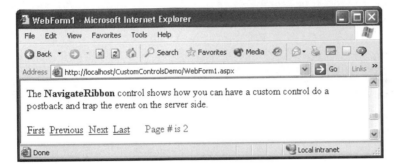

Figure 28-8   The NavigateRibbon custom control

In general, you can't use plain <A HREF="url"> tags when working with custom controls because a click on these hyperlinks doesn't post the values in the form's fields. However, the solution is easy—let the __doPostBack routine perform the post for you:

```
<A HREF="javascript:__doPostBack('NavigateRibbon1', 'first')">First</A>
```

Once you understand the trick, it's easy to write the code for the Render method of the NavigateRibbon custom control. Here's the control's source code, after I omit a couple of property procedures to save space. Notice that this control implements the IPost-BackEventHandler interface but doesn't need to implement IPostBackDataHandler:

```
Public Class NavigateRibbon
    Inherits System.Web.UI.WebControls.WebControl
    Implements IPostBackEventHandler

    ' ...(The implementation of these properties is omitted here)...
    Property PageCount() As Integer
        ⋮
    End Property
    Property PageNumber() As Integer
        ⋮
    End Property
```

```
Protected Overrides Sub Render(ByVal output As HtmlTextWriter)
    Dim items() As String = {"First", "Previous", "Next", "Last"}
    For Each s As String In items
        ' Create the <A HREF="javascript:__doPostBack(....)"> tag
        output.AddAttribute("id", Me.ClientID)
        output.AddAttribute("href", "javascript:" & _
            Page.GetPostBackEventReference(Me, s))
        output.RenderBeginTag("a")
        ' Display the caption and close the tag.
        output.Write(s)
        output.RenderEndTag()
        ' Add a couple of spaces.
        output.Write("  ")
    Next
End Sub


' Process the postback.
Public Sub RaisePostBackEvent(ByVal eventArgument As String) _
    Implements IPostBackEventHandler.RaisePostBackEvent

    ' Update the page number, but keep it within valid range.
    Dim pageNum As Integer = PageNumber
    Select Case eventArgument.ToLower
        Case "first"
            pageNum = 1
        Case "previous"
            pageNum = Math.Max(pageNum - 1, 1)
        Case "next"
            pageNum = Math.Min(pageNum + 1, PageCount)
        Case "last"
            pageNum = PageCount
    End Select

    If PageNumber <> pageNum Then
        ' If the page number changed, fire a PageChanged event.
        PageNumber = pageNum
        OnPageChanged(EventArgs.Empty)
    End If
End Sub

' An alternative way to define an event that takes (object, EventArgs).
Event PageChanged As EventHandler

' Raise the event in the client page.
Protected Overridable Sub OnPageChanged(ByVal e As EventArgs)
    RaiseEvent PageChanged(Me, e)
End Sub
End Class
```

A client page can react to a click on the four navigation links as follows:

```
Private Sub NavigateRibbon1_PageChanged(ByVal sender As Object, _
    ByVal e As EventArgs) Handles NavigateRibbon1.PageChanged
    ' (Just update a Label control in this demo.)
    lblMessage.Text = "Page #" & NavigateRibbon1.PageNumber
End Sub
```

Composite Controls

Custom controls that render themselves by emitting HTML in the Render method are efficient but fail to take advantage of the functionality embedded in standard ASP.NET controls. For example, say you want to create a control that contains 10 text fields. Wouldn't it be simpler to instantiate 10 TextBox controls and rely on their properties instead of emitting HTML code for each one? Composite controls exist exactly to fulfill this purpose.

A composite control is a custom control that inherits from Control or WebControl, with a few differences from the examples seen so far:

- It overrides the CreateChildrenControls protected method of the base class. Inside this method, it instantiates all the constituent controls and adds them to its own Controls collection.

- It implements the INamingContainer interface. This interface is just a marker interface that exposes no methods. Its only purpose is to inform ASP.NET that this control has child controls, and each control must receive a unique ID.

From a conceptual point of view, composite custom controls are similar to user controls in that you build them by composing simpler controls. Unlike user controls, however, composite controls have all the advantages of custom controls: they are compiled, they can be used in Visual Studio designers in a WYSIWYG fashion, and they give you better control over how they render HTML code to the client.

Creating a composite control is generally simpler than creating a regular custom control with the same functionality, for at least a couple of reasons. First, you don't have to worry about rendering each child control; you just call the RenderChildren method and each child control will render itself. Second, you don't have to take any special steps for persisting the state of child controls or implementing additional interfaces, such as IPostBackDataHandler and IPostBackEventHandler.

The key to building composite controls is the CreateChildControls method. ASP.NET invokes this method on all the controls on a page when it's time for them to create child controls, if they have any. This method wasn't a concern in previous examples because the controls had no child controls, but in this case it can't be ignored it any longer.

The problem with composite controls is that you can't be sure about *when* the collection of child controls must be created. Depending on many factors, it might occur early in the life cycle of the control or just when the Render method is called. For this reason, you can't assume that a child control is available when you reference it in code. To avoid null reference exceptions, you should always call the EnsureChildControls method before accessing any child control. This method invokes the CreateChildControls method if it hasn't been invoked already. Or you can check the ChildControlsCreated property, a Boolean that tells whether the collection of child controls has been created already. (You can also reset this property to False if you want the control to refresh itself.)

To illustrate how to create a composite control, I wrote a Multiplier control that multiplies the numbers entered in two text fields and shows the result in a third field. (See Figure 28-9.) This control contains (in this order) a TextBox control, a Label control, another TextBox control, a Button, and finally a third TextBox control with its Read-Only property set to True.

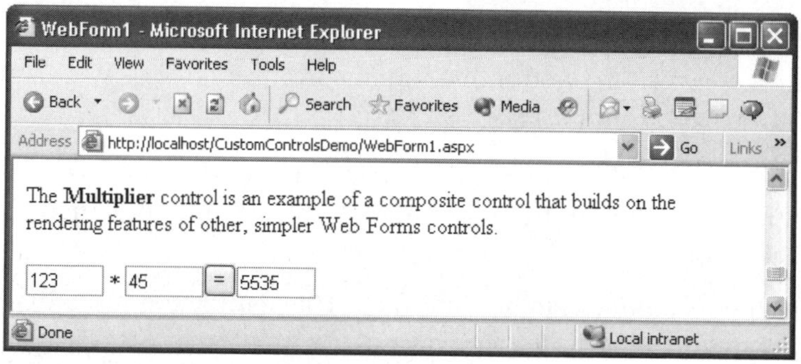

Figure 28-9 The Multiplier composite custom control

Here's the complete source code of the Multiplier control:

```
Public Class Multiplier
    Inherits System.Web.UI.WebControls.WebControl
    Implements INamingContainer

    ' These variables hold a reference to child controls.
    Dim txtFirst As TextBox
    Dim txtSecond As TextBox
    Dim txtResult As TextBox
    Dim WithEvents btnEval As Button

    Sub New()
        MyBase.New()
        Me.Width = Unit.Pixel(200)
    End Sub

    Protected Overrides Sub CreateChildControls()
        ' Create all child controls.
        txtFirst = New TextBox()
        txtSecond = New TextBox()
        Dim lblAsterisk As New Label()
        btnEval = New Button()
        txtResult = New TextBox()

        ' Set their properties.
        lblAsterisk.Text = " * "
        btnEval.Text = " = "
        txtResult.ReadOnly = True
        ' Establish correct width for text controls.
        AdjustControlWidth()
```

```
            ' Add to the Controls collection.
            Controls.Add(txtFirst)
            Controls.Add(lblAsterisk)
            Controls.Add(txtSecond)
            Controls.Add(btnEval)
            Controls.Add(txtResult)
        End Sub

        Protected Overrides Sub Render(ByVal output As HtmlTextWriter)
            ' Ensure the child controls exist and then render them.
            EnsureChildControls()
            RenderChildren(output)
            ' Adjust their width.
            AdjustControlWidth()
        End Sub

        ' Adjust controls' width.
        Private Sub AdjustControlWidth()
            ' Evaluate the space available for the three text boxes.
            Dim w As Unit = Unit.Pixel(CInt(Me.Width.Value - 50) \ 3)
            txtFirst.Width = w
            txtSecond.Width = w
            txtResult.Width = w
        End Sub

        Private Sub btnEval_Click(ByVal sender As Object, ByVal e As EventArgs) _
            Handles btnEval.Click
            EnsureChildControls()
            Try
                ' Multiply the two numbers.
                Dim res As Double = CDbl(txtFirst.Text) * CDbl(txtSecond.Text)
                txtResult.Text = res.ToString
            Catch
                ' Do nothing if there's an error.
            End Try
        End Sub

        ' The value of the result field
        <Browsable(False)> _
        Property Result() As Double
            Get
                EnsureChildControls()
                Try
                    Return CDbl(txtResult.Text)
                Catch
                    Return 0
                End Try
            End Get
            Set(ByVal Value As Double)
                EnsureChildControls()
                txtResult.Text = Value.ToString
            End Set
        End Property
    End Class
```

Several details in this listing are worth noticing:

- You must create class-level variables for all the controls that you want to later reference in code, and use the WithEvents keyword if you also want to trap events raised by them. All the other controls—typically Literal and Label controls—can be created on the fly in the CreateChildControls method.

- You must invoke the EnsureChildControls method before accessing any control's property to prevent NullReference exceptions being thrown because the object hasn't been created yet.

- Your code inside the Render method must ensure that controls have been created and then call the RenderChildren method, which in turn will call the CreateChild-Controls method if necessary.

You must arrange the dimension and position of children controls from inside both the CreateChildControls method and the Render method; otherwise, your control won't react to resizing operations inside the Visual Studio designer. For this reason, I encapsulated the resizing logic in the AdjustControlWidth private procedure, which the code calls from both the CreateChildControls method and the Render method.

Client-Side Script Code

Custom controls can be greatly enhanced with blocks of script code that run on the client machine. For example, all the ASP.NET validation controls take advantage of client-side script blocks. Client-side scripts improve performance and scalability because they lessen the workload on the server and make for a better user experience.

Client-side code should be written in JavaScript language, which is the only script language supported by all major browsers, but you can also use VBScript if you know that your application will be seen only on Internet Explorer. In general, custom controls that use client-side script code should work correctly even when the end user has disabled client-side scripting. These custom controls usually expose an EnableClientScript property; in most applications, developers will leave this property set to True, but it's useful to test how the control behaves on down-level browsers, such as earlier versions of Internet Explorer.

The example I prepared to illustrate how you can leverage client-side scripting is a custom control that expands on the Multiplier control you saw in the preceding section. If the browser supports scripting and the programmer has left the EnableClientScript property set to True (its default value), this control performs the multiplication on the client without firing a postback on the server.

HTML and JavaScript Code on the Client

Because the real action occurs on the client in this case, let's see the HTML and script code that the MultiplierEx class has to generate first. Only when it's clear what we need to produce will we have a look at the source code of the class. This is the text produced by an HTML form that contains an instance of the MultiplierEx control:

```
<form name="Form1" method="post" action="WebForm1.aspx" id="Form1">
<input type="hidden" name="__VIEWSTATE" value="dDw2MzYwNDk3MTk70z4=" />

<script language="javascript"><!--
function MultiplierExecute(txt1, txt2, txt3) {
   var op1 = parseFloat( txt1.value );
   var op2 = parseFloat( txt2.value );
   txt3.value = (op1 * op2).toString();
   }
--></script>

<input name="MultiplierEx1:_ctl0" type="text" id="MultiplierEx1__ctl0"
   style="width:82px;" />
<span> * </span>
<input name="MultiplierEx1:_ctl2" type="text" id="MultiplierEx1__ctl2"
   style="width:82px;" />
<input type="button" name="MultiplierEx1__ctl3" value=" = "
   onClick="javascript:MultiplierExecute(MultiplierEx1__ctl0,
   MultiplierEx1__ctl2, MultiplierEx1__ctl4);" />
<input name="MultiplierEx1:_ctl4" type="text" readonly="readonly"
   id="MultiplierEx1__ctl4" style="width:82px;" /></P>
</form>
```

As you see, the key to client-side functionality of the control is the onClick attribute of the button control, which cancels the default submit action and redirects the execution to the MultiplierExecute JavaScript procedure. This procedure receives a reference to the three text fields, so it can multiply the value of the first control by the value of the second control and store the result in the third control. Before you can correctly generate this HTML from inside the MultiplierEx class, you must solve the following problems:

■ How do you generate the MultiplierExecute procedure and send it to the browser? How do you ensure that this procedure appears only once in the page, even if the form contains multiple MultiplierEx controls?

■ How do you force ASP.NET to generate the id attribute for the three text fields?

The second point is important: without the id attribute, the JavaScript code wouldn't have a valid reference for accessing the controls' values. Unfortunately, you can't use the name attribute that ASP.NET generates for this purpose because the default name attribute string contains a colon, which is an invalid character inside JavaScript variables.

The MultiplierEx Custom Control

Let's see how to address the first issue, the one related to the generation of the client-side code block. The Page class exposes several methods that help developers implement client-side functionality in custom controls. (See Table 28-1.) The Register*xxxx* methods can add pieces of script code in specific positions on the page, and above all they ensure that the same piece of script is sent to the client only once, even if there are multiple instances of the same control on the page. Needless to say, you should select an unlikely name for the key value passed to the first argument, in the hope that no other custom control from a different author uses it.

The best place to output pieces of client-side scripts is in the OnPreRender method. This method is defined in the base Control class and is called by ASP.NET immediately before it calls the Render method of all the controls on the form.

Table 28-1   Members of the Page Class That Are Related to Client-Side Script Generation

Syntax	Description
RegisterClientScriptBlock(key,script)	Emits a block of script code immediately after the <form> tag. It registers the code with a key so that subsequent requests with the same key are ignored.
IsClientScriptBlockRegistered(key)	Returns True if a script block with a given key has been registered for this page.
RegisterStartupScript(key,script)	Emits a block of script code at the bottom of the page so that the elements it references are guaranteed to exist when the script runs.
IsStartupScriptRegistered(key)	Returns True if a script block with a given key has been registered as a start-up script for this page.
RegisterHiddenField (fieldname,initialvalue)	Creates and registers a hidden field on the page. The field is accessible to client script and to server-side code as postback data. (This method is useful when a server control must make a value visible to client scripts.)
RegisterOnSubmitStatement (key,script)	Associates a script code with the onSubmit attribute of the form so that the code runs when the form is submitted. The code can be an inline statement or a call to a script routine registered separately.
RegisterArrayDeclaration (arrayname,value)	Registers the name of a client-side array that will be declared in the page and adds the specified value to the array. (This method is useful when all the instances of a given custom control must be processed together, as is the case with validation controls.)

The design of the MultiplierEx class poses an interesting design problem that comes up regularly when you're attaching client-side script functionality to composite controls. On the one hand, you must override the custom control's Render method to insert the correct value for the onClick attribute of the btnEval constituent control. On the other hand, overriding the Render method means that you give up the convenience offered by composite controls, revert to using the IPostBackDataHandler interface to trap postbacks, manage the state of individual constituent controls manually, and so on.

Fortunately, you can implement custom code generation for a single constituent control—the Button, in the example—while continuing to use the composition technique for all others. The trick is actually simple: instead of instantiating a regular Button object, you create an instance of a custom Button class that you have defined. This custom Button class derives its functionality from the "real" Button, but overrides two methods: in the Render method you output the custom <input> tag with a proper onClick attribute, while in the OnPreRender method you emit the code for the MultiplierExecute script routine.

The custom Button class appears as a nested class inside the main MultiplierEx class so that the name Button now refers to the nested custom class instead of the standard Button class in the System.Web.UI.WebControls namespace. This trick enables you to reuse all the code in the main class because the nested Button class shadows the ASP.NET Button class.

Not counting the implementation of the EnableClientScript property, which is just a wrapper around an element in the ViewState collection, the only addition to the main MultiplierEx class is a block of three lines in the CreateChildControls routine (emphasized in boldface in the following listing). These statements ensure that the name attribute that ASP.NET generates for the three text fields is a valid variable name in JavaScript. This can be achieved easily by assigning the ClientID property to the ID property.

```
<ToolboxData("<{0}:MultiplierEx runat=server></{0}:MultiplierEx>")> _
Public Class MultiplierEx
    Inherits System.Web.UI.WebControls.WebControl
    Implements INamingContainer

    ' ...(All variable declarations and procedures as in Multiplier class
    '     except the ones that follow)...

    Protected Overrides Sub CreateChildControls()
        ' Create all child controls.
        txtFirst = New TextBox()
        txtSecond = New TextBox()
        btnEval = New Button()    ' <= It refers to the nested class!!
        txtResult = New TextBox()
        Dim lblAsterisk As New Label()

        ' This is necessary to achieve syntactically correct ID properties.
        txtFirst.ID = txtFirst.ClientID
        txtSecond.ID = txtSecond.ClientID
        txtResult.ID = txtResult.ClientID

        ' ...(The remainder of the procedure as in Multiplier control)...
    End Sub

    Property EnableClientScript() As Boolean
        Get
            Dim objValue As Object = Me.ViewState("EnableClientScript")
            If objValue Is Nothing Then
                Return True             ' The default value
            Else
                Return CBool(objValue)
```

```
                End If
            End Get
        Set(ByVal Value As Boolean)
            Me.ViewState("EnableClientScript") = Value
        End Set
End Property


' The custom Button control

Friend Class ButtonEx
    Inherits System.Web.UI.WebControls.Button

    Protected Overrides Sub Render(ByVal writer As HtmlTextWriter)
        ' If client scripts are disabled, render as usual and exit.
        If Not IsClientScriptEnabled() Then
            MyBase.Render(writer)
            Exit Sub
        End If

        ' Get a reference to the parent control.
        Dim parCtrl As MultiplierEx = DirectCast(Me.Parent, MultiplierEx)
        ' Prepare the code that invokes the script.
        Dim scriptInvoke As String = _
            String.Format("javascript:MultiplierExecute({0},{1},{2});", _
            parCtrl.txtFirst.ClientID, parCtrl.txtSecond.ClientID, _
            parCtrl.txtResult.ClientID)

        ' Output standard attributes plus the onClick attribute.
        writer.AddAttribute("type", "button")
        writer.AddAttribute("name", Me.ClientID)
        writer.AddAttribute("value", Me.Text)
        writer.AddAttribute("onClick", scriptInvoke)
        ' Enclose attributes in <input> tag.
        writer.RenderBeginTag("input")
        writer.RenderEndTag()
    End Sub

    ' Output the client script code if requested.
    Protected Overrides Sub OnPreRender(ByVal e As EventArgs)
        ' Let the base class do what it needs to do.
        MyBase.OnPreRender(e)
        ' Nothing else to do if client scripts are disabled.
        If Not IsClientScriptEnabled() Then Exit Sub

        ' Prepare the script routine.
        Dim s As String
        s &= "<script language=""javascript""><!--" & ControlChars.CrLf
        s &= "function MultiplierExecute(txt1, txt2, txt3) {" & _
            ControlChars.CrLf
        s &= "    var op1 = parseFloat( txt1.value );" & ControlChars.CrLf
        s &= "    var op2 = parseFloat( txt2.value );" & ControlChars.CrLf
        s &= "    txt3.value = (op1 * op2).toString(); " & _
            ControlChars.CrLf
        s &= "    }" & ControlChars.CrLf
        s &= "--></script>" & ControlChars.CrLf
        ' Register the script on the page.
        Page.RegisterClientScriptBlock("MultiplierExecute", s)
    End Sub
```

```
' Return True if client script support is requested and possible.
Private Function IsClientScriptEnabled() As Boolean
    ' We need a Try block because accessing the Browser
    ' property at design time may throw an exception.
    Try
        ' Return False if DOM version is too low.
        If Page.Request.Browser.W3CDomVersion.Major < 1 Then
            Return False
        End If

        ' Return False if EcmaScript version is too low.
        If Page.Request.Browser.EcmaScriptVersion.CompareTo( _
            New Version(1, 2)) < 0 Then
            Return False
        End If

        ' If all tests passed, return the EnableClientScript property
        ' of the parent MultiplierEx control
        Return DirectCast(Me.Parent, MultiplierEx).EnableClientScript
    Catch
        ' Return False if any error occurs.
        Return False
    End Try
End Function
    End Class                    ' ButtonEx class

End Class                        ' MultiplierEx class
```

Because it's a nested class, the custom Button class is able to access Private variables in its container class, which it must do to read the ClientID property of the txtFirst, txt-Second, and txtResult controls.

You can use the IsClientScriptEnabled auxiliary to decide whether the client-side script code should be emitted or not. For example, you must not output script code when the control is running inside the designer, when the request comes from a browser that doesn't support scripting, and of course when the developer using your control has set the EnableClientScript property to False. You can easily reuse this code in all your controls that rely on client-side scripting.

Client-side script programming is a complex topic, and I've just scratched the surface here. For example, you can use the Page.Request.Browser object to test specific browser features and generate HTML and the client-side script code that take advantage of these features. You can perform sophisticated validation chores right in the browser to increase your site's scalability even more. You can take advantage of Dynamic HTML to do eye-catching animations. You can open secondary windows for showing help messages or subforms, and so on.

You now know enough to create valuable user and custom controls, and it's time to move to the chapter about Web Services, where we'll apply many of the concepts learned in this chapter and the previous chapter. We can do this because Web services are just a different kind of ASP.NET application, as you'll see in a moment.

29 Web Services

As you might remember from Chapter 1, a Web service is a .NET component that replies to HTTP requests that are formatted using the SOAP syntax. Web services are one of the cornerstones of the .NET initiative in that they allow a degree of interoperability among applications over the Internet that was inconceivable before.

Given the importance of Web services, you might be surprised by the relatively little space devoted to them in this book. The explanation is simple, however: Web services leverage many features of the Microsoft .NET Framework that I've already covered in depth in previous chapters. First and foremost, Web services are just ASP.NET applications—more precisely, they're implemented as HTTP handlers that intercept requests for .asmx files—so you can apply most of what you've learned in Chapter 26 and Chapter 27, including state management, output caching, and authentication. You'll also see that you can create better Web services by applying your knowledge of XML serialization from Chapter 23 and of asynchronous operations from Chapter 12.

> **Note** To keep the code as concise as possible, all the code samples in this chapter assume the use of the following Imports statements at the file or project level:
>
> ```
> Imports System.Web.Services
> Imports System.Web.Services.Protocols
> Imports System.Net
> Imports System.Threading
> Imports System.Web.Security
> Imports System.IO
> Imports System.Xml.Serialization
> Imports System.Text.RegularExpressions
> ```

Introduction to Web Services

Instead of illustrating the Web service theory first, I'll start by showing you how to create a simple Web service and access it from a Microsoft Visual Basic .NET program. As with any other .NET application, you can build a Web service by using Notepad and the command-line tools provided with the .NET Framework. However, Microsoft Visual Studio .NET makes everything so easy that it's difficult to resist the temptation to use it exclusively. In the following sections, I'll show how to create a simple Web service for converting from dollar to euro currencies and back. (To keep things simple, I hardcoded the conversion rate in code.)

Building the Web Service Project

Launch Visual Studio, and create a new ASP.NET Web service project named Money-Converter, as shown in Figure 29-1. Visual Studio creates a subdirectory under IIS's main directory and names it after your project, exactly as it does when you create an ASP.NET Web Forms project. Like Web Forms applications, the new project contains its own web.config and global.asax files. However, instead of the WebForm1.aspx file, it contains a file named Service1.asmx.

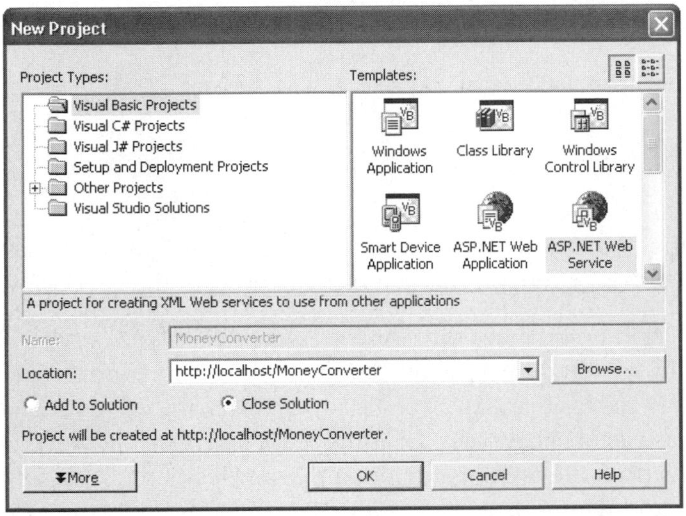

Figure 29-1   Creating an ASP.NET Web service project

The Service1.asmx file contains the code for your Web service that—once again—is just a .NET component that's accessed through the Internet via HTTP. Before continuing with our example, you should give this file a more descriptive name, such as Converter.asmx.

Like Web Forms files, .asmx files each have a designer's surface on which you can drop .NET components. Because a Web service doesn't have a user interface, you'll use this feature only for nonvisual components, such as ADO.NET connections or FileSystem-Watcher objects. Next, press the F7 key and switch to the code editor: as you see, Visual Studio has already created a working Web service class named Service1, with a sample HelloWorld method ready to be uncommented.

Let's rename the class Converter to keep it in sync with the file name, and let's add two methods that convert currencies, patterned after the commented sample procedure. Following is the source code for our first Web service. To save space, I omitted the automatically generated code in the #Region block:

```
<WebService(Description:="A web service for converting currencies", _
    Namespace:="http://tempuri.org/MoneyConverter/Service1") > _
Public Class Converter
    Inherits System.Web.Services.WebService
```

```
#Region " Web Services Designer Generated Code "
    ⋮
#End Region

    <WebMethod(Description:="Convert from Euro to Dollar currency")> _
    Function EuroToDollar(ByVal amount As Decimal) As Decimal
        Return amount * GetEuroToDollarConversionRate()
    End Function

    <WebMethod(Description:="Convert from Dollar to Euro currency")> _
    Function DollarToEuro(ByVal amount As Decimal) As Decimal
        Return amount / GetEuroToDollarConversionRate()
    End Function

    Private Function GetEuroToDollarConversionRate() As Decimal
        ' A real application would read this number from a file or a database.
        Return 01.1@
    End Function
End Class
```

The actual code for the two worker methods is so simple that I won't comment on it. Instead, I want to draw your attention to the attributes used in the preceding listing:

- The WebService attribute qualifies the Converter class as a Web service class. This attribute isn't really required because the .asmx file extension and the fact that the Converter class inherits from System.Web.Services.WebService is enough to inform the ASP.NET infrastructure that we're building a Web service. However, the WebService attribute is useful for setting additional properties of the Web service, such as its description and namespace, and as a rule you should never omit it.

- The WebMethod attribute makes a method of the class accessible through the Internet. Only methods marked with this attribute are seen from remote clients, so you can't omit it. You can use this attribute to associate a description with the method and to define other important properties, such as session-state support and caching. (See the section "The WebMethod Attribute," later in this chapter.)

Testing the Web Service Within the Browser

The simplest way to test the Web service that you've just created is by running the project, after ensuring that Converter.asmx is defined as its start page. Visual Studio will then launch a new instance of Microsoft Internet Explorer and have it point to the .asmx page. Figure 29-2 shows what you see in the browser. The title of the page is the name of the class, and the description property of the WebService attribute appears immediately below it, followed by the list of all available methods and their descriptions.

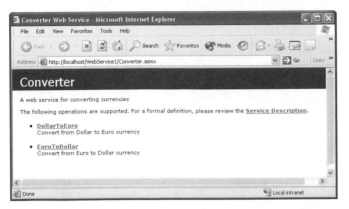

Figure 29-2   The HTML page that ASP.NET creates on the fly when accessing an .asmx file without passing any parameters

Where does this information come from? When ASP.NET intercepts a request for an .asmx page without anything on the query string, it uses reflection to extract the attributes and the method names of the first class in the .asmx file, and then it synthesizes this HTML page for you. (If the file contains multiple classes deriving from System.Web.Services.WebService, only the first class is visible in the browser.) In a real application, clients access the service programmatically, but this nice feature lets you test the service interactively during the debugging phase.

The page that produces the output you've seen is nothing but an .aspx page. More precisely, it's the DefaultWsdlHelpGenerator.aspx file stored in the C:\Windows\Microsoft.NET\Framework*v.x.y.zzzz*\Config directory. Because it's a standard .aspx page, you can customize it if you want. You could add your own company logo, for example, or change the the page to hide information about your Web services. You can also modify a few constants defined near the top of this page to enable debugging mode or other features.

Changing the DefaultWsdlHelpGenerator.aspx file affects all the Web services running on the machine. For a more granular control of which page should be used, you can add a <wsdlHelpGenerator> tag to the web.config file in your application's root directory or in the directory that contains the .asmx file:

```
<configuration>
   <system.web>
      <webServices>
         <wsdlHelpGenerator href="LocalWsdlHelpGenerator.aspx" />
      </webServices>
   </system.web>
</configuration>
```

The standard help page offers more than just a description of the Web service and its methods: it also lets you interactively call individual methods and pass them all the required attributes. Not all methods can be tested in this way—for example, you can't test methods that take object or ByRef arguments—but it's surely a great bonus when you're testing the service.

Figure 29-3 shows the page that appears when you click a method's name (Dollar-ToEuro, in this example). You can enter any value in the Amount box and click the Invoke button. The return value from the method is displayed as XML inside a new instance of Internet Explorer. (See Figure 29-4.) Notice that the URL used to get the result is in the following format:

```
http://servername/webservicename/pagename.asmx/methodname
```

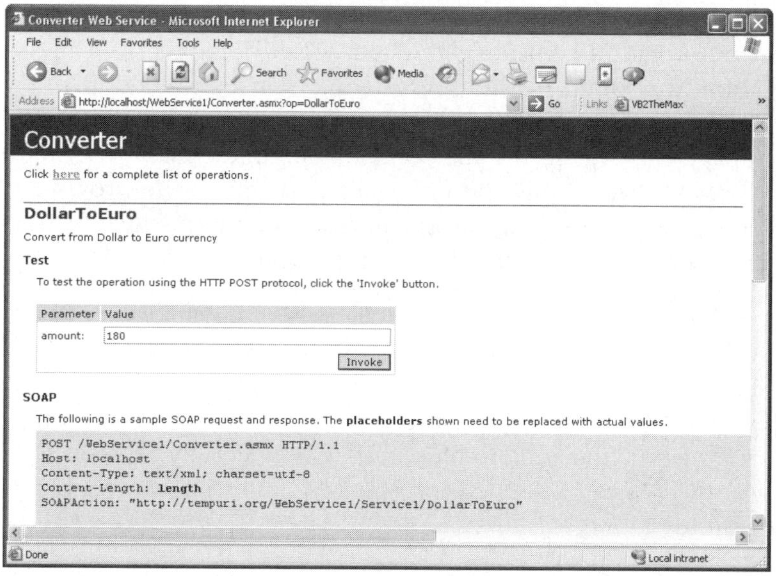

Figure 29-3   You can invoke a Web service method from inside the browser.

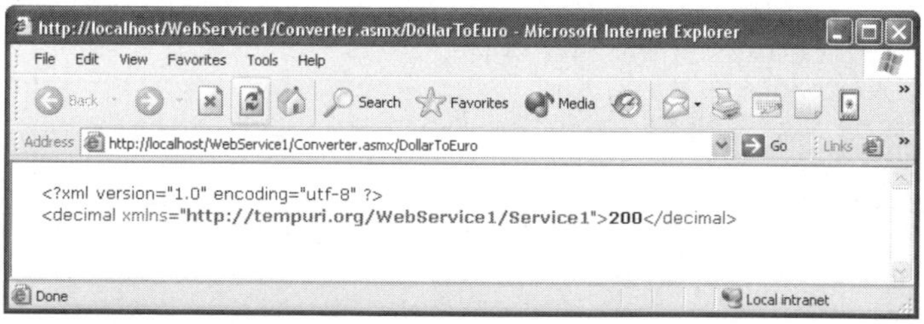

Figure 29-4   The return value from a Web service method is formatted as XML.

Any local client that knows where to look for this Web service and what arguments to pass can call a method by posting an HTTP POST request. As you'll learn later in this chapter, this is just one of the three protocols you can use to query a Web service through the Internet, the other two being HTTP GET and SOAP.

The main Web service help page contains one more link of interest. If you click the Service Description link, the browser displays the Web Service Description Language (WSDL) contract. This is a file that describes the Web service you've just created, with information about each method and the arguments it expects. You can browse the WSDL contract for an .asmx page directly from the browser by appending the ?WSDL argument to the .asmx page's URL.

Although Web services rely heavily on WSDL files, most of the time you don't have to worry about them and the information they contain because Visual Studio .NET can handle these files transparently for you.

> **Note** To learn more about the WSDL contract and the action of discovering which Web services are available on a Web site, read the topics "Web Service Description Language Tool (Wsdl.exe)" and "Web Service Discovery Tool (Disco.exe)" in MSDN documentation.

Creating a Web Service Client

Now that you know that the MoneyConverter Web service works correctly from inside a browser, let's see how to create a client application that uses it. Any application that can post an HTTP request can be a client of the Web service, and it doesn't need to be a .NET application or even a Windows application. If we limit our attention to managed applications only, typically a Web service client is one of the following application types: a Windows Forms application, a Web Forms application, or another Web service application. In the following steps, I'll show how to create a Windows Forms client, but keep in mind that you'll follow the same procedure when you're creating other types of clients.

1. Add a Windows Forms project to the current solution, name it MoneyConverter-Client, and make it the start-up project of the solution.

2. Choose the Add Web Reference command from the Project menu or from the shortcut menu that you open by right-clicking the project's node in the Solution Explorer.

3. The dialog box that appears lets you select a Web service from among those registered in the local machine or in a Universal Description, Discovery, and Integration (UDDI) directory stored on your network or managed by Microsoft or someone else. (See Figure 29-5.) UDDI directories are a bit like the Web services' yellow pages in that they list Web services distributed across the Internet. (Visit *http://www.uddi.org* for more information about UDDI.)

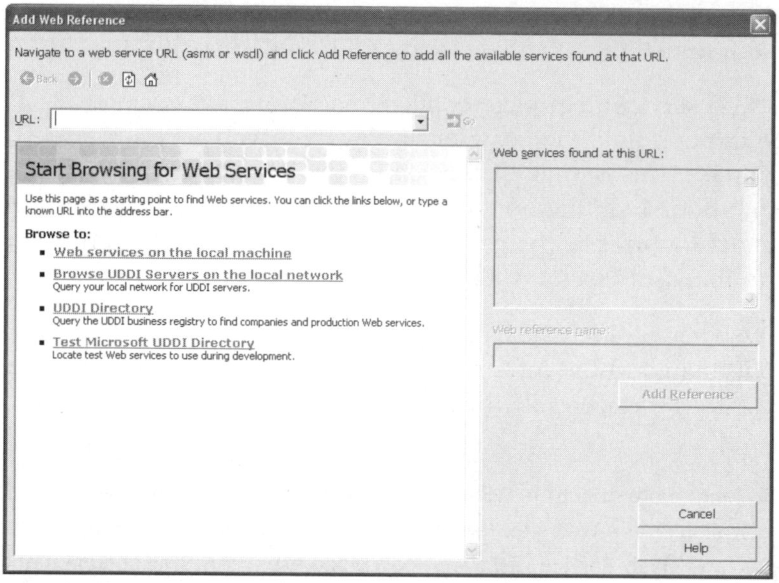

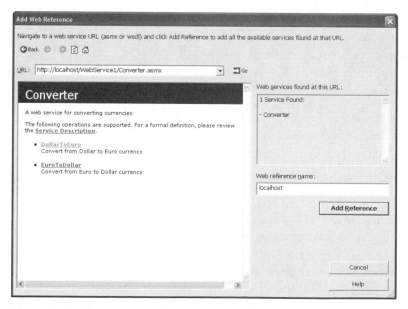

Figure 29-5   The Add Web Reference dialog box

4. Select the Web Services On The Local Machine link and the Converter Web service from the list that appears, or just type the path to the .asmx file on the local machine—that is, **http:// localhost/MoneyConverter/converter.asmx**—in the URL box, and press the Enter key. The left pane will display the description page associated with the Web service. (See Figure 29-6.)

Figure 29-6   Entering the address of an .asmx page enables the Add Reference button.

5. You can use the left pane to test the Web service, but you already know that your Web service works correctly, so you can go ahead and click the Add Reference button. (For this first experiment, accept the default Web reference name localhost, even though you will usually change this name to a more descriptive one in a real-world project.)

Visual Studio adds a new Web References folder to the project, with a localhost node that gathers all the files that Visual Studio has created or downloaded from the Web service—for example, the WSDL contract file. The most important file, from the perspective of the client application, is the Reference.vb file. (You must click the Show All Files button in the Solution Explorer and expand Web References, Localhost, and Reference.map to access this file.) This file contains a Converter class that exposes the same methods as the original Web services (and a few additional ones) and that works as a proxy between the Windows Forms application and the Web service running somewhere in the Internet. (See Figure 29-7.) Instead of sending the HTTP requests directly to the Web service, the client application invokes the methods of this proxy class, and the proxy class routes the call to the Web service through the HTTP protocol.

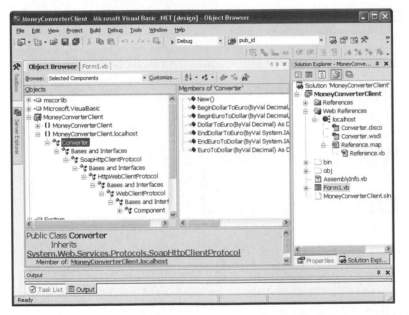

Figure 29-7 How a Web reference appears in the Solution Explorer and in the Object Browser

As often happens in the .NET world, this little bit of magic is made possible by inheritance. The Converter proxy class inherits many of its methods from the System.Web.Services.Protocols.SoapHttpClientProtocol base class. The most important of these inherited methods is Invoke, which performs a sort of late-bound call to the remote Web service class. The class that Visual Studio has generated automatically contains wrapper procedures that allow the client application to call remote methods using a strongly typed syntax:

```
' ...(From inside the Converter class in Reference.vb file)...

Public Function EuroToDollar(ByVal amount As Decimal) As Decimal
    Dim results() As Object = Me.Invoke("EuroToDollar", New Object() {amount})
    Return CType(results(0), Decimal)
End Function
```

Once you understand how the mechanism works, invoking the Web service is just a matter of creating an instance of the proxy class and calling one of its methods, without worrying about what happens behind the scenes. Figure 29-8 shows a simple form that lets you convert dollars to euros and back. This is the code behind the two push buttons:

```
Private Sub btnToEuros_Click(ByVal sender As Object, ByVal e As EventArgs) _
    Handles btnToEuros.Click
    Dim conv As New localhost.Converter()            ' Create the proxy.
    Dim value As Decimal = CDec(txtDollars.Text)     ' Get the argument.
    Dim result As Decimal = conv.DollarToEuro(value) ' Call the remote method.
    txtEuros.Text = result.ToString                  ' Display the result.
End Sub

Private Sub btnToDollars_Click(ByVal sender As Object, ByVal e As EventArgs) _
    Handles btnToDollars.Click
    Dim conv As New localhost.Converter()            ' Create the proxy.
    Dim value As Decimal = CDec(txtEuros.Text)       ' Get the argument.
    Dim result As Decimal = conv.EuroToDollar(value) ' Call the remote method.
    txtDollars.Text = result.ToString                ' Display the result.
End Sub
```

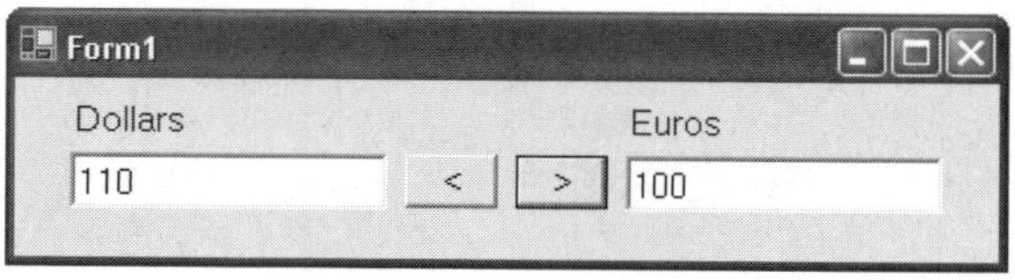

Figure 29-8   The demo client application

> **Note**   During the test phase, you'll often change the structure of the Web service class—for example, by adding new methods or changing the signature of existing ones. After any change to the class interface, you should rebuild the proxy class in the client project. The easiest way to do this is with the Update Web Reference command on the shortcut menu of the individual reference (localhost, if you haven't renamed it) in the Web References folder of the Solution Explorer window.

Understanding Web Services Protocols

Web services built with ASP.NET support three protocols: HTTP GET, HTTP POST, and SOAP. To improve security, the .NET Framework version 1.1, however, disables the GET protocol and leaves the POST protocol enabled only for local calls (for you to test Web services from within the browser). Here's the portion of the machine.config files that defines which protocols are supported. (Notice that the HttpPost and HttpGet protocols are commented out.)

```
<configuration>
  <system.web>
    <webServices>
      <protocols>
        <add name="HttpSoap1.2"/>
        <add name="HttpSoap"/>
        <!-- <add name="HttpPost"/> -->
        <!-- <add name="HttpGet"/> -->
        <add name="HttpPostLocalhost"/>
        <add name="Documentation"/>
      </protocols>
    </webServices>
  </system.web>
</configuration>
```

You can reenable the GET and POST protocols by modifying your machine.config file or by overriding these settings in a local Web.config file. (Use the <remove> tag in the Web.config file to disable a protocol enabled in machine.config.) You rarely need to do so, however, because in practice you'll use the SOAP protocol in virtually all your applications.

The HTTP GET and POST protocols, in fact, aren't powerful enough for most real applications. They prevent you from passing structures and objects as arguments, and they won't let you pass ByRef arguments either (even though it's legal to return an object if it can be serialized to XML).

The SOAP protocol, on the other hand, employs SOAP messages for both the input arguments and the return value and doesn't have any of the limitations of the HTTP GET and POST protocols. For this reason, I'll focus on the SOAP protocol exclusively in the remainder of this chapter.

The root node of any SOAP message is the message envelope, which contains the message body; in turn, the body contains an XML tag named after the target method, and all arguments are sent inside this block. For example, this is the text sent to the Web service when the DollarToEuro method is invoked through the SOAP protocol:

```
POST /MoneyConverter/Converter.asmx HTTP/1.1
Host: localhost
Content-Type: text/xml; charset=utf-8
Content-Length: 341
SOAPAction: "http://tempuri.org/DollarToEuro"
```

```
<?xml version="1.0" encoding="utf-8"?>
<soap:Envelope xmlns:xsi="http://www.w3.org/2001/XMLSchema-instance"
    xmlns:xsd="http://www.w3.org/2001/XMLSchema"
    xmlns:soap="http://schemas.xmlsoap.org/soap/envelope/">
  <soap:Body>
    <DollarToEuro xmlns="http://tempuri.org/">
      <amount>110</amount>
    </DollarToEuro>
  </soap:Body>
</soap:Envelope>
```

The text returned from the method is another SOAP message with its own envelope and body blocks. In this case, however, the body contains a tag named MethodName-Response, which in turn contains a nested tag named MethodNameResult, whose text is the return value:

```
HTTP/1.1 200 OK
Content-Type: text/xml; charset=utf-8
Content-Length: 381

<?xml version="1.0" encoding="utf-8"?>
<soap:Envelope xmlns:xsi="http://www.w3.org/2001/XMLSchema-instance"
    xmlns:xsd="http://www.w3.org/2001/XMLSchema"
    xmlns:soap="http://schemas.xmlsoap.org/soap/envelope/">
  <soap:Body>
    <DollarToEuroResponse xmlns="http://tempuri.org/">
      <DollarToEuroResult>100</DollarToEuroResult>
    </DollarToEuroResponse>
  </soap:Body>
</soap:Envelope>
```

Any SOAP message can contain an optional header, which might contain additional information not strictly related to the method being called. For example, a client might use the header to send its credentials so that the Web service can record who accessed its methods and when. The body of a SOAP message can be replaced by a <soap:Fault> section if the message is carrying error information, such as when you call a method with the wrong number of arguments or when the code in the method has thrown an exception.

SOAP is the only protocol that supports objects and structures as arguments. The only requirement for an object fed to or returned from a Web service is that it must be serializable as XML. (See the note at the end of Chapter 23 for more details about XML serialization.) In addition, only the SOAP protocol supports output arguments. In other words, if the method takes one or more ByRef arguments, you can invoke that method only by using the SOAP protocol.

Web Services Up Close

In the sections that follow, you'll see how you can improve the performance of Web services through caching, how to deal with exceptions, and how to take advantage of the ASP.NET infrastructure.

The Web Service Class

The class that exposes the methods of the Web service usually inherits from the System.Web.Services.WebService class, even though this isn't a requirement because the presence of the WebMethod attribute is enough to make one or more methods of the class callable by remote clients. In practice, however, you always build a Web service class that inherits from the WebService base class because this arrangement lets you access the ASP.NET context and other useful objects, such as Application and Session variables.

The WebService Attribute

The WebService attribute is optional in the sense that ASP.NET can determine that a class can work as a Web service without it. The constructor of the WebService attribute can take three arguments: Description, Namespace, and Name. You've already seen how to use the first two:

```
<WebService(Description:="A web service for converting currencies",
    Namespace:="http://www.vb2themax.com/") > _
Public Class Converter
    Inherits System.Web.Services.WebService
    ⋮
End Class
```

Remember that the namespace value is only a means to make the Web service name unique and doesn't have to correspond to a physical URL. The common convention of using the URL of your company's Web site ensures that the namespace+name combination is unique.

The Name argument affects the name of the class as it appears in the WSDL contract, and it ultimately becomes the name of the proxy class that you create with the Add Web Reference command in Visual Studio or with the Wsdl utility. If you omit this argument, the proxy class has the same name as the original Web service class:

```
<WebService(Description:="A web service for converting currencies",
    Namespace:="http://www.vb2themax.com/", Name:="MoneyConv") > _
Public Class Converter
    Inherits System.Web.Services.WebService
    ⋮
End Class
```

Access to ASP.NET Objects

One of the benefits of creating a Web service by deriving a class from System.Web.Services.WebService is the ability to access any ASP.NET intrinsic object from inside the class. More precisely, the WebService base class exposes the following properties:

- The Application, Session, and Server properties return the ASP.NET object of the same name. You can use the Application object to cache values in common to all clients, as you do in a Web Forms application. Keep in mind that the Session object is available only if you have specified the EnableState argument in the Web-Method attribute, as I'll explain in the section "Enabling Session State," later in this chapter.

- The User property returns the IPrincipal object that represents an authenticated user. For example, this property returns a Windows Principal object if users are authenticated through Windows authentication. You can decide which authentication method the Web service supports by editing the web.config file for the Web service application, exactly as you do for Web Forms applications. (See Chapter 27 for details about ASP.NET authentication.)

- The Context property returns the HttpContext object for the current request. This object exposes the five ASP.NET intrinsic objects, the Trace object, the Error object, and a few other properties.

Among the most useful objects you can access from inside a Web service are Application and Cache, which can cache values and share them among clients. Here's a very simple example that uses an Application variable to keep track of how many times a given method has been called:

```
<WebMethod(Description:="Return the server time")> _
Function GetTime(ByVal arg As Integer) As Date
    Me.Application.Lock()
    Me.Application("GetTimeCounter") = GetTimeCounter() + 1
    Me.Application.Unlock()
    Return Date.Now
End Function

<WebMethod(Description:="The number of times GetTime has been called")> _
Function GetTimeCounter() As Integer
    Dim o As Object = Me.Application("GetTimeCounter")
    If o Is Nothing Then
        Return 0
    Else
        Return CInt(o)
    End If
End Function
```

You can review how to use the Application and Cache objects in the sections "The HttpApplicationState Class" and "The Cache Class," in Chapter 26.

Simple and Complex Data Types

The great thing about Web services is their ability to receive and return any .NET data type, including your custom type, provided that it's serializable to XML. For example, you can pass and return ADO.NET DataSet objects—either generic or strongly typed— because they're serializable to XML.

Most of the time, you don't have to do anything special to marshal a data type because the definition of all the types taken or returned by the Web service project and exposed as arguments or return values is included in the WSDL contract. When you add a Web reference in Visual Studio or run the Wsdl utility, a proxy class for each of these types is generated and the client can therefore use them. In a few cases, however, you must force Visual Studio or the Wsdl utility to include the correct types in the WSDL contract. For example, consider the following Web service class:

```
Public Class SampleService
    Inherits System.Web.Services.WebService

    <WebMethod()> _
    Function GetDocument(ByVal docname As String) As Document
        Select Case docname.ToLower
            Case "invoice"
                Return New Invoice()
            Case "purchaseorder"
                Return New PurchaseOrder()
        End Select
    End Function
End Class

Public MustInherit Class Document
    Public [Date] As Date
    Public Number As Integer
End Class

Public Class Invoice
    Inherits Document
    Public Total As Decimal
End Class

Public Class PurchaseOrder
    Inherits Document
    Public AuthorizedBy As String
End Class
```

The problem in the preceding listing is that the GetDocument method can return either an Invoice or a PurchaseOrder object, although the WSDL contract will contain the definition of only the Document abstract class. To force the WSDL contract to include the definition of the two concrete classes, you must flag the method with the SoapRpc-Method attribute and add two instances of the SoapInclude attribute, as follows:

```
<WebMethod(),SoapRpcMethod(),SoapInclude(GetType(Invoice)), _
    SoapInclude(GetType(PurchaseOrder))> _
Function GetDocument(ByVal docname As String) As Document
    ⋮
End Function
```

You should use the SoapInclude attribute in other similar cases—for example, when a method takes or returns an ArrayList or a collection of objects and the actual class name of the returned object doesn't appear explicitly anywhere in public method signatures:

```
' The following method takes an ArrayList of Book objects
' but no other method explicitly takes or returns a Book object.

<WebMethod(),SoapRpcMethod(),SoapInclude(GetType(Book)) > _
Sub ProcessProducts(ByVal books As ArrayList)
    ⋮
End Function
```

The System.Xml.Serialization namespace includes other Soap*xxxx* attributes, such as SoapType, SoapElement, SoapAttributeAttribute, SoapIgnore, and SoapEnum. These attributes can be used to define how structures and classes are serialized to XML. Unless you need to control the shape of the XML sent or received from the Web service, you don't need to apply these attributes to work with Web services.

The WebMethod Attribute

Unlike the optional WebService attribute, the WebMethod attribute is mandatory, and you must use it to flag all the methods that must be accessible to clients. This arrangement lets you build a component that exposes a set of methods to its local clients, but it makes only a subset of those methods available to remote clients that connect to it through a Web service. All the arguments for this attribute are optional, but in practice you should at least specify the Description for the method, which appears in the Web service help page:

```
<WebMethod(Description:="Convert from Euro to Dollar currency")> _
Function EuroToDollar(ByVal amount As Decimal) As Decimal
    Return amount * GetEuroToDollarConversionRate()
End Function
```

Working with Overloaded Methods

The MessageName argument specifies the name clients can use to invoke the method. This argument is necessary only when the Web service class exposes overloaded methods of the same name. Because the Web service infrastructure can't resolve calls to overloaded methods, you must specify different external names for them:

```
<WebMethod (Description:="Add two Integers")> _
Public Function Add(ByVal n1 As Integer, ByVal n2 As Integer) _
```

```
    As Integer
    Return n1 + n2
End Function

<WebMethod (Description:="Add two floating point numbers", _
    MessageName:="AddDouble")> _
Public Function Add(ByVal n1 As Double, ByVal n2 As Double) _
    As Double
    Return n1 + n2
End Function
```

Buffering the Response

The BufferResponse argument is similar to the BufferOutput property of the HttpResponse object in that it affects whether the output from the Web service is sent to the client as a single XML block or split into smaller chunks that are sent while the returned object is being serialized to XML. In practice, you'll want to leave this argument set to True (its default value) and set it to False only when you're returning large quantities of XML, as when you're returning a large DataSet to the client:

```
<WebMethod(BufferResponse:="False")> _
Public Function GetPublishers() As DataSet
    ⋮
End Function
```

When BufferResponse is False, SOAP extensions are disabled for the method. (See the section "SOAP Extensions," later in this chapter, for a description of SOAP extensions.)

Caching Results

Because they're ASP.NET applications, Web services support output caching, much like Web Forms and Web User controls. Web services don't support the @OutputCache directive, however, and the output from each individual method can be cached with a different duration by means of the CacheDuration argument of the WebMethod attribute. For example, the following code caches the output of the GetPublishers method for 1 minute:

```
<WebMethod(CacheDuration:=60)> _
Public Function GetPublishers() As DataSet
    ⋮
End Function
```

If the method takes arguments, ASP.NET maintains a different cached version for each combination of argument values. For example, the following method stores a cached image for each distinct value of the State argument passed to the method in its argument:

```
<WebMethod(CacheDuration:=60, MesssageName:="GetPublishersByState")> _
Public Function GetPublishers(ByVal State As String) As DataSet
    ⋮
End Function
```

If used wisely, the CacheDuration attribute can improve the Web service performance more than any other technique available. However, you should always consider carefully the impact on resource consumption on the server. This technique is especially effective for small results that require a lot of processing on the server—for example, computation of database statistics—and can become a bottleneck if the method takes arguments whose value can vary greatly or if the method returns a large amount of data.

Enabling Session State

Web services can take advantage of session-state support, like all ASP.NET applications, even though session support is disabled for Web services by default because most Web service calls are stateless and don't need to store data in a session variable. This arrangement avoids the need to populate the Session collection at each call, reduces memory consumption on the server, and avoids server affinity.

Sometimes, however, enabling session variables can be useful or desirable—for example, in a Web service that has a method for ordering individual products and another method that confirms the order, evaluates shipping charges, and returns the total cost. Such a Web service isn't stateless and has to store details of the order being built in one or more session variables. You enable session support by setting the EnableSession argument of the WebMethod attribute to True; if you omit this argument or set it to False, any reference to the Session object throws a NullReference exception. Here's a simple example of a Web service method that relies on session variables:

```
<WebMethod(EnableSession:=True)> _
Function IncrementCounter() As Integer
    If Session("counter") Is Nothing Then
        Session.Add("counter", 1)
    Else
        Session("counter") = CInt(Session("counter")) + 1
    End If
    Return CInt(session("counter"))
End Function

<WebMethod(EnableSession:=True)> _
Function GetSessionID() As String
    Return Session.SessionId
End Function
```

Web services that rely on session state have a serious shortcoming. If you test the IncrementCounter method from the browser by using the standard help page, you'll see that each call to the method increments the result, which proves that session state is correctly preserved between method invocations. You can double-check that this feature works well by seeing that the return value from the GetSessionID method doesn't change, at least until you close the browser or the session expires after its natural timeout (20 minutes of inactivity, by default).

However, be prepared for an unpleasant surprise when you call the method from a Windows Forms application that uses a proxy class. In this case, the IncrementCounter method always returns 1, and the GetSessionID method returns a different string at each invocation. To explain this odd behavior, you must remember that session support depends on a nonpersistent cookie sent to the client the first time the client sends a request to the ASP.NET application. If the client is a browser, the session cookie is preserved in the browser's memory and resubmitted at each subsequent request so that the application can recognize the client and associate it with the proper set of session variables. If the client is a Windows Forms application, however, the session cookie can't be stored anywhere, and each new request appears as if it were the first request coming from that client. In the section "The CookieContainer Property," later in this chapter, you'll see how to work around this issue.

Building Transactional Web Services

You can use the TransactionOption argument of the WebMethod attribute to create transactional Web services, which can call transactional COM+ components and take advantage of Microsoft Distributed Transaction Coordinator (MS DTC) support. (You can read more about transactional components in Chapter 31.)

Due to the stateless nature of Web services, a Web service method can be only the root of a transaction. In other words, you can't start a transaction in a client—which might be a Windows Forms application, a Web Forms page, or another Web service method—and propagate the transaction through a call to the Web service.

The TransactionOption argument can take five different values—Disabled, NotSupported, Supported, Required, and RequiresNew—but because of the limitation I just mentioned, only two different behaviors are available. You have a transactional Web service if you specify Required or RequiresNew, and a regular, nontransactional Web service if you use any other value for this argument. Here's the typical structure of a transactional Web service method:

```
<WebMethod(TransactionOption:=TransactionOption.RequiresNew)> _
Function UpdateDatabase() As Boolean
    Dim cn As New System.Data.OleDb.OleDbConnection(myConnString)
    Try
        cn.Open()
        ' Perform all the required update operations.
        ⋮
        ' If everything went well, commit the transaction.
        ContextUtil.SetComplete()
        ' Let the client know that everything is OK.
        Return True
    Catch
        ' If an update error occurred, abort the transaction.
        ContextUtil.SetAbort()
        ' Let the client know that something went wrong.
        Return False
```

```
        Finally
            ' Close the connection in all cases.
            cn.Close()
        End Try
    End Function
```

You can also flag the method with the AutoComplete attribute, in which case the transaction is rolled back if the method throws an exception but committed otherwise, so you can omit the call to the SetComplete and SetAbort methods.

The Web Service Proxy Class

By default, Visual Studio .NET hides the proxy class that it creates. To make it visible, you must click on the Show All Files button on the Solution Explorer window's toolbar, expand the Web References element, and then expand the Reference.map element. In addition to the specific methods that mirror those that the Web server exposes, the proxy class inherits several useful properties and methods from the System.Web.Protocols.SoapHttpClientProtocol class. For example, you can use the Timeout and Url properties to invoke a different Web service with the same interface, should the default Web service be unavailable. UserAgent is the user agent header used in the request to the Web service; the default is Mozilla/4.0 (compatible; MSIE 6.0; MS Web Services Client Protocol w.x.yyyy.z, where w.x.yyyy.z is the version of the common language runtime).

Two properties have to do with user credentials. If the PreAuthenticate property is True, all the requests must contain authentication credentials; if it is False (the default), the credentials are sent only if the Web service disallows anonymous access and returns a 401 HTTP return code when the request is initially attempted. If AllowAutoRedirect is False (the default), the proxy class throws an exception if a server redirection is attempted; this setting is appropriate if the message contains authentication information or other confidential information and a redirection to another server would compromise security.

Late-Bound and Early-Bound Method Calls

All proxy classes inherit from the SoapHttpClientProtocol base class the ability to invoke methods synchronously and asynchronously by means of the Invoke, BeginInvoke, and EndInvoke protected methods.

In addition to these generic, late-bound methods, Visual Studio and the Wsdl utility create three strongly typed methods in the proxy class for each method in the Web service component. These methods are public and can be invoked from the client application. For example, the EuroToDollar method in the Converter.asmx file causes the following methods to be created in the proxy class:

```
' (In client's proxy class...)
' Strongly typed method for synchronous calls
```

```
Public Function DollarToEuro(ByVal amount As Decimal) As Decimal
    Dim results() As Object = Me.Invoke("DollarToEuro", New Object() {amount})
    Return CType(results(0),Decimal)
End Function

' Strongly typed method for starting asynchronous calls
Public Function BeginDollarToEuro(ByVal amount As Decimal, _
    ByVal callback As AsyncCallback, ByVal asyncState As Object) _
    As IAsyncResult
    Return Me.BeginInvoke("DollarToEuro", _
        New Object() {amount}, callback, asyncState)
End Function

' Strongly typed method for ending asynchronous calls
Public Function EndDollarToEuro(ByVal asyncResult As IAsyncResult) As Decimal
    Dim results() As Object = Me.EndInvoke(asyncResult)
    Return CType(results(0),Decimal)
End Function
```

Let's see how you can make a synchronous and an asynchronous call to a Web service.

Synchronous Method Calls

Because you're making a call to a Web service running on a computer across the Internet, you should always protect your synchronous calls with a timeout. If the timeout specified by the Timeout property is exceeded, a System.Net.WebException object is thrown. So you should protect the method invocation with a Try…End Try block:

```
' (In client's proxy class...)
Dim service As New localhost.SampleService
Try
    ' Set a timeout of 5 seconds.
    service.Timeout = 5000
    ' Invoke a method that takes 10 seconds to complete.
    service.LengthyMethodCall(10)
Catch ex As WebException
    If ex.Status = WebExceptionStatus.Timeout Then
        ' The operation timed out.
        ⋮
    End If
Catch ex As Exception
    ' Another exception has occurred.
End Try
```

The LengthyMethodCall method in the SampleService.asmx Web service contains just a Thread.Sleep method, so we can use it to test how the proxy class behaves when the call times out:

```
' (In server's Web service class...)
<WebMethod(Description:="A lengthy method")> _
Sub LengthyMethodCall(ByVal seconds As Integer)
    ' Wait for the specified number of seconds.
    Thread.Sleep(seconds * 1000)
End Sub
```

You can use the Timeout property in combination with the Url property to provide alternative addresses. Suppose, for example, that you have a list of Web services that offer the same functionality (and have the same WSDL contract). You can then call the default Web service—whose URL is stored in the WSDL and hard-coded into the proxy class's source code—after setting an adequate timeout. If the timeout expires, you can have the Url property point to an alternative Web service and retry the method call.

The proxy class also exposes the Abort method, which allows you to cancel a synchronous Web service method call. Because a synchronous call blocks the thread, you can call the Abort method only from another thread, so this technique makes sense if your application has at least two threads. (If you create the additional thread with the only purpose of calling the Abort method, you should consider calling the method asynchronously.) If a synchronous method call is canceled, the thread on which it runs receives a WebException object.

The Abort method enables you to cancel a synchronous method call depending on conditions other than timeout expiration, as in the following example:

```
' (In client's proxy class...)
Dim service As New localhost.SampleService

Sub RunTheMethod()
    ' Run another thread.
    Dim tr As New Thread(AddressOf CallWebMethod)
    tr.Start()
    ' Abort the method call when a condition becomes true. For example,
    ' a file is updated or a process is terminated.
    ⋮
    ' (In this demo we just wait for some seconds.)
    Thread.Sleep(5000)
    service.Abort()
End Sub

Sub CallWebMethod()
    Try
        ' Invoke a method that takes 10 seconds to complete.
        service.LengthyMethodCall(10)
    Catch ex As WebException
        If ex.Status = WebExceptionStatus.RequestCanceled Then
            ' The method call has been canceled.
            ⋮
        End If
    End Try
End Sub
```

Asynchronous Method Calls

As I've shown you before, the proxy class exposes a Begin*xxxx* and End*xxxx* pair of methods for each procedure in the Web service component marked with the WebMethod attribute. You can use these two methods for calling the Web service asynchronously.

The actions necessary to invoke a Web service method asynchronously are identical to the actions needed to invoke an asynchronous delegate. I covered asynchronous delegates in Chapter 12, so in this section I'll give you just an example of asynchronous invocation of a Web service method.

```
Sub CallAsyncMethod()
    Dim service As New localhost.SampleService
    ' Call a lengthy method that takes about 5 seconds to complete.
    ' Note that the proxy object is passed in the third argument.
    Dim ar As IAsyncResult = service.BeginLengthyMethodCall(5, _
        AddressOf MethodCallback, service)
End Sub

' This is the callback method.
Sub MethodCallback(ByVal ar As IAsyncResult)
    ' Retrieve the proxy object from the AsyncState property.
    Dim service As localhost.SampleService = _
        DirectCast(ar.AsyncState, localhost.SampleService)
    ' Complete the method call.
    service.EndLengthyMethodCall(ar)
End Sub
```

Aborting a Web service asynchronous call is slightly more difficult than aborting a synchronous call. You must cast the IAsyncResult object returned by the Begin*xxxx* method to a WebClientAsyncResult object and then call the Abort method of the WebClientAsyncResult object:

```
' Run a method that takes 5 seconds to complete.
Dim service As New localhost.SampleService()
Dim ar As IAsyncResult = service.BeginLengthyMethodCall(5, _
    Nothing, Nothing)
' Do something else here.
⋮
If ar.IsCompleted Then
    ' If the method completed, complete the call.
    service.EndLengthyMethodCall(ar)
Else
    ' Else, cast to WebClientAsyncResult to abort the call.
    DirectCast(ar, WebClientAsyncResult).Abort()
End If
```

One-Way Methods

A special case of asynchronous calls occurs when the client doesn't really care about the return value from the Web service. For example, you might build a Web service that exposes one or more methods that clients call only to signal that something has occurred or to issue commands (for example, to start a lengthy batch compilation). In such a case, you can reach perfect asynchronicity by flagging the Web service method using a SoapDocumentMethod attribute with its OneWay argument set to True:

```
<WebMethod(), SoapDocumentMethod(OneWay:=True)> _
Sub OneWayLengthyMethodCall(ByVal seconds As Integer)
    ' Simulate a lengthy method.
    Thread.Sleep(seconds * 1000)
End Sub
```

Methods flagged in this way must have neither a return value nor ByRef arguments. Also, they can't access their HttpContext object, and any property of the Web service class returns Nothing.

Working with Proxy Servers

If the client is behind a proxy server, calls to a Web service might fail. In most cases, you can solve this problem by creating a System.Net.WebProxy object and assigning it to the Proxy property of the client's proxy object:

```
Dim service As New localhost.SampleService
' True means that we want to bypass the proxy for local addresses.
service.Proxy = New WebProxy("http://proxyserver:80", True)
service.LengthyMethodCall(10)
```

The CookieContainer Property

Remember from the section "Enabling Session State," earlier in this chapter, the standard proxy class doesn't work well with Web service methods that rely on session state—that is, methods whose EnableSession attribute is set to True—because the proxy class can't work as a cookie container. Therefore, it can't store the session cookie that ASP.NET sends to the client when a new session is detected.

Fortunately, making the proxy class a valid cookie container is just a matter of ensuring that its CookieContainer property holds a reference to a System.Net.CookieContainer object:

```
Dim service As New localhost.SampleService()

' Each time this method is called, the value in the Label
' control is incremented by 1.
Sub TestIncrementCounterMethod()
    ' Make the proxy object a cookie container, if necessary.
    If service.CookieContainer Is Nothing Then
        service.CookieContainer = New CookieContainer()
    End If
    Label1.Text = service.IncrementCounter()
End Sub
```

After setting the CookieContainer property, the proxy object is able to store the session cookie. The session is terminated when the proxy object is set to Nothing or when the session timeout expires without invoking any method in the Web service. (The default session timeout is 20 minutes.)

The CookieContainer property returns a collection of cookies, so you can read the cookies it contains and you can add your own cookies. In particular, you can read the special session cookie named ASP.NET_SessionId, save it in a variable or on disk, and add it to the cookies collection in a subsequent call:

```
Dim saveCookie As Cookie

Sub CallStatefulWebServiceMethod()
    Dim service As New localhost.SampleService()
    ' Make the proxy object a cookie container.
    service.CookieContainer = New CookieContainer()

    ' If we already have the cookie, let's add it to the cookies collection.
    If Not (saveCookie Is Nothing) Then
        service.CookieContainer.Add(saveCookie)
    End If
    ' Call the  Web service method.
    Label1.Text = service.IncrementCounter()

    ' Save the cookie if this is the first call.
    If saveCookie Is Nothing Then
        ' Replace the argument with the actual  Web service's URL.
        Dim cookieUri As New Uri("http://localhost")
        ' Save the ASP.NET_SessionId cookie belonging to the localhost URI.
        saveCookie = service.CookieContainer.GetCookies(cookieUri).Item _
            ("ASP.NET_SessionId")
    End If
End Sub
```

This technique has two important applications. First, two Windows Forms applications can share the same session, regardless of whether they're running on the same or different client machines, as long as they have a means for exchanging the contents of the session cookie. Second, all the pages in a Web Forms ASP.NET application can invoke methods in a Web service and share the same set of session variables. (In this case, the individual .aspx pages should save the cookie in a Session or Application variable.)

SOAP Exceptions

Web services methods can throw exceptions, either directly with a Throw statement or indirectly when they perform an invalid operation. When interacting with a Web service, you must account for other types of errors as well, such as those caused by a client using an outdated version of the WSDL contract (and of the proxy class).

Whenever an error occurs while a Web service is processing a request, the SOAP message returned to the client contains a <soap:Fault> block inside its body instead of the usual <soap:Body> block. On the client side, this fault block is translated into a SoapException object, which is the type to look for in the Catch clause of the Try...End Try block. The SoapException class inherits from SystemException all the usual properties, to which it adds a few specific ones. The most significant members of the SoapException class are the following:

- Message is the message property of the original exception.

- Actor is the URL of the Web service that threw the exception.

- Code is an XmlQualifiedName object that specifies the SOAP fault code that describes the general cause of the error.

- Detail is an XmlNode object representing application-specific error information. This property is set only if the error occurred when the Web service was processing the body of the message and is Nothing in other cases (such as when the problem was in the header or in the format of the message).

Most of the time, the properties you should focus your attention on are Message and Code. A minor problem is that the original error string is buried inside the value returned by the Message property. For example, if the Web service method throws a NullReferenceException, this is the string you'll find in the Message property:

```
System.Web.Services.Protocols.SoapException: Server was unable to
process request. ---> System.NullReferenceException: Object reference
not set to an instance of an object.
   at MoneyConverter.SampleService.ThrowAnException()
   --- End of inner exception stack trace ---
```

The simplest way to extract the name of the real exception is to use regular expressions. Here's a reusable routine that does the job:

```
' Extract the name of the "inner" exception.
Function GetWSException(ByVal ex As SoapException) As String
    ' Parse the exception's Message property.
    Dim mc As MatchCollection = Regex.Matches(ex.Message, "---> ([^:]+):")
    If mc.Count >= 1 Then
        ' We've found a match - the first group contains the value.
        Return mc.Item(0).Groups(1).Value
    End If
End Function
```

You can use the GetWSException function inside a Try...End Try block that uses a When clause, as follows:

```
Try
    Dim service As New localhost.SampleService()
    service.ThrowAnException()
Catch ex As SoapException _
    When GetWSException(ex) = "System.NullReferenceException"
    ' A null reference exception
    ⋮
Catch ex As SoapException _
    When GetWSException(ex) = "System.DivideByZeroException"
    ' A divide-by-zero exception
    ⋮
End Try
```

The Code property of the SoapException class is useful in that it lets you quickly classify the type of exception you've received. This property returns an XmlQualifiedName object, whose Name property can be one of the following:

- **VersionMismatch**   An invalid namespace was found.

- **MustUnderstand**   The client sent an element whose MustUnderstand attribute was 1, but the server was unable to process it.

- **Client**   The client request wasn't formatted properly or didn't contain appropriate information. This exception is an indication that the message shouldn't be sent again without change.

- **Server**   An error occurred on the server but wasn't caused by the message contents; this is the value returned by the Code property when the code running in the Web service throws an exception.

To help you test the Code property, the SoapException class defines four constants, named VersionMismatchFaultCode, MustUnderstandFaultCode, ClientFaultCode, and ServerFaultCode. The following code uses these constants to determine what kind of error occurred, by means of the When clause of the Try...End Try block:

```
Try
    Dim service As New localhost.SampleService()
    service.ThrowAnException()
Catch ex As SoapException _
    When ex.Code.Equals(SoapException.VersionMismatchFaultCode)
    ' An invalid namespace has been used.
    ⋮
Catch ex As SoapException _
    When ex.Code.Equals(SoapException.ServerFaultCode)
    ' An invalid namespace has been used.
    ⋮
End Try
```

Advanced Topics

In the last part of this chapter, I cover three advanced topics that can be useful when implementing real-world Web services: SOAP headers, security, and SOAP extensions.

SOAP Headers

Remember from the section "Understanding Web Services Protocols," near the beginning of this chapter, a SOAP message can contain additional information in its header. The message header is optional, and in fact all the examples I've shown you so far haven't used this portion of the SOAP message.

I've prepared an example that shows how you can pass a SOAP header and how a Web service can use this header to format date and other information in the format expected by the client. To prepare a Web service class to work with a SOAP header, you must do three things:

1. Define a class that contains the fields that you want to pass through the header. This class must inherit from the System.Web.Services.Protocols.SoapHeader class.

2. Define a public field in the class typed after the class defined in the previous step.

3. Add a SoapHeader attribute to all the methods that you want to read the SOAP header. The argument of this attribute is the name of the field defined in the previous step.

Here's an example of a Web service that exposes a method named GetClientTime, which returns the client's local time formatted according to the client's locale. The locale information and the offset from the Universal Time Coordinates (UTC) are passed in an instance of the UserInfoHeader class:

```
Public Class SampleService
    Inherits System.Web.Services.WebService

    ' This is the Public variable that receives the userInfo header.
    Public userInfo As UserInfoHeader

    <WebMethod(), SoapHeader("userInfo")> _
    Function GetClientTime() As String
        ' The server's local time in Coordinated Universal Time
        Dim serverTime As Date = Date.Now.ToUniversalTime
        ' Convert to client's time zone.
        Dim clientTime As Date = serverTime.AddHours(userInfo.TimeOffset)
        ' Create a CultureInfo object with proper locale information.
        Dim ci As New System.Globalization.CultureInfo(userInfo.Culture)
        ' Return the time formatted using client's formatting rules.
        Return clientTime.ToString(ci)
    End Function
End Class


' This class defines the information carried with the SOAP header.

Public Class UserInfoHeader
    Inherits SoapHeader

    ' This member contains the culture name of the user.
    Public Culture As String = ""
    ' This member contains the time difference from UTC time.
    Public TimeOffset As Single = 0
End Class
```

When you produce the WSDL contract and use it to generate the proxy class, the client definition of the UserInfoHeader class is generated as well, so the client code can create an instance of this class and initialize it as required. Moreover, the proxy class is extended with a field named *headerclass*Value—UserInfoHeaderValue in this example—so the client can assign the UserInfoHeader object to this field. Here's how you call a Web service method that takes a SOAP header:

```
' Create a header.
Dim userInfo As New localhost.UserInfoHeader()
' This is the identifier for the Italian language.
userInfo.Culture = "it-it"
' Italian time is one hour ahead of Greenwich time.
userInfo.TimeOffset = 1

' Create an instance of the proxy class.
Dim service As New localhost.SampleService()
' Assign the header to the special xxxxValue field.
service.UserInfoHeaderValue = userInfo
' Call the Web service.
Dim res As String = service.GetClientTime()
```

Under .NET 1.0, the SoapHeader attribute makes the header mandatory, and the client gets an exception if no header is associated with the proxy object, but you can make the header optional by adding a Required argument set to False. Under .NET 1.1, the Required argument is ignored, and SOAP headers are always optional. Therefore, under .NET 1.1, either you must ensure that the code in the Web service method works well even if the client doesn't send a header or you must manually throw an exception if the client didn't send a header that is strictly necessary to process the method call:

```
' You can omit the Required argument under .NET 1.1.

<WebMethod(), SoapHeader("userInfo", Required:=False)> _
Function GetClientTime() As String
    ' Provide a default userInfo object if the client omitted it.
    If userInfo Is Nothing Then
        userInfo = New UserInfoHeader()
        ' In this case, UTC time is returned to the client.
    End If
    ⋮
End Function
```

By default, headers are sent to the Web service but aren't returned to the client to save bandwidth. In other words, the header object works as an input-only argument for the Web service method. It doesn't have to be so, however, and you have complete control over how headers are sent back and forth. The key to this feature is the Direction argument of the SoapHeader attribute: its default value is In, but you can set it to InOut or Out. .NET Framework 1.1 supports a fourth value, Fault; you can add this value to any of the other three if you want to return the SOAP header to the client even when the Web service throws an exception.

```
<WebMethod(), SoapHeader("userInfo", Required:=False, _
    Direction:=SoapHeaderDirection.InOut)> _
Function GetClientTime() As String
    ' Provide a default userInfo object if the client omitted it.
    If userInfo Is Nothing Then
        ' (This header is returned to the client.)
        userInfo = New UserInfoHeader()
        userInfo.Culture = "EN-US"        ' American English
        userInfo.TimeOffset = -5          ' U.S. eastern time
```

```
      End If
        ⋮
End Function
```

I'll illustrate other uses for SOAP headers shortly, in the section "Custom Authentication."

Web Service Security

Web service security doesn't differ noticeably from standard ASP.NET security, and all the security mechanisms you saw in Chapter 27 are valid with Web services. The peculiarities in Web service security stem from their noninteractive nature. For example, if you disable anonymous access for an .asmx file from inside IIS, any client request for that .asmx file fails, but no dialog box is displayed.

Another consequence of the programmatic nature of Web services: you can use Forms authentication and redirect all nonauthenticated requests to a given URL (using the LoginURL entry in web.config), but this tactic is of no practical use because the Web service client would receive HTML instead of the SOAP message it's expecting. Although this obstacle might be removed if you provided a custom function that manually creates the authentication cookie, in general Forms authentication isn't recommended as a viable authentication method for Web services, and I won't cover it in this book.

Windows Authentication

Windows authentication is the simplest authentication method you can use for a Web service that can't accept anonymous requests. Whether or not you've protected the .asmx page with Basic, Digest, or Integrated Windows authentication, you can provide your credentials to IIS by assigning a NetworkCredential object to the proxy object's Credential property, as in this code snippet:

```
' Create a System.Net.NetworkCredential object.
Dim nc As New NetworkCredential()
nc.UserName = "username"
nc.Password = "userpwd"
nc.Domain = "domainname"

' Create the proxy object and assign it the user credentials.
Dim service As New localhost.Converter()
service.Credentials = nc
' Make the call.
Dim euros As Decimal = service.DollarToEuro(100)
```

If the .asmx page requires Windows authentication and you pass invalid credentials (or no credentials at all), the client application receives a WebException object whose Message property is this:

```
The request failed with HTTP status 401: Access Denied.
```

If the client application has a user interface, you might catch this exception, display a dialog box, and ask the user to enter her name and password to submit in a second attempt.

Everything I said in Chapter 27 about the various Windows authentication methods holds true for Web services. For example, when Basic authentication is used, the username and password are sent in clear text (in Base64-encoded format), and you should use Integrated Windows security if possible.

Custom Authentication

As happens with regular ASP.NET applications, Windows authentication has a major drawback: often you don't want to create one Windows account for each user of your Web service. In this section, I show how you can leverage SOAP headers to implement a custom authentication mechanism.

The idea is simple: each call from the client application must include a SOAP header that contains username and password. All the Web service methods that require authentication—for example, methods that require some form of subscription—invoke a central function, named ValidateUser, which checks the credentials in the header and throws an exception if the credentials aren't valid or the subscription has expired. Here's the source code for a Web service class that contains such a method:

```
Public Class SampleService
    Inherits System.Web.Services.WebService

    Public accountInfo As AccountInfoHeader

    <WebMethod(), SoapHeader("accountInfo")> _
    Function ProtectedMethod() As Boolean
        ' Check that credentials are OK; throw exception if not.
        ValidateAccount()
        ' Return a value (always True in this demo).
        Return True
    End Function

    ' Validate username and password (private function).
    Private Sub ValidateAccount()
        ' Throw exception if missing header.
        If accountInfo Is Nothing Then
            Throw New SoapException("Missing user info header", _
                SoapException.ClientFaultCode)
        End If

        ' Throw exception if header members aren't set.
        If accountInfo.UserName = "" Or accountInfo.Password = "" Then
            Throw New SoapException("Missing user info", _
                SoapException.ClientFaultCode)
        End If

        ' Throw exception if invalid user.
        If Not CheckUser(accountInfo.UserName, accountInfo.Password) Then
            Throw New SoapException("Insufficient subscription level", _
                SoapException.ClientFaultCode)
        End If
```

```
            ' Exit regularly if everything is OK.
        End Sub

        ' Check that user credentials are valid.
        Function CheckUser(ByVal username As String, ByVal password As String) _
            As Boolean
            ' (A real-world application would use a database.)
            If username = "JoeDoe" And password = "jdpwd" Then
                Return True
            ElseIf username = "AnnSmith" And password = "aspwd" Then
                Return True
            Else
                ' Unknown user or invalid credentials
                Return False
            End If
        End Function
End Class


' This is the SOAP Header class.

Public Class AccountInfoHeader
        Inherits SoapHeader
    Public UserName As String
    Public Password As String
End Class
```

The client-side code is similar to the code you saw in the section "SOAP Headers," earlier in this chapter:

```
' Prepare the SOAP header with account information.
Dim accountInfo As New localhost.AccountInfoHeader()
accountInfo.UserName = "JoeDoe"
accountInfo.Password = "jdpwd"

' Pass account information to the proxy class.
Dim service As New localhost.SampleService()
service.AccountInfoHeaderValue = accountInfo
' Call the protected  Web service method.
Dim res As Boolean = service.ProtectedMethod()
```

The beauty of this approach is that you can easily expand the ValidateUser procedure in the Web service class to implement sophisticated authorization policies. For example, the procedure can use reflection techniques to retrieve the name of the method that called it—that is, the Web service method invoked by the client—and ensure that users have a subscription level that allows them to make the call. Here's an implementation of this concept:

```
    ' Validate username and password. (Private procedure)
    Private Sub ValidateAccount()
        ' Throw exception if missing header.
        If accountInfo Is Nothing Then
            Throw New SoapException("Missing user info header", _
                SoapException.ClientFaultCode)
        End If
```

```
' Throw exception if header members aren't set.
If accountInfo.UserName = "" Or accountInfo.Password = "" Then
    Throw New SoapException("Missing user info", _
        SoapException.ClientFaultCode)
End If

' Retrieve the subscription level of this user.
Dim thisUserSubscriptionLevel As Integer = GetUserSubscriptionLevel _
    (accountInfo.UserName, accountInfo.Password)
' Exit if credentials are invalid.
If thisUserSubscriptionLevel < 0 Then
    Throw New SoapException("Unknown user", _
        SoapException.ClientFaultCode)
End If

' Retrieve the name of the method that called this procedure.
Dim st As New System.Diagnostics.StackTrace(False)
' GetFrame(0) describes the running procedure,
' GetFrame(1) describes the calling procedure.
Dim sf As System.Diagnostics.StackFrame = st.GetFrame(1)
Dim mb As System.Reflection.MethodBase = sf.GetMethod

' Retrieve the required subscription level for the calling method.
Dim requiredSubscriptionLevel As Integer
Select Case mb.Name
    Case "ProtectedMethod"
        requiredSubscriptionLevel = 1
    Case "AnotherProtectedMethod"
        requiredSubscriptionLevel = 2
End Select

' Throw exception if subscription level isn't sufficient.
If thisUserSubscriptionLevel < requiredSubscriptionLevel Then
    Throw New SoapException("Insufficient subscription level", _
        SoapException.ClientFaultCode)
End If

' Exit regularly if everything is OK.
End Sub

' Get user subscription level, or -1 if credentials are invalid.
Function GetUserSubscriptionLevel(ByVal username As String, _
    ByVal password As String) As Integer
    ' (A real application would use a database instead.)
    If username = "JoeDoe" And password = "jdpwd" Then
        Return 1
    ElseIf username = "AnnSmith" And password = "aspwd" Then
        Return 2
    Else
        ' Unknown user or invalid credentials
        Return -1
    End If
End Function
```

Now you have a centralized place in which you can control all access to your Web service, so you can change your subscription and charge policy without editing the code in any other Web service method.

You can improve this mechanism even more by creating a SOAP extension that reads the SOAP header and does the authentication and authorization before the execution flow ever reaches the method, as I explain in the following section.

SOAP Extensions

The Web service architecture can be completely redefined by the programmer, if necessary, by means of *SOAP extensions*. A SOAP extension is a software module that can execute custom code before the SOAP message reaches the Web service method. More precisely, there are four points at which a SOAP extension has a chance of executing custom code. They correspond to the four possible stages of a SOAP message. (See the right side of Figure 29-9.)

- **BeforeDeserialize**   The SOAP message has been received from the client, is still in XML format, and hasn't been deserialized into an in-memory object yet.

- **AfterDeserialize**   The SOAP message has been serialized into an object, and the actual Web service method is about to be called.

- **BeforeSerialize**   The Web service method has completed its execution, and the result object is about to be serialized into XML.

- **AfterSerialize**   The result object has been serialized into a SOAP message, and the XML text is about to be sent to the client.

Interestingly, a SOAP message leaving a client—that is, the proxy object on the client—undergoes the same four stages, but they occur in a different order. (See the left side of Figure 29-9.)

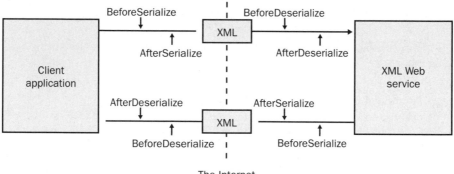

The Internet

Figure 29-9   The four stages a SOAP message undergoes on the server and on the client

A SOAP extension can read the XML data being sent from the client to the server and back and can modify it if necessary. So, for example, you might save the XML for logging or debugging reasons or encrypt return values to avoid eavesdropping and tampering—even though this task would require a SOAP extension running on the client that decrypts the result.

From the perspective of a developer, a SOAP extension is just a class that inherits from the System.Web.Services.Protocols.SoapExtension abstract class and overrides a few of its methods. However, before you can see how to build this class, you should learn how to associate a SOAP extension with a Web service. You can choose from two methods for doing so:

■   Add an entry to the configuration file. (In this case, the SOAP extension is invoked for all the methods associated with a WebMethod attribute.)

■   Define a custom attribute, and use it to flag only the methods for which you want to activate the SOAP extension. This method is more flexible because you can pass one or more arguments to the custom attribute's constructor and make these arguments available to the SOAP extension class. (This mechanism might be used, for example, to associate a fee with each Web service method.)

Let's see how to implement these two activation methods.

Activating a SOAP Extension from a Configuration File

You can install a SOAP extension by adding an <add> tag in the <soapExtension-Types> block in web.config:

```
<configuration>
 <system.web>
   <webServices>
     <soapExtensionTypes>
      <add type="Logger.LoggerExtension, logger"
           Priority="1" Group="0" />
     <soapExtensionTypes>
    <webServices>
 <system.web>
<configuration>
```

Here type is the name of the SOAP extension class, Group is the SOAP extension group (can be 0 or 1), and Priority is the priority inside the group (0 being the highest priority). A SOAP extension can belong to one of three groups:

■   **Group 0**   SOAP extensions in this group have the highest priority and can process the message before extensions belonging to the other two groups.

■   **Medium group**   These are the SOAP extensions activated through custom attributes applied to methods in the Web service class. (I explain how to activate these extensions in the next section.)

■   **Group 1**   SOAP extensions in this group have the lowest priority and process the message after extensions that belong to the first two groups.

Activating a SOAP extension by editing the web.config class is the best solution when the extension must be applied to all the methods in the Web service and when no argument must be passed to the extension. For example, you might use this technique to activate a SOAP extension that traces all incoming requests or that encrypts the result from all Web service methods.

Activating a SOAP Extension with a Custom Attribute

The second and more flexible method for activating a SOAP extension is by means of a custom attribute used to flag the methods in the Web service for which the SOAP extension must be used. This technique lets you apply the extension to just a subset of all the existing methods and allows you to define arguments that are passed to the SOAP extension, on a method-by-method basis.

In the following sections, I'll show you how to implement a SOAP extension that monitors access to any Web service method marked with a special SoapCustomAuthenticationAttribute. The constructor for this attribute takes an integer that defines the minimum subscription level required for a client to invoke the method that has been flagged with the attribute. (This is the SOAP extension version of the authentication and authorization method described in the section "Custom Authentication," earlier in this chapter.) For example, a method in SampleService.asmx that can be called only by clients whose subscription level is 2 or higher would look like this:

```
<WebMethod(), SoapCustomAuthentication(2), SoapHeader("accountInfo")> _
Function YetAnotherProtectedMethod() As Boolean
    ⋮
End Function
```

The SoapCustomAuthenticationAttribute class must inherit from the SoapExtensionAttribute abstract class. All classes that derive from this abstract class must override its Priority and ExtensionType properties. The latter property is especially important in that it returns the System.Type object that defines the SOAP extension class (named SoapExtensionAuthentication in this example). In the example that follows, the attribute class exposes also an additional property, RequiredSubscriptionLevel, which defines the minimum subscription level that's necessary to invoke the method to which this attribute is applied. The minimum subscription level is the only argument you must pass to the attribute's constructor:

```
' The custom attribute you must use to flag methods that require
' a given subscription level.

<AttributeUsage(AttributeTargets.Method)> _
Public Class SoapCustomAuthenticationAttribute
    Inherits SoapExtensionAttribute

    ' The attribute constructor
    Sub New(ByVal requiredSubscriptionLevel As Integer)
        Me.RequiredSubscriptionLevel = requiredSubscriptionLevel
    End Sub

    ' You must override the Priority property.
```

```vb
    Dim m_Priority As Integer

    Public Overrides Property Priority() As Integer
        Get
            Return m_Priority
        End Get
        Set(ByVal Value As Integer)
            m_Priority = Value
        End Set
    End Property

    ' The ExtensionType property returns the type of the SoapExtension class.

    Public Overrides ReadOnly Property ExtensionType() As System.Type
        Get
            Return GetType(SoapCustomAuthentication)
        End Get
    End Property

    ' RequiredSubscriptionLevel is a custom property for this attribute.

    Dim m_RequiredSubscriptionLevel As Integer

    Property RequiredSubscriptionLevel() As Integer
        Get
            Return m_RequiredSubscriptionLevel
        End Get
        Set(ByVal Value As Integer)
            m_RequiredSubscriptionLevel = Value
        End Set
    End Property
End Class
```

The SOAP Extension Class

The actual SOAP extension is contained in a class that inherits from the System.Web.Services.Protocols.SoapExtension abstract class and overrides a few of its members. Because the structure of this class is complex, I'll show and comment its listing one method at a time, in the order in which these methods are called by the ASP.NET infrastructure.

The GetInitializer method is called only once during the life of the SOAP extension. There are two overloaded versions for this method, depending on whether the extension is activated by means of an entry in the configuration file or by means of a custom attribute in the Web service class. In the former instance, the method receives a System.Type object corresponding to the type of the Web service class. (This argument is necessary because a SOAP extension can serve multiple Web service classes.) In the latter instance, the GetInitializer method receives a reference to the custom attribute and a MethodInfo object that describes the method to which the attribute has been applied.

In both cases, the GetInitializer method is expected to return an Object value. This value is then passed as an argument to the Initialize method. This double-initialization approach makes the developer's job a bit more complicated, but it improves performance. In our specific example, the GetInitializer method returns the RequiredSubscriptionLevel property of the custom attribute or the value 1 if the SOAP extension has been activated by means of an entry in the configuration file:

```
' The Soap extension class

Class SoapCustomAuthentication
    Inherits SoapExtension

    ' This overload is called if the SOAP extension is installed
    ' in web.config; it receives the Type of the WebService class.

    Public Overloads Overrides Function GetInitializer( _
        ByVal serviceType As System.Type) As Object
        ' In this case, we just return 1, the lowest subscription level
        ' required to access methods in the  Web service.
        If serviceType Is GetType(SampleService) Then
            Return 1
        End If
    End Function

    ' This overload is called if the SOAP extension is activated because the client
    ' called a method that was flagged with a SoapExtensionAttribute.

    Public Overloads Overrides Function GetInitializer( _
        ByVal methodInfo As LogicalMethodInfo, _
        ByVal attribute As SoapExtensionAttribute) As Object
        ' Get a strongly typed reference to the attribute.
        Dim scaAttr As SoapCustomAuthenticationAttribute = _
            DirectCast(attribute, SoapCustomAuthenticationAttribute)
        ' Return its RequiredSubscriptionLevel property.
        Return scaAttr.RequiredSubscriptionLevel
    End Function

    ' ...(Other methods of this class are described later)...
    ⋮
End Class
```

Unlike the GetInitializer method—which is called only once in the SOAP extension's lifetime—the Initialize method is called every time ASP.NET receives a request that must be passed to the SOAP extension. The Initialize method receives an Object argument equal to the return value of the GetInitializer method. In our example, this value is the minimum subscription level necessary to access the Web service method being invoked. Typically, the code in the Initialize method saves this value in a private variable to make it accessible from other methods in the class:

```
' The Initialize method is called with the RequiredSubscriptionLevel
' integer in its argument.
Dim RequiredSubscriptionLevel As Integer

Public Overrides Sub Initialize(ByVal initializer As Object)
```

```
        ' Save the required subscription level for later.
        RequiredSubscriptionLevel = CInt(initializer)
    End Sub
```

The third overridden method is ChainStream, which receives the stream used to move the XML text from the client to the Web service and back. It can be the original stream used by ASP.NET to read and output data, or it can be a stream created by another SOAP extension. The ChainStream method is called before each processing stage the SOAP message goes through. Because the purpose of most SOAP extensions is to read and possibly modify the XML being transmitted from and to the client, you must create a new stream, save both the original and the new stream in a pair of local variables, and return the stream just created:

```
Dim oldStream As Stream, newStream As Stream

' The ChainStream is called when the SoapExtension class is instantiated.
Public Overrides Function ChainStream(ByVal stream As Stream) As Stream
    ' Save the old stream.
    oldStream = stream
    ' Create a new stream and return it.
    newStream = New MemoryStream()
    Return newStream
End Function
```

The last overridden method that ASP.NET calls into your SOAP extension is also the most important of the group because it's where the real action is. The ProcessMessage method is called once for each possible state the message can be in, and you can tell what these states are by means of the Stage property of the SoapMessage object passed as an argument:

```
' This method is called multiple times for each message.

Public Overrides Sub ProcessMessage(ByVal message As SoapMessage)
    Select Case message.Stage
        Case SoapMessageStage.BeforeDeserialize
            ' Copy from old stream to new stream.
            CopyStream(oldStream, newStream)
            newStream.Position = 0
        Case SoapMessageStage.AfterDeserialize
            ' The message is deserialized, so we can read message headers.
            If EvalSubscriptionLevel(message) < RequiredSubscriptionLevel Then
                ' Throw an exception if subscription level isn't adequate.
                Throw New SoapException("Insufficient subscription level", _
                    SoapException.ClientFaultCode)
            End If
        Case SoapMessageStage.BeforeSerialize
        Case SoapMessageStage.AfterSerialize
            ' Copy from new to old stream.
            newStream.Position = 0
            CopyStream(newStream, oldStream)
    End Select
End Sub
```

```
' This is a helper routine that moves data from one stream to another.

Private Sub CopyStream(ByVal source As Stream, ByVal dest As Stream)
    Dim sr As New StreamReader(source)
    Dim sw As New StreamWriter(dest)
    sw.WriteLine(sr.ReadToEnd)
    sw.Flush()
End Sub
```

The EvalSubscriptionLevel is a private function that analyzes all the headers of the
SoapMessage object and looks for an AccountInfoHeader object. If such a header is
found, the function can determine whether the client's username and password are
valid and returns the client's subscription level:

```
Private Function EvalSubscriptionLevel(ByVal message As SoapMessage) _
    As Integer
    ' Check whether there is a header of type AccountInfoHeader.
    For Each header As SoapHeader In message.Headers
        If TypeOf header Is AccountInfoHeader Then
            ' Cast to the proper type.
            Dim accountInfo As AccountInfoHeader = _
                DirectCast(header, AccountInfoHeader)
            ' Check user credentials and return subscription level.
            Return GetUserSubscriptionLevel(accountInfo.UserName, _
                accountInfo.Password)
        End If
    Next
    ' If we get here, credentials were missing or invalid.
    Return -1
End Function
```

(I omitted the source code for the GetUserSubscriptionLevel class because it is the
same as the class illustrated in the section "Custom Authentication," earlier in this chapter.)

Here's the client-side code that invokes a method protected with a SoapCustomAu-
thentication attribute:

```
' Prepare account information in the header.
Dim accountInfo As New localhost.AccountInfoHeader()
accountInfo.UserName = "JoeDoe"
accountInfo.Password = "jdpwd"
' Associate account info with the proxy object.
Dim service As New localhost.SampleService()
service.AccountInfoHeaderValue = accountInfo

Try
    ' This call succeeds only if user JoeDoe has a subscription
    ' level of 2 or higher.
    Dim res As Boolean = service.YetAnotherProtectedMethod()
Catch ex As Exception
    MsgBox(ex.Message, MsgBoxStyle.Critical)
End Try
```

Client-Side SOAP Extensions

So far, I've described what are called server-side SOAP extensions, which are by far the most common types of SOAP extensions. However, you can also implement client-side SOAP extensions. For example, a client-side SOAP extension might be necessary to decrypt the XML sent by a Web service and encrypted by a server-side SOAP extension. You can activate a client-side SOAP extension via custom attributes, exactly as you do for server-side extensions, except the custom attribute is applied to the methods in the proxy class.

A client-side SOAP extension goes through the same four stages that server-side extensions do, but their order is different: BeforeSerialize and AfterSerialize when the SOAP message is being sent to the Web service; BeforeDeserialize and AfterDeserialize when the result XML is being received from the Web service. (See Figure 29-9.)

Web Service Extensions (WSE)

The Web services story doesn't end with the techniques I have illustrated in this chapter. Instead, I'd dare to say that this is just the beginning of a saga that will keep developers occupied for many years to come.

If you are serious about learning Web services, you should visit *http://www.msdn.microsoft.com/webservices* and download the most recent version of the Web Services Enhancement (WSE) library, which implements great features such as authentication, encryption, and binary attachments. As of this writing, the Technology Preview version of WSE 2.0 is available, which adds many other useful characteristics, including role-based security and transactions. These features are implemented as SOAP extensions, so you can leverage what you've learned in this chapter.

When I began to write the second edition of this book, I was determined to add one chapter on WSE, but the fast pace at which Web services technology is evolving would have made that information stale after a few months (or even weeks). Instead of chasing this new and exciting technology, I decided to devote the new chapters of this edition to other portions of the .NET Framework that are quite stable and that aren't going to change remarkably in the short run, starting with PInvoke and COM Interop.

Part VII
Advanced Topics

30 PInvoke and COM Interop

The Microsoft .NET Framework is a revolution in the programming world. Managed applications are going to become the most common type of Microsoft Windows software—or at least this is what Microsoft hopes. However, even the most enthusiastic .NET fan—inside or outside Microsoft—can't reasonably expect that unmanaged code is going to disappear anytime soon, for at least three reasons. First, rewriting all existing software as managed code can be cost-prohibitive, and the advantage of having it running as a .NET application might not justify migration costs. Second, many services are available today to Windows programmers only as COM components, such as Microsoft Word or Excel object libraries. Third, the .NET platform encompasses many but not all features of the operating system. You still need unmanaged code to write shell extensions, work with memory mapped files, or perform cross-process window subclassing, just to mention a few Windows features not yet encapsulated in .NET classes.

For these and other reasons, Microsoft correctly assumed that the ability to call unmanaged code was crucial for the success of the .NET platform, and therefore they provided two distinct yet related mechanisms to extend .NET in that direction: Platform Invoke (also known as PInvoke) and COM Interop. PInvoke technology lets .NET code call "traditional" DLLs, such as those that make up the Windows kernel or those written in C or C++, whereas COM Interop lets you reuse COM components from .NET or call .NET components from COM applications.

Despite their different goals, these two technologies have a lot in common, and it makes sense to discuss them in the same chapter. For example, with only a few exceptions, they share the marshaling rules that dictate how data can be moved from the managed world to the unmanaged world and back. PInvoke is the simpler of the two technologies, so I'll cover it first. I'll defer COM Interop to the second part of this chapter.

> **Note** To keep the code as concise as possible, all the code samples in this chapter assume the use of the following Imports statements at the file or project level:
>
> ```
> Imports System.Runtime.InteropServices
> Imports System.Reflection
> Imports System.Text
> Imports System.Threading
> Imports Microsoft.Win32
> ```

Using PInvoke

Before you can call a function in an external DLL, you must declare the function's name and syntax. Microsoft Visual Basic .NET provides two different ways to do so: the Declare keyword and the DllImport attribute. The former provides backward compatibility with earlier versions of the language; the latter is the mechanism adopted by all .NET languages. Except for the different syntax, the two approaches are broadly equivalent, with DllImport being slightly more flexible.

The Declare Keyword

Visual Basic has supported the Declare keyword since version 1, so odds are that you are already familiar with it. In a difference from previous language versions, you can use a public Declare statement anywhere in your application, including module, form, and class blocks. Here's its complete syntax:

```
Declare [Ansi|Unicode|Auto] [Sub|Function] procedurename Lib "dllname"
[Alias "entrypoint"] ( arglist ) [As returntype]
```

where procedurename is the name of the procedure as seen in the Visual Basic program, dllname is the name of the DLL, and entrypoint is the name of the procedure in the DLL. (This name can be different from procedurename and can include characters that are invalid in Visual Basic.) In most cases, you can convert Declare statements written for Visual Basic 6 to Visual Basic .NET without any change other than adjusting data types (for example, translating Long to Integer).

Visual Basic .NET has introduced the optional Ansi, Unicode, and Auto keywords, which dictate how .NET strings are passed to the external DLL. Ansi specifies that strings are passed as ANSI strings (the default behavior); Unicode forces strings to be passed as Unicode; Auto causes strings to be passed as ANSI strings under Windows 98 and Windows Me or as Unicode strings under more recent versions of the operating system.

The following code snippet declares two functions in the Windows User32.dll and invokes them to retrieve the handle of a window titled Untitled - Notepad, resize the window, and move the window to the upper left corner of the screen. You should launch Notepad on an empty document before trying this code.

```
' (The Ansi qualifier is optional.)
Private Declare Ansi Function FindWindow Lib "user32" Alias "FindWindowA" _
    (ByVal lpClassName As String, ByVal lpWindowName As String) As Integer
Private Declare Function MoveWindow Lib "user32" Alias "MoveWindow" _
    (ByVal hWnd As Integer, ByVal x As Integer, ByVal y As Integer, _
    ByVal nWidth As Integer, ByVal nHeight As Integer, _
    ByVal bRepaint As Integer) As Integer
```

```
Sub TestFindWindow()
    ' This works only on English and US versions of Windows.
    Dim hWnd As Integer = FindWindow(Nothing, "Untitled - Notepad")
    If hWnd <> 0 Then
        MoveWindow(hWnd, 0, 0, 600, 300, 1)
    Else
        MessageBox.Show("Window not found", "Error")
    End If
End Sub
```

As this snippet demonstrates, you can use Nothing to pass a null string. In earlier versions of Visual Basic, you would have passed the vbNullString constant in these circumstances. (This constant is still supported but is superfluous under Visual Basic .NET.) Remember that a null string is always different from an empty string—that is, a string that contains no characters—when calling a function in a DLL.

A Declare statement can include optional arguments; if you omit an optional argument when calling the function, its default value is pushed on the stack anyway. If the external function receives an incorrect number of arguments, your application is likely to crash.

> **See Also**   You can learn more about the Declare keyword and see many advanced examples of how to use it in Appendix of Programming Microsoft Visual Basic 6, available on the companion CD. All examples are for Visual Basic 6; you need to adapt them to Visual Basic .NET.

The DllImport Attribute

Although the Declare keyword is still supported, you should abandon it in favor of the DllImport attribute. This attribute is preferable because it offers additional options and also because it works in virtually all .NET languages, including C#, so it makes your code more readable to other developers and more easily ported to other languages.

The DllImport attribute is defined in the System.Runtime.InteropServices namespace and can be applied only to static methods—namely, methods defined in a module or class methods flagged with the Shared keyword. The method marked with this attribute is used only as a blueprint for deriving the type of arguments and the type of the return value (if there is one); a compilation error occurs if the method contains executable code. In the simplest case, the DllImport attribute specifies only the name of the DLL that contains the external function:

```
Class WindowsFunctions
    <DllImport("user32")> _
    Public Shared Function FindWindow(ByVal lpClassName As String, _
        ByVal lpWindowName As String) As Integer
        ' No code here
    End Function
```

```
        <DllImport("user32")> _
        Shared Function MoveWindow(ByVal hWnd As Integer, ByVal x As Integer, _
            ByVal y As Integer, ByVal nWidth As Integer, ByVal nHeight As Integer, _
            ByVal bRepaint As Integer) As Integer
            ' No code here
        End Function
    End Class
```

As you see, the .dll extension in the DLL name can be omitted. If the path is also omitted, the DLL must be in a system folder or another directory listed in the PATH environment variable.

Once you have declared an external function, you can invoke it as if it were defined in managed code:

```
    Dim hWnd As Integer = WindowsFunctions.FindWindow(Nothing, "Untitled - Notepad")
    If hWnd <> 0 Then
        WindowsFunctions.MoveWindow(hWnd, 0, 0, 600, 300, 1)
    Else
        MessageBox.Show("Window not found", "Error")
    End If
```

The DllImport attribute supports several optional arguments, which let you precisely define how the external procedure should be called and how it returns a value to the caller.

```
<DllImport("filename.dll", CharSet:=charsetoption, ExactSpelling:=bool, _
    EntryPoint:="procname", CallingConvention:=calloption, _
    SetLastError:=bool, BestFitMapping:=bool, ThrowOnUnmappableChar:=bool>
⋮
```

The CharSet argument tells how strings are passed to the external routine; it can be CharSet.Ansi (the default), CharSet.Unicode, or CharSet.Auto. This argument has the same meaning as the Ansi, Unicode, or Auto qualifier in the Declare statement. In addition, if you specify the Ansi setting and a function with that name isn't found in the DLL, Visual Basic appends the *A* character to the function name and tries again. If you specify the Unicode setting, Visual Basic appends the *W* character to the function name before searching for it; if this first search fails, Visual Basic searches for the name you've provided. Notice the subtle difference between the Ansi and Unicode settings—the latter works as described because .NET uses Unicode strings, so a function that takes Unicode strings is preferable because it is more efficient than one that doesn't.

The ExactSpelling argument is a Boolean value that determines whether the method name must match exactly the name in the DLL; if True (the default setting), the CharSet setting has no effect on the function name being searched.

The EntryPoint argument specifies the actual function name in the DLL and is therefore equivalent to the Alias clause in a Declare statement. In practice, you use this argument if the entry point name is an invalid or a reserved name in Visual Basic (such as Friend), if it duplicates a name already defined in the application, or if it's an ordinal entry point (such as *#123*).

The CallingConvention argument specifies the calling convention for the entry point. Available values are WinApi (the default), CDecl, FastCall, StdCall, and ThisCall. You rarely need to specify this option.

The SetLastError argument indicates whether the called function sets the Win32 last error code. If this argument is True, the compiler emits additional code that saves the last error code; therefore, you should leave this argument False (its default value) if you know that the function you're calling doesn't set the Win32 error. (Beware that the documentation incorrectly states that the value for this argument is True for Visual Basic .NET.)

When the .NET runtime converts Unicode strings to ANSI, each Unicode character is translated to the matching ANSI character, or to "?" if no closely matching character exists. This approach is usually desirable, but it might cause problems if the matching character is a character that might have a special meaning for the called procedure. For example, if the matching character is the backslash character, a string representing a path might point to the wrong place. Under version 1.1 of the .NET Framework, you can disable the default behavior by setting the BestFitMapping argument to False (the default is True), and you can have the .NET runtime throw an exception if a Unicode character in the string has no close match in the ANSI set by setting the ThrowOnUn-mappableChar argument to True. (The default is False.)

The following example shows how you can use the DllImport attribute to call a method named Friend in a DLL named myfunctions.dll, which takes Unicode strings and affects the Win32 error code:

```
' We must use an aliased name because Friend is a reserved keyword.
<DllImport("myfunctions.dll", EntryPoint:="Friend", _
    CharSet:=CharSet.Unicode, SetLastError:=True)> _
Function MakeFriends(ByVal s1 As String, ByVal s2 As String) As Integer
    ' No implementation code
End Function
```

If the external routine sets the Win32 error code and you passed True to the SetLastError argument, you can read this error code when the call returns, by means of either the Err.LastDllError method or the Marshal.GetLastWin32Error method:

```
Dim res As Integer = MakeFriends("first", "second")
If Err.LastDllError <> 0 Then
    ' Deal here with the error.
End If
```

You can read the last error code only once. External routines declared with the Declare keyword always set the Win32 error code; therefore, using DllImport provides a slight optimization if the external routine doesn't set the error code or if you aren't going to test it after the call.

Marshaling Data

To successfully invoke a function in an external DLL, you must be familiar with how data is passed from .NET to the external DLL, and how results are passed back to .NET. This mechanism is known as *data marshaling*, and it works similarly under both PInvoke and COM Interop. (I will point out a few minor differences in how these two technologies marshal data only when it makes sense to do so.)

Most data types can be passed from managed to unmanaged code without much concern on your part because these data types have the same memory representation in the two worlds. These types are known as *blittable types*, a group that includes Byte, Short, Integer, Long, Single, Double, and Date types, as well as one-dimensional arrays thereof and structures that contain only blittable elements. You should pass blittable types, if possible, because they can cross the boundary between managed and unmanaged code very efficiently.

Nonblittable types are those that have a different representation in the two worlds, or that might have many representations in the unmanaged world, and must undergo marshaling when they cross the border between the managed and unmanaged worlds.

The most common nonblittable types are Boolean, Char, String, Decimal, and Array. The Boolean type is nonblittable because it can be 1, 2, or 4 bytes in the unmanaged world and because the True value can be represented as either 1 or –1. The Char type can be translated to either an ANSI or a Unicode character. The String type can be transformed in a variety of unmanaged formats, including null-terminated strings or length-prefixed BSTRs (each with the ANSI and Unicode variants). The Decimal type must be converted to Currency. Arrays are nonblittable because they can be translated either to SAFEARRAYS or to C-style arrays. You can determine exactly how nonblittable data is passed to or returned from managed code by means of the MarshalAs attribute, which I cover later.

Many Windows API functions that are designed to send a string value back to the caller don't actually return a string in the return value; instead, they take a string buffer as an argument and fill it with zero or more characters. (The actual return value is often an integer that specifies how many characters have been placed in the buffer.)

When passing a String to such external methods, you have a problem to solve: .NET strings are immutable, and you wouldn't see a different value in the string when the call returns. To see the actual returned string, you must pass a StringBuilder object instead. Here's an example of how you can define the GetClassName API function:

```
' Add these lines to the WindowsFunctions class.
<DllImport("user32")> _
Public Shared Function GetClassName(ByVal hWnd As IntPtr, _
  ByVal buffer As StringBuilder, _
    ByVal charcount As Integer) As Integer
End Function
```

The first argument, a 32-bit integer, is declared as an IntPtr element. Using an IntPtr instead of an Integer gives you two benefits. First, you can pass the value of a form's Handle property without any conversion. Second, the IntPtr type automatically matches the size of CPU registers and works well under 64-bit versions of Windows. Here's how you can retrieve the class name of the current form:

```
Dim buffer As New StringBuilder(512)
' The last argument is the max number of characters in the buffer.
WindowsFunctions.GetClassName(Me.Handle, buffer, buffer.Capacity)
Dim classname As String = buffer.ToString()
```

The MarshalAs Attribute

.NET provides a default marshaling mechanism for each nonblittable type, but you modify the default behavior by means of the MarshalAs attribute. The following code shows how to use this attribute to let the compiler know that the (fictitious) Check-String procedure takes an ANSI null-terminated string and returns a Boolean value as a 2-byte integer that uses –1 to represent the True value:

```
<DllImport("mydll")> _
Shared Function CheckString( _
    <MarshalAs(UnmanagedType.LPWStr)> ByVal s As String) _
    As <MarshalAs(UnmanagedType.VariantBool)> Boolean
End Function
```

You can apply the MarshalAs attribute to parameters, fields, and return values. In most cases, the attribute takes only the UnmanagedType enumerated value that determines how the value is converted during the marshaling operation. Some UnmanagedType values, however, might require additional arguments, such as ArraySubType and Size-Const. See Table 30-1 for more details.

Table 30-1   UnmanagedType Enumerated Values

Value	Description
AnsiBStr	A length-prefixed ANSI character string. (Length is single byte.)
AsAny	A dynamic type that determines the type of an object at run time and marshals the object as that type. (Not valid for COM Interop.)
Bool	A 4-byte Boolean value, corresponding to the Win32 BOOL type. (0 is False; any other value is True.) This is the default way of passing Boolean values for PInvoke.
BStr	A length-prefixed double-byte Unicode character string. (The default way of passing strings for COM Interop.)
ByValArray	A fixed-length array field inside a structure. The SizeConst field must specify the number of elements in the array; the ArraySubType field can specify the UnmanagedType enumerated value that corresponds to the type of the array elements, if array elements aren't blittable.

Table 30-1 UnmanagedType Enumerated Values *(continued)*

Value	Description
ByValTStr	A fixed-length string field in a structure. The SizeConst argument must contain the size of the buffer in bytes. The CharSet attribute in the class determines the type of the characters.
Currency	A COM Currency value. (Can be used only with Decimal values.)
I1, I2, I4, I8	A 1-byte, 2-byte, 4-byte, or 8-byte signed integer.
IDispatch	A COM IDispatch interface pointer (same as the As Object variable in Visual Basic 6).
Interface	A COM interface pointer that specifies the exact interface type or the default interface type when applied to a class. The GUID of the interface is obtained from the class metadata.
IUnknown	A COM IUnknown interface pointer. (Can be used with Object values.)
LPArray	A pointer to the first element of a C-style array. When marshaling from .NET to unmanaged code, the array length is determined at run time. When marshaling from unmanaged code to .NET, the array length is determined from the SizeConst or SizeParamIndex arguments, optionally followed by the unmanaged type of array elements if they aren't blittable.
LPStr	A single-byte, null-terminated ANSI character string. (Can be used with String and StringBuilder elements.)
LPTStr	A platform-dependent character string. ANSI on Windows 98 and Windows Me, Unicode on Windows NT and later versions. (Not valid with COM Interop.)
LPWStr	A 2-byte, null-terminated Unicode character string.
R4, R8	A 4-byte or 8-byte floating point number.
SafeArray	An OLE Automation SafeArray. You can use the SafeArraySubType field to define the default element type.
Struct	A Variant used to marshal a structure or a formatted reference type.
SysInt, SysUInt	A platform-independent signed or unsigned integer. 4 bytes on 32-bit Windows, 8 bytes on 64-bit Windows.
U1, U2, U4, U8	A 1-byte, 2-byte, 4-byte, or 8-byte unsigned integer.
VariantBool	A 2-byte OLE Boolean value, also known as VARIANT_BOOL (-1 for True; 0 for False). This is the default way of passing Boolean values for COM Interop.
VBByRefStr	Allows Visual Basic to correctly receive the new value of a string modified in unmanaged code. (Not valid for COM Interop.)

The following code shows how you can use the MarshalAs attribute to pass a Unicode string to the Windows API function that changes the current directory. This example is for illustration purposes only; you can achieve the same result by using the CharSet.Unicode setting in the DllImport attribute.

```
<DllImport("kernel32", EntryPoint:="SetCurrentDirectoryW")> _
Function SetCurrentDirectory( _
   <MarshalAs(UnmanagedType.LPWStr)> ByVal lpPathName As String) As Integer
End Function
```

The following structure containing two string fields flagged with the MarshalAs attribute. When this structure is passed to an external procedure, the first field is translated to a null-terminated ANSI string, whereas the second field becomes a 256-characters fixed-length string.

```
Structure MyStructure
    <MarshalAs(UnmanagedType.LPStr)> Public f1 As String
    <MarshalAs(UnmanagedType.ByValTStr, SizeConst:=256)> Public f2 As String
End Structure
```

Here's another example that uses the SizeConst optional argument:

```
Structure Employee
    ' Marshal the Name string as an ANSI fixed-length string of 100 chars.
    ' (We must account for the extra null character.)
    <MarshalAs(UnmanagedType.ByValTStr, SizeConst:=101)> _
    Dim Name As String
    ⋮
End Structure
```

The StructLayout Attribute

Visual Basic .NET defines a couple of attributes that let you control how the elements of a Structure block are arranged in memory and how the runtime should marshal them when they're passed to a function in an external DLL.

Fields of a structure are arranged in memory in the order in which they appear in source code, even though the compiler is free to insert padding bytes to arrange members so that 16-bit values are aligned with word boundaries, 32-bit values are aligned with double-word boundaries, and so on. This arrangement—known as an *unpacked layout*—delivers the best performance because Intel processors work faster with aligned data.

Visual Basic .NET lets you finely control where each member of the structure or the class is located by means of the StructLayout attribute. The allowed values for this attribute are StructLayout.Auto (the compiler can reorder elements for best performance—for example, by grouping value types together), StructLayout.Sequential (elements are laid out and properly aligned sequentially in memory), and StructLayout.Explicit.

```
<StructLayout(LayoutKind.Explicit)> _
Structure ARGBColor
    ⋮
End Structure
```

By default, Visual Basic .NET uses the StructLayout.Auto setting for classes and Struct-Layout.Sequential for structures.

The StructLayout attribute supports three additional fields: CharSet, Pack, and Size. CharSet defines how string members in the structure are marshaled when the structure is passed to a DLL and can be Unicode, Ansi, or Auto. This argument, which defaults to Auto, has the same meaning as the DllImport argument with the same name.

The Pack field defines the packing size for the structure, and can be 1, 2, 4, 8 (the default), 16, 32, 64, 128, or the special value 0 that uses the default packing size for the current platform. A structure whose LayoutKind is Sequential always aligns elements to this number of bytes; if you omit the StructLayout attribute, elements align to their natural boundary (2-byte words for Short elements, 4-byte double words for Integer and Single, addresses that are multiples of 8 for Long and Double, and so forth).

The Size field determines the total length of the structure when passed to unmanaged code; you can use this argument to increase the length of a structure. (You can reach the same goal by appending dummy, unused fields to the structure.)

```
<StructLayout(LayoutKind.Sequential, CharSet:=CharSet.Unicode, Pack:=4)> _
Structure ARGBColor
    ⋮
End Structure
```

By default, the Visual Basic compiler is free to arrange class members in a way that optimizes memory usage and performance. This corresponds to the StructLayout.Auto setting. When passing an object—as opposed to a structure—to unmanaged code, you must apply the StructLayout attribute with a different setting, typically StructLayout.Explicit. Classes flagged in this way are known as *formatted classes*. PInvoke supports classes as arguments only if they are formatted classes, with only a few exceptions such as the String and StringBuilder types; conversely, COM Interop doesn't enforce any limitation in passing a reference type.

In practice, you will rarely pass a reference to an object other than String or StringBuilder as an argument to an external DLL via PInvoke. If you do, however, remember that the DLL receives a *pointer* to the data in the object. From the perspective of the called routine, an object reference passed with ByVal is similar to a structure passed with ByRef because in both cases the routine receives an address. If you pass an object reference to a ByRef argument, the routine receives the address of a pointer that points to the object's data.

The FieldOffset Attribute

When you opt for an explicit layout, the definition of all the fields in a structure must include a FieldOffset attribute, whose argument specifies the distance in bytes from the beginning of the structure:

```
<StructLayout(LayoutKind.Explicit)> _
Structure ARGBColor
    <FieldOffset(0)> Dim Red As Byte
    <FieldOffset(1)> Dim Green As Byte
    <FieldOffset(2)> Dim Blue As Byte
    <FieldOffset(3)> Dim Alpha As Byte
End Structure
```

The StructLayout and the FieldOffset attributes let you implement a *union*, a language feature that many languages, such as C and C++, have had for years but that has always been out of reach for Visual Basic developers. A union is a structure in which two or more elements overlap in memory. Or, if you prefer, a union permits you to refer to the same memory location in a structure using different names. The key to unions in .NET is the support for explicit structure layout. Consider the following example:

```
<StructLayout(LayoutKind.Explicit)> _
Structure RGBColor
    <FieldOffset(0)> Dim Red As Byte
    <FieldOffset(1)> Dim Green As Byte
    <FieldOffset(2)> Dim Blue As Byte
    <FieldOffset(3)> Dim Alpha As Byte
    <FieldOffset(0)> Dim Value As Integer
End Structure
```

Figure 30-1 illustrates how these elements are located in memory:

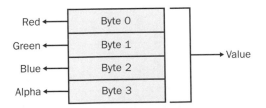

Figure 30-1   Locating elements in memory

In other words, you can access the 4 bytes as a whole through the Value field, or individually via the Red, Green, Blue, and Alpha fields. The following code shows how useful this feature can be:

```
' Split a color into its components.
Dim rgb As RGBColor
rgb.Value = &H112233              ' This is equal to 1122867.
Console.WriteLine("Red={0}, Green={1}, Blue={2}", rgb.Red, rgb.Green, rgb.Blue)
    ' => Red=51, Green=34, Blue=17
```

You can also combine the three RGB components into a single color:

```
rgb.Red = 51
rgb.Green = 34
rgb.Blue = 17
Console.WriteLine("RGB color = {0}", rgb.Value)    ' => 1122867
```

Unions make it possible to implement some tricky conversion routines far more efficiently than using standard math operators. Consider the following structure:

```
<StructLayout(LayoutKind.Explicit)> _
Structure IntegerTypes
    ' A 64-bit integer
    <FieldOffset(0)> Dim Long0 As Long
    ' Two 32-bit integers
    <FieldOffset(0)> Dim Integer0 As Integer
    <FieldOffset(4)> Dim Integer1 As Integer
    ' Four 16-bit integers
    <FieldOffset(0)> Dim Short0 As Short
    <FieldOffset(2)> Dim Short1 As Short
    <FieldOffset(4)> Dim Short2 As Short
    <FieldOffset(6)> Dim Short3 As Short
    ' Eight 8-bit integers
    <FieldOffset(0)> Dim Byte0 As Byte
    <FieldOffset(1)> Dim Byte1 As Byte
    <FieldOffset(2)> Dim Byte2 As Byte
    <FieldOffset(3)> Dim Byte3 As Byte
    <FieldOffset(4)> Dim Byte4 As Byte
    <FieldOffset(5)> Dim Byte5 As Byte
    <FieldOffset(6)> Dim Byte6 As Byte
    <FieldOffset(7)> Dim Byte7 As Byte
End Structure
```

This structure takes exactly 8 bytes, but you can refer to those bytes in multiple ways. For example, you can extract the low and high bytes of a 16-bit integer:

```
Dim it As IntegerTypes
it.Short0 = 517                     ' Hex 0205
Console.WriteLine(it.Byte0)         ' => 5
Console.WriteLine(it.Byte1)         ' => 2
```

This technique works also if the structure fields are declared as Private. However, you should use it only with integer member types, such as Byte, Short, Integer, and Long; trying to interpret locations as Single or Double values often returns the special NaN (Not-a-Number) value. Trying to map a reference type (such as a String) throws an exception because the Visual Basic .NET compiler rejects structures in which reference types overlap with other members or aren't aligned properly.

Most of the structures used by Windows API functions are unpacked and don't require any special attribute. Others, most notably those in the Shell32.dll library, might require you to define an explicit layout. One such example is the SHFILEOPSTRUCT structure that you pass as an argument to the SHFileOperation function:

```
Private Declare Ansi Function SHFileOperation Lib "shell32.dll" _
    Alias "SHFileOperationA" (ByRef lpFileOp As SHFILEOPSTRUCT) As Integer

<StructLayout(LayoutKind.Explicit)> _
Private Structure SHFILEOPSTRUCT
    <FieldOffset(0)> Public hwnd As IntPtr
    <FieldOffset(4)> Public wFunc As Integer
    <FieldOffset(8)> Public pFrom As String
```

```
<FieldOffset(12)> Public pTo As String
<FieldOffset(16)> Public fFlags As Short
<FieldOffset(18), MarshalAs(UnmanagedType.Bool)> _
    Public fAnyOperationsAborted As Boolean
<FieldOffset(22)> Public hNameMappings As Integer
<FieldOffset(26)> Public lpszProgressTitle As IntPtr
    ' (It was String, only used if FOF_SIMPLEPROGRESS.)
End Structure
```

By carefully examining the previous structure, you can see that the fFlag field (a 2-byte integer) is immediately followed by a 4-byte Boolean value. If this structure were unpacked, two padding bytes would be inserted between these two fields. Unfortunately, the Shell32.dll library expects a packed structure, so we must resort to explicit layout. Notice also that the last element in the structure is defined as a string in the SDK documentation, but we must use an IntPtr or an Integer in Visual Basic .NET because strings are reference types and must be aligned to the double word.

Here's a procedure that uses the SHFileOperation API function to copy one or more files while displaying the standard Windows dialog box (shown in Figure 30-2). This API function automatically manages name collisions and allows undelete operations.

```
' Copy a file using the SHFileOperation API function.
' It can return 0 (ok), 1 (user canceled the operation), or 2 (error).
Function CopyFile(ByVal source As String, ByVal dest As String) As Integer
    ' Fill an SHFILEOPSTRUCT structure.
    Dim sh As SHFILEOPSTRUCT
    sh.wFunc = 2              ' = FO_COPY, a file copy operation
    sh.hwnd = IntPtr.Zero     ' No owner window
    sh.pTo = dest
    ' Ensure source file ends with an extra null char. (See SDK docs.)
    sh.pFrom = source & ControlChars.NullChar
    sh.fFlags = &H48          ' = ALLOWUNDO Or RENAMEONCOLLISION

    ' The API functions returns non-zero if there is a problem.
    Dim res As Integer = SHFileOperation(sh)
    If res = 0 Then
        Return 0              ' 0 means everything was OK.
    ElseIf sh.fAnyOperationsAborted Then
        Return 1             ' 1 means user aborted the operation.
    Else
        Return 2             ' 2 means an error has occurred.
    End If
End Function
```

Here's how you can use the CopyFile function to copy all the files in the C:\Docs directory to the C:\Backup directory:

```
Select Case CopyFile("c:\Docs\*.*", "c:\Backup")
    Case 0: MessageBox.Show("All files were copied correctly.")
    Case 1: MessageBox.Show("User canceled the operation.")
    Case 2: MessageBox.Show("An error occurred.")
End Select
```

Figure 30-2   The standard window that the SHFileOperation API function displays when deleting files

Delegates and Callback Procedures

A method in an external DLL can take the address of a *callback procedure*. A callback procedure is a procedure in your program that the external method calls to notify your code that something has happened. For example, the EnumWindows API function enumerates all the upper top-level windows in the system and invokes a callback method for each found window. You can write code in the callback procedure that uses this information—for example, by displaying the name of the window in a ListBox control or by filling an array of structures for later processing.

Visual Basic 6 applications can call EnumWindows, EnumFonts, and other Enum*xxxx* functions in the Windows API and pass them the address of a local callback function (using the AddressOf operator). This technique is unsafe because the application crashes if the callback routine doesn't comply with the expected syntax for arguments and return values. (You can learn about the expected syntax of Enum*xxxx* procedures from the Windows SDK documentation.) Visual Basic .NET lets you call any Windows API function in a safe way, by means of delegates.

Before you can declare an external procedure that uses a callback mechanism, you must create a delegate class that defines the syntax of the callback routine:

```
' This is the syntax for a EnumWindows callback procedure.
Delegate Function EnumWindowsCBK(ByVal hWnd As Integer, _
    ByVal lParam As Integer) As Integer
```

In the definition of the API function, you specify the callback argument using the delegate type (instead of a 32-bit integer, as is the case with Visual Basic 6):

```
Declare Function EnumWindows Lib "user32" (ByVal lpEnumFunc As EnumWindowsCBK, _
    ByVal lParam As Integer) As Integer
```

Finally, you can write the actual callback procedure and pass its address to the external method. The delegate argument forces you to pass the address of a procedure that complies with the delegate's syntax. This mechanism makes the Visual Basic .NET approach inherently safer than that of Visual Basic 6, even though the call syntax is exactly the same:

```
Sub TestAPICallback()
    EnumWindows(AddressOf ListWindows, 0)
End Sub
```

```
' The second argument to the callback function is ignored in
' this demo--in a real application, it helps discern the
' reason why this procedure has been called.
Function ListWindows(ByVal hWnd As Integer, ByVal lParam As Integer) As Integer
    ' Display the handle of this top-level window.
    ListBox1.Items.Add(hWnd)
    ' Return 1 to continue enumeration.
    Return 1
End Function
```

The preceding code snippet displays the 32-bit handle of all the top-level windows in the system. The complete demo on the companion CD shows how you can display the handle and other pieces of information about all the open windows in the system, by using the EnumWindows and EnumChildWindows API functions in a recursive fashion. (See Figure 30-3.)

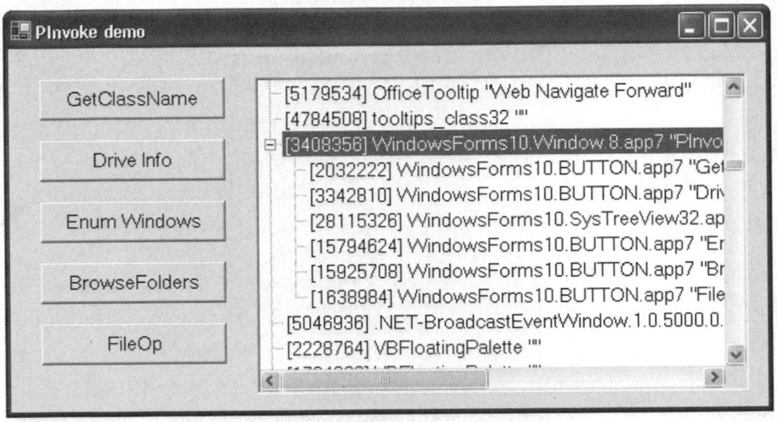

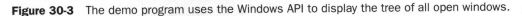

Figure 30-3   The demo program uses the Windows API to display the tree of all open windows.

The In and Out Attributes

The .NET marshaler always copies a parameter's values from .NET to the unmanaged DLL, but it copies the value back only if the parameter is passed by reference. This means that you see the new value if the callee changes the value of a ByRef parameter. At first glance, therefore, the semantics of the ByVal and ByRef keywords are preserved when working with PInvoke and COM Interop. However, things aren't always so smooth, and you must be prepared to work around a few potential problems you might have with reference types.

As I explained earlier, the PInvoke marshaler can pass a reference type only if the type is a formatted class (that is, it uses an explicit layout), with String and StringBuilder types being among the few exceptions. The PInvoke marshaler copies the fields of a formatted structure to unmanaged memory instead of just passing a pointer to the managed object. (The COM Interop marshaler, however, simply passes the object pointer, as you'd expect.)

As you know, if you pass a ByVal object to a Visual Basic .NET routine that modifies the object's fields, you see the new fields' values when the call returns. Conversely, the PInvoke marshaler doesn't copy data back to the object when you pass a reference type to an external DLL, to achieve better performance. In other words, by default, reference types are passed as input-only arguments. You can change this behavior by flagging the argument with explicit In and Out attributes, as follows:

```
' "In" is a reserved word, so you can't omit the Attribute portion.
Declare Sub TestRoutine Lib "mydll" (<InAttribute, Out> objref As Object)
```

The StringBuilder class is an exception to this rule because the PInvoke marshaler copies it back even if you pass it by value and without the Out attribute. You can omit the In attribute when passing a ByRef argument that doesn't have to be initialized; in some circumstances, this omission can save a few CPU cycles when passing the object to a COM object in another apartment.

In its quest for greater efficiency, under certain circumstances the marshaler can decide to *pin* the passed argument, a detail that makes things a bit more complicated. When an argument is pinned, the marshaler passes the address of the original value in the managed heap rather than the address of a copy. (The word *pinning* is used because the object is pinned in memory and doesn't move even if a garbage collection occurs in the meantime.) Data can be pinned in both PInvoke calls and intra-apartment COM Interop calls.

For example, under PInvoke, a .NET string passed by value to a Unicode string argument is pinned: the callee receives the address of the internal character buffer, and no copy occurs. If the callee doesn't abide by the by-value semantics and mistakenly changes the passed string, the managed heap might be corrupted. (This happens, for example, if a longer string is assigned.)

Pinning occurs also when you pass a blittable formatted class because the marshaler can improve performance by passing a pointer to the .NET object's memory in the managed heap. Pinning happens regardless of whether you use the Out attribute. (In other words, the Out attribute forces a copy of the value back to .NET only if the argument isn't pinned.) Pinning can occur only with strings passed by value. The PInvoke marshaler always copies ByRef string arguments to a temporary buffer and then passes the address of this buffer to the external routine. When the call returns, the marshaler creates a new string with the characters found in the buffer and passes the new string back to the caller. (This double copy is necessary to preserve .NET string immutability.)

Arrays are reference types and can be pinned too. More precisely, an array is pinned if its elements are blittable and you make either a PInvoke call or a COM Interop call to an object that lives in the same apartment as the caller. Arrays defined as part of a structure are dealt with as other objects, but they can be passed by value by flagging them with a MarshalAs attribute, as follows:

```
<StructLayout(LayoutKind.Sequential)> Structure MyStruct
    <MarshalAs(UnmanagedType.ByValArray, SizeConst:=64)> _
    Public s1() As Short
End Structure
```

The structure in the preceding code takes 128 bytes when it is passed by value on the stack because the MarshalAs attribute specifies that the s1 array has 64 elements. Without this attribute, the array would have been marshaled as any other object reference, and the structure would take only 4 bytes.

The Marshal Class

You've seen that you can affect the behavior of the PInvoke marshaler by means of a few attributes, but in the most intricate cases, you must resort to so-called *manual marshaling* techniques, which require that you manually allocate and deallocate unmanaged memory and copy your data into it.

The basis for manual marshaling is the Marshal class, a container for static methods that let you do virtually anything you might need to do with unmanaged memory. I mentioned this class when I described the Marshal.GetLastWin32Error method in "The DllImport Attribute" section; in this section, I will describe its most useful methods and provide a complete example.

The SizeOf method takes an object or a structure (or a System.Type that identifies a structure or a class) and returns the number of bytes that object or structure would take when marshaled to unmanaged code:

```
' These statements display the same value.
Console.WriteLine(Marshal.SizeOf(GetType(Person)))
Console.WriteLine(Marshal.SizeOf(New Person))
```

The OffsetOf method takes two arguments: a System.Type that identifies either a structure or a class flagged with the StructLayout attribute, and the name of one of the type's members. The method returns the offset of the member in the unmanaged representation of the structure or class:

```
Console.WriteLine(Marshal.OffsetOf(GetType(Person), "FirstName"))
```

You can allocate three kinds of unmanaged memory with the methods of the Marshal class; each kind must be deallocated later with a different method.

The AllocHGlobal method allocates memory by invoking the GlobalAlloc API function and returns a pointer to the allocated memory. You can resize the memory block with the ReAllocHGlobal method and release it with the FreeHGlobal method:

```
' Allocates and then releases 10K of memory using GlobalAlloc API function.
Dim ptr As IntPtr = Marshal.AllocHGlobal(10240)
  ⋮
Marshal.FreeHGlobal(ptr)
```

Notice that memory allocated in this way isn't controlled by garbage collection. If you forget to release it, it will be freed only when the application terminates.

When working with COM, you typically use a different allocating technique, based on the CoTaskMemAlloc function. You can deal with this kind of memory via the AllocCo-TaskMem, ReAllocCoTaskMem, and FreeCoTaskMem shared methods:

```
' Allocates and then releases 10K of memory using CoTaskMemAlloc OLE function.
Dim ptr As IntPtr = Marshal.AllocCoTaskMem(10240)
 ⋮
Marshal.FreeCoTaskMem(ptr)
```

Once you have allocated a block of unmanaged memory, you usually want to store some data in it before calling an unmanaged function, or read data from it when the call returns. If the memory block contains an array of numeric, Char, or DateTime elements, you can use the Copy method:

```
' Pass an array of integers to a procedure that expects a pointer.
Dim values() As Integer = {1, 3, 5, 9, 11, 13, 15}
Dim bytes As Integer = values.Length * 4
' Allocate a block of memory and copy array elements into it.
Dim ptr As IntPtr = Marshal.AllocHGlobal(bytes)
Marshal.Copy(values, 0, ptr, bytes)
' Call the external routine.
TheExternalProc(ptr)
' Copy array elements back to the .NET array and release memory.
Marshal.Copy(ptr, values, 0, bytes)
Marshal.FreeHGlobal(ptr)
```

You often have to allocate a block of unmanaged memory and copy a .NET string into it, possibly after converting the string to ANSI. You can perform this operation in a single step by using one of the following techniques: use StringToHGlobalAnsi, StringTo-HGlobalUni, and StringToHGlobalAuto when copying a .NET string into a block allocated with GlobalAlloc API function; or use StringToCoTaskMemAnsi, StringToCo-TaskMemUni, and StringToCoTaskMemAuto when copying a .NET string into a block allocated with the CoTaskMemAlloc function. The last portion of the method name indicates whether the string is converted to ANSI during the copy process:

```
' Use GlobalAlloc to allocate unmanaged memory and copy a .NET string
' after converting it to ANSI if running on a Windows 98 or ME system.
Dim s As String = "A .NET string passed to COM"
Dim ptr As IntPtr = Marshal.StringToHGlobalAuto(s)
 ⋮
Marshal.FreeHGlobal(ptr)
```

You can also allocate a BSTR—which is the standard format for a COM string—and copy a .NET string into it with the StringToBSTR method; memory allocated in this fashion must be released with the FreeBSTR method:

```
Dim s As String = "A .NET string passed to COM"
Dim ptr As IntPtr = Marshal.StringToBSTR(s)
 ⋮
Marshal.FreeBSTR(ptr)
```

The Marshal class offers methods that write individual values into a block of unmanaged memory (WriteByte, WriteInt16, WriteInt32, WriteInt64, WriteIntPtr) and that read them back (ReadByte, ReadInt16, ReadInt32, ReadInt64, ReadIntPtr). The first argument to these methods is the IntPtr value returned by an allocation method, and the second (optional) argument is an offset into the memory block:

```
' Write an integer at offset 10 in a block of unmanaged memory.
Dim oldValue As Integer = 1234
Marshal.WriteInt32(ptr, 10, oldValue)
' Call the unmanaged function.
⋮
' Read the integer back.
Dim newValue As Integer = Marshal.ReadInt32(ptr, 10)
```

To show what you can do in practice with the allocation methods of the Marshal class, I have prepared an enhanced version of the CopyFile procedure that I introduced in the section "The FieldOffset Attribute." As you might remember, the last element of the SHFILEOPSTRUCT structure that the SHFileOperation Windows API function uses is a string field that isn't aligned to the 4-byte boundary. The lack of alignment forces us to declare this element as an IntPtr instead of a string, or the program would throw a runtime exception. This element is used to display a user-defined message in the Copy File dialog box instead of the name of the file being copied. The enhanced version of the CopyFile function takes this user-defined message as an optional argument:

```
Function CopyFile(ByVal source As String, ByVal dest As String, _
    Optional ByVal progressText As String = Nothing) As Integer
    ' Fill an SHFILEOPSTRUCT structure.
    Dim sh As SHFILEOPSTRUCT
    sh.wFunc = 2              ' = FO_COPY, a file copy operation
    sh.hwnd = IntPtr.Zero    ' No owner window
    sh.pTo = dest
    ' Ensure source filename ends with an extra null char. (See SDK docs.)
    sh.pFrom = source & ControlChars.NullChar
    sh.fFlags = &H48          ' = ALLOWUNDO Or RENAMEONCOLLISION

    If Not (progressText Is Nothing) Then
        ' Allocate an ANSI string in memory and store its pointer here.
        sh.lpszProgressTitle = Marshal.StringToHGlobalAnsi(progressText)
        sh.fFlags = sh.fFlags Or &H100    ' &H100 = SIMPLEPROGRESS
    End If
    Dim res As Integer = SHFileOperation(sh)
    If Not (progressText Is Nothing) Then
        ' Release any memory taken for the progressText string.
        Marshal.FreeHGlobal(sh.lpszProgressTitle)
        sh.lpszProgressTitle = IntPtr.Zero
    End If

    ' The API function returns non-zero if there is a problem.
    If res = 0 Then
        Return 0              ' 0 means everything was OK.
    ElseIf sh.fAnyOperationsAborted Then
        Return 1              ' 1 means user aborted the operation.
```

```
        Else
            Return 2            ' 2 means an error has occurred.
        End If
    End Function
End Function
```

For more details, see the demo program included on the companion CD.

Calling COM Components from .NET

There are three ways to enable a .NET application to call a COM object: you can use the Microsoft Visual Studio .NET Add Reference command, you can run the TlbImp SDK utility, or you can code against the TypeLibConverter class. Before looking at the practical details, however, it is important to understand what happens behind the scenes when a .NET client uses a COM object.

The Runtime Callable Wrapper (RCW)

Calling a COM component from .NET is made possible by an object named the Runtime Callable Wrapper, or RCW. (See Figure 30-4.) This object "wraps" the COM component and makes it look like a regular managed component to .NET clients. The RCW is in charge of several tasks, all of which are necessary to make the COM component appear to its clients as a .NET component. Such tasks include the marshaling of data, the conversion of COM's HRESULT values to .NET exceptions, and the management of the COM component's lifetime (which is based on reference counting instead of garbage collection).

The RCW consumes several important COM interfaces—including IUnknown, IDispatch, IDispatchEx, IProvideClassInfo, ISupportErrorInfo, and IErrorInfo—and hides them from .NET clients. For example, a .NET client can use a COM component through late binding because the RCW consumes the IDispatch interface behind the scenes to dispatch these calls to the actual object. The RCW is also responsible for object identity: there is one and only one RCW for each distinct COM object, regardless of how references to the COM object have been returned to the managed client(s). This requirement is necessary for the Is operator to work correctly with references pointing to a COM object.

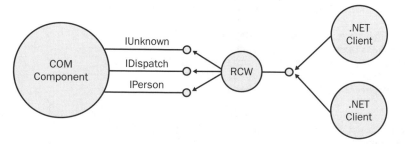

Figure 30-4   The Runtime Callable Wrapper object

The .NET Framework creates an RCW not only when a managed client explicitly instantiates a COM object, but also when a COM method returns a reference to a new object (more precisely, a reference to a COM object that isn't already known to the .NET Framework). Object identity works also in this case because the COM Interop infrastructure always creates one distinct RCW for each COM object accessed from .NET, regardless of whether it was instantiated by your code or returned by another method. The COM Interop infrastructure correctly preserves identity even in the most intricate cases. For example, when a managed client passes a .NET object as an argument to a COM method and the unmanaged code later returns that object to .NET, COM Interop correctly recognizes that the returned object is actually a managed object and returns a reference to that managed object, without creating an RCW.

A .NET client can create a COM object in two different ways: as an early-bound object or as a late-bound object. You usually create an early-bound object by calling its constructor (with New) and assigning the result to a specific variable; you create a late-bound object by using Activator.CreateInstance and assigning the result to a generic Object variable.

The difference in how the object is created affects the type of the RCW object that COM Interop creates behind the scenes. In the early-binding case, the RCW is a well-defined .NET type, and you can invoke its methods using the "dot" syntax, as you do with all .NET types. In the late-binding case, the type of the RCW is System.__ComObject, and you can invoke the methods of the wrapped COM object only via reflection (including reflection methods that Visual Basic transparently calls for you when Option Strict is off and you use late-bound calls).

The .NET runtime can early-bind a COM component only if metadata is available for it. This metadata must be available both at compile time (to generate the IL code) and at run time (to create the RCW object). The metadata for a COM component is similar to the metadata associated with standard .NET types, except for a few attributes that identify that type as a COM component. In general, this metadata is extracted from the COM object's type library, implicitly if you use Visual Studio.NET or explicitly if you use the TlbImp utility.

> **See Also**   Because this is a book on .NET programming, I am not going to assume that you are familiar with basic COM-related concepts, such as interface programming and type libraries. You can refresh your memory by reading Chapter 16 of my book *Programming Microsoft Visual Basic 6*, provided on the companion CD. That chapter includes a tutorial on COM component creation using Visual Basic 6 and can prove useful when you're creating test COM components for use from managed applications.

Importing a COM Component with Visual Studio .NET

The simplest way to create metadata for a COM component is to let Visual Studio.NET do it for you. Right-click on the References node in the Solution Explorer window (or choose the Add Reference command from the Project menu) to display the Add Reference dialog box, and then click the COM tab. It might take several seconds to fill this window the first time you run this command because Visual Studio parses the system registry and looks for all the registered COM components. When this process is completed, you see a list of components like the one shown in Figure 30-5. In the next section I will describe a code sample that uses COM Interop to access Microsoft Word, so you'll need to add a reference to the Microsoft Word library to compile the sample. Select the library from the list and click OK to start the type library import process. When the dialog box disappears, you will see new nodes in the References subtree in the Solution Explorer window; you can right-click on them to display their Properties.

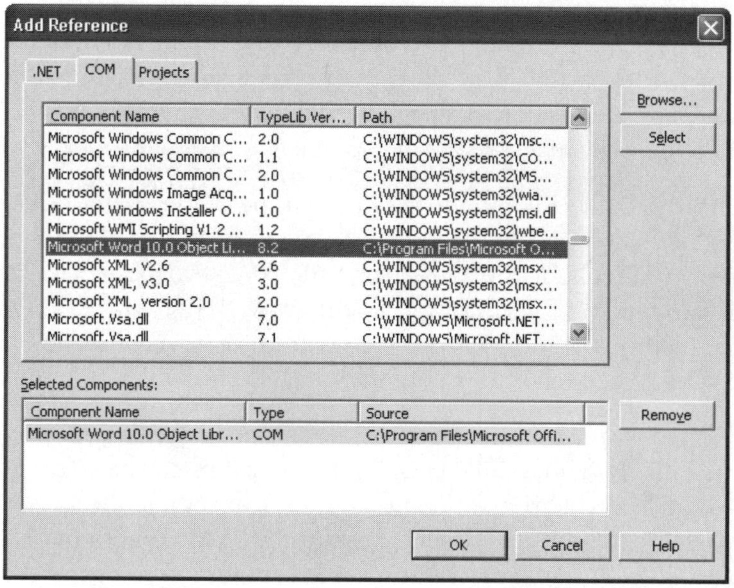

Figure 30-5   The COM tab of the Add Reference dialog box

You can explore the metadata created by importing the type libraries in the Object Browser window. In this case, Visual Studio has created as many as three new assemblies: Interop.Word.dll, Interop.VBIDE.dll, and Interop.Microsoft.Office.Core.dll (or Interop.Office.dll, depending on the Word version installed on your machine). These DLLs are known as *interop assemblies*. By expanding these nodes, you can see how fields and properties have been converted and all the methods that have been created to make COM interoperability do its magic. If you use ILDASM to peek into an interop assembly, you'll see that it contains a lot of metadata but no executable code.

Using the Imported Interop Assembly

The main goal of COM Interop is to let the developer use COM objects as if they were .NET components. The Microsoft Word library you've just imported provides a great example of this concept. The following code, taken from the demo application shown in Figure 30-6, shows how you can use Word's spelling checker from inside your applications:

```
Dim msword As Word.Application

Private Sub btnCheck_Click(ByVal sender As Object, ByVal e As EventArgs) _
    Handles btnCheck.Click
    ' Create an instance of the Word component, if not done yet.
    If msword Is Nothing Then
        msword = New Word.Application
        ' Add a document, if there aren't any (necessary to get suggestions).
        If msword.Documents.Count = 0 Then msword.Documents.Add()
    End If


    ' Retrieve the word to be spellchecked from the user interface.
    Dim word As String = txtWord.Text
    ' Clear the list of suggestions.
    lstSuggestions.Items.Clear()
    If msword.CheckSpelling(word) Then
        lstSuggestions.Items.Add("(Word is correct)")
    Else
        ' The word is incorrect. Display the list of suggested words.
        For Each sug As Word.SpellingSuggestion In msword.GetSpellingSuggestions(word)
            lstSuggestions.Items.Add(sug.Name)
        Next
    End If
End Sub

Private Sub Form1_Closing(ByVal sender As Object, ByVal e As System.ComponentModel.Can
celEventArgs) _
    Handles MyBase.Closing
    ' Tell Word to close when we don't need it any longer.
    msword.Quit()
    msword = Nothing
End Sub
```

In addition to doing something useful, the preceding code snippet shows that you can use an imported COM object exactly as if it were a .NET object. The only way a programmer could determine whether an object is a COM object is by using the *Marshal.IsComObject* method or by reflecting on the object's attributes.

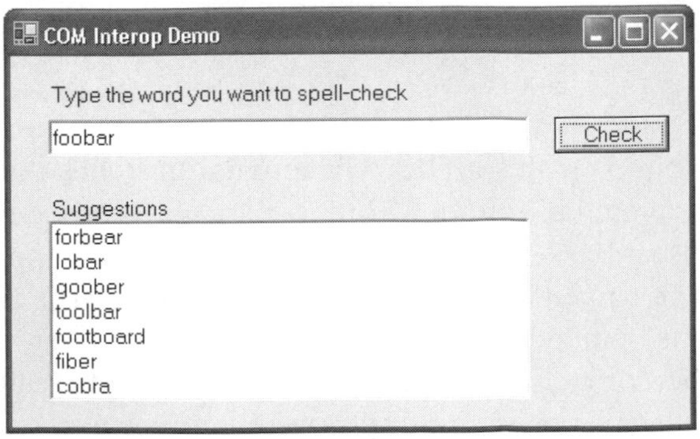

Figure 30-6   The demo application lets you check the spelling of a word and ask for spelling suggestions.

On the other hand, if you know that you're dealing with an imported COM object, you can often optimize your code's behavior and avoid subtle bugs that derive from the different nature of COM and .NET components. The different ways that .NET and COM manage object lifetime offers an example of what I mean.

A "true" COM component is destroyed as soon as the last variable that points to it is set to Nothing. However, a managed client has a reference to the RCW, which is a .NET object that works as a proxy for the COM component. Even if the managed client sets all the references to the COM object to Nothing, the RCW will not be garbage-collected until some time afterward. If the COM performs critical cleanup code in its destructor—such as closing a file or unlocking a record—the actual cleanup will occur later, and you might get an error when trying to access that specific file or record.

You can force the immediate release of a COM object by invoking the Marshal.ReleaseComObject method just before setting the object reference to Nothing:

```
' Modify the Form_Closing event handler in previous example...
msword.Quit()
Marshal.ReleaseComObject(msword)
msword = Nothing
```

In more advanced scenarios, you can also use the AddRef, Release, and QueryInterface methods of the Marshal class to directly access the object's IUnknown interface and manage its internal reference counter.

Importing a COM Component with TlbImp

Although Visual Studio's Add Reference dialog box offers a quick-and-dirty method to create metadata for a COM component, in some cases, you need to use the Type Library Importer (TlbImp) command-line utility provided with the .NET Framework SDK. For example, this utility is necessary when you want to perform the conversion from a batch or MAKE program or when you import the COM component as a strong-name assembly. (Strong name is required if you want to reference it from another strong name assembly). The syntax for the TlbImp is simple:

```
TLBIMP source.dll [/OUT:dest.dll]
```

If the /out option is omitted, TlbImp creates a DLL whose name matches the internal name of the type library, which might be different from its filename. For example, the type library associated with a Visual Basic 6 component is named after the project, not the DLL file (which in fact can be renamed before registering the type library). If the /out option is used, its argument affects both the name of the assembly being created and the namespace of the types inside it. For example, the following command creates a DLL named MyApp.Data.dll that contains types such as MyApp.Data.Invoice:

```
TLBIMP MyApp.dll [/OUT:MyApp.Data]
```

If the internal name of the type library matches its filename, you must use the /out switch because TlbImp correctly refuses to overwrite the source file. If the source DLL contains multiple type libraries (as is the case with the Visual Basic 6 type library, msvbvm60.dll), TlbImp extracts only the first type library, but you can append *N* to the filename to extract the *N*th type library. For example, the following command imports the VBRUN type library (which is the third type library embedded in msvbvm60.dll):

```
TLBIMP c:\Windows\System32\msvbvm60.dll\3 /OUT:vbrun.dll
```

As I've already mentioned, you must use TlbImp instead of Visual Studio's Add Reference command to generate interop assemblies with a strong name and a version number. Another good reason for using TlbImp is to generate classes in a namespace different from the default one. You can accomplish these tasks with the /keyfile, /asmversion, and /namespace options:

```
TLBIMP source.dll /KEYFILE:c:\codearchitects.snk /ASMVERSION:2.0.0.0 /
NAMESPACE:CodeArchitects
```

Here the .snk file containing the public/private key pair has been generated previously with the option –k of the SN utility, as I explain in Chapter 13. By default, TlbImp recursively imports all the type libraries referenced by the type library you specify. You can avoid this behavior by providing one or more /reference options pointing to other assemblies—in which case, TlbImp will attempt to solve external types in the assemblies you specify before it imports them. You can also specify the /strictref option if you want to cause an error if one or more external references could not be resolved without importing another type library:

```
TLBIMP source.dll /REFERENCE:Interop.Office.dll /STRICTREF
```

You can find additional details on TlbImp and its options in the MSDN documentation.

Primary Interop Assemblies

When working with COM Interop assemblies, you might bump into the following problem. Let's say that you create an interop assembly for the Microsoft Word type library, and you sign it to obtain a strong name assembly. As a consequence, all the objects in this assembly have an identity that depends on your assembly's name and version and your publisher key. Let's further suppose that your program interacts with another .NET application that uses Word via COM Interop and that has been authored by another company. Here's the problem: If the other company has created *another* interop assembly for Word and has signed it with *their* public key, their Word objects and your Word objects have different identities. For example, if a method in the other application returns a Word.Document object, your code throws a type mismatch exception when it attempts to store the return value to a Word.Document variable.

Microsoft has anticipated this problem and has introduced the concept of Primary Interop Assembly (PIA). A PIA is the "official" interop assembly for a COM component.

It should be created by the manufacturer of the COM component itself, and it should be installed in the GAC and registered in the registry. Here's how you can create a PIA for a COM component that you've authored:

1. Use the /primary option of TlbImp to create the primary interop assembly, as follows:

   ```
   TLBIMP mylib.dll /OUT:mypia.dll /PRIMARY /KEYFILE:mycompany.snk
   ```

2. Run the AsmReg utility to add the PrimaryInteropAssembly registry key under the HKEY_CLASSES_ROOT\TypeLib\{tlbguid}\Version key related to the COM component:

   ```
   ASMREG mypia.dll
   ```

3. Run the GacUtil tool to install the interop assembly in the GAC:

   ```
   GACUTIL -i mypia.dll
   ```

4. Copy the assembly file to the C:\Program Files\Microsoft.NET\Primary Interop Assemblies folder, to make it appear in Visual Studio .NET's Add Reference dialog box. (This step is optional.)

Visual Studio .NET deals with PIAs in a special way: when you add a reference to a type library for which a PIA exists, Visual Studio .NET doesn't import the type library as it normally would; instead, it uses the PIA installed in the system. Notice that a PIA can reference only other PIAs.

Microsoft provides the PIAs for a few important type libraries, such as adodb, Microsoft.mshtml, Microsoft.stdformat, office, and stdole. Other PIAs might be available on Microsoft Web site.

Late Binding and Reflection

In most real-world situations, you will import the metadata for a COM component and use it through early binding, but it's good to know that you don't strictly have to. In fact, managed code can access COM objects by using late binding and reflection techniques, without having to import their type library. This technique can be useful when you use a COM object only once in a while, or when you don't know at compile time which objects your application will use.

Creating a COM component in a late-bound fashion requires that you use the Type.GetTypeFromProgID or Type.GetTypeFromCLSID static methods to retrieve the Type object corresponding to the COM component with a given ProgID or CLSID. You can then pass this Type object to the Activator.CreateInstance method to create an instance of the component, which you typically assign to an Object variable. Finally, you use the Type.InvokeMember method to call a method, set a property, or read a property of the object, as you learned in Chapter 14.

The following code shows you how to create an ADODB.Connection object in a late-bound fashion and then query it for its Version property and open a connection to a SQL Server database:

```
' Get the Type object for the ADODB.Connection COM component.
Dim ty As Type = Type.GetTypeFromProgID("ADODB.Connection")
' Create a Connection object through late binding.
Dim cn As Object = Activator.CreateInstance(ty)
' Use InvokeMember to retrieve the connection's Version property.
Dim version As String = CStr(ty.InvokeMember("Version", _
    BindingFlags.GetProperty, Nothing, cn, Nothing))

' Open the connection. (Open method takes one argument.)
Dim args() As Object = {"Provider=SQLOLEDB.1;Integrated Security=SSPI;" _
    & "Initial Catalog=pubs;Data Source=."}
ty.InvokeMember("Open", Reflection.BindingFlags.InvokeMethod, Nothing, cn, args)
```

When you invoke a method through late binding, you are implicitly relying on the COM object's IDispatch interface. This detail has a number of consequences. For example, the method name is case-insensitive because IDispatch works in this way, and all arguments are converted to Variant before being passed to the COM object. All COM components written with Visual Basic 6 support IDispatch and can be accessed in this fashion, but you can't use this technique with a few vtable-only components written in some other languages.

The BinderFlags value passed to InvokeMember is transparently converted to IDispatch flags. For example, BinderFlags.InvokeMethod corresponds to the DISPATCH_METHOD flag, and BinderFlags.GetProperty corresponds to DISPATCH_PROPERTYGET. Binder-Flags.SetProperty might pose a problem, however, because it is translated to DISPATCH_PROPERTYPUT or DISPATCH_PROPERTYPUTREF, so it is unclear whether the property being assigned has both a Property Let and a Property Set procedure. In this case, you can precisely describe which Property procedure you're calling by using either the BinderFlags.PutDispProperty value (DISPATCH_PROPERTYPUT, for Property Let) or the BinderFlags.PutRefDispProperty value (DISPATCH_PROPERTYPUTREF, for Property Set).

The System.Type class has a few members that are useful when working with COM objects. You can use the IsComObject readonly property to check whether a .NET type is actually a wrapper for a COM class and the GUID property to retrieve the component's GUID. The BaseType property of a COM object created via late binding is System.__ComObject, whereas the BaseType property of an early-bound COM object is Nothing.

> **Note** The next two sections assume that you're familiar with advanced COM programming topics, such as HRESULTs, VT_* Variant subtypes, and apartments. If you aren't familiar with these concepts, you might want to skip these sections.

COM Interop Marshaling

I covered data marshaling in the section "Using PInvoke," but there are a few issues left to be discussed that concern COM Interop only.

To begin with, you must learn how COM errors are returned to the .NET caller. The .NET runtime checks the HRESULT 32-bit value returned from all COM methods: if the COM method returns an error, this value is negative. In this case, the runtime attempts to generate the .NET exception that matches the returned HRESULT value. It can find the matching exception type by looking for a known mapping or by calling methods of the IErrorInfo interface to retrieve additional information about the error, if the COM object supports this interface. If both these attempts fail, the .NET runtime throws a generic COMException object. The ErrorCode property of this COMException object contains the original HRESULT value, so you can use it in a Select Case block to provide different recovery actions for different error codes.

Variant arguments are another common source of problems. When you import a type library, all arguments and return values of Variant type are converted to Object values by the type library import process. If you pass a value to one of these Object arguments, the .NET runtime dynamically determines the internal type of the Variant that is actually passed to COM. For example, Integer values are converted to VT_I4 Variants, Boolean values to VT_BOOL Variants, Nothing values to VT_EMPTY Variants, and DBNull values to VT_NULL Variants. (The internal type of a Variant corresponds to the value returned by the VarType function under Visual Basic 6.)

However, not all COM types correspond to .NET types, so you might need to resort to one of the following auxiliary classes to force the marshaler to convert your Object value to a specific VT_* type: CurrencyWrapper (VT_CY), UnknownWrapper (VT_UNKNOWN), DispatchWrapper (VT_DISPATCH), and ErrorWrapper (VT_ERROR). For example, here's how you can pass a .NET Decimal value to a Variant argument that is expected to receive a Currency value:

```
Dim cw As New CurrencyWrapper(2.5@)
obj.MyMethod(cw)
```

Objects passed to Variant arguments pose other problems, too, because the runtime must copy the Object into a brand-new Variant. If the object is passed by value and the COM method changes one or more object properties, these changes can't be seen by the .NET caller. A similar thing happens when a COM method returns a Variant value that contains an object: in this case, the runtime copies the Variant into a brand-new Object value, but changes to this object's properties aren't propagated to the original Variant seen by the COM component.

Changes in both directions are seen if a .NET caller passes an object to a ByRef Variant argument, but keep in mind that the COM method might assign a completely different type of object to the argument. Therefore, you can't assume that, when the method returns, the argument still contains the same type of object it did before the call.

The situation is even more complicated if the Variant returned from COM has the VT_BYREF bit set, which indicates that the Variant contains a 32-bit pointer to the data. (For example, a Variant that contains a VT_BYREF+VT_DISPATCH value is actually a pointer to an object.) If the Variant is passed by value, the marshaler correctly recognizes the BT_BYREF bit and is able to retrieve the object reference, but any changes to this .NET object aren't propagated to the original COM object (unlike what would happen if the client were a true COM application). If the Variant is passed with the ByRef keyword, however, changes to the .NET object are correctly propagated to the original COM object, but only if the COM method hasn't changed the type of the object. If the COM method has changed the object's type, an InvalidCastException occurs on return from the method.

The bottom line: Steer clear of COM objects that take and return Variant arguments, if possible. If you can't avoid them, read the documentation carefully, and use the preceding notes as a guideline for troubleshooting code that doesn't behave as expected.

Threading Issues

One more issue must be taken into account when accessing COM from a .NET client. COM components live either in a Single Thread Apartment (STA) or in a Multi Thread Apartment (MTA), even though there are a few components that can live in both apartment types. By comparison, .NET applications always run as free-threaded code, don't use apartments, and implement synchronization by other means (for example, synchronized regions and locks).

The .NET runtime must initialize either an STA or an MTA before a managed client can call a COM object. The type of the apartment being initialized affects all subsequent calls: if the apartment isn't compatible with the apartment where the COM component resides, COM has to create a proxy/stub pair between them, which in turn has a serious negative effect on performance. As you probably know, all Visual Basic 6 components can live only in an STA; therefore, calls to these components coming from .NET applications that have initialized an MTA will be slowed by an intermediate proxy/stub.

Visual Basic .NET console and Windows Forms applications initialize an STA by default, but other types of applications initialize an MTA by default. You can affect the apartment type that a managed thread creates by setting the Thread object's ApartmentState property, before the first call to COM is made:

```
If Thread.CurrentThread.ApartmentState = ApartmentState.Unknown Then
    ' Apartment hasn't been created yet.
    Thread.CurrentThread.ApartmentState = ApartmentState.STA
End If
' Now you can call a Visual Basic 6 component.
Dim sc As New SampleComponent.SampleObject
```

You can't change the apartment type after the thread has initialized the apartment. Further attempts to modify the ApartmentState property are simply ignored, without raising any exception. Another way to tell .NET which apartment type should be created is by flagging the Sub Main procedure with either the STAThread or the MTAThread attribute:

```
<STAThread()> _
Sub Main
    ⋮
End Sub
```

ASP.NET applications create MTA apartments by default, but you can set the *Page.Asp-CompatMode* property or the *AspCompat* attribute in an @Page directive to *True* to force the page to execute in an STA. This setting is also necessary to call COM+ objects that access built-in objects such as *Request* or *Response* either through the *ObjectContext* object or through the argument passed to the *OnStartPage* method. For this property or attribute to work correctly, however, the COM or COM+ object must be created from inside the *Page_Init* or *Page_Load* event handler, as opposed to from inside the page's constructor or by means of a field initializer. Setting this property or attribute to *True* degrades the page's performance, so you should weigh the tradeoff of having an ASP.NET page running in an STA vs. going through a proxy/stub when the page calls an STA-only COM object.

Calling .NET Objects from COM

When porting a large Visual Basic 6 application to .NET, you might decide to leave the bulk of the application as unmanaged code while rewriting selected components as Visual Basic .NET classes. In this scenario, roles are reversed: unmanaged COM-based code works as the client of managed components. The COM Interop portion of the .NET Framework makes this scenario feasible.

The COM Callable Wrapper (CCW)

A COM Callable Wrapper (CCW) works as a wrapper for a .NET component exposed to a COM client. (See Figure 30-7.) It synthesizes any COM interface that clients expect to find, most notably IUnknown ("the mother of all COM interfaces") and IDispatch (which makes the object accessible from languages such as VBScript or through late binding in Visual Basic 6 and earlier versions). The CCW is also responsible for the object identity, so there is always at most one CCW instance for each instance of the .NET component, even if multiple clients have a reference to the same object. The CCW also protects the .NET object from garbage collections and morphs .NET exceptions into HRESULT codes when the method call returns to the COM client.

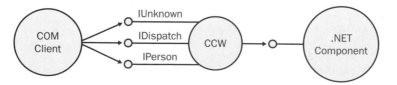

Figure 30-7   The COM Callable Wrapper object

For the .NET Framework to be able to create a suitable CCW object, you must create a type library for each component you want to expose to the COM world. Providing a type library helps COM developers code against the .NET class—for example, by leveraging the Visual Basic 6 Object Browser and the Microsoft IntelliSense feature—and lets the .NET object expose richer information at run time. A type library is also necessary at run time to let OleAut32 marshal remote instances of the objects.

Creating a Sample .NET Component

To see in practice how you can expose a .NET component to the COM world, let's create a sample .NET class and see how a COM client can access it. Start by creating a new Class Library project, name it SampleNetComponent, and delete the default Class1.vb file.

When creating a .NET class meant to be exposed to COM clients, you can save time by using the Add New Item command from the Project menu and selecting the COM Class template. Name the new component NetComponent, and click the OK button. Visual Studio .NET creates a new class that is already decorated with some key attributes that make the .NET class visible to COM clients. Here's an abridged version of what Visual Studio creates if you select the COM Class template:

```
<ComClass(NetComponent.ClassId, NetComponent.InterfaceId, NetComponent.EventsId)> _
Public Class NetComponent
    ' (These GUIDs will surely be different in your case.)
    Public Const ClassId As String = "FC0B96B3-E719-4CD7-816B-BB3DCAD8BD97"
    Public Const InterfaceId As String = "7B8BA729-6B1D-4AB2-9FDE-75632CFC200E"
    Public Const EventsId As String = "948576A4-15BB-4EE3-A8AE-C22CF652CC56"

    Public Sub New()
        MyBase.New()
    End Sub
End Class
```

You can now add members to this class. For illustration purposes, the class in the demo application on the companion CD exposes sample fields, properties, methods, events, and interface members, including some methods that take arrays or return exceptions. I don't include the entire source code here, but you can browse it on the companion CD.

.NET assemblies meant to be used by COM clients are usually registered in the GAC, and for this reason, they should be signed with a strong name. Remember to add an AssemblyKeyFile attribute to the AssemblyInfo.vb file to make the DLL a signed assembly.

Open the Project Properties dialog box, switch to the Build page, and ensure that the Register For COM Interop option is selected. The Register For COM Interop setting forces Visual Studio .NET to create a type library with the same name as the DLL (SampleNetComponent.tlb in this example) and to register this type library in the system registry.

Build the project, create a DLL named SampleNetComponent.dll, and then create another project that references and uses the NetComponent class. This second project can be as simple as a console application; it serves only to verify that the class works as expected. You'll notice that all the extra attributes in the NetComponent class don't affect the way the class can be used by a managed client.

Now you can bring up Visual Basic 6, add a reference to this NetComponent.tlb file, and use the .NET class as if it were a standard COM component. (See the companion CD for a demo client written in Visual Basic 6.)

> **Important**   .NET components undergo all the usual binding and probing rules, even when they are accessed by COM clients. If you don't install the assembly in the GAC, the assembly should be stored as a private assembly in the unmanaged application's directory. If the client is a Visual Basic 6 running inside the IDE (as opposed to compiled on disk), the application's directory is C:\Program Files\Microsoft Visual Studio\VB98—namely, the directory where the VB6.EXE executable resides.

The RegAsm and TlbExp Utilities

You can also use a couple of utilities in the .NET SDK to export a .NET assembly to a type library. You should become familiar with these utilities because they offer some extra flexibility that you can't achieve solely with Visual Studio .NET's export capabilities.

The Assembly Registration Tool (RegAsm) takes the name of an assembly and registers all the classes it contains in the system registry:

```
REGASM samplenetcomponent.dll /tlb:netcomp.tlb
```

The /tlb switch is optional, but you'll want to use it so that RegAsm produces a type library that COM clients can use to reference .NET objects through early binding. In practice, you can omit the /tlb switch and not create a type library for the component only if COM clients create and use instances of the .NET class exclusively via late binding, by means of the CreateObject function and Object (or Variant) variables.

You can think of RegAsm as a RegSvr32 utility that works with .NET components instead of COM components. As with the RegSvr32 utility, you can unregister a component from the registry with the /u option:

```
REGASM samplenetcomponent.dll /u
```

Figure 30-8 shows all the registry keys that RegAsm has created for the sample assembly. As you see, .NET components appear to be exposed to COM clients by the mscoree.dll. The InProcServer32 key contains three additional values that let mscoree.dll find the assembly: Assembly, Class, and RuntimeVersion.

The RegAsm utility supports two more useful switches. The /codebase option adds a CodeBase registry entry, and should be used only if the .NET assembly isn't shared or isn't going to be registered in the GAC. (Visual Studio .NET uses the /codebase option when exporting an assembly.)

```
REGASM samplenetcomponent.dll /codebase
```

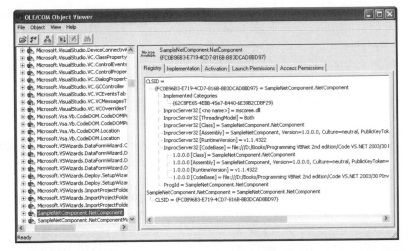

Figure 30-8   The .NET component displayed in the OleView utility. All .NET components exposed to COM can be found in the .NET category subtree.

The other option is /regfile, which doesn't register the component but creates a .reg file that you can later use to create all the necessary registry keys. (You can't use this option with /u or /tlb, and you can't duplicate its effect from inside Visual Studio.)

```
REGASM samplenetcomponent.dll /regfile:netcomp.reg
```

The .NET SDK offers another tool that you can use to export a type library, the Type Library Exporter utility (TlbExp). TlbExp has the same effect as using the /tlb option with RegAsm, except the component isn't registered:

```
TLBEXP samplenetcomponent.dll /OUT:netcomp.tlb
```

If you omit the /out option, TlbExp creates a type library with the same name as the source DLL but with a .tlb extension. In practice, you'll use TlbExp far less frequently than RegAsm.

Conversion Details

.NET assemblies embed more metadata than COM type libraries; therefore, it is unavoidable that some information is lost in the conversion process from .NET to COM. In most cases, you don't need to care about these details, but there are a few things that you should keep in mind. In this section, I'll summarize what you should be careful about.

Assembly version information consists of a 4-part number, whereas type libraries support only major and minor version numbers. During the conversion process, the assembly's revision and build version numbers are discarded. If the assembly had no version information—that is, the version is 0.0.0.0—the type library is assigned version 1.0; otherwise, it couldn't be loaded correctly by a COM client.

A .NET class or interface is exported to a coclass or interface with the same name as the .NET type. The namespace portion of the class or interface name is discarded because type libraries don't support the concept of nested classes or interfaces. For example, a type named Animal.Mammal.Mouse is exported to a coclass named Mouse. When a name collision would result—for example, because there is another class named Hardware.Peripheral.Mouse—the type is exported with its full name, but periods are replaced by underscores.

A .NET class must be nonabstract (that is, not marked with the MustInherit keyword) and must expose a public parameterless constructor, either explicit or implicit, for it to be converted to a COM creatable class. (COM doesn't support constructors with arguments.) Creatable classes are assigned a ProgID equal to their complete namespace+name path. This ProgID generation process usually works flawlessly because ProgIDs can contain periods, except when the complete class name is longer than 39 characters or contains punctuation symbols other than periods. In such cases, you should specify a ProgID attribute in your .NET source code. (See the next section.) Noncreatable classes are marked with the noncreatable attribute in the type library. Only creatable classes are registered by the RegAsm utility.

Any coclass generated by the conversion process is assigned a CLSID calculated using a hash function on the complete class name (including its namespace). This technique ensures that different classes generate different CLSIDs, and therefore each .NET class is converted to a distinct COM class. This technique also ensures that the same CLSID is generated regardless of how many times the conversion process is performed. You can also assign a custom ID if you need to, as explained in the following section.

The conversion process generates one *class interface* for each .NET class. Interfaces generated by the conversion process are assigned an IID calculated using a hash function on the complete interface name (including its namespace) as well as the signatures of its methods. The hash function ensures that a different IID is generated if the interface name, the order of its methods, or the signature of any method changes. The generation of a new IID is necessary to comply with the immutable interface concept in COM. Notice that method names aren't taken into account by the hash function and that you can control the IID value using the Guid attribute, as explained in the next section.

Only public instance members are exposed through a class interface; shared members, nondefault constructors, and members with a scope other than Public aren't exported to COM. You can selectively hide one or more public methods to COM by means of the ComVisible attribute, as I explain in the next section.

Methods preserve their name when they are exported to a class interface (or any interface, for that matter). However, .NET supports method overloading, whereas COM doesn't. To let COM clients call overloaded versions of a method, TlbExp generates a distinct method for each overloaded variant and decorates the name of additional methods with an ordinal number, starting at 2, so that each method is assigned a unique name. For example, three overloaded versions of a method named MyMethod are exported as MyMethod, MyMethod_2, and MyMethod_3. There is no guarantee that numbers will be assigned always in the same order if you repeat the export process.

Marshaling data from COM to .NET works along the same general guidelines described earlier in this chapter. However, you should be careful about .NET method signatures when working with Visual Basic 6 as a client. A Visual Basic 6 client can't call a .NET method that takes an array by value. You should change the method signature so that the array is passed ByRef, which is the only legal way to pass array arguments in earlier Visual Basic versions.

Using Attributes to Control the Conversion

Now that you have a broad idea of how the conversion from assemblies to type libraries works, let's see how you can decorate the .NET class with attributes to gain control of the conversion process and solve some of the problems I mentioned in the previous section.

The ComVisible, Progid, and Guid Attributes

By default, public .NET assemblies, classes, and interfaces are exported and made visible to COM clients. However, you can make a specific public element invisible to COM with the ComVisible attribute, which can be applied at the assembly, class, or member level. If applied at the assembly level, the attribute affects the visibility of all classes in the assembly, unless a class-level attribute forces a different visibility. Likewise, an attribute at the class level affects all the methods in the class that aren't flagged with a ComVisible attribute. Consider this code:

```
<Assembly: ComVisible(False)>

<ComVisible(True)> _
Public Class Person          ' This class is visible to COM.
    ⋮
    <ComVisible(False)> _
    Sub DoSomething()        ' This method isn't visible to COM.
        ⋮
    End Sub
End Class

Public Class Employee        ' This class isn't visible to COM.
    ⋮
End Class
```

Interestingly, if a method takes or returns a type that isn't visible to COM, the argument or the return value is exported to COM as an IUnknown value; if a method takes or returns a structure (as opposed to a class) that isn't visible to COM, the method isn't exported at all.

You can explicitly assign a ProgID to a class by using the ProgId attribute in the .NET source code. For example, the following code assigns the MouseCollection class a ProgID equal to Animal.Mice:

```
<ProgID("Animal.Mice")> _
Public Class MouseCollection
    ⋮
End Class
```

You can also assign a specific GUID to a class or an interface, with the Guid attribute. When you apply this attribute at the assembly level, it is taken as the TLBID identifier for the entire type library:

```
' This is the TLBID for the exported type library.
<Assembly: Guid("3DC10475-92DB-4E52-A3D2-925AA4E8BA17")>

' This is the CLSID for the class.
<Guid("{E6A2200A-5869-4C89-83A1-D0FE8540020B}")> _
Public Class MouseCollection
    ⋮
End Class
```

The DispId Attribute

All the members of a COM IDispatch interface must be marked with a DISPID value, and these values are generated automatically in the conversion from .NET to COM. In general, you never see these DISPIDs and don't need to control their generation. The only exception worth mentioning is the special 0 value, which is reserved for the class default member.

As you might remember from your Visual Basic 6 days, most controls and objects have a default member—for example, the Text property for TextBox controls and the Caption property for Label controls. The default member of .NET classes exported to COM is the ToString method that all classes inherit from System.Object, but you can make any property or method the default class member by applying the DispId attribute, as in:

```
<DispId(0)> Property Name() As String
    ⋮
End Property
```

The ComClass and ClassInterface Attributes

You can be in control of the CLSID and the IID of the class interface generated for a .NET class as well as the IID of the generated interface that handles events by means of the ComClass attribute. (Visual Studio .NET automatically inserts this attribute when it generates a COM class, as explained in the section "Creating a Sample .NET Component.") Interestingly, the ComClass attribute belongs to the Microsoft.VisualBasic namespace, unlike all other attributes related to COM Interop (which belong to the System.Runtime.InteropServices namespace).

Any public .NET class can be exposed to COM, provided that its source code contains a ComVisible(True) attribute at the class or the assembly level. A class exposed to COM with a ComVisible attribute but without a ComClass attribute exports its class interface—that is, the interface that contains all the properties and methods defined in the class—as an IDispatch interface. This means that COM clients can access the class's members only by means of late binding. Late binding is slow, isn't robust, and doesn't allow you to trap events. In spite of these shortcomings, Microsoft decided to make class interfaces accessible through IDispatch by default. Late binding ensures that you don't incur versioning problems. Flagging a .NET class with this Visual Basic–specific ComClass attribute has many advantages and a few disadvantages. On the pro side, .NET classes flagged with this attribute correctly expose properties, methods, and events to both early-bound and late-bound COM clients, with very little effort on your part. On the con side, however, these classes don't expose their public fields, nor do they expose methods inherited from System.Object, including the useful ToString method.

```
Dim o As Object
Set o = CreateObject("SampleNetComponent.NetComponent")
o.MyMethod()
```

You can control which type of class interface the export process generates by means of the ClassInterface attribute. This attribute can take one of the following ClassInterface-Type enumerated values: AutoDispatch (the default—methods are accessible via late binding only), AutoDual (methods are accessible through early and late binding), and None (no class interface is created and only methods in secondary interfaces can be accessed). Here's how you must decorate a class to offer support for both early binding and late binding:

```
<ClassInterface(ClassInterfaceType.AutoDual)> _
Public Class NetComponent
   :
End Class
```

Clients of a class flagged with the ClassInterface attribute that specifies an AutoDual interface type can access public fields and the four instance methods that all .NET classes inherit from System.Object; these two kinds of members aren't visible if you decorate the class with the ComClass attribute.

However, a class flagged with just the ClassInterface attribute doesn't make its events visible to clients. To solve this problem, I need to introduce two more attributes.

The InterfaceType and ComSourceInterfaces Attributes

Let's say that you have the following .NET class:

```
Public Class Person
    Public Event GotEmail(ByVal msg As String)
    Public Event TodayIsMyBirthday(ByVal age As Integer)
    :
End Class
```

As I've just explained, these events aren't automatically exposed to COM clients if the class isn't flagged with the ComClass attribute. To make events visible to COM clients, you must define a separate interface that contains the event signature and mark the interface with an InterfaceType attribute to make it an IDispatch interface, as follows:

```
<InterfaceType(ComInterfaceType.InterfaceIsDispatch)> _
Public Interface Person_Events
    Sub GotEmail(ByVal msg As String)
    Sub TodayIsMyBirthday(ByVal age As Integer)
End Interface
```

Next you must flag the Person class with a ComSourceInterfaces attribute that informs COM Interop that the class events are defined in the Person_Events interface:

```
<ClassInterface(ClassInterfaceType.AutoDual), _
 ComSourceInterfaces(GetType(Person_Events))> _
Public Class Person
    Public Event GotEmail(ByVal msg As String)
    Public Event TodayIsMyBirthday(ByVal age As Integer)
    ⋮
End Class
```

After these edits, Visual Basic 6 clients can assign an instance of the Person class to a WithEvents variable and correctly trap events.

Caution   Event support is quite weak in versions 1.0 and 1.1 of the .NET Framework. For example, assigning the same object reference to two WithEvents variables crashes the application when these variables are later set to Nothing. Also, if a .NET object raises an event but there is no WithEvents variable pointing to that object—in other words, the client isn't trapping the event—the client can occasionally receive an Unknown Name error.

The ComRegisterFunction and ComUnregisterFunction Attributes

At times, you might need to perform a custom action when the .NET class is registered as a COM component by RegAsm (or by Visual Studio .NET, if you have selected the Register For COM Interop option). For example, you might want to ask the end user for a password or add some keys to the registry (in addition to those added by the registration process). Accomplishing these tasks is as easy as adding a shared procedure to the class and marking it with the ComRegisterFunction attribute:

```
Const COMPANYKEY As String = "Software\CodeArchitects\MyApp"

<ComRegisterFunction()> _
Private Shared Sub Register(ByVal ty As Type)
    Dim key As RegistryKey = Registry.CurrentUser.CreateSubKey(COMPANYKEY)
    key.SetValue("InstallDate", Now.ToLongDateString)
    key.Close()
End Sub
```

If you add a registry key at installation time, you should remove it when the .NET class is unregistered as a COM component. In this case, you create another static procedure and mark it with the ComUnregisterFunction attribute:

```
<ComUnregisterFunction()>_
Private Shared Sub UnRegister(ByVal ty As Type)
    Registry.CurrentUser.DeleteSubKey(COMPANYKEY)
End Sub
```

Both these procedures can be private or public, provided that they are marked with the Shared keyword and take a System.Type argument; this Type value identifies the class being registered or unregistered.

Working with Exceptions

Most .NET exceptions are automatically translated to the corresponding HRESULT codes when they are marshaled back to COM clients. For example, a DivideByZeroException object is translated to an HRESULT code equal to COR_E_DIVIDEBYZERO, which a Visual Basic 6 client can trap with an On Error statement and interpret as an error whose Err.Number code is 11.

In those rare cases when you need to return a more specific HRESULT code, you can use a couple of techniques. The first and simplest one relies on the ThrowException-ForHR method of the Marshal class:

```
' Throw an exception whose HRESULT is hex 80001234.
Marshal.ThrowExceptionForHR(&H80001234)
```

The second, more elegant technique consists of the definition of a custom exception class whose constructor assigns the desired error code to its HResult protected property:

```
Public Class CustomException
    Inherits Exception

    Sub New(ByVal message As String)
        MyBase.New(message)
        Me.HResult = &H80001234
    End Sub
End Class
```

Your .NET class can then throw an exception with a given HRESULT by throwing this custom exception as it would any standard exception:

```
Throw New CustomException("File not found")
```

Writing COM-Friendly .NET Components

.NET components that are meant to be exposed to COM clients shouldn't use features that COM-based clients can't see. Or they should provide alternative ways for COM clients to access those features. Here's a brief summary of the dos and don'ts of COM-friendly .NET components:

- Only public and nonabstract classes can be exposed to COM; use ComVisible(False) for public MustInherit classes.

- Avoid deep hierarchies in .NET classes, such as nested classes or namespaces with more than two levels.

- The class must expose an implicit or explicit parameterless constructor; constructors with parameters can't be accessed via COM Interop.

- The class shouldn't expose shared members, as they aren't visible to COM clients.

- The class shouldn't expose overloaded members because they can create confusion when used by COM clients.

- If the class exposes events, define them in a separate interface, and use the ComSourceInterfaces attribute to let COM Interop export them correctly.

- For simplicity's sake, use the ComClass attribute if COM clients don't need to access fields, trap events, or invoke methods inherited from System.Object.

- Use custom exception classes that set the HResult property for returning non-standard error codes to COM clients.

The .NET Framework offers superb support for the transition from the unmanaged world to the .NET world, thanks to PInvoke and COM Interop. In most cases, these two worlds can communicate quite easily, but you must be familiar with the techniques I have covered in this chapter to solve some of the problems you might bump into when writing real-world applications. However, never forget that a .NET application that relies on COM components inherits many of the issues that have plagued COM programming—for example, the tendency to leak memory.

There are other ways to leverage pre-.NET technologies. One of them is using serviced components that build on COM+ services, as I explain in the next chapter.

31 Serviced Components

As you might remember from Chapter 1, the Microsoft .NET Framework doesn't replace COM+ and the built-in features portion of the Microsoft Windows operating system known as Component Services. As a matter of fact, COM+ has been greatly improved even after the inception of .NET and has evolved from version 1.0 (the version provided with Windows 2000) to version 1.5 (the version introduced with Windows XP and enhanced with Windows Server 2003). You can leverage COM+ features from a .NET application by writing one or more serviced components.

A Quick Introduction to COM+

Many books have been written about COM+ and I can't even begin to do this technology justice in just one chapter. Nevertheless, an introduction is in order for those programmers who have never worked with COM+ in previous versions of Microsoft Visual Basic.

The COM+ story began when Microsoft released the Option Pack for Windows NT; among its other products, that Option Pack included Microsoft Transaction Server (MTS), which enabled you to instantiate and invoke a component hosted in a DLL, on either the same or another computer. The most intriguing new feature was the ability to create *transactional components*, which can perform transactions that spawn different databases.

A few years later, Microsoft released Windows 2000, which included a new module officially named Component Services but that is known among developers as COM+. This operating system module offered everything MTS did and a lot more, including object pooling, queued components, and loosely coupled events. At last developers could create enterprise-level, distributed applications with relatively little effort, as they could rely on the COM+ infrastructure for services such as distributed transactions, security, synchronization, resource management, and deployment. Programmers could focus on building the application's logic, thus saving a lot of time in development and debugging.

Windows XP and Windows Server 2003 come with version 1.5 of COM+, which adds new features, such as the ability to access a COM+ component via SOAP (as if it were a Web service) and the ability to run a component as a Windows NT service. You can adjust the isolation level used by transactional components, register a given component under multiple COM+ applications, and create application partitions. COM+ applications can be configured to automatically restart after a given timeout or after a given number of objects are created.

Regardless of the Windows version you're using, you can administer COM+ by means of the Component Services snap-in, an MMC applet that you can reach from the Administrative Tools menu. (See Figure 31-1.) You can create a custom MMC configuration that includes the Component Services plug-in by running the mmc.exe application with the /a switch (for Author mode) and then choosing the Add/Remove Snap-In command from the File menu.

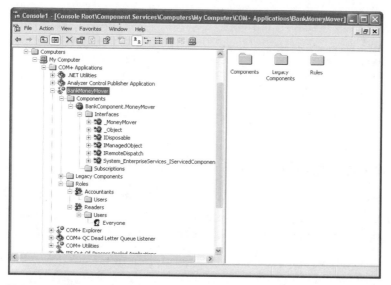

Figure 31-1   The Component Services MMC snap-in

The MMC application gives you a visual front end to the COM+ catalog. The COM+ catalog contains essential information about all registered COM+ components, such as whether they run in the client's memory or in the server's memory, which users can instantiate them or call their methods, and under which account they run. You can expand the Running Process element to list the COM+ applications that are currently running, actually *see* their components spinning, and determine how many objects are running and how many methods have been called on them.

.NET Serviced Components Overview

Instead of describing how to leverage COM+ features from Visual Basic .NET in an abstract fashion, I will begin by showing you how to create a simple serviced component with Visual Basic .NET and how to use it from a client application. I will then implement new features—in most cases by just adding attributes—and explain how you can leverage them to create better applications.

COM+ transactions are used in portions of the .NET Framework other than serviced components. You might want to review the Transaction attribute in the @Page directive of Web Forms (which I briefly mentioned in Chapter 24) and the TransactionOption argument of the WebMethod for Web services (which I covered in Chapter 29).

Remember that serviced components are supported only under Windows 2000, Windows XP, and Windows Server 2003—that is, all platforms that support COM+. Serviced components aren't supported under MTS running under Windows NT 4.

> **Note** To keep the code as concise as possible, all the code samples in this chapter assume the use of the following Import statements at the file or project level:
>
> ```
> Imports System.EnterpriseServices
> Imports System.Runtime.InteropServices
> Imports System.Messaging
> Imports System.Data.SqlClient
> ```

Introducing Serviced Components

A serviced component is a public class that inherits from System.EnterpriseServices.ServicedComponent:

```
Public Class MoneyMover
    Inherits ServicedComponent
    ⋮
End Class
```

The ServicedComponent class, in turn, inherits indirectly from System.MarshalByRefObject, a type that defines a marshal-by-reference (MBR) object. An MBR object is an object that never leaves the AppDomain where its assembly runs. When a client in another assembly receives a reference to an MBR object, the reference is actually a pointer to a *proxy* object that looks like the MBR object but runs in the client's AppDomain. When the client invokes a method, the proxy transparently dispatches the call to the remote object, using the .NET infrastructure.

Notice that .NET serviced components support remote method invocation of their instance methods only. A serviced component can expose shared methods, but they can't be called by COM+ clients.

Creating the Test Database

The sample COM+ component I'll develop lets client applications move money from one bank account to another in a safe manner and updates a SQL Server database.

To make the sample code work correctly, create a new SQL Server database named BankAccounts, and add a table named Accounts. This table has three fields: ID (the primary key, a 32-bit integer), Name (the user name, a 40-character field), and Balance (a decimal value that tells you how much money a given user has). The companion CD comes with a SQL script that creates this database for you. After you create the table, you should add a couple of records to experiment with:

```
INSERT Accounts (ID, Name, Balance) VALUES(1, 'Joe Doe', 10000)
INSERT Accounts (ID, Name, Balance) VALUES(2, 'Ann Smith', 10000)
```

Once the database is ready, you can focus on the COM+ component itself.

Creating the COM+ Application

Create a Class Library project named BankComponent, rename the default Class1 class as MoneyMover, and add a reference to the System.EnterpriseServices.dll assembly. This assembly contains all the base classes and attributes that you need when building .NET serviced components. Alternatively, you can delete the default Class1.vb file and use the Add New Item command from the Project menu to add a Transactional Component named MoneyMover. By using the latter approach, a reference to System.EnterpriseServices.Dll is added automatically to the current project.

> **Note**   This first sample relies on automatic registration of the COM+ component. This feature works only if the interactive user has administrative privileges on the system. Later in this chapter, you'll learn how to register the component manually so that any user can instantiate COM+ components.

All serviced components must live in a strongly named assembly (even though they must not necessarily be installed in the GAC), so you must define a few attributes in the AssemblyInfo.vb file:

```
' It's better to use a fixed version number during development.
<Assembly: AssemblyVersion("1.0.0.0")>
' Replace the .snk filename as necessary.
<Assembly: AssemblyKeyFile("c:\codearchitects.snk")>
```

(See Chapter 13 for details about creating a .snk file with the SN utility.)

Serviced components also require additional attributes that affect how the component is registered in the COM+ catalog the first time you instantiate them:

```
<Assembly: ApplicationName("BankMoneyMover")>
<Assembly: Description("Components for moving money between accounts")>
<Assembly: ApplicationID("F088FCFF-6FF0-496B-9121-DC9EB9DAEFFA")>
<Assembly: ApplicationActivation(ActivationOption.Library)>
```

The ApplicationName attribute is the name that identifies the application in the Component Services administration snap-in; the Description attribute is used to better describe the application itself. The ApplicationID attribute assigns an explicit ID to the application. (If omitted, this ID is generated automatically when the component is registered.). An explicit ApplicationID value is especially useful to have multiple assemblies share the same COM+ application (and therefore the same server-side process), which in turn dramatically optimizes cross-component communication and marshaling. The ApplicationName and ApplicationID attributes affect what you see on the General tab of the application's Properties window, shown in the left portion of Figure 31-2.

The ApplicationActivation attribute is crucial, as it determines whether the COM+ component runs as a library application (in the creator's process) or as a server application (in a distinct process hosted in the DllHost.exe executable). In this first example, we'll create a library application, but you'll later learn that you need server applications to enable a few important features, such as the ability to run on a remote system or as an NT service, or to implement more robust security checks. (See right portion of Figure 31-2.)

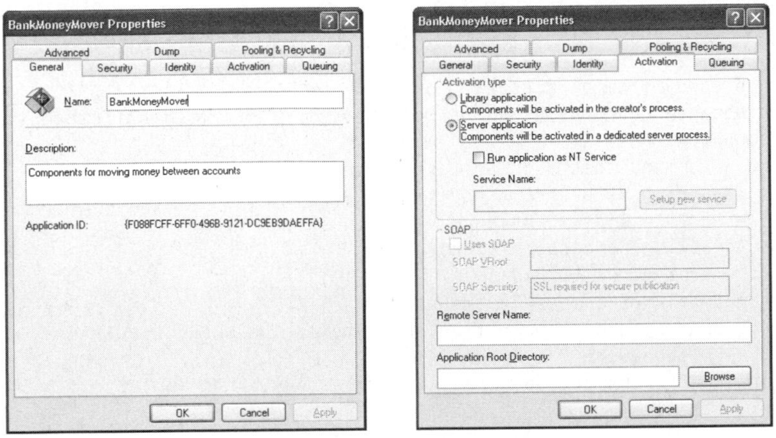

Figure 31-2 The General and Activation tabs of the Properties window of a COM+ component; you can display this window by choosing the Properties command from the component's context menu.

> **Note** The Disable Deletion and Disable Changes check boxes on the Advanced tab of the component's Properties window must be deselected for you to be allowed to change any application setting or delete the application from the COM+ catalog.

Defining a Transactional Class

You can now turn your attention to the MoneyMover class, which contains a public method named TransferMoney and a private method named UpdateAccount. The latter method adds or takes money from a given account but throws an exception if the account ID isn't valid or if the new balance for that account would be negative.

```
<Transaction(TransactionOption.Required), JustInTimeActivation()> _
Public Class MoneyMover
    Inherits ServicedComponent

    Sub TransferMoney(ByVal senderID As Integer, ByVal receiverID As Integer, _
        ByVal amount As Decimal)
        ' Open the connection.
        Dim cn As New SqlConnection("Data Source=.;" _
            & "Initial Catalog=BankAccounts;Integrated Security=SSPI;")
        Try
            cn.Open()
            UpdateAccount(cn, senderID, -amount)
            UpdateAccount(cn, receiverID, amount)
            ' Tell COM+ that transaction can be committed.
            ContextUtil.SetComplete()
        Catch ex As Exception
            ' Tell COM+ that the transaction must be aborted, then rethrow.
```

```
            ContextUtil.SetAbort()
            Throw ex
        Finally
            ' Close the connection in all cases.
            cn.Close()
        End Try
    End Sub


    ' Add or take money from an account.
    Private Sub UpdateAccount(ByVal cn As SqlConnection, ByVal id As Integer, _
        ByVal amount As Decimal)
        ' Create a command that adds or takes money in a safe manner.
        Dim sql As String = "UPDATE Accounts SET Balance = Balance + @amount " _
            & "WHERE ID = @id AND Balance + @amount >= 0"
        Dim cmd As New SqlCommand(sql, cn)
        cmd.Parameters.Add("@id", id)
        cmd.Parameters.Add("@amount", amount)
        ' Execute the command, throw if no row matched the WHERE condition
        If cmd.ExecuteNonQuery() = 0 Then
            Throw New Exception("Unable to update account# " & id.ToString)
        End If
    End Sub
End Sub
End Class
```

The Transaction attribute is what makes—or can make, at least—the MoneyMover class a transactional class. This attribute takes a TransactionOption enumerated value, which can be one of the following:

- **NotSupported**   COM+ ignores the transactional attributes when determining the transactional context for the object.

- **Disabled**   The object isn't a transactional object and never participates in a transaction, even if the caller has one.

- **Supported**   The object can participate in a transaction, if the caller has one, but doesn't require a transaction if no transaction exists.

- **Required**   The object will participate in a transaction, and a new transaction will be created for it if the caller has no transaction.

- **RequiresNew**   The object always runs in a new transaction, even if the caller already has a transaction.

All transactional objects—that is, objects marked with the Required or RequiresNew value for the Transaction attribute—must vote for the outcome of the transaction they live in. If something goes wrong, they should tell COM+ to abort the transaction they live in, which they do by invoking the ContextUtil.SetAbort method. If everything is OK, they should tell COM+ to commit the transaction, which they do by invoking the ContextUtil.SetComplete method. (See boldface statements in previous code snippet.)

Notice that the SetComplete and SetAbort methods aren't symmetrical. All the components that live in the transaction must vote with SetComplete for a transaction to be committed successfully, whereas just a single SetAbort method is enough to doom the transaction.

The JustInTimeActivation attribute enables an important feature of COM+ components. A JIT-activated component isn't created when the client calls the New operator and is actually instantiated only later, when the client makes the first call to it. COM+ components can be instantiated only by means of a parameterless constructor; therefore, no code needs to actually run when the client uses the New keyword. JIT-activated components make a distributed application more scalable, because they don't take memory until one of their methods is actually invoked.

JIT activation is a prerequisite for transactional objects and is a desired feature for poolable objects, as I'll explain in the section "Enabling Object Pooling," later in this chapter. As a matter of fact, JIT activation is automatically enabled if you use the Transaction attribute to specify that the component is transactional, even though I have added it explicitly to the MoneyMover class for clarity.

If a method in a transactional object votes for the transaction outcome, the object is immediately deactivated when the method returns. The client continues to keep an object reference, but the actual object doesn't exist any longer. If the client makes a new call into the object, COM+ transparently creates a fresh new instance of the object. This mechanism ensures that fewer resources are taken on the computer where the object runs and, more important, guarantees that the semantics of the transaction are satisfied.

To understand why this is necessary, consider this scenario. Object A votes "commit" and then returns to the client. At this point in time, the state of the object (its fields and properties) reflects the state of the database. Object B, which is enrolled in the same transaction as Object A, votes "abort" and forces the transaction to roll back. If Object A weren't a JIT-activated object, clients could mistakenly use its public fields and properties and make wrong assumptions about values stored in the database. By requiring that transactional objects be JIT-activated and by destroying them immediately after they vote for the transaction outcome, COM+ prevents clients from using the previous state of the object.

Transactional objects manage two internal bits that reflect the state of the object: the *consistent* bit and the *done* bit. The done bit tells COM+ whether a JIT-activated object can be deactivated; the consistent bit tells COM+ whether the transaction can be committed (if True) or must be rolled back (if False). When the method returns, COM+ checks these bits and decides what to do.

If a method in a transactional object performs an action on a database and leaves the database in a consistent state—for example, it takes money from one account and successfully moves it to another account—it should set the done bit to True as well as set the consistent bit to True to inform COM+ that the transaction can be committed. If the database update attempted by the object can't be completed correctly—for example, there isn't enough money in the first account or the second account doesn't exist—the object should set the consistent bit to False to tell COM+ to immediately roll back the transaction the object lives in. The exact behavior depends on whether the object is the root of the transaction—that is, whether the object initiated a new transaction. (The transaction root is any object whose Transaction attribute is set to RequiresNew or the first object in a call chain whose Transaction attribute is set to Required.) If the object is the root of the transaction and the done bit is True, the transaction is committed or rolled back, depending on the consistent bit. The transaction is also rolled back if the transaction timeout expires.

Regardless of the transaction outcome, if the done bit is True when a method call returns, the JIT activation feature ensures that, even if the client maintains an object reference, the object is destroyed and a new object instance is silently created at the next method invocation. It bears repeating that a JIT-activated object should never rely on values assigned to class-level fields and properties, because these values are gone when the object is deactivated and reactivated at the next method call. For all practical purposes, JIT-activated objects should be regarded as *stateless objects*.

If the transaction can't be completed in a single method call, the object should leave the done bit set to False. In this case, COM+ keeps the object instance alive, and the client must invoke another method to complete the transaction. If the client never calls such a method, the transaction will stay active and you can see it in the Transaction List node of the MMC snap-in. If the transaction has a timeout, COM+ will roll it back automatically when the timeout expires.

An object that hasn't set its done bit to True can reliably save values in its private fields and properties between calls. If the client releases the object that hasn't set the done bit, the current value of the consistent bit determines whether the transaction is committed or aborted when the garbage collection actually releases the object. The transaction is actually committed or rolled back only when the GC releases the object, which might happen at a random time. For this reason, a client should *never* release a reference to a transaction COM+ object whose done bit is True.

The SetComplete and SetAbort methods let you affect the consistent and done bits by executing a single statement. Both these methods set the done bit to True but they differ for value assigned to the consistent bit (True for SetComplete; False for SetAbort). The ContextUtil class exposes other members that let you affect the consistent and the done bit individually, as I explain later in this chapter.

> **Note**   The transactional features of COM+ really shine when multiple databases are involved. Without a coordinator such as COM+ it is extremely difficult—if not impossible—to correctly implement a distributed transaction between different databases. COM+ transactions use the two-phase transactional support from the Microsoft Distributed Transaction Coordinator (MS DTC), which adds significant overhead. If you are working with a single database and don't require other COM+ features—such as object pooling and synchronization—you might want to implement standard transactions by using the BeginTransaction method of the ADO.NET Connection object or by manually sending SQL commands to your database.

Testing the Component

Building a client application that uses the TransferMoney transactional class isn't different from creating a client that uses any other .NET class in a separate assembly. Create a new Windows Forms application in the same or another Microsoft Visual Studio .NET solution, make it the startup project, and then add a reference to the BankComponent project. Next build a minimal user interface that lets the user provide the details of a money transfer (as shown in Figure 31-3). This is the code that runs when the user clicks the Update button:

```
Dim senderID As Integer = CInt(txtSender.Text)
Dim receiverID As Integer = CInt(txtReceiver.Text)
Dim amount As Decimal = CDec(txtAmount.Text)

Try
    Dim mover As New BankComponent.MoneyMover
    mover.TransferMoney(senderID, receiverID, amount)
Catch ex As Exception
    MessageBox.Show(ex.Message, "Error", MessageBoxButtons.OK, MessageBoxIcon.Error)
End Try
```

As you see, the client doesn't need to be aware that the MoneyMover class is a serviced component, nor that it internally uses COM+. It just uses the class as any regular .NET component.

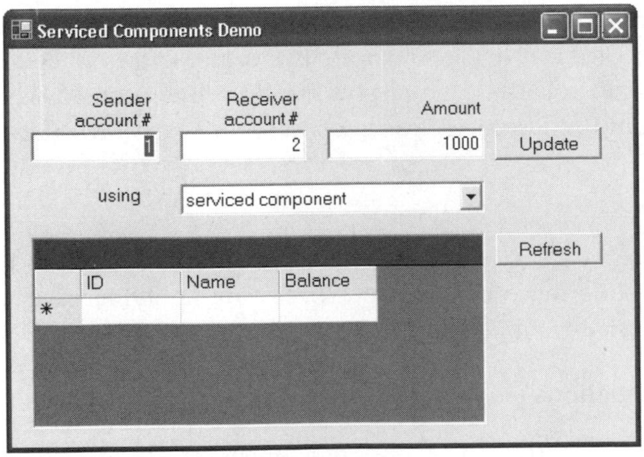

Figure 31-3   A client Windows Forms application for the BankComponent COM+ component

COM+ can keep track of how many objects have been instantiated at any given time and how many are in the pool or have a call in progress. You can look at this statistics information by right-clicking the Components folder and choosing the Status menu command. This feature is enabled by default, but you can explicitly turn it off with an EventTrackingEnabled attribute set to False at the class level:

```
<EventTrackingEnabled(False)> _
Public Class MoneyMover
    ⋮
```

Don't confuse this event tracking feature with statistics information about successful, failed, and pending information that is available by clicking on the Transaction Statistics node below the Distributed Transaction Coordinator folder (See Figure 31-4.) Transaction statistics are managed by the MS DTC and can't be turned off from the MMC snap-in.

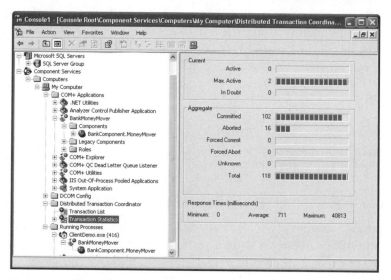

Figure 31-4   The Transaction Statistics page in the Component Services MMC snap-in

During the test phase, it frequently happens that COM+ keeps a lock on the assembly DLL, which prevents Visual Studio .NET from correctly compiling a new version of the serviced component. You can release this lock by shutting down the COM+ application, which you can do from the Running Processes folder in the MMC snap-in.

Improving the Application

Now that you have seen the basics of .NET serviced components, you're ready to learn about ways to make your code more concise and robust, by applying other attributes in the System.EnterpriseServices namespace.

Using AutoComplete Transactions

As a rule, the component should throw an exception whenever the transaction is aborted so that the client can detect the problem and take appropriate steps. To encourage this practice, the .NET Framework provides a method-level attribute named AutoComplete. If a method is flagged with this attribute, COM+ transparently calls ContextUtil.SetAbort on your behalf if the method throws an exception, or it calls ContextUtil.SetComplete if the method doesn't throw any exception. This attribute often simplifies the structure of transactional methods, reduces the margin for programming mistakes—such as omitting a call to SetComplete—and is therefore the recommended way to vote for a transaction. Here's how you can rewrite the TransferMoney method to use this attribute:

```
<AutoComplete()> _
Sub TransferMoney(ByVal senderID As Integer, ByVal receiverID As Integer, _
    ByVal amount As Decimal)
    ' Open the connection.
    Dim cn As New SqlConnection("Data Source=.;" _
        & "Initial Catalog=BankAccounts;User ID=sa;Password=sa;")
    Try
        cn.Open()
        UpdateAccount(cn, senderID, -amount)
        UpdateAccount(cn, receiverID, amount)
    Finally
        cn.Close()
    End Try
End Sub
```

Any exception from the inner UpdateAccount private method is correctly returned to the client, but the AutoComplete attribute ensures that the TransferMoney method correctly votes for the transaction it runs in.

Changing the Transaction Isolation Level and Timeout

COM+ initiates a new transaction when a transactional component opens a database connection or any other resource managed by the MS DTC. By default, these automatic transactions run at the highest isolation level available, the serializable level. Any action performed by a component on the database (including reads) at this isolation level is completely isolated from actions performed by other components running in a different transaction. The serializable level ensures that transactions are carried out in perfect isolation and that no rows are unexpectedly added, removed, or changed in the database while the transaction is running. In practice, it's as if the component is the only user of the database for the entire duration of the transaction. As you can imagine, such a complete isolation can slow down your application and dramatically reduce its scalability.

As it happens with standard database transactions, in many cases, you don't need such a high level of isolation. COM+ 1.5 supports the following isolation levels (from less isolated to more isolated): ReadUncommitted, ReadCommitted, RepeatableRead, and Serializable, plus the special Any setting (which I'll describe shortly). I have described the four canonical isolation levels in the section "Selecting the Isolation Level," in Chapter 21, so I won't repeat myself here. It's interesting to know what happens, however, when a transactional component invokes other transactional components with a different isolation level.

The isolation level of a transaction is determined by the root component—that is, the first transactional component in the call chain. If this root component calls a child component whose isolation level is equal to or higher than the root's isolation level, everything will work smoothly; otherwise, the cross-component call will fail with an E_ISOLATIONLEVELMISMATCH error.

The TransactionIsolationLevel.Any setting is special and should be used only with components that aren't the root of a transaction. When this setting is used, the component doesn't care for the isolation level and uses whatever isolation level has been set up by the component that created the transaction. The Any setting is often useful with transactional components that might not be the root of a transaction—namely, components marked with TransactionOption.Required rather than with TransactionOption.RequiresNew. (The latter components are always the root of a new transaction.)

Let's see how you can use optional arguments of the Transaction attribute to change the isolation level and set the transaction timeout:

```
<Transaction(TransactionOption.Required, _
 Isolation:=TransactionIsolationLevel.ReadUncommitted, Timeout:=10) _
Public Class MoneyMover
    ⋮
```

The Timeout value is in seconds and overrides the machine-level default value (60 seconds) specified on the Options tab of the My Computer node Properties window in the Component Services MMC snap-in. You need to work with Windows XP or Windows Server 2003 to change the default isolation level and timeout.

The Transaction attribute, like most of the attributes that interact with the COM+ catalog, is effective only if the COM+ application hasn't been created yet. Therefore, you must switch to the MMC snap-in and delete the BankMoneyMover application to force .NET to create a brand-new application with the transaction settings that you've specified. Or you can change these values after installing the COM+ application from the Transactions tab of the component's Properties dialog box. (See the left portion of Figure 31-5.)

> **Note**   The only attributes that are always read from the metadata in the component and that supersede the attributes in the COM+ catalog are: JustInTimeActivation, AutoComplete, and ObjectPooling, plus the SecurityRole attribute when used at the method level. The ObjectPooling attribute in source code can enable or disable object pooling, but it always uses the pool size defined in the COM+ catalog.

The isolation level applies to all the methods in the transactional component: if a method opens a database connection or interacts with another resource managed by the MS DTC, a transaction with the specified isolation level is automatically created (and your code *must* vote for its outcome, either by invoking the SetComplete or SetAbort method or implicitly by means of an AutoComplete attribute). It often happens that different methods in a component require different isolation levels, but unfortunately you can't apply the Transaction attribute at the method level.

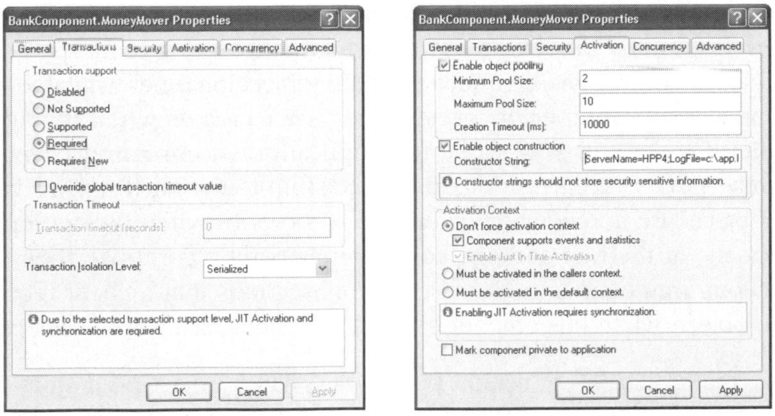

Figure 31-5 The Transaction and Activation tabs of the Properties window of a COM+ component

For example, if one method updates a database and requires the RepeatableRead level, whereas another method performs a read operation for which a ReadCommitted level would be enough, the best you can do is use a Transaction attribute at the class level that specifies a RepeatableRead isolation level and accept the unnecessary overhead that results when the latter method is invoked. To avoid this unnecessary overhead, you must create two additional classes: one that performs all the write operations at the RepeatableRead level, and one that performs all read operations at the ReadCommitted level. The original component would have no Transaction attribute and would be responsible only for dispatching calls to one of the two components, depending on whether it's a write or a read operation. A component that behaves in this way is known as a *facade component*.

Enabling Object Pooling

Object pooling can help improve your COM+ applications in many ways. For example, if your objects take a relatively long time to initialize themselves, it makes sense not to release them when the first client has completed its job, so that they can serve requests from other clients. Object pooling is also useful to limit the number of objects that can be alive at any given moment, so that they don't take too much memory on the server. Another good occasion for adopting pooling is when you have a well-defined number of resources—be they database connections, parallel or serial ports, or other peripheral devices—and each resource is managed by a single instance of your component.

As with most serviced component features, you can enable object pooling from the MMC snap-in, as shown in the right portion of Figure 31-5, or by means of an attribute in source code at the class level:

```
<Transaction(TransactionOption.Required), JustInTimeActivation(), _
   ObjectPooling(MinPoolSize:=2, MaxPoolSize:=10, CreationTimeout:=10000)> _
Public Class MoneyMover
   :
```

The MaxPoolSize argument is the maximum number of objects in the pool; if the pool already contains this number of objects and all of them are serving requests from clients, all subsequent client requests will be queued until an object becomes available. The Min-PoolSize argument is the number of objects that COM+ creates when the application starts and that are kept in the pool while the application is running. If client requests exceed this number, COM+ creates additional objects (up to the MaxPoolSize value), but the additional objects are immediately taken out of the pool when they complete their job (more precisely, at the first garbage collection after they complete their job). The ConnectionTimeout argument is the number of milliseconds that a client request waits for an available object; when this timeout expires, the client receives an exception.

It is strongly advisable that JIT activation be enabled when object pooling is used; this setting lets the .NET runtime move the object back to the pool as soon as the method returns and the object is deactivated. If a pooled object isn't configured to use JIT activation, the object will be put back in the pool only when the garbage collector reclaims it.

Defining an Initialization String

In real-world applications, you can rarely hard-code values such a connection string into the component's source code. In Chapter 13, you saw that .NET provides a simple way to retrieve these configuration values from the configuration file associated with the assembly. In addition, serviced components can easily retrieve the object constructor string that the end user has typed in the Activation tab of the component's Properties window. This feature must be explicitly enabled, either by selecting a check box in the MMC snap-in or from code with the ConstructionEnabled attribute at the class level. (This attribute is ignored if the application is already registered in the COM+ catalog.) In both cases, your component retrieves the construction string by overriding the protected Construct method inherited from the ServicedComponent base class:

```
<ConstructionEnabled(True, Default:="ServerName=.;LogFile:=c:\app.log")> _
Public Class MoneyMover
    Inherits ServicedComponent

    Protected Overrides Sub Construct(ByVal s As String)
        ' Process the construct string here.
        ⋮
    End Sub
End Class
```

The Default optional argument sets the initial construct string and is ignored if the COM+ application is already registered or if the user has typed a different string in the Activation tab of the component's Properties window, as shown in the right portion of Figure 31-5.

Typically, the construct string is a semicolon-delimited series of values that you can easily extract by means of a String.Split method or a regular expression pattern.

Enforcing Role-Based Security

In a typical enterprise-level application, security can't be an afterthought. Developers should have a clear idea of who can use the object and which actions should be considered legal. Robust applications should check the identity of the client trying to use an object (the authentication phase), and they should verify that the client is authorized to perform the specific action (the authorization phase).

Implementing authentication and authorization in a robust way used to require a lot of code, until Microsoft released MTS and then COM+. The Component Services snap-in lets administrators define one or more roles for the application and specify which roles can create a given component or invoke one of its methods. The .NET Framework made this process even easier, because you can add a few attributes to your source code to automatically set a few entries in the COM+ catalog when the application is registered.

Let me show you how to enforce COM+ security by using the Component Services MMC snap-in. Right-click on the Roles folder under the BankMoneyMover application, choose the New command, and add a role named Accountants. This command creates a new element, whose Properties window lets you assign a description for the role. Next expand the new Accountants element, right-click on the Users folder, and choose the Add command. This action displays the dialog box shown in Figure 31-6, where you can define which Windows users and groups belong to the COM+ role you've just defined.

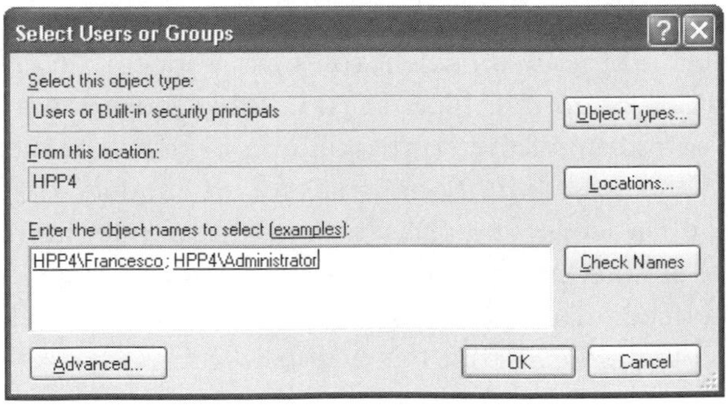

Figure 31-6   Adding Windows users and groups to a COM+ role

After you've defined one or more roles, you can switch to the Security tab of the COM+ application's Properties window (shown in the left portion of Figure 31-7), which contains the master security switch for the application. If you select the Enforce Access Checks For This Application check box, only clients whose identity matches one of the roles you've defined for the application can launch the application and instantiate one of its components.

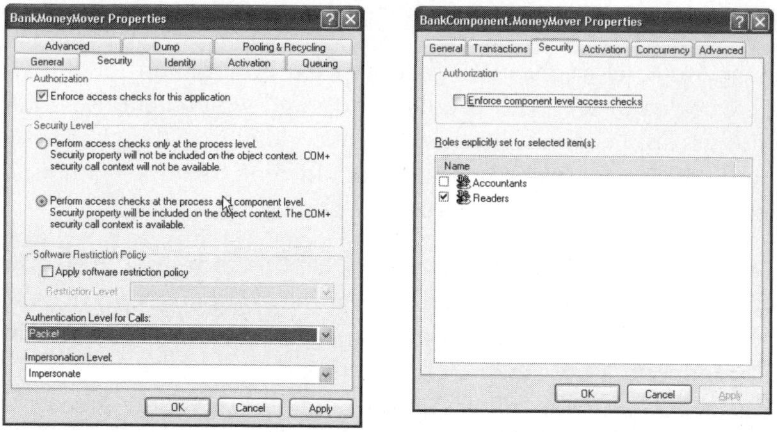

Figure 31-7   The Security tab in the application's Properties window (left) and in the component's Properties window (right)

COM+ can perform access checks at two levels: at the process level or at the process and component level. (In the latter case, COM+ enforces security at each method call.) These options correspond to the two radio buttons in the Security Level frame. If you decide to perform access checks at both the process and the component level, you can still enable or disable access checks for a specific component on the Security tab of the Properties window for that component, as shown in the right portion of Figure 31-7. On this tab, you can also decide which roles can access the component.

COM+ security is very granular, and you can select roles for a specific interface level and even for individual methods of an interface. (You enforce these settings on the Security tab of the Properties window of the corresponding interface or method element.) Notice, however, that you can set *additional* roles for an interface or a method, but you can prevent a role that has access to a class from calling an interface. Similarly, if you have specified a role for an interface, you can't prevent that role from calling any method belonging to that interface. (The MMC snap-in permits you to deselect a role that has been inherited from a higher level, but this action is ignored.)

All the public methods of a class belong to an interface whose name is the class name prefixed by an underscore (_MoneyMover in our sample serviced component). When you expand the node that corresponds to this interface in the MMC snap-in, you'll be surprised to find no methods in there. Here's the reason: as you learned in Chapter 30, by default a .NET class exposes only the IDispatch interface to the unmanaged world, and serviced components are no exceptions. To actually see the public methods of your class (including those inherited by the ServicedComponent base class), you must apply this attribute at the class level:

```
<ClassInterface(ClassInterfaceType.AutoDual)> _
Public Class MoneyMover
    ⋮
```

Using the ClassInterface attribute causes all the class methods to appear in the MMC snap-in, which in turn lets you enforce role-based security at the method level. There is one more reason for specifying the ClassInterface attribute: without this attribute, late-bound calls from unmanaged clients would ignore the AutoComplete attribute, and you'd be forced to explicitly commit or abort the transaction via code.

Let's see now how you can apply attributes to the Visual Basic .NET project so that all these security settings are applied automatically when the application is registered for the first time. (As usual, remember to delete the application to force a brand-new registration, if you want to see these attributes in action.). To enforce access checks and set the security level, you must apply the ApplicationAccessControl attribute at the assembly level:

```
<Assembly: ApplicationAccessControl(True, _
    AccessChecksLevel:=AccessChecksLevelOption.ApplicationComponent)>
<Assembly: SecurityRole("Accountants", False)>
```

Notice that in .NET Framework version 1.1, the COM+ security is enabled by default if the ApplicationAccessControl attribute is omitted; in version 1.0, COM+ security was disabled by default.

Even if you have enabled access checks at the component level, you must flag individual classes with a ComponentAccessControl attribute to enable access checks for that specific component. (This attribute is ignored if access checks are enabled only at the application level.) This attribute corresponds to the Enforce Component Level Access Checks check box on the Security tab of the component's Properties window.

```
<ComponentAccessControl()> _
Public Class MoneyMover
    ⋮
```

When applied at the assembly level, the SecurityRole attribute defines a role for the entire application; the second argument passed to this attribute specifies whether the Everyone user is a member of the defined role. For simplicity, you might want to pass True in this argument during the test phase; otherwise, the role will initially contain no users, and requests from any users are doomed to fail.

You can also apply the SecurityRole attribute at the class level, in which case you both define a role for the COM+ application and specify that only users in that role can instantiate the class and invoke its methods:

```
<SecurityRole("Readers", True, Description:="Users who can read")> _
Public Class MoneyMover
    ⋮
```

There is no way to create a role and add users and groups to it (other than the Everyone user) by means of attributes.

You can now launch the client application (which runs in the identity of the interactive user); you'll see that it receives an *Access denied* error if the client identity isn't among those that are allowed to run the BankMoneyMover application, instantiate the Money-Mover component, or call methods in its _MoneyMover interface.

You can also apply the SecurityRole attribute at the interface level, to decide who can call methods in a given interface, and even at the method level. Applying the Security-Role attribute to a method level, however, works correctly only if the method belongs to a secondary interface implemented by the class. This constraint makes declarative security at the method level a bit more contorted:

```
Public Interface TransferMoney
    Sub TransferMoney(ByVal senderID As Integer, ByVal receiverID As Integer, _
        ByVal amount As Decimal)
End Interface

<Transaction(TransactionOption.Required, SecurityRole("Readers", True)> _
Public Class MoneyMover
    Inherits ServicedComponent
    Implements TransferMoney

    <SecurityRole("AllReaders", True)> _
    Sub TransferMoney (ByVal senderID As Integer, ByVal receiverID As Integer, _
        ByVal amount As Decimal) Implements TransferMoney.TransferMoney
        ⋮
    End Sub
End Class
```

When applied at the method level, the SecureRole attribute supersedes any existing setting in the COM+ catalog.

Not all security checks can be done in a declarative manner by means of attributes. For example, let's assume you want to bar Accountants from valid roles during weekends, or you want to have a transaction fail if the amount is higher than a given threshold and the user isn't in the Managers role. Programmatically checking the role of the current user is as easy as calling the IsCallerInRole shared method of the ContextUtil class:

```
If amount > 10000 And Not ContextUtil.IsCallerInRole("Managers") Then
    Throw New Exception("Only managers can do this!")
End If
```

IsCallerInRole always returns True if role-based security is disabled; therefore, you might want to ensure that role-based security is active for the current context, by means of the IsSecurityEnabled method:

```
If Not ContextUtil.IsSecurityEnabled Then
    Throw New Exception("This method requires role-based security")
ElseIf amount > 10000 And Not ContextUtil.IsCallerInRole("Managers") Then
    Throw New Exception("Only managers can do this!")
End If
```

Using Synchronization

The COM+ infrastructure helps developers to build multithreaded applications by introducing the concept of logical threads, also known as *activity*. The concept of activity is important because COM+ objects and .NET serviced components can run inside multiple threads and even inside different physical processes. In these scenarios, synchronizing cross-component calls would be extremely difficult if it weren't for the synchronization features of COM+.

To understand what kind of problems you might face, envision the following situation. Object A (a multithreaded component) calls Object B in a separate process and expects to be called back via an interface method; it is crucial that only B be able to call back A, and A should reject calls from other objects. There are several ways to manually solve this problem, but all of them are quite complex. (For example, Object A might pass Object B a special token value that Object B can use in the callback to let Object A know where the callback comes from.)

Fortunately, you never need to write such complex code with COM+ and serviced components, thanks to automatic synchronization with *activities*. You can enforce automatic synchronization by means of the Synchronization attribute, which you apply at the class level:

```
<Synchronization()> _
Public Class MoneyMover
   ⋮
```

The Synchronization attribute can take one of the following SynchronizationOption enumerated values: Disabled (COM+ ignores the synchronization requirements of the component, which might or might not live in its creator's activity), NotSupported (the object never participates in synchronization), Supported (the object participates in its creator's activity, if it exists), Required (all calls to the object are synchronized, using the creator's activity if possible or creating a new one), and RequiresNew (the object always creates a new activity). Here's how you define an object that always creates a new activity:

```
<Synchronization(SynchronizationOption.RequiresNew)> _
Public Class MoneyMover
   ⋮
```

You typically select Disabled or NotSupported when using components that provide their own synchronization mechanism, but these settings are rarely useful with .NET serviced components. The Supported setting is useful only if you are absolutely certain that the component can correctly handle calls from multiple clients on multiple threads—for example, if the object adopts one of the techniques I illustrated in Chapter 12, and you don't need the synchronization services that COM+ provides.

If you decide to use COM+ synchronization, you must decide which of the remaining settings is better for you. In most cases, Required is the most suitable setting, and in fact, it is the default value used when the Synchronization attribute has no arguments. You should use RequiresNew in special cases, such as when this object is created by a factory component and then passed to a client that lives in another activity. In such a situation, a component marked as Required would reject all calls coming from clients because they don't share its creator activity.

If you use JIT activation and transactional components, you have only a limited choice. Such components can serve only one client at a time, and therefore their synchronization attribute can be set only to Required or RequiresNew. (If the Synchronization attribute is omitted, the Required setting is enforced by default.)

> **Note**   You might want to compare the Synchronization attribute described in this section with the attribute with same name in the System.Runtime.Remoting.Contexts namespace, which I introduced in Chapter 12. These attributes serve the same broad purpose and even take a similar set of arguments, the main difference being that the former implements synchronization at the COM+ activity level, whereas the latter accomplishes the same tasks on physical threads by means of synchronization objects provided by the operating system.

Registering and Deploying the COM+ Application

In all the examples seen so far, we've been using a library application running on the same computer as its client. You know, however, that one of the main goals of the COM+ technology is to create distributed applications that can run on remote systems. In this section, you'll learn how to purse these objectives.

Creating a Server Application

The first step in creating a COM+ application that can run on a remote computer is to make the application a server application. You can accomplish this from the Activation tab of the application's Properties window or by inserting an appropriate attribute at the assembly level:

```
<Assembly: ApplicationActivation(ActivationOption.Server)>
```

COM+ server applications running as .NET serviced components have one additional requirement: they must be registered in the GAC. Thus, you must rebuild the application and use the GacUtil tool to install the BankComponent.Dll assembly in the GAC:

```
GACUTIL -i BankComponent.Dll
```

(See Chapter 13 for additional information about registering an assembly in the GAC.) Delete the BankMoneyMover application from the COM+ catalog for the new attributes to be applied in a fresh registration, and then run the client as usual. If everything works correctly, this first step has been completed successfully.

In many real-world cases, however, you'll need to do more than just change the ApplicationActivation attribute in the source code to transform a client application into a server application. For example, all the objects passed to (or returned from) a serviced component running in a server application must either be marked as serializable or derive from the MarshalByRefObject class. (You'll read more about these constraints in Chapter 32.)

As I'll explain later in this chapter, COM+ server applications have other advantages in addition to being able to run remotely. For example, if you're running under COM+ 1.5, you can create an application pool and automatically restart an application under certain conditions, but only if the application is a server application.

Using the Regsvcs Utility

All the examples seen so far have relied on *dynamic registration*, a procedure that the .NET runtime runs to ensure that a COM+ application is automatically created and registered in the COM+ catalog the first time the component is instantiated, if it isn't there yet. Dynamic registration is useful during the development phase and allows developers and administrators to leverage XCOPY deployment. However, dynamic registration is rarely practical or feasible in most real-world situations, for a number of reasons.

First, the client can register a COM+ application in a dynamic fashion only if the client runs under an account that belongs to the Administrators group. This requirement is too limiting in most cases. (For example, few ASP.NET applications have administrative privileges.) Second, the dynamic registration of a large COM+ application can take several seconds; thus, the very first call from a client would take too long and might even cause a timeout error. Third, components belonging to COM+ server applications must be registered in the GAC, and therefore you need an installation procedure that is more complex than plain XCOPY deployment.

The .NET Services Installation Tool (Regsvcs) provides a way to manually register an application in the COM+ catalog. This tool registers the assembly for COM Interop, generates its type library, and configures a new COM+ application (or reconfigures an existing application) that contains the components in your assembly. In the simplest case, you pass Regsvcs only the name of the assembly containing the serviced components:

```
REGSVCS BankComponent.Dll
```

Regsvcs extracts the name and the ID of the COM+ application from the attributes in the assembly and creates a type library named after the assembly (BankComponent.tlb in this example). You can also specify the application name with the /appname option and choose another name for the type library with the /tlb option:

```
REGSVCS BankComponent.Dll /appname:BankApp /tlb:BankApp.tlb
```

You must be a member of the Administrators group to run the Regsvcs tool. Please read the MSDN documentation for a description of the other options you can use with this tool.

> **Note**   All the services offered by the Regsvcs tool are available to your code via the RegistrationHelper class, which is especially valuable when used from inside a Visual Studio .NET deployment project. For more information, read the MSDN documentation.

Setting the Application Identity

Unlike a library application, which runs in the same process as the client that started it, a server application runs in a separate process and is hosted by the DllHost.exe executable. This process runs under a Windows account that might be different from the client's account. By default, a new server application runs under the identity of the interactive user, which greatly simplifies testing and debugging (for example, a component running in the interactive user's account can display a message box). However, in most cases, you'll need to change this default setting on the Identity tab of the application's Properties window (as shown in Figure 31-8). You have the following options:

- **Interactive User**   This setting greatly simplifies testing and debugging and is the default setting for new applications. In general, however, this setting shouldn't be used for deployment, because any attempt to instantiate the component would fail if no user has logged onto the system. In addition, an application configured to run as an NT service can't use this account.

- **Local Service**   This built-in account has limited rights on the local system and virtually no network permissions. It doesn't have authenticated access, it doesn't belong to the Authenticated Users group, and it runs under the anonymous account (even though it doesn't have the same identity as the anonymous IIS account—namely, IUSR_machinename).

- **Network Service**   This built-in account is similar to Local Service, but it can also access network resources using the credentials of the machine account (as can the Local System account, which is described next). In general, a component running under this identity can access any resource that is accessible to the Everyone and Authenticated Users accounts.

- **Local System**   This built-in account has full control on local resources, being a hidden member of the Administrators group, and can do virtually anything on the local computer, including interacting with the desktop. It also has limited access to network resources (which it does under the computer's domain identity). Only applications that run as NT services can use this account, although very few services need all this access power.

■ **This User**   The component runs under the account you specify and therefore has the same access rights as that account (except that it can't access the desktop). In many cases, you should create an account that has exactly the privileges that the component needs and run the component under that account. This setting can be used also for components running as NT services.

The complete list of settings is available only if you're running COM+ 1.5 under Windows Server 2003. If you're working with Windows XP, the Local Service and Network Service options are available only for COM+ applications running as NT services. If you're working with Windows 2000, only the Interactive User and This User options are available.

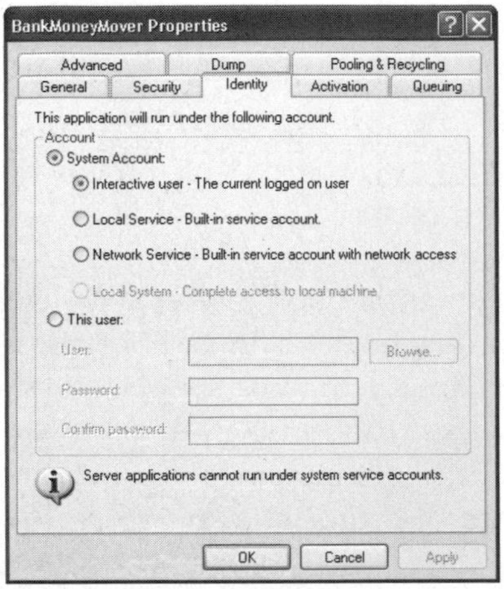

Figure 31-8   The Identity tab of a COM+ server application

Exporting the COM+ Application

When the server application is correctly configured, you can export it to a remote client machine by right-clicking on the application's node in the MMC snap-in and choosing the Export command. This command starts the COM+ Application Export Wizard, whose only interesting page is shown in Figure 31-9. On this page, you select the path of the .msi file that you want to create and specify whether you want to create a complete copy of the entire application (which is useful when moving the application from your development machine to the end user's server) or just an application proxy that allows remote systems to access this instance of the application. When creating a complete copy of the application, you can also export user identities and roles, but this option isn't available when creating a proxy, because the roles you've defined in the COM+ application will remain valid. Finally, you have the option to export the application to Windows 2000 clients in COM 1.0 format, which might result in a loss of information.

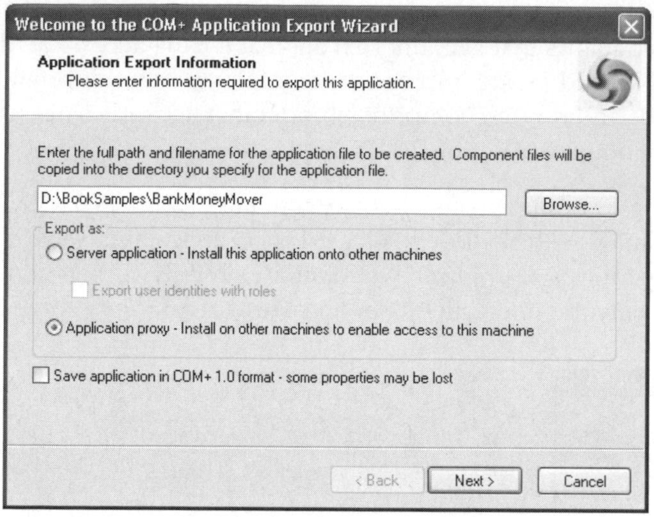

Figure 31-9   The COM+ Application Export Wizard

For our purposes, specify that you're creating an application proxy, and save the .msi file in a location that is accessible to the client machine you'll use for your tests. You can then either physically move to the client computer or, more simply, administer that computer remotely from the Component Services MMC snap-in that you use for the local machine by adding a new element under the Computers folder. (You must have administrative privileges on the client computer, of course.)

Regardless of whether you are physically working at the remote client or just administering it from the MMC snap-in running on the server, you should expand the computer node: right-click on the COM+ Applications folder, and choose the New Application command. This command runs the COM+ Application Install Wizard. On the second page of this wizard, you click the Install Pre-built Application(s) option, which brings you to a new page, where you select the .msi file. (See the left portion of Figure 31-10, which shows how you can import the application on a Windows 2000 system.) Click Next to proceed to the next page, where you can specify a target directory (see right portion of Figure 31-10), and finally click Finish to complete the wizard. The directory you've selected now contains both the application proxy and a .tlb file for Visual Basic 6 and other pre-.NET clients.

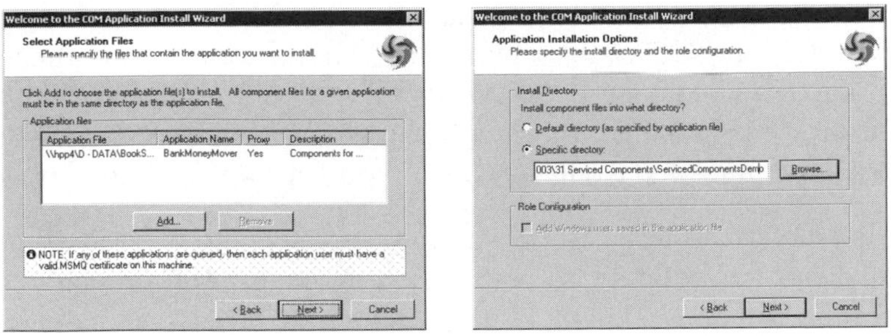

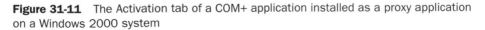

Figure 31-10 Two pages of the COM+ Application Install Wizard, when it runs on a Windows 2000 system

If the COM+ application has been installed correctly on the client, you can find it under the COM+ Applications folder in the MMC snap-in. (You might need to click the Refresh icon to see the new element.) The Activation tab of the application's Properties window should contain the name of the server when the application is actually running, as shown in Figure 31-11. You can change this value to have the client point to another server if necessary, but this is the only setting you can change from the MMC snap-in for an application proxy, because all other values depend on how the application is configured on the server.

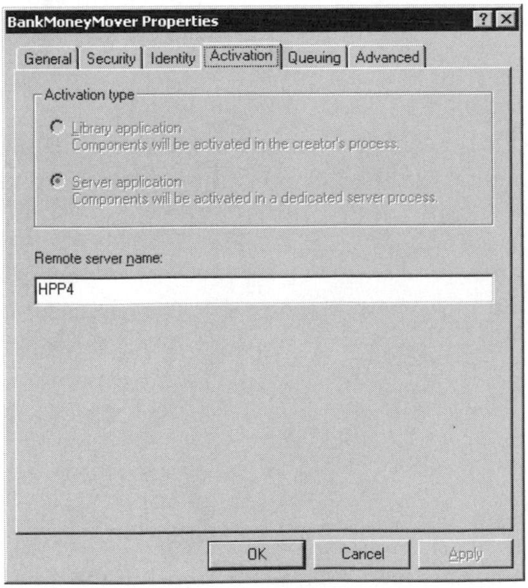

Figure 31-11 The Activation tab of a COM+ application installed as a proxy application on a Windows 2000 system

The simplest way to test the BankMoneyMover application remotely is to copy the ClientDemo.exe executable to the client machine and run it from there. If everything has been installed properly, you'll see the icons representing the MoneyMover component spinning in the server's MMC snap-in when the client invokes the component's methods.

Note that the .NET Framework must be installed on client computers to access serviced components remotely, regardless of whether the client application is managed or unmanaged. In additional, Service Pack 3 is also required for Windows 2000 clients. The installation process installs all the involved assemblies in the client's GAC, but these assemblies aren't removed from the GAC if you later uninstall the application.

The managed assemblies are installed on the client because the client must access the assembly's metadata—for example, to read the value of the AutoComplete attribute. This implies that the component might behave incorrectly if you change the assembly on the server without re-exporting it to all clients.

Serviced Components Up Close

Now that you are familiar with the basics of COM+ programming under .NET, you're ready to dive into more advanced topics, such as interacting with the call context via code and leveraging COM+ 1.5 features.

Classes and Interfaces

Most of the techniques I've described so far are based on attributes, but a good programmer should be able to code against the objects and the interfaces that COM+ provides. In this section, I'll illustrate some of these techniques.

The ServicedComponent Class

The author of a .NET serviced component can interact with some of the features COM+ exposes by overriding protected methods in the ServicedComponent base class. The two most important of these methods are Activate and Deactivate, which fire when a JIT-activated object is brought to life and terminated:

```
Protected Overrides Sub Activate()
    ' Initialize the object here.
    ⋮
End Sub

Protected Overrides Sub Deactivate()
    ' Clean up the object here.
    ⋮
End Sub
```

The Activate method fires immediately after the Construct method (if the ConstructionEnabled attribute is present), whereas the Deactivate method fires immediately before the Dispose protected method:

```
Protected Overloads Overrides Sub Dispose(ByVal disposing As Boolean)
    ⋮
End Sub
```

Unlike normal .NET objects—which are released when the garbage collector collects them—JIT-activated objects are disposed of automatically by the .NET runtime when the object is deactivated. You can therefore use the Dispose protected method as a sort of deterministic finalizer for serviced components. (You can create an explicit Finalize method, but you would incur an unnecessary performance penalty in doing so.)

Clients should explicitly dispose of objects that aren't JIT-activated. The suggested way to do so is invoking the DisposeObject shared method of the ServicedComponent class:

```
' In the client application
ServicedComponent.DisposeObject(obj)
```

The ContextUtil Class

You've already seen how to use the ContextUtil object to programmatically commit or abort a transaction, or to determine whether the caller is in a given role. This object exposes several other properties and methods of interest. All its members are shared.

Most of the shared properties of this class are read-only and return a System.Guid value: ApplicationId (the current application), TransactionId (the current transaction), ActivityId (the current activity), ContextId (the current context), PartitionId (the current partition), and ApplicationInstanceId (the current application's instance). All the properties in this group are useful mostly for reporting purposes—for example, to easily identify a specific transaction in the list of running transactions in the MMC snap-in. The PartitionId and ApplicationInstanceId properties are supported only under Windows XP and Windows Server 2003.

The IsInTransaction read-only property returns True if the object is running in a transaction. This property is useful for objects that support transactions but don't require them. Such objects should vote for the transaction outcome only if necessary:

```
If ContextUtil.IsInTransaction Then
    ContextUtil.SetComplete()
End If
```

The ContextUtil class lets you read and set the done bit and the consistent bit that all COM+ objects manage. (See the section "Defining a Transactional Class," earlier in this chapter.) You already know that the SetComplete method sets both these bits to True (the transaction can be committed and the object can be deactivated), whereas the SetAbort method sets the done bit to True and the consistent bit to False (the transaction is doomed). You can also vote for a transaction outcome without deactivating the object, by means of the EnableCommit method (which sets the consistent bit to True and the done bit to False) and the DisableCommit method (which sets both bits to False); these methods can be useful if the client can perform multiple calls into the object to complete the task at hand.

You can read and set the two bits individually by means of the MyTransactionVote property (the consistent bit) and the DeactivateOnReturn property (the done bit):

```
Sub MyMethod()
    ' The object will be deactivated at the end of this method
    ' (unless the DeactivateOnReturn is set to False later in this code).
    ContextUtil.DeactivateOnReturn = True
    ⋮
End Sub
```

Notice, however, that you can't prevent a JIT object from being deactivated on return from a method that has been flagged with the AutoComplete attribute.

The SecurityCallContext Class

The ContextUtil class exposes only a couple of methods that are related to COM+ security; for more serious work, you must use the methods of the SecurityCallContext class. First you need to get a reference to an object of this class by means of the CurrentCall shared property:

```
Dim scc As SecurityCallContext = SecurityCallContext.CurrentCall
```

You are already familiar with two members of this class, the IsCallerInRole method and the IsSecurityEnabled property, which return the same values as the ContextUtil class's members with same name:

```
If scc.IsSecurityEnabled And scc.IsCallerInRole("Managers") Then
    ⋮
End If
```

You can check whether a specific user is in a role with the IsUserInRole method:

```
If scc.IsUserInRole("HPP4\Francesco", "Managers") Then ...
```

Three properties return information about callers of the current method: OriginalCaller, DirectCaller, and the Callers collection. The caller identity is returned as a SecurityIdentity object, which has properties such as AccountName, AuthenticationLevel, and ImpersonationLevel:

```
' Display information about all callers of this method.
For Each si As SecurityIdentity In scc.Callers
    Debug.WriteLine(String.Format("AccountName={0}, " _
        & "AuthenticationLevel={1}, ImpersonationLevel={2}", _
        si.AccountName, si.AuthenticationLevel, si.ImpersonationLevel))
Next
```

The BYOT (Bring Your Own Transaction) Class

The preferred way to perform transactional works in COM+ is by leveraging the automatic transactions enforced by the Transaction attribute. In some circumstances, however, your application might receive a reference to an object that is already running inside an MS DTC transaction, and you might need to enroll one of your components in the same transaction.

You can enroll a component in a preexisting transaction if you can obtain a reference to the ITransaction object that represents the transaction itself. If the object is a serviced component that you have authored, you can implement a public function that returns the value of the ContextUtil.Transaction property:

```
Public Class TxComponent
    ' Return the current transaction object.
    Public Function GetTransaction() As ITransaction
        Return ContextUtil.Transaction
    End Function

    ' Commit or abort the current transaction.
    Sub CompleteTransaction(ByVal vote As TransactionVote)
        ContextUtil.MyTransactionVote = vote
        ContextUtil.DeactivateOnReturn = True
    End Sub
    ⋮
    ' Plus all the usual transactional methods.
End Class
```

You can then instantiate an object and have it run in the same transaction by means of the CreateWithTransaction shared method of the BYOT class, as in this code:

```
Dim c1 As New TxComponent
Try
    ' This method keeps the transaction open.
    c1.UpdateAccount(1)
    ' Get a reference to the transaction.
    Dim tx As ITransaction = c1.GetTransaction()
    ' Create another object in the same transaction.
    Dim c2 As TxComponent = DirectCast(BYOT.CreateWithTransaction(tx, _
        GetType(TxComponent)), TxComponent)
    ' Run method from the new object in the same transaction.
    c2.UpdateAccount(2)
    ' If no exception, commit the transaction.
    c1.CompleteTransaction(TransactionVote.Commit)
Catch ex As Exception
    ' Else, rollback the transaction.
    c1.CompleteTransaction(TransactionVote.Abort)
    MsgBox(ex.Message, MsgBoxStyle.Critical, "Error")
End Try
```

In this example, the TxComponent exposes two methods for retrieving the current transaction and for committing (or aborting) it. The latter method isn't strictly required, however, because the client can control the transaction directly through the reference to the ITransaction object.

The BYOT class exposes another method, named CreateWithTipTransaction, which lets you enlist an object in a Transaction Internet Protocol (TIP) transaction.

The Connection.EnlistDistributedTransaction Method

Another way to leverage the ContextUtil.Transaction property is to pass its value to the EnlistDistributedTransaction method exposed by Connection objects in all the ADO.NET managed providers that come with version 1.1 of .NET Framework. This method forces the Connection object to take part in a specific MS DTC transaction:

```
Dim c1 As New TxComponent
Dim tx As ITransaction = c1.GetTransaction()
' The connection must be open before enrolling in MS DTC transaction.
Dim cn As New SqlConnection(SqlPubsConnString)
cn.Open()
cn.EnlistDistributedTransaction(tx)
⋮
```

The EnlistDistributedTransaction method throws an exception if the connection is already enrolled in a transaction started with the BeginTransaction ADO.NET method. However, no error occurs if you've opened a local transaction on the connection with the BEGIN TRANSACTION SQL statement—in this case, the local transaction is silently rolled back and the connection is enlisted in the distributed transaction.

The IProcessInitializer Interface

At times, you'd like to allocate resources when the first component in a COM+ application is created and release them when the application terminates. The simplest way to do so is by having one component in the application implement the IProcessInitializer interface. This interface has been introduced with version 1.1 of the .NET Framework and has only two methods: Startup and Shutdown.

```
Public Class TxComponent
    Inherits ServicedComponent
    Implements IProcessInitializer

    Sub Startup(ByVal punk As Object) Implements IProcessInitializer.Startup
        ' Allocate resources here, write to the event log, etc.
        ' Under Windows XP and later the argument points to the first object
        ' being instantiated; under Windows 2000 the argument is always Nothing.
        ⋮
    End Sub

    Public Sub Shutdown() Implements IProcessInitializer.Shutdown
        ' Release resources here, write to the event log, etc.
        ⋮
    End Sub
End Class
```

When the DllHost.exe executable runs, COM+ creates one instance of each component that implements the IProcessInitializer interface and invokes the Startup method. This instance is kept alive until the DllHost process is terminated, and when this happens, COM+ invokes its Shutdown method. Because the object lives for the entire application lifetime, you can store values in shared private fields, and possibly make them available to other objects in the applications by means of shared members. If the application contains multiple components that implement this interface, the order in which their Startup and Shutdown methods are called is unpredictable.

The IProcessInitializer interface works correctly only with server COM+ applications, because library applications don't launch a new instance of the DllHost executable. This interface is available under Windows 2000 Service Pack 3 and later, but it is fully working only under COM+ 1.5. Read MSDN articles Q319776 and Q303890 for more details about this feature.

COM+ 1.5 Features

Version 1.5 of COM+ has several new features that can greatly improve the scalability and robustness of your applications, especially if they're running under Windows Server 2003. In previous chapters, I have described some of these new features—for example, configurable isolation levels and new accounts under which a COM+ server application can run—but there is more to be covered. Only a fraction of these features can be configured in code by means of attributes; in all other cases, you'll have to activate them manually from inside the MMC snap-in or by authoring an administrative script.

> **Important**   For security reasons, COM+ network access is initially disabled under Windows Server 2003, so you can use COM+ components only locally. To verify that network access is enabled, open the Add/Remove Windows Components dialog box of Control Panel, select Application Server, click the Details button, and verify that the Enable Network COM+ Access option is selected.

Application Pooling

By default, all the requests for components in a given COM+ server application are hosted in a single instance of the DllHost process. COM+ 1.5, however, lets you create a pool of two or more host processes that serve the same application, up to the number you specify on the Pooling & Recycling tab of the application's Properties window. (See Figure 31-12.) When the maximum number of processes has been reached, subsequent client requests are dispatched to the existing processes, using a round-robin algorithm.

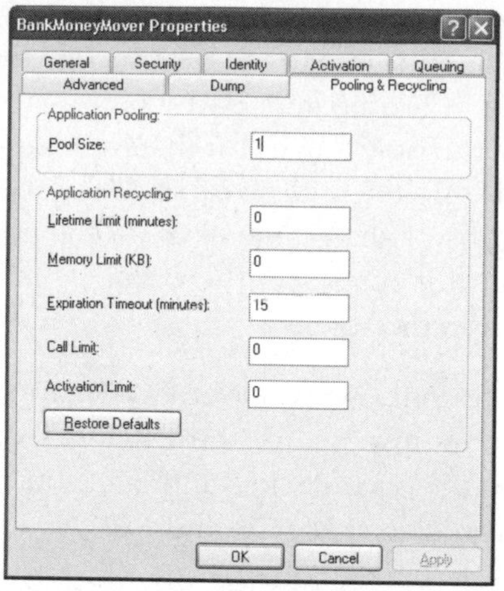

Figure 31-12   The Pooling & Recycling tab in a COM+ application's Properties window

Application pooling provides a way to improve isolation among components: if a component crashes, only the DllHost instance that hosts the component is shut down; clients served by the other instances aren't affected. Application pooling is also useful for legacy single-threaded COM components. All such components are created in the main Single-Thread Apartment (STA) of a given process, which tends to negatively affect performance. Creating multiple hosting processes can reduce this performance penalty.

Application pooling has a few limitations too. For example, a COM+ application that runs as an NT service can't use application pooling. Also, you can't use the Shared Property Manager (SPM) to share data among all the instances of a given component because the SPM can't span multiple processes. In general, you should never assume that two instances of a given component run in the same process. (Read the MSDN documentation for more information about the SPM.)

When you shut down a pooled application from the MMC snap-in, COM+ terminates all the DllHost instances that are serving that application. Similarly, when you manually start a pooled application from the snap-in, COM+ creates a number of processes equal to the pool size. (Conversely, when the application is started by a client request, only one process is initially created.)

Application Recycling

One recurring complaint from developers (and end users) is that COM+ applications have a tendency to degrade performance in the long run. In many cases, the blame belongs to the developers themselves—as this performance degradation is typically caused by bugs, memory leaks, or unreleased resources—but this surely doesn't help solve the problem.

COM+ 1.5 supports automatic application recycling, which you define in the same tab you use for application pooling. (See Figure 31-12.) You can decide to recycle the application after a given number of minutes (the Lifetime Limit field in the user interface), when a given amount of virtual memory is exceeded for longer than 1 minute (the Memory Limit field), after a specified number of method calls (the Call Limit field), or after a specified number of activations (the Activation Limit field).

When one of these limits is exceeded, COM+ waits for existing objects to complete their job and then shuts down the application. If not all objects have completed their tasks within the number of minutes specified in the Expiration Timeout field, COM+ shuts down the application on the assumption that these objects have entered an endless loop or that their clients haven't correctly released their references.

As soon as the Expiration Timeout period starts, COM+ creates a new DllHost process that serves incoming requests from clients while the original process is waiting for existing objects to complete their tasks. This mechanism ensures that clients won't notice any delay while the application is being recycled. If you have enabled recycling for a pooled application, COM+ spreads shutdowns evenly over time, in an attempt to avoid situations in which two or more applications are recycling at the same time.

An application marked for recycling ignores the Leave Running When Idle setting on the Advanced tab of the application's Properties window. Because recycling affects the lifetime of the DllHost process, you can use it only for COM+ server applications, and only for applications that aren't configured to run as NT services. (See the next section.) You can also manually recycle an application by right-clicking the application icon under the Running Processes folder in the MMC snap-in.

Applications Running as NT Services

In a welcome improvement from the first version of COM+, you can configure a COM+ 1.5 server application to run as an NT service. Even better, you don't have to change your source code to activate this feature; you just need to select the Run Application As NT Service check box on the Activation tab of the application's Properties window. (See the left portion of Figure 31-13.)

In most cases, you should click the Setup New Service button to create and configure the new service. Clicking this button displays the dialog box shown in the right portion of Figure 31-13. If you set the Startup Type to Automatic. the service will start when the computer completes the bootstrap sequence; however, setting the Startup Type to Manual doesn't mean that you have to activate it manually, because COM+ will automatically activate the service when the first activation requests comes from a client. (The only disadvantage in setting Startup Type to Manual is that the first client will have to wait until COM+ launches the service.)

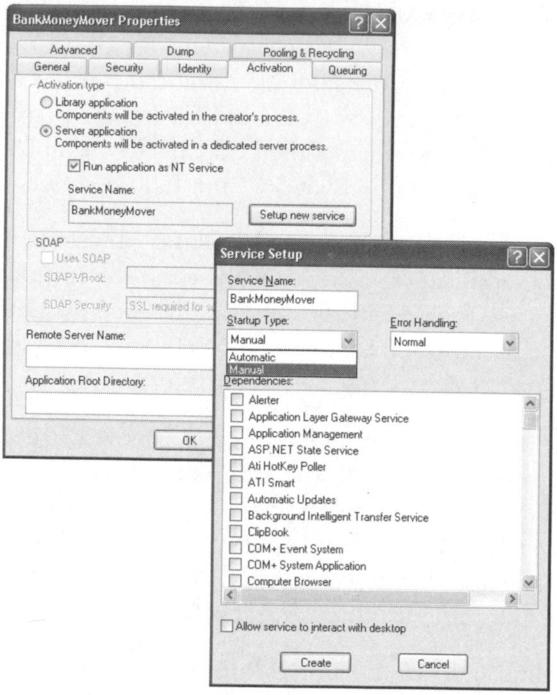

Figure 31-13   You can configure an application to run as an NT service on the Application tab (on the left) and create the new service by clicking the Setup New Service button (which brings up the window shown on the right).

Another advantage of applications configured as NT services is that they can run under the Local System account, which isn't available to other types of COM+ applications. On the other hand, applications configured as NT services can't use application pooling and recycling, as I've explained in previous sections.

Legacy Components

COM+ components can use the so-called *unconfigured* COM components (also known as *legacy components*), but you can't add them to applications under version 1.0 of COM+. This limitation made the deployment of applications that use legacy components overly complicated and has been lifted in COM+ 1.5.

You can add a legacy component to a COM+ 1.5 application by right-clicking on the Legacy Components folder in the MMC snap-in and choosing the Legacy Component command from the New submenu. This action starts the Legacy Component Import Wizard. On the second page of this wizard, you can select one or more COM components from the list of installed components (as shown in Figure 31-14); these components will appear in the Legacy Components folder when you complete the wizard.

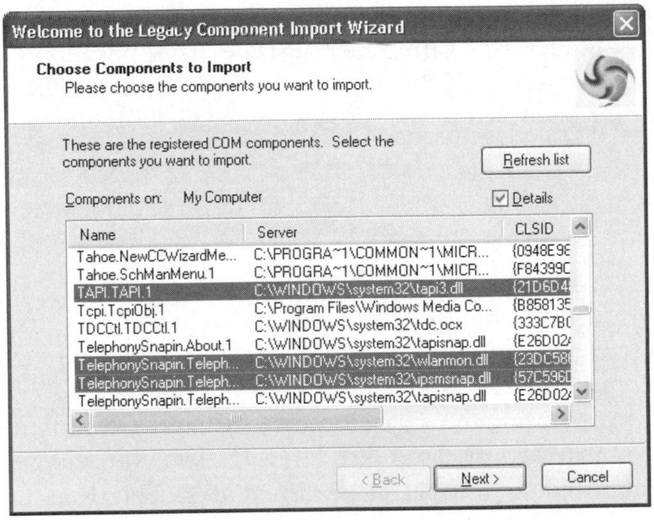

Figure 31-14 The second page of the Legacy Component Import Wizard

A component added to a COM+ application in this way remains a legacy component and can't make use of any COM+ feature. Its Properties window is different from that of configured components, and in practice it only lets you browse and change the registry keys related to the component, set its launch and access permissions, and specify the identity the component runs under.

You can use the commands on the legacy component's context menu to promote the component to a configured COM+ component or to disable it. In-process legacy components are always instantiated in the client process and never cause a new instance of DllHost to be launched, whereas out-process legacy components always run in their own process. You can also change the setting of any legacy component in the system, not just those that you associate with a COM+ application. All legacy components, in fact, are listed under the DCOM Config folder in the MMC snap-in. (Under Windows 2000 and earlier versions, you can change these settings by running the DCOMCNFG utility; under Windows XP and Windows Server 2003, typing **DCOMCNFG** at the system prompt displays the Component Services MMC.)

Private and Aliased Components

Under COM+ 1.0, a component added to an application can always be called from client applications. If this component is inherently private to the application—for example, it offers services to other components but is not meant to be used from outside the application—the only way to prevent clients from using it is to enable security for that component but assign no roles to it. (This mechanism works because security isn't enforced on calls from within the same application.)

Under COM+ 1.5, you can make such components private to the application they belong to simply by selecting the Mark Component Private To Application check box on the Activation tab of the component's Properties window. (See the right portion of Figure 31-5.) You can also make a component private by means of the PrivateComponent attribute:

```
<PrivateComponent()> _
Public Class MoneyMover
    ⋮
```

COM+ 1.5 overcomes another limitation of previous versions in that a component can belong to more than just one application on the same machine. The feature that allows you to do this is called *component aliasing*. You can create an alias for a component in a different application by choosing the Alias command from the component's context menu. The dialog box that appears (see Figure 31-15) lets you select the target application, the new ProgID, and the new CLSID for the component. (You rarely need to change the latter.)

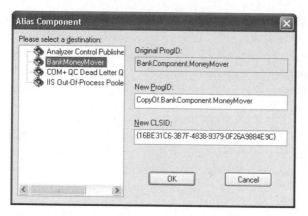

Figure 31-15   The Alias Component dialog box

An aliased component initially has the same set of properties as the component it originates from, but it can be configured as if it were a completely new component. For example, it can take a different configuration string, different transaction isolation levels, and so forth. You can even apply the Alias command to an aliased component to create another alias that initially has the same properties as the aliased component rather than the original component.

Application Pausing and Disabling

The Component Services MMC snap-in under COM+ 1.0 lets you start and shut down a server application by right-clicking on it and choosing the appropriate command from the context menu. In addition, you can control whether idle applications stay up and running or automatically shut down after a given time. (You can change these settings on the Advanced tab of the application's Properties window.) COM+ 1.5 extends these options with the ability to pause or disable a given application. These commands have slightly different effects and goals.

You can pause an application by right-clicking on its icon inside the Running Processes folder of the MMC snap-in, as shown in Figure 31-16. You can then attach a debugger to the paused application and be sure that client requests don't modify the application's state while you're examining it. If the application is pooled, you can individually pause any of its DllHost processes, and processes that aren't paused will continue to serve incoming requests (which is extremely important when debugging a COM+ application in a production environment). A paused application won't be recycled by COM+, but the application won't be in a paused state after a computer reboot. You can resume a paused application by right-clicking on it from inside the MMC snap-in.

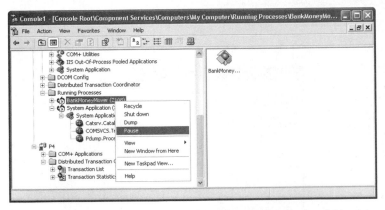

Figure 31-16 The context menu in the Running Processes folder lets you pause, recycle, or shut down an application.

You can disable an entire COM+ application or its individual components by right-clicking on them in the COM+ Applications folder of the MMC snap-in. Disabling an application is especially useful when you want to update its components on a production server, because in this case shutting down the application wouldn't prevent clients from restarting it immediately afterwards. Unlike pausing, the disabled state survives a system reboot. In addition, you can disable both server and library applications. (In comparison, you can pause only server applications.)

If a pooled application is disabled, all its processes are disabled. On the other hand, if only an individual component is disabled, the running process (or processes, in the case of pooled applications) that contains instances of that component will continue to serve clients holding a reference to those instances, but no new instances of that component can be created.

Application Partitions

In COM+ 1.0, a configured component can belong to exactly one application on a given computer. This limitation has been lifted in COM+ 1.5 if you enable application partitions from the Options tab of the My Computer Properties window in the Component Services MMC snap-in. When partitions are enabled, the tree structure of the MMC snap-in changes slightly, as applications must now belong to one (and only one) partition. (See the left portion of Figure 31-17.) Initially, only the Base Application Partition exists (this partition contains all preexisting COM+ applications), but you can easily create new partitions and new applications inside each partition. When using multiple partitions, you should create one or more users under the COM+ Partition Users folder and define the default partition for each user. (See right portion of Figure 31-17.)

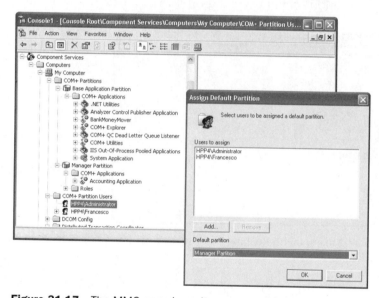

Figure 31-17   The MMC snap-in as it appears after enabling COM+ partitions (on the left), and the dialog box that lets you define the default partition for each user (on the right)

Correctly defining users and their default partition is crucial. When a user requests a component, COM+ first looks in the applications belonging to the default partition for that user. If the component can't be found there, COM+ searches for it in the applications belonging to the Base Application Partition. The request fails if the component can't be found in either partition. Interestingly, a component can reside in multiple partitions, but each partition can contain only one copy of the component (although you can alias the component if necessary).

You shouldn't use an ApplicationID attribute at the assembly level when using COM+ partitions. A component can determine at run time the partition it lives in by means of the PartitionId property of the ContextUtil object.

Services Without Components

Version 1.1 of the .NET Framework introduces a new feature that lets regular clients take advantage of the many features of COM+ 1.5 running under Windows Server 2003—for example, automatic transactions, pooling, and synchronization—without creating a serviced component that has been previously registered in the COM+ catalog.

You leverage the Services Without Components feature by invoking the Enter shared method of the ServiceDomain class. This method takes a ServiceConfig object, which serves to configure all the characteristics of the COM+ context to be created on the fly:

```
' (In the client application...)
Dim sc As New ServiceConfig
' Set transaction properties.
sc.Transaction = TransactionOption.Required
sc.IsolationLevel = TransactionIsolationLevel.Serializable
sc.TransactionTimeout = 60                        ' One minute
sc.Synchronization = SynchronizationOption.Required  ' Not really necessary
' Prepare values for tracking purposes only.
sc.TrackingAppName = "ServicesWithoutComponentsDemo"
sc.TrackingComponentName = "UpdateAccounts"
sc.TrackingEnabled = True
sc.TransactionDescription = "UpdateAccounts Transaction"

' Create the COM+ context.
ServiceDomain.Enter(sc)
' Do your transactional work here.
UpdateAccount(1)
UpdateAccount(2)
' Complete the transaction and display its outcome.
Dim status As TransactionStatus = ServiceDomain.Leave()
MsgBox("Transaction Status = " & status.ToString)
```

Notice that it's up to the client to correctly pair the calls to the Enter and Leave methods of the ServiceDomain class.

Components as Web Services

COM+ 1.5 provides a great way to simplify the migration of existing COM and COM+ applications toward the .NET platform, by allowing components to be exposed as Web services. As with most COM+ services, you can leverage this feature either from inside the MMC snap-in or via code.

To manually expose a COM+ server application as a Web service, you just select the Uses SOAP check box on the Activation tab of the application's Properties window and type a name of a virtual directory in the SOAP VRoot field. This action creates a physical directory named C:\Windows\System32\Com\SoapVRoots*vrootname* (where *vrootname* is the name you have typed) and exposes it as a virtual directory named *vrootname* under the root directory for the IIS default Web site. Additionally, COM+

creates a few files that are necessary for the Web service to work correctly: a Web.config file, a default.disco file, and a default.aspx file that returns the WSDL for the Web service. If the component had been created with a .NET language, the assembly is registered in the GAC; otherwise, a .NET interoperability assembly is created in the new directory.

To expose a serviced component as a Web service via code, you must add a SoapVRoot argument to the ApplicationActivation attribute. The value of this argument is the name of the virtual directory.

```
<assembly: ApplicationActivation(ActivationOption.Server, SoapVRoot:="BankApp">
```

You can then test all the methods in the component by creating a client that adds a reference to the Web service, as you would do with regular Web services. You can simplify the test phase by clearing the Enforce Access Checks For This Application check box on the Security tab of the application's Properties window.

Remote clients don't necessarily have to reach the component via SOAP, as they can continue to use the component as if it were a regular COM+ component. However, the protocol used by remote clients depends on whether the Uses SOAP check box was selected when the application was exported to create the proxy. If SOAP was enabled, calls from the remote client use the SOAP protocol and flow over HTTP on port 80; if SOAP was disabled, remote calls use RPC and DCOM protocols.

> **Note**   The Uses SOAP check box is disabled by default under Windows Server 2003. To enable it, you must display the Security tab of the application's Properties window, deselect the Enforce access checks for this application option and select None in the Authentication level for calls, and then click OK to close the window. Next, reopen the Properties window and display the Activation tab, where you'll see that the Uses Soap check box is now enabled.
>
> Also note that regardless of the operating system you're using, you'll have problems passing and returning complex .NET types such as DataSets. For this reason, you might consider the ability to expose COM+ components as a Web service mainly a quick and simple way to reuse your legacy COM+ components for .NET clients.

Asynchronous Method Invocation

In this section, I will focus on two programming techniques that you can use to invoke a method or pass data to another application in an asynchronous way.

Queued Components

Not all method calls require an immediate response. For example, let's say your application accepts an order from a remote client and must notify the the shipping department and the accounting department of the new order. The notification to the shipping department requires a confirmation, to let the client know when the product is expected to ship. The purpose of the notification to the accounting department is to have an invoice prepared. You don't really need a return value from such a notification—what really matters is that you can be absolutely certain that the notification reaches the intended recipient. This is the ideal situation for using COM+ queued components (QC).

Introducing the QC Architecture

The COM+ Queued Components service relies on Microsoft Message Queuing for executing methods on COM+ components asynchronously in a reliable manner. A client application can instantiate a queued component and invoke one or more of its methods. These method calls aren't immediately dispatched to the real component; instead, they are intercepted by an intermediate object on the client computer known as the recorder, as shown in Figure 31-18. When the client application releases the reference to the queued component (more precisely, to the proxy that points to the queued component), the recorder object serializes all the method calls and stores them in a Microsoft Message Queue (MSMQ) queue on the client. Microsoft Message Queuing then moves this data to a queue on the server machine—immediately or after some time, depending on whether the server machine is reachable. A listener object on the server reads data from the server and passes it to a player object, which makes the calls into the actual object.

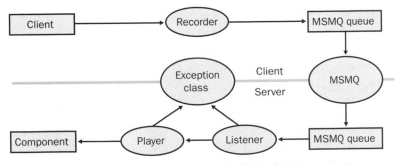

Figure 31-18   The queued components architecture

This short description of the roles of the recorder and listener objects reveals a few important points about the queued components architecture. First, the server application doesn't need to be running (or even be physically reachable) when the client calls the method. (It must be running to process the data coming from MSMQ, however, so you might want to install it as an NT service.) Second, because of their asynchronous nature, QCs can only expose Sub methods that don't take any ByRef arguments. Finally, any object passed to a QC must be serializable in the COM sense of the word, which means that the object must implement the IPersistStream interface. Serializable .NET objects don't implement this interface, so the simplest way to send a .NET object in one of the method's arguments is to serialize the object to an array of bytes with the BinaryFormatter (or to a string with the SoapFormatter) and send the array of bytes (or the string) instead.

By default, all the queues used for QCs are transactional, which means that the action of retrieving the message from the queue and the action of invoking the method on the component can be considered as an atomic operation; this atomicity ensures that if the method can't be called for some reason, the message won't be lost. If the component is transactional and the method invokes the SetAbort method, the message is moved to the next retry queue. For this mechanism to work correctly, the QC shouldn't be marked with the TransactionOption.RequiresNew attribute, because this setting would create a separate transaction. It is interesting to note what happens if the code in the component throws an exception during the playback phase. In this case, no exception can be returned to the client because the client might not be running; instead, the playback process is interrupted, and the MSMQ message that represents the method call is moved to the first retry queue. After 1 minute, COM+ retries the playback process: if the component throws an exception, COM+ moves the message to the second retry queue, and then it waits for 2 minutes and retries the playback process. There are five retry queues: the message stays 4 minutes in the third retry queue, 8 minutes in the fourth retry queue, and 16 minutes in the fifth retry queue. If even the fifth attempt fails because of an exception, the message is moved to the *dead letter queue*, from which an administrator can delete it or move it to the main queue.

If a client can't deliver a message to the queue or if the server can't correctly play back a method even after all the retries, COM+ creates an instance of the *exception class* associated with the application and calls its methods instead of those of the intended target of the call. An exception class might notify an administrator by e-mail or some other means that something went wrong. You can specify the ProgID of the exception class to be used for each QC on the Advanced tab of the class's Properties window. You can find additional information about exception classes in the MSDN documentation.

Queued components honor role-based security, so you can protect their methods by means of attributes or calls to IsCallerInRole methods, as you do with regular components. For role-based security to work correctly, however, callers must be authenticated; this implies that the playback process will fail if the client disables authentication. In addition, MSMQ can't authenticate queued calls if it has been installed in workgroup configuration.

Enabling the Queued Component

Two settings on the Queuing tab of the application's Properties window are crucial for enabling QCs, as shown in Figure 31-19: the Queued setting must be activated for the application to be reachable via MSMQ queues, and the Listen setting must be activated for the listener object to be instantiated on the server. You can enable the former but leave the latter disabled to avoid server components being activated only during certain time periods (for example, on weekends or at night). If you're working with COM+ 1.5, you can also set the maximum number of concurrent players—that is, the maximum number of threads that will process incoming messages.

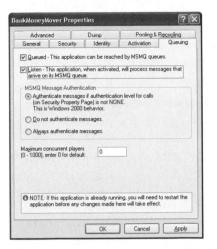

Figure 31-19   The Queuing tab of the application's Properties window

When you click OK to apply your changes, COM+ creates all the MSMQ queues that are needed to process incoming messages, as shown in Figure 31-20.

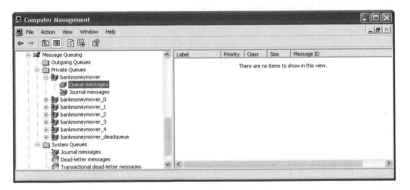

Figure 31-20   The queues created for a COM+ application that can contain queued components

When creating a .NET serviced component, you can enable queuing and set all relevant values by means of an ApplicationQueuing attribute at the assembly level:

```
' This syntax lets you control all values.
<Assembly: ApplicationQueuing(Enabled:=True, QueueListenerEnabled:=True, _
    MaxListenerThreads:=10)>

' This syntax enables queuing but disables the listener object and uses
' zero for MaxListenerThreads (the default, no limit is enforced).
<Assembly: ApplicationQueuing()>
```

Defining the Queued Interface

Clients can call asynchronously only the methods that belong to an interface for which queuing is enabled, and therefore you must define an interface that contains such methods:

```
Public Interface IMoveMoney
    Sub MoveMoney(ByVal senderID As Integer, ByVal receiverID As Integer, _
        ByVal amount As Decimal)
End Interface
```

Notice that the interface must be visible through COM Interop, and therefore it must be public and not marked with a ComVisible(False) attribute. Next you use the Interface-Queuing attribute on the class that contains the methods to be invoked asynchronously:

```
<InterfaceQueuing(Interface:="IMoveMoney"), EventTrackingEnabled() > _
Public Class AsyncMoneyMover
    Inherits ServicedComponent
    Implements IMoveMoney

    Sub MoveMoney(ByVal senderID As Integer, ByVal receiverID As Integer, _
        ByVal amount As Decimal) Implements IMoveMoney.MoveMoney
        UpdateAccount(senderID, -amount)
        UpdateAccount(receiverID, amount)
    End Sub
End Class
```

You can also mark an interface as queued from the MMC snap-in, on the Queuing tab of the interface's Properties window. Notice that you can even mark individual methods of the interface as queued. All the methods in the interface undergo the limitations I explained previously—that is, they must be Subs and take only ByVal arguments. If one or more methods don't comply with these limitations, you get an error when the component is registered in the COM+ catalog.

When you've completed the definition of the queued component, you should compile the project, install the assembly in the GAC, and register it with the Regsvcs tool.

Using the Queued Component

Clients don't instantiate queued components as they do regular COM+ components. Instead, they use the Marshal.BindToMoniker shared method with the following syntax:

```
' Create an instance of the component, and cast to the queued interface.
Dim mover As BankComponent.IMoveMoney = DirectCast(Marshal.BindToMoniker( _
    "queue:/new:BankComponent.AsyncMoneyMover"), BankComponent.IMoveMoney )
' Invoke the method(s) asynchronously.
mover.MoveMoney(1, 2, 12000)
mover.MoveMoney(1, 3, 7000)
⋮
' Activate the QC by forcing the release of the component.
Marshal.ReleaseComObject(mover)
mover = Nothing
```

The string that you pass to the BindToMoniker method can include optional values that let you decide the computer on which the QC is instantiated. For example, the following string creates the QC on a computer whose name is MyServer:

```
queue:ComputerName=MyServer/new:BankComponent.AsyncMoneyMover
```

See the MSDN documentation for additional arguments you can pass in this string.

MSMQ Messages

Queued components hide the complexity of asynchronous programming by offering a high-level view of MSMQ and its messages. If you need to exert more control over your application, however, you can manipulate MSMQ messages directly.

Creating a Queue

You can create an MSMQ queue either manually from the Computer Manager MMC snap-in or via code. In the first case, you right-click on the Private Queues node, choose the New command, and assign the new queue a name. (See the left portion of Figure 31-21.) After creating the queue, you can set a few more attributes in its Properties window, most notably its label, as shown in the right portion of Figure 31-21.

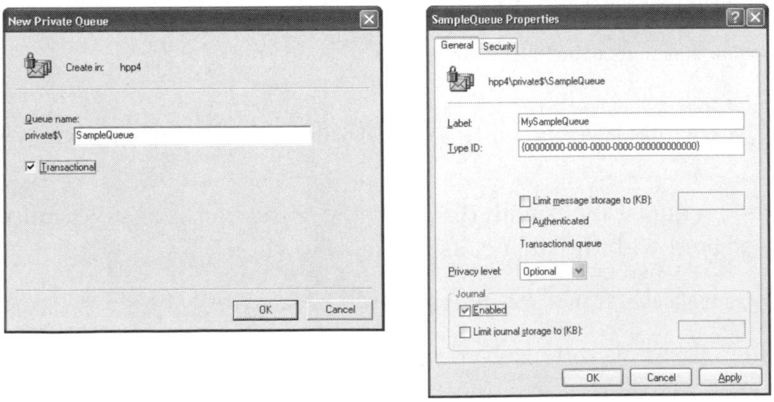

Figure 31-21   Creating a new private queue (on the left) and setting its properties (on the right)

To access MSMQ queues programmatically, you must add a reference to the System.Messaging.Dll library and insert an Imports statement in the System.Messaging namespace. The most important class in this namespace is MessageQueue, which exposes shared methods for creating a queue, checking whether a queue exists, and enumerating all the public and private queues on a machine. This class also exposes instances of read-only properties that return information about a specific queue, such as FormatName, Id, Transactional, and CreateTime:

```
' The machine "." is the local computer.
For Each q As MessageQueue In MessageQueue.GetPrivateQueuesByMachine(".")
    Debug.WriteLine(String.Format("FormatName={0}, Id={1}, Transactional={2}", _
        q.FormatName, q.Id, q.Transactional))
Next
```

The FormatName property of a queue is a GUID that identifies the queue or a string in the form DIRECT=OS:*servername*\private$*queuename*, as in

```
FormatName=DIRECT=OS:myserver\private$\samplequeue
```

You can also create a public queue by using the *servername**queuename* syntax, but this syntax isn't supported if MSMQ is installed in workgroup mode. You typically create a queue by using a piece of code like the following:

```
Const QUEUE_NAME As String = ".\private$\SampleQueue"
Dim queue As MessageQueue

Try
    ' Create the queue if it doesn't exist already.
    If Not MessageQueue.Exists(QUEUE_NAME) Then
        ' False means the queue isn't transactional.
        queue = MessageQueue.Create(QUEUE_NAME, False)
        queue.Label = "MySampleQueue"
        ' Optional means that accepts but doesn't require encrypted messages.
        queue.EncryptionRequired = EncryptionRequired.Optional
    Else
        queue = New MessageQueue(QUEUE_NAME)
    End If
Catch ex As Exception
    MessageBox.Show(ex.Message, "Error", MessageBoxButtons.OK, MessageBoxIcon.Error)
End Try
```

You can reference a queue by its path (for example, myserver\private$\samplequeue) or the label associated with the queue, as in the following:

```
Dim q2 As New MessageQueue("Label:MySampleQueue")
```

The path and the label must be resolved internally to the format name, however, and therefore they add a little overhead. Moreover, the Format Name Direct syntax is the only syntax that allows access to private queues on remote computers, so it is the recommended one.

You can use the Purge instance method to delete all the messages in the queue or the Delete shared method to remove the entire queue:

```
' Delete all messages from the queue.
queue.Purge()

' Delete the queue from MSMQ.
MessageQueue.Delete(queue.Path)
```

In general, only an administrator can create and delete queues; if the previous code runs under a nonadministrator account, it raises an Access Denied error.

> **Note**   You can also create a MessageQueue object at design time, by dragging and dropping it either from the Server Explorer window or from the Components tab of the Toolbox. One of the benefits of design-time creation is the ability to create an installer class that automates the process of creating the queue on the target machine.

Sending Messages

You send a message to a queue by calling the Send method of a MessageQueue object. This method takes the message body in its first argument and a second, optional argument that specifies a label for the message (not to be confused with the label of the queue):

```
Dim msg As String = "This is my first MSMQ message"
queue.Send(msg, "Sample Message")
```

You can see actual sent messages in the MMC snap-in, and you can double-click a message to browse its properties, including the actual bytes of the message body. (See Figure 31-22.)

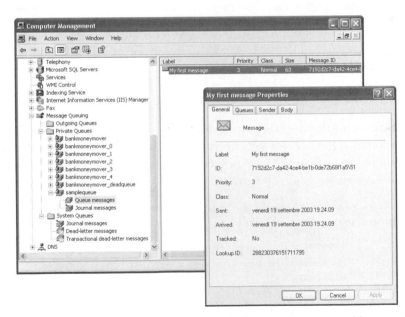

Figure 31-22   Looking at messages and their properties in the Message Queuing MMC snap-in

The value that you pass to the first argument of the Send method can be any primitive value or any .NET object that can be serialized to XML—for example, a DataSet or a public class that you define and that has a public default constructor. (See the note at the end of Chapter 23 for more details about XML serialization.) A single MSMQ message can't contain more than 4 megabytes of data.

You can better control the message and its other properties by explicitly creating a Message object, as in this code:

```
Dim m As New Message
' Set label, body, and priority.
m.Label = txtLabel.Text
m.Body = txtMessage.Text
m.Priority = MessagePriority.High
' Send the message in binary format.
m.Formatter = New BinaryMessageFormatter
' This message must be received within one hour.
m.TimeToBeReceived = New TimeSpan(1, 0, 0)
' The message must be recoverable in case of system failure.
m.Recoverable = True
' Send the message to the queue.
queue.Send(m)
```

Using the BinaryMessageFormatter instead of the XmlMessageFormatter (the default formatter) usually improves performance but makes debugging harder. You can also set a default formatter for the queue instead of creating it for each individual message:

```
queue.Formatter = New BinaryMessageFormatter
```

You should use only one type of formatter in a given application, because the receiver program must set the Formatter property of the queue or the message in advance to match the formatter used when sending the message.

Receiving Messages

An application can read the messages in a queue by using one of the following two techniques: the Receive method for synchronous retrieval of messages, or the Receive-Completed event of the MessageQueue object for asynchronous retrieval of messages. Retrieving a message synchronously is trivial:

```
' Get a reference to the queue. (QUEUE_NAME has been defined previously.)
Dim queue As New MessageQueue(QUEUE_NAME)
Try
    ' Receive the next message, wait up to 10 seconds.
    Dim m As Message = queue.Receive(New TimeSpan(0, 0, 10))
    ' Read the body as a string.
    Dim targetTypes() As Type = {GetType(String)}
    m.Formatter = New XmlMessageFormatter(targetTypes)
    ' Display the message body and label in TextBox controls.
    txtLabel.Text = m.Label
    txtMessage.Text = CStr(m.Body)
Catch ex As Exception
    ' Often this is a MessageQueueException caused by a timeout.
    MsgBox(ex.Message, MsgBoxStyle.Critical)
End Try
```

The formatter being used to retrieve the body of the message—BinaryMessageFormatter or XmlMessageFormatter—must match the formatter applied when sending the message.

The constructors of these two formatter classes take an array of System.Type objects that represent the types expected in the message's body. (In the previous example, we expect only strings.) The receiver application can discern among different types using the TypeOf operator, as in the following:

```
Dim targetTypes() As Type = {GetType(String), GetType(DataSet)}
m.Formatter = New XmlMessageFormatter(targetTypes)
Dim body As Object = m.Body
If TypeOf body Is String Then
    txtMessage.Text = CStr(body)
Else
    ' Display the DataSet as XML.
    txtMessage.Text = CType(body, DataSet).GetXml
End If
```

The Receive method extracts the message from the queue, and you can't undo its action. Alternatively, you can use the Peek method to get the next message in the queue while leaving it in the queue:

```
    ' Peek the next message, wait up to 5 seconds.
    Dim m As Message = queue.Peek(New TimeSpan(0, 0, 5))
```

You aren't limited to reading messages one at a time. If you expect to find several messages in the queue, you can collect all of them more efficiently in one operation by means of the GetAllMessages method:

```
Dim messages() As Message = queue.GetAllMessages()
```

Retrieving messages in an asynchronous fashion requires that you set up a handler for the ReceiveCompleted event of a MessageQueue object—by using either a WithEvents variable or the AddHandler keyword—and then start listening for events by means of the BeginReceive method:

```
Dim queue As New MessageQueue(Form1.QUEUE_NAME)
AddHandler queue.ReceiveCompleted, AddressOf NewMessage
' Start listening to events.
queue.BeginReceive()
```

The handler for the event can access the incoming message by using one of the properties of the ReceiveCompletedEventArgs object passed to its second argument:

```
Private Sub NewMessage(ByVal sender As Object, ByVal e As ReceiveCompletedEventArgs)
    Dim m As Message = e.Message
    Dim targetTypes() As Type = {GetType(String)}
    m.Formatter = New XmlMessageFormatter(targetTypes)
    Dim body As String = CStr(m.Body)
    ' Just display body and label in this demo program.
    MsgBox(body, MsgBoxStyle.Information, m.Label)
    ' Wait for the next message.
    queue.BeginReceive()
End Sub
```

As the previous routine illustrates, the code in the event handler must call the Begin-Receive method to receive subsequent events. (The MessageQueue object also exposes a PeekCompleted event, which you activate with a BeginPeek method.)

Transactional Queues

MSMQ supports transactional queues, which can take part in two types of transactions: *internal transactions* and *external transactions*. Internal transactions are managed directly by MSMQ, are more efficient, and have a simple programming model. External transactions require the presence of MS DTC (or another transaction coordinator), add more overhead, and are more complex. Only external transactions can involve other types of resources, such as databases. (For information about external transactions, read the MSDN documentation.)

Regardless of the transition type, MSMQ can guarantee either that all the messages in the transaction are sent (or received), or that none of them is sent (or received). Additionally, MSMQ guarantees that all the messages inside a transaction are received in the same order in which they were sent. The following example shows how you can create a transactional queue, send a group of messages, and then commit or roll back the transaction:

```
' True means that the queue is transactional.
Dim tq As MessageQueue = MessageQueue.Create(QUEUE_NAME, True)
' Create an internal transaction.
Dim tran As New MessageQueueTransaction
Try
    ' Open the transaction.
    tran.Begin()
    ' Send a bunch of messages.
    tq.Send("First message", "Label 1", tr)
    tq.Send("Second message", "Label 2", tr)
    ⋮
    ' Commit the transaction if no error so far.
    tran.Commit()
Catch ex As Exception
    tran.Abort()
End Try
```

MSMQ also supports a simpler type of internal transaction that wraps a single message and ensures that the message is delivered exactly once. You specify this type of transactional message by passing a second argument to the Send method:

```
queue.Send(m, MessageQueueTransactionType.Single)
```

Because this statement defines a transaction of its own, it can't be executed while another transaction is active.

The .NET platform provides three technologies to implement distributed computing. You learned about Web services in Chapter 29 and serviced components in this chapter. The third way to execute an object on a remote system is .NET remoting, which I'll describe in the next chapter.

32 Remoting

One of the main goals of the Microsoft .NET Framework is to promote the creation of *n*-tiered, enterprise-level distributed applications. In such applications, you typically have a *user tier* (a Windows Forms or Web Forms application that interacts with the user), a *business tier* (with objects that embed the logic of the application), and a *data tier* (with objects that encapsulate data access and hide the database implementation to the user and business tiers). A typical prerequisite for a distributed architecture is the ability to run objects on remote systems; this capability is necessary, for example, to move data objects as physically near as possible to the database.

> **See Also** To keep the code as concise as possible, all the code samples in this chapter assume the use of the following Import statements at the file or project level:
>
> ```
> Imports System.Runtime.Remoting
> Imports System.Runtime.Remoting.Channels
> Imports System.Runtime.Remoting.Channels.Tcp
> Imports System.Runtime.Remoting.Channels.Http
> Imports System.Runtime.Remoting.Services
> Imports System.Runtime.Remoting.Lifetime
> ```

Remoting Essentials

The .NET Framework offers several technologies that allow objects to run on a remote computer. You can expose remote components as Web services, you can use serviced components if you need to leverage existing COM+ services, or you can create your solutions by means of .NET remoting.

.NET Technologies for Distributed Computing

It's important to understand the peculiarities of .NET remoting and how it compares with the other two technologies. .NET remoting lets you invoke a method on an object that has been instantiated and is physically running on a different machine. By default, the caller and the callee can use HTTP or TCP as the communication medium, but other channel types can be used. The support for HTTP and TCP channels means that the remote object can reside as near as on another machine of your LAN or as far as a server located across the Internet. Data can be encoded in different ways. Binary format and SOAP format are provided by the .NET Framework, but you can implement your own.

Regardless of the communication channel and the encoding mechanism you adopt, .NET remoting lets you use a remote object as if it were a local object. You can use configuration files to specify the channel and the encoding (and other settings) and change the way your application works without recompiling it.

.NET remoting has a few limitations as well, the two most serious being the lack of built-in support for security and for transactions. You can circumvent the first problem if you run your remote object inside IIS (see the section "Hosting Using Internet Information Services," later in this chapter), but there's no way to enroll a remote object in a transaction. In this respect, remoting is similar to Web service components, which can leverage the security capabilities offered by IIS but can't participate in a transaction initiated by the client. You can create transactional components only by means of COM+ and .NET serviced components, although transactions should be available in the next version of Web Services Extensions (WSE 2.0), in beta version as of this writing.

Another thing to consider when selecting a technology for distributed applications is that .NET remoting requires that the .NET Framework be installed on both server and client machines. In comparison, Web services offer a better degree of interoperability with other platforms and operating systems, as they rely exclusively on nonproprietary standards such as SOAP and HTTP.

The .NET remoting architecture is quite complex, but it is also extremely customizable. (See Figure 32-1.) For example, you can plug in your own formatters—to encrypt messages and compress large amounts of data—and your custom channels if you can't use HTTP or TCP. Fortunately, you seldom need to know more than what I cover in this chapter to use remoting effectively.

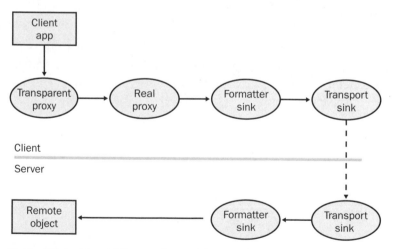

Figure 32-1   The .NET remoting architecture

Remotable Object Types

In spite of the intricacies of its internal architecture, creating and using a remote object with .NET remoting is quite simple. Before I show you a practical example, however, I need to introduce a few concepts.

Marshaling is an important concept that you have already encountered in previous chapters. In the .NET Framework, you implicitly use marshaling whenever you must pass an object between two applications that live in two distinct AppDomains (including applications that live in the same process but in different AppDomains).

When marshaling is involved, you typically describe the two involved programs as the *client application* and the *server application*. (The latter is also known as the *host application*, because it hosts the objects exposed to remote clients.) Because these applications can live on the same machine, in this chapter I will use the terms *client* and *server* in quite a loose way. For most practical purposes, the server application is the application that exposes the remotable object, whereas the client application is the one that uses the object and invokes its methods.

You can classify all objects passed between the client and the server according to a couple of criteria, depending on which of the two applications activates and is responsible for the object and whether the object is passed by reference or by value when it moves across AppDomains.

Server-Activated Objects and Client-Activated Objects

Remotable components can be of two types: *server-activated objects* (SAOs) and *client-activated objects* (CAOs). The server-activated objects category includes two subtypes: single-call objects and singleton objects. In total, therefore, you must learn about three kinds of remotable objects:

- **Single-call server-activated objects (single-call SAOs)**   These objects are created on the server when a request arrives from the client and are destroyed at the end of the method call. Because the object is released after each call, the object can't store any information between calls, and you should consider the object as stateless. Invoking a method on a single-call SAOs is similar to calling an Auto-Complete method in a serviced component—in both cases, the object is immediately released after each call, although the client still has a reference to it.

- **Singleton server-activated objects (singleton SAOs)**   There is at most one instance of such objects running on the server in any given moment. The first request from clients creates the instance; subsequent client requests receive a reference to the instance already running. The object is disposed of when its *lease time* expires, or it lives until the host application destroys it if you set an infinite lease time for it. (For details on the lease mechanism, see the section "Object Lifetime," later in this chapter.) Singleton objects are stateful objects, and they can be used to share information among remote clients. (When sharing state among clients, you must account for threading issues, however.)

- **Client-activated objects (CAOs)**   These objects are similar to classic DCOM and non-JIT-activated COM+ objects. Each request from a client creates a new object running on the server, and that object is kept alive until the client releases the reference. CAOs can maintain the state between consecutive method calls. (Unlike singleton SAOs, you don't have to worry about threading, because each client references a different instance.)

The distinction between SAOs and CAOs is quite confusing at first. Server-activated objects are so named because the client has no control of when the object is instantiated and released. When the client creates an instance of an SAO with the New keyword, nothing actually happens on the server; the object is physically instantiated only when the client invokes a method on the object. For this reason, a client receives a RemotingException if it attempts to create an SAO by calling a constructor with arguments. (Parameterized constructors are OK with CAOs.) Server-activated objects are also called *Well Known Objects* (WKO).

Single-call SAOs are quite scalable, because they take resources on the host only for a limited amount of time, and should be used whenever you don't need stateful objects. Singleton SAOs might or might not scale well, depending on whether they need a synchronization mechanism to handle simultaneous calls from multiple clients. If the singleton SAO wraps a shared resource, you must protect the resource with one of the synchronization lock techniques I demonstrated in Chapter 12; these synchronization locks can easily become a bottleneck for the entire distributed application.

CAOs tend to tax the server system's memory, so they suffer from the same scalability problems that DCOM objects had. You should exercise caution when using CAOs in applications with lots of clients that create many objects and keep them alive for a long time.

A class can be exposed as a local object, an SAO, or a CAO, without any change in the source code of the class itself. The only difference is in how the class is published or registered. In practice, a class meant to be accessed as a remote object is designed differently from a class meant to be used locally. For example, objects designed to be accessed from remote clients expose few or no properties and are less "chatty" than regular objects. In other words, clients must be able to complete a task by calling very few methods.

Marshal-by-Reference and Marshal-by-Value Objects

An object meant to be accessed from a different AppDomain must be of the marshal-by-reference (MBR) type, which implies that it inherits from the System.MarshalByRefObject class. (You already encountered MBR objects in Chapter 31.)

You use an MBR object when you want the object to execute on a specific machine. When the client application creates an MBR object, the object is instantiated in the AppDomain that hosts its assembly, and a reference to the (remote) object is marshaled back to the client. The reference held by the client points to a so-called transparent proxy. When the client invokes a method on this proxy, the .NET remoting infrastructure dispatches the call to the remote object running in another AppDomain (possibly on another machine).

The opposite of an MBR object is a *marshal-by-value* (MBV) object. When such an object is marshaled between the client and the server, only a copy of the object is actually transferred. For this to happen, the object must be serialized into a stream and shipped along the channel.

In distributed applications based on .NET remoting, MBV objects are typically used as arguments or return values from methods exposed by MBR objects. You use MBV objects to move information from the client to the server and back. For example, the client might create an Order object (an MBV object) and pass it to the PlaceOrder method of the OrderManager class (an MBR object).

Once an MBV object has been marshaled to another AppDomain, the object behaves like any other object: its methods run in the local instance, and .NET remoting isn't involved in any way. An MBV object must be marked with the <Serializable> attribute and possibly implement the ISerializable interface. (See Chapter 10 for details about .NET serialization.)

> **Important**   If a remotable method returns an object that can be marshaled both by reference and by value—that is, a serializable object that inherits from MarshalByRefObject—the MBR nature has a higher priority, and the client application receives a reference to a proxy object, not a serialized copy of the original object. This MBR object is always marshaled back to the client as a client-activated object.

If an object is neither an MBR nor an MBV object—in other words, it isn't serializable and doesn't derive from MarshalByRefObject—it can't be marshaled between two applications living in different AppDomains. You get an error if you attempt to pass such an object to a method of a remote component.

The ObjRef Class

The ObjRef type is crucial for the .NET remoting architecture. An ObjRef object represents a serializable pointer to an MBR object that lives in another AppDomain. An ObjRef contains all the information that is necessary to reach the remote object and invoke its methods. Being serializable, the .NET remoting infrastructure can move an ObjRef through a transport channel from the host to the client application.

Interestingly, because the ObjRef object embeds the exact URI of the remote object, a client might pass the ObjRef to another client (possibly on a different computer) and the new client would be still able to reach and use the remote object, provided that there are no obstacles of a different nature, such as a firewall, between the new client and the host application that exposes the object.

A .NET Remoting Example

Our first example of a remotable component is an object that evaluates a math operation on a remote server and returns the result to the client.

In this example—as in all applications based on .NET remoting—you must be concerned about three pieces of code: the server application that hosts the object, the DLL that contains the object, and the client application that uses the object. The first two pieces of code run in the same process on the server machine; the client application runs in a different AppDomain (possibly on a different machine). The following figure shows the relations among these three entities:

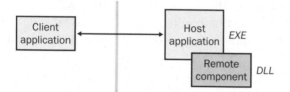

For the remoting mechanism to work correctly, the client application must have access to the metadata of the remotable object; otherwise, the .NET runtime can neither resolve the New operator nor invoke the object's members. The simplest way to let the client access the object's metadata is to deploy the component DLL on the client system. This approach is fine for our initial experiments but is clearly contrary to the principles of distributing programming. Providing clients with a copy of the object's DLL makes deployment more difficult and opens up a security hole, as malicious clients can decompile and reverse-engineer the component.

I'll tackle this problem in the section "Metadata Deployment," later in this chapter, but for now let's agree on deploying the DLL on both the server and the client machine. This unrealistic assumption will greatly simplify the explanation that follows.

.NET remoting differs from both COM+ and Web services architectures in one important detail. When a client calls a serviced component in a server application, the COM+ infrastructure can intercept the call and instantiate the object inside the DllHost.exe executable. A similar thing happens with Web services—in this case, the aspnet_isapi.dll filter intercepts the request and creates the object on behalf of the client.

In a sense, you could say that DllHost.exe is the host application for COM+ components and IIS is the host application for Web services components. If COM+ and IIS are up and running, they can serve incoming requests for serviced components and Web service components, respectively. Alas, the .NET remoting infrastructure doesn't offer a similar service and doesn't come with a predefined host application. You have to create your own host application and ensure that this application is running when the request from the client arrives; otherwise, the request fails.

The main goal of the host application is to inform the .NET remoting subsystem that the component in the DLL can be accessed by remote clients and to provide an address space in which the DLL can be loaded. From that point on, the .NET runtime will respond to requests from clients without any intervention by the host application. Even if the host application doesn't play any active role after it registers the remote object, the application must be running for this mechanism to work; otherwise, the .NET runtime would have no AppDomain in which the DLL can run.

The host can be any managed application. Real-world remoting systems typically use either a Windows NT service or IIS as the host application. Both these solutions have a great advantage over other types of programs: they can run even if no user has logged onto the system, which is a requirement if the distributed application must run in unattended mode.

For our experiments, however, we'll adopt a simpler approach and use a console application as the host application. It is therefore essential that you run the console application on the server machine *before* the client requests the object; otherwise, the request will fail.

The Remotable Object

Create a new Class library project, name it RemoteComponents, rename the Class1.vb file as Calculator.vb, and type this code:

```
Public Class Calculator
    Inherits MarshalByRefObject
    ' This variable holds the total number of calls.
    Dim Counter As Integer = 0

    ' Return the sum of two numbers
    Function Add(ByVal n1 As Double, ByVal n2 As Double) As Double
        Add = n1 + n2
        ' Display a diagnostic message on the console window.
        Counter += 1
        Console.WriteLine("Call #{0} : {1} + {2} = {3}", Counter, n1, n2, Add)
    End Function

    ' Return information the process that hosts this object.
    Function GetProcessID() As String
        Return String.Format("Process #{0} on {1}", _
            Process.GetCurrentProcess.Id, Environment.MachineName)
    End Function
End Class
```

Admittedly, except for the Inherits keyword that makes this an MBR class, this code isn't very interesting. The Add method displays a diagnostic message that contains the value of the Counter member variable, a piece of information useful for understanding what's going on behind the scenes. Both methods are instance methods: like serviced components, .NET remoting doesn't support remote invocation of shared methods. (Calls to shared methods seem to work correctly, but some debugging proves that they are run in the local assembly, not the remote assembly.)

Also, notice that you neither need to reference additional DLLs nor add Imports statements. It makes no difference to the Calculator object that it will be accessed remotely. Except for the Inherits keyword, a remotable class looks exactly like a regular .NET class.

Remember to compile the RemoteComponents project before continuing, as you need to reference its assembly from both the host and the client applications.

The Host Application

You can develop and test the host application in the same Microsoft Visual Studio .NET solution that contains the RemoteComponent project. This process simplifies debugging. Create a new Console application, name it ServerApp, and add a reference to the RemoteComponents project. The host application uses types in the System.Runtime.Remoting assembly, so you must add a reference to that DLL and include a few Imports statements:

```
Imports System.Runtime.Remoting
Imports System.Runtime.Remoting.Channels
Imports System.Runtime.Remoting.Channels.Tcp
Imports System.Runtime.Remoting.Channels.Http
Imports RemoteComponents

Module Module1
    Sub Main()
        Console.WriteLine("Starting ServerApp...")
        ' Create and register a TCP server channel that listens to port 50000.
        Dim channel As New TcpChannel(50000)
        ChannelServices.RegisterChannel(channel)

        ' Create and publish the Calculator object.
        Dim calc As New Calculator
        RemotingServices.Marshal(calc, "calculator.rem")

        ' Wait until the operator terminates the program.
        Console.ReadLine()
        ' Unregister the channel. (Optional in this demo.)
        ChannelServices.UnregisterChannel(channel)
    End Sub
End Module
```

Before it can expose an object through remoting, the host application must create and register a server TCP channel. The constructor of this class takes the port number that you want to associate with the channel, as shown in previous code:

```
Dim channel As New TcpChannel(50000)
ChannelServices.RegisterChannel(channel)
```

You should use a port number equal to or higher than 1024 to avoid clashes with ports used by common protocols such as HTTP (port 80) or FTP (port 21). Even better, you should use a number equal to or higher than 48152 to stay clear of ports used by other commercial software such as SQL Server (port 1433).

Next, the host application creates an instance of the Calculator class and makes it available for remoting as a singleton SAO by calling the Marshal shared method of the RemotingServices class:

```
Dim calc As New Calculator
RemotingServices.Marshal(calc, "calculator.rem")
```

The second argument is the URI at which clients can request the object. For example, if the IP address of the server machine is 192.168.0.212 and you've chosen a port number equal to 50000, the published Calculator object can be reached at this address:

```
tcp://192.168.0.212:50000/Calculator.rem
```

If the server machine has a name, you can use it in lieu of the IP address, as in this code:

```
tcp://www.vb2themax:50000/Calculator.rem
```

And of course you can use localhost if the client and the host application are running on the same computer:

```
tcp://localhost:50000/Calculator.rem
```

The URI doesn't require an extension, but it is advisable that you use a URL that ends with .rem or .soap, because IIS recognizes these extensions. This means that you can later decide to host these objects inside IIS without having to modify remote clients.

The Client Application

Start another instance of Visual Studio .NET—on the same or a different machine—and create a new Windows Forms project. The client application needs to interact with .NET remoting services, so you must add a reference to the System.Runtime.Remoting assembly and include the same Imports statements you used for the host application. The client application must also have a reference to the RemoteComponents.dll assembly, which is necessary to declare a strongly typed variable of the Calculator type.

Drop a button on the default Form1 form, name it btnAdd, and write this code in its Click event handler:

```
' Connect to the remote object (running on local computer in this demo).
Dim url As String = "tcp://localhost:50000/calculator.rem"
Dim calc As Calculator = DirectCast(RemotingServices.Connect( _
    GetType(Calculator), url), Calculator)

' Invoke the Add method and display its return value.
Dim result As Double = calc.Add(11, 22)
' Call GetProcessID to prove that the object is running in another process.
MsgBox("Result is " & result.ToString, MsgBoxStyle.Information, calc.GetProcessID)
```

As I've explained previously, the URL to the remote object is formed by combining the protocol (tcp: or http:), the server name or address, the port number, and the URI string (as specified in the host application).

The Connect shared method of the RemotingServices object is where the client asks the .NET Framework to create a remote instance of the Calculator object; this method returns an Object value, and so you need to cast it to a strongly typed variable. Once you have a reference to the remote Calculator object, you can call its methods as if it were a local object.

Running the Example

You're now ready to see .NET remoting in action. First run the ServerApp console application, which will register the remote object. You should see an empty console window with the *Starting ServerApp...* message in it. The host application will run and keep the Calculator object available to remote clients until you press the Enter key.

Next run the ClientApp, and click the Add button. A message box confirms that the Add method has been invoked on an instance of the Calculator class, and a message in the console window proves that the object ran in the host process. (See Figure 32-2.)

> **Note**   The client application can programmatically determine whether it's dealing with a local or remote object by means of the RemotingServices.IsTransparentProxy method, as in this line of code:
>
>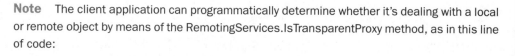
> ```
> If RemotingServices.IsTransparentProxy(obj) Then ...
> ```

Figure 32-2   The message in the console window shows that the Calculator object is running in the host application process.

Click the Add button a few times, and notice that the value of the Counter variable displayed in the console window increases with each click. This behavior confirms that the same instance of the remote object is used for all calls and that the object retains the value of its variables between calls.

Switch to the console application, and press Enter to terminate the host application. If you now click the Add button in the client application, you get a SocketException error, because the connection with the remote object no longer exists.

Object and Channel Registration

In the preceding example, you saw how the host application can explicitly create an object and make it available to remote clients by means of the RemotingServices.Marshal method. Although this technique has its merits and can be quite useful in some cases (as I explain in the section "Publishing a Singleton Server-Activated Object," later in this chapter), usually you want to register the class with the remoting infrastructure so that an instance of the object (Calculator in this case) is automatically instantiated when a request from a remote client arrives.

The host application registers a type for being accessed remotely by calling one of the Register*xxxx* shared methods of the RemotingConfiguration class. The exact method to be called depends on whether you want to expose the object as a server-activated object or a client-activated object.

In addition, the .NET remoting architecture supports declarative registration by means of configuration files, which let you change all registration settings by simply modifying the .config file associated with the client and the host application. I'll cover registration through configuration files in the section "Registration through Configuration Files," later in this chapter.

Registering a Single-Call Server-Activated Object

Registering a type as a single-call server-activated object requires that the host application invokes the RegisterWellKnownServiceType method of the RemotingConfiguration class, as in this code:

```
' (In the host application.)
ChannelServices.RegisterChannel(New TcpChannel(50000))
' Register the object as a single-call SAO.
RemotingConfiguration.RegisterWellKnownServiceType(GetType(Calculator), _
    "calculator.rem", WellKnownObjectMode.SingleCall)
```

(The call to the RegisterWellKnownServiceType must replace the call to RemotingServices.Marshal method in first example.) The client application can register an SAO—of either the single-call or the singleton type—by means of a call to the RegisterWellKnownClientType shared method. This registration can be done only once during the life of the client application, so our sample Windows Forms client program does it in the Form_Load event handler. After this step, the object can be used as if it were a local object:

```
' (In the client application.)
Private Sub Form1_Load(ByVal sender As Object, ByVal e As EventArgs) _
    Handles MyBase.Load
    ' Register the remote object.
    Dim url As String = "tcp://localhost:50000/calculator.rem"
    RemotingConfiguration.RegisterWellKnownClientType(GetType(Calculator), url)
End Sub
```

If you now run the host application and then the client application, you'll see that repeated calls to the Add method are all labeled as *Call #1*, as shown in Figure 32-3. This happens because single-call SAOs are created and destroyed at each method invocation; therefore, their member variables are reset each time.

Figure 32-3   Private members of a single-call SAO are initialized at each method invocation.

Registering a Singleton Server-Activated Object

Registering a singleton SAO requires the same steps as registering single-call SAOs, both in the host and in the client application. The only difference is the last argument that the host application passes to the RegisterWellKnownServiceType method:

```
' (In the host application.)
ChannelServices.RegisterChannel(New TcpChannel(50000))
' Register the object as a singleton SAO.
RemotingConfiguration.RegisterWellKnownServiceType(GetType(Calculator), _
    "calculator.rem", WellKnownObjectMode.Singleton)
```

The client application works the same way, regardless of whether it accesses a single-call or a singleton SAO:

```
' (In the client application.)
Dim url As String = "tcp://localhost:50000/calculator.rem"
RemotingConfiguration.RegisterWellKnownClientType(GetType(Calculator), url)
```

You must run two or more instances of the client application to see how a singleton SAO differs from a single-call SAO. All the various clients receive a reference to the same singleton object, thus you'll get the result shown in Figure 32-2 even if the method is called by different clients.

Instead of registering an SAO and then instantiating the proxy with a regular New keyword, the client application can use the Activator.GetObject method, as in this code snippet:

```
' (In the client application.)
Dim calc As Calculator = DirectCast(Activator.GetObject( _
    GetType(Calculator), url), RemoteComponent.Calculator)
```

This technique makes it clear that the object is instantiated remotely and is especially useful when the client application needs to instantiate the object on a specific remote system. Additionally, this technique can greatly simplify the deployment of the distributed application, as I'll explain in the section "Shared Interfaces with SAOs," later in this chapter.

Publishing a Singleton Server-Activated Object

Instead of registering a singleton SAO and then letting the .NET remoting instantiate a singleton of that type when a client request arrives, you can use the RemotingServices.Marshal shared method to publish a *specific* instance of an object as a singleton SAO. (This is the technique used in the first example in this chapter.) In this case, the server doesn't register the class; rather, it publishes a specific instance that it has created previously:

```
' (In the host application.)
ChannelServices.RegisterChannel(New TcpChannel(50000))
Dim calc As New Calculator
RemotingServices.Marshal(calc, "calculator.rem")
```

The client is oblivious to the fact that it is accessing a published or registered object, so it accesses the remote instance as any SAO, either by registering it and then using New or by getting a reference with the RemotingServices.Connect method, as shown by the following equivalent declarations:

```
' 1. The registration method.
RemotingConfiguration.RegisterWellKnownClientType(GetType(Calculator), url)
Dim calc As New Calculator

' 2. The publishing method (no registration is necessary).
Dim calc As Calculator = DirectCast(RemotingServices.Connect( _
    GetType(Calculator), url), Calculator)
```

Publishing a specific object instance has two advantages over the registration techniques described earlier. First, the host application can use parameterized constructors when creating the object. Second, the host application can publish different objects at different times, as in this code:

```
' This code assumes that the Calculator class has a constructor
' that takes one integer value.
Dim calc0 As New Calculator(0)
Dim calc1 As New Calculator(1)

RemotingServices.Marshal(calc0, "calculator.rem")
' Client applications will connect to calc0.
⋮
' Disconnect calc0 and publish calc1.
RemotingServices.Disconnect(calc0)
RemotingServices.Marshal(calc1, "calculator.rem")
' Client applications will connect to calc1.
⋮
' Disconnect calc1.
RemotingServices.Disconnect(calc1)
' Clients receive an exception if they attempt to create an object now.
```

Registering a Client-Activated Object

The host application registers a CAO by means of the RegisterActivatedServiceType shared method of the RemotingConfiguration class. An important difference from SAOs is that you don't specify any URI when registering a client-activated object:

```
' (In the host application.)
ChannelServices.RegisterChannel(New TcpChannel(50000))
RemotingConfiguration.ApplicationName = "Calculator"
RemotingConfiguration.RegisterActivatedServiceType(GetType(Calculator))
```

The client application registers a CAO with the RegisterActivatedClientType method. The string you pass to the second argument of this method is the concatenation of the URL of the remote machine and the application name:

```
' (In the client application.)
Dim url As String = "tcp://localhost:50000/Calculator"
RemotingConfiguration.RegisterActivatedClientType(GetType(Calculator), url)
```

Instead of registering the object on the client and then instantiating it with a New keyword, the client application can explicitly create an instance of a CAO with the Activator.CreateInstance method:

```
' (In the client application.)
Dim attrs() As Object = {New System.Runtime.Remoting.Activation.UrlAttribute( _
    "tcp://localhost:50000/Calculator")}
Dim calc As Calculator = DirectCast(Activator.CreateInstance( _
    GetType(Calculator), Nothing, attrs), Calculator)
```

You see the difference between CAOs and singleton SAOs by launching two or more instances of the client application. Each application receives a reference to a different remote object; intermixed method calls from different clients produce a result similar to what you see in Figure 32-4.

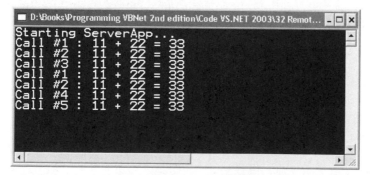

Figure 32-4   Client application receives references to distinct instances of a CAO, and each instance maintains its own member variables. Here we have three calls from client A, two calls from client B, and then two more calls from client A.

Registering a Channel

As I explained previously, a .NET remoting application can use a TCP channel or an HTTP channel to move data across AppDomains, plus any custom channel you might have defined for your purposes.

In general, using the TCP channel is advisable, both because the protocol is more efficient and because by default the TCP channel uses a binary formatter to encode data. The HTTP channel, on the other hand, is the only available channel when you host your objects in IIS (see the section "Hosting Using Internet Information Services," later in this chapter); the HTTP channel uses the SOAP formatter by default, but you can configure it to use the binary formatter to improve performance.

Modifying our example to use the HTTP channel instead of the TCP channel is trivial. In the host application, you simply create an HttpChannel object instead of a TcpChannel:

```
' (In the host application.)
Dim channel As New HttpChannel(50000)
ChannelServices.RegisterChannel(channel)
```

In the client application, you need to modify only the protocol portion of the URL used to reach the remote object:

```
' (In the client application.)
' Connect to the remote object (running on local computer in this demo).
Dim url As String = "http://localhost:50000/calculator.rem"
Dim calc As Calculator = DirectCast(RemotingServices.Connect( _
    GetType(Calculator), url), Calculator)
```

When you pass a port number to the constructor of the TcpChannel or the HttpChannel, you create a server channel; when you call the constructor without parameters, you are implicitly creating a client channel. Instead of using a generic TcpChannel object, you can be more specific about whether the channel is to be used on the server (host) or the client machine, by instantiating a TcpServerChannel or a TcpClientChannel object. Likewise, you can use an HttpServerChannel or an HttpClientChannel in lieu of the more generic HttpChannel.

Both the TcpServerChannel and the HttpServerChannel classes expose a constructor that allows you to change the default behavior of the channel itself. The first argument you pass to this constructor is an IDictionary object (usually a Hashtable) that contains one or more property/value pairs. At the very minimum, you must specify the port number, and you can optionally define the channel's name (to later retrieve the channel with a call to the ChannelServices.GetChannel method) and its priority (high numbers indicate a higher chance of being chosen to connect first; the default is 1). By default, the channel uses the IP address in the publication URL, but you can change this behavior by assigning False to the useIpAddress property, and you can specify the machine name to be used in publication by setting the machineName property equal to the name of the computer used with the channel:

```
' An HTTP channel on port 50000 that publishes an URL containing the machine name.
Dim props As New Hashtable
props("port") = 50000
props("useIpAddress") = False
props("machineName") = "MyServer"
Dim channel As New HttpServerChannel(props, Nothing)
ChannelServices.RegisterChannel(channel)
```

The second argument in the constructor specifies the formatter to be used with the channel. By default, the TCP channel uses the binary formatter and the HTTP channel uses the SOAP formatter, but you can change this default behavior. For example, you can have an HTTP channel use a binary formatter for better performance:

```
' (props is defined as in previous example.)
Dim channel As New HttpServerChannel(props, New BinaryServerFormatterSinkProvider)
ChannelServices.RegisterChannel(channel)
```

(You can also use the SoapServerFormatterSinkProvider to specify a SOAP formatter with a TCP channel, should you need to do so.)

If you register a server channel that uses a nondefault formatter, you must also register a client channel of the same type and that uses the same type of formatter. Notice that in this case, the names of the channel class and of the formatter class contain the string *client* rather than *server*:

```
' (In the client application.)
' Register an HTTP client channel that uses a binary formatter.
Dim props As New Hashtable
props("port") = 0                    ' port=0 is used for client channels.
Dim channel As New HttpClientChannel(props, New BinaryClientFormatterSinkProvider)
ChannelServices.RegisterChannel(channel)
' Register the remote object (as a CAO, in this case).
RemotingConfiguration.RegisterActivatedServiceType(GetType(Calculator))
```

Registration through Configuration Files

The code examples you've seen so far register a remote object and a channel programmatically, a technique that provides the highest flexibility and the capability to change configuration settings at run time. In many real-world applications, however, you might want to store these settings in the configuration file so that you can change them without recompiling the application.

Both the client and the host application can use the RemotingConfiguration.Configure shared method to have the .NET remoting architecture read a given configuration file and apply all the settings it defines:

```
' (This code assumes that the current application is named MyHostApp.)
RemotingConfiguration.Configure("MyHostApp.Exe.Config")
```

The configuration file can have any name, so you can switch to a different set of values simply by selecting another configuration file, but it's advisable that you use the application's main .config file. You aren't forced to use the same registration method on the client and on the server system—for example, the host application can use a configuration file, whereas the client application can do the registration via code.

These are the portions of the configuration file that affect the .NET remoting infrastructure:

```xml
<?xml version="1.0" encoding="utf-8" ?>
<configuration>
  <system.runtime.remoting>
    <application name="applicationname" >
      <channels>
        <!-- Define all the channels used by the application. -->
        <channel>
          :
        </channel>
      </channels>

      <!-- Define all server objects exposed by this application. -->
      <service>
        :
      </service>

      <!-- Define all client objects used by this application. -->
      <client>
        :
      </client>

      <!-- Define the default lifetime for exposed MBR objects. -->
      <lifetime .... />
    </application>

    <!-- Specify how much error information is returned to clients. -->
    <customErrors .... />

  </system.runtime.remoting>
</configuration>
```

In the following sections, you'll learn how to use all the tag elements in the preceding listing, except the <lifetime> tag (which I'll cover in the section "Changing Lease Settings for the Server Application"). In most cases, an application uses either the <service> tag (if it's a host application) or the <client> tag (if it's a client application). In more complex scenarios, however, an application can expose one or more objects to remoting and consume remote objects exposed by other applications at the same time; therefore, its configuration file can include both types of tags.

The <channel> Tag

The <channel> tag lets you define both the server channel and the client channel. The ref attribute specifies the type of the channel—tcp or http—and the port attribute is the port number:

```xml
<configuration>
  <system.runtime.remoting>
```

```
    <application>
      <channels>
        <!-- A server TCP channel on port 50000 -->
        <channel ref="tcp" port="50000"/>
      </channels>
    </application>
  </system.runtime.remoting>
</configuration>
```

The previous configuration file defines a server channel. When defining a client channel, you omit the port number:

```
<channels>
  <!-- A client TCP channel -->
  <channel ref="tcp" />
</channels>
```

The <channel> tag supports a few optional attributes, such as name (the name, which defaults to tcp or http), priority (default is 1), and machine Name (the name of the server machine; will be used instead of the IP address when publishing the channel). The HTTP channel supports the clientConnectionLimit attribute (the number of connections that can be open in a given moment; the default is 2), the timeout attribute (in milliseconds; use   1 for infinite timeout), and the proxyName and proxyPort attributes (name and port of your proxy server):

```
<!-- A server HTTP channel that supports up to 10 simultaneous connections -->
<channel ref="http" port="50000" clientConnectionLimit="10" />
```

Server-side TCP channels support the rejectRemoteConnection attribute. If you set this attribute to true, .NET remoting will allow only communication among AppDomains on the local machine and will reject requests from remote computers:

```
<channel ref="tcp" port="50000" rejectRemoteRequests="true" />
```

You can specify a nondefault formatter for a channel by nesting a <serverProviders> or a <clientProviders> section in the <channel> tag:

```
<!-- A server HTTP channel that uses a binary formatter. -->
<channel ref="http" port="50000" >
  <serverProviders>
    <formatter ref="binary" />
  </serverProviders>
</channel>
```

This is how such an HTTP channel would be configured on the client:

```
<!-- A client HTTP channel that uses a binary formatter. -->
<channel ref="http" >
  <clientProviders>
    <formatter ref="binary" />
  </clientProviders>
</channel>
```

The <formatter> tag supports several other attributes—for example, type (the type of a custom formatter), includeVersions (true, the default, if the formatter sends complete information about the type and the assembly version), and strictBinding (false, the default, if the .NET runtime will allow to deserialize the object by ignoring versioning information when an exact match can't be found).

To protect applications from deserialization attacks, version 1.1 of the .NET Framework added the typeFilterLevel attribute, which can take two values: Low and Full. When this attribute is omitted or the Low default value is used, only primitive types and types associated with the most basic remoting functionality are deserialized. To allow deserialization of all types, you must set the typeFilterLevel attribute equal to Full:

```
<channel ref="http" port="50000" >
  <serverProviders>
    <formatter ref="binary" typeFilterLevel="Full" />
  </serverProviders>
</channel>
```

You must set this attribute to Full to marshal any ObjRef pointing to a remote MBR if the ObjRef is passed as a method argument. This is necessary, for example, when the client passes an object to the server that the server uses to call back the client (an advanced technique that I don't cover in this chapter).

The <service> Tag

The <service> tag contains the definitions of all objects exposed by the application to remote clients. More precisely, it contains one nested <wellknown> tag for each server-activated object and one <activated> tag for each client-activated object.

The <wellknown> tag takes three attributes: the type of the object being published, the mode (which can be Singleton or SingleCall), and the objectUri (the URI where this object can be found). For example, here is a configuration file that exposes the RemoteComponents.Calculator object as a singleton SAO:

```
<configuration>
  <system.runtime.remoting>
    <application>
      <channels>
        <channel ref="tcp" port="50000" />
      </channels>
      <service>
        <!-- Expose a singleton SAO at tcp://<hostip>:50000/Calculator.rem -->
        <wellknown type="RemoteComponents.Calculator, RemoteComponents"
          mode="Singleton" objectUri="Calculator.rem" />
      </service>
    </application>
  </system.runtime.remoting>
</configuration>
```

The type attribute is in the format *namespace.classname, assemblyname*. If the assembly is a strong name assembly registered in the GAC, the assembly name includes version, culture, and publisher key, as in this code:

```
<!-- Next line has been split in two to fit the page width. -->
<wellknown type="RemoteComponents.Calculator, RemoteComponents,
        Version=1.0.0.0, Culture=neutral, PublicKeyToken=c89a5D5de938e0ab"/>
    mode="SingleCall" objectUri="Calculator.rem" />
```

The <activated> tag defines a client-activated object and supports only the type attribute:

```
<service>
  <!-- Expose the RemoteComponents.Calculator as a CAO -->
  <activated type="RemoteComponents.Calculator, RemoteComponents" />
</service>
```

As for the <wellknown> tag, the type attribute for objects registered in the GAC must include the assembly's version, culture, and publisher key.

The <client> Tag

The <client> tag contains the definitions of all remote objects that the application uses. More precisely, it contains one nested <wellknown> tag for each server-activated object and one <activated> tag for each client-activated object.

The <wellknown> tag takes two attributes: the type of the object being published and the URL of the remote object. For example, here is a client-side configuration file that defines the RemoteComponents.Calculator object as an SAO:

```
<configuration>
  <system.runtime.remoting>
    <application>
      <channels>
        <channel ref="http" />
      </channels>
      <client>
        <!-- Define a remote SAO at specified URL -->
        <wellknown type="RemoteComponents.Calculator, RemoteComponents"
            url="http://localhost:50000/Calculator.rem" />
      </client>
    </application>
  </system.runtime.remoting>
</configuration>
```

(Notice that you don't specify the mode—Singleton or SingleCall—of an SAO in the configuration file used by the client application.) As usual, if the assembly containing the definition of the remote component is strong named, the type attribute must include the assembly's version, culture, and publisher key.

To register a remote CAO, you use an <activated> tag nested in the <client> tag. All the CAOs used by this client application use the URL defined as an attribute of the <client> tag. (This URL is ignored by remote SAOs.) Here's an example of a client-side configuration file that defines a remote CAO:

```
<client url="http://localhost:50000" >
  <!-- Define a remote CAO -->
  <activated type="RemoteComponents.Calculator, RemoteComponents" />
</client>
```

The <customErrors> Tag

Unlike the tags you've seen so far, which were nested in the <application> block, the <customErrors> tag appears in the <system.runtime.remoting> section. The mode attribute of this tag specifies whether clients received filtered exception information. Filtered exception information includes neither the exact exception type nor stack details about where the exception was thrown.

If the mode attribute is equal to remoteOnly (the default), only clients from the local computer receive complete exception information. Other valid values for the mode attribute are on (all callers receive filtered error information) and off (all callers receive complete, unfiltered error information). You typically use the on setting only if you're debugging your application from a remote computer, whereas you should use remoteOnly or on settings in production applications.

```
<configuration>
  <system.runtime.remoting>
    <application>
       ⋮
    </application>
    <!-- Prevent all clients from seeing details about exceptions. -->
    <customErrors mode="on" />
  </system.runtime.remoting>
</configuration>
```

A host application can determine whether the client is about to receive regular or filtered error information by querying the CustomErrorsEnabled shared method of the RemotingConfiguration class:

```
' Pass True if the client is running on the same computer.
If RemotingConfiguration.CustomErrorsEnabled(False) Then
    ' Remote clients receive filtered error information.
End If
```

The Microsoft .NET Framework Configuration Tool

You can view and edit some of the settings in the configuration file by means of the Microsoft .NET Framework Configuration tool, which you can reach from the Administrative Tools menu.

Before you can edit the remoting settings of an application with this tool, you must add the application to the list of configured applications. You can do this by right-clicking on the Applications element and choosing the Add command. You can configure both host and client applications. (See left portion of Figure 32-5.)

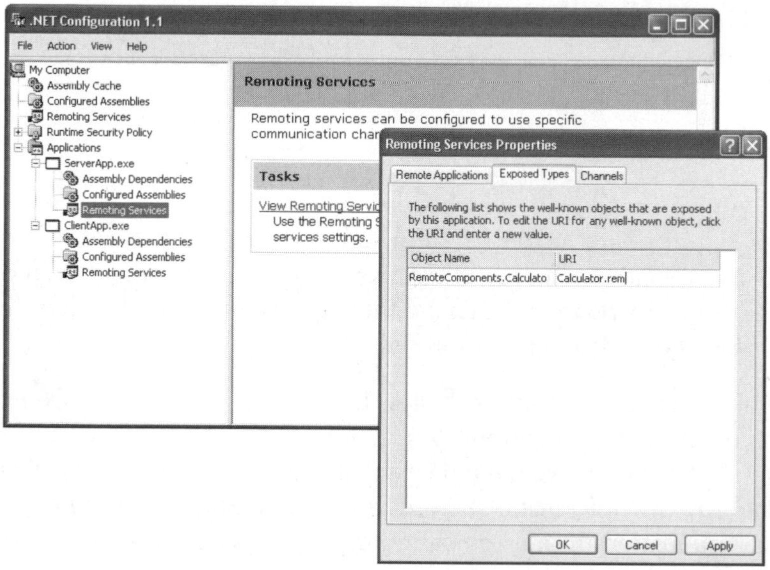

Figure 32-5   The .NET Framework Configuration tool

Next you click on the View Remoting Services Properties link in the right pane to open a dialog box that lets you set both client settings (on the Remote Applications tab) and server settings (on the Exposed Types tab).

Object Lifetime

All remotable architectures must implement a mechanism to detect when a remote object should be released. For example, DCOM uses distributed reference counting: the object is released only when all the references held in remote clients are set to Nothing. However, DCOM must also account for possible system and network failures, by having clients periodically ping the server to say "I am alive." If the server doesn't receive a ping from a client in a given timeout, it assumes that the client has crashed or is unreachable, and consequently decreases the reference counter of all the objects the client has a reference to.

The DCOM pinging mechanism suffers from performance and scalability problems, as well as other issues. For example, this mechanism doesn't work well with firewalls and proxies, which makes DCOM unfit for Internet scenarios.

For these and other reasons, the developers at Microsoft opted for a different solution when they came up with a remoting infrastructure for the .NET Framework. .NET remoting manages the lifetime of remote objects via a *lease-based* mechanism. When the object is created, it is assigned a lease object. The initial lease time is 5 minutes, but you can change this default value in a number of ways. Each time the object receives a remote call, the lease time is extended, if necessary, by a configurable time value. (The default is 2 minutes.) Each AppDomain has a lease manager object that checks whether the lease time of each object has expired, and if so, it releases the object. (By default, this check occurs every 10 seconds, but this value can be configured.)

Before releasing the object whose lease has expired, the lease manager checks whether the server or client application has registered a *sponsor* for that specific object. If a sponsor does exist, the .NET remoting infrastructure tries to contact the sponsor (via remoting, if the sponsor doesn't reside on the server machine) and asks it whether the lease period should be renewed. If the sponsor fails to respond within a given timeout (the default is 2 minutes), the lease manager assumes that the sponsor isn't working or reachable and proceeds to release the object.

The lease mechanism doesn't apply to single-call SAOs. These objects live for the duration of one method call and don't have any lease objects associated with them.

Singleton SAOs are subject to the lease mechanism, but in most cases, you can use the default lease time. If a singleton SAO is released by the remoting infrastructure because its lease has expired, client applications don't receive any error when they later invoke a method of the object, because .NET transparently creates a new instance behind the scenes. However, if the singleton object is used to share data among clients, you might want to associate it with a lease object that never expires. (In this case, the object will live as long as its host application.)

The lease mechanism is quite critical with client-activated objects. As a matter of fact, many of the techniques I demonstrate in the following sections make sense only if applied to CAOs.

Changing Lease Settings for the Server Application

The easiest way to change the default timeout settings used by the host application is by adding a <lifetime> tag in the application's configuration file:

```
<configuration>
  <system.runtime.remoting>
    <application>
      <lifetime leaseManagerPollTime="30s" sponsorshipTimeout="1m"
        leaseTime="1m" renewOnCallTime="20s" />
    </application>
  </system.runtime.remoting>
</configuration>
```

The default unit for time values is seconds, but you can specify other time units by using a character suffix: *D* for days, *H* for hours, *M* for minutes, *S* for seconds, or *MS* for milliseconds.

The leaseManagerPollTime attribute is the interval at which the lease manager checks the lease time of a remote object (the default is 10 seconds); the sponsorshipTimeout attribute is the amount of time the lease manager is willing to wait when it contacts a sponsor (the default is 2 minutes); the leaseTime is the initial lease time granted to a remote object (the default is 5 minutes); the renewOnCallTime attribute specifies the minimum amount of time granted to a remote object after a remote client invokes one of its methods (the default is 2 minutes).

The renewOnCallTime value is used only if it is higher than the value of the lease time when a method is invoked. For example, let's say that the server publishes an object using the default values of 5 minutes for leaseTime and 2 minutes for newOnCallTime. If the first method call arrives after 1 minute, the lease time has become 4 minutes, and therefore the renewOnCallTime value is ignored. If the next call from a client arrives after 3 minutes, the lease time has become 1 minute, but the renewOnCallTime setting brings it up to 2 minutes. If these 2 minutes elapse without the client making a method call, the object expires, and the .NET runtime throws a RemotingException (whose message reads *Requested service not found*) the next time the client attempts to use the object reference. (Notice that an expired object isn't necessarily physically destroyed, because it might be kept alive by local references in the host application.)

Instead of using a configuration file, the host application can adjust lease settings by assigning a TimeSpan value to shared properties of the LifetimeServices class. For example, this code has the same effect as the <lifetime> tag in the previous configuration file:

```
' You can create a TimeSpan value in many ways.
LifetimeServices.LeaseManagerPollTime = TimeSpan.FromSeconds (30)
LifetimeServices.SponsorshipTimeout = TimeSpan.FromMinutes (1)
Lifetimeservices.LeaseTime = new TimeSpan(0,0,10)
LifetimeServices.RenewOnCallTime = New TimeSpan(0, 0, 5)
```

Changing Lease Settings for a Specific Class

You can control the lease time of a specific type of remote object—as opposed to all the objects exposed by the host application—by overriding the InitializeLifetimeService method that all MBR classes inherit from MarshalByRefObject. This method is expected to return the lease associated with the MBR object. You can change the properties of the lease object before returning it to the .NET runtime, but you can do so only the first time this method is called:

```
Public Class Calculator
    Inherits MarshalByRefObject
    ⋮
    Public Overrides Function InitializeLifetimeService() As Object
        ' Get a reference to the lease object returned by the base class.
        Dim lease As ILease = DirectCast(MyBase.InitializeLifetimeService, ILease)
        ' Set the lease properties, but only if initializing.
        If lease.CurrentState = LeaseState.Initial Then
```

```
            lease.InitialLeaseTime = TimeSpan.FromSeconds(30)
            lease.RenewOnCallTime = TimeSpan.FromSeconds(10)
            lease.SponsorshipTimeout = TimeSpan.FromSeconds(20)
        End If
        Return lease
    End Function
End Class
```

As a special case, you can return Nothing if you want to keep the remote object alive forever, which corresponds to an infinite lease time:

```
    Public Overrides Function InitializeLifetimeService() As Object
        Return Nothing            ' (Not really necessary)
    End Function
```

Accessing the Lease Object

Code running in the host application can retrieve the lease associated with a remotable object either by invoking the object's GetLifetimeService method (which all MBR objects inherit from MarshalByRefObject) or by passing the object to the RemotingServices.GetLifetimeService shared method:

```
' These two statements are equivalent.
Dim lease As ILease = DirectCast(calc.GetLifetimeService(), ILease)
Dim lease2 As ILease = _
    DirectCast(RemotingServices.GetLifetimeService(calc), ILease)
```

You can determine the state of the lease by querying its CurrentState property, which can be Null (the lease hasn't been initialized), Initial (the lease is created but not active yet), Active (the lease is active and hasn't expired yet), Renewing (the lease has expired and is attempting to find a sponsor), or Expired (the lease has expired). If the lease is active, you can use the CurrentLeaseTime property to determine how long the remote object will live.

You can use the lease to perform two important operations: you can extend the lifetime of the remote object, and you can associate the lease with a sponsor. Extending the object lifetime is trivial:

```
' Renew the lease for one minute.
lease.Renew(TimeSpan.FromMinutes(1))
```

You'll see how to associate a sponsor with the lease in the next section.

Defining a Sponsor

A sponsor is an object that implements the ISponsor interface. This interface exposes only one method, Renewal, which is called by the lease manager when the lease of the remote object associated with the sponsor is about to expire. The Renewal method must return a TimeSpan value that specifies how long the object will live or return the value TimeSpan.Zero to refuse to extend the remote object's lifetime. A remote object can be associated with multiple sponsors; in this case, the .NET runtime will call the Renewal method for each one of them.

Building the Sponsor Class

A sponsor object can run on the server machine or the client machine. The following sponsor class exposes a method named SetState, which lets clients affect the value of a private Active field. If this field is True, the sponsor renews the lease of the associated remote object; otherwise, the sponsor refuses to extend the object's lifetime:

```
Public Class CalculatorSponsor
    Inherits MarshalByRefObject                    ' This is an MBR object.
    Implements ISponsor

    ' If True the sponsor renews the object's lease.
    Private Active As Boolean = True

    ' Let remote clients set the sponsor's active state.
    Public Sub SetState(ByVal active As Boolean)
        Me.Active = active
    End Sub

    Public Function Renewal(ByVal lease As ILease) As TimeSpan _
        Implements ISponsor.Renewal
        If Active Then
            Return New TimeSpan(0, 1, 0)              ' One minute
        Else
            Return TimeSpan.Zero
        End If
    End Function
End Class
```

Implementing the ISponsor interface is what makes the CalculatorSponsor class work as a sponsor. In addition, sponsor classes usually derive from MarshalByRefObject to make them accessible to clients via remoting.

Using the Sponsor Class

The Calculator class registers its sponsor in its InitializeLifetimeService procedure by invoking the lease's Register method and makes the sponsor available to clients through its Sponsor read-only property:

```
Public Class Calculator
    Inherits MarshalByRefObject
    ⋮
    Public Overrides Function InitializeLifetimeService() As Object
        Dim lease As ILease = DirectCast(MyBase.InitializeLifetimeService, ILease)
        If lease.CurrentState = LeaseState.Initial Then
            lease.InitialLeaseTime = TimeSpan.FromSeconds(30)
            lease.RenewOnCallTime = TimeSpan.FromSeconds(10)
            lease.SponsorshipTimeout = TimeSpan.FromSeconds(20)
            m_Sponsor = New CalculatorSponsor
            lease.Register(m_Sponsor)
```

```
        End If
        Return lease
    End Function

    Private m_Sponsor As CalculatorSponsor

    ' A readonly property that exposes the object's sponsor.
    Public ReadOnly Property Sponsor() As CalculatorSponsor
        Get
            Return m_Sponsor
        End Get
    End Property
End Class
```

(You can disconnect a sponsor from a lease object by means of the lease's Unregister method.)

The Calculator class exposes its sponsor object as a public read-only property, so clients can call the sponsor's SetState method to tell the sponsor "I am alive":

```
' (In the client application.)
calc.Sponsor.SetState(True)
```

Improving the Sponsor Class

The CalculatorSponsor sponsor class doesn't correctly handle cases in which the client application crashes or a problem on the channel prevents the client from communicating with the server. In such situations, the Active field is never set to False, and the sponsor keeps the remote object alive forever.

The simplest way to account for such cases is by remembering when the last call to the SetActive method occurred and checking this timestamp at the top of the Renewal method. Here's an improved implementation of the sponsor that uses this strategy:

```
Public Class CalculatorSponsorEx
    Inherits System.MarshalByRefObject
    Implements ISponsor

    ' If True the sponsor will renew the object's lease time.
    Private Active As Boolean = True
    ' Timestamp of last call to SetActive
    Private LastCallDateTime As Date = Now

    Public Sub SetState(ByVal active As Boolean)
        Me.Active = active
        Me.LastCallDateTime = Now
    End Sub

    Public Function Renewal(ByVal lease As ILease) As TimeSpan _
        Implements ISponsor.Renewal
        ' Disable renewing if last call was more than 10 minutes ago.
        If Me.LastCallDateTime.AddMinutes(10) < Now Then Active = False
        If Active Then
```

```
            Return New TimeSpan(0, 0, 10)
        Else
            Return TimeSpan.Zero
        End If
    End Function
End Class
```

Using the CalculatorSponsorEx class is conceptually similar to having the client manually call the lease's Renew method but offers more flexibility. For example, you can have one sponsor for each distinct client application, and thus a single call to the SetState method from a client would extend the lifetime of all the remote objects that have been returned to that specific client.

The ClientSponsor Class

Interestingly, the .NET Framework defines a class named ClientSponsor that works much like the initial version of the CalculatorSponsor class. This generic sponsor extends the lease time of the associated object by the TimeSpan value that you pass to its constructor or assign to its RenewalTime property. For example, here's how you might use this generic sponsor with a remotable object from inside the Calculator class:

```
' Get a reference to the lease object.
Dim lease As ILease = DirectCast(calc.GetLifetimeService(), ILease)
' Create a generic sponsor that will renew for half a minute, and register it.
Dim mysponsor As New ClientSponsor(New TimeSpan(0, 0, 30)
lease.Register(mysponsor)
⋮
' If you later want to double the renewal time...
mysponsor.RenewalTime = New TimeSpan(0, 1, 0)
⋮
' This is what you do to prevent the sponsor from renewing the lease.
mysponsor.RenewalTime = TimeSpan.Zero
```

Defining a Tracking Handler

A *tracking handler* is an object that receives a notification when an object is marshaled, unmarshaled, or disconnected. From the developer's perspective, a tracking handler is a public class that implements the System.Runtime.Remoting.Services.ITrackingHandler interface. Here's a simple tracking handler that displays diagnostic messages in the console window:

```
Public Class CustomTracker
    Implements ITrackingHandler

    Public Sub DisconnectedObject(ByVal obj As Object) _
        Implements ITrackingHandler.DisconnectedObject
        Console.WriteLine("CustomTracker.DisconnectedObject {0}", obj)
    End Sub

    Public Sub MarshaledObject(ByVal obj As Object, ByVal ref As ObjRef) _
        Implements ITrackingHandler.MarshaledObject
```

```
        Console.WriteLine("CustomTracker.MarshaledObject {0}", obj)
        If Not ref.URI Is Nothing Then Console.WriteLine("    URI = {0}", ref.URI)
    End Sub

    Public Sub UnmarshaledObject(ByVal obj As Object, ByVal ref As ObjRef) _
        Implements ITrackingHandler.UnmarshaledObject
        Console.WriteLine("CustomTracker.UnmarshaledObject {0}", obj)
        If Not ref.URI Is Nothing Then Console.WriteLine("    URI = {0}", ref.URI)
    End Sub
End Class
```

The URI information displayed when an object is marshaled or unmarshaled is a path that the .NET remoting architecture generates for internal use; it can be useful in the debug phase to distinguish objects of the same class. (See Figure 32-6.)

Figure 32-6   Tracking handlers let you display notification messages when a remote object is marshaled, unmarshaled, or disconnected.

The host application must register the handler object by passing it to the RegisterTrackingHandler method of the TrackingServices class, also in the System.Runtime.Remoting.Services namespace:

```
' (In the host application.)
Dim tracker As New CustomTracker
TrackingServices.RegisterTrackingHandler(New tracker)
```

You can later unregister the handler by calling the UnregisterTrackingHandler method and retrieve the array of all the registered handlers with the RegisteredHandlers property.

Metadata Deployment

For simplicity's sake, all the samples you've seen so far assumed that the client application has access to the DLL containing the remote object (RemoteComponents.dll in this case). In real-world distributed applications, this assumption is quite unrealistic, for at least a couple of reasons. First, distributing the DLL containing the remote objects makes deployment a nightmare, especially if you plan to frequently release new versions. Second, in many cases you don't want to give your remote clients the real DLL that runs on the server, because malicious users might reverse-engineer the assembly and "borrow" your code for use in other projects or access data that should be kept secret.

There are three solutions to this issue: using the SoapSuds utility, creating an assembly that defines a public interface, or creating an assembly that defines a public base class. Let's examine the pros and cons of each.

Using the SoapSuds Tool

The client application needs to access the object's metadata for two reasons: to instantiate the object with a New keyword and to reference the object using a strongly typed variable. If the client can't access the remote object's metadata, these operations would fail with an error at run time.

You can provide your clients with the remote object's metadata without giving them the actual assembly by compiling an assembly (known as proxy assembly) that contains the same classes with the same methods as the real assembly, but without any code inside those methods. Once compiled, all the classes in this proxy assembly would have the same identity as the actual assembly, and a strongly typed object could be assigned a reference to the remote object without a glitch.

While in theory this approach is feasible, in practice maintaining two source code sets (or using compilation constants and tons of #If statements) to generate the two assemblies is problematic at the least. Fortunately, the SoapSuds tool can create the proxy assembly for you.

Generating Metadata from a Compiled Assembly

Let's see how we can use the SoapSuds utility to generate a proxy for RemoteComponents.dll:

```
SOAPSUDS /ia:remotecomponents /oa:metadata.dll /nowp
```

The /ia (Input Assembly) option must be followed by the name of the assembly without the .exe or .dll, whereas the /oa (Output Assembly) option specifies the complete name of the metadata-only assembly you want to create. The /nowp (No Wrapped Proxy) tells SoapSuds to include only the metadata instead of generating a wrapped proxy. (Read on for more information about wrapped proxies.) You can also sign the assembly with a strong name, by using the /sn option:

```
SOAPSUDS /ia:remotecomponents /oa:metadata.dll /nowp /sn:mykeyfile.snk
```

If you explore the new metadata.dll assembly with ILDASM, you'll see that it contains all the classes and methods in RemoteComponents.dll, but method bodies contain only a minimum amount of code. For all practical purposes, the proxy.dll exposes only metadata.

Open the client application with Visual Studio .NET, remove the reference to Remote-Components.dll, and add a reference to the new metadata.dll. Because the old and the new assembly expose classes with the same name (including the namespace) and the same methods, the client application will recompile flawlessly.

What happens when you run the program, however, depends on whether the client application registers the remote object programmatically or by means of a configuration file. If you register the remote type programmatically, you don't have to change anything in the client application to have it work with the remote object. In this case, in fact, the client contains a block of code like this:

```
Dim url As String = "tcp://localhost:50000/calculator.rem"
RemotingConfiguration.RegisterWellKnownClientType(GetType(Calculator), url)
:
Dim calc As New Calculator
```

The Calculator class is now the one defined in metadata.dll; therefore, the type passed to the RegisterWellKnownClientType method and the type passed to the New keyword match perfectly.

If the client application registers the object via a configuration file, you must adjust the identity of the assembly containing the type that is to be requested to the remote server. For example, if the configuration file is

```
<client>
  <wellknown type="RemoteComponents.Calculator, RemoteComponents"
    url="tcp://localhost:50000/Calculator.rem" />
</client>
```

you must edit it as follows to have it work with the SoapSuds-generated assembly:

```
<client>
  <wellknown type="RemoteComponents.Calculator, Metadata"
    url="tcp://localhost:50000/Calculator.rem" />
</client>
```

After this edit, the client application will work correctly.

Generating Metadata from a Running Server

When you expose a remote object through an HTTP channel, the .NET remoting architecture can intercept requests at the object's URL and react accordingly. If you append *?WSDL* to the object's URL, the .NET Framework responds by sending you a block of XML text that defines the object. You can prove this easily by launching Internet Explorer and typing this URL in its Address field (after starting the host application if necessary):

```
http://localhost:50000/Calculator.rem?wsdl
```

The XML text returned to the browser is in the same format as the WSDL document that Web services expose. (See Figure 32-7.) The SoapSuds utility can use this WSDL document to generate a metadata-only assembly from a type that is exposed by a remote server, even if you don't have the original compiled DLL at hand. This feature is especially useful if you expose a remote object on your Internet Web site and want to give remote clients the ability to use it.

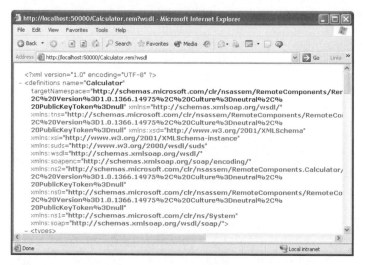

Figure 32-7   The WSDL contract that describes the metadata of a remote object

When using SoapSuds to generate the metadata for a remote assembly, you specify the /url option instead of the /ia option:

```
SOAPSUDS /url:http://localhost:50000/Calculator.rem?wsdl /oa:metadata.dll /nowp
```

Check the .NET Framework documentation for more information about other options you can use with SoapSuds—for example, the /domain, /username, and /password options that are necessary when accessing a server that requires authentication, or the /httpproxyname and /httpproxyport options that you must use when accessing a remote system through a proxy server.

Generating a Wrapped Proxy

The two examples illustrated in the previous sections used the /nowp option to tell SoapSuds not to generate a *wrapped proxy*. A wrapped proxy is a local class that the client application can use in lieu of the remote class, because all its methods and properties automatically dispatch the call to the remote object. Here's how you can generate a wrapped proxy for an object at a given URL:

```
SOAPSUDS /url:http://localhost:50000/Calculator.rem?wsdl /oa:wrappedproxy.dll
```

If you now remove the reference to the metadata.dll and add a reference to the wrappedproxy.dll, your client application can work with the remote object *exactly* as if the object were defined locally. A client application that uses a wrapped proxy doesn't even need to register the object as remote.

You're probably wondering why you can't use SoapSuds-generated proxy assemblies in all cases and get rid of all the intricacies related to object registration. The answer to this question is twofold: performance and flexibility. A proxy wrapper, in fact, can be used only if the remote object is reachable through SOAP over an HTTP channel, and so you can't use the more efficient binary formatter (not to mention the TCP channel). A wrapped proxy is also less flexible, because the URL of the remote object is burned into the proxy assembly. You must regenerate the wrapped proxy and redeploy it on all your clients if you want to move the remote object to another server.

In spite of these severe limitations, the ability to generate wrapped proxies is a great bonus in the prototyping phase and for the simplest remoting scenarios.

Generating the Source Code

The SoapSuds tool gives you yet another option: the ability to generate the source code of the metadata-only class, rather than generate a compiled assembly. In this case, you specify the /gc (Generate Code) option or the /od (Output Directory) option instead of the /oa option:

```
SOAPSUDS /url:http://localhost:50000/Calculator.rem?wsdl /gc
```

SoapSuds can generate only C# code; therefore, it is of limited use to Microsoft Visual Basic .NET developers. Fortunately, even if you aren't a C# wizard, translating the source code to Visual Basic .NET is a simple process that doesn't take too long, unless the assembly contains a lot of classes and methods. For example, this is a Visual Basic .NET class that I obtained by converting the C# source code produced by the previous command:

```
' IMPORTANT: all the attributes in this listing must be typed on one line.

Imports System.Runtime.Remoting.Messaging
Imports System.Runtime.Remoting.Metadata
Imports System.Runtime.Remoting.Metadata.W3cXsd2001

<SoapType(XmlNamespace:= "http://schemas.microsoft.com/clr/nsassem/RemoteComponents/
RemoteComponents%2C%20Version%3D1.0.0.0%2C%20Culture%3Dneutral%2C%20PublicKeyToken%3Dn
ull", XmlTypeNamespace:= "http://schemas.microsoft.com/clr/nsassem/RemoteComponents/
RemoteComponents%2C%20Version%3D1.0.0.0%2C%20Culture%3Dneutral%2C%20PublicKeyToken%3Dn
ull")> _
Public Class Calculator
    Inherits System.Runtime.Remoting.Services.RemotingClientProxy

    Public Sub New()
        MyBase.ConfigureProxy(Me.GetType(), "http://localhost:50000/Calculator.rem")
    End Sub

    Public ReadOnly Property RemotingReference() As Object
        Get
            Return (_tp)
```

```
            End Get
    End Property

    <SoapMethod(SoapAction:= "http://schemas.microsoft.com/clr/nsassem/RemoteCompo-
nents.Calculator/RemoteComponents#InitializeLifetimeService")> _
    Public Overrides Function InitializeLifetimeService() As Object
            Return DirectCast(_tp, Calculator).InitializeLifetimeService()
    End Function

    <SoapMethod(SoapAction:= "http://schemas.microsoft.com/clr/nsassem/RemoteCompo-
nents.Calculator/RemoteComponents#Add")> _
    Public Function Add(ByVal n1 As Double, ByVal n2 As Double) As Double
            Return DirectCast(_tp, Calculator).Add(n1, n2)
    End Function

    <SoapMethod(SoapAction:= "http://schemas.microsoft.com/clr/nsassem/RemoteCompo-
nents.Calculator/RemoteComponents#GetProcessID")> _
    Public Function GetProcessID() As String
            Return DirectCast(_tp, Calculator).GetProcessID()
    End Function
End Class
```

The values assigned to the XmlNamespace and XmlTypeNamespace attributes of the SoapType attribute associated with the class might be puzzling at first, until you realize that they are just the URL-encoded strings that define the complete name of the remote object:

```
http://schemas.microsoft.com/clr/nsassem/RemoteComponents/
RemoteComponents, Version=1.0.0.0, Culture=neutral, PublicKeyToken=null
```

All methods are marked with a SoapMethod attribute and delegate the execution to _tp, a protected field that they inherit from the RemotingClientProxy base class. Once you understand the rationale behind this code, you can create your proxy class quite easily.

The main advantage of translating the wrapped proxy to Visual Basic .NET source code is the ability to get rid of the external metadata DLL and include the class in your project.

Regardless of whether it is compiled inside the client application or deployed as separate DLL, you need to recompile a wrapped proxy if the URL of the remote object changes, because the URL is used as an argument of the SoapMethod attribute and therefore must be a constant string.

Using Shared Interfaces

Many developers don't recommend using SoapSuds for generating metadata assemblies for two reasons. First, the SoapSuds utility has a few problems with methods that take or return complex objects, such as a typed DataSet. Second, many seasoned developers don't like the *location transparency* feature of the .NET remoting architecture—that is, the ability to make a remote object appear as if it were local—and prefer to make the source code access the remote object explicitly. In this section, I'll explain how you can use shared interfaces to avoid the deployment of a SoapSuds-generated metadata-only assembly.

Shared Interfaces with SAOs

The idea behind the shared interface technique is quite simple, and I'll show how to apply it to our Calculator example. You define an interface—say, ICalculator—that defines all the methods that should be exposed to remote clients:

```
' (In the RemoteInterfaces project.)
Public Interface ICalculator
    Function Add(ByVal n1 As Double, ByVal n2 As Double) As Double
    Function GetProcessID() As String
End Interface
```

This interface must reside in a separate assembly, RemoteInterfaces, which you compile to a DLL named RemoteInterfaces.dll.

Next switch to the RemoteComponents project, add a reference to the RemoteInterfaces.dll, and extend the Calculator class so that it implements the ICalculator interface. You don't need to create new procedures, because you can simply append an Implements keyword to existing methods:

```
Public Class Calculator
    Inherits MarshalByRefObject
    Implements RemoteInterfaces.ICalculator

    ' Return the sum of two numbers.
    Function Add(ByVal n1 As Double, ByVal n2 As Double) As Double _
        Implements RemoteInterfaces.ICalculator.Add
        Add = n1 + n2
    End Function

    ' Return information about the process that hosts this object.
    Function GetProcessID() As String _
        Implements RemoteInterfaces.ICalculator.GetProcessID
        Return String.Format("Process #{0} on {1}", _
            Process.GetCurrentProcess.Id, Environment.MachineName)
    End Function
End Class
```

Next open the client project, delete the reference to the RemoteComponents.dll or metadata.dll assembly, and add a reference to the RemoteInterfaces.dll. After this change, the client application can no longer use the New keyword to instantiate a Calculator object. Instead it must use an Activator.GetObject method and cast the result to an ICalculator variable:

```
' This code assumes that the remote object is exposed as an SAO.
Dim url As String = "tcp://localhost:50000/calculator.rem"
Dim calc As ICalculator = _
    DirectCast(Activator.GetObject(GetType(ICalculator), url), ICalculator)
```

```
' Use the remote calculator.
Dim result As Double = calc.Add(10, 20)
```

Because the ICalculator interface exposes exactly the same methods as the original Calculator class, you don't have to modify the source code of the client application anywhere else. As you learned in the section "Registering a Singleton Server-Activated Object," the Activator.GetObject method doesn't require that the remote object be registered—either by code or via configuration files—so the structure of the client application is simpler.

The most serious drawbacks of the deployment technique based on shared interfaces are that it works only with SAOs and that the client application can't pass the interface reference to programs running in other AppDomains. You can't do much to solve the latter problem, but at least I can show you a way to work around the former issue.

Shared Interfaces and Factory Classes for CAOs

You learned in the section "Registering a Client-Activated Object" that you can create a remote CAO with the Activator.CreateInstance method without having to register it. The Type object you pass to the first argument of CreateInstance must be an MBR, so this argument can't be an interface reference. This limitation means that we can't directly apply the shared interface technique to CAOs. Fortunately, you can work around this limitation using an approach based on *factory methods*.

The idea is simple: you define an SAO that works as a factory for your CAOs. The client application can create CAO instances by calling a method in the SAO. This technique works well because all objects returned by remote methods are marshaled to the client as CAOs.

The server-activated factory class might expose one public method for each exposed CAO—for example, CreateCalculator, CreateInvoice, and so on—or it might expose a generic CreateInstance method that takes the name of the object to be created as an argument. In this section, I'll focus on the latter, more generic approach.

To further refine the concept, the client should access the CreateInstance method through an interface, so let's define the IRemoteFactory interface, which exposes only one method:

```
' (In the RemoteInterfaces project.)
Public Interface IRemoteFactory
    Function CreateInstance(ByVal assemblyName As String, _
        ByVal typeName As String) As Object
End Interface
```

This interface goes in the RemoteInterfaces.dll assembly, because it must be accessible to client applications.

Next switch to the host ServerApp project, add a reference to the RemoteInterfaces.dll assembly, and type the code for the RemoteFactory class. This factory class must be an

MBR class because it is accessed remotely as a singleton SAO, and its CreateInstance method is just a wrapper for the Activator.CreateInstance method.

```
' (In the ServerApp host application.)
Public Class RemoteFactory
    Inherits MarshalByRefObject
    Implements RemoteInterfaces.IRemoteFactory

    ' This object will live forever.
    Public Overrides Function InitializeLifetimeService() As Object
        Return Nothing
    End Function

    ' A wrapper for Activator.CreateInstance method
    Function CreateInstance(ByVal assemblyName As String, ByVal typeName As String) _
        As Object Implements RemoteInterfaces.IRemoteFactory.CreateInstance
        ' Unwrap the return value to return the real object, not the wrapper.
        Return Activator.CreateInstance(assemblyName, typeName).Unwrap
    End Function
End Class
```

The client application must register the RemoteFactory class as a remote object. It can perform the registration programmatically, as in this code:

```
RemotingConfiguration.RegisterWellKnownServiceType(GetType(RemoteFactory), _
    "RemoteFactory.rem", WellKnownObjectMode.Singleton)
```

Or the client can register the RemoteFactory class in the configuration file:

```
<service>
  <wellknown type="ServerApp.RemoteFactory, ServerApp"
    mode="Singleton" objectUri="RemoteFactory.rem" />
</service>
```

Here's the code that runs on the client and uses the RemoteFactory class to create remote objects:

```
' (In the client application.)
' Get a reference to the remote factory class.
'    (You can cache this reference for future calls.)
Dim url As String = "tcp://localhost:50000/RemoteFactory.rem"
Dim factory As IRemoteFactory = DirectCast(Activator.GetObject( _
    GetType(IRemoteFactory), url), IRemoteFactory)
' Create an instance of the remote Calculator as a CAO, cast to known interface.
Dim calc As ICalculator = DirectCast(factory.CreateInstance( _
    "RemoteComponents", "RemoteComponents.Calculator"), ICalculator)
' Use it.
Dim result As Double = calc.Add(10, 20)
```

You can easily extend the factory pattern to support constructors with arguments. Here's a better version of the IRemoteFactory interface with an overload of the CreateInstance method that takes one or more arguments to be passed to the constructor:

```
Public Interface IRemoteFactory
    Function CreateInstance(ByVal assemblyName As String, _
        ByVal typeName As String) As Object
    Function CreateInstance(ByVal assemblyName As String, _
        ByVal typeName As String, ByVal ParamArray args() As Object) As Object
End Interface
```

The RemoteFactory class implements the new method as follows:

```
Function CreateInstance(ByVal assemblyName As String, ByVal typeName As String, _
    ByVal ParamArray args() As Object) As Object _
    Implements RemoteInterfaces.IRemoteFactory.CreateInstance

    ' Load the assembly with given name
    Dim asm As [Assembly] = [Assembly].Load(assemblyName)
    ' Load the type, in case-insensitive mode.
    Dim ty As Type = asm.GetType(typeName, True, True)
    ' Call the constructor and pass all the arguments.
    Return ty.InvokeMember("", BindingFlags.CreateInstance, Nothing, Nothing, _
        args)
End Function
```

Here's how the client can use the overloaded version of the CreateInstance method to pass a couple of arguments to the constructor of the remote class:

```
Dim calc As ICalculator = DirectCast(factory.CreateInstance( _
    "RemoteComponents", "RemoteComponents.Calculator", 10, 20), ICalculator)
```

Using Shared Base Classes

The third technique for deploying metadata to clients without giving them the real assembly is actually a variation of the technique based on shared interfaces. Instead of having the remote class implement an interface, you derive it from a base abstract class that is defined in a separate DLL. Because all remotable classes must inherit from MarshalByRefObject, this base class should also inherit from MarshalByRefObject. Here's an example of such a base class:

```
' (In the RemoteInterfaces project.)
Public MustInherit Class CalculatorBase
        Inherits MarshalByRefObject
    MustOverride Function Add(ByVal n1 As Double, ByVal n2 As Double) As Double
    MustOverride Function GetProcessID() As String
End Class
```

You should slightly modify the source code of the Calculator class to have it inherit from CalculatorBase instead of MarshalByRefObject. The client application must use the Activator.GetObject method to instantiate an instance of the Calculator object and then cast the object reference to a variable of type CalculatorBase (instead of type ICalculator, as we did in the previous section). I leave these minor edits to you as an exercise.

The main advantage of the technique based on shared base classes is that the client now has a reference to an MBR object and can marshal it to applications living in other AppDomains.

Hosting Remote Objects

I've already explained that console applications rarely work well as hosts in real-world scenarios, because you typically want to make remotable objects available as soon as the server machine completes the bootstrap sequence, without having an interactive user to log in and manually run the host application.

The .NET Framework gives you two useful options for hosting remotable objects: Windows NT services and Internet Information Services.

Hosting Using a Windows NT Service

I covered the creation of Windows NT services quite extensively in Chapter 20, and I won't repeat myself here. In practice, the only thing you need to do to employ a Windows NT service as a host is to register remote objects in the OnStart protected method, either programmatically or by means of a configuration file:

```
Protected Overrides Sub OnStart(ByVal args() As String)
    RemoteConfiguration.Configure("myservice.exe.config")
End Sub
```

You can add flexibility to this solution by passing arguments to the service from the Services MMC snap-in. The service can retrieve such values in the args array passed to the OnStart method.

With Windows NT services out of the way, we can now focus on using IIS as a host for remotable objects.

Hosting Using Internet Information Services

Using IIS to host your remotable objects is really the simplest solution. In fact, this kind of hosting complies with XCOPY deployment: you can install a .NET remoting solution by simply copying a directory tree from your system to the end user's machine. In addition, all the traffic with clients occurs on port 80 (the default port used by HTTP), and so you rarely need to configure your firewall when you expose remote objects through IIS.

The IIS solution is also very flexible, as you can change a setting in the configuration file and the new values will be applied immediately, without the need to restart the IIS application. (You must use a FileSystemWatcher component to achieve the same behavior when you use a Windows NT service as a host.)

Hosting inside IIS gives you another important benefit: security. You can use Basic authentication and Integrated Windows authentication, and you can even encrypt data flowing to and from clients by using an HTTPS channel.

The only serious drawback of IIS as a host for your remotable object is performance. IIS supports only the HTTP channel and prevents you from using the more efficient TCP channel. You can mitigate this problem by adopting a binary formatter, however, but you can't go as fast as a plain TCP channel (which uses the binary formatter by default).

Modifying Existing Solutions to Work with IIS

In most cases, you don't need to change the source code of your remote class to expose it through IIS instead of a console-based or a Windows NT service–based host. There are, however, several differences in how you register the object as well as a few limitations on the configuration values you can use with remote objects hosted in IIS. Here's a short list of the most important differences to account for:

- The host program is neither necessary nor allowed, because IIS itself works as the host. For example, you can't publish a specific instance of a singleton object with the RemotingServices.Marshal method.

- Server-side objects can be registered only by means of a configuration file, because no custom host program can register the objects programmatically. As I mentioned in the previous section, you can change registration settings and other configuration values by simply saving a new version of the configuration file, without having to stop and restart the IIS application. (There is an exception to this rule, as noted after the last item of this list.)

- The objectUri attribute used for SAOs can have only a .rem or .soap extension because these are the only extensions that IIS maps to the .NET remoting infrastructure.

- Only the HTTP channel can be used. As I explained previously, you can use a binary formatter instead of the default SOAP formatter for increased performance.

- You can't specify the port used for the server-side HTTP channel, because it would interfere with IIS settings. This also affects the URL used by clients to reach SAOs.

- You can't specify the name attribute for the <application> tag in the configuration file. The name of the application is automatically set equal to the name of the virtual directory where the object resides.

- All the considerations on the lifetime of remote objects apply when the object is hosted in IIS. In addition, ASP.NET processes can be recycled, so you might need to take this factor into account, especially if you work with CAOs.

Because the ASP.NET infrastructure intercepts the very first call to the remote object, you can also use the Application_Start event handler in Global.asax to run any initialization code. You can use this approach to register a configuration file with a name other than Web.config or register your server-side remotable objects programmatically.

Configuring IIS for Hosting

Let's review the simple steps for hosting the RemoteComponents.dll assembly in IIS and letting remote clients access the objects that this assembly exposes:

1. Create an appropriate configuration file for the remote objects, and save it as Web.config in a directory of your local hard disk. (IIS configuration files must have this name.) Remember that you can specify an HTTP channel but omit the port number, and you must not specify an application name.

2. Create a directory named bin as a subdirectory of the directory that contains the Web.config file; save the RemoteComponents.dll into this bin directory. Alternatively, you can sign the assembly with a strong name and register it in the GAC. (If you do so, remember that the configuration file should refer to the assembly using its complete name, including version, culture, and publisher key.)

3. Right-click on the folder that contains the Web.config file, choose the Sharing And Security command, switch to the Web Sharing tab, and select the Share This Folder option to create an IIS virtual directory that maps to this folder. (See Figure 32-8.) Alternatively, you can create the virtual directory from inside the IIS MMC snap-in, by right-clicking the Default Web Site element and choosing the Virtual Directory command from the New submenu.

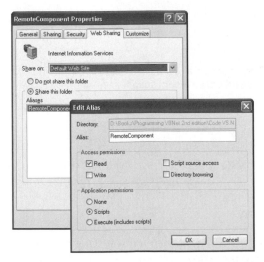

Figure 32-8   Creating an IIS virtual directory that hosts the Web.config configuration file

4. Locate the new virtual directory in the IIS MMC snap-in, right-click on it to display the Properties window, switch to the Directory Security tab, and click the Edit button in the Authentication And Access Control area. This action displays the Authentication Methods dialog box, where you should verify that the Enable Anonymous Access check box is selected. (See Figure 32-9.)

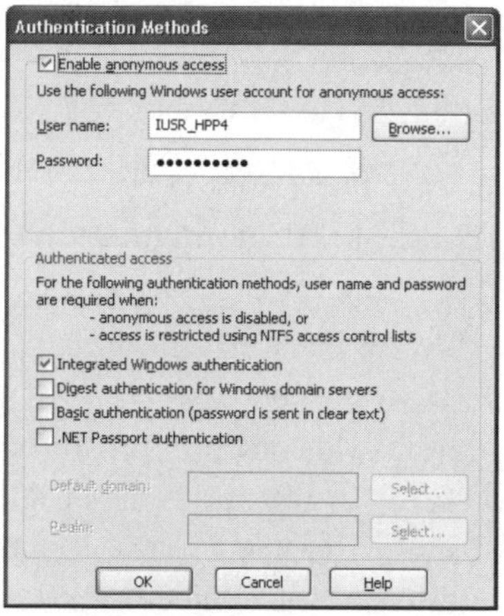

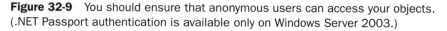

Figure 32-9   You should ensure that anonymous users can access your objects. (.NET Passport authentication is available only on Windows Server 2003.)

Here's an example of a Web.config file that you can deploy together with the Remote-Component.dll assembly. I have used the .soap extension for the objectUri attribute of the <wellKnown> tag, which emphasizes the fact that the object will be serialized via SOAP. (You can use the .rem extension without any problem, however.)

```
<configuration>
  <system.runtime.remoting>
    <application>
      <service>
        <wellknown type="RemoteComponents.Calculator, RemoteComponents"
          mode="Singleton" objectUri="Calculator.soap" />
      </service>
    </application>
  </system.runtime.remoting>
</configuration>
```

Notice also that you can drop the <channels> section entirely, unless you need to specify a binary formatter or some other custom attribute for the HTTP default channel.

Configuring the Client Application

Very few changes are necessary in the client application to let it use a remote object hosted in IIS. In practice, assuming that the application is already configured to use the HTTP channel, the only significant change is in the URL that references the remote object. The new URL doesn't specify the port number, but it must include the name of the virtual directory that you've created for the object. Here's an example of the configuration file that the client can use to reach the object exposed with the Web.config file listed in the previous section:

```
<configuration>
  <system.runtime.remoting>
    <application>
      <client>
        <wellknown type="RemoteComponents.Calculator, RemoteComponents"
          url="http://localhost/RemoteComponent/Calculator.soap" />
      </client>
    </application>
  </system.runtime.remoting>
</configuration>
```

Implementing Security

I've mentioned that IIS offers built-in security, in the form of one of the authentication mechanisms shown in Figure 32-9. (As you might remember from previous sections, you had to *disable* IIS security and accept requests from anonymous clients.) In this section, I'll show you how you can take advantage of the most common authentication mechanisms that IIS provides: Basic authentication and Integrated Windows authentication.

Enabling Integrated Windows authentication is actually quite simple, so I'll start with that. Go back to the IIS dialog box shown in Figure 32-9 and verify that only the Integrated Windows Authentication check box is selected. If you now rerun the client, you'll see that an exception occurs. If the client machine is in the same domain or in a trusted domain, you can authenticate the client application by just adding the useDefaultCredentials attribute to the <channel> tag in the client's configuration file:

```
<!-- In the client configuration file -->
<channels>
  <channel ref="http" useDefaultCredentials="true" />
</channels>
```

If the client resides outside your domain (which is the case when your objects can be reached from the Internet), you can't use Integrated Windows authentication exclusively and must enable Basic authentication. Let's see how the client application can pass its credentials to the server:

```
' Create an SAO object.
Dim calc As New Calculator
' Specify username and password in the channel properties.
Dim props As IDictionary = ChannelServices.GetChannelSinkProperties(calc)
props("username") = "myusername"
props("password") = "mypassword"
' Use the object as usual.
Dim result As Double = calc.Add(10, 20)
```

Another thing you can do with IIS is use an encrypted HTTPS channel. This requires that you install a certificate on the server, as you would do to protect your Web site. Read the .NET Framework documentation for more information.

Space constraints prevent me from describing advanced remoting techniques, such as asynchronous method invocation, events, custom formatters, and sinks. Suffice it to say that you can replace virtually every object in the .NET remoting architecture with your own custom classes and implement, for example, encrypted and compressed channels.

Another reason for not covering remoting in too much detail is because Microsoft is going to abandon remoting in favor of the Web services infrastructure in the next version of the .NET Framework, with the clear purpose of focusing its efforts on a single object remoting technology. For this reason, weigh your options very carefully when deciding about the remoting technology to use in your applications.

An important aspect of all enterprise-level applications is security. Most developers love to forget about security until the application is about to go to production. Implementing security in code is a notoriously tedious and difficult task. The .NET Framework doesn't make writing security code more fun, but at least it surely makes it easier, as you'll learn in the next chapter.

33 Security

As you remember from Chapter 1, the .NET Framework was built with security in mind. It implements a security model that integrates with Windows security and addresses the new types of security attacks that operating-system designers never had to worry about in the pre-Internet era. The portion of the .NET Framework that implements this new security model is called *Code Access Security*, or CAS for short.

> **Note** To keep the code as concise as possible, all the code samples in this section assume the use of the following Imports statements at the file or project level:
>
> ```
> Imports System.Security
> Imports System.Security.Permissions
> Imports System.Security.Policy
> Imports System.Security.Principal
> Imports System.Security.Cryptography
> Imports System.Reflection
> Imports System.Threading
> Imports System.IO
> ```

Basic .NET Code Access Security Concepts

As a developer and user, the odds are that you're already familiar with fundamental security concepts such as authentication, authorization, and Access Control Lists (ACLs). So I'll take these concepts for granted and focus exclusively on what .NET adds to the picture.

Looking at CAS in Action

For an example that illustrates what .NET security is all about, compile this simple console application to an executable file on your local disk:

```
Sub Main()
    Console.Write("Username: {0}", Environment.UserName)
End Sub
```

Open a command prompt window and run the application to check that it correctly displays the name of the current user. Next, copy the executable to a network share on your LAN and attempt to run it. Instead of the expected result, you get an exception, as shown in Figure 33-1.

Figure 33-1   By default, an application that resides on a remote disk can't access local environment variables.

What happened? The demo application internally reads an environment variable to return the current user's name, but this operation triggers a SecurityException if the code has been loaded from a location other than a local disk. It's worth noting that choosing a different location for the executable didn't change the Windows account under which the application runs because in each case it's the current user's account. What does change is that the .NET runtime detects that the assembly was launched from a location that's potentially insecure, and consequently the .NET runtime applies a different security policy.

This introductory description highlights an important difference between "traditional" Windows security and the new .NET Code Access Security. The former is mainly concerned with protecting the system from untrusted and potentially malicious users. It supports authentication and uses ACLs to protect vital resources. It doesn't, however, prevent legitimate users from unwittingly compromising the system by running unknown and potentially dangerous code.

.NET CAS deals with code privileges rather than user privileges—for example, managed code loaded from the Internet has restricted permissions and isn't able to harm your system, even if you are the machine's administrator and the code runs under your identity.

As a .NET developer, you need to be familiar with the basic concepts of CAS in order to resolve situations where .NET security will prevent your code from working correctly—for example, when it has been loaded from the Internet. Component authors must be prepared to deal with potentially harmful client applications attempting to use their components to perform operations that would be otherwise prohibited.

CAS is based on several concepts, and at first it is difficult to understand how they fit together. The best way to get started is to define some of the terms you're going to meet frequently in this chapter. Instead of describing these concepts in a purely abstract way, I'll show how they map to the elements of the .NET Configuration tool, which you reach from the Administrative Tools menu. (See Figure 33-2.)

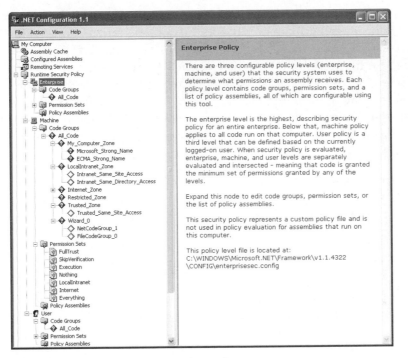

Figure 33-2 The .NET Configuration tool

Policy Levels

Security policy is divided into four levels: Enterprise, Machine, User, and AppDomain. In this section, I'll focus on the first three levels, the ones that are configurable via configuration files or interactively with the .NET Configuration tool.

The most commonly used policy level is Machine, which dictates which security rules are enforced for all the assemblies running on the local machine. An example of such a security rule is "Code downloaded from the Internet cannot execute on this machine." Different rules can be enforced for all the computers in the enterprise or for a specific user by using the Enterprise policy level and the User policy level, respectively.

An assembly is allowed to perform a specific operation—for example, write a file on the C:\ directory—only if the operation is allowed by all policy levels. In other words, the .NET runtime uses the most restrictive policy level among those defined for the Enterprise, Machine, User, and AppDomain levels. In its default configuration, however, the Enterprise and User policy levels give full trust to all assemblies (including those run from the Internet); thus, in practice the Machine policy level dictates which operations can be performed.

The Enterprise and Machine policy levels are stored in configuration files named enterprisesec.config and security.config, respectively, which you can find in the

C:\Windows\Microsoft.NET\Framework\v*x.y.zzzz*\config folder. The User policy level is stored in the security.config file in the C:\Documents and Settings\<*user-name*>\Application Data\Microsoft\CLR Security Config\v*x.y.zzzz* folder. You can easily copy these files to another machine (or another user's directory) either manually or by selecting the Create Deployment Package command from the Runtime Security Policy element's context menu. The .NET Configuration tool gives you an intuitive and simple way to interpret and edit these configuration files, but you can also use the Caspol.exe tool if you like working at the command prompt and using cryptic options.

The AppDomain policy level can be set only programmatically. For example, an App-Domain might set its own policy level so that all the external (and potentially harmful) assemblies that AppDomain loads are prevented from messing with the registry or the file system.

Evidence

All assemblies running in an AppDomain are associated with their *evidence* when they are loaded from disk or from the Internet. *Evidence is* a collection of values that the .NET runtime uses to keep track of the assembly identity and the location it was loaded from. You can further classify evidence as *assembly evidence* and *host evidence.*

Assembly evidence is intrinsic to the compiled assembly and doesn't depend on where the assembly is loaded from; it includes the assembly's strong name, hash, and publisher's Authenticode signature.

Host evidence is assigned by the .NET runtime when the assembly is loaded; this category includes the URL, the site, and the zone. The zone can be My Computer, Local Intranet, Trusted Sites, Internet, or Untrusted Sites; the last four values correspond to the four security zones you can define in Microsoft Internet Explorer. (See Figure 33-3.)

The six standard evidence types correspond to the following classes in the System.Security.Policy namespace: Hash, StrongName, Publisher, Url, Site, and Zone. You'll see how to use them later in this chapter.

> **Note**   The .NET Framework offers two wizards that let you adjust the security policy in a simple way. The Adjust .NET Security wizard changes the security level for each of the five zones an assembly can be loaded from (My Computer, Local Intranet, Internet, Trusted Sites, and Untrusted Sites), both at the machine and the user level. The Trust an Assembly wizard changes the level of trust for a specific assembly (or for all the assemblies with a given publisher public key), both at the machine and the user level. I'll explain these wizards in more detail in Chapter 34.

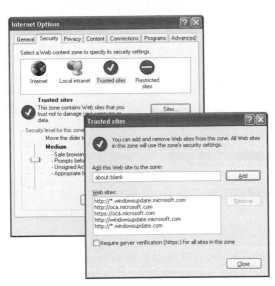

Figure 33-3 Internet Explorer lets you define which sites belong to its security zones.

Permissions

A permission object represents the authorization to use a system resource—for example, the permission to read files in the C:\Temp directory and its subfolders or to use the default printer. The .NET Framework defines several permission classes in the System.Security.Permissions namespace whose names clearly indicate the resource they protect. All CAS-related permission classes derive from the CodeAccessPermission type.

The most important of these classes are FileIOPermission (file system), RegistryPermission (system registry), EnvironmentPermission (environment variables), UIPermission (full access to screen), FileDialogPermission (File Open and File Save common dialog boxes), ReflectionPermission (reflection objects and their methods), and IsolatedStoragePermission (isolated storage, which I cover in Chapter 34). This namespace also contains the SecurityPermission class, which indicates what security features the running code can access and change—for example, the right to run unmanaged code or create an AppDomain.

Other namespaces contain more specific permission classes—for example, System.Diagnostics.LogEventPermission (the event log), System.Diagnostics.PerformanceCounterPermission (performance counters), System.Data.OleDb.OleDbPermission (the OLE DB .NET Data Provider), System.Data.SqlClient.SqlClientPermission (the SQL Server .NET Data Provider), System.Drawing.Printing.PrintingPermission (the printer), and System.Net.SocketPermission (sockets for making or accepting connections).

Each specific permission class exposes its own constructors, properties, and methods. In some cases, these members let you precisely indicate which portion of the system resource can be used, and in what manner. For example, here's how you create a File-IOPermission object that grants the permission to read files in the C:\Temp directory tree:

```
Dim perm As New FileIOPermission(FileIOPermissionAccess.Read, "c:\Temp")
```

Permission classes that map to compound resources such as the file system and the registry expose methods that can precisely determine which portions of the resource are protected:

```
' Create a permission that grants access to two directories.
Dim perm2 As New FileIOPermission(PermissionState.None)
perm2.AddPathList(FileIoPermissionAccess.Read, "c:\templates")
perm2.AddPathList(FileIoPermissionAccess.AllAccess, "c:\temp")
```

Permission Sets

Specifying what each assembly is or isn't allowed to do by means of individual permission objects would be a difficult and error-prone task, so it's preferable to reason in terms of *permission sets*. A permission set is a collection of permission objects. A programmer can manipulate permission sets through instances of the PermissionSet class or the NamedPermissionSet class if the permission set has a name. (Both of these classes are in the System.Security namespace.)

To ease the job of both the developer and the administrator, the .NET Framework defines seven named permission sets. (You can browse them if you expand the Permission Sets node under the Machine element in the .NET Configuration tool.) Here are more details on each of them, from the least restricted to the most restricted:

- **FullTrust**   An assembly that is granted this permission set has no restriction at all and can do absolutely everything. In practice, CAS is disabled on such assemblies. In the default configuration, this permission set is associated with all assemblies running from a local drive.

- **Everything**   This permission set includes all the permissions defined for the .NET Framework, but it doesn't include any custom permission you might have defined. If you haven't defined any custom permission, this permission set is the same as Full Trust. In the default configuration, no assembly is associated with this permission set.

- **SkipVerification**   An assembly associated with this permission set isn't verified by the .NET runtime. (For more details, see the "Code Verification" section in Chapter 1.) This permission is only useful for assemblies written with Managed C++ because Visual Basic .NET and C# always generate fully verifiable assemblies.

- **LocalIntranet**   In the default configuration, assemblies loaded from your local intranet are associated with this permission set, which grants the permission to create user interface elements and use the printer, but prevents full disk access and type discovery via reflection. An assembly associated with this permission set can only read files in the directory it was loaded from or access the Web site it was executed from, and it can use an unlimited amount of isolated storage.

- **Internet**   In the default configuration, assemblies loaded from the Internet, including the Trusted Sites zone but excluding the Untrusted Sites zone, are assigned this permission set. As you might guess, these assemblies have more restricted permissions than those coming from the local intranet. They can use up to 10 KB of isolated storage, access the Web site they were loaded from, and use the Clipboard (but only paste data copied there from the same AppDomain). They can use the printer only through a restricted printer dialog box, and can't display user interface elements, except for Open File dialog boxes and safe top-level windows. (A safe top-level window is a Windows form whose location, size, and opacity are restricted.)

- **Execution**   This permission set corresponds to the right to execute code. Assemblies associated with this permission set can execute, but they can't access any system resources. This permission set isn't used in the default configuration, but it could be useful—for example, for code libraries that contain only math, string, and financial functions.

- **Nothing**   This permission set is empty and assemblies associated with it are prevented from executing, let alone accessing system resources. At a first glance, a Nothing permission set might seem useless, but it's actually quite handy to explicitly prevent an assembly from being loaded. In the default configuration, assemblies loaded from the Untrusted Sites zone are associated with this permission set.

If you need to be more specific about what an assembly can and can't do, you must create a custom permission set. You can do that in the .NET configuration tool by selecting the New command from the context menu of the Permission Sets element. For example, you might define a permission set named DataReaders that specifies the right to read from C:\Data directory and its subfolders, use the default printer, and display user interface elements. (See Figure 33-4.)

You can also create a PermissionSet object via code, as I'll explain in "The Permission-Set Class" section later in this chapter.

CAS policy often gets in the way when you're running a Visual Studio .NET project loaded from a network drive. In this case, the compiled assembly is granted the LocalIntranet permission set, which prevents it from accessing the file system and discovering type information through reflection. Visual Studio .NET anticipates this problem and displays the warning shown in Figure 33-5. The simple solution is to change the output path in the Project Properties window so that Visual Studio .NET saves the compiled assembly on a local disk.

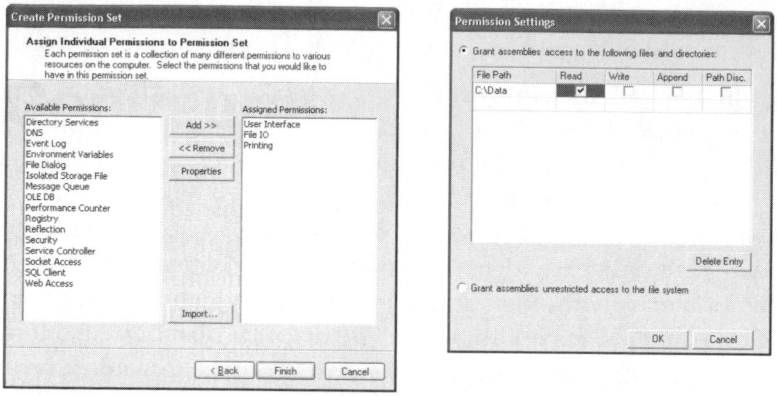

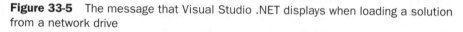

Figure 33-4   The .NET Configuration tool lets you build a permission set that combines one or more permission objects (left) and set the individual properties of each permission object (right).

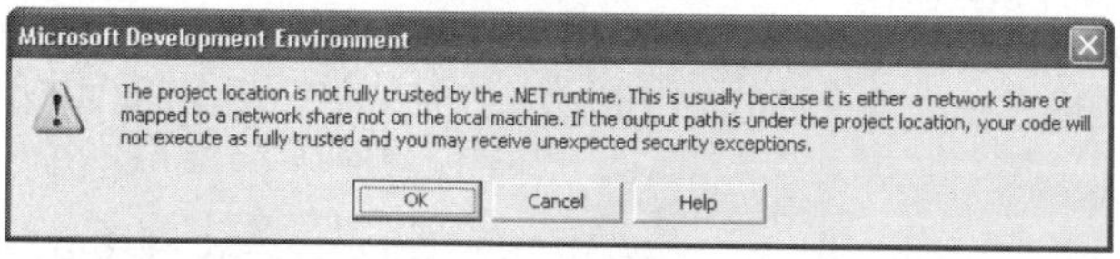

Figure 33-5   The message that Visual Studio .NET displays when loading a solution from a network drive

Code Groups

Each policy level has a tree of code group elements below it. (See the Machine policy level in Figure 33-2.) Each code group is a combination of a group of evidence objects and a permission set. The group of evidence objects determines the *membership condition* for the code group—for example, "All assemblies loaded from the local machine" or "All assemblies loaded from a Microsoft Web site and signed with the publisher's signature."

The permission set determines which operations are allowed for the assemblies in the code group—so, for example, you can define a code group that corresponds to the following security policy: "All assemblies loaded from a Microsoft Web site and signed with the publisher's signature are assigned the DataReaders custom permission set." Therefore, they can read from C:\Data, display user interface elements, and use the default printer.

The code groups immediately below the Enterprise and User policy levels are named All_Code; their membership condition is true for all assemblies and their permission set is FullTrust—therefore, in the default configuration these policy levels don't contribute to limiting what permissions are granted to code. With the Enterprise and User policy levels out of the way, we can focus on the Machine policy level.

The first code group below the Machine policy level is also named All_Code and has a membership condition that is true for all assemblies, but its permission set is Nothing.

This means that an assembly won't be allowed to execute unless it also belongs to another code group with sufficient permissions.

There are six child code groups under the All_Code group, the first five of which correspond to one of the security zones defined for Internet Explorer: My_Computer_Zone, LocalIntranet_Zone, Internet_Zone, Restricted_Zone, and Trusted_Zone. (The sixth code group, Wizard_0, is for use by the .NET Configuration tool only.)

In the default configuration, the My_Computer_Zone group is associated with the Full-Trust permission set; LocalIntranet_Zone is associated with the LocalIntranet permission set; Trusted_Zone and Internet_Zone are associated with the Internet permission set; and the Restricted_Zone is associated with the Nothing permission set. (In other words, assemblies from sites in the Restricted zone aren't allowed to run by default.)

You can organize code groups in a hierarchy to express quite sophisticated membership conditions. For example, let's say you want to associate the DataReaders custom permission set with a strong name assembly named SampleNetComponent when this assembly is downloaded from the Internet. You already have a code group that matches the condition "any assembly loaded from the Internet," so it makes sense to create a new code group as a child of the Internet_Zone code group.

Right-click on the Internet_Zone group and select New to start the Create Code Group wizard. On the first page, enter a name for the code group—for example, Data_Reader—and a short description. On the second page you can set all the membership conditions for this group. In this specific case, you specify the strong name an assembly must have to be part of this code group, as shown in the left portion of Figure 33-6. (The easiest way to fill the Public Key field is clicking on the Import button and point to an existing DLL.) In the third and last page, you select which permission set is assigned to assemblies in this code group (DataReaders, in this case).

The list in the combo box shown in the right portion of Figure 33-6 matches the list of permission sets defined for the current policy level (Machine, in this case). You can't assign the custom DataReaders permission set to a code group at the Enterprise or User level unless you copy the DataReaders permission set under another policy level. (You can copy and paste or just drag the element while you press the Ctrl key, as you'd do in Windows Explorer.)

The hierarchical nature of the policy level requires that the membership condition of a nested code group *narrows* the membership condition of its parent code group, rather than making it less restrictive. For example, the Data_Readers code group is a child of the Internet_Zone code group and therefore inherits the Zone = Internet membership condition from its parent code group. If you accidentally change the Zone condition to Local Intranet, the policy manager will ignore the new Data_Readers code group because it never will be reached when comparing assembly evidence with the membership conditions of the hierarchy under the All_Code element.

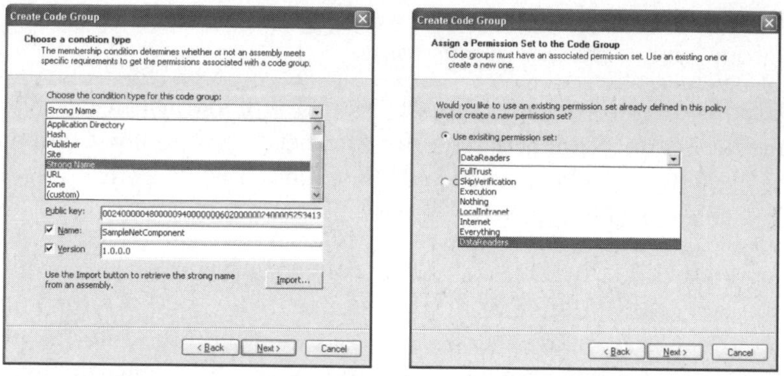

Figure 33-6   You can set the membership condition of a new code group (left) and associate all the assemblies in this group with a given permission set among those defined for the current policy level (right).

Custom Code Groups

There are code groups whose membership or permission set can't be established in terms of standard evidence and standard permission objects. For example, assemblies running from a directory on the local intranet should be allowed to read files from that directory, but this condition can't be expressed with a standard FileIOPermission object because the path would be different for each assembly. Likewise, it looks impossible to grant the right to connect back to the Web site the assembly was loaded from (but not to other Web sites). In cases like these, you can only use a *custom code group* class.

A custom code group is a class that you define in a strong name assembly installed in the GAC. You then inform the .NET policy manager that your custom code group is part of the policy level hierarchy by creating a piece of XML text and importing that text in the correct position of the code group hierarchy. Figure 33-7 clearly shows that the property window of a custom code group has no Membership Condition or Permission Set tabs because this information is defined via code. Read the MSDN documentation for more information about creating a custom code group.

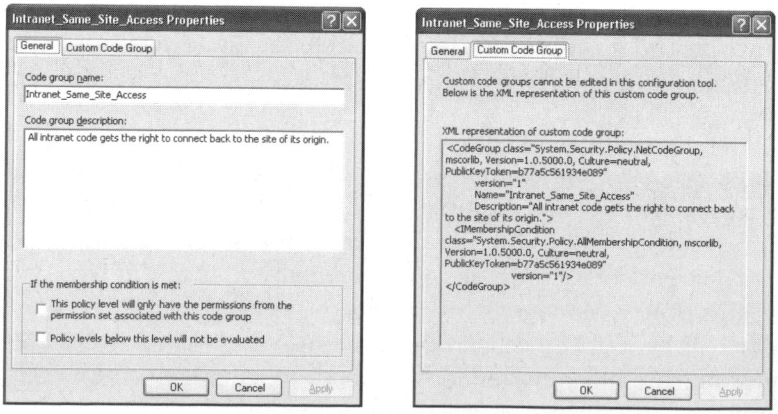

Figure 33-7   The property window of the Intranet_Same_Site_Access code group

Code Group Options

By default, the .NET runtime visits all the sublevels of a policy level when the membership condition is true. For example, if the assembly comes from the MyComputer zone and has the Microsoft strong name, the runtime first searches the My_Computer_Zone group and then continues into the Microsoft_Strong_Name group. (See Figure 33-2.) You can avoid this recursive search by telling the policy manager that policy levels below a given policy level should be ignored when searching a membership condition that matches the assembly in question. This option is named *flag level final* and corresponds to the bottommost check box in the General tab of a code group's Properties window. (See Figure 33-7.)

None of the scenarios illustrated so far consider the case when an assembly belongs to two or more code groups at the same level in the hierarchy. For example, say that you define the following code group structure under the Machine policy level:

```
All_Code
    ⋮
    Internet_Zone
        Microsoft_Strong_Name    (assemblies signed by Microsoft)
        VB2TheMax_Site           (assemblies downloaded from www.vb2themax.com)
    ⋮
```

For illustration purposes, let's say that assemblies in the Microsoft_Strong_Name group can read files and that assemblies in the VB2TheMax_Site group can access the registry. What happens to an assembly signed by Microsoft and downloaded from the www.vb2themax.com Web site? By default, the .NET runtime grants the assembly the union of the permissions granted by all the individual code groups the assembly belongs to, and in most cases this is what you want. (In this example, a strong name Microsoft assembly downloaded from the VB2TheMax site would be granted permission to both read files and access the registry.) However, you can override this default behavior and force the .NET runtime to associate the assembly with only one code group. This option is termed *flag exclusive*. You enforce it by selecting the topmost check box in the General tab of the property window of that code group. In this specific example, you should select this check box in the property window for the Microsoft_Strong_Name code group if strong name Microsoft assemblies should be granted permission to read files *only*, even if they are downloaded from the VB2TheMax site (or, more in general, if they satisfy the membership condition of other code groups).

Stack Walks

Now that you have a better idea of code groups, permissions, and permission sets, it is easy to understand how the CAS mechanism works.

The .NET runtime uses the assembly evidence to assign the assembly to a code group, which in turn lets the runtime discover the set of permissions associated with the assembly itself. This process occurs both when you launch a stand-alone executable (for example, a Windows Forms application) and when a running application loads an assembly, either implicitly by accessing one of the types defined in the assembly or explicitly via reflection (for example, by means of the Assembly.LoadFrom method).

If the permission set associated with the assembly doesn't include at least the Execute permission set, the .NET runtime refuses to load the assembly. Otherwise, the CAS subsystem quietly waits until the code in the assembly attempts to access one of the system resources that require permission. What happens at this point, however, is a bit more complicated than you might expect.

When the current assembly attempts to create an object or invoke a method that is protected by CAS—for example, one of the objects that interact with the registry or the file system—the .NET runtime triggers a stack walk and visits all the assemblies in the call stack. (See Figure 33-8.) The .NET runtime grants the permission to complete the operation only if all the assemblies in the stack have the necessary permission. As soon as the .NET runtime finds one caller that doesn't have the permission being demanded, the stack walk is interrupted and the operation fails with a security exception.

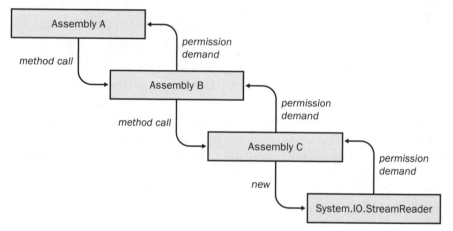

Figure 33-8   The stack walk

The stack walk mechanism is what makes CAS extremely secure and often transparent for the developer. For example, say you're writing a library of functions that manipulate files. Thanks to the stack walk mechanism you can confidently deploy the assembly on your system without any risk to your valuable files because your file library can be used only by assemblies that have the right to access the file system anyway. If any assembly in the call chain lacks the FileIOPermission permission, the .NET runtime throws an exception.

On the downside, stack walks add a noticeable overhead to many common operations, such as writing files or opening database connections. The more callers in the stack, the longer such operations take. In the remainder of this chapter, I'll present a few techniques for reducing this overhead.

> **Note**   If the code is running in a secondary thread—for example, a thread created with the Thread class or taken from the thread pool—the stack walk includes the callers in the current thread as well as all the callers in the thread that created the current thread. There is one exception to this rule, though. If the secondary thread is launched with the Thread-Pool.UnsafeQueueUserWorkItem shared method, then the stack walk includes only callers in the secondary thread. This technique might speed up your code a little, but it also makes it less secure. Your code needs a SecurityPermission with ControlEvidence and ControlPolicy flags to be allowed to invoke the UnsafeQueueUserWorkItem method.

Partially Trusted Assemblies

You rarely have to care about CAS if you're writing applications and libraries that are loaded from a local drive because these assemblies are fully trusted and are allowed to do virtually anything. On the other hand, security plays an important role when an assembly that isn't fully trusted (for example, an executable launched from a network drive) attempts to access a system resource. These assemblies are also known as *untrusted* or *partially trusted assemblies.*

.NET applications can access a system resource in one of two ways: by calling unmanaged code directly or, more often, by creating a managed object in the .NET Framework that wraps the resource (for example, a FileStream object).

.NET assemblies must have a special permission to call unmanaged code. This special permission corresponds to a SecurityPermission object whose UnamangedCode flag is set. This permission should be granted only to the assemblies you trust completely because an assembly that can call unmanaged code can sidestep CAS and damage your system. Only assemblies that run from the My Computer zone have this permission.

Let's examine the more common case of a .NET assembly that accesses system resources by creating and using an object in the .NET Framework. By default, the CAS subsystem prevents a partially trusted assembly from accessing a strong name assembly stored inside or outside the GAC, unless the strong name assembly is flagged with the AllowPartiallyTrustedCallers attribute. This attribute is defined at the assembly level and takes no arguments:

```
' Add this statement to the AssemblyInfo.vb file.
<Assembly: AllowPartiallyTrustedCallers()>
```

This attribute has no effect if applied to assemblies that lack a strong name and are therefore private to an application (because these assemblies can't be accessed by untrusted code outside the application itself). An application that is launched from a network drive can always access a private assembly that is stored in the application's directory or another subdirectory that is searched by the .NET runtime via probing. (I covered probing in Chapter 13.)

If you're developing an assembly that you intend to install in the GAC, you must decide whether to use the AllowPartiallyTrustedCallers attribute. If you omit it, your library can't be invoked by partially trusted assemblies and you don't have worry about CAS. If you apply the attribute, you're implicitly telling the .NET Framework that you understand that your library might be used by untrusted (and potentially dangerous) code and that you have taken all the necessary precautions to prevent callers from tricking your code into doing anything harmful to your system. (This kind of attack, by the way, is known as a *luring attack.*)

In the remainder of this chapter, you'll learn how to write CAS-aware code that ensures your library can be used safely by partially trusted callers. Also, remember that untrusted applications are still subject to any restrictions enforced by the code group they belong to, because all attempts to use a CAS-protected system resource trigger a stack walk, which will eventually check the permissions associated with the untrusted application.

This is the complete list of the assemblies marked with the AllowPartiallyTrustedCallers attribute in version 1.1 of the .NET Framework:

- Accessibility.dll

- IEExecRemote.dll

- Microsoft.VisualBasic.dll

- Mscorlib.dll

- System.dll

- System.Data.dll

- System.Drawing.dll

- System.Web.dll

- System.Web.Mobile.dll

- System.Web.Services.dll

- System.Web.RegularExpressions.dll

- System.Windows.Forms.dll

- System.Xml.dll

As you see, a few key assemblies are missing from this list, most notably System.Data.dll. This absence means that a partially trusted assembly can't use ADO.NET objects. (The System.Data.dll assembly was flagged with the AllowPartiallyTrustedCallers attribute in version 1.0 of the .NET Framework so you might have to account for this change when migrating your database code to version 1.1.)

Policy Levels in ASP.NET Applications

The policy level applied to an ASP.NET application is determined by a completely different mechanism, which allows Internet Service Providers (ISPs) to run multiple ASP.NET applications on the same machine without interfering with each other or with the system.

The web.config files (at both the application and directory level) and the machine.config file can include a <trust> element that specifies the policy level for the all the ASP.NET applications, a specific application, or a portion of an application:

```
<trust level="Levelname" originUrl="Url"/>
```

Levelname can be Full, High, Medium, Low, or Minimal under .NET Framework 1.1, whereas Url can be any well-formed URL. Each level corresponds to a different .config file stored in the C:\Windows\Microsoft.NET\Framework\v1.1.4322\Config folder. The association between the level name and the .config file is held in the <securityPolicy> element of machine.config:

```
<securityPolicy>
    <trustLevel name="Full" policyFile="internal"/>
    <trustLevel name="High" policyFile="web_hightrust.config"/>
    <trustLevel name="Medium" policyFile="web_mediumtrust.config"/>
    <trustLevel name="Low" policyFile="web_lowtrust.config"/>
    <trustLevel name="Minimal" policyFile="web_minimaltrust.config"/>
</securityPolicy>
```

The Full level is special because it assigns full trust to all ASP.NET applications and doesn't correspond to any .config file. This is the default policy level for a brand new installation of ASP.NET. Each successive level, from High to Minimal, grants fewer permissions:

- The High level grants unlimited access to file system, environment variables, and Web sites. Applications can use the default printer, access the SQL Server .NET Data Provider, and assert permissions. (See "The Assert Method" section later in this chapter.) Reflection permissions are limited to the ability to emit code dynamically.

- The Medium level grants unrestricted use of isolated storage, read/write access to files in the application's directory, read access of a few environment variables, access to the default printer, the ability to assert, and permission to connect back to the URL specified in the originUrl attribute. Applications can use the SQL Server .NET Data Provider, but it is required that the user password be nonblank.

- The Low level grants only 1 MB of isolated storage and read access to files in the application's directory.

- The Minimal level grants only execution rights.

Isolated storage is a .NET mechanism that gives access only to a portion of the system drive and optionally puts a higher limit on the number of bytes that can be used. (You can read more information about isolated storage in Chapter 34.)

You have several ways to change the policy level for an ASP.NET application:

■ You can change the value of the <trust> element in the machine.config file to affect all ASP.NET applications running in the system that don't include a <trust> element.

■ You can change the value of the <trust> element in the web.config file to affect only a specific ASP.NET application (or a portion of it if you modify a secondary web.config file).

■ You can change the association between level name and configuration file by editing the <securityPolicy> block in the machine.config file.

■ You can edit one of the web_*.config files to change the policy level of all the ASP.NET applications associated with a given trust level. (You can restore the default settings anytime by copying one of the web_*.config.default files over the .config file.)

■ You can create a brand-new .config file and associate it with a given trust level, to change the policy level of all the ASP.NET applications associated with that trust level.

ISPs should add a <location> element in machine.config with the allowOverride attribute set to False so that the author of an ASP.NET application can't arbitrarily increase the application's trust level:

```
<location path="MyApp" allowOverride="false">
    <trust level="High" originUrl="http://www.contoso.com"/>
</location>
```

CAS in Action

All the CAS concepts illustrated so far—including evidence, permissions, and permission sets—correspond to well-defined objects in the .NET Framework. In this section, you'll learn how you can write code that handles these objects.

Working with Evidence

You typically have to work with evidence objects for a couple of reasons: to discover the evidence associated with an assembly or to explicitly load an assembly with the evidence that you define.

Showing Assembly Evidence

The Reflection.Assembly object exposes the Evidence read-only property, which returns the collection of all the evidence associated with the assembly. This property makes it possible to write a routine that displays information about a given assembly:

```
Sub ShowAssemblyEvidence(ByVal asm As [Assembly])
    ' Enumerate all the evidence objects in this assembly.
    For Each ev As Object In asm.Evidence
        ' Display the name of this evidence
        Console.WriteLine(ev.GetType().FullName)

        ' Display more detailed information, depending on the evidence type
        If TypeOf ev Is StrongName Then
            Dim evSn As StrongName = DirectCast(ev, StrongName)
            Console.WriteLine("    Name={0}, Version={1}, PublicKey={2}", _
                evSn.Name, evSn.Version, evSn.PublicKey)
        ElseIf TypeOf ev Is Publisher Then
            Dim evPub As Publisher = DirectCast(ev, Publisher)
            Dim cert As X509Certificates.X509Certificate = evPub.Certificate
            Console.WriteLine("    Name={0}, Issuer={1}, Algorithm={2}", _
                cert.GetName, cert.GetIssuerName, cert.GetKeyAlgorithm)
        ElseIf TypeOf ev Is Hash Then
            Dim evHash As Hash = DirectCast(ev, Hash)
            Console.WriteLine("    SHA1={0}, MD5={1}", _
                BytesToHex(evHash.SHA1), BytesToHex(evHash.MD5))
        ElseIf TypeOf ev Is Zone Then
            Dim evZone As Zone = DirectCast(ev, Zone)
            Console.WriteLine("    SecurityZone={0}", evZone.SecurityZone)
        ElseIf TypeOf ev Is Url Then
            Dim evUrl As Url = DirectCast(ev, Url)
            Console.WriteLine("    Url={0}", evUrl.Value)
        ElseIf TypeOf ev Is Site Then
            Dim evSite As Site = DirectCast(ev, Site)
            Console.WriteLine("    Site={0}", evSite.Name)
        Else
            Console.WriteLine("    (custom evidence)")
        End If
    Next
End Sub


' Helper routine for showing a byte array as hex values
Function BytesToHex(ByVal arr() As Byte) As String
    Dim res As New System.Text.StringBuilder
    For Each b As Byte In arr
        res.AppendFormat("{0:X2}", b)
    Next
    Return res.ToString
End Function
```

For example, here's how you can display evidence information about the executing assembly:

```
ShowAssemblyEvidence([Assembly].GetExecutingAssembly())
```

You can also use the ShowAssemblyEvidence routine to create a command line utility that displays information on the assembly you pass as an argument, which can be a useful tool to solve security problems:

```
Sub Main(ByVal args() As String)
    ShowAssemblyEvidence([Assembly].LoadFile(args(0)))
End Sub
```

Loading an Assembly with Custom Evidence

Imagine the following scenario: you've downloaded an assembly from the Internet and saved it on your local drive. You are wary about the assembly and the real intentions of its author, but you know that the assembly will receive full trust and will be granted enough permission to damage your system if you run the executable from where it currently resides.

In cases like this, you can load the assembly explicitly through reflection and pass it a custom evidence object that informs the .NET runtime that the assembly was originally downloaded from the Internet.

```
Sub TestCustomEvidence()
    Dim ev As New Evidence
    Dim evZone As New Zone(SecurityZone.Internet)
    Dim evUrl As New Url("http://www.vb2themax.com")
    ' Use AddHost because Zone and Url are host evidence objects.
    ' (You must use AddAssembly for assembly evidence objects.)
    ev.AddHost(evZone)
    ev.AddHost(evUrl)
    ' Load the assembly as if it were downloaded from www.vb2themax.com.
    Dim asm As [Assembly] = [Assembly].LoadFile("C:\Downloaded\Library.dll", ev)
    ' Access objects in the DLL via reflection.
    ⋮

    ' Uncomment next statement to see what happens if the DLL is referenced
    ' by current project and you access its classes via early binding.
    ' Dim obj As New Library.SampleClass
End Sub
```

A minor problem in this approach is that it forces you to access all the classes and methods in the assembly through reflection and late binding, as seen in the previous code snippet. In fact, if you add a reference to the DLL and uncomment the statement that uses the New keyword to instantiate the object, the LoadFile method throws a File-LoadException. The reason for this is subtle: the .NET runtime resolves the reference to the external assembly when it JIT-compiles the TestCustomEvidence method, and loads the Library.dll in memory with its default evidence, which states it's a local assembly. When the LoadFile method attempts to reload the same assembly with different evidence, the runtime throws the exception.

Once you understand the problem, finding the solution its simple. You should load all the assemblies that require custom evidence as soon as the program starts so that all the strongly typed references to them use the preloaded assembly and honor the custom evidence. Here's a possible skeleton of such a program:

```
Sub Main(ByVal args() As String)
    ' Here you preload all assemblies with custom evidence.
    ⋮
    ' Call the "real" entry point of the assembly.
    RealMain(args)
End Sub
```

```
Sub RealMain(ByVal args() As String)
    ' Here you can use strongly typed references to types in the assemblies.
    ⋮
End Sub
```

Using the LoadFrom method to assign a custom evidence object works only with DLLs. Loading an .exe assembly with custom evidence requires a technique based on the AppDomain.ExecuteAssembly method:

```
' (This code assumes that EV is a custom evidence object.)
Dim appdom As AppDomain = AppDomain.CreateDomain("newappdom")
appdom.ExecuteAssembly("AnotherAssembly.exe", ev)
```

Working with Imperative Security

You already know that a stack walk is performed whenever you access one of the system resources that are protected with a permission object (for example, the file system). The stack walk ensures that all the assemblies in the call chain have the permission to access the resource. Most of the CAS-related code you'll write in your applications has to do with stack walks.

You can affect how stack walks are performed by adopting *imperative* or *declarative* coding style. In the former case, you create permission objects and then invoke one of their methods; in the latter case, you apply security attributes at the class or method level.

The Demand Method

All the permission objects in the .NET Framework expose the Demand method, which forces a stack walk to verify that all callers have that specific permission and throws a security exception if this isn't the case. You can use the Demand method to verify that your code has been granted the permission to access a given resource:

```
' Verify that code has unrestricted permission on the registry.
Dim regPerm As New RegistryPermission(PermissionState.Unrestricted)
Try
    regPerm.Demand()
    Console.WriteLine("Access to registry is granted.")
Catch ex As Exception
    Console.WriteLine("Access to registry is forbidden.")
End Try
```

A permission object can only test CAS-related constraints, not ACL-related permissions enforced by the operating system. For example, your executable is prevented from reading or writing to the registry if it is running under a user account that doesn't have enough privileges to do so, even if CAS settings allow registry access.

You can encapsulate a Demand method in a function that checks whether a given permission is available:

```
Function IsFilePermissionGranted() As Boolean
    Try
        Dim filePerm As New FileIOPermission(PermissionState.Unrestricted)
        filePerm.Demand()
        Return True
    Catch ex As Exception
        Return False
    End Try
End Function
```

You might wonder why you should force a stack walk with a Demand method instead of just waiting for the exception to be thrown when the code accesses the protected resource. There are actually a few reasons why an induced stack walk is desirable or even necessary. For example, knowing whether your code can access the file system or the printer lets you create a more consistent user interface. (End users prefer to know immediately that they can't save or print a document rather than discovering this limitation after hours of editing work.)

Here's another case where the Demand method is not only useful, it's also essential to enforce security correctly. Let's suppose you've written the following method, which reads an .ini file and caches it in a string variable:

```
Shared iniText As String
Function GetIniFile() As String
    ' Read the .ini file only if it hasn't been cached already.
    If iniText Is Nothing Then
        Dim sr As New StreamReader("C:\myapp\data.ini")
        iniText = sr.ReadToEnd()
        sr.Close()
    End If
    Return iniText
End Function
```

Let's say that the GetIniFile method is invoked by a fully trusted caller. The reference to the StreamReader object causes a stack walk, which succeeds because the caller has the right to access the file system. So far, so good.

Can you predict what happens if an assembly with no permission on the file system calls the GetIniFile method now? The call should fail but it doesn't because the code returns a value without using the StreamReader object and without causing a stack walk. To fix this security hole, you must make an explicit demand for permission:

```
Dim iniText As String
Function GetIniFile() As String
    ' Read the .ini file only if it hasn't been cached already.
    If iniText Is Nothing Then
        Dim sr As New StreamReader("c:\myapp\data.ini")
        iniText = sr.ReadToEnd()
        sr.Close()
    Else
        ' Throw a security exception if callers can't read from this directory.
```

```
      Dim filePerm As New FileIOPermission(FileIOPermissionAccess.Read, "C:\myapp")
      filePerm.Demand()
   End If
   Return iniText
End Function
```

> **Note**   If you just want to check whether a given permission is granted to your assembly (as opposed to your assembly *and* all its callers) as the result of the policy level and the evidence assigned to your assembly, you can use the IsGranted shared method of the SecurityManager class:
>
> ```
> Dim filePerm As New FileIOPermission(PermissionState.Unrestricted)
> If SecurityManager.IsGranted(filePerm) Then
>     ' This assembly has been granted unrestricted access to file system.
>     ⋮
> End If
> ```
>
> In most cases, however, this information has little value because it doesn't ensure that the protected resource can be accessed. The IsGranted method is more useful when applied to identity permissions, as I'll explain in the "Identity Permission Classes" section later in this chapter.

The Deny and PermitOnly Methods

When you are calling an assembly that you haven't authored yourself and don't trust completely, it is a good idea to reduce the permission set for that assembly. For example, let's say you are calling an assembly that should be prevented from doing anything but displaying user interface elements. You can enforce this security rule by invoking the PermitOnly method of the UIPermission object:

```
' From now on, permit only UI operations
Dim uiPerm As New UIPermission(PermissionState.Unrestricted)
uiPerm.PermitOnly()
' Any resource except UI elements is now forbidden.
Console.WriteLine(IsFilePermissionGranted)        ' => False
⋮
' Undo the effect of the most recent PermitOnly method.
CodeAccessPermission.RevertPermitOnly()
' Prove that the file system is reachable again.
Console.WriteLine(IsFilePermissionGranted)        ' => True
```

In most cases, you don't need to explicitly call the RevertPermitOnly shared method of the CodeAccessPermission class to undo the effect of the PermitOnly method because the permission object will be removed from the stack when the current procedure terminates. However, the RevertPermitOnly method is mandatory if you plan to invoke the PermitOnly method on a different permission from inside the same procedure because only one PermitOnly method can be active at a given time:

```
Dim uiPerm As New UIPermission(PermissionState.Unrestricted)
uiPerm.PermitOnly()
⋮
' If no RevertPermitOnly method is used, the following PermitOnly method throws an exc
eption.
Dim regPerm As New RegistryPermission(PermissionState.Unrestricted)
regPerm.PermitOnly()
```

The Deny method is similar to the PermitOnly method in that it reduces the permission granted to the assemblies your code calls. The Deny method tells the .NET runtime that a specific permission object isn't granted. Its effect can be undone with the RevertDeny shared method of the CodeAccessPermission class:

```
' From now on, deny UI operations.
Dim uiPerm As New UIPermission(PermissionState.Unrestricted)
uiPerm.Deny()
' UI is not permitted now.
⋮
' Undo the effect of the Deny method.
CodeAccessPermission.RevertDeny()
' UI is permitted again from now on.
```

In general, however, the Deny method is less useful than the PermitOnly method because it's easier to enumerate the permission objects that an assembly needs than those that the assembly doesn't need.

The Assert Method

The stack walk mechanism ensures that no untrusted callers can use your assembly to perform an operation for which they have no permission. In some circumstances, however, this mechanism might prevent operations that would be legitimate otherwise. For example, let's say you've written a financial math library that reads some critical values—for example, currency exchange ratios—from an .ini file. This library does nothing dangerous, yet calling its methods throws an exception if the caller has no permission to access the file system.

Let's use Figure 33-8 as a guideline and assume you are the author of Assembly B. Your assembly has the right to read files, and it passes this right along to Assembly C. However, the stack walk fails when Assembly C creates a FileReader object if your caller (Assembly A) has no permission to read files.

To work around this problem, you can use the Assert method of a permission object. This method tells the .NET runtime not to go past your assembly when walking up the stack while checking for a given permission object:

```
' Assert the permission of accessing the file system.
Dim filePerm As New FileIOPermission(PermissionState.Unrestricted)
filePerm.Assert()
' Access the file system here.
Dim sr As New StreamReader("c:\myapp\vars.ini")
⋮
```

As for the PermitOnly and Deny methods, there can be only one active Assert in the current procedure at any given time. You must use the CodeAccessPermission.RevertAssert shared method before you can assert a different permission inside the same procedure.

By default, only assemblies in the My_Computer_Zone and LocalIntranet_Zone code groups can call the Assert method because the permission set associated with these zones includes a SecurityPermission object with the Assertion flag enabled. As you might expect, an assembly can only assert a permission object that the assembly owns—for example, an assembly from the local intranet can assert the permission for printing to the default printer and displaying UI elements, but it can't assert the right to enumerate types and methods via reflection.

If your assembly calls unmanaged code via either PInvoke or COM Interop, you should assert an appropriate SecurityPermission object, as follows:

```
Dim secPerm As New SecurityPermission(SecurityPermissionFlags.UnmanagedCode)
secPerm.Assert()
' Access unmanaged code here.
⋮
```

If you fail to do this assertion, your assembly can't be used by untrusted code. In addition, if your assembly has a strong name, it must be marked with the AllowPartiallyTrustedCallers attribute, otherwise untrusted code won't be able to even load it. (See the "Partially Trusted Assemblies" section earlier in this chapter.)

It's crucial that you use the Assert method judiciously. By asserting a permission you are claiming that callers can't trick your assembly into doing anything dangerous. Let's suppose you need to provide users with the ability to read and write files only in the C:\MyApp directory. You might be tempted to use the following approach:

```
Public Sub DeleteFile(ByVal filename As String)
    ' Ensure that filename begins with C:\MyApp\.
    If Not filename.ToLower().StartsWith("c:\myapp\") Then
        Throw New ArgumentException("Path not allowed")
    End If
    ' Assert the right to access the file system.
    Dim filePerm As New FileIOPermission(PermissionState.Unrestricted)
    filePerm.Assert()
    ' Delete the file.
    File.Delete(filename)
End Sub
```

Alas, a smart (and wicked) caller can delete a system file by providing a string argument that passes your validation test:

```
DeleteFile("C:\MyApp\..\Windows\Soap Bubbles.bmp")
```

Of course, you might suffer from problems far more serious than just losing your favorite wallpaper. Here's a better approach, which is also more concise:

```
Public Sub DeleteFile(ByVal filename As String)
    ' Assert the right to access the C:\MyApp.
    Dim filePerm As New FileIOPermission(FileIOPermissionAccess.AllAccess, "C:\MyApp")
    filePerm.Assert()
    ' Delete the file.
    File.Delete(filename)
End Sub
```

The Demand and Assert methods are often used together on the same permission object to improve the performance of your code. Let's say you are authoring a library that repeatedly accesses the file system from inside a method. Each time your assembly accesses a file, the .NET runtime must check the permission objects associated with your assembly, your caller, the caller of your caller, and so on. The greater the number of callers that are above your assembly in the stack, the longer this operation takes. You can reduce this overhead by demanding and then asserting a specific permission object:

```
Dim filePerm As New FileIOPermission(PermissionState.Unrestricted)
' Ensure that all callers in the stack have this permission.
filePerm.Demand()
' Tell the .NET runtime that you have checked.
filePerm.Assert()
' File operations from now on fire a *partial* stack walk.
⋮
```

By demanding and then asserting a permission object, you are telling the .NET runtime, "I checked that my callers have this permission, so you don't have to recheck them each time this resource is accessed."

The PermissionSet Class

The PermitOnly, Deny, and Demand methods can grant, deny, or demand one permission at a time. In real-world applications, however, an assembly typically accesses multiple resources—for example, the registry, the file system, and the user interface. To work with such compound permission, you need to define a custom permission set:

```
Sub TestPermissionSet()
    ' Define three permission objects.
    Dim filePerm As New FileIOPermission(FileIOPermissionAccess.AllAccess, "c:\myapp")
    Dim regPerm As New RegistryPermission(PermissionState.Unrestricted)
    Dim uiPerm As New UIPermission(PermissionState.Unrestricted)
    ' Combine them in a permission set.
    Dim ps As New PermissionSet(PermissionState.None)
    ps.AddPermission(filePerm)
    ps.AddPermission(regPerm)
    ps.AddPermission(uiPerm)
    ' Permit only those actions, until the end of the procedure.
    ps.PermitOnly()
    ⋮
    ' The permission set is discarded when the procedure returns.
End Sub
```

The PermissionSet class also exposes the Demand, Deny, and Assert methods, which behave as they do with individual permission objects. You can undo the effect of these methods with the Revert*xxxx* shared methods of the CodeAccessPermission class, as you do when you demand, permit, and deny individual permission objects.

The previous code example shows how to create a permission set by creating a PermissionSet object that is initially empty, and then adding individual permission objects to it by means of the AddPermission method. You can also start with a PermissionSet object that contains all the available permission objects and then remove specific types of permissions with the RemovePermission method:

```
' Create a permission set that contains all available permission objects.
Dim ps1 As New PermissionSet(PermissionState.Unrestricted)
' Remove all permissions to access the file system.
ps1 = DirectCast(ps1.RemovePermission(GetType(FileIOPermission)), PermissionSet)
ps1.PermitOnly()
```

This code has broadly the same effect as denying one or more permissions, but you can't be very granular about which permission to deny because you can only remove all the permissions of a given type (FileIOPermission, in this example).

You also combine two permission sets with the Union and Intersect methods, and check whether a permission set contains all the permission objects that are defined in another permission set with the IsSubsetOf method:

```
' (This code assumes that ps1 and ps2 are PermissionSet objects.)
' ps3 contains the permission objects defined either in ps1 or ps2.
Dim ps3 As PermissionSet = DirectCast(ps1.Union(ps2), PermissionSet)
' ps4 contains only the permission objects defined both in ps1 and ps2.
Dim ps4 As PermissionSet = DirectCast(ps1.Intersect(ps2), PermissionSet)

' Check that ps4 contains a subset of the permission objects in ps1.
Console.WriteLine(ps4.IsSubsetOf(p1))          ' => True
```

The PermissionSet class can be serialized and deserialized to and from XML with the ToXml and FromXml methods, respectively. However, you usually invoke these methods on NamedPermissionSet objects, so I'll illustrate them in the following section.

The NamedPermissionSet Class

A NamedPermissionSet object is nothing but a permission set with a name and an optional description. The main reason to create such an object is to demand all the permissions defined in one of the predefined permission sets, that is: FullTrust, Everything, LocalIntranet, and Internet. This is a quick and simple way to ensure that your code runs under the level of trust you need:

```
' Ensure that all our callers are fully trusted.
Dim nps As New NamedPermissionSet("FullTrust")
nps.Demand()
```

Another reason for creating a NamedPermissionSet object is to save an XML file that you later import using the .NET Configuration tool:

```
' Create a named permission set and assign a description.
Dim nps As New NamedPermissionSet("LimitedFileReaders", PermissionState.None)
nps.Description = "Allows reading files in directory C:\MyData " _
    & "and displaying UI elements"
' Add three permission objects to the permission set.
nps.AddPermission(New FileIOPermission(FileIOPermissionAccess.AllAccess, _
    "c:\MyData"))
nps.AddPermission(New RegistryPermission(PermissionState.Unrestricted))
nps.AddPermission(New UIPermission(PermissionState.Unrestricted))
```

This class doesn't expose methods that read and write files directly, and you must use the ToXml method together with a StreamWriter object:

```
' Save definition of permission set to an XML file.
Dim sw As New StreamWriter("c:\custom permission.xml")
sw.Write(nps.ToXml)
sw.Close()
```

You can also deserialize an XML file with the FromXml method and a StreamReader object.

Permission sets imported in the .NET Configuration tool can be later associated with code groups. You can't change the permissions in the permission set once you have imported it, but you can rename it and add a description in its Properties window. (See Figure 33-9.)

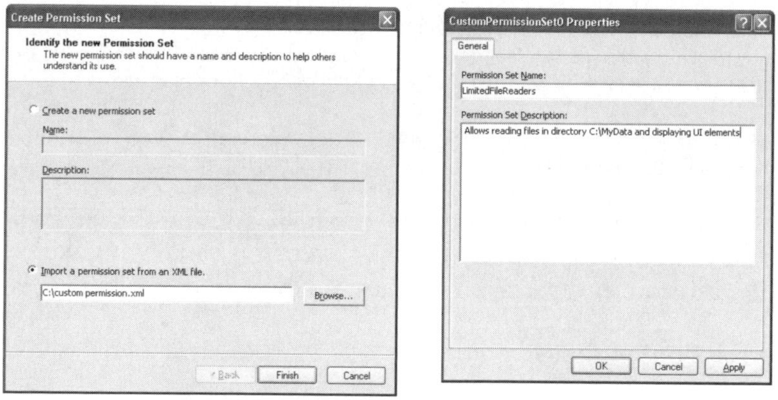

Figure 33-9 You can create a custom permission set by importing an XML file (left) and later assign the permission set object a name and a description (right).

Working with Declarative Security

You can control many facets of CAS by means of attributes. In some cases, these attributes let you achieve the same effect you can reach by invoking methods of Permission and PermissionSet objects. In other cases, these attributes provide functionality that can't be obtained in other ways. This is true for attributes that the .NET runtime checks when it loads the assembly—that is, when no code in the assembly is running yet.

Demand, PermitOnly, Deny, and Assert Actions

All the permission objects defined in the .NET Framework have a corresponding permission attribute that allows you to use the permission object in a declarative fashion. For example, you can use the FileIOPermissionAttribute object to replace a method call on the FileIOPermission object and an EventLogPermissionAttribute in lieu of a method call on the EventLogPermission object.

All these permission attributes take a SecurityAction enumerated value in their first argument; this value corresponds to the method that you would call if you were using the permission object in an imperative fashion. For example, let's say you have a procedure that uses the PermitOnly method of the FileIOPermission object:

```
Sub ProcessDirectory()
    ' From now on, permit only file operations
    Dim filePerm As New FileIOPermission(PermissionState.Unrestricted)
    filePerm.PermitOnly()
    ' (Only file operations are allowed from here to the end of method.)
    ⋮
End Sub
```

Here's how you can rewrite the procedure with declarative security instead of imperative security:

```
<FileIOPermission(SecurityAction.PermitOnly, Unrestricted:=True)> _
Sub ProcessDirectory()
    ' (Only file operations are allowed from here to the end of method.)
    ⋮
End Sub
```

Permission attributes can take optional arguments to further define the scope of the permission. These arguments correspond to the values you would pass to the permission object's constructor:

```
' Assert the right to call unmanaged code.
<SecurityPermission(SecurityAction.PermitOnly, _
    Flags:=SecurityPermissionFlags.UnmanagedCode)> _
Sub DoSomething()
    ⋮
End Sub

' Deny read operations in directory C:\MyApp.
' (In a real application you would rarely burn a path name in code.)
<FileIOPermission(SecurityAction.Deny, Read:="C:\MyApp")> _
Sub DoSomething2()
    ⋮
End Sub
```

You can protect a method with two or more attributes:

```
<FileIOPermission(SecurityAction.PermitOnly, Unrestricted:=True), _
    RegistryPermission(SecurityAction.Demand, Unrestricted:=True)> _
Sub ProcessDirectory()
    ' (Only file and registry operations are allowed from here to the end of method.)
    ⋮
End Sub
```

A great advantage of using permission attributes rather than permission objects is that you can apply attributes at the class level—for example:

```
<ReflectionPermission(SecurityAction.PermitOnly, _
    Flags:=ReflectionPermissionFlag.TypeInformation> _
Class ReflectionDemoClass
    ' All procedures in this class have only the permission to use
    ' reflection to access type information.
    ⋮
End Class
```

A permission attribute applied at the class level protects all the methods in the class as well as the action of creating an instance of the class. (It doesn't protect nested types, though.) For example, achieving the same effect as the previous code snippet without declarative security requires that you instantiate a ReflectionPermission object and call its PermitOnly method in each constructor, property, and method of the class.

It is also possible to demand all the permissions that are associated with one of the named permission sets defined in the default policy (FullTrust, Everything, LocalIntranet, and Internet). In this case, you must use a PermissionSet attribute at the class or method level:

```
<PermissionSet(SecurityAction.Demand, Name:="FullTrust")> _
Sub DoSomething
    ' This method requires full trust.
    ⋮
End Sub
```

Using a PermissionSet attribute in this fashion corresponds to demanding permission for a named permission set:

```
Sub DoSomething
    Dim nps As New NamedPermissionSet("FullTrust")
    nps.Demand()
    ⋮
End Sub
```

Here's an important detail about declarative security: permission attributes at the method level *replace* class-level attributes of the same type and with the same SecurityAction value. They don't merge together, as you might expect. However, attributes of the same type defined at the class and method level combine their effect if their SecurityAction argument is different.

LinkDemand Action

Both the Demand method (for imperative security) and the SecurityAction.Demand action (for declarative security) ensure that all your callers have a given set of permissions. Each time a procedure protected with the Demand method or action is invoked, the CAS subsystem triggers a stack walk. If the CPU time required by the stack walk is a significant fraction of the total time spent in the procedure and if the procedure is invoked many times during the application's lifetime, then the overall stack walk overhead becomes remarkable.

You can reduce this overhead by using a declarative LinkDemand action, as in this code:

```
<ReflectionPermission(SecurityAction.LinkDemand, Unrestricted:=True)> _
Sub DoSomething()
    ' This method makes heavy use of reflection.
    ⋮
End Sub
```

It's crucial that you understand the two main differences between the Demand and LinkDemand actions. First, a permission flagged with LinkDemand is checked only when the .NET runtime JIT-compiles the piece of code that references the class or invokes the method marked with the attribute, as in these lines of code:

```
' The LinkDemand permission on DoSomething is checked when this
' method is JIT-compiled.
Sub TestLinkDemand(ByVal o As SampleClass)
    ' (Assumes that DoSomething is defined in SampleClass.)
    o.DoSomething()
End Sub
```

For example, if the DoSomething method is invoked from three different procedures in the caller assembly the LinkDemand permission is checked three times. This detail explains why the LinkDemand action is faster than a regular Demand action (the .NET runtime checks the permission a relatively small number of times) and why the LinkDemand action is only available in a declarative fashion (the permission is checked at JIT-compilation time, before the procedure runs for the first time).

The second important difference is that the .NET runtime checks only the permission objects associated with the immediate caller of the method marked with a LinkDemand action instead of doing a complete stack walk. This behavior makes the LinkDemand action somewhat less safe than a Demand action; it's up to you to decide whether the gain on the performance side is worth the loss on the security side.

Using the LinkDemand action with overridable methods and methods that implement an interface member isn't recommended. If the DoSomething method shown in the previous code example were a virtual method, a malicious assembly could wait until a trusted assembly invokes (and indirectly JIT-compiles) the TestLinkDemand procedure, and then pass the procedure an object whose class derives from SampleClass but overrides the DoSomething method.

Another problem of the LinkDemand action is that, in the case of insufficient permissions, the code doesn't throw when the target method is invoked; instead, it throws when the caller is JIT-compiled. This makes it harder to use a Try block to catch the error and to interpret the state of the call stack when the exception occurs.

The LinkDemand action behaves differently if a method protected with a permission attribute is invoked via reflection. In this case, the immediate caller is the mscorlib.dll assembly, which is already JIT-compiled, therefore, the LinkDemand action has no effect. For this reason, the .NET runtime transforms the link demand action into a full demand action and performs a complete stack walk.

While we're on the topic of reflection, it should be noted that the .NET runtime correctly prevents the invocation of security-related methods—such as the Assert and Demand methods of permission objects—via reflection. Such attempts fail with an ArgumentException error.

InheritanceDemand Action

You can mark a class or a method with a permission attribute that has the Inheritance-Demand action if you want to enforce some constraints in how the class or the method can be used by derived types in a different assembly. When the InheritanceDemand action is applied at the class level it ensures that all the derived types have the requested permission:

```
<RegistryPermission(SecurityAction.InheritanceDemand, Unrestricted:=True> _
Class RegistryExplorer
    ' This class can be inherited only by assemblies with full registry permission.
    ⋮
End Class
```

You typically apply the InheritanceDemand action if the class can be safely used by untrusted callers but has protected methods that access a resource in a potentially dangerous way.

If the InheritanceDemand action is applied at the method level, then only assemblies with the request permission can override that method in a derived type:

```
<RegistryPermission(SecurityAction.InheritanceDemand, Unrestricted:=True> _
Protected Overridable Sub DoSomething()
    ⋮
End Sub
```

(The InheritanceDemand action has no effect on nonoverridable methods.)

The .NET runtime checks the permission only once, either the first time the derived class is used or the first time the overridden method is invoked. The InheritanceDemand action also works with indirect inheritance when there are multiple levels of inheritance.

RequestMinimum, RequestOptional, and RequestRefuse Actions

Permission attributes support three more actions, all of which can be specified only for attributes defined at the assembly level:

- **RequestMinimum**   This action specifies the permissions that are strictly necessary for the assembly to work correctly. If the .NET runtime can't grant these permissions, the assembly won't be loaded and a System.Security.Policy.PolicyException is thrown.

- **RequestOptional**   This action specifies the permissions that the assembly would like to use but that aren't crucial for its operations. For example, an assembly might request the ability to write to disk as an optional permission. If this permission isn't granted, the assembly loads all the same, but its user interface should disable or hide all commands that let the user save files.

- **RequestRefuse**   This action specifies permissions that the .NET runtime should never grant to the assembly. By reducing the permission set assigned to the assembly you make it harder for malicious code to exploit your assembly to access protected resources.

The following code shows the attributes that can be applied to an assembly that requires permission to create user interface elements and access files by means of common file dialogs, that wants to be granted permission to use performance counters (but can run without them), and that explicitly refuses to receive the permission to call unmanaged code:

```
<Assembly: UIPermission(SecurityAction.RequestMinimum, Unrestricted:=True)>
<Assembly: FileDialogPermission(SecurityAction.RequestMinimum, Unrestricted:=True)>
<Assembly: PerformanceCounterPermission(SecurityAction.RequestOptional, _
  Unrestricted:=True)>
<Assembly: SecurityPermission(SecurityAction.RequestRefuse, UnmanagedCode:=True)>
```

The RequestOptional action works in a way that might be considered counterintuitive. It actually *restricts* the permission set granted to the assembly even though its name suggests differently. (If the assembly doesn't specify this action, it is granted all the permissions that aren't explicitly refused.) For example, the previous code snippet could be simplified by dropping the RequestRefuse action on the SecurityPermission object because the permission to call unmanaged code will be denied anyway.

To recap, the permission set granted to the assembly consists of all the permissions marked with the RequestMinimum action, plus all the permissions marked with the RequestOptional action, minus all the permissions marked with the RequestRefuse action. In all cases, however, an assembly will be given permissions that aren't granted by the policy level and the code group the assembly belongs to.

Using attributes to precisely specify which permissions your code requires or refuses is useful for the system administrator, who can then decide whether it's necessary to give the compiled assembly more permissions than it would normally have. Administrators can list the minimal, optional, and refused permission sets of an assembly with the PermView utility:

```
PERMVIEW myapp.exe
```

The optional /decl switch also lists all the declarative security attributes associated with classes and methods (see Figure 33-10), information that is useful to developers who want to use the types defined in an assembly:

```
PERMVIEW /decl mylibrary.dll
```

Figure 33-10   The PermView utility

Identity Permission Classes

A group of five permission classes in the System.Security.Permissions namespace and their corresponding attributes don't map to any system resource. You recognize these classes because their names end with IdentityPermission: StrongNameIdentityPermission, PublisherIdentityPermission, UrlIdentityPermission, SiteIdentityPermission, and ZoneIdentityPermission. You typically use these classes to ensure that your code can be called only by assemblies with a given identity—for example, assemblies coming from a given zone, site, or URL.

```
<ZoneIdentityPermission(SecurityAction.LinkDemand, Zone:=SecurityZone.MyComputer)> _
Class SampleClass
    ⋮
End Class

<UrlIdentityPermission(SecurityAction.LinkDemand, Url:="www.vb2themax.com")> _
Class SampleClass2
    ⋮
End Class
```

You can use identity permission objects to demand permissions—by using either an imperative or a declarative coding style—but this technique is rarely useful because it requires that all the assemblies in the call stack have the same identity. Instead, these permission objects are typically used with a LinkDemand action and declarative security (which explains why I deferred the explanation of these objects until now).

The StrongNameIdentityPermission class is especially useful to ensure that an assembly can be used only by a specific assembly. This class exposes the Name, PublicKey, and Version properties, but you often omit the last one so that it works with any version of the caller. In addition, you can omit the Name value to grant access to all the assemblies coming from the same publisher (more specifically, all the assemblies with a given public key):

```
<Assembly: StrongNameIdentityPermission(SecurityAction.RequestMinimum, _
   PublicKey:="002400683011af5799aced238935f32ab125790aa787786343440023410" & _
   "073958138838746ac86ef8732623f87978223aced6767169876acde74e59a6457be26ee0" & _
   "045467467ce68a123cdef89648292518478536964ace47852361985636487523b7e0e25b" & _
   "71ad39acef23457893574852568eac5863298de685de69124de56eded66978425008142e" & _
   "f723bfe602345459574568790b365852cdead454585c6")>
```

Used in conjunction with the SecurityManager.IsGranted shared method, identity permissions objects are useful to let the assembly know which zone, site, or URL it was launched from:

```
If SecurityManager.IsGranted( _
     New ZoneIdentityPermission(SecurityZone.Intranet)) Then
     ' This assembly has been launched from a network drive.
     ⋮
End If
```

The SuppressUnmanagedCodeSecurity Attribute

When managed code calls unmanaged code—through either PInvoke or COM Interop—the .NET runtime fires a stack walk demanding a SecurityPermission object with the SecurityPermissionFlag.UnmanagedCode flag. You can reduce the overhead by flagging the method that calls into unmanaged code with a SuppressUnmanaged-CodeSecurity attribute. This attribute forces a link demand when the method is JIT-compiled but suppresses the full stack walk at each method invocation:

```
<SuppressUnmanagedCodeSecurity()> _
Sub DoSomething()
     ' Calls to unmanaged code through PInvoke don't cause a demand at runtime.
     ⋮
End Sub
```

You can also narrow the scope of the attribute to a specific unmanaged procedure by applying it together with the DllImport attribute

```
<System.Runtime.InteropServices.DllImport("kernel32", EntryPoint:="Beep"), _
    SuppressUnmanagedCodeSecurity()> _
    Function WinBeep(ByVal freq As Integer, ByVal duration As Integer) As Integer
    End Function
```

You can also apply the SuppressUnmanagedCodeSecurity attribute at the class level, in which case it affects all the methods in the class.

The story is completely different when you call unmanaged code via COM Interop. In this case, you must apply the attribute to the interface through which you invoke the methods in the COM class. (Applying the attribute to just the method that accesses the COM object has no effect.) This requirement forces you to explicitly access COM objects though a managed interface they implement, which is an unnatural coding style. More frequently, you ask the TlbImp utility to apply this attribute to all unmanaged interfaces being imported by specifying the /unsafe option:

```
TLBIMP /unsafe mycomponent.dll
```

Disabling CAS

This long discussion about code access security demonstrated the amount of activity that goes on under the hood whenever your code accesses a protected resource, either directly or indirectly. Stack walks are performed in all cases, even if all the assemblies involved are fully trusted.

In general, most developers are willing to trade some performance in exchange for better security, but there are times when you don't really need to protect your code with CAS. This is the case, for example, when you run a stand-alone Windows Forms application that uses only local assemblies on a computer that isn't connected to the Internet or that is protected by a firewall. In cases such as these, you can decide to turn code access security off. You can do this from the command prompt with the –s switch of the CasPol utility:

```
CASPOL -s off
```

Needless to say, this is a very dangerous operation and should be performed with extreme care because it disables CAS for all the managed applications and all the versions of the .NET Framework installed on the computer.

You can also turn off CAS via code using the SecurityEnabled shared property of the SecurityManager class. Setting this property doesn't affect other applications:

```
' Turn CAS off at the application level.
SecurityManager.SecurityEnabled = False
```

Notice that disabling CAS in one of these two ways doesn't disable role-based security, which I'll illustrate in the next section.

Role-Based Security

.NET programs running under Windows undergo two different types of security: code access security (.NET security) and role-based security (Windows security). CAS is concerned with the origin of the running code, whereas role-based security grants or denies permissions depending on the identity of the user account under which the code is running.

Luckily, the .NET Framework exposes several classes for dealing with the latter type of security. Role-based security revolves around two concepts:

- **Identity** An identity object represents an individual user and exposes properties such as the user name, whether the user has been authenticated, and the security provider used to authenticate the user. (Users of ASP.NET applications can be anonymous users, namely users that haven't been authenticated.) An identity object is used in the authentication phase of the login.

- **Principal** A principal object is a combination of a user identity plus all the roles assigned to the user. These roles are the Windows groups the user belongs to, if the user is the interactive Windows user or is an ASP.NET user authenticated with Windows authentication. A principal object is used when deciding whether one or more resources should be granted to a user (the authorization phase).

Role-based security under .NET is extendible, and you can create a custom identity and principal objects. More in general, .NET role-based security can use any authentication mechanism, including but not limited to Windows authentication. (Form authentication and Passport authentication under ASP.NET are two examples of authentication models that don't rely on Windows identity.) The great thing is that security-aware code works in a similar way, regardless of the authentication model used in a specific case.

For example, a login form for a credit card application might validate user credentials against a database and generate a custom identity object that includes information such as the login date and time. Then the application might use this custom identity object to associate the user with all its application roles and include information such as the maximum amount of money a user can withdraw in a given day.

All the classes and interfaces that are related to role-based security are in the System.Security.Principal namespace.

Working with Identity Objects

The current version of the .NET Framework exposes four identity classes: GenericIdentity (a generic user), WindowsIdentity (a Windows user or an ASP.NET user authenticated with Windows authentication), FormsIdentity (an ASP.NET user authenticated with Forms authentication), and PassportIdentity (an ASP.NET user authenticated via Passport authentication).

All identity classes implement the IIdentity interface. This interface exposes the following read-only properties:

- IsAuthenticated returns True if the user has been authenticated.

- AuthenticationType returns a string that specifies which authentication method has been used; it can be NTLM, Basic, Forms, Passport, or any other string passed to the .NET runtime by the authentication provider (Kerberos, for instance).

- Name returns the user name under which the user logged in. For a Windows user, this is a string in the format *domainname\username* or *machinename\username*; for an ASP.NET user authenticated via Forms, this is the username typed on the login page.

The WindowsIdentity Class

The most commonly used identity object is the WindowsIdentity object. This object exposes the three properties defined in the IIdentity interface, plus the following: IsAnonymous (True if the user is anonymous), IsGuest (True if the user is identified as a Guest account), IsSystem (True if the user is identified as a System account), and Token (an IntPtr that represents the Windows account token for the user).

You retrieve the WindowsIdentity object that corresponds to the currently logged user by means of the GetCurrent shared method. Here's a piece of code that displays information about the interactive user currently logged on:

```
Sub TestWindowsIdentity()
    Dim wi As WindowsIdentity = WindowsIdentity.GetCurrent()
    Console.WriteLine("Name = {0}", wi.Name)                '=> MyMachine\Francesco
    Console.WriteLine("IsAuthenticated = {0}", wi.IsAuthenticated)     ' => True
    Console.WriteLine("AuthenticationType = {0}", wi.AuthenticationType) ' => NTLM
    Console.WriteLine("IsAnonymous = {0}", wi.IsAnonymous)             ' => False
    Console.WriteLine("IsGuest = {0}", wi.IsGuest)                    ' => False
    Console.WriteLine("IsSystem = {0}", wi.IsSystem)                  ' => False
Console.WriteLine("Token = {0}", wi.Token)                          ' => 1632
End Sub
```

Only fully trusted code can access information about the current user because this sort of information would be valuable to malicious code trying to access system resources.

Impersonating a Windows User

The WindowsIdentity object exposes both an instance and a shared method named Impersonate, which allows your code to impersonate a different user. Impersonating a user other than the user who launched the application can be useful for several reasons. For example, you might need to temporarily impersonate a user with higher privileges (such as an administrator) before accessing a resource protected by an ACL, or you might want to impersonate a user with fewer privileges before loading an assembly or launching an external unmanaged application (to prevent that application from accessing critical resources). Here's an example that shows how to use the LogonUser API function to impersonate a user and then revert to the previous identity.

```
Declare Function LogonUser Lib "advapi32" Alias "LogonUserA" ( _
    ByVal username As String, ByVal domain As String, ByVal password As String, _
    ByVal logonType As Integer, ByVal logonProvider As Integer, _
    ByRef token As IntPtr) As Boolean
Declare Auto Function CloseHandle Lib "kernel32.dll" _
    (ByVal handle As IntPtr) As Boolean


<SecurityPermission(SecurityAction.Demand, ControlPrincipal:=True, _
    UnmanagedCode:=True)> _
Sub TestImpersonation()
    Const LOGON32_LOGON_INTERACTIVE As Integer = 2
    Const LOGON32_LOGON_NETWORK As Integer = 3
    Const LOGON32_PROVIDER_DEFAULT As Integer = 0
    Dim token As IntPtr = IntPtr.Zero

    Dim username As String = "JoeDoe"
    Dim password As String = "jd"
    ' The name of domain or server whose account database contains the username.
    ' Can be "." for the local account database.
    Dim machinename As String = "."

    ' Attempt to log on as the user, exit if fails.
    If Not LogonUser(username, machinename, password, LOGON32_LOGON_INTERACTIVE, _
        LOGON32_PROVIDER_DEFAULT, token) Then
        Console.WriteLine("Unable to impersonate user {0}", username)
        Exit Sub
    End If

    ' Create a new WindowsIdentity corresponding to the returned token.
    Dim wi As New WindowsIdentity(token)
    ' Impersonate the new identity, remember returned context.
    Dim context As WindowsImpersonationContext = wi.Impersonate()
    ' Prove that it worked.
    TestWindowsIdentity()

    ' Revert to previous identity and release handle.
    context.Undo()
    CloseHandle(token)
End Sub
```

You can use the previous code to impersonate a specific user under ASP.NET. This technique is especially useful with Internet Web sites, where remote clients don't directly map to one of the Windows users defined on the server. In this case, you might authenticate the client using Form authentication, Passport authentication, or a custom authentication mechanism, and then use the LogonUser API and the Impersonate method to map the client to a known Windows identity and leverage ACLs and other Windows-specific authorization mechanisms.

Version 1.1 of the .NET Framework solves a problem that occurred with ASP.NET 1.0 running under Windows 2000. This version of the operating system requires code to have a special administrative privilege to call the LogonUser API function, a privilege that the default ASPNET account doesn't have. Therefore, if you are working with ASP.NET 1.0 under Windows 2000 you have to run ASP.NET under a more privileged account to use impersonation, but this more privileged account opens up a security risk. Now impersonation is fully supported under ASP.NET 1.1 with the default ASPNET identity.

Working with Principal Objects

You typically use programmatic security to implement some form of authorization—for example, to authorize only users in the Administrators group to use a class that wraps a critical resource. Information about the roles a user belongs to is contained in principal objects.

By definition, a principal object is an object that implements the IPrincipal interface. This interface exposes only two members: the Identity read-only property (which returns an IIdentity object holding information about the user) and the IsInRole method, which returns True if the current user is in the role whose name is passed as an argument.

Only two classes in the .NET Framework implement the IPrincipal interface: GenericPrincipal and WindowsPrincipal. As you can imagine, the latter is the more interesting of the two. You can also define your own principal classes, a technique that can be useful to implement a custom authorization mechanism.

The AppDomain.SetPrincipalPolicy Method

You can retrieve the principal object associated with the current thread with the CurrentPrincipal shared property of the Thread class. However, contrary to what you might expect, in a console or Windows Forms application this property returns by default a GenericPrincipal representing an unauthenticated user instead of a WindowsPrincipal representing the user account the application is running under. (In an ASP.NET application that uses Windows authentication, the Thread.CurrentPrincipal property returns a WindowsPrincipal object even if the user is anonymous.) You can easily prove this point by running the following code snippet in a console or Windows Forms project:

```
' Prove that, by default, the current principal is a GenericPrincipal object.
Dim ip As IPrincipal = Thread.CurrentPrincipal
' Cast to Object to retrieve its Type.
Debug.WriteLine(CObj(ip).GetType)
                    ' => System.Security.Principal.GenericPrincipal
Debug.WriteLine(ip.Identity.Name)              ' => (null string)
Debug.WriteLine(ip.Identity.IsAuthenticated)   ' => False
Debug.WriteLine(ip.Identity.AuthenticationType) ' => (null string)
```

The .NET runtime presumably behaves in this way to reveal as little information about the current user as possible so that malicious code can't exploit this information for finding security holes in your application.

A console or Windows Form application can ask the .NET security subsystem to have the Thread.CurrentPrincipal property return the actual Windows user by calling the SetPrincipalPolicy method of the current AppDomain, as follows:

```
' Change the security policy for the current AppDomain.
AppDomain.CurrentDomain.SetPrincipalPolicy(PrincipalPolicy.WindowsPrincipal)

Dim ip As IPrincipal = Thread.CurrentPrincipal
' Cast to Object to retrieve its Type.
Console.WriteLine(CObj(ip).GetType)
                           ' => System.Security.Principal.WindowsPrincipal
Console.WriteLine(ip.Identity.Name)                ' => MyMachine\JoeDoe
Console.WriteLine(ip.Identity.IsAuthenticated)     ' => True
Console.WriteLine(ip.Identity.AuthenticationType)  ' => NTLM
```

The SetPrincipalPolicy method should be invoked *before* accessing the principal object, otherwise it has no effect (and no exception is thrown). Also, you should bracket the call to this method in a Try...End Try block because calling this method fires a stack walk demanding a SecurityPermission object with the ControlPrincipal flag. (Only fully trusted code has this permission.)

The WindowsPrincipal Class

Once you have a WindowsPrincipal object you can use its IsInRole method to determine whether the current user belongs to a given role or group:

```
AppDomain.CurrentDomain.SetPrincipalPolicy(PrincipalPolicy.WindowsPrincipal)
Dim wp As WindowsPrincipal = DirectCast(Thread.CurrentPrincipal, WindowsPrincipal)
If wp.IsInRole("BUILTIN\Administrators") Then
    Console.WriteLine("User is in the Administrators group")
End If
```

The ability to check a role lets you implement sophisticated security policies:

```
If Today.DayOfWeek = DayOfWeek.Saturday Or Today.DayOfWeek = DayOfWeek.Sunday Then
    If Not wp.IsInRole("BUILTIN\Backup Operators") Then
        ' On weekends, grant access only to backup operators.
        Throw New SecurityException("Access denied")
    End If
End If
```

The argument you pass to the IsInRole method can be a string in one of the following formats: BUILTIN\groupname (for built-in roles), machinename\groupname (for machine-specific roles), or domainname\groupname (for domain-specific roles):

```
If wp.IsInRole("MyMachine\Power Users") Then
    Console.WriteLine("Current user is a power user.")
End If
```

You can also use an overloaded version of the method that takes a WindowsBuiltIn-Role enumerated value, which can be one of the following: AccountOperator, Administrator, BackupOperator, Guest, PowerUser, PrintOperator, Replicator, SystemOperator, or User. (This overload isn't exposed by the IPrincipal interface and the GenericPrincipal object.)

```
' Same effect as previous code snippet
If wp.IsInRole(WindowsBuiltInRole.PowerUser) Then
    Console.WriteLine("Current user is a power user.")
End If
```

Principal Objects under ASP.NET

The key to programmatic security under ASP.NET is the User property of the Page object, which returns an object that implements the IPrincipal interface. Code that isn't running inside a Page class can access this object through the HttpContext.Current.User property.

The User.Identity property returns an object that implements the IIdentity interface. The actual object being returned depends on the type of authentication that has been performed, and can be WindowsIdentity, FormsIdentity, PassportIdentity, or Generic-Identity:

```
Dim msg As String
If Not User.Identity.IsAuthenticated Then
    ' You can see this only if the site doesn't require authentication.
    msg = "Unauthenticated user"
Else
    msg = "User name = " & User.Identity.Name & "<br />"
    msg &= "Authentication type = " & User.Identity.AuthenticationType & "<br />"
End If
' Display user information in a Label control.
lblUserInfo.Text = msg
```

The ASP.NET user is authenticated only if you enforce Windows authentication and reject anonymous users, by using a web.config file like this:

```
<configuration>
  <system.web>
    <authentication mode="Windows" />
    <authorization>
      <deny users="?" />
      <allow users="*" />
    </authorization>
  </system.web>
</configuration>
```

If the page request has been authenticated with Windows authentication, you can cast the object returned by the User property to a WindowsPrincipal variable and access the overloaded method that takes a WindowsBuiltInRole enumerated value:

```
If Page.User.Identity.IsAuthenticated AndAlso _
    TypeOf User.Identity Is WindowsIdentity Then
    Dim wp As WindowsPrincipal = DirectCast(Page.User, WindowsPrincipal)
    If Not wp.IsInRole(WindowsBuiltInRole.Administrator) Then
        ' Refuse access to nonadministrators.
        Response.Redirect("/AccessDenied.htm")
    End If
End If
```

The PrincipalPermission Class

The code samples presented earlier in this chapter show how to retrieve information about the current user and possibly customize the behavior of the application depending on the user. However, in many cases you just want to grant access to some users and refuse access to others.

To help you with this task, the System.Security.Permissions namespace includes a PrincipalPermission class. This class doesn't inherit from CodeAccessPermission, yet it exposes a similar set of members and can be used like a CAS-related permission. For example, the following code uses the Demand method to throw an exception if the current user isn't an administrator:

```
' We need the following statement.
AppDomain.CurrentDomain.SetPrincipalPolicy(PrincipalPolicy.WindowsPrincipal)
' Throw an exception if the user isn't an administrator.
Dim pp As New PrincipalPermission(Nothing, "BUILTIN\Administrators")
pp.Demand()
```

You can also check for a specific user account (as opposed to a group) by passing a non-Nothing string in the first argument:

```
' (Continuing previous example.)
Dim pp2 As New PrincipalPermission("MyMachine\JoeDoe", Nothing)
pp2.Demand()
```

(You can also demand both a user name and a role.) You can use the Union method to combine multiple permissions together, as you'd do with a CAS-related permission object:

```
Dim pp1 As New PrincipalPermission(Nothing, "BUILTIN\Administrators")
Dim pp2 As New PrincipalPermission(Nothing, "BUILTIN\Power Users")
pp1.Union(pp2).Demand()
```

There are two important differences between the PrincipalPermission class and CAS-related permission classes that derive from CodeAccessSecurity. First, the PrincipalPermission class supports only demand actions because it makes no sense to assert or deny a principal permission. Second, a demand for a PrincipalPermission object doesn't trigger a full stack walk. Instead, only the principal associated with the current user is checked.

You can demand a PrincipalPermission object in a declarative fashion by means of the PrincipalPermissionAttribute type, which can be applied at the method and the class level. The attribute constructor can take either a Name or a Role argument (or both):

```
<PrincipalPermission(SecurityAction.Demand, Role:="BUILTIN\Administrators")> _
Class SampleClass
    <PrincipalPermission(SecurityAction.Demand, Name:="MyMachine\JoeDoe")> _
    Sub DoSomething()
        ' This method can be called only if current user is JoeDoe.
    End Sub

    ' All other methods in the class can be only called by administrators.
    ⋮
End Class
```

Cryptography

The .NET Framework includes many classes that let you encrypt and decrypt data, sign data with a hash code to ensure that nobody can silently tamper with it, and authenticate data to prove that it originates from a given party.

The System.Security.Cryptography Namespace

Most of the classes in the System.Security.Cryptography namespace are organized in a logical way and rely heavily on inheritance, as shown in Figure 33-11. Instead of just delivering concrete classes that implement a cryptographic algorithm, the .NET Framework provides three main abstract classes from which all other classes inherit: SymmetricAlgorithm (for algorithms that use the same secret key for encrypting and decrypting, such as DES and Rijndael), AsymmetricAlgorithm (for algorithms that use a public key for encrypting and a private key for decrypting, such as RSA), and HashAlgorithm (for algorithms that provide a hash value that can be used to ensure that data hasn't been tampered with). A fourth class, RandomNumberGenerator, defines algorithms that generate random bytes in an unpredictable fashion.

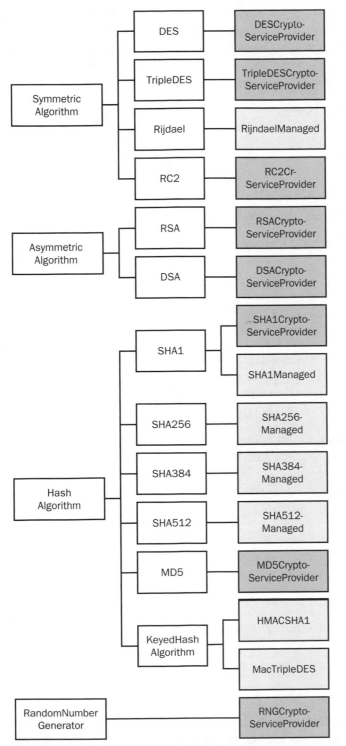

Figure 33-11   The hierarchy of the most important classes in the System.Security.Cryptography namespace

Below the three main abstract classes you find another layer of abstract classes that define how a specific algorithm should behave. For example, the TripleDES and Rijndael classes derive from SymmetricAlgorithm and define the properties and the methods that should be exposed by a class that implements the TripleDES and the Rijndael algorithms, respectively.

Concrete Cryptographic Classes

A third and final layer (near the right edge of Figure 33-11) contains the concrete classes that implement the actual encryption or hash algorithm. In most cases, the name of a concrete class denotes whether the class uses the Microsoft Cryptographic Service Providers (CSPs, which in turn use the unmanaged CryptoAPI library) or whether the class is a managed C# implementation of the algorithm. For example, the TripleDESCryptoServiceProvider and RSACryptoServiceProvider classes use the CryptoAPI library, whereas the RiijdaelManaged and the SHA512Managed classes are implemented in managed code. The current version of the .NET Framework provides both a fully managed class and a class that uses the CryptoAPI only in the case of the SHA-1 hash algorithm.

The organization in abstract and concrete classes has several advantages. For example, once you know how to use one symmetrical algorithm class you can easily adapt your code to work with another class of the same type. Even better, the inheritance relations that exist let you use variables typed after the base SymmetricAlgorithm class so that you only have to change the statement where you create the concrete class that contains the actual encryption code.

In addition, all the abstract classes expose a Create shared method that returns an instance of the default implementation for that algorithm, so in most cases you don't strictly need to specify which class you want to instantiate and you can make your code absolutely generic:

```
' Create an instance of the default concrete class for SHA-1 hash algorithm.
Dim hash As SHA1 = SHA1.Create()
Console.WriteLine(hash.GetType().Name)      ' => SHA1CryptoServiceProvider

' Create an instance of the default concrete class for symmetrical encryption.
Dim encr As SymmetricAlgorithm = SymmetricAlgorithm.Create()
Console.WriteLine(encr.GetType().Name)      ' => RijndaelManaged
```

The type of concrete class returned by the Create method can be changed by adding a <cryptographySetting> element in the machine.config file. Read the MSDN documentation for more details.

The CryptoStream Class

Even though the classes that implement encryption and hashing can work on an array of bytes, in most cases you will use them to encrypt, decrypt, or hash a flux of bytes while these bytes are being sent to or read from a stream, such as a FileStream. To help you apply cryptography concepts in real applications, the .NET Framework offers the CryptoStream object. Your code typically wraps a CryptoStream object around a regular stream (a file stream, a memory stream, a network stream, and so on) and specifies which algorithm the CryptoStream is associated with. For example, here's how you can create a CryptoStream object that uses the default algorithm for symmetrical encryption to encrypt data sent to a memory stream:

```
Dim encr As SymmetricAlgorithm = SymmetricAlgorithm.Create()
Dim ms As New MemoryStream
Dim encStream As New CryptoStream(ms, encr.CreateEncryptor, CryptoStreamMode.Write)
```

Figure 33-12 shows how the CryptoStream object works to encrypt and decrypt data. The application writes the unencrypted data to the CryptoStream object, which in turn encrypts it using the associated algorithm and then outputs the encrypted data via the inner Stream object.

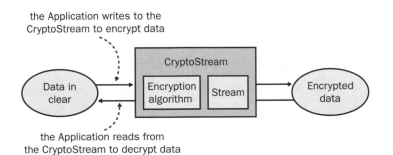

Figure 33-12   The CryptoStream object encrypting and decrypting data

Some time later, the same or another application can read back the data by creating another CryptoStream object in read mode: the CryptoStream object will use the internal Stream object to retrieve the data and will pass it to the encryption algorithm, and will finally return the decrypted bytes. The following code shows how you can encrypt and decrypt an array of bytes in memory:

```
' (This code reuses the BytesToHex procedure
'  introduced in the "Working with Evidence" section.)

' This is the data to be encrypted.
Dim originalData() As Byte = {1, 3, 5, 9, 11, 13, 15}
Console.WriteLine("Original data : " & BytesToHex(originalData))

' The object used to encrypt and decrypt
Dim encr As SymmetricAlgorithm = SymmetricAlgorithm.Create()
' The destination of encrypted data
Dim memStream As New System.IO.MemoryStream(10000)
' The CryptoStream that encrypts with symmetrical algorithm _
  and writes to the destination
Dim encStream As New CryptoStream(memStream, encr.CreateEncryptor, _
  CryptoStreamMode.Write)
```

```
' Write to the CryptoStream to encrypt data.
encStream.Write(originalData, 0, originalData.Length)
' Ensure bytes have been written and padding bytes have been added, if necessary.
encStream.FlushFinalBlock()

' Retrieve encrypted data and display it.
Dim encryptedData() As Byte = memStream.ToArray()
Console.WriteLine("Encrypted data: " & BytesToHex(encryptedData))

' We can reuse the MemoryStream, as it already contains the data to be decrypted.
memStream.Seek(0, SeekOrigin.Begin)
' The CryptoStream that reads data from the stream and decrypts it.
' (We reuse the same SymmetricAlgorithm object to create the decryptor.)
Dim decStream As New CryptoStream(memStream, encr.CreateDecryptor, CryptoStreamMode.Re
ad)

' Read the decrypted data from the CryptoStream object.
' (In this demo a 1024-byte read buffer will suffice)
Dim buffer(1023) As Byte
Dim count As Integer = decStream.Read(buffer, 0, 1024)
' Copy the bytes that have been actually read into the result array.
Dim decryptedBytes(count - 1) As Byte
Array.Copy(buffer, decryptedBytes, count)
Console.WriteLine("Decrypted data: " & BytesToHex(decryptedBytes))
```

Here's an example of what you might see in the console window when you run this code:

```
Original data : 010305090B0D0F
Encrypted data: BA327819FAD7AE9127620C81124053FD
Decrypted data: 010305090B0D0F
```

Encrypted data can be longer than original (and decrypted) data because the encryptor can add one or more padding bytes to make the length of the block a multiple of the value returned by the BlockSize property of the encryption object (16 bytes, in this case). It's crucial that you invoke the FlushFinalBlock method after writing the last bytes of the data to be encrypted, otherwise these padding bytes aren't added and data can't be decrypted correctly.

There are two more things you should know about CryptoStream objects. First, they don't support the Seek method and can be accessed only sequentially. Second, when you close a CryptoStream object the inner Stream object is closed as well. If you close the inner Stream manually, you'll get an exception when closing the CryptoStream object.

The structure of the previous code is simple because it uses a single SymmetricAlgorithm-derived object so both the encryption and decryption phases use the same random key that is generated when such an object is created. In most real-world cases, however, encrypted data is stored in a file that's later processed by a different program (or another instance of the same program). In this more realistic scenario, it's up to you to either store the random key in a safe place or reinitialize the Key property with a well-known sequence of bytes. The steps you take to accomplish this task depend on the type of encryption algorithm you're using.

Symmetrical Encryption

You can create an instance of a class that implements a symmetrical algorithm in many ways:

```
' The default symmetrical algorithm, as defined at the machine level
Dim encr As SymmetricAlgorithm = SymmetricAlgorithm.Create()

' The default implementation of a symmetrical algorithm (Rijndael in this case)
Dim encr2 As Rijndael = Rijndael.Create()

' A specific implementation of a symmetrical algorithm (TripleDES in this case)
Dim encr3 As New TripleDESCryptoServiceProvider
```

Although using the New keyword is OK in most cases, it is recommended that you invoke the Create method so that your code is generic and can work with different machine-level default values.

All symmetric algorithm objects require that you assign their Key and IV properties before encrypting and decrypting data. The Key property is the password that the algorithm uses in the encryption process and must be assigned an array of bytes of a given length. Each specific symmetric algorithm supports keys of different lengths—for example, 128, 192, or 256 bits in the case of Rijndael or 192 bits for TripleDES. By default, the .NET Framework uses the longest key size among those available for increased security:

```
Dim encr As Rijndael = Rijndael.Create()
Console.WriteLine(encr.KeySize)            ' => 256
```

As I mentioned in the previous section, symmetric algorithm objects use a randomly generated key if you don't assign a specific value to the Key property. If you use a self-generated key, you have to store it in a safe place, such as a file inside an ACL-protected directory, so that you can later reassign it when decrypting the data. Or you can burn it in code, as follows:

```
' (Continuing previous example...)
encr.Key = New Byte() {23, 45, 98, 231, 244, 5, 89, 33, 44, 23, 45, 78, 123, 222, _
    47, 56, 230, 59, 77, 2, 74, 254, 45, 76, 3, 70, 60, 58, 101, 35, 40, 9}
```

The IV property holds the so-called initialization vector. By default, the encrypting object processes one chunk of bytes at a time and uses the previous encrypted block to make the data look even more random. The Byte array assigned to the IV property is used to add randomness to encrypted blocks. Unlike the Key property, you don't need to store the IV property in a safe place, but it is essential that you use random values for its bytes. If you don't assign this property explicitly, a random Byte array is generated for you when the encrypting process starts. It is crucial that you reuse the same value when decrypting the data.

The following routine initializes a symmetrical algorithm object with the Key and IV values stored on a file; the file is created the first time you call the procedure:

```
Sub InitializeSymmetricAlgorithm(ByVal encr As SymmetricAlgorithm, _
    ByVal filename As String)
    Dim fs As FileStream
    Dim ivLength As Integer = encr.IV.Length

    Try
        fs = New FileStream(filename, FileMode.OpenOrCreate)
        If fs.Length = 0 Then
            ' The file wasn't there. Save randomly generated key and IV.
            fs.Write(encr.Key, 0, encr.Key.Length)
            fs.Write(encr.IV, 0, ivLength)
        Else
            ' Else, read the key from file.
            Dim bytes(encr.KeySize \ 8 - 1) As Byte
            fs.Read(bytes, 0, bytes.Length)
            encr.Key = bytes
            ' Read the initialization vector.
            ReDim bytes(ivLength - 1)
            fs.Read(bytes, 0, ivLength)
            encr.IV = bytes
        End If
    Finally
        If Not fs Is Nothing Then fs.Close()
    End Try
End Sub
```

The following code shows how you can use the preceding procedure to save a Byte array to an encrypted file and read it back later.

```
' Create a byte array for testing.
Dim data(1023) As Byte
For i As Integer = 0 To data.Length - 1
    data(i) = CByte(i Mod 256)
Next

' ****** ENCRYPTION ******
' Encrypt data and write it to C:\ENCRYPTED.DAT file.

Dim encr As Rijndael = Rijndael.Create()
InitializeSymmetricAlgorithm(encr, "c:\key.dat")

Dim fs As FileStream
Dim cs As CryptoStream
Try
    ' Open the file for writing.
    fs = New FileStream("c:\encrypted.dat", FileMode.Create)
    ' Create the CryptoStream that can write to that file.
    cs = New CryptoStream(fs, encr.CreateEncryptor(), CryptoStreamMode.Write)
    ' Write and encrypt the bytes in the input buffer.
    cs.Write(data, 0, data.Length)
    cs.FlushFinalBlock()
```

```
Finally
    If Not cs Is Nothing Then
        cs.Close()            ' This also closes the underlying FileStream.
    ElseIf Not fs Is Nothing Then
        fs.Close()
    End If
End Try


' ****** DECRYPTION ******
' Create another SymmetricAlgorithm object, initialize it with same key and IV.

Dim encr2 As SymmetricAlgorithm = SymmetricAlgorithm.Create()
InitializeSymmetricAlgorithm(encr2, "c:\key.dat")

' Read and decrypt the C:\ENCRYPTED.DAT file.
Dim fs2 As FileStream
Dim cs2 As CryptoStream
Dim data2() As Byte
Try
    ' Open the file for reading.
    fs2 = New FileStream("c:\encrypted.dat", FileMode.Open)
    ' Create the CryptoStream that can read from that file.
    cs2 = New CryptoStream(fs2, encr2.CreateDecryptor(), CryptoStreamMode.Read)
    ' Read and decrypt the contents of the file.
    ReDim data2(CInt(fs2.Length) - 1)
    cs2.Read(data2, 0, data2.Length)
Finally
    If Not cs2 Is Nothing Then
        cs2.Close()               ' This also closes the underlying FileStream.
    ElseIf Not fs2 Is Nothing Then
        fs2.Close()
    End If
End Try
```

A better technique consists of using a different, randomly generated initialization vector for each file. In this case, you must store the IV property at the top of the encrypted file (but in an unencrypted format) so that you can restore it correctly when you decrypt the file. These two reusable routines let you apply this technique and show how to encrypt and decrypt large files in chunks:

```
' Encrypt a file, optionally including the IV in the output.
' (Pass True to last argument to store IV in file.)
Sub EncryptFile(ByVal encr As SymmetricAlgorithm, ByVal sourceFile As String, _
    ByVal destFile As String, ByVal includeIV As Boolean)
    Dim souFs, desFs As FileStream
    Dim cs As CryptoStream
    Const BUFFERSIZE As Integer = 4096

    Try
        ' Open source and destination streams.
        souFs = New FileStream(sourceFile, FileMode.Open)
        desFs = New FileStream(destFile, FileMode.Create)
        ' Write the (unencrypted) IV to the output file, if so requested.
```

```
        If includeIV Then
            desFs.Write(encr.IV, 0, encr.IV.Length)
        End If
        ' Create the CryptoStream that encrypts data and writes it to file.
        cs = New CryptoStream(desFs, encr.CreateEncryptor, CryptoStreamMode.Write)

        Dim bytes(BUFFERSIZE - 1) As Byte
        Do
            ' Read bytes from source file, exit if no more bytes.
            Dim bytesRead As Integer = souFs.Read(bytes, 0, bytes.Length)
            If bytesRead = 0 Then Exit Do
            ' Encrypt and write bytes to the destination file.
            cs.Write(bytes, 0, bytesRead)
        Loop
        cs.FlushFinalBlock()
    Finally
        ' Close all streams.
        If Not souFs Is Nothing Then souFs.Close()
        If Not cs Is Nothing Then
            cs.Close()
        ElseIf Not desFs Is Nothing Then
            desFs.Close()
        End If
    End Try
End Sub

' Decrypt a file. (The file might contain an IV value.)
Sub DecryptFile(ByVal encr As SymmetricAlgorithm, ByVal sourceFile As String, _
    ByVal destFile As String, ByVal includeIV As Boolean)
    Dim souFs, desFs As FileStream
    Dim cs As CryptoStream
    Const BUFFERSIZE As Integer = 4096

    Try
        ' Open source and destination streams.
        souFs = New FileStream(sourceFile, FileMode.Open)
        desFs = New FileStream(destFile, FileMode.Create)

        ' Read the (unencrypted) IV from source file, if so requested.
        If includeIV Then
            Dim iv(encr.IV.Length - 1) As Byte
            souFs.Read(iv, 0, iv.Length)
            encr.IV = iv
        End If
        ' Create the CryptoStream that can read and decrypt data from source stream.
        cs = New CryptoStream(souFs, encr.CreateDecryptor, CryptoStreamMode.Read)

        Dim bytes(BUFFERSIZE - 1) As Byte
        Do
            ' Read and decrypt bytes from source file, exit if no more bytes.
            Dim bytesRead As Integer = cs.Read(bytes, 0, bytes.Length)
            If bytesRead = 0 Then Exit Do
            ' Write decrypted bytes to the destination file.
            desFs.Write(bytes, 0, bytesRead)
        Loop
```

```
        Finally
            ' Close all streams.
            If Not desFs Is Nothing Then desFs.Close()
            If Not cs Is Nothing Then
                cs.Close()
            ElseIf Not souFs Is Nothing Then
                souFs.Close()
            End If
        End Try
    End Sub
```

Asymmetric Encryption

As you can see in Figure 33-11, the System.Security.Cryptography namespace contains two abstract classes that derive from AsymmetricAlgorithm, namely RSA and DSA, and two concrete classes that implement these algorithms by wrapping the CryptoAPI, namely RSACryptoServiceProvider and DSACryptoServiceProvider. By default, the Create shared method of the AsymmetricAlgorithm class creates an RSACryptoServiceProvider object:

```
Dim asym As AsymmetricAlgorithm = AsymmetricAlgorithm.Create()
Console.WriteLine(asym.GetType().Name)      ' => RSACryptoServiceProvider
```

Asymmetric encryption algorithms work with two distinct keys: a private key and a public key. You can generate a key pair and give away the public key so that anyone can use it to encrypt a message that only you can decrypt.

As with a symmetric algorithm, a freshly created AsymmetricAlgorithm object contains randomly generated keys. You can export them to XML (and possibly save them on file) with the ToXmlString method and import them with the FromXmlString method:

```
' (Continuing previous example...)
Dim publicKey As String = asym.ToXmlString(False)
Dim bothKeys As String = asym.ToXmlString(True)

' Create a new object that contains only the public key.
Dim asym2 As AsymmetricAlgorithm = AsymmetricAlgorithm.Create()
asym2.FromXmlString(publicKey)
```

It's easy to create a procedure that initializes an AsymmetricAlgorithm object with the key pair (or just the public key) stored in an XML file, similar to what we did with SymmetricAlgorithm objects:

```
' Initialize an AsymmetricAlgorithm object from an XML file and create
' the file if necessary. (includePrivateKey is ignored if the file exists.)
Sub InitializeAsymmetricAlgorithm(ByVal asym As AsymmetricAlgorithm, _
        ByVal filename As String, ByVal includePrivateKey As Boolean)
    Dim fs As FileStream
    Try
        ' Open the file, create it if not there.
        fs = New FileStream(filename, FileMode.OpenOrCreate, FileAccess.ReadWrite)
```

```
            If fs.Length = 0 Then
                ' File didn't exist, export both keys or just the public key.
                Dim sw As New StreamWriter(fs)
                sw.Write(asym.ToXmlString(includePrivateKey))
                sw.Close()
            Else
                ' File exists, import whatever key is there.
                Dim sr As New StreamReader(fs)
                asym.FromXmlString(sr.ReadToEnd())
            End If
        Finally
            If Not fs Is Nothing Then fs.Close()
        End Try
End Sub
```

Unlike objects for symmetric encryption, which expose a uniform interface, the methods that asymmetric encryption objects expose vary with the specific algorithm. In the remainder of this section, I'll show how you can use an RSACryptoServiceProvider object to encrypt and decrypt data:

```
Dim rsaCSP As New RSACryptoServiceProvider
' Save both keys to file the first time you run this code.
InitializeAsymmetricAlgorithm(rsaCSP, "c:\rsakey.xml", True)
```

You can encrypt data with this object only if it has been initialized with both the private and the public key; if only the public key has been assigned, this object can only decrypt data.

Encrypting data is as simple as invoking the Encrypt method, which takes the Byte array to be encrypted and a Boolean that specifies OAEP padding (can be True only on Windows XP and later). The size of the data that can be encrypted is limited, however. On most systems it can't be higher than 64 bits:

```
' Create a byte array for testing.
Dim data(1023) As Byte
For i As Integer = 0 To data.Length - 1
    data(i) = CByte(i Mod 256)
Next

' 2nd argument enables OAEP padding. It can be True only on Windows XP and later.
Dim encryptedBytes() As Byte = rsaCSP.Encrypt(data, False)
```

Notice that the result array might be longer than the original array. In addition, each time you run this code you will see different values in the result array because the RSA algorithm uses randomly generated numbers.

You can decrypt an encrypted array with the Decrypt method:

```
' Create another object for the decryption step.
Dim rsaCSP2 As RSACryptoServiceProvider = New RSACryptoServiceProvider
InitializeAsymmetricAlgorithm(rsaCSP2, "c:\rsakey.xml", True)

' Second argument enables OAEP padding. (Must match padding used by encryption.)
Dim data2() As Byte = rsaCSP2.Decrypt(encryptedBytes, False)
```

The limit to the size of the data that can be encrypted in one operation and the relatively slow performance of asymmetric algorithms make them unfit to work with large files. However, you can adopt the following compromise: generate a large random key, use that key to encrypt the file with a more efficient symmetric algorithm, and then use the more secure RSA algorithm only to encrypt the large random key.

For example, the HTTPS protocol uses asymmetric encryption to encode the key used by the symmetric algorithm that encrypts the actual data.

Hash Algorithms

Figure 33-11 shows several classes that inherit directly or indirectly from HashAlgorithm. These objects let you analyze a block of data to compute its hash value, which could be considered as the signature of the data. Even though two different blocks of data—for example, two files—might coincidentally provide the same hash value, in practice the chance that this will happen is negligible. Even more importantly, the hash function can't be reversed; therefore, it's virtually impossible to create a block of data that corresponds to a known hash value. This feature can ensure that you can detect any change in a file whose original hash value is known.

The most frequently used concrete class in the list is SHA1CryptoServiceProvider, which is also the default object returned by a Create shared method:

```
Dim hash As HashAlgorithm = HashAlgorithm.Create()
Console.WriteLine(hash.GetType().Name)      ' => SHA1CryptoServiceProvider
```

Once you have an object that derives from HashAlgorithm, you can compute the hash of a block of data with the ComputeHash method. This method exposes three overloaded versions, which can take a Byte array, a portion of a Byte array, or a stream. The return value from the ComputeHash method is another Byte array that represents the hash value for the data. Here's a simple routine that uses this method to calculate the hash value of a given file:

```
Function ComputeHashFromFile(ByVal filename As String) As Byte()
    Dim sha1 As SHA1 = sha1.Create()
    Dim fs As FileStream
    Try
        fs = New FileStream(filename, FileMode.Open)
        Return sha1.ComputeHash(fs)
    Finally
        If Not fs Is Nothing Then fs.Close()
    End Try
End Function
```

Using this function is trivial:

```
Dim hash() As Byte = ComputeHashFromFile("c:\mydatafile.txt")
Console.WriteLine(BytesToHex(hash))
```

You can invoke the ComputeHash method of a SHA1CryptoServiceProvider object multiple times, without having to reinitialize the object.

The ComputeHash method works well when data you want to hash is in a buffer or a stream, but it isn't flexible enough when you want to hash from multiple sources—for example, to generate a hash value for all the files in a directory. In this case, you must create a CryptoStream that wraps another stream and that evaluates the hash of any data written to it. If you associate a CryptoStream object with an object that derives from HashAlgorithm, bytes aren't modified in any way while they are read from or written to the underlying stream; instead, their hash value is computed and will be available at the end of the operation. If the CryptoStream doesn't need to send data anywhere, you can wrap it around a do-nothing stream, such as the following NullStream:

```
Class NullStream
    Inherits MemoryStream
    Public Overrides Sub Write(ByVal buffer() As Byte, _
        ByVal offset As Integer, ByVal count As Integer)
        ' Do nothing here.
    End Sub
End Class
```

Here's a complete and reusable routine that uses a SHA1 object and a CryptoStream to compute a single hash value for all the files in a given directory:

```
' Generate a single hash value for all the files in a directory.
Function ComputeHashFromDirectory(ByVal path As String) As Byte()
    Dim sha1 As SHA1 = sha1.Create()
    ' A CryptoStream that wraps a null stream but hashes data sent to it.
    Dim cs As New CryptoStream(New NullStream, sha1, CryptoStreamMode.Write)

    ' Iterate over all the files in the directory.
    For Each file As String In Directory.GetFiles(path)
        Dim fs As FileStream
        Try
            ' Open the file for input
            fs = New FileStream(file, FileMode.Open)
            Dim buffer(4095) As Byte
            Do
                ' Read this file in chunks, exit when no more bytes.
                Dim readBytes As Integer = fs.Read(buffer, 0, buffer.Length)
                If readBytes = 0 Then Exit Do
                ' Send to null stream, but compute hash at the same time.
                cs.Write(buffer, 0, readBytes)
            Loop
        Finally
            If Not fs Is Nothing Then fs.Close()
        End Try
    Next

    ' We can now evaluate the hash of all files.
    cs.FlushFinalBlock()
    cs.Close()
    Return sha1.Hash
End Function
```

Keyed Hash Algorithms

The ComputeHashFromFile and ComputeHashFromDirectory functions introduced in previous sections let you easily detect whether a file has been tampered with, without having to store a copy of the original file. However, they assume that you save the hash value in a safe place so that attackers can't simply recompute the hash value of the new version of the file and replace the original hash value with the recomputed value. This assumption is unrealistic if you're transmitting data over the wire because the hash value must travel with the data itself.

You can solve this problem with one of the two concrete classes that inherit from the KeyedHashAlgorithm abstract class, namely HMACSHA1 and MacTripleDES. (See Figure 33-11.) A keyed hash algorithm is similar to a regular hash algorithm, except you initialize the hash function with a secret key. This mechanism prevents attackers from recomputing the hash value because they don't know the key used by the hash function. I prepared a pair of reusable methods that wrap this algorithm. AppendHash evaluates the keyed hash value of a file and appends this value to the file itself; VerifyHash verifies a file signed by the previous routine and optionally removes the hash value. The source code for AppendHash is quite linear:

```
' Append the keyed hash value of a file to end of the file itself.
Sub AppendHash(ByVal filename As String, ByVal key() As Byte)
    ' Create a keyed hash object with given key.
    Dim keyhash As New HMACSHA1(key)
    Dim fs As FileStream

    Try
        ' Open the file
        fs = New FileStream(filename, FileMode.Open)
        ' Evaluate hash value.
        Dim hash() As Byte = keyhash.ComputeHash(fs)
        ' Append hash at the end of the file.
        fs.Write(hash, 0, hash.Length)
    Finally
        If Not fs Is Nothing Then fs.Close()
    End Try
End Sub
```

The VerifyHash procedure can't use a ComputeHash method on the input stream because this method would include the hash value at the end of the file. Instead, this procedure uses a CryptoStream that wraps a NullStream object to evaluate the hash code of data as it is being read from the file, but stops reading just before the trailing hash code.

```
' Return True if a file signed with AppendHash hasn't been modified,
' and optionally deletes the hash value.
Function VerifyHash(ByVal filename As String, ByVal key() As Byte, _
    ByVal discardHash As Boolean) As Boolean
    ' Create a keyed hash object with given key.
```

```
        Dim keyhash As New HMACSHA1(key)
        Dim fs As FileStream
        Dim cs As CryptoStream

        Try
            ' Open the file.
            fs = New FileStream(filename, FileMode.Open)
            ' Create a CryptoStream that just evaluates the hash value.
            cs = New CryptoStream(New NullStream, keyhash, CryptoStreamMode.Write)
            ' The number of bytes in the file excluding hash at the end
            Dim bytesToRead As Integer = CInt(fs.Length) - keyhash.HashSize \ 8

            ' Read the file contents while evaluating its hash code.
            Dim buffer(4095) As Byte
            Do
                Dim bytesRead As Integer = fs.Read(buffer, 0, _
                    Math.Min(bytesToRead, buffer.Length))
                If bytesRead = 0 Then Exit Do
                bytesToRead -= bytesRead
                ' Send data to null stream just to evaluate the hash code.
                cs.Write(buffer, 0, bytesRead)
            Loop
            ' Evaluate the hash value of data read so far.
            cs.FlushFinalBlock()
            Dim realHash() As Byte = keyhash.Hash

            ' Read the hash value stored at the end of the file.
            Dim storedHash(keyhash.HashSize \ 8 - 1) As Byte
            fs.Read(storedHash, 0, storedHash.Length)
            ' Discard hash value if so requested.
            If discardHash Then fs.SetLength(fs.Length - storedHash.Length)

            ' Compare real and stored hash bytes, return False if they don't match.
            For i As Integer = 0 To realHash.Length - 1
                If realHash(i) <> storedHash(i) Then Return False
            Next
            ' All bytes match, hash is verified.
            Return True
        Finally
            If Not cs Is Nothing Then cs.Close()
            If Not fs Is Nothing Then fs.Close()
        End Try
    End Function
```

Random Values

Many of the cryptographic classes seen so far require a key containing random bytes. For obvious reasons, the more random the key is, the more secure the encryption. For a robust encryption mechanism, however, you can't just use the System.Random class to generate random keys because this class generates sequences of values that are reproducible and aren't random enough for cryptographic purposes. Instead, you should use the RNGCryptoServiceProvider class, which wraps the CryptoAPI library. Using this class to generate a random sequence of bytes is trivial:

```
Dim rng As New RNGCryptoServiceProvider
Dim bytes(63) As Byte
rng.GetBytes(bytes)
```

You can also explicitly request that no byte in the sequence be zero:

```
Dim bytes2(1023) As Byte
rng.GetNonZeroBytes(bytes2)
```

Another common way to generate a key to be used for encryption purposes is to derive it from a textual password. For example, you can ask your user for a readable password such as "ILoveDotNet" and your program generates a seemingly random sequence of bytes using some sort of transformation over each character in the string. This technique makes an attacker's job much harder while letting the end user use a human-readable password.

You can easily transform a human-readable password into an apparently disordered sequence of bytes by means of a PasswordDerivedBytes object. The constructor for this object takes a string and a Byte array. This byte array is known as the *salt* and it has more or less the same purpose that initialization vectors have with symmetric encryption algorithms: they help hide any pattern in the input data.

```
Dim password As String = "ILoveDotNet"
Dim salt() As Byte = {3, 45, 78, 123, 9, 77}
Dim pdb As New PasswordDeriveBytes(password, salt)
Dim bytes() As Byte = pdb.GetBytes(32)
```

This code creates the same byte sequence for each given password (provided that you use the same salt array, of course).

Security is a complex matter. It has always been complex, and the .NET Framework makes it even more complicated, if possible, because of the new CAS features. There is more about security than I could cover in this chapter (which is already one of the longest in the book), but the concepts you learned here are more than sufficient to become a security-wise developer. You'll see some of these concepts in action in the next chapter, where I'll show how you can invoke forms over the HTTP protocol.

34 Programming for the Internet

You can take advantage of the opportunities that the Internet offers in ways other than creating Web Forms and Web Services applications. For example, you could have a Windows Forms application read and process Web pages (thereby creating a Web crawler), send e-mail, or communicate via TCP or directly through sockets.

Just as interesting, the .NET Framework offers a completely new and quite revolutionary way of deploying your Windows Forms application. This technique combines the power of Windows Forms applications—with their support for menus, drag-and-drop operations, complex controls, and so on—with the ease of deployment that Web Forms applications have.

> **Note** To keep the code as concise as possible, all the code samples in this section assume the use of the following Imports statements at the file or project level:
>
> ```
> Imports System.Reflection
> Imports System.IO
> Imports System.IO.IsolatedStorage
> Imports System.Security.Permissions
> Imports System.Net
> Imports System.Net.Sockets
> Imports System.Web.Mail
> ```

Windows Forms Applications over HTTP

Instead of installing your executables on the end user's machine, you can have your users access them over HTTP by typing the complete URL of the main executable in the address bar of Microsoft Internet Explorer. This deployment mechanism doesn't require that the server be Internet Information Services (IIS) or that the .NET Framework be installed on the server. As a matter of fact, the server machine might even run on an operating system other than Windows. The entire magic, in fact, is done on the client, where you must install the .NET Framework and Internet Explorer 5.01 or later.

Deploying a Windows Forms application over HTTP isn't difficult once you account for a few details. You begin by creating a simple Windows Forms application using Visual Studio .NET, or use the demo application I built for you, named HttpFormDemo.exe. (See Figure 34-1.)

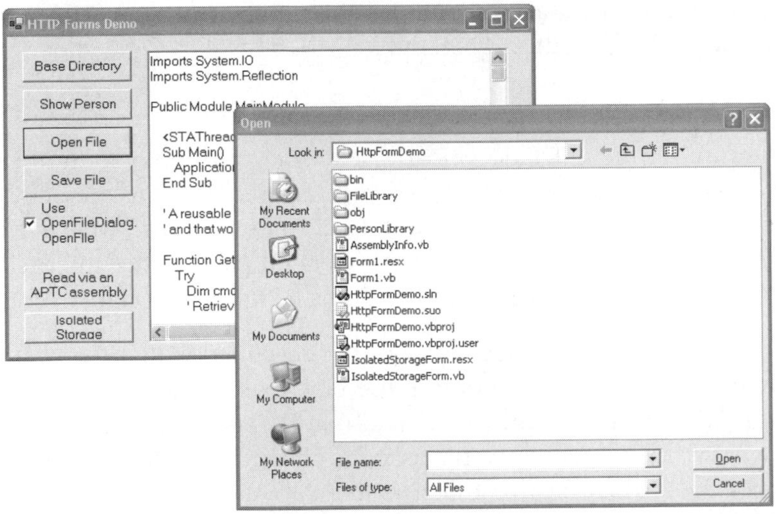

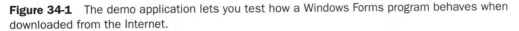

Figure 34-1   The demo application lets you test how a Windows Forms program behaves when downloaded from the Internet.

In the next step, you must make the executable accessible from the Internet. The following directions assume that you have IIS installed on your development machine, but any Web server will do in a production environment. Go to Windows Explorer, right-click on the Bin directory that contains the executable, and select the Sharing and Security menu command. Switch to the Web Sharing tab, select the Share this folder option, and assign this share the name HttpDemo under the Default Web Site. (You need to grant only read access.) If you're running on Windows Server 2003, you must also ensure that the new virtual directory grants access to unauthorized users if you want to access the executable from the Internet.

Finally, you can run your application by navigating to *http://localhost/HttpForm/ HttpFormDemo.exe* from inside Internet Explorer or by means of the Run command on the Start menu. It's that easy!

The demo application uses a Person object defined in a separate DLL that's stored in the same directory as the main executable. As you can see by clicking on the Show Person button, the .NET assembly loader is able to locate this DLL and correctly instantiate the object. (You can review the way the .NET runtime looks for assemblies in Chapter 13.)

The .NET Download Cache

All the executable files that make up your applications are cached in the .NET download cache. This caching mechanism makes all subsequent downloads much faster. In fact, when you ask for the same .exe file again (and when the .exe file tells .NET to load a .dll file), the .NET runtime checks the timestamp of the file in its cache and uses an If-Modified-Since HTTP header when sending the request. If the file hasn't been modified in the meantime, the .NET runtime uses the cached version. You can browse the .NET download cache with this command:

```
GACUTIL /ldl
```

At times, you must clear the .NET download cache for your deployment tests, which you do with the /cdl option of the Gacutil tool. Just remember that to correctly simulate a "clean" user machine, you should also delete all files from the Internet Explorer cache, an action that you can perform from the General page of the Internet Options dialog box. (You can reach this page from the Tools menu of Internet Explorer.)

An important consequence of the mechanism I just described is that Internet Explorer downloads a new version of the .exe only if the new executable file has a timestamp later than the one downloaded previously, and that the assembly version number is ignored. However, when the main .exe file asks for one or more strong name DLLs, the version number is checked. You can redirect requests for an assembly as you'd do with a standard .NET application—that is, by means of a configuration file in the same directory as the main .exe file.

A Visual Basic .NET application can indirectly check whether it is being executed from a local directory or downloaded from the Web by looking at the BaseDirectory property of the current AppDomain object:

```
Dim appbase As String = AppDomain.CurrentDomain.BaseDirectory
```

This property returns a string such as *http://localhost/HttpForm/* when the application has been accessed via HTTP.

Debugging

In general, you should debug a Windows Forms application intended to be launched via HTTP before you actually deploy it on the Web server and ensure that the application works correctly when run from a local disk. In this way, you'll fix most bugs and only have to deal with problems deriving from the different environment a .NET application runs in when it is running from a system other the local computer. Most of the differences you have to account for are related to security.

When you're finally ready to load the application via HTTP, you discover an unpleasant surprise: the Visual Studio .NET debugger simply doesn't work. The reason is simple. The instance of your .exe that Visual Studio .NET can debug isn't the same instance that you reach through HTTP. Never fear, however; you can use the Debug Processes command in the Debug menu to attach the debugger to any executable running on your machine. You must select the Show system processes option to see the process and look for a process named IEExec.exe. This application (located in the C:\Windows\Microsoft.NET\Framework*vx.y.zzzz* directory) is used by the .NET Framework to load executables downloaded from the Web and to ensure that they run in a correct security environment. (This tool is poorly documented. I found it by searching the list of processes running in my system after launching an .exe via HTTP.) After you attach the debugger to the IEExec.exe application, you can debug your application as usual. Even if you don't want to debug the application, knowing that your executable runs under IEExec.exe is important if you want to kill your application by using the Windows Task Manager—for example, if it enters an endless loop.

You can simplify the debugging phase by changing the action that Visual Studio .NET performs when you invoke the Start command from the Debug menu (or just press the F5 key). In the Debugging page of the Project Properties dialog box, select the Start external program option and type the complete path to IEExec.exe, then type the URL of the .exe program in the Command line argument field—for example, *http://localhost /HttpForm/HttpFormDemo.exe*. (See Figure 34-2.) This way your application will run as if it had been downloaded from an intranet site.

By the way, here's a little-known trick to simulate the security settings applied to an application (or any resource, for that matter) loaded from the Internet (as opposed to loaded from an intranet site): just use the 127.0.0.1 IP address instead of localhost. For example, you can debug the demo application as if it were loaded from the Internet by typing *http://127.0.0.1/HttpForm/HttpFormDemo.exe* in the Debugging page of the Project Properties dialog box.

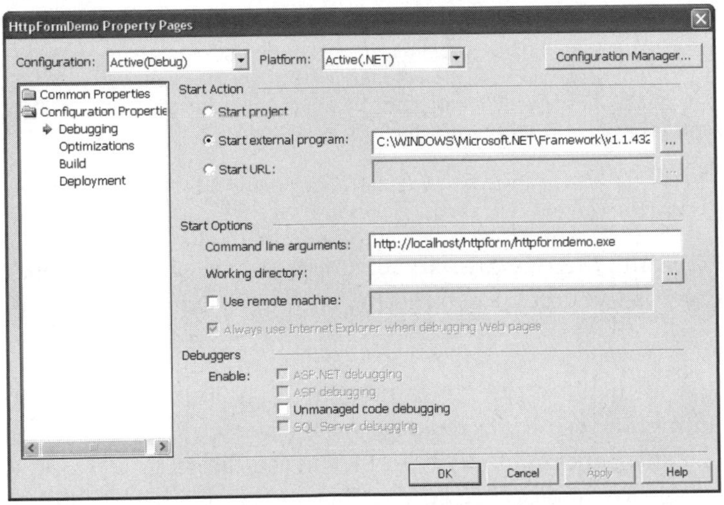

Figure 34-2 The Debugging tab of the Project Properties dialog box lets you easily debug a Windows Forms application launched from the Web.

Security Issues

You must be prepared to solve a few problems if your application reads and writes files and, more in general, accesses resources on the client machine. (You might want to review the "Permission Sets" section in Chapter 33 to get more details about how CAS works with untrusted assemblies.)

Working with Files

For starters, if your application reads files in the same directory as its executable—for example, a bitmap or an XML file—you can't use a standard Stream or StreamReader object because they don't support remote URI arguments. (Remember that the application is now running on the client, not on the server where the .exe file resides.) If the files you're working with are read-only—for example, the bitmaps and icons used by the application—you should embed them as resources in your application. (See "Working with Embedded Resources" section in Chapter 15.) Or you can use a satellite DLL so that the .NET assembly loader can locate them on the server.

If the files you want to work with are on the end user's machine, you must solve a completely different category of problems, all coming from the security restrictions that .NET poses to assemblies that don't reside on a local drive. In the default configuration, an assembly launched from the intranet can both read and write files on the client machine, but it can open those files only via the OpenFile method of the OpenFileDialog or Save-FileDialog control. An assembly downloaded from the Internet has stricter permissions and can only read a file, again only by means of the OpenFile method of the OpenFile-Dialog control. (In addition, you might need to include the specific Internet domain in the list of trusted sites; otherwise such an assembly isn't downloaded at all.) The rationale behind this setting is that an assembly launched from the Web should access a file on the local machine only after the explicit approval of the end user:

```
' This code succeeds if the assembly is downloaded from the Intranet,
' but fails if it has been downloaded from the Internet.
Dim sw As New StreamWriter(SaveFileDialog1.OpenFile)

' This code always fails if the assembly is downloaded over HTTP.
Dim sw2 As New StreamWriter(SaveFileDialog1.Filename)
```

If you attempt to open the file directly—for example, by passing the filename to the StreamWriter constructor—you get a SecurityException, which you can trap like any other exception.

Instead of working with files on the client machine, a Windows Forms application deployed via HTTP might access data residing on the server. By default an assembly launched from the local intranet can only read files in the directory it was loaded from. Likewise, an assembly downloaded from the Internet and Trusted Sites zones can access the Web site it was loaded from. In either case, modifying data in the original directory or site isn't allowed.

You can work around this limitation by setting up a Web service that the assembly can use to both read and write data that is shared by all other clients, including data stored in a database. Remember, however, the limitation that an assembly can only access the Web site it comes from applies to Web services as well.

Yet another option you have for working with data files is based on isolated storage. I'll discuss this technique later in this chapter.

Increasing Security Permissions

In Chapter 33, you learned how to increase the permissions assigned to an assembly launched from the Web by means of the .NET Configuration tool. In this section I'll show you how to change the level of trust for the specific assembly by using the Adjust .NET Security wizard, which you can reach from the Administrative Tools menu of the Windows task bar. On the first page of this wizard, you decide whether your changes apply to the Machine or to the User level. On the second page, you select the level of trust given to assemblies coming from one of the five Internet Explorer zones. The four ticks on the vertical trackbar correspond to the FullTrust, LocalIntranet, Internet, and Nothing permissions. (See Figure 34-3.)

In some cases, it makes sense to give full trust to all the applications originating from the local intranet; if the assembly is launched from a site outside the intranet, you can include the site in the list of Internet Explorer's trusted sites (accessed from the Security page of Internet Explorer's Internet Options dialog box) and then give full trust to the trusted sites group. (You could also give full trust to assemblies launched from anywhere on the Internet, but I strongly advise you against doing so, for obvious reasons.)

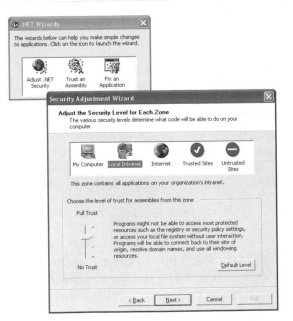

Figure 34-3   The Adjust .NET Security wizard lets you change the trust assigned to downloaded assemblies for the entire machine or a specific user.

You can also increase the trust level for a specific assembly, which in most cases is the preferred way to let downloaded assemblies perform their chores. In this case, you use the Trust an Assembly wizard, which lets you specify a given assembly by its network path or URL, as shown in Figure 34-4. Once again, you can change the trust level at the machine level or just for the current user only. It is advisable that you apply this technique only to strong name assemblies.

Once you give full trust to the *http://localhost/HttpForm/HttpFormDemo.exe* assembly, you can unselect the Use OpenFileDialog.OpenFile check box in the demo application and try the Open File and Save File buttons, which now will work without a glitch.

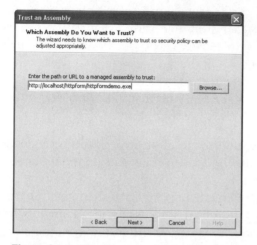

Figure 34-4   The Trust an Assembly wizard lets you change the trust level for a specific assembly.

Using the AllowPartiallyTrustedCallers Attribute

Another way to work around the limitations of downloaded assemblies is to gather all the routines that require full trust into a separate strong name library that's installed in the GAC and marked with the AllowPartiallyTrustedCallers attribute. As you learned in Chapter 33, by default strong name libraries refuse to be linked from partially trusted code, which is any code that doesn't have full trust. This happens because an implicit LinkDemand action is performed on the library, and this demand fails if the caller isn't fully trusted. The assembly-level AllowPartiallyTrustedCallers attribute disables this implicit LinkDemand and makes a strong name DLL accessible from any other assembly:

```
<Assembly: System.Security.AllowPartiallyTrustedCallers() >
```

It's important to remember that this attribute only disables the implicit LinkDemand on all the methods in the assembly, but if your assembly uses one or more .NET types that request a special permission, you need to assert that permission. For example, here is the source code of the FileReader class in the demo FileLibrary.dll; this class lets untrusted callers read any text file on the local system:

```
Public Class FileReader
    <FileIOPermission(SecurityAction.Assert, Unrestricted:=True)> _
    Public Shared Function ReadFile(ByVal filename As String) As String
        Dim st As StreamReader
        Try
            ' In a real application, you might enforce some restrictions on file
            ' name. For example, allow access only to files with given extension
            ' and residing in selected directories.
            st = New StreamReader(filename)
            Return st.ReadToEnd
```

```
        Finally
            If Not (st Is Nothing) Then st.Close()
        End Try
    End Function
End Class
```

The AllowPartiallyTrusted Callers attribute works only with strong name assemblies, so it must include an AssemblyKeyFile attribute and must be registered in the GAC with the GACUTIL tool.

Of course, the FileLibrary.dll must be installed on the client machine using a standard installation routine and can't be just downloaded from the Web, so this mechanism makes the deployment of your Windows Forms application less transparent to the end user. However, once this library is in the client's GAC you can use its classes and methods from any untrusted assembly.

> **Warning** As I explained in Chapter 33, you should apply the AllowPartiallyTrustedCallers attribute only if you're absolutely certain that no malicious code can cheat your assembly into damaging the system or stealing information. You can reach this degree of certainty only after carefully reviewing your code and understanding all the security implications of the methods you expose to your callers. For example, the sample FileLibrary.dll doesn't meet all these requirements because it lets an untrusted caller read any file in your system. For this reason, you should uninstall it from the GAC as soon as you've completed your tests. Leaving it in the GAC might make your system vulnerable to assemblies loaded from the Internet that are aware of this library. It isn't likely to happen, but it could.

You'll recall from Chapter 33 that only a subset of the assemblies in the .NET Framework have been flagged with the AllowPartiallyTrustedCallers attribute. This group includes mscorlib.dll, System.dll, System.Windows.Forms.dll, System.Drawing.dll, System.XML.dll, System.Data.dll, System.Web.dll, System.Web.Services.dll, and Microsoft.VisualBasic.dll. No other .NET Framework DLLs can be called by untrusted callers.

No-Touch Deployment

The ability to launch Windows Forms applications over the HTTP protocol is often dubbed *no-touch deployment*. To achieve real no-touch deployment, however, you must take into account the problem of how you automatically update the application to use the latest version of its components.

Using Windows Forms applications over HTTP gives you a great bonus: the actual executable files—both the main .exe file and all its DLLs—are never locked and you can overwrite them with newer versions without having to wait until all clients shut down their instances of the application. Even so, however, you can't simply overwrite all the application's files at once because a client might launch the application while you're updating the directory and might end up with files belonging to different versions.

The simple solution to this problem is to disable client access during the few seconds that you need to replace all the files in the application. However, you can never be sure that you won't stop the server while a user is in the middle of a download. Besides, not all users are willing to switch to a new version without being warned in advance, especially if the new version has a slightly different user interface or behavior; therefore, you need another, more flexible solution to this problem.

An easy way to solve the versioning problem relies on a small application on the client whose purpose is to read an XML file on the server that keeps track of the most recent versions of the application. Having this launcher program on the client partially defies the usefulness of no-touch deployment, but greatly simplifies your job and opens up a few interesting options.

To illustrate, let's suppose that you have both version 1.0 and 1.1 of the HttpForm-Demo.exe sample application. You should deploy these versions in two distinct subdirectories under the main application directory on the server—for example, in Ver10 and Ver11. The XML file containing versioning information can be as simple as this one:

```xml
<?xml version="1.0" encoding="utf-8" ?>
<configuration>
    <versioning latestVersion="1.1">
        <version number="1.0">
            <url>Ver10/HttpFormDemo10.exe</url>
        </version>
        <version number="1.1">
            <url>Ver11/HttpFormDemo11.exe</url>
        </version>
    </versioning>
</configuration>
```

You should name this file versioninfo.xml and deploy it in the virtual directory. The complete directory structure on the server now looks like this:

```
C:\MyApplication    (accessible from clients as http://yourservername/HttpDemo/)
    versioninfo.xml
    Ver10 (folder)
        HttpFormDemo10.exe
        ⋮
    Ver11 (folder)
        HttpFormDemo11.exe
        ⋮
```

The launcher program that clients must run is a Windows Forms application that doesn't display any window. (You can't use a console application because its empty console window would disorient users.) It connects to the specified Web site, reads the versioninfo.xml configuration file, reads the URL for the most recent version, and executes that assembly. Here's the complete source code for a simple launcher:

```
Imports System.Net
Imports System.IO
Imports System.Xml
```

```
Module Module1
    Const BASEURL As String = "http://localhost/HttpDemo/"

    Sub Main()
        ' Request the versioninfo.xml file.
        Dim versionUrl As String = BASEURL & "versioninfo.xml"
        Dim webReq As WebRequest = WebRequest.Create(versionUrl)
        Dim webRes As WebResponse = webReq.GetResponse()
        ' Read its contents as XML text.
        Dim xmlDoc As New XmlDocument
        xmlDoc.Load(webRes.GetResponseStream)

        ' Get the latest version number, using an XPath query.
        Dim node As XmlNode = xmlDoc.SelectSingleNode("//configuration/versioning")
        Dim latestVersion As String = node.Attributes("latestVersion").Value
        ' Read information about the latest version, using an XPath query.
        Dim xpathExpr As String = "//configuration/versioning/version[@number='" _
            & latestVersion & "']/url"
        Dim node2 As XmlNode = xmlDoc.SelectSingleNode(xpathExpr)
        Dim url As String = CType(node2, XmlElement).InnerText
        ' Convert to absolute path if needed.
        If Not url.StartsWith("/") Then url = BASEURL & url

        ' Run the assembly from there.
        Dim appDom As AppDomain = AppDomain.CreateDomain("newappdom")
        appDom.ExecuteAssembly(url, Nothing, Nothing)
    End Sub
End Module
```

Except for the WebRequest and WebResponse objects, which I'll cover later in this chapter, this is all familiar stuff that I won't explain in more detail. (You might want to review the XPath search expressions in Chapter 23.) Thanks to this launcher program, you can now prepare a new set of application files and store them in a separate directory, and then replace only the versioninfo.xml file with a new version. Replacing this XML file can be considered an atomic operation, and clients will never download files from mixed versions. (You don't even need to temporarily stop the Web server while you update these files.)

You can improve this mechanism in many ways. For example, if you believe it's safe to do so, you can pass an evidence object to the ExecuteAssembly method to load the assembly as if it were executing from a local disk (which would make it fully trusted). In another improvement, the launcher might take the value of BASEURL from the command line so that you can reuse the same launcher with all the Windows Applications you run from an HTTP address. The launcher can also keep track of the version number used in the last version. If a newer version is available, the launcher can inform the end user and ask whether the newer version should be used.

As I mentioned previously, the launcher must be installed on a local drive and run from there. This requirement stems from the implicit permission demand that fires when the launcher creates another AppDomain. This permission is necessary only when loading and running an EXE in another AppDomain because loading DLLs with LoadFrom doesn't cause a permission demand.

Isolated Storage

Isolated storage is a .NET Framework feature that enables assemblies to access a well-defined area of the file system, even if they don't have full permissions on the entire file system.

Assemblies manage isolated storage by means of *stores*. Each store contains one or more files or subdirectories and is distinct from the store that another user (or even another assembly running in the same user account) uses. This isolation ensures that an untrusted assembly can't read or modify the store used by another assembly. In addition, the system administrator can set a higher limit to the amount of data that can be written to a store (the so-called *quota*) so that an assembly can't compromise the client system by writing too much data to its hard drive.

Isolated storage was primarily designed for partially trusted assemblies that are loaded from the Internet—either as Windows Forms applications launched via an HTTP URL or Windows Forms controls running inside Internet Explorer—but it can have other uses as well. An ASP.NET application can use isolated storage on the server to maintain a user's data between sessions; the only prerequisite in this latter case is that the ASP.NET application must impersonate the remote user so that each remote user has a distinct store.

Isolated data is perfect for storing user preferences but not for configuration settings—such as an ADO.NET connection string—because the latter type of settings should be under the control of the administrator, not the end user. Likewise, isolated storage should *not* be used to store secret data because any unmanaged or fully trusted application can access the area of the file system where the store is held.

Creating a Store

All the classes you need to use isolated storage in your applications can be found in the System.IO.IsolatedStorage namespace. The most important of such classes are IsolatedStorageFile (which represents a store) and IsolatedStorageFileStream (which represents an open file in the store). The following example shows how you get a reference to a store, write a text file into it, and then read the file back:

```
' Create a store for current user/assembly.
Dim store1 As IsolatedStorageFile = IsolatedStorageFile.GetStore( _
    IsolatedStorageScope.User Or IsolatedStorageScope.Assembly Or _
    IsolatedStorageScope.Domain, Nothing, Nothing)
' Create a file in the store.
Dim ifs1 As New IsolatedStorageFileStream("file1.txt", FileMode.Create, store1)
' Write a string to it.
Dim sw As New StreamWriter(ifs1)
```

```
sw.WriteLine("This is a test string")
sw.Close()
' This statement ensures that the store is written to disk.
store1.Close()

' Create another store for current user/assembly.
Dim store2 As IsolatedStorageFile = IsolatedStorageFile.GetStore( _
    IsolatedStorageScope.User Or IsolatedStorageScope.Assembly Or _
    IsolatedStorageScope.Domain, Nothing, Nothing)
' Read a file in the store.
Dim ifs2 As New IsolatedStorageFileStream("file1.txt", FileMode.Open, store2)
' Display its contents.
Dim sr As New StreamReader(ifs2)
MsgBox(sr.ReadToEnd, MsgBoxStyle.Information)
sr.Close()
store2.Close()
```

In most cases you don't need to know where the actual files in a store are saved, but this information can be useful during the debug phase. The path of the directory that holds isolated storage files depends on the Windows version, the isolation scope being used (see next section), the user identity, whether the store is enabled for roaming users, and in some cases whether the operating system was installed on a clean machine or was an update from a previous version.

For example, on Windows XP and Windows Server 2003, isolated storage files are held under the C:\Document and Settings*username*\Local Settings\Application Data directory for nonroaming stores and C:\Document and Settings*username*\Application Data for roaming-enabled stores. (See Figure 34-5.)

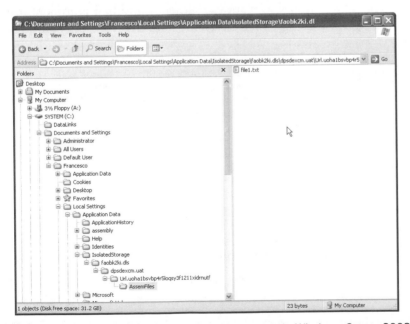

Figure 34-5   The actual directory used for a store in Windows Server 2003

Understanding Isolation Scope

Different users always access different stores and there is no way to change this default behavior, even though an application with sufficient permissions can impersonate a different user and therefore access a different store. Stores are further isolated at the assembly level, which means that assembly A and assembly B always access a different store, even if they run under the same user identity and in the same AppDomain.

Again, you can't change the way stores are isolated at the user or assembly level. However, you can decide whether two instances of the same assembly running under the same user identity but in different AppDomains share the same store or access different stores. You can make this decision by selecting one of the following two isolation levels for the store you create:

- **Isolation by User and Assembly**   If this isolation type is selected, two instances of the same assembly running under the same user identity share the same store, even if the two instances are running in different AppDomains. You should use this isolation type for data that is to be shared among applications, such as user name and general preferences (colors, fonts, and so on). By default, code loaded from the local intranet can select this type of isolation, but code loaded from the Internet can't.

- **Isolation by User, Domain, and Assembly**   If this isolation type is selected, two instances of the same assembly running under the same user identity always access different stores and can't share data via isolated storage. This setting is more secure and should be adopted unless applications must share data.

You select the type of isolation you want to enforce in the first argument to the GetStore shared method or by using either the GetUserStoreForAssembly or the GetUserStoreForDomain shared methods:

```
' These two statements create a store that is isolated by user and assembly.
Dim store1 As IsolatedStorageFile = IsolatedStorageFile.GetStore( _
    IsolatedStorageScope.User Or IsolatedStorageScope.Assembly, Nothing, Nothing)
Dim store2 As IsolatedStorageFile = IsolatedStorageFile.GetUserStoreForAssembly()

' These two statements create a store that is isolated by user, domain, and assembly.
Dim store3 As IsolatedStorageFile = IsolatedStorageFile.GetStore( _
    IsolatedStorageScope.User Or IsolatedStorageScope.Assembly Or _
    IsolatedStorageScope.Domain, Nothing, Nothing)
Dim store4 As IsolatedStorageFile = IsolatedStorageFile.GetUserStoreForDomain()
```

Stores that support roaming users—that is, users who can log on to any machine on the network and still access their isolated storage data—require that you specify the IsolatedStorageScope.Roaming bit in the first argument of the GetStore shared method:

```
' Create a roaming-enabled store that is isolated by user, domain, and assembly.
Dim store5 As IsolatedStorageFile = IsolatedStorageFile.GetStore( _
    IsolatedStorageScope.User Or IsolatedStorageScope.Assembly Or _
    IsolatedStorageScope.Domain Or IsolatedStorageScope.Roaming, Nothing, Nothing)
```

You can use neither the GetUserStoreForAssembly nor the GetUserStoreForDomain shared methods for roaming-enabled stores.

Working with Isolated Storage Security

Whenever a store is created or used, the .NET runtime triggers a stack walk to ensure that all the callers have enough permissions to perform the requested operation. This stack walk can fail because the user has exceeded his or her quota or because operations of that type aren't allowed.

Quotas

In the default configuration, assemblies loaded from the local intranet can store as much data as they want in a store (subject to physical free space on the system drive, of course), whereas assemblies loaded from the Internet can write no more than 10 KB of data in their store. When an assembly attempts to write more data than allowed, an IsolatedStorageException is thrown. You can change these security settings or enforce different quotas on an assembly-by-assembly basis by creating a custom permission set with the .NET Configuration utility and associating it to a specific code group. (See Figure 34-6.)

Quotas are never enforced on roaming stores. For this reason, code requires a slightly higher level of permission to create such stores.

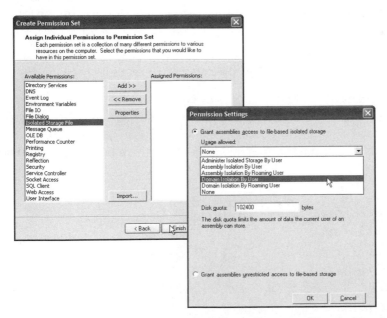

Figure 34-6   Creating a permission set to enforce a nonstandard quota for isolated storage.

The IsolatedStorageFilePermission Class

If managed code uses isolated storage, the .NET runtime transparently invokes a Demand method on an IsolatedStorageFilePermission object. When creating a custom permission set that includes this permission object, you must specify which kind of usage is allowed, as shown in the right portion of Figure 34-6. These are the meanings of the available choices:

- **None**   Isolated storage isn't permitted.

- **DomainIsolationByUser**   Isolation by user, domain, and assembly is allowed, but isolation by user and assembly isn't; quotas are enforced.

- **DomainIsolationByRoamingUser**   Like DomainIsolationByUser, but the store is saved to a network drive and will be available to roaming users; quotas aren't enforced.

- **AssemblyIsolationByUser**   Isolation by user and assembly is allowed; quotas are enforced.

- **AssemblyIsolationByRoamingUser**   Like AssemblyIsolationByUser, but the store is saved to a network drive and will be available to roaming users; quotas aren't enforced.

- **AdministerIsolatedStorageByUser**   Isolation by user only; code can access and delete any file associated with the user. Only code in administrative tools should use this isolation type.

- **UnrestrictedIsolatedStorage**   Isolation by all users, domains, and assemblies. Only code in administrative tools should use this isolation type.

The Isolated Storage tool (Storeadm.exe) is a .NET Framework utility that lets a user administer personal stores. You can use the /list option to display all existing stores for the current user and the /remove option to delete all the stores for the current user. If you also specify the /roaming option, the list or delete action extends to the roaming store. (See Figure 34-7.)

Figure 34-7   The Storeadm /list command displays all the stores for the current user.

Working with Stores, Directories, and Files

In most cases, the actions that are necessary to create, delete, and enumerate directories and files inside a store resemble those that you perform with the standard file system, but you always need to account for the particular nature of isolated storage.

Stores

I already showed a code sample that creates a store, writes a file to it, and reads it back, so in this section I'll focus on the tasks of enumerating and deleting a store. You can't enumerate stores using a standard For Each loop; instead you must invoke the GetEnumerator method on a store object and then use the returned enumerator object to list all the stores associated with the current user. The following code lists all the stores owned by the current user and their properties:

```
' Create a store for current user/assembly.
Dim store As IsolatedStorageFile = IsolatedStorageFile.GetStore( _
    IsolatedStorageScope.User Or IsolatedStorageScope.Assembly, Nothing, Nothing)
' Get an IEnumerator object.
Dim ienum As IEnumerator = store.GetEnumerator(IsolatedStorageScope.User)
Dim totalSize As Long = 0
Dim sb As New System.Text.StringBuilder
Dim CrLf As String = ControlChars.CrLf

Do While ienum.MoveNext
    ' Convert the current enumerated object to a store.
    Dim thisStore As IsolatedStorageFile = DirectCast(ienum.Current, IsolatedStorageFi
le)
    ' Display information about this store.
    sb.AppendFormat("AssemblyIdentity = {0}{1}", _
        thisStore.AssemblyIdentity.ToString, CrLf)
    ' NOTE: you can't use MaximumSize on stores obtained through enumeration.
    sb.AppendFormat("   CurrentSize = {0}{1}", thisStore.CurrentSize, _
    CrLf)
    ' Scope is always assembly in this case.
    sb.AppendFormat("   Scope = {0}{1}", thisStore.Scope.ToString, CrLf)
    sb.Append(CrLf)
    ' Add to total size. (Must convert because CurrentSize is UInt64.)
    totalSize += Convert.ToInt32(thisStore.CurrentSize)
Loop
sb.AppendFormat("TotalSize = {0}", totalSize)
Console.WriteLine(sb.ToString)
```

The AssemblyIdentity property returns a string that identifies the assembly associated with the current store, whereas the CurrentSize property returns the number of bytes currently used in the store.

The IsolatedStorageFile object exposes another interesting property, MaximumSize, which returns the quota allowed to the store. You can't read this property with objects returned by enumeration, but you can use it on the store object returned by the GetStore method. Combining this property and the CurrentSize property, you can anticipate out-of-space conditions:

```
' Create a store for current user/assembly.
Dim store As IsolatedStorageFile = IsolatedStorageFile.GetStore( _
    IsolatedStorageScope.User Or IsolatedStorageScope.Assembly, Nothing, Nothing)
Dim availableBytes As Long = Convert.ToInt64(store.MaximumSize) _
    - Convert.ToInt64(store.CurrentSize)
Console.WriteLine("Available bytes = {0}", availableBytes)
```

The IsolatedStorageFile class exposes both an instance version and a static version of the Remove method. The instance version removes a specific store, whereas the static version deletes all the stores for the current user:

```
' Create a store for current user/assembly.
Dim store As IsolatedStorageFile = IsolatedStorageFile.GetStore( _
    IsolatedStorageScope.User Or IsolatedStorageScope.Assembly, Nothing, Nothing)
⋮
' Remove the store.
store.Remove()

' Delete all the stores associated with the current user.
IsolatedStorageFile.Remove(IsolatedStorageScope.User)
```

Directories and Files

You can create a directory inside a store by calling the CreateDirectory method. The argument you pass to this method can specify multiple directory levels; the command ensures that all intermediate directories are created if necessary. If the directory exists already, no exception is thrown. For example, look at the following code:

```
' Create a store for current user/assembly.
Dim store As IsolatedStorageFile = IsolatedStorageFile.GetStore( _
    IsolatedStorageScope.User Or IsolatedStorageScope.Assembly, Nothing, Nothing)
' Create the AAA directory.
store.CreateDirectory("AAA")
' Create the BBB directory and the BBB\CCC directory.
store.CreateDirectory("BBB\CCC")
' Create a file in BBB\CCC directory.
Dim st As New IsolatedStorageFileStream("BBB\CCC\Example.txt", FileMode.Create, store)
```

Enumerating directories and files in a store requires that you use the GetDirectoryNames and GetFileNames instance methods of the IsolatedStorageFile object. Both methods take a search argument, which can include * and ? wildcards in the last portion of the path—for example, \AAA* or \BBB\CCC\demo*.txt. Thanks to this feature, you can build a recursive routine that retrieves the directory tree in a store:

```
Function GetSubDirectories(ByVal store As IsolatedStorageFile, ByVal path As String) _
    As ArrayList
    Dim res As New ArrayList
    ' Add all subdirectories to result.
    For Each dir As String In store.GetDirectoryNames(path & "\*")
        res.Add(path & "\" & dir)
        ' Recurse on this subdirectory.
        res.AddRange(GetSubDirectories(store, path & "\" & dir))
    Next
    Return res
End Function
```

Using this function to list all files and directories in a store is a trivial task:

```
For Each dir As String In GetSubDirectories(store, "")
    Console.WriteLine("Directory: {0}", dir)
    For Each file As String In store.GetFileNames(dir & "\*")
        Console.WriteLine("  File: {0}", file)
    Next
Next
```

You can delete an individual directory or file with the DeleteDirectory or DeleteFile method, respectively. These methods don't take wildcards and the DeleteDirectory method throws an exception if the directory isn't empty. However, you can solve both problems by using the GetFileNames method and the GetSubDirectories function. Here's a routine that deletes a subdirectory tree:

```
Sub DeleteDirectoryTree(ByVal store As IsolatedStorageFile, ByVal path As String)
    ' Delete all files in this directory.
    For Each file As String In store.GetFileNames(path & "\*")
        store.DeleteFile(path & "\" & file)
    Next
    ' Delete all directory trees in this directory.
    For Each dir As String In GetSubDirectories(store, path)
        DeleteDirectoryTree(store, dir)
    Next
    ' Finally, delete the directory, if it isn't the root.
    If path.Length > 0 Then store.DeleteDirectory(path)
End Sub
```

Common Tasks for Internet-Aware Applications

The .NET Framework includes many classes that let you add Internet-related functionality to your applications—for example, to read Web pages or communicate over the TCP protocol. I'll cover some of these classes in this section.

Notice that, unlike all the previous samples in this chapter, the code in this section is assumed to run in a trusted assembly.

Requesting a Web Page

Requesting a Web page is the most frequent operation you perform in many Internet-related applications. You can post an HTTP request to a Web page with the WebClient class, or you can use the WebRequest and WebResponse types for more articulated requests. All these classes are in the System.Net namespace.

The WebClient Class

The simplest technique for posting an HTTP request to a Web page is by means of the WebClient class and its DownloadFile method.

```
' Read the home page of www.vb2themax.com and save it in C:\home.html.
Dim client As New WebClient
client.DownloadFile("http://www.vb2themax.com/default.asp", "C:\homepage.htm")
```

If the contents of the page don't go to a file (as in the demo application shown in Figure 34-8), you must open a stream with the OpenRead method and use the returned Stream object as you'd use any .NET stream:

```
Dim client2 As New WebClient
' (In a real-world application you should use a Try block here.)
Dim stream As Stream = client2.OpenRead("http://www.vb2themax.com/default.asp")
Dim sr As New StreamReader(stream)
' Read the HTML in the page.
Dim html As String = sr.ReadToEnd()
' Always close streams.
stream.Close()
```

The WebClient class can be used with the http:, https:, and file: protocols. If the page takes a query string, you can embed it in the URL you pass to the DownloadFile or Open-Read methods, or you can feed the QueryString collection with name/value pairs. The latter method is more convenient when you build the query string programmatically:

```
' Download the page at www.vb2themax.com/item.asp?PageID=TipBank&Cat=101&ID=557
client.QueryString.Add("PageID", "TipBank")
client.QueryString.Add("Cat", "101")
client.QueryString.Add("ID", "557")
client.DownloadFile("http://www.vb2themax.com/Item.asp", "C:\homepage.html")
```

You can also send data to the page—for example, to implement an application that uploads files to a Web server. Please read the MSDN documentation for details about the UploadFile and UploadData methods.

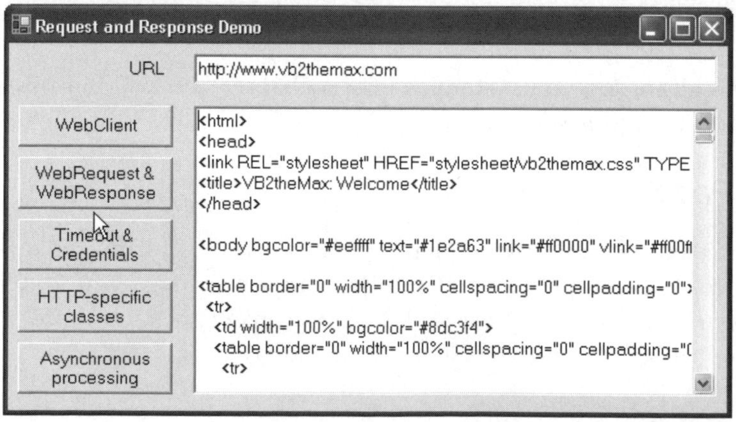

Figure 34-8   The demo application lets you experiment with WebClient, WebRequest, and WebResponse classes.

The WebRequest and WebResponse Classes

The WebRequest and WebResponse classes work together, as the following listing demonstrates:

```
' Read the home page of www.vb2themax.com.
Dim webReq As WebRequest = WebRequest.Create("http://www.vb2themax.com")
Dim webResp As WebResponse = webReq.GetResponse()
Dim sr As New StreamReader(webResp.GetResponseStream, Encoding.ASCII)
Dim html As String = sr.ReadToEnd()
sr.Close()
' Display the result in the console window.
Console.WriteLine(html)
```

The WebRequest and WebResponse classes are virtual and don't expose any constructors. The WebRequest.Create shared method parses the URI passed as an argument and returns a concrete class whose type depends on the protocol part: HttpWebRequest for HTTP requests and FileWebRequest for the file: protocol. Both these classes derive from WebRequest, so the code in the previous example works regardless of the actual concrete object being returned. Likewise, the GetResponse method returns a protocol-specific object—HttpWebResponse if the request object is an HttpWebRequest or a FileWebResponse if the request object is a FileWebRequest. The WebRequest and WebResponse types are at the heart of .NET Framework's *pluggable protocol* mechanism, which ensures that new protocols can be added without having to modify the source code in applications that use these classes.

The WebRequest class allows a few operations that the simpler WebClient doesn't. For example, you can set a timeout for the request and you can send client credentials if the page doesn't grant anonymous access:

```
Try
    Dim webReq As WebRequest = WebRequest.Create("http://www.vb2themax.com")
    ' Set a 10-second timeout.
    webReq.Timeout = 10000
    ' Access a password-protected page. (Just an example in this demo)
    webReq.Credentials = New NetworkCredential("JoeDoe", "joepassword")
    Dim webResp As WebResponse = webReq.GetResponse
    Dim sr As New StreamReader(webResp.GetResponseStream, Encoding.ASCII)
    Dim html As String = sr.ReadToEnd()
    sr.Close()
    ' Display the page
    Console.WriteLine(html)
Catch ex As WebException
    If ex.Status = WebExceptionStatus.Timeout Then
        ' Deal with timeout errors.
        ⋮
    Else
        ' Display a message for other types of errors.
        Console.WriteLine(ex.Message)
    End If
End Try
```

The classes in System.Net throw a WebException object when a Web-related error occurs. The WebException has a Status-enumerated property that lets you understand what went wrong without having to parse the Message property. Common status values are Timeout, ConnectFailure, RequestCancel, and ConnectionClosed.

You can leverage the Proxy property to have requests sent through a proxy server, as follows:

```
Dim webReq As WebRequest = WebRequest.Create("http://www.vb2themax.com")
' The proxy server is named "altproxy" and communicates on port 80.
webReq.Proxy = New WebProxy("http://altproxy:80/")
```

The WebRequest class (as well as the HttpWebRequest class, which I'll discuss shortly) exposes the BeginGetResponse and EndGetResponse methods, which allow you to retrieve data from the page by using the standard .NET programming model for asynchronous operation. Here's an example that uses a simple polling technique:

```
' Use an Uri object to specify the URL, just for variety.
Dim uri As New Uri("http://www.vb2themax.com")
Dim webReq As WebRequest = WebRequest.Create(uri)
' Start the asynchronous operation.
Dim ar As IAsyncResult = webReq.BeginGetResponse(Nothing, Nothing)
Do Until ar.IsCompleted
    ' Do something else until the operation completes.
    ⋮
Loop
' Complete the operation and display the response.
Dim webRes As WebResponse = webReq.EndGetResponse(ar)
Dim sr As New StreamReader(webRes.GetResponseStream)
Console.Write(sr.ReadToEnd())
sr.Close()
```

Of course, you can use all the programming techniques described in Chapter 12, including callback methods.

The HttpWebRequest and HttpWebResponse Classes

I already explained that the WebRequest and WebResponse abstract classes should be used whenever possible because they ensure that your code works with any recognized protocol specified in the URI. In some cases, however, you should cast the return value of the WebRequest.Create and the WebRequest.GetResponse methods to a more specific variable. When you're working with the HTTP protocol, the target variable can be declared of the HttpWebRequest and HttpWebResponse type, as appropriate:

```
' A specific HTTP request can use HttpWebRequest and HttpWebResponse objects.
Dim httpReq As HttpWebRequest = DirectCast( _
    WebRequest.Create("http://www.vb2themax.com"), HttpWebRequest)
Dim httpRes As HttpWebResponse = DirectCast(httpReq.GetResponse, HttpWebResponse)
```

The main reason for using a specific HttpWebRequest object is to leverage the properties it exposes in addition to those inherited from the WebRequest abstract class. Most of these properties correspond to HTTP headers that are sent with the request, such as Accept, ContentType, IfModifiedSince, Referer, and UserAgent. You can set the AllowAutoRedirect to True if the response can be redirected and you can assign False to the KeepAlive property to disable persistent connections:

```
Dim httpReq As HttpWebRequest = DirectCast( _
    WebRequest.Create("http://www.vb2themax.com"), HttpWebRequest)
' The user agent sent by Internet Explorer
httpReq.UserAgent = "Mozilla/4.0 (compatible; MSIE 6.0; Windows NT 5.0)"
' Accept only HTML and XML and turn off keep-alive connections.
httpReq.Accept = "text/html, text/xml"
httpReq.KeepAlive = False
```

(You can also use the Headers collection to specify HTTP header values that don't correspond to any property.) The HttpWebRequest object exposes properties derived from WebResponse (such as ContentType, ContentLength, and Headers) plus those specific for the HTTP protocol—for example, ContentEncoding, LastModified, Server, StatusCode, and StatusDescription:

```
' (Continuing previous example...)
Dim httpRes As HttpWebResponse = DirectCast(httpReq.GetResponse, HttpWebResponse)
Console.WriteLine("StatusCode = {0}", httpRes.StatusCode)
Console.WriteLine("StatusDescription = {0}", httpRes.StatusDescription)
Console.WriteLine("LastModified = {0}", httpRes.LastModified)
Console.WriteLine("ContentEncoding = {0}", httpRes.ContentEncoding)
```

The GET and POST Methods

If the page you are requesting expects data from HTML fields, you must pass these values either on the query string or in the body of the request, depending on whether the page is processing a form that uses the GET or POST method, respectively. Sending data to a page that expects values on the query string is trivial and only requires that you correctly encode data after the ? symbol, as in this code:

```
' Pass data for the txtUserName and txtCity fields on the query string.
Dim uri As New Uri("http://localhost/GetPage.asp?txtUserName=Joe Doe&txtCity=Bari")
Dim httpReq As HttpWebRequest = DirectCast(WebRequest.Create(Uri), HttpWebRequest)
```

Sending data with the POST method is slightly more complex because you must set the Method, ContentType, and ContentLength properties and then write the field values to the request stream after encoding them. Here's an example that you can easily adapt to real world cases:

```
' This is the URL of a page that processes a form with POST method.
Dim uri As New Uri("http://localhost/ProcessPost.asp")
Dim httpReq As HttpWebRequest = DirectCast(WebRequest.Create(Uri), HttpWebRequest)
' Post values to txtUserName and txtCity fields.
Dim formData As String = "txtUserName=Francesco&txtCity=Bari&txtCountry=Italy"
' You must set method, content type, and content length.
httpReq.Method = "POST"
httpReq.ContentType = "application/x-www-form-urlencoded"
httpReq.ContentLength = formData.Length
```

```
' Write the data to the request stream.
Dim sw As New StreamWriter(httpReq.GetRequestStream)
sw.Write(formData)
sw.Close()
' Read the page as usual.
  ⋮
```

Cookies and Cookie Containers

Most Web sites heavily rely on cookies. For example, ASP and ASP.NET sites use cookies to store a client's session ID so that all requests from that client can be associated with its session variables. Working with cookies requires that you assign a CookieContainer object to the CookieContainer property of the HttpWebRequest object and optionally fill this cookie container with one or more cookies. On return from the call, you can read the Cookies collection of the HttpWebResponse object and possibly use the elements of this collection to fill the CookieContainer object the next time you visit a page from the same site. This is how your code might be structured:

```
' Use an Uri object to set the address of page.
Dim uri As New Uri("http://localhost/cookies.asp")
Dim httpReq As HttpWebRequest = DirectCast(WebRequest.Create(uri), HttpWebRequest)
' Prepare to receive cookies.
httpReq.CookieContainer = New CookieContainer
' Read the page.
Dim httpRes As HttpWebResponse = DirectCast(httpReq.GetResponse, HttpWebResponse)

' Display cookies received from page (optional).
For Each coo As Cookie In httpRes.Cookies
    Console.WriteLine("COOKIE {0} = {1}", coo.Name, coo.Value)
Next

' Process the page here.
  ⋮

' Make another request to same page (or another page from same site)
httpReq = DirectCast(WebRequest.Create(uri), HttpWebRequest)
httpReq.CookieContainer = New CookieContainer
' Reuse cookies received from last response.
For Each coo As Cookie In httpRes.Cookies
    httpReq.CookieContainer.Add(coo)
Next
' Read the page again.
httpRes = DirectCast(httpReq.GetResponse, HttpWebResponse)
' (and so on...)
  ⋮
```

Using cookie containers in this fashion is similar to what you do to support cookies and ASP.NET sessions when working with Web services, as I explained in Chapter 29.

Working with the TCP Protocol

Data transferred over the Internet doesn't have to be HTML or XML, and a Web server can and usually does offer more services than just serving HTML pages. In this section, you'll see how you can have two machines communicate through the Transmission Control Protocol (TCP) using the System.Net.Sockets.TcpClient class. The System.Net.Sockets namespace also contains the UdpClient class (for working with the User Datagram Protocol, or UDP) and the Socket class (for working directly with socket services). I won't cover these classes here, but you can find several examples in the MSDN documentation.

You can have two applications—on the same or different machines—communicate through TCP. This protocol ensures that data is either correctly received or an exception is thrown, and for this reason it is the preferred protocol when you can't afford to lose data. You can apply these techniques to programs running on the same LAN or the same machine as a simple alternative to other communication techniques, such as remoting.

The TCP protocol assumes you have a server application that listens to requests coming from clients. Writing the client application is simpler, so I'll begin there. The client code must instantiate a TcpClient object that references the server application by means of the server application's URL and port number. (The port number should be in the range of 1024 to 65535.) Next, the client invokes the TcpClient.GetStream method to retrieve the NetworkStream object that can be used to send and receive data from the server.

It's obvious that the client and the server application must agree on the port number as well as the format of the data being sent over the wire. In the following example, I'll use the simple rule that the client sends and receives a string terminated with a CR-LF character so that I can perform the actual write and read operations by means of the StreamWriter and StreamReader objects:

```
' This code assumes a server on local machine is listening to port 2048.
Dim tcpCli As New TcpClient("localhost", 2048)
' Retrieve the stream that can send and receive data.
Dim ns As NetworkStream = tcpCli.GetStream
' Send a CR-LF-termined string to the server.
Dim sw As New StreamWriter(ns)
sw.WriteLine(txtSendData.Text)
sw.Flush()                          ' This is VERY important!

' Receive data from the server application and display it.
Dim sr As New StreamReader(ns)
Dim result As String = sr.ReadLine()
Console.WriteLine(result)
' Release resources.
sr.Close()
sw.Close()
ns.Close()
```

The server application must create a TcpListener object that listens to a given port and accepts incoming requests from clients. The AcceptTcpClient method waits until a connection is made and returns the TcpClient object that represents the client making the request. The GetStream method of this TcpClient object returns a NetworkStream that the server application can use to read data from clients and send them a result.

```
Dim listening As Boolean = False

Sub ListenToClients()
    ' Listen to port 2048.
    Dim localhostAddress As IPAddress = IPAddress.Loopback
    Dim tcpList As New TcpListener(localhostAddress, 2048)
    tcpList.Start()
    listening = True

    Do
        ' Wait for the next client to make a request.
        Dim tcpCli As TcpClient = tcpList.AcceptTcpClient()
        ' Read data sent by the client (a CR-LF separated string in this case).
        Dim ns As NetworkStream = tcpCli.GetStream
        Dim sr As New StreamReader(ns)
        Dim receivedData As String = sr.ReadLine()

        ' Process the data (just convert to upper case in this demo).
        Dim resultData As String = receivedData.ToUpper
        ' Send it back to the client.
        Dim sw As New StreamWriter(ns)
        sw.WriteLine(resultData)
        sw.Flush()                              ' This is VERY important.
        ' Release resources.
        sr.Close()
        sw.Close()
        ns.Close()
        tcpCli.Close()

        ' Exit the loop if another thread set the listening variable to False.
    Loop While listening

    ' Reject client requests from now on.
    tcpList.Stop()
End Sub
```

You should call the ListenToClients procedure on a secondary thread so that another portion of the program has the opportunity to set the listening variable to False to exit the loop—for example, when the operator clicks a button. (See Figure 34-9.)

The problem with the naive approach used in the previous code example is that the AcceptTcpClient method blocks the thread until a client actually connects. Even if another thread sets the listening variable to False, the thread in which the ListenToClients procedure is running is blocked until a client makes a request. You can cope with this situation by using the Pending method of the TcpListener object, which returns False if no connections are waiting to be processed:

```
Do
    ' Wait until a connection is made or user decided to quit.
    Do While tcpList.Pending = False And listening = True
        ' Yield the CPU for a while.
```

```
        Thread.Sleep(10)
    Loop
    ' Exit if user decided to quit.
    If Not listening Then Exit Do

    ' Accept the pending client request.
    Dim tcpCli As TcpClient = tcpList.AcceptTcpClient()
    ' Remainder of procedure as before.
    ⋮
Loop While listening
```

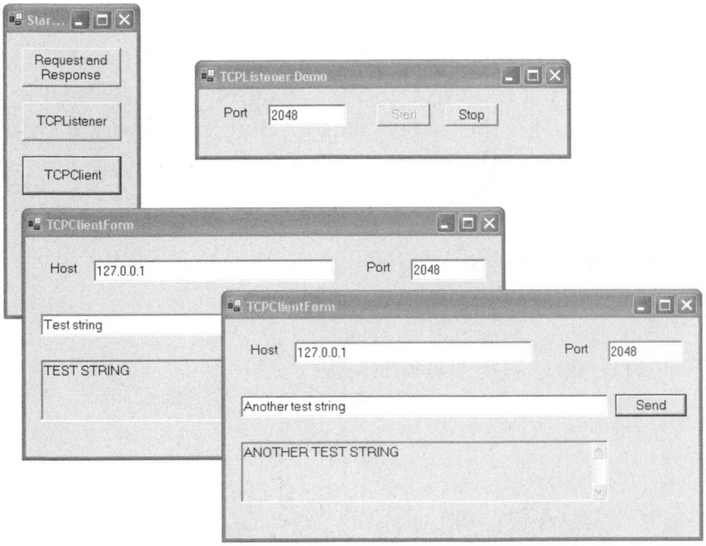

Figure 34-9   The demo application shows how to communicate with the TcpClient and TcpListener classes.

Sending E-mail

Sending e-mail from a Visual Basic .NET application—be it a Windows Forms, Web Forms, or Web Services program—is embarrassingly simple thanks to the classes in the System.Web.Mail namespace. (If you aren't working on an ASP.NET application, you must add a reference to the System.Web.dll assembly to use these classes.) In practice, you just have to create a MailMessage object, set its properties, and then pass the object to the Send shared method of the SmtpMail class. All the message properties have the same name and meaning of the fields you usually fill when working with a client mail program such as Microsoft Outlook. The following code is excerpted from the demo application shown in Figure 34-10:

```
Dim msg As New MailMessage
' The following four fields can be a semicolon-delimited list of addresses.
msg.From = txtFrom.Text        ' Who sends the mail
msg.To = txtTo.Text            ' Who receives the mail
msg.Cc = txtCC.Text            ' Carbon-copy receivers
```

```
msg.Bcc = txtBCC.Text                       ' Blind carbon-copy receivers
msg.Priority = MailPriority.Normal          ' This is the default priority
msg.Subject = txtSubject.Text               ' The subject of the message
msg.Body = txtBody.Text                      ' The message body (can be HTML)

Try
    ' Uncomment next statement to use a specific SMTP relay mail server.
    ' SmtpMail.SmtpServer = "mailservername"
    SmtpMail.Send(msg)
Catch ex As System.Web.HttpException
    MsgBox(ex.Message)
End Try
```

The SmtpMail class uses the Collaboration Data Objects for Windows 2000 (CDOSYS) component. The message is delivered through the SMTP mail service that comes with the operating system or through the SMTP server that you specify in the Smtp-Mail.SmtpServer shared property. In the former case, the message is queued so that the program doesn't block network traffic.

You can send attachments by adding one or more MailAttachment objects to the Attachments property of MailMessage:

```
' msg is a MailMessage object.
Dim attachment As New MailAttachment("C:\myfile.dat")
msg.Attachments.Add(attachment)
' (Continue as in previous code example.)
⋮
```

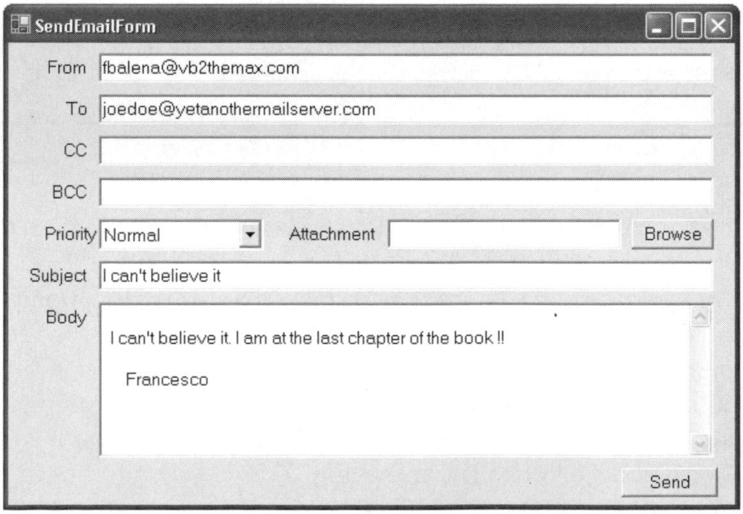

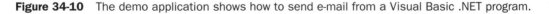

Figure 34-10   The demo application shows how to send e-mail from a Visual Basic .NET program.

As an alternative to the SmtpMail class, the mailto: protocol provides a quick-and-dirty way to let the end user send e-mail using a client mail program, such as Microsoft

Outlook. For example, here's how you can prepare a message that the user can send from inside the application that's registered as the default client mail program:

```
' All fields after the question mark are optional.
Dim url As String = "mailto:frank@contoso.com?CC=johnny@contoso.com&"_
  & "BCC=ann@contoso.com&SUBJECT=Greetings&BODY=Hello Frank") _
  System.Diagnostics.Process.Start(url)
⋮
```

You can use the mailto: protocol to activate the client mail program also from inside Web Form applications by assigning the URL string to the NavigateUrl property of a Hyperlink control or to the href attribute of an <A> HTML element:

```
<A HREF="mailto:info@contoso.com?SUBJECT=Info request">
    Click here to request additional info</A>
```

Using the WebBrowser Control

As I explained in "The LinkLabel Control" section of Chapter 16, you can display a Web page inside Internet Explorer quite simply by means of the Start shared method of the System.Diagnostic.Process object:

```
' Run Internet Explorer and display VB2TheMax's home page.
Process.Start("http://www.vb2themax.com/default.asp")
```

In many cases, however, you'd like to display a Web page inside a form of your application and interact with the page's element from code.

The .NET Framework doesn't include a control for browsing Web pages, but you can use the WebBrowser ActiveX control available with Visual Basic 6 after importing it into Visual Studio .NET. To do so, right-click the Toolbox control to select the Add/Remove Items command, switch to the COM Components tab, and add the Microsoft Web Browser control (stored in C:\Windows\System32\shdocvw.dll). Visual Studio .NET creates a wrapper for the control named AxWebBrowser, but I'll continue to refer to it as the WebBrowser control.

Once you have dropped an instance of the WebBrowser control on a form, you surely will want to navigate to a Web page, which couldn't be simpler:

```
Dim url As Object = "www.vb2themax.com"
' Optional arguments of Navigate2 method let you select the destination
' frame, define headers, post data, etc.
AxWebBrowser1.Navigate2(url)
```

(See Figure 34-11.) Other methods of the WebBrowser control let you navigate in the browser history (GoBack, GoForward) or jump to predefined pages (GoHome, GoSearch):

```
Private Sub btnBack_Click(ByVal sender As Object, ByVal e As EventArgs) _
    Handles btnBack.Click
    AxWebBrowser1.GoBack()
End Sub
```

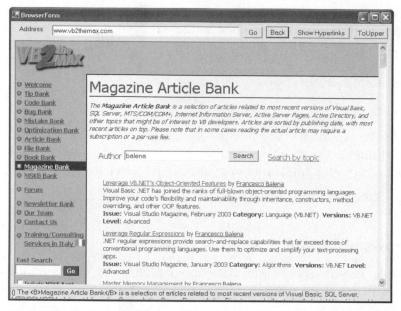

Figure 34-11   You can use the WebBrowser control for your personalized browser (and access VB2TheMax's index of articles appearing in major programming magazines, as this particular one does).

Many properties and methods of the WebBrowser control—including Toolbar, Status-Bar, and Resizable—are actually members of Internet Explorer and do not effect the appearance of the control.

The most important property is undoubtedly Document, which gives you access to the contents and structure of the Web page currently displayed in the control. The Document property returns an object that you must cast to the mshtml.HTMLDocument type, which is defined in the mshtml.dll COM library. Microsoft opportunely provides a Primary Interop Assembly (PIA) for this library, which you can find in the .NET tab of the Add Reference dialog box. (Even if you select the component in the COM tab, the PIA library is used anyway.)

The Document property takes a non-Nothing value only when the Web page has been completely read and parsed. The best place to read the Document property is in the NavigateComplete2 event handler of the WebBrowser control:

```
Private Sub AxWebBrowser1_NavigateComplete2(ByVal sender As Object, _
    ByVal e As AxSHDocVw.DWebBrowserEvents2_NavigateComplete2Event) _
    Handles AxWebBrowser1.NavigateComplete2
    Dim doc As mshtml.HTMLDocument = _
      DirectCast(AxWebBrowser1.Document, mshtml.HTMLDocument)
    ' Use the Document property here.
    :
End Sub
```

The HTMLDocument object returned by the Document property is the entry point to the Dynamic HTML structure of the page. By using the many properties and collections that this object exposes, you can reach any element in the page (images, hyperlinks, client-side scripts, forms, and so on), read their properties, and even change their appearance. For example, you can retrieve the textual or HTML contents of the page with just one line:

```
' (doc holds a reference to the HTMLDocument object.)
' This is the body of the page as plain text.
Dim bodyText As String = doc.Body.InnerText
' This is the body of the page as HTML.
Dim bodyHtml As String = doc.Body.documentElement.OuterHtml
```

The HTMLDocument class exposes several collections, such as forms, anchors, images, and styleSheets. The form collection, in turn, exposes the elements collection, which gives you access to all the controls in a given HTML form. The following code enumerates all the hyperlinks on the page and displays information on their anchor text and destination URL in the Debug window:

```
' (doc holds a reference to the HTMLDocument object.)
For Each link As mshtml.HTMLAnchorElement In doc.links
    Debug.WriteLine(link.innerText & " -> " & link.href)
Next
```

The Selection property of the HTMLDocument class returns a TextRange DHTML object that describes the text currently selected in the browser. Here's the code that lets you retrieve the selection:

```
' (doc holds a reference to the HTMLDocument object.)
Dim txtRange As mshtml.IHTMLTxtRange = CType(doc.selection.createRange(), mshtml.IHTML
TxtRange)
Dim selectedText As String = txtRange.text
```

The *dynamic* in Dynamic HTML means that the contents of the Web page can be changed after the page has been loaded. For example, you could convert the selected text to uppercase (admittedly a silly thing to do, but it's just for the sake of brevity):

```
' (Continuing previous example...)
If Not (txtRange Is Nothing) AndAlso Not (txtRange.Text Is Nothing) Then
    txtRange.text = txtRange.text.ToUpper()
End If
```

> **See Also**   To learn more about Dynamic HTML, the Document object, and all its countless properties, members, and collections, read Chapter 19 of *Programming Microsoft Visual Basic 6* on the companion CD with this book.

You can trap events from the HTMLDocument object, even though the syntax isn't intuitive:

```
Private Sub AxWebBrowser1_NavigateComplete2(ByVal sender As Object, _
    ByVal e As AxSHDocVw.DWebBrowserEvents2_NavigateComplete2Event) Handles _
```

```
    AxWebBrowser1.NavigateComplete2
    ' Cast to the interface that defines the event you're interested in
    Dim docevents As mshtml.HTMLDocumentEvents2_Event = _
        DirectCast(AxWebBrowser1.Document, mshtml.HTMLDocumentEvents2_Event)
    ' Define a handler for onmouseover event.
    AddHandler docevents.onmousemove, AddressOf onmousemove
End Sub

' Must use Overloads because the Form has a protected method with same name.
Private Overloads Sub onmousemove(ByVal obj As mshtml.IHTMLEventObj)
    ' Get a reference to the HTML element under the mouse cursor.
    Dim el As mshtml.IHTMLElement = obj.srcElement
    ' Display the HTML text in a label.
    lblStatus.Text = el.innerHTML
End Sub
```

The WebBrowser control doesn't expose any method to directly print its contents. You can achieve this effect via the ExecWB method by passing the OLECMDID_PRINT constant in its first argument. The second argument for this method determines whether a dialog box must be displayed prior to printing the document:

```
' Display the Print dialog.
AxWebBrowser1.ExecWB(SHDocVw.OLECMDID.OLECMDID_PRINT, _
    SHDocVw.OLECMDEXECOPT.OLECMDEXECOPT_PROMPTUSER)
' Print without displaying any dialog.
AxWebBrowser1.ExecWB(SHDocVw.OLECMDID.OLECMDID_PRINT, _
    SHDocVw.OLECMDEXECOPT.OLECMDEXECOPT_DONTPROMPTUSER)
```

The ExecWB method raises an error if the WebBrowser control doesn't contain any document, so in production code the previous statements should be protected with a Try…Catch block. The ExecWB method supports several other constants that let you access additional WebBrowser features—for example, you can display the Page Setup dialog box with the following code:

```
AxWebBrowser1.ExecWB(SHDocVw.OLECMDID.OLECMDID_PAGESETUP, _
    SHDocVw.OLECMDEXECOPT.OLECMDEXECOPT_DODEFAULT)
```

Read the MSDN documentation for more options.

That's all, folks! No more chapters, no more Visual Basic, no more concepts to grasp or tricks to learn! This is the end for now, although the next version of Visual Studio .NET is already on the programmers' horizon. I'll surely write a book about the forthcoming version soon, but I don't want to worry about it right now. I'm just too happy to return to my circadian cycles and go to bed at a decent time for the first time in months. A good night to you, too!

Index

Symbols & Numeric

<%#...%> syntax, 910
<< operator, 47–49
>> operator, 47–49
\= operator, 53
^= operator, 53
2-D vector graphics (GDI+), 554–567

A

Abort method
  threads, 329
  Web service proxy class, 1106
abstract classes. *See* virtual classes (inheritance)
Accept property, HtmlInputFile class, 882
AcceptButton property
  Button control, 491
  forms, 448
AcceptChanges method, DataRow class, 754, 758
AcceptRejectRule property, ForeignKeyConstraint object, 768
AcceptReturns property, multiline TextBox controls, 487
AcceptTabs property, multiline TextBox controls, 487
access
  resources, 1013
  interfaces, 175–176
  Lease object, 1240
  Visual Studio .NET user controls, 1053
ACLs (Access Control Lists), 1259
AcquireReaderLock method, ReaderWriterLock class, 348
AcquireRequestState event, 997–999
AcquireWriterLock method, ReaderWriterLock class, 348
Activate method, ServicedComponent class, 1192
Activated event (forms), 440
<activated> tag, 1235
ActivateMdiChild method, 461
Activation Limit field, 1199
activation methods, SOAP extensions, 1119–1121
Activation property, ListView control, 512
Activation tab (Properties window), 1170, 1191
Activator.CreateInstance method, RegisteringConfiguration class, 1229
Activator.GetObject method, RemotingConfiguration class, 1227
Active Server Pages. *See* ASP (Active Server Pages)
ActiveControl property, ContainerControl class, 422
ActiveLinkColor property, LinkLabel control, 489
ActiveX controls, 439–440
ActiveX Data Objects. *See* ADO (ActiveX Data Objects)
activity (logical threads), 1185–1186
Actor property, SoapException class, 1110
Adapter shared method, ArrayList class, 257

AdCreated event, AdRotator control, 906
<add> blocks, 1008
Add Components command (Project menu), 362
Add Inherited Form command (Project menu), 466
Add method
  Application object, 974
  ArrayList class, 254
  Cache class, 988
  CollectionBase abstract class, 264, 265
Add New Item command (Project menu), 479, 600, 843
Add New Item dialog box, 466, 1058
Add procedures, 15
Add Project command (File menu), 360
Add Reference dialog box, 35, 360, 372, 1148
Add UserControl command (Project menu), 603
Add value (MergeType property), 463
Add Web Reference command (Project menu), 1091
Add Web Reference dialog box, 1091
AddAttribute method, HtmlTextWriter class, 1061
AddAttributesToRender method, WebControl class, 1068
Add/Edit Application Extension Mapping dialog box, 1006
AddHandler command, 450
AddHandler keyword, 116–119, 458
AddLine method, GraphicPath objects, 558
AddOwnedForm method, 446
AddPermission method, PermissionSet class, 1283
AddRange method
  ArrayList class, 256
  MenuItem objects, 454
AddRef method, 157
Add/Remove Items command (Customize Toolbox window), 362
Address objects, 625–627
AddressControl class, 630
AddressControl custom control, 625–627
AddressOf operators, 186
AddressTypeConverter class, 627
AddValue method, 302
Adjust .NET Security wizard, 1321
ADO (ActiveX Data Objects), 9, 200
  COM Interop, 707–708
  compared to ADO.NET, 702–711
ADO.NET, 9
  Classes. *See* DataAdapter class
  COM Interop, 707–708
  compared to ADO, 702–711
  connection mode
    Command object. *See* Command object (ADO.NET)
    Connection object. *See* Connection object (ADO.NET)
    DataReader object. *See* DataReader object
  data binding, 527–532

D

Francesco Balena

Francesco Balena began his software studies in the 70s and had to fight for a while against huge IBM mainframes and tons of punched cards while he waited for the PC to be invented. From those good old days—when the word *megabyte* made little sense and *gigabyte* was pure blasphemy—he has retained the taste for writing the most efficient and resource-aware code possible.

In more recent years, Francesco became contributing editor and member of the Technical Advisory board of *Visual Studio Magazine* (formerly *Visual Basic Programmer's Journal*), for which he writes features articles and columns. He's the author of *Programming Microsoft Visual Basic 6* and coauthor of *Applied .NET Framework Programming with Microsoft Visual Basic .NET* (with Jeffrey Richter) both from Microsoft Press. Francesco teaches Visual Basic .NET courses for Wintellect (*www.wintellect.com*) and is a regular speaker at developer conferences such as VBITS, SQL2TheMax, WinDev, and WinSummit. He is the founder of the popular VB-2-The-Max site (*www.vb2themax.com*), where you can find hundreds of articles, tips, and routines.

Francesco is the lead author of VBMaximizer, an add-in for Visual Basic 6 that has won an award from readers of *Visual Studio Magazine*, and coauthor of *CodeBox.NET*, a code repository tool for .NET programming languages. He has been appointed Microsoft's MSDN Regional Director for Italy and is cofounder of Code Architects, an Italian company that specializes exclusively in .NET programming, training, and consulting.

Francesco lives in Bari, Italy, with his wife Adriana and his son Andrea, but spends a lot of his time abroad. In his previous life, he had a lot of good times playing his alto sax with big bands and jazz combos, until he found that computer programming can be just as fun and doesn't require that he be awake and blowing until 4 A.M. each and every night. Only later he realized that—to write code and meet deadlines—he couldn't go to sleep before 4 A.M. anyway, but it was too late to change his mind. He currently plays with the Band on The Runtime, together with musicians of the caliber of David Chappell, Don Box, and Ted Pattison.

Keep Your Copy of Programming Microsoft Visual Basic .NET 2003 Up-to-date

Visit *www.codearchitects.com/programmingvbnet* to read any updates, errata, or additions to this book, including a special index for programmers who already have the first edition of the book and are switching from .NET Framework 1.0 to version 1.1

You can also subscribe to the Code Architects newsletter to access our collection of utilities, add-ins, and components for all Visual Studio .NET developers.

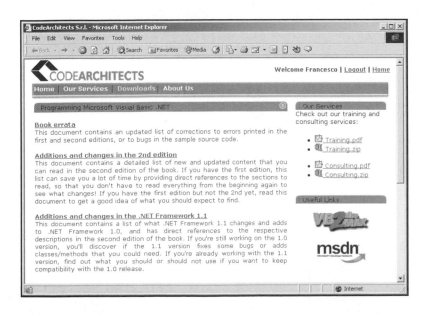

Get a **Free**
e-mail newsletter, updates,
special offers, links to related books,
and more when you
register online!

Register your Microsoft Press® title on our Web site and you'll get a FREE subscription to our e-mail newsletter, *Microsoft Press Book Connections*. You'll find out about newly released and upcoming books and learning tools, online events, software downloads, special offers and coupons for Microsoft Press customers, and information about major Microsoft® product releases. You can also read useful additional information about all the titles we publish, such as detailed book descriptions, tables of contents and indexes, sample chapters, links to related books and book series, author biographies, and reviews by other customers.

Registration is easy. Just visit this Web page and fill in your information:

http://www.microsoft.com/mspress/register

Microsoft